Contents

2006/2007

AFRICANAMERICANYEARBOOK

CAREER & BUSINESS OPPORTUNITIES

THE US DEPARTMENT OF DEFENSE AND THE INTERNATIONAL SCENE

RELIGION•EDUCATION•HEALTH•ORGANIZATIONS AND MEDIA

DEFINITION OF AFRICA*

Africa is the world's second-largest continent in both area and population, after Eurasia.

Separated from Europe by the Mediterranean Sea, it is joined to Asia at its northeast extremity by the Isthmus of Suez. From the most northerly point, Ras ben Sakka in Morocco, to the most southerly point, Cape Agulhas in South Africa, is a distance approximately of 8,000 km (5,000 miles); from Cape Verde, the westernmost point, to Ras Hafun in Somalia, the most easterly projection, is a distance of 7,400 km (4,600 miles) approximately.

DEFINITION OF BLACK OR AFRICAN-AMERICAN**

The term "Black or African American" refers to people having origins in any of the Black race groups of Africa. It includes people who reported "Black, African Am., or Negro" or wrote in entries such as African American, Afro American, Nigerian, or Haitian.

*Source: Wikipedia. http://en2.wikipedia.org
**Source: US Census Bureau

AFRICAN AMERICAN YEARBOOK

PUBLISHER
Juan Ovidio Zavala

EDITOR
Angela E. Zavala

ASSOCIATE PUBLISHER
John Zavala

**GOVERNMENT RELATIONS
& CIRCULATION**
Jess Quintero

**ADVERTISING & PUBLIC
RELATIONS**
Evelyn Day
Robert James

PRODUCTION
Ramón Palencia-Calvo
Kim Chi Un
Jordan L. Dansby
Fatoki Olayinka

RESEARCH
Fredalyn Bardaje
Helena V. Pisano
Lorena Quintana

CONTRIBUTING EDITORS
Thomas Brunton
Linda Burnette
Aimée Winegar
Stephen J. Winegar

DESIGN
Caruso Creative, LLC
Babak Shahbodaghloo

Trademark No. 78159159
Library of Congress Control No:
87-64-1284
Call Main No. HD2346.u 52 W 352
ISSN: 1067-330X
ISBN:0-9777254-0-5

AFRICAN-AMERICAN YEARBOOK
is an annual publication of
TIYM Publishing Company, Inc. a current
8(a) certified business, qualified as a Small
Disadvantaged Business (SDB) under
the SBA's Office of Small Disadvantaged
Business Certification and Eligibility.

TIYM Publishing Company
FOUNDED IN 1985
The Origin of TIYM:
The acronym and commercial name of
the publishing company, TIYM, recalls
its roots in Argentina

Headquarters
6718 Whittier Avenue Suite 130
McLean, Virginia 22101 USA
Tel: (703) 734-1632
Fax: (703) 356-0787

Florida Office
814 Ponce de León Suite 510
Coral Gables, FL 33134 USA
Tel: (305) 442-7003
Fax: (305) 442-7013
tiym@tiym.com
www.tiym.com

Angela E. Zavala, President & CEO
DUNS:161904669

DISTRIBUTION NETWORK
Circulation 50,000
Distributed to many of the groups and
organizations listed in this edition:
Throughout the United States:
- US Senate and House of Representatives
- US Department of Defense
- Historically Black Colleges and Universities
- High Schools, Colleges and Universities with
  high proportion of African Americans
- Libraries
- The Congress of National Black Churches, Inc.
- African American Churches
- Sponsors of AFRICAN-AMERICAN
  YEARBOOK
- Retail Outlets in Association with the
  Independent Publishers Group (IPG)

At Conferences and Conventions:
- American Council on Education
- NAACP
- Minority Business Development Agency
  (MED WEEK)
- Congressional Black Caucus Conference
- G.I. Forum
- African American Chambers of Commerce
- National Council for Community and
  Education Partnerships (NCCEP)
- Blacks in Government
- Urban League

International:
- US Embassies and Consulates in
  Africa

THE WHITE HOUSE

WASHINGTON

November 22, 2005

I send greetings to readers of the African-American Yearbook.

Throughout our history, America has been a land of diversity and has benefited from the contributions of people of different backgrounds brought together by a love of liberty. African Americans have strengthened our country through their achievements in all walks of life, including business, politics, education, the military, community service, the arts, and science. Their hard work, strong values, and devotion to community set a positive example for others and add to the success and prosperity of America.

My Administration is committed to ensuring that our Nation remains the land of hope and opportunity for every citizen. By working to make tax relief permanent, address the growing burden of frivolous lawsuits, reduce excessive Federal regulations, and confront the rising costs of health care, we are building an environment for economic growth and vitality that encourages all Americans to achieve their dreams.

I appreciate all those involved with the African-American Yearbook for your efforts to recognize the achievements of African Americans and the significant role they have played in making our country prosperous and free. As a resource for business, employment, educational, and health needs, this yearbook helps strengthen the African-American community and extend the great promise of America to all our citizens.

Laura and I send our best wishes.

Congressional Black Caucus
of the United States Congress

2236 Rayburn Building • Washington, DC 20515 • (202) 226-9776 • fax (202) 225-1512
www.congressionalblackcaucus.net

January 6, 2006

Ms. Angela Zavala
Editor
African-American Yearbook
TIYM Publishing Company, Inc.
6718 Whittier Avenue – Suite 130
McLean, Virginia 22101

Dear Ms. Zavala,

Congratulations to TIYM Publishing Company, Inc. on publishing its 6th annual edition of the African-American Yearbook. The Yearbook is an excellent resource and guide on business, health, education and other topics relevant to the African-American community.

On behalf of the members of the Congressional Black Caucus (CBC), I congratulate you again on the 6th annual publication of the African-American yearbook.

Sincerely,

Melvin L. Watt

Melvin L. Watt
Chair, CBC

THE DEPUTY SECRETARY OF DEFENSE
WASHINGTON

JAN 1 3 2006

Congratulations on the 20th anniversary edition of the Anuario Hispano – Hispanic Yearbook. This annual guide, together with the African and Asian yearbooks that followed, have effectively highlighted the vital contributions to peace, prosperity and progress made by our friends around the world and by Americans of many diverse backgrounds. Year after year, these reference resources have played an important role in connecting leaders in business, government, education and the public to build the close personal relationships that are the foundation of strong international ties and to provide a roadmap to opportunities in employment, business and education.

From the first edition, the Armed Forces of the United States have been part of each of these yearbooks. The yearbooks have aided in our recruiting efforts and highlighted the work of the many thousands of Soldiers, Sailors, Airmen, Marines, Coast Guardsmen and civilian employees who proudly serve in the defense of freedom and liberty.

America's military reflects the diverse people and intrinsic values of our blessed country. Our men and women in uniform protect and defend all Americans, our friends and allies, and our way of life. The Armed Services have earned the respect and admiration of a grateful Nation.

My very best wishes to the readers of these informative yearbooks and my thanks to the dedicated staff who each year compiles these valuable guides.

Again, congratulations on 20 years of success!

Gordon England

Letter from the Editor

Our various publications allow us to get a glimpse of this Nation's increasingly diverse population. Among this great diversity, African Americans are the second-largest minority group in the United States, now totaling more than 34 million. The constant achievement of this community clearly contributes to the success of the country as a whole.

African Americans weave an indispensable thread through the Nation's collective story. They have gained prominent positions in all levels and branches of politics, are teaching and learning at the finest educational institutions, and represent some of our most talented artists, musicians and athletes. Happily, the continuing integration and consolidation of the cultural components of our country has not diminished the wonderful African American heritage and identity.

The men and women of the African American community have contributed as much, if not more, than any other group in the United States. This contribution is quite evident with respect to the Armed Forces, where they have shown a level of commitment to the country that is beyond reproach. From privates to generals, the entire country can take pride in the achievements, valor, and selflessness of African Americans serving at home and abroad.

It is impossible to portray the country in any way without mentioning the wide range of contributions made by this group. TIYM Publishing humbly accepts the acknowledgement of the African American community, and I present this product in the great hope of its continued usefulness and service.

Warmest Regards,

Angela Elizalde Zavala

General Michael W. Hagee (center) made history in June of 2005 when he became the first Commandant of the US Marine Corps to visit the African and Middle East Division of the Library of Congress. General Hagee was in attendance with his wife and Major General Walter E. Gaskin for the dedication of the 2005 African-American Yearbook.

NATIONAL ASSOCIATION FOR THE ADVANCEMENT OF COLORED PEOPLE
4805 MT. HOPE DRIVE • BALTIMORE, MD 21215-3297 • (410) 580-5777

Bruce S. Gordon, President and CEO

BRUCE S. GORDON
President & Chief Executive Officer

JULIAN BOND
Chairman, Board of Directors

December 1, 2005

Greetings:

Congratulations to TIYM Publishing on it 6th *Annual African American Yearbook.*

This unique guide of resource information on business, health, education, and other opportunities for and about the African American community is a most worthwhile and useful publication that is distributed to corporations, businesses and the national government.

The National Association for the Advancement of Colored People (NAACP), as the largest and oldest civil rights advocacy organization in the nation, thanks you for providing copies to our National Convention delegates and visitors and our units across the country.

We wish you continued success in your endeavor.

Sincerely,

Bruce S. Gordon
President & CEO

/sah

Interview

BARACK OBAMA

UNITED STATES SENATOR FOR ILLINOIS

Senator Barack Obama has dedicated his life to public service as a community organizer, civil rights attorney, and leader in the Illinois state Senate. Obama now continues his fight for working families following his recent election to the United States Senate.

Sworn into office January 4, 2005, Senator Obama is focused on promoting economic growth and bringing good paying jobs to Illinois. Obama serves on the important Environment and Public Works Committee, which oversees legislation and funding for the environment and public works projects throughout the country, including the national transportation bill. He also serves on the Veterans ' Affairs Committee where he is focused on investigating the disability pay discrepancies that have left thousands of Illinois veterans without the benefits they earned. Senator Obama will also serve on the Foreign Relations Committee.

During his seven years in the Illinois state Senate, Obama worked with both Democrats and Republicans to help working families get ahead by creating programs like the state Earned Income Tax Credit, which in three years provided over $100 million in tax cuts to families across the state. Obama also pushed through an expansion of early childhood education, and after a number of inmates on death row were found innocent, Senator Obama enlisted the support of law enforcement officials to draft legislation requiring the videotaping of interrogations and confessions in all capital cases.

Obama is especially proud of being a husband and father of two daughters, Malia, 7 and Sasha, 4. Obama and his wife, Michelle, married in 1992 and live on Chicago 's South Side where they attend Trinity United Church of Christ.

Barack Obama was born on August 4th, 1961, in Hawaii to Barack Obama, Sr. and Ann Dunham. Obama graduated from Columbia University in 1983, and moved to Chicago in 1985 to work for a church-based group seeking to improve living conditions in poor neighborhoods plagued with crime and high unemployment. In 1991, Obama graduated from Harvard Law School where he was the first African American editor of the Harvard Law Review.

AAY: In your opinion what are the major issues facing the African American community?

Obama Obviously we have a variety of issues that we confront. The single issue that I think has the most important long term impact is boosting our educational achievement. Ultimately, many of the problems that we face — whether it's the problem of incarceration, substandard housing, inadequate health care — flows from the fact that too many of us aren't participating in the mainstream economy. Unfortunately, there are a majority of African Americans that don't have good jobs that pay decent wages, and in today's economy the best way of assuring that you are in that mainstream is to have a good educational base. Too many of our kids just don't have that.

AAY: As the only African American member of the US Senate, do you feel that you have a responsibility that you have to live up to, [in terms of] expectations from the African American community?

Obama Obviously my first job is to represent the state of Illinois and the people of Illinois, whether black, white, Hispanic or Asian. But I don't shy away from serving as one of many African American leaders who can help highlight some of the specific issues that we face as a community.

AAY: You continually emphasize the importance of cohesive unity rather than stress differences such as race and political affiliation. Why is it vital for Americans to understand the common denominator within us? What do you feel is that common denominator?

Obama I stress unity because it's good politics and also because I think it's genuinely what I believe. I think that all of us as Americans share certain core values. I don't care if you go to the inner city, or to a farm somewhere in downstate Illinois, you'll hear the same things. People want honesty, hard work, discipline, upward mobility. There are a set of values that we share that transcend whatever immediate differences we may have. I also think it's just necessary in terms of politics. We are not going to be able to move a major healthcare initiative forward in this country if it's only going to benefit black people, or if it's only going to benefit Hispanic people. It has to be a program that benefits all people, otherwise we're just not going to be able to round up the votes.

AAY: How do you propose getting African American youth more involved in politics and public service? What needs to be done to increase voter registration among African Americans?

Obama The problem today is not so much voter registration. I've worked on those issues for a long time. The problem is actually getting people to turn out to vote and also getting people engaged and interested in politics in between elections

so that they can hold their elected officials accountable. And I think young people can serve as a critical component to that. The main way to get young people involved in politics and public service is to make it relevant to their lives. Talk about the issues that they face in terms of trying to get an education, trying to pay for an education, trying to get a foothold in the economy. Speaking to the issues that they're dealing with on a day-in, day-out basis and giving them opportunities for real responsibility. A lot of times young people aren't interested in getting involved in politics because the only possibilities that are given to them are going and fetching things as opposed to taking in their ideas and their insights about what needs to happen.

AAY: What role will the African American community play in shaping the direction of the country?

Obama The African American community has always been at the forefront of insisting that America lives up to its creed, and I don't see that changing.

AAY: What has been your greatest accomplishment, and what would you like your legacy to be?

Obama It's too early for me to talk about legacies or accomplishments at this point. I've only been in office a year. I'm proud that I have so far, at least, represented my constituents in a way that I think brings honor to the office.

The State of the Community: A Republican's Perspective

Written by:

JENNIFER CARROLL

Jennifer Carroll won election to the Florida State House of Representatives in 2003 and was reelected without opposition in 2004. She is the first African-American female Republican ever to be elected to the Florida Legislature. Representative Carroll is the Vice-Chair of the Ethics and Elections Committee and Majority Whip.

During the 2004 Legislative Session, Jennifer was able to pass meaningful legislation that protects members of Neighborhood Crime Watch Programs from harassment and intimidation. She also sponsored the "Live the Dream" specialty license plate, which pays tribute to Dr. Martin Luther King, Jr., by using his likeness.

Jennifer is the former Executive Director of the Florida Department of Veterans' Affairs. She was responsible for the claims and benefits of over 1.8 million veterans. She was also the Chairperson for Florida's Council on Homelessness.

Jennifer holds a Bachelor's Degree in Political Science from the University of New Mexico and an Honorary Doctorate Degree from Florida Metropolitan University.

Jennifer enlisted in the Navy in 1979, and rose through the ranks from an enlisted Jet Mechanic to retire as a highly decorated Lieutenant Commander Aviation Maintenance Officer after 20 years of service.

In May 2004, Jennifer was appointed to the Veterans' Disability Benefits Commission by President Bush, which she currently serves.

Jennifer resides in Clay County and is married to Nolan Carroll. They have three children.

The Republican Party is delivering for the African American community on issue after issue. While Democrats have spent decades taking our votes for granted, the GOP is dedicated toward addressing the concerns at the heart of our community. Republicans will continue to work hard to present African Americans with a clear choice if only we give the GOP a chance.

President Bush's ambitious homeownership agenda has enabled more Americans to own a piece of the American Dream than ever before. Homeownership is important because it is such an essential step on the path to success in our nation. Three years ago, the President unveiled his goal of 5.5 million more minority homeowners by the end of the decade. We are now more than halfway to meeting that goal, with 2.3 million new minority households.

Homeownership is not the only area where President Bush supports our community's values and aspirations. Ever since his time as Governor of Texas, the President has worked hard to promote the faith-based initiatives that are the essence of compassionate conservatism.

The basic philosophy behind the President's faith-based initiative is that having a cross or other religious symbol on the wall should not prevent an organization from receiving government funding. The government's complicated rules and regulations that put these organizations at a disadvantage are an unfortunate roadblock, and the Administration is working to enable these groups to compete with others for government funding. Religious organizations shouldn't be given an upper hand in receiving this funding, but they deserve an equal playing field.

President Bush is also leveling the playing field when it comes to education, fulfilling his promise to end the soft bigotry of low expectations and ensure no child is left behind. Recently released data shows No Child Left Behind (NCLB) is fulfilling its goal of holding students and teachers accountable. Known as the "Nation's Report Card," the National Assessment of Education Progress (NAEP) is a clear standard for judging NCLB's progress, and this year's report shows the achievement gap between white and African American nine-year olds is the smallest in the history of the testing. African American nine year olds have seen their reading scores increase 14 points and math scores

increase 13 points in the past five years.

Historically Black Colleges and Universities (HBCUs) are another area where the Bush Administration is making real progress. The President's 2006 budget requested nearly $300 million for HBCUs. This record level of funding represents a 30 percent spending increase since the President took office.

Some saw Hurricane Katrina as demonstrating what is wrong with America but President Bush is determined to make Katrina an example of what is right with our nation by spearheading an aggressive response to rebuild New Orleans. The President is leading a comprehensive effort to revitalize one of America's great cities.

The first priority is making sure that those affected by Hurricane Katrina receive the care and attention they need in rebuilding their lives. More than half a million evacuated families received financial help from the federal government to purchase essential items. Congress has allocated more than $60 billion for these efforts. Nobody can imagine America without New Orleans, and the Bush administration has launched an incredibly broad effort in rebuilding the Gulf Coast and caring for the storm's victims. From rebuilding the levies to rebuilding the lives of those impacted by Katrina, we will not relent until the job is done and we will never again allow America to be unable to respond immediately to citizens in need.

The federal government will ensure that minority-owned businesses play a major role in a revitalized New Orleans. The President's pro-growth agenda has worked to lower taxes and reduce the burdens that excessive

regulations and frivolous lawsuits place on small businesses. Minority businesses in New Orleans and across the country are benefiting from the President's economic policies.

The devastation caused by Hurricane Katrina is not the only challenge facing our community. As with the rebuilding in the aftermath of Katrina, there is hope when it comes to stopping the AIDS pandemic. AIDS is crippling sub-Sahara Africa, and the Bush Administration is making every effort to stem the disease's tide. After committing $15 billion to fight AIDS, the President's dedication to combating the disease remains strong, and his Administration is committed to providing much needed drugs and education across the continent.

2005 has been a remarkable year for the relationship between Republicans and the African American community. 2006 will see President Bush continue to fulfill the promises he has made regarding homeownership, faith-based initiatives, education, economic development, and Hurricane recovery, as well as combating AIDS across the globe. The 'Party of Lincoln' will continue presenting African Americans with a clear choice in the coming year and simply ask that we give them a chance.

AFRICAN AMERICAN
Population

FIG 1. Black or African American Population: 2004

In 2004, the population of those people who identified themselves as being African American (either alone or in combination with another race) was 36.6 million or 12.8 percent of the total population.

Source: U.S. Census Bureau, 2004 American Community Survey

Race	Number	Percent of total population
Total Population	**285,691,501**	**100**
Black or African American alone or in combination with one or more races	36,597,015	12.8
Black or African American alone	34,772,381	12.2
Black or African American in combination with one or more other races	1,824,634	0.6
Black or African American; White	1,141,232	0.4
Black or African American; American Indian and Alaska Native	204,832	0.1
All other combinations including Black or African American	478,570	0.2
Not Black or African American alone or in combination with one or more other races	249,094,486	87.2

FIG 2. Projected Population Change in the United States, by Race and Hispanic Origin: 2000 to 2050 (In thousands except as indicated. As of July 1. Resident population.)

By 2050, the African American population is expected to grow by 25.5 million people — a 71 percent increase. During that same time period, however, the rate of growth will decline from 12.9 percent to 9.8 percent.

[1] Includes American Indian and Alaska Native alone, Native Hawaiian and Other Pacific Islander alone, and Two or More Races.

Source: U.S. Census Bureau, 2004, "U.S. Interim Projections by Age, Sex, Race, and Hispanic Origin, Internet Release Date: March 18, 2004

POPULATION IN THOUSANDS	2000-2010	2010-2020	2020-2030	2030-2040	2040-2050
NUMERICAL CHANGE TOTAL	**26,811**	**26,869**	**27,779**	**28,362**	**27,908**
White alone	16,447	15,634	15,102	13,959	12,936
Black alone	**4,636**	**4,911**	**5,077**	**5,434**	**5,485**
Asian alone	3,557	3,747	4,592	5,412	5,438
All other races [1]	2,171	2,576	3,009	3,557	4,049
Hispanic (of any race)	12,134	12,000	13,299	14,530	14,975
White alone, not Hispanic	5,383	4,824	3,240	1,155	-48
PERCENT CHANGE TOTAL	**9.5**	**8.7**	**8.3**	**7.8**	**7.1**
White alone	7.2	6.4	5.8	5.1	4.5
Black alone	**12.9**	**12.1**	**11.2**	**10.8**	**9.8**
Asian alone	33.3	26.3	25.5	24.0	19.4
All other races [1]	30.7	27.9	25.5	24.0	22.0
Hispanic (of any race)	34.1	25.1	22.3	19.9	17.1
White alone, not Hispanic	2.8	2.4	1.6	0.6	0.0

FIG 3. Population by Selected Age, and Race Groups: 2003

African Americans are young compared to non-Hispanic Whites, although still older on average than the Hispanic population. The percentage of African Americans under 18 was 30.6 in 2003, a slight decrease from the previous year.

Source: U.S. Census Bureau, Statistical Abstract of the United States, 2004-2005

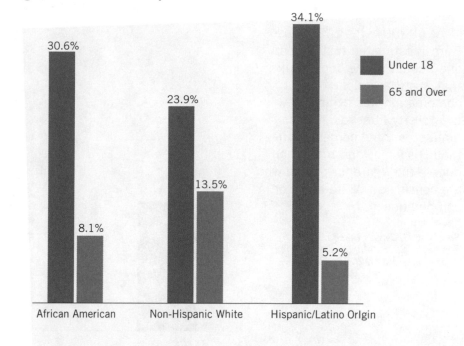

FIG 4. Family and Nonfamily Household Type by Race and Hispanic Origin of Householder (Numbers in thousands)

According to the U.S. Census Bureau, Black families had a far higher percentage (52%) of single parent families than other racial or ethnic groups. Of those single parent homes, over 43 percent were single mothers, more than twice as high as any other group in the sample.

[1] *Hispanic refers to people whose origin is Mexican, Puerto Rican, Cuban, South or Central American, or other Hispanic/Latino origin, regardless of race.*

[2] *The data in this table do not include families in group quarters.*

Source: U.S. Census Bureau, Current Population Survey, March 2002, Racial Statistics Branch, Population Division

| Family and nonfamily household type | Total Population | | Race and Hispanic Origin[1] | | | | | |
| | | | Black | | Hispanic Origin | | Other | |
	Number	Percent	Number	Percent	Number	Percent	Number	Percent
Family households/Total[2]	74,329	100.0	8,844	100.0	53,619	100.0	11,865	100.0
Married-couple families	56,747	76.3	4,233	47.9	44,117	82.3	8,397	70.8
Male householder	4,438	6.0	773	8.7	2,618	4.9	1,047	8.8
Female householder	13,143	17.7	3,838	43.4	6,884	12.8	2,422	20.4
Nonfamily households Total	34,969	100.0	4,470	100.0	27,200	100.0	3,299	100.0
Male householder	15,579	44.6	1,903	42.6	11,861	43.6	1,814	55.0
Female householder	19,390	55.4	2,567	57.4	15,338	56.4	1,484	45.0

FIG 5. Percentage of Population Below Poverty Level by Race/Ethnicity: 2004

As of 2004, the U.S. Census Bureau estimated that almost one-quarter of the population that was Black alone or in combination was living below the poverty threshold. This number is three percent higher than Hispanics and more than double the figure for people who are considered White alone or in combination.

Source: U.S. Census Bureau, Current Population Survey, Annual Demographic Supplement, March 2004

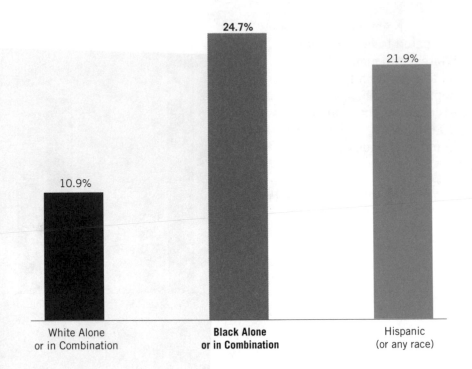

FIG 6. U.S. States with African American Population Greater than 25 Percent: 2004

In 2004, African Americans comprised 25 percent or more of the population in six U.S. states.

Source: U.S. Census Bureau, Population Estimates 2004

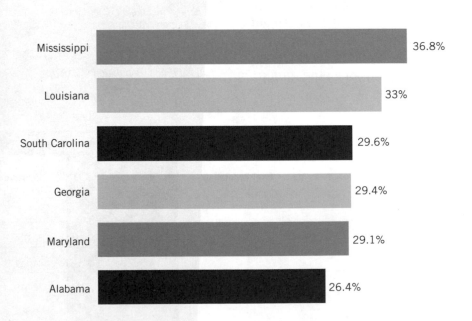

FIG 7a. Region of Residence by Race: 2004

The majority of African Americans (60.4%) resided in the South in 2004, followed by the Midwest (20.6%).

Source: U.S. Census Bureau, Population Estimates, 2004

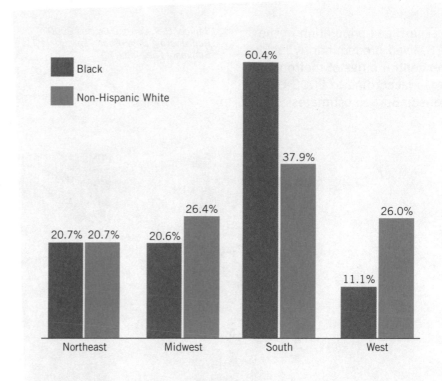

FIG 7b. Rate of Population Growth by Region and Race: 2000-2004

Although the majority lived in the South in 2004 (see previous figure), the West had the fastest growing African American population.

Source: U.S. Census Bureau, Population Estimates, 2004

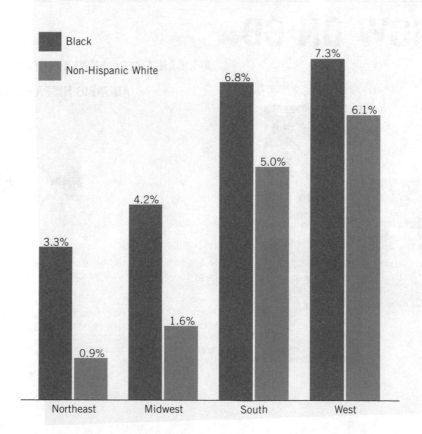

FIG 8. Metropolitan and Nonmetropolitan Residence by Race: 2002
(Percent distribution of population)

The Black population in the U.S. lived predominantly inside the central cities of metropolitan areas, according to 2002 U.S. Census Bureau estimates.

Source: U.S. Census, Census 2000 Redistricting Data (Public Law 94-171) Summary File, Table PL1

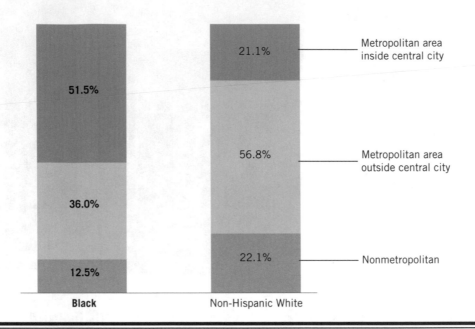

Black
- 51.5%
- 36.0%
- 12.5%

Non-Hispanic White
- 21.1% — Metropolitan area inside central city
- 56.8% — Metropolitan area outside central city
- 22.1% — Nonmetropolitan

Environmental Justice

Environmental Justice is the fair treatment and meaningful involvement of all people regardless of race, color, national origin, or income with respect to the development, implementation, and enforcement of environmental laws, regulations, and policies. Fair treatment means that racial, ethnic or socioeconomic groups should not bear a disproportionate share of negative environmental consequences resulting from the execution of Federal, state, local and tribal programs and policies. Environmental justice is not an outcome but a process. Communities fostering meaningful and knowing participation in environmental decisions that affect their children, homes, health and jobs successfully achieve environmental justice. The Department of Energy (DOE) has made Environmental Justice an integral part of doing business. Community and public involvement in decision-making provides for more reasonable and just outcomes. Here are a number of examples of Environmental Justice in action at DOE.

On November 17, 2005, DOE and the National Small Town Alliance conducted a symposium to examine the ways Hurricanes Katrina and Rita impacted environmental justice and economic development efforts in small towns in the southeast. Small town mayors and community representatives from Mississippi, Alabama, North Carolina and Oklahoma joined Federal representatives from DOE, the Environmental Protection Agency, the United States Department of Agriculture, academic institutions, and the private sector for the discussion. The mayors and other representatives gave accounts of inadequate responses from Federal agencies with response requirements. There were accounts of little or no communication, little or no directions and a reluctance to accept local knowledge recommendations. One of the positives from the discussion was the fact that computers distributed in small towns through DOE's environmental justice project were placed in evacuee shelters. In some cases, the computers were the only ones available to the evacuees. The evacuees were able to use computers to learn about their benefits and communicate with family and agencies.

DOE partnered with the Congressional Black Caucus (CBC) to support "Listening Sessions" which allowed members of the CBC to take public comment that were used to develop forward-thinking, comprehensive environmental and health policies that recognize and foster the unique relationship between environmental protection, human health, environmental justice and economic development. Listening Sessions were held in various locations throughout the U.S. and the Virgin Islands.

As a member of the Federal Interagency Working Group on Environmental Justice (IWG), DOE collaborates with other Federal agencies to coordinate Federal environmental justice efforts and develop a dialogue and strategy for future environmental justice projects in communities around Federal sites. These agencies have joined forces to promote collaboration among stakeholders in environmentally and economically disadvantaged communities - rural, urban and Tribal - to achieve integrated solutions that result in environmental improvements, economic development, and neighborhood revitalization.

DOE is also participating in 'Tribal Wind Power – A Viable Strategy for Community Revitalization and Capacity in the Northern Great Plains." DOE has partnered with other Federal Agencies and the Intertribal Council on Utility Policy (ICOUP), a confederation of Federally recognized tribes in the Northern Great Plains, to demonstrate that the development of wind energy can be a viable strategy to provide for future economic, cultural, and community revitalization through development of sustainable homeland tribal economies.

DOE has taken a lead role in the IWG & Environmental Justice Training Collaborative. This generic Environmental Justice training was developed for all agencies and private sector use.

DOE entered into a cooperative agreement with the National Small Town Alliance to build capacity for energy and environmental planning and for monitoring and responding to energy and environmental issues in small towns and rural areas across America. The program utilizes computer-based technology, Internet access, training and formal relationships with the Dr. Samuel P. Massie Chairs of Excellence and Historically Black Colleges and Universities (HBCUs) as sources of technical assistance and guidance.

DOE developed a community capacity-building project in partnership with Howard University in Washington, DC, to provide disadvantaged citizens with access to computers and the Internet. By creating community technology centers and providing excess DOE computers, this project offers citizens the opportunity to explore environmental cleanup information and obtain technical assistance using internet-based sources and computer-based information and models.

Another activity initiated through the Howard University partnership involves working with HBCUs and other environmental professionals to ensure community stakeholders receive the best technical assistance available. The HBCUs provide technical assistance online and in person through conferences, workshops and direct one-to-one interaction. This puts stakeholders in a position to make positive contributions to environmental decisions, and to make sure that environmental decisions are made in the best interests of the community.

DOE has expanded the community capacity building partnership with Tennessee State University to provide technical assistance to the communities around DOE facilities in Oak Ridge (Scarboro Community) and the Savannah River Site (Augusta and Savannah, Georgia). The partnership with Tennessee State University has enabled these communities to build community centers that provide access to computers, the Internet, training and technical assistance in order to expand and develop capacity to participate in environmental decision-making.

Taken together, DOE and partners have distributed more than 3,000 computers to small towns, limited resource farmers and community groups across America.

Another DOE community capacity building partner is the Medical University of South Carolina, which has convened Community Leaders' Institutes to introduce small, rural and minority community leaders to resources and information that will help them address environmental and other issues in their communities. Community Leaders' Institutes have been held in South Carolina towns for communities near the Savannah River Site.

Academic Institutions, Communities and Agencies Network (ACA-Net) is a collaborative approach involving communities, academia and government that helps develop the capacity of environmentally impacted communities to solve environmental problems through education and technical assistance. In addition to promoting dialogue among all stakeholders, ACA-Net helps communities respond to both short- and long-term environmental problems by using specially designed response teams with expertise drawn from academic institutions.

The Dr. Samuel P. Massie Chairs of Excellence are a team of world-class scholars, researchers and educators from nine Historically Black Colleges and Universities and one Hispanic-Serving Institution who conduct research; provide advice and assistance to municipalities; mentor young scientists and serve as role models for students; and promote collaboration among Federal agencies, the private sector, research institutions, and other HBCUs. The Massie Chairs are a key element in DOE's community capacity building efforts and support projects.

DOE and the United Negro College Fund have entered into a Memorandum of Agreement that builds upon Historically Black Colleges and Universities (HBCUs) and Minority Institutions (MIs) efforts in the fields of environment, life sciences, computing, and engineering. A total of 40 students in the MES Internship Program will receive internships during their undergraduate study and will spend 10-12 weeks interning at a DOE national laboratory or facility. Each scholar is partnered with a laboratory or facility scientist to assist/mentor the student in his or her distinctly designed research project.

DOE believes in and supports Environmental Justice.

Melinda Downing is DOE's Environmental Justice Program Manager. She can be reached at (202) 586-7703 or Melinda.Downing@hq.doe.gov.

ANTHONY A. WILLIAMS

MAYOR OF THE DISTRICT OF COLUMBIA

Anthony A. Williams began serving as the fourth Mayor of the District of Columbia on January 4, 1999, twenty five years after the city was granted Home Rule in 1974. On January 2, 2003, Mayor Williams was inaugurated and began serving his second term in office. His second term extends through December 2006. During his first term in office, Mayor Williams and his administration have consistently produced a balanced budget, while generating economic stability and affordable housing. One of the cornerstones of Mayor Williams' tenure has been creating a friendly government that listens to citizens through town hall meetings and citizen summits. During his second term, the Mayor has set education, public safety, and expanding opportunities for all the District's citizens as his top priorities.

Born on July 28, 1951, in Los Angeles, California, Anthony Williams is the adopted son of Virginia and the late Lewis Williams, and is one of eight children. He graduated magna cum laude with a Bachelor of Arts in Political Science from Yale College, earned a Juris Doctorate from Harvard Law and a master's degree in Public Policy from the Kennedy School of Government at Harvard University.

AAY In your opinion, what is the key issue or area of concern for the majority of African Americans residing in Washington, D.C.? What initiatives have you taken to ensure the needs of the African American community are being addressed?

Williams The District is a densely urban population with many vital social services needs—from affordable housing to health and human services. The majority of our city is African American, and the city government works hard to ensure that the needs of that community are addressed. While we are making tremendous progress in our city, too many people –yes, many of them African American— have not fully reaped the progress of the last six years. They are still going to crumbling schools, still surrounded by the twin tragedies of poverty and violence, still without a place to live or work. This year, we are launching our New Communities Initiative to transform our most distressed neighborhoods and help citizens begin new lives. We're not talking about a few more dollars here or there. We are not just talking about bricks and mortar. It is truly an innovative and holistic approach to creating healthier neighborhoods across our city.

AAY There are 326,910 African Americans living in the District of Columbia, which constitutes 58% of the city's total population. Of the 58%, 33% live in poverty, according to Urban Institute and the Kaiser Commission on Medicaid and the Uninsured. What is being done to address this problem?

Williams Our poorest residents are certainly our city's homeless. So I have a ten-year plan, called Homeless No More. This year alone, I am investing $20 million in new funds to provide shelter for those who need it, subsidized housing,

Mayor Williams helps new homeowner Mila Hernandez cut the ribbon on her new redeveloped house which is part of the District's Home Again Initiative.

Mayor Williams plays a short game of baseball during the *22nd Annual National Night Out* against crime in August 2005.

and preventative services –from substance abuse to mental health treatment. When it comes to jobs for our neediest residents, the good news is that as our country lost jobs over the past six years, our city created them. The bad news is, as unemployment decreased nationwide, it rose in the District from 7% to 8%. But that is only an average. In some neighborhoods, as many as 30% of residents are unemployed. In September we did receive some positive news that unemployment decreased in our city in recent months. Either way, we must continue to find new and innovative ways to put residents to work and I have full confidence in Gregg Irish, Director of our city's Department of Employment Services.

AAY There is a deadly AIDS epidemic among African Americans. African Americans represent about half of the over one million people living with HIV in the U.S., even though African Americans make up only 12% of the country's population. In the nation's Capital, the numbers are even more staggering. African Americans

constitute 76.7 % of all AIDS cases in D.C., according to the Centers for Disease Control and Prevention. How do you propose tackling the AIDS epidemic on a local and national level?

Williams On a local level, our city's HIV/AIDS Administration (HAA) partners with health and community-based organizations to provide HIV/AIDS prevention and care services to District residents. Services include medical support, HIV counseling and testing, data and information on HIV/AIDS programs and services as well as on the impact of HIV/AIDS on the community, education, information, referrals, and intervention services. A drug assistance program (ADAP) provides drugs at no cost to eligible District residents who are HIV positive or have AIDS. HAA administers the District's budget for HIV/AIDS programs, provides grants to service providers, monitors programs, and tracks the incidence of HIV and AIDS in the District of Columbia. In September, I named Marsha Martin as the new director of the HIV/AIDS Administration. She brings with her a wealth of knowledge and

Mayor Williams speaks at the District's Home Again Initiative.

AAY As Mayor of Washington, D.C., what accomplishment are you most proud of? What would you like your legacy to be?

I believe we have made tremendous progress as a city since I first took office in 1999. We are safer today. The number of police officers in the District has grown to 3,800 and violent crime has gone down in our toughest neighborhoods. We are healthier—24,000 citizens who were once just an illness away from bankruptcy now have the security of health insurance. We are going to college in record numbers. Last year our college attendance jumped 30%—the biggest increase in the

considerable expertise in the field of HIV/AIDS.

AAY You are the Vice Chair of the Metropolitan Washington Council of Governments. What is the objective of this council?

Williams I am pleased to be part of the Metropolitan Washington Council of Governments, known in our region as COG. The Council is made up of nineteen local governments surrounding our city—plus members from the Maryland and Virginia legislatures, the U.S. Senate, and the U.S. House of Representatives. The group is truly a way for our region to find better methods for solving the critical problems that face us—particularly in the realm of homeland security. National tragedies like September 11 and Hurricane Katrina have taught us the great need to work together in order to be prepared for any event that may befall us.

Founded in 1957, COG is an independent, nonprofit association. It is supported by contributions from its participating local governments, federal and state grants and contracts, and donations from foundations and the private sector.

AAY What role will the African American community play in shaping the general direction of our Nation's Capital?

Williams The African American community has played and will play a huge role in shaping the direction of the Nation's Capital. Our city government is made up of some of the finest minds in the African American community—and as long as I am mayor, that will not change. The District of Columbia is steeped in black history. It's always been my stated goal to help our young people learn about that history, while at the same time continuing the traditions that have made us such a strong community.

"The District of Columbia is steeped in black history. It's always been my stated goal to help our young people learn about that history, while at the same time continuing the traditions that have made us such a strong community."

U.S. We are becoming the place to live: Last year, *Black Enterprise* magazine rated Washington, D.C. the second best city for African Americans in the entire country. We are more prosperous and have a more efficient government. We have a double A grade investment rating from Wall Street for the first time in fifteen years, a $1.2 billion rainy-day fund, and only better fiscal news on the horizon. We should all be proud of the District of Columbia. We are strong. And we are only getting better.

Politics

FIG 1. Reasons for Not Voting by Race/Ethnicity: 2004 (Percent distribution)

Reported voting problems and reasons for not voting in the 2004 elections varied significantly among racial and ethnic groups. One noteworthy difference in the Black community versus other groups was the difficulty associated with finding transportation to the polls. People who identified themselves as Black alone or in combination were more than twice as likely than any other group to have trouble getting to voting stations.

Source: U.S. Census Bureau Population Survey, November 2004

Reason	Total	Illness or disability	Out of town	Registration problems	Not interested	Did not like candidates or campaign issues	Transportation problems	Don't know or refused
TOTAL	**16,334**	**15.4**	**9.0**	**6.8**	**10.7**	**9.9**	**2.1**	**8.5**
Race and Hispanic origin								
White alone	13,341	15.6	9.4	6.8	10.8	10.6	1.9	7.9
White non-Hispanic alone	11,752	16.2	9.9	6.2	10.8	11.1	1.9	7.6
White alone or in combination	13,597	15.5	9.4	6.8	10.8	10.7	1.8	7.9
White non-Hispanic alone	11,977	16.1	9.9	6.2	10.8	11.2	1.9	7.7
Black alone	**2,019**	**16.5**	**5.5**	**7.2**	**10.0**	**6.4**	**4.2**	**13.0**
Black alone or in combination	**2,084**	**16.5**	**5.9**	**7.3**	**9.9**	**6.6**	**4.1**	**12.9**
Asian alone or in combination	528	7.2	10.5	5.7	7.7	5.4	1.2	9.1
Asian alone	479	6.1	11.6	6.1	7.9	4.4	1.3	9.0
Hispanic (of any race)	1,721	10.7	6.3	10.9	10.5	7.3	1.6	9.8

FIG 2. Reported Voting and Registration by Citizenship, Race and Hispanic Origin: November 2000 and 2004 (Numbers in thousands)

All voting measurements increased for the Black community from 2000 to 2004, including registrations and actual voting. Among non-Whites, Blacks had by far the highest percentage of citizens registered. This same category also saw a higher increase

for Blacks than any other non-White group, from 56.8 percent in 2000 to 60 percent in 2004. Among any group, including Whites, the Black population also experienced the highest increase in the percentage of registered voters actually voting.

[1] This figure added to or subtracted from the estimate provides the 90-percent confidence interval

Source: U.S. Census Bureau, Current Population Survey, November 2004 and 2000

Characteristic	Total population				Citizens				Registered	
	Total	Citizen	Reported registered	Reported voted	Percent reported registered	Margin of error[1]	Percent reported voted	Margin of error[1]	Percent reported voted	Margin of error[1]
2004										
Total, 18 years and over	215,694	197,005	142,070	125,736	72.1%	0.3	63.8%	0.3	88.5%	0.3
Race and Hispanic origin										
White	176,618	162,958	119,929	106,588	73.6%	0.2	65.4%	0.3	88.9%	0.3
White non-Hispanic	151,410	148,159	111,318	99,567	75.1%	0.1	67.2%	0.3	89.4%	0.3
Black	**24,910**	**23,346**	**16,035**	**14,016**	**68.7%**	**0.5**	**60.0%**	**1**	**87.4%**	**1.1**
Asian and Pacific Islander	9,291	6,270	3,247	2,768	51.8%	1.7	44.1%	1.8	85.2%	1.7
Hispanic (of any race)	27,129	16,088	9,308	7,587	57.9%	1.3	47.2%	1.3	81.5%	1.2
2000										
Total, 18 years and over	202,609	186,366	129,549	110,826	69.5%	0.3	59.5	0.3	85.5	0.3
Race and Hispanic origin										
White	168,733	157,291	110,773	95,098	70.4%	0.3	60.5	0.4	85.8	0.3
White non-Hispanic	148,035	144,732	103,588	89,469	71.6%	0.4	61.8	0.4	86.4	0.3
Black	**24,132**	**22,753**	**15,348**	**12,917**	**67.5%**	**1.1**	**56.8**	**1.2**	**84.2**	**1.1**
Asian and Pacific Islander	8,041	4,718	2,470	2,045	52.4%	2.7	43.3	2.7	82.8	2.9
Hispanic (of any race)	21,598	13,158	7,546	5,934	57.3%	2.0	45.1	2.0	78.6	2.2

FIG 3. Top Ten States for Black Voter Turnout as a Percentage of Total Registered: 2004

Some of the states that were responsible for the increases in Black voter turnout (see Fig. 2) can be seen in Figure 3. Missouri had the highest rate with 74.7 percent, followed by Kentucky and Wisconsin.

Source: U.S. Census Bureau, Current population survey, November 2004

Missouri	74.7%
Kentucky	68.5%
Wisconsin	68.1%
Illinois	66.9%
Mississippi	66.8%
Ohio	65.5%
Minnesota	64.7%
Alabama	63.9%
North Carolina	63.1%
Michigan	62.6%

Coast Guard Response to Hurricane Katrina

By U.S. Coast Guard

In August 2005, a huge Category 5 storm was bearing down on the Gulf Coast of the U.S. By Aug 29, Hurricane Katrina, struck land as a powerful Category 4 hurricane, resulting in perhaps the worst natural disaster in American history. True to its motto, Semper Paratus–Always Ready, the United States Coast Guard responded quickly, decisively and professionally to the devastating impacts of the storm. As one of the nation's five military services, the United States Coast Guard has the unique capability, capacity and authority that allow it to play a critical role in disaster response. The Coast Guard is a first responder, one of very few federal first responders and the only national maritime first responder.

Despite having two critical Air Stations in the area severely damaged by the storm, the U.S. Coast Guard made the first rescue only six hours after the Hurricane made landfall. In the next seven days, the Coast Guard would rescue seven times the number of people it normally does in one year. Working around the clock, dedicated Coast Guard personnel tirelessly prevailed thru such adverse conditions as the lack of power, running water, and air conditioning, and worked long arduous days. By Sept. 11, 2005, the Coast Guard rescued more than 24,000 people, roughly half by helicopter and half by boat, and assisted with the joint-agency evacuation of an additional 9,462 patients and medical personnel from hospitals in the Gulf Coast region. As a result of the Coast Guard's quick response, dedication and professionalism,

more than 33,735 lives were saved or evacuated. That's more in two weeks than is normally handled in six years.

Most of the helicopter hoist rescues were completed in obstacle-strewn environments, often in conditions of reduced visibility with the pilots wearing night vision goggles, over dangerous power lines and downed trees with outside temperatures near 100 degrees. Coast Guard rescue swimmers, an important member of the helicopter crew, had to contend with flooded houses, steep slippery roofs, foul and contaminated water, and at times even had to cut through roofs to free survivors.

At the height of rescue operations, the Coast Guard had at least 62 aircraft, 30 cutters, 111

small boats, 5,290 active duty personnel and 400 reservists from all over the Coast Guard performing rescue and recover operations. Approximately one-third of the Coast Guard's entire air fleet was deployed to the region to support rescue operations in the immediate aftermath of the storm.

The storm also caused widespread environmental damage. Katrina impacted 6,400 miles of shoreline. The Coast Guard responded to 1,380 Aids to Navigation discrepancies, handled 3,806 pollution cases, including seven major pollution incidents, and catalogued 2,500 salvage cases with more than 500 grounded vessels and numerous offshore structures that were adrift, damaged, or sunk.

In the case of Hurricane Katrina, the unique capability and capacity of the Coast Guard allowed the service to play a critical role in disaster response. "Coast Guard forces have several key strengths that allow a quick and effective response to natural disasters. That strength begins with our people whose dedication to response and adaptability to changing circumstances never ceases to fill me with pride and admiration," said Admiral Thomas H. Collins, Commandant of the Coast Guard. When asked by Senate Committee on Homeland Security and Governmental Affairs on how the Coast Guard was so effective at its response, Rear Admiral Robert F. Duncan, Commander, Eighth Coast Guard District stated, "We routinely delegate authority to qualified people at the lowest possible level because it facilitates rapid response and maximizes effectiveness in dynamic environments. Coast Guard personnel are trained, almost from the day they come aboard, to use Coast Guard doctrine and regulations, an institutionalized operational risk management process, and their own professional and personal experience to make appropriate decisions at the scene of the operation." The leadership of the Coast Guard was never more visible than when Department of Homeland Security Secretary Michael Chertoff designated Vice Admiral Thad Allen, Coast Guard Chief of Staff, as the Principal Federal Official for rescue and recovery operations within the region.

Coast Guard personnel are diverse heroes who make up our American community. They are your neighbors who save lives and protect our homeland. They make extraordinary things look ordinary every day.

The United States Coast Guard is America's Shield of Freedom. They are always there and they are ALWAYS READY–Semper Paratus.

Interview

CLAUDE ALLEN

ASSISTANT TO THE PRESIDENT FOR DOMESTIC POLICY

Claude A. Allen currently serves as the Assistant to the President for Domestic Policy, in which capacity he advises the President on all domestic, non-economic issues. The Domestic Policy Council handles topics that range from health care to education and job training to space and veterans affairs and is one of the lead White House offices in promoting the President's second-term agenda.

Allen previously served as the Deputy Secretary for the Department of Health and Human Services. As Deputy Secretary, Allen worked closely with the Secretary on all major policy and management issues, and he served as the department's chief operating officer.

Prior to joining HHS, Allen was Secretary of Health and Human Resources for the Commonwealth of Virginia from 1997 - 2001, leading 13 agencies and 15,000 employees. Allen led initiatives for Virginia's Patients Bill of Rights, allowing patient appeals for adverse coverage decisions made by health plans, and direct access to physician specialists. Allen also spearheaded Virginia's welfare reform initiative in the Gilmore Administration and provided leadership to overhaul Virginia's mental health institutions and community services. Additionally, Allen was responsible for implementing Virginia's private health insurance program for children and families, offering lower-cost coverage options to thousands of uninsured Virginians.

Before joining the Gilmore administration, Allen was Counsel to the Attorney General, and later, Deputy Attorney General for the Civil Litigation Division in the Office of the Attorney General, Virginia. He reported directly to then-Attorney General Gilmore on legal, legislative, and policy matters, including all health, education and welfare issues. Before joining the Office of the Attorney General, Allen practiced law in Washington, D.C., specializing in government contracts, litigation, and legislative affairs.

Allen holds both a Juris Doctorate and a Masters of Law in International and Comparative Law from Duke University Law School. He completed his undergraduate education at the University of North Carolina at Chapel Hill, earning degrees in Political Science and Linguistics.

Allen and his wife are the parents of four children.

AAY As the chief domestic advisor, how do your views concerning domestic policies affect the President's decisions?

Allen As Domestic Policy Advisor, my job is to advise the President on all non-economic domestic policy. That covers a wide range of issues: health, education, labor, housing, veterans' issues, Justice Department issues. It covers energy issues, faith-based issues. We also work on drug control policy, HIV/AIDS, and with US Freedom Corps on volunteer issues. My role is to advise the President. So, he takes my advice and weighs that with other White House senior staff to formulate the policies for his administration. My expectation is that the President listens to all of his advisors, and I'm privileged to be one of them.

AAY What issues are of particular concern to the African American community?

Allen I think the issues that we are dealing with today—I'll start with some that really stand out to me, that really have an impact on our communities. Clearly, education is an issue that is very important to the African American community. We have seen in the last national Report Card that was put out on how our kids are doing in the fourth and the eighth grade that African Americans have had the greatest increase in closing the gap between African Americans and the greater white community in terms of reading and math scores. And that's important because we know the future of our community lies in our youth and the future of our youth lies in their ability to read, write, to get jobs, and to be contributing citizens of the United States. So that's a major issue. Additionally, I think housing

issues are very important. Even in a post-Katrina era, we see that one of the major challenges is housing, and yet there's a lot of great news in the housing area. Once again, minority home ownership is up. African Americans—just under about 50 percent of African Americans—own their homes and what that says is that we have a stake in our communities. Other issues that stand out that I think are important on the health front are critical. We need to address the rampant epidemic of HIV/AIDS in our community that is killing so many of our people, both African American men and African American women. And that has a real impact on our future. Other health issues include chronic disease. We need to be focused on having good health, which means addressing prevention issues—that is, living healthy lifestyles, eating well, accessing quality health care, including, for example, the new prescription drug program that rolled out this year for our seniors and the disabled: the Medicare Modernization Act. For the first time, many African American seniors will have a physical examination that can tell them whether they've got diabetes, or whether they're pre-diabetic or hypertensive, and then be able to do something

about it, and be able to afford the prescription drugs. And so these are some of the issues that are very important. Some other areas I'll mention: The family is vitally important to the African American community and the future of our community. And by that I mean we need to be making sure that we have fathers involved with their children. We need to make sure that young people are connected with adults. And this President has really promoted helping America's youth, which is helping our young people avoid risk behaviors that expose them to alcohol, drugs, tobacco, sex, and violence; and helping them to have the tools and the ability to make good decisions with the involvement of adults in their lives—beginning with parents, then going on to coaches, pastors, teachers, and other community leaders. So these are a few of the areas that are very important, and faith-based issues are important as well.

AAY As an African American Republican, how do your views coincide and conflict with a majority of African Americans who are Democrats?

Allen First of all, I don't think it's an issue of partisanship; I think my views are very much in the mainstream of the African American community. We're concerned about education; we're concerned about jobs, the opportunities that are presented to us in order to make a living, concerned about a strong national defense that protects us on the home front. So many of our young men and women are fighting around the world, defending what every American—hopefully every American—believes, and that is that our way of life is protected as we are willing to defend our freedoms abroad in the war theaters. I think my views are very consistent with African Americans'. I think where we may differ, sometimes, is not in the end: it's the means of getting there. I think the President strongly believes, and I strongly believe, that giving people the ability to be self-determining, to be self-sufficient, to be personally responsible, is vitally important for us and the longevity of our community. Others look to the government as the primary source of those decisions, but I think the average American family—African American or otherwise—believes that they want to be able to make choices for themselves, and have the government be a safety net for those who cannot provide for themselves, as again we saw in the post-Katrina situation.

AAY Your reputation as a morally conscious Christian has led some to categorize you as an extreme conservative. What is your view on this? And how would you define yourself in terms of your political and social views?

Allen Well, I think again my views are very consistent with the majority of the African American community. I come out of a strong family and community that believes that faith is a vital element and a key aspect of our lives. And I think if you look at any given Sunday, the vast majority of Americans—African Americans particularly—are in church somewhere. And so my faith, which is important to me personally, had an impact on my life and has provided me with a quality of life that I think most African Americans share. I think in many ways I typically define myself not by political party, but I define myself based on being a person who believes in protecting the rights of individuals, while also promoting the good of our community. And that means very specifically that we need to be seeking justice, fairness, having a system of government that provides individuals opportunities that allowed me—as a young man who grew up here in Washington, DC, in a neighborhood that few people got out of—to one day be able to sit and be the Domestic Policy Advisor to a president. That only happens in America. And so as an African American I'm very grateful

for the opportunities that I've been afforded—not because of my race, but because of my talent and skill—that accrue to the benefit of my people and to my race. It began with education, and education begins with making sure that parents are empowered to make decisions on behalf of their children and for us to be involved with our children. I think the one thing that stands out about education, that comes out of the national Report Card, is that African Americans have begun to do so much better—and Latinos are doing so much better—because of several things. First, it begins in the home. We're finding more and more parents are reading to their children at younger ages. That is so critically important—that we set the example with our kids. But secondly, we are not allowing our school systems to say because you are black, because you are Latino, because you have a disability, we're going to lower the standards for you. The President's No Child Left Behind initiative, supported by Congress, has produced tremendous results that say we will no longer accept the soft-bigotry of low expectations that comes along with suggesting that some people are not able to benefit from a quality education. And so we're pushing for that. Soft-bigotry of low expectations is what our President calls it, and we're not going to have low expectations for any of our kids.

AAY African Americans have statistically lower college graduation rates and lower incomes than whites, according to the U.S. Census Bureau. How do you propose that this administration address these realities, in order to enhance the standard of living for the African American community?

Allen Well, I think a couple of things are very important for us to focus on. First and foremost, interestingly enough there was a time within the very recent past when African Americans had the highest matriculation rate—that is, there were more African Americans per capita going into college than whites. What we've seen happen, though—as we've seen more and more of our young men not engaged and not doing well in school and more and more of them at risk of engaging in violence and therefore being incarcerated—we've actually seen the numbers going down for African American men. And so some of the things that we're focused on are: first of all, reaching young people before they're college-aged, to first of all make sure that they have the tools that they need to succeed. And there again, No Child Left Behind is the key area in making sure that young kids at a very early age are able to read and write. One of the greatest predictors of whether a young person will be able to navigate life successfully is how early they learn to read and write. Then, beyond that, making sure that our schools are accountable to provide an education that does more than simply say at the end of the day, you've graduated, here's your piece of paper; but you can't read, you can't write, you can't apply for a job, you can't fill out a job application. We're going to hold them accountable to equip men and women to be able to compete. Then we are focused on our colleges and universities to make sure that as these young people transition, we are also holding them accountable in the higher education years. Right now, No Child Left Behind focuses on elementary education. We need to have the same rigorous standards for high school so that, for the young man or young woman who graduated from high school, that diploma is more than a piece of paper on the wall that says this is where I went to school. Rather, that young person will be able to compete in a twenty-first-century economy. We have done some things because many African Americans choose to go to Historically Black Colleges and Universities, as many Latinos go to Hispanic-serving institutions. We're making sure that our Historically Black Colleges and Universities are able to recruit and retain low-income students and those from disadvantaged backgrounds who otherwise might not receive a college education. We have provided some $299 million for Historically Black Colleges and Universities, and I think about $96 million for Hispanic-serving institutions. And this is a way of saying we want to make sure that you're connected. And then lastly, making sure that people see the vision before them, that there are jobs available for them to access and compete for when they finish college. One of the other pieces in making sure that young men and women are able to matriculate and graduate is to make sure that they have mentors along the way. Again, the President's Helping America's youth initiative, and our matching up young entrepreneurs with successful businesses and successful businessmen and women is key to ensuring that these young people are able to go to college or start a business and thereby compete effectively.

> "The family is vitally important to the African American community and the future of our community. And by that I mean we need to be making sure that we have fathers involved with their children."

AAY What has been your greatest achievement as chief domestic advisor?

Allen *[laughs]* You have to ask the President that question! My greatest achievement is actually being a part of a team that is able to work on issues that President Bush is passionate about and I'm passionate about too. I have the privilege every day to come to work and to make a difference in the lives of Americans. And that's not something that someone can talk about every day. There are some decisions that I make or some activity I'm involved with that will have an impact on my community as an African American, and to me that's the greatest achievement—that if I can go home at the end of the day after working hard, and I can point to something that accrues to the benefit of my people, then I will say that I've had a good day. That is also when it is consistent with helping the President to fulfill his mission as being the President of all the people—not just those who voted for him, but of all Americans—and to do that well, then I will serve our President well and our country well.

African American Mayors of Big Cities

Name	Municipality	State	Population	% African Americans
John F. Street	Philadelphia	PA	1,517,550	43.2
Kwame Kilpatrick	Detroit	MI	951,270	81.6
Michael B. Coleman	Columbus	OH	711,470	24.5
Willie W. Herenton	Memphis	TN	650,100	61.4
Anthony A. Williams	Washington	DC	572,059	60.0
C. Ray Nagin	New Orleans	LA	484,674	67.3
Shirley Franklin	Atlanta	GA	416,474	61.4
Jack Ford	Toledo	OH	313,619	23.5
Sharpe James	Newark	NJ	273,546	53.5
Bernard Kincaid	Birmingham	AL	242,820	73.5
Glenn D. Cunningham	Jersey City	NJ	240,055	28.3
Melvin Kip Holden	Baton Rouge	LA	227,818	50.0
William A. Johnson	Rochester	NY	219,773	38.5
William E. Ward	Chesapeake	VA	199,184	28.5
Rudolph C. McCollum Jr.	Richmond	VA	197,790	57.2
William V. Bell	Durham	NC	187,035	43.8
Harvey Johnson, Jr.	Jackson	MS	184,256	70.6
Rhine McLin	Dayton	OH	166,179	19.9
Terry Johnson	Oceanside	CA	161,029	7.4
Johns Marks	Tallahassee	FL	150,624	34.2
Mamie E. Locke	Hampton	VA	146,437	44.7
Otis Johnson	Savannah	GA	131,510	57.1
William D. Euille	Alexandria	VA	128,283	22.5
Woodrow Stanley	Flint	MI	124,943	53.3
Marshall B. Pitts, Jr.	Fayetteville	NC	121,015	34.9
Mae J. Jackson	Waco	TX	113,726	22.6
Roosevelt F. Dorn	Inglewood	CA	112,580	47.1
James Holley	Portsmouth	VA	100,565	50.6
Shirley Gibson	Miami Gardens	FL	100,000	90.0
Irma Anderson	Richmond	CA	99,216	9.4
Jack Ellis	Macon	GA	97,255	62.5
Eric Perrodin	Compton	CA	93,493	40.3
Douglas Palmer	Trenton	NJ	85,403	52.1
Gwendolyn A. Faison	Camden	NJ	79,904	53.3
Brenda L. Lawrence	Southfield	MI	78,296	54.2

Note: This list includes US cities with more than 50,000 residents.

Source: National Conference of Black Mayors, Inc. (NCBM). www.ncbm.org.

Name	Municipality	State	Population	% African Americans
Robert Jones	Kalamazoo	MI	77,145	20.6
Willie Adams Jr.	Albany	GA	76,939	64.8
Lorraine Morton	Evanston	IL	74,239	22.5
James M. Baker	Wilmington	DE	72,664	56.4
Robert Bowser	East Orange	NJ	69,824	89.5
Ernest D. Davis	Mount Vernon	NY	68,381	59.6
Willie Payne	Pontiac	MI	66,337	47.9
Wilmer Jones-Ham	Saginaw	MI	61,799	43.3
Wayne Smith	Irvington	NJ	60,695	81.7
Josaphat "Joe" Celestin	North Miami	FL	59,880	54.9
Carl Redus	Pine Bluff	AR	55,085	65.9
James Mayo	Monroe	LA	53,107	61.1

The 14 users currently in the teen chat room.

good2hug:	14, female, Daytona, FL
joey16:	16, male, Hackensack, NJ
robbieW:	38, male, Daytona, FL
b-ball_tommy:	15, male, Pocatello, ID
tu_tu:	16, female, Burlington, VT
duffme:	44, male, Minneapolis, MN
QTpie:	30, male, Chicago, IL
ty1989:	15, female, Naperville, IL
harrys_grl:	12, female, Appleton, MN
slugger20:	17, male, Jackson, MS
qtrback21:	26, male, Brooklyn, NY
suzie14:	14, female, Portland, OR
hiphopper:	13, female, Plano, TX
paperboy:	41, male, Beaverton, OR

1 in 5 children is sexually solicited online.

African American Mayors

ALABAMA

AKRON
Henry Miles, Mayor
P.O. Box 132
Akron, AL 35441
Tel: (256) 372-3148 Fax: (256) 372-0837

ATTALA
Bessie D. Twine, Mayor
P.O. Box 423
Attala, AL 35954
Tel: (256) 538-6978 Fax: (256) 538-8947

BESSEMER
Edward E. May, Mayor
1800 North 3rd Ave.
Bessemer, AL 35020
Tel: (205) 424-4060 Fax: (205) 424-4372

BIRMINGHAM
Bernard Kincaid, Mayor
710 North 20th St.
Birmingham, AL 35203
Tel: (205) 254-2700 Fax: (205) 254-2105

BOLIGEE
Walter Taylor, Mayor
Arrowood Apts.
Boligee, AL 35443
Tel: (205) 336-8563 Fax: (205) 336-8563

BRIGHTON
Eddie Cooper, Mayor
3700 Main St.
Brighton, AL 35020
Tel: (256) 428-9547 Fax: (256) 428-0470

CAMP HILL
Danny Evans, Mayor
P.O. Box 100, 309 Holly Ave.
Camp Hill, AL 36850
Tel: (256) 896-4148 Fax: (256) 896-4480

COLONY, TOWN OF
Earlene Johnson, Mayor
65 Byars Rd.
Hanceville, AL 35077
Tel: (256) 287-1192 Fax: (256) 287-1131

EMELLE
Roy Willingham, Mayor
P.O. Box 97
Emelle, AL 35459
Tel: (205) 652-7529 Fax: (205) 652-7529

EPES
Larry Yates, Sr., Mayor
P.O. Box 126
Epes, AL 35460
Tel: (205) 652-2223 Fax: (205) 392-4700

EUTAW
Raymond Steele, Mayor
P.O. Box 431
Eutaw, AL 35462
Tel: (205) 372-4212 Fax: (205) 372-0748

FAUNSDALE
Sadie Stanford, Mayor
P.O. Box 211
Faunsdale, AL 36738
Tel: (334) 628-4871

FIVE POINTS
Geneva Bledsoe, Mayor
P.O. Box 147
Five Points, AL 36855
Tel: (334) 864-7733

FORKLAND
Eddie Woods, Mayor
P.O. Box 126
Forkland, AL 36740
Tel: (334) 289-3032 Fax: (334) 289-3032

FORT DEPOSIT
Fletcher Fountain, Sr., Mayor
P.O. Box 260
Fort Deposit, AL 36032
Tel: (334) 227-4331 Fax: (334) 227-4800

FRANKLIN, TOWN OF
Rufus Carson, Mayor
1660 Alabama Highway 49
Tuskegee, AL 36083
Tel: (334) 727-2111

GAINESVILLE
Carrie Fulgham, Mayor
P.O. Box 73
Gainesville, AL 35464
Tel: (205) 652-7551

GEIGER
Herbert H. Payne, Sr., Mayor
201 BRd.way
Geiger, AL 35459
Tel: (205) 455-2811 Fax: (205) 758-3205

GORDON
Ozell Smith, Mayor
692 Tifton Rd.
Gordon, AL 36343
Tel: (334) 522-3113 Fax: (334) 522-1305

GREENSBORO
Johnnie B. Washington, Mayor
1101 Main St.
Greensboro, AL 36744
Tel: (334) 624-8119 Fax: (334) 624-0500

HAYNEVILLE
Helenor Bell, Mayor
P.O. Box 365
Hayneville, AL 36040
Tel: (334) 548-2128 Fax: (334) 548-2129

HILLSBORO
Billy Young, Mayor
P.O. Box 10
Hillsboro, AL 35643
Tel: (256) 637-2070 Fax: (256) 637-2070

HOBSON CITY
Ralph Woods, Mayor
610 MLK, Jr. Dr., City Hall
Hobson City, AL 36201
Tel: (256) 831-0441 Fax: (256) 831-4242

LAFAYETTE
Robert Finley, Mayor
P.O. Box 87
LaFayette, AL 36862
Tel: (334) 864-7181 Fax: (334) 864-2205

LEIGHTON
Robert Ricks, Mayor
2295 Lee High Circle
Leighton, AL 35646
Tel: (256) 627-7001

LIPSCOMB
Albert Mason, Mayor
5515 Ave. H, Town Hall
Lipscomb, AL 35020
Tel: (205) 428-6374 Fax: (205) 428-6373

LISMAN
Thomas Jackson, Mayor
P.O. Box 157, City Hall
Lisman, AL 36912
Tel: (205) 398-3889

MADISON
Marvalene Freeman, Mayor
640 6th St.
Madison, AL 35758
Tel: (256) 772-0151 Fax: (256) 464-5099

MARION
Edward Daniel, Mayor
P.O. Drawer 959
Marion, AL 36756
Tel: (334) 683-6545 Fax: (334) 683-4326

MCMULLEN, TOWN OF
Essie R. Madison, Mayor
170 Cleveland Cir.
Aliceville, AL 35442
Tel: (205) 373-8959

MOSSES, TOWN OF
William Scott, Mayor
P.O. Box 296
Hayneville, AL 36040
Tel: (334) 563-9141 Fax: (334) 563-7559

MT. VERNON
Cleon Bolden, Mayor
P.O. Box 309
Mt. Vernon, AL 0.3656
Tel: (334) 829-6632 Fax: (334) 829-5546

NEW BROCKTON
Charles B. Cole, Mayor
P.O. Box 70
New Brockton, AL 36351
Tel: (334) 894-5550 Fax: (334) 894-5686

NORTH COURTLAND
Fred James, Mayor
P.O. Box 93, City Hall
North Courtland, AL 35618
Tel: (256) 637-8460 Fax: (256) 637-8460

PRICHARD
Ron Davis, Mayor
P.O. Box 10427
Prichard, AL 36610
Tel: (251) 452-7800 Fax: (251) 452-2875

SELMA
James Perkins, Jr, Mayor
P.O. Box 450, City Hall
Selma, AL 36701
Tel: (334) 874-2100 Fax: (334) 874-2402

SHORTER
Willie Mae Powell, Mayor
P.O. Box 117
Shorter, AL 36075
Tel: (334) 727-9190 Fax: (334) 727-9298

SLOCOMB
Vicki Moore, Mayor
P.O. Box 1147
Slocomb, AL 36375
Tel: (334) 886-3333 Fax: (334) 886-3695

TUSKEGEE
Johnny Ford, Mayor
101 Fonville, Municipal Complex
Tuskegee, AL 36083
Tel: (334) 727-2180 Fax: (334) 727-4820

UNION, TOWN OF
Loyddetta Wabbington, Mayor
Route 3, Box 300-A
Eutaw, AL 35462
Tel: (205) 372-2688

Source: National Conference of Black Mayors, Inc. (NCBM). www.ncbm.org.

UNIONTOWN
Phillip White, Mayor
P.O. Box 1069
Uniontown, AL 36786
Tel: (334) 628-2011 Fax: (334) 628-2028

VRENDENBURGH
Cynthia Evans, Mayor
P.O. Box 285
Vrendenburgh, AL 36481

WHITE HALL, TOWN OF
John Jackson, Mayor
625 Freedom St.
Hayneville, AL 36040
Tel: (334) 875-5703 Fax: (334)875-5708

YELLOW BLUFF, TOWN OF
Sharon Nicholson, Mayor
80 Park Ave.
Pine Hill, AL 36769
Tel: (334) 963-4881 Fax: (334) 963-9551

YORK
Carolyn Gosa, Mayor
P.O. Box 37
York, AL 36925
Tel: (256) 392-5231 Fax: (256) 392-7202

ARKANSAS

ALEXANDER
Shirley Johnson, Mayor
P.O. Box 610, 15412 Main Street
Alexander, AR 72002
Tel: (501) 455-2585 Fax: (501) 455-5531

ALLPORT, TOWN OF
Kervin Dolphin, Mayor
P.O. Box 58
England, AR 72046

ALTHEIMER
Leo Rasberry, Mayor
P.O. Box 206
Altheimer, AR 72004
Tel: (870) 766-8229 Fax: (870) 766-4875

BIRDSONG, TOWN OF
Robert Johnson, Mayor
123 Shumpert St.
Tyronza, AR 72386
Tel: (870) 537-4293

BUCKNER
Charlie Tyson, Mayor
P.O. Box 56
Buckner, AR 71827
Tel: (870) 533-2260 Fax: (870) 533-2260

CARTHAGE
Willie Toney, Jr., Mayor
P.O. Box 17
Carthage, AR 71725
Tel: (870) 254-2463 Fax: (870) 254-2124

COTTON PLANT
Eddie Johnson, Mayor
P.O. Box 220, City Hall
Cotton Plant, AR 72036
Tel: (870) 459-2121 Fax: (870) 459-3650

DERMOTT
Floyd E. Gray, Mayor
P.O. Box 371, 112 N. Freeman
Dermott, AR 71638
Tel: (870) 538-5251 Fax: (870) 538-5252

EARLE
Sherman Smith, Mayor
215 Alabama
Earle, AR 72331
Tel: (870) 792-8477 Fax: (870) 792-8477

EDMONDSON
Patricia Henderson, Mayor
P.O. Box 300
Edmondson, AR 72332
Tel: (870) 735-6946

FORREST CITY
Larry S. Bryant, Mayor
224 N. Rosser St., City Hall
Forrest City, AR 72335
Tel: (870) 633-1315 Fax: (870) 261-1424

GARLAND CITY
Yvonne Smith-Dockery, Mayor
P.O. Box 9
Garland City, AR 71839
Tel: (870) 683-2289 Fax: (870) 683-2491

GILMORE
Christine Brownlee, Mayor
P.O. Box 253
Gilmore, AR 72339
Tel: (870) 343-2697 Fax: (870) 343-2601

GOULD
Eddye Wilson, Mayor
P.O. Box 638
Gould, AR 71643
Tel: (870) 263-4417

HELENA
Robert Miller, Mayor
226 Perry St.
Helena, AR 72342
Tel: (870) 338-6439 Fax: (870) 338-9832

HOLLY GROVE
Lula Tyler, Mayor
P.O. Box 430
Holly Grove, AR 72069
Tel: (870) 462-3422 Fax: (870) 462-3580

JENNETTE, TOWN OF
Plez Frank Lucas, Mayor
2333 Jennette Circle
Crawfordville, AR 72327

JERICHO, TOWN OF
Helen Adams, Mayor
P.O. Box 10
Crawfordville, AR 72327
Tel: (870) 739-4918 Fax: (870) 739-4918

LAKEVIEW, CITY OF
Leon A. Phillips, Jr., Mayor
14264 Hwy. 44
Helena, AR 72342
Tel: (870) 827-6341 Fax: (870) 827-6357

LEXA
Ethel Westbrook, Mayor
114 McKee St.
Lexa, AR 72355
Tel: (870) 295-5254

MADISON
James Lee Brooks, Mayor
P.O. Box 109, City Hall
Madison, AR 72359
Tel: (870) 633-2172 Fax: (870) 630-0935

MARIANNA
Robert P. Taylor, Mayor
45 W. Mississippi St.
Marianna, AR 72360
Tel: (870) 295-6089 Fax: (870) 295-5726

MCNEIL
Henry Warren, Mayor
P.O. Box 130
McNeil, AR 71752
Tel: (870) 695-3641 Fax: (870) 695-3638

MENIFEE
Stanley Morris, Mayor
P.O. Box 148
Menifee-, AR 72107-0038
Tel: (501) 354-2818 Fax: (501) 354-0799

MITCHELLVILLE, TOWN OF
Bobbie Norman, Mayor
P.O. Box 568
Dumas, AR 71639
Tel: (870) 382-2121 Fax: (870) 382-3043

OZAN
Willie C. Carringan, Mayor
P.O. Box 21
Ozan, AR 71855
Tel: (870) 983-2820

PINE BLUFF
Carl Redus, Mayor
P.O. Box 3119
Pine Bluff, AR 71611
Tel: (870) 543-1855 Fax: (870) 536-9877

PROCTOR
Leroy C. Wright, Mayor
P.O. Box 140, 197 Luke, Jr. Ave.
Proctor, AR 72376
Tel: (870) 732-3975 Fax: (870) 733-9306

REED, TOWN OF
Tommie Smith, Mayor
P.O. Box 139
Tillar, AR 71670
Tel: (870) 392-2610 Fax: (870) 392-2000

SUNSET
Kirby Massey, Mayor
300 John H. Johnson Blvd.
Sunset, AR 72364
Tel: (870) 739-3233 Fax: (870) 739-3234

TOLLETTE
Martha Hendrix, Mayor
301 Peach St.
Tollette, AR 71851
Tel: (870) 287-4273 Fax: (870) 287-7233

TURRELL
Chester McGee, Mayor
P.O. Box 249
Turrell, AR 71851
Tel: (870) 343-2537 Fax: (870) 343-2537

TWIN GROVES
Richard Ealy, Mayor
101 Twin Groves Lane
Twin Groves, AR 72039
Tel: (501) 335-7733

WABBASEKA
James Murry, Sr., Mayor
P.O. Box 141
Wabbaseka, AR 72175
Tel: (870) 766-4962

WEST HELENA
Johnny Weaver, Mayor
98 Plaza St.
West Helena, AR 72390
Tel: (870) 572-3421

WILMAR
Curly Jackson, Mayor
P.O. Box 397
Wilmar, AR 71675
Tel: (870) 469-5609 Fax: (870) 469-8309

WILTON
Spencer Nixon, Mayor
P.O. Box 10
Wilton, AR 71865
Tel: (870) 898-3230

WRIGHTSVILLE
Lorraine Smith, Mayor
P.O. Box 237
Wrightsville, AR 72183
Tel: (501) 897-4547 Fax: (501) 897-5647

CALIFORNIA

COMPTON
Eric Perrodin, Mayor
205 South Willowbrook, City Hall
Compton, CA 90220
Tel: (310) 605-5500 Fax: (310) 605-5449

EAST PALO ALTO
David Woods, Mayor
2415 University Ave
East Palo Alto, CA 94303
Tel: (650) 835-3100 Fax: (650) 853-3115

FOSTER CITY
Jim Lawrence, Mayor
610 Foster City Blvd., City Hall
Foster City, CA 94404
Tel: (415) 286-3219 Fax: (415) 574-3483

INGLEWOOD
Roosevelt F. Dorn, Mayor
One Manchester Blvd., City Hall
Inglewood, CA 90301
Tel: (310) 412-5300 Fax: (310) 330-5733

LYNWOOD
Louis Byrd, Mayor
11330 Bullis Rd.
Lynwood, CA 90262
Tel: (310) 603-0220 Fax: (310) 764-4908

OCEANSIDE
Terry Johnson, Mayor
300 N. Coast Highway
Oceanside, CA 92054
Tel: (760) 966-4435

RICHMOND
Irma Anderson, Mayor
2600 Barrett Ave.
Richmond, CA 94804
Tel: (510) 620-6503 Fax: (510) 620-6542

SAN RAMON
H. Abram Wilson, Mayor
2222 Camino Ramon, City Hall
San Ramon, CA 94583
Tel: (925) 973-2530 Fax: (925) 275-0650

SEASIDE
Jerry Smith, Mayor
P.O. Box 810, City Hall
Seaside, CA 93955
Tel: (408) 899-6200 Fax: (408) 899-6227

DELAWARE

WILMINGTON
James M. Baker, Mayor
800 French St., City Hall
Wilmington, DE 19801
Tel: (302) 571-4100 Fax: (302) 571-4102

DISTRICT OF COLUMBIA

WASHINGTON, DC
Anthony A. Williams, Mayor
441 4th St. NW, 11th Fl. #1100
Washington, DC 20001
Tel: (202) 727-2643 Fax: (202) 727-6561

FLORIDA

COTTONDALE
Riley Henderson, Mayor
4490 Jackson Rd.
Cottondale, FL 32431
Tel: (850) 263-6636

EATONVILLE
Anthony Grant, Mayor
307 E. Kennedy
Eatonville, FL 32431
Tel: (407) 623-1318 Fax: (407) 623-1319

EL PORTAL
Audrey M. Edmonson, Mayor
500 N.E. 87th St.
El Portal, FL 33138
Tel: (305) 795-7880 Fax: (305) 759-5341

FLORIDA CITY
Otis T. Wallace, Mayor
404 West Palm Dr.
Florida City, FL 33034
Tel: (305) 247-8221 Fax: (305) 242-8133

GRETNA
Earnest O. Barkley, Mayor
P.O. Drawer 220
Gretna, FL 32332
Tel: (850) 856-5257 Fax: (850) 856-9454

HOMESTEAD
Roscoe Warren, Mayor
790 N. Homestead Blvd., City Hall
Homestead, FL 33030
Tel: (305) 247-1801 Fax: (305) 246-3241

LAUDERDALE LAKES
Samuel S. Brown, Mayor
4300 NW 36th St.
Lauderdale Lakes, FL 33319
Tel: (954) 535-2730 Fax: (954) 731-5857

MIAMI GARDENS
Shirley Gibson, Mayor
1515 NW 167th St. #5-200
Miami Gardens, FL 33169
Tel: (305) 622-8010 Fax: (305) 622-8001

MIDWAY
Delores Madison, Mayor
P.O. Box 408
Midway, FL 32343
Tel: (850) 488-1049

NORTH MIAMI
Josaphat "Joe" Celestin, Mayor
776 N.E. 125th St., City Hall
North Miami, FL 33161
Tel: (305) 895-8931 Fax: (305) 892-9899

OAKLAND PARK
Allegra Webb Murphy, Mayor
3650 NE 12th Ave.
Oakland Park, FL 33334
Tel: (954) 561-6231 Fax: (954) 567-7129

OPA-LOCKA
Joseph L. Kelly, Mayor
777 Sharazad Blvd.
Opa-locka, FL -33054
Tel: (305) 688-4611 Fax: (305) 953-2834

PALATKA
Karl Nathaniel Flagg, Mayor
201 North 2nd St., City Hall
Palatka, FL 32177
Tel: (386) 329-0100 Fax: (386) 329-0106

RIVIERA BEACH
Michael D. Brown, Mayor
600 W. Blue Heron Blvd.
Riviera Beach, FL 33404
Tel: (561) 845-4145 Fax: (561) 863-3236

SOUTH BAY
Clarence Anthony, Mayor
335 SW 2nd Ave.
South Bay, FL 33493
Tel: (561) 996-6751 Fax: (561) 996-7950

TALLAHASSEE
John Marks, Mayor
300 S. Adams St., City Hall
Tallahassee, FL 32301
Tel: (850) 891-8181 Fax: (850) 891-8542

WEST PARK
Eric H. Jones, Jr., Mayor
4702 SW 23rd St.
West Park, FL 33023

GEORGIA

ALBANY
Willie Adams, Jr., Mayor
P.O. Box 447
Albany, GA 31702
Tel: (229) 431-3244 Fax: (229) 878-3198

ATLANTA
Shirley Franklin, Mayor
55 Trinity Ave., SW, City Hall
Atlanta, GA 30335
Tel: (404) 330-6100 Fax: (404) 658-7292

BACONTON
Tholen Edwards, Mayor
P.O. Box 7, Town Hall
Baconton, GA 31716
Tel: (912) 787-5511 Fax: (912) 787-5513

BARNESVILLE
Dewaine T. Bell, Mayor
109 Forsyth St.
Barnesville, GA 30204
Tel: (770) 358-6893 Fax: (770) 358-6805

BRONWOOD
Ruben Hawkins, Mayor
P.O. Box 56
Bronwood, GA 31226
Tel: (229) 995-5708 Fax: (229) 995-5085

BUENA VISTA
Ralph Brown, Jr., Mayor
P.O. Box 158
Buena Vista, GA 31803
Tel: (912) 649-7888 Fax: (912) 649-2177

CUTHBERT
Willie R. Martin, Mayor
P.O. Box 100
Cuthbert, GA 31740
Tel: (229) 732-3164 Fax: (229) 732-3115

DAWSON
Robert Albritten, Mayor
P.O. Box 486
Dawson, GA 31742
Tel: (912) 995-5895 Fax: (912) 995-3713

EAST POINT
Patsy Jo Hilliard, Mayor
3350 Sir Henry St.
East Point, GA 30344
Tel: (404) 765-1004 Fax: (404) 209-5100

EATONTON
John Reid, Mayor
201 North Jefferson Ave.
Eatonton, GA 31024
Tel: (706) 485-3311

FLOVILLA
Harvey Norris, Mayor
P.O. Box 39
Flovilla, GA 30216
Tel: (770) 775-5661 Fax: (770) 775-1909

GREENSBORO
Glenn Wright, Mayor
212 N. Main St., City Hall
Greensboro, GA 30642
Tel: (706) 453-7967 Fax: (760) 453-2912

GREENVILLE
Ruby Byrd, Mayor
P.O. Box 548
Greenville, GA 30222
Tel: (706) 672-1216 Fax: (706) 672-1940

IRWINTON
Edna Brown, Mayor
P.O. Box 359
Irwinton, GA 31042
Tel: (478) 946-7144 Fax: (478) 946-2873

JEFFERSONVILLE
Sonja A. Mallory, Mayor
200 Church St.
Jeffersonville, GA 31044
Tel: (478) 945-3191 Fax: (478) 945-6894

KEYSVILLE
Emma Gresham, Mayor
P.O. Box 159
Keysville, GA 30816
Tel: (706) 547-3007 Fax: (706) 547-3875

KINGSLAND
Kenneth E. Smith, Sr., Mayor
P.O. Box 250
Kingsland, GA 31548
Tel: (912) 729-5613 Fax: (912) 729-7618

LITHONIA
Darold Honoroe, Jr., Mayor
6980 Main St.
Lithonia, GA 30058
Tel: (770) 482-8136 Fax: (678) 526-0267

MACON
Jack Ellis, Mayor
P.O. Box 247
Macon, GA 31202
Tel: (478) 751-7170 Fax: (478) 751-2749

MIDWAY
James C. Shipman, Mayor
P.O. Box 125
Midway, GA 31320
Tel: (912) 884-3344 Fax: (912) 884-5107

MILLEDGEVILLE
Floyd L. Griffin Jr., Mayor
P.O. Box 1900
Milledgeville, GA 31061
Tel: (478) 414-4010 Fax: (478) 414-4011

MONTEZUMA
Willie J. Larry, Mayor
P.O. Box 388
Montezuma, GA 31063
Tel: (478) 472-8144 Fax: (478) 472-5873

MORGAN
Fred Oliver, Mayor
P.O. Box 36
Morgan, GA 31766
Tel: (912) 849-4045 Fax: (912) 849-0045

OLIVER
Justine Thomas Brown, Mayor
P.O. Box 82
Oliver, GA 30449
Tel: (912) 857-3789 Fax: (912) 857-4663

RICEBORO
Gregory Richardson, Mayor
P.O. Box 269
Riceboro, GA 31323
Tel: (912) 884-2986 Fax: (912) 884-2988

RICHLAND
Olan Faulk, Mayor
P.O. Box 126
Richland, GA 31825
Tel: (912) 887-3323 Fax: (912) 887-3939

RIVERDALE
Phaedra Graham, Mayor
6690 Church St., City Hall
Riverdale, GA 30274
Tel: (770) 997-8989 Fax: (770) 997-8992

SAVANNAH
Otis S. Johnson, Mayor
P.O. Box 1027
Savannah, GA 31402
Tel: (912) 651-6444 Fax: (912) 651-6805

SMITHVILLE
Jerry Myrick, Mayor
P.O. Box 208
Smithville, GA 31787
Tel: (229) 846-2101

SPARTA
William Evans, Jr., Mayor
P.O. Box H
Sparta, GA 31087
Tel: (706) 444-5753 Fax: (706) 444-6722

STILLMORE
Roxie L. Wilkins, Mayor
P.O. Box 70
Stillmore, GA 30464
Tel: (912) 562-3529 Fax: (912) 562-3868

TOOMSBORO, TOWN OF
Roger Smith, Mayor
P.O. Box 67
Toomsboro, GA 31090
Tel: (478) 933-5257 Fax: (478) 290-2488

UNION CITY
Ralph Moore, Mayor
5047 Union St., City Hall
Union City, GA 30291
Tel: (770) 964-2288 Fax: (770) 306-6861

VIENNA
Willie J. Davis, Mayor
P.O. Box 436, City Hall
Vienna, GA 31092
Tel: (229) 268-4744 Fax: (229) 268-6172

WADLEY
Herman Baker, Mayor
P.O. Box 219
Wadley, GA 30477
Tel: (478) 252-1116 Fax: (478) 252-9954

WALTHOURVILLE
Henry Frasier, Sr., Mayor
P.O. Box K
Walthourville, GA 31313
Tel: (912) 368-7501 Fax: (912) 368-2803

WASHINGTON
Willie Burns, Mayor
P.O. Box 9
Washington, GA 30673
Tel: (706) 678-3277 Fax: (706) 678-3752

WAYCROSS
John N. Fluker, Mayor
P.O. Drawer 99, City Hall
Waycross, GA 31502-0099
Tel: (912) 287-2912 Fax: (912) 287-2990

WOODLAND
James Carter, Mayor
P.O. Box 187
Woodland, GA 31836
Tel: (706) 674-2700 Fax: (706) 674-2200

IDAHO

MOUNTAIN HOME
Joe B. McNeal, Mayor
P.O. Box 10
Mountain Home, ID 83647
Tel: (208) 587-2104

ILLINOIS

ALORTON
Carolyn Williams, Mayor
4821 Bond Ave.
Alorton, IL 62207
Tel: (618) 271-4586 Fax: (618) 874-7088

BROOKLYN
Dennis Miller, Mayor
312 North 5th St., City Hall
Brooklyn, IL 62059
Tel: (618) 271-8424 Fax: (618) 271-7910

CENTREVILLE
Frankie J. Seaberry, Mayor
5800 Bond Ave., City Hall
Centreville, IL 62207
Tel: (618) 332-8822 Fax: (618) 332-8698

DIXMOOR
Martha Loggins, Mayor
170 West 145 St.
Dixmoor, IL 60426
Tel: (708) 385-0319 Fax: (708) 389-9717

DOLTON
William Shaw, Mayor
14014 Park Ave.
Dolton, IL 60419
Tel: (708) 201-3268 Fax: (708) 201-3388

EAST ST. LOUIS
Carl E. Officer, Mayor
301 River Park Dr., City Hall
East St. Louis, IL 0.62201
Tel: (618) 482- 6601 Fax: (612) 482-6629

EVANSTON
Lorraine Morton, Mayor
2100 Ridge Ave.
Evanston, IL 60201
Tel: (847) 866-2979 Fax: (847) 866-2978

FORD HEIGHTS
Saul L. Beck, Mayor
1343 Ellis Ave.
Ford Heights, IL 60411
Tel: (708) 758-3131 Fax: (708) 758-6741

HARVEY
Eric Kellogg, Mayor
15320 BRd.way Ave., City Hall
Harvey, IL 60426
Tel: (708) 210-5300 Fax: (708) 210-5366

HAZELCREST
William A. Browne, Mayor
3000 West 170th Place, City Hall
Hazelcrest, IL 60429
Tel: (708) 335-9600 Fax: (708) 335-9622

HOPKINS PARK
Jon E. Dyson, Mayor
P.O. Box AK
Hopkins Park, IL 60944
Tel: (815) 944-8625 Fax: (815) 944-6809

MARKHAM
David Webb, Jr., Mayor
16313 Kedzie Ave.
Markham, IL 60426
Tel: (708) 596-3450

MAYWOOD
Ralph W. Conner, Mayor
125 South 5th Ave.
Maywood, IL 60153
Tel: (708) 450-4486 Fax: (708) 450-0657

NORTH CHICAGO
Bette Thomas, Mayor
1850 Lewis Ave., City Hall
North Chicago, IL 60064
Tel: (847) 596-8610 Fax: (847) 578-8619

OLYMPIA FIELDS
Linzey D. Jones, Mayor
20701 Governor Hwy., City Hall
Olympia Fields, IL 60461
Tel: (708) 503-8000 Fax: (708) 503-8002

PHOENIX
Terry R. Wells, Mayor
650 E. Phoenix Cte., Office of the Mayor
Phoenix, IL 60426
Tel: (708) 331-2636

ROBBINS
Irene H. Brodie, Ph.D., Mayor
3327 W. 137th St.
Robbins, IL 60472
Tel: (708) 385-8606 Fax: (708) 385-0542

ST. ANNE
Shirley Byrd, Mayor
7267 East Chicago St., City Hall
St. Anne, IL 60964
Tel: (815) 937-1200 Fax: (815) 937-9930

UNIVERSITY PARK
Alvin R. McCowan, Mayor
698 Burnham Dr., Village Hall
University Park, IL 60466
Tel: (708) 534-4237 Fax: (708) 534-2956

VENICE
Tyrone Echols, Mayor
Kline & Broadway, City Hall
Venice, IL 62090
Tel: (618) 877-2412 Fax: (618) 877-2412

WASHINGTON PARK
Sherman Sorrell, Mayor
5005 Forest Blvd.
Washington Park, IL 62204
Tel: (618) 874-2040 Fax: (618) 874-1218

IOWA

CLINTON
Lametta K. Wynn, Mayor
611 South Third St., City Hall
Clinton, IA 52733-2958
Tel: (563) 242-2144 Fax: (563) 242-7775

LOUISIANA

BAKER, CITY OF
Harold Rideau, Mayor
3325 Groom Rd.
Baker, LA 70714
Tel: (225) 778-0300 Fax: (225) 775-5598

BASTROP, CITY OF
Clarence W. Hawkins, Mayor
P.O. Box 431
Bastrop, LA 71220
Tel: (318) 283-3301 Fax: (318) 281-5783

BATON ROUGE
Melvin Kip Holden, Mayor
222 St. Louis St., City Hall
Baton Rouge, LA 70802
Tel: (225) 389-3100 Fax: (225) 389-5203

BIENVILLE, VILLAGE OF
Dennis Boston, Mayor
P.O. Box 207
Bienville, LA 71008
Tel: (318) 385-7532

BOYCE, TOWN OF
Julius Patrick, Jr., Mayor
P.O. Box 146
Boyce, LA 71409
Tel: (318) 793-2175 Fax: (318) 793-5978

CAMPTI, TOWN OF
Donald R. Davis, Mayor
P.O. Box 427
Campti, LA 71411
Tel: (318) 476-3321 Fax: (318) 476-2622

CHATAIGNER, VILLAGE OF
Herman Malveaux, Mayor
P.O. Box 70
Chataigner, LA 70524
Tel: (337) 885-2500 Fax: (337) 885-2077

CLARENCE, VILLAGE OF
Bobby Braxton, Mayor
P.O. Box 214
Clarence, LA 71414
Tel: (318) 357-0440 Fax: (318) 356-9700

CLAYTON, TOWN OF
Wilbert Washington, Mayor
P.O. Box 277
Clayton, LA 71326
Tel: (318) 757-8540 Fax: (318) 757-8543

CULLEN, TOWN OF
Bobby Washington, Mayor
P.O. Box 149
Cullen, LA 71021
Tel: (318) 994-2731 Fax: (318) 994-2189

DONALDSONVILLE, CITY OF
Leroy Sullivan, Sr., Mayor
P.O. Box 470
Donaldsonville, LA 70346
Tel: (225) 473-4247 Fax: (225) 473-0630

EAST HODGE, VILLAGE OF
Harry Mims, Mayor
P.O. Drawer 10
East Hodges, LA 71247
Tel: (318) 259-9127 Fax: (318) 259-9127

FARMERVILLET, TOWN OF
Willie Davis, Mayor
P.O. Box 427
Farmerville, LA 71241
Tel: (318) 368-9242 Fax: (318) 368-7142

FENTON, VILLAGE OF
Frank D. Broxton, Mayor
P.O. Box 310
Fenton, LA 70640
Tel: (337) 756-2321 Fax: (337) 756-2242

FOLSOM
Marshall Brumfield, Mayor
P.O. Box 609, 2428 Hay Hollow Rd.
Folsom, LA 70437
Tel: (985) 796-5607 Fax: (985) 796-5701

FRANKLIN
Ramon Harris, Jr., Mayor
P.O. Box 567
Franklin, LA 70538
Tel: (337) 828-6305 Fax: (337) 828-6359

GIBSLAND, TOWN OF
Odell Odis Key, Mayor
P.O. Box 309
Gibsland, LA 71028
Tel: (318) 843-6141 Fax: (318) 843-9409

GRAMBLING, CITY OF
Martha Andrus, Mayor
P.O. Box 108
Grambling, LA 71245
Tel: (318) 247-6120 Fax: (318) 247-0940

GRAND COTEAU, TOWN OF
Jean Coco, Mayor
P.O. Drawer G
Grand Coteau, LA 70541
Tel: (337) 662-5246 Fax: (337) 662-5701

GREENWOOD
Ernest Lampkins, Mayor
P.O. Box 195
Greenwood, LA 71033
Tel: (318) 938-7261 Fax: (318) 938-1512

KENTWOOD
Harold J. Smith, Mayor
308 Ave. G
Kentwood, LA 70444
Tel: (985) 229-3451 Fax: (985) 229-3451

LECOMPTE, TOWN OF
Rosa S. Jones, Mayor
P.O. Box 1007
LeCompte, LA 71346
Tel: (318) 776-5488 Fax: (318) 776-5495

LUCKY, VILLAGE OF
Bobby Joe Boston, Mayor
P.O. Box 216
Castor, LA 71016
Tel: (318) 576-3912 Fax: (318) 576-3912

MANSFIELD, CITY OF
Curtis McCoy, Mayor
P.O. Box 773
Mansfield, LA 71052
Tel: (318) 872-4113 Fax: (318) 872-0402

MARINGOUIN, TOWN OF
John Overton, Jr., Mayor
P.O. Box 10
Maringouin, LA 70757
Tel: (225) 625-2630 Fax: (225) 625-2359

MELVILLE, TOWN OF
Willie Haynes, Mayor
P.O. Box 483
Melville, LA 71353
Tel: (337) 623-4226 Fax: (337) 623-3620

MONROE, CITY OF
Jamie Mayo, Mayor
P.O. Box 123
Monroe, LA 71210
Tel: (318) 329-2310 Fax: (318) 329-3300

NAPOLEONVILLE, VILLAGE OF
Darrell C. Jupiter, Sr., Mayor
P.O. Box 6
Napoleonville, LA 70390
Tel: (985) 369-6365 Fax: (985) 369-6361

NATCHEZ, VILLAGE OF
Lloyd Benjamin, Sr., Mayor
P.O. Box 229
Natchez, LA 71456
Tel: (318) 352-1414 Fax: (318) 352-6266

NEW ORLEANS
C. Ray Nagin, Mayor
1300 Perdido St. #2E04, Mayor's Office
New Orleans, LA 70112
Tel: (504) 565-6400 Fax: (504) 565-7742

NEW ROADS, CITY OF
Sylvester Muckelroy, Mayor
PO Box 280
New Roads, LA 70760
Tel: (225) 638-5360 Fax: (225) 638-5368

NEWELLTON, TOWN OF
Alex Davis, Mayor
P.O. Box 477
Newellton, LA 71357
Tel: (318) 467-5051 Fax: (318) 467-9984

OPELOUSAS
Anna C. Simmons, Mayor
P.O. Box 1879, 318 N. Court St.
Opelousas, LA 70571-1879
Tel: (337) 948-2520 Fax: (337) 948-2593

PINEVILLE, CITY OF
Clarence Fields, Mayor
P.O. Box 3820
Pineville, LA 71361
Tel: (318) 449-5658 Fax: (318) 442-8373

PLEASANT HILL, TOWN OF
Betty Thomas, Mayor
P. O. Box 125
Pleasant Hill, LA 71065
Tel: (318) 796-3680 Fax: (318) 796-3366

POWHATAN, VILLAGE OF
Margie Davenport, Mayor
P.O. Box 91
Powhatan, LA 71066
Tel: (318) 352-8549 Fax: (318) 352-7791

RAYVILLE, TOWN OF
Harry "Kayo Lewis, Mayor
P.O. Box 878
Rayville, LA 71269
Tel: (318) 728-2011 Fax: (318) 728-7503

RICHWOOD, TOWN OF
Edward L. Harris, Mayor
5130 -A Brown Rd.
Richwood, LA 71202-7004
Tel: (318) 322-2104 Fax: (318) 323-3254

SICILY ISLAND, TOWN OF
Gloria Anderson, Mayor
P.O. Box 45
Sicily Island, LA 71368
Tel: (318) 389-4472 Fax: (318) 389-4473

SOUTH MANSFIELD, TOWN OF
Dessie Lee Patterson, Mayor
P.O Box 995
South Mansfield, LA 71052
Tel: (318) 872-3960 Fax: (318) 872-9198

ST. GABRIEL, TOWN OF
George L. Grace, Mayor
5035 Iberville St.
St. Gabriel, LA 0.70776
Tel: (225) 642-9600 Fax: (225) 642-9670

ST. JOSEPH, TOWN OF
Edward L. Brown, Mayor
P.O. Box 217
St. Joseph, LA 0.71366
Tel: (318) 766-3713 Fax: (318) 766-3063

TALLULAH, CITY OF
Theodore Lindsey, Mayor
204 North Cedar St.
Tallulah, LA 71282
Tel: (318) 574-0964 Fax: (318) 574-2773

TANGIPAHOA, VILLAGE OF
Clarence J. Fultz, Mayor
P.O. Box 156
Tangipahoa, LA 70465
Tel: (504) 229-8300 Fax: (504) 229-4423

VINTON, TOWN OF
David Riggins, Mayor
1200 Horridge St.
Vinton, LA 70668
Tel: (337) 589-7453 Fax: (337) 589-6127

WASHINGTON
Joseph A. Pitre, Mayor
P.O. Box 218
Washington, LA 70589
Tel: (337) 826-3626 Fax: (337) 826-3601

WATERPROOF, TOWN OF
Mariah J. Cooper, Mayor
P.O. Box 248
Waterproof, LA 71375
Tel: (318) 749-5233 Fax: (318) 749-3131

WHITE CASTLE, TOWN OF
Maurice Brown, Mayor
P.O. Box 488
White Castle, LA 70788
Tel: (225) 545-3012 Fax: (225) 545-8456

WILSON, VILLAGE OF
Bennie C. Jones, Jr., Mayor
P.O. Box 40
Wilson, LA 70789
Tel: (225) 629-5415 Fax: (225) 629-5129

MARYLAND

CAPITOL HEIGHTS, TOWN OF
Joyce Ayers Nixon, Mayor
1 Capitol Heights Blvd.
Capitol Heights, MD 20743
Tel: (301) 336-0626 Fax: (301) 336-8706

COLMAR MANOR
Diana Fennell, Mayor
3707 Lawrence St.
Colmar Manor, MD 20722
Tel: (301) 277-4920 Fax: (301) 699-5245

DISTRICT HEIGHTS
Carol Johnson, Mayor
2000 Marbury Drive
District Heights, MD 20747
Tel: (301) 336-1402 Fax: (301) 350-3660

EAGLE HARBOR
Joseph C. Lomax, Jr., Mayor
P.O. Box 28
Aquasco, MD 20608
Tel: (301) 292-0941 Fax: (301) 888-2410

FAIRMOUNT HEIGHTS, TOWN OF
Lillie Thompson Martin, Mayor
6100 Jost St.
Fairmount Heights, MD 20743
Tel: (301) 925-8585 Fax: (301) 925-8977

FOREST HEIGHTS
Paula R. Noble, Mayor
5508 Arapahoe Drive
Forest Heights, MD 20745
Tel: (301) 839-1030 Fax: (301) 839-9236

GLENARDEN
Elaine Carter, Mayor
8600 Glenarden Pkwy., Municipal Building
Glenarden, MD 20706
Tel: (301) 773-2100 Fax: (301) 773-7329

LANDOVER HILLS, TOWN OF
Lee P. Walker, Mayor
P.O. Box 3833
Capitol Heights, MD 20791
Tel: (301) 773-6401 Fax: (301) 773-9145

MORNINGSIDE
Irving L. Robinson, Mayor
6901 Ames St.
Suitland, MD 20746
Tel: (202) 528-2760 Fax: (301) 736-7440

NORTH BRENTWOOD
Lillian K. Beverly, Mayor
P.O. Box 196, 4707 Church St.
North Brentwood, MD 20722
Tel: (301) 699-9699 Fax: (301) 699-1824

SEAT PLEASANT
Eugene W. Grant, Mayor
6301 Addison Rd.
Seat Pleasant, MD 20743
Tel: (301) 336-2600 Fax: (301) 336-0029

MICHIGAN

BENTON HARBOR
Wilce Cooke, Mayor
200 Wall St.
Benton Harbor, MI 49022
Tel: (269) 927-8400 Fax: (269) 927-6070

BUENA VISTA TOWNSHIP
Dwayne A. Parker, Mayor
1160 S. Outer Dr.
Saginaw, MI 48601
Tel: (989) 754-6536 Fax: (989) 759-1607

CASSOPOLIS
Julia Bell, Mayor
139 N. Broadway, Village Hall
Cassopolis, MI 49031
Tel: (269) 445-8648 Fax: (269) 445-2992

DETROIT
Kwame Kilpatrick, Mayor
1126 City County Blvd.
Detroit, MI 48226
Tel: (313) 224-3400 Fax: (313) 224-4433

HIGHLAND PARK
Titus W. McClary, Mayor
12050 Woodward Ave.
Highland Park, MI 48203
Tel: (313) 867-4598 Fax: (313) 865-5422

INKSTER
Hilliard L. Hampton, Jr., Mayor
2121 Inkster Rd., City Hall
Inkster, MI 48141
Tel: (313) 563-0249 Fax: (313) 563-9844

KALAMAZOO
Robert Jones, Mayor
241 W. South St., City Hall
Kalamazoo, MI 49007
Tel: (616) 381-8659 Fax: (616) 337-8182

MUSKEGON HEIGHTS
Rillastine Wilkins, Mayor
2724 Peck St.
Muskegon Heights, MI 49442
Tel: (231) 733-8870 Fax: (231) 733-5229

PONTIAC
Willie W. Payne, Mayor
47450 Woodward Ave.
Pontiac, MI 48342
Tel: (248) 758-3033 Fax: (248) 758-3166

SAGINAW
Wilmer Jones-Ham, Mayor
1315 S. Washington Ave., City Hall
Saginaw, MI 48601
Tel: (517) 759-1400 Fax: (517) 759-1607

SOUTHFIELD
Brenda L. Lawrence, Mayor
26000 Evergreen Rd.
Southfield, MI 48037
Tel: (248) 354-9600 Fax: (248) 208-8048

VANDALIA
Beverly Young, Mayor
18035 State St., Village Hall
Vandalia, MI 49095-0057
Tel: (616) 476-2344 Fax: (616) 476-2072

YATES TOWNSHIP
Donel Brown, Mayor
P.O. Box 115
Idlewild, MI 49642
Tel: (231) 745-3940 Fax: (231) 745-3940

MISSISSIPPI

ABERDEEN
Cecil Belle, Mayor
125 West Commerce St., City Hall
Aberdeen, MS 39730
Tel: (662) 369-8588 Fax: (662) 369-3103

ANGUILLA
Emma Cooper Harris, Mayor
P.O. Box 217
Anguilla, MS 38721
Tel: (662) 873-4573 Fax: (662) 873-4978

ARCOLA
Clifton Harris, Mayor
P.O. Box 25
Arcola, MS 38722
Tel: (662) 827-2063 Fax: (662) 827-0451

ATESIA
Jimmy L. Sanders, Mayor
Front St., City Hall
Atesia, MS 39736
Tel: (662) 272-5104

BEAUMONT
Lucinda Dailey, Mayor
P.O. Box 605
Beaumont, MS 39423
Tel: (601) 784-3352

BEAUREGARD, CITY OF
Linda F. Harris, Mayor
P.O. Box 427
Wesson, MS 39191
Tel: (601) 643-0020

BEULAH
Luscius Tucker, Mayor
P.O. Box 14
Beulah, MS 38726
Tel: (662) 759-3758 Fax: (662) 759-3607

BOLTON
Lawrence Butler, Mayor
P.O. Box 7, 202 Bolton-Raymond Rd.
Bolton, MS 39041
Tel: (601) 866-2221 Fax: (601) 866-2100

BROOKSVILLE
William W. Smith, Mayor
P.O. Box 256, City Hall
Brooksville, MS 39739
Tel: (662) 738-5531 Fax: (662) 738-5020

BUDE
Arthur MacLittleton, Mayor
P.O. Box 448
Bude, MS 39630
Tel: (601) 384-2600 Fax: (601) 384-4193

CANTON
Fred Esco, Jr., Mayor
P.O. Box 1605, 226 East Peace St.
Canton, MS 39046
Tel: (601) 859-4331 Fax: (601) 859-4379

CLARKSDALE
Henry Espy, Mayor
P.O. Box 353
Clarksdale, MS 38614
Tel: (662) 621-8164 Fax: (662) 621-8163

COAHOMA
W.J. Jones, Mayor
P.O. Box 23
Coahoma, MS 38617
Tel: (662) 337-2964 Fax: (662) 337-2964

COLDWATER
Roseber Thomas, Mayor
P.O. Box 352
Coldwater, MS 38618
Tel: (662) 622-7241 Fax: (662) 622-7242

COMO
Azria Lewers, Mayor
P.O. Box 118, 204 North Main St.
Como, MS 38619
Tel: (662) 526-9647 Fax: (662) 526-0210

CRAWFORD
Helen O'Neal, Mayor
P.O. Box 136, 365 Main St.
Crawford, MS 39743
Tel: (662) 272-5164 Fax: (662) 272-5164

CROSBY
James Bateaste, Mayor
P.O. Box 338
Crosby, MS 39743
Tel: (601) 639-4516

CRUGER
Mary L. Ajoku, Mayor
P.O. Box 214, City Hall
Cruger, MS 38924
Tel: (662) 455-0009 Fax: (662) 455-9908

DODDSVILLE
Torrey Bell, Mayor
P.O. Box 7, City Hall
Doddsville, MS 38736
Tel: (662) 756-2242 Fax: (662) 756-2700

DUCK HILL
Joey Cooley, Mayor
Main St.
Duck Hill, MS 38935
Tel: (601) 565-7200

DUNCAN
Charles Harvey, Mayor
West Front St., Town Hall
Duncan, MS 38740
Tel: (662) 395-8358

DURANT
Eddie Logan, Mayor
P.O. Box 272, 253 W. Mulberry St.
Durant, MS 39063
Tel: (662) 653-3221 Fax: (662) 653-6847

EDWARDS
Darron Pritchard, Mayor
101 Front St.
Edwards, MS 39066
Tel: (601) 852-5461

FALCON
Alvin Hodo, Mayor
P.O. Box 79, 226 Railroad Ave.
Falcon, MS 38628
Tel: (662) 382-7669 Fax: (662) 382-7669

FAYETTE
Rogers King, Mayor
P.O. Box 637
Fayette, MS 39069
Tel: (662) 786-3682 Fax: (662) 786-3910

FRIARS POINT
Herbert Thomas, Mayor
P.O. Box 185
Friars Point, MS 38631
Tel: (662) 383-2233 Fax: (662) 383-2403

GLENDORA
Johnny B. Thomas, Mayor
P.O. Box 90
Glendora, MS 38928
Tel: (662) 375-7333 Fax: (662) 375-7250

GOODMAN
Debra A. Mabry, Mayor
P.O. Box 397, 9912 Main St.
Goodman, MS 39079
Tel: (662) 472-2263 Fax: (662) 472-2513

GREENVILLE
Heather Hudson, Mayor
P.O. Box 897, City Hall
Greenville, MS 38702-0897
Tel: (662) 378-1501 Fax: (662) 378-1564

GRENADA
Diana Freelon-Foster, Mayor
P.O. Box 310, City Hall
Grenada, MS 38902
Tel: (662) 226-8820 Fax: (662) 227-3412

GUNNISON
Erma Williams, Mayor
P.O. Box 278, 404 Main St.
Gunnison, MS 38746
Tel: (662) 747-2213 Fax: (662) 747-2263

HATTIESBURG
Johnny L. DuPree, Mayor
P.O. Box 1898, 200 Forrest St.
Hattiesburg, MS 39403
Tel: (601) 545-4501 Fax: (601) 545-4608

HEIDELBERG
Juan Barnett, Mayor
P.O. Box 372
Heidelberg, MS 39439
Tel: (601) 787-3000 Fax: (601) 787-3700

HOLLY SPRINGS
Andre DeBerry, Mayor
160 South Memphis St.
Holly Springs, MS 38635
Tel: (662) 252-4280 Fax: (662) 252-4651

INDIANOLA
Arthur Marble, Mayor
P.O. Box 269
Indianola, MS 38751
Tel: (662) 887-1825

ISOLA
Willie Tanner, Mayor
203 Julia St., City Hall
Isola, MS 38754
Tel: (662) 962-7725 Fax: (662) 962-6133

JACKSON
Harvey Johnson, Jr., Mayor
219 S. President St., City Hall
Jackson, MS 39205-0017
Tel: (601) 960-1084 Fax: (601) 960-1813

JONESTOWN
Patrick Campbell, Mayor
P.O. Box 110
Jonestown, MS 38639
Tel: (662) 358-4328 Fax: (662) 358-4337

KILMICHAEL
Mary McAskil-Young, Mayor
P.O. Box 296, 503 Guinea Tom Ave.
Kilmichael, MS 39747-0296
Tel: (662) 262-4242 Fax: (662) 262-4400

LAMBERT
Reginald G. Griffin, Mayor
P.O. Box 198, 709 Mike Omar St.
Lambert, MS 38643
Tel: (662) 326-8018 Fax: (662) 326-8017

LUMBERTON
Gregory Cooley, Mayor
P.O. Box 211
Lumberton, MS 39455
Tel: (601) 565-7200

MARKS
Dwight A. Barfield, Mayor
P.O. Box 315
Marks, MS 38646
Tel: (662) 326-3161 Fax: (662) 326-3164

MAYERSVILLE
Linda Williams Short, Mayor
P.O. Box 162, 132 Court St.
Mayersville, MS 39113
Tel: (662) 873-6439 Fax: (662) 873-4671

MCLAIN
Mary Bolton, Mayor
P.O. Box 5
McLain, MS 39456
Tel: (601) 753-2205

METCALFE
Shirley S. Allen, Mayor
P.O. Box 250, 315 Bayou St.
Metcalfe, MS 38760
Tel: (662) 335-0212 Fax: (662) 378-8041

MOORHEAD
John E. Carpenter, Mayor
P.O. Box 578, 801 Johnny Russell Dr.
Moorhead, MS 38761
Tel: (662) 246-5461 Fax: (662) 246-5037

MOUND BAYOU
Kennedy Johnson, Mayor
P.O. Box 680, 106 W. Green St.
Mound Bayou, MS 38762
Tel: (662) 741-2194 Fax: (662) 741-2195

MT. OLIVER
Robert McNair, Mayor
P.O. Box 510
Mt. Oliver, MS 0.39119
Tel: (601) 797-3496 Fax: (601) 797-3035

NATCHEZ
Phillip C. West, Mayor
P.O. Box 1185
Natchez, MS 39121
Tel: (601) 445-7555 Fax: (601) 442-2536

OAKLAND
James R. Swearengen, Mayor
Highway 330 West, City Hall
Oakland, MS 38948
Tel: (662) 623-8668 Fax: (662) 623-9726

OKOLONA
Sherman Carouthers, Mayor
P.O.Box 111
Okolona, MS 38860
Tel: (662) 447-5461

PACE
Mae Rosie Williams, Mayor
P.O. Box 216, 333 Jenny Washington Ave.
Pace, MS 38764
Tel: (662) 723-6292 Fax: (662) 723-6198

PICKENS
Jonathan Moore, Mayor
P.O. Box 297
Pickens, MS 39146
Tel: (662) 468-2171 Fax: (662) 468-2172

PLANTERSVILLE
Viola Foster, Mayor
P.O. Box 507
Plantersville, MS 38862
Tel: (662) 844-2012 Fax: (662) 840-9565

PORT GIBSON
Amelda Arnold, Mayor
P.O. Box 607
Port Gibson, MS 39150
Tel: (601) 437-4234 Fax: (601) 437-8667

POTTS CAMP
Jimmie Collins, Mayor
P.O. Box 57, 24 South Cardinal St., City Hall
Potts Camp, MS 38659
Tel: (662) 333-7285 Fax: (662) 333-7287

RENOVA
Maurice Lucas, Mayor
5 Second Ave.
Renova, MS 38732
Tel: (662) 843-8233

ROLLING FORK
Eldridge Walker, Mayor
P.O. Box 310
Rolling Fork, MS 39159
Tel: (662) 873-2814 Fax: (662) 873-2920

RULEVILLE
Shirley Edwards, Mayor
P.O. Box 428, 200 East Floyce
Ruleville, MS 38771
Tel: (662) 756-2791 Fax: (662) 756-4590

SHAW
Roger D. Carter, Mayor
P.O. Box 679, 202 Main St.
Shaw, MS 38773
Tel: (662) 754-3131 Fax: (662) 754-5744

SHELBY
Robert Patton, Mayor
P.O. Box 43
Shelby, MS 38774
Tel: (662) 398-5156 Fax: (662) 398-7878

SHUBUTA
Clyde Brown, Mayor
P.O. Box 416, 179 Eucutta St., City Hall
Shubuta, MS 39360
Tel: (662) 678-1536

SHUQUALAK
Velma Jenkins, Mayor
P.O. Box 64, 204 Pine St.
Shuqualak, MS 39361
Tel: (662) 793-4521

SLEDGE
Lorenzo Windless, Mayor
P.O. Box 276, City Hall
Sledge, MS 38670
Tel: (662) 382-7716

SUMMIT
Charles Carter, Mayor
P.O. Box 315
Summit, MS 39666
Tel: (601) 276-7548

SUNFLOWER
Betty Fowler, Mayor
P. O. Box 127
Sunflower, MS 38778
Tel: (662) 569-3387

TCHULA
Yvonne Brown, Mayor
P.O. Box 356, City Hall
Tchula, MS 39169
Tel: (662) 235-5112 Fax: (662) 235-4925

TUTWILER
Robert Grayson, Mayor
209 Hancock Ave.
Tutwiler, MS 38963
Tel: (662) 345-8321 Fax: (6) 623-4599

UTICA
Charles E. Stokes, Mayor
P.O. Box 335, City Hall
Utica, MS 39175
Tel: (601) 885-8718 Fax: (601) 885-2807

WEBB
Ernestine Dixon, Mayor
P.O. Box 305, 338 E. Main St.
Webb, MS 38966
Tel: (662) 375-8164 Fax: (662) 375-9494

WINSTONVILLE
Milton Tutwiler, Mayor
P.O. Box 151, City Hall
Winstonville, MS 38781
Tel: (662) 741-2106 Fax: (662) 741-2107

YAZOO CITY
Wardell Leach, Mayor
421 Cluster St., City Hall
Yazoo City, MS 39194
Tel: (662) 746-1401 Fax: (662) 746-6506

MISSOURI

BERKELEY
Kyra Watson, Mayor
6140 No. Hanley Rd., City Hall
Berkeley, MO 63134
Tel: (314) 524-3313 Fax: (314) 524-1860

BEVERLY HILLS, CITY OF
Clarence King, Mayor
7150 Natural Bridge
St. Louis, MO 63121
Tel: (314) 382-6544 Fax: (314) 382-7332

COOL VALLEY
Randolph E. Toles, Mayor
100 Signal Hill Dr., City Hall
Cool Valley, MO 63121
Tel: (314) 521-3500 Fax: (314) 521-8135

COUNTRY CLUB HILLS, CITY OF
Felton L. Flagg, Mayor
7422 Eunice Ave.
St. Louis, MO 63136
Tel: (314) 261-0845 Fax: (314) 389-4933

GREENDALE, CITY OF
Monica Huddleston, Mayor
7717 Natural Bridge
St. Louis, MO 63121
Tel: (314) 383-3664 Fax: (314) 383-3664

HANLEY HILLS, VILLAGE OF
Roger Mason, Mayor
7713 Utica Drive
St. Louis, MO 63133
Tel: (314) 725-0909 Fax: (314) 727-7669

HAYTI HEIGHTS, CITY OF
Alex Green, Mayor
P.O. Box 426
Hayti, MO 63851
Tel: (573) 359-2680 Fax: (573) 359-2682

HAYWOOD CITY
Johnny Avance, Mayor
258 Pine St., City Hall
Haywood City, MO 63771
Tel: (573) 471-6511

HOMESTOWN, CITY OF
Reginald Grant, Mayor
P.O. Box 142
Wardell, MO 63879
Tel: (573) 688-2137

HOWARDVILLE
Jim Farr, Mayor
Box 6916, Hwy 61
Howardville, MO 36869
Tel: (573) 688-2137 Fax: (573) 688-2139

KINLOCH
Keith Conway, Mayor
5990 Kinloch Ave.
Kinloch, MO 63140
Tel: (314) 521-3335 Fax: (314) 521-3851

MOLINE ACRES
George H. Murphy, Mayor
2449 Cambers Rd., City Hall
Moline Acres, MO 63136
Tel: (314) 868-2433 Fax: (314) 868-2590

NORTH LILBOURN, VILLAGE OF
James Anderson, Mayor
P.O. Box 327
North Lilbourn, MO 63862
Tel: (573) 688-2584

NORTHWOODS
Evertt R. Thomas, Mayor
7121 Farley Ave., City Hall
Northwoods, MO 63121
Tel: (314) 385-8000 Fax: (314) 385-8144

PAGEDALE
Mary Louise Carter, Mayor
1420 Ferguson Ave., City Hall
Pagedale, MO 63133
Tel: (314) 726-1200 Fax: (314) 725-1756

PINE LAWN
Adrian Wright, Mayor
6250 Steve Marr Ave., City Hall
Pine Lawn, MO 63121
Tel: (314) 261-5500 Fax: (314) 261-4412

UNIVERSITY CITY
Joseph Adams, Mayor
6801 Delmar Blvd.
University City, MO 63130
Tel: (314) 862-6767 Fax: (314) 863-9146

UPLAND PARK
Carmen McClendon, Mayor
6390 Natural Bridge Ave., Village Hall
Upland Park, MO 63121
Tel: (314) 383-1856 Fax: (314) 383-1856

VELDA CITY
Robert Hensley, Mayor
2803 Maywood
Velda City, MO 63121
Tel: (314) 382-6600 Fax: (314) 382-7988

VELDA VILLAGE HILLS, CITY OF
Earlene Luster, Mayor
3501 Avondale Ave
Velda Village Hills, MO 63121
Tel: (314) 261-7221 Fax: (314) 261-7225

WELLSTON
James A. Harvey, Mayor
1414 Evergreen
Wellston, MO 63133
Tel: (314) 385-1015 Fax: (314) 381-4096

WILSON CITY, VILLAGE OF
Nichole Ghant, Mayor
P.O. Box 366
Wyatt, MO 63882
Tel: (573) 675-3400 Fax: (573) 675-3400

NEW JERSEY

ASBURY PARK
Kevin G. Sanders, Mayor
One Municipal Plaza
Asbury Park, NJ 07712
Tel: (732) 502-5755 Fax: (732) 775-1483

ATLANTIC CITY
Lorenzo Langford, Mayor
1301 Bacharach Blvd.
Atlantic City, NJ 08401
Tel: (609) 347-5400 Fax: (609) 347-5638

CAMDEN
Gwendolyn A. Faison, Mayor
P.O. Box 95120, 4th Fl., City Hall
Camden, NJ 08101-5120
Tel: (856) 757-7000 Fax: (856) 963-1841

CHESILHURST
Arland W. Poindexter, Mayor
201 Grant Ave.
Chesilhurst, NJ 08089
Tel: (856) 767-4153 Fax: (856) 753-1696

EAST ORANGE
Robert L. Bowser, Mayor
44 City Hall Plaza, City Hall
East Orange, NJ 07019
Tel: (973) 266-5151 Fax: (973) 266-5135

HILLSIDE, TOWNSHIP OF
Karen McCoy Oliver, Mayor
Hillside and Liberty Ave.
Hillside, NJ 07205
Tel: (973) 926-3000 Fax: (973) 926-9232

IRVINGTON
Wayne Smith, Mayor
Town Hall, Municipal Bldg.
Irvington, NJ 07111
Tel: (973) 399-6797 Fax: (973) 399-7321

JERSEY CITY
L. Harvey Smith, Mayor
280 Grove St., City Hall
Jersey City, NJ 07302
Tel: (201) 547-5200 Fax: (201) 547-4288

LAWNSIDE
Mark Bryant, Mayor
4 Douglas Ave., Borough Hall
Lawnside, NJ 8045
Tel: (609) 573-6200 Fax: (609) 546-3232

NEWARK
Sharpe James, Mayor
920 BRd. St. #200, , City Hall
Newark, NJ 07102
Tel: (973) 733-6400 Fax: (973) 733-5325

ORANGE
Mims Hackett, Mayor
29 N. Day St., City Hall
Orange, NJ 07050
Tel: (973) 266-4000 Fax: (973) 676-7458

PLAINFIELD
Albert I. McWilliams, Mayor
515 Watchung Ave., City Hall
Plainfield, NJ 07060
Tel: (908) 753-3310 Fax: (908) 753-3634

PLEASANTVILLE
Ralph Peterson, Sr., Mayor
18 North 1st St., City Hall
Pleasantville, NJ 08232
Tel: (609) 484-3610 Fax: (609) 641-8642

SOUTH BRUNSWICK TOWNSHIP
Deborah Johnson, Mayor
P.O. Box 190
Mommouth Jun., NJ 0.08852
Tel: (908) 329-4000

TRENTON
Douglas Palmer, Mayor
319 East State St., City Hall
Trenton, NJ 08608
Tel: (609) 989-3030 Fax: (609) 989-3939

WILLINGBORO
Jeffery E. Ramsey, Mayor
Salem Rd., Borough Hall
Willingboro, NJ 08046
Tel: (609) 877-2200 Fax: (609) 835-0782

NEW YORK

HEMPSTEAD
James A. Garner, Mayor
99 Nichols Court, Village Hall
Hempstead, NY 11550
Tel: (516) 489-3400 Fax: (516) 489-4285

MT.VERNON
Ernest D. Davis, Mayor
Roosevelt Square, City Hall
Mt.Vernon, NY 10550
Tel: (914) 665-2361 Fax: (914) 665-6173

OWEGO
Edward L. Arrington, Mayor
178 Main St.
Owego, NY 13827
Tel: (607) 687-1710 Fax: (607) 687-1787

ROCHESTER
William A. Johnson, Mayor
30 Church St. #307, Mayor's Office
Rochester, NY 14614
Tel: (585) 428-7045 Fax: (585) 428-6059

SPRING VALLEY
George Darden, Mayor
200 North Main St.
Spring Valley, NY 10977
Tel: (845) 352-1100 Fax: (845) 352-1164

NORTH CAROLINA

BAYBORO
John Gyalog, Mayor
P.O. Box 519
Bayboro, NC 28515
Tel: (252) 745-4238

BOLTON
Frank A. Wilson, Mayor
P.O. Box 327, 221 9th St.
Bolton, NC 28423
Tel: (910) 655-8945 Fax: (910) 655-4366

COFIELD
Hermea Pugh, Sr., Mayor
P.O. Box 99
Cofield, NC 27922
Tel: (252) 358-8611 Fax: (252) 358-0367

CREEDMOOR
Darryl Moss, Mayor
P.O. Box 765
Creedmoor, NC 27522
Tel: (919) 528-3332

DOBBINS HGTS, TOWN OF
William M. Ward, Sr., Mayor
P.O. Box 151
Hamlet, NC 28345
Tel: (910) 582-6002 Fax: (910) 582-1268

DOVER
Malcolm Johnson, Mayor
P.O. Box 128
Dover, NC 28526
Tel: (252) 523-9610

DURHAM
William V. Bell, Mayor
101 City Hall Plaza
Durham, NC 27701
Tel: (919) 560-4333 Fax: (919) 560-4801

EAST ARCADIA, TOWN OF
Willie Dixon, Mayor
1516 East Arcadia Rd.
Riegelwood, NC 28456
Tel: (910) 655-4388

EAST SPENCER
Erma Jefferies, Mayor
P.O. Box 339
East Spencer, NC 28039
Tel: (704) 636-7111 Fax: (704) 636-8903

ELM CITY
Grady N. Smith, Mayor
P.O. Box 717
Elm City, NC 27822
Tel: (252) 236-4917 Fax: (252) 291-7281

ENFIELD
Edward W. Jones, Mayor
P.O. Box 699
Enfield, NC 27823
Tel: (252) 445-3146 Fax: (252) 445-1019

EUREKA
Richard Worrells, Mayor
P.O. Box 3105
Eureka, NC 27830
Tel: (919) 242-5064

FAIR BLUFF
J.B. Evans, Mayor
P.O. Box 157
Fair Bluff, NC 28439
Tel: (910) 649-7426 Fax: (910) 649-7151

FAIRMONT
Nedward Graddy, Mayor
P.O. Box 248
Fairmont, NC 28340
Tel: (910) 628-9766

FAYETTEVILLE
Marshall B. Pitts, Jr., Mayor
433 Hay St.
Fayetteville, NC 28301
Tel: (910) 433-1992 Fax: (910) 433-1948

FOUNTAIN
Shirley Mitchell, Mayor
P.O. Box 134
Fountain, NC 27829
Tel: (252) 749-2881

GARYSBURG
Roy Bell, Mayor
P.O. Box 278
Garysburg, NC 27831
Tel: (252) 536-2167

GIBONSVILLE
Leonard Williams, Mayor
129 W. Main St.
Gibonsville, NC 27249
Tel: (336) 449-4144

GOLDSBORO
Alfonzo King, Mayor
P.O. Box A
Goldsboro, NC 27533
Tel: (919) 735-6121

GRANITE QUARRY
Mary Ponds, Mayor
P.O. Box 351
Granite Quarry, NC Q28072
Tel: (704) 279-5596

GREEN LEVEL, TOWN OF
Algene Tarpley, Mayor
P.O. Box 729
Haw River, NC 27258
Tel: (336) 578-3443 Fax: (336) 578-5373

GREENEVERS, CITY OF
Alfred Dixon, Mayor
314 E. Charity Rd.
Rose Hill, NC 28458
Tel: (910) 289-2927 Fax: (910) 289-2608

HOFFMAN
Jo-Ann Thomas, Mayor
P.O. Box 40
Hoffman, NC 28347
Tel: (910) 281-3576

JACKSON
John McKellar, Mayor
P.O. Box 614
Jackson, NC 27845
Tel: (252) 534-3811

KINGSTOWN, TOWN OF
Clarence Withrow, Mayor
2014 Kingstown
Kingstown, NC 28150
Tel: (704) 484-9776 Fax: (704) 484-8612

KINSTON
Johnnie Mosley, Mayor
P.O. Box 339
Kinston, NC 28502
Tel: (252) 939-3115 Fax: (252) 939-3388

KNIGHTDALE
Doug Boyd, Mayor
P.O. Box 640
Knightdale, NC 27545-0640
Tel: (919) 217-2220 (919) 217-2209

LILESVILLE
James Harrington, Mayor
P.O. Box 451
Lilesville, NC 28091
Tel: (704) 848-4711

MAXTON
Lillie McKoy, Mayor
P.O. Box 10
Maxton, NC 28364
Tel: (910) 844-5231 Fax: (910) 844-5802

MAYSVILLE
James Harper, Mayor
P.O. Box 265
Maysville, NC 28555
Tel: (910) 743-4441

MORVEN
Theodore Carr, Mayor
P.O. Box 295
Morven, NC 28119
Tel: (704) 851-9321

NAVASSA
Eulis A. Willis, Mayor
334 Main St.
Navassa, NC 28451
Tel: (910) 371-2432 Fax: (910) 371-0041

NEW BERN
Tom A. Bayliss, Mayor
3021 River Lane
New Bern, NC 28562
Tel: (252) 636-4000 Fax: (252) 636-1848

NORTHWEST, TOWN OF
James S. Knox, Mayor
P.O. Box 1509
Leland, NC 28451
Tel: (910) 655-3110 Fax: (910) 655-8853

PARMELE
Lula H. Council, Mayor
P. O. Box 98
Parmele, NC 27861
Tel: (919) 795-4242 Fax: (919) 795-4242

PRINCEVILLE
Priscilla Everette-Oates, Mayor
P.O. Box 1527, Town Hall
Princeville, NC 27886-1057
Tel: (252) 641-6816 Fax: (252) 823-5388

RENNERT, TOWN OF
Emmett McRae, Mayor
62 Park St.
Shannon, NC 28336
Tel: (910) 843-2162

RICH SQUARE
John Pellan, Mayor
P.O. Box 336
Rich Square, NC 27869
Tel: (252) 539-2315 Fax: (252) 539-3945

ROPER
Bunny Sanders, Mayor
P.O. Box 217
Roper, NC 27970-0217
Tel: (252) 793-5527 Fax: (252) 793-4396

ROWLAND
Harris McCall, Mayor
P.O. Box 127
Rowland, NC 28383
Tel: (910) 422-3333

SANDYFIELD, TOWN OF
Perry Dixon, Mayor
P.O. Box 907
Riegelwood, NC 28456
Tel: (910) 655-9877 Fax: (910) 655-9914

SEABOARD
Melvin Broadnax, Mayor
P.O. Box 327
Seaboard, NC 27876
Tel: (252) 589-5061 Fax: (252) 589-1099

SEDALIA
Jeanne Rudd, Mayor
P.O. Box C
Sedalia, NC 27342
Tel: (336) 449-1132

SHARPSBURG
Sheila Williams, Mayor
P.O. Box 1759
Sharpsburg, NC 27878
Tel: (252) 446-9441 Fax: (252) 977-7488

SNOW HILL
Donald Davis, Mayor
201 N. Greene St.
Snow Hill, NC 28580
Tel: (252) 747-3414

SPEED
Wilbert Harrison, Mayor
P.O. Box 327
Speed, NC 27781
Tel: (252) 823-4596

SPRING LAKE
Ethel Clark, Mayor
P.O. Box 617
Spring Lake, NC 28390
Tel: (910) 436-0241

TAYLORTOWN, TOWN OF
Ulysses Barrett, Jr., Mayor
P.O. Box 1274
Pinehurst, NC 28370
Tel: (910) 295-4010

TRENTON
Sylvia Willie, Mayor
P.O. Box 339
Trenton, NC 28585
Tel: (252) 448-1784

WADE
Aekins Huell, Mayor
P.O. Box 127
Wade, NC 28395
Tel: (910) 485-3502

WAGRAM
Milton Farmer, Mayor
P.O. Box 118
Wagram, NC 28396
Tel: (910) 369-2776 Fax: (910) 369-2776

WINFALL
Fredrick L. Yates, Mayor
P.O. Box 275
Winfall, NC 27985
Tel: (252) 426-5051 Fax: (252) 326-1763

OHIO

COLUMBUS
Michael B. Coleman, Mayor
90 West BRd. St.
Columbus, OH 43215
Tel: (614) 645-7671 Fax: (614) 645-1970

DAYTON
Rhine McLin, Mayor
101 W. Third St., City Commission Office
Dayton, OH 45401
Tel: (937) 333-3636 Fax: (937) 333-4299

DELAWARE

Dennis D. Davis, Mayor
1 South Sandusky St.
Delaware, OH 43015-4316
Tel: (614) 363-1965

EAST CLEVELAND

Saratha A. Goggins, Mayor
14340 Euclid Ave.
East Cleveland, OH 44112
Tel: (216) 681-2210 Fax: (216) 681-2650

FOREST PARK

Stephanie S. Dumas, Mayor
1201 W. Camper Rd.
Forest Park, OH 45240
Tel: (513) 595-5200 Fax: (513) 595-5285

HIGHLAND HILLS

Robert Nash, Mayor
4019 Northfield Rd., Village Hall
Highland Hills, OH 44122
Tel: (216) 283-3000 Fax: (216) 283-3005

LEBANON

James Mills, Mayor
50 South Broadway, City Hall
Lebanon, OH 45036
Tel: (513) 932-3060 Fax: (513) 932-2493

LINCOLN HEIGHTS

LaVerne Mitchell, Mayor
1201 Steffens Ave., City Hall
Lincoln Heights, OH 45215
Tel: (513) 733-5900 Fax: (513) 733-4190

NORTH RANDALL

Shelton Richardson, Mayor
21937 Miles Rd.
North Randall, OH 44128
Tel: (216) 662-0430 Fax: (216) 587-9280

TOLEDO

Jack Ford, Mayor
1 Government Ctr Ste 2200
Toledo, OH 43604
Tel: (419) 245-1001 Fax: (419) 245-1370

URBANCREST

Marlin West, Mayor
3357 Central Ave., Adminstration Bldg.
Urbancrest, OH 43123
Tel: (614) 875-1279 Fax: (614) 875-1359

WARRENSVILLE HGHTS

Marcia L. Fudge, Mayor
4301 Warrensville Ctr. Rd., City Hall
Warrensville Hghts, OH 44128
Tel: (216) 587-6500 Fax: (216) 587-6594

WOODLAWN

Raymond Terrell, Mayor
10141 Woodlawn Blvd.
Woodlawn, OH 45215
Tel: (513) 771-6130 Fax: (513) 771-3066

WOODMERE VILLAGE

Yolanda Broadie, Mayor
27899 Chargin Blvd.
Woodmere Village, OH 44122
Tel: (216) 831-9511 Fax: (216) 292-7023

OKLAHOMA

ARCADIA

Marilyn Murrell, Mayor
P.O. Box 268
Arcadia, OK 73007
Tel: (405) 396-2899 Fax: (405) 396-2869

BOLEY

Mary Joan Matthews, Mayor
P.O. Box 352
Boley, OK 74829
Tel: (918) 667-9790 Fax: (918) 667-9790

BROOKSVILLE, TOWN OF

Lee Oliver, Mayor
Route 1, Box 774
Brooksville, OK 74873
Tel: (405) 598-3497

CLEARVIEW

Tom Lucas, Mayor
Rt. 1- Box 1219, Town Hall
Clearview, OK 74880
Tel: (405) 786-2955

FT. COFFEE, TOWN OF

DeNay Burris, Mayor
Rt. 2 - Box 203
Spiro, OK 74959
Tel: (918) 962-5636

GRAYSON, TOWN OF

Helen JoAnn Fox, Mayor
24160 Martin Luther King
Grayson, OK 74437
Tel: (918) 652-3127 Fax: (918) 652-2823

LANGSTON

Jake Spencer, Mayor
P.O. Box 1256, Town Hall
Langston, OK 73050-1256
Tel: (405) 466-2271 Fax: (405) 466-3835

LIMA, TOWN OF

Tammie Hill, Mayor
Route 1, Box 106-A
Wewoka, OK 74884
Tel: (405) 257-6905

MERIDIAN

Anna B. Brooks, Mayor
P.O. Box 57, Town Hall
Meridian, OK 73058-0057
Tel: (405) 586-2282 Fax: (405) 586-2488

OKAY

Clarence Ashley, Mayor
P.O. Box 505
Okay, OK 74446-0505
Tel: (918) 687-6585 Fax: (918) 687-6454

OKEMA

Clyde Shaver, Mayor
Rte. 4 - Box 194
Okema, OK 74859

REDBIRD

Eugene Osborn, Mayor
P.O. Box 65
Redbird, OK 74458
Tel: (918) 483-7381 Fax: (918) 483-1801

RENTIESVILLE

Mildred Burkhalter, Mayor
P.O. Box 58
Rentiesville, OK 74459-0025
Tel: (918) 473-1577 Fax: (918) 473-0173

SPENCER

Marsha Jefferson, Mayor
P.O. Box 660, City Hall
Spencer, OK 73084
Tel: (405) 771-3226 Fax: (405) 771-3228

SUMMIT

Greg Smith, Mayor
5110 West 66th St.
Summit, OK 74401

TAFT

Essie McIntosh, Mayor
P.O. Box 312, 208 W. Seminole
Taft, OK 74463-0312
Tel: (918) 683-0568 Fax: (918) 686-9459

TATUMS

Cecil Jones, Mayor
P.O. Box 47, Town Hall
Tatums, OK 73087-0147
Tel: (580) 856-3833 Fax: (580) 856-3731

TULLAHASSEE

Benice Joy Gaines, Mayor
P.O. Box 1119
Tullahassee, OK 74454
Tel: (918) 483-2129 Fax: (918) 483-2128

OREGON

DEPOE BAY

James White, Mayor
P.O. Box 1040
Depoe Bay, OR 97341
Tel: (541) 765-2361

SHANIKO

Booker T. Pannell, Mayor
P.O. Box 17
Shaniko, OR 97057
Tel: (541) 489-3226

PENNSYLVANIA

PHILADELPHIA

John F. Street, Mayor
Room 215, 15 Market St., City Hall
Philadelphia, PA 19107
Tel: (215) 686-2181 Fax: (215) 686-2180

WILKINSBURG

Wilbert A. Young, Mayor
605 Ross St., Municipal Bldg.
Wilkinsburg, PA 15221
Tel: (412) 244-2920 Fax: (412) 243-1786

SOUTH CAROLINA

ANDREWS

Curtis Dorsey, Mayor
15 Laurie St.
Andrews, SC 29510

ATLANTIC BEACH

Irene Armstrong, Mayor
P.O. Box 1425
Atlantic Beach, SC 29582
Tel: (843) 663-2284 Fax: (843) 272-3727

AWENDAW

William H. Alston, Mayor
6470 Highway 17N
Awendaw, SC 29429
Tel: (843) 928-3378 Fax: (843) 928-3713

BLACKVILLE

Jackie T. Holman, Mayor
5983 Lartigue St.
Blackville, SC 29817
Tel: (803) 284-2444 Fax: (803) 284-3243

BOWMAN

Zelda Pelzer, Mayor
P.O. Box 37
Bowman, SC 29018

BRUNSON

Terry Wright, Mayor
P.O. Box 300
Brunson, SC 29911
Tel: (843) 632-3633 Fax: (843) 632-3023

CALHOUN FALLS

Johnnie Waller, Mayor
P.O. Box 501
Calhoun Falls, SC 29628
Tel: (864) 447-8512 Fax: (864) 447-9299

CARLISLE

Janie G. Goree, Mayor
P.O. Box 305
Carlisle, SC 29031
Tel: (864) 427-1505 Fax: (864) 427-3155

CHESTER

Wanda Stringfellow, Mayor
103 Wanda Ln., City Hall
Chester, SC 29706
Tel: (803) 581-2123 Fax: (803) 377-1116

CLIO

Leroy Woods, Mayor
P.O. Box 554
Clio, SC 29525

EASTOVER

Christopher K. Campbell, Mayor
P.O. Box 58
Eastover, SC 29044
Tel: (803) 353-2281 Fax: (803) 353-8178

ESTILL

Thomas Owens, Mayor
P.O. Box 415
Estill, SC 29918
Tel: (803) 625-3243 Fax: (803) 625-3106

FAIRFAX

Moses L.Cohen, Jr., Mayor
P.O. Box Drawer 8
Fairfax, SC 29827
Tel: (803) 632-3111 Fax: (803) 632-3799

GIFFORD

James Risher, Sr., Mayor
P.O. Box Drawer 189
Gifford, SC 29923
Tel: (803) 625-2712 Fax: (803) 625-2712

GRAY COURT

John R. Carter, Mayor
P.O. Box 438
Gray Court, SC 29645
Tel: (864) 876-2581 Fax: (864) 876-3999

GREELEYVILLE

German Glasscho, Mayor
P.O. Box 212
Greeleyville, SC 29056
Tel: (843) 426-2111 Fax: (843) 426-2298

GREENWOOD

Floyd Nicholson, Mayor
P.O. Box 40
Greenwood, SC 29648
Tel: (864) 942-8400 Fax: (864) 942-8470

LAKE CITY

Carl LaRue Alford, Mayor
202 Kelley St.
Lake City, SC 29560
Tel: (843) 374-5421 Fax: (843) 374-1704

LINCOLNVILLE

Tyrone Aiken, Mayor
P.O. Box 536
Lincolnville, SC 29484
Tel: (843) 873-3261 Fax: (843) 873-3267

LIVINGSTON
Bobby Gordon, Mayor
129 Shop Rd.
Livingston, SC 29107
Tel: (803) 247-5271

MANNING
Kevin Johnson, Mayor
P.O. Box 155
Manning, SC 29102

MAYESVILLE
Willie Jefferson, Mayor
P.O. Box 156
Mayesville, SC 29104
Tel: (803) 453-5482

MCBEE
Levorn Von Mack, Mayor
P.O. Box 248
McBee, SC 20101-0248
Tel: (803) 335-8474 Fax: (803) 335-8393

PORT ROYAL
Samuel E. Murray, Mayor
Drawer 9
Port Royal, SC 29935
Tel: (843) 986-2200 Fax: (843) 986-2210

SANTEE
Silas Seabrooks, Mayor
P.O. Box 424-A
Santee, SC 29142
Tel: (803) 854-2154 Fax: (803) 854-3233

SELLERS
Levenia Wright, Mayor
P.O. Box 116
Sellers, SC 29592
Tel: (843) 752-5009 Fax: (843) 752-9338

TIMMONSVILLE
Henry B. Peoples, Mayor
P.O. Box 342
Timmonsville, SC 29161
Tel: (803) 346-7942 Fax: (803) 346-7942

VANCE
Sylvia G. Shinger, Mayor
P.O. Box 410
Vance, SC 29163
Tel: (803) 492-3114 Fax: (803) 492-4166

WATERLOO
Harvey Henderson, Mayor
P.O. Box 108A
Waterloo, SC 29384
Tel: (803) 677-9505

WELLFORD
Sallie Peake, Mayor
P.O. Box 215
Wellford, SC 29385-0099
Tel: (864) 439-4875 Fax: (864) 439-2437

WILLIAMS
Wilmot Hayes, Mayor
P.O. Box 67
Williams, SC 29493

TENNESSEE

HENNING
Mary Ann Jarrett, Mayor
P.O. Box 488
Henning, TN 38041
Tel: (731) 738-5055 Fax: (731) 738-5056

MEMPHIS
Willie W. Herenton, Mayor
125 Mid-American Mall
Memphis, TN 38103
Tel: (901) 576-6000 Fax: (901) 576-6012

NEWPORT
Roland Dykes, Jr., Mayor
P.O. Box 370
Newport, TN 37822
Tel: (423) 623-1063 Fax: (423) 623-4060

TEXAS

AMES, CITY OF
John White, Mayor
P.O. Box 8094
Liberty, TX 77575-8094
Tel: (936) 336-7278 Fax: (936) 336-8856

ANNONA
George English, Mayor
P.O. Box 707
Annona, TX 75550-0107
Tel: (903) 697-3691 Fax: (903) 697-2601

BELLMEAD
Carl Swanson III, Mayor
3015 Bellmead Drive
Bellmead, TX 76705
Tel: (254) 799-2436 Fax: (254) 799-5969

BROOKSHIRE
Keith Woods, Mayor
P.O. Box 160
Brookshire, TX 77423-0160
Tel: (281) 375-5050 Fax: (281) 375-5045

BUFFALO
Charlie S. Scott, Mayor
P.O. Box 219
Buffalo, TX 75831
Tel: (903) 322-4741 Fax: (903) 322-2142

CANEY CITY
Joe Barron, Mayor
15241 Barron Rd.
Caney City, TX 75148
Tel: (903) 489-1844 Fax: (903) 489-2576

CHINA
Herman Edwards, Mayor
P.O. Box 248
China, TX 77613-0248
Tel: (409) 752-5403 Fax: (409) 752-5184

CLEVELAND
Monique McDuffie Davis, Mayor
203 East Boothe St.
Cleveland, TX 77327
Tel: (281) 592-2667 Fax: (281) 592-6624

COFFEE CITY
Michael Warren, Mayor
P.O. Box 716
Coffee City, TX 75763-0716
Tel: (903) 876-3414 Fax: (903) 876-2433

CRAWFORD
Robert Campbell, Mayor
P.O. Box 7, City Hall
Crawford, TX 76638
Tel: (254) 486-2125 Fax: (254) 486-2125

CUNEY, CITY OF
Oscar Birdow, Mayor
P.O. Box 42
Cuney, TX 75759-0068
Tel: (903) 876-2655 Fax: (903) 876-4705

DETROIT
Travis Bronner, Mayor
190 East Garner Ave.
Detroit, TX 75436
Tel: (903) 674-4573 Fax: (903) 674-6029

DOMINO, TOWN OF
Marvin Campbell, Mayor
14555 FM 3129
Queen City, TX Q75572
Tel: (903) 796-2843 Fax: (903) 796-1056

EASTON
Willis Sammons, Mayor
P.O. Box 007
Easton, TX 75641-0007
Tel: (903) 643-7819 Fax: (903) 643-2219

FOREST HILL
James Gosey, Mayor
6800 Forest Hill Drive
Forest Hill, TX 76140
Tel: (817) 568-3000 Fax: (817) 568-3049

FULSHEAR
Viola Randle, Mayor
P.O. Box 182
Fulshear, TX 77441-0182
Tel: (713) 346-1796 Fax: (713) 346-2556

GLENN HEIGHTS
Jesus Humphrey, Mayor
1938 South Hampton
Glenn Heights, TX 75154
Tel: (972) 223-1690 Fax: (972) 223-9307

GOLINDA
Ennis Degrate, Jr., Mayor
7021 Golinda Dr., City Hall
Golinda, TX 76658
Tel: (254) 881-6998

GOODLOW, CITY OF
Willie H. Washington, Mayor
P.O. Box 248
Kerens, TX 75144-0001
Tel: (903) 396-7862

GREENVILLE
Kathy Wilson, Mayor
2469 County Rd. 4311, City Hall
Greenville, TX 75401
Tel: (903) 455-5776

HEMPSTEAD
Michael Wolfe, Mayor
1125 Austin
Hempstead, TX 77445
Tel: (979) 826-2486 Fax: (979) 826-6703

HIGHLAND VILLAGE
Bill Lawrence, Mayor
1000 Highland Village Rd
Highland Village, TX 75077
Tel: (972) 317-5558 Fax: (972) 317-0237

HUTCHINS
Artis Johnson, Mayor
P.O. Box 500
Hutchins, TX 75141
Tel: (972) 225-6121 Fax: (972) 225-5559

ITALY
Frank Jackson, Mayor
101 W. Main, City Hall
Italy, TX 76654
Tel: (972) 483-7329 Fax: (972) 483-2800

JASPER
R.C. Horn, Mayor
P.O. Box 610
Jasper, TX 75951
Tel: (409) 384-4651 Fax: (409) 384-3790

KENDLETON
Carolyn Jones, Mayor
P.O. Box 809
Kendleton, TX 77451-0809
Tel: (979) 532-8240 Fax: (979) 282-2055

KOUNTZE
Fred Williams, Mayor
P.O. Box 188
Kountze, TX 77625
Tel: (409) 246-3352 Fax: (409) 246-2319

KYLE
James Adkins, Mayor
P.O. Box 40
Kyle, TX 78640-0040
Tel: (512) 268-5341 Fax: (512) 268-0675

LARUE
Arthur Earl, Mayor
Route 1, Box 133
LaRue, TX 75770
Tel: (903) 852-3431

LEANDER
Charles Eaton, Mayor
P.O. Box 319, City Hall
Leander, TX 78646
Tel: (512) 259-1178

LEROY
David Williams, Mayor
P.O. Box 164
Leroy, TX 76654-0164
Tel: (254) 822-0407 Fax: (254) 757-3622

LEXINGTON
Robert L. Willrich, Sr., Mayor
P.O. Box 154
Lexington, TX 78947-0154
Tel: (979) 773-2221

MANCHACA
John Linton, Mayor
11919 Bluebonnet Lane
Manchaca, TX 78652
Tel: (512) 282-2493

MINERAL WELLS
Clarence Holliman, Mayor
P.O. Box 460
Mineral Wells, TX 76068
Tel: (940) 328-7700 Fax: (940) 328-7704

OLD RIVER-WINFREE, TOWN OF
Joe Landry, Mayor
P.O. Box 1169
Mount Belview, TX 77580
Tel: (281) 385-1735 Fax: (281) 576-2655

ORANGE
Essie Bellfield, Mayor
P.O. Box 520
Orange, TX 77630
Tel: (409) 886-3611 Fax: (409) 886-9096

PITTSBURG
Noble Smith, Mayor
P.O. Box 795
Pittsburg, TX 75157-0795
Tel: (903) 856-7889

PRAIRIE VIEW
Frank D. Jackson, Mayor
P.O. Box 817
Prairie View, TX 77446-0817
Tel: (936) 857-3711 Fax: (936) 857-5836

ROSSER
Albert L. Davis, Mayor
P.O. Box 31
Rosser, TX 75157-0031
Tel: (972) 486-3360

SAN FELIPE
Bobby Byars, Mayor
927 Sixth St.
San Felipe, TX 77473
Tel: (929) 885-7035 Fax: (929) 885-7396

SEVEN OAKS, TOWN OF
Calvin Cooper, Mayor
P.O. Box 32
Leggett, TX 77350
Tel: (936) 398-5026

SOUR LAKE
Bruce Robinson, Mayor
P.O. Box 208
Sour Lake, TX 77659-0208
Tel: (408) 287-3573

TAYLOR
Donald Hill, Mayor
400 Porter St.
Taylor, TX 76574
Tel: (512) 352-3676 Fax: (512) 352-8256

TERRELL
Frances Anderson, Mayor
201 East Nash
Terrell, TX 75160
Tel: (972) 551-6600 Fax: (972) 551-2743

THE COLONY
Bernetta Shannon, Mayor
6800 Main St.
The Colony, TX 75056
Tel: (972) 625-3184

THOMPSONS
Freddie Newsome, Jr., Mayor
P.O. Box 29
Thompsons, TX 77481
Tel: (281) 343-9929 Fax: (281) 343-7786

THORNDALE
Gary Williams, Mayor
P.O. Box 308
Thorndale, TX 76577-0308
Tel: (512) 898-2523

VAN ALSTYNE
Willie Boddie, Mayor
P.O. Box 247
Van Alstyne, TX 75495
Tel: (903) 482-5426 Fax: (903) 482-5122

WACO
Mae J. Jackson, Mayor
P.O. Box 2570
Waco, TX 76702-2570
Tel: (254) 750-5640 Fax: (254) 754-3949

WHITEWRIGHT
Bill Goodson, Mayor
P.O. Box 516
Whitewright, TX 75491-0516
Tel: (903) 364-2219 Fax: (903) 364-5241

WILLIS
Leonard Reed, Mayor
P.O. Box 436
Willis, TX 77378
Tel: (936) 856-3099 Fax: (936) 890-7414

WOLFE CITY
Robert C. Lewis, Jr., Mayor
101 Main St.
Wolfe City, TX 75496
Tel: (903) 496-2251 Fax: (903) 496-7181

UTAH

SOUTH ODGEN
George Garwood, Jr., Mayor
560 39th St.
South Odgen, UT 84403
Tel: (801) 622-8585 Fax: (801) 399-4410

VIRGINIA

ALEXANDRIA
William D. Euille, Mayor
301 King St., Rm. 2300, City Hall
Alexandria, VA 22314
Tel: (703) 838-4501 Fax: (703) 838-6433

CHESAPEAKE
William E. Ward, Mayor
P.O. Box 15225
Chesapeake, VA 23328
Tel: (757) 382-6462 Fax: (757) 382-6678

PETERSBURG
Annie M. Mickens, Mayor
135 N. Union St.,Rm 210, City Hall
Petersburg, VA 23803
Tel: (804) 733-2323 Fax: (804) 863-2171

PORTSMOUTH
James Holley, Mayor
P.O. Box 820
Portsmouth, VA 23705
Tel: (757) 393-8639 Fax: (757) 393-5378

RICHMOND
Douglas Wilder, Mayor
900 East Brd. St. #201, City Hall
Richmond, VA 23219
Tel: (804) 646-7977 Fax: (804) 646-3027

Prominent
African Americans

Arts

B.B. KING
Blues Musician

Throughout the 1990s, as well as the 1980s, 1970s, 1960s and 1950s, there has been only one King of the Blues—Riley B. King, affectionately known as B.B. King. Since King started recording in the late 1940s, he has released over fifty albums, many of them considered blues classics.

Riley B. King was born on September 16, 1925, on a cotton plantation in Itta Bena, Mississippi. He used to play on the corner of Church and Second Street for dimes and would sometimes play in as many as four towns on a Saturday night. In 1947, with his guitar and $2.50, he hitchhiked north to Memphis, Tennessee, to pursue his musical career. King stayed with his cousin, Bukka White, one of the most renowned rural blues performers of his time, who schooled King further in the art of the blues.

King's first big break came in 1948 when he performed on Sonny Boy Williamson's radio program on KWEM. This led to steady performance engagements at the Sixteenth Avenue Grill in West Memphis and later to a ten-minute spot on WDIA. King's Spot, sponsored by Pepticon, became so popular that it was increased in length and became the Sepia Swing Club. Soon, King

needed a catchy radio name. What started out as Beale Street Blues Boy was shortened to Blues Boy King, and eventually B.B. King. Incidentally, King's middle initial "B" is just that; it is not an abbreviation.

Soon after his number-one hit, *Three O'Clock Blues*, King began touring nationally, and he has never stopped, performing an average of 275 concerts a year. In 1956, King and his band played an astonishing 342 one-night stands. From small-town cafes to prestigious concert halls, King has become the most renowned blues musician of the past forty years.

King's technique is nonetheless complex, featuring delicate filigrees of single-string runs punctuated by loud chords, subtle vibratos, and bent notes. The technique of rock guitar playing is to a large degree derived from King's playing.

Over the years, King has developed one of the world's most readily identified guitar styles. He borrowed from Lonnie Johnson, Blind Lemon Jefferson, T-Bone Walker, and others, integrating his precise vocal-like string bends and his left-hand vibrato, both of which have become indispensable components of rock guitarists' vocabulary. His economy and every-note-counts phrasing have been a model for thousands of players, including Eric Clapton, George Harrison, and Jeff Beck.

King has mixed traditional blues, jazz, swing, mainstream, pop, and jump into a unique sound. His singing is richly melodic, both vocally and in the singing that comes from his guitar.

King has influenced Eric Clapton, Mike Bloomfield, Albert Collins, Buddy Guy, Freddie King, Jimi Hendrix, Otis Rush, Johnny Winter, Albert King, and many others; and he himself was influenced by Charles Brown, Lowell Fulsom, Elmore James, Blind Lemon Jefferson, Jimmy Rushing, T-Bone Walker, Bukka White, and others.

In 1969, King was chosen by the Rolling Stones to open eighteen American concerts for them; Ike and Tina Turner also played on eighteen shows. King also made the first of his numerous appearances on Johnny Carson's *The Tonight Show*. In 1970, King premiered in Las Vegas at Caesar's Palace and at the Royal Box in the American Hotel in New York City, as well as on *The Ed Sullivan Show*.

On February 23, 1990, PBS started televising *All Day & All Night: Memories From Beale Street Musicians*, which featured B.B. King and captured the lifestyles of musicians who performed on Beale Street from the 1920s to the 1950s, when being on Beale Street was like living in paradise.

In 1990, King and Ray Charles co-headlined the Philip Morris Superband five-continent world tour. The final concert was recorded and *Live At The Apollo* became King's first big band album. In 1991, King headlined the Philip Morris Superband International Tour again with Diane Reeves featured. Also in 1991, King participated in the all-star Guitar Legends concert in Seville, Spain, where practically every guitar hero performed.

In 1990, King received the Songwriter's Hall of Fame Lifetime Achievement Award, and in 1991, the Orville H. Gibson Lifetime Achievement Award from Gibson Guitar Company. In 1989, King's imprint was added to the Amsterdam, Holland, Walk of Fame and in 1991, to the Hollywood Walk of Fame. In 1973, King received the B'nai Brith Humanitarian Award from the Music and Performance Lodge of New York.

In 1990, King received the prestigious Presidential Medal of the Arts in Washington, DC, with President Bush presiding. In 1991, King received the National Heritage Fellowship from the National Endowment of the Arts. In 1995, he received the Kennedy Center Honors.

Over the years, King has been bestowed eight Grammy Awards by his peers: Best Rhythm & Blues Vocal Performance, Male in 1970 for "The Thrill Is Gone," Best Ethnic or Traditional recording in 1981 for *There Must Be A Better World Somewhere*, and Best Traditional Blues Recording in 1983 for *Blues 'N' Jazz* and in 1985 for "My Guitar Sings the Blues" from *Six Silver Strings*. In 1970, King's *Indianola Mississippi Seeds* won an art director's award for Best Album Cover. In 1989, King received two more nominations: Best Contemporary Blues Recording *King Of The Blues* 1989, and Best Rock Performance by a duo or group with vocal for "When Love Comes To Town" with U2 from U2's *Rattle And Hum*. In 1990, King received another Grammy for the album *Live At San Quentin* as Best Traditional Blues Recording. In 1991, King was bestowed Best Traditional Blues Recording for *Live At The Apollo* and in 1993 the same award for *Blues Summit*. And in 1996, along with Eric Clapton, Jimmie Vaughn, Robert Cray, Bonnie Raitt, Buddy Guy, Dr. John, and Art Neville, King received the Best Rock Instrumental Performance for "SRV Shuffle" from *A Tribute to Stevie Ray Vaughan*.

King was inducted into the Blues Foundation Hall of Fame in 1984 and into the Rock and Roll Hall of Fame in 1987, where Sting, of the Police, made the induction speech. King was the recipient of the 1986 National Association For Campus Activities Hall of Fame Award. He was Blues Act of the Year in 1985, 1987, and 1988 Performance Award Polls. He is a founding member of the John F. Kennedy Performing Arts Center. King received the Grammy Lifetime Achievement Award in December of 1987 at the first televised awards in May 1990. He won the Lifetime Achievement Award from the Blues Foundation in 1997. He has received four honorary doctorates: Tougaloo College (L.H.D.) in 1973; Yale University (D. Music) in 1977; Berklee College of Music (D. Music) in 1982; and Rhodes College of Memphis (D. Fine Arts) in 1990. In 1992, he received the National Award of Distinction from the University of Mississippi.

Business

ARTHUR H. HARPER
President and CEO, GE Equipment Services

Arthur H. ("Art") Harper is President and Chief Executive Officer of GE Equipment Services, based in Stamford, Connecticut. The Company's primary business units include Rail Services, Trailer Fleet Services/Modular Space, Equipment Services Europe, Asset Intelligence, and Penske Truck Leasing.

Harper also oversees the GE SeaCo joint venture. Previously Harper was an Executive Vice President and a member of the Office of the Chief Executive Officer at GE Capital. He is also a member of GE's Corporate Executive Council.

Harper joined GE Plastics in 1984 as a market development specialist in the ULTEM business, where he also worked as an aerospace application field programs specialist and as the aircraft application program manager. In 1987, he was appointed district sales manager for GE Silicones in Brea, CA, which he held until he was named plant manager in 1991 at the Plastics plant in Oxnard. In 1992, Harper was named business leader for crystalline materials in Pittsfield, Massachusetts, and in 1994, moved to business leader of the LEXAN business. He became President of GE Plastics of Greater China in 1996. Harper was appointed Vice President of Global Manufacturing for GE Plastics in Bergen Op Zoom, the Netherlands, in 1998.

In May 2000, Harper became President and Senior Managing Director for GE Plastics Europe at the company's European headquarters in Bergen op Zoom. Harper had full responsibility and accountability for the entire operation and financial results of GE Plastics Europe, Middle East, India, and Africa.

Harper received his Bachelor's Degree in Chemical Engineering from Stevens Institute of Technology in 1978. In recognition of his many accomplishments, he received the Black Achievers in Industry Award in 1994 and the 1998 Career Achievement Award at Stevens Institute of Technology. In 2004, Harper received the

Social Justice Hero Award from the Fairfield County Region National Conference for Community and Justice, and the Whitney M. Young, Jr. Service Award from the Boy Scouts of America Greater New York Councils. He is a member of the Executive Committee of GE's African American Forum and serves as Chair of the Stamford Commission on Education Achievement, a volunteer community organization working to eliminate the achievement gap among public school children in Stamford, Connecticut. He is also a board member of the Yerwood Center, a non-profit community center in Stamford.

Harper's hobbies include golf, collecting jazz recordings, and African American art.

JOHNATHAN RODGERS
President and CEO, TV One

In March 2003, Johnathan Rodgers was named President and CEO of TV One, the new lifestyle and entertainment channel targeting adult African American viewers that was launched January 19, 2004, by Radio One, the largest radio broadcaster primarily targeting African American and urban

listeners; Comcast Corporation, the nation's largest cable operator; and four other investors.

Previously, Rodgers was President of Discovery Networks, U.S., for six years, and was responsible for all aspects of the domestic television division of Discovery Communications, including programming, affiliate sales, advertising sales, marketing, research, business development and communications. Discovery Networks owns, operates, and manages the Discovery Channel, TLC (The Learning Channel), Animal Planet, Travel Channel, Discovery Health Channel, Discovery en Español, Discovery Kids Channel, Discovery Science Channel, Discovery Home & Leisure Channel, Discovery Civilization Channel (now Discovery Times Channel), and Discovery Wings Channel.

Prior to joining Discovery Communications, Inc., in 1996, Rodgers had a successful twenty-year career at CBS, Inc., where he held a variety of executive positions, including serving at the President of CBS' highly profitable Television Stations Division. During his career at CBS Television, Rodgers also served as an award-winning news director and general manager and as an executive producer for CBS News.

Rodgers began his professional career as a print journalist working as a writer-reporter for *Sports Illustrated*. He later worked for *Newsweek* magazine as an associate editor.

Rodgers is a trustee of the University of California (Berkeley) Foundation. He also serves on the Board of Directors of the Procter & Gamble Company and the National Cable Television Association. He received his undergraduate degree in journalistic studies from the University of California at Berkeley and his Masters in Communications from Stanford University.

JOHN ROGERS

Chairman and CEO, Ariel Capital Management, LLC

John W. Rogers, Jr,. is Chairman and Chief Executive Officer of Ariel Capital Management, LLC, an institutional money management firm that he founded in 1983. With over $21 billion in assets under management, the firm manages separate accounts for institutional clients and also serves individual investors and 401(k) plans through its no-load mutual funds. As the firm's Chief Investment Officer, Rogers has direct responsibility for the management of Ariel's small- and mid-cap value portfolios as well as the publicly traded Ariel Fund and Ariel Appreciation Fund. Prior to founding Ariel, Rogers worked for two and a half years for the investment banking firm of William Blair & Company.

Rogers serves as a corporate board member of organizations that include Aon Corporation, Bally Total Fitness Holding Corporation, Exelon Corporation, and McDonald's Corporation. Also dedicated to giving back to the community, Rogers' civic affiliations include serving as a Director of the Chicago Urban League and as a Trustee of the University of Chicago. In addition, he is a former President of the Board of the Chicago Park District. He received an A.B. in

Economics in 1980 from Princeton University, where he was also Captain of the Varsity Basketball Team.

Rogers' investment expertise has brought him to the forefront of media attention. He is frequently quoted in business publications. In addition, he has made guest appearances on television shows ranging from Louis Rukeyser's *Wall Street* to *The Oprah Winfrey Show* and has also spoken at many academic institutions. In 1995, Rogers was profiled in The Mutual Fund Masters alongside Peter Lynch and John Templeton. In 1994, he was named by *Time* magazine as one of its 50 for the Future, a roster of the country's most promising leaders under age forty. Additionally, in 1988, he was named Mutual Fund Manager of the Year by Sylvia Porter's *Personal Finance* magazine.

Community

ANDREW YOUNG

Chairman, Goodworks International

Ambassador Andrew Young is chairman of Goodworks International, a specialty consulting group based in Atlanta, Georgia, that provides strategic services to corporations and governments operating in the global economy. Ambassador Young serves as a member of the boards of directors of numerous organizations and businesses, including Delta Airlines, Argus, Host Marriott Corporation, Archer Daniels Midland, Cox Communications, and Thomas Nelson Publishers.

Now the National Council of Churches'(NCC's) Immediate Past President, Ambassador Young served as NCC President—a part-time, non-salaried leadership post—in 2000-2001. His NCC presidency brought him full circle, as he had served as associate director of the Department of Youth Work of the NCC's Division of Christian Education from 1957 to 1961.

Ambassador Young is an ordained minister in the United Church of Christ. He has published two books: *A Way Out of No Way* (Thomas Nelson), and *An Easy Burden* (Harper Collins). His awards include the Presidential Medal of Freedom and many honorary degrees. He served three terms in the U.S. Congress from the Fifth District of Georgia. In 1977, President Jimmy Carter named him Ambassador to the United Nations. He served two terms as Mayor of Atlanta and was Co-Chairman of the Centennial Olympic Games in 1996.

Ambassador Young was a top aide to Dr. Martin Luther King, Jr., during the Civil Rights Movement, was involved in its inception, and served as Vice-President of the Southern Christian Leadership Conference. He presently serves on the Board of the Dr. Martin Luther King, Jr. Center for Non-Violent Social Change.

Andrew Young, born March 12, 1932, was ordained a United Church of Christ (UCC) minister and worked on the NCC staff before serving as a civil rights leader, mayor, congressman and ambassador. His history with the NCC stretches back to its beginning years.

VIRGIL ROBERTS
Activist

Virgil Roberts' activist career began early. At UCLA, he helped create the trailblazing African American Studies Center. Upon graduation, he received a Ford Foundation Foreign Affairs Scholar Fellowship. Instead of a career in diplomacy, however, Roberts decided to become a civil rights attorney.

A Felix Frankfurter Scholar at Harvard, Roberts received his Juris Doctor degree in 1972. He began his legal career as a civil litigator with a prominent Los Angeles law firm, Pacht, Ross, Warne, Bernard & Sears.

In 1976, Roberts formed the law firm of Manning & Roberts. Notable among the civil rights matters handled by the firm was Roberts' representation of the NAACP in the Los Angeles school desegregation case, *Crawford vs. Board of Education.*

Roberts joined Solar Records as Executive Vice President and General Counsel in 1981, and in 1990 became President of Solar Records, the most successful African American-owned record company in the 1980s.

In 1996, Roberts formed the law firm of Bobbitt & Roberts, which specializes in representing entertainment industry clients, concentrating on television, film, and music.

The active attorney has served as Chairman of the Los Angeles Education Partnership, Treasurer of the Los Angeles Private Industry Council, Vice Chairman of the Public Education Fund Network, Trustee of the Committee for Economic Development, and Trustee of Marlborough School. He has served on the boards of BESLA, Los Angeles Education Alliance for Restructuring Now, and the CORO Foundation.

Past Chairman of the California Community Foundation board, Roberts also was board chair of the Los Angeles Annenberg Metropolitan Project, which under his leadership raised and spent more than $120 million to reform public education in the Los Angeles Basin.

Roberts' current commitments include, among others, the boards of Community Build, Occidental College, Families in Schools, and the Alliance of Artists and Record Companies.

Roberts has been honored by the Los Angeles Urban League, the NAACP Legal Defense and Education Fund, the University of Southern California School of Education, and the UCLA Black Alumni Association.

Education

MARVALENE HUGHES
President, Dillard University, New Orleans, Louisiana

The Dillard University Board of Trustees unanimously elected Dr. Marvalene Hughes of Modesto, California, as the Institution's ninth and first woman President-elect on March 4, 2005. She officially began her presidency on July 1, 2005.

Dr. Hughes served as President of California State University, Stanislaus, from 1994 to 2005. There, she served as the first woman and first president of color. During her extensive career in higher education, Dr. Hughes has served in a number of high-level leadership positions at major research universities.

Exhibiting strong leadership and integrity, combined with her passion and commitment to providing educational opportunities to America's young scholars, Dr. Hughes has served as Vice President for Student Affairs/Vice Provost, and Professor of Educational Psychology at the University of Minnesota's Twin Cities campus, and system-wide administrator for all four University of Minnesota campuses (1990-1994). She was a vice president and professor at the University of Toledo (1988-90), Associate Vice President for Student Affairs at Arizona State University (1986-1988), and Director of Counseling Services and Placement at San Diego State University (1977-1986), where she also served as a professor and counselor (1972-1977).

Underscoring her dedication to building global educational opportunities, Dr. Hughes initiated international partnerships with the Arab American University in Jenin (Palestinian Territory), Ethiopian-African American University (Addis Ababa), Hanseo University in South Korea, Evora University in Portugal, the University of the Azores, and Tamkang University in Taiwan.

Dr. Hughes has published and conducted research in the areas of education, managing organizations, human behavior, and diversity. She has made hundreds of presentations globally throughout the United States, Austria, South Africa, Russia, Lithuania, China, Bermuda, Jordan, the United Arab Emirates, and Ethiopia. She has been the recipient of several professional and community service awards from both national and international groups and agencies.

Dr. Hughes' educational background includes earning a Ph.D. in Counseling and Administration from Florida State University, and Bachelor of Science and Master of Science degrees from Tuskegee University. She has pursued post-doctoral studies at Harvard, New York University, and Columbia University.

FREEMAN A. HRABOWSKI

President, University of Maryland, Baltimore County

Freeman A. Hrabowski III has served as President of the University of Maryland, Baltimore County, since May 1992. His research and publications focus on science and math education, with special emphasis on minority participation and performance.

Dr. Hrabowski serves as a consultant to the National Science Foundation, the National Institutes of Health, and universities and school systems nationwide. He also sits on several corporate and civic boards, including the Baltimore Museum of Art; Constellation Energy Group; France-Merrick Foundation; Marguerite Casey Foundation; McCormick & Company, Inc.; Mercantile Safe Deposit & Trust Company; University of Maryland Medical System, and the Urban Institute.

Dr. Hrabowski's recent awards and honors include election to the American Academy of Arts and Sciences and the American Philosophical Society; receiving the prestigious McGraw Prize in Education and the U.S. Presidential Award for Excellence in Science, Mathematics, and Engineering Mentoring; being named Marylander of the Year by the editors of the *Baltimore Sun*; and being listed among *Fast Company* magazine's Fast 50 Champions of Innovation in business and technology. He also holds a number of honorary degrees, including, most recently, from Duke University, the University of Illinois, Gallaudet University, the Medical University of South Carolina, and Binghamton University.

Dr. Hrabowski has co-authored two books, *Beating the Odds* and *Overcoming the Odds*, focusing on parenting and high-achieving African American males and females in science. Both books are used by universities, school systems, and community groups around the country.

A child-leader in the Civil Rights Movement, Dr. Hrabowski was prominently featured in Spike Lee's 1997 documentary *Four Little Girls*, on the 1963 racially motivated bombing of Birmingham's Sixteenth Street Baptist Church.

Born in 1950 in Birmingham, Alabama, Dr. Hrabowski graduated at nineteen from Hampton Institute with highest honors in mathematics. At the University of Illinois at Urbana-Champaign, he received his M.A. in Mathematics and four years later, at age 24, his Ph.D. in Higher Education Administration/Statistics.

ISIAH WARNER

Boyd Professor, Louisiana State University

Isiah M. Warner received his B.S. in Chemistry from Southern University (Baton Rouge) in 1968. He entered graduate school at the University of Washington in 1973 and received his Ph.D. in 1977.

Dr. Warner was assistant professor of chemistry at Texas A&M University from 1977 to 1982. He joined Emory University in 1982 as associate professor and was promoted to full professor in 1986. He was named Samuel Candler Dobbs Professor of Chemistry in 1987. In August 1992, Dr. Warner joined Louisiana State University (LSU) as Philip W. West Professor of Analytical and Environmental Chemistry. He was Chair of the Chemistry Department from July 1994 to 1997. He was appointed Boyd Professor of the LSU System in July 2000, Vice Chancellor for Strategic Initiatives in April 2001, and Howard Hughes Medical Institute Professor in 2002.

Dr. Warner has more than 250 publications and has been issued six patents for his work. He has chaired thirty-five doctoral dissertations. His honors include: Marquette University Honorary Doctor of Science degree (May 22, 2005); Charles E. Coates Award; ACS local section (May 12, 2005); Tuskegee University George Washington Carver Achievement Award (January 27, 2005); University of Washington College of Arts & Sciences Distinguished Alumnus Award (2004); ACS Award for Encouraging Disadvantaged Students into Careers in the Chemical Sciences, and Council for Chemical Research Diversity Award (2003). He was elected to the status of Fellow of the

American Association for the Advancement of Science (2003); Howard Hughes Medical Institute Professor (2002); and was named CASE Louisiana Teacher of the Year. He also received the LSU Distinguished Faculty Award; AAAS Lifetime Mentor Award; Eastern Analytical Symposium Award for Achievements in the Fields of Analytical Science (2000); 1998 Fulbright Fellowship for Research/Teaching in Kenya; and the 1997 Presidential Award for Excellence in Science, Mathematics, and Engineering Mentoring from President Clinton.

Government

MELINDA DOWNING

Environmental Justice Program Manager, U.S. Department of Energy

Melinda Downing currently serves as the U.S. Department of Energy's (DOE's) Environmental Justice Program Manager. She carries out her duties in the Office of Stakeholder Relations in the Office of Legacy Management (LM). Prior to transferring to LM, Downing carried out her duties in the Internal/External Coordination Group within the Office of Environmental Management at DOE headquarters in Washington, DC. During this tenure, she served as the Director of the Office of Environmental Management's Center for Environmental Management Information, which is a clearinghouse for environmental management information. Downing also represents the DOE as a member of the Federal Interagency Working Group on Environmental Justice. She has managed and conducted Public Participation and Environmental Justice training at DOE headquarters and field offices across the nation.

In October 1989, Downing began her assignment in the DOE's Office of Environmental Management—which was called the Office of Environmental Restoration and Waste Management at that time—as Program Review Coordinator and Assistant to the Assistant Secretary of Environmental Management.

Prior to joining the Office of Environmental Management, she was on the staff of the Secretary of Energy's office, serving as the Administrative Specialist for the Secretary's Chief of Staff.

Downing has thirty-six years of federal service in various agencies. She has served on many committees, was Employee of the Year for 1990, and has received numerous Awards of Excellence for her work in Public Participation.

SHIRLEY FRANKLIN
Mayor, Atlanta, Georgia

Shirley Franklin became the fifty-eighth Mayor of Atlanta, winning in a landslide victory in November 2001. Having never been an elected official, Shirley Franklin re-defined history, being elected as the city's first woman mayor and the first African American woman to serve as mayor of a major southern city. She was inaugurated on January 7, 2002.

Franklin's public service career began in 1978, when she served as the Commissioner of Cultural Affairs under Mayor Maynard Jackson. Under the leadership of Mayor Andrew Young, she was later appointed as the nation's first woman Chief Administrative Officer or City Manager, with responsibility for all the daily operations of a city.

In 1991, Franklin joined the Atlanta Committee for the Olympic Games, Inc. (ACOG) as the top-ranking female executive, serving as Senior Vice President for External Relations. While in this position, she was instrumental in the development of such legacies as the Centennial Olympic Park and served as ACOG's primary liaison with various labor unions, civil rights groups, neighborhood/community organizations, and environmentalists.

In 1997, Franklin formed Shirley Clarke Franklin & Associates, a management and consulting firm for public affairs, community affairs and strategic

planning, and in 1998 became a majority partner in Urban Environmental Solutions, LLC.

Following Governor Barnes' election in 1998, Ms. Franklin served on his three-person transition team and in 1999 accepted the Governor's invitation to serve on the Georgia Regional Transportation Authority (GRTA), where she was elected vice-chair. In April 2000, Franklin resigned from the GRTA and officially declared her candidacy for Mayor of Atlanta.

Since her inauguration on January 7, 2002, Franklin has taken on the challenges of governing in the new millennium. Her first task as Mayor was to fill a budget gap of $82 million and deliver the 2002 Balanced Budget to the City Council. In order to balance the budget, she cut her own salary by $40,000, cut the Mayor's department staff by fifty percent, cut 277 jobs, eliminated 605 vacancies, and raised taxes. She recalled non-essential city-owned cars, cell phones, and credit cards; and issued an administrative order to freeze vacancies, except in public safety.

Franklin proposed sweeping ethics reform legislation, which was passed by the Atlanta City Council, keeping her pledge to restore trust and integrity in City Hall. The new ethics legislation bans gifts to employees, including the Mayor and Council, from companies doing business with the city; establishes a full-time Ethics Officer; and bans the Mayor from accepting any outside income, including speaking fees.

Franklin focused on improving daily government operations with initiatives like the Pothole Posse (seven street repair crews dedicated to repairing potholes and maintaining streets and sidewalks) and the TIPS Hotline, established to gain information that may be relevant to reports of misconduct involving city officials, city employees, or any business entities that contract with the City of Atlanta.

Franklin moved quickly and decisively to repair relationships with regional, state, and national officials, actively working with the Atlanta Regional Council, the Georgia General Assembly, and the Georgia congressional delegation. She got the Hartsfield Airport Expansion project back on track, secured the funding for the Multi-Modal Transportation Facility, gained approval for a referendum for a one percent sales tax to fund improvements to the sewer system, and a Homestead Exemption to freeze property taxes for senior citizens who make less than $39,000.

Currently, Franklin serves as a member of the Democratic National Committee and Treasurer of the Democratic Party of Georgia. She has served on a variety of other boards, including Atlanta Life Insurance Company, Spelman College, East Lake Community Foundation, Charles Drew Charter School, King Baudouin-U.S. Foundation, United Way, Paideia School, the Atlanta Symphony Orchestra, the National Black Arts Festival, the Community Foundation, Georgia State Arts Council, and the Atlanta Convention and Visitor's Bureau.

Franklin has received numerous awards and honors during her career, including the 1995 Legacy Award from the Big Brothers-Big Sisters of Metro Atlanta; the 1996 Woman of the Year Award from the YWCA; the Georgia Women's Policy Group's Outstanding Women of 2001; awards from the League of Women Voters; and the Abercrombie Lamp of Learning Award. Most recently, she received the 2002 Woman of Achievement Award from the YWCA.

Over the course of her career, Franklin has been featured in *Business to Business* magazine, the *New York Times*, *Ebony* magazine, *Jet* magazine, *Heart & Soul* magazine, *Savoy* magazine, *Glamour*, *Time* magazine, *Women Looking Ahead* magazine, *Atlanta Good Life* magazine, *Atlanta Woman* magazine, *Georgia Trend* magazine; and was recently chosen as one of Atlanta's movers and shakers in *Jezebel* magazine.

A native of Philadelphia, Franklin earned her Bachelor of Arts degree in Sociology from Howard University and her Master of Arts degree in Sociology from the University of Pennsylvania. In May 2002, she delivered the commencement address and was awarded an honorary Doctor of Laws degree from her alma mater Howard University.

Franklin has lived in southwest Atlanta for more than thirty years and has three adult children.

CLARENCE A. JOHNSON

Principal Director, Civilian Equal Employment Opportunity, U.S. Department of Defense

Since February 2003, Clarence A. Johnson has served as Principal Director and Director for Civilian Equal Employment Opportunity, Office of the Deputy Under Secretary of Defense (Equal Opportunity) at the Pentagon. He is responsible for the development

and coordination of equal opportunity policies and programs affecting all U.S. Department of Defense (DoD) civilian employees and military personnel within DoD worldwide. He also provides staff supervision of the Defense Equal Opportunity Management Institute (DEOMI), a 100-member institution, located at Patrick Air Force Base, Florida, which is the premiere DoD school in equal opportunity and equal employment opportunity training, education, and research. Johnson serves as principal advisor to the Deputy Under Secretary of Defense (Equal Opportunity) on equal opportunity and equal employment opportunity matters.

Before serving the DoD in his present capacity, Johnson was an active duty Air Force colonel serving in the Office of the Deputy Assistant Secretary of Defense for Equal Opportunity as Director, Military Equal Opportunity. In that capacity, he formulated and provided policy guidance to the military components regarding policies and programs which prescribe, promote, coordinate, and enforce equal opportunity and treatment of active duty and Reserve component military personnel; oversaw policy implementation and evaluated/monitored the performance of DoD component programs; and provided staff oversight for DEOMI.

Johnson entered active duty service as a C141 navigator. In addition to global airlift and contingency operations, his tours of duty included the Military Airlift Command Plans staff and Air Staff Training (ASTRA). He was a squadron commander three times and a group commander twice. Additionally, he held increasingly responsible positions at the headquarters and installation levels His decorations include the Defense Superior Service Medal (with one oak-leaf cluster), the Legion of Merit, and the Meritorious Service Medal (with three oak-leaf clusters).

Johnson holds a Master's Degree in Human Resource Management from Webster University, Missouri, and a Bachelor's Degree in Biology from Tuskegee Institute, Alabama. Johnson is also a graduate of Air Command and Staff College and the Air War College, Alabama; and the National Security Management Course, National Defense University.

Johnson and his wife, Gloria, reside in Waldorf, Maryland. They have three children: Clarence Jr. (USAF major and fighter pilot), Joi, and Daniel.

CHARLES H. RAMSEY
Chief of Police, Metropolitan Police Department, District of Columbia

Charles H. Ramsey was appointed chief of the Metropolitan Police Department of the District of Columbia (MPDC) on April 21, 1998. A nationally recognized innovator, educator, and practitioner of community policing, Chief Ramsey has refocused the MPDC on crime fighting and crime prevention through a more accountable organizational structure, new equipment and technology, and an enhanced strategy of community policing.

A native of Chicago, Illinois, Chief Ramsey served in the Chicago Police Department for nearly three decades in a variety of assignments. He began his career in 1968, at the age of eighteen, as a Chicago police cadet. He became a police officer in February 1971, and was promoted through the ranks, eventually serving as commander of patrol, detectives and narcotics units. In 1994, he was named Deputy Superintendent of the Bureau of Staff Services, where he managed the department's education and training, research and development, labor affairs, crime prevention, and professional counseling functions.

Chief Ramsey was instrumental in designing and implementing the Chicago Alternative Policing Strategy (CAPS), the city's nationally acclaimed model of community policing. As co-manager of the CAPS project in Chicago, Chief Ramsey was one of the principal authors of the police department's strategic vision. He also designed and implemented the CAPS operational model and helped to develop new training curricula and communications efforts to support implementation.

As head of the 4,600-member Metropolitan Police Department, Chief Ramsey has worked to improve police services, enhance public confidence in the police, and bring down the District of Columbia's crime rate. In September 1998, the Chief announced a major reorganization of the Department that has put more police resources in the community, cut bureaucracy, and enhanced accountability by creating a system of Regional Operations Commands that are responsible for the quality of police services throughout the District. Through enhanced recruiting, including Internet-based advertising and a first-ever lateral-hiring program, the Department has brought its sworn strength back up to 3,600 officers for the first time in several years, with plans to expand to 3,800 officers.

Chief Ramsey has also overseen a multi-million-dollar upgrade to district stations and other Department facilities, as well as new communications and information technology, including mobile data computing and the 3-1-1 non-emergency system. Expanded training programs for both police recruits and veteran members — including a unique diversity management course at the United States Holocaust Memorial Museum — are enhancing officer performance. And the MPDC has received international acclaim for its handling of recent major events, including the April 2000 protests against the International Monetary Fund/World Bank Group meetings and the NATO Fiftieth Anniversary Summit a year earlier.

In the area of community policing, Chief Ramsey has redefined the Department's mission to focus on crime prevention. Policing for Prevention, the Department's new community policing strategy, encompasses focused law enforcement, neighborhood-based partnerships and problem solving, and systemic prevention efforts. The new strategy is supported not only by enhanced training for officers and supervisors, but also by a unique community training initiative called Partnerships for Problem Solving.

The result of these and other initiatives has been an overall reduction in crime in the Nation's Capital. Between 1997 and 2001, serious crime in the District declined by approximately fifteen percent, and is at one of its lowest levels in three decades.

Chief Ramsey holds both a Bachelor's and a Master's degree in Criminal Justice from Lewis University in Romeoville, Illinois. A graduate of the FBI National Academy and the National Executive Institute, Chief Ramsey has lectured nationally on community policing as an adjunct faculty member of both the Northwestern University Traffic Institute's School of Police Staff and Command and Lewis University. His national honors have included the 1994 Gary P. Hayes Award from the Police Executive Research Forum (PERF), the 2001 Robert Lamb Humanitarian Award from the National Organization of Black Law Enforcement Executives (NOBLE), the 2001 Civil Rights Award from the International Association of Chiefs of Police (IACP), and the 2003 John Carroll Society Medal.

Media/Literature

ED BRADLEY
60 MINUTES, CBS News Correspondent

The 2005-2006 season marks Ed Bradley's 25th on *60 MINUTES*. He joined the broadcast during the 1981-1982 season. He also anchors and reports hour-long specials.

Bradley's consummate skills as a broadcast journalist and his distinctive body of work have been recognized with numerous awards, including nineteen Emmys, the latest for a segment that reported the reopening of the fifty-year-old racial murder case of Emmett Till. He was just honored with the Lifetime Achievement award from the National Association of Black Journalists. Three of his Emmys came at the 2003 awards: a Lifetime Achievement Emmy; one for a *60 MINUTES* report on brain cancer patients, "A New Lease on Life" (April 2002); and another for his hour on *60 MINUTES II* about sexual abuse in the Catholic Church, "The Catholic Church on Trial" (June 2002). Bradley's *60 MINUTES* interview with condemned Oklahoma City bomber Timothy McVeigh (March 2000) was the only television interview ever given by the man guilty of one of the worst terrorist acts on American soil; it also earned Bradley an Emmy. His reporting on the worst school shooting in American history, "Columbine" (April 2001), revealed on *60 MINUTES II* that authorities ignored telling evidence with which they might have prevented the massacre. Other hour-long reports by Bradley have prompted praise and action: "Death by Denial" (June

2000) won a Peabody Award for focusing on the plight of Africans dying of AIDS and helped convince drug companies to donate and discount AIDS drugs; "Unsafe Haven" (April 1999) spurred federal investigations into the nation's largest chain of psychiatric hospitals; and "Town Under Siege" (December 1997), about a small town battling toxic waste, was named one of the Ten Best Television Programs of 1997 by *Time* magazine.

Bradley's significant contribution to electronic journalism was also recognized by the Radio/Television News Directors Association when it named him its Paul White Award winner for 2000. He joins other distinguished journalists, such as Edward R. Murrow, Walter Cronkite, and Peter Jennings as a Paul White recipient. More recently, the Denver Press Club awarded him its 2003 Damon Runyon Award for career journalistic excellence. Another prestigious honor received by Bradley is the Robert F. Kennedy Journalism Awards grand prize and television first prize for "CBS Reports: In the Killing Fields of America" (January 1995), a documentary about violence in America, for which he was co-anchor and reporter.

Bradley's work on *60 MINUTES* has gained much recognition, including a George Foster Peabody Award for "Big Man, Big Voice" (November 1997), the uplifting story of a German singer who became successful despite birth defects. In 1995, he won his eleventh Emmy Award for a *60 MINUTES* segment on the cruel effects of nuclear testing in the town of Semipalatinsk, Kazakhstan, a report that also won him an Alfred I. DuPont-Columbia University Award in 1994. Also in 1994, he was honored with an Overseas Press Club Award for two *60 MINUTES* reports that took viewers inside sensitive military installations in Russia and the United States. In 1985, he received an Emmy Award for "Schizophrenia," a *60 MINUTES* report on that misunderstood brain disorder. In 1983, two of Bradley's reports for *60 MINUTES* won Emmy Awards: "In the Belly of the Beast," an interview with Jack Henry Abbott, a convicted murderer and author; and "Lena," a profile of singer Lena Horne. He received an Alfred I. DuPont-Columbia University Silver Baton and a 1991 Emmy Award for his *60 MINUTES* report "Made in China," a look at Chinese forced-labor camps; and another Emmy for "Caitlin's Story" (November 1992), an examination of the controversy between the parents of a deaf child and a deaf association.

In addition to "In the Killing Fields," Bradley's work for *CBS Reports* has included: "Enter the Jury Room"

(April 1997), an Alfred I. duPont-Columbia University Award winner that revealed the jury deliberation process for the first time in front of network cameras; "The Boat People" (January 1979), which won duPont, Emmy, and Overseas Press Club Awards; "The Boston Goes to China" (April 1979), a report on the historic visit to China by the Boston Symphony Orchestra, which won Emmy, Peabody, and Ohio State Awards; and "Blacks in America: With All Deliberate Speed?" (July 1979), which won Emmy and duPont Awards.

Bradley's coverage of the plight of Cambodian refugees, broadcast on the *CBS Evening News with Walter Cronkite* and *CBS NEWS SUNDAY MORNING*, won a George Polk Award in journalism. He also received a DuPont citation for a segment on the Cambodian situation broadcast on CBS News' "Magazine" series. He covered the presidential campaign of Jimmy Carter during Campaign '76, served as a floor correspondent for CBS News' coverage of the Democratic and Republican National Conventions from 1976 through 1996, and has participated in CBS News' election-night coverage.

Prior to joining *60 MINUTES*, Bradley was a principal correspondent for *CBS Reports* (1978-81), after serving as CBS News' White House correspondent (1976-1978). He was also anchor of the *CBS Sunday Night News* (November 1976-May 1981) and of the CBS News magazine *Street Stories* (January 1992-August 1993).

Bradley joined CBS News as a stringer in its Paris bureau in September 1971. A year later, he was transferred to the Saigon bureau, where he remained until he was assigned to the CBS News Washington bureau in June 1974. He was named a CBS News correspondent in April 1973 and, shortly thereafter, was wounded while on assignment in Cambodia. In March 1975, he volunteered to return to Indochina and covered the fall of Cambodia and Vietnam.

Prior to joining CBS News, Bradley was a reporter for WCBS Radio, the CBS-owned station in New York (August 1967-July 1971). He had previously been a reporter for WDAS Radio Philadelphia (1963-1967).

Bradley was born June 22, 1941, in Philadelphia and graduated from Cheyney (Pa.) State College in 1964 with a B.S. in Education. He lives in New York with his wife, Patricia Blanchet.

DEREK MCGINTY
Anchor, W*USA Tonight and Host, Eye on Washington

Eye On Washington debuted on Saturday, November 13, at 7:00 p.m. The program is a politically based roundtable talk show that provides analysis and perspectives on top stories from our Nation's Capital. Each week, McGinty is joined by three to five panelists to discuss current issues.

From March 2001 to June 2003, he was co-anchor of *ABC NEWS'* overnight broadcast, *World News Now*, and anchor of *World News This Morning*.

Additionally, McGinty was a correspondent for HBO's *Real Sports* for four years. Prior to joining ABC, McGinty worked for two years as a reporter and anchor for WJLA. Before that, he was a correspondent for the nationally broadcast program, *Public Eye with Bryant Gumbel* on CBS.

McGinty previously hosted the nationally broadcast *Straight Talk with Derek McGinty* for PBS. At WETA, he had a similar role for the station's Emmy-nominated *Here and Now*, a weekly half-hour local program focusing on issues, events, and people in metropolitan Washington, DC.

From 1991 to 1998, McGinty became increasingly popular on a nationwide basis with *The Derek McGinty Show* on WAMU. His guests have included D.C. Mayor Marion Barry; former Secretary of State James Baker; former House Speaker Newt Gingrich; jazz musician Wynton Marsalis; rapper Ice-T; and author Robert Ludlum. In 1994, the show received the highest programming honor in public radio, when it won the Gold Award for Public Affairs Programming from the Corporation of Public Broadcasting.

Prior to his work at WAMU, McGinty co-hosted *The Daily Drum*, a news and interview program covering local politics on WHUR-FM. Derek was a reporter/editor for UPI's Washington metro desk and a news editor at WTOP radio. He began his professional career as a desk assistant for *ABC Radio News* in the Washington bureau. Articles by McGinty have appeared in the *New York Times,* the *Washington Post,* the *New York Daily News,* and *Washingtonian Magazine.*

A native of Washington, DC, McGinty is a graduate of American University, where he received a Bachelor's Degree in Communications.

NTOZAKE SHANGE
Author

Ntozake Shange is the author of the Obie-winning and Tony-, Grammy-, and Emmy-nominated *for colored girls who have considered suicide/when the rainbow is enuf: a choreopoem.* Shange has published three novels: *Sassafrass, Cypress and Indigo* (a Pen-Faulkner nominee); *Betsey Brown;* and *Liliane: Resurrection of the Daughter.* Her poetry collections include *A Daughter's Geography; nappy edges; Ridin' the Moon in Texas: Word Paintings;* and *The Love Space Demands (a continuing saga).*

While she was an artist-in-residence at Philadelphia's Freedom Theatre, Shange directed Keith Antar Mason's *Mississippi Gulag.* In addition, Freedom Theatre presented a stage version of Shange's novel *Liliane: Resurrection of the Daughter,* as well as her adaptation of *Sparkle.*

Shange's work for children includes *Ellington Was Not a Street, Float Like a Butterfly, i live in music,* and the Humantitas-winning *Whitewash.* Shange's oeuvre also includes *A Photograph: Lovers-in-Motion; Spell # 7; Where the Mississippi Meets the Amazon,* with Hagadon and Davis; *Betsey Brown The Musical,* with Mann and Carroll; *Nomathamba,* with Simonsen and Shabalala; *Hydraulics /Phat like Mean;* and most recently, *lavender lizards and lilac land mines: layla's dream.* She adapted Willy Russell's *Educating Rita* and won an Obie for her adaptation of Bertolt Brecht's *Mother Courage and her Children.*

Shange has performed with many Jazz musicians, such as David Murray, Max Roach, Oliver Lake, Kahil L Zabar, Billy Bang, Craig Harris, Malachi Savors, Lester and Joe Bowie, and Jean-Paul Bourrelly. Throughout her career, Shange has danced and studied dance with such notables as Pearl Primes, Beryl McBurney, Mercedes Baptista, Eleo Pomare, Dianne McIntyre, Raymond Sawyer, Ed Mock, Pepsi Bethel, Thelma Hill, Stanze Peterson, Chuck Davis, Halifu Osumare, and Fred Benjamin. Her most recent work, with Frank Stuart, is entitled *The Sweet Breath of Life.*

Shange's current projects include works on paper with Wopo Holup and Lewis Delsarte, as well as a dance drama with choreographer Otis Sallid. *Shange's* is currently associated with the Center for Women's Studies and Gender Research of the University of Florida.

Military

ADMIRAL D.C. CURTIS
Director, Navy Europe Programs, Resources, and Support

Rear Admiral D.C. Curtis is a native of Chicago, Illinois, where he attended Chicago Vocational High School. He graduated from the United States Naval Academy in 1976, receiving a Bachelor's Degree in Political Science. Following commissioning, he attended the Surface Warfare Basic School in Newport, Rhode Island, and was awarded the Arleigh Burke Award.

Rear Adm. Curtis served in a variety of sea and shore assignments. At sea, his assignments include USS *Moinster* (FF-1097); USS *Thorn* (DD-988); USS *Dahlgren* (DDG-43); Executive Officer, USS *Scott* (DD-995); Cruiser-Destroyer Group Two/George Washington Battle Group; Chief of Staff to Commander, Second Fleet/Commander, Striking Fleet Atlantic/Task Force 120; and Deputy Commander, U.S Naval Forces Southern Command. He served as Commanding Officer,

USS *Wainwright* (CG 28); Commanding Officer, USS *Donald B Beary* (FFT 1085); Commander, Destroyer Squadron Fourteen; Commander, Naval Surface Group Two; and Commander, Carrier Strike Group Eleven/ Nimitz Strike Group.

Rear Adm. Curtis' shore assignments include the U. S. Naval Academy as a Brigade Officer; the Bureau of Naval Personnel as the Senior Year Group Detailer; the Chief of Naval Operations Aegis/DDG-51 Program Office; Senior Military Assistant in the Office of Naval Warfare; and Executive Assistant and Naval Aide to the seventy-first and seventy-second Secretaries of the Navy.

Rear Adm. Curtis currently serves the Commander of Naval Forces Europe and the Commander of Sixth Fleet as the Director, Navy Europe Programs, Resources, and Support/Director, Transformation Activities.

Rear Adm. Curtis' personal decorations include the Legion of Merit, Defense Meritorious Service Medal, Meritorious Service Medal, Navy Commendation Medal, Navy Achievement Medal, and other awards. He holds a Master of Science in Administration from Central Michigan University and is a graduate of the National Defense University and NATO Defense College. He also attended the Flag Officers Executive Business course in Monterey, and the Joint Flag Officers' Warfighter and Joint Forces Air Component Commander's Courses at Maxwell Air Force Base.

BRIGADIER GENERAL ANTHONY L. JACKSON

Deputy Commander, U.S. Marine Forces Central Command

Brigadier General Anthony L. Jackson is currently serving as the Deputy Commanding General, U.S. Marine Corps Forces Central Command.
Brig. Gen. Jackson was born in Fort Lewis, Washington. He graduated from Oakland High School, Oakland, California, in 1967 and San Jose State University, San Jose, California, 1971. In 1973, he completed his Master's in History at San Jose State.

In May 1975, Brig. Gen. Jackson enlisted in the Marine Corps to attend Officer Candidate School. Upon graduating from the Basic School in June 1976, he was assigned to 1st Battalion, 5th Marines, 1st Marine Division, Camp Pendleton, California. While there, Brig. Gen. Jackson served as a Rifle and Weapons

Platoon Commander and Battalion Adjutant. In 1978, he left the regular Marine Corps; however, he continued to serve in the reserves as the Weapons Platoon Commander, "L" Company, 3rd Battalion, 25th Marines, Pittsburgh, Pennsylvania.

Upon returning to the regular Marine Corps in December 1979, Brig. Gen. Jackson was again assigned to 1st Battalion, 5th Marines. During this tour, he served as the Assistant Operations Officer and as a Rifle and Weapons Company Commander. In February 1982, he was transferred to the Marine Corps Recruit Depot, San Diego, California. While there, he served as a Battalion Operations Officer, Company Commander, and Officer-in-Charge, Recruit Field Training Division. In June 1984, Brig. Gen. Jackson was assigned as the Commanding Officer, Marine Detachment, USS *Long Beach* (CGN-9), which was home ported in San Diego, California. In July 1988, he was transferred to 1st Marine Expeditionary Brigade (MEB), Kaneohe Bay, Hawaii. While in 1st MEB, he served consecutively as a Company Commander, as a Combat Serviced Support Plans Officer, as the Operations Officer, and Executive Officer of 3rd Batallion/3rd Marines.

After completing his tour with 1st MEB, Brig. Gen. Jackson attended the Armed Forces Staff College, Norfolk, Virgnia. Upon graduation in June 1990, he served as a Senior Emergency Action Officer in the National Military Command Center, J-3, Joint Staff, Washington, DC, until July 1992. Upon transfer, Brig. Gen. Jackson served as the Chief of Instructors, The Basic School, Marine Corps Combat Development Command, Quantico, Virginia. From July 1993 to June 1995, he was the Commanding Officer, Marine Security Forces, Naval Submarine Base, Kings Bay, Georgia. In June 1997, he completed an assignment as the Advisor to the Commandant of the Marine Corps on Equal Opportunity matters as the Head, Equal Opportunity Branch, Headquarters, Marine Corps.

In June 1998, Brig. Gen. Jackson graduated from the United States Army War College, Carlisle, Pennsylvania. Upon graduation from the War College, he was assigned as the Assistant Chief of Staff, G-

7, I Marine Expeditionary Force. He served in that billet from June 1998 to June 2000. He then served as the Commanding Officer, 1st Marine Regiment, and 1st Marine Division. After that assignment, Brig. Gen. Jackson was assigned to the 3rd Marine Division, Okinawa, Japan, where he was the Division's Chief of Staff. During that assignment, he served concurrently as the Chief of Staff, Joint Task Force-555, in support of Operation Enduring Freedom-Philippines. From August 2003 until March 2005, he served as the Assistant Chief of Staff (G-5), First Marine Expeditionary Force, and deployed in support of Operation Iraqi Freedom II.

Brig. Gen. Jackson completed both the Amphibious Warfare School and the Marine Corps Command and Staff College by correspondence.

Brig. Gen. Jackson's personal decorations include the Legion of Merit (with two gold stars in lieu of second and third award), Bronze Star, Defense Meritorious Medal, Meritorious Service Medal (with two gold stars in lieu of second and third award), Navy and Marine Corps Commendation Medal (with gold star in lieu of second award), the Navy and Marine Corps Achievement Medal, the Iraqi Campaign Medal, the Global War on Terrorism Expeditionary Medal, Global War on Terrorism Service Medal, and the Korea Defense Service Medal.

JAMES E. LOVE

Acting Director, Military Equal Opportunity, U.S. Department of Defense

James E. Love currently serves as the Acting Director of Military Equal Opportunity in the Office of the Deputy Under Secretary of Defense for Equal Opportunity.

In his current position, Love advises and assists senior Department of Defense officials in formulating and monitoring DoD equal opportunity policy for the active duty and reserve forces. He analyzes trends and identifies equal opportunity issues for resolution to the Military Departments, senior officials, and the Defense Equal Opportunity Council, which is the senior advisory board to the Secretary of Defense on equal opportunity matters. He serves also as the Department's liaison with the Defense Equal Opportunity Management Institute.

Love graduated from the United States Air Force Academy and holds a Master of Arts degree in

Personnel Management/Human Relations. His military education includes completion of Squadron Officer School in residence, the Air Force Professional Personnel Management Course, Air Command and Staff College in residence, the Air War College seminar program, and the Defense Race Relations Institute (currently the Defense Equal Opportunity Management Institute).

Love retired in 1993 from the Air Force in the grade of lieutenant colonel. As a military officer, he served in a variety of command, personnel and special duty assignments. He returned to DoD in 1994 after serving as the director of program operations with a private contracting firm.

Among Love's several distinguished awards are the Secretary of Defense Award for Outstanding Achievement, the Defense Meritorious Service Medal, the Air Force Meritorious Service Medal, the Air Force Commendation Medal, the Outstanding Unit Award, and the National Association for the Advancement of Colored People (NAACP) Benjamin Hooks Distinguished Leadership Award.

Love is married to the former Beryl Elizabeth Cook of Dothan, Alabama. They have three daughters and four grandsons.

Science

VIVIAN PINN

Director, Office of Research on Women's Health, National Institutes of Health

In her role as director of the Office of Research on Women's Health (ORWH), Vivian Pinn is in a unique position to help ensure that women's health issues and women are well represented in National Institutes of Health (NIH) research efforts.

Before coming to NIH, Dr. Pinn was professor and chair of the Department of Pathology at Howard

Sports

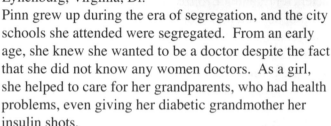

University. Previously, she held teaching appointments at Tufts University and Harvard Medical School. At Tufts, she was Assistant Dean for Student Affairs and an advocate for minority students.

Born to modest circumstances in Lynchburg, Virginia, Dr. Pinn grew up during the era of segregation, and the city schools she attended were segregated. From an early age, she knew she wanted to be a doctor despite the fact that she did not know any women doctors. As a girl, she helped to care for her grandparents, who had health problems, even giving her diabetic grandmother her insulin shots.

Dr. Pinn's interest in women's health and women's issues grew out of this experience and from a profound personal loss. When Pinn was , nineteen, her mother became ill. The medical professionals who attended to her did not take her health complaints seriously. The doctor who examined her mother, Pinn recalls, "dismissed my mother's complaints, prescribing special shoes and exercise for her painful backaches." Shortly thereafter, her mother died of bone cancer.

Fueled by her deep loss, Dr. Pinn was determined to become a doctor, and her family supported her dream. She earned a scholarship to Wellesley College, a women's college with a supportive environment; graduated in 1962; and enrolled in medical school at the University of Virginia. As the only African American and only woman in her class, she was doubly distinguished.

While Dr. Pinn intended to become a pediatrician, during a summer internship at Massachusetts General Hospital in Boston, she developed a passion for research.

The recipient of numerous awards and honors, Dr. Pinn is past president of the National Medical Association. She received the Elizabeth Blackwell Award from the American Medical Women's Association in 1995, the year she was elected to the National Academies of Science Institute of Medicine. She is a fellow of the American Academy of Arts and Sciences as well.

JEANETTE JENKINS
Founder and President, The Hollywood Trainer

Jeanette Jenkins, founder and President of The Hollywood Trainer, is one of the country's leading fitness professionals, known best for her cutting-edge style, results-driven cross-training techniques, and supreme ability to motivate.

One of seventeen experts chosen for Nike Corporation's Elite Athletes program, Jenkins is in the company of top Olympians and other premiere fitness personalities. A resident expert on the Food Network's weight-loss show *Weighing In*, and official Spokesperson for the BET Foundation's A Healthy BET Campaign, she has also been featured on numerous other television programs, including *The Oprah Winfrey Show, The Jay Leno Show, The Best Damn Sports Show...Period, E! Entertainment Television, Extra, Access Hollywood, Celebrity Fit Club and Good Day Live*. Her work has also been profiled in such leading publications as *In Style, People, Self, Redbook, In-Touch, Glamour, Fitness, EDiets, Oxygen, Ebony, Women's Health & Fitness, Us Weekly,* the *Los Angeles Times,* the *Los Angeles Daily News, Entertainment Weekly, Sister to Sister, Hollywood Life, Essence, InStyle Weddings,* and more.

Jenkins' knowledge and ability to get results is what attracts a client roster that includes A-list actors, professional athletes, swimsuit models, and Hollywood executives. It is also what keeps her group classes at L.A.'s top fitness clubs jam-packed with celebrity regulars and Hollywood's hottest bodies. In fact, in addition to working with Taryn Manning, Mara Brock Akil (creator of UPN's *Girlfriends*) and Tom Arnold, Jeanette is credited with training Queen Latifah for roles in her hit movies *Bringing Down The House, Beauty Shop,* and most recently, Paramount Pictures' *The Last Holiday*. The NFL's Terrell Owens describes Jenkins as being "high-energy, passionate and knowledgeable." Says Owens, "Jeanette knows how to draw you in and keep you motivated."

Jenkins' fitness philosophy is simple. "I am passionate about fitness and I try to share that passion with my clients," she says. "I know what it takes to achieve results, but I also want them to have fun, stay motivated and keep them coming back for more."

Growing up in Canada, Jenkins was one of three children raised by a single mother, and fitness is what kept her focused. A natural athlete, Jeanette found a safe haven in sports, one that taught her the value of discipline and team work, and, most importantly, instilled self-confidence and a "can do" attitude. Jenkins studied Human Kinetics at the University of Ottawa and has earned over seventeen international certifications in various methods of training.

MALVIN G. WHITFIELD
CEO, The Whitfield Foundation

World Records Halls of Fame competitive track and field star Mal Whitfield was born in humble beginnings in 1924 to Mary and Esaw Whitfield in Bay City, Texas. At an early age, following the death of his mother and father, Whitfield was adopted by his sister, Elizabeth, who lived in Los Angeles, California.

While growing up in the city of Los Angeles, Whitfield watched athletic greats such as Eddie Tolan win a Gold Medal in the 100-meters and the 200-meters during the 1932 Olympic Games in Los Angeles Coliseum; and the great Jessie Owens win a Gold Medal in the 1936 Olympic Games in Berlin, Germany. This fueled Whitfield's ambitions; and his sister would also eventually help to mold his destiny.

In 1943, Whitfield was inducted into the Army Air Force. Following World War II (1945), while still in the military service and on active duty (1946), he was accepted into Ohio State University for undergraduate matriculation.

Whitfield became a Sergeant in the U.S. Air Force during his tenure at Ohio State University. It was here

that his perseverance earned him an Olympic Gold Medal as an athlete on military duty. This combination turned out to be a giant step towards a golden athletic career. He soon earned the name of "Marvelous Mal" for his winning style. While at Ohio State and while in the U.S. Air Force, his fortitude won him the national collegiate 880-800-meters titles in 1948 and 1949. This inspiration took him to his first U.S. Olympic team in 1948 in London, England, where he won the 800-meters Gold Medal, setting an Olympic record. He won another Gold Medal in the 4 x 400-meters relay, and a Bronze Medal in the 400-meters. In 1950, he set a new world record in the 800-meters. Two years later, he won a Gold Medal, sustaining his world record in the 800-meters at the Helsinki, Finland Olympic Games. In addition to the Gold Medal, he took home a Silver Medal in the 4 x 400-meters.

In 1952, Whitfield received an honorable discharge from the U.S. Air Force and received an Honorable Veterans of Foreign Wars Award. He then went on to continue his academics at the Los Angeles State University, where he received his B.S.

From 1953 to 1963, Whitfield served as a Goodwill Ambassador for the United States, where he promoted sports as a tool for gaining and maintaining global friendship among allied countries. In 1964, he attended the School of Foreign Service. He became a Sports Specialist in the U.S. Information Service under the auspices of the U.S. Department of State, in the Office of Cultural Affairs. His 35-year tenure working within the mission of the United States Government took him to nations in eastern, western, southern, and central Africa; as well as to European and Middle Eastern nations and Asia. His dedication to utilizing his skills to produce results was a winning posture, resulting in trusted American friendship, Olympic champions, enhanced teaching techniques in academia, and physical dexterity in sports.

Recently, Whitfield promoted an American/Kenyan Golf Safari Tournament in Nairobi, Kenya (October 10-23, 2005). This special project captures twenty-five years of Whitfield's historic efforts in Africa to promote economic wealth in countries where the people are prepared to enter the global corporate market.

African American Conventions and Events 2006

Email: info@ncbm.org
Web: www.ncbm.org

NATIONAL ASSOCIATION OF MINORITY MEDIA EXECUTIVES
NAMME Awards Banquet
April 27, 2006/Seattle, WA
Contact: Toni F. Laws
Tel: (703) 893-2410 Fax: (703) 893-2414
Email: tlaws@namme.org
Web: www.namme.org

THE ARTHUR ASHE INSTITUTE FOR URBAN HEALTH
12th Annual Black Tie and Sneakers Gala
April 27, 2006/New York, NY
Contact: Leeann Hicks
Tel: (718) 222-5953 Fax: (718) 222-4462
Web: www.arthurasheinstitute.org

NEW YORK UNIVERSITY CENTER FOR MARKETING
Marketing to the New Majority: How to Reach the Multicultural Consumer
April 28-29, 2006/New York, NY
Contact: Lisa Skriloff
Tel: (212) 242-3351 Fax: (212) 691-5969
Email: lisa@multicultral.com
Web: www.multicultural.com

IQPC
4th Annual Multicultural Branding Conference
April, 2006 TBA/New York City, NY
Tel: (212) 885-2700 Fax: (212) 885-2703
Email: info@iqpc.com
Web: www.iqpc.com

MAY

NATIONAL ASSOCIATION OF BLACK OWNED BROADCASTERS
30th Annual Spring Broadcast Management Conference
May 5-10, 2006/St. Maarten, Netherlands Antilles,
Contact: Ellen McClain
Tel: (202) 463-8970 Fax: (202) 429-0657
Email: info@nabob.org
Web: www.nabob.org

MULTICULTURAL EDUCATION DEPARTMENT
Ethnic Festival 2006
May 6, 2006/Oak Park, IL
Contact: Lynn Allen
Tel: (708) 524-7700 Fax: (708) 524-7703
Email: lallen@op97.org
Web: www.op97.org

NORTH ALABAMA AFRICAN AMERICAN CHAMBER OF COMMERCE
2006 Business Opportunity Expo
May 11-12, 2006/Huntsville, AL
Contact: Jerry Mitchell
Tel: (256) 564-7574 Fax: (256) 564-7344
Email: info@thenaaacc.org
Web: www.thenaaacc.org

NATIONAL ORGANIZATION OF CONCERNED BLACK MEN, INC.
CBM Convention
May 11-14, 2006/Washington, DC
Tel: (202) 783-6119 Fax: (202) 783-2480
Email: info@cbmnational.org
Web: www.cbmnational.org

THE FRIENDS OF SWEET AUBURN
Sweet Auburn SpringFest 2006
May 12-14, 2006/Atlanta, GA
Contact: Charles E. Johnson
Tel: (404) 886-4469 Fax: (404) 870-0883

Email: charles@sweetauburn.com
Web: www.sweetauburn.com

CORNELL'S DIVERSITY MANAGEMENT PROGRAM
Advanced Diversity Strategies
May 17-18, 2006/New York, NY
Contact: Christopher J. Metzler
Tel: (212) 340-2852 Fax: (212) 340-2890
Email: cm277@cornell.edu
Web: www.ilr.cornell.edu/mgmtprog/dm/certificates.html

BLACK ENTERPRISE MAGAZINE
11th Annual Black Enterprise/General Motors Entrepreneurs Conference
May 17-21, 2006/Dallas, TX
Contact: Sherry Herbert
Tel: (212) 886-9559 Fax: (212) 886-9509
Email: herberts@blackenterprise.com
Web: www.blackenterprise.com

NATIONAL MULTICULTURAL INSTITUTE
Cultural Liberty: The Elusion of Inclusion Beyond Heroic to Sustainable Future
May 18-21, 2006/Bethesda, MD
Contact: Melinda Chow
Tel: (202) 483-0700 X232 Fax: (202) 483-5233
Email: nmci@nmci.org
Web: www.nmci.org

URBAN FINANCIAL SERVICES COALITION
32nd Annual National Conference
May 29-June 4, 2006/Dallas, TX
Contact: Andrew Carr
Tel: (202) 289-8335 Fax: (202) 682-3058
Email: ufsc@ufscnet.org
Web: www.ufscnet.org

BLACK COACHES ASSOCIATION
BCA National Convention and Expo
May 31-June 3, 2006/Miami, FL
Contact: Glenda K. Wilson
Tel: (317) 829-5603 Fax: (317) 829-5601
Email: gwilson@bcasports.org
Web: www.bcasports.org

JUNE

100 BLACK MEN OF AMERICA, INC.
20th Annual Conference
June 7-11, 2006/Atlanta, GA
Contact: Dorita Treadwell
Tel: (404) 688-5100 Fax: (404) 688-1028
Email: dorita.treadwell@100bmoa.org
Web: www.100blackmen.org

THE LAGRANT FOUNDATION
8th Annual Recognition Reception/Awards Program
June 12, 2006/New York, NY
Contact: Melissa Lopez
Tel: (323) 469-8680 Fax: (323) 469-8683
Email: melissalopez@lagrant.com
Web: www.lagrantfoundation.org

NATIONAL ASSOCIATION OF BLACK ACCOUNTANTS, INC.
2006 NABA Convention
June 13-17, 2006/Hollywood, FL
Contact: Darryl R. Matthews, Sr.
Tel: (301) 474-6222 Fax: (301) 474-3114
Web: www.nabainc.org

REAL MEN COOK
Real Men Cook Father's Day Celebration 2006
June 18, 2006/Atlanta, GA
Contact: Diane Powell-Larche
Tel: (404) 273-3227
Email: realmencookatl@yahoo.com

Web: www.realmencook.com

REAL MEN COOK
Real Men Cook Father's Day Celebration 2006
June 18, 2006/Chicago, IL
Contact: Rael Jackson
Tel: (773) 651-8008
Email: raeljackson@mobe.com
Web: www.realmencook.com

REAL MEN COOK
Real Men Cook Father's Day Celebration 2006
June 18, 2006/Dallas, TX
Contact: Terry Allen
Tel: (214) 376-6530 Fax: (214) 376-6535
Web: www.realmencook.com

REAL MEN COOK
Real Men Cook Father's Day Celebration 2006
June 18, 2006/Detroit, MI
Contact: Carmen Carter
Tel: (313) 592-0057
Email: cacar2003@yahoo.com
Web: www.realmencook.cóm

REAL MEN COOK
Real Men Cook Father's Day Celebration 2006
June 18, 2006/Los Angeles, CA
Contact: Cynthia Bolden
Tel: (661) 250-7300
Email: bolden@realmencook.com
Web: www.realmencook.com

REAL MEN COOK
Real Men Cook Father's Day Celebration 2006
June 18, 2006/Miami, FL
Contact: Hasan Brown
Tel: (305) 610-4441
Email: info@realmencook.com
Web: www.realmencook.com

REAL MEN COOK
Real Men Cook Father's Day Celebration 2006
June 18, 2006/New York, NY
Contact: Carolyn Dunn
Tel: (917) 359-3835
Email: dunwad@aol.com
Web: www.realmencook.com

REAL MEN COOK
Real Men Cook Father's Day Celebration 2006
June 18, 2006/Philadelphia, PA
Contact: Bruce Rush
Tel: (215) 924-6263 Fax: (215) 242-4737
Email: marketstor@aol.com
Web: www.realmencook.com

REAL MEN COOK
Real Men Cook Father's Day Celebration 2006
June 18, 2006/Houston, TX
Tel: (773) 651-8008
Web: www.realmencook.com

REAL MEN COOK
Real Men Cook Father's Day Celebration 2006
June 18, 2006/Minneapolis, MN
Contact: Deborah Watts
Email: wattsfive@aol.com
Web: www.realmencook.com

TURNING POINT COMMUNICATIONS
9th Annual African American Business Summit 2006
June 22-25, 2006/Palm Springs, CA
Contact: Sean Ransom

Tel: (323) 299-6000 Fax: (310) 299-6006
Email: info@turningpointmagazine.com
Web: www.turningpointmagazine.com

INTERNATIONAL SOCIETY ON HYPERTENSION IN BLACKS
ISHIB 2006 Annual International Convention
June 23-26, 2006/Atlanta, GA
Contact: Noni Redding
Tel: (404) 880-0343 Fax: (404) 880-0347
Email: ishib2005@ishib.org
Web: www.ishib.org

NIA ENTERPRISES
2006 Nia Enterprises Leadership Summit Series
June 2006 TBA/Chicago, IL
Contact: Sheryl Huggins
Tel: (312) 222-0943 Fax: (312) 222-0944
Email: info@niaonline.com
Web: www.niaonline.com

JULY

NATIONAL ORGANIZATION OF BLACK LAW ENFORCEMENT EXECUTIVES
2006 NOBLE Conference
July 5-12, 2006/Cincinnati, OH
Tel: (703) 658-1529 Fax: (703) 658-9479
Email: noble@noblenatl.org
Web: www.noblenatl.org

CONFERENCE OF MINORITY TRANSPORTATION OFFICIALS
2006 National Meeting & Training Conference
July 8-12, 2006/Austin, TX
Contact: Patrea' Cheatham-Logan
Tel: (202) 530-0551 Fax: (202) 530-0617
Email: comto@comto.org
Web: www.comto.org

ALPHA KAPPA ALPHA SORORITY, INC.
63rd Annual Boule
July 12-16, 2006/Detroit, MI
Contact: Allyson Talbert
Tel: (773) 684-1282 Fax: (773) 684-3702
Email: atalbert@aka1908.com
Web: www.aka1908.com

NATIONAL BLACK ARTS FESTIVAL
National Black Arts Festival
July 14-23, 2006/Atlanta, GA
Contact: Melody Fuller
Tel: (404) 730-7315 Fax: (404) 730-7104
Email: info@nbaf.org
Web: www.nbaf.org

NATIONAL ASSOCIATION FOR THE ADVANCEMENT OF COLORED PEOPLE
2006 Annual Convention
July 15-20, 2006/Washington, DC
Contact: Ana Aponte
Tel: (410) 580-5780
Web: www.naacp.org

NATIONAL ASSOCIATION OF BLACKS IN CRIMINAL JUSTICE
33rd Annual Conference and Training Institute
July 16-20, 2006/Denver, CO
Tel: (919) 683-1801 Fax: (919) 683-1903
Email: office@nabcj.org
Web: www.nabcj.org

WORKING MOTHER MEDIA
Professional Women of Color: Patterns In The Tapestry of Difference
July 18-19, 2006/Boston, MA
Contact: Carol Evans
Tel: (212) 351-6401 Fax: (212) 351-6480
Email: carolevans@workingmother.com
Web: www.workingmother.com

NATIONAL ASSOCIATION OF BLACK HOTEL OWNERS, OPERATORS & DEVELOPERS
2006 National Summit
July 19-22, 2006
Contact: Andy Ingraham
Tel: (954) 797-7102 Fax: (954) 337-2877
Email: horizons@gate.net
Web: www.nabhood.com

ZETA PHI BETA SORORITY, INC.
86th Anniversary Celebration
July 20-26, 2006/Hollywood, FL
Contact: Barbara C. Moore
Tel: (202) 387-3103
Email: ihq@zphib1920.org
Web: www.zphib1920.org

ASSOCIATION OF BLACK PSYCHOLOGISTS
38th ABPsi Annual International Convention
July 26-30, 2006/Cleveland, OH
Tel: (202) 722-0808 Fax: (202) 722-5941
Email: abpsi_office@abpsi.org
Web: www.abpsi.org

NATIONAL URBAN LEAGUE, INC.
2006 Annual Conference
July 26-30, 2006/Atlanta, GA
Contact: Michael Thompson
Tel: (212) 558-5433 Fax: (212) 344-8925
Email: info@nul.org
Web: www.nul.org

DELTA SIGMA THETA SORORITY, INC.
2006 National Convention
July 26-August 2/Philadelphia, PA
Contact: Roseline McKinney
Tel: (202) 986-2400 Fax: (202) 986-2513
Email: dstemail@deltasigmatheta.org
Web: www.deltasigmatheta.org

AUGUST

BLACK DATA PROCESSING ASSOCIATES
28th Annual National Conference
August 2-5, 2006/Los Angeles, CA
Contact: Vercilla Brown
Tel: (301) 220-2180 Fax: (301) 220-2185
Email: conference@bdpa.org
Web: www.bdpa.org

BLACK CAUCUS OF THE AMERICAN LIBRARY ASSOCIATION, INC.
6th National Conference
August 2-6, 2007/Forth Worth, TX
Contact: Karolyn S. Thompson
Tel: (601) 266-5111 Fax: (601) 266-4410
Email: karolyn.thompson@usm.edu
Web: www.bcala.org

ASSOCIATION OF BLACK CARDIOLOGISTS, INC.
18th Annual Dr. Walter M. Booker, Sr. Memorial Symposium
August 5, 2006/Dallas, TX
Contact: Angela Flannigan
Tel: (678) 302-4222 Fax: (678) 302-4223
Email: abcardio@abcardio.org
Web: www.abcardio.org

ANCIENT EGYPTIAN ARABIC ORDER NOBLES MYSTIC SHRINE, INC.
Imperial Session 2006
August 7-10, 2006
Tel: (901) 395-0150 Fax: (901) 395-0115
Web: www.aeaonms.org

PROGRESSIVE NATIONAL BAPTIST CONVENTION, INC.
44th Annual Conference
August 8-11, 2006/Cincinnati, OH
Contact: Dr. Tyrone S. Pitts
Tel: (202) 396-0558 Fax: (202) 398-4998
Email: tspitts@pnbc.org
Web: www.pnbc.org

NATIONAL ASSOCIATION OF BLACK JOURNALISTS
31st Annual NABJ Convention and Career Fair
August 16-20, 2006/Indianapolis, IN
Tel: (317) 925-2702 Fax: (317) 925-6624
Email: contact@iabj.net
Web: www.iabj.net

BLACKS IN GOVERNMENT
28th Annual National Training Conference
August 21-25, 2006/New York, NY
Tel: (202) 667-3280 Fax: (202) 667-3705
Email: big@bignet.org
Web: www.bignet.org

SEPTEMBER

CONGRESSIONAL BLACK CAUCUS FOUNDATION, INC.
36th Annual Legislative Conference
September 6-9, 2006/Washington, DC
Tel: (202) 263-2800 Fax: (202) 775-0773
Email: info@cbcfinc.org
Web: www.cbcfinc.org

BLACK WOMEN'S AGENDA, INC.
29th Annual Luncheon
September 8, 2006/Washington, DC
Contact: Dottie McNeill
Tel: (202) 216-5797 Fax: (202) 408-9888
Web: www.blackwomensagenda.org

BLACK WOMEN UNITED FOR ACTION
Slave Wreath Laying Memorial Ceremony
September 23, 2006/Alexandria, VA
Contact: Sheila B. Coates
Tel: (703) 922-5757 Fax: (703) 922-7681
Email: events@bwufa.org
Web: www.bwufa.org

NATIONAL COLLEGE ACCESS NETWORK
2006 Annual Conference
September 25-27, 2006/Orlando, FL
Contact: Christina R. Milano
Tel: (216) 241-6122 Fax: (216) 241-6140
Web: www.collegeaccess.org

ASSOCIATION FOR THE STUDY OF AFRICAN AMERICAN LIFE AND HISTORY
2006 Annual Convention
September 26-October 1, 2006/Atlanta, GA
Contact: Dr. Gloria Harper Dickinson
Tel: (202) 865-0053 Fax: (202) 265-7920
Email: asalh@earthlink.net
Web: www.asalh.org

NATIONAL BLACK MBA ASSOCIATION, INC.
28th Annual Conference & Exposition
September 26-October 1, 2006/Atlanta, GA
Contact: Barbara L. Thomas
Tel: (312) 236-2622 Fax: (312) 236-0390
Email: conference@nbmbaa.org
Web: www.nbmbaa.org

SICKLE CELL DISEASE ASSOCIATION OF AMERICA, INC.
34th Annual Convention
September 27-30, 2006/Dallas, TX
Tel: (410) 528-1555 Fax: (410) 528-1495
Email: scdaa@sicklecelldisease.org
Web: www.sicklecelldisease.org

OCTOBER

AMERICAN CIVIL LIBERTIES UNION OF THE NATIONAL CAPITAL AREA
2006 ACLU Membership Conference
October 15-18, 2006/Washington, DC
Contact: Anthony D. Romero
Tel: (202) 457-0800
Web: www.aclu.org

DIVERSITY BEST PRACTICES
2006 Diversity and Women Summit & Gala
October 25-26, 2006/Washington, DC
Contact: Edie Fraser
Tel: (202) 466-8209 Fax: (202) 833-1808
Email: inquire@tpag.com
Web: www.diversitybestpractices.com

AFRO-AMERICAN HISTORICAL AND GENEALOGICAL SOCIETY, INC.
Annual National Conference
October 26-29, 2006/Salt Lake City, UT
Contact: Pamela Tenpenny-Lewis
Tel: (501) 425-5578 Fax: (202) 722-9113
Email: info@aahgs.org
Web: www.aahgs.org

NATIONAL MINORITY SUPPLIER DEVELOPMENT COUNCIL, INC.
NMSDC Conference
October 29-November 1, 2006/San Diego, CA
Contact: Suzannet Eaddy
Tel: (212) 944-2430 Fax: (212) 719-9611
Web: www.nmsdcus.org

AKRON URBAN MINORITY ALCOHOLISM AND DRUG ABUSE OUTREACH PROGRAM
15th Annual Conference
October 2006 TBA/Akron, OH
Contact: Janice Bourda Mercier
Tel: (330) 379-3467 Fax: (330) 379-3465
Email: info@akronumadaop.org
Web: http://umadaops.com

NOVEMBER

MINORITY CORPORATE COUNSEL ASSOCIATION
Creating Pathways to Diversity Conference
November 8, 2006/New York City, NY
Contact: Shawn Boynes
Tel: (202) 739-5909 Fax: (202) 216-9040
Email: info@mcca.com
Web: www.mcca.com

ASSOCIATION OF NATIONAL ADVERTISERS, INC.
2006 Multicultural Marketing Conference
November 12-14, 2006/Los Angeles, CA
Contact: Patricia Hanlon
Tel: (212) 697-5950 Fax: (212) 661-8057
Email: phanlon@ana.net
Web: www.ana.net

DECEMBER

GLOBAL DIVERSITY GROUP, INC.
Business Exchange 2006 Tour for Success
December 8, 2006/Miami, FL
Tel: (410) 730-6906 Fax: (410) 730-6908
Email: corporate@globaldiversitygroup.com
Web: www.mpbnetwork.com

African American Web Sites

BUSINESS

AFRICAN AMERICAN BUSINESS ALLIANCE
www.a-aba.com
Provides information and resources for business.

AFRICAN AMERICAN BUSINESS DIRECTORY
www.africanamericabusiness.com
Directory of African American businesses in major US cities.

AFRICAN AMERICAN BUSINESS EXCHANGE
http://groups.yahoo.com/group/AfricanAmericanBusinessExchange/
Bulletin board.

AFRICAN AMERICAN BUSINESS LINK
www.aabl.com
Offers a business directory, online catalog shopping, and a complete line of web publishing and communication products that link businesses, consumers, manufacturers and vendors both African American and others.

AFRICAN AMERICAN BUSINESSES AND STORES
www.math.buffalo.edu/~sww/circle/CL_aastores.html
Offers links to African American sites.

BLACK CAREER WOMEN
www.bcw.org
Designs and implements annual programs which provide enrichment and encouragement to black women as they deal with institutional barriers as well as economic, political, and societal forces.

BLACK ENTERPRISE
www.blackenterprise.com
A virtual desktop for African Americans, dedicated to unlocking profitable business opportunities in the affluent African American market.

BLACKONOMICS.COM
www.blackonomics.com
Offers information about business, careers, and economics.

CLARK INTERNET PUBLISHING, INC.
www.aabl.com
An index of African American-owned businesses, news, and information about colleges, as well as employment opportunities.

EINFONEWS
www.einfonews.com
To help business people become more familiar with information technology.

FEDERAL ACCESS
www.fedaccess.com
To focus on the special needs of small businesses seeking opportunities in the multi-billion dollar government contracts sector.

IMDIVERSITY.COM
www.imdiversity.com
Career and self-development site.

KB ENTERPRISES
www.africanamericanbusinessdirectory.com
Searchable directory of businesses and professional firms owned by African Americans.

THE BLACK COLLEGIAN ONLINE
www.black-collegian.com
To provide cutting-edge information on career, resources for Black collegians.

US DEPARTMENT OF COMMERCE
www.mbda.gov
As part of the US Department of Commerce, the MBDA offers free services through this web site.

WORKSHOP IN BUSINESS OPPORTUNITIES
www.wibo.org
Seeks to educate people in disadvantaged neighborhoods about business and jobs.

COMMUNITY

BLACK AMERICA ONLINE
www.blackamericaonline.com
Information about the black community.

BLACK AMERICA WEB
www.blackamericaweb.com
To develop, acquire and partner in quality media and marketing opportunities targeting the African American community.

BLACK NATIVE AMERICAN ASSOCIATION
www.bnaa.org
An intertribal group of people with African-American and Native American heritage.

BLACKPLANET.COM
www.blackplanet.com
Chat room.

UNIVERSAL NEGRO IMPROVEMENT ASSOCIATION AND AFRICAN COMMUNITIES LEAGUE
www.unia-acl.org
Network of people of African ancestry.

CULTURAL

AFRICAN AMERICAN BIOGRAPHICAL DATABASE
http://aabd.chadwyck.com
Online resource for biographical information, photographs, and illustrations.

AFROFUTURISM.NET
www.afrofuturism.net
Considers futurist themes in black cultural production and the ways in which technological innovation is changing the face of black art and culture.

BLACK QUEST
www.blackquest.com
Black Quest is an African American and Black History resource web site.

BLACKUSA.COM
www.blackusa.com
To offer cultural, historical information and links.

BROWN UNIVERSITY
http://lcweb2.loc.gov/ammem/award97/rpbhtml/aasmhome.html
An online collection of over 1,000 pieces of sheet music related to the African-American experience.

COLUMBIA COLLEGE CHICAGO
www.cbmr.org
An internationally recognized center devoted to research into the music of the global African Diaspora.

JOHN G. RILEY FOUNDATION, INC.
http://tfn.net/Riley
Online historical information.

MELANET, LC
www.melanet.com
A platform for the intellectual, economic and spiritual expression of peoples throughout the African Diaspora.

NATIONAL ASSOCIATION OF NEGRO MUSICIANS
http://facstaff.morehouse.edu/~cgrimes
Dedicated to the preservation, encouragement, and advocacy of all genres of the music of African-Americans in the world.

NEW YORK PUBLIC LIBRARY
www.nypl.org/research/sc/sc.html
Features exhibits at the Center, a national research library documenting the experiences of peoples of African descent.

SOULOFAMERICA.COM
www.SoulOfAmerica.com
Information on African American cultural sites.

EDUCATION

BLACK HISTORY HOTLIST
www.kn.pacbell.com/wired/BHM/bh_hotlist.html
List of Internet resources that may be used as raw material for a study of African American history and issues.

DUKE UNIVERSITY
http://scriptorium.lib.duke.edu/collections/african-american-women.html
An online collection of letters and memoirs of 19th century slave women.

FILAMENTALITY
www.kn.pacbell.com/wired/BHM/AfroAm.html
Educational resource for young readers and teachers, the site explores ways to learn about African American history, literature, and social issues.

LIBRARY OF CONGRESS
http://lcweb2.loc.gov/ammem/snhtml/snhome.html
A searchable collection of pamphlets about African American history and culture from the A.P. Murray Collection. Contains more than 2300 first-person accounts of slavery and 500 black and white photographs of former slaves.

UNIVERSITY OF MARYLAND
www.academy.umd.edu/scholarship/aali/
To enhance the performance of established, emerging, and potential African American leaders.

EMPLOYMENT

BLACK EMPLOYMENT AND ENTREPRENEUR JOURNAL
www.blackeoejournal.com
Assists minorities by providing career opportunities, community awareness, and higher education.

EQUAL OPPORTUNITY NEWS
www.equalopportunitynews.com
A retired federal civil rights investigator offers guidance and assistance on filing and processing charges of employment discrimination.

HIREDIVERSITY
www.hirediversity.com
Employment assistance.

MINORITY CAREER NETWORK
www.minoritycareernet.com
Assists job seekers.

ENTERTAINMENT

AJENTE.COM
http://usablackent.com
Web site for urban entertainment.

BET
www.bet.com
A subsidiary of BET.

BLACKFILM.COM
www.BlackFilm.com
An online resource which links the Black film community while cultivating national and international audiences interested in their work.

BLACKFLIX.COM
www.blackflix.com
A site dedicated to continuing to develop a Black theme movie web site on the internet.

GENEALOGY

AFRICAN AMERICAN CEMETERIES ONLINE
www.prairiebluff.com/aacemetery
Genealogical information for African Americans.

AFRICAN AMERICAN GENEALOGICAL SOCIETY OF NORTHERN CALIFORNIA
www.aagsnc.org
Information on African American genealogy resources.

AFRICAN-AMERICAN GENEALOGY RING
http://afamgenealogy.ourfamily.com
Dedicated to genealogists who are re-searching African-American family histories.

AFRICAN-NATIVE AMERICAN HISTORY AND GENEALOGY WEB PAGE
www.african-nativeamerican.com
Devoted to genealogists who are research-ing African-American and Native American family histories.

AFRIGENEAS
www.afrigeneas.com
Devoted to African ancestors genealogy.

CHRISTINE'S GENEALOGY WEB SITE
www.ccharity.com
Offers links and resources for family history.

CYNDI'S LIST OF GENEALOGY SITES ON THE INTERNET
www.cyndislist.com/african.htm
Offers links and resources to research family history.

USGENWEB ARCHIVES
www.rootsweb.com/%7Eusgenweb/la/afamer.htm
Information on African American genealogy resources.

USGENWEB PROJECT
www.usgenweb.org
Information on African American genealogy resources.

INTERNET SERVICE PROVIDER

NUBONYX.COM
www.nubonyx.com
An ISP for people of color.

SUCCESSNET
www.successnet.net

LITERARY

A DIFFERENT BOOKLIST
www.adifferentbooklist.com
A site focusing on African American writers.

AFRICAN AMERICAN YEARBOOK
www.africanamericanyearbook.com
A reference guide for the African-American community.

QBR: THE BLACK BOOK REVIEW ONLINE
www.qbr.com
Dedicated to books about the African American experience.

TIMBOOKTU.COM
www.timbooktu.com
Offers stories, poetry and essays related to the African American experience.

MEDICAL

BLACKHEALTHNETWORK.COM
www.BlackHealthNetwork.com
Features articles on health trends, fitness, and illnesses; includes a search engine for Black doctors.

NEWS

BLACK VOICES
http://blackvoices.aol.com
News, lifestyle, career, and entertainment online destination.

BLACKNEWS
www.blacknews.com
The online portal for Black news.

BLACKPRESSUSA.COM
www.BlackPressUSA.com
Independent source of news for the African American community.

GLOBAL BLACK NEWS
www.globalblacknews.com
An Internet news organization.

THEODORE MYLES PUBLISHING, INC.
www.afrocentricnews.com
An web site for Afrocentric network.

POLITICAL ACTION

BLACK CONGRESS ON HEALTH, LAW AND ECONOMICS
www.bchle.org

LEADERSHIP CONFERENCE ON CIVIL RIGHTS
www.civilrights.org
A collaboration of the Leadership Confer-ence on Civil Rights and the Leadership Conference on Civil Rights Education Fund. Its mission is to serve as the site of record for relevant and up-to-the minute civil rights news and information.

PORTAL

AFRICAN AMERICAN WEB CONNECTION
www.aawc.com
Directory and links.

AFRONET WIRELESS
www.afronet.com
An Afrocentric resource center.

BEST BLACK WEBSITES.COM
www.bestblackwebsites.com
A searchable list of African American web sites.

BLACK DIRECTORY
www.blackdirectory.net
Information and resources.

BLACKSEEK
www.blackseek.com
Includes a search engine for businesses and employment.

BLACKWORLD
www.blackworld.com
A global Internet communications, com-merce and media company offering a branded network of web services to people of African origin and descent.

IAFRICA.COM
www.iafrica.com
Content and services.

MYBLACKWEB.COM
www.myblackweb.com
An Afrocentric resource center.

NIAONLINE
http://niaonline.com
Seeks to meet the needs of African-Ameri-can women.

THE BLACK WORLD TODAY
www.tbwt.org
An online Black community.

PROFESSIONAL

ASSOCIATION OF AFRICAN AMERICAN WEB DEVELOPERS
www.aaawd.org
To promotes camaraderie, collaboration, and professional growth among profession-als in all phases of web development and design.

REDIBIS
www.redibis.com
To connect technology industry profession-als of color.

THE DIGITAL SISTAS NETWORK
http://digitalsistas.net
An on and offline professional network of African American women in new media and technology.

RELIGIOUS

A.M.E. TODAY
www.ame-today.com
To cover topics relevant to members of A.M.E. churches.

BLACKANDCHRISTIAN.COM
www.blackandchristian.com
An online community for people of African descent and others interested in the African and African American Christian experience.

NATIONAL BAPTIST CONVENTION, USA, INC.
www.nationalbaptist.com
Information and links about the National Baptist Convention.

THE AFRICAN AMERICAN PULPIT
www.theafricanamericanpulpit.com
To cover topics relevant to today's African American pastor.

SHOPPING

AFRICAN AMERICAN SHOPPER ONLINE
www.africanamericanshopperonline.com
An online marketplace.

AFRICAN AMERICAN SHOPPING MALL
www.aasm.com
An Internet mall including more than 200 Black-owned businesses.

AFRICANSISTERS
www.africansisters.com
An online marketplace for women.

BUYITBLACK.COM
www.buyitblack.com
An online shopping network.

IT'S A BLACK THANG
www.itsablackthang.com
Online shopping.

LITTLEAFRICA.COM
www.LittleAfrica.com
An online shopping network.

SPORTS

AFRICAN AMERICANS IN MOTOR SPORTS
www.aaim1.com
Information on African Americans in racing.

BLACK ATHLETE SPORTS NETWORK
http://blackathlete.com
Sports focus.

NATIONAL COWBOYS OF COLOR MUSEUM AND HALL OF FAME
www.cowboysofcolor.org
Information on African Americans in the sport of rodeo.

Congressional Black Caucus Foundation, Inc.

Congressional Black Caucus Foundation, Inc.

The Congressional Black Caucus Foundation, Inc. (CBCF) was established in 1976 as a non-partisan, non-profit, public policy, research and educational institute. Our mission is to serve as the non-partisan policy-oriented catalyst that educates future leaders and promotes collaboration among legislators, business leaders, minority-focused organizational leaders, and organized labor to effect positive and sustainable change in the African American community. To that end, CBCF works to broaden and elevate the influence of African Americans in the political, legislative, and public policy arenas.

With a focus on Education, Public Health, Economic Development and African Globalism, CBCF is the premier organization that creates, identifies, analyzes and disseminates policy-oriented information critical to advancing African Americans and people of African descent towards equity in economics, health and education.

All CBCF and CBC Spouses programs are supported by fundraising events and corporate underwriting. Each year, CBCF sponsors the Annual Legislative Conference (ALC) which provides a national forum to develop strategies and viable solutions to public policy issues facing Black America.
In addition, CBCF produces regional symposiums throughout the country to explore public policy concerns and to solicit opinions and recommendations of citizens at the local community level.

Congressional Black Caucus Foundation, Inc.

1720 Massachusetts Avenue, NW
Washington, DC 20036
Phone: (202) 263-2800
Fax: (202) 775-0773

Email us at info@cbcfonline.org

Source: Congressional Black Caucus Foundation, Inc. www.cbcfinc.org.

NOV 2 5 2005

Dear Colleagues:

Each year as TIYM publishes its AFRICAN AMERICAN YEARBOOK, the Minority
Business Development Agency (MBDA) looks forward to the opportunity to send
greetings to its readers.

MBDA considers this publication to be an excellent resource for information on minority
establishments in the United States. In fact, MBDA has ties to many individuals and
organizations featured in this YEARBOOK, as we share a common goal of promoting the
growth of African American businesses and communities.

As the only federal agency created solely to foster the establishment and growth of
minority businesses in this country, MBDA is delighted to report that there are now over
4.1 million minority firms in the United States. The number of African American firms
has grown 45% since 1997 and now exceeds 1.1 million firms. Their receipts are $92.7
billion, and together they employ over 800,000 people. These numbers indicate that
African American businesses have a significant impact on the economic landscape of our
Nation. MBDA predicts even greater growth ahead for minority enterprises.

Everyone at TIYM is to be commended for your dedication to strengthening the
foundation upon which African American entrepreneurs can build powerful business
collaborations. Thank you for your commitment, and you have our best wishes for many
more years of success with the YEARBOOK.

Sincerely,

Ronald N. Langston
National Director

The State of the Community
A Democrat's Perspective

Written by:

CHARLES B. RANGEL

Congressman Charles B. Rangel is serving his seventeenth term as the Representative from the 15th Congressional District of New York, located in New York City and comprising East and Central Harlem, the Upper West Side, and Washington Heights/Inwood. Congressman Rangel is the Ranking Member of the Committee on Ways and Means, Deputy Democratic Whip of the House of Representatives, a Co-Chair of the Democratic Congressional Campaign Committee, and Dean of the New York State Congressional Delegation.

Congressman Rangel is the principal author of the $5 billion Federal Empowerment Zone demonstration project to revitalize urban neighborhoods in America. He also authored the Low Income Housing Tax Credit, which is responsible for financing ninety percent of the affordable housing built in the U.S. in the last ten years. The Work Opportunity Tax Credit, also championed by Congressman Rangel, has provided thousands of jobs for underprivileged youth, veterans, and ex-offenders. In additon, Congressman Rangel serves as chairman of the Congressional Narcotics Abuse and Control Caucus.

Congressman Rangel is a founding member and former chairman of the Congressional Black Caucus; he was also chairman of the New York State Council of Black Elected Democrats and was a member of the House Judiciary Committee during the hearings on the articles of impeachment of President Richard Nixon.

Congressman Rangel served in the U.S. Army in Korea, 1948-52, and was awarded the Purple Heart and Bronze Star. Congressman Rangel has authored several pieces of legislation to benefit minority and women veterans, including a successful bill that established the Office of Minority Affairs within the Department of Veterans Affairs.

In 1987, at the height of the battle against apartheid, Congressman Rangel led the effort to include in the Internal revenue Code one of the most effective anti-apartheid measures, denial of tax credits for taxes paid to South Africa. This measure resulted in several Fortune 500 companies leaving South Africa. In addition, Congressman Rangel played a vital role in restoring the democratic government in Haiti.

Congressman Rangel is a graduate of New York University and St. John's University School of Law. He has spent his entire career in public service, first as an Assistant U.S. attorney for the Southern District of New York, and later ion the New York State Assembly. He was elected to Congress on November 3, 1970, and has been re-elected to each succeeding congress.

Congressman Rangel lives in Harlem with his wife Alma, a founding member of the Congressional Black Caucus Spouses and participant in many civic and community organizations. Congressman and Mrs. Rangel have two children

The Bush Administration has been disastrous for the poor. The financial health of a significant number of American families has worsened since 2000. Real household income fell for the fourth year in a row in 2004, for a drop of $1,669 in the median household income since the beginning of the Bush Administration. And in the past year, average hourly earnings have decreased 1.5 percent, after adjusting for inflation. In fact, since 2000, while real incomes have declined for all income levels, the declines have been most severe at the bottom – implying that the gap between the haves and have nots has widened.

In addition, job growth has slowed in recent years. In the last 5 years, our nation has experienced the slowest job growth in over 70 years – a paltry pace of just 34,000 total jobs/month and 16,000 private jobs/month. This compares quite unfavorably with the 1992-2000 pace of 240,000 total jobs/month and 217,000 private jobs/month.

Perhaps most telling in evaluating the economic health of American families is the number of these individuals who comprise our nation's poor. At the end of President Bush's first term, there were 37.0 million Americans in poverty – 5.4 million more than just before the start of the his administration in 2000. The number of persons in poverty has risen every year for the last four years. Further, the value of the minimum wage as a percentage of poverty has fallen to its lowest level on record – going all the way back to 1959. Earnings from full-year, full-time minimum wage work now equal less than 70% of the poverty level for a family of three.

The situation of African Americans is even worse. Their unemployment rate of 9.3% is higher than that of any other ethnic group. Nine million African Americans live in poverty, an increase of 1 million over the last four years, that includes 3.8 million children.

While incomes have fallen for all Americans, the costs of living have risen, including a 60 percent increase in health care costs. Meanwhile, 45.8 million Americans are without health insurance – 6 million more than in 2000. Last year, working Americans faced record gas prices, and continue to deal with skyrocketing energy costs. Home prices rose at the fastest pace in a quarter century.

Unfortunately, Republican policies in Congress and the White House are making matters worse. Instead of addressing growing income disparities and trying to reduce health care costs, they have focused on extending tax breaks that benefit the wealthiest households. Fifty percent of the benefit of extending rate reductions for capital gains and dividend income will go to households with annual incomes over $1 million while middle-income families will receive only 2% of the annual savings.

Congress recently voted for a bill that cuts foster care payments, delays assistance to the disabled and slashes Medicaid and Medicare, ultimately raising health care costs and reducing benefits for our nation's most vulnerable citizens. At the same time, Congress has failed to tackle outrageous energy costs or to crack down on price gouging by the oil and gas industry.

In addition to worsening the economic insecurity of working families, Congress has endangered their retirement security as well. Last year, Democrats were successful in beating back efforts to privatize Social Security, a program which currently benefits 4.8 million African Americans. That said, we must continue to fight efforts to privatize Social Security, as President Bush and Republican leaders continue to advocate for private accounts.

Congress can no longer afford to ignore the harsh economic realities facing Americans of all races. We must appreciate that our failures to address the financial, educational, and health needs of Americans have measurable costs, in lost productivity, economic competitiveness, tax receipts, as well as crime, drug abuse, and the variety of symptoms brought about by poverty. As a nation, we can and must do better.

AFRICAN AMERICAN
Business

FIG 1. U.S. Buying Power by Race: 1990-2009 (Numbers in billions)

The real median income of Black households was $30,134 in 2004, according to the Census Bureau. This change represents a one percent decrease from 2003, the highest loss of any racial or ethnic group in real median income.

Buying power of the African American population, however, will continue to increase throughout this decade. From 1990 to 2000, the Selig Center for Economic Growth estimates that the buying power of the U.S. Black population increased 83.8 percent. Based on Selig Center projections, by 2009 African American buying power will increase to almost $965 billion, a sixty-five percent increase from 2000.

Source: Selig Center for Economic Growth, Terry College of Business, The University of Georgia, May 2004

Race or Ethnicity	1990	2000	Percent Increase 1990 - 2000	2009	Percent Increase 2000 - 2009
Total	4,277.2	7,113.6	66.3%	11,068.8	55.6%
White	3,736.4	5,919.9	58.4%	8,967.5	51.5%
Black	318.3	584.9	83.8%	964.6	64.9%
Hispanic	221.9	503.9	127.1%	992.3	96.9%
Asian	118.2	268.7	127.3%	528.2	96.6%
Other	85.0	195.7	130.2%	371.8	90.0%
American Indian	19.3	37.2	92.7%	65.6	76.3%
Multiracial	NA	107.2	NA	170.9	59.4%

FIG 2. Distribution of African American Women-Owned Firms by Industry

Between 1997 and 2004, the number of African American women-owned firms increased by 32.5 percent, according to a study by the Center for Women's Business Research. The same study revealed that an overwhelming majority of those businesses owned by African American women were in the services sector.

Source: Center for Women's Business Research Using U.S. Census Bureau Data

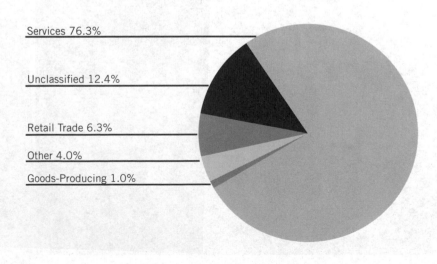

Services 76.3%

Unclassified 12.4%

Retail Trade 6.3%

Other 4.0%

Goods-Producing 1.0%

FIG 3. States With the Largest Number of African American-Owned Firms: 2002

The percentage of African American-owned businesses rose from 1997 to 2002. According to the newly released Survey of Business Owners by the U.S. Census Bureau, the percentage of Black-owned businesses increased from 3.6 to 5.2 percent during this period. New York, California and Florida topped the list of states for total number of firms, while Maryland, Georgia and North Carolina had the highest percentage of firms owned by African Americans.

Source: U.S. Census Bureau, Survey of Business Owners, 2002

State	African American-owned firms (number)	Percent of total firms owned by African Americans
U.S. total	1,197,988	5.2%
New York	129,339	7.6%
California	113,003	3.9%
Texas	88,777	5.1%
Florida	102,074	6.6%
Georgia	90,480	13.4%
Maryland	69,428	15.7%
Illinois	68,708	7.2%
North Carolina	52,134	8.1%
Michigan	44,367	6.0%
Virginia	41,158	7.8%

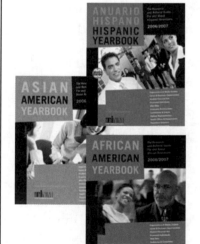

WYNTON MARSALIS

ARTISTIC DIRECTOR, JAZZ AT LINCOLN CENTER

Wynton Marsalis is the Artistic Director of Jazz at Lincoln Center (JALC). Born in New Orleans, Louisiana in 1961, Mr. Marsalis began his classical training on trumpet at age twelve and soon began playing in local bands of diverse genres. He entered The Juilliard School at age seventeen and joined Art Blakey and the Jazz Messengers. Mr. Marsalis made his recording debut as a leader in 1982, and since then he has made more than thirty jazz and classical recordings, which have won him nine Grammy Awards. In 1997, Mr. Marsalis became the first jazz artist to be awarded the prestigious Pulitzer Prize in Music, for his oratorio *Blood on the Fields*. Mr. Marsalis is also an internationally respected teacher and spokesman for music education, and has received honorary doctorates from dozens of universities and colleges. He has also written two books: *Sweet Swing Blues on the Road* in collaboration with photographer Frank Stewart, and the recently released *Jazz in the Bittersweet Blues of Life,* with Carl Vigeland. In 2001, Mr. Marsalis was appointed Messenger of Peace by Kofi Annan, Secretary-General of the United Nations, and he has also been designated Cultural Ambassador to the United States by the U.S. State Department through its Culture Connect program.

AAY When did you first get involved in music?

Marsalis I started playing music when I was six years old. My father was a musician. My brother, who was seven at that time, he had been playing piano and clarinet, and I started playing trumpet.

AAY When did you know that music would be a major part of your life?

Marsalis When I was twelve I got serious about playing music. I began practicing quite a lot. I was interested in jazz musicians to learn how to play like [John] Coltrane, Miles Davis, Clifford Brown, Freddie Hubbard.

AAY How did the artistic and musical culture of New Orleans influence you?

Marsalis In New Orleans we have a lot of different styles of music. Music is very popular, so I had the opportunity to play in a lot of places. I played in clubs, places like Lou and Charlie's. Funk music we played a lot, New Orleans funk and straight-up funk. I played with a lot of brass bands—marching bands. I played with the Fairview Baptist Church Marching Band when I was eight years old. I played a lot of traditional music. I had the opportunity to play modern jazz with people in clubs, like the Bar and Tyler's Beer Gardens. I had the opportunity to play in churches and things like that—classical music. I played in this cathedral. I played with this symphony brass quintet and also with the New Orleans Symphony; I played solos with them. I played with the New Orleans Youth Orchestra and the Civic Orchestra. I played with the band directors, even though I was

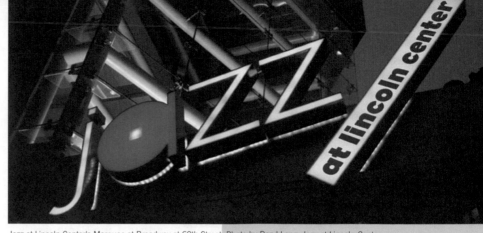

Jazz at Lincoln Center's Marquee at Broadway at 60th Street. Photo by Daryl Long, Jazz at Lincoln Center.

in high school, a thing called the Community Band. I don't think that is around now. I played with my father at gigs where they played just jazz. I played a lot of auxiliary gigs like the circus, ballet and stuff like that. We just had a lot of music in the city. It gave me the opportunity to play in a lot of places. And also we had a tradition of music, so music is a part of our everyday life.

AAY What are your thoughts on the destruction of New Orleans by Hurricane Katrina?

Wynton Marsalis, Artistic Director, Jazz at Lincoln Center.

Marsalis I think it is a tragic occurrence, but it showed us a lot about what we need to work on and I think we'll come back strong. It exposed the poverty and the racism and ignorance of the city, but it also exposed the beauty of the city and it brought to the forefront the nature of New Orleans culture and how special it is. So I feel like, in the long run, it was good that the ignorance was exposed. Of

course, I'm devastated by all the loss of all the homes and all the many lives. It is going to be worse if the real count ever comes out.

AAY In your opinion, what type of impact has music, and in particular jazz, had on the African American community and on American culture?

Marsalis Jazz music has had a great impact on American culture because the rhythm section came out of jazz. Jazz went all over the world and introduced so many great artists. Jazz objectified a lot about Afro-American life, and jazz musicians have always been in the front of social protest. They came before civil rights leaders. The first integrated ensembles in America were jazz bands. Jazz bands were integrated before baseball was integrated. The first Afro-American genius that would go all around the world and be recognized was a jazz musician and that was Louis Armstrong. He, along with Duke Ellington, brought the message of jazz and the sophistication of Afro-American life to the world. And their music was often at odds with the way Afro-Americans were forced to live here at home. So it was an eye-opening music. Nowadays, it has less impact on the Afro-American community because African Americans are not that much into the arts, or really not into musical arts. A vast majority of Afro-Americans have not really been interested in arts and are mainly interested in entertainment. So I think Afro-Americans would see a great increase in our productivity as citizens if we were to embrace the arts, and most specifically the art of jazz. But as of right now, we are a long way from that. It might change with education, but we have a long way to go.

AAY How do you feel about the state of jazz music today?

Marsalis I think jazz music is an art form—music that stays around. Some generations pick up on the best of it and some don't, but the music is so deep in the soil and the consciousness of the country that it remains. Each generation redefines the greatness of the greatest artists. Like Beethoven's greatness is redefined by every generation. We just saw an upsurge in Shakespeare over the last ten years or so. This tends to happen with great things—they stay around because of the profundity of the idea. Jazz will be around. People all over the world are trying to play it. It's been redefined in many ways, and the recordings are the definitive statement on the music. And those recordings have been disseminated all over the world and people love it all over the world. In terms of predicting where jazz will be—I don't know. I don't think you can tell what decision people are going to make. I couldn't have predicted that gangster rap would become popular. If you had asked me ten years before that music calling people "niggers" and "bitches" was going to be popular, there's no way I would have been able to predict that. So I don't know. Just like [rap] was able to come in, I feel that something of significance and substance can also come in.

AAY How do you feel about the level of participation of African Americans in the music industry?

Marsalis I feel that we provide a kind of performance. I feel we are still tied to the minstrel position— we provide comic relief. It's how the minstrels would play out what it was like to be on the plantation for the entertainment of people. Now, black America plays out—the plantation now is the ghetto. In many cases we play out ghetto stereotypes for the entertainment of people. In current Afro-America, in the music industry, I feel that's gotten better because at least we have been able to make some money off of it. In the minstrel shows, black people really didn't make money off of it, whereas today, they can make money off of it.

AAY Do you think African American artists are shaping the direction of the music industry?

Marsalis No. I don't feel that African American artists are shaping the direction of the music industry. I feel that the business people are shaping it; they exploit the talent of Afro-Americans. In this case, the talents of minstrels, the talent that they want to promote. I feel like a vast bulk of the music that is sold is not Afro-American music. There is a lot of music being sold all over

The Marsalis family performs at the October 18th grand opening concert of Jazz at Lincoln Center's new home, Frederick P. Rose Hall.

Cabaret and jazz singer Bobby Short with Artistic Director Wynton Marsalis at the Ertegun Jazz Hall of Fame induction ceremony.

the world and there's many kinds of music. If you look at touring, a rock group can still sell stadiums out, Afro-American groups have not been able to do that. The Rolling Stones still can make all kinds of money. The number of white groups that can sell out stadiums, Bruce Springsteen can sell out the Meadowlands for a week. There is no Afro-American artist that can do that. Afro-Americans are part of it and we provide the cutting edge in the rush. In terms of real elevation of the music industry, I don't find that, but I am sure there are some Afro-Americans that are doing great things. I don't see them getting most of the headlines.

AAY How do you feel about the direction music is headed in?

Marsalis I think there are a lot of really great musicians, but I just don't think people know who they are. I am not pleased with the direction that commercial music is heading. It is going too far in the direction of pornography and ignorance, which I don't endorse, on any level.

AAY What advice can you provide young Afro-American artists interested in pursuing a career in music?

Marsalis Be very clear whether you want to be in the entertainment side of music or the music side. If you're on the entertainment side, you have to get into the gym, you have to look a certain way or you have to have a certain type of tattoo, you have to have your publicity thing. You have to have good taste, and a feeling for hooks and things like that. If you're going to be on the music side, you have to practice and study and get knowledge of music from a historical standpoint. And you have to have a level of integrity and a desire to change the world with your music. You have to be kind of anti-cliché and be willing to stand alone. That's the most painful part of it. You have to stand against your own people for their good: it's hard. But it's worth it if you want to do it. It's not worth it if you don't.

AAY In your opinion, what role will the Afro-American community play in shaping the general direction of the country?

Marsalis I don't feel that there's too much in recent years. If we ever wake up maybe we could do something, but in this current state of slumber, not too much. We're more like a national joke at this point. The future depends on whether we as a people wake up and get control of our young people. If we could

just, myself included, if we could just get control of our language first. It is the vulgarity…public vulgarity. If we could just get our language together, then we could start to deal with our people. This is not a bright period in Afro-American history. For some people, yes. Some people will always survive. But as a group, we are having a rough time right now. We've accepted a vision of ourselves that's not real. My only hope is that we'll come out from underneath this by constructing a vision of ourselves that celebrates the grandeur of our survival of slavery and our contributions to this country and to the world, and that we know what those things are. We follow the best of those things, the best of our religious traditions, the best of our music, the best of the work of our intellectuals, the best of our political figures, the best of our law figures. I find that too often we don't know what any of these things are, so we accept the worst. The question is: Will we identify with the best of our contributions and embrace those things and begin to ascend as a people? Or will we continue to be an international joke through videos and these other things, calling ourselves "niggers" and all of that?

Lincoln Center Jazz Orchestra with Wynton Marsalis. Photo by Keith Major.

Federal and State Employment Offices

ALABAMA

AIR FORCE, DEPT. OF THE
Maxwell AFB
Maxwell AFB, AL 36112-6334
Tel: (800) 423-8723
Web: www.airforce.com

ARMY, DEPT. OF
US Army Recruiting Battalion Montgomery
Public Affairs Office
775 McDonald St., Bldg. 1510
MAFB-Gunter Annex, AL 36114
Tel: (334) 271-3059

EQUAL EMPLOYMENT OPPORTUNITY COMMISSION
Birmingham District Office
1130 22nd St., Ridge Park Pl. #2000 South
Birmingham, AL 35205
Bernice Williams-Kimbrough, Director
Tel: (205) 212-2100 Fax: (205) 212-2105
Web: www.eeoc.gov

HOMELAND SECURITY, DEPT. OF
USCG Recruiting Office Birmingham
Eastwood Festival Ctr., 7001 Crestwood
Blvd. #612
Birmingham, AL 35201
BMC Jose Rodriquez, Recruiter in Charge
Tel: (205) 592-8923 Fax: (205) 592-9826
Email: jrodriquez@cgrc.uscg.mil
Web: www.gocoastguard.com

USCG Recruiting Office Mobile
Mobile Festival Ctr., 3725 Airport Blvd.
#148
Mobile, AL 36608-1633
SKC Charles L. Miles, Recruiter in Charge
Tel: (251) 441-5171 Fax: (251) 441-5173
Email: cmiles@cgrc.uscg.mil
Web: www.gocoastguard.com

USCG Recruiting Office Montgomery
Armed Forces Career Ctr., 2933 Eastern
Blvd.
Montgomery, AL 36116
AMTC Tim Lucas, Recruiter in Charge
Tel: (334) 279-4880 Fax: (334) 279-3129
Email: tlucas@cgrc.uscg.mil
Web: www.gocoastguard.com

NAVY, DEPT. OF THE
Navy Recruiting District, Montgomery
2400 President South Dr.
Montgomery, AL 36116
Tel: (334) 279-8543

USMC Recruiting Station, Montgomery
2853 Fairlane Dr. #64, Bldg. G
Montgomery, AL 36116-1698
Tel: (334) 647-3110
Web: www.marines.com

POSTAL SERVICE
Alabama District
351 24th St. North
Birmingham, AL 35203-9989
April M. Williams, Diversity Specialist
Tel: (205) 521-0256 Fax: (205) 521-0935
Email: april.m.williams@usps.gov
Web: www.usps.gov

ALASKA

AIR FORCE, DEPT. OF THE
Eielson AFB
Eielson AFB, AK 99702-1720
Tel: (800) 423-8723
Web: www.airforce.com

Elmendorf AFB
Elmendorf AFB, AK 99506-2400
Tel: (800) 423-8723
Web: www.airforce.com

HOMELAND SECURITY, DEPT. OF
USCG Recruiting Office Anchorage
800 Diamond Blvd. Space 3-205
Anchorage, AK 99515
AETC Frank L. Brown, Recruiter in Charge
Tel: (907) 271-2447 Fax: (907) 271-5075
Email: flbrown@cgrc.uscg.mil
Web: www.gocoastguard.com

INTERIOR, DEPT. OF THE
National Park Service
Alaska Region
240 W. 5th Ave. #114
Anchorage, AK 99501
Darwin Aho, Human Resources Manager
Tel: (907) 644-3336
Email: darwin_aho@nps.gov
Web: www.nps.gov/akso

ARIZONA

AIR FORCE, DEPT. OF THE
Davis-Monthan AFB
Davis-Monthan AFB, AZ 85707-3018
Tel: (800) 423-8723
Web: www.airforce.com

Luke AFB
Luke AFB, AZ 85309-1514
Tel: (800) 423-8723
Web: www.airforce.com

ARMY, DEPT. OF
US Army Recruiting Battalion Phoenix
Public Affairs Office
1 N. 1st St. #400
Phoenix, AZ 85004-2357
Tel: (602) 254-1981

EQUAL EMPLOYMENT OPPORTUNITY COMMISSION
Phoenix District Office
3300 N. Central Ave. #690
Phoenix, AZ 85012-2504
Chester V. Bailey, Director
Tel: (602) 640-5000 Fax: (602) 640-5071
Web: www.eeoc.gov

HOMELAND SECURITY, DEPT. OF
USCG Recruiting Office Phoenix
826 N. Central Ave.
Phoenix, AZ 85004-2003
SKC Zeke Witherspoon, Recruiter in Charge
Tel: (602) 379-3834 Fax: (602) 379-3843
Email: zwitherspoon@cgrc.uscg.mil
Web: www.gocoastguard.com

USCG Recruiting Office Tucson
Mission Plz., 4679 E. Speedway
Tucson, AZ 85714
AMT1 Mickey Winchel, Recruiter in Charge
Tel: (520) 323-5546 Fax: (520) 323-5587
Email: mwinchel@cgrc.uscg.mil
Web: www.gocoastguard.com

INTERIOR, DEPT. OF THE
Bureau Indian Affairs
Western Region, Personnel Office
400 N. 5th St., 12th Fl.
Phoenix, AZ 85004
Marcelnia Hills, Acting Personnel Officer
Tel: (602) 379-6739 Fax: (602) 379-4966
Web: www.bia.gov

NAVY, DEPT. OF THE
Navy Recruiting District, Phoenix
P.O. Box 25368
Phoenix, AZ 85002
Tel: (602) 256-6026

USMC Recruiting Station, Phoenix
1 N. 1st St. #302
Phoenix, AZ 85004
Tel: (602) 256-7819
Web: www.marines.com

POSTAL SERVICE
Arizona District
4949 E. VanBuren
Phoenix, AZ 85026
Aida Murrieta-Penn, Diversity Development
Specialist
Tel: (602) 225-5451 Fax: (602) 225-5432
Email: amurriet@email.usps.gov
Web: www.usps.gov

STATE OF ARIZONA
Governors Office
EEO Office
1700 W. Washington St. #156
Phoenix, AZ 85007
Patti Campbell, Specialist
Tel: (602) 542-3711 Fax: (602) 542-3712
Email: pcampbell@az.gov
Web: www.governor.state.az.us

ARKANSAS

AGRICULTURE, DEPT. OF
Natural Resources Conservation Service
700 W. Capital Ave., Federal Bldg. #3416
Little Rock, AR 72201
Rose Webb, Federal Women's Program
Manager
Tel: (501) 301-3174 Fax: (501) 301-3189
Email: rose.webb@ar.usda.gov
Web: www.ar.nrcs.usda.gov

AIR FORCE, DEPT. OF THE
Little Rock AFB
Little Rock AFB, AR 72099-5052
Tel: (800) 423-8723
Web: www.airforce.com

EQUAL EMPLOYMENT OPPORTUNITY COMMISSION
Little Rock Area Office
820 Louisiana St. #200
Little Rock, AR 72201
Kay Klugh, Director
Tel: (501) 324-5060 Fax: (501) 324-5991
Web: www.eeoc.gov

HOMELAND SECURITY, DEPT. OF
USCG Recruiting Office Little Rock
Ashley Sq. Shopping Ctr., 9108 N. Rodney
Parham Rd.
Little Rock, AR 72205-1648
AMTC James Lawson, Recruiter in Charge
Tel: (501) 217-9446 Fax: (501) 217-3858
Email: jlawson@cgrc.uscg.mil
Web: www.gocoastguard.com

POSTAL SERVICE
Arkansas District
420 Natural Resources Dr.
Little Rock, AR 72205-9001
Judy E. Gurkin, Diversity Development
Specialist
Tel: (501) 228-4263 Fax: (501) 228-4249
Email: jgurkin@email.usps.gov
Web: www.usps.gov

STATE OF ARKANSAS
Department of Finance and Administration
Administrative Services Office
1515 W. 7th St. #102
Little Rock, AR 72201
Jenette S. Manno, DSA Manager of Human
Resources
Tel: (501) 371-6009 Fax: (501) 683-2174
Email: jenette.manno@dfa.state.ar.us
Web: www.arkansas.gov/dfa

CALIFORNIA

AGRICULTURE, DEPT. OF
Forest Service
Region 5, Pacific Southwest Region
1323 Club Dr.
Vallejo, CA 94592
Sandra Wallace, Director of Civil Rights
Tel: (707) 562-8752 Fax: (707) 562-9208
Email: sandrawallace@fs.fed.us
Web: www.fs.fed.us

AIR FORCE, DEPT. OF THE
Forest Service
Region 5, Pacific Southwest Region
2550 Riverside Dr.
Susanville, CA 96130
Dan Gonzalez, Forest Civil Rights Officer
Tel: (530) 252-6603 Fax: (530) 252-6646
Email: dgonzalez@fs.fed.us
Web: www.fs.fed.us

Beale AFB
Beale AFB, CA 95903-1533
Tel: (800) 423-8723
Web: www.airforce.com

Edwards AFB
Edwards AFB, CA 93524-1470
Tel: (800) 423-8723
Web: www.airforce.com

Los Angeles AFB
Los Angeles AFB, CA 90245-4677
Tel: (800) 423-8723
Web: www.airforce.com

March AFB
March AFB, CA 92518-1723
Tel: (800) 423-8723
Web: www.airforce.com

Onizuka Air Station
Sunnyvale, CA 94089-1233
Tel: (800) 423-8723
Web: www.airforce.com

Travis AFB
Travis AFB, CA 94535-2406
Tel: (800) 423-8723
Web: www.airforce.com

Vandeburg AFB
Vandeburg AFB, CA 93437-6252
Tel: (800) 423-8723
Web: www.airforce.com

ARMY, DEPT. OF
US Army Recruiting Battalion Los Angeles
Public Affairs Office
5051 Rodeo Rd. #2087
Los Angeles, CA 90016-4793
Tel: (323) 293-7317

US Army Recruiting Battalion Sacramento
Public Affairs Office
2880 Sunrise Blvd. #230
Rancho Cordova, CA 95742-6549
Tel: (916) 638-0970

US Army Recruiting Battalion Southern California
Public Affairs Office
27401 Los Altos #330
Mission Viejo, CA 92691-6316
Tel: (949) 367-1159

CITY OF LOS ANGELES
LA Unified School District/Human Resources
Certificated Recruitment and Selection
Section
333 S. Beaudry Ave., 15th Fl.

Los Angeles, CA 90017
Deborah Ignagni, Director
Tel: (213) 241-5300 Fax: (213) 241-8412
Email: deborah.ignagni@lausd.net
Web: www.teachinla.com

ENVIRONMENTAL PROTECTION AGENCY
Human Resources Office
Region 9, Pacific Southwest
75 Hawthorne St. M/C PMD-12
San Francisco, CA 94105
Kim Driver, Outreach and Recruitment
Coordinator
Tel: (415) 972-3830 Fax: (415) 947-8024
Email: driver.kim@epa.gov
Web: www.epa.gov

EQUAL EMPLOYMENT OPPORTUNITY COMMISSION
Fresno Local Office
1265 W. Shaw Ave. #103
Fresno, CA 93711
Adria Boetig, Acting Director
Tel: (559) 487-5793 Fax: (559) 487-5053
Web: www.eeoc.gov

Los Angeles District Office
255 E. Temple St., Roybal Federal Bldg.
4th Fl.
Los Angeles, CA 90012
Olophius E. Perry, Director
Tel: (213) 894-1000 Fax: (213) 894-1118
Web: www.eeoc.gov

Oakland Local Office
1301 Clay St. #1170N
Oakland, CA 94612-5217
Joyce Hendy, Director
Tel: (510) 637-3230 Fax: (510) 637-3235
Web: www.eeoc.gov

San Diego Area Office
401 B St.Wells, Fargo Bank Bldg. #510
San Diego, CA 92101
Tel: (619) 557-7235 Fax: (619) 557-7274
Web: www.eeoc.gov

San Francisco District Office
350 The Embarcadero #500
San Francisco, CA 94105-1260
H. Joan Ehrlich, Director
Tel: (415) 625-5600 Fax: (415) 625-5609
Web: www.eeoc.gov

San Jose Local Office
96 N. 3rd St. #200
San Jose, CA 95112
Adria Boetig, Acting Director
Tel: (408) 291-7352 Fax: (408) 291-4539
Web: www.eeoc.gov

GENERAL SERVICES ADMINISTRATION
Office of Equal Employment Opportunity
Region 9, 10
450 Golden Gate Ave. #6577
San Francisco, CA 94102-3434
Tel: (415) 522-2711 Fax: (415) 522-2710
Web: www.gsa.gov

HOMELAND SECURITY, DEPT. OF
USCG Recruiting Office Fresno
3749 W. Shaw Ave.
Fresno, CA 93711
HSC Richard Garcia, Recruiter in Charge
Tel: (559) 221-6600 Fax: (559) 229-5608
Email: rgarcia@cgrc.uscg.mil
Web: www.gocoastguard.com

USCG Recruiting Office Hawthorne
12620 Hawthorne Plz. #C
Hawthorne, CA 90250
YNC Rodney Weiss, Recruiter in Charge

Tel: (310) 675-7562 Fax: (310) 675-7739
Email: twilbert@cgrc.uscg.mil
Web: www.gocoastguard.com

USCG Recruiting Office Humboldt Bay
Victoria Place Shopping Ctr., 3220 S.
Broadway St. #A-4
Eureka, CA 95501-3854
SK1 Tim Crothers, Recruiter in Charge
Tel: (707) 268-2471 Fax: (707) 268-2473
Email: tcrothers@cgrc.uscg.mil
Web: www.gocoastguard.com

USCG Recruiting Office Lakewood
Lakewood Center., 4431 Candlewood St.
Lakewood, CA 90712
HSC James Anderson, Recruiter in Charge
Tel: (562) 790-2318 Fax: (562) 790-2478
Email: wbulman@cgrc.uscg.mil
Web: www.gocoastguard.com

USCG Recruiting Office Montebello
2350 W. Beverly Blvd. #100
Montebello, CA 90640
HSC Diana Bullwinkle, Recruiter in Charge
Tel: (323) 887-7558 Fax: (323) 887-7576
Email: dbullwikle@cgrc.uscg.mil
Web: www.gocoastguard.com

USCG Recruiting Office Riverside
1090 E. Washington St. #A
Colton, CA 92324-8180
AMTCS Wayne Campbell, Recruiter in Charge
Tel: (909) 783-2772 Fax: (909) 783-3158
Email: wcampbell@cgrc.uscg.mil
Web: www.gocoastguard.com

USCG Recruiting Office Sacramento
Antelope Plz., 6456 Tupelo Dr. #A-5
Citrus Heights, CA 95621
MKC Thomas Pitock, Recruiter in Charge
Tel: (916) 721-6877 Fax: (916) 721-7857
Email: tpitock@cgrc.uscg.mil
Web: www.gocoastguard.com

USCG Recruiting Office San Diego
Point Loma Plz., 3663 E. Midway Dr.
San Diego, CA 92110-3224
FSCS Randy Washington, Recruiter in Charge
Tel: (619) 226-8222 Fax: (619) 226-8234
Email: rwashington@cgrc.uscg.mil
Web: www.gocoastguard.com

USCG Recruiting Office San Diego South
703 H St. #3
Chula Vista, CA 91910-4056
FSCS Randy Washington, Recruiter in Charge
Tel: (619) 427-1678 Fax: (619) 427-0585
Email: rwashington@cgrc.uscg.mil
Web: www.gocoastguard.com

USCG Recruiting Office San Francisco
14410 Washington Ave. #118
San Leandro, CA 94578
GMC Rick Ward, Recruiter in Charge
Tel: (510) 352-8992 Fax: (510) 352-0359
Email: rickward@cgrc.uscg.mil
Web: www.gocoastguard.com

USCG Recruiting Office San Jose
3381 Stevens Creek Blvd.
San Jose, CA 95117-1070
YNC Carlos Rosario, Recruiter in Charge
Tel: (408) 246-8724 Fax: (408) 246-8729
Email: crosario@cgrc.uscg.mil
Web: www.gocoastguard.com

USCG Recruiting Office Ventura
4202 S. Victoria Ave.
Oxnard, CA 93035
OSCS Thomas Buccowich, Recruiter in Charge
Tel: (805) 984-6893 Fax: (805) 984-5925
Email: tbuccowich@cgrc.uscg.mil
Web: www.gocoastguard.com

INTERIOR, DEPT. OF THE
Bureau of Land Management
California State Office, EEO Office
2800 Cottage Way #W-1834
Sacramento, CA 95825-1886
Mario Gonzalez, EEO Manager
Tel: (916) 978-4492 Fax: (916) 978-4498
Web: www.ca.blm.gov

Bureau of Reclamation
Mid-Pacific Region
2800 Cottage Way, M/C MP500
Sacramento, CA 95825
Leila Horibata, Special Emphasis Coordinator
Tel: (916) 978-5032 Fax: (916) 978-5496
Email: lhoribata@mp.usbr.gov
Web: www.usbr.gov/mp

LABOR, DEPT. OF
Employment and Training Administration
Office of Youth Programs/Job Corps
71 Stevenson St. #1015
San Francisco, CA 94105-3768
Tel: (415) 975-4683 Fax: (415) 975-4715
Web: www.dol.gov

NAVY, DEPT. OF THE
Naval Reserve Recruiting Command Area Pacific
960 N. Harbor Dr.
San Diego, CA 92132-5000
Tel: (619) 532-3157

Navy Recruiting District, San Diego
33055 Nixie Way
San Diego, CA 92147
Tel: (619) 571-8782

USMC Recruiting Station, Los Angeles
5051 Rodeo Rd. #2061
Los Angeles, CA 90016-4794
Tel: (323) 294-3679
Web: www.marines.com

USMC Recruiting Station, Orange County
1921 E. Alton Ave. #150
Santa Anna, CA 92705
Tel: (949) 261-0331
Web: www.marines.com

USMC Recruiting Station, Sacramento
3870 Rosin Ct. #110
Sacramento, CA 95834-1633
Tel: (916) 646-6980
Web: www.marines.com

USMC Recruiting Station, San Diego
2221 Camino del Rio South #212
San Diego, CA 92108-3610
Tel: (619) 688-1508
Web: www.marines.com

USMC Recruiting Station, San Francisco
Moffet Federal Airfield, 546 Vernon Ave. #212
Mountain View, CA 94043
Tel: (650) 603-8953
Web: www.marines.com

POSTAL SERVICE
Oakland District
1675 7th St. #306
Oakland, CA 94615-9512

Elmira A. Walton, Diversity Development
Specialist
Tel: (510) 874-8665 Fax: (510) 433-7643
Email: ewalton@usps.gov
Web: www.usps.gov

Pacific Area Office
1675 7th St.
Oakland, CA 94615-9998
Henrietta Clark Goldsby, Senior Diversity
Program Coordinator
Tel: (510) 874-8650 Fax: (510) 874-8596
Email: hgoldsby@email.usps.gov
Web: www.usps.gov

San Diego District
11251 Rancho Carmel Dr. #341
San Diego, CA 92199-9461
Hector Baca, Diversity Development
Specialist
Tel: (858) 674-0256 Fax: (619) 674-2711
Email: hector.baca@usps.gov
Web: www.usps.gov

San Francisco District
P.O. Box 885348
San Francisco, CA 94188-5348
Abel E. Sanchez, Diversity Development
Specialist
Tel: (415) 550-5710 Fax: (415) 550-5283
Email: asanche4@email.usps.gov
Web: www.usps.gov

Santa Ana District
15421 Gale Ave.
City of Industry, CA 91715-9347
Norma Diaz, Diversity Development
Specialist
Tel: (626) 855-6354 Fax: (626) 855-6696
Email: normadiaz@usps.com
Web: www.usps.gov

Van Nuys District
28201 Franklin Pkwy.
Santa Clarita, CA 91383-9994
Tyrone Washington, Diversity Development
Specialist
Tel: (661) 775-7055 Fax: (661) 775-7190
Email: tyrone.d.washington@usps.gov
Web: www.usps.gov

STATE OF CALIFORNIA
Employment Development Department
EEO Office
P.O. Box 826880
Sacramento, CA 94280-0001
Walter Johnson, Chief
Tel: (916) 654-8434 Fax: (916) 654-9371
Email: wjohnson@edd.ca.gov
Web: www.edd.ca.gov

COLORADO

AGRICULTURE, DEPT. OF
Forest Service
Region 2, Rocky Mountain Region
740 Simms Ave.
Golden, CO 80401
Angela Baca, Equal Employment Specialist
Tel: (303) 275-5343 Fax: (303) 275-5502
Email: abaca@fs.fed.us
Web: www.fs.fed.us

Natural Resources Conservation Service
State of Colorado
655 Parset St. #E200C
Lakewood, CO 80215-5517
Dave Ueda, African American Program
Manager
Tel: (720) 544-2860 Fax: (720) 544-2862

Email: david.ueda@co.usda.gov
Web: www.co.nrcs.usda.gov

AIR FORCE, DEPT. OF THE
Buckley AFB
Buckley AFB, CO 80011-9542
Tel: (800) 423-8723
Web: www.airforce.com

Headquarters Air Force Space Command
Peterson AFB, CO 80914-4450
Tel: (800) 423-8723
Web: www.airforce.com

Schriever AFB
Schriever AFB, CO 80912
Tel: (800) 423-8723
Web: www.airforce.com

USAF Academy
USAF Academy, CO 80840-2215
Tel: (800) 423-8723
Web: www.airforce.com

ARMY, DEPT. OF
US Army Recruiting Battalion Denver
Public Affairs Office
225 E. 16th St. #400
Denver, CO 80203-1620
Tel: (303) 894-9804

COMMERCE, DEPT. OF
National Oceanic and Atmospheric
Administration
EEO Office
325 Broadway, Bldg. 22
Boulder, CO 80305
Anthony Tafoya, EEO Manager
Tel: (303) 497- 6731 Fax: (303) 497-7283
Email: anthony.j.tafoya@noaa.gov
Web: www.noaa.gov

EQUAL EMPLOYMENT OPPORTUNITY
COMMISSION
Denver District Office
303 E. 17th Ave. #510
Denver, CO 80203
Jeanette Leino, Acting Director
Tel: (303) 866-1300 Fax: (303) 866-1085
Web: www.eeoc.gov

HOMELAND SECURITY, DEPT. OF
USCG Recruiting Office Denver
7355 W 88th Ave. #H
Westminister, CO 80021
MKC Charles Rowland, Recruiter in Charge
Tel: (303) 252-0919 Fax: (303) 252-1763
Email: crowland@cgrc.uscg.mil
Web: www.gocoastguard.com

INTERIOR, DEPT. OF THE
Bureau of Reclamation
Human Resources Office
P.O. Box 25007
Denver, CO 80225-0007
Laurie Johnson, Manager
Tel: (303) 445-2656 Fax: (303) 445-6349
Email: ljohnson@do.usbr.gov
Web: www.usbr.gov

Geological Survey
Central Region
P.O. Box 25046
Denver, CO 80225-0046
Deborah Douglas, Human Resources
Officer
Tel: (303) 236-9562 Fax: (303) 236-5973
Email: ddouglas@usgs.gov
Web: www.usgs.gov

National Park Service
Intermountain Region, Office of Human
Resources

P.O. Box 25287
Denver, CO 80225-0287
John Crowley, Assistant Regional Director
Tel: (303) 969-2506 Fax: (303) 969-2785
Email: john_crowley@nps.gov
Web: www.nps.gov

NAVY, DEPT. OF THE
Naval Reserve Recruiting Command Area
West
791 Chambers Rd. #502
Aurora, CO 80011-7152
Tel: (303) 361-0631 Fax: (303) 361-0648

Navy Recruiting District, Denver
225 E. 16th Ave.
Denver, CO 80203
Tel: (303) 866-1984

USMC Recruiting Station, Denver
225 E. 16th Ave. #500
Denver, CO 80203-9860
Tel: (303) 832-2515
Web: www.marines.com

CONNECTICUT

HOMELAND SECURITY, DEPT. OF
USCG Recruiting Office Hartford
William Cotter Bldg.,135 High St. #G
Hartford, CT 06103
ETC Randall Davidson, Recruiter in Charge
Tel: (860) 240-4260 Fax: (860) 240-4302
Email: rdavidson@cgrc.uscg.mil
Web: www.gocoastguard.com

USCG Recruiting Office New London
New London Shopping Plz., 260 Frontage
Rd. #202
New London, CT 06320
AETI Darrin Merrill, Recruiter in Charge
Tel: (860) 444-4947 Fax: (860) 444-4946
Email: dmerrill@cgrc.uscg.mil
Web: www.gocoastguard.com

POSTAL SERVICE
Connecticut District
24 Research Pkwy.
Wallingford, CT 06492-9632
Karen Kucharczyk, Diversity Development
Specialist
Tel: (203) 949-3129 Fax: (203) 265-9462
Web: www.usps.gov

Northeast Area Office
6 Griffin Rd. North
Windsor, CT 06006-7110
Michelle D. Collins, Senior Diversity
Program Coordinator
Tel: (860) 285-7246 Fax: (860) 285-1203
Email: michelle.d.collins@usps.gov
Web: www.usps.gov

DELAWARE

AGRICULTURE, DEPT. OF
Natural Resources Conservation Service
East Region
1221 College Park Dr. #100
Dover, DE 19904-8713
William Bell, Black Employment Program
Manager (BEPM)
Tel: (302) 678-4169 Fax: (302) 678-0843
Email: william.bell@de.usda.gov
Web: www.nrcs.usda.gov

AIR FORCE, DEPT. OF THE
Dover AFB
Dover AFB, DE 19902-5520

Tel: (800) 423-8723
Web: www.airforce.com

DISTRICT OF COLUMBIA

AGENCY FOR INTERNATIONAL
DEVELOPMENT
Equal Opportunity Programs Office
1300 Pennsylvania Ave. NW, Ronald
Reagan Bldg. #2.9
Washington, DC 20523-2901
Gloria Blackwell, Equal Employment
Specialist
Tel: (202) 712-0376 Fax: (202) 216-3524
Email: gblackwell@usaid.gov
Web: www.usaid.gov

AGRICULTURE, DEPT. OF
Civil Rights Office
1400 Independence Ave. SW
Washington, DC 20250-9410
Sadhna G. True, Director
Tel: (202) 720-5212 Fax: (202) 720-0953
Email: sadhna.true@usda.gov
Web: www.usda.gov

Agricultural Marketing Service
Civil Rights Office
1400 Independence Ave. SW #3074, South
Bldg.
Washington, DC 20250-0206
Kenneth R. Johnson, Affirmative
Employment Manager
Tel: (202) 720-0583 Fax: (202) 690-0476
Email: kennethr.johnson@usda.gov
Web: www.ams.usda.gov

Marketing and Regulatory Programs
1400 Independence Ave. SW, South Bldg.
#3074
Washington, DC 20250
Rose Moye, African American Employment
Manager
Tel: (202) 720-2702 Fax: (202) 690-0476
Web: www.ams.usda.gov

Agricultural Research Service
Civil Rights Office
1400 Independence Ave. SW, South Bldg.
#3552
Washington, DC 20250-0304
Korona Prince, Director
Tel: (202) 720-6161 Fax: (202) 690-0109
Email: kprince@ars.usda.gov
Web: www.ars.usda.gov

Assistant of Civil Rights
Civil Rights Office
300 7th St. SW #250
Washington, DC 20250
Jack Nelson, African American
Departmental Manager
Tel: (202) 720-7933 Fax: (202) 690-2345
Email: jacke.nelson@usda.gov
Web: www.usda.gov

Assistant Secretary of Civil Rights
Civil Rights Office
1400 Independence Ave. SW #4045,
Washington, DC 20250
Shirley Harrington, Senior Specialist
Tel: (202) 720-2983
Email: shirley.harrington-watson@usda.gov
Web: www.usda.gov

Cooperative State Research, Education, and
Extension Service
Civil Rights Office
800 9th St. SW, #1230
Washington, DC 20024
Curtiland Deville, Director

Tel: (202) 720-2700 Fax: (202) 720-6954
Email: cdeville@csrees.usda.gov
Web: www.csrees.usda.gov

Equal Opportunity Office
800 9th St. SW,#1230
Washington, DC 20024
Richard G. Chavez, Equal Opportunity
Specialist
Tel: (202) 690-2051 Fax: (202) 720-6954
Email: rchavez@csrees.usda.gov
Web: www.csrees.usda.gov

Economic Research Service
Civil Rights Office
1800 M St. NW #4152
Washington, DC 20036-5831
Joyce Key, Director
Tel: (202) 694-5005 Fax: (202) 694-5757
Email: jkey@ers.usda.gov
Web: www.ers.usda.gov

Farm Service Agency
Civil Rights Office
1280 Maryland Ave. SW, #580-B
Washington, DC 20024
John Toles, Director
Tel: (202) 401-7220 Fax: (202) 401-7100
Email: john.toles@usda.gov
Web: www.fsa.usda.gov

Foreign Agricultural Service
Outreach and Exporter Assistance Office
1400 Independence Ave. SW, South Bldg.
#4949
Washington, DC 20250
Karl Hampton, Foreign Service Officer
Tel: (202) 690-0188 Fax: (202) 205-9728
Email: hamptonk@fas.usda.gov
Web: www.fas.usda.gov

Forest Service
Civil Rights Office
201 14th St. SW #4-SW
Washington, DC 20250
Kathleen Gause, Director
Tel: (202) 205-1585 Fax: (202) 690-1025
Email: kgause@fs.fed.us
Web: www.fs.fed.us/cr

National Agricultural Statistics Service
1400 Independence Ave. SW, South Bldg.
#4833
Washington, DC 20250
Klara L. Greene, African American Program
Manager
Tel: (202) 720-5805 Fax: (202) 690-1995
Email: k_greene@nass.usda.gov
Web: www.nass.usda.gov

National Agricultural Statistics Service
Research, Education and Economics
1400 Independence Ave. SW, South Bldg.
Capital A #5041
Washington, DC 20250-2000
Rafael Sanchez, Director of Civil Rights
Tel: (202) 720-8257 Fax: (202) 720-9013
Email: rsanchez@nass.usda.gov
Web: www.nass.usda.gov

Risk Management Agency
EEO Office
1400 Independence Ave. SW
Washington, DC 20250
Sae Mi Hong, EEO Specialist
Tel: (202) 690-1687 Fax: (202) 690-2496
Email: shong@wdc.usda.gov
Web: www.rma.usda.gov

AIR FORCE, DEPT. OF THE
Headquarters US Air Force

Washington, DC 20330-1460
Tel: (800) 423-8723
Web: www.airforce.com

AMTRAK (NATIONAL RAILROAD PASSENGER CORPORATION)
Business Diversity and Strategic Initiatives
60 Massachusetts Ave. NE
Washington, DC 20002
Rodney Ruffin, Director External Affairs
Tel: (202) 906-3753 Fax: (202) 906-2889
Web: www.amtrak.com

COMMERCE, DEPT. OF
International Trade Administration
14th & Constitution Ave. NW #7417
Washington, DC 20230
Tina James, Recruitment Manager
Tel: (202) 482-0653 Fax: (202) 482-1903
Email: tina_james@ita.doc.gov
Web: www.ita.doc.gov

Office of Civil Rights
Policy & Evaluation Division
14th & Constitution Ave. NW #6003
Washington, DC 20230
Tel: (202) 482-5691 Fax: (202) 482-5375
Web: www.commerce.gov

Office of Inspector General
Human Resources Office
14th & Constitution Ave. NW #7713
Washington, DC 20230
Tel: (202) 482-4948 Fax: (202) 482-3006
Web: www.oig.doc.gov/oig/

COMMISSION ON CIVIL RIGHTS
Human Resources Division
624 9th St. NW #510
Washington, DC 20425
Myrna Hernandez, Human Resources
Specialist
Tel: (202) 376-8364 Fax: (202) 376-7577
Email: mhernandez@usccr.gov
Web: www.usccr.gov

Office of EEO
3 Lafayette Ctr., 1155 21st St. NW
Washington, DC 20581
Sandra J. Canery, Director
Tel: (202) 418-5400 Fax: (202) 418-5546
Email: scanery@cftc.gov
Web: www.cftc.gov

CORPORATION FOR NATIONAL AND COMMUNITY SERVICE
Civil Rights/Inclusiveness Office
1201 New York Ave. NW #10800
Washington, DC 20525
Jonathan Williams, Director
Tel: (202) 606-7053 Fax: (202) 606-3465
Email: eo@cns.gov
Web: www.americorps.org

DEFENSE, DEPT. OF
Defense Intelligence Agency
Diversity Management/Equal Opportunity
Office
Bolling AFB, Bldg. 6000 #D4-938
Washington, DC 20340
Marilyn McCabe, Deputy Chief
Tel: (202) 231-8178 Fax: (202) 231-3865
Email: marilyn.mccabe@dia.mil
Web: www.dia.mil

Deputy Assistant Secretary of Defense for Equal Opportunity
Military Equal Opportunity
400 Defense Pentagon #5D641
Washington, DC 20301-4000
James Love, Acting Director
Tel: (703) 571-9331 Fax: (703) 571-3338

Email: james.love@osd.mil
Web: www.osd.mil

DEFENSE NUCLEAR FACILITIES SAFETY BOARD
625 Indiana Ave. NW #700
Washington, DC 20004
Kenneth Pusateri, EEO Director
Tel: (202) 694-7000 Fax: (202) 208-6515
Email: kenp@dnfsb.gov
Web: www.dnfsb.gov

DISTRICT OF COLUMBIA
DC Office of Personnel
441 4th St. NW #300 South
Washington, DC 20001
Lisa Marin, Director
Tel: (202) 442-9600 Fax: (202) 727-6827
Email: lisa.marin@dc.gov
Web: www.dc.gov

Fire Department
1923 Vermont Ave. NW #201 South
Washington, DC 20001
Tel: (202) 673-3320 Fax: (202) 462-0807
Web: www.dc.gov

EDUCATION, DEPT. OF
Equal Employment Opportunity Group
400 Maryland Ave. SW FOB-6 #2W228
Washington, DC 20202
James R. White, Director
Tel: (202) 205-0518 Fax: (202) 205-5760
Web: www.ed.gov

Equal Employment Opportunity Group
Diversity and Workforce Planning Programs
400 Maryland Ave. SW #2W228
Washington, DC 20202
Gwendolyn Washington, Team Leader
Tel: (202) 401-3577 Fax: (202) 205-5760
Email: gwendolyn.washington@ed.gov
Web: www.ed.gov

ELECTION ASSISTANCE COMMISSION
1225 New York Ave. NW #1100
Washington, DC 20005
Tel: (202) 566-3100 Fax: (202) 566-3127
Email: www.eac.gov
Web: havainfo@eac.gov

ENVIRONMENTAL PROTECTION AGENCY
Office of Civil Rights
1200 Pennsylvania Ave. NW, M/C 1201-A
Washington, DC 20004
Tel: (202) 564-7272 Fax: (202) 501-1836
Web: www.epa.gov

EQUAL EMPLOYMENT OPPORTUNITY COMMISSION
Washington Field Office
1801 L St. NW #100
Washington, DC 20507
Dana Hutter, Director
Tel: (202) 419-0700 Fax: (202) 419-0740
Web: www.eeoc.gov

EXECUTIVE OFFICE OF THE PRESIDENT
Office of Administration
EEO Office
725 17th St. NW #2200
Washington, DC 20503
Linda Sites, Director
Tel: (202) 395-3996

FEDERAL COMMUNICATIONS COMMISSION
Office of Workplace Diversity
445 12th St. SW
Washington, DC 20554
Barbara J. Douglas, Director
Tel: (202) 418-1799 Fax: (866) 418-0232
Email: ccinfo@fcc.gov
Web: www.fcc.gov

FEDERAL COURTS
Administrative Office
Employee Relations Office
1 Columbus Cir. NE #5-265
Washington, DC 20544
Trudi M. Morrison, Chief, Employee
Relations Office
Tel: (202) 502-1380 Fax: (202) 502-1433
Email: trudi_morrison@ao.uscourts.gov

FEDERAL DEPOSIT INSURANCE CORPORATION
Office of Diversity and Economic Opportunity
FDIC #201-1215
Washington, DC 20434-0001
Janice Williams, EEO Specialist
Tel: (202) 416-2475 Fax: (202) 416-2841
Email: jwilliams@fdic.gov
Web: www.fdic.gov

FEDERAL ELECTION COMMISSION
EEO Office
999 E St. NW #436
Washington, DC 20463
Lola Hatcher-Capers, Director
Tel: (202) 694-1228 Fax: (202) 219-3880
Email: eeo@fec.gov
Web: www.fec.gov

FEDERAL HOUSING FINANCE BOARD
Department of Human Resources
1625 Eye St. NW
Washington, DC 20006
David Lee, Associate Director
Tel: (202) 408-2514 Fax: (202) 408-2530
Email: david.lee@fhfb.gov
Web: www.fhfb.gov

FEDERAL LABOR RELATIONS AUTHORITY
EEO
1400 K St. NW, 2nd Fl.
Washington, DC 20424-0001
Bridget Sisson, Director
Tel: (202) 218-7919 Fax: (202) 482-6629
Email: bsisson@flra.gov
Web: www.flra.gov

FEDERAL MARITIME COMMISSION
EEO Office
800 N. Capitol St. NW #1052
Washington, DC 20573
Carmen Cantor, Director
Tel: (202) 523-5806 Fax: (202) 523-4224
Email: ccantor@fmc.gov
Web: www.fmc.gov

FEDERAL MEDIATION AND CONCILIATION SERVICE
Human Resources Office
2100 K St. NW, 7th Fl.
Washington, DC 20427
Dan Ellerman, Director
Tel: (202) 606-5460 Fax: (202) 606-4216
Email: dellerman@fmcs.gov
Web: www.fmcs.gov

FEDERAL MINE SAFETY AND HEALTH REVIEW COMMISSION
Office of EO
200 Constitution Ave. NW
Washington, DC 20210
Daliza Salas, Director
Tel: (202) 693-7719 Fax: (202) 693-7716
Web: www.msha.gov

FEDERAL RETIREMENT THRIFT INVESTMENT BOARD
Personnel Office
1250 H St. NW
Washington, DC 20005-3952
Susan Smith, Acting Director
Tel: (202) 942-1670 Fax: (202) 942-1674
Email: ssmith@tsp.gov
Web: www.frtib.gov

GENERAL SERVICES ADMINISTRATION
Office of Civil Rights
Central Office
1800 F St. NW, GSA Bldg. #5127
Washington, DC 20405
Madeline Caliendo, Associate Administrator
Tel: (202) 501-0767 Fax: (202) 219-3369
Email: madeline.caliendo@gsa.gov
Web: www.gsa.gov

Office of EEO
1800 F St. NW #5123
Washington, DC 20405
Bernadette Butler, EE Officer
Tel: (202) 501-0767 Fax: (202) 219-3369
Email: bernadette.butler@gsa.gov
Web: www.gsa.gov

Office of Equal Employment Opportunity
National Central Region
7th & D St. SW #7002
Washington, DC 20407
Avis B. Johnson, EEO Officer
Tel: (202) 708-8588 Fax: (202) 205-0656
Email: avis.johnson@gsa.gov
Web: www.gsa.gov

GOVERNMENT ACCOUNTABILITY OFFICE
Talent Acquisition/Human Capital
Consulting Center
441 G St. NW #1165
Washington, DC 20548
Phyllis Hughes, Director
Tel: (202) 512-3000 Fax: (202) 512-2539
Email: phughes@gao.gov
Web: www.gao.gov

HEALTH AND HUMAN SERVICES, DEPT. OF
Administration for Children and Families
Office of Intergovernmental Affairs
370 L'Enfant Promenade SW, Aerospace
Bldg., 6th Fl. West
Washington, DC 20447
Carl Montoya, Intergovernmental Affairs
Tel: (202) 205-8557 Fax: (202) 401-5727
Email: cmontoya@acf.dhhs.gov
Web: www.acf.dhhs.gov

Office of the Secretary
EEO Office
200 Independence Ave. SW #536-E, HHH
Bldg.
Washington, DC 20201
Bonita V. White, Esq., Director
Tel: (202) 690-6555 Fax: (202) 690-8328
Email: bonita.white@hhs.gov
Web: www.hhs.gov

Office of the Secretary
EEO Office
200 Independence Ave. SW #709-D, HHS
Bldg.
Washington, DC 20201
David L. Shorts, Manager
Tel: (202) 619-8215 Fax: (202) 619-0823
Email: david.shorts@hhs.gov
Web: www.hhs.gov

HOMELAND SECURITY, DEPT. OF
US Citizenship and Immigration Services
EEO Office
800 K St. NW #200
Washington, DC 20536
Tel: (202) 514-1246 Fax: (202) 514-9866
Web: www.uscis.gov

USCG Recruiting Office Washington DC
3204A Pennsylvania Ave. SE
Washington, DC 20020
MKC Joseph Geter, Recruiter in Charge
Tel: (202) 583-3641 Fax: (202) 583-3645

Email: jgeter@cgrc.uscg.mil
Web: www.gocoastguard.com

US Coast Guard, Headquarters
Civil Rights Office
2100 2nd St. SW #2400
Washington, DC 20593
Arlene J. Gonzalez, Director
Tel: (202) 267-0042 Fax: (202) 267-4282
Email: agonzalez@comdt.uscg.mil
Web: www.uscg.mil

US Customs and Border Protection
EEO Office
1300 Pennsylvania Ave. NW #3.3D
Washington, DC 20229
Christopher Rodriguez, EEO Specialist
Tel: (202) 344-1481 Fax: (202) 344-1476
Email: christopher.rodriguez@dhs.gov
Web: www.cbp.gov

US Immigration and Customs Enforcement
EEO Office
800 K St. NW #200
Washington, DC 20536
Maria Jackson, Black Affairs Program
Manager
Tel: (202) 514-1246 Fax: (202) 514-9866
Email: maria.jackson1@dhs.gov
Web: www.dhs.gov

HOUSING AND URBAN DEVELOPMENT, DEPT. OF
EEO Office
451 7th St. SW #2134
Washington, DC 20410
Linda Bradford Washington, Acting Director
Tel: (202) 708-3362 Fax: (202) 401-2843
Email: linda_b_washington@hud.gov
Web: www.hud.gov

INSTITUTE OF MUSEUM AND LIBRARY SERVICES
Office of Administration and Budget
1800 M St. NW, 9th Fl.
Washington, DC 20036-5802
Teresa LaHaie, Director
Tel: (202) 653-4633 Fax: (202) 653-4625
Web: www.imls.gov

INTERIOR, DEPT. OF THE
EEO Office
1849 C St. NW, M/S 5214
Washington, DC 20240
Sharon Eller, Director
Tel: (202) 208-5693 Fax: (202) 208-6112
Email: sharon_eller@ios.doi.gov
Web: www.doi.gov

Bureau of Reclamation
The Commissioner's Office
1849 C St. NW #7060-MIB
Washington, DC 20240-0001
Janice Johnson, Chief of Administrative
Services
Tel: (202) 513-0522 Fax: (202) 513-0310
Email: jjohnson@usbr.gov
Web: www.usbr.gov

National Park Service
Employment Office
1849 C St. NW
Washington, DC 20240
Tel: (202) 354-1993 Fax: (202) 219-1786
Web: www.nps.gov

National Park Service
National Capital Region, Department of
Human Resources
1100 Ohio Dr. SW
Washington, DC 20242
Kym Elder, Special Emphasis Recruitment
Officer

Tel: (202) 619-7246 Fax: (202) 619-7244
Email: kym_elder@nps.gov
Web: www.nps.gov

National Park Service
WAFO Area, Office of Human Resources
1201 Eye St. NW, 12th Fl.
Washington, DC 20005
Adele Singer, Personnel Specialist
Tel: (202) 354-1985 Fax: (202) 371-1762
Email: adele_singer@nps.gov
Web: www.nps.gov

Office of Surface Mining
EEO Office
1951 Constitution Ave. NW #138
Washington, DC 20240
Diane Wood-Medley, Diversity Program
Manager
Tel: (202) 208-2997 Fax: (202) 219-3109
Email: dwood@osmre.gov
Web: www.osmre.gov

EEO Office
1951 Constitution Ave. NW #20240
Washington, DC 20240
James E. Joiner, EEO Officer
Tel: (202) 208-5897 Fax: (202) 219-3109
Email: jjoiner@osmre.gov
Web: www.osmre.gov

INTERNATIONAL BROADCASTING BUREAU
Office of Civil Rights
EEO Office
330 C St. SW #1086
Washington, DC 20237
Delia L. Johnson, Director
Tel: (202) 619-5151 Fax: (202) 260-0406
Email: djohnso@ibb.gov
Web: www.ibb.gov

JUSTICE, DEPT. OF
Bureau of Alcohol, Tobacco, Firearms, and Explosives
EEO Office
650 Massachusetts Ave. NW #8210
Washington, DC 20226
Dora Salas, Special Emphasis Programs
Manager
Tel: (202) 927-7760 Fax: (202) 927-8835
Web: www.atf.gov

Executive Office for US Attorneys
EEO Office
1331 Pennsylvania Ave. NW #524
Washington, DC 20530
Hilda Hudson, EEO Specialist
Tel: (202) 514-3982 Fax: (202) 305-1431
Web: www.usdoj.gov/usao/eousa/

Federal Bureau of Investigation
EEO Office
935 Pennsylvania Ave. NW #7901
Washington, DC 20535-0001
Kimberlee Swain, Black Affairs Program
Manager
Tel: (202) 324-6603 Fax: (202) 324-3976
Web: www.fbi.gov

Federal Bureau of Prisons
Discriminations, Complaints and Ethics
320 1st St. NW #437
Washington, DC 20534
Carlos V. Rivera, Diversity Management
Administrator
Tel: (202) 307-3175 Fax: (202) 370-0828
Email: info@bop.gov
Web: www.bop.gov

Discriminations, Complaints and Ethics
320 1st St. NW #770
Washington, DC 20534

Sandra Burks-Farrior, Chief, Affirmative
Action Programs
Tel: (202) 307-3175 Fax: (202) 514-9650
Email: sfarrior@bop.gov
Web: www.bop.gov

Headquarters
EEO Office
1110 Vermont Ave. NW #620
Washington, DC 20530
Carmen Mendez, EEO Program Manager
Tel: (202) 616-4812 Fax: (202) 616-4823
Email: carmen.g.mendez@smojmed.usdoj.
gov
Web: www.usdoj.gov/jmd/eeos

Marshals Service
EEO Office
US Marshals Services Office Washington DC
Department of EEO
Washington, DC 20530-1000
Annalisa D. Lee, Affirmative Employment
Manager
Tel: (202) 307-9048 Fax: (202) 307-8765
Email: annalisa.lee@usdoj.gov
Web: www.usdoj.gov/marshals

Office of Justice Programs
EEO Office
810 7th St. NW #6109
Washington, DC 20531
Stacie D. Brockman, EEO Officer
Tel: (202) 307-6013 Fax: (202) 616-5963
Email: stacie.brockman@usdoj.gov
Web: www.usdoj.gov

LABOR, DEPT. OF
Bureau of Labor Statistics
EEO Office, Human Resources
2 Massachusetts Ave. NE #4280
Washington, DC 20212
Dorothy Wigglesworth, EEO Officer
Tel: (202) 691-6604 Fax: (202) 691-6610
Email: wigglesworth_d@bls.gov
Web: www.bls.gov

Employment Standards Administration
EEO Unit
200 Constitution Ave. NW #C-3315
Washington, DC 20210
Tel: (202) 693-0328 Fax: (202) 693-1455
Web: www.dol.gov

Occupational Safety and Health Administration
EEO Office
200 Constitution Ave. NW #N-3425
Washington, DC 20210
William Burke, Acting Director
Tel: (202) 693-2150 Fax: (202) 693-1626
Email: william.burke@bol.gov
Web: www.osha.gov

Office of the Assistance Secretary for Administration and Management
Worklife Center
200 Constitution Ave. NW #C5515
Washington, DC 20210
Thomasina McPhail, Events Program
Manager
Tel: (202) 693-7774 Fax: (202) 693-7611
Email: tmcphail@dol.gov
Web: www.dol.gov

Office of the Assistant Secretary for Administration & Management
Business Operation Center, EEO Office
200 Constitution Ave. NW #S1514
Washington, DC 20210
Milton Blount, Manager
Tel: (202) 693-4031 Fax: (202) 219-5138
Email: blount.milton@dol.gov
Web: www.dol.gov

MERIT SYSTEMS PROTECTION BOARD
EEO Office
1615 M St. NW
Washington, DC 20419
Janice Pirkle, Director
Tel: (202) 653-6180 Fax: (202) 653-7130
Email: janice.pirkle@mspb.gov
Web: www.mspb.gov

METROPOLITAN POLICE DEPT.
Office of Police Recruiting
EEO Office
6 DC Village Ln. SW, Bldg. #1A
Washington, DC 20032
Kevin Anderson, Director
Tel: (202) 645-0445 Fax: (202) 645-0444
Email: mpd@dc.gov
Web: www.mpdc.dc.gov

NATIONAL AERONAUTICS AND SPACE ADMINISTRATION
Headquarters
Office of Diversity and Equal Opportunity Programs
300 E St. SW
Washington, DC 20546
Dr. Dorothy Hayden-Watkins, Assistant Administrator for Diversity and Equal Opportunity Programs
Tel: (202) 358-2167 Fax: (202) 358-3336
Email: dhaydenw@hq.nasa.gov
Web: www.hq.nasa.gov

NATIONAL CAPITAL PLANNING COMMISSION
401 9th St. NW, North Lobby #500
Washington, DC 20004
Barry Socks, Executive Office
Tel: (202) 482-7200 Fax: (202) 482-7272
Email: info@ncpc.gov
Web: www.ncpc.gov

NATIONAL COUNCIL ON DISABILITY
1331 F St. NW #850
Washington, DC 20004
Tel: (202) 272-2004 Fax: (202) 272-2022
Email: info@ncd.gov
Web: www.ncd.gov

NATIONAL ENDOWMENT FOR THE ARTS
Office of Human Resources
EEO Office
1100 Pennsylvania Ave. NW #627
Washington, DC 20506
Craig McCord, Director
Tel: (202) 682-5470 Fax: (202) 682-5666
Email: mccordc@arts.endow.gov
Web: www.arts.endow.gov

NATIONAL ENDOWMENT FOR THE HUMANITIES
Administrative Services
EEO Office
1100 Pennsylvania Ave. NW #202
Washington, DC 20506
Willie V. McGhee, Jr., Officer
Tel: (202) 606-8233 Fax: (202) 606-8243
Email: wmcghee@neh.gov
Web: www.neh.fed.us

Office of Human Resources
EEO Office
1100 Pennsylvania Ave. NW #418
Washington, DC 20506
Tim Connelly, Director
Tel: (202) 606-8415 Fax: (202) 606-8656
Email: tconnelly@neh.gov
Web: www.neh.fed.us

NATIONAL LABOR RELATIONS BOARD
EEO Office
1099 14th St. NW #6300
Washington, DC 20570-0001

Robert Poindexter, Director
Tel: (202) 273-3891 Fax: (202) 273-4473
Email: robert.poindexter@nlrb.gov
Web: www.nlrb.gov

NATIONAL TRANSPORTATION SAFETY BOARD
EEO Office
490 L'Enfant Plz. SW
Washington, DC 20594
Tel: (202) 314-6190 Fax: (202) 314-6018
Web: www.ntsb.gov

NAVY, DEPT. OF THE
Computer and Telecommunications Command
EEO Office
1014 N. St. SE #1
Washington, DC 20374-5050
Tel: (202) 685-1879 Fax: (202) 433-2653
Web: www.navy.mil

Military Sealift Command
EEO Office
914 Charles Morris Ct. SE
Washington, DC 20398
Wanda Watson-Mays, Command Deputy EEO Officer
Tel: (202) 685-5563 Fax: (202) 685-5514
Email: wanda.watson-mays@navy.mil
Web: www.navy.mil

Naval Criminal Investigative Service
EEO Office
716 Sicard St. SE #2000
Washington, DC 20388-5380
Ruth Leichter, Command Deputy Officer
Tel: (202) 433-9140 Fax: (202) 433-9619
Email: rleichter@ncis.navy.mil
Web: www.ncis.navy.mil

Naval Facilities Engineering Command
EEO Office
1322 Patterson Ave. SE, Washington Navy Yard
Washington, DC 20374-5065
Keith Kirkpatrick, Command Deputy EEO Officer
Tel: (202) 685-9280 Fax: (202) 685-1475
Web: www.navy.mil

Office of Naval Intelligence
Office of the EEO Director (ONI-OCE)
4251 Suitland Rd. #2A129
Washington, DC 20359-5720
Antoinette Brady, Command Deputy Officer
Tel: (301) 669-5119 Fax: (301) 669-3991
Email: abrady@nmic.navy.mil
Web: www.nmic.navy.mil

Secretariat/HQ Human Resources Office
Office EEO
2 Navy Annex #2052
Washington, DC 20370-5240
Deborah McCormick, Command Deputy EEO Officer
Tel: (703) 693-0202 Fax: (703) 693-1333

OCCUPATIONAL SAFETY & HEALTH REVIEW COMMISSION
1120 20th St. NW, 9th Fl.
Washington, DC 20036
Barbara Ligon, Administrative Assistant
Tel: (202) 606-5380 Fax: (202) 606-5050
Email: Lg_gpo@oshrc.gov
Web: www.oshrc.gov

OFFICE OF BILINGUAL EDUCATION
District of Columbia
4301 13th St. NW
Washington, DC 20011
Elba Garcia, Interim Director

Tel: (202) 576-8850 Fax: (202) 576-8860
Email: elba.garcia@k12.dc.us
Web: www.k12.dc.us

OFFICE OF GOVERNMENT ETHICS
1201 New York Ave. NW #500
Washington, DC 20005-3917
Tel: (202) 482-9300
Email: contactoge@oge.gov
Web: www.usoge.gov

OFFICE OF HUMAN RIGHTS
District of Columbia
441 4th St. NW #570 North
Washington, DC 20001
Kenneth L. Saunders, Director
Tel: (202) 727-4559 Fax: (202) 727-9589
Email: kenneth.saunders@dc.gov
Web: www.ohr.dc.gov

OFFICE OF PERSONNEL MANAGEMENT
EEO Office
1900 E St. NW #6460
Washington, DC 20415
Stephen Shih, Director
Tel: (202) 606-2460 Fax: (202) 606-1841
Web: www.opm.gov

EEO Office
1900 E St. NW #6460
Washington, DC 20415
Terry Coleman, EEO Specialist
Tel: (202) 606-2460 Fax: (202) 606-1841
Web: www.opm.gov

OFFICE OF SPECIAL COUNSEL
EEO
1730 M St. NW #218
Washington, DC 20036-4505
Bill Reukauf, Director
Tel: (202) 254-3600 Fax: (202) 653-5161
Web: www.osc.gov

OFFICE OF THE NATIONAL COUNTERINTELLIGENCE EXECUTIVE
National Counterintelligence Executive (NCIX), CS5 #380
Washington, DC 20505
Ann Johnson, Director of Administration
Tel: (703) 682-4555 Fax: (703) 682-4510
Email: aannfj@ncix.gov
Web: www.ncix.gov

PEACE CORPS
Minority Recruitment
EEO Office
1111 20th St. NW, 6th Fl.
Washington, DC 20526
Wilfredo Sauri, Director
Tel: (202) 692-1819 Fax: (202) 692-1801
Email: wsauri@peacecorps.gov
Web: www.peacecorps.gov

PENSION BENEFIT GUARANTY CORPORATION
EEO
1200 K St. NW #1080
Washington, DC 20005
Lori Bledsoe, EEO Manager
Tel: (202) 326-4000 Fax: (202) 326-4016
Web: www.pbgc.gov

POSTAL SERVICE
Affirmative Employment Program
475 L'Enfant Plz. SW #3821
Washington, DC 20260-3821
Young Chung-Hall, Special Emphasis Program Specialist
Tel: (202) 268-5844 Fax: (202) 268-6573
Email: ychung@email.usps.gov
Web: www.usps.gov

Headquarters
475 L'Enfant Plz. SW #3821
Washington, DC 20260-3821
Chester Cross, Jr., Manager, Affirmative Employment Program
Tel: (202) 268-7456 Fax: (202) 268-6573
Web: www.usps.gov

Headquarters
475 L'Enfant Plz. SW #3821
Washington, DC 20260-3821
William Farley, Diversity Development Specialist
Tel: (202) 268-6716 Fax: (202) 268-6573
Email: william.r.farley@usps.gov
Web: www.usps.gov

SECURITIES AND EXCHANGE COMMISSION
EEO Office
100 F St. NE #212
Washington, DC 20549
Deborah Balducchi, Director
Tel: (202) 551-6006 Fax: (202) 942-9547
Email: deborahbalducchi@sec.gov
Web: www.sec.gov

SMALL BUSINESS ADMINISTRATION
EEO Office
409 3rd St. SW #5100
Washington, DC 20416
Harriett Tyler, Specialist
Tel: (202) 205-6750 Fax: (202) 205-7580
Email: hariett.tyler@sba.gov
Web: www.sba.gov

Human Resources
Personnel Office
409 3rd St. SW #5300
Washington, DC 20416
Judy Mitchell, Lead Human Resource Specialist
Tel: (202) 205-6786 Fax: (202) 205-6172
Email: judy.mitchell@sba.gov
Web: www.sba.gov/dc

SMITHSONIAN INSTITUTION
Office of Equal Employment Opportunity and Minority Affairs
750 9th St. NW #8100
Washington, DC 20013-7012
Pauline Fletemeyer, Special Emphasis Program Manager
Tel: (202) 275-0145 Fax: (202) 275-2055
Email: fletemey@si.edu
Web: www.si.edu

Office of Human Resources and Recruitment
Chief Executive Resources Branch
750 9th St. NW #6100, MRC 912
Washington, DC 20560-0912
Darrell Caldwell, Chief Executive Resources Officer
Tel: (202) 275-1055 Fax: (202) 275-1115
Email: caldwelld@hr.si.edu
Web: www.si.edu

STATE, DEPT. OF
Human Resources
Recruitment, Examination Employment
2401 E St. NW #518H
Washington, DC 20522
Janice Barnett, African American Coor.
Tel: (202) 261-8052 Fax: (202) 261-8841
Email: barnettj@state.gov
Web: www.state.gov

TRANSPORTATION, DEPT. OF
Federal Highway Administration
Human Resources Office
400 7th St. SW #4317
Washington, DC 20590

Patricia Tool, Director
Tel: (202) 366-0530 Fax: (202) 366-3749
Email: patricia.tool@fhwa.dot.gov
Web: www.fhwa.dot.gov

Office of the Secretary
Departmental Office of Civil Rights
400 7th St. SW #5420A
Washington, DC 20590
Patrice Wilson , Program Manager HBCU
Tel: (202) 366-9256 Fax: (202) 366-7717
Email: patrice.wilson@ost.dot.gov
Web: www.dot.gov/ost/docr

Bureau of Engraving and Printing
EEO Office & Employee Counseling Services
14th & C St. SW #639-17 PD
Washington, DC 20228
Arthur W. Hicks, Chief Officer
Tel: (202) 874-2460 Fax: (202) 874-3311
Email: arthurw.hicks@bep.trea.gov
Web: www.bep.treas.gov

Internal Revenue Service
EEO Office
1111 Constitution Ave. NW #2422
Washington, DC 20224
John M. Robinson, Chief EEO and Diversity
Officer
Tel: (202) 622-5400 Fax: (202) 622-6529
Email: john.m.robinson@irs.gov
Web: www.irs.gov

TREASURY, DEPT. OF THE
Office of the Comptroller of the Currency
250 E St. SW
Washington, DC 20219
Joyce Cofield, Director, Employment/
Diversity Management
Tel: (202) 874-5359 Fax: (202) 874-4656
Email: joyce.cofield@occ.treas.gov
Web: www.occ.treas.gov

Office of Thrift Supervision
1700 G St. NW, 5th Fl.
Washington, DC 20552
Douglas Mason, Senior Contract Specialist
and Advocate/Outreach Program
Tel: (202) 906-7624 Fax: (202) 906-5648
Email: douglas.mason@ots.treas.gov
Web: www.ots.treas.gov

**UNITED STATES INTERNATIONAL TRADE
COMMISSION**
Office EEO
500 E St. SW #4000
Washington, DC 20436
Jacqueline Waters, Director
Tel: (202) 205-2240 Fax: (202) 205-3004
Web: www.usitc.gov

**WASHINGTON METRO TRANSIT
AUTHORITY**
Human Resources Office
600 5th St. NW #806-A
Washington, DC 20001
Cassandra Graves, Employee Programs/
Worklife Coordinator
Tel: (202) 962-1365 Fax: (202) 962-2263
Email: cgraves@wmata.com
Web: www.wmata.com

FLORIDA

AGRICULTURE, DEPT. OF
Natural Resources Conservation Service
6191 Orange Dr. #6183Q
Davie, FL 33314
Thaddeus Hamilton, Urban Conservationist
Director
Tel: (954) 792-1984 Fax: (954) 792-3996

Email: thaddeus.hamilton@usda.gov
Web: www.nrcs.usda.gov

AIR FORCE, DEPT. OF THE
Eglin AFB
Eglin AFB, FL 32542-6825
Tel: (800) 423-8723
Web: www.airforce.com

Homestead AFB
Homestead AFB, FL 33039-1299
Tel: (800) 423-8723
Web: www.airforce.com

Macdill AFB
Macdill AFB, FL 33621-5321
Tel: (800) 423-8723
Web: www.airforce.com

Patrick AFB
Patrick AFB, FL 32925-3303
Tel: (800) 423-8723
Web: www.airforce.com

Tyndall AFB
Tyndall AFB, FL 32403-5538
Tel: (800) 423-8723
Web: www.airforce.com

ARMY, DEPT. OF
US Army Recruiting Battalion Jacksonville
Public Affairs Office
1851 Executive Center Dr. #130
Jacksonville, FL 32207-2350
Tel: (904) 396-2673

US Army Recruiting Battalion Miami
Public Affairs Office
8685 NW 53rd Terr., The Augusta Bldg.
#200
Miami, FL 33166-4611
Tel: (305) 591-1833

Public Affairs Office
3350 Buschwood Park Dr. #140
Tampa, FL 33618-4312
Tel: (813) 935-5657/8955

**EQUAL EMPLOYMENT OPPORTUNITY
COMMISSION**
Miami District Office
2 S. Biscayne Blvd., 1 Biscayne Tower
#2700
Miami, FL 33131
Federico Costales, Director
Tel: (305) 536-4491 Fax: (305) 536-4011
Web: www.eeoc.gov

Tampa Area Office
501 E. Polk St. #1000
Tampa, FL 33602
Manuel Zurita, Director
Tel: (813) 228-2310 Fax: (813) 228-2841
Web: www.eeoc.gov

HOMELAND SECURITY, DEPT. OF
USCG Recruiting Office Daytona
Ormond Interchange Complex., 1568 W.
Granada Blvd.
Ormond Beach, FL 32174
YNC David DePietro, Recruiter in Charge
Tel: (386) 672-2945 Fax: (386) 672-8104
Email: ddepietro@cgrc.uscg.mil
Web: www.gocoastguard.com

USCG Recruiting Office Jacksonville
Manderini Landing Shopping Ctr., 10601
San Jose Blvd. #215
Jacksonville, FL 32257
TCC Julius Tatum, Recruiter in Charge
Tel: (904) 232-1561 Fax: (904) 232-2760

Email: jtatum@cgrc.uscg.mil
Web: www.gocoastguard.com

USCG Recruiting Office Miami Central-
Lakes
Royal Oak Plaza Ctr., 15466 NW 77th Ct.
Miami Lakes, FL 33016
PAC Harry Craft, Recruiter in Charge
Tel: (305) 819-3330 Fax: (305) 819-7484
Email: hcraft@cgrc.uscg.mil
Web: www.gocoastguard.com

USCG Recruiting Office Miami North-
Broward
West Broward Shopping Ctr., 3939 W.
Broward Blvd.
Ft. Lauderdale, FL 33312
SKC Jim Council, Recruiter in Charge
Tel: (954) 321-8172 Fax: (954) 321-8776
Email: jcouncil@cgrc.uscg.mil
Web: www.gocoastguard.com

USCG Recruiting Office Miami South-Dade
18867 S. Dixie Hwy.
South Miami, FL 33157
MSTC Miguel Flores, Recruiter in Charge
Tel: (786) 242-2148 Fax: (305) 255-7956
Email: mflores@cgrc.uscg.mil
Web: www.gocoastguard.com

USCG Recruiting Office Orlando
8427 S. John Young Pkwy.
Orlando, FL 32819
ETC Jeffery Locklair, Recruiter in Charge
Tel: (407) 352-3897 Fax: (407) 352-9017
Email: jlocklair@cgrc.uscg.mil
Web: www.gocoastguard.com

USCG Recruiting Office Panama City
1714 W. 23rd St. #C
Panama City, FL 32405-2928
BMC Daniel J. Undieme, Recruiter in
Charge
Tel: (850) 763-1950 Fax: (850) 763-9018
Email: dundieme@cgrc.uscg.mil
Web: www.gocoastguard.com

USCG Recruiting Office Tampa Bay
Bayview Shopping Ctr., 11022 4th St. North
St. Petersburg, FL 33716-2945
MSTC Rodolpho Lopez, Recruiter in Charge
Tel: (727) 579-3849 Fax: (727) 579-8079
Email: rlopez@cgrc.uscg.mil
Web: www.gocoastguard.com

NAVY, DEPT. OF THE
**Naval Reserve Recruiting Command Area
Southeast**
5850 T.G. Lee Blvd. #210
Orlando, FL 32822-4437
Tel: (407) 856-4424 Fax: (407) 856-4424

Navy Recruiting District, Miami
8523 53rd Terrace, Savannah Bldg. #201
Miami, FL 33166-4521
Tel: (954) 845-0101

USMC Recruiting Station, Ft. Lauderdale
7820 Peters Rd. Rm. 109, Bldg. E
Plantation, FL 33324-4006
Tel: (954) 452-0113
Web: www.marines.com

USMC Recruiting Station, Jacksonville
3728 Phillips Hwy. #229
Jacksonville, FL 32207
Tel: (904) 858-9698
Web: www.marines.com

USMC Recruiting Station, Orlando
5886 S. Semoran Blvd., Air Business Ctr.
Orlando, FL 32822-4817

Tel: (407) 249-5870
Web: www.marines.com

PANAMA CANAL AUTHORITY
P.O. Box 526725
Miami, FL 33152-6725
Web: www.pancanal.com

POSTAL SERVICE
Central Florida District
P.O. Box 999237
Mid Florida, FL 32799-9237
Annie P. Seabrooks, Diversity Development
Specialist
Tel: (407) 333-4892 Fax: (407) 333-8467
Email: annie.p.seabrooks@usps.gov
Web: www.usps.gov

North Florida District
P.O. Box 40005
Jacksonville, FL 32203-0005
Mary L. Alston, Diversity Development
Specialist
Tel: (904) 858-6575 Fax: (904) 858-6528
Email: malston@email.usps.gov
Web: www.usps.gov

South Florida District
2200 NW 72nd Ave. #204
Miami, FL 33152-9461
Dorothy (Dottie) Johnson, Diversity
Development Specialist
Tel: (305) 470-0622 Fax: (305) 470-0647
Web: www.usps.gov

Sun Coast District
2203 N. Lois Ave. #1070
Tampa, FL 33607-7170
Regla M. Watts, Diversity Development
Specialist
Tel: (813) 354-6023 Fax: (813) 877-8656
Email: rwatts@email.usps.gov
Web: www.usps.gov

GEORGIA

AGRICULTURE, DEPT. OF
Natural Resources Conservation Service
205 E. Jefferson St.
Madison, GA 30650
Dennis Brooks, Black Emphasis Program
Manager (BEPM)
Tel: (706) 342-1315 Fax: (706) 342-2051
Email: dennis.brooks@ga.usda.gov
Web: www.ga.nrcs.usda.gov

AIR FORCE, DEPT. OF THE
Dobbins AFB
Dobbins AFB, GA 30069-5010
Tel: (800) 423-8723
Web: www.airforce.com

Headquarters Air Force Reserve Command
Robins AFB, GA 31098
Tel: (800) 423-8723
Web: www.airforce.com

Moody AFB
Moody AFB, GA 31699-1518
Tel: (800) 423-8723
Web: www.airforce.com

Robins AFB
Robins AFB, GA 31098-1662
Tel: (800) 423-8723
Web: www.airforce.com

ARMY, DEPT. OF
US Army 2nd Recruiting Brigade
Southeast Region, Public Affairs Office
1295 Hood Ave.

Forest Park, GA 30297-5104
Tel: (404) 469-3192/3194
US Army Recruiting Battalion Atlanta
Public Affairs Office
2400 Herodian Way #490
Smyrna, GA 30080-8500
Tel: (770) 951-2815/2834

ENERGY, DEPT. OF
Southeastern Power Association
1166 Athens Tech Rd.
Elberton, GA 30635-6711
Joel Seymour, Diversity Program Manager
Tel: (706) 213-3810 Fax: (706) 213-3884
Email: joels@sepa.doe.gov
Web: www.sepa.doe.gov

ENVIRONMENTAL PROTECTION AGENCY
Region 4, Human Capitol Management
Branch, Civil Rights Office
61 Forsyth St. SW
Atlanta, GA 30303-8960
Freda Lockhart, EEO Officer
Tel: (404) 562-8142 Fax: (404) 562-8152
Email: lockhart.freda@epa.gov
Web: www.epa.gov

EQUAL EMPLOYMENT OPPORTUNITY COMMISSION
Atlanta District Office
100 Alabama St. SW #4R30, Sam Nunn
Atlanta Federal Ctr.
Atlanta, GA 30303
Bernice Williams-Kimbrough, Director
Tel: (404) 562-6800 Fax: (404) 562-6909
Web: www.eeoc.gov

Savannah Local Office
410 Mall Blvd. #G
Savannah, GA 31406-4821
Lynn Jordan, Director
Tel: (912) 652-4234 Fax: (912) 652-4248
Web: www.eeoc.gov

FEDERAL RESERVE BANK
Atlanta District Office
Human Resources/EEO
1000 Peachtree St. NE
Atlanta, GA 30309-4470
Mary Kepler, Director
Tel: (404) 498-8500 Fax: (404) 498-8997
Email: mkeplar@frbatlanta.org
Web: www.frbatlanta.org

GENERAL SERVICES ADMINISTRATION
Office of Equal Employment Opportunity
Region 4
77 Forsyth St. #660
Atlanta, GA 30303
Ouida Cosey, EEO Officer
Tel: (404) 331-5127 Fax: (404) 331-7080
Email: ouida.cosey@gsa.gov
Web: www.gsa.gov

HEALTH AND HUMAN SERVICES, DEPT. OF
Centers for Disease Control and Prevention
Human Resources Management Office
4770 Buford Hwy., M/S K15
Atlanta, GA 30341
Ramona Ramsey, Human Resources
Management Consultant
Tel: (770) 488-1894 Fax: (770) 488-1991
Web: www.cdc.gov

HOMELAND SECURITY, DEPT. OF
USCG Recruiting Office Atlanta East
2375 Westley Chapel Rd. #9
Decatur, GA 30035
YNC Dexter Lindsey, Recruiter in Charge
Tel: (770) 808-0329 Fax: (770) 808-0794
Email: dlindsey@cgrc.uscg.mil
Web: www.gocoastguard.com

USCG Recruiting Office Atlanta North

3983 Lavista Rd. #189
Tucker, GA 30084
YNC Dexter Lindsey, Recruiter in Charge
Tel: (770) 934-9686 Fax: (770) 934-7022
Email: clindsey@cgrc.uscg.mil
Web: www.gocoastguard.com

USCG Recruiting Office Savannah
46 Abercorn St.
Savannah, GA 31401
AMTC David Medeiros, Recruiter in Charge
Tel: (912) 447-0832 Fax: (912) 352-9748
Email: dmedeiros@cgrc.uscg.mil
Web: www.gocoastguard.com

INTERIOR, DEPT. OF THE
Geological Survey
Southeast Region, Personnel Office
3850 Holcomb Bridge Rd. #160
Norcross, GA 30092
Connie Smith, Chief Human Resources
Officer
Tel: (770) 409-7706 Fax: (770) 409-7771
Email: connie.smith@usgs.gov
Web: www.usgs.gov

National Park Service
Southeast Region, Office of EEO/Diversity
Programs
100 Alabama St. SW, Bldg.1924, 5th Fl.
Atlanta, GA 30303
Gwen Evans, Special Emphasis Program
Manager
Tel: (404) 562-3103 Fax: (404) 562-3269
Email: gwen_evans@nps.gov
Web: www.nps.gov

LABOR, DEPT. OF
Atlanta Regional Office
Personnel Office
61 Forsyth St. SW #6B50
Atlanta, GA 30303
Betty McPherson, Personnel Manager
Specialist
Tel: (404) 562-2008 Fax: (404) 562-2050
Web: www.dol.gov

Employment and Training Administration
South East Job Corps
61 Forsyth St. SW #6T95
Atlanta, GA 30303
Wenomia Person, Outreach Coordinator
Tel: (404) 562-2382 Fax: (404) 562-2396
Email: person.wenomia@dol.gov
Web: www.doleta.gov

NAVY, DEPT. OF THE
Navy Recruiting District, Atlanta
2400 Herodian #400
Smyrna, GA 30080
Tel: (770) 612-4384

USMC Recruiting Station, Atlanta
4855 Peachtree Industrial Rd. #225
Norcross, GA 30071-1251
Tel: (770) 246-9029
Web: www.marines.com

POSTAL SERVICE
Atlanta District
P.O. Box 599390
Duluth, GA 30026-9390
Barbara Danzy, Diversity Development
Specialist
Tel: (770) 717-2992 Fax: (770) 717-2993
Email: barbara.a.danzy@usps.com
Web: www.usps.gov

South Georgia District
451 College St.
Macon, GA 31213-9800

Alberta Lawson, Diversity Development
Specialist
Tel: (478) 752-8494 Fax: (478) 752-8685
Web: www.usps.gov

SMALL BUSINESS ADMINISTRATION
Disaster Assistance-Disaster Area 2
Disaster Personnel Office
1 Baltimore Pl. #300
Atlanta, GA 30308
Henriquetta Wessman, Acting Personnel
Officer
Tel: (404) 347-3771 Fax: (404) 347-5487
Email: henriquetta.wessman@sba.gov
Web: www.sba.gov

AIR FORCE, DEPT. OF THE
Andersen AFB
Andersen AFB, GU 96543-4001
Tel: (800) 423-8723
Web: www.airforce.com

GUAM

HOMELAND SECURITY, DEPT. OF
USCG Recruiting Office Guam
Baltej Pavillion., 415 Chalan San Antonio
Rd. #314
Tamuning, GU 96911
CPO Kevin Hiro, Recruiter in Charge
Tel: (671) 647-6156 Fax: (671) 647-6169
Email: khiro@cgrc.uscg.mil
Web: www.gocoastguard.com

HAWAII

AIR FORCE, DEPT. OF THE
Hickam AFB
Hickam AFB, HI 96853-5398
Tel: (800) 423-8723
Web: www.airforce.com

EQUAL EMPLOYMENT OPPORTUNITY COMMISSION
Honolulu Local Office
300 Ala Moana Blvd. #7-127
Honolulu, HI 96850-0051
Timothy Riera, Director
Tel: (808) 541-3120 Fax: (808) 541-3390
Web: www.eeoc.gov

HOMELAND SECURITY, DEPT. OF
USCG Recruiting Office Honolulu
Pearl Ridge Mall Phase III., 98-151 Pali
Momi St. #106
Aiea, HI 96701
BMC Calvin Williams, Recruiter in Charge
Tel: (808) 486-8677 Fax: (808) 487-3640
Email: cwilliams@cgrc.uscg.mil
Web: www.gocoastguard.com

NAVY, DEPT. OF THE
Pacific Fleet (Code NO1CP)
Commander in Chief
250 Makalapa Dr.
Pearl Harbor, HI 96860-3131
Maureen Kleintop, Deputy Chief Director for
Total Staff and Personnel
Tel: (808) 471-9393 Fax: (808) 474-9662
Email: maureen.kleintop@navy.mil
Web: www.navy.mil

IDAHO

AIR FORCE, DEPT. OF THE
Mountain Home AFB
Mountain Home AFB, ID 83648-5298
Tel: (800) 423-8723
Web: www.airforce.com

ENERGY, DEPT. OF
Idaho Operations Office
1955 Fremont Ave.
Idaho Falls, ID 83401
LaDonna Foster, Black Employment
Program Manager
Tel: (208) 526-8698 Fax: (208) 526-7407
Email: fosterlr@id.doe.gov

HOMELAND SECURITY, DEPT. OF
USCG Recruiting Office Boise
Overland Park., 6907 Overland Rd.
Boise, ID 83709-1908
PO Gary Armstrong, Recruiter in Charge
Tel: (208) 376-7655 Fax: (208) 376-1180
Email: garmstrong@cgrc.uscg.mil
Web: www.gocoastguard.com

INTERIOR, DEPT. OF THE
Bureau of Reclamation
Pacific Northwest Region, Human
Resources
1150 N. Curtis Rd. #100
Boise, ID 83706-1234
Max Gallegos, Human Resources Officer
Tel: (208) 378-5140 Fax: (208) 378-5023
Email: mgallegos@pn.usbr.gov
Web: www.usbr.gov/pn

ILLINOIS

AGRICULTURE, DEPT. OF
Natural Resources Conservation Service
Midwest Region
2118 W. Park Ct.
Champaign, IL 61821
James Johnson, African American
Employment Program Manager
Tel: (217) 353-6641 Fax: (217) 353-6678
Email: james.johnson@il.usda.gov
Web: www.il.nrcs.usda.gov

AIR FORCE, DEPT. OF THE
Scott AFB
Scott AFB, IL 62225-5002
Tel: (800) 423-8723
Web: www.airforce.com

ARMY, DEPT. OF
US Army Recruiting Battalion Chicago
Public Affairs Office
P.O. Box 1130
Sheridan US Army Reserve Center Bldg.
142
Highland Park, IL 60035-7130
Tel: (847) 266-1359/1360

EQUAL EMPLOYMENT OPPORTUNITY COMMISSION
Chicago District Office
500 W. Madison St. #2800
Chicago, IL 60661
John P. Rowe, Director
Tel: (312) 353-2713 Fax: (312) 886-1168
Web: www.eeoc.gov

FEDERAL RESERVE BANK
Chicago District Office
Human Resources/EEO
230 S. La Salle St.
Chicago, IL 60604-1413
Michael H. Moskow, President/CEO

Tel: (312) 322-5322 Fax: (312) 322-5332
Email: information.chi@chi.frb.org
Web: www.chicagofed.org

HOMELAND SECURITY, DEPT. OF
USCG Recruiting Office Chicago
Chatham Village Sq., 716 E. 87th St.
Chicago, IL 60619
DCC Tyrone Hughes, Recruiter in Charge
Tel: (773) 723-8751 Fax: (773) 994-3857
Email: thughes@cgrc.uscg.mil
Web: www.gocoastguard.com

LABOR, DEPT. OF
Employment and Training Administration
Office of Job Corps
230 S. Dearborn St., Federal Bldg. #676
Chicago, IL 60604
Tom Deuschle, Regional Director
Tel: (312) 596-5475 Fax: (312) 596-5471
Email: tdeuschle@doleta.gov
Web: www.doleta.gov

NAVY, DEPT. OF THE
Naval Reserve Recruiting Command Area Central
2834B Green Bay Rd., Bldg. 3400, Rm. 266
Great Lakes, IL 60088-5709
Tel: (847) 688-2548

Navy Recruiting District, Chicago
3400 Patten Rd. #300
Ft. Sheridan, IL 60037
Tel: (847) 688-2024

USMC Recruiting Station, Chicago
1700 S. Wolf Rd.
Des Plaines, IL 60018-5912
Tel: (847) 803-6371
Web: www.marines.com

POSTAL SERVICE
Central Illinois District
6801 W. 73rd St.
Bedford Park, IL 60499-9311
Sharon Murphy, Diversity Development Specialist
Tel: (708) 563-7343 Fax: (708) 563-7638
Email: sharon.t.murphy@usps.gov
Web: www.usps.gov
Chicago District
433 W. Harrison St., 4th Fl.
Chicago, IL 60607-3296
Iloma Perkins, Diversity Development Specialist
Tel: (312) 983-8039 Fax: (312) 983-8033
Email: iperkins@usps.gov
Web: www.usps.gov

POSTAL SERVICE
Great Lakes Area Office
244 Knollwood Dr., 4th Fl.
Bloomingdale, IL 60117-3050
Jaime Claudio, Jr., Senior Diversity Program Coordinator
Tel: (630) 539-8338 Fax: (630) 539-7095
Web: www.usps.gov

Northern Illinois District
500 E. Fullerton Ave.
Carol Stream, IL 60199-9601
Marquetta Tisdell, Diversity Development Specialist
Tel: (630) 260-5203 Fax: (630) 260-5841
Email: mtisdell@email.usps.gov
Web: www.usps.gov

RAILROAD RETIREMENT BOARD
EEO Office
844 N. Rush St. #60611-2092
Chicago, IL 60611-2092
Lynn Cousins, Director

Tel: (312) 751-4942 Fax: (312) 751-7136
Email: lynn.cousins@rrb.gov
Web: www.rrb.gov

STATE OF ILLINOIS
Department of Commerce and Community Affairs
EEO Office
620 E. Adams St.
Springfield, IL 62701
Victoria Benn-Rochelle, Compliance Manager
Tel: (217) 524-2997 Fax: (217) 524-0189
Email: vbennroc@commerce.state.il.us
Web: www.commerce.state.il.us

INDIANA

AGRICULTURE, DEPT. OF
Natural Resources Conservation Service
Indiana Office
6013 Lakeside Blvd.
Indianapolis, IN 46278
Bennie Clark, African American Employment Program Manager
Tel: (317) 290-3200 x394
Fax: (317) 290-3225
Email: bennie.clark@in.usda.gov
Web: www.nrcs.usda.gov

AIR FORCE, DEPT. OF THE
Grissom ARB
Grissom ARB, IN 46971-5000
Tel: (800) 423-8723
Web: www.airforce.com

ARMY, DEPT. OF
US Army Recruiting Battalion Indianapolis
Public Affairs Office
9152 Kent Ave.
Indianapolis, IN 46216
Tel: (317) 549-0338/1738

EQUAL EMPLOYMENT OPPORTUNITY COMMISSION
Indianapolis District Office
101 W. Ohio St. #1900
Indianapolis, IN 46204
Danny G. Harter, Director
Tel: (317) 226-7212 Fax: (317) 226-7953
Web: www.eeoc.gov

HOMELAND SECURITY, DEPT. OF
USCG Recruiting Office Indianapolis
Metroplex Ctr., 8255 Craig St. #130
Indianapolis, IN 46250-4583
DCC Thomas Huffman, Recruiter in Charge
Tel: (317) 596-0833 Fax: (317) 596-1097
Email: thuffman@cgrc.uscg.mil
Web: www.gocoastguard.com

NAVY, DEPT. OF THE
Naval Reserve Center Indianapolis
3010 White River Pkwy.
Indianapolis, IN 46208
Tel: (317) 921-2024

Navy Recruiting District, Indianapolis
9152 Kent Ave., Bldg. 401 #352
Indianapolis, IN 46216
Tel: (317) 842-9168

USMC Recruiting Station, Indianapolis
9152 Kent Ave. #C-200
Indianapolis, IN 46216-2036
Tel: (317) 554-0506
Web: www.marines.com

POSTAL SERVICE
Greater Indiana District
3939 Vincennes Rd.

Indianapolis, IN 46298-9855
Patricia A. Proctor, Diversity Development Specialist
Tel: (317) 870-8562 Fax: (317) 837-8686
Email: patricia.proctor@usps.gov
Web: www.usps.gov

IOWA

AGRICULTURE, DEPT. OF
Natural Resources Conservation Service
State of Iowa
210 Walnut St. #693
Des Moines, IA 50309
James Ceigler, African American Employment Program Manager
Tel: (515) 284-4519 Fax: (515) 284-4767
Email: james.ceigler@ia.usda.gov
Web: www.nrcs.usda.gov

ARMY, DEPT. OF
US Army Recruiting Battalion Des Moines
Public Affairs Office
210 Walnut St., Federal Bldg. #557
Des Moines, IA 50309-2108
Tel: (515) 280-7401

HOMELAND SECURITY, DEPT. OF
USCG Recruiting Office Davenport
Old Town Mall., 901 E Kimberly Rd. #20
Davenport, IA 52807-1622
AST1 Kirk Machovec, Recruiter in Charge
Tel: (563) 388-2002 Fax: (319) 388-1090
Email: kmachovec@cgrc.uscg.mil
Web: www.gocoastguard.com

NAVY, DEPT. OF THE
USMC Recruiting Station, Des Moines
4725 Merle Hay Rd. #209
Des Moines, IA 50322
Tel: (515) 253-9508
Web: www.marines.com

KANSAS

AIR FORCE, DEPT. OF THE
McConnell AFB
McConnell AFB, KS 67221-3614
Tel: (800) 423-8723
Web: www.airforce.com

ENVIRONMENTAL PROTECTION AGENCY
Human Resources Office
Region 7
901 N. 5th St. M/C PLMGHROD
Kansas City, KS 66101
Jackie Beard, Director
Tel: (913) 551-7407 Fax: (913) 551-7267
Email: beard.jackie@epa.gov
Web: www.epa.gov

EQUAL EMPLOYMENT OPPORTUNITY COMMISSION
Kansas City Area Office
4th & State Ave., Gateway Tower II, 9th Fl.
Kansas City, KS 66101
George Dixon, Director
Tel: (913) 551-5655 Fax: (913) 551-6957
Web: www.eeoc.gov

KENTUCKY

ARMY, DEPT. OF
HQ Army, Second Region (ROTC)
US Army Cadet Command
Attn: Public Affairs Office
Fort Knox, KY 40121-5610
Tel: (502) 624-8149

US Army 3rd Recruiting Brigade
Upper Midwest Region, Public Affairs Office
Bldg. 6580
Fort Knox, KY 40121-2726
Tel: (502) 626-1030/1041

US Army Recruiting Command G5
1307 3rd Ave., Rm. 3078
Fort Knox, KY 40121-2726
Julia Bobick, Public Information Specialist
Tel: (502) 626-0172 Fax: (502) 626-0924
Email: julia.bobick@usarec.army.mil

EQUAL EMPLOYMENT OPPORTUNITY COMMISSION
Louisville Area Office
600 Dr. Martin Luther King, Jr. Pl. #268
Louisville, KY 40202
Marcia Hall-Craig, Director
Tel: (502) 582-6082 Fax: (502) 582-5895
Web: www.eeoc.gov

HOMELAND SECURITY, DEPT. OF
USCG Recruiting Office Louisville
3201 Fern Valley Rd. #112
Louisville, KY 40213-3535
BMC Jess W. Farmer, Recruiter in Charge
Tel: (502) 969-4006 Fax: (502) 969-3572
Email: jfarmer@cgrc.uscg.mil
Web: www.gocoastguard.com

NAVY, DEPT. OF THE
Naval Reserve Center Lexington
151 Votech Rd.
Lexington, KY 40511
Tel: (859) 422-8767

USMC Recruiting Station, Louisville
600 Martin Luther King Jr., Pl. #221
Louisville, KY 40202-2269
Tel: (502) 582-6601
Web: www.marines.com

LOUISIANA

AGRICULTURE, DEPT. OF
Office of Chief Financial Officer
13800 Old Gentilly Rd.
New Orleans, LA 70160
Patricia A. Bachemin, African American Program Manager
Tel: (504) 426-6206 Fax: (504) 253-5801
Email: patricia.bachemin@usda.gov
Web: www.usda.gov

National Finance Center
Civil Rights Office
13800 Old Gentilly Dr.
New Orleans, LA 70129
Donald Lewis, Director
Tel: (504) 426-6221 Fax: (504) 426-9710
Email: donald.lewis@usda.gov
Web: www.nfc.usda.gov

AIR FORCE, DEPT. OF THE
Barksdale AFB
Barksdale AFB, LA 71110-2073
Tel: (800) 423-8723
Web: www.airforce.com

ARMY, DEPT. OF
US Army Recruiting Battalion New Orleans
Public Affairs Office
4400 Dauphine St., Bldg. 602-2C
New Orleans, LA 70146-1699
Tel: (504) 678-8531/8533

COMMERCE, DEPT. OF
National Oceanic and Atmospheric Administration
National Weather Service - Southern Region
5655 Hollywood Ave.
Shreveport, LA 71109

Bill Parker, EEO Program Manager
Tel: (318) 631-3669 Fax: (318) 636-9620
Email: Bill.Parker@noaa.gov
Web: www.noaa.gov

EQUAL EMPLOYMENT OPPORTUNITY COMMISSION
New Orleans District Office
701 Loyola Ave. #600
New Orleans, LA 70113-9936
Keith T. Hill, Acting Director
Tel: (504) 589-2329 Fax: (504) 589-6861
Web: www.eeoc.gov

INTERIOR, DEPT. OF THE
Minerals Management Service
Personnel Office
1201 Elmwood Park Blvd., M/S 2620
New Orleans, LA 70123
Sarah Schlumbrecht, Personnel Staffing Classification Specialist
Tel: (504) 736-2884 Fax: (504) 736-2478
Email: sarah.schlumbrecht@mms.gov
Web: www.mms.gov

NAVY, DEPT. OF THE
Navy Recruiting District, New Orleans
4400 Dauphine St.
New Orleans, LA 70146
Tel: (504) 678-5520
Web: www.navy.mil

USMC Recruiting Station, New Orleans
Naval Support Station, 4400 Dauphine St. 602-2-C
New Orleans, LA 70146-0800
Tel: (504) 678-5095
Web: www.marines.com

POSTAL SERVICE
Louisiana District
701 Loyola Ave. #10021
New Orleans, LA 70113-9813
Hedy H. Duplessis, Diversity Development Specialist
Tel: (504) 589-1283 Fax: (504) 589-1467
Email: hduples1@email.usps.gov
Web: www.usps.gov

MAINE

ARMY, DEPT. OF
US Army Recruiting Battalion New England
Public Affairs Office
33 Canam Dr.
Topsham, ME 04086-1117
Tel: (207) 725-8637

HOMELAND SECURITY, DEPT. OF
USCG Recruiting Office Portland
Brighton Avenue Plz., 1041 Brighton Ave.
Portland, ME 04102
YNC Don Hodgdon, Recruiter in Charge
Tel: (207) 761-4307 Fax: (207) 874-6058
Email: dhodgdon@cgrc.uscg.com
Web: www.gocoastguard.com

NAVY, DEPT. OF THE
Naval Reserve Center Brunswick
500 Sewall St.
Brunswick, ME 04011
Tel: (207) 921-1534

POSTAL SERVICE
Maine District
P.O. Box 7800
Portland, ME 04104-7800
Debbie Woods, Diversity Development Sp.
Tel: (207) 828-8400 Fax: (207) 828-8447
Web: www.usps.com

MARYLAND

AGRICULTURE, DEPT. OF
Animal and Plant Health Inspection Service
Marketing and Regulatory Programs
4700 River Rd. #92-5C17
Riverdale, MD 20737
Terry A. Henson, National HEPM
Tel: (301) 734-5555 Fax: (301) 734-3698
Email: terry.henson@aphis.usda.gov
Web: www.aphis.usda.gov

Food Safety and Inspection Service
Civil Rights Office
5601 Sunnyside Ave. #5261 M/S 5261
Beltsville, MD 20705-5000
Steven Newbold, Director
Tel: (301) 504-7759 Fax: (301) 504-2141
Email: steven.newbold@fsis.usda.gov
Web: www.fsis.usda.gov

Natural Resources Conservation Service
Civil Rights Office
5601 Sunnyside Ave. #1-1123
Beltsville, MD 20705-5000
Andrew Johnson, Jr., Director
Tel: (301) 504-2181 Fax: (301) 504-2175
Email: andrew.johnson@usda.gov
Web: www.nrcs.usda.gov

AIR FORCE, DEPT. OF THE
Andrews AFB
Andrews AFB, MD 20762-7002
Tel: (800) 423-8723
Web: www.airforce.com

ARMY, DEPT. OF
US Army 1st Recruiting Brigade
Northeast Region, Public Affairs Office
4550 Llewelyn Ave.
Fort George Meade, MD 20755-5380
Tel: (301) 677-2380/2378

US Army Recruiting Battalion Baltimore
Public Affairs Office
4550 Llewelyn Ave.
Fort George Meade, MD 20755-5390
Tel: (301) 677-7034/7029

COMMERCE, DEPT. OF
National Institute of Standards and Technology
Civil Rights Office/Diversity Division
100 Bureau Dr., M/S 1740
Gaithersburg, MD 20899-1740
Mirta-Marie M. Keys, Director
Tel: (301) 975-2042
Email: keys@nist.gov
Web: www.nist.gov

National Oceanic and Atmospheric Administration
Civil Rights Office
1305 East-West Hwy., Bldg. SSMC4 #12222
Silver Spring, MD 20910
Terri Belle, African American Coordinator
Tel: (301) 713-0500 Fax: (301) 713-0983
Email: terri.l.belle@noaa.gov
Web: www.noaa.gov

CONSUMER PRODUCT SAFETY COMMISSION
EEO and Minority Enterprise Office
4330 East-West Hwy. #712
Bethesda, MD 20814
Kathleen Buttrey, Director
Tel: (301) 504-7771 Fax: (301) 504-0107
Email: kbuttrey@cpsc.gov
Web: www.cpsc.gov

DEFENSE, DEPT. OF
Defense Security Service
Office of Diversity Management
881 Elkridge Landing Rd.
Linthicum, MD 21090
Lori A. Simmons, EEO Director
Tel: (410) 865-2477 Fax: (410) 865-3438
Email: oaaeop.questions@mail.dss.mil
Web: www.dss.mil

National Security Agency
Diversity and Disability Affairs
9800 Savage Rd.
Ft. Meade, MD 20755-1100
Carla Downs, Black Employment Program Manager
Tel: (301) 688-6961 Fax: (443) 479-6690
Email: cjdowns@nsa.gov
Web: www.nsa.gov

Uniformed Services University of the Health Sciences
EEO Office
4301 Jones Bridge Rd.
Bethesda, MD 20814-4799
Karen Moore, Employment Program Manager
Tel: (301) 295-9388 Fax: (301) 295-5194
Email: kmoore@usuhs.mil
Web: www.usuhs.mil

EQUAL EMPLOYMENT OPPORTUNITY COMMISSION
Baltimore District Office
10 S. Howard St.,
City Crescent Bldg., 3rd Fl.
Baltimore, MD 21201
Marie Tomasso, Acting Director
Tel: (410) 962-3932 Fax: (410) 962-4270
Web: www.eeoc.gov

HEALTH AND HUMAN SERVICES, DEPT. OF
Centers for Medicare and Medicaid Services
Office of Equal Opportunity/Civil Rights
7500 Security Blvd. #N2-22-17
Baltimore, MD 21244-1850
Patricia Lamond, Director
Tel: (410) 786-5110 Fax: (410) 786-9549
Email: patricia.lamond@cms.hhs.gov
Web: www.cms.hhs.gov

Food and Drug Administration
EEO Office
5600 Fishers Ln., Parklawn Bldg. #883
Rockville, MD 20857
Cheryl Kelley, EEO Specialist
Tel: (301) 827-6737 Fax: (301) 827-9675
Email: cheryl.kelley@fda.gov
Web: www.fda.gov

Office of Minority Health
Resource Center
1101 Wootton Pkwy. #650
Rockville, MD 20852
José T. Carneiro, Project Director
Tel: (301) 251-1797 Fax: (301) 251-2160
Email: jcarneiro@omhrc.gov
Web: www.omhrc.gov

HOMELAND SECURITY, DEPT. OF
USCG Recruiting Office Baltimore
6499 Baltimore National Pike
Catonsville, MD 21228-3904
YNC Kenneth Starnes, Recruiter in Charge
Tel: (410) 747-3963 Fax: (410) 747-9264
Email: kstarnes@cgrc.uscg.mil
Web: www.gocoastguard.com

USCG Recruiting Office Salisbury
1506 S. Salisbury Blvd. #7
Salisbury, MD 21801
MKC Bernard Graham, Recruiter in Charge
Tel: (410) 742-3778 Fax: (410) 543-2621

Email: bgraham@cgrc.uscg.mil
Web: www.gocoastguard.com

MONTGOMERY COUNTY GOVERNMENT
Minority & Multi-Cultural Affairs
99 Maryland Ave., Administrative Office Bldg.
Rockville, MD 20850
Betty Valdes, Community Affairs Officer for Montgomery County Public Libraries
Tel: (240) 777-0017 Fax: (301) 217-2517
Email: betty.valdes@montgomerycountymd.gov
Web: www.montgomerylibrary.org

Montgomery County Department of Police
Personnel Section
2350 Research Blvd. #203
Rockville, MD 20850
Brian Walker, Recruitment Officer
Tel: (240) 773-5310 Fax: (240) 773-5302
Email: brian.walker@montgomerycountymd.gov
Web: www.montgomerycountymd.gov

NATIONAL ARCHIVES AND RECORDS ADMINISTRATION
EEO and Diversity Programs
8601 Adelphi Rd. #4400
College Park, MD 20740-6001
Allison Darnaby, AEP/Diversity Manager
Tel: (301) 837-0295 Fax: (301) 837-0869
Web: www.archives.gov

EEO and Diversity Programs
8601 Adelphi Rd. #4400
College Park, MD 20740-6001
Robert D. Jew, Director
Tel: (301) 837-1849 Fax: (301) 837-0869
Email: robert.jew@nora.gov
Web: www.archives.gov

NAVY, DEPT. OF THE
Naval Reserve Center Baltimore
Ft. McHenry
Baltimore, MD 21230-5392
Tel: (410) 547-1915

USMC Recruiting Station, Baltimore
6845 Deerpath Rd., Dorsey Business Ctr.
Elk Ridge, MD 21227-6221
Tel: (410) 379-0800
Web: www.marines.com

USMC Recruiting Station, Frederick
5112 Pegasus Ct. #B
Frederick, MD 21704
Tel: (301) 668-2025
Web: www.marines.com

NUCLEAR REGULATORY COMMISSION
Office of Human Resources
11555 Rockville Pike
Rockville, MD 20852-2738
Peggy Etheridge, Recruitment Manager
Tel: (301) 415-2294 Fax: (301) 415-3818
Email: opa@nrc.gov
Web: www.nrc.gov

POSTAL SERVICE
Baltimore District
900 E. Fayette St. #327
Baltimore, MD 21233-9989
Thomasine A. Adams, Diversity Development Specialist
Tel: (410) 347-4265 Fax: (410) 234-8260
Email: thomasine.a.adams@usps.gov
Web: www.usps.gov

Capital Metro Operations
16501 Shady Grove
Gaithersburg, MD 20898-9998
Penny L. Fleury, Manager, Diversity/Human Capital Management

Tel: (301) 548-1432 Fax: (301) 548-1434
Web: www.usps.gov

SOCIAL SECURITY ADMINISTRATION
Center for Personnel Policy and Staffing
6401 Security Blvd., 2720 Annex Bldg.
#G-120
Baltimore, MD 21235
Sandy Eckert, Director
Tel: (410) 965-4506
Web: www.ssa.gov

MASSACHUSETTS

AIR FORCE, DEPT. OF THE
Hanscom AFB
Hanscom AFB, MA 01731-2800
Tel: (800) 423-8723
Web: www.airforce.com

Otis ANGB
Otis ANGB, MA 02542-5028
Tel: (800) 423-8723
Web: www.airforce.com

Westover AFB
Westover AFB, MA 01022-1843
Tel: (800) 423-8723
Web: www.airforce.com

ENVIRONMENTAL PROTECTION AGENCY
Human Resources Office
Region 1
1 Congress St. #1100
Boston, MA 02114-2023
Frank Harris, Acting Director
Tel: (617) 918-1981 Fax: (617) 918-1183
Email: harris.frank@epa.gov
Web: www.epa.gov

EQUAL EMPLOYMENT OPPORTUNITY COMMISSION
Boston Area Office
John F. Kennedy Federal Bldg., 475
Government Ctr.
Boston, MA 02203
Robert L. Sanders, Director
Tel: (617) 565-3200 Fax: (617) 565-3196
Web: www.eeoc.gov

HOMELAND SECURITY, DEPT. OF
USCG Recruiting Office Boston
Capt. John Foster Williams Bldg., 408
Atlantic Ave. #548
Boston, MA 02110-3350
ETC William Slauenwhite, Recruiter in
Charge
Tel: (617) 565-8656 Fax: (617) 565-8460
Email: wslauenwhite@cgrc.uscg.mil
Web: www.gocoastguard.com

USCG Recruiting Office Springfield
New Federal Office Bldg., 1550 Main St.
#110
Springfield, MA 01103-1422
MSTC Timothy Ryan, Recruiter in Charger
Tel: (413) 785-0324 Fax: (413) 785-0326
Email: tryan@cgrc.uscg.mil
Web: www.gocoastguard.com

LABOR, DEPT. OF
Employment and Training Administration
Office of Youth Programs/Job Corps
JFK Federal Bldg., #E-350
Boston, MA 02203
Tel: (617) 788-0170 Fax: (617) 788-0101
Web: www.dol.gov

NAVY, DEPT. OF THE
Naval Reserve Center Quincy

85 Sea St.
Quincy, MA 02169
Tel: (617) 753-4669 Fax: (617) 753-4642

Navy Recruiting District, New England
495 Summer St. #316
Boston, MA 02210
Tel: (617) 753-4599

USMC Recruiting Station, Springfield
105 East St.
Chicopee Falls, MA 01020-3400
Tel: (413) 594-2033
Web: www.marines.com

POSTAL SERVICE
Boston District
25 Dorchester Ave. #3013
Boston, MA 02205-9431
Lillian J. Buckley, Diversity Development
Specialist
Tel: (617) 654-5933 Fax: (617) 654-5932
Email: lillian.j.buckley@usps.gov
Web: www.usps.gov

Middlesex-Central Cluster
74 Main St.
North Reading, MA 01889-9402
Andrea Marshall, Diversity Development
Specialist
Tel: (978) 664-7652 Fax: (978) 664-5998
Email: andrea.v.marshall@usps.gov
Web: www.usps.gov

SOCIAL SECURITY ADMINISTRATION
Boston Region
EEO Office
JFK Federal Bldg. #1900
Boston, MA 02203
Linda Tuttle, Manager
Tel: (617) 565-2879 Fax: (617) 723-0460
Email: linda.tuttle@ssa.gov
Web: www.ssa.gov

MICHIGAN

AIR FORCE, DEPT. OF THE
Selfridge ANGB
Selfridge ANGB, MI 48045-5399
Tel: (800) 423-8723
Web: www.airforce.com

ARMY, DEPT. OF
US Army Recruiting Battalion Great Lakes
Public Affairs Office
Holiday Office Park N., 6545 Mercantile
Way #11
Lansing, MI 48911-5974
Tel: (517) 887-5782

EQUAL EMPLOYMENT OPPORTUNITY COMMISSION
Detroit District Office
477 Michigan Ave., Patrick V. McNamara
Bldg. #865
Detroit, MI 48226
James R. Neely, Jr., Director
Tel: (313) 226-4600 Fax: (313) 226-4610
Web: www.eeoc.gov

HOMELAND SECURITY, DEPT. OF
USCG Recruiting Office Detroit
26097 John R. Rd.
Madison Heights, MI 48071-3607
OSC Fred Napoleon, Recruiter in Charge
Tel: (248) 582-8364 Fax: (248) 582-8375
Email: fnapoleon@cgrc.uscg.mil
Web: www.gocoastguard.com

USCG Recruiting Office Lansing

2515 E. Jolly Rd. #1
Lansing, MI 48910
MKC Andrew Hiester, Recruiter in Charge
Tel: (517) 377-1719 Fax: (517) 377-1731
Email: ahiester@cgrc.uscg.mil
Web: www.gocoastguard.com

INTERIOR, DEPT. OF THE
National Park Service
Sleeping Bear Dunes National Lake Shore
9922 Front St.
Empire, MI 49630-9797
Gale Purifoy, Personnel Management
Specialist
Tel: (231) 326-5134 Fax: (231) 326-5382
Email: gale_purifoy@nps.gov
Web: www.nps.gov/slbe

NAVY, DEPT. OF THE
Naval Reserve Center Detroit
Bldg. 1410, 25154 Plattsburg
Selfridge Angb, MI 48045-4911
Tel: (586) 307-6638 Fax: (586) 307-6985

Navy Recruiting District, Michigan
1155 Brewery Park Blvd. #320
Detroit, MI 48207
Tel: (313) 259-1004 Fax: (313) 259-2296

USMC Recruiting Station, Detroit
580 Kirts Blvd. #307
Troy, MI 48084
Tel: (248) 269-9058
Web: www.marines.com

USMC Recruiting Station, Lansing
6545 Mercantile Way #12
Lansing, MI 48933
Tel: (517) 882-8762
Web: www.marines.com

POSTAL SERVICE
Detroit District
1401 W. Fort St., 10th Fl.
Detroit, MI 48233-9998
Alzana Braxton, Diversity Development
Specialist
Tel: (313) 226-8131 Fax: (313) 226-8005
Email: abraxton@email.usps.gov
Web: www.usps.gov

Greater Michigan District
678 Front St. NW, 3rd Fl.
Grand Rapids, MI 49599-9997
Susan Pfeifer, Diversity Development
Specialist
Tel: (616) 776-6139 Fax: (616) 336-5399
Email: susan.d.pfeifer@usps.gov
Web: www.usps.com

MINNESOTA

ARMY, DEPT. OF
US Army Recruiting Battalion Minneapolis
Public Affairs Office
1 Federal Dr., BHW Federal Bldg. #3700
Fort Snelling, MN 55111-4007
Tel: (612) 725-3122/3121

EQUAL EMPLOYMENT OPPORTUNITY COMMISSION
Minneapolis Area Office
330 S. 2nd Ave., Towle Bldg. #430
Minneapolis, MN 55401-2224
Cornelius Sheppard, Acting Director
Tel: (612) 335-4040 Fax: (612) 335-4044
Web: www.eeoc.gov

HOMELAND SECURITY, DEPT. OF
USCG Recruiting Office Minneapolis
8575 Lyndale Ave. South

Bloomington, MN 55420
AMTC Tad Gentile, Recruiter in Charge
Tel: (612) 725-3222 Fax: (612) 725-3238
Email: tgentile@cgrc.uscg.mil
Web: www.gocoastguard.com

NAVY, DEPT. OF THE
Navy Recruiting District, Minneapolis
6020 28th Ave. South
Minneapolis, MN 55450
Tel: (612) 725-0414

USMC Recruiting Station, Twin Cities
Bishop Henry Whipple Federal Bldg., 1
Federal Dr. #1
Ft. Snelling, MN 55111
Tel: (612) 725-3193
Web: www.marines.com

POSTAL SERVICE
Northland District
P.O. Box 645001
St. Paul, MN 55164-5001
Andrew S. Fisher, Diversity Development
Specialist
Tel: (651) 293-3716 Fax: (651) 293-3000
Email: andrew.s.fishers@usps.gov
Web: www.usps.gov

MISSISSIPPI

AIR FORCE, DEPT. OF THE
Columbus AFB
Columbus AFB, MS 39710-6801
Tel: (800) 423-8723
Web: www.airforce.com

Keesler AFB
Keesler AFB, MS 39534-2547
Tel: (800) 423-8723
Web: www.airforce.com

ARMY, DEPT. OF
US Army Recruiting Battalion Jackson
Public Affairs Office
3780 I-55 N. Frontage Rd., Howie Bldg.
Jackson, MS 39211-6323
Tel: (601) 366-0895

EQUAL EMPLOYMENT OPPORTUNITY COMMISSION
Jackson Area Office
100 W. Capitol St., Dr. A.H. McCoy Federal
Bldg. #207
Jackson, MS 39269
Benjamin Bradley, Director
Tel: (601) 965-4537 Fax: (601) 965-5272
Web: www.eeoc.gov

HOMELAND SECURITY, DEPT. OF
USCG Recruiting Office Jackson
4229 Lakeland Dr.
Flowood, MS 39232
AMTC Don Fortin, Recruiter in Charge
Tel: (601) 933-4901 Fax: (601) 939-9757
Email: dfortin@cgrc.uscg.mil
Web: www.gocoastguard.com

NAVY, DEPT. OF THE
Naval Reserve Center Meridian
434 Rosenbaum Ave.
Meridian, MS 39309
Tel: (601) 679-7105 Fax: (601) 679-8609

POSTAL SERVICE
Mississippi District
P.O. Box 99987
1461 Lakeover Rd.
Jackson, MS 39205-9987
Fannie B. Smith, Diversity Development
Specialist
Tel: (601) 351-7251 Fax: (601) 351-7504

Email: fannie.b.smith@usps.gov
Web: www.usps.gov

MISSOURI

AIR FORCE, DEPT. OF THE
Jefferson Barracks ANGS
Jefferson Barracks ANGS, MO 63125-4193
Tel: (800) 423-8723
Web: www.airforce.com
Whiteman AFB
Whiteman AFB, MO 65305-5021
Tel: (800) 423-8723
Web: www.airforce.com

ARMY, DEPT. OF
US Army Recruiting Battalion Kansas City
Public Affairs Office
10300 NW Prairie View Dr.
Kansas City, MO 64153-1350
Tel: (816) 891-8721/8729

US Army Recruiting Battalion St. Louis
Public Affairs Office
1222 Spruce St., Robert Young Bldg.,
10th Fl.
St. Louis, MO 63102-2815
Tel: (314) 331-4131/4145

COMMERCE, DEPT. OF
National Oceanic and Atmospheric
Administration
Human Resources Office
601 E. 12th St. #1737
Kansas City, MO 64106
Paul Kountzman, Acting Manager
Tel: (816) 426-5016 Fax: (816) 426-7177
Email: paul.j.kountzman@noaa.gov
Web: www.rdc.noaa.gov/~casc/main.html

DEFENSE, DEPT. OF
National Geospatial-Intelligence Agency
EEO Office
3838 Vogel Rd., M/S L11
Arnold, MO 63010
Margaret Brown, Deputy Director
Tel: (314) 263-4385 Fax: (314) 263-4252
Web: www.nga.mil

EQUAL EMPLOYMENT OPPORTUNITY
COMMISSION
St. Louis District Office
1222 Spruce St., Robert A. Young Federal
Bldg. #8100
St. Louis, MO 63103
Lynn Bruner, Director
Tel: (314) 539-7800 Fax: (314) 539-7894
Web: www.eeoc.gov

FEDERAL RESERVE BANK
Kansas City District
Human Resources/EEO
925 Grand Blvd.
Kansas City, MO 64198-0001
Debra Bronston, Assistant VP
Tel: (816) 881-2463 Fax: (816) 881-6742
Web: www.kc.frb.org

GENERAL SERVICES ADMINISTRATION
Office of Equal Employment Opportunity
Region 6
1500 E. Bannister Rd. #1181
Kansas City, MO 64131
Pinkie Mason, EEO Officer
Tel: (816) 926-7349 Fax: (816) 823-1970
Email: pinkie.mason@gsa.gov
Web: www.gsa.gov

HOMELAND SECURITY, DEPT. OF
USCG Recruiting Office Kansas City
6228 NW Barry Rd.

Kansas City, MO 64154-2530
MSTC Thomas Kimberling, Recruiter in
Charge
Tel: (816) 746-9924 Fax: (816) 746-9927
Email: tkimberling@cgrc.uscg.mil
Web: www.gocoastguard.com

USCG Recruiting Office St. Louis
5445 Telegraph Rd. #125
St. Louis, MO 63129-3500
MSTC Greg Cable, Recruiter in Charge
Tel: (314) 845-0807 Fax: (314) 845-1805
Email: gcable@cgrc.uscg.mil
Web: www.gocoastguard.com

NAVY, DEPT. OF THE
Navy Recruiting District, Kansas City
10306 Prairie View Rd.
Kansas City, MO 64153
Tel: (816) 880-1105
Web: www.navy.mil

Navy Recruiting District, St. Louis
1222 Spruce St., 10th Fl.
St. Louis, MO 63103
Tel: (314) 331-4296

USMC Recruiting Station, Kansas City
10302 NW Prairie View Rd.
Kansas City, MO 64153-1350
Tel: (816) 891-7577
Web: www.marines.com

USMC Recruiting Station, St. Louis
1222 Spruce St. #1031
St. Louis, MO 63103-2817
Tel: (314) 331-4555
Web: www.marines.com

POSTAL SERVICE
Gateway District
1720 Market St. #2022
St. Louis, MO 63155-9756
Glenda Fields, Diversity Development
Specialist
Tel: (314) 436-3868 Fax: (314) 436-6424
Email: glenda.d.fields@usps.gov
Web: www.usps.com

Mid-America District
300 W. Pershing Rd.
Kansas City, MO 64108
Rita A. Hamilton, Diversity Development
Specialist
Tel: (816) 374-9131 Fax: (816) 374-9487
Email: rita.a.hamilton@usps.gov
Web: www.usps.gov

SOCIAL SECURITY ADMINISTRATION
Civil Rights/Equal Opportunity Office
Region 7
601 E. 12th St. #436
Kansas City, MO 64106
Wanda McIntosh, Civil Rights/Equal
Opportunity Manager
Tel: (816) 936-5720 Fax: (816) 936-5727
Email: wanda.mcintosh@ssa.gov
Web: www.ssa.gov

MONTANA

AIR FORCE, DEPT. OF THE
Malmstrom AFB
Malmstrom AFB, MT 59402-6857
Tel: (800) 423-8723
Web: www.airforce.com

INTERIOR, DEPT. OF THE
Bureau of Indians Affairs
Rocky Mountain Region, Personnel Office
316 N. 26th St.

Billings, MT 59101
Sharon Limberhand, Human Resource
Officer
Tel: (406) 247-7956 Fax: (406) 247-7902
Email: sharonlimberhand@bia.gov
Web: www.bia.gov

Bureau of Reclamation
Great Plains Region
P.O. Box 36900
Billings, MT 57401
Sue McCannel, Personnel Manager
Tel: (406) 247-7614 Fax: (406) 247-7741
Web: www.usbr.gov/gp

POSTAL SERVICE
Big Sky District
841 S. 26th St.
Billings, MT 59101-9437
Leslie L. Denny, Diversity Development
Specialist
Tel: (406) 657-5660 Fax: (406) 657-5788
Web: www.usps.com

NEBRASKA

AIR FORCE, DEPT. OF THE
Offutt AFB
Offutt AFB, NE 68113-4015
Tel: (800) 423-8723
Web: www.airforce.com

HOMELAND SECURITY, DEPT. OF
USCG Recruiting Office Omaha
Montclair Ctr., 2758 S. 129th Ave.
Omaha, NE 68144
SKC Mark G. Floerchinger, Recruiter
Tel: (402) 334-0607 Fax: (402) 334-0260
Email: mfloerchinger@cgrc.uscg.mil
Web: www.gocoastguard.com

INTERIOR, DEPT. OF THE
National Park Service
Midwest Region, Office of Human
Resources
601 Riverfront Dr.
Omaha, NE 68102-4226
Carol Solnosky, Human Resources
Specialist
Tel: (402) 661-1650 Fax: (402) 661-1985
Email: carol_solnosky@nps.gov
Web: www.nps.gov

NAVY, DEPT. OF THE
Navy Recruiting District, Omaha
6910 Pacific St. #400
Omaha, NE 68106
Tel: (402) 558-7909

STATE OF NEBRASKA
Equal Opportunity Commission
EEO Office
P.O. Box 94934
Lincoln, NE 68509-4934
Anne Hobbs, Executive Director
Tel: (402) 471-2024 Fax: (402) 471-4059
Email: ahobbs@neoc.state.ne.us
Web: www.neoc.state.ne.us

NEVADA

AIR FORCE, DEPT. OF THE
Nellis AFB
Nellis AFB, NV 89191-6526
Tel: (800) 423-8723
Web: www.airforce.com

ARMY, DEPT. OF
US Army 6th Recruiting Brigade
Western Region, Public Affairs Office

4539 N. 5th St.
North Las Vegas, NV 89031
Tel: (702) 639-2071/2072

ENVIRONMENTAL PROTECTION AGENCY
Radiation and Indoor Environments
Human Resources Office
P.O. Box 98517
Las Vegas, NV 89193-8517
Robert Mosley, Black Employment Program
Manager
Tel: (702) 784-8266 Fax: (702) 784-8231
Email: mosley.robert@epa.gov
Web: www.epa.gov

HOMELAND SECURITY, DEPT. OF
USCG Recruiting Office Las Vegas
Tropicana Gardens., 3510 E Tropicana
Blvd. #L
Las Vegas, NV 89121-7341
AMT1 JD Lawrence, Recruiter in Charge
Tel: (702) 898-2226 Fax: (702) 898-3026
Email: jlawrence@cgrc.uscg.mil
Web: www.gocoastguard.com

INTERIOR, DEPT. OF THE
Bureau of Reclamation
Lower Colorado Region, Personnel Office
P.O. Box 61470
Boulder City, NV 89006-1470
Bob Johnson, Regional Director
Tel: (702) 293-8412 Fax: (702) 293-8614
Email: bjohnson@usbr.gov
Web: www.usbr.gov

NAVY, DEPT. OF THE
Armed Forces Reserve Center Las Vegas
Navy Reserve, Area III
Nellis Air Force Base, 5095 Range Rd.
Las Vegas, NV 89115
Tel: (702) 632-1468

NEW HAMPSHIRE

HOUSING AND URBAN DEVELOPMENT,
DEPT. OF
New Hampshire State Office
1000 Elm St., 8th Fl.
Manchester, NH 03101-1730
Robert A. Grenier, Operations Specialist
Tel: (603) 666-7510 Fax: (603) 666-7667
Email: robert_grenier@hud.gov
Web: www.hud.gov

NAVY, DEPT. OF THE
USMC Recruiting Station, Portsmouth
875 Greenland Rd. #A9
Portsmouth, NH 03801-4123
Tel: (603) 436-0890
Web: www.marines.com

POSTAL SERVICE
New Hampshire District
955 Goffs Falls Rd.
Manchester, NH 03103-9994
Harry H. Figueroa, Diversity Development
Specialist
Tel: (603) 644-3890 Fax: (603) 644-3896
Email: hfigueroa@email.usps.gov
Web: www.usps.gov

NEW JERSEY

AIR FORCE, DEPT. OF THE
McGuire AFB
McGuire AFB, NJ 08641-5000
Tel: (800) 423-8723
Web: www.airforce.com

ARMY, DEPT. OF
US Army Recruiting Battalion Mid-Atlantic
Public Affairs Office
Lakehurst Naval Air Station, Hwy. 547,
Bldg. 120
Lakehurst, NJ 08733
Tel: (732) 323-7380/7376

EQUAL EMPLOYMENT OPPORTUNITY COMMISSION
Newark Area Office
1 Newark Ctr., 21st Fl.
Newark, NJ 07102-5233
Corrado Gigante, Director
Tel: (973) 645-6383 Fax: (973) 645-4524
Web: www.eeoc.gov

HOMELAND SECURITY, DEPT. OF
USCG Recruiting Office Atlantic City
1333 New Rd. #8
Northfield, NJ 08225-1202
FSC George Lopez, Recruiter in Charge
Tel: (609) 484-8260 Fax: (609) 484-9471
Email: glopez@cgrc.uscg.mil
Web: www.gocoastguard.com

NAVY, DEPT. OF THE
Naval Reserve Center Fort Dix
5994 New Jersey Ave.
Fort Dix, NJ 08650-7810
Tel: (609) 723-6582 Fax: (609) 723-4832

USMC Recruiting Station, New Jersey
Naval Weapons Station Earle, 201 Hwy.
34 South
Colts Neck, NJ 07722
Tel: (732) 866-2933
Web: www.marines.com

POSTAL SERVICE
Northern New Jersey District
494 Broad St.
Newark, NJ 07102-9300
Florina Cordero, Diversity Development
Specialist
Tel: (973) 468-7203 Fax: (973) 468-7254
Email: florina.cordero@usps.gov
Web: www.usps.gov

NEW MEXICO

AIR FORCE, DEPT. OF THE
Cannon AFB
Cannon AFB, NM 88103-5326
Tel: (800) 423-8723
Web: www.airforce.com

Holloman AFB
Holloman AFB, NM 88330-8060
Tel: (800) 423-8723
Web: www.airforce.com

Kirtland AFB
Kirtland AFB, NM 87117-5625
Tel: (800) 423-8723
Web: www.airforce.com

ENERGY, DEPT. OF
**National Nuclear Security Administration
Service Center**
EEO/Diversity Office
P.O. Box 5400
Albuquerque, NM 87185-5400
Yolanda Giron, EEO & Diversity Program
Manager
Tel: (505) 845-5517 Fax: (505) 845-4963
Email: ygiron@doeal.gov
Web: www.doeal.gov

EQUAL EMPLOYMENT OPPORTUNITY COMMISSION
Albuquerque Area Office
505 Marquette NW #900
Albuquerque, NM 87102
Georgia M. Marchbanks, Director
Tel: (505) 248-5201 Fax: (505) 248-5239
Web: www.eeoc.gov

HOMELAND SECURITY, DEPT. OF
USCG Recruiting Office Albuquerque
6001 San Mateo Blvd. NE #B-2A
Albuquerque, NM 87109-3348
EMCS James Richey, Recruiter in Charge
Tel: (505) 883-5396 Fax: (505) 883-5721
Email: jrichey@cgrc.uscg.mil
Web: www.gocoastguard.com

INTERIOR, DEPT. OF THE
Bureau of Indian Affairs
Southwest Region, Personnel Office
P.O. Box 26567
Albuquerque, NM 87102
Karen Tarrish, Personnel Officer
Tel: (505) 563-3170 Fax: (505) 563-3040
Web: www.bia.com

NAVY, DEPT. OF THE
USMC Recruiting Station, Albuquerque
5338 Montgomery Blvd. NE #30
Albuquerque, NM 87109
Tel: (505) 248-5274
Web: www.marines.com

STATE OF NEW MEXICO
Energy Minerals and Natural Resources
State Parks Division-Personnel Office
1220 S. Saint Francis Dr.
Santa Fe, NM 87505
Faye Barela, Personnel Officer
Tel: (505) 476-3375 Fax: (505) 476-3361
Email: fbarela@state.nm.us
Web: www.state.nm.us

NEW YORK

AIR FORCE, DEPT. OF THE
Niagara Falls ARS
Niagara Falls ARS, NY 14304-5001
Tel: (800) 423-8723
Web: www.airforce.com

ARMY, DEPT. OF
US Army Recruiting Battalion Albany
Public Affairs Office
21 Aviation Rd.
Albany, NY 12205-1131
Tel: (518) 438-5536/1615

US Army Recruiting Battalion New York City
Public Affairs Office
407 Pershing Loop North
Fort Hamilton, NY 11252-7000
Tel: (718) 630-4386/4387

US Army Recruiting Battalion Syracuse
Public Affairs Office
The Atrium, 2 Clinton Sq. #230
Syracuse, NY 13202-1042
Tel: (315) 479-8534

ENVIRONMENTAL PROTECTION AGENCY
Water Compliance Branch
Region 2
290 Broadway, 20th Fl.
New York, NY 10007-1866
Larry R. Parker, African American Program
Manager
Tel: (212) 637-4243 Fax: (212) 637-3953
Email: parker.larry@epa.gov
Web: www.epa.gov

EQUAL EMPLOYMENT OPPORTUNITY COMMISSION
Buffalo Local Office
6 Fountain Plz. #350
Buffalo, NY 14202
Elizabeth Cadle, Director
Tel: (716) 551-4441 Fax: (716) 551-4387
Web: www.eeoc.gov

New York District Office
33 Whitehall St.
New York, NY 10004
Elizabeth Grossman, Acting Director
Tel: (212) 336-3620 Fax: (212) 336-3622
Web: www.eeoc.gov

FEDERAL RESERVE BANK
New York District
Human Resources/EEO
33 Liberty St., 7th Fl.
New York, NY 10045-0001
Renoka Singh, EEO Officer
Tel: (212) 720-6040 Fax: (212) 720-6947
Web: www.ny.frb.org

GENERAL SERVICES ADMINISTRATION
Office of Equal Employment Opportunity
Region 2
26 Federal Plz. #18-130
New York, NY 10278
Francine Blyther, EEO Officer
Tel: (212) 264-7600 Fax: (212) 264-6729
Email: francine.blyther@gsa.gov
Web: www.gsa.gov

HOMELAND SECURITY, DEPT. OF
USCG Recruiting Office Albany
Loudon Plz., 324 Northern Blvd.
Albany, NY 12204-1028
Troy Timmons,
Tel: (518) 465-6182 Fax: (518) 465-6319
Email: ttimmons@cgrc.uscg.mil
Web: www.gocoastguard.com

USCG Recruiting Office Bronx
46 Westchester Square Plz.
Bronx, NY 10461
OSC Paul Gladding, Recruiter in Charge
Tel: (718) 904-8585 Fax: (718) 904-1900
Email: pgladding@cgrc.uscg.mil
Web: www.gocoastguard.com

USCG Recruiting Office Brooklyn
7810 Flatlands
Brooklyn, NY 11236
PO Craig Reid, Recruiter in Charge
Tel: (718) 251-1636 Fax: (718) 251-1660
Email: creid@cgrc.uscg.mil
Web: www.gocoastguard.com

USCG Recruiting Office Buffalo
1526 Walden Ave. #500
Cheektowaga, NY 14225
MKC Bernard Tobolski, Recruiter in Charge
Tel: (716) 893-2429 Fax: (716) 893-0570
Email: btobolski@cgrc.uscg.mil
Web: www.gocoastguard.com

USCG Recruiting Office Long Island
Wantagh Plz., 747 Wantagh Ave.
Wantagh, NY 11793-3133
FSC Dana Jewett, Recruiter in Charge
Tel: (516) 796-3339 Fax: (516) 796-3344
Email: djewett@cgrc.uscg.mil
Web: www.gocoastguard.com

USCG Recruiting Office New York
Battery Park Bldg., 1 South St. #109
New York, NY 10004-1466
YN1 Kevin Brathwaite, Recruiter in Charge
Tel: (212) 668-7036 Fax: (212) 668-7866

Email: kbrathwaite@cgrc.uscg.mil
Web: www.gocoastguard.com

USCG Recruiting Office Queens
116-18 Queens Blvd.
Forest Hills, NY 11375
PO Esther Martinez, Recruiter in Charge
Tel: (718) 793-4962 Fax: (718) 793-0540
Email: emartinez@cgrc.uscg.mil
Web: www.gocoastguard.com

USCG Recruiting Office Syracuse
Shop City Shopping Ctr., 386 Grant Blvd.
Syracuse, NY 13206
ETC Lawrence McLaren, Recruiter in
Charge
Tel: (315) 437-6135 Fax: (315) 437-2953
Email: lmclaren@cgrc.uscg.mil
Web: www.gocoastguard.com

NAVY, DEPT. OF THE
Naval Reserve Center Brooklyn
Floyd Bennett Field
Brooklyn, NY 11234-7097
Tel: (718) 258-0324 Fax: (718) 258-0780

Navy Recruiting District, Buffalo
300 Pearl St. #200
Buffalo, NY 14202
Tel: (716) 551-5816

Navy Recruiting District, New York
1975 Hempstead Turnpike
East Meadow, NY 11554
Tel: (800) 451-8758

USMC Recruiting Station, Albany
US Army Watervliet Arsenal Bldg. 40-3,
2nd Fl.
Watervliet, NY 12189-4050
Tel: (518) 266-6113
Web: www.marines.com

USMC Recruiting Station, Buffalo
100 Corporate Pkwy.
Buffalo, NY 14226
Tel: (716) 551-4915
Web: www.marines.com

USMC Recruiting Station, New York
605 Stewart Ave.
Garden City, NY 11530-4761
Tel: (516) 228-3684
Web: www.marines.com

POSTAL SERVICE
Albany District
30 Old Karner Rd.
Albany, NY 12288-9291
Josephine D. Grimes, Diversity
Development Specialist
Tel: (518) 452-2219 Fax: (518) 512-4525
Email: jgrimes1@email.usps.gov
Web: www.usps.gov

Long Island District
P.O. Box 7700
Islandia, NY 11760-9997
Betsy Diaz, Diversity Development
Specialist
Tel: (631) 582-7478 Fax: (631) 582-7595
Email: betsy.diaz-konstanzer@usps.gov
Web: www.usps.com

New York District
421 8th Ave. #3028
New York, NY 10199-9811
Evette Corchado, Diversity Development
Specialist
Tel: (212) 330-3935 Fax: (212) 330-2575
Web: www.usps.com

New York Metro Area Office
142-02 20th Ave.
Flushing, NY 11351-0600
Bruce Lederman, Manager of Diversity and
Human Capital Development
Tel: (718) 321-5723 Fax: (718) 463-8243
Email: bruce.lederman@usps.gov
Web: www.usps.gov

Westchester District
1000 Westchester Ave. #3130
White Plains, NY 10610-9411
Enid M. Samuels, Diversity Development
Specialist
Tel: (914) 697-7102 Fax: (914) 697-7152
Email: esamuels@email.usps.gov
Web: www.usps.com

Western New York District
1200 William St. #304
Buffalo, NY 14240-9431
Mary Quinn, Diversity Development
Specialist
Tel: (716) 846-2484 Fax: (716) 846-2407
Web: www.usps.com

SMALL BUSINESS ADMINISTRATION
Disaster Assistance-Disaster Area 1
Disaster Personnel Office
130 S. Elmwood Ave.
Buffalo, NY 14202
Jina M. Koop, Personnel Management
Specialist
Tel: (716) 843-4100 Fax: (716) 282-6151
Email: da1.hr@sba.gov
Web: www.sba.gov

TRANSPORTATION, DEPT. OF
**St. Lawrence Seaway Development
Corporation**
Civil Rights Office
P.O. Box 520
Massena, NY 13662-0520
Vicki Garcia, Director
Tel: (315) 764-3208 Fax: (315) 764-3235
Email: vicki.garcia@sls.dot.gov
Web: www.seaway.dot.gov

NORTH CAROLINA

AIR FORCE, DEPT. OF THE
Pope AFB
Pope AFB, NC 28308-2372
Tel: (800) 423-8723
Web: www.airforce.com

Seymour Johnson AFB
Seymour Johnson AFB, NC 27531-2469
Tel: (800) 423-8723
Web: www.airforce.com

ARMY, DEPT. OF
HQ Army, First Region (ROTC)
US Army Cadet Command
Attn: Public Affairs Office
Fort Bragg, NC 28307-5000
Tel: (910) 396-9415

US Army Recruiting Battalion Raleigh
Public Affairs Office
3117 Poplarwood Ct., Cypress Bldg. #218
Raleigh, NC 27604-1041
Tel: (919) 872-9147/3441

**EQUAL EMPLOYMENT OPPORTUNITY
COMMISSION**
Charlotte District Office
129 W. Trade St. #400
Charlotte, NC 28202
Reuben Daniels, Jr., Director

Tel: (704) 344-6682 Fax: (704) 344-6734
Web: www.eeoc.gov

Greensboro Local Office
2303 W. Meadowview Rd. #201
Greensboro, NC 27407
Michael A. Whitlow, Director
Tel: (336) 547-4188 Fax: (336) 547-4032
Web: www.eeoc.gov

HOMELAND SECURITY, DEPT. OF
USCG Recruiting Office Charlotte
Sugar Creek Professional Bldg., 537 W
Sugar Creek Rd.
Charlotte, NC 28213-6159
PAC Renee E. Gordon, Recruiter in Charge
Tel: (704) 598-2424 Fax: (704) 598-2426
Email: rgordon@cgrc.uscg.mil
Web: www.gocoastguard.com

USCG Recruiting Office Greensboro
4411 High Point Rd. #103
Greensboro, NC 27407-4315
MST1 Daniel Moore, Recruiter in Charge
Tel: (336) 294-6975 Fax: (336) 323-0592
Email: dmoore@cgrc.uscg.mil
Web: www.gocoastguard.com

USCG Recruiting Office Raleigh
2917 Brentwood Rd.
Raleigh, NC 27604-2464
ETC Chad Willits, Recruiter in Charge
Tel: (919) 878-4303 Fax: (919) 878-4460
Email: cwillits@cgrc.uscg.mil
Web: www.gocoastguard.com

USCG Recruiting Office Wilmington
Cornerstone Shopping Ctr., 1616 Shipyard
Blvd. #15
Wilmington, NC 28412
MKC Richard Lyons, Recruiter in Charge
Tel: (910) 791-2593 Fax: (910) 791-5247
Email: rlyons@cgrc.uscg.mil
Web: www.gocoastguard.com

NAVY, DEPT. OF THE
Navy Recruiting District, Raleigh
801 Oberlin Rd.
Raleigh, NC 27605
Tel: (919) 873-1284

USMC Recruiting Station, Raleigh
5000 Falls of Neuse Rd. #404
Raleigh, NC 27609-5408
Tel: (919) 790-3039
Web: www.marines.com

POSTAL SERVICE
Greensboro District
P.O. Box 27499
Greensboro, NC 27498-9000
Patricia H. Gray, Acting Diversity
Development Specialist
Tel: (336) 668-1268 Fax: (336) 668-1218
Web: www.usps.gov

NORTH DAKOTA

AIR FORCE, DEPT. OF THE
Grand Forks AFB
Grand Forks AFB, ND 58205-6338
Tel: (800) 423-8723
Web: www.airforce.com

Minot AFB
Minot AFB, ND 58705-5038
Tel: (800) 423-8723
Web: www.airforce.com

OHIO

AIR FORCE, DEPT. OF THE
Wright Patterson AFB
Wright Patterson AFB, OH 45433-5006
Tel: (800) 423-8723
Web: www.airforce.com

Youngstown Air Reserve Station
Vienna, OH 44473-5904
Tel: (800) 423-8723
Web: www.airforce.com

ARMY, DEPT. OF
US Army Recruiting Battalion Cleveland
Public Affairs Office
1240 E. 9th St. #1269
Cleveland, OH 44199
Tel: (216) 802-1409

US Army Recruiting Battalion Columbus
Public Affairs Office
200 N. High St., New Federal Bldg. #114
Columbus, OH 43215-2483
Tel: (614) 469-2343/2345

ENVIRONMENTAL PROTECTION AGENCY
Human Resources Office
Cincinnati Office
26 W. Martin Luther King Dr.
Cincinnati, OH 45268
Ken Briggs, Director
Tel: (513) 569-7801 Fax: (513) 569-7826
Email: briggs.ken@epa.gov
Web: www.epa.gov

**EQUAL EMPLOYMENT OPPORTUNITY
COMMISSION**
Cincinnati Area Office
550 Main St., John W. Peck Federal Office
Bldg., 10th Fl.
Cincinnati, OH 45202
Wilma L. Javey, Director
Tel: (513) 684-2851 Fax: (513) 684-2361
Web: www.eeoc.gov

Cleveland District Office
1660 W. 2nd St., Tower City Skylight Office
Tower #850
Cleveland, OH 44113-1412
Michael C. Fetzer, Director
Tel: (216) 522-2003 Fax: (216) 522-7395
Web: www.eeoc.gov

FEDERAL RESERVE BANK
Cleveland District Office
Human Resources
1455 E. 6th St.
Cleveland, OH 44114
Elizabeth Robinson, Asst. Vice Pres.
Tel: (216) 579-2000 Fax: (216) 579-3198
Web: www.clevelandfed.org

HOMELAND SECURITY, DEPT. OF
USCG Recruiting Office Cincinnati
7255 Dixie Hwy.
Fairfield, OH 45014-8504
ETC Randy Evans, Recruiter in Charge
Tel: (513) 942-3145 Fax: (513) 942-3149
Email: revans@cgrc.uscg.mil
Web: www.gocoastguard.com

USCG Recruiting Office Cleveland
912 Great Northern Mall
North Olmstead, OH 44070-3394
ETC Kevin Riggs, Recruiter in Charge
Tel: (440) 734-4400 Fax: (440) 734-1643
Email: kriggs@cgrc.uscg.mil
Web: www.gocoastguard.com

USCG Recruiting Office Columbus
6046 Huntley Rd.

Columbus, OH 43229-2508
SCPO Harry Rosa, Recruiter in Charge
Tel: (614) 431-0270 Fax: (614) 431-0368
Email: hrosa@cgrc.uscg.mil
Web: www.gocoastguard.com

NAVY, DEPT. OF THE
Naval Reserve Center Cleveland
1089 E. 9th St.
Cleveland, OH 44114
Tel: (216) 861-3406

Navy Recruiting District, Ohio
200 N. High St. #609
Columbus, OH 43215
Tel: (614) 469-6672

USMC Recruiting Station, Cleveland
7261 Engle Rd. #110
Middleburg Heights, OH 44130-3479
Tel: (440) 243-4010
Web: www.marines.com

POSTAL SERVICE
Cincinnati District
1623 Dalton St. #423
Cincinnati, OH 45234-9431
Jo Ann Hutton, Diversity Development
Specialist
Tel: (513) 684-5250 Fax: (513) 684-5240
Email: jhutton@usps.gov
Web: www.usps.com

Cleveland District
2200 Orange Ave. #238
Cleveland, OH 44101
Gloria Jennings, Diversity Development
Specialist
Tel: (216) 443-4235 Fax: (216) 443-4879
Email: gloria.m.jennings@usps.gov
Web: www.usps.gov

Columbus District
850 Twin River Dr.
Columbus, OH 43216-9402
Deborah O'Neal, Diversity Development
Specialist
Tel: (614) 722-9629 Fax: (614) 722-9649
Email: doneal@email.usps.gov
Web: www.usps.gov

STATE OF OHIO
Attorney's General Office
EEO Office
30 E. Broad St., 16th Fl.
Columbus, OH 43215-3428
Megan Kish, Director
Tel: (614) 466-8911 Fax: (614) 728-7582
Email: mkish@ag.state.oh.us
Web: www.ag.state.oh.us

OKLAHOMA

AIR FORCE, DEPT. OF THE
Altus AFB
Altus AFB, OK 73523-5001
Tel: (800) 423-8723
Web: www.airforce.com

Tinker AFB
Tinker AFB, OK 73145-3014
Tel: (800) 423-8723
Web: www.airforce.com

Vance AFB
Vance AFB, OK 73705-5011
Tel: (800) 423-8723
Web: www.airforce.com

ARMY, DEPT. OF
US Army Recruiting Battalion Oklahoma City

Public Affairs Office
301 NW 6th St. #218
Oklahoma City, OK 73102
Tel: (405) 609-8792/8794

EQUAL EMPLOYMENT OPPORTUNITY COMMISSION
Oklahoma Area Office
210 Park Ave. #1350
Oklahoma City, OK 73102
Donald Stevens, Director
Tel: (405) 231-4911 Fax: (405) 231-4140
Web: www.eeoc.gov

HOMELAND SECURITY, DEPT. OF
USCG Recruiting Office Oklahoma City
7329 S. Western Ave.
Oklahoma City, OK 73139
MKC Brent Divine, Recruiter in Charge
Tel: (405) 231-4483 Fax: (405) 231-4486
Email: bdivine@cgrc.uscg.mil
Web: www.gocoastguard.com

INTERIOR, DEPT. OF THE
Bureau of Indian Affairs
Southern Plains Region, Personnel Office
P.O. Box 1487
Anadarko, OK 73005
Jeannie Cooper, Human Resources Officer
Tel: (405) 247-6673 Fax: (405) 247-3920
Web: www.bia.gov

NAVY, DEPT. OF THE
Naval Reserve Center Oklahoma City
5316 Douglas Blvd.
Oklahoma City, OK 73150-9702
Tel: (405) 733-3368

USMC Recruiting Station, Oklahoma City
301 NW 6th St. #211
Oklahoma City, OK 73102
Tel: (405) 787-1635
Web: www.marines.com

POSTAL SERVICE
Oklahoma District
3030 NW Expressway St. #1042
Oklahoma City, OK 73198-9807
Eugene Talley, Diversity Development Specialist
Tel: (405) 553-6217 Fax: (405) 553-6107
Email: eugene.talley@usps.gov
Web: www.usps.com

OREGON

AIR FORCE, DEPT. OF THE
Portland IAP
Portland IAP, OR 97218-2797
Tel: (800) 423-8723
Web: www.airforce.com

ARMY, DEPT. OF
US Army Recruiting Battalion Portland
Public Affairs Office
6130 NE 78th Ct.
Portland, OR 97218-2853
Tel: (503) 256-1436/1433

INTERIOR, DEPT. OF THE
Bureau of Indians Affairs
Northwest Region, Personnel Office
911 NE 11th Ave.
Portland, OR 97232-4169
Danielle Dutt, Personnel Officer
Tel: (503) 231-6710 Fax: (503) 231-6110
Web: www.bia.gov

NAVY, DEPT. OF THE
Navy Recruiting District, Portland
Airport Business Ctr., 7028 NE 79th Ct.,
Bldg. 2

Portland, OR 97218
Tel: (503) 258-2017

USMC Recruiting Station, Portland
Federal Bldg., 1220 SW 3rd Ave. #519
Portland, OR 97204-2888
Tel: (503) 326-3016
Web: www.marines.com

PENNSYLVANIA

AIR FORCE, DEPT. OF THE
Pittsburgh IAP-ARS
Pittsburgh IAP-ARS, PA 15108-4403
Tel: (800) 423-8723
Web: www.airforce.com

Willowgrove ARS
Willowgrove ARS, PA 19090-5203
Tel: (800) 423-8723
Web: www.airforce.com

ARMY, DEPT. OF
US Army Recruiting Battalion Harrisburg
Public Affairs Office
M Ave., Bldg. 54 #11, New Cumberland
Army Depot
New Cumberland, PA 17070-5099
Tel: (717) 770-6721/7252

US Army Recruiting Battalion Pittsburgh
Public Affairs Office
1000 Liberty Ave., Wm. Moorhead Federal
Bldg., #1404
Pittsburgh, PA 15222-4197
Tel: (412) 395-5879/5786

BOARD OF PROBATION AND PAROLE
Commonwealth of Pennsylvania
EO Office
1101 S. Front St.
Harrisburg, PA 17104-2522
Brenda Kates, Director
Tel: (717) 787-6897 Fax: (717) 772-4185
Email: bkates@state.pa.us
Web: www.pbpp.state.pa.us

DEPARTMENT OF BANKING
Commonwealth of Pennsylvania
Human Resources Office
333 Market St., 16th Fl.
Harrisburg, PA 17101
Kevin Hoffman, Director
Tel: (717) 787-4129 Fax: (717) 705-5492
Email: khoffman@state.pa.us
Web: www.banking.state.pa.us

DEPARTMENT OF COMMUNITY AND ECONOMIC DEVELOPMENT
Commonwealth of Pennsylvania
EEO Office
Keystone Bldg., 4th Fl.
Harrisburg, PA 17120
Brenda Longacre, Human Resources
Analyst/EEO Manager
Tel: (717) 346-7786 Fax: (717) 787-6939
Email: blongacre@state.pa.us
Web: www.newpa.com

DEPARTMENT OF CORRECTIONS
Commonwealth of Pennsylvania
EEO Office
P.O. Box 598
Camp Hill, PA 17001-0598
Rafael Chieke, Director
Tel: (717) 975-4905 Fax: (717) 731-7115
Email: rchieke@state.pa.us
Web: www.cor.state.pa.us

DEPARTMENT OF LABOR AND INDUSTRY
Commonwealth of Pennsylvania
Equal Opportunity Office

L&I Bldg. #514
Harrisburg, PA 17120
Autro Heath, Jr., Director
Tel: (717) 787-1182 Fax: (717) 772-2321
Email: aheath@state.pa.us
Web: www.dli.state.pa.us

DEPARTMENT OF PUBLIC WELFARE
Commonwealth of Pennsylvania
Bureau of Equal Opportunity
H&W Bldg. #223
Harrisburg, PA 17105
Merry Grace Majors, Director
Tel: (717) 787-1146 Fax: (717) 772-4366
Email: mmajors@state.pa.us
Web: www.dpw.state.pa.us

DEPARTMENT OF THE TREASURY
Commonwealth of Pennsylvania
Human Resources Office
103 Finance Bldg.
Harrisburg, PA 17120-0018
Patrick C. Tighe, Director
Tel: (717) 787-5979 Fax: (717) 787-3026
Email: ptighe@state.pa.us
Web: www.patreasury.org

EDUCATION, DEPT. OF
Commonwealth of Pennsylvania
Human Resources Bureau
333 Market St., 11th Fl., Harristown 2
Harrisburg, PA 17126-0333
Susan Shatto, Human Resources Analyst
Tel: (717) 705-2672 Fax: (717) 783-9348
Email: sshatto@state.pa.us
Web: www.state.pa.us

ENERGY, DEPT. OF
National Energy Technology Laboratory
EEO Office
P.O. Box 10940, M/S 922-105
Pittsburgh, PA 15236-0940
Nancy Vargas, EEO Diversity Officer
Tel: (412) 386-4654 Fax: (412) 386-4604
Email: nancy.vargas@netl.doe.gov
Web: www.netl.doe.gov

ENVIRONMENTAL PROTECTION AGENCY
Human Resources Management Branch
Region 3
1650 Arch St. M/C 3PM00
Philadelphia, PA 19103-2029
Cynthia Burrows, EEO Officer
Tel: (215) 814-5326 Fax: (215) 814-5108
Email: burrows.cynthia@epa.gov
Web: www.epa.gov

EQUAL EMPLOYMENT OPPORTUNITY COMMISSION
Philadelphia District Office
21 S. 5th St., The Bourse Bldg. #400
Philadelphia, PA 19106
Marie Tomasso, Director
Tel: (215) 440-2600 Fax: (215) 440-2632
Web: www.eeoc.gov

Pittsburgh Area Office
1001 Liberty Ave. #300, Liberty Ctr.
Pittsburgh, PA 15222-4187
Joseph Hardiman, Director
Tel: (412) 644-3444 Fax: (412) 644-2664
Web: www.eeoc.gov

FISH AND BOAT COMMISSION
Commonwealth of Pennsylvania
Human Resources Office
1601 Elmerton Ave.
Harrisburg, PA 17110
Bernard Matscavage, Personnel Officer
Tel: (717) 705-7820 Fax: (717) 705-7802
Email: bmatscavage@state.pa.us
Web: www.fish.state.pa.us

GENERAL SERVICES ADMINISTRATION
Office of Equal Employment Opportunity
Region 1, 3
20 N. 8th St., The Strawbridges Bldg.
9th Fl.
Philadelphia, PA 19107
Kelly Ann Williams, EEO Officer
Tel: (215) 446-4906 Fax: (215) 446-5126
Email: kellyann.williams@gsa.gov
Web: www.gsa.gov

HOMELAND SECURITY, DEPT. OF
USCG Recruiting Office Harrisburg
4337A Union Deposit Rd., Union Ct.
Harrisburg, PA 17111-2883
BMC Joe Colonna, Recruiter in Charge
Tel: (717) 561-0972 Fax: (717) 561-0975
Email: bcolonna@cgrc.uscg.mil
Web: www.gocoastguard.com

USCG Recruiting Office Philadelphia North
Haverford Avenue Shops.,
2327 Cottman Ave. #48
Philadelphia, PA 19149
BMC Marshall Miller, Recruiter in Charge
Tel: (215) 331-2788 Fax: (215) 473-8956
Email: mmiller@cgrc.uscg.mil
Web: www.gocoastguard.com

USCG Recruiting Office Philadelphia West
Haverford Avenue Shops.,
7567 Haverford Ave.
Philadelphia, PA 19151
BMC Marshal Miller, Recruiter in Charge
Tel: (215) 473-8497 Fax: (215) 473-8956
Email: mmiller@cgrc.uscg.mil
Web: www.gocoastguard.com

USCG Recruiting Office Pittsburgh
7206 McKnight Rd. #104
Pittsburgh, PA 15237-3510
AMTC Troy Klabach, Recruiter in Charge
Tel: (412) 369-2870 Fax: (412) 369-2873
Email: ssnyder@cgrc.uscg.mil
Web: www.gocoastguard.com

HUMAN RELATIONS COMMISSION
Commonwealth of Pennsylvania
Personnel Office
301 Chestnut St. #300
Harrisburg, PA 17101
Richard Fairfax, Director
Tel: (717) 787-4410 Fax: (717) 214-0587
Email: rfairfax@state.pa.us
Web: www.phrc.state.pa.us

INSURANCE DEPARTMENT, BUREAU OF ADMINISTRATION
Commonwealth of Pennsylvania
Human Resources/EEO Office
1326 Strawberry Sq.
Harrisburg, PA 17120
Kathy Culbertson, Director
Tel: (717) 705-4194 Fax: (717) 705-3873
Email: kculbertso@state.pa.us
Web: www.state.pa.us

INTERIOR, DEPT. OF THE
National Park Service
Northeast Region, Office of Human
Resources, Staffing Division
200 Chestnut St., 3rd Fl.
Philadelphia, PA 19106
Tel: (215) 597-7067 Fax: (215) 597-5747
Web: www.nps.gov

LABOR, DEPT. OF
Employment and Training Administration
Office of Youth Programs/Job Corps
The Curtis Center #815 East., 170
Independence Mall West
Philadelphia, PA 19106-3315

Lynn Intrepidi, Regional Director
Tel: (215) 861-5501 Fax: (215) 861-5520
Email: intrepidi.lynn@dol.gov
Web: www.dol.gov

LIQUOR CONTROL BOARD
Commonwealth of Pennsylvania
EO Office
408 Northwest Office Bldg.
Harrisburg, PA 17124-0001
Kathy Blatt, Equal Opportunity Specialist
Tel: (717) 705-6958 Fax: (717) 705-6218
Email: kblatt@state.pa.us
Web: www.lcb.state.pa.us

MILITARY AND VETERANS AFFAIRS, DEPT. OF
Bureau of Administrative Services
EEO Office
DMVA Fishers Ave.
Annville, PA 17003-5002
Kristy L. Smith, Director
Tel: (717) 861-8796 Fax: (717) 861-8628
Email: krsmith@state.pa.us
Web: www.state.pa.us

MILK MARKETING BOARD
Commonwealth of Pennsylvania
Human Resources Office
2301 N. Cameron St., #110
Harrisburg, PA 17110
Timothy Moyer, Chief of Support Services/
Personnel
Tel: (717) 787-4231 Fax: (717) 783-6492
Email: tmoyer@state.pa.us
Web: www.mmb.state.pa.us

NAVY, DEPT. OF THE
Navy Recruiting District, Philadelphia
700 Robbins Ave., Bldg. 2D
Philadelphia, PA 19111
Tel: (215) 697-3984

Navy Recruiting District, Pittsburgh
1000 Liberty Ave. #713
Pittsburgh, PA 15222
Tel: (412) 395-5895

USMC Recruiting Station, Harrisburg
Bldg. 54, #5DDC
New Cumberland, PA 17070-5006
Tel: (717) 770-4227
Web: www.marines.com

USMC Recruiting Station, Pittsburgh
New Federal Bldg., 1000 Liberty Ave.
#1512
Pittsburgh, PA 15222-4179
Tel: (412) 395-4917
Web: www.marines.com

OFFICE OF ADMINISTRATION
Bureau of Equal Employment Opportunity
Finance Bldg. #222
Harrisburg, PA 17120-1005
Beverly LaVia, Director
Tel: (717) 783-1130 Fax: (717) 472-3302
Web: www.state.pa.us

PENNSYLVANIA HISTORICAL AND MUSEUM COMMISSION
Division of Personnel Services
300 N. St.
Harrisburg, PA 17120
Jane Peyton, Personnel Director
Tel: (717) 787-3362 Fax: (717) 783-9924
Email: jpeyton@state.pa.us
Web: www.phmc.state.pa.us

PENNSYLVANIA PUBLIC SCHOOL EMPLOYEES' RETIREMENT SYSTEM
Human Resources Division
5 N. 5th St.

Harrisburg, PA 17101-1905
Maribel Laluz, Director
Tel: (717) 720-4737 Fax: (717) 783-7275
Email: ra-ps-contact@state.pa.us
Web: www.psers.state.pa.us

POSTAL SERVICE
Eastern Area Office
5315 Campbells Run Rd.
Pittsburgh, PA 15277-7050
Sue Marsh, Senior Diversity Program
Coordinator
Tel: (412) 494-2567 Fax: (650) 357-6375
Email: susan.l.marsh@usps.gov
Web: www.usps.com

Erie District
2709 Legion Rd.
Erie, PA 16515-9741
Wendy Nelson-Smith, Diversity
Development Specialist
Tel: (814) 678-6574 Fax: (814) 836-7215
Email: wnelsons@email.usps.gov
Web: www.usps.com

Harrisburg District
1425 Crooked Hill Rd.
Harrisburg, PA 17107-0041
Bobbi Reid, Diversity Development
Specialist
Tel: (717) 257-5380 Fax: (717) 257-2152
Email: breid1@email.usps.gov
Web: www.usps.com

Philadelphia District
P.O. Box 7237
Philadelphia, PA 19101-7237
Linda Kelley, Diversity Development
Specialist
Tel: (215) 895-8040 Fax: (215) 895-8611
Web: www.usps.com

Pittsburgh District
1001 California Ave. #2358A
Pittsburgh, PA 15290-9600
Clarissa A. Scott-Jones, Diversity
Development Specialist
Tel: (412) 359-7510 Fax: (412) 359-7535
Email: clarissa.scott-jones@usps.gov
Web: www.usps.gov

PUBLIC TELEVISION NETWORK
Commonwealth of Pennsylvania
EEO Office
24 Northeast Dr.
Hershey, PA 17033
Barb Frantz, Administrative Assistant
Tel: (717) 534-1502 Fax: (717) 533-4236
Email: bfrantz@state.pa.us
Web: www.pptn.state.pa.us

SECURITIES COMMISSION
Commonwealth of Pennsylvania
Personnel Office
Eastgate Office Bldg., 2nd Fl.
Harrisburg, PA 17102-1410
Margaret Hivner, Director
Tel: (717) 783-4689 Fax: (717) 783-5122
Email: mahivner@state.pa.us
Web: www.psc.state.pa.us

SOCIAL SECURITY ADMINISTRATION
Philadelphia Region
Civil Rights and Equal Employment Office
P.O. Box 8788
Philadelphia, PA 19101
Agnes T. Sampson, Manager
Tel: (215) 597-1694 Fax: (215) 597-2827
Web: www.ssa.gov

STATE EMPLOYEES' RETIREMENT SYSTEM
Commonwealth of Pennsylvania
Human Resources Office
30 N. 3rd St., 3rd Fl.
Harrisburg, PA 17108-1147
Cheryl Krchnar, Personnel Officer
Tel: (717) 783-8085 Fax: (717) 783-0581
Email: ckrchnar@state.pa.us
Web: www.sers.state.pa.us

PUERTO RICO

HOMELAND SECURITY, DEPT. OF
USCG Recruiting Office Aguadilla
USCG Air Station Borinquen, 260 Guard
Rd.
Aguadilla, PR 00603
GM1 Reynaldo Gonzalez, Recruiter in
Charge
Tel: (787) 890-8400 X8020
Fax: (787) 890-8407
Email: rgonzalez@cgrc.uscg.mil
Web: www.gocoastguard.com

USCG Recruiting Office San Juan
100 Gran Bulevar Los Paseos. #102
San Juan, PR 00926
SKC Alfredo Rodríguez, Recruiter in Charge
Tel: (787) 292-0210 Fax: (787) 292-0405
Email: arodriguez@cgrc.uscg.mil
Web: www.gocoastguard.com

OFFICE OF PERSONNEL MANAGEMENT
San Juan Service Center
Torre de Plaza las Americas #1114, 525
F.D., Roosevelt Ave.
San Juan, PR 00918-8026
Vivian Fernandez, Senior Personnel
Specialist
Tel: (787) 766-5620 Fax: (787) 766-5598
Email: lxrodrig@opm.gov
Web: www.opm.gov

RHODE ISLAND

HOMELAND SECURITY, DEPT. OF
USCG Recruiting Office Providence
380 Westminster St.
Providence, RI 02903-3246
AET1 Darrin Merrill, Recruiter in Charge
Tel: (401) 421-1291 Fax: (401) 528-4371
Email: dmerrill@cgrc.uscg.mil
Web: www.gocoastguard.com

POSTAL SERVICE
Southeast New England District
24 Corliss St.
Providence, RI 02904
Mary Hahnen, Diversity Development
Specialist
Tel: (401) 276-6905 Fax: (401) 276-6968
Web: www.usps.gov

STATE OF RHODE ISLAND
EEO Office
1 Capitol Hill
Providence, RI 02908
A. Vincent Igliozzi, Administrator
Tel: (401) 222-3090 Fax: (401) 222-2490

SOUTH CAROLINA

AIR FORCE, DEPT. OF THE
Charleston AFB
Charleston AFB, SC 29404-5021
Tel: (800) 423-8723
Web: www.airforce.com

Shaw AFB
Shaw AFB, SC 29152-5028
Tel: (800) 423-8723
Web: www.airforce.com

ARMY, DEPT. OF
US Army Recruiting Battalion Columbia
Public Affairs Office
1835 Assembly St., Strom Thurmond
Federal Bldg., #733
Columbia, SC 29201-2491
Tel: (803) 765-5640

EQUAL EMPLOYMENT OPPORTUNITY COMMISSION
Greenville Local Office
301 N. Main St. #1402
Greenville, SC 29601-9916
Patricia B. Fuller, Director
Tel: (864) 241-4400 Fax: (864) 241-4402
Web: www.eeoc.gov

HOMELAND SECURITY, DEPT. OF
USCG Recruiting Office Charleston
1650 Sam Rittenberg Blvd. #1
Charleston, SC 29407-4933
SC Charles Franklin, Recruiter in Charge
Tel: (843) 766-7315 Fax: (843) 766-7630
Email: cfranklin@cgrc.uscg.mil
Web: www.gocoastguard.com
USCG Recruiting Office Columbia
Capitol Center Shopping Ctr.,
201 Columbia Mall Blvd. #207
Columbia, SC 29223
SKCS Glenda Smith-Leeth, Recruiter in
Charge
Tel: (803) 699-7230 Fax: (803) 699-6149
Email: gleeth@cgrc.uscg.mil
Web: www.gocoastguard.com

NAVY, DEPT. OF THE
Naval Reserve Center Columbia
513 Pickens St.
Columbia, SC 29201-4198
Tel: (803) 256-7167 Fax: (803) 156-7096

USMC Recruiting Station, Columbia
9600 2 Notch Rd. #17
Columbia, SC 29223-4379
Tel: (803) 788-9251
Web: www.marines.com

POSTAL SERVICE
Greater South Carolina District
P.O. Box 929801
Columbia, SC 29292-9801
Mary Ellen Padin, Diversity Development
Specialist
Tel: (803) 926-6429 Fax: (803) 926-6434
Email: maryellen.padin@usps.gov
Web: www.usps.gov

SOUTH CAROLINA STATE WIDE
Minority Business Development Center
Columbia MBDC
1515 Richland St. #C
Columbia, SC 29201
Greg Davis, Director
Tel: (803) 779-5905 Fax: (803) 779-5915
Email: davisg@desainc.com
Web: www.scmbdc.com

SOUTH DAKOTA

AIR FORCE, DEPT. OF THE
Ellsworth AFB
Ellsworth AFB, SD 57706-4700
Tel: (800) 423-8723
Web: www.airforce.com

STATE OF SOUTH DAKOTA
Bureau of Personnel
500 E. Capitol Ave.
Pierre, SD 57501
Jeff Bloomberg, Attorney
Tel: (605) 773-3148 Fax: (605) 773-4344
Web: www.state.sd.us/bop

TENNESSEE

AIR FORCE, DEPT. OF THE
Arnold AFB
Arnold AFB, TN 37389-3314
Tel: (800) 423-8723
Web: www.airforce.com

ARMY, DEPT. OF
US Army Recruiting Battalion Nashville
Public Affairs Office
2517 Perimeter Place Dr.
Nashville, TN 37214
Tel: (615) 871-4172

EQUAL EMPLOYMENT OPPORTUNITY COMMISSION
Memphis District Office
1407 Union Ave. #621
Memphis, TN 38104
Shirley Richardson, Director
Tel: (901) 544-0115 Fax: (901) 544-0111
Web: www.eeoc.gov
Nashville Area Office
50 Vantage Way #202
Nashville, TN 37228-9940
Sarah L. Smith, Director
Tel: (615) 736-5820 Fax: (615) 736-2107
Web: www.eeoc.gov

HOMELAND SECURITY, DEPT. OF
USCG Recruiting Office Knoxville
Blue Grass Landing., 9321 Northshore Dr.
Knoxville, TN 37922
OSCS Paul Hunyady, Recruiter in Charge
Tel: (865) 690-1164 Fax: (865) 690-4544
Email: phunyady@cgrc.uscg.mil
Web: www.gocoastguard.com

USCG Recruiting Office Memphis
2830 Coleman Rd. #G
Memphis, TN 38128
OSC Gerald Jett, Recruiter in Charge
Tel: (901) 380-9873 Fax: (901) 380-1395
Email: gjett@cgrc.uscg.mil
Web: www.gocoastguard.com

USCG Recruiting Office Nashville
The Market at Bell Forge., 5308 Mount
View Rd. #C
Antioch, TN 37013-2307
BMC Randy L. Price, Recruiter in Charge
Tel: (615) 731-3408 Fax: (615) 731-4992
Email: rprice@cgrc.uscg.mil
Web: www.gocoastguard.com

NAVY, DEPT. OF THE
Naval Reserve Center Memphis
5722 Integrity Dr., Bldg. N-930
Millington, TN 38128
Tel: (901) 874-5056 Fax: (901) 874-5841

Navy Recruiting District, Nashville
640 Grassmere Park #104

Nashville, TN 37211
Tel: (615) 332-0824

USMC Recruiting Station, Nashville
2519 Perimeter Place Dr.
Nashville, TN 37214-3681
Tel: (615) 627-1526
Web: www.marines.com

POSTAL SERVICE
Area District
225 N. Humphreys Blvd.
Memphis, TN 38166-0840
Betty J. Davis-Smith, Manager, Diversity/
Human Capital Development
Tel: (901) 747-7209 Fax: (901) 747-7206
Web: www.usps.gov

Tennessee District
811 Royal Pkwy.
Nashville, TN 37229-9771
Sheila Baskins, Diversity Development
Specialist
Tel: (615) 872-5693 Fax: (615) 885-9374
Web: www.usps.com

TENNESSEE VALLEY AUTHORITY
400 W Summit Hill Dr.
Knoxville, TN 37902-1499
Tel: (865) 632-8981
Email: tvainfo@tva.com
Web: www.tva.gov

TEXAS

AIR FORCE, DEPT. OF THE
Brooks AFB
Brooks AFB, TX 78235-5358
Tel: (800) 423-8723
Web: www.airforce.com
Dyess AFB
Dyess AFB, TX 79607-1517
Tel: (800) 423-8723
Web: www.airforce.com

Goodfellow AFB
Goodfellow AFB, TX 76908-3216
Tel: (800) 423-8723
Web: www.airforce.com

Lackland AFB
Lackland AFB, TX 78236-5226
Tel: (800) 423-8723
Web: www.airforce.com

Laughlin AFB
Laughlin AFB, TX 78843-5230
Tel: (800) 423-8723
Web: www.airforce.com

Sheppard AFB
Sheppard AFB, TX 76311-2927
Tel: (800) 423-8723
Web: www.airforce.com

ARMY, DEPT. OF
US Army 5th Recruiting Brigade
South Central Region, Public Affairs Office
P.O. Box 8277
Bldg. 2064, Fort Sam Houston
Wainwright Station, TX 78277
Tel: (210) 221-1900/0176

US Army Recruiting Battalion Dallas
Public Affairs Office
1350 Walnut Hill Ln. #150
Irving, TX 75038-3025
Tel: (972) 756-0842

US Army Recruiting Battalion Houston
Public Affairs Office
1919 Smith St. #1529
Houston, TX 77002
Tel: (713) 209-3220/3222

US Army Recruiting Battalion San Antonio
Public Affairs Office
1265 Buck Rd., Bldg. 2003
Fort Sam Houston, TX 78234-5034
Tel: (210) 295-0624/0626

ENVIRONMENTAL PROTECTION AGENCY
Human Resources Office
Region 6
1445 Ross Ave., #1200 M/C 6MD-A
Dallas, TX 75202-2733
Richard Martinez, Human Resource
Manager
Tel: (214) 665-6563 Fax: (214) 665-6538
Email: martinez.richard@epa.gov
Web: www.epa.gov

EQUAL EMPLOYMENT OPPORTUNITY COMMISSION
Dallas District Office
207 S. Houston St., 3rd Fl.
Dallas, TX 75202
Mike Fetzer, Director
Tel: (214) 253-2700 Fax: (214) 253-2720
Web: www.eeoc.gov

El Paso Area Office
300 E. Main St. #500
El Paso, TX 79901
Robert Calderon, Director
Tel: (915) 534-6700 Fax: (915) 534-6701
Web: www.eeoc.gov

Houston District Office
1919 Smith St., Mickey Leland Federal
Bldg. #600 & 700
Houston, TX 77002-8049
Mike Fetzer, Director
Tel: (713) 209-3320 Fax: (713) 209-3381
Web: www.eeoc.gov

San Antonio District Office
5410 Fredericksburg Rd., Mockingbird
Plz. II, #200
San Antonio, TX 78229
Pedro Esquivel, Director
Tel: (210) 281-7600 Fax: (210) 281-7690
Web: www.eeoc.gov

FEDERAL RESERVE BANK
Dallas District Office
Human Resources/EEO
2200 N. Pearl St.
Dallas, TX 75201-2272
Bob Williams, Assistant Vice President
Tel: (214) 922-5270 Fax: (214) 922-6355
Email: info@dallasfed.org
Web: www.dallasfed.org

GENERAL SERVICES ADMINISTRATION
Office of Equal Employment Opportunity
819 Taylor St. #7A12
Fort Worth, TX 76102-6105
James Hood, EEO Officer
Tel: (817) 978-3838 Fax: (817) 978-4179
Email: james.hood@gsa.gov
Web: www.gsa.gov

Immigration and Naturalization Service
San Antonio District Office, Administrative
Office
8940 Fourwinds Dr.
San Antonio, TX 78239
Annie Ross, Program Manager/Special
Emphasis Programs

Tel: (210) 967-7125 Fax: (210) 967-7099
Email: annie.ross@dhs.gov
Web: www.dhs.gov

USCG Recruiting Office Corpus Christi
Wind Chase Shopping Ctr., 2033 Airline
Rd. #E-4
Corpus Christi, TX 78412
AET1 David Ozuna, Recruiter in Charge
Tel: (361) 993-6977 Fax: (361) 993-9810
Email: dozuna@cgrc.uscg.mil
Web: www.gocoastguard.com

USCG Recruiting Office Dallas
Beltline Village Shopping Center., 3455 N.
Beltline Road
Irving, TX 75062
BMC Brian Lee, Recruiter in Charge
Tel: (972) 255-0165 Fax: (972) 255-6397
Email: blee@cgrc.uscg.mil
Web: www.gocoastguard.com

USCG Recruiting Office El Paso
9100 Viscount Blvd. #E
El Paso, TX 79925
ETC Jarrod Purseglove, Recruiter in Charge
Tel: (915) 591-6741 Fax: (915) 591-6766
Email: jpurseglove@cgrc.uscg.mil
Web: www.gocoastguard.com

USCG Recruiting Office Houston Central
Gulfgate Center Mall., 3111 Woodridge
Ave. #160
Houston, TX 77087
HSC Travis Biggerstaff, Recruiter in Charge
Tel: (713) 641-3559 Fax: (713) 641-5341
Email: tbiggerstaff@cgrc.uscg.mil
Web: www.gocoastguard.com

USCG Recruiting Office Houston West
12807 Westheimer Rd.
Houston, TX 77077
PS1 Patrick Zinck, Recruiter in Charge
Tel: (281) 556-1460 Fax: (281) 556-1534
Email: pzinck@cgrc.uscg.mil
Web: www.gocoastguard.com

USCG Recruiting Office San Antonio East
River Oaks Plz., 8347 Perrin Beitel
San Antonio, TX 78218
YNC Bruce Crawford, Recruiter in Charge
Tel: (210) 590-9760 Fax: (210) 590-9763
Email: bcrawford@cgrc.uscg.mil
Web: www.gocoastguard.com

USCG Recruiting Office San Antonio West
Ingram Place Shopping Ctr., 3227
Wurzbach Rd.
San Antonio, TX 78238
YNC Bruce Crawford, Recruiter in Charge
Tel: (210) 680-5475 Fax: (210) 680-5509
Email: bcrawford@cgrc.uscg.mil
Web: www.gocoastguard.com

INTERIOR, DEPT. OF THE
National Park Service
San Antonio Missions National Historical
Parks
2202 Roosevelt Ave.
San Antonio, TX 78210-4919
Karen Steed, Human Resources Specialist
Tel: (210) 534-8875 X240 Fax: (210)
534-1106
Email: karen_steed@nps.gov
Web: www.nps.gov/saan

JUSTICE, DEPT. OF
Attorney's Office
816 Congress Ave. #1000
Austin, TX 78701
Barbara Brown, African American
Employment Program Manager

Tel: (512) 916-5858 Fax: (512) 916-5854
Email: barbara.brown@usdoj.gov
Web: www.usdoj.gov

LABOR, DEPT. OF
Employment and Training Administration
Office of Youth Programs/Job Corps
525 Griffin St. #403
Dallas, TX 75202
Joan Boswell, Regional Director
Tel: (214) 767-2114 Fax: (214) 767-2148
Web: www.dallasregioncdss.org

NAVY, DEPT. OF THE
Naval Reserve Recruiting Command Area South
1564 Headquarters Ave.
Ft. Worth, TX 76127-1564
Tel: (817) 782-6131/69

Navy Recruiting District, Dallas
6440 N. Beltline Rd. #150
Irving, TX 75063
Tel: (972) 714-8300

USMC Recruiting Station, Dallas
207 S. Houston St. #146
Dallas, TX 75202-4703
Tel: (214) 655-3481
Web: www.marines.com

USMC Recruiting Station, Ft. Worth
3313 Pioneer Pkwy.
Pantego, TX 76013
Tel: (817) 303-3488
Web: www.marines.com

USMC Recruiting Station, Houston
701 San Jacinto St. #230
Houston, TX 77002-3622
Tel: (713) 718-4282
Web: www.marines.com

USMC Recruiting Station, San Antonio
1265 Buck Rd. #MC
Fort Sam Houston, TX 78234-5034
Tel: (210) 295-1006
Web: www.marines.com

POSTAL SERVICE
Dallas District
951 W. Bethel Rd.
Coppell, TX 75099-9852
Gail Lofton, Diversity Development Specialist
Tel: (972) 393-6665 Fax: (972) 393-6502
Web: www.usps.gov

Forth Worth District
4600 Mark IV Pkwy.
Fort Worth, TX 76161-9100
Linda A. Brantley, Diversity Development Specialist
Tel: (817) 317-3333 Fax: (817) 317-3320
Web: www.usps.gov

Rio Grande District
1 Post Office Dr.
San Antonio, TX 78284-9425
Alice A. Orta, Diversity Development Specialist
Tel: (210) 368-5563 Fax: (210) 368-8409
Email: aorta@email.usps.com
Web: www.usps.com

Southwest Area Office
P.O. Box 225459
Dallas, TX 75222-5459
Vickie Tovar, Senior Diversity Program Coordinator
Tel: (214) 819-8736 Fax: (214) 819-8956
Email: vickie.a.tovar@usps.gov
Web: www.usps.com

SMALL BUSINESS ADMINISTRATION
Disaster Assistance-Disaster Area 3
Disaster Personnel Office
14925 Kingport Rd.
Ft. Worth, TX 76155
Kandye Wells, Personnel Officer
Tel: (817) 868-2300 Fax: (817) 684-5621
Email: kandye.wells@sba.gov
Web: www.sba.gov

SOCIAL SECURITY ADMINISTRATION
Dallas Region
EEO Office
1301 Young St. #500
Dallas, TX 75202
Emerson Lattimore, Manager
Tel: (214) 767-3036 Fax: (214) 767-4338
Email: emerson.lattimore@ssa.gov
Web: www.ssa.gov

STATE OF TEXAS
Office of the Governor
Human Resources
P.O. Box 12428
Austin, TX 78711
Edna Jackson, Director
Tel: (512) 463-1740 Fax: (512) 463-8464
Email: humanresources@governor.state.tx.us
Web: www.governor.state.tx.us

Texas Workforce Commission
Human Resources
101 E. 15th St. #230
Austin, TX 78778-0001
Brenda Nickles, Acting Director
Tel: (512) 463-2314 Fax: (512) 463-2832
Email: brenda.nickles@twc.state.tx.us
Web: www.twc.state.tx.us

VETERANS AFFAIRS, DEPT. OF
South Texas Veterans Health Care System
EEO Office
7400 Merton Minter Blvd., Audie L. Murphy VA.
San Antonio, TX 78229-4404
Laura Faust, Manager
Tel: (210) 617-5300 Fax: (210) 949-3304
Email: laura.faust@med.va.gov
Web: www.vasthcs.med.va.gov

UTAH

AIR FORCE, DEPT. OF THE
Hill AFB
Hill AFB, UT 84056-5819
Tel: (800) 423-8723
Web: www.airforce.com

ARMY, DEPT. OF
US Army Recruiting Battalion Salt Lake City
Public Affairs Office
2830 S. Redwood Rd.
Salt Lake City, UT 84119-4708
Tel: (801) 974-9518/9519

DEPARTMENT OF COMMUNITY AND CULTURE
State of Utah
State Office of African Affairs
324 S. State St. #500
Salt Lake City, UT 84111
Michael Styles, Director
Tel: (801) 538-8791 Fax: (801) 538-8678
Email: mstyles@utah.gov
Web: http://ethnicoffice.utah.gov

HOMELAND SECURITY, DEPT. OF
USCG Recruiting Office Salt Lake City
Roy Shopping Ctr., 5639 S. 1900 W. #302
Roy, UT 84067-2301

HSC David Holcomb, Recruiter in Charge
Tel: (801) 525-1904 Fax: (801) 525-1925
Email: dholcomb@cgrc.uscg.mil
Web: www.gocoastguard.com

INTERIOR, DEPT. OF THE
Bureau of Reclamation
Upper Colorado Regional Office
125 S. State St. #6107
Salt Lake City, UT 84138-1147
Kathy Nicholson, Acting Human Resources Officer
Tel: (801) 524-3656 Fax: (801) 524-3187
Email: knicholson@uc.usbr.gov
Web: www.usbr.gov

NAVY, DEPT. OF THE
USMC Recruiting Station, Salt Lake City
1279 W. 2200 South Bldg. #A
West Valley City, UT 84119-1471
Tel: (801) 954-0418
Web: www.marines.com

POSTAL SERVICE
Salt Lake City District
1760 W. 2100 South
Salt Lake City, UT 84199-2922
Pania Heimuli, Diversity Development Specialist
Tel: (801) 974-2922 Fax: (801) 974-2975
Email: pania.heimuli@usps.gov
Web: www.usps.com

VIRGINIA

AIR FORCE, DEPT. OF THE
Langley AFB
Langley AFB, VA 23665-2096
Tel: (800) 423-8723
Web: www.airforce.com

ARLINGTON COUNTY GOVERNMENT
Human Resources Department
2100 Clarendon Blvd. #511
Arlington, VA 22201
Hilaria Heilman, Human Resources Analyst
Tel: (703) 228-3506 Fax: (703) 228-3265
Email: hheilm@arlingtonva.us
Web: www.arlingtonva.us

ARMY, DEPT. OF
Fort Myer, EEO Office
204 Lee Ave.
Fort Myers, VA 22211-1199
James Winbush, EEO Specialist
Tel: (703) 696-3545 Fax: (703) 696-8588
Email: james.winbush@fmmc.army.mil
Web: www.fmmc.army.mil

EEO & Civil Rights Office
1901 S. Bell St. #207
Arlington, VA 22202-4508
Peguine Taylor, Black Employment Program Manager
Tel: (703) 607-2339 Fax: (703) 607-0084
Email: peguine.taylor@hqda.army.mil

HQ Army
2531 Jefferson David Hwy. #9E22
Arlington, VA 22202-3905
Jim Halloran, Special Program Manager
Tel: (703) 604-2945 Fax: (703) 602-3491
Email: hallojm@hqda.army.mil

HQ Army
US Army Cadet Command
Bldg. 56 Patch Rd.
Fort Monroe, VA 23651-5000
Tel: (757) 788-4610

Military Surface Deployment and Distribution Command
200 Stovall St. #12S71
Alexandria, VA 22332-5000
Emma Ruffin, Acting EEO Director
Tel: (703) 428-2105 Fax: (703) 428-3318
Email: Emma.Ruffin@hqda.army.mil

DEFENSE, DEPT. OF
Defense Commissary Agency
EEO Office
1300 E Ave.
Ft. Lee, VA 23801-1800
Claudie Grant, Jr., Diversity Manager
Tel: (804) 734-8579 Fax: (804) 734-8028
Email: claudie.grant@deca.mil
Web: www.commissaries.com

Defense Contract Audit Agency
EEO Office
8725 John J. Kingman Rd. #2135
Ft. Belvoir, VA 22060
Vicky O'Donnell, Director
Tel: (703) 767-1240 Fax: (703) 767-1228
Email: vicky.o'donnell@dcaa.mil
Web: www.dcaa.mil

Inspector General
EEO Office
400 Army Navy Dr. #336
Arlington, VA 22202
Kerry Brown, Acting Director
Tel: (703) 604-9710 Fax: (703) 604-0044
Email: kbrown@dodig.osd.mil
Web: www.dodig.osd.mil

National Guard Bureau
Equal Employment Opportunity Division
1411 Jefferson Davis Hwy. #2400
Arlington, VA 22202
Phyllis Brantley, Special Emphasis Program Manager
Tel: (703) 607-0782 Fax: (703) 607-0790
Email: phyllis.brantley@ngb.ang.af.mil
Web: www.ngb.army.mil

EQUAL EMPLOYMENT OPPORTUNITY COMMISSION
Norfolk Area Office
200 Granby St., Federal Bldg. #739
Norfolk, VA 23510
Herbert Brown, Director
Tel: (757) 441-3470 Fax: (757) 441-6720
Web: www.eeoc.gov

Richmond Area Office
830 E. Main St., 6th Fl.
Richmond, VA 23219
Gloria L. Underwood, Director
Tel: (804) 771-2200 Fax: (804) 771-2222
Web: www.eeoc.gov

FAIRFAX COUNTY PUBLIC SCHOOLS
Human Resources Recruitment Office
6815 Edsall Rd.
Springfield, VA 22151
Pamela McKnight, Recruitment Coordinator
Tel: (703) 750-8519 Fax: (703) 750-8593
Email: pamela.mcknight@fcps.edu
Web: www.fcps.edu

FARM CREDIT ADMINISTRATION
EEO and Office of the Ombudsman
1501 Farm Credit Dr.
McLean, VA 22102-5090
Eric Howard, Director
Tel: (703) 883-4481 Fax: (703) 734-5784
Email: howarde@fca.gov
Web: www.fca.gov

HOMELAND SECURITY, DEPT. OF
USCG Recruiting Office Fredericksburg
4300 Plank Rd. #160
Fredericksburg, VA 22408
BMC Howard McCarthy, Recruiter in Charge
Tel: (540) 785-4068 Fax: (540) 785-4085
Email: cthompson@cgrc.uscg.mil
Web: www.gocoastguard.com

USCG Recruiting Office Hampton Roads
1011 Eden Wy. North #A
Chesapeake, VA 23320-2768
YNC Rhonda Killmon, Recruiter in Charge
Tel: (757) 312-0514
Email: jhoesli@cgrc.uscg.mil
Web: www.gocoastguard.com

USCG Recruiting Office Potomac Mills
2700 Potomac Mills Cir. #832
Woodbridge, VA 22193
YN1 Justin Batton, Recruiter in Charge
Tel: (703) 492-3949
Email: jbatton@cgrc.uscg.mil
Web: www.gocoastguard.com

USCG Recruiting Office Richmond
10447 Midlothian Trnpk.
Richmond, VA 23235
MK2 Jeffery Keim, Recruiter in Charge
Tel: (804) 771-8635 Fax: (804) 771-8076
Email: jkeim@cgrc.uscg.mil
Web: www.gocoastguard.com

INTER-AMERICAN FOUNDATION
901 N. Stuart St., 10th Fl.
Arlington, VA 22203
Tel: (703) 306-4301 Fax: (703) 306-4365
Email: info@iaf.gov
Web: www.iaf.gov

INTERIOR, DEPT. OF THE
Bureau of Land Management
Virginia State Office, EEO Office
7450 Boston Blvd.
Springfield, VA 22153
Lynda Nix, EEO Manager
Tel: (703) 440-1593 Fax: (703) 440-1797
Email: lynda_nix@es.blm.gov
Web: www.blm.gov

Fish and Wildlife Service
Directorate of Civil Rights
4401 N. Fairfax Dr. #200
Arlington, VA 22203
Pedro De Jesus, EEO Manager
Tel: (703) 358-2552 Fax: (703) 358-2030
Email: pedro_dejesus@fws.gov
Web: www.fws.gov

Forest Service, Jefferson National Forest
Human Resources
5162 Valley Pointe Pkwy.
Roanoke, VA 24019
Laura Germaine, Personnel Manager
Tel: (540) 265-5245 Fax: (540) 265-5250
Email: lgermaine@fs.fed.us
Web: www.fs.fed.us

Minerals Management Service
EEO Office
381 Elden St. M/S 2900
Herndon, VA 20170
Rosa Thomas, EEO Specialist
Tel: (703) 787-1314 Fax: (703) 787-1601
Email: rosa.thomas@mms.gov
Web: www.mms.gov

JUSTICE, DEPT. OF
Executive Office for Immigration Review
EEO Office
5107 Leesburg Pike #1902

Falls Church, VA 22041
Wanda Owens, EEO Manager
Tel: (703) 305-0994 Fax: (703) 605-0367
Email: wanda.owens@usdoj.gov
Web: www.usdoj.gov

LABOR, DEPT. OF
Mine Safety and Health Administration
Office of Diversity Outreach and Employee Safety
1100 Wilson Blvd. #2407
Arlington, VA 22209-3939
Michael Thompson, Director
Tel: (202) 693-9882 Fax: (202) 693-9881
Email: thompson.michael@dol.gov
Web: www.msha.gov

NATIONAL CREDIT UNION ADMINISTRATION
EEO Office
1775 Duke St. #4093
Alexandria, VA 22314-3401
Marilyn Gannon, Director
Tel: (703) 518-6325 Fax: (703) 518-6319
Email: mggannon@ncua.gov
Web: www.ncua.gov

NATIONAL SCIENCE FOUNDATION
Equal Opportunity Programs
EEO Office
255 S. Wilson Blvd.
Arlington, VA 22230
Ronald Branch, Director
Tel: (703) 292-8020 Fax: (703) 292-9072
Email: rbranch@nsf.gov
Web: www.nsf.gov

NAVY, DEPT. OF THE
Navy Recruiting District, Richmond
411 E. Franklin St. #101
Richmond, VA 23219-2243
Tel: (804) 771-2001 Fax: (804) 771-2082

USMC Recruiting Station, Richmond
9210 Arboretum Pkwy. #220
Richmond, VA 23236-3472
Tel: (804) 272-0227
Web: www.marines.com

OFFICE OF PERSONNEL MANAGEMENT
Norfolk Service Center
200 Granby St., Federal Bldg. #500
Norfolk, VA 23510-1886
Alan Nelson, Director
Tel: (757) 441-3373 Fax: (757) 441-6280
Email: norfolk@opm.gov
Web: www.opm.gov

POSTAL SERVICE
Northern Virginia District
8409 Lee Hwy. #216A
Merrifield, VA 22116-9996
Julie Lane, Diversity Development Specialist
Tel: (703) 698-6614
Email: jlane3@email.usps.gov
Web: www.usps.gov

Richmond District
1801 Brook Rd.
Richmond, VA 23232
Doreen Williams, Diversity Development Specialist
Tel: (804) 775-6362
Web: www.usps.com

SELECTIVE SERVICE SYSTEM
EEO Office
1515 Wilson Blvd. #400
Arlington, VA 22209-2425
Richard S. Flahavan, Officer
Tel: (703) 605-4100 Fax: (703) 605-4106

Email: richard.flahavan@sss.gov
Web: www.sss.gov

TRADE AND DEVELOPMENT AGENCY
1000 Wilson Blvd. #1600
Arlington, VA 22209-3901
Tel: (703) 875-4357 Fax: (703) 875-4009
Email: info@ustda.gov
Web: www.tda.gov

WASHINGTON

AIR FORCE, DEPT. OF THE
Fairchild AFB
Fairchild AFB, WA 99011-8524
Tel: (800) 423-8723
Web: www.airforce.com

McChord AFB
McChord AFB, WA 98438-1109
Tel: (800) 423-8723
Web: www.airforce.com

ARMY, DEPT. OF
HQ Army, Fourth Region (ROTC)
US Army Cadet Command
Attn: Public Affairs Office
Fort Lewis, WA 98433-7100
Tel: (253) 967-7473

US Army Recruiting Battalion Seattle
Public Affairs Office
P.O. Box 3957
4735 E. Marginal Way South
Seattle, WA 98124-3957
Tel: (206) 764-3599

EDUCATION, DEPT. OF
Human Resources Services Office
915 2nd Ave., Jackson Federal Bldg. #3388
Seattle, WA 98174
Ike Gilbert, Human Resources Officer
Tel: (206) 220-7813 Fax: (206) 220-7949
Email: ike.gilbert@ed.gov
Web: www.ed.gov

ENVIRONMENTAL PROTECTION AGENCY
Civil Rights, Calma Enforcement and Environmental Justice
Region 10, Pacific Northwest
1200 6th Ave. M/C CRE-164
Seattle, WA 98101
Victoria Plata, EEO Officer
Tel: (206) 553-8580 Fax: (206) 553-7176
Email: plata.victoria@epa.gov
Web: www.epa.gov

EQUAL EMPLOYMENT OPPORTUNITY COMMISSION
Seattle District Office
909 1st Ave., Federal Office Bldg. #400
Seattle, WA 98104-1061
Jeanette M. Leino, Director
Tel: (206) 220-6883 Fax: (206) 220-6911
Web: www.eeoc.gov

HOMELAND SECURITY, DEPT. OF
USCG Recruiting Office Portland
8109 F NE Vancouver Mall Dr.
Vancouver, WA 98662-6422
AMTC Thomas F. Brunney, Recruiter in Charge
Tel: (360) 699-1047 Fax: (360) 699-1048
Email: tbrunney@cgrc.uscg.mil
Web: www.gocoastguard.com

USCG Recruiting Office Seattle
10712 5th Ave. NE
Seattle, WA 98125
BMC Randall Dennis, Recruiter in Charge

Tel: (206) 364-4667 Fax: (206) 365-0866
Email: rdennis@cgrc.uscg.mil
Web: www.gocoastguard.com

USCG Recruiting Office Spokane
11516-A E. Sprague Ave.
Spokane, WA 99206-5135
GMC Mark Brown, Recruiter in Charge
Tel: (509) 927-0993 Fax: (509) 927-8026
Email: mebrown@cgrc.uscg.mil
Web: www.gocoastguard.com

USCG Recruiting Office Tacoma
Tacoma Office Mall Bldg., 4301 S. Pine St. #102
Tacoma, WA 98409-7264
MKC Steve Fisk, Recruiter in Charge
Tel: (253) 476-5939 Fax: (253) 476-8382
Email: sfisk@cgrc.uscg.mil
Web: www.gocoastguard.com

USCG Recruiting Office Yakima
1200 Chesterly Dr. #110, Plz. II
Yakima, WA 98902-7338
AMTC Russel Kirkham, Recruiter in Charge
Tel: (509) 452-1356 Fax: (509) 452-1375
Email: rkirkham@cgrc.uscg.mil
Web: www.gocoastguard.com

NAVY, DEPT. OF THE
Navy Recruiting District, Seattle
2901 3rd Ave. #250
Seattle, WA 98121
Tel: (800) 832-0258

USMC Recruiting Station, Seattle
South Federal Center South, 4735 E. Marginal Way
South Seattle, WA 98134-2379
Tel: (206) 762-1645
Web: www.marines.com

POSTAL SERVICE
Seattle District
P.O. Box 90309
Seattle, WA 98109-8872
Carol V. Peoples-Proctor, Diversity Development Specialist
Tel: (206) 442-6293 Fax: (206) 378-2537
Email: carol.v.peoples-proctor@usps.gov
Web: www.usps.com

Spokane District
707 W. Main St. #600
Spokane, WA 99299-1000
Gail Meredith, Diversity Development Specialist
Tel: (509) 626-6714 Fax: (509) 626-6918
Email: gmeredi1@email.usps.gov
Web: www.usps.com

STATE OF WASHINGTON
Social and Health Services, Dept. of
Aging and Adult Services Administration-State Unit on Aging
P.O. Box 45600
Olympia, WA 98504-5600
Patty McDonald, Diversity Program Manager
Tel: (360) 725-2559 Fax: (360) 438-8633
Email: mcdonpm@dshs.wa.gov
Web: www.aasa.dshs.wa.gov

WEST VIRGINIA

ARMY, DEPT. OF
US Army Recruiting Battalion Beckley
Public Affairs Office
21 Mallard Ct.
Beckley, WV 25801-3615
Tel: (304) 252-0422/0459

INTERIOR, DEPT. OF THE
National Park Service
Harpers Ferry Center, EEO Office
P.O. Box 50
Harpers Ferry, WV 25425
Magaly M. Green , Manager
Tel: (304) 535-6003 Fax: (304) 535-6295
Email: magaly_green@nps.gov
Web: www.nps.gov/hfc

NAVY, DEPT. OF THE
USMC Recruiting Station, Charleston
4216 State Rt. 34
Hurricane (Teays Valley), WV 25526
Tel: (304) 757-5028
Web: www.marines.com

POSTAL SERVICE
Appalachian District
P.O. Box 59000
Charleston, WV 25350-9000
Lora M. Moles, Diversity Development
Specialist
Tel: (304) 561-1269 Fax: (304) 561-1268
Email: lora.m.moles@usps.gov
Web: www.usps.com

TREASURY, DEPT. OF THE
Bureau of the Public Debt
EEO Office
200 3rd St. #415
Parkersburg, WV 26106
Cheryl D. Adams, Officer
Tel: (304) 480-6527 Fax: (304) 480-6074
Email: cheryl.adams@bpd.treas.gov
Web: www.publicdebt.treas.gov

WISCONSIN

ARMY, DEPT. OF
US Army Recruiting Battalion Milwaukee
Public Affairs Office
310 W. Wisconsin Ave. #600
Milwaukee, WI 53203-2211
Tel: (414) 297-4596/1193

**EQUAL EMPLOYMENT OPPORTUNITY
COMMISSION**
Milwaukee District Office
310 W. Wisconsin Ave., Reuss Federal
Plz. #800
Milwaukee, WI 53203-2292
John P. Rowe, Director
Tel: (414) 297-1111 Fax: (414) 297-4133
Web: www.eeoc.gov

HOMELAND SECURITY, DEPT. OF
USCG Recruiting Office Milwaukee
Woodland Ct., 3953 S. 76th St.
Milwaukee, WI 53220-2320
MKC David Shuart, Recruiter in Charge
Tel: (414) 321-4220 Fax: (414) 321-3527
Email: dshuart@cgrc.uscg.mil
Web: www.gocoastguard.com

NAVY, DEPT. OF THE
USMC Recruiting Station, Milwaukee
310 Wisconsin Ave. #480
Milwaukee, WI 53203-2216
Tel: (414) 297-1796
Web: www.marines.com

POSTAL SERVICE
Milwaukee District
350 W. St. Paul Ave. #650
Milwaukee, WI 53201-5027
Terri Jordan, Diversity Development
Specialist
Tel: (414) 287-2577 Fax: (414) 287-2296
Email: terri.l.jordan@usps.gov
Web: www.usps.com

SOCIAL SECURITY ADMINISTRATION
Wisconsin Recruiting Office
425 State St.
La Crosse, WI 54601
Ricardo Acevedo, District Manager
Tel: (608) 784-6838 Fax: (608) 784-6838
Email: ricardo.acevedo@ssa.gov
Web: www.ssa.gov

WYOMING

AIR FORCE, DEPT. OF THE
FE Warren AFB
FE Warren AFB, WY 82005-3905
Tel: (800) 423-8723
Web: www.airforce.com

THE DEPARTMENT OF JUSTICE EMPLOYMENT OPPORTUNITIES

- ATTORNEYS
- CRIMINAL INVESTIGATORS
- SPECIAL AGENTS
- CORRECTIONAL OFFICERS
- CLERK TYPISTS
- SECRETARY STENOGRAPHERS
- PARALEGAL SPECIALISTS
- DEPUTY U.S. MARSHALS
- COMPUTER SPECIALISTS/SCIENTIST AND MANY OTHER ADMINISTRATIVE AND TECHNICAL POSITION

The Department of Justice employs over 102,000 persons throughout the Nation, foreign countries, and in U.S. Territories. Through its thousands of lawyers, investigators, agents and support staffs, the Department plays a key role in protecting against crime; in ensuring healthy competition of business; in safeguarding the consumer; in enforcing civil rights laws. The Department also plays a significant role in protecting citizens through its efforts in areas of prosecution and rehabilitation of offenders and represents the Government in legal matters generally, rendering legal advice and opinions upon request to the President and to the Heads of Executive Department and agencies.

For more information about career opportunities, please visit our website at

www.USDOJ.GOV/JMD/EEOS

United States Department of Justice
An Equal Opportunity Employer

Private Sector Employment Opportunities

ALABAMA

REGIONS FINANCIAL
Human Resources
471 N. 20th St.
Birmingham, AL 35203
John M. Daniel, Director, Human Resources
Tel: (205) 944-1289
Web: www.regions.com

SAKS INCORPORATED
Human Resources
750 Lakeshore Pkwy
Birmingham, AL 35211
Marilyn Tipton, Director of Trainer
Tel: (601) 968-5348
Web: www.saksincorporated.com

ARIZONA

ALLIED WASTE INDUSTRIES
Human Resources
15880 N. Greenway-Hayden Loop
Scottsdale, AZ 85260
Stephanie Kalivas, Recuiter, Human
Resources
Tel: (480) 627-2700
Web: www.alliedwaste.com

ARKANSAS

ALLTEL
Human Resources
1 Allied Dr.
Little Rock, AR 72202
C. J. Duvall, Human Resources
Tel: (501) 905-8000 Fax: (501) 905-5444
Web: www.alltel.com

AVNET
Human Resources
2211 S. 47th St.
Phoenix, AR 85034
Tel: (480) 643-2000
Web: www.avnet.com

DILLARD'S
Human Resources
1600 Cantrell Rd
Little Rock, AR 72201
Tel: (501) 376-5200
Web: www.dillards.com

MURPHY OIL CORPORATION
200 Peach St.
El Dorado, AR 71731
Matt Angelette, Manager Personnel
Tel: (870) 864-6435 Fax: (870) 864-6511
Email: matt_angelette@murphyoilcorp.com
Web: www.murphyoilcorp.com

PHELPS DODGE
Human Resources
1 N. Central Ave.
Phoenix, AR 85004
David L. Pulatie, Senior Vice President,
Human Resources
Tel: (602) 366-8100
Web: www.phelpsdodge.com

TYSON FOODS INC.
Human Resources
2210 W. Oaklawn Dr.
Springdale, AR 72762
Kenneth J. Kimbro, Senior Vice President,
Human Resources
Tel: (479) 290-4000
Web: www.tysonfoodsinc.com

WAL-MART STORES
Arkansas
702 S.W. Eighth St
Bentonville, AR 72716
Lawrence V. Jackson, Executive Vice
President People Division
Tel: (479) 273-4000 Fax: (479) 273-4329
Web: www.walmart.com

CALIFORNIA

ADVANCED MICRO DEVICES
Human Resources
1 AMD Place
Sunnyvale, CA 94088
Tel: (408) 749-4000
Web: www.amd.com

AGILENT TECHNOLOGIES
Human Resources
395 Page Mill Rd.
Palo Alto, CA 94306
Jean M. Halloran, Senior Vice President,
Human Resources
Tel: (650) 752-5000
Web: www.agilent.com

AMGEN
Human Resources
1 Amgen Center Dr.
Thousand Oaks, CA 91320
Brian McNamee, Senior Vice President,
Human Resources
Tel: (805) 447-1000 Fax: (805) 447-1010
Web: www.amgen.com

APPLE COMPUTER
Human Resources
1 Infinite Loop #301-1RC
Cupertino, CA 95014
Shelly Hoefer, Director of Human Resources
Tel: (408) 974-2852 Fax: (408) 996-1010
Email: college@apple.com
Web: www.apple.com/jobs

APPLIED MATERIALS
Human Resources
3050 Bowers Ave.
Santa Clara, CA 95054
Jeannette Liebman, Vice President, Global
Human Resources
Tel: (408) 727-5555
Web: www.appliedmaterials.com

AVERY DENNISON
Human Resources
150 N. Orange Grove Blvd.
Pasadena, CA 91103
Tel: (626) 304-2000
Web: www.averydennison.com

CALPINE
Human Resources
50 W. San Fernando St.
San Jose, CA 95113
John Miller, Senior Vice President, Human
Resources and Safety
Tel: (408) 995-5115 Fax: (408) 995-0505
Web: www.calpine.com

CHARLES SCHWAB
Human Resources
120 Kearny St.
San Francisco, CA 94108
Tel: (415) 627-7000
Web: www.schwab.com

CHEVRONTEXACO
Chevron Headquarters
6001 Bollinger Canyon Rd.
San Ramon, CA 94583
Candy Gubauich, Head of Human
Resources
Tel: (888) 825-5247 Fax: (888) 239-8647
Web: www.chevrontexaco.com

CISCO SYSTEMS
Human Resources
170 W. Tasman Dr.
San Jose, CA 95134
Kate D'Camp, Senior Vice President,
Human Resources
Tel: (408) 526-4000
Web: www.cisco.com

CLOROX
Human Resources
1221 Broadway
Oakland, CA 94612
Tel: (510) 271-7000
Web: www.clorox.com

CNF
Human Resources
3240 Hillview Ave.
Palo Alto, CA 94304
David L. Slate, Vice President, Human
Resources

Tel: (650) 424-2900
Web: www.cnf.com

COMPUTER SCIENCES
Corporate Headquarters
2100 E. Grand Ave.
El Segundo, CA 90245
Tel: (310) 615-0311
Web: www.csc.com

COUNTRYWIDE FINANCIAL
Corporate Headquarters
4500 Park Granada
Calabasas, CA 91302
Leora I. Goren, Senior Managing Director
and Chief Human Resources Officer
Web: www.countrywide.com

DIRECTV GROUP
Corporate Headquarters
2250 E. Imperial Highway
El Segundo, CA 90245
Tel: (310) 964-5000
Web: www.directv.com

DOLE FOOD
Human Resources
1 Dole Dr
Westlake Village, CA 91362
Yvonne Myenon, Recruiter, Human
Resources
Tel: (818) 879-6600
Web: www.dole.com

EDISON INTERNATIONAL
Corporate Headquarters
2244 Walnut Grove Ave.
Rosemead, CA 91770
Tel: (626) 302-2222
Web: www.edison.com

FIRST AMERICAN CORP.
Human Resources
1 First American Way
Santa Ana, CA 92707
Tel: (714) 800-3000
Web: www.firstam.com

FLUOR
Human Resources
1 Enterprise Dr.
Aliso Viejo, CA 92656
H. Steven Gilbert, Senior Vice President,
Human Resources and Administration
Tel: (949) 349-2000 Fax: (949) 349-2585
Web: www.fluor.com

GAP
Corporate Headquarters
2 Folson St.
San Francisco, CA 94105
Eva Sage-Gavin, Executive Vice President,
Human Resources
Tel: (650) 952-4400
Web: www.gapinc.com

GATEWAY
Human Resources
7565 Irvine Center Dr.
Irvine, CA 92618
Mike Tyler, Vice President, Administration
Tel: (949) 491-7000
Web: www.gateway.com

GOLDEN WEST FINANCIAL
Human Resources
1901 Harrison St.
Oakland, CA 94612
Tel: (510) 446-3420
Web: www.worldsavings.com

HEALTH NET
Corporate Headquarters
21650 Oxnard St.
Woodland Hills, CA 91367
Steven Sell, Vice President, Employer Services
Tel: (818) 676-6000
Web: www.healthnet.com

HEWLETT-PACKARD
Headquarters
3000 Hanover St
Palo Alto, CA 94304
Marcela Perez de Alonso, Executive Vice President, Human Resources
Tel: (650) 857-1501 Fax: (650) 857-5518
Web: www.hp.com

INGRAM MICRO
Human Resources
1600 E. St. Andrews Pl.
Santa Ana, CA 92705
Matthew A Suaer, Senior Vice President, Human Resources
Tel: (714) 566-1000
Web: www.ingrammicro.com

INTEL
Corporate Headquarters
2200 Mission College Blvd
Santa Clara, CA 95052
Patricia Murray, Senior Vice President, Human Resources
Tel: (408) 765-8080
Web: www.intel.com

JACOBS ENGINEERING GRP.
Human Resources
1111 S. Arroyo Pkwy
Pasadena, CA 91105
Tel: (626) 578-3500
Web: www.jacobs.com

KB HOME
Human Resources
10990 Wilshire Blvd.
Los Angeles, CA 90024
Laurel Osborne, Client Service Manager
Email: losborne@kbhome.com
Web: www.kbhome.com

LEVI STRAUSS
Human Resources
1155 Battery St.
San Francisco, CA 94111
Fred Paulenich, Senior Vice President, Human Resources
Tel: (415) 501-6000
Web: www.levistrauss.com

LONGS DRUG STORES
Human Resources
141 N. Civic Dr.
Walnut Creek, CA 94596
Linda M. Watt, Senior Vice President, Human Resources
Tel: (925) 937-1170
Web: www.longs.com

MATTEL
Human Resources
333 Continental Blvd
El Segundo, CA 90245
Alan Kaye, Senior Vice President, Human Resources
Tel: (310) 252-2000 Fax: (310) 252-2180
Web: www.mattel.com

MAXTOR
Human Resources
500 McCarthy Blvd
Milpitas, CA 95035
Lina George, Senior Vice President, Human Resources
Tel: (408) 894-5000
Web: www.maxtor.com

MCKESSON
Corporate Headquarters
1 Post St.
San Francisco, CA 94104
Paul E. Kirincic, Executive Vice President, Human Resources
Tel: (415) 983-8300
Web: www.mckesson.com

NORTHROP GRUMMAN
Corporate Headquarters
1840 Century Park E.
Los Angeles, CA 90067
J. Michael Hately, Corporate Vice President and Chief Human Resources and Administrative Officer
Tel: (310) 553-6262
Web: www.northropgrumman.com

OCCIDENTAL PETROLEUM
Corporate Headquarters
10889 Wilshire Blvd
Los Angeles, CA 90024
Tel: (310) 208-8800
Web: www.oxy.com

ORACLE CORPORATION
Corporate Headquarters
500 Oracle Pkwy
Redwood City, CA 94065
Tel: (650) 506-7000
Web: www.oracle.com

PACIFIC LIFE
Human Resources
700 Newport Center Dr.
Newport Beach, CA 92660
Anthony J. Bonno, Senior Vice President, Human Resources
Tel: (949) 219-3011
Web: www.pacificlife.com

PACIFICARE HEALTH SYS.
Human Resources
5995 Plaza Dr.
Cypress, CA 90630
Carol Black, Senior Vice President, Human Resources
Tel: (714) 952-1121
Web: www.pacificare.com

PG&E CORP.
Corporate Headquarters
1 Market St.
San Francisco, CA 94105
Russell M. Jackson, Senior Vice President, Human Resources
Tel: (415) 267-7000
Web: www.pgecorp.com

QUALCOMM
Human Resources
5775 Morehouse Dr.
San Diego, CA 92121
Dr. Daniel L. Sullivan, Executive Vice President, Human Resources
Tel: (858) 587-1121
Web: www.qualcomm.com

ROSS STORES
Human Resources
4440 Rosewood Dr
Pleasanton, CA 94588
D. Jane Marvin, Senior Vice President, Human Resources
Tel: (925) 965-4400
Web: www.rossstores.com

RYLAND GROUP
Human Resources
24025 Park Sorrento
Calabasas, CA 91302
Robert J. Cunnion, III, Senior Vice President, Human Resources
Tel: (818) 223-7500
Web: www.ryland.com

SAFEWAY
Corporate Headquarters
5918 Stoneridge Mall Rd.
Pleasanton, CA 94588
James Derosier, Manager Supplier Human Resources
Tel: (925) 467-3000
Web: www.safeway.com

SANMINA-SCI
Corporate Headquarters
2700 N. First St.
San Jose, CA 95143
Carmine Renzilli, Senior Vice President, Global Human Resources
Tel: (408) 964-3500 Fax: (408) 964-3779
Web: www.sanmina-sci.com

SCIENCE APPLICATIONS INTL.
Human Resources Dept.
102260 Campus Point Dr.
San Diego, CA 92121
Tel: (858) 826-6000
Web: www.saic.com

SEMPRA ENERGY
Human Resources
101 Ash St.
San Diego, CA 92101
G. Joyce Rowling, Senior Vice President, Human Resources
Tel: (619) 696-2000
Web: www.sempra.com

SOLECTRON
Human Resources
847 Gibratlar Dr.
Milpitas, CA 95053
Kevin O'Connor, Executive Vice President, Human Resources
Tel: (408) 957-8500
Web: www.solectron.com

STARTER BROS. HOLDINGS
Human Resources
21700 Barton Rd.
Cotton, CA 92324
Cathy Finazzo, Vice President Diversity and Corporate EEO
Tel: (909) 783-5000
Web: www.starterbros.com

SUN MICROSYSTEMS
Human Resources
4150 Network Circle
Santa Clara, CA 95054
Bill MacGowan, Senior Vice President, Human Resources
Tel: (650) 960-1300
Web: www.sun.com

UNOCAL CORPORATION
Corporate Headquarters

2141 Rosecrans Ave.
El Segundo, CA 90245
Tel: (310) 726-7600
Web: www.unocal.com

WALT DISNEY
Corporate Headquarters
500 S. Buena Vista Dr.
Burbank, CA 91521
John M. Rentro, Senior Vice President and Chief Human Resources
Tel: (818) 560-1000
Web: www.disney.com

WELLS FARGO
Corporate Headquarters
420 Montgomery Rd.
San Francisco, CA 94104
Avid Modtjabai, Executive Vice President, Human Resources
Tel: (800) 333-0343
Web: www.wellsfargo.com

COLORADO

BALL
Human Resources
10 Longs Peak Dr.
Broomfield, CO 80021
Tel: (303) 469-3131
Web: www.ball.com

ECHOSTAR COMMUNICATIONS
Human Resources
9601 S. Meridian Blvd.
Englewood, CO 80112
Tel: (303) 723-1000
Web: www.echostar.com

FIRST DATA
Human Resources
6200 S. Quebec St.
Greenwood Village, CO 80111
Mike D'Ambrose, Executive Vice President, Human Resources
Tel: (303) 488-8000
Web: www.firstdata.com

LEVEL 3 COMMUNICATIONS
Human Resources
1025 Eldorado Rd
Broomfield, CO 80021
Tel: (720) 888-1000
Web: www.level3.com

LIBERTY MEDIA
Human Resources
12300 Liberty Blvd.
Englewood, CO 80112
Tel: (720) 875-5400
Web: www.libertymedia.com

MDC HOLDINGS
Human Resources
3600 S. Yosemite St.
Denver, CO 80237
Sharon S. Brown, Vice President, Human Resources
Tel: (303) 773-1100
Web: www.richmondamerican.com

MOLSON COORS BREWING
Human Resources
311 Tenth St.
Golden, CO 80401
Tel: (303) 279-6565
Web: www.molsoncoors.com

NEWMONT MINING
Human Resources
1700 Lincoln St.
Denver, CO 80203

Darla Caudie, Vice President, Human
Resources
Tel: (303) 863-7414
Web: www.newmont.com

QWEST COMMUNICATIONS
Corporate Headquarters
1801 California St.
Denver, CO 80202
Teresa Taylor, Executive Vice President/
Chief Human Resources
Tel: (303) 992-1400 Fax: (303) 896-8515
Web: www.quest.com

TRANSMONTAIGNE
Human Resources
1670 Broadway
Denver, CO 80202
Nico Soreno, Human Resources
Tel: (303) 626-8200 Fax: (303) 626-8228
Web: www.transmontaigne.com

CONNECTICUT

AETNA
Corporate Headquarters
151 Farmington Ave
Hartford, CT 06156
Elease Wright, Head of Human Resources
Tel: (860) 273-0123
Web: www.aetna.com

EMCOR GROUP
Human Resources
301 Merritt 7 Corporate Pk.
Norwalk, CT 06851
Christine Names, Vice President, Human
Resources
Tel: (203) 849-7800
Web: www.emcorpgroup.com

GENERAL ELECTRIC
Corporate Headquarters
3135 Easton Turnpike
Fairfield, CT 06828
Julie Grzee, Managing Director, Human
Resources
Tel: (203) 373-2211
Web: www.ge.com

HARTFORD FINANCIAL SERVICES
Human Resources
690 Asylum Ave.
Hartford, CT 06115
Ann M. de Raismes, Executive Vice
President, Human Resources
Tel: (860) 547-5000
Web: www.thehartford.com

INTERNATIONAL PAPER
Corporate Headquarters
400 Atlantic st.
Stamford, CT 06921
Jerome N. Carter, Senior Vice President,
Human Resources
Tel: (203) 451-8000
Web: www.ipaper.com

NORTHEAST UTILITIES
Human Resources
107 Selden St.
Berlin, CT 06037
Jean M. LaVecchia, Vice President, Human
Resources
Tel: (860) 665-5000
Web: www.nu.com

PITNEY BOWES
Human Resources
1 Elmcroft Rd.
Stamford, CT 06926
Johnna G. Torsone, Senior Vice President,
Human Resources

Tel: (203) 356-5000
Web: www.pb.com

PRAXAIR
Human Resources
39 Old Ridgebury Rd.
Danbury, CT 06810
Sally A. Savoia, Vice President, Human
Resources
Tel: (203) 837-2000
Web: www.praxair.com

PREMCOR
Corporate Headquarters
1700 E. Putnam Ave.
Old Greenwich, CT 06870
Peter Terenzio, Vice President, Human
Resources
Tel: (203) 698-7500 Fax: (203) 698-7925
Web: www.premcor.com

TEREX
Human Resources
500 Post Rd. E.
Westport, CT 06880
Kevin A. Barr, Vice President, Human
Resources
Tel: (203) 222-7170
Web: www.terex.com

UNITED TECHNOLOGIES
Corporate Headquarters
1 Financial Plz.
Hartford, CT 06103
William L. Bucknall Jr., Senior Vice
President, Human Resources and
Organization
Tel: (860) 678-5454
Web: www.utc.com

W.R. BERKLEY
Human Resources
475 Steamboat Rd.
Greenwich, CT 06830
Joseph M. Pennachio, Vice President,
Human Resources
Tel: (203) 629-3000
Web: www.wrbc.com

XEROX
Corporate Headquarters
800 Long Ridge Rd.
Stamford, CT 06904
Patricia M. Nazemetz, Vice President,
Human Resources
Tel: (203) 968-3000
Web: www.xerox.com

DELAWARE

DUPONT
Corporate Headquarters
1007 Market St.
Wilmington, DE 19898
James C. Borel, Senior VP- Dupont Global
Human Resources
Tel: (302) 774-1000
Web: www.dupont.com

MBNA
Corporate Headquarters
1100 N. King St.
Wilmington, DE 19884
Tel: (800) 362-6255
Web: www.mbna.com

DISTRICT OF COLUMBIA

DANAHER
Human Resources
2099 Pennsylvannia Ave, N.W.

Washington, DC 20006
Tel: (202) 828-0850
Web: www.danaher.com

PEPCO HOLDINGS, INC.
Corporate Headquarters
701 9th St. NW
Washington, DC 20068
Freda Gray, Staffing Supervisor
Tel: (202) 872-2101 Fax: (202) 331-6850
Web: www.pepcoholdings.com

FLORIDA

AUTONATION
Human Resources
110 S.E. Sixth St.
Fort Lauderdale, FL 33301
Andrea Dawkins, Manager, Human
Resources
Tel: (954) 769-2757
Web: www.autonation.com

CSX
Human Resources
500 Water St.
Jacksonville, FL 32202
Robert J. Haulter, Senior Vice President,
Human Resources and Labor Relations
Tel: (904) 359-3200
Web: www.csx.com

DARDEN RESTAURANTS
Human Resources
5900 Lake Ellenor Dr.
Orlando, FL 32809
Daniel M. Lyons, Senior Vice President,
Human Resources
Tel: (407) 245-4000
Web: www.darden.com

FIDELITY NATIONAL FINANCIAL
Human Resources
601 Riverside Ave.
Jacksonville, FL 32204
Pete Pennella, Staffing Manager
Tel: (904) 854-8100 Fax: (904) 854-4282
Web: www.fnf.com

FPL GROUP
Corporate Headquarters
700 Universe Blvd
Juno Beach, FL 33408
Robert H. Escoto, Vice President, Human
Resources
Tel: (561) 694-4000
Web: www.fplgroup.com

HUGHES SUPPLY
Human Resources
1 Hughes Way
Orlando, FL 32805
Jay Romans, Senior Vice President, Human
Resources
Tel: (407) 841-4755
Web: www.hughessupply.com

JABIL CIRCUIT
Human Resources
10560 Dr. Martin Luther King Jr. St. N.
St. Petersburg, FL 33716
Thomas T. O'Connor, Vice President,
Human Resources-Americas
Tel: (727) 577-9749
Web: www.jabil.com

LENNAR
Corporate Headquarters
700 N.W. 107th Ave.
Miami, FL 33172
Frank Matthews, Human Resources
Tel: (305) 559-4000
Web: www.lennar.com

OFFICE DEPOT
Human Resources
2200 Old Germantown Rd.
Delray Beach, FL 33445
Frank Scruggs, Executive Vice President,
Human Resources
Tel: (561) 438-4800
Web: www.officedepot.com

PUBLIX SUPER MARKETS
Corporate Headquarters
3300 Publix Corporate Pkwy.
Lakeland, FL 33811
John Harabusa, Vice President, Human
Resources
Tel: (863) 688-1188
Web: www.publix.com

RYDER SYSTEM
Human Resources
3600 N.W. 82nd Ave.
Miami, FL 33166
Jennifer Thomas, Senior Vice President,
Human Resources
Tel: (305) 500-3726
Web: www.ryder.com

TECH DATA
Corporate Headquarters
5350 Tech Data Dr.
Clearwater, FL 33760
Lawrence W. Hamilton, Senior Vice
President, Human Resources
Tel: (727) 539-7429
Web: www.techdata.com

WINN-DIXIE STORES
Corporate Headquarters
5050 Edgewood Ct.
Jacksonville, FL 32254
Tel: (904) 783-5000
Web: www.winn-dixie.com

WORLD FUEL SERVICES
Human Resources
9800 NW 41st St.
Miami, FL 33178
Tel: (305) 428-8000 Fax: (305) 392-5600
Web: www.wfscorp.com

GEORGIA

AFLAC
Human Resources
1932 Wynnton Rd.
Columbus, GA 31999
Audrey Tillman, Director, Human Resources
Tel: (706) 323-3431
Web: www.aflac.com

AGCO
Human Resources
4205 River Green Pkwy.
Duluth, GA 30096
Norman L. Boyd, Senior Vice President,
Human Resources
Tel: (770) 813-9200 Fax: (770) 232-8001
Web: www.agcocorp.com

BEAZER HOMES USA
Human Resources
1000 Abernathy Rd.
Atlanta, GA 30328
Fred Fratto, Senior Vice President, Human
Resources
Tel: (770) 829-3700
Web: www.beazer.com

BELLSOUTH
Corporate Headquarters
1155 Peachtree St. N.E.,
Atlanta, GA 30309

Tel: (404) 249-2000
Web: www.bellsouth.com

COCA-COLA
Corporate Headquarters
1 Coca-Cola Plz.
Atlanta, GA 30313
Cynthia P. McCague, Director, Human Resources
Tel: (404) 676-2121
Web: www.coca-cola.com

Human Resources
2500 Windy Ridge Pkwy.
Atlanta, GA 30339
Daniel S. Bowling, III, Senior Vice President, Human Resources
Tel: (770) 989-3000
Web: www.cokecce.com

COX COMMUNICATIONS
Human Resources
1400 Lake Hearn Dr.
Atlanta, GA 30319
Monica Johnson, Director of Recruiting
Tel: (404) 843-5000
Web: www.cox.com

DELTA AIR LINES
Corporate Heaquarters
1030 Delta Blvd
Atlanta, GA 30320
Lee Macenczak, Senior Vice President and Chief Customer Service Officer
Tel: (404) 715-2600
Web: www.delta.com

GENUINE PARTS
Human Resources
2999 Circle 75 Pkwy.
Atlanta, GA 30339
Kathy McCort, Human Resources
Tel: (770) 953-1700
Web: www.genpt.com

GEORGIA-PACIFIC
Corporate Headquarters
133 Peachtree St. N.E.
Atlanta, GA 30303
Patricia A. Bernard, Executive Vice President, Human Resources
Tel: (404) 652-4000
Web: www.gp.com

HOME DEPOT
Corporate Headquarters
2455 Paces Ferry Rd. N.W.
Atlanta, GA 30339
Dennis Donovan, Executive Vice President, Human Resources
Tel: (770) 433-8211
Web: www.homedepot.com

MIRANT
Human Resources
1155 Perimeter Center W.
Atlanta, GA 30338
Tel: (678) 579-5000
Web: www.mirant.com

MOHAWK INDUSTRIES
Human Resources
160 S. Industrial Blvd
Calhoun, GA 30701
Tel: (706) 629-7721
Web: www.mohawkind.com

NEWELL RUBBERMAID
Human Resources
10 B Glenlake Pkwy. #600
Atlanta, GA 30328
James M. Sweet, Vice President, Human Resources
Tel: (770) 407-3800
Web: www.newellrubbermaid.com

SOUTHERN
Corporate Headquarters
270 Peachtree St. N.W.
Atlanta, GA 30303
Tel: (404) 506-5000
Web: www.southernco.com

SUNTRUST BANKS
Human Resources
303 Peachtree St. N.E.
Atlanta, GA 30308
Mary T. Steele, Director, Human Resources
Tel: (404) 588-7711
Web: www.suntrust.com

UNITED PARCEL SERVICE
Corporate Headquarters
55 Glenlake Pkwy, N.E.
Atlanta, GA 30328
Lea N. Soupata, Senior Vice President, Human Resources
Tel: (404) 828-6000
Web: www.ups.com

IDAHO

ALBERTSON'S
Corporate Headquarters
250 Parkcenter Blvd
Boise, ID 83642
Jennifer Giro, Director of Corporate Human Resources
Tel: (208) 395-3853
Web: www.albertsons.com

MICRON TECHNOLOGY
Human Resources
8000 S. Federal Way
Boise, ID 83716
Jo Anne S. Arnold, Vice President, Human Resources
Tel: (208) 368-4000
Web: www.micron.com

ILLINOIS

ABBOTT LABORATORIES
Corporate Headquarters
100 Abbott Park Rd.
Abbott Park, IL 60064
Stephen R. Fusell, Senior Vice President, Human Resources
Tel: (847) 937-6100
Web: www.abbott.com

ALLSTATE
Corporate Headquarters
2775 Sanders Rd.
Northbrook, IL 60062
Joan M. Crockett, Senior Vice President, Human Resources
Tel: (847) 402-5000
Web: www.allstate.com

AON
Corporate Headquarters
200 E. Randolph St.
Chicago, IL 60601
Jeremy G.O. Farmer, Senior Vice President and Head, Human Resources
Tel: (312) 381-1000
Web: www.aon.com

ARCHER DANIELS MIDLAND
Corporate Headquarters
4666 Faries Pkwy
Decatur, IL 62525
Randy Moon, Human Resources
Tel: (217) 424-5200 Fax: (217) 451-4383
Web: www.admworld.com

BAXTER INTERNATIONAL
Human Resources
1 Baxter Pkwy
Deerfield, IL 60015
Karen J. May, Corporate Vice President, Human Resources
Tel: (847) 948-2000
Web: www.baxter.com

BOEING
Corporate Headquarters
100 N. Riverside Park
Chicago, IL 60606
Richard Stephens, Senior Vice President, Internal Services
Tel: (312) 544-2000
Web: www.boeing.com

BRUNSWICK
Human Resources
1 N. Field Court
Lake Forest, IL 60045
B. Russell Lockridge, Vice President and Chief Human Resources Officer
Tel: (847) 735-4700
Web: www.brunswick.com

CATERPILLAR
Corporate Headquarters
100 N.E. Adams St.
Peoria, IL 61629
Sidney C. Bandwart, Vice President Human Resources
Tel: (309) 675-1000
Web: www.cat.com

CDW
Corporate Headquarters
200 N. Milwaukee Ave.
Vernon Hills, IL 60061
Maria M. Sullivan , Vice President, Learning and Development
Tel: (847) 465-6000
Web: www.cdw.com

EXELON
Corporate Headquarters
10 S. Dearborn St.
Chicago, IL 60680
S. Gary Snodgrass, Executive Vice President and Chief Human Resources Officer
Tel: (312) 394-7398
Web: www.exeloncorp.com

FORTUNE BRANDS
Human Resources
300 Tower Pkwy
Lincolnshire, IL 60069
Tel: (847) 484-4400
Web: www.fortunebrands.com

ILLINOIS TOOL WORKS
Human Resources
3600 W. Lake Ave.
Glenview, IL 60026
Barbara Morris, Manager, Human Resources
Tel: (847) 724-7500
Web: www.itw.com

JOHN DEERE
Corporate Headquarters
1 John Deere Pl.
Moline, IL 61265
Mertroe B. Hornbuckle, VP/Human Resources
Tel: (309) 765-8000
Web: www.deere.com

LAIDLAW INTERNATIONAL
Human Resources
55 Shuman Blvd.
Naperville, IL 60563
Alice Wright, Human Resources

Tel: (630) 848-3000
Web: www.laidlaw.com

MCDONALD'S
Corporate Headquarters
1 McDonald's Plaza
Oak Brook, IL 60523
Richard Floersch, Executive Vice President, Worldwide Human Resources
Tel: (630) 623-3000
Web: www.mcdonalds.com

MOTOROLA
Corporate Headquarters
1303 E. Algonquin Rd.
Schaumburg, IL 60196
Ruth Fattori, Executive Vice President, Human Resources
Tel: (847) 576-5000
Web: www.motorola.com

NAVISTAR INTERNATIONAL
Corporate Headquarters
4201 Winfield Rd.
Warrenville, IL 60555
Tel: (630) 753-5000
Web: www.navistar.com

OFFICEMAX
Corporate Headquarters
150 Pierce Rd.
Itasca, IL 60143
Lorene Flewellen, Senior Vice President, Human Relations
Tel: (630) 438-7800
Web: www.officemax.com

R.R. DONNELLEY & SONS
Human Resources Department
111 S.Wacker Dr.
Chicago, IL 60601
Stan Jaworski
Tel: 312-326-8396
Web: www.rrdonnelley.com

SARA LEE
Human Resources
3 First National Plaza
Chicago, IL 60602
Lois M. Huggins, Senior Vice President, Global Human Resources
Tel: (312) 726-2600
Web: www.saralee.com

SEARS ROEBUCK
Corporate Headquarters
3333 Beverly Rd
Hoffman Estates, IL 60179
Tel: (847) 286-2500
Web: www.sears.com

SERVICEMASTER
Human Resources
3250 Lacey Rd.
Downers Grove, IL 60515
Lisa Goettel, Senior Vice President, Human Resources
Tel: (630) 663-2000
Web: www.svm.com

SMURFIT-STONE CONTAINER
Human Resources
150 N. Michigan Ave.
Chicago, IL 60601
Marissia Ayala, Human Resources
Tel: (312) 346-6600
Web: www.smurfit-stone.com

STATE FARM INSURANCE COS
Corporate Headquarters
1 State Farm Plaza
Bloomington, IL 61710
Margie Southard, Assistant Vice President, Diversity/Human Resources

Tel: (309) 766-2311
Web: www.statefarm.com

TELEPHONE & DATA SYS.
Human Resources
30 N. LaSalle St.
Chicago, IL 60602
C. Theordore Herbert, Vice President,
Human Resources
Tel: (312) 630-1990
Web: www.teldta.com

TENNECO AUTOMOTIVE
Human Resources
500 N. Field Dr.
Lake Forest, IL 60045
Barb Kluch, Director, Human Resources
Tel: (847) 482-5000
Web: www.tenneco-automotive.com

TRIBUNE
Human Resources
435 N. Michigan Ave.
Chicago, IL 60611
Luis E. Lewin, Senior Vice President,
Human Resources
Tel: (312) 222-9100
Web: www.tribune.com

UNITED AIRLINES INC.
Corporate Headquarters
1200 E. Algonquin Rd.
Elk Grove Township, IL 60007
Sara A. Fields, Senior Vice President,
People
Tel: (847) 700-4000
Web: www.united.com

UNITED STATIONERS
Human Resources
2200 E. Golf Rd.
Des Plaines, IL 60016
John T. Sloan, Senior Vice President,
Human Resources
Tel: (847) 699-5000
Web: www.unitedstationers.com

USG
Human Resources
125 S. Franklin St.
Chicago, IL 60606
Brian J. Cook, Senior Vice President,
Human Resources
Tel: (312) 606-4000
Web: www.usg.com

W.W. GRAINGER
Human Resources
100 Grainger Pkwy
Lake Forest, IL 60045
Tel: (847) 535-1000
Web: www.grainger.com

WALGREEN
Corporate Headquarters
200 Wilmot Rd.
Deerfield, IL 60015
Jennifer Briscoe, Human Resources
Recruiting Manager
Tel: (847) 914-2500
Web: www.walgreens.com

WM. WRIGLEY JR.
Human Resources
410 N. Michigan Ave.
Chicago, IL 60611
Dushan Petrovich, Senior Vice President,
Administrative
Tel: (312) 644-1212
Web: www.wrigley.com

INDIANA

CONSECO
Human Resources
11825 N. Pennsylvania St.
Carmel, IN 46032
Susan L. Menzel, Executive Vice President,
Human Resources
Tel: (317) 817-6100
Web: www.conseco.com

CUMMINS
Human Resources
500 Jackson St.
Columbus, IN 47201
Felecia Roseburgh, Manager, Corporate
Compliance
Tel: (317) 610-2481

ELI LILLY
Corporate Headquarters
Lilly Corporate Center
Indianapolis, IN 46285
Anthony Murphy, Senior Vice President
Tel: (317) 276-2000
Web: www.lilly.com

GUIDANT
Human Resources
111 Monument Circle
Indianapolis, IN 46204
Roger Marchetti, Vice President, Human
Resources
Tel: (317) 971-2000
Web: www.guidant.com

NISOURCE
Human Resources
801 E. 86th Ave.
Merrillville, IN 46410
S. LaNette Zimmerman, Executive Vice
President, Human Resources
Tel: (219) 647-6200
Web: www.nisource.com

WELLPOINT
Human Resources
120 Mounment Circle
Indianapolis, IN 46204
Randy Brown, Senior Vice President,
Human Resources
Tel: (317) 523-6000
Web: www.wellpoint.com

IOWA

MAYTAG
Human Resources
403 W. Fourth St. N.
Newton, IA 50208
Mark W. Krivoruchka, Senior Vice President,
Human Resources
Tel: (641) 792-7000 Fax: (641) 787-8376
Web: www.maytagcorp.com

PRINCIPAL FINANCIAL
Human Resources
711 High St.
Des Moines, IA 50392
James D. DeVries, Senior Vice President,
Human Resources
Tel: (571) 247-5111
Web: www.principal.com

KANSAS

HUMANA
Human Resources
500 W. Main St.

Louisville, KS 40202
Bonita C. Hathcock, Senior Vice President,
Chief Human Resources Officer
Tel: (502) 580-1000
Web: www.humana.com

SPRINT
Corporate Headquarters
6200 Sprint Pkwy
Overland Park, KS 66251
Jim Kessinger, Vice President, Human
Resources
Tel: (800) 829-0965
Web: www.sprint.com

YELLOW ROADWAY
Human Resources
10990 Roe Ave.
Overland Park, KS 66211
Steven T. Yamasaki, Senior Vice President,
Human Resources
Tel: (913) 696-6100
Web: www.yellowroadway.com

KENTUCKY

KINDRED HEALTHCARE
Human Resources
680 S. Fourth St.
Louisville, KY 40202
Terry Montgomery, Recruiting Services
Tel: (502) 596-7300
Web: www.kindredhealthcare.com

LEXMARK INTERNATIONAL
Human Resources
740 W. Circle Rd.
Lexington, KY 40550
Jeri Stromquist, Vice President, Human
Resources
Tel: (859) 232-2000
Web: www.lexmark.com

OMNICARE
Human Resources
100 E. River Center Blvd.
Covington, KY 41011
J. Michael Roberts, Vice President, Human
Resources
Tel: (859) 392-3300
Web: www.omnicare.com

YUM BRANDS
Human Resources
1441 Gardiner Ln.
Louisville, KY 40213
Anne P. Byerlein, Chief People Officer
Tel: (502) 874-8300
Web: www.yum.com

LOUISIANA

ENTERGY
Human Resources
639 Loyola Ave.
New Orleans, LA 70113
William E. Madison, Senior Vice President,
Human Resources and Adminsitration
Tel: (504) 576-4000
Web: www.entergy.com

MARYLAND

BLACK & DECKER
Human Resources
701 E. Joppa Rd.
Towson, MD 21286
Paul F. McBride, Senior Vice President,
Human Resources and Corporate Initiatives

Tel: (410) 716-3900
Web: www.bdk.com

CONSTELLATION ENERGY
Human Resources
750 E. Pratt St.
Baltimore, MD 21202
Marc L. Ugol, Senior Vice President
Tel: (410) 783-2800
Web: www.constellation.com

COVENTRY HEALTH CARE
Human Resources
6705 Rockledge Dr.
Bethesda, MD 20817
Clarie Connors, Director, Executive
Recruiting Human Resources
Tel: (301) 581-0600
Web: www.cvty.com

HOST MARRIOTT
Human Resources
6903 Rockledge Rd.
Bethesda, MD 20817
Pamela K. Wagoner, Senior Vice President,
Human Resources and Leadership
Development
Tel: (240) 744-1000
Web: www.hostmarriott.com

LOCKHEED MARTIN
Corporate Headquarters
6801 Rockledge Dr.
Bethesda, MD 20817
Jean Carr, Diversity, Human Resources
Manager
Tel: (301) 897-6000
Web: www.lockheedmartin.com

MARRIOTT INTERNATIONAL
Corporate Headquarters
10400 Fernwood Rd.
Bethesda, MD 20817
Brendan M. Keegan, Executive Vice
President, Human Resources
Tel: (301) 380-3000
Web: www.marriott.com

MASSACHUSETTS

BJ'S WHOLESALE CLUB
Human Resources
1 Mercer Rd.
Natick, MA 01760
Tel: (508) 651-7400
Web: www.bjs.com

BOSTON SCIENTIFIC
Human Resources
1 Boston Scientific Pl.
Natick, MA 01760
Tel: (508) 650-8000
Web: www.bostonscientific.com

EMC CORPORATION
Human Resources
176 South St.
Hopkinton, MA 01748
John T. Mollen, Senior VP, Human
Resources
Tel: (508) 435-1000 Fax: (508) 497-6912
Web: www.emc.com

LIBERTY MUTUAL INS. GROUP
Corporate Headquarters
175 Berkeley St.
Boston, MA 02116
Helen E.R. Sayles, Senior Vice President,
Human Resources and Administration
Tel: (617) 357-9500
Web: www.libertymutual.com

MASS. MUTUAL LIFE INS.
Corporate Headquarters
1295 State St.
Springfield, MA 01111
Tel: (413) 788-8411
Web: www.massmutual.com

RAYTHEON
Human Resources
870 Winter St.
Waltham, MA 02451
David Freeman, Director, Human Resources
Tel: (781) 522-3000
Web: www.raytheon.com

REEBOK INTERNATIONAL
Human Resources
1891 J.W. Foster Blvd
Canton, MA 02021
Tel: (781) 401-5000
Web: www.reebok.com

STAPLES
Corporate Headquarters
500 Staples Dr.
Framingham, MA 01702
Tel: (508) 253-5000 Fax: (508) 305-1300
Web: www.staples.com

STATE ST. CORP.
Human Resources
1 Lincoln St.
Boston, MA 02111
Luis J. de Ocejo, Executive Vice President, Human Resources and Organizational Performance
Tel: (617) 786-3000
Web: www.statestreet.com

THE GILLETTE COMPANY
Human Resources
Prudential Tower Bldg.
Boston, MA 02199
Edward E. Guillet, Vice President, Human Resources
Tel: (617) 421-7000
Web: www.gillette.com

THE TJX COMPANIES INC.
Human Resources
770 Cochituate Rd.
Framingham, MA 01701
Mary Beth Kelly, Manager Human Resources
Tel: (508) 390-1000
Web: www.tjx.com

MICHIGAN

ARVINMERITOR
Human Resources
2135 W. Maple Rd.
Troy, MI 48084
Ernie Whitus, Senior Vice President, Human Resources
Tel: (248) 435-1000 Fax: (248) 435-1393
Web: www.arvinmeritor.com

AUTO-OWNERS INSURANCE
Human Resources
6101 Anacapri Blvd
Lansing, MI 48917
Amy Baker, Manager, Recruiting Services
Tel: (517) 323-1200 Fax: (512) 323-8796
Web: www.auto-owners.com

BORDERS GROUP
Human Resources
100 Phoenix Dr.
Ann Arbor, MI 48108
Daniel Smith, Senior Vice President, Human Resources
Tel: (734) 477-1100
Web: www.bordersgroupinc.com

CMS ENERGY
Human Resources
1 Energy Plaza
Jackson, MI 49201
John F. Drake, Senior Vice President, Human Resources and Administrative Services
Tel: (517) 788-0550
Web: www.cmsenergy.com

COLLINS & AIKMAN
Human Resources
250 Stephenson Hwy
Troy, MI 48083
Tel: (248) 824-2500 Fax: (248) 824-1613
Web: www.collinsaikman.com

DELPHI
Corporate Headquarters
5725 Delphi Dr.
Troy, MI 48098
Mark R. Weber, Executive Vice President, Operations, Human Resources Management and Corporate Affairs
Tel: (248) 813-2000
Web: www.delphi.com

DOW CHEMICAL
Corporate Headquarters
2030 Dow Center
Midland, MI 48674
Luciano Respini, Corporate Vice President, Geography, Human Resources/Public Affairs
Tel: (989) 636-1000
Web: www.dow.com

DTE ENERGY
2000 2nd Ave.
Detroit, MI 48226
Theresa Alfafara, Director of Human Resources
Tel: (313) 235-6520
Email: theresaalfafara@dtenergy.com
Web: www.dtenergy.com

FEDERAL-MOGUL
Human Resources
26555 Northwestern Hwy.
Southfield, MI 48034
Pam Mitchell, Director, Diversity
Tel: (248) 354-7700 Fax: 248-354-8100
Web: www.federal-mogul.com

FORD MOTOR
Corporate Office
1 American Rd.
Dearborn, MI 48126
Felicia J. Fields, Vice President, Human Resources
Tel: (313) 322-3000
Web: www.ford.com

GENERAL MOTORS
300 Renaissance Center
Detroit, MI 48265
Kathleen S. Barclay, Human Resources
Tel: (313) 556-5000 Fax: (517) 272-3709
Web: www.gm.com

KELLOGG
Human Resources
1 Kellogg Square
Battle Creek, MI 49016
Annuciata Cerioli, Vice President, Human Resources
Tel: (269) 961-2000
Web: www.kelloggcompany.com

KELLY SERVICES
Human Resources
999 W. Big Beaver Rd.
Troy, MI 48084
Michael L. Durik, Executive Vice President, Administration.
Tel: (248) 362-4444
Web: www.kellyservices.com

KMART HOLDING
Human Resources
3100 W. Big Beaver Rd.
Troy, MI 48084
Robert Luse, Senior Vice President, Human Resources
Tel: (248) 463-1000
Web: www.searsholdings.com

LEAR
Human Resources
21557 Telegraph Rd.
Southfield, MI 48034
Mary-Ann Churchwell, Director Human Resources
Tel: (248) 447-1500 Fax: (248) 447-5944
Web: www.lear.com

MASCO
Corporate Headquarters
21001 Van Born Rd.
Taylor, MI 48180
Tel: (313) 274-7400
Web: www.masco.com

PULTE HOMES
Corporate Headquarters
100 Bloomfields Hill Pkwy
Bloomfield Hills, MI 48304
Tel: (248) 647-2750
Web: www.pulte.com

STRYKER
Human Resources
2725 Fairfield Rd.
Kalamazoo, MI 49002
Michael W. Rude, Vice President, Human Resources
Tel: (269) 385-2600 Fax: (269) 385-1062
Web: www.stryker.com

TRW AUTOMOTIVE HOLDINGS
Human Resources
12025 Tech Center Dr.
Livonia, MI 48150
Neil Marchuk, Human Resources
Tel: (734) 855-2600
Web: www.trwauto.com

UNITED AUTO GROUP
Corporate Headquarters
2555 Telegraph Rd.
Bloomfield Hills, MI 48302
Randolph Johnson, Vice President, Human Resources
Tel: (248) 648-2500
Web: www.unitedauto.com

VISTEON
Corporate Headquarters
1 Village Center Dr.
Van Buren Township, MI 48111
Charles Hudson, Vice President, Corporate Human Resources
Tel: (800) 847-8366
Web: www.visteon.com

WHIRLPOOL
Corporate Headquarters
2000 North M-63
Benton Harbour, MI 49022
David A. Binkley, Senior Vice President, Global Human Resources
Tel: (269) 923-5000
Web: www.whirlpoolcorp.com

MINNESOTA

3M
Human Resources
3M Center
St. Paul, MN 55144
M. Kay Grenz, Senior Vice President, Human Resources
Tel: (651) 733-1110
Web: www.3m.com

BEST BUY
Corporate Headquarters
7601 Penn Ave. South
Richfield, MN 55423
Shari Ballard, Executive Vice President, Human Capital and Leadership
Tel: (621) 291-1000
Web: www.bestbuy.com

C.H. ROBINSON WORLDWIDE
Human Resources
8100 Mitchell Rd.
Eden Prairie, MN 55344
Laura Guillund, Vice President, Human Resources
Tel: (952) 937-8500
Web: www.chrobinson.com

CHS INC.
Corporate Headquarters
5500 Cenex Dr.
Inver Grove Hghts., MN 55077
John Schmitz, Executive ViP/CFO
Tel: (651) 355-6000
Web: www.chsinc.com

ECOLAB
Human Resources
370 Wabasha St. N.
St. Paul, MN 55102
Tel: (651) 293-2233
Web: www.ecolab.com

GENERAL MILLS
Human Resources
1 General Mills Blvd.
Minneapolis, MN 55426
Michael A. Peel, Senior Vice President, Human Resources and Corporate Services
Tel: (763) 764-7600
Web: www.generalmills.com

HORMEL FOODS
Corporate Headquarters
1 Hormel Place
Austin, MN 55912
Tel: (507) 437-5611
Web: www.hormel.com

LAND O'LAKES
Human Resources
4001 Lexington Ave. N.
Arden Hills, MN 55126
Kasey Comnick, Recruitment Coordinator
Tel: (651) 766-1778 Fax: (651) 766-1376
Web: www.landolakesinc.com

MEDTRONIC
Human Resources
710 Medtronic Pkwy.
Minneapolis, MN 55423
Janet Fiola, Senior Vice President, Human Resources
Tel: (763) 514-4000
Web: www.medtronic.com

NASH FINCH
Human Resources
7600 France Ave. S.
Minneapolis, MN 55435
Joe R. Eulberg, Senior Vice President, Human Resources

Tel: (952) 832-0534
Web: www.nashfinch.com

NORTHWEST AIRLINES
Human Resources
2700 Lone Oak Pkwy.
Eagan, MN 55121
Michael J. Becker, Senior Vice President,
Human Resources and Labor Relations
Tel: (612) 726-2111
Web: www.nwa.com

ST. PAUL TRAVELERS COS.
Corporate Headquarters
385 Washington St
St. Paul, MN 55102
John Clifford, Senior Vice President, Human
Resources
Tel: (651) 310-7911
Web: www.stpaultravelers.com

SUPERVALU
Human Resources
11840 Valley View Rd
Eden Prairie, MN 55344
Rick Talmersheim, Manager, Human
Resources
Tel: (952) 828-4000
Web: www.supervalu.com

TARGET
Corporate Headquarters
1000 Nicollet Mall
Minneapolis, MN 55403
Todd V. Blackwell, Executive Vice President,
Human Resources, Assets Protection,
Target Sourcing Services
Tel: (612) 304-6073
Web: www.target.com

THRIVENT FINANCIAL FOR LUTHERANS
Human Resources
625 Fourth Ave. S.
Minneapolis, MN 55415
Deb Palmer, Staffing Manager
Tel: (800) 847-4836 Fax: (612) 340-6897
Email: deb.palmer@thrivent.com
Web: www.thrivent.com

U.S. BANCORP
Corporate Headquarters
800 Nicollett Mall
Minneapolis, MN 55402
Jennie P. Carlson, Executive vice
President, Human Resources
Tel: (651) 466-3000
Web: www.usbank.com

UNITEDHEALTH GROUP
Corporate Headquarters
9900 Bren Rd. E.
Minnetonka, MN 55343
L. Robert Dapper, Senior Vice President,
Human Capital
Tel: (952) 936-1300
Web: www.unitedhealthgroup.com

XCEL ENERGY
Human Resources
414 Nicollet Mall
Minneapolis, MN 55402
Mark Sauerbrey, Corporate Recruiter
Tel: (612) 330-5724 Fax: (612) 330-7935
Email: mark.w.sauerbrey@xcelenergy.com
Web: www.xcelenergy.com

MISSOURI

AMEREN
Human Resources
1901 Chouteau Ave.
St. Louis, MO 63103

Donna K. Martin, Senior Vice President,
Human Resources
Tel: (314) 621-3222
Web: www.ameren.com

ANHEUSER-BUSCH
Human Resources
1 Busche Pl.
St. Louis, MO 63118
Tel: (314) 577-2000
Web: www.anheuser-busch.com

CHARTER COMMUNICATIONS
Human Resources
12405 Powerscourt Dr.
St. Louis, MO 63131
Lynne F. Ramsey, Senior Vice President,
Human Resources
Tel: (314) 965-0555
Web: www.charter.com

EMERSON ELECTRIC
Human Resources
8000 W. Florissant Ave.
St. Louis, MO 63136
Charles Kelly, Vice President, Human
Resources
Tel: (314) 553-2000
Web: www.gotoemerson.com

EXPRESS SCRIPTS
Corporate Headquarters
13900 Riverport Rd.
Maryland Heights, MO 63043
Glenda Knebel, Director Human Resources
Tel: (314) 770-1666
Web: www.express-scripts.com

GRAYBAR ELECTRIC
Human Resources
34 N. Meramec Ave.
St. Louis, MO 63105
Kathleen M. Mazzarella, Vice President,
Human Resources and Strategic Planning
Tel: (314) 573-9200
Web: www.graybar.com

H&R BLOCK
Human Resources
4400 Main St.
Kansas City, MO 64111
Tammy S Serati, Senior Vice President,
Human Resources
Tel: (816) 753-6900
Web: www.hrblock.com

LEGGETT & PLATT
Human Resources
1 Leggett Rd.
Carthage, MO 64836
Cathleen Garrison, Recruiting Manager,
Human Resources
Tel: (417) 358-8131
Web: www.leggett.com

MAY DEPT. STORES
Human Resources
611 Olive St.
St. Louis, MO 63101
Marian Wagner, Vice President, Human
Resources
Tel: (314) 342-6300
Web: www.mayco.com

MOSANTO
Human Resources
800 N. Lindbergh Blvd
St. Louis, MO 63167
Steven C. Mizell, Senior Vice President,
Human Resources
Tel: (314) 694-1000
Web: www.mosanto.com

PEABODY ENERGY
Human Resources
701 Market St.
St. Louis, MO 63101
Sharon D. Fiehler, Executive Vice President,
Human Resources
Tel: (314) 342-3400
Web: www.peabodyenergy.com

NEBRASKA

BERKSHIRE HATHAWAY
Corporate Headquarters
1440 Kiewit Plaza
Omaha, NE 68131
Tel: (402) 346-1400
Web: www.berkshirehathaway.com

CONAGRA FOODS
Human Resources
1 ConAgra Dr.
Omaha, NE 68102
Peter M. Perez, Senior Vice President,
Human Resources
Tel: (402) 595-4000
Web: www.conagrafoods.com

MUTUAL OF OMAHA INS.
Human Resources
Mutual of Omaha Plaza
Omaha, NE 38175
Deborah Woods, Diversity Program
Coordinator
Tel: (402) 351-3044
Web: www.mutualofomaha.com

UNION PACIFIC
Corporate Headquarters
1400 Douglas St.
Omaha, NE 68179
Barbara W. Schaefer, Senior Vice President,
Human Resources and Corporate Secretary
Tel: (402) 544-5000
Web: www.up.com

NEVADA

CAESARS ENTERTAINMENT
Human Resources
3930 Howard Hughes Pkwy
Las Vegas, NV 89109
Jerry Boone, Senior Vice President, Human
Resources
Tel: (702) 699-5000
Web: www.caesars.com

HARRAH'S ENTERTAINMENT
Human Resources
1 Harrah's Court
Las Vegas, NV 89119
Jerry Boone, Senior Vice President, Human
Resources
Tel: (702) 407-6000
Web: www.harrah's.com

MGM MIRAGE
Human Resources
3600 Las Vegas Blvd S.
Las Vegas, NV 89109
Tel: (702) 693-7120
Web: www.mgmmirage.com

NEW HAMPSHIRE

FISHER SCIENTIFIC INTL.
Human Resources
1 Liberty Lane
Hampton, NH 03842
Mariam Quast, Recruiter

Tel: (603) 926-5911
Web: www.fisherscientific.com

NEW JERSEY

AMERICAN STANDARD
Human Resources
1 Centennial Ave.
Piscataway, NJ 08855
Lawrence B. Costello, Senior Vice
President, Human Resources
Tel: (732) 980-6000
Web: www.americanstandard.com

AT&T
Corporate Headquarters
1 AT&T Way
Bedminster, NJ 07921
Mirian Graddick-Weir, Executive Vice
President, Human Resources
Tel: (908) 221-2000
Web: www.att.com

AUTOMATIC DATA
1 ADP Blvd
Roseland, NJ 07068
Tel: (973) 974-5000 Fax: (973) 422-4323
Web: www.adp.com

AVAYA
Human Resources
211 Mount Airy Rd.
Basking Ridge, NJ 07920
Maryanne DiMarzo, Senior Vice President,
Human Resources
Tel: (908) 953-6000
Web: www.avaya.com

BECTON DICKINSON
Human Resources
1 Becton Dr.
Franklin Lakes, NJ 07417
Jean-Marc Dageville, Vice President,
Human Resources
Tel: (201) 847-6800
Web: www.bd.com

BED BATH & BEYOND
Human Resources
650 Liberty Ave.
Union, NJ 07083
Concetta Van Dyke, Vice President, Human
Resources
Tel: (908) 688-0888
Web: www.bedbathandbeyond.com

CAMPBELL SOUP
Human Resources
1 Campbell Place
Camden, NJ 08103
Marlon Doles, Sr. Manager Global Staffing
and Diversity
Tel: (856) 342-4800 Fax: (856) 342-3765
Email: marlon_doles@campbellsoup.com
Web: www.campbellsoupcompany.com

CHUBB
Corporate Headquarters
15 Mountain View Rd.
Warren, NJ 07061
Tel: (908) 903-2000 Fax: (908) 903-2027
Web: www.chubb.com

CIT GROUP
Human Resources
1 CIT Dr.
Livingston, NJ 07039
Gail Hardenburg, Manager, Human
Resources
Tel: (973) 740-5000
Web: www.cit.com

ENGELHARD
Human Resources
101 Wood Ave
Iselin, NJ 08830
Shamika Williams, Manager, Human Resources
Tel: (732) 205-5000
Web: www.englehard.com

HONEYWELL INTL.
Corporate Headquarters
101 Columbia Rd.
Morristown, NJ 07962
Thomas W. Weidenkopf, Senior Vice President, Human Resources and Communication
Tel: (973) 455-2000 Fax: (973) 455-4807
Web: www.honeywell.com

HOVNANIAN ENTERPRISES
Human Resources
10 Highway 35
Red Bank, NJ 07701
Robyn T. Mingle, Senior Vice President, Human Resources
Tel: (732) 747-7800
Web: www.khov.com

JOHNSON & JOHNSON
Corporate Headquarters
1 Johnson & Johnson Plz.
New Brunswick, NJ 08933
Tel: (732) 524-0400
Web: www.jnj.com

LUCENT TECHNOLOGIES
Human Resources
600 Mountain Ave.
Murray Hill, NJ 07974
Pamela Kimmet, Senior Vice President, Human Resources
Tel: (908) 582-8500
Web: www.lucent.com

MEDCO HEALTH SOLUTIONS
Corporate Headquarters
100 Parsons Pond Dr.
Franklin Lakes, NJ 07417
Laury Lawsky, Recruiter, Human Resources
Tel: (201) 269-3400 Fax: (201) 269-1204
Web: www.medco.com

MERCK
Corporate Headquarters
I Merck Rd.
Whitehouse Station, NJ 08889
Marcia J. Avedon, Senior Vice President, Human Resources
Tel: (908) 423-1000
Web: www.merck.com

PATHMARK STORES
200 Milk St.
Carteret, NJ 07008
Tony Parisi, Manager for Employment/Recruiting
Tel: (732) 499-3000 Fax: (732) 499-3500
Web: www.pathmark.com

PRUDENTIAL FINANCIAL
Corporate Headquarters
751 Broad St.
Newark, NJ 07102
Peter Rienzi, Director, Human Resources
Tel: (973) 802-6000
Web: www.prudential.com

PUBLIC SERVICE ENTERPRISE GROUP
Corporate Headquarters
80 Park Plaza
Newark, NJ 07102
Tel: (973) 430-7565
Web: www.pseg.com

QUEST DIAGNOSTICS
Human Resources
1290 Wall St. W.
Lyndhurst, NJ 07071
Tel: (201) 393-5000
Web: www.questdiagnostics.com

SCHERING-PLOUGH CORPORATION
Human Resources
2000 Galloping Hill Rd.
Kenilworth, NJ 07033
Carmelina Passante, HR Coordinator
Tel: (908) 298-2728 Fax: (908) 298-6756
Web: www.Schering-Plough.com

SEALED AIR
Human Resources
Park 80 E.
Saddle Brook, NJ 07663
Nadine Maffucci, Recruiter, Human Resources
Tel: (201) 791-7600
Web: www.sealedair.com

TOYS `R` US
Human Resources
1 Geoffrey Way.
Wayne, NJ 07470
Deborah Derby, Executive Vice President, Human Resources
Tel: (973) 617-3500
Web: www.toysrusinc.com

WYETH
Corporate Headquarters
5 Giraida Farms
Madison, NJ 07940
Rene R. Lewin, Senior Vice President
Tel: (973) 660-5000
Web: www.wyeth.com

NEW YORK

ALTRIA GROUP
Corporate Headquarters
120 Park Ave.
New York, NY 10017
Kenneth Murphy, Senior Vice President, Human Resources and Administration
Tel: (917) 663-2144 Fax: (917) 663-5544
Web: www.altria.com

AMERADA HESS
Corporate Headquarters
1185 6th Ave
New York, NY 10036
Lawrence Fox, Director, Human Resources
Tel: (212) 997-8500
Web: www.hess.com

AMERICAN EXPRESS
Corporate Headquarters
200 Vesey St.
New York, NY 10285
Bet Franzone, Manager, Public Affairs and Communications, Human Resources
Tel: (212) 640-1850 Fax: (212) 640-0332
Email: betfranzone@aexp.com
Web: www.americanexpress.com

AMERICAN INTL. GROUP
Corporate Headquarters
70 Pine St.,
New York, NY 10270
Alex I. Freudmann, Senior Vice President, Human Resources
Tel: (212) 770-7000
Web: www.aig.com

ARROW ELECTRONICS
Human Resources
50 Marcus Dr.
Melville, NY 11747

Susan M. Suver, Senior Vice President, Global Human Resources
Tel: (631) 847-2000
Web: www.arrow.com

ASBURY AUTOMOTIVE GROUP
Human Resources
622 Third Ave.
New York, NY 10017
Mr. Phil Johnson, Vice President, Human Resources
Tel: (212) 885-2500
Web: www.ashburyauto.com

ASSURANT
Human Resources
1 Chase Manhattan Center
New York, NY 10005
Robert Haertel, Senior Vice President, Compensation and Benefits
Tel: (212) 859-7000
Web: www.assurant.com

AVON PRODUCTS
Human Resources
1345 Sith Ave.
New York, NY 10105
Mae Eng, Global Recruiting
Tel: (212) 282-5000
Web: www.avoncompany.com

BANK OF NEW YORK CO.
Human Resources
1 Wall St.
New York, NY 10286
Gerry Gallashaw, Manager of Affirmative Action and Diversity
Tel: (212) 635-7479 Fax: (212) 635-7470
Email: ggallashaw@bankofny.com
Web: www.bankofny.com

BARNES & NOBLE
Human Resources
122 Fifth Ave.
New York, NY 10011
Michelle Smith, Vice President, Human Resources
Tel: (212) 633-3300
Web: www.barnesandnobleinc.com

BEAR STEARNS
Human Resources Department
383 Madison Ave.
New York, NY 10179
Tony Brown, Senior Managing Director
Tel: (212) 272-2000
Email: hresources_internetbear.com@bear.com
Web: www.bearstearns.com

BRISTOL-MYERS SQUIBB
Corporate Headquarters
345 Park Ave.
New York, NY 10154
Stephen E. Bear, Senior Vice President, Human Resources
Tel: (212) 546-4000
Web: www.bms.com

CABLEVISION SYSTEMS
Human Resources
1111 Stewart Ave.
Bethpage, NY 11714
Cara Mancini, Recruiting Manager, Human Resources
Tel: (516) 803-2300
Web: www.cablevision.com

CENDANT
Corporate Headquarters
9 W. 57th St.
New York, NY 10019
Terence P. Conley, Executive Vice President, Human Resources and Corporate Services

Tel: (212) 413-1800
Web: www.cendent.com

CITIGROUP
Corporate Headquarters
399 Park Ave.
New York, NY 10043
Michael Schlein, Senior Vice President, Global Corporate Affairs, Human Resources and Business Practices Citigroup Inc.
Tel: (212) 559-1000
Web: www.citigroup.com

COLGATE-PALMOLIVE
Human Resources
300 Park Ave.
New York, NY 10022
Paul T. Parker, Vice President, Human Resources
Web: www.colgate.com

CONSOLIDATED EDISON
Human Resources
4 Irving Pl.
New York, NY 10003
Claude Trahan, Vice President, Human Resources
Tel: (212) 460-4600
Web: www.conedison.com

CORNING
1 Riverfront Plz.
Corning, NY 14831
Tel: (607) 974-9000
Web: www.corning.com

DOVER
Human Resources
280 Park Ave.
New York, NY 10017
Tel: (212) 922-1640
Web: www.dovercorporation.com

EASTMAN KODAK COMPANY
Corporate Headquarters
343 State St.
Rochester, NY 14650
Tel: (800) 254-7923
Web: www.kodak.com

ENERGY EAST
Human Resources
Albany, NY 12212
Tel: (518) 434-3049
Web: www.energyeast.com

ESTÉE LAUDER
Human Resources
767 Fifth Ave.
New York, NY 10153
May Digeso, Senior Vice President, Human Resources
Tel: (212) 572-4200
Web: www.elcompanies.com

FOOT LOCKER
Human Resources
112 W. 34th St.
New York, NY 10120
Paticia A. Peck, Vice President, Human Resources
Tel: (212) 720-3700
Web: www.footlocker-inc.com

GOLDMAN SACHS GROUP
Corporate Headquarters
85 Broad St.
New York, NY 10004
Tel: (212) 902-1900
Web: www.gs.com

GUARDIAN LIFE OF AMERICA
Human Resources Department
7 Hanover Square

New York, NY 10004
Steven Smith, Recruitment Manager
Tel: (212) 598-8407
Web: www.guardianlife.com

HENRY SCHEIN
Human Resources
135 Duryea Rd.
Melville, NY 11747
Gerald A. Benjamin, Vice President
Tel: (631) 843-5500
Web: www.henryschein.com

IAC/INTERACTIVE
Human Resources
152 W. 57th St.
New York, NY 10019
Tel: (212) 314-7300
Web: www.iac.com

INTERPUBLIC GROUP
Human Resources
1114 Sixth Ave.
New York, NY 10036
James Simmons, Manager
Tel: (212) 704-1200
Web: www.interpublic.com

INTL. BUSINESS MACHINES
Corporate Headquarters
New Orchard Rd.
Armock, NY 10504
J. Randall McDonald, Human Resources
Tel: (914) 499-1900
Web: www.ibm.com

ITT INDUSTRIES
Human Resources
4 W. Red Oak Ln.
White Plains, NY 10604
Lucille Hill, Manager, Human Resources
Tel: (914) 641-2077
Web: www.itt.com

J.P. MORGAN CHASE & CO.
Corporate Headquarters
270 Park Ave.,
New York, NY 10017
John Farrell, Human Resources
Tel: (212) 270-6000
Web: www.jpmorganchase.com

L-3 COMMUNICATIONS
Human Resources
600 Third Ave
New York, NY 10016
Kenneth W. Manne, Human Resources
Tel: (212) 697-1111
Web: www.L-3com.com

LEHMAN BROTHERS HLDGS.
Human Resources
745 Seventh Ave.
New York, NY 10019
Lori Blankstein, Human Resources
Tel: (212) 526-7000
Email: humanresources.us@lehman.com
Web: www.lehman.com

LIZ CLAIBORNE
Human Resources
1441 Broadway
New York, NY 10018
Lawrence D. McClure, Senior Vice
President, Human Resources
Tel: (212) 354-4900
Web: www.lizclaiborne.com

LOEWS CORPORATION
Human Resources
655 Madison Ave. 7th Fl.
New York, NY 10021
Alan Moneyer, Director, Human Resources
Tel: (212) 521-2000 Fax: (212) 521-2466

Email: hrrep@newposition.com
Web: www.loews.com

MARSH & MCLENNAN
Corporate Headquarters
1166 Sixth Ave.
New York, NY 10036
Brian M. Storms, President/CEO
Tel: (212) 345-5000
Web: www.mmc.com

MCGRAW-HILL
Human Resources
1221 Sixth Ave.
New York, NY 10020
David L. Murphy, Executive Vice President,
Human Resources
Tel: (212) 512-2000
Web: www.mcgraw-hill.com

MERRILL LYNCH
Corporate Headquarters
4 Financial Center
New York, NY 10080
Terry Kasel, Head of Human Resources
Tel: (212) 449-1000
Web: www.ml.com

METLIFE
Corporate Headquarters
200 Park Ave.
New York, NY 10166
Denise Singleton, Minority Diversity
Manager
Tel: (908) 253-1068
Web: www.metlife.com

MORGAN STANLEY
Corporate Headquarters
1585 Broadway
New York, NY 10036
Marilyn Booker, Global Head of Diversity
Tel: (212) 761-4000
Email: diversityrecruiting@morganstanley.
com
Web: www.morganstanley.com

NEW YORK LIFE INSURANCE
Corporate Headquarters
51 Madison Ave
New York, NY 10010
Craig Gill, Senior Vice President, Human
Resources
Tel: (212) 576-7000
Web: www.newyorklife.com

NEWS CORP.
Human Resources
1211 Sixth Ave.
New York, NY 10036
Margaret Smith, Manager, Human
Resources
Tel: (212) 852-7000
Web: www.newscorp.com

NTL
Human Resources
909 Third Ave
New York, NY 10022
Carolyn Walker, Director, Human Resources
Tel: (212) 906-8440
Web: www.ntl.com

OMNICOM GROUP
Human Resources
437 Madison Ave.
New York, NY 10022
Tel: (212) 415-3600 Fax: (212) 415-3530
Web: www.omnicompgroup.com

PEPSI BOTTLING
Corporate Headquarters
1 Pepsi Way
Somers, NY 10589

John L. Berisford, Senior Vice President,
Human Resources
Tel: (914) 767-6000
Web: www.pbg.com

PEPSICO
700 Anderson Hill Rd.
Purchase, NY 10577
Margaret D. Moore, Senior Vice President,
Human Resources
Tel: (914) 253-2000
Web: www.pepsico.com

PFIZER
Corporate Headquarters
235 E. 42nd St.
New York, NY 10017
Sylvia M. Montero, Senior Vice President,
Human Resources
Tel: (212) 573-2323 Fax: (212) 573-7851
Web: www.pfizer.com

STARWOOD HOTELS & RSRTS.
Human Resources
1111 Westchester Ave.
White Plains, NY 10604
Randal Tucker, Manager MBE and Diversity
Tel: (914) 640-8100
Web: www.starwoodhotels.com

TIAA-CREF
Corporate Headquarters
730 Third Ave.
New York, NY 10017
Dermot J. O'Brien, Executive Vice
President, Human Resources
Tel: (212) 490-9000
Web: www.tiaa-cref.org

TIME WARNER
Corporate Headquarters
1 Time Warner Center
New York, NY 10019
Patricia Fili-Krushel, Executive Vice
President, Administration
Tel: (212) 484-8000
Web: www.timewarner.com

VERIZON COMMUNICATIONS
Corporate Headquarters
1095 Sixth Ave.
New York, NY 10036
Marc C. Reed, Executive Vice President,
Human Resources
Tel: (212) 395-1525 Fax: (212) 597-2721
Web: www.verizon.com

VIACOM
Corporate Headquarters
1515 Broadway
New York, NY 10036
William A. Roskin, Executive Vice President.
Human Resources
Tel: (212) 258-6000
Web: www.viacom.com

WELLCHOICE
Human Resources
11 W. 42nd St.
New York, NY 10036
Robert Lawrence, Senior Vice President,
Human Resources and Services
Tel: (212) 476-7800
Web: www.wellchoice.com

NORTH CAROLINA

BANK OF AMERICA CORP.
Corporate Headquarters
100 N. Tryon St.
Charlotte, NC 28255
Steele Alphin, Global Personnel Executive

Tel: (704) 386-8486
Web: www.bankofamerica.com

BB&T CORP.
200 W. 2nd St.
Winston-Salem, NC 27101
Laura Wingate, Administrator Assistance
Tel: (336) 733-2000
Web: www.bbandt.com

DUKE ENERGY
Corporate Headquarters
526 S. Church St.
Charlotte, NC 28202
Jim W. Moggs, Group Vice President and
Chief Development Officer
Tel: (704) 594-6200
Web: www.duke-energy.com

FAMILY DOLLAR STORES
Human Resources
10401 Monroe Rd.
Matthews, NC 28105
Samuel N. McPherson, Senior Vice
President, Human Resources
Tel: (704) 847-6961
Web: www.familydollar.com

GOODRICH
Human Resources
2730 W. Tyvola Rd.
Charlotte, NC 28217
Jennifer Pollino, Senior Vice President,
Human Resources
Tel: (704) 423-7000
Web: www.goodrich.com

JEFFERSON-PILOT
Human Resources
100 N. Greene St.
Greensboro, NC 27401
Brenda Lawrence, Manager, Recruiting
Tel: (336) 691-4061
Email: gsojobs@jpfinancial.com
Web: www.jpfinancial.com

LOWE'S
Corporate Headquarters
100 Loews Blvd
Mooresville, NC 28117
Maureen Ausura, Senior Vice President,
Human Resources
Tel: (704) 758-1000
Web: www.loews.com

NUCOR
Human Resources
2100 Rexford Rd.
Charlotte, NC 28211
James M. Coblin, Vice President, Human
Resources
Tel: (704) 366-7000 Fax: (704) 362-4208
Web: www.nucor.com

PROGRESS ENERGY
Human Resources
410 S. Wilmington St.
Raleigh, NC 27601
Anne M. Huffman, Vice President, Human
Resources
Tel: (919) 546-6111
Web: www.progress-energy.com

REYNOLDS AMERICAN
Corporate Headquarters
401 N. Main St.
Winston-Salem, NC 27102
Ann A. Johnston, Executive Vice President,
Human Resources
Tel: (336) 741-5500
Web: www.reynoldsamerican.com

SONIC AUTOMOTIVE
Human Resources

6415 Idlewild Rd
Charlotte, NC 28212
Tel: (704) 566-2400 Fax: (704) 536-4665
Web: www.sonicautomotive.com

SPX
Human Resources
13515 Ballantyne Corporate Place
Charlotte, NC 28277
Robert B. Foreman, Senior Vice President,
Human Resources
Tel: (704) 752-4400
Web: www.spx.com

VF CORPORATION
Human Resources
105 Corporate Center Blvd.
Greeensboro, NC 27408
Joann Otto, Manager, Human Resources
Tel: (336) 332-4143 Fax: (336) 332-4118
Email: joann_otto@vfc.com
Web: www.vfc.com

WACHOVIA CORP.
Corporate Headquarters
301 S. College St.
Charlotte, NC 28288
Shannon McFayden, Head of Human
Resources and Corporate Relations
Tel: (704) 374-6161
Web: www.wachovia.com

OHIO

AK STEEL HOLDING
Human Resources
703 Curtis St.
Middletown, OH 45043
Lawrence Zizzo, Human Resources
Tel: (513) 425-5000
Web: www.aksteel.com

AMERICAN ELECTRIC POWER
Human Resources
1 Riverside Rd.
Columbus, OH 43215
Steven Jamison, Human Resources
Tel: (614) 716-1000 Fax: (614) 716-1864
Web: www.aep.com

AMERICAN FINANCIAL GRP.
Human Resources
1 E. Fourth St.
Cincinnati, OH 45202
Michelle Young, Recruiting Manager
Tel: (513) 579-2121
Web: www.afginc.com

ASHLAND
Human Resource Department
PO Box 2219
Columbus, OH 43216
Tel: (800) 782-4669 Fax: (614) 790-3973
Web: www.ashland.com

BIG LOTS
Human Resources
300 Phillipi Rd.
Columbus, OH 43228
Paulie McCormick, Manager
Tel: (614) 278-6800
Web: www.biglots.com

CARDINAL HEALTH
Corporate Headquarters
7000 Cardinal Pl.
Dublin, OH 43017
Carole Watkins, Human Resources
Tel: (614) 757-5000
Web: www.cardinal.com

CINCINNATI FINANCIAL
Human Resources
6200 Gilmore Rd.
Fairfield, OH 45014
Dave Karas, Manager, Recruiting
Tel: (513) 870-2000
Web: www.cinfin.com

CINERGY
139 E. 4th St.
Cincinnati, OH 45202
Tel: (513) 421-9500
Web: www.cinergy.com

COOPER TIRE & RUBBER
Human Resources
701 Lima Ave
Findlay, OH 45840
Linda Gallant, Recruiting Manager
Tel: (419) 423-1321
Web: www.coopertire.com

DANA
Corporate Headquarters
4500 Dorr St.
Toledo, OH 43615
Richard W. Spriggle, Vice President,
Human Resources
Web: www.dana.com

EATON
Human Resources
1111 Superior Ave.
Cleveland, OH 44114
Susan J. Cook, Vice President, Human
Resources
Tel: (216) 523-5000
Web: www.eaton.com

FEDERATED DEPT. STORES
Human Resources
7 W.Seventh St.
Cincinnati, OH 45202
David W. Clark, Human Resources
Tel: (513) 579-7000
Web: www.fds.com

FIFTH THIRD BANCORP
Human Resources
38 Fountain Square Pl.
Cincinnati, OH 45263
Rachel Klink, Employment Process
Manager
Tel: (513) 534-5300 Fax: (534) 534-8621

FIRST ENERGY
Human Resources
76 S. Main St.
Akron, OH 44308
Renee Spino, Director, Human Resources
Tel: (800) 736-3402 Fax: (330) 384-2455
Web: www.firstenergycorp.com

GOODYEAR TIRE & RUBBER
Human Resources
1144 E. Market St.
Akron, OH 44316
Kathleen T. Geier, Senior Vice President,
Human Resources
Tel: (330) 796-2121 Fax: (330) 796-2222
Web: www.goodyear.com

INTERNATIONAL STEEL GROUP
Human Resources
4020 Kinross Lakes Pkwy.
Richfield, OH 44286
Karen A. Smith, Vice President, Human
Resources
Tel: (330) 659-9100
Web: www.intlsteel.com

KEYCORP
Human Resources
127 Public Square
Cleveland, OH 44114
Thomas E. Helfrich, Executive Vice
President, Human Resources
Tel: (216) 689-6300
Web: www.key.com

KROGER
Corporate Headquarters
1014 Vine St.
Cincinnati, OH 45202
Caroline Growl, Human Resources
Tel: (513) 762-4000 Fax: (513) 762-1160
Web: www.kroger.com

LIMITED BRANDS
Human Resources
3 Limited Pkwy.
Columbus, OH 43230
Sandra West, Executive Vice President
Tel: (614) 415-7000
Web: www.limitedbrands.com

NATIONAL CITY CORP.
Corporate Headquarters
1900 E. 9th St.
Cleveland, OH 44114
Jon N. Couture, Senior Vice President,
Tel: (216) 222-2000
Web: www.nationalcity.com

NATIONWIDE
Human Resources
1 Nationwide Plaza
Columbus, OH 43215
Tel: (614) 249-7111
Web: www.nationwide.com

NCR CORPORATION
Human Resources
1700 S. Patterson Blvd.
Dayton, OH 45479
Tel: (937) 445-5000
Web: www.ncr.com

OWENS CORNING
Human Resources
1 Owens Corning Pkwy
Toledo, OH 43659
Joseph C. High, Senior Vice President
Tel: (419) 248-8000
Web: www.owenscorning.com

OWENS-ILLINOIS
Human Resources
1 Seagate
Toledo, OH 43666
Stephen Malia, Senior Vice President
Tel: (419) 247-5000
Web: www.o-i.com

PARKER HANNIFIN
Human Resources
6035 Parkland Blvd.
Cleveland, OH 44124
Patti Sfero, HR Manager
Tel: (216) 896-3000 Fax: (216) 896-4024
Web: www.parker.com

PROCTER & GAMBLE
1 Procter & Gamble Plz.
Cincinnati, OH 45202
Richard L. Antoine, Global Human
Resources Officer
Tel: (513) 983-1100
Web: www.pg.com

PROGRESSIVE
Human Resources
6300 Wilson Mills Rd.
Mayfield Village, OH 44143
Susan Patricia Griffith, COO

Tel: (440) 461-5000
Web: www.progressive.com

SHERWIN-WILLIAMS
Human Resources
101 Prospect Ave. N.W.
Cleveland, OH 44115
Neil Ghanen, Human Resources Manager
Tel: (216) 566-2000 Fax: (216) 566-3670
Web: www.sherwin.com

TIMKEN
Human Resources
1835 Dueber Ave S.W.
Canton, OH 44706
Donald L. Walker, Human Resources
Tel: (330) 438-3000
Web: www.timken.com

WENDY'S INTERNATIONAL
Human Resources
4288 W. Dublin-Granville Rd.
Dublin, OH 43017
Kim Anderson, Administrator
Tel: (614) 764-3100
Web: www.wendys.com

WESTERN & SOUTHERN FINANCIAL
Human Resources
400 Broadway
Cincinnati, OH 45202
Noreen J. Hayes, Senior Vice President
Tel: (513) 629-1800 Fax: (513) 629-1220
Web: www.westernsouthern.com

OKLAHOMA

DEVON ENERGY CORPORATION
Human Resources
20 N. Broadway
Oklahoma City, OK 73102
Paul R. Poley, Human Resources
Tel: (405) 235-3611 Fax: (405) 552-4550
Web: www.devonenergy.com

KERR-MCGEE
Human Resources
Kerr-McGee Center
Oklahoma, OK 73125
Fran G. Heartwell, Vice President, Human
Resources
Tel: (405) 270-1313
Web: www.kerr-mcgee.com

OGE ENERGY
Human Resources
321 N. Harvey Ave.
Oklahoma City, OK 73102
Kevin Maxwell, Recruiting Coordinator
Tel: (405) 553-3000
Web: www.oge.com

ONEOK
Human Resources
100 W. Fifth St.
Tulsa, OK 74103
Manning, Manager, Human Resources
Tel: (918) 588-7000
Web: www.oneok.com

WILLIAMS
Human Resources
1 Williams Center
Tulsa, OK 74172
John C. Fischer, Vice President, Human
Resources
Tel: (918) 573-2000
Web: www.williams.com

OREGON

NIKE
Human Resources
1 Bowerman Dr.
Beaverton, OR 97005
Julia Law, Vice President
Web: www.nike.com

PENNSYLVANIA

AIR PRODUCTS & CHEM.
Central Staffing Group
7201 Hamilton Blvd.
Allentown, PA 18195
Robin Lysek, Director of Central Staffing
Tel: (610) 481-4911 X8787
Web: www.airproducts.com

ALCOA
Corporate Headquarters
201 Isabella St.
Pittsburgh, PA 15212
Regina M. Hitchery, Human Resources
Tel: (412) 553-4545 Fax: (412) 553-4498
Web: www.alcoa.com

AMERISOURCEBERGEN
Corporate Headquarters
1300 Morris Dr.
Chesterbrook, PA 19087
Gab Holdman, Human Resources Manager
Tel: (610) 727-7000 Fax: (617) 727-3611
Web: www.amerisourcebergen.com

ARAMARK
Human Resources
1101 Market St.
Philadelphia, PA 19107
Lynn B. McKee, Human Resources
Tel: (215) 238-3000
Web: www.aramark.com

CIGNA
Corporate Headquarters
1 Liberty Pl.
Philadelphia, PA 19192
John M. Murabito, Executive Vice
President, Human Resources and Services
Tel: (215) 761-1000
Web: www.cigna.com

COMCAST
Human Resources
1500 Market St.
Philadelphia, PA 19102
Chaisse Lillie, Vice President, Human
Resources
Tel: (215) 665-1700
Web: www.comcast.com

CROWN HOLDINGS
Human Resources
1 Crown Way
Philadelphia, PA 19154
Douglass McLaughlin, Cooporate Manager
Tel: (215) 698-5100 Fax: (215) 676-7245

ERIE INSURANCE GROUP
Human Resources
100 Erie Insurance Pl.
Erie, PA 16530
Ann Scott, Manager, Human Resources
Tel: (814) 870-2000
Web: www.erieinsurance.com

H.J. HEINZ
World Headquarters
357 6th Ave.
Pittsburgh, PA 152222
Thomas DiDonato, Chief People Officer

Tel: (412) 456-5700
Web: www.heinz.com/jsp/careers_f.jsp

HERSHEY FOODS
Human Resources
100 Crystal A Dr.
Hershey, PA 17033
Marcella K. Arline, Senior Vice President
Tel: (717) 534-6799

IKON OFFICE SOLUTIONS
Human Resources
70 Valley Stream Pkwy
Malvern, PA 19355
Beth B. Sexton, Senior Vice President
Tel: (610) 296-8000
Web: www.ikon.com

JONES APPAREL GROUP
Human Resources
250 Rittenhouse Circle
Bristol, PA 19007
Jackie Mallory, Recruiting Manager
Tel: (215) 785-4000
Web: www.jny.com

LINCOLN NATIONAL
Human Resources
1500 Market St.
Philadelphia, PA 19102
Elizabeth L. Reeves, Senior Vice President
Tel: (215) 448-1400
Web: www.lfg.com

MELLON FINANCIAL CORP.
Human Resources
1 Melon Center
Pittsburgh, PA 15258
Tel: (412) 234-5000
Web: www.mellon.com

PNC FINANCIAL SERVICES
249 5th Ave.
Pittsburgh, PA 15222
Tel: (412) 762-2000
Web: www.pnc.com

PPG INDUSTRIES
Human Resources
1 PPG St.
Pittsburgh, PA 15272
Charles W. Wise, Vice President, Human
Resources
Tel: (412) 434-3131
Web: www.ppg.com

PPL
Human Resources
2 N. Ninth St.
Allentown, PA 18101
Tel: (610) 774-5836
Web: www.pplweb.com

RITE AID
Corporate Headquarters
30 Hunter Lane
Camp Hill, PA 17011
Stephanie Naito, Human Resources
Tel: (717) 761-2633
Web: www.riteaid.com

ROHM & HAAS
Human Resources
100 Independence Mall W.
Philadelphia, PA 19106
Tel: (212) 679-0000
Web: www.rohmhaas.com

SUNOCO
Corporate Headquarters
1801 Market Pl.
Philadelphia, PA 19103
Rolf D. Naku, Human Resources
Tel: (215) 977-6106
Web: www.sunocoinc.com

TOLL BROTHERS
250 Gibraltar Rd.
Horsham, PA 19044
Jay Lehnan, Director of Recruiting
Tel: (215) 938-8130 Fax: (215) 938-3060
Web: www.tollbrothers.com

UGI
Human Resources
460 N. Gulph Rd.
King of Prussia, PA 19406
Rose Mary
Tel: (610) 337-1000
Web: www.unicorp.com

UNITED STATES STEEL
Human Resources
600 Grant St.
Pittsburgh, PA 15219
Thomas W. Sterling, Senior Vice President
Tel: (412) 433-6748
Web: www.ussteel.com

UNIVERSAL HEALTH SVCS.
Human Resources
367 S. Gulph Rd.
King of Prussia, PA 19406
Coleen Johns, Recruiter, Human Resources
Tel: (610) 768-3300
Web: www.uhsinc.com

WESCO INTERNATIONAL
Human Resources
225 West Station Square Dr.
Pittsburgh, PA 15219
Bob Henshaw, Director, Human Resources
Tel: (412) 454-2200
Web: www.wesco.com

YORK INTERNATIONAL
Human Resources
631 S. Richland Ave.
York, PA 17403
Jeffret Gard, Vice President, Human
Resources
Tel: (717) 771-7890
Web: www.york.com

RHODE ISLAND

CVS
Corporate Headquarters
1 CVS Dr.
Woonsocket, RI 02895
V. Michael Ferdinandi, Senior Vice
President, Human Resources
Tel: (401) 765-1500
Web: www.cvs.com

TEXTRON
Human Resources
40 WestMinster St.
Providence, RI 02903
George E. Metzger, Vice President
Tel: (401) 421-2800
Web: www.textron.com

SOUTH CAROLINA

SCANA
Human Resources
1426 Main St.
Columbia, SC 29201
Joseph C. Bouknight, Human Resources
Tel: (803) 217-9000
Web: www.scana.com

TENNESSEE

AUTOZONE
Human Resources
123 S. Front St.
Memphis, TN 38103
Daisy L. Vanderlinde, Senior Vice President
Tel: (901) 495-6500
Web: www.autozone.com

CAREMARK RX
Human Resources
211 Commerce St.
Nashville, TN 37201
Kirk McConnell, Executive Vice President
Tel: (615) 743-6600
Web: www.caremark.com

DOLLAR GENERAL
Human Resources
100 Mission Ridge
Goodlettsville, TN 37072
Jeffrey Rice, Vice President
Tel: (615) 855-4000
Web: www.dollargeneral.com

EASTMAN CHEMICAL
Human Resources
100 N. Eastman Rd.
Kingsport, TN 37660
Norris P. Sneed, Senior Vice President,
Human Resources
Tel: (423) 229-2000
Web: www.eastman.com

FEDEX
Corporate Headquarters
924 S. Shady Grove Rd.
Memphis, TN 38120
Larry C. Miller, President, Chief Executive
Officer, FedEx Freight East
Tel: (901) 369-3600
Web: www.fedex.com

HCA
Corporate Headquarters
1 Park Plz.
Nashville, TN 37203
John M. Steele, Senior Vice President,
Human Resources
Tel: (615) 344-9551
Web: www.hcahealthcare.com

UNUMPROVIDENT
Human Resources
1 Fountain Sq.
Chattanooga, TN 37402
Aileen Farrah, Director, Human Resources
Tel: (423) 755-1011
Web: www.unumprovident.com

TEXAS

AFFILIATED COMPUTER SVCS.
Human Resources
2828 N. Haskell Ave
Dallas, TX 75204
Denettra Quintanilla, Manager, Recruiting
Tel: (214) 841-6111
Web: www.acs-inc.com

AMR
Corporate Headquarters
4333 Amon Carter Dr.
Fort Worth, TX 76155
Jeffery J. Brunage, Senior Vice President,
Human Resources
Tel: (817) 963-1234
Web: www.aa.com

ANADARKO PETROLEUM
Human Resources

1201 Lake Robbins Dr.
The Woodlands, TX 77380
Susan Cleveland, Staff Specialist
Tel: (832) 636-1000 Fax: (832) 636-5653
Email: susan_cleveland@andarko.com
Web: www.anadarko.com

APACHE
Human Resources
2000 Post Oak Blvd.
Houston, TX 77056
Jeffrey M. Bender, Human Resources
Tel: (713) 296-6000
Web: www.apachecorp.com

BAKER HUGHES
Human Resources
3900 Essex Lane
Houston, TX 77027
Greg Nakanishi, Vice President
Tel: (713) 439-8600
Web: www.bakerhughes.com

BRINKER INTERNATIONAL
Human Resources
6820 L.B.J. Freeway
Dallas, TX 75240
Valerie L. Davisson, Executive Vice
President, Human Resources
Tel: (972) 980-9917
Web: www.brinker.com

BURLINGTON NO. SANTA FE
Corporate Headquarters
2650 Lou Menk Dr.
Fort Worth, TX 76131
Jeanna E. Michalski, Vice President
Tel: (800) 795-2673
Web: www.bnsf.com

BURLINGTON RESOURCES
Human Resources
717 Texas Ave.
Houston, TX 77002
William Usher, Vice President
Tel: (817) 347-2000 Fax: (817) 347-2229
Web: www.br-inc.com

CENTERPOINT ENERGY
Corporate Headquarters
1111 Louisiana St.
Houston, TX 77002
Preston Johnson, Jr., Senior Vice President,
Tel: (713) 207-1111
Web: www.centerpointenergy.com

CENTEX
Human Resources
2728 N. Harwood St.
Dallas, TX 75201
Wilemia Shaw, Director, Human Resources
Tel: (214) 981-5000
Web: www.centex.com

CLEAR CHANNEL COMMUNICATIONS
Human Resources
200 E. Basse Rd.
San Antonio, TX 78209
Bill Hamersly, Senior Vice President
Tel: (210) 822-2828
Email: billhamersly@clearchannel.com
Web: www.clearchannel.com

COMMERCIAL METALS
Human Resources
6565 N. MacArthur Blvd
Irving, TX 75039
Keith Shull, Vice President, Human
Resources
Tel: (214) 689-4300
Web: www.commercialmetals.com

CONOCOPHILLIPS
Corporate Headquarters
600 N. Dairy Ashford Rd.

Houston, TX 77079
Carin S. Knickel, Vice President, Human
Resources
Tel: (281) 293-1000
Web: www.conocophillips.com

CONTINENTAL AIRLINES
Human Resources
1600 Smith St.
Houston, TX 77002
Mike Bonds, Senior Vice President
Tel: (713) 324-5000
Web: www.continental.com

D.R. HORTON
Corporate Headquarters
301 Commerce St.
Fort Worth, TX 76102
Tel: (817) 390-8200
Web: www.drhorton.com

DEAN FOODS
Human Resources
2515 McKinney Ave.
Dallas, TX 75201
Robert Dunn, Senior Vice President
Tel: (214) 303-3400
Web: www.deanfoods.com

DELL
Corporate Headquarters
1 Dell Way
Round Rock, TX 78682
Paul D. McKinnon, Senior Vice President
Tel: (512) 338-4400
Web: www.dell.com

DYNEGY
Human Resources
1000 Louisiana St.
Houston, TX 77002
R. Blake Young, Executive Vice President,
Administration and Technology
Tel: (713) 507-6400
Web: www.dynegy.com

EL PASO
Human Resources
1001 Louisana St.
Houston, TX 77002
Tel: (713) 420-2600
Email: staffing@elpaso.com
Web: www.elpaso.com

ELECTRONIC DATA SYSTEMS
Human Resources
5400 Legacy Dr.
Plano, TX 75024
Tina M. Sivinski, Executive Vice President,
Human Resources
Tel: (972) 604-6000
Web: www.eds.com

ENBRIDGE ENERGY PARTNERS
Human Resources
1100 Louisiana St.
Houston, TX 77002
Tel: (713) 821-2000 Fax: (713) 821-2229
Web: www.enbridgepartners.com

ENTERPRISE PRODUCTS
Human Resources
2727 N. Loop West
Houston, TX 77008
David Scott, Manager of Benefits
Tel: (713) 880-6500
Web: www.epplp.com

EXXON MOBIL
Exxon Mobil Corporation
5959 Las Colinas Blvd.
Irving, TX 75039-2298
L. J. Cavanaugh, Vice President
Tel: (972) 444-1000 Fax: (972) 444-1883
Web: www.exxon.mobil.com

GROUP 1 AUTOMOTIVE
Human Resources
950 Echo Lane
Houston, TX 77024
J. Brooks O'Hara, Vice President, Human
Resources
Tel: (713) 647-5700 Fax: (713) 647-5858
Web: www.group1auto.com

J.C. PENNEY
Corporate Headquarters
6501 Legacy Dr.
Plano, TX 75024
Gary L. Davis, Executive Vice President,
Chief Human Resources
Tel: (973) 431-1000
Web: www.jcpenney.net

KIMBERLY-CLARK
Corporate Headquarters
351 Phelps Dr.
Irving, TX 75038
Lizanne C. Gottung, Senior Vice President,
Human Resources
Tel: (972) 281-2000
Web: www.kimberley-clark.com

KINDER MORGAN ENERGY
Human Resources
500 Dallas St. #1000
Houston, TX 77002
Roger Mosby, VP of HR
Tel: (713) 369-9000 Fax: (713) 369-9411
Web: www.kindermorgan.com

LYONDELL CHEMICAL
Human Resources
1221 McKinney St.
Houston, TX 77010
John A. Hollinshead, Vice President,
Human Resources
Tel: (713) 652-7200
Web: www.lyondell.com

MARATHON OIL
Corporate Headquarters
5555 San Felipe Rd.
Houston, TX 77056
Eileen Campbell, Vice-President, Human
Resources
Tel: (713) 629-6600
Web: www.marathon.com

PILGRIM'S PRIDE
Human Resources
110 S. Texas St.
Pittsburg, TX 75686
Peg Patton, Recuiter, Human Resources
Tel: (903) 855-1000
Web: www.pilgrimspride.com

PLAINS ALL AMERICAN PIPELINE
Human Resources
333 Clay St.
Houston, TX 77002
Connie Emerson, Recuitment, Human
Resources
Tel: (713) 646-4100 Fax: (713) 646-4147
Web: www.paalp.com

RADIO SHACK
Human Resources
300 Radio Shack Circle
Fort Worth, TX 76102
James R. Fredericks, Senior Vice President,
Human Resources
Web: www.radioshackcorporation.com

RELIANT ENERGY
Human Resources
1000 Main St.
Houston, TX 77002
Karen D. Taylor, Senior Vice President,
Human Resources and Administration

Tel: (713) 497-3000 Fax: (713) 488-5925
Web: www.reliant.com

SBC COMMUNICATIONS
Corporate Headquarters
175 E. Houston St.
San Antonio, TX 78205
Karen Jennings, Senior Executive Vice
President, Human Resources and
Communications
Tel: (210) 821-4105
Web: www.sbc.com

SMITH INTERNATIONAL
Human Resources
411 N. Sam Houston Pkwy.
Houston, TX 77060
Malcolm W. Anderson, Vice President,
Human Resources
Tel: (281) 443-3370
Web: www.smith.com

SOUTHWEST AIRLINES
Human Resources
2702 Love Field Dr.
Dallas, TX 75235
Willie Edwards, Director, Human Resources
Tel: (214) 792-6192 Fax: (214) 792-5015
Email: willieedwards@wnco.com
Web: www.southwest.com

SYSCO
Corporate Headquarters
1390 Enclave Pkwy
Houston, TX 77077
K. Susan Billiot, Assistant Vice President,
Human Resources
Tel: (281) 584-1390
Web: www.sysco.com

TEMPLE-INLAND
Human Resources
1300 MoPac Expressway S.
Austin, TX 78746
Tel: (512) 434-5800
Web: www.templeinland.com

TENET HEALTHCARE
Human Resources
13737 Noel Rd.
Dallas, TX 75240
Joseph A. Bosch, Senior Vice President,
Human Resources
Tel: (469) 893-2200 Fax: (469) 893-8600
Web: www.tenethealth.com

TESORO
Corporate Headquarters
300 Concord Plaza Dr.
San Antonio, TX 78216
Susan A. Lerette, Vice President, Human
Resources
Tel: (210) 828-8484
Web: www.tsocorp.com

TEXAS INSTRUMENTS
Corporate Headquarters
12500 TI Blvd
Dallas, TX 75266
Steve Leven, Senior Vice President,
Manager of Worldwide Human Resources
Web: www.ti.com

TRIAD HOSPITALS
Human Resources
5800 Tennyson Pkwy
Plano, TX 75024
Rick Thomason, Vice President
Tel: (214) 473-7000
Web: www.triadhospitals.com

TXU
Diversity
1601 Bryan St.

Dallas, TX 75201
Cheryl Stevens, Vice President, Workforce
and Supplier Diversity
Tel: (214) 812-6923 Fax: (214) 812-5597
Web: www.txucorp.com

USAA
Corporate Headquarters
9800 Fredericksburg Rd.
San Antonio, TX 78288
Tel: (210) 498-2211
Web: www.usaa.com

VALERO ENERGY
Human Resources
1 Valero Way
San Antonio, TX 78249
Pat Dullie, Human Resources
Tel: (210) 345-2000 Fax: (210) 345-2646
Web: www.valero.com

WASTE MANAGEMENT
Human Resources
1001 Fannin St.
Houston, TX 77002
Carlton Yearwood, Vice President
Tel: (713) 512-6200
Web: www.wm.com

WHOLE FOODS MARKET
Human Resources
550 Bowie St.
Austin, TX 78703
Mark Ehrstein, Director, Human Resources
Tel: (512) 477-4455
Web: www.wholefoodsmarket.com

UTAH

AUTOLIV
Human Resources
3350 Airport Rd.
Ogden, UT 84405
Brian Peterson, Human Resources
Manager
Tel: (801) 625-9200
Web: www.autoliv.com

VIRGINIA

ADVANCE AUTO PARTS
Human Resources
5673 Airport Rd.
Roanoke, VA 24012
Keith A. Oreson, Senior Vice President
Tel: (540) 362-4911
Web: www.advanceautoparts.com

AES
Human Resources
4300 Wilson Blvd
Arlington, VA 22203
Jay Kloosterboer, Vice President
Tel: (703) 522-1315
Web: www.aes.com

BRINK'S
Human Resources
1801 Bayberry Ct
Richmond, VA 23226
Joe Verostic, Director Human Resources
Tel: (804) 289-9700 Fax: (804) 289-9758
Web: www.brinkscompany.com

CAPITAL ONE FINANCIAL
Corporate Headquarters
1680 Capital One Dr.
McLean, VA 22102
Tel: (703) 720-1000
Web: www.capitalone.com

CARMAX
Human Resources
4900 Cox Rd.
Glen Allen, VA 23060
Scott Rivas, Vice President
Tel: (804) 747-0422
Web: www.carmax.com

CIRCUIT CITY STORES
Human Resources
9950 Maryland Dr.
Richmond, VA 23233
Eric A. Jonas, Jr., Senior Vice President
Tel: (804) 527-4000
Web: www.circuitcity.com

DOMINION RESOURCES
Corporate Heaquarters
120 Tredegar St
Richmond, VA 23219
Tel: (804) 819-2000
Web: www.dom.com

GANNETT
Human Resources
7950 Jones Branch Dr.
McLean, VA 22107
Jose Berrios, VP of Leadership
Tel: (703) 854-6224 Fax: (703) 854-2009
Web: www.gannett.com

GENERAL DYNAMICS
2941 Fairview Park Dr
Falls Church, VA 22042
Walter M. Oliver, Senior Vice President
Tel: (703) 876-3000 Fax: (703) 876-3125
Web: www.gd.com

MCI
Human Resources
22001 Loundon County Pkwy,
Ashburn, VA 20147
Daniel Casaccia, Executive Vice President
Tel: (703) 866-5600
Web: www.mci.com

MEADWESTVACO CORPORATION
Human Resources/Staffing
1011 Boulder Spring Dr.
Richmond, VA 23225
Cynda Berger, Staffing Director
Tel: (804) 327-7900 Fax: (804) 327-7205
Web: www.meadwestvaco.com

NEXTEL COMMUNICATIONS
Human Resources
2001 Edmund Halley Dr
Reston, VA 20191
Randy Harris, Senior Vice President
Tel: (703) 433-4000
Web: www.nextel.com

NORFOLK SOUTHERN
3 Commercial Pl.
Norfolk, VA 23510
Ricky Morris, Management Recruiting
Tel: 757-664-5066 Fax: 757-664-5069
Email: ricky.morris@nscorp.com
Web: www.nscorp.com

NVR
Human Resources
7601 Lewinsville Rd
McLean, VA 22102
Tel: (703) 956-4000 Fax: (703) 956-4750
Web: www.nvrinc.com

OWENS & MINOR
Human Resources
4800 Cox Rd.
Glen Allen, VA 23060
Erika T. Davis, Senior Vice President
Tel: (804) 747-9794 Fax: (804) 270-7281
Web: www.owens-minor.com

PERFORMANCE FOOD GROUP
Human Resources
12500 W. Creek Pkwy.
Richmond, VA 23238
Pauline Donato, Regional Vice President
Tel: (804) 484-7700 Fax: (804) 484-7940
Email: pdonato@pfgc.com
Web: www.pfgc.com

SLM
Human Resources
12061 Bluemont Way
Reston, VA 20190
Joni Reich, Senior Vice President
Tel: (703) 810-3000
Web: www.salliemae.com

SMITHFIELD FOODS
Corporate Headquarters
200 Commerce St.
Smithfield, VA 23430
Denise Sweat, Employee Relations Manager
Tel: (757) 365-3000
Web: www.smithfieldfoods.com

WASHINGTON

AMAZON.COM
Human Resources
1200 12th Ave. South
Seattle, WA 98144
Tel: (206) 266-2171 Fax: (206) 266-1355
Web: www.amazon.com

COSTCO WHOLESALE
Corporate Headquarters
999 Lake Dr.
Issaquah, WA 98027
John Matthews, Senior Vice President,
Human Resources and Risk Management
Tel: (425) 313-8100
Web: www.costco.com

MICROSOFT
Corporate Headquarters
1 Microsoft Way
Redmond, WA 98052
Lisa Brummel, Corporate Vice President,
Human Resources
Tel: (425) 882-8080
Web: www.microsoft.com

NORDSTROM
Human Resources
1671 Sixth Ave.
Seattle, WA 98101
Johnnetta Rowsey, Washing/Alaska Diversity
Affairs Director
Tel: (206) 628-2111
Web: www.nordstrom.com

PACCAR
Human Resources
777 106th Ave.
Bellevue, WA 98004
Tel: (425) 468-7400 Fax: (425) 468-8216
Web: www.paccar.com

SAFECO
Human Resources
Safeco Plaza
Seattle, WA 98185
Kevin Carter, Director of Diversity
Tel: (206) 545-5000 Fax: (206) 925-0165
Web: www.safeco.com

STARBUCKS
Human Resources
2401 Utah Ave.
Seattle, WA 98134
Tel: (206) 447-1575
Web: www.starbucks.com

WASHINGTON MUTUAL
Human Resources
1201 Third Ave.
Seattle, WA 98101
Daryl D. David, Executive Vice President,
Human Resources
Tel: (206) 461-2000
Web: www.wamu.com

WEYERHAEUSER
Human Resources
33633 Weyerhaeuser Way St.
Federal Way, WA 98063
Edward Rogel, Senior Vice President,
Human Resources
Tel: (253) 924-2345
Web: www.weyerhaeuser.com

WISCONSIN

AMERICAN FAMILY INS. GRP.
Strategic Staffing
6000 American Pkwy.
Madison, WI 53783
Tel: (608) 249-2111 Fax: (608) 243-6529
Web: www.amfam.com

HARLEY-DAVIDSON
Human Resources
3700 Juneau Ave.
Milwaukee, WI 53208
Ryan Smith, Recuiter, Human Resources
Tel: (414) 342-4680
Web: www.harley-davidson.com

JOHNSON CONTROLS
Corporate Headquarters
5757 N. Green Bay Ave.
Milwaukee, WI 53201
Susan Davis, Vice President, Human
Resources
Tel: (414) 524-1200
Web: www.johnsoncontrols.com

KOHL'S
Human Resources
N56 W. 17000 Ridgewood Dr.
Menomonee Falls, WI 53051
Genny Shields, Vice President, Human
Resources
Tel: (262) 703-7000 Fax: (262) 703-7115
Web: www.kohls.com

MANPOWER
Human Resources
5301 N. Ironwood Rd.
Milwaukee, WI 53217
Charles Pugh, Director of Human
Resources
Tel: (414) 961-1000 Fax: (414) 961-7985
Web: www.manpower.com

NORTHWESTERN MUTUAL
Corporate Headquarters
720 E. Wisconsin Ave.
Milwaukee, WI 53202
Susan A. Lueger, Vice President
Tel: (414) 271-1444
Web: www.northwesternmutual.com

ROUNDY'S
Human Resources
875 E. Wisconsin Ave.
Milwaukee, WI 53202
John Quincannon, Senior Recruiter
Tel: (414) 231-5000
Web: www.roundys.com

WISCONSIN ENERGY
Human Resources
231 W. Michigan St.
Milwaukee, WI 53203

121: one to one ADN: any day now AFAIK: as far as I know AFK: away from keyboard **A/S/L: age, sex, location** B4: before B4N: bye for now BAK: back at the keyboard BBIAB: be back in a bit BBL: be back later BBN: bye bye now BBS: be back soon BEG: big evil grin **BF: boyfriend** BFN: bye for now BG: big grin BL: belly laughing BMTIPG: brilliant minds think in parallel gutters BRB: be right back BTA: but then again BTW: by the way BWL: bursting with laughter BWTHDIK: but what the heck do I know C&G: chuckle & grin CID: crying in disgrace CNP: continued (in my) next post CP: chat post CRBT: crying real big tears CSG: chuckle, snicker, grin CU: see you CUL: see you later CYO: see you online DBAU: doing business as usual DIKU: do I know you? DL: dead link DLTBBB: don't let the bed bugs bite DQMOT: don't quote me on this EG: evil grin EMFBI: excuse me for butting in EMSG: email message EOT: end of thread F2F: face to face FC: fingers crossed FISH: first in, still here FMTYEWTK: far more than you ever wanted to know FOMCL: falling off my chair laughing FTBOMH: from the bottom of my heart FUD: fear, uncertainty, and doubt FWIW: for what it's worth G2G: got to go G: grin GA: go ahead GAL: get a life GD&R: grinning, ducking, and running GF: girlfriend GFN: gone for now GIWIST: gee, I wish I'd said that GMBO: giggling my butt off GMTA: great minds think alike GOL: giggling out loud GTRM: going to read mail GTSY: glad to see you H&K: hug and kiss HAGN: have a good night **HDOP: help delete online predators** HHIS: hanging head in shame HTH: hope this helps HUB: head up butt IAC: in any case IANAL: I am not a lawyer (but) IC: I see IDK: I don't know IHA: I hate acronyms IIRC: if I remember correctly ILU: I love you IM: instant message IMHO: in my humble opinion IMNSHO: in my not so humble opinion IMO: in my opinion IOW: in other words IPN: I'm posting naked IRL: in real life IWALU: I will always love you IYSWIM: if you see what I mean JIC: just in case JK: just kidding JMO: just my opinion JTLYK: just to let you know K: okay KIT: keep in touch KOC: kiss on cheek KOL: kiss on lips KOTC: kiss on the cheek KWIM: know what I mean? L8R: later LD: later, dude LDR: long distance relationship LLTA: lots and lots of thunderous applause **LMIRL: let's meet in real life** LMSO: laughing my socks off LOL: laughing out loud LSHMBB: laughing so hard my belly is bouncing LTM: laugh to myself LTNS: long time, no see LTR: long-term relationship LULAB: love you like a brother **LULAS: love you like a sister** LUWAMH: love you with all my heart LY: love you M/F: male or female MOSS: member of same sex MOTOS: member of the opposite sex MSG: message MTF: more to follow MUSM: miss you so much NADT: not a darn thing NIFOC: naked in front of computer NP: no problem NRN: no reply necessary OIC: oh I see **OLL: online love** OM: old man OTF: off the floor OTOH: on the other hand OTTOMH: off the top of my head P2P: peer to peer PDA: public display of affection PEBCAK: problem exists between chair and keyboard PLZ: please PM: private message PMFJIB: pardon me for jumping in but POAHF: put on a happy face **POS: parent over shoulder** PU: that stinks QT: cutie RL: real life ROTFL: rolling on the floor laughing RPG: role playing games RSN: real soon now S4L: spam for life SETE: smiling ear to ear SHCOON: shoot hot coffee out of nose SHID: slaps head in disgust SF: surfer friendly SNERT: snot nosed egotistical rude teenager SO: significant other SOMY: sick of me yet? SOT: short of time STW: search the web SWAK: sealed with a kiss SWL: screaming with laughter SYS: see you soon TA: thanks again TCOB: taking care of business TCOY: take care of yourself TIA: thanks in advance TILII: tell it like it is TMI: too much information TOY: thinking of you TTYL: talk to you later UW: you're welcome WB: welcome back WFM: works for me WIBNI: wouldn't it be nice if **WTGP: want to go private?** WTG: way to go WU: what's up WUF: where are you from? YBS: you'll be sorry YL: young lady YM: young man

1 in 5 children is sexually solicited online.

Public Sector Minority Business Opportunites

ALABAMA

AGRICULTURE, DEPT. OF
Natural Resources Conservation Service
Alabama State Office
3381 Skyway Dr.
Auburn, AL 36830-6443
Lynn Thomas, Contracting Officer
Tel: (334) 887-4507 Fax: (334) 887-4551
Email: lynn.thomas@al.usda.gov
Web: www.al.nrcs.usda.gov

COMMERCE, DEPT. OF
Minority Business Development Agency
Birmingham Minority Business Opportunity
Committee
710 20th St. North
Birmingham, AL 35203
Andrew Mayo, Administrative
Tel: (205) 254-2799 Fax: (205) 254-7741
Email: ajmayo@ci.birmingham.al.us
Web: www.birminghammboc.com

DEFENSE, DEPT. OF
US Air Force, 42nd Contracting Squadron/
LGC-Air Education and Training Command
Small Business Office
50 Lemay Plz. South
Maxwell AFB, AL 36112-6334
Gladys Johnson, Small Business Specialist
Tel: (334) 953-5457 Fax: (334) 953-2453
Email: gladys.johnson@maxwell.af.mil
Web: www.maxwell.af.mil

**US Air Force, HQ Standard Systems Group/
AQP-Air Force Materiel Command**
Small Business Office
490 E. Moore Dr., Gunter Annex
Maxwell AFB, AL 36114-3004
Rosa Shanon, Small Business Specialist
Tel: (334) 416-5415
Email: rosa.shanon@gunter.af.mil
Web: www.selltoairforce.org

US Army Engineer & Support Center
Small Business Office
4820 University Sq.
Huntsville, AL 35816-1822
Judy Griggs, Small Business Specialist
Tel: (256) 895-1179 Fax: (256) 895-1049
Email: Judy.K.Griggs@hnd01.usace.army.
mil
Web: www.hnd.usace.army.mil

**NATIONAL AERONAUTICS & SPACE
ADMINISTRATION (NASA)**
Marshall Space Flight Center
Small Business Office
MSFC PS01
Huntsville, AL 35812
David Brock, Small Business Specialist
Tel: (256) 544-0267 Fax: (256) 544-5851
Email: david.e.brock@nasa.gov
Web: http://ec.msfc.nasa.gov/msfc/doin_
bus.html

ALASKA

AGRICULTURE, DEPT. OF
Forest Service, State of Alaska
Contracting Office
P.O. Box 21628
Juneau, AK 99802
Caroline Wallace, Supervisory Contracting
Officer
Tel: (907) 586-7912 Fax: (907) 586-7090
Web: www.fs.fed.us/r10

COMMERCE, DEPT. OF
Minority Business Development Agency,
Alaska Statewide County Minority Business
Development Center
122 1st Ave. #600
Fairbanks, AK 99701
Project Director
Tel: (907) 452-8251 Fax: (907) 459-3851
Email: lallen@tananachiefs.org
Web: www.mbda.gov

DEFENSE, DEPT. OF
US Air Force, 354th Contracting Squadron/
CONS DBO-Pacific Air Forces
Small Business Office
3112 Broadway Ave. #5B
Eielson AFB, AK 99702-1887
Sharon Cobb, Small Business Specialist
Tel: (907) 377-4183 Fax: (907) 377-4647
Email: sharon.cobb@eielson.af.mil
Web: www.eielson.af.mil

**US Air Force, 3rd Contracting Squadron/
LGC-Pacific Air Forces**
Small Business Office
10480 22nd St.
Elmendorf AFB, AK 99506
Della Simmons, Small Business Specialist
Tel: (907) 552-1419 Fax: (907) 552-7497
Email: della.simmons@elmendorf.af.mil
Web: www.elmendorf.af.mil

VETERANS AFFAIRS, DEPT. OF
Alaska VA Healthcare System and Regional
Office
2925 DeBarr Rd.
Anchorage, AK 99508-2989
Sandra Magers, Small Business Specialist
Tel: (907) 257-6945 Fax: (907) 257-6711
Email: sandra.magers2@med.va.gov
Web: www.va.gov

ARIZONA

COMMERCE, DEPT. OF
Minority Business Development Agency
Arizona Statewide Minority Business
Development Center
255 E. Osborn Rd. #202
Phoenix, AZ 85012
Roy B. Laos, Project Director
Tel: (602) 248-0007 Fax: (602) 279-8900
Email: royl@azhcc.com
Web: www.mbda.gov

DEFENSE, DEPT. OF
CECOM Acquisition Center, SW Operations
Attn.: AMSEL-IE-SB, Greeley Hall #3212,
Bldg. 61801
Fort Huachuca, AZ 85613-5300
Chuck Collins, Small Business Advisor
Tel: (520) 538-7870 Fax: (520) 533-0360
Email: charles.collins@netcom.army.mil

**US Air Force, 355th Contracting Squadron/
LGC-Air Combat Command**
Small Business Office
3180 S. Craycroft Rd.
Davis-Monthan AFB, AZ 85707-3522
Joanne Squire, Small Business Specialist
Tel: (520) 228-3131 Fax: (520) 228-7834
Email: joanne.squire@dm.af.mil
Web: www.dm.af.mil/355cons2/355cons.
htm

**US Air Force, 56th Contracting Squadron/
CC-Air Education and Training Command**
Small Business Office
14100 W. Eagle St.
Luke AFB, AZ 85309-1217
Teresa Hendrix, Small Business Specialist
Tel: (623) 856-7121 Fax: (623) 856-4969
Email: teresa.hendrix@luke.af.mil
Web: www.luke.af.mil

VETERANS AFFAIRS, DEPT. OF
Carl T. Hayden VA Medical Center
650 E. Indian School Rd. M/C 90C
Phoenix, AZ 85012
Pat Amidon, Small Business Specialist
Tel: (602) 212-2163 Fax: (602) 212-2155
Email: pat.amidon@med.va.gov
Web: www.phoenix.med.va.gov

Southern Arizona VA Health Care System
3601 S. 6th Ave.
Tucson, AZ 85723
Carlene S. Rush, Acquisition Manager/
Small Business Specialist
Tel: (520) 629-4610 Fax: (520) 629-1817
Email: carlene.rush@med.va.gov
Web: www.va.gov

ARKANSAS

DEFENSE, DEPT. OF
US Air Force, 314th Contracting Squadron/
CCD-Air Education and Training Command
Small Business Office
642 Thomas Ave.
Little Rock AFB, AR 72099-5019
Steven R. West, Small Business Specialist
Tel: (501) 987-3836 Fax: (501) 987-6624
Email: steven.west@littlerock.af.mil
Web: www.littlerock.af.mil

VETERANS AFFAIRS, DEPT. OF
Fayetteville VA Medical Center
1100 N. College Ave.
Fayetteville, AR 72703
Donna Lenz, Small and Disadvantaged
Business Specialist
Tel: (479) 444-5035 Fax: (479) 444-5031
Email: donna.lenz@med.va.gov
Web: www.va.gov

Central Arkansas Veterans Healthcare
System
2200 Fort Roots Dr.
North Little Rock, AR 72114
Michael D. Barger, Small Business
Specialist
Tel: (501) 257-1047 Fax: (501) 257-1055
Email: mike.barger@med.va.gov

CALIFORNIA

AGRICULTURE, DEPT. OF
Agricultural Research Service
Pacific West Area
800 Buchanan St. #2021
Albany, CA 94710-1105
Jack Nelson, Supervisory Procurement
Analyst
Tel: (510) 559-6016 Fax: (510) 559-6023
Email: jnelson@pw.ars.usda.gov
Web: www.pwa.ars.usda.gov

Forest Service
IBET Province
100 Forni Rd.
Placerville, CA 95667
Kathryn Griffin, Contracting Officer
Tel: (530) 622-5061 Fax: (530) 621-5297
Email: kgriffin@fs.fed.us
Web: www.fs.fed.us

Tahoe National Forest
631 Coyote St.
Nevada City, CA 95959-2250
Alan James, Contracting Officer
Tel: (530) 478-6121 Fax: (530) 478-6126
Email: amjames@fs.fed.us
Web: www.fs.fed.us/r5/tahoe

Natural Resources Conservation Service
California State Office
430 G St. #4164
Davis, CA 95616
Brian Hallet, Administrative Services Officer
Tel: (530) 792-5675 Fax: (530) 792-5795
Email: brian.hallet@ca.usda.gov
Web: www.usda.gov

COMMERCE, DEPT. OF
Minority Business Development Agency
East Los Angeles Minority Business
Development Center
5271 E. Beverly Blvd.
Los Angeles, CA 90022
Sal Carlos, Project Director
Tel: (323) 726-4072 Fax: (323) 721-9794
Email: scarlos@elambdc.org
Web: www.mbda.gov

Los Angeles Metro Minority Business
Development Center
3550 Wilshire Blvd. #905
Los Angeles, CA 90010
Ramesh N. Swamy, Project Director
Tel: (213) 368-1450 Fax: (213) 368-1454
Email: rswamy@usc.edu
Web: www.mbda.gov

San Francisco Regional Office
221 Main St. #1280
San Francisco, CA 94105
Linda Marmolejo, Regional Director
Tel: (415) 744-3001 Fax: (415) 744-3061
Email: lmarmolejo@mbda.gov
Web: www.mbda.gov

DEFENSE, DEPT. OF
Fleet & Industrial Supply Center/San Diego
937 N. Harbor Dr., M/C 260
San Diego, CA 92132
Gary Thomas, Small Business Specialist
Tel: (619) 532-3439 Fax: (619) 532-2575
Email: gary.p.thomas@navy.mil
Web: www.nor.fisc.navy.mil

Naval Air Warfare Center Weapons Division
Code 500000, 1 Administration Cir.
China Lake, CA 93555-6001
Pam Lochhead, Small Business Officer
Tel: (760) 939-2712 Fax: (760) 939-8329
Email: pamela.lochhead@navy.mil
Web: www.nawcwpns.navy.mil

Space and Missile Systems Center
2420 Bela Way #1467
El Segundo, CA 90245-4692
Willard Strozer, Small Business Specialist
Tel: (310) 363-2855 Fax: (310) 363-1189
Email: willard.strozer@losangeles.af.mil
Web: www.losangeles.af.mil

**Defense Contract Management Command
West**
18901 S. Wilmington Ave., Bldg. DH2
Carson, CA 90746
Tel: (310) 900-6028 Fax: (310) 900-6029
Email: renee.deavens@dcma.mil
Web: www.dcma.mil/DCMAHQ/dcma-sb/
index.htm

**US Air Force, 30th Space Wing/BZ-Air Force
Space Command**
Small Business Office
806 13th St., Bldg. 7015 #113
Vandenberg AFB, CA 93437-5228
Charles Painter, Small Business Specialist
Tel: (805) 605-7265 Fax: (805) 606-5662
Email: charles.painter@vandenberg.af.mil
Web: www.vandenberg.af.mil

**US Air Force, 452nd LSS/LGC-Air Force
Reserve Command**
Small Business Office
1940 Graeber St.
March ARB, CA 92518-1650

Mary Boswell, Small Business Specialist
Tel: (951) 655-3116 Fax: (951) 655-3772
Email: mary.boswell@march.af.mil
Web: www.selltoairforce.org

**US Air Force, 60th Air Mobility Wing/LGC-Air
Mobility Command**
Small Business Office
350 Hangar Ave., Bldg. 549
Travis AFB, CA 94535-2632
John Clarke, Director
Tel: (707) 424-7713 Fax: (707) 424-8456
Email: john.clarke@travis.af.mil
Web: http://public.travis.amc.af.mil/
pages/60cons

**US Air Force, 9th Contracting Squadron/LGC-
Air Combat Command**
Small Business Office
6500 B St. #101
Beale AFB, CA 95903-1712
Sandra Turzak, Small Business Specialist
Tel: (530) 634-2872 Fax: (530) 368-3311
Email: sandra.turzak@beale.af.mil
Web: www.beale.af.mil

**US Air Force, Flight Test Center/BC-Air Force
Materiel Command**
Small Business Office
5 S. Wolfe Ave., Bldg. 2800
Edwards AFB, CA 93524-1185
Donna L. Thomason, Director
Tel: (661) 277-3640 Fax: (661) 277-8443
Email: donna.thomason@edwards.af.mil
Web: www.edwards.af.mil

**US Air Force, Space and Missile Systems
Center/BC-Air Force Space Command**
Small Business Office
155 Discoverer Blvd. #2017
El Segundo, CA 90245-4962
Charles R. Willett, Director
Tel: (310) 363-2855 Fax: (310) 363-1189
Email: charles.willett@losangeles.af.mil
Web: www.losangeles.af.mil/SMC/BC/home.
htm

ENERGY, DEPT. OF
Lawrence Livermore National Laboratory/
University of California
P.O. Box 5012
Livermore, CA 94561
Stan Howell, Small Business Program
Manager
Tel: (925) 422-8997 Fax: (925) 422-3253
Email: howell6@llnl.gov
Web: www.llnl.gov

Lawrence Berkeley National Laboratory
Procurement Office
1 Cyclotron Rd., M/S 937R-0200
Berkeley, CA 94720
David T. Hen, Team Leader
Tel: (510) 486-4506 Fax: (510) 486-4380
Email: dtchen@lbl.gov
Web: http://procurement.lbl.gov

Stanford Linear Accelerator Center
2575 Sand Hill Rd., M/S 01
Menlo Park, CA 94025
Robert Todaro, Small Business Program
Manager
Tel: (650) 926-2425 Fax: (650) 926-2000
Email: rocker@slac.stanford.edu
Web: www.slac.stanford.edu

ENVIRONMENTAL PROTECTION AGENCY
Region IX-Office of Small and
Disadvantaged Business Utilization
75 Hawthorne St. PMD 1
San Francisco, CA 94105
Joe Ochab, Officer
Tel: (415) 972-3761 Fax: (415) 947-3556
Email: ochab.joe@epa.gov
Web: www.epa.gov/region09

75 Hawthorne St. PMD 8
San Francisco, CA 94105
Barbara Bycsek, Contracting Specialist
Tel: (415) 972-3716 Fax: (415) 947-3558
Email: bycsek.barbara@epa.gov
Web: www.epa.gov/osdbu

**NATIONAL AERONAUTICS AND SPACE
ADMINISTRATION**
Ames Research Center
M/S 241-1
Moffett Field, CA 94035-1000
Thomas J. Kolis, Field Installation/Small
Minority Business Specialist
Tel: (650) 604-4690 Fax: (650) 604-4646
Email: t.kolis@nasa.gov
Web: www.hq.nasa.gov

Dryden Flight Research Center
P.O. Box 273
M/S D-1422
Edwards, CA 93523-0273
Robert Medina, Field Installation/Small
Minority Business Specialist
Tel: (661) 276-3343 Fax: (661) 276-2904
Email: robert.medina@nasa.gov
Web: www.hq.nasa.gov

Jet Propulsion Laboratory
4800 Oak Grove Dr., M/S 190-205
Pasadena, CA 91109-8099
Martin Ramirez, Field Installation Small/
Minority Business Specialist
Tel: (818) 354-6093 Fax: (818) 393-1746
Email: martin.m.ramirez@jpl.nasa.gov
Web: www.hq.nasa.gov

Jet Propulsion Laboratory
Business Opportunity Office
M/C 190-205
Pasadena, CA 91109
Tom May, Manager
Tel: (818) 354-2121 Fax: (818) 393-1746
Email: thomas.h.may@jpl.nasa.gov
Web: http://acquisition.jpl.nasa.gov

Jet Propulsion Laboratory
NASA Management Office
M/C 180-802K
Pasadena, CA 91109
Robert DeMack, Field Installation Small/
Minority Business Specialist
Tel: (818) 354-6050 Fax: (818) 354-6051
Web: www.hq.nasa.gov

TREASURY, DEPT. OF THE
Internal Revenue Service
Western Area Field Office
333 Market St. #1400
San Francisco, CA 94105
Jan Janson, Small Business Specialist
Tel: (415) 848-4716 Fax: (415) 848-4711
Email: jan.janson@irs.gov
Web: www.treas.gov

VETERANS AFFAIRS, DEPT. OF
VA Medical Center 22
VA Network Business Ctr., 5901 E. 7th St.,
Bldg. 149
Long Beach, CA 90822
Wayne Keen, Small Business Specialist
Tel: (562) 826-8154 Fax: (562) 826-5828
Email: wayne.keen@med.va.gov
Web: www.long-beach.med.va.gov

COLORADO

AGRICULTURE, DEPT. OF
Agricultural Research Service
Northern Plains Area
2150 Center Ave., Bldg. D #310
Ft. Collins, CO 80526-8119

Richard Jansen, Supervisory Contract
Specialist
Tel: (970) 492-7017 Fax: (970) 492-7031
Email: dick.jansen@ars.usda.gov
Web: www.ars.usda.gov

Forest Service
Central Administrative Zone
240 W. Prospect Rd.
Fort Collins, CO 80526
Katherine Padilla, Procurement Technician
Tel: (970) 498-1285 Fax: (970) 498-1166
Web: www.fs.fed.us

Rocky Mountain Acquisition Service Team
P.O. Box 25127
Lakewood, CO 80225
Tom Turner, Procurement Analyst
Tel: (303) 275-5556 Fax: (303) 275-5453
Email: tnturner@fs.fed.us
Web: www.fs.fed.us

Natural Resources Conservation Service
Colorado State Office
655 Parfet St. #E200C
Lakewood, CO 80215
Tony K. Doxtater, Contract Specialist
Tel: (720) 544-2826 Fax: (720) 544-2962
Email: tony.doxtater@co.usda.gov
Web: www.co.nrcs.usda.gov

COMMERCE, DEPT. OF
**Minority Business Development Agency,
Denver Minority Business Development
Center**
3840 York St. #230B
Denver, CO 80211
Sara Fuentes, Director
Tel: (303) 455-3099 Fax: (303) 455-3076
Email: sfuentes@dmbdg.com

**National Oceanic and Atmospheric
Administration**
Acquisition Management Division
325 Broadway, M/C 3
Boulder, CO 80305-3328
Janet Clark, Small Business Specialist
Tel: (303) 497-6320 Fax: (303) 497-3163
Email: jan.clark@noaa.gov
Web: www.noaa.gov

325 Broadway, M/C 3
Boulder, CO 80305-3328
David Barr, Chief
Tel: (303) 497-3515 Fax: (303) 497-3163
Email: david.m.barr@noaa.gov
Web: www.noaa.gov

DEFENSE, DEPT. OF
**US Air Force, 10th MSG/LGC-United States
Air Force Academy**
Small Business Office
8110 Industrial Dr.
USAF Academy, CO 80840-2315
Sherry Pittinger, Director
Tel: (719) 333-4561 Fax: (719) 333-4404
Email: sherry.pittinger@usafa.af.mil
Web: www.usafa.af.mil

**US Air Force, 21st Contracting Squadron/
LGC-Air Force Space Command**
Small Business Office
700 Suffolk St.
Peterson AFB, CO 80914-1200
Jim Redd, Small Business Specialist
Tel: (719) 556-4669 Fax: (719) 556-4321
Email: jim.redd@peterson.af.mil
Web: www.peterson.af.mil

US Air Force, 50th Contracting Squadron
Small Business Office
210 Falcon Pkwy. #2116
Schriever AFB, CO 80912-2116
Detrice Shields, Small Business Specialist
Tel: (719) 567-3805 Fax: (719) 567-4974

Email: detrice.shields@schriever.af.mil
Web: www.schriever.af.mil

US Air Force, 821st SPTS/LGC-Air Force Space Command
Small Business Office
320 N. Beaver Creek, M/S 70
Buckley AFB, CO 80011
Elizabeth Bryant, Small Business Specialist
Tel: (720) 847-6735 Fax: (720) 847-6443
Email: elizabeth.bryant@buckley.af.mil
Web: www.buckley.af.mil

ENERGY, DEPT. OF
Golden Field Office
1617 Cole Blvd.
Golden, CO 80401
John Olsen, Small Business Program
Manager
Tel: (303) 275-4722 Fax: (303) 275-4750
Email: john.olsen@go.doe.gov
Web: www.go.doe.gov

CH2M Hill Companies
9191 S. Jamaica St.
Englewood, CO 80112
Willie T. Franklin, III, Small Business
Program Manager
Tel: (720) 286-2274 Fax: (720) 286-9121
Email: wfrankli@ch2m.com
Web: www.ch2m.com

National Renewable Energy Laboratory
1617 Cole Blvd.
Golden, CO 80401-3393
Nancy Gardner, Small Business
Development Liaison
Tel: (303) 384-7335 Fax: (303) 275-3109
Email: nancy_gardner@nrel.gov
Web: www.nrel.gov

Western Area Power Administration
12155 W. Alameda Pkwy.
Lakewood, CO 80228
Judy Madsen, Small Business Program
Manager
Tel: (720) 962-7154 Fax: (720) 962-7161
Email: madsen@wapa.gov
Web: www.wapa.gov

ENVIRONMENTAL PROTECTION AGENCY
Region VIII-Office of Small and
Disadvantaged Business Utilization
999 18th St. #300, M/C TMS-G
Denver, CO 80202-2466
Marshell Pullman, Officer
Tel: (303) 312-6499 Fax: (303) 312-6685
Email: pullman.marshell@epa.gov
Web: www.epa.gov/osdbu

GENERAL SERVICES ADMINISTRATION
Small Business Utilization Center/Rocky
Mountain Region
P.O. Box 25006, 8AB
Denver Federal Center Bldg. 41 #234
Denver, CO 80225
Pennie Estrada, Business Specialist
Tel: (303) 236-7409 Fax: (303) 236-7552
Email: pennie.estrada@gsa.gov
Web: http://rmrbsc.gsa.gov

VETERANS AFFAIRS, DEPT. OF
Denver Distribution Center (905)
P.O. Box 25166
Denver, CO 80225-0166
Tim Grauer, Small Business Specialist
Tel: (303) 914-5180 Fax: (303) 914-5424
Email: tim.grauer@med.va.gov
Web: www.va.gov

Denver VA Medical Center
1055 Clermont St.
Denver, CO 80220
Mary Anne Achen, Small Business
Specialist

Tel: (303) 393-2846 Fax: (303) 393-2860
Email: maryanneachen@med.va.gov
Web: www.va.gov

Grand Junction VA Medical Center
2121 North Ave.
Grand Junction, CO 81501
Denise Boren, Contract Specialist
Tel: (970) 263-5004 Fax: (970) 244-7721
Email: denise.boren@med.va.gov
Web: www.va.gov

VA Health Administration Center
300 S. Jackson St. #444
Denver, CO 80206-9020
James Davis, Small Business Specialist
Tel: (303) 331-7556 Fax: (720) 889-2387
Email: james.davis7@med.va.gov
Web: www.va.gov

CONNECTICUT

VETERANS AFFAIRS, DEPT. OF
VA Connecticut Healthcare System West
Haven Campus
950 Campbell Ave.
West Haven, CT 06516
Bruce Fortuna, Small Business Specialist
Tel: (203) 937-3881 Fax: (203) 937-4347
Email: bruce.fortuna@med.va.gov
Web: www.visn1.med.va.gov/vact

DELAWARE

DEFENSE, DEPT. OF
US Air Force, 436 CONS/LGCD-Airlift Wing
Small Business Office
639 Atlantic St. #243
Dover AFB, DE 19902-5639
Thelma Gabrielson, Small Business
Specialist
Tel: (302) 677-2184 Fax: (302) 677-5105
Email: thelma.gabrielson@dover.af.mil
Web: http://public.dover.amc.af.mil

VETERANS AFFAIRS, DEPT. OF
Stars & Stripes Healthcare Network
VA Medical Center/Regional Office
1601 Kirkwood Hwy.
Wilmington, DE 19805
Toni A. Wilson, Small Business Specialist
Tel: (302) 633-5371 Fax: (302) 633-5377
Email: toni.wilson@med.va.gov
Web: www.va.gov/osdbu

DISTRICT OF COLUMBIA

AGENCY FOR INTERNATIONAL DEVELOPMENT
Office of Small and Disadvantaged Business
Utilization/Minority Resource Center
1300 Pennsylvania Ave. NW #78E, Ronald
Reagan Bldg.
Washington, DC 20523-7800
Marilyn Marton, Director
Tel: (202) 712-1500 Fax: (202) 216-3056
Email: mmarton@usaid.gov
Web: www.usaid.gov/business

1300 Pennsylvania Ave. NW #7.8-E,
Ronald Reagan Bldg.
Washington, DC 20523-7800
Rhoda Isaac, Women Business
Representative
Tel: (202) 712-0609 Fax: (202) 216-3056
Email: risaac@usaid.gov
Web: www.usaid.gov

AGRICULTURE, DEPT. OF
Office of Operations/Procurement Division
300 7th St. SW #377, Reporters Bldg.
Washington, DC 20250
Brantt Lindsey, Contracting Officer
Tel: (202) 720-4674 Fax: (202) 720-4529
Email: brantt.lindsey@usda.gov
Web: www.usda.gov/oo

Office of Procurement/Property
Management
300 7th St. SW #367, Reporters Bldg.
Washington, DC 20024
Richard Storie, Contracting Officer
Tel: (202) 720-3211 Fax: (202) 720-4529
Email: richard.storie@usda.gov
Web: www.usda.gov

Office of Small and Disadvantaged
Business Utilization
1400 Independence Ave. SW #1323 South
Bldg.
Washington, DC 20250-9400
James E. House, Director
Tel: (202) 720-7117 Fax: (202) 720-3001
Email: house.jamese@usda.gov
Web: www.usda.gov/osdbu

1400 Independence Ave. SW #1566S
Washington, DC 20250-9501
Sherry Cohen, Program Analyst
Tel: (202) 720-7117 Fax: (202) 720-3001
Email: sherryr.cohen@usda.gov
Web: www.usda.gov/osdbu

1400 Independence Ave. SW #1566S
Washington, DC 20250-9501
Stella Hughes, Veteran Business
Representative
Tel: (202) 720-7117 Fax: (202) 720-3001
Email: stella.hughes@usda.gov
Web: www.usda.gov/osdbu

Office of the Chief Economist
1400 Independence Ave. #4419 South
Bldg.
Washington, DC 20250-3812
Kyra Toland, Administrative Officer
Tel: (202) 720-4793 Fax: (202) 690-1805
Email: ktoland@oce.usda.gov
Web: www.usda.gov/oce

Office of the Chief Information Office, ITS
1400 Independence Ave. SW #S-106
Washington, DC 20250
Diana Mack, Resource Manager
Tel: (202) 720-5342 Fax: (202) 720-8274
Email: diana.mack@usda.gov
Web: www.ocio.usda.gov

Office of the Inspector General/
Procurement Management Branch
1400 Independence Ave. SW #40-E, Jamie
L. Whitten Bldg.
Washington, DC 20250
Tina Jones, Coordinator
Tel: (202) 720-5931 Fax: (202) 690-1282
Email: tmjones@oig.usda.gov
Web: www.usda.gov/oig

Agricultural Marketing Service
CPB, Fruit & Vegetable Programs
1400 Independence Ave. SW M/S 0239
Washington, DC 20250
Michellee Warren, Contract Specialist
Tel: (202) 720-4517 Fax: (202) 720-2782
Email: michellee.warren@usda.gov
Web: www.ams.usda.gov

Livestock and Seed Program
1400 Independence Ave. #1566 South
Bldg.
Washington, DC 20250
Ondray James, Small Business Specialist
Tel: (202) 690-0404 Fax: (202) 720-9538

Email: ondray.james@usda.gov
Web: www.ams.usda.gov

Poultry Division
1400 Independence Ave. SW #3941 M/S
0260
Washington, DC 20250
Valerie Dinkel, Agricultural Marketing
Specialist/OSDBU Coordinator
Tel: (202) 720-7693 Fax: (202) 720-5871
Email: valerie.dinkel@usda.gov
Web: www.ams.usda.gov

Agricultural Research Service
1280 Maryland Ave. SW #580C
Washington, DC 20024
Tony S. Wimbush, Contract Specialist
Tel: (202) 720-3998 Fax: (202) 720-3987
Email: twimbush@ars.usda.gov
Web: www.ars.usda.gov

Farm Service Agency
Procurement/Donations Division
1400 Independence Ave. SW #5754S,
M/S 0551
Washington, DC 20013
Lisa Brown, Coordinator
Tel: (202) 720-0956 Fax: (202) 205-3702
Email: lisa_brown@wdc.usda.gov
Web: www.fsa.usda.gov

AGRICULTURE, DEPT. OF
Farm Service Agency
Contracting and Acquisitions Management
Division
1280 Maryland Ave. SW #6957
Washington, DC 20024
Scott P. Cook, Small Business Coordinator
Tel: (202) 720-7349 Fax: (202) 690-0689
Email: Scott.cook@wdc.usda.gov
Web: www.fsa.usda.gov/amb

Forest Service
Acquisition Management Branch
P.O. Box 96090, #706, Rosslyn Plaza East
Washington, DC 20090-6090
James G. McDonald, Director of Small
Business Outreach
Tel: (703) 605-5144 Fax: (703) 605-5100
Email: jmcdonald04@fs.fed.us
Web: www.fs.fed.us

Natural Resources Conservation Service
Administrative Services Division
1400 Independence Ave. SW #0106
Washington, DC 20250
Terry Kirby, Small Business Coordinator
Tel: (202) 720-8758 Fax: (202) 720-2899
Email: terry.kirby@usda.gov
Web: www.nrcs.usda.gov

Office of Communications Budget &
Operations
1400 Independence Ave. SW #434-A,
Jamie L. Whitten Bldg.
Washington, DC 20250
Terry Logan, Financial Management
Specialist
Tel: (202) 720-3118 Fax: (202) 690-1131
Email: Terry.Logan@usda.gov
Web: www.usda.gov

Rural Development
1400 Independence Ave. SW, M/S 0741
Washington, DC 20250-0741
Erin Anderson, Contract Specialist
Tel: (202) 692-0017 Fax: (202) 692-0235
Email: erin.anderson@wdc.usda.gov
Web: www.rurdev.usda.gov

Procurement Management Division
1400 Independence Ave. SW M/C 0742
Washington, DC 20250
Donna Douglas, Contracting Officer
Tel: (202) 692-0016 Fax: (202) 692-0013

Email: donna.douglas@usda.gov
Web: www.rurdev.usda.gov

Rural Business Cooperative Service
1400 Independence Ave. SW #5801A
Washington, DC 20250
Peter J. Thomas, Administrator
Tel: (202) 690-4730 Fax: (202) 690-4737
Email: peter.thomas@wdc.usda.gov
Web: www.rurdev.usda.gov/rbs

COMMERCE, DEPT. OF
Office of Small and Disadvantaged Business
Utilization
14th & Constitution Ave. NW Herbert C.
Hoover Bldg. #6411
Washington, DC 20230
La Juene Desmukes, Acting Director
Tel: (202) 482-1472 Fax: (202) 482-0501
Email: ldesmukes@doc.gov
Web: www.commerce.gov/osdbu

Office of the Secretary/Office of Acquisition
Management
14th & Constitution Ave. NW #H6521
Washington, DC 20230
Biba Inoussa, Small Business Specialist
Tel: (202) 482-5240 Fax: (202) 482-4988
Email: binoussa@doc.gov
Web: http://oamweb.osec.doc.gov

Minority Business Development Agency
14th & Constitution Ave. NW #5053
Washington, DC 20230
Ronald N. Langston, National Director
Tel: (202) 482-5061 Fax: (202) 501-4698
Email: rlangston@mbda.gov
Web: www.mbda.gov

Office of the Secretary
Office of Acquisition Management,
Acquisition Services
14th & Constitution Ave. NW #H6521
Washington, DC 20230
Patty Stang, Acting Director/Head of
Contracting
Tel: (202) 482-3416 Fax: (202) 482-4988
Email: dlocke@doc.gov
Web: http://oamweb.osec.doc.gov

US Census Bureau
Procurement Office
4700 Silver Hill Rd. #G-314
Washington, DC 20233-0001
Jacqueline V. Wilson, Small Business
Specialist
Tel: (301) 763-1864 Fax: (301) 457-1785
Email: jacqueline.v.wilson@census.gov
Web: www.census.gov

**COMMODITY FUTURES TRADING
COMMISSION**
Office of Financial Management
Three Lafayette Ctr., 1155 21st St. NW
Washington, DC 20581
Steven Grossman, Deputy Director for
Procurement Operations and Policy
Tel: (202) 418-5192 Fax: (202) 418-5529
Web: www.cftc.gov

**COMMODITY FUTURES TRADING
COMMISSION**
Office of Financial Management
1155 21st St. NW
Washington, DC 20581
Nicholas Graham, Contracting Officer
Tel: (202) 418-5191 Fax: (202) 418-5529
Email: ngraham@cftc.gov
Web: www.cftc.gov

1155 21st St. NW
Washington, DC 20581
Sonda Owens, Contracting Officer
Tel: (202) 418-5182 Fax: (202) 418-5529

Email: sowens@cftc.gov
Web: www.cftc.gov

DEFENSE, DEPT. OF
Military Sealift Command
Small Business Office
914 Charles Morris Ct. SE, Bldg. 210
Washington Navy Yard, DC 20398-5540
Brad Taylor, Associate Director
Tel: (202) 685-5554 Fax: (202) 685-5515
Email: brad.taylor@navy.mil
Web: www.msc.navy.mil

US Air Force
Office of Small and Disadvantaged Business
Utilization
SASSB, 1060 Air Force, The Pentagon
Washington, DC 20330-1060
Joseph Diamond, Director
Tel: (703) 696-1103 Fax: (703) 696-1170
Email: joseph.diamond@pentagon.af.mil
Web: www.selltoairforce.org

SASSB, 1060 Air Force, The Pentagon
Washington, DC 20330-1060
Sara Mitcho, Women Business
Representative
Tel: (703) 696-1103 Fax: (703) 696-1170
Email: sara.mitcho@pentagon.af.mil
Web: www.selltoairforce.org

Small Business Office, AFDW/A7K
110 Luke Ave. #200
Bolling AFB, DC 20032
Everett Carter, Director
Tel: (202) 767-8086 Fax: (202) 404-7006
Email: everett.carter@bolling.af.mil
Web: www.bolling.af.mil

US Army
Office of Small and Disadvantaged Business
Utilization
106 Army Pentagon #3B514
Washington, DC 20310-0106
Tracey L. Pinson, Director
Tel: (703) 697-2868 Fax: (703) 693-3898
Email: tracey.pinson@hqda.army.mil
Web: www.sellingtoarmy.info

US Army Corps of Engineers
Small Business Office
441 G St. NW, 3rd Fl.
Washington, DC 20314-1000
Judith Blake, Director
Tel: (202) 761-0732 Fax: (202) 761-4609
Email: smallbusinessoffice@usace.army.mil
Web: www.hq.usace.army.mil/hqhome

EDUCATION, DEPT. OF
Office of Small and Disadvantaged Business
Utilization
400 Maryland Ave. SW
Washington, DC 20202
Dr. Kristi Wilson, Director
Tel: (202) 245-6300 Fax: (202) 245-6304
Email: small.business@ed.gov
Web: www.ed.gov

ENERGY, DEPT. OF
Office of Congressional and
Intergovernmental Affairs, CI-3
1000 Independence Ave. SW #8G096
Washington, DC 20585
Laura Brown, Small Business Program
Manager
Tel: (202) 586-5524 Fax: (202) 586-0230
Email: laura.brown@hq.doe.gov
Web: www.doe.gov

Office of Science, CH-64
1000 Independence Ave. SW #CH-64
Washington, DC 20585
Martin P. Rubenstein, Procurement Analyst/
Grants and Contracts

Tel: (301) 903-4946 Fax: (301) 903-4194
Email: martin.rubenstein@science.doe.gov
Web: www.sc.doe.gov

Office of Small and Disadvantaged
Business Utilization
1000 Independence Ave. SW #5B-148
Washington, DC 20585
Yosef Patel, Deputy Director
Tel: (202) 586-7377 Fax: (202) 586-5488
Email: yosef.patel@hq.doe.gov
Web: www.doe.gov

Office of the Inspector General, IG-12
1000 Independence Ave. SW #5D-031
Washington, DC 20585
Gloria Jennings, Small Business Program
Manager
Tel: (202) 586-1930 Fax: (202) 586-7851
Email: gloria.jennings@hq.doe.gov
Web: www.ig.doe.gov

Energy Information Administration, EI-20
1000 Independence Ave. SW #2H055
Washington, DC 20585
Gwenne Goodwin, Small Business Program
Manager
Tel: (202) 586-6307 Fax: (202) 586-0552
Email: gwenne.goodwin@eia.doe.gov
Web: www.eia.doe.gov

Environmental Management, EM42
1000 Independence Ave. SW #1H050
Washington, DC 20585
Kay Rash, Small Business Program
Manager
Tel: (202) 586-5420 Fax: (202) 586-9469
Email: kay.rash@em.doe.gov
Web: www.em.doe.gov

National Nuclear Security Administration
1000 Independence Ave. SW
Washington, DC 20585
Gary Lyttek, Small Business Program
Manager
Tel: (202) 586-8304 Fax: (202) 586-7535
Email: nnsa.smallbusiness@nnsa.doe.gov
Web: www.nnsa.doe.gov

Office of Counter Intelligence, CN-1
1000 Independence Ave. SW #8F089
Washington, DC 20585
Sharon Steffe, Procurement and Budget
Specialist
Tel: (202) 586-5218 Fax: (202) 586-0551
Email: sharon.steffe@cn.doe.gov
Web: www.doe.gov

Office of Management & Budget Evaluation
Office of Procurement & Assistance
Management
950 L'Enfant Plz. #710 MA60
Washington, DC 20585
Richard Hopf, Director
Tel: (202) 287-1310 Fax: (202) 287-1305
Email: richard.hopf@hq.doe.gov
Web: www.mbe.doe.gov

ENVIRONMENTAL PROTECTION AGENCY
Grants/Management Division
1300 Pennsylvania Ave. NW M/C 3903R
Washington, DC 20460
Lupe Saldaña, Officer
Tel: (202) 564-5353 Fax: (202) 565-2467
Email: saldana.lupe@epa.gov
Web: www.epa.gov

Office of Small and Disadvantaged
Business Utilization
1200 Pennsylvania Ave. NW M/C 1230N
Washington, DC 20460
Jeanette L. Brown, Director
Tel: (202) 564-4100 Fax: (202) 501-0756
Email: brown.jeanettel@epa.gov
Web: www.epa.gov/osdbu

1200 Pennsylvania Ave. NW Code 1230A
Washington, DC 20460
David Sutton, Deputy Director
Tel: (202) 564-4100 Fax: (202) 501-0756
Email: sutton.david@epa.gov
Web: www.epa.gov\osdbu

EXECUTIVE OFFICE OF THE PRESIDENT
Office of Small and Disadvantaged Business
Utilization
1725 17th St. NW
Washington, DC 20503
Brenda Spriggs, Contract Specialist
Tel: (202) 395-7669
Email: bspriggs@oa.eop.gov
Web: www.whitehouse.gov

1725 17th St. NW
Washington, DC 20503
John Strub, Director
Tel: (202) 395-7669 Fax: (202) 456-6512
Web: www.whitehouse.gov

FEDERAL COMMUNICATIONS COMMISSION
Office of Communications Business
Opportunities
445 12th St. SW #4A624
Washington, DC 20054
Carolyn Fleming Williams, Director
Tel: (202) 418-0990 Fax: (202) 418-0235
Email: carolyn.williams@fcc.gov
Web: www.fcc.gov/ocbo

445 12th St. SW #4A624
Washington, DC 20054
Karen Beverly, Consumer Industry Affairs
Specialist/Assistant for Management
Tel: (202) 418-0990 Fax: (202) 418-0235
Email: karen.beverly@fcc.gov
Web: www.fcc.gov/ocbo

**FEDERAL DEPOSIT INSURANCE
CORPORATION**
Division of Administration, Acquisitions
Services Branch, Headquarters
550 17th St. NW #PA1700-4002
Washington, DC 20429
Ann Bridges Steely, Associate Director
Tel: (202) 942-3010 Fax: (202) 942-3544
Email: asteely@fdic.gov
Web: www.fdic.gov/buying

FEDERAL TRADE COMMISSION
Acquisition Office
600 Pennsylvania Ave. NW #H-706
Washington, DC 20580
Jean Sefcheck, Women Business
Representative
Tel: (202) 326-2258 Fax: (202) 326-3529
Web: www.ftc.gov/procurement

GENERAL SERVICES ADMINISTRATION
Office of Small Business Utilization
1800 & F St. NW #6029
Washington, DC 20405
Felipe Mendoza, Associate Administrator
Tel: (202) 501-1021 Fax: (202) 501-2590
Email: felipe.mendoza@gsa.com
Web: www.gsa.gov

1800 F St. NW #6029
Washington, DC 20405
Elizabeth Ivey, Women Business
Representative
Tel: (202) 501-1021 Fax: (202) 208-5938
Email: elizabeth.ivey@gsa.gov
Web: www.gsa.gov

Small Business Utilization Center
7th & D St. SW #1050, WCAB
Washington, DC 20407
Shaunta Johnson, Director
Tel: (202) 708-5804 Fax: (202) 205-2872
Email: shaunta.johnson@gsa.gov
Web: www.gsa.gov

HEALTH AND HUMAN SERVICES, DEPT. OF

Office of Small and Disadvantaged Business
Utilization
200 Independence Ave. SW #360-G
Washington, DC 20201
Debbie Ridgely, Director
Tel: (202) 690-7300 X4
Fax: (202) 260-4872
Email: debbie.ridgely@hhs.gov
Web: www.hhs.gov/osdbu

Office of the Secretary/Office of Small and
Disadvantaged Business Utilization
200 Independence Ave. SW #360G
Washington, DC 20201
Arthuretta Martin, Deputy Director
Tel: (202) 690-6845 Fax: (202) 260-4872
Email: arthuretta.martin@hhs.gov
Web: www.hhs.gov/osdbu

HOMELAND SECURITY, DEPT. OF

Federal Emergency Management Agency
Financial and Acquisitions Management
Division/ Flood Fire and Mitigation Branch
Office
500 C St. SW #350
Washington, DC 20472
Brenda Thomas, Small Business and
Disadvantaged Utilization Specialist
Tel: (202) 646-4584 Fax: (202) 646-3846
Email: brenda.d.thomas@dhs.gov
Web: www.dhs.gov

US Coast Guard
Office of Procurement Management
2100 2nd St. SW #2606
Washington, DC 20593
Phyllis Miriashtiani, Small Business
Program Manager
Tel: (202) 267-1172 Fax: (202) 267-4011
Email: pmiriashtiani@comdt.uscg.mil
Web: www.dhs.gov

**US Customs Service, National Office,
Procurement Division**
1300 Pennsylvania Ave. NW #1310
Washington, DC 20229
William Bickelman, Small Business
Specialist
Tel: (202) 344-1168 Fax: (202) 344-1190
Email: william.bickelman@dhs.gov
Web: www.customs.gov

US Secret Service
Procurement Division
950 H St. NW #6700
Washington, DC 20223
Marcia Rodriguez, Small Business
Specialist
Tel: (202) 406-6129 Fax: (202) 406-6801
Email: marcia.rodriguez@usss.dhs.gov
Web: www.ustreas.gov/usss

HOUSING AND URBAN DEVELOPMENT, DEPT. OF

Office of Small and Disadvantaged Business
Utilization
451 7th St. SW #3130
Washington, DC 20410-1000
Valerie Hayes, Director
Tel: (202) 708-1428 Fax: (202) 708-7642
Email: valerie_t._hayes@hud.gov
Web: www.hud.gov

451 7th St. SW #3130
Washington, DC 20410-1000
Keira Buggs, Women Business
Representative
Tel: (202) 708-1428 Fax: (202) 708-7642
Email: Keira_C._Buggs@hud.gov
Web: www.hud.gov

INTERIOR, DEPT. OF THE

Office of Small and Disadvantaged Business
Utilization
1849 C St. NW #2252
Washington, DC 20240
Robert W. Faithful, Director
Tel: (202) 208-3493 Fax: (202) 208-7444
Email: robert_faithful@ios.doi.gov
Web: www.doi.gov/osdbu

INTERNATIONAL TRADE COMMISSION

Facilities Management/Procurement
Division
500 E St. SW #414
Washington, DC 20436
Jonathan Brown, Director
Tel: (202) 205-2741 Fax: (202) 205-2337
Email: jonathan.brown@usitc.gov
Web: www.usitc.gov

JUSTICE, DEPT. OF

Justice Management Division
1331 Pennsylvania Ave. NW #1000
Washington, DC 20530
Kenneth Freeman, Procurement Services
Staff
Tel: (202) 307-1971 Fax: (202) 307-1931
Email: kenneth.h.freeman@usdoj.gov
Web: www.usdoj.gov/jmd

Office of Detention Trustee
1331 Pennsylvania Ave. NW #1210
Washington, DC 20530
Lori A. Ray, Small Business Representative
Tel: (202) 353-4601 Fax: (202) 353-4611
Email: lori.ray@usdoj.gov
Web: www.usdoj.gov/ofdt

Office of Justice Program
810 7th St. NW #3621
Washington, DC 20531
Raymond German, Small Business
Representative
Tel: (202) 307-0613 Fax: (202) 307-0086
Email: raymond.german@usdoj.gov
Web: www.ojp.usdoj.gov

Office of Small and Disadvantaged
Business Utilization
1331 Pennsylvania Ave. NW #1010
Washington, DC 20530
David Sutton, Director
Tel: (202) 616-0521 Fax: (202) 616-1717
Email: david.sutton@usdoj.gov
Web: www.usdoj.gov/jmd/osdbu

Bureau of Alcohol, Tobacco, Firearms and
Explosives
Acquisition/Property Management Division
650 Massachusetts Ave. NW #3290
Washington, DC 20226
Grace Foster, Small Business Specialist
Tel: (202) 927-8332 Fax: (202) 927-7311
Email: grace.foster@atf.gov
Web: www.atf.gov

Federal Bureau of Prisons
Acquisition Management Section
320 1st St. NW #5006
Washington, DC 20534
Lenard Foust, Small Business Administrator
Tel: (202) 307-0985 Fax: (202) 307-1146
Email: len.g.foust@usdoj.gov
Web: www.usdoj.gov

US Marshals Service
Procurement Office
#932, CS3
Washington, DC 20530-1000
Elizabeth Howard, Small Business
Specialist
Tel: (202) 307-9349 Fax: (202) 307-9695
Email: elizabeth.howard@usdoj.gov
Web: www.usdoj.gov/marshals

LABOR, DEPT. OF

Office of Small Business Programs/
Procurement Services Center
200 Constitution Ave. NW #C2318
Washington, DC 20210
Frederick Trakowski, Small Business
Advisor
Tel: (202) 693-6465 Fax: (202) 693-6485
Email: trakowski.frederick@dol.gov
Web: www.dol.gov

NATIONAL AERONAUTICS AND SPACE ADMINISTRATION

NASA Headquarters
Office of Small and Disadvantaged Business
Utilization
300 E St. SW #9K70
Washington, DC 20546-0001
Ralph C. Thomas, III, Assistant
Administrator
Tel: (202) 358-2088 Fax: (202) 358-3261
Email: rthomas@hq.nasa.gov
Web: www.osdbu.nasa.gov

300 E St. SW #9K70
Washington, DC 20546-0001
Shirley Perez, Program Manager for
Aeronautics Research Mission
Tel: (202) 358-0640 Fax: (202) 358-3261
Email: shirley.a.perez@nasa.gov
Web: www.hq.nasa.gov

300 E St. SW #9K70
Washington, DC 20546-0001
Lamont O. Hames, Program Manager for
Space Science/Earth Science
Tel: (202) 358-0644 Fax: (202) 358-3261
Email: lamont.hames@hq.nasa.gov
Web: www.hq.nasa.gov

300 E St. SW #9K70
Washington, DC 20546-0001
Eleanor N. Chiogioji, Ph.D., Program
Manager for Education
Tel: (202) 358-2088 Fax: (202) 358-3261
Email: echiogioji@nasa.gov
Web: www.hq.nasa.gov

NAVY, DEPT. OF THE

Office of Small and Disadvantaged Business
Utilization
720 Kennon St. SE #207 Navy Yard
Washington, DC 20374-5015
Paulette Widmann, Acting Director
Tel: (202) 685-6485 Fax: (202) 685-6865
Email: paulette.widmann@navy.mil
Web: www.hq.navy.mil/sadbu

SMITHSONIAN INSTITUTION

Office of Equal Employment/Minority Affairs
P.O. Box 37012
Washington, DC 20013-7012
Rudy D. Watley, Supplier Diversity Program
Manager
Tel: (202) 275-0157 Fax: (202) 275-2055
Email: watleyr@si.edu
Web: www.si.edu

STATE, DEPT. OF

Office of Small and Disadvantaged Business
Utilization
A/SDBU, SA-6 #L500
Washington, DC 20522-0602
Gregory N. Mayberry, Acting Operations
Director
Tel: (703) 875-6822 Fax: (703) 875-6825
Email: mayberryg@state.gov
Web: www.state.gov/m/a/sdbu

A/SDBU, SA-6 #L500
Washington, DC 20522-0602
Patricia B. Culbreth, Women-Owned
Business Representative
Tel: (703) 875-6881 Fax: (703) 875-6825

Email: culberthpb@state.gov
Web: www.state.gov/m/a/sdbu

TRANSPORTATION, DEPT. OF

Office of Small and Disadvantaged Business
Utilization
400 7th St. SW #9414
Washington, DC 20590
Jose Gutierrez, Acting Director
Tel: (202) 366-1930 Fax: (202) 366-7228
Email: jose.gutierrez@dot.gov
Web: http://osdbuweb.dot.gov

400 7th St. SW #9414 M/S S40
Washington, DC 20590
Pat Hodge, Women Business
Representative
Tel: (202) 366-1930 Fax: (202) 366-7228
Email: pat.hodge@dot.gov
Web: www.dot.gov

Office of the Secretary of Transportation/
Administrative Service Center
400 7th St. SW #5106
Washington, DC 20590
Cyndy Blackmon, Small Business Specialist
Tel: (202) 366-4968 Fax: (202) 366-9848
Email: cyndy.blackmon@ost.dot.gov
Web: www.dot.gov

TRANSPORTATION, DEPT. OF

Federal Aviation Administration
Small Business Development Office
800 Independence Ave. SW #715
Washington, DC 20591
Fred Dendy, Small Business Program
Analyst
Tel: (202) 267-7454 Fax: (202) 493-4380
Email: fred.dendy@faa.gov
Web: www.faa.gov

400 7th St. SW #4404
Washington, DC 20590
Frank Waltos, Small Business Specialist
Tel: (202) 366-4205 Fax: (202) 366-3705
Email: frank.waltos@fhwa.dot.gov
Web: www.fhwa.dot.gov

Federal Railroad Administration
Office of Acquisition/Grants Services
(RAD-30)
1120 Vermont Ave. #6062
Washington, DC 20005
Illona Williams, Director
Tel: (202) 493-6130 Fax: (202) 493-6171
Email: illona.williams@fra.dot.gov
Web: www.fra.dot.gov

Federal Transit Administration
400 7th St. SW
Washington, DC 20590
Dale Johnson, Small Business Specialist
Tel: (202) 366-2512 Fax: (202) 366-3808
Email: dale.johnson@fta.dot.gov
Web: www.fta.dot.gov

Maritime Administration
400 7th St. SW #7310
Washington, DC 20590
Rita Thomas, Small Business Specialist
Tel: (202) 366-2802 Fax: (202) 366-3237
Email: rita.thomas@dot.gov
Web: www.marad.dot.gov

National Highway Traffic Safety Administration
400 7th St. SW #5301
Washington, DC 20590
Lloyd Blackwell, Small Business Specialist
Tel: (202) 366-9564 Fax: (202) 366-9555
Email: lloyd.blackwell@nhtsa.dot.gov
Web: www.nhtsa.dot.gov

Research/Special Programs Administration
400 7th St. SW #7118

Washington, DC 20590
Nauman Ansari, Small Business Specialist
Tel: (202) 366-5513 Fax: (202) 366-7974
Email: nauman.ansari@rspa.dot.gov
Web: http://osdbuweb.dot.gov/index.cfm

TREASURY, DEPT. OF THE
Office of Small and Disadvantaged Business
Utilization
1500 Pennsylvania Ave. NW M/C 655, 15th
St. #6097
Washington, DC 20220
Virginia Bellamy-Graham, Director
Tel: (202) 622-2826 Fax: (202) 622-4963
Email: va.bellamy-graham@do.treas.gov
Web: www.treas.gov/offices/management/
dcfo/osdbu

Office of Thrift Supervision/Procurement
Management
1700 G St. NW, 2nd Fl.
Washington, DC 20552
Douglas Mason, Small Business Specialist
Tel: (202) 906-7624 Fax: (202) 906-5648
Email: douglas.mason@ots.treas.gov
Web: www.ots.treas.gov

Bureau of Engraving and Printing
14th & C Sts. SW #708A-06
Washington, DC 20228
Kimberly Witcher, Small Business Specialist
Tel: (202) 874-2451 Fax: (202) 874-2200
Email: kimberly.witcher@bep.treas.gov

Comptroller of the Currency
Acquisitions
AQS 4-13 250 E. St. SW
Washington, DC 20219
Karen Galloway, Small Business Specialist
Tel: (202) 874-4567 Fax: (202) 874-5625
Email: karen.galloway@occ.treas.gov
Web: www.treas.gov

Departmental Offices
Procurement Office
1425 New York Ave. #2100
Washington, DC 20220
Sheryl Smith, Small Business Specialist
Tel: (202) 927-1031 Fax: (202) 622-2343
Email: sheryl.smith@do.treas.gov
Web: www.treas.gov

Financial Management Service
Small Business Office
401 14th St. SW #457F
Washington, DC 20227
Sonya Steebley, Small Business Specialist
Tel: (202) 874-0639 Fax: (202) 874-7275
Email: fms.sb@fms.treas.gov
Web: www.treas.gov

US Mint
801 9th St. NW
Washington, DC 20220
Melissa James, Small Business Specialist
Tel: (202) 354-7823 Fax: (202) 756-6562
Email: melissa.james@usmint.treas.gov
Web: www.usmint.gov

US Secret Service
Procurement Division
950 H St. NW
Washington, DC 20223
Robert Petrosky, Branch Chief
Tel: (202) 406-6940 Fax: (202) 406-6801
Email: rpetrosky@usss.treas.gov
Web: www.usss.treas.gov

US POSTAL SERVICE
Supplier Diversity Office
475 L'Enfant Plz. SW #4320
Washington, DC 20260-4320
Janice B. Williams-Hopkins, Program
Manager
Tel: (202) 268-4633 Fax: (202) 268-7288

Email: janice.b.williams-hopkins@usps.gov
Web: www.usps.com

VETERANS AFFAIRS, DEPT. OF
Office of Small and Disadvantaged Business
Utilization
810 Vermont Ave. NW, M/C 20S2
Washington, DC 20420
Patricia Stanford, Director of Acquisition
Tel: (202) 273-6818 Fax: (202) 275-1283
Email: patricia.stanford@mail.va.gov
Web: www.va.gov/osdbu

810 Vermont Ave. NW
Washington, DC 20420
Scott F. Denniston, Director
Tel: (202) 565-8124 Fax: (202) 565-8156
Email: scott.denniston@mail.va.gov
Web: www.va.gov/osdbu

810 Vermont Ave. NW
Washington, DC 20420
John Blake, Small Business Specialist
Tel: (202) 565-5784 Fax: (202) 565-4921
Email: john.blake@mail.va.gov
Web: www.va.gov/osdbu

Washington DC, VA Medical Center
50 Irving St. NW
Washington, DC 20422
Joan F. Van Middlesworth, Small Business
Specialist
Tel: (202) 745-8000 X8413 Fax: (202)
754-8530
Email: joan.vanmiddlesworth@med.va.gov
Web: www.va.gov

FLORIDA

COMMERCE, DEPT. OF
Minority Business Development Agency
District Office
51 SW 1st Ave. #1314, Box 25
Miami, FL 33130
Robert M. Henderson, Regional Director
Tel: (305) 536-5054 Fax: (305) 530-7068
Email: rhenderson@mbda.gov
Web: www.mbda.gov

Florida Minority Supplier Development
Council
6880 Lake Eleanor Dr. #104A
Orlando, FL 32809
Malik Ali, Executive Director
Tel: (407) 245-6062 Fax: (407) 857-8647
Email: malik@fmsdc.org
Web: www.nmsdcfl.com

Miami/Ft. Lauderdale Minority Business
Development Center
3050 Biscayne Blvd. #201
Miami, FL 33137
Andrew Byer, Small Business Specialist
Tel: (786) 316-0888 Fax: (786) 316-0090
Email: abyer@mbdcsouthflorida.org
Web: www.mbdcsouthflorida.org

Miami/Ft. Lauderdale Minority Business
Development Center
Bank of America Bldg., 3800 W. Broward
Blvd. #101
Ft. Lauderdale, FL 33313
Ricardo Martinez, Small Business Specialist
Tel: (954) 660-7601 Fax: (954) 587-3703
Email: rmartinez@mbdcsouthflorida.org
Web: www.mbdcsouthflorida.org

DEFENSE, DEPT. OF
**Naval Air Warfare Center Training Systems
Division**
Small Business Office
12350 Research Pkwy. Code 253D

Orlando, FL 32826-3224
Argentina V. Thompson, Deputy of Small
Business
Tel: (407) 380-8253 Fax: (407) 380-4487
Email: argentina.thompson@navy.mil
Web: www.ntsc.navy.mil

**US Air Force, 16th Contracting Squadron/
LGC-Air Force Special Operations Command**
Small Business Office
350 Tully St., Bldg. 90339
Hurlburt Field, FL 32544-9190
Ron Siniscalchi, Small Business Specialist
Tel: (850) 884-5376 X1250 Fax: (850)
884-2001
Email: ron.siniscalchi@hurlburt.af.mil
Web: www.selltoairforce.org

**US Air Force, 325 Contracting Squadron/CC-
Air Education and Training Command**
Small Business Office
501 Illinois Ave. #5
Tyndall AFB, FL 32403-5526
Norma Myers, Small Business Specialist
Tel: (850) 283-3670 Fax: (850) 283-1222
Email: norma.myers@tyndall.af.mil
Web: www.selltoairforce.org

US Air Force, 45th Space Wing/BZ (AFSPC)
Small Business Office
1201 Edward White St.
Patrick AFB, FL 32925-3237
Linda Sherod, Small Business Specialist
Tel: (321) 494-2207 Fax: (321) 494-5599
Email: linda.sherod@patrick.af.mil
Web: www.patrick.af.mil

**US Air Force, 482nd LSS/LGC-Air Force
Reserve Command**
Small Business Office
29050 Coral Sea Blvd.
Homestead ARS, FL 33039-1299
John Marshburn, Small Business Specialist
Tel: (305) 224-7474 Fax: (305) 224-7055
Email: john.marshburn@homestead.af.mil
Web: www.selltoairforce.org

**US Air Force, 6th Air Refueling Wing/LGC
(AF)-Air Mobility Command**
Small Business Office
2606 Brown Pelican Ave.
MacDill AFB, FL 33621-5000
Judy Hall, Director of Contract Operations
Tel: (813) 828-4752
Email: hallj@macdill.af.mil
Web: http://public.macdill.amc.
af.mil/6contracting.html

**US Air Force, Air Armament Center/BC-Air
Force Materiel Command**
Small Business Office
205 W. D Ave. #449
Eglin AFB, FL 32542-6863
Gina L. Holman, Director
Tel: (850) 882-2843 X3 Fax: (850) 882-
4836
Email: gina.holman@eglin.af.mil
Web: www.eglin.af.mil/org-busopp.htm

**US Air Force, HQ AFSOC/PKM-Air Force
Special Operations Command**
Small Business Office
427 Cody Ave.
Hurlburt Field, FL 32544
Molly Yow, Small Business Director
Tel: (850) 884-2376 Fax: (850) 884-2476
Email: Molly.Yow@Hurlburt.af.mil
Web: www.selltoairforce.org

US Special Operations Command
7701 Tampa Point Blvd.
Tampa, FL 33621-5323
Karen Para, Small Business Specialist
Tel: (813) 828-7549 Fax: (813) 828-7504
Web: www.socom.mil

**NATIONAL AERONAUTICS AND SPACE
ADMINISTRATION**
Kennedy Space Center
M/C OP-CIAO
Kennedy Space Center, FL 32899
David A. Wansley, Field Installation Small/
Minority Business Specialist
Tel: (321) 867-7346 Fax: (321) 867-8599
Email: david.a.wansley@nasa.gov
Web: www.hq.nasa.gov
M/C OP-CIAO
Kennedy Space Center, FL 32899
Gloria Marsh, Small Business Specialist
Tel: (321) 867-7349 Fax: (321) 867-7999
Email: gloria.marsh-1@nasa.gov
Web: www.nasa.gov

VETERANS AFFAIRS, DEPT. OF
Miami VA Medical Center
1201 NW 16th St.
Miami, FL 33125
Gwendolyn Moore, Assistant Chief of
Acquisition/Material Management
Tel: (305) 575-7000 X3221 Fax: (305)
575-3280
Email: gwen.moore@med.va.gov
Web: www.visn8.med.va.gov/miami

St. Petersburg VA Medical Center
10,000 Bay Pines Blvd.
St. Petersburg, FL 33708
James Robert, Small Business Specialist
Tel: (727) 398-6661 X1278 Fax: (727)
398-9536
Web: www.va.gov

West Palm Beach VA Medical Center
7305 N. Military Trail
West Palm Beach, FL 33410
Dinora Bruno, Chief of Acquisitions
Tel: (561) 422-8262 X6511 Fax: (561)
422-6507
Email: dinora.bruno@med.va.gov
Web: www.visn8.med.va.gov/westpalm

VA Medical Center
1601 SW Archer Rd.
Gainesville, FL 32608-1197
Susan Little, Small Business Specialist
Tel: (386) 755-3016 x2095 Fax: (386)
758-3211
Email: susan.little@med.va.gov
Web: www.va.gov/osdbu

VA Medical Center 90C
Contracting Office
13000 Bruce B. Downs Blvd.
Tampa, FL 33612
Cathy Pridlides, Small Business Specialist
Tel: (813) 972-7515 Fax: (813) 903-4838
Email: Cathy.Pridlides2@med.va.gov
Web: www.va.gov/osdbu

GEORGIA

AGRICULTURE, DEPT. OF
Agricultural Research Service
South Atlantic Area
P.O. Box 5677
Athens, GA 30604
Mary LaRue, Supervisory Procurement
Analyst
Tel: (706) 546-3532 Fax: (706) 546-3444
Email: laruem@saa.ars.usda.gov
Web: www.saa.ars.usda.gov

Natural Resources Conservation Service
Georgia State Office
Federal Bldg. #200, 355 E. Hancock Ave.
Athens, GA 30601
Sharon Gipson, State Administrative Officer
Tel: (706) 546-2272 Fax: (706) 546-2120

Public Sector Minority Business Opportunities - Georgia

Email: sharon.gipson@ga.usda.gov
Web: www.nrcs.usda.gov

Federal Bldg. #225, 355 E. Hancock Ave.
Athens, GA 30601
Carolyn Adams, Contracting Officer
Tel: (706) 546-2280 Fax: (706) 546-2157
Email: carolyn.adams@ga.usda.gov
Web: www.nrcs.usda.gov

COMMERCE, DEPT. OF
Minority Business Development Agency
Atlanta Regional Office
401 W. Peachtree St. NW #1715
Atlanta, GA 30308
Robert Henderson, Regional Director
Tel: (404) 730-3300 Fax: (404) 730-3313
Email: rhenderson@mbda.gov
Web: www.mbda.gov

760 Spring St. NW #319
Atlanta, GA 30332-0640
Donna Ennis, Project Director
Tel: (404) 894-2096 Fax: (404) 894-1192
Email: donna.ennis@edi.gatech.edu
Web: www.georgiambdc.org

DEFENSE, DEPT. OF
US Air Force, 347th Contracting Squadron/ CC-Special Operations Command
Small Business Office
4380B Alabama Rd.
Moody AFB, GA 31699-1793
Ailene B. Duff, Small Business Specialist/ Director of Business Operations
Tel: (229) 257-4706 Fax: (229) 257-2738
Email: ailene.duff@moody.af.mil
Web: www.moody.af.mil

US Air Force, 94 CONF/LGC
Small Business Office
1538 Atlantic Ave.
Dobbins ARB, GA 30069-4824
Linda K. Lewis, Chief of Contracting
Tel: (678) 655-4981 Fax: (678) 655-5612
Email: linda.lewis@dobbins.af.mil
Web: www.selltoairforce.org

US Air Force, Warner-Robins Air Logistics Center/BC-Air Force Materiel Command
Small Business Office
180 Page Rd.
Robins AFB, GA 31098-1600
James A. Lovett, Jr., Director
Tel: (478) 926-5873 Fax: (478) 926-2929
Email: jim.lovett@robins.af.mil
Web: www.robins.af.mil/smallbusiness/ index.htm

ENERGY, DEPT. OF
Southeastern Power Administration
1166 Athens Tech Rd.
Elberton, GA 30635-6711
Frances Deal, Small Business Program Manager
Tel: (706) 213-3825 Fax: (706) 213-3884
Email: francesd@sepa.doe.gov
Web: www.sepa.doe.gov

ENVIRONMENTAL PROTECTION AGENCY
Region IV-Office of Small and Disadvantaged Business Utilization/Minority Business Enterprise/Women Business Enterprise
61 Forsyth St. SW
Atlanta, GA 30303-8960
Rafael Santamaria, MBE/WBE Coordinator
Tel: (404) 562-8110 Fax: (404) 562-8370
Email: santamaria.rafael@epa.gov
Web: www.epa.gov/osdbu

HEALTH AND HUMAN SERVICES, DEPT. OF
Centers for Disease Control and Prevention
Procurement/Grants Office

2920 Brandywine Rd. #1142
Atlanta, GA 30341
Curtis L. Bryant, Small Business Program Manager
Tel: (770) 488-2806 Fax: (770) 488-2828
Email: ckb9@cdc.gov
Web: www.cdc.gov

HOMELAND SECURITY, DEPT. OF
Federal Law Enforcement Training Center
Office of Small and Disadvantaged Business Utilization/Procurement Division
1131 Chapel Crossing Rd. Bldg. 93
Glynco, GA 31524
Beverly Nesmith, Small Business Specialist
Tel: (912) 267-2449 Fax: (912) 267-3132
Email: beverly.nesmith@dhs.gov
Web: www.fletc.gov

TREASURY, DEPT. OF THE
Internal Revenue Service
Southeast Area Field Office
2888 Woodcock Blvd. #300
Atlanta, GA 30341
Pat Hewitt, Small Business Specialist (alternate)
Tel: (404) 338-9205 Fax: (404) 338-9203
Email: patricia.hewitt@irs.gov
Web: www.treas.gov

TREASURY, DEPT. OF THE
Internal Revenue Service
Southeast Area Field Office
2888 Woodcock Blvd. #300
Atlanta, GA 30341
Lori Johnson, Small Business Specialist
Tel: (404) 338-9204 Fax: (404) 338-9203
Email: Lori.Johnson@irs.gov
Web: www.treas.gov

US POSTAL SERVICE
Atlanta District/Diversity Office
P.O. Box 599390
North Metro, GA 30026-9390
Barbara A. Danzy, Diversity Development Specialist Manager
Tel: (770) 717-2992 Fax: (770) 717-2993
Email: barbara.a.danzy@usps.gov
Web: www.usps.gov

VETERANS AFFAIRS, DEPT. OF
Augusta VA Medical Center
1 Freedom Way
Augusta, GA 30904
Cindy Rogers, Procurement Analyst
Tel: (706) 481-6724 Fax: (706) 481-6741
Email: cindy.rogers2@med.va.gov
Web: www.va.gov

HAWAII

COMMERCE, DEPT. OF
Minority Business Development Agency
Honolulu Minority Business Development Center
2404 Maile Way, D307
Honolulu, HI 96822
David M. Gillespie, Project Director
Tel: (808) 956-0850 Fax: (808) 956-0851
Email: info@honolulu-mbdc.org
Web: www.honolulu-mbdc.org

DEFENSE, DEPT. OF
US Air Force, 15th Contracting Squadron
Small Business Office
90 G St.
Hickam AFB, HI 96853-5320
Jim Watanabe, Small Business Specialist
Tel: (808) 449-6860 X103 Fax: (808) 449-7026
Email: james.watanabe@hickam.af.mil
Web: www2.hickam.af.mil

IDAHO

AGRICULTURE, DEPT. OF
Forest Service
Region IV-Boise National Forest
1249 S. Vinnell Way #200
Boise, ID 83709
Diana J. Early, Procurement Assistant
Tel: (208) 373-4150 Fax: (208) 373-4197
Email: dearly@fs.fed.us
Web: www.fs.fed.us

DEFENSE, DEPT. OF
US Air Force, 366th Contracting Squadron/ CCD-Air Combat Command
Small Business Office
366 Gunfighter Ave. #498
Mountain Home AFB, ID 83648-5296
Marilyn Lemmon, Small Business Specialist
Tel: (208) 828-3106 Fax: (208) 828-2485
Email: marilyn.lemmon@mountainhome. af.mil
Web: www.mountainhome.af.mil

ENERGY, DEPT. OF
Idaho Operations Office
1955 N. Fremont Ave.
Idaho Falls, ID 83401-1221
Trudy A. Harmel, Small Business Program Manager
Tel: (208) 526-9519 Fax: (208) 526-5548
Email: harmelta@id.doe.gov
Web: www.id.doe.gov

VETERANS AFFAIRS, DEPT. OF
Boise VA Medical Center
500 W. Fort St.
Boise, ID 83702-4598
Amanda Glade, Purchasing Agent
Tel: (208) 422-1000 X1363 Fax: (208) 422-1139
Email: amanda.glade@med.gov
Web: www.va.gov

ILLINOIS

AGRICULTURE, DEPT. OF
Agricultural Research Service
Midwest Area
1815 N. University St.
Peoria, IL 61604
Rebecca Holzinger, Area Procurement Officer
Tel: (309) 681-6616 Fax: (309) 681-6683
Email: rholzinger@mwa.ars.usda.gov
Web: www.mwa.ars.usda.gov

COMMERCE, DEPT. OF
Minority Business Development Agency
Chicago Minority Business Development Council
1 E. Wacker Dr. #1200
Chicago, IL 60601
Tracye E. Smith, Executive Director
Tel: (312) 755-8880 X15 Fax: (312) 755-8890
Email: tsmith@cmbdc.org
Web: www.cmbdc.org

Illinois Statewide Minority Business Development Agency
1 E. Wacker Dr.
Chicago, IL 60601
Hans Bonner, Project Director
Tel: (312) 755-8889 Fax: (312) 755-8891
Email: hbonner@chiventures.org
Web: www.mbda.gov

National Enterprise Center
55 E. Monroe St. #1406
Chicago, IL 60603
Eric Dobyne, Regional Director

Tel: (312) 353-0182 Fax: (312) 353-0191
Email: edobyne@mbda.gov
Web: www.mbda.gov

DEFENSE, DEPT. OF
US Air Force, 375th Contracting Squadron, Air Mobility Command
Small Business Office
201 E. Winters St., Bldg. 50
Scott AFB, IL 62225-5015
Garth Sanginiti, Small Business Specialist
Tel: (618) 256-9322 Fax: (618) 256-2649
Email: garth.sanginiti@scott.af.mil
Web: www.selltoairforce.org

US Air Force, AMC Contracting Flight/LGCF- Air Mobility Command
Small Business Office
507 Symington Dr. #W202
Scott AFB, IL 62225-5015
Jeannine Kinder, Small Business Specialist
Tel: (618) 256-9995 Fax: (618) 256-5724
Email: jeannine.kinder@scott.af.mil
Web: http://public.amc.af.mil

US Air Force, Contract Airlift Division/DOY- Air Mobility Command
Small Business Office
402 Scott Dr. Unit 3A1
Scott AFB, IL 62225-5302
Joyce Pavlak, Small Business Specialist
Tel: (618) 229-2460 Fax: (618) 256-8316
Email: joyce.pavlak@scott.af.mil
Web: http://public.amc.af.mil

ENERGY, DEPT. OF
Chicago Office/Office of Acquisition Assistance
9800 S. Cass Ave.
Argonne, IL 60439
Larry Thompson, Small Business Program Manager
Tel: (630) 252-2711 Fax: (630) 252-5045
Email: larry.thompson@ch.doe.gov
Web: www.ch.doe.gov

Argonne National Laboratory
Procurement Department
9700 S. Cass Ave., Bldg. 201
Argonne, IL 60439-4873
Diana Thompson, Small Business Liaison Officer
Tel: (630) 252-6920 Fax: (630) 252-4517
Email: dlthompson@anl.gov
Web: www.anl.gov

Fermi National Accelerator Laboratory
Chicago Operations Office
P.O. Box 500
Batavia, IL 60510
Joe Collins, Small Business Program Manager
Tel: (630) 840-4169 Fax: (630) 840-2457
Email: jcollins@fnal.gov
Web: www.fnal.gov

Region 5
Office of Small and Disadvantaged Business Utilization
77 W. Jackson Blvd., M/C 10J
Chicago, IL 60604-3507
Adrianne Callahan, Officer
Tel: (312) 353-5556 Fax: (312) 353-9096
Email: callahan.adrianne@epa.gov
Web: www.epa.gov/region05/

GENERAL SERVICES ADMINISTRATION
Region V-Office of Small Business Utilization
230 S. Dearborn St. #3718
Chicago, IL 60604
Beverly Coley, Small Business Specialist
Tel: (312) 353-1100 Fax: (312) 886-9893
Email: beverly.coley@gsa.gov
Web: www.gsa.gov

VETERANS AFFAIRS, DEPT. OF
VA National Acquisition Center
P.O. Box 76
Hines, IL 60141
Jay McLain, Small Business Specialist
Tel: (708) 786-5154 Fax: (708) 786-5148
Email: jay.mclain@med.va.gov
Web: www.va.gov

INDIANA

COMMERCE, DEPT. OF
Minority Business Development Agency
Northwest Indiana Minority Business
Opportunity Committee
839 Broadway, 2nd Fl.
Gary, IN 46402
Lucia Dotson, Executive Director
Tel: (219) 886-9572 Fax: (219) 881-4999
Email: ldotson@nimboc.com
Web: www.nimboc.com

US Census Bureau
Procurement Office
1201 E. 10th St. #149, Bldg. 66
Jeffersonville, IN 47132
Connie Smith, Chief
Tel: (812) 218-3351 Fax: (812) 218-3937
Email: connie.smith@census.gov
Web: www.census.gov

DEFENSE, DEPT. OF
US Air Force, 34 LG/LGC-Air Force Reserve
Command
Operations Contracting Office
448 Mustang Ave.
Grissom ARB, IN 46971-5320
Patricia Craddock, Small Business
Specialist
Tel: (765) 688-2801 Fax: (765) 688-2803
Email: patricia.craddock@grissom.af.mil
Web: www.selltoairforce.org

DEPARTMENT OF ADMINISTRATION
State of Indiana
Minority and Women's Business Enterprises
Division
402 W. Washington St. #W-469
Indianapolis, IN 46204
Claudia Cummings, Deputy Commissioner
Tel: (317) 232-3061 Fax: (317) 233-6921
Email: mwdbe@idoa.in.gov
Web: www.in.gov/idoa/minority

HOMELAND SECURITY, DEPT. OF
Customs and Border Protection
Regional Office
6650 Telecom Dr. #300
Indianapolis, IN 46278
Clarence Abernathy, Small Business
Specialist
Tel: (317) 614-4562 Fax: (317) 298-1344
Email: clarence.abernathy@dhs.gov
Web: www.ready.gov

VETERANS AFFAIRS, DEPT. OF
Indianapolis VA Medical Center
1481 W. 10th St.
Indianapolis, IN 46202
Craig Earles, Small Business Specialist
Tel: (317) 554-0265 Fax: (317) 554-0200
Email: craig.earles@med.va.gov
Web: www.va.gov

VA Northern Indiana Health Care System
2121 Lake Ave.
Ft. Wayne, IN 46805
Robert Nash, Small Business Specialist
Tel: (260) 426-5431 X71205
Fax: (260) 460-1336
Email: robert.nash@med.va.gov
Web: www.va.gov

IOWA

ENERGY, DEPT. OF
Chicago Operations Office/Ames Laboratory
Iowa State University, 211 TASF
Ames, IA 50011
Connie Heim, Small Business Program
Manager
Tel: (515) 294-4191 Fax: (515) 294-6166
Email: heimc@ameslab.gov
Web: www.ameslab.gov

VETERANS AFFAIRS, DEPT. OF
Central Plains Health Network, VA Medical
Center/Contracting Office
601 Hwy. 6 West
Iowa City, IA 52240
Patricia K. Parker, Contracting Officer
Tel: (319) 338-7157 Fax: (319) 339-7121
Email: patricia.parker@med.va.gov
Web: www.va.gov

VA Medical Center
1515 W. Pleasant St.
Knoxville, IA 50138
Steven Ethell, Small Business Specialist
Tel: (641) 828-5043 Fax: (641) 828-5083
Email: steven.ethell@med.va.gov
Web: www.va.gov/osdbu

KANSAS

DEFENSE, DEPT. OF
US Air Force, 22nd Air Refueling Wing/LGC-
Air Mobility Command
Small Business Office
53147 Kansas St. #102
McConnell AFB, KS 67221-3606
Edward W. Harvell, Small Business
Specialist
Tel: (316) 759-4505 Fax: (316) 759-4507
Email: ed.harvell@mcconnell.af.mil
Web: www.selltoairforce.org

ENVIRONMENTAL PROTECTION AGENCY
Region VII-Office of Small and
Disadvantaged Business Utilization
901 N. 5th St.
Kansas City, KS 66101
Chester Stovall, Officer
Tel: (913) 551-7549 Fax: (913) 551-7579
Email: stovall.chester@epa.gov
Web: www.epa.gov/osdbu

VETERANS AFFAIRS, DEPT. OF
VA Eastern Kansas Health Care System-
Dwight D. Eisenhower VA Medical Center
4101 S. 4th St., Traffic Way
Leavenworth, KS 66048
Marcus A. Clayton, Small Business
Specialist
Tel: (913) 758-4281 Fax: (913) 758-6495
Email: marcus.clayton@med.va.gov
Web: www.va.gov

KENTUCKY

AGRICULTURE, DEPT. OF
Natural Resources Conservation Service
Kentucky State Office
771 Corporate Dr. #210
Lexington, KY 40503-5479
Connie McKinney, Contract Specialist
Tel: (859) 224-7395 Fax: (859) 224-7393
Email: connie.mckinney@ky.usda.gov
Web: www.ky.nrcs.usda.gov

LOUISIANA

AGRICULTURE, DEPT. OF
National Finance Center
Contracting Support Team
13800 Old Gentilly Rd.
New Orleans, LA 70129
Deidre V. Phillips, Head
Tel: (504) 426-0281 Fax: (504) 426-9722
Email: deidre.phillips@usda.gov
Web: www.nfc.usda.gov

Natural Resources Conservation Service
Louisiana State Office
3737 Government St.
Alexandria, LA 71302
Ralph E. Broome, Contracting Officer
Tel: (318) 473-7781 Fax: (318) 473-7831
Email: ralph.broome@la.usda.gov
Web: www.la.nrcs.usda.gov

DEFENSE, DEPT. OF
US Air Force, 2nd Contracting Squadron/
CCD-Air Combat Command
Small Business Office
841 Fairchild Ave. #205
Barksdale AFB, LA 71110-2271
Connie Shirley, Small Business Specialist
Tel: (318) 456-6940 Fax: (318) 456-2629
Email: connie.shirley@barksdale.af.mil
Web: www.barksdale.af.mil

ENERGY, DEPT. OF
Strategic Petroleum Reserve
Project Management Office
900 Commerce Rd. East
New Orleans, LA 70123
Geralyn "Geri" Champagne-Funk, Small
Business Program Manager
Tel: (504) 734-4766 Fax: (504) 818-5766
Email: geralyn.champagne@spr.doe.gov
Web: www.spr.doe.gov

Strategic Petroleum Reserve Project
Management Office
Dyn McDermott Petroleum Operations
Company
850 S. Clearview Pkwy.
New Orleans, LA 70123
Steven E. Haines, Diversity Subcontracting
Program Administrator
Tel: (504) 734-4394 Fax: (504) 818-5394
Email: steve.haines@spr.doe.gov
Web: www.spr.doe.gov

VETERANS AFFAIRS, DEPT. OF
Alexandria VA Medical Center
P.O. Box 69004
Alexandria, LA 71306-9004
Herman Chelette, Small Business Specialist
Tel: (318) 473-0010 X12239 Fax: (318)
483-5063
Email: herman.chelette@med.va.gov
Web: www.va.gov

New Orleans VA Medical Center
1601 Perdido St.
New Orleans, LA 70112
Robert Forbes, Small Business Specialist
Tel: (504) 589-5280 Fax: (504) 589-5289
Email: robert.forbes@med.va.gov
Web: www.va.gov

Overton Brooks VA Medical Center
510 E. Stoner Ave.
Shreveport, LA 71101-4295
Beverly Lockett, Chief of Acquisitions/
Material Management
Tel: (318) 424-6034 Fax: (318) 424-6078
Email: beverly.lockett@med.va.gov
Web: www.va.gov

MAINE

VETERANS AFFAIRS, DEPT. OF
VA Medical Center
Augusta VA Medical Center
1 VA Ctr.
Augusta, ME 04330
Kathleen Burnham, Small Business
Specialist
Tel: (207) 623-5717 Fax: (207) 621-7325
Email: kathy.burnham@med.va.gov
Web: www.va.gov

MARYLAND

AGRICULTURE, DEPT. OF
Agricultural Research Service
Acquisition and Property Division
5601 Sunnyside Ave., M/S 5116
Beltsville, MD 20705-5116
Meghan Ryan, Section Head for Acquisition
Branch
Tel: (301) 504-1744 Fax: (301) 504-1717
Email: mryan@ars.usda.gov
Web: www.afm.ars.usda.gov

5601 Sunnyside Ave.
Beltsville, MD 20705-5117
Theresa Stephens, Procurement Analyst
Tel: (301) 504-1729 Fax: (301) 504-1739
Email: tstephens@ars.usda.gov
Web: www.nps.ars.usda.gov

Beltsville Area
10300 Baltimore Blvd. 003 #329
Beltsville, MD 20705
Michael Wyckoff, Supervisory Procurement
Analyst
Tel: (301) 504-7019 X452 Fax: (301)
504-5009
Email: wyckoffm@ba.ars.usda.gov
Web: www.ba.ars.usda.gov

Food Safety and Inspection Service
5601 Sunnyside Ave., M/S 5230
Beltsville, MD 20705-5230
Madonna Langley, Contracting Officer
Tel: (301) 504-4228 Fax: (301) 504-4276
Email: madonna.langley@usda.gov
Web: www.fsis.usda.gov

COMMERCE, DEPT. OF
Minority Business Development Agency
National Capital Minority Business
Opportunity Committee
1100 Mercantile Ln.
Largo, MD 20774
Thomas McLamore, Executive Director
Tel: (301) 583-4605 Fax: (301) 772-8540
Email: tmclamore@ncmboc.com
Web: www.mbda.gov

National Institute of Standards and
Technology
Acquisitions and Management Division
100 Bureau Dr. #1640
Gaithersburg, MD 20899
Phyllis Bower, Chief of Acquisition Division
Tel: (301) 975-6336
Web: www.nist.gov

100 Bureau Dr., Bldg. 301 #B-129
Gaithersburg, MD 20899-1640
Henry M. Levy, Small Business Specialist
Tel: (301) 975-6343 Fax: (301) 975-8884
Email: henry.levy@nist.gov
Web: www.nist.gov

National Oceanic and Atmospheric
Administration
Acquisition and Grants Management
1315 East-West Hwy. #10100

Silver Spring, MD 20910
Tom Genovese, Director
Tel: (301) 713-3478 X170
Fax: (301) 713-4155
Email: tom.genovese@noaa.gov
Web: www.rdc.noaa.gov

1305 East-West Hwy. #6206
Silver Spring, MD 20910-3281
Robert Ransom, Head of Contracting
Tel: (301) 713-1055 X159 Fax: (301)
713-3599
Email: robert.ransom@noaa.gov
Web: www.rdc.noaa.gov

Acquisition/Grants Office
1335 East-West Hwy. #6300
Silver Spring, MD 20910
Helen Hurcombe, Director
Tel: (301) 713-0325 Fax: (301) 713-1974
Email: helen.hurcombe@noaa.gov
Web: www.rdc.noaa.gov

National Weather Service/Acquisition
Division
1325 East-West Hwy., SSMC2 #1530
Silver Spring, MD 20910
Daniel L. Clever, Division Chief
Tel: (301) 713-3405 X153
Fax: (301) 713-1024
Email: daniel.l.clever@noaa.gov
Web: www.rdc.noaa.gov

Staff, Offices/External Clients Acquisition
Division
1305 East-West Hwy. #7604
Silver Spring, MD 20910
Gary Rice, Director
Tel: (301) 713-0839 X190
Fax: (301) 713-0809
Email: gary.rice@noaa.gov
Web: www.rdc.noaa.gov

COMMERCE, DEPT. OF
US Census Bureau
Procurement Office
4700 Silver Hill Rd. #G-314
Suitland, MD 20746
Michael Palensky, Chief
Tel: (301) 763-1818 Fax: (301) 457-1785
Email: michael.l.palensky@census.gov
Web: www.census.gov

DEFENSE, DEPT. OF
Naval Air Warfare Center Aircraft Division
Small Business Office
21983 Bundy Rd., Bldg. 441
Patuxent River, MD 20670-1127
Estella Balmaceda, Deputy for Small
Business
Tel: (301) 757-9087 Fax: (301) 757-9093
Email: estella.balmaceda@navy.mil
Web: www.navair.navy.mil

US Air Force, 89th Airlift Wing/LGC-Air
Mobility Command
Small Business Office
1419 Menoher Dr.
Andrews AFB, MD 20762-6500
Sandra Foster, Small Business Specialist
Tel: (301) 981-6509 Fax: (301) 981-6538
Email: sandra.foster@andrews.af.mil
Web: http://public.andrews.amc.af.mil/
index.asp

US Army
Office of Small Business
Attn: AMSRD-SB, Aberdeen Proving
Ground, Bldg. E-4455
Aberdeen, MD 21010-5424
John Rasmusen, Small Business Officer
Tel: (410) 436-3136 Fax: (410) 436-7744
Web: www.rdecom.army.mil

HEALTH AND HUMAN SERVICES, DEPT. OF
Centers for Medicare & Medicaid Services
7500 Security Blvd. Code C2-21-15
Baltimore, MD 21244-1850
Alice Roache, Small Business Specialist
Tel: (410) 786-9319 Fax: (410) 786-9922
Web: http://cms.hhs.gov

Program Support Center/Division of
Acquisition Management
5600 Fishers Ln. #5C-26, Parklawn Bldg.
Rockville, MD 20857
Linda Danley, Small Business Specialist
Tel: (301) 443-1715 Fax: (301) 443-7593
Email: linda.danley@psc.hhs.gov
Web: www.psc.gov

Agency for Healthcare Research and Quality
Substance Abuse and Mental Health
Services Administration
Office of Small and Disadvantaged Business
Utilization
1 Choke Cherry Rd. #L-1053
Rockville, MD 20857
Vivian Kim, Small Business Specialist
Tel: (240) 276-1017 Fax: (240) 276-1232
Email: vivian.kim@samhsa.hhs.gov
Web: www.samhsa.gov

Centers for Medicare & Medicaid Services
Office of Acquisition/Grants Management
7500 Security Blvd. Code C2-21-15
Baltimore, MD 21244-1850
Alice Roache, Small Business Program
Manager
Tel: (410) 786-9319 Fax: (410) 786-9922
Email: alice.roache@cms.hhs.gov
Web: http://cms.hhs.gov

**Health Resources and Services
Administration**
Acquisition Branch
5600 Fishers Ln. #13A-19 Parklawn Bldg.
Rockville, MD 20857
Steve Zangwill, Small Business Adviser
Tel: (301) 443-2750 Fax: (301) 443-8254
Email: steve.zangwill@hrsa.hhs.gov
Web: www.hrsa.gov

Indian Health Service
Office of the Secretary/Office of Small and
Disadvantaged Business Utilization
12300 Twinbrook Pkwy. #450-A
Rockville, MD 20852
Nelia K. Holder, Small Business Specialist
Tel: (301) 443-1480 Fax: (301) 443-0929
Email: nelia.holder@ihs.gov
Web: www.ihs.gov

National Institutes of Health
Office of Small and Disadvantaged Business
Utilization
Executive Plz. South, 6120 Executive Blvd.
#6038
Bethesda, MD 20892
Joseph Bowe, Small Business Program
Manager
Tel: (301) 435-3810 Fax: (301) 480-0309
Email: jb166i@nih.gov
Web: www.nih.gov

National Institutes of Health
Small Business Office
6100 Executive Blvd. #6D05, M/S 7540
Bethesda, MD 20892-7540
Annett Owens-Scarboro, Small Business
Specialist
Tel: (301) 496-9639 Fax: (301) 480-2506
Email: sbocalender@mail.nih.gov
Web: http://sbo.od.nih.gov

Food & Drug Administration
Office of Facilities, Acquisition and Central
Services

5600 Fishers Ln. #12A43 M/C HFA630
Rockville, MD 20857
Doug Smith, Small Business Specialist
Tel: (301) 827-1994 Fax: (301) 827-7233
Email: rloube@oc.fda.gov
Web: www.fda.gov

NATIONAL AERONAUTICS AND SPACE ADMINISTRATION
Goddard Space Flight Center
M/C 210
Greenbelt, MD 20771
Rosa Acevedo, Small Business Specialist
Tel: (301) 286-4679 Fax: (301) 286-0237
Email: rosa.e.acevedo@nasa.gov
Web: http://procurement.nasa.gov

Goddard Space Flight Center
Greenbelt Rd. M/C 210
Greenbelt, MD 20771
Gilberto Del Valle, Procurement Analyst
Tel: (301) 286-8136 Fax: (301) 286-0732
Email: gilberto.delvalle-1@nasa.gov
Web: http://procurement.nasa.gov

NUCLEAR REGULATORY COMMISSION
Office of Small Business/Civil Rights
11545 Rockville Pike
Rockville, MD 20852
Mauricio Vera, Small Business Program
Manager
Tel: (301) 415-7160 Fax: (301) 415-5953
Email: mxv@nrc.gov
Web: www.nrc.gov/who-we-are/small-
business.html

11545 Rockville Pike, M/S T2D56
Rockville, MD 20555
Corenthis B. Kelley, Director
Tel: (301) 415-7380 Fax: (301) 415-5953
Email: cbk@nrc.gov
Web: www.nrc.gov

SOCIAL SECURITY ADMINISTRATION
Office of Small and Disadvantaged Business
Utilization
7111 Security Blvd.
Baltimore, MD 21244
Wayne Mcdonald, Director
Tel: (410) 965-7467 Fax: (410) 965-2965
Email: wayne.mcdonald@ssa.gov
Web: www.ssa.gov/oag

7111 Security Blvd., 1st Fl.
Baltimore, MD 21244
Pat Bullock, Small Business Specialist
Tel: (410) 965-9457 Fax: (410) 965-2965
Email: pat.bullock@ssa.gov
Web: www.ssa.gov/oag

TREASURY, DEPT. OF THE
Internal Revenue Service
National Office
Constellation Ctr., 6009 Oxon Hill Rd.
Oxon Hill, MD 20745
Jodie L. Paustian, Small Business Specialist
Tel: (202) 283-1350 Fax: (202) 283-1529
Email: jodie.l.paustian@irs.gov
Web: www.irs.gov

MASSACHUSETTS

DEFENSE, DEPT. OF
**US Air Force, 439th LSS/LGC-Air Force
Reserve Command**
Small Business Office
250 Airlift Dr.
Westover AFB, MA 01022-1525
Michael LaFortune, Small Business
Specialist
Tel: (413) 557-3508 Fax: (413) 557-2017

Email: michael.lafortune@westover.af.mil
Web: www.selltoairforce.org

**US Air Force, Electronic Systems Center/BC-
Air Force Materiel Command**
Small Business Office
275 Randolph Rd.
Hanscom AFB, MA 01731-2818
Bill Donaldson, Small Business Specialist
Tel: (781) 377-4973 Fax: (781) 377-3015
Email: bill.donaldson@hanscom.af.mil
Web: www.herbb.hanscom.af.mil

US Army Soldiers Systems Center
Research, Development and Engineering
Command/Small Business Office
258 Kansas St.
Natick, MA 01760-5008
David Condon, Small Business Specialist
Tel: (508) 233-4995 Fax: (508) 233-8676
Email: david.condon@natick.army.mil
Web: www.natick.army.mil/soldier/business

ENVIRONMENTAL PROTECTION AGENCY
Region I-Office of Small and Disadvantaged
Business Utilization
John F. Kennedy Federal Bldg., 1 Congress
St. #1100, M/C MCP
Boston, MA 02114
Sharon Molden, Officer
Tel: (617) 918-1062 Fax: (617) 918-1909
Email: molden.sharon@epa.gov
Web: www.epa.gov/osdbu

GENERAL SERVICES ADMINISTRATION
Region I-Small Business Utilization
O'Neil Federal Bldg., 10 Causeway St. #901
Boston, MA 02222
Grace Saenz, Small Business Director
Tel: (617) 565-8100 Fax: (617) 565-8101
Email: grace.saenz@gsa.gov
Web: www.gsa.gov

VETERANS AFFAIRS, DEPT. OF
Bedford VA Medical Center
200 Springs Rd.
Bedford, MA 01730
Richard Terramagra, Contract Specialist
Tel: (781) 687-2368 Fax: (781) 687-2661
Email: richard.terramagra@med.va.gov
Web: www.va.gov

Northampton VA Medical Center
421 N. Main St.
Leeds, MA 01053
Douglas Brown, Small Business Specialist
Tel: (413) 582-3093 Fax: (413) 582-3119
Email: douglas.brown2@med.va.gov
Web: www.va.gov

MICHIGAN

AGRICULTURE, DEPT. OF
Natural Resources Conservation Service
Michigan State Office
3001 Coolidge Rd. #250
East Lansing, MI 48823
Bonnie Kilgore, Contract Specialist
Tel: (517) 324-5243 Fax: (517) 324-5287
Email: bonnie.kilgore@mi.usda.gov
Web: www.mi.nrcs.usda.gov

VETERANS AFFAIRS, DEPT. OF
Aleda E. Lutz VA Medical Center
1500 Weiss St.
Saginaw, MI 48602
Joseph Roberts, Small Business Specialist
Tel: (989) 497-2500 X3806 Fax: (989)
791-2886
Email: joseph.roberts@med.va.gov
Web: www.va.gov

Battle Creek VA Medical Center
5500 Armstrong Rd.
Battle Creek, MI 49015
Kathy Young, Small Business Specialist
Tel: (269) 966-5600 X3076 Fax: (269) 966-5483
Email: kathy.young@med.va.gov
Web: www.va.gov

VA Medical Center
2215 Fuller Rd.
Ann Arbor, MI 48105
Brenda M. Johnson, Small Business Specialist
Tel: (734) 769-7100 x5246 Fax: (734) 213-3833
Email: brenda.johnson3@med.va.gov
Web: www.va.gov/osdbu

MINNESOTA

AGRICULTURE, DEPT. OF
Forest Service
North Central Research Station
1992 Folwell Ave.
St. Paul, MN 55108
Cindy Johnson, Group Leader/Acquisitions Manager
Tel: (651) 649-5203 Fax: (651) 649-5285
Email: cjohnson06@fs.fed.us
Web: www.fs.fed.us

1992 Folwell Ave.
St. Paul, MN 55108
Carol A. Hulstrom, Contract Specialist
Tel: (651) 649-5201 Fax: (651) 649-5285
Email: chulstrom@fs.fed.us
Web: www.fs.fed.us

DEFENSE, DEPT. OF
US Air Force, 934th LG/LGC-Air Force Reserve Command
Small Business Office
760 Military Hwy.
Minneapolis ARS, MN 55450-2100
Darcee Copus-Sabart, Small Business Specialist
Tel: (612) 713-1432 Fax: (612) 713-1425
Email: darcee.copus-sabart@minneapolis.af.mil
Web: www.selltoairforce.org

VETERANS AFFAIRS, DEPT. OF
Minneapolis VA Medical Center
1 Veterans Dr.
Minneapolis, MN 55417
Linda Kelly, Small Business Specialist
Tel: (612) 725-2183 Fax: (612) 725-2072
Email: linda.kelly2@va.gov
Web: www.va.gov

VA Medical Center
4801 Veterans Dr.
St. Cloud, MN 56303
Wendy Hoeschen, Small Business Specialist
Tel: (320) 255-6307 Fax: (320) 255-6341
Email: wendy.hoeschen@med.va.gov
Web: www1.va.gov

MISSISSIPPI

AGRICULTURE, DEPT. OF
Agricultural Research Service
P.O. Box 225
Stoneville, MS 38776
Terry Krutz, Supervisory Procurement/Realty Specialist
Tel: (662) 686-5361 Fax: (662) 686-5373
Email: tkrutz@ars.usda.gov
Web: www.ars.usda.gov

Forest Service
Region VIII/IX-Western Operations Center/Procurement
A.H. McCoy Federal Bldg. #1141, 100 W. Capitol St.
Jackson, MS 39269-1199
Byron Brown, Procurement Officer
Tel: (601) 965-4391 X155 Fax: (601) 965-6029
Email: bbbrown@fs.fed.us
Web: www.fs.fed.us

Natural Resources Conservation Service
Mississippi State Office
A.H. McCoy Federal Bldg. #1321, 100 W. Capitol St.
Jackson, MS 39269
Matleaner B. Spann, State Administrative Officer
Tel: (601) 965-5183 Fax: (601) 965-4940
Email: matleaner.spann@ms.usda.gov
Web: www.ms.nrcs.usda.gov

COMMERCE, DEPT. OF
National Oceanic and Atmospheric Administration
National Data Buoy Center/Program Support Division
Bldg. 1100 #360
Stennis Space Center, MS 39529-6000
Dennis E. Morris, Small Business Specialist/Small Purchases
Tel: (228) 688-1705 Fax: (228) 688-3153
Email: dennis.morris@noaa.gov
Web: www.noaa.gov

DEFENSE, DEPT. OF
US Air Force, 14th Contracting Squadron/CC-Air Education and Training Command
Small Business Office
555 7th St. #113
Columbus AFB, MS 39710-1006
Neo Cole, Small Business Specialist
Tel: (662) 434-7802 Fax: (662) 434-7764
Email: neo.cole@columbus.af.mil
Web: www.selltoairforce.org

US Air Force, 81st Contracting Squadron/CC1-Air Education and Training Command
Small Business Office
310 M St. #102
Keesler AFB, MS 39534-2147
Linda Falks, Small Business Specialist
Tel: (228) 377-3131 Fax: (228) 377-9775
Email: linda.falks@keesler.af.mil
Web: www.selltoairforce.org

NATIONAL AERONAUTICS AND SPACE ADMINISTRATION
John C. Stennis Space Center/Procurement Office
M/C BA30
Stennis Space Center, MS 39529-6000
Jane Gipson, Small Minority Business Specialist
Tel: (228) 688-3681 Fax: (228) 688-1141
Email: jane.a.gipson@ssc.nasa.gov
Web: www.ssc.nasa.gov

VETERANS AFFAIRS, DEPT. OF
Jackson VA Medical Center
1500 E. Woodrow Wilson Dr.
Jackson, MS 39216
Brenda Stewart, Small Business Specialist
Tel: (601) 364-1361 Fax: (601) 364-1346
Email: brenda.stewart@med.va.gov
Web: www.va.gov

VA Medical Center, Acquisitions
400 Veterans Blvd.
Biloxi, MS 39531
Kenneth W. Johns, Small Business Specialist
Tel: (228) 563-2692 X2692

Fax: (228) 563-2675
Email: kenneth.johns@med.va.gov
Web: www.va.gov/osdbu

MISSOURI

AGRICULTURE, DEPT. OF
National Information Technology Center
8930 Ward Pkwy.
Kansas City, MO 64114
Regina Allen, Management Specialist
Tel: (816) 926-2719 Fax: (816) 926-2804
Email: regina.allen@usda.gov
Web: www.usda.gov

AGRICULTURE, DEPT. OF
Farm Service Agency
6501 Beacon Dr. Stop 8698
Kansas City, MO 64133
Betty Kunkel, Small Business Specialist
Tel: (816) 926-3295 Fax: (816) 823-4034
Email: betty.kunkel@kcc.usda.gov
Web: www.fsa.usda.gov/mo

Kansas City Commodity Office
P.O. Box 419205, M/S 8748
Kansas City, MO 64141-6205
Todd Shuck, Contract Officer
Tel: (816) 823-1114 Fax: (816) 823-1804
Email: tashuck@kcc.usda.gov
Web: www.fsa.usda.gov

6501 Beacon Dr., M/S 8738
Kansas City, MO 64133
Nelson Randall, Chief, Export Operations Division
Tel: (816) 926-6658 Fax: (816) 823-1640
Email: nelson.randall@kcc.usda.gov
Web: www.fsa.usda.gov/daco/kcco.htm

Natural Resources Conservation Service
Missouri State Office
601 Business Loop 70 W. #250
Columbia, MO 65203-2546
Joan Gibbs, Contract Specialist
Tel: (573) 876-0906 Fax: (573) 876-0914
Email: joan.gibbs@mo.usda.gov
Web: www.mo.nrcs.usda.gov

601 Business Loop 70 W. #250
Columbia, MO 65203
Renee Gardner, Contract Specialist
Tel: (573) 876-9374 Fax: (573) 876-0914
Email: renee.gardner@mo.usda.gov
Web: www.mo.nrcs.usda.gov

Missouri State Office/Water Resources Division
601 Business Loop 70 W. #250
Columbia, MO 65203
Harold L. Deckerd, Assistant State Conservationist/Small Business Specialist
Tel: (573) 876-9421 Fax: (573) 876-0913
Email: harold.deckerd@mo.usda.gov
Web: www.mo.nrcs.usda.gov

COMMERCE, DEPT. OF
National Oceanic and Atmospheric Administration
Central Administrative Support Center/Acquisition Management Division
601 E. 12th St. #1756
Kansas City, MO 64106
Sharon Webster Tyson, Small Business Specialist
Tel: (816) 426-7469 Fax: (816) 426-7530
Email: sharon.k.tyson@noaa.gov
Web: www.ofa.noaa.gov

601 E. 12th St. #1756
Kansas City, MO 64106
Jean M. Jennings, Chief
Tel: (816) 426-7458 Fax: (816) 426-7530

Email: jeanie.m.jennings@noaa.gov
Web: www.noaa.gov

DEFENSE, DEPT. OF
US Air Force, 509th Contracting Squadron/CCV-Air Combat Command
Small Business Office
727 2nd St. #124A
Whiteman AFB, MO 65305-5344
Bill Krause, Small Business Specialist
Tel: (660) 687-3641 Fax: (660) 687-5418
Email: william.krause@whiteman.af.mil
Web: www.whiteman.af.mil/509cons/509cons.html

ENERGY, DEPT. OF
Albuquerque Operations Office, Honeywell Federal Manufacturing & Technologies, LLC
Small Business Office
P.O. Box 419159, Dept. 626, M/S 0C44
Kansas City, MO 64141-6159
C. J. Warrick, Small Business Program Manager
Tel: (816) 997-2874 Fax: (816) 997-5063
Email: cwarrick@kcp.com
Web: www.kcp.com

GENERAL SERVICES ADMINISTRATION
Region VI-Office of Small Business Utilization
1500 E. Bannister Rd.
Kansas City, MO 64131
Ruby Rice, Small Business Specialist
Tel: (816) 926-7203 Fax: (816) 823-1167
Email: ruby.rice@gsa.gov
Web: www.r6.gsa.gov

1500 E. Bannister Rd.
Kansas City, MO 64131
Lois Phillips, Small Business Specialist
Tel: (816) 926-7203 Fax: (816) 823-1167
Email: lois.phillips@gsa.gov
Web: www.r6.gsa.gov

MONTANA

DEFENSE, DEPT. OF
US Air Force, 341st Contracting Squadron/LGC-Air Force Space Command
Small Business Office
7015 Goddard Dr.
Malmstrom AFB, MT 59402-6863
Lynn Huggins, Small Business Specialist
Tel: (406) 731-3123 Fax: (406) 731-3748
Email: merry.huggins@malmstrom.af.mil
Web: www.malmstrom.af.mil

VETERANS AFFAIRS, DEPT. OF
Fort Harrison Medical/Regional Office
1892 Williams St.
Fort Harrison, MT 59636
Daniel Herrera, Chief Logistic Officer
Tel: (406) 447-7305 Fax: (406) 447-7916
Email: daniel.herrera@med.va.gov
Web: www.va.gov

NEBRASKA

DEFENSE, DEPT. OF
US Air Force, 55th Contracting Squadron/CCD-Air Combat Command
Small Business Office
101 Washington Sq.
Offutt AFB, NE 68113-2107
Cindy Beyer, Small Business Specialist
Tel: (402) 232-5676 Fax: (402) 232-6375
Email: cindy.beyer@offutt.af.mil
Web: www.offutt.af.mil

VETERANS AFFAIRS, DEPT. OF
Grand Island VA Medical Center
2201 N. Broadwell Ave.
Grand Island, NE 68801
Leigh Porter, Small Business Specialist
Tel: (308) 382-3660 X7915 Fax: (308) 385-2712
Email: leigh.porter@med.va.gov
Web: www.va.gov

NEVADA

DEFENSE, DEPT. OF
US Air Force, 99th Contracting Squadron/ CC-Air Combat Command
Small Business Office
5865 Swaab Blvd.
Nellis AFB, NV 89191-7063
George Salton, Small Business Specialist
Tel: (702) 652-4003 Fax: (702) 652-4003
Email: george.salton@nellis.af.mil
Web: www.selltoairforce.org

ENERGY, DEPT. OF
Office of Civilian Radioactive Waste Management
Office of Repository Developments
1551 Hillshire Dr.
Las Vegas, NV 89134
Marcelle Brown, Small Business Program Manager
Tel: (702) 794-5530 Fax: (702) 794-5557
Email: marcelle_brown@ymp.gov
Web: www.ocrwm.doe.gov

NEW HAMPSHIRE

DEFENSE, DEPT. OF
Naval Shipyard, Purchasing Division
Portsmouth Naval Shipyard, Code 530SB
Portsmouth, NH 03801-2590
Michael Levesque, Deputy for Small Business
Tel: (207) 438-1630 Fax: (207) 438-1251
Email: levesquemj@mail.ports.navy.mil
Web: www.ports.navy.mil

VETERANS AFFAIRS, DEPT. OF
Manchester VA Medical Center
718 Smyth Rd.
Manchester, NH 03104
Richard Marino, Contracting Specialist
Tel: (603) 624-4366 X6506 Fax: (603) 626-6511
Email: richard.marino@med.va.gov
Web: www.va.gov

NEW JERSEY

COMMERCE, DEPT. OF
Minority Business Development Agency
New Jersey Statewide Minority Business Development Center
744 Broad St. #1812
Newark, NJ 07102
Lorraine Kelsey, Project Director
Tel: (973) 297-1142 Fax: (973) 297-1439
Email: lkelsey@newjersey-mbdc.com
Web: www.mbda.gov

DEFENSE, DEPT. OF
Naval Air Warfare Center Aircraft Division
Small Business Office
Hwy. 547 Code Air-09c4
Lakehurst, NJ 08733-5082
Dawn Chartier, Deputy for Small Business
Tel: (732) 323-2933 Fax: (732) 323-2908
Email: patricia.kohanyi@navy.mil

Web: http://wingspan.navair.navy.mil

US Air Force, 305th Air Mobility Wing/LGC-Air Mobility Command
Small Business Office
2402 Vandenberg Ave.
McGuire AFB, NJ 08641-1712
Lidija Erazo, Small Business Specialist
Tel: (609) 754-5929 Fax: (609) 724-3735
Email: lidija.erazo@mcguire.af.mil
Web: http://public.mcguire.amc.af.mil

US Army Armament Research Development/ Engineering Center
AMSRD-AAR-SB, Bldg. 323
Picatinny Arsenal, NJ 07860-5000
Richard A. Burdett, Small Business Specialist
Tel: (973) 724-4106 Fax: (973) 724-3002
Email: rick.burdett@us.army.mil
Web: www.pica.army.mil

US Army Communications-Electronic Command
Small and Disadvantaged Business Utilization Office
Commander-USA Base C-E LCMC AMSEL-SB, Bldg. 1208 E. Grand Fl.
Fort Monmouth, NJ 07703-5005
Kevin Loesch, Chief
Tel: (732) 532-4511 Fax: (732) 532-8732
Email: kevin.loesch@mail1.monmouth.army.mil
Web: www.sadbu.cecom.army.mil/sadbu

NEW MEXICO

COMMERCE, DEPT. OF
Minority Business Development Agency
New Mexico Statewide Minority Business Development Center
718 Central Ave. SW
Albuquerque, NM 87102
Anna Muller, Project Director
Tel: (505) 843-7114 Fax: (505) 242-2030
Email: inso@nedainc.net
Web: www.mbda.gov

DEFENSE, DEPT. OF
US Air Force, 27th CONS/CD-Air Combat Command
Small Business Office
511 N. Torch Blvd.
Cannon AFB, NM 88103-5109
Eddie West, Small Business Specialist
Tel: (505) 784-2321 Fax: (505) 784-4791
Email: eddie.west@cannon.af.mil
Web: www.cannon.af.mil

US Air Force, 49th Contracting Squadron/ COV-Air Combat Command
Small Business Office
1210 Forty Niner Ave.
Holloman AFB, NM 88330-7908
Frank Eggert, Small Business Specialist
Tel: (505) 572-3048 Fax: (505) 572-5456
Email: frank.eggert@holloman.af.mil
Web: www.holloman.af.mil

US Air Force, AFRL/VS
Small Business Office
2000 Wyoming Blvd. SE, Bldg. 20604
Kirtland AFB, NM 87117-5060
Joan Fulkerson, Small Business Specialist
Tel: (505) 846-8515 Fax: (505) 846-4919
Email: joan.fulkerson@kirtland.af.mil
Web: www.de.afrl.af.mil

US Air Force, HQ AFOTEC/Air Force Operational Test and Evaluation Center
Small Business Office
8500 Gibson Blvd. SE
Kirtland AFB, NM 87117-5558

Sherry Freeman, Small Business Specialist
Tel: (505) 846-5627 Fax: (505) 846-2414
Email: sherry.freeman@afotec.af.mil
Web: www.afotec.af.mil

US Army White Sands Missile Range
Small Business Office
Bldg. 143 Crozier St.
White Sands Missile Range, NM 88002
Ron Taft, Small Business Advisor
Tel: (505) 678-1401 Fax: (505) 678-3883
Email: taftr@wsmr.army.mil
Web: www.wsmr.army.mil/docpage/docpage.htm

ENERGY, DEPT. OF
Albuquerque Operations Office/Los Alamos Site Office
P.O. Box 1663, M/S P222
Los Alamos, NM 87545
Dennis Roybal, Small Business Program Manager
Tel: (505) 667-4410 Fax: (505) 667-9819
Email: business@lanl.gov
Web: www.lanl.gov

Sandia National Laboratories
P.O. Box 5800, M/S 0201
Albuquerque, NM 87185-0201
Elizabeth Gonzales, Business Consultant
Tel: (505) 284-3205 Fax: (505) 844-7468
Email: ecgonza@sandia.gov
Web: www.sandia.gov/supplier

Albuquerque Operations Office, Westinghouse TRU Solutions, Waste Isolation Pilot Plant
P.O. Box 2078
Carlsbad, NM 88220
Bob Prentiss, Small Business Program Manager
Tel: (505) 234-7507 Fax: (505) 234-7050
Email: bob.prentiss@wipp.ws
Web: www.wipp.ws

National Nuclear Security Administration
Service Center
P.O. Box 5400
Albuquerque, NM 87185
Greg Gonzales, Small Business Program Manager
Tel: (505) 845-5420
Email: ggonzales@doeal.gov
Web: www.doeal.gov

NEW YORK

AGRICULTURE, DEPT. OF
Natural Resources Conservation Service
New York State Office
441 S. Salina St. #354
Syracuse, NY 13202
Laureen M. Eipp, Contract Specialist
Tel: (315) 477-6522 Fax: (315) 477-6560
Email: laureen.eipp@ny.usda.gov
Web: www.ny.nrcs.usda.gov

COMMERCE, DEPT. OF
Minority Business Development Agency
Jamaica Business Resource Center
90-33 160th St.
Jamaica, NY 11432
Timothy H. Marshall, President/CEO
Tel: (718) 206-2255 Fax: (718) 206-3693
Email: tmarshall@jbrc.org
Web: www.jbrc.org

Manhattan/Bronx Minority Business Development Center
350 5th Ave.
New York, NY 10118
Lora Trimingham, Assistant Director
Tel: (212) 947-5351 Fax: (212) 947-1506

Email: ltrimingham@manhattan-bronx-mbdc.com
Web: www.manhattan-bronx-mbdc.org

New York Regional Office
26 Federal Plz. #3720
New York, NY 10278
Heyward Davenport, Regional Director
Tel: (212) 264-3262 Fax: (212) 264-0725
Email: hdavenport@mbda.gov
Web: www.mbda.gov

Queens/Brooklyn Minority Business Development Center
90-33 160th St.
Jamaica, NY 11432
Earl Francis, Project Director
Tel: (718) 206-2255 Fax: (718) 206-3693
Email: jbrc@jbrc.org
Web: www.mbda.gov

Williamsburg-Brooklyn Minority Business Development Center
12 Heyward St.
Brooklyn, NY 11211
Deborah Charnas, Project Director
Tel: (718) 522-5620 Fax: (718) 522-5931
Email: oda@odabdc.org
Web: www.odabdc.org

DEFENSE, DEPT. OF
US Air Force, 914th AW/LGC-Air Force Reserve Command
Small Business Office
2720 Kirkbridge Dr.
Niagara Falls, NY 14304-5001
Barbara Mansfield, Small Business Specialist
Tel: (716) 236-2216 Fax: (716) 236-2357
Email: barbara.mansfield@niagarafalls.af.mil
Web: www.selltoairforce.org

US Air Force, AFRL/IFB-Air Force Materiel Command
Small Business Office
26 Electronic Pkwy.
Rome, NY 13441-4514
Janis Norelli, Small Business Specialist
Tel: (315) 330-3311 Fax: (315) 330-7043
Email: janis.norelli@rl.af.mil
Web: www.if.afrl.af.mil/div/IFK/bc-main.html

ENERGY, DEPT. OF
Brookhaven National Laboratory
50 Brookhaven Ave., Bldg. 355
Upton, NY 11973
Jill Clough-Johnston, Small Business Program Manager
Tel: (631) 344-3173 Fax: (631) 344-5878
Email: clough@bnl.gov
Web: www.bnl.gov

Ohio Field Office/West Valley Nuclear Services Company
10282 Rock Springs Rd.
West Valley, NY 14171-9799
Lynn Whiting, Small Business Utilization Officer
Tel: (716) 942-4477 Fax: (716) 942-4110
Web: www.wvnsco.com

Schenectady Naval Reactors Office
P.O. Box 1069
Schenectady, NY 12301
Marie Pastor, Small Business Program Manager
Tel: (518) 395-6375 Fax: (518) 395-6670
Email: smbus@snrmail.kapl.gov

ENVIRONMENTAL PROTECTION AGENCY
Region II-Office of Small and Disadvantaged Business Utilization
290 Broadway, 27th Fl.
New York, NY 10007-1866

Otto Salamon, Officer
Tel: (212) 637-3417 Fax: (212) 637-3518
Email: salamon.otto@epa.gov
Web: www.epa.gov/osdbu

GENERAL SERVICES ADMINISTRATION
Region II-Small Business Utilization
26 Federal Plz. #18-110
New York, NY 10278
Janice Bracey, Small Business Specialist
Tel: (212) 264-1235 Fax: (212) 264-2760
Email: janice.bracey@gsa.gov
Web: www.gsa.gov

TRANSPORTATION, DEPT. OF
Saint Lawrence Seaway Development Corporation
P.O. Box 520
Massena, NY 13662-0520
Linda M. Harding, Contracting Officer
Tel: (315) 764-3244 Fax: (315) 764-3268
Email: linda.harding@sls.dot.gov
Web: www.seaway.dot.gov

TREASURY, DEPT. OF THE
Internal Revenue Service
Northeast Area Field Office
290 Broadway
New York, NY 10007-1867
Pamela King-Doran, Small Business Specialist
Tel: (212) 436-1776 Fax: (212) 436-1849
Email: pamela.k.doran@irs.gov
Web: www.treas.gov

TREASURY, DEPT. OF THE
Internal Revenue Service
Northeast Area Field Office
290 Broadway
New York, NY 10007-1867
Deborah Paulin-Foster, Small Business Specialist
Tel: (212) 436-1481 Fax: (212) 436-1849
Email: deborah.e.foster@irs.gov
Web: www.treas.gov

VETERANS AFFAIRS, DEPT. OF
VA Western New York Healthcare System at Buffalo
3495 Bailey Ave.
Buffalo, NY 14215
Nancy Holdaway, Small Business Specialist
Tel: (716) 862-6389 Fax: (716) 862-8893
Email: nancy.holdaway@med.va.gov
Web: www.va.gov

NORTH CAROLINA

COMMERCE, DEPT. OF
Minority Business Development Agency
North Carolina Institute of Minority Economic Development
114 W. Parrish St., 6th Fl.
Durham, NC 27702
Andrea Harris, President
Tel: (919) 956-8889 Fax: (919) 688-7668
Email: andreah@ncimed.com
Web: www.ncimed.com

Raleigh/Durham/Charlotte Minority Business Development Center
114 W. Parrish St.
Durham, NC 27702
Dan Stafford, Director of Information Technology/Compliance
Tel: (919) 287-3198 Fax: (919) 688-8478
Email: dstafford@ncimed.com
Web: www.mbda.gov

DEFENSE, DEPT. OF
US Air Force, 43rd Contracting Squadron/ LGC-Air Mobility Command
Small Business Office
1443 Reilly Rd. #C
Pope AFB, NC 28308-2896
Leslie L. Crawley, Small Business Specialist
Tel: (910) 394-6244 Fax: (910) 394-7040
Email: leslie.crawley@pope.af.mil
Web: http://public.pope.amc.af.mil

US Air Force, 4th Contracting Squadron/CD- Air Combat Command
Small Business Office
1695 Wright Bros Ave.
Seymour Johnson AFB, NC 27531-2459
Laverne Miller, Small Business Specialist
Tel: (919) 722-5411 Fax: (919) 722-5414
Email: laverne.miller@seymourjohnson. af.mil
Web: www.seymourjohnson.af.mil/4fwunits/ msg/cons/default.htm

HEALTH & HUMAN SERVICES, DEPT. OF
National Institute of Environmental Health Sciences
Acquisitions Management Branch, OM
Small Business Office
P.O. Box 12874, M/D NH-02
Research Triangle Park, NC 27709
Stephen Cannon, Small Business Manager
Tel: (919) 541-0377 Fax: (919) 541-5117
Email: cannons@niehs.nih.gov
Web: www.niehs.nih.gov

NORTH DAKOTA

DEFENSE, DEPT. OF
US Air Force, 319th Air Refueling Wing/LGC- Air Mobility Command
Small Business Office
575 6th Ave., Bldg. 418
Grand Forks AFB, ND 58205-6436
Duane Mann, Small Business Specialist
Tel: (701) 747-5256 Fax: (701) 747-4215
Email: duane.mann@grandforks.af.mil
Web: http://public.grandforks.amc.af.mil

US Air Force, 5th Contracting Squadron/LGC- Air Combat Command
Small Business Office
211 Missile Ave.
Minot AFB, ND 58705-5027
Dwight Slotto, Small Business Specialist
Tel: (701) 723-4188 Fax: (701) 723-4172
Email: dwight.slotto@minot.af.mil
Web: www.minot.af.mil

OHIO

AGRICULTURE, DEPT. OF
Natural Resources Conservation Service
Ohio State Office
200 N. High St. #522
Columbus, OH 43215
Barbara S. Clayton, Contracting Specialist
Tel: (614) 255-2502 Fax: (614) 255-2548
Email: barbara.clayton@oh.usda.gov
Web: www.oh.nrcs.usda.gov

COMMERCE, DEPT. OF
Minority Business Development Agency
Ohio Statewide Minority Business Development Center
7162 Reading Rd. #630
Cincinnati, OH 45237-3844
Onnie R. Martin, Executive Director
Tel: (513) 631-7666 Fax: (513) 631-7613
Email: omartin@ohiostatewidembdc.org
Web: www.ohiostatewidembdc.org

DEFENSE, DEPT. OF
US Air Force, 910th CONF/LGC-Air Force Reserve Command
Small Business Office
3976 King Graves Rd. Unit 31
Vienna, OH 44473-5931
Jacqueline Rogers, Small Business Specialist
Tel: (330) 609-1155 Fax: (330) 609-1042
Email: jacqueline.rogers@youngstown.af.mil
Web: www.selltoairforce.org

US Air Force, Aeronautical Systems Center/ BC-Air Force Materiel Command
Small Business Office
2196 D St. #109
Wright-Patterson AFB, OH 45433-7201
Teresa Rendon, Small Business Specialist
Tel: (937) 255-5322 Fax: (937) 656-4306
Email: teresa.rendon@wpafb.af.mil
Web: www.wpafb.af.mil/pk

US Air Force, Air Force Research Laboratory-Air Force Materiel Command
Small Business Office
1981 Monahan Way, Bldg. 12 #107
Wright-Patterson AFB, OH 45433-5209
Patricia Deschaine, Small Business Specialist
Tel: (937) 904-7130 Fax: (937) 656-9619
Email: patricia.deschaine@wpafb.af.mil
Web: www.afrl.af.mil

US Air Force, Contracting Division ASC/BCL- Air Force Materiel Command
Small Business Office
1940 Allbrook Dr. #3
Wright-Patterson AFB, OH 45433-5309
Sandy Haught, Small Business Specialist
Tel: (937) 257-2324 X4506 Fax: (937) 656-1288
Email: sandy.haught@wpafb.af.mil
Web: www.wpafb.af.mil/bc

ENERGY, DEPT. OF
Environmental Management Consolidated Business Center
250 E. 5th St.
Cincinnati, OH 45202
Karen Bahan, Small Business Program Manager
Tel: (513) 246-0555 Fax: (513) 246-0529
Email: karen.bahan@emcbc.doe.gov
Web: www.doe.gov

Ohio Field Office/Battelle Memorial Institute
505 King Ave.
Columbus, OH 43201
Warren K. Weaver, Small Business Officer
Tel: (614) 424-4515 Fax: (614) 424-6311
Email: weaverwk@battelle.org
Web: www.battelle.org

CH2M HILL Mound, Inc.
1 Mound Rd.
Miamisburg, OH 45343
Don Liepold, Small Business Program Manager
Tel: (937) 865-3074 Fax: (937) 865-3816
Email: liepda@doe-md.gov
Web: www.doe-md.gov

Earthline Technologies, Inc.
Ohio Field Office
1601 21st St.
Ashtabula, OH 44004
Cathleen Drew, Purchasing/Administrative Support
Tel: (440) 993-1962 Fax: (440) 993-2046
Email: cathleen_drew@rmies.com
Web: www.earthlinetech.com

ENVIRONMENTAL PROTECTION AGENCY
Contracts Procurement Operations Division
26 W. Martin Luther King Dr.

Cincinnati, OH 45220
Norman G. White, Officer
Tel: (513) 487-2024 Fax: (513) 487-2004
Email: white.norman@epa.gov
Web: www.epa.gov

NATIONAL AERONAUTICS AND SPACE ADMINISTRATION
Glenn Research Center
M/C 500-313
Cleveland, OH 44135
Carl L. Silski, Field Installation Small/ Minority Business Specialist
Tel: (216) 433-2786 Fax: (216) 433-5489
Email: carl.l.silski@nasa.gov
Web: www.hq.nasa.gov

Glenn Research Center
M/C 3-9
Cleveland, OH 44135
Sunil Dutta, SDB/HBCU/OMI Program Manager
Tel: (216) 433-8844 Fax: (216) 433-2946
Email: sunil.dutta-1@nasa.gov
Web: www.hq.nasa.gov

VETERANS AFFAIRS, DEPT. OF
Brecksville VA Medical/Regional Office Center (541/90C)
10000 Brecksville Rd.
Brecksville, OH 44141
Sabrina Sommerville, Small Business Specialist
Tel: (440) 526-3030 X7440 Fax: (440) 838-6052
Email: sabrina.sommerville@med.va.gov
Web: www.va.gov

Chillicothe VA Medical Center
17273 State Route 104
Chillicothe, OH 45601
Sharon Kempton, Small Business Specialist
Tel: (740) 773-1141 X7011 Fax: (740) 772-7008
Email: sharon.kempton@med.va.gov
Web: www.va.gov

VA Outpatient Clinic
543 Taylor Ave.
Columbus, OH 43203-1278
Richard T. Hardy, Small Business Specialist
Tel: (614) 257-5520 Fax: (614) 257-5526
Email: richard.hardy@med.va.gov
Web: www.va.gov

Cincinnati VA Medical Center
Management and Acquisition Section
3200 Vine St.
Cincinnati, OH 45220
Joseph Boggs, Small Business Specialist
Tel: (513) 475-6336 Fax: (513) 475-6500
Web: www.va.gov

VA Medical Center
4100 W. 3rd St.
Dayton, OH 45428
Kathy Laffey-Miller
Tel: (937) 268-6511 X3388 Fax: (937) 262-5974
Web: www.va.gov/osdbu

OKLAHOMA

COMMERCE, DEPT. OF
Minority Business Development Agency
Oklahoma City Minority Business Development Center
4205 Lincoln Blvd. #109
Oklahoma City, OK 73105
Nancy Alexander, Project Director
Tel: (405) 962-1623 Fax: (405) 962-1639
Email: nhalexander@lunet.edu
Web: www.mbda.gov

DEFENSE, DEPT. OF

US Air Force, 38th Engineering Installation Group
Small Business Office
4064 Hilltop Rd. #101 M/S 38
Tinker AFB, OK 73145-2713
Karen Nobles, Small Business Specialist
Tel: (405) 734-9394 Fax: (405) 734-1615
Email: karen.nobles@tinker.af.mil
Web: www.tinker.af.mil

US Air Force, 71st CONF/LGC-Air Education and Training Command
Small Business Office
246 Brown Pkwy. #205
Vance AFB, OK 73705-5037
Thomas Patton, Small Business Specialist
Tel: (580) 213-7565 Fax: (580) 213-6397
Email: thomas.patton@vance.af.mil
Web: www.selltoairforce.org

US Air Force, 97th Contracting Squadron CONS/CD-Air Education and Training Command
Small Business Office
303 J Ave., Bldg. 302
Altus AFB, OK 73523-5132
Michael Pierce, Small Business Specialist
Tel: (580) 481-7320 Fax: (580) 481-7472
Email: michael.pierce@altus.af.mil
Web: www.altus.af.mil

US Air Force, DynCorp, Local Purchase, Vance Support Division
273 Scott Rd. #123
Vance AFB, OK 73705-5514
Jerry D. Cornwell, Small Business Specialist
Tel: (580) 213-7174 Fax: (580) 213-6047
Email: jerry.cornwell@vance.af.mil
Web: www.selltoairforce.org

US Air Force, OC-ALC/BC
Small Business Office
3001 Staff Dr. #1AG85A
Tinker AFB, OK 73145-3009
Sandra Geib, Small Business Director
Tel: (405) 739-2601 Fax: (405) 739-7085
Email: sandra.geib@tinker.af.mil
Web: www.tinker.af.mil

US Air Force, Oklahoma City Air Logistics Center-Air Force Materiel Command
Small Business Office
3001 Staff Dr. #1AG85A
Tinker AFB, OK 73145-3009
Carole Wanish, Small Business Specialist
Tel: (405) 739-5242 Fax: (405) 739-7085
Email: carole.wanish@tinker.af.mil
Web: www.tinker.af.mil

US Air Force, Oklahoma City Air Logistics Center-Air Force Materiel Command
Small Business Office
3001 Staff Dr. #1AG84A
Tinker AFB, OK 73145-3009
Renaye Tyce, Small Business Specialist
Tel: (405) 739-2604 Fax: (405) 739-7085
Email: renaye.tyce@tinker.af.mil
Web: www.tinker.af.mil

ENERGY, DEPT. OF

Southwestern Power Administration
Division of Acquisition and Facilities Services
1 W. 3rd St.
Tulsa, OK 74103
Gary Bridges, Small Business Program Manager
Tel: (918) 595-6671
Email: gary.bridges@swpa.gov
Web: www.swpa.gov

VETERANS AFFAIRS, DEPT. OF

Muskogee VA Medical Center
1011 Honor Heights Dr.
Muskogee, OK 74401
Kris Kelly, Small Business Specialist
Tel: (918) 680-3616 Fax: (918) 680-3852
Email: kris.kelly@med.va.gov
Web: www.va.gov

Oklahoma City VA Medical Center
921 NE 13th St.
Oklahoma City, OK 73104
Danny M. Drennan, Small Business Specialist
Tel: (405) 270-0501 X5110 Fax: (405) 270-5115
Email: danny.drennan@med.va.gov
Web: www.va.gov

OREGON

AGRICULTURE, DEPT. OF

Forest Service
Ochoco National Forest
3160 NE 3rd St.
Prineville, OR 97754
Jeanette Young, Contract Specialist
Tel: (541) 416-6533 Fax: (541) 416-6661
Email: jayoung@fs.fed.us
Web: www.fs.fed.us/r6/centraloregon

Region VI-Deschutes National Forest
1001 SW Emkay Dr.
Bend, OR 97702
Ben McGrane, Contract Specialist
Tel: (541) 383-5550 Fax: (541) 383-5544
Email: bmcgrane@fs.fed.us
Web: www.fs.fed.us/r6/centraloregon

Region VI-Mt. Hood National Forest
16400 Champion Way
Sandy, OR 97055
Lois Tate, Contract Specialist
Tel: (503) 668-1768 Fax: (503) 668-1763
Email: ltate@fs.fed.us
Web: www.fs.fed.us/r6

Region VI-Rogue River-Siskiyou National Forest
P.O. Box 520
Medford, OR 97501
John Owen, Supervisory Contract Specialist
Tel: (541) 858-2209 Fax: (541) 858-2224
Email: jowen@fs.fed.us
Web: www.fs.fed.us/r6

Umatilla National Forest
2517 SW Hailey Ave.
Pendleton, OR 97801
Gary Dillavou, Contract Specialist
Tel: (541) 278-3841 Fax: (541) 278-3845
Email: gdillavou@fs.fed.us
Web: www.fs.fed.us

Willamette National Forest
P.O. Box 10607
Eugene, OR 97440
Maurica Owen, Contract Specialist
Tel: (541) 225-6325 Fax: (541) 225-6220
Email: mowen@fs.fed.us
Web: www.fs.fed.us

VETERANS AFFAIRS, DEPT. OF

Portland VA Medical Center
3710 SW US Veterans Hospital Rd.
Portland, OR 97239
Guin Peterson, Small Business Specialist
Tel: (503) 402-2865 Fax: (503) 402-2914
Email: guinevere.peterson@med.va.gov
Web: www.va.gov

VA Roseburg Healthcare System
913 NW Garden Valley Blvd.
Roseburg, OR 97470-6513
Terry Albertus, Small Business Specialist
Tel: (541) 440-1000 X44250 Fax: (541) 440-1276
Email: terry.albertus2@med.va.gov
Web: www.va.gov

VA Southern Oregon Rehabilitation Center and Clinics
8495 Crater Lake Hwy.
White City, OR 97503
Katherine A. Baughman, Small Business Specialist
Tel: (541) 826-2111 X3213
Fax: (541) 830-3511
Email: kathy.baughman@med.va.gov
Web: www1.va.gov

PENNSYLVANIA

AGRICULTURE, DEPT. OF

Agricultural Research Service
North Atlantic Area
600 E. Mermaid Ln.
Wyndmoor, PA 19038
Eileen LeGates, Supervisor/Procurement Analyst
Tel: (215) 233-6551 Fax: (215) 233-6558
Email: eileen.legates@ars.usda.gov
Web: www.naa.ars.usda.gov

COMMERCE, DEPT. OF

Minority Business Development Agency
Pennsylvania Minority Business Development Center
4548 Market St.
Philadelphia, PA 19139
Jacqueline Hill, Project Director
Tel: (215) 895-4099 Fax: (215) 895-4001
Email: jhill@pambdc.com
Web: www.mbda.gov

DEFENSE, DEPT. OF

Naval Inventory Control Point/Small Business Office
700 Robbins Ave. Bldg. 1
Philadelphia, PA 19111-5098
Nina Evans, Small Business Specialist
Tel: (215) 697-4950 Fax: (215) 697-2986
Email: phil_sadbusphiladelphia@navy.mil

P.O. Box 2020
Mechanicsburg, PA 17055-0788
Helen Katz, Small Business Specialist
Tel: (717) 605-6625 Fax: (717) 605-4858
Web: www.navicp.navy.mil

Fleet & Industrial Supply Center, Philadelphia Detachment
Small Business Office
700 Robins Ave., Bldg. 2B
Philadelphia, PA 19111-5083
Gerald Furey, Small Business Specialist
Tel: (215) 697-9555 Fax: (215) 697-9738
Email: Gerald.Furey@navy.mil
Web: www.nor.fisc.navy.mil

US Air Force, 911th AW/LGC-Air Force Reserve Command
Small Business Office
Pittsburgh IAP-ARS, 2375 Defense Ave.
Coraopolis, PA 15108-4495
Dan Lucci, Small Business Specialist
Tel: (412) 474-8119 Fax: (412) 474-8410
Email: daniel.lucci@pittsburgh.af.mil
Web: www.afrc.af.mil/911aw

US Air Force, 913th MSG/CONF-Air Force Reserve Command
Small Business Office
1051 Fairchild St.
Willow Grove ARS, PA 19090-5203
John Golasa, Small Business Specialist
Tel: (215) 443-1057 Fax: (215) 443-1956
Email: john.golasa@willowgrove.af.mil
Web: www.afrc.af.mil/913aw

ENERGY, DEPT. OF

National Energy Technology Laboratory
P.O. Box 10940
Pittsburgh, PA 15236-0940
Larry R. Sullivan, Small Business Specialist
Tel: (412) 386-6115 Fax: (412) 386-6137
Email: larry.sullivan@netl.doe.gov
Web: www.netl.doe.gov

Pittsburgh Naval Reactors Office/Bechtel Bettis Atomic Power Laboratory
P.O. Box 79
West Mifflin, PA 15122-0079
Mark Prescott, Small Business Program Manager
Tel: (412) 476-6003 Fax: (412) 476-7320
Email: smallbizinfocenter@bettis.gov
Web: www.bettis.gov

ENVIRONMENTAL PROTECTION AGENCY

Region III-Office of Small and Disadvantaged Business Utilization
1650 Arch St.
Philadelphia, PA 19103
Romona McQueen, Officer
Tel: (215) 814-5155 Fax: (215) 814-5108
Email: mcqueen.romona@epa.gov
Web: www.epa.gov/osdbu

VETERANS AFFAIRS, DEPT. OF

Altoona VA Medical Center
2907 Pleasant Valley Blvd.
Altoona, PA 16602-4377
Jean Gelbke, Small Business Specialist
Tel: (814) 943-8164 X7233 Fax: (814) 942-9253
Email: jean.gelbke@med.va.gov
Web: www.va.gov

Butler VA Medical Center
325 New Castle Rd.
Butler, PA 16001
Sharon Leszczynski, Small Business Specialist
Tel: (724) 287-4781 X2523 Fax: (724) 477-5026
Email: sharon.leszczynski@med.va.gov
Web: www.va.gov

Lebanon VA Medical Center
1700 S. Lincoln Ave.
Lebanon, PA 17042
Ben Grogg, Acquisition Manager
Tel: (717) 228-5939 Fax: (717) 228-5936
Email: benjamin.grogg@med.va.gov
Web: www.va.gov

VA Pittsburgh Healthcare Systems
7180 Highland Dr. M/C 04A-H
Pittsburgh, PA 15206
Linda Glancy, Small Business Specialist
Tel: (412) 365-5436 Fax: (412) 365-5471
Email: linda.glancy@med.va.gov
Web: www.va.gov/pittsburgh/highland.htm

VA Medical Center
135 E. 38th St.
Erie, PA 16504-1596
Susan Lang, Small Business Specialist
Tel: (814) 860-2091 Fax: (814) 860-2990
Email: susan.lang@med.va.gov
Web: www1.va.gov

PUERO RICO

COMMERCE, DEPT. OF

Minority Business Development Agency
Puerto Rico Minority Business Opportunity Committee

Atrium Office Ctr., 530 Ponce de Leon
Ave. #320
San Juan, PR 00901
Gloribel Garcia, Project Director
Tel: (787) 289-7878 Fax: (787) 289-7877
Email: gloribel@puertoricomboc.com
Web: www.puertoricomboc.com

Minority Business Development Agency of
Puerto Rico
P.O. Box 363631
San Juan, PR 00936-3631
Teresa Berrios, Project Director
Tel: (787) 753-8484 Fax: (787) 753-0855
Email: teresaberrios@mbdcpr.com
Web: www.mbdcpr.com

VETERANS AFFAIRS, DEPT. OF
VA Medical Center (B03)
Business Office
10 Casia St.
San Juan, PR 00921-3201
Elisa Cruz, Small Business Specialist
Tel: (787) 781-8700 X4710 Fax: (787)
781-8721
Email: elisa.cruz@med.va.gov
Web: www.va.gov/osdbu

RHODE ISLAND

DEFENSE, DEPT. OF
**Naval Undersea Warfare Center, Small
Business Office**
NUWC Bldg. 11 Code 00SB
Newport, RI 02841-1708
David Rego, Small Business Advocate
Tel: (401) 832-1766 Fax: (401) 832-4820
Email: regodj@npt.nuwc.navy.mil
Web: www.npt.nuwc.navy.mil

VETERANS AFFAIRS, DEPT. OF
Providence VA Medical Center
830 Chalkstone Ave.
Providence, RI 02908
Mary Herman, Small Business Specialist
Tel: (401) 457-3035 Fax: (401) 457-3079
Email: mary.herman2@med.va.gov
Web: www.va.gov

SOUTH CAROLINA

COMMERCE, DEPT. OF
Minority Business Development Agency
South Carolina Statewide Minority Business
Development Center
1515 Richland St.
Columbia, SC 29201
Greg Davis, Director
Tel: (803) 779-5905 X28 Fax: (803)
779-5915
Email: davisg@scmbdc.com
Web: www.scmbdc.com

DEFENSE, DEPT. OF
**Naval Facilities Engineering Command,
Southern Division/Code 09J**
Small Business Office
P.O. Box 190010
North Charleston, SC 29419-9010
Robin Brown, Small Business Specialist
Tel: (843) 820-5935 Fax: (843) 820-7438
Email: robin.brown1@navy.mil
Web: www.efdsouth.navfac.navy.mil

**US Air Force, 20th Contracting Squadron/
CC-Air Combat Command**
Small Business Office
305 Blue Jay St.
Shaw AFB, SC 29152-5004

Judith Croxton, Director of Business
Operations
Tel: (803) 895-6834 Fax: (803) 895-6019
Email: Judith.Croxton@shaw.af.mil
Web: www.shaw.af.mil

**US Air Force, 437th Airlift Wing/LGC-Air
Mobility Command**
Small Business Office
101 E. Hill Blvd.
Charleston AFB, SC 29404-5021
Donna R. Barber, Small Business Specialist
Tel: (843) 963-3328 Fax: (843) 963-5880
Email: donna.barber@charleston.af.mil
Web: http://public.charleston.amc.af.mil

ENERGY, DEPT. OF
Savannah River Operations
P.O. Box A
Bldg. 730-B #2250
Aiken, SC 29802
David W. Hepner, Sr., Small Business
Manager
Tel: (803) 952-9354 Fax: (803) 952-9452
Email: david.hepner@srs.gov
Web: www.srs.gov

Wackenhut Services, Inc.
Savannah River Site
P.O. Box W
Aiken, SC 29802
Lorri Wright, Procurement Administrator
Tel: (803) 952-7598 Fax: (803) 952-6020
Email: lorri.wright@srs.gov
Web: www.srs.gov

Westinghouse Savannah River Company
Bldg. 730-4B #225
Aiken, SC 29802
Bob Harris, Small Business Program
Manager
Tel: (803) 952-6162 Fax: (803) 952-6159
Email: bob.harris@srs.gov
Web: www.srs.gov

VETERANS AFFAIRS, DEPT. OF
Ralph H. Johnson VA Medical Center
109 Bee St.
Charleston, SC 29403
Cindy Rogers, Small Business Specialist
Tel: (706) 481-6724 Fax: (706) 481-6741
Email: cindy.rogers2@med.va.gov
Web: www.va.gov

SOUTH DAKOTA

AGRICULTURE, DEPT. OF
Natural Resources Conservation Service
South Dakota State Office
Federal Bldg. #308 200 4th St. SW
Huron, SD 57350
Joe Volesky, Contract Specialist
Tel: (605) 352-1169 Fax: (605) 352-1187
Email: joe.volesky@sd.usda.gov
Web: www.sd.nrcs.usda.gov

DEFENSE, DEPT. OF
**US Air Force, 28th Contracting Squadron/
LGCD-Air Combat Command**
Small Business Office
1000 Ellsworth St. #1200
Ellsworth AFB, SD 57706-4904
Larry Bulman, Director of Business
Operations
Tel: (605) 385-1719 Fax: (605) 385-1726
Email: lawrence.bulman@ellsworth.af.mil
Web: www.ellsworth.af.mil

VETERANS AFFAIRS, DEPT. OF
VA Black Hills Healthcare System
113 Comanche Rd.

Ft. Meade, SD 57741
Neil Ondriezek, Small Business Specialist
Tel: (605) 347-7027 Fax: (605) 720-7029
Email: neil.ondriezek@med.va.gov
Web: www.va.gov

TENNESSEE

DEFENSE, DEPT. OF
**US Air Force, Arnold Engineering
Development Center/BC-Air Force Materiel
Command**
Small Business Office
100 Kindel Dr. #A332
Arnold AFB, TN 37389-1332
Alan Fudge, Small Business Specialist
Tel: (931) 454-4406 Fax: (931) 454-7330
Email: alan.fudge@arnold.af.mil
Web: www.arnold.af.mil/aedc/contracting/
smallbus.htm

ENERGY, DEPT. OF
Oak Ridge Associated Universities
P.O. Box 117
Oak Ridge, TN 37381-0117
John Bennett, Procurement Manager
Tel: (865) 241-4887 Fax: (865) 576-9385
Email: whitakee@orau.gov
Web: www.orau.org

Oak Ridge Operations Office/Bechtel
Jacobs Company, LLC/Supplier Advocate
Office
East Tennessee Technology Park Hwy. 58,
M/S 7596, Bldg. K-1007
Oak Ridge, TN 37831-7596
McArthur Moore, Small Business Program
Manager
Tel: (865) 576-3847 Fax: (865) 241-9330
Email: mzo@bechteljacobs.org
Web: www.bechteljacobs.com

Oak Ridge National Laboratory
1009 Commerce Park #350
Oak Ridge, TN 37830
Kimberly Hinton, Small Business Program
Manager
Tel: (865) 576-5484 Fax: (865) 576-0096
Email: hintonkc@ornl.gov
Web: www.ornl.gov

Oak Ridge National Laboratory
P.O. Box 2008, M/S 6293
Oak Ridge, TN 37831
Al Guidry, Operations Manager
Tel: (865) 241-4161 Fax: (865) 576-1523
Email: guidrya@ornl.gov
Web: www.ornl.gov

Oak Ridge Operations
Socioeconomic Programs/Acquisition and
Asset Management
P.O. Box 2009 M/S 6501
Oak Ridge, TN 37831-6501
Gloria Mencer, Small Business Program
Manager
Tel: (865) 576-2090 Fax: (865) 576-3664
Email: mencergd@y12.doe.gov
Web: www.y12.doe.gov

Oak Ridge Operations Office
P.O. Box 2001
Oak Ridge, TN 37831
Freda H. Hopper, Small Business Program
Manager
Tel: (865) 576-9430 Fax: (865) 576-9188
Email: hopperfh@oro.doe.gov
Web: www.oro.doe.gov

Oak Ridge Operations Office, Wackenhut
Services, Inc., Oak Ridge Team
Small Business Office

161 Mitchell Rd.
Oak Ridge, TN 37830
Katherine McMillan, Small Business
Program Manager
Tel: (865) 276-9281 Fax: (865) 276-9318

VETERANS AFFAIRS, DEPT. OF
VA Acquisition Service Center
3400 Lebanon Pike
Murfreesboro, TN 37129
Patricia McKay, Network Contract Manager
Tel: (615) 867-6091 Fax: (615) 867-5429
Email: patricia.mckay@med.va.gov
Web: www.va.gov

TEXAS

AGRICULTURE, DEPT. OF
Agricultural Research Service
Southern Plains Area
1001 Holleman Dr. East
College Station, TX 77840
Michael C. Downing, Area Procurement/
Realty Officer
Tel: (979) 260-9446 Fax: (979) 260-9413
Email: mdowning@spa.ars.usda.gov
Web: www.spa.ars.usda.gov

COMMERCE, DEPT. OF
Minority Business Development Agency
Dallas Regional Office
1100 Commerce St. #726
Dallas, TX 75242
John F. Iglehart, Regional Director
Tel: (214) 767-8001 Fax: (214) 767-0613
Email: jiglehart@mbda.gov
Web: www.mbda.gov

Dallas/Ft. Worth/Arlington/Minority
Business Development Center
545 E. John Carpenter Frwy. #100
Irving, TX 75062
Joseph Newton, Project Director
Tel: (214) 688-1612 Fax: (214) 688-1753
Email: jnewton@dmbdc.com
Web: www.mbda.gov

El Paso Minority Business Development
Center
5959 Gateway Blvd. West #425
El Paso, TX 79925
Jose Rocha, Project Director
Tel: (915) 774-0626 Fax: (915) 774-0680
Email: epneda@aol.com
Web: www.nedainc.net

South Texas Minority Business Opportunity
Committee
2412 S. Closner St. #160
Edinburg, TX 78539
Johnny Cisneros, Project Director
Tel: (956) 292-7555 Fax: (956) 292-7521
Email: jrcisneros@utpa.edu
Web: www.mbda.gov

Minority Business Development Agency
of Houston
4801 Woodway #210
Houston, TX 77056
Milton Thibodeaux, Director
Tel: (713) 644-0821 Fax: (713) 644-3523
Email: mthibodeaux@gacompanies.com
Web: www.mbda.gov

Minority Business Development Agency of
San Antonio
501 W. Durango Blvd.
San Antonio, TX 78207
Fletcher M. Parks, Director
Tel: (210) 458-2480 Fax: (210) 458-2481
Email: fparks@utsa.edu
Web: www.mbda.gov

DEFENSE, DEPT. OF

US Air Force, 12th Contracting Squadron
Small Business Office
395 B St. West #2
Randolph AFB, TX 78150-4525
Estella Calvillo, Small Business Specialist
Tel: (210) 652-5460 X3064
Fax: (210) 652-4673
Email: estella.calvillo@randolph.af.mil
Web: www.randolph.af.mil/12ftw/12lg/12cons

US Air Force, 17th Contracting Squadron/ CC-Air Education and Training Command
Small Business Office
210 Schertz Blvd.
Goodfellow AFB, TX 76908-4705
Philip Kirby, Small Business Specialist
Tel: (325) 654-3821 Fax: (325) 654-5052
Email: philip.kirby@goodfellow.af.mil
Web: www.goodfellow.af.mil

US Air Force, 301 MSG/LGC-Air Force Reserve Command
Small Business Office
1710 Burke St. #100, NAS/JRB
Ft. Worth, TX 76127-6200
Small Business Specialist
Tel: (817) 782-7315 x237
Fax: (817) 782-5371
Email: nancy.audelo@carswell.af.mil
Web: www.selltoairforce.org

US Air Force, 311th Human Systems Wing/ BC-Air Force Materiel Command
Small Business Office
8046 Crouch Rd.
Brooks AFB, TX 78235-5366
Mary Urey, Small Business Specialist
Tel: (210) 536-4348 Fax: (210) 536-4363
Email: mary.urey@brooks.af.mil
Web: www.brooks-smallbusiness.com

US Air Force, 37th Contracting Squadron/ CC-Air Education and Training Command
Small Business Office
1655 Selfridge Ave.
Lackland AFB, TX 78236-5253
Arthur Dinwiddie, Small Business Specialist
Tel: (210) 671-1723 Fax: (210) 671-0674
Email: arthur.dinwiddie@lackland.af.mil
Web: www.lackland.af.mil

US Air Force, 47th Contracting Squadron/ CC1-Air Education and Training Command
Small Business Office
171 Alabama Ave. Bldg., 7
Laughlin AFB, TX 78843-5102
Jesús N. Martinez, Small Business Specialist
Tel: (830) 298-5641 Fax: (830) 298-4178
Email: jesus.martinez@laughlin.af.mil
Web: www.laughlin.af.mil

US Air Force, 7th Contracting Squadron/CC
Small Business Office
381 3rd St.
Dyess AFB, TX 79607-1581
William Banks, Small Business Specialist
Tel: (325) 696-2285 Fax: (325) 696-3676
Email: william.banks@dyess.af.mil
Web: www.dyess.af.mil

US Air Force, 82nd Contracting Squadron/ CCB-Air Education and Training Command
Small Business Office
136 K Ave. #1
Sheppard AFB, TX 76311-2746
Tandy Weaver, Small Business Specialist
Tel: (940) 676-4138 Fax: (940) 676-7829
Email: tandy.weaver@sheppard.af.mil
Web: www.sheppard.af.mil

US Air Force, AETC Contracting Squadron/ LGCB-Air Education and Training Command
Small Business Office
2021 1st St. West, Bldg. 853
Randolph AFB, TX 78150-4302
Floyd Taylor, Small Business Specialist
Tel: (210) 652-3407 Fax: (210) 652-7665
Email: floyd.taylor@randolph.af.mil
Web: www.randolph.af.mil

ENERGY, DEPT. OF

BWXT Pantex
P.O. Box 30020
Pantex Plant
Amarillo, TX 79120
Marilyn Daves, Small Business Program Manager
Tel: (806) 477-3850 Fax: (806) 477-3839
Email: mdaves@pantex.com
Web: www.pantex.com

ENVIRONMENTAL PROTECTION AGENCY

Region VI-Office of Small and Disadvantaged Business Utilization
1445 Ross Ave. #1200
Dallas, TX 75202-2733
Debora N. Bradford, Officer
Tel: (214) 665-7406 Fax: (214) 665-8505
Email: bradford.debora@epa.gov
Web: www.epa.gov

GENERAL SERVICES ADMINISTRATION

Region VII-Office of Small Business Utilization
819 Taylor St. #1E13A
Fort Worth, TX 76102
Willie Heath, Jr., Director
Tel: (817) 978-0800 Fax: (817) 978-0440
Email: willie.heath@gsa.gov
Web: www.gsa.gov

NATIONAL AERONAUTICS AND SPACE ADMINISTRATION

Johnson Space Center
2101 Nasa Pkwy.
Houston, TX 77058
Jeffrey Cullen, Small Business Advocate
Tel: (281) 483-0248 Fax: (281) 483-5100
Email: jeffrey.m.cullen@nasa.gov
Web: www.nasa.gov

Johnson Space Center/Industry Assistant Office
2101 Nasa Pkwy. M/C BD3
Houston, TX 77058
Cheryl Harrison, Field Installation Small/ Minority Business Specialist
Tel: (281) 483-3734 Fax: (281) 483-4326
Email: cheryl.a.harrison@nasa.gov
Web: www.hq.nasa.gov

TREASURY, DEPT. OF THE

Internal Revenue Service
Mid-States Area Field Office
4050 Alpha Rd., M/SRO 1800
Dallas, TX 75244-4203
Jeff Schraeder, Small Business Specialist
Tel: (972) 308-1637 Fax: (972) 308-1928
Email: jeff.l.schraeder@irs.gov
Web: www.treas.gov

VETERANS AFFAIRS, DEPT. OF

Amarillo VA Health Care System
6010 Amarillo Blvd. West
Amarillo, TX 79106
Robert Auffrey, Small Business Specialist
Tel: (806) 354-7845 Fax: (806) 354-7875
Email: robert.auffrey@med.va.gov
Web: www.va.gov

Big Springs VA Medical Center
300 Veterans Blvd.
Big Springs, TX 79720-5500

Beverly Atwell, Small Business Specialist
Tel: (432) 264-4866 X7471 Fax: (432) 264-4887
Email: beverly.atwell@med.va.gov
Web: www.va.gov

Houston VA Medical Center (580/90C)
2002 Holcombe Blvd.
Houston, TX 77030-4298
Linda B. Dean, Small Business Specialist
Tel: (713) 794-7405 Fax: (713) 794-7869
Email: linda.dean@med.va.gov
Web: www.va.gov

South Texas Veterans Health Care System
7400 Merton Minter Blvd.
San Antonio, TX 78229
Frank M. Caraballo, Chief Purchasing/ Contracting
Tel: (210) 617-5152 Fax: (210) 949-3777
Email: frank.caraballo@med.va.gov
Web: www.va.gov

VA Automation Center
1615 E. Woodward St.
Austin, TX 78772
Dave W. Peterson, Small Business Specialist
Tel: (512) 326-6020 Fax: (512) 326-6028
Email: david.peterson@mail.va.gov
Web: www.va.gov

VA Healthcare System (138/90C)
5001 N. Piedras St.
El Paso, TX 79930-4211
Daniel Portillo, Small Business Specialist
Tel: (915) 564-6112 Fax: (915) 564-6109
Email: daniel.portillo@med.va.gov
Web: www.va.gov

VA North Texas Health Care System
4500 S. Lancaster Rd. M/C 90C
Dallas, TX 75216
Donald Knight, Chief of Acquisitions
Tel: (214) 857-0028 Fax: (214) 857-0027
Email: donald.knight@med.va.gov
Web: www.va.gov

UTAH

AGRICULTURE, DEPT. OF

Forest Service
Intermountain Region
2222 W. 2300 South
Salt Lake City, UT 84119
Jo Lippire, Head Contracting Officer
Tel: (801) 975-3444 Fax: (801) 975-3483
Email: jlippire@fs.fed.us
Web: www.fs.fed.us/r4

Region IV-Acquisition Management
324 25th St.
Ogden, UT 84401
Carleen Ashbaker, Supervisory Contract Specialist
Tel: (801) 625-5137 Fax: (801) 625-5365
Email: cashbaker@fs.fed.us
Web: www.fs.fed.us

DEFENSE, DEPT. OF

US Air Force, OO-ALC/BC
6038 Aspen Ave., Bldg. 1289
Hill AFB, UT 84056-5805
Marsha Peterson, Management Assistant
Tel: (801) 777-4143
Email: marsha.peterson@hill.af.mil
Web: http://contracting.hill.af.mil/ newcontracting/Opportunities/ SmallBusiness/SmallBusiness.asp

VETERANS AFFAIRS, DEPT. OF

VA Salt Lake City Health Care System
500 Foothill Blvd.
Salt Lake City, UT 84148
Brenda Alverson, Small Business Specialist
Tel: (801) 584-1201 Fax: (801) 584-2506
Email: brenda.alverson@med.va.gov
Web: www.va.gov

VERMONT

VETERANS AFFAIRS, DEPT. OF

White River Junction VA Medical Center
215 N. Main St.
White River Junction, VT 05009
Susanne Rybczyk, Small Business Specialist
Tel: (802) 295-9363 X5790 Fax: (802) 296-5103
Email: susanne.rybczyk@med.va.gov
Web: www.va.gov

VIRGINIA

AGRICULTURE, DEPT. OF

Food and Nutrition Services
Administrative Services Division
Contract Management Branch
3101 Park Center Dr. #228
Alexandria, VA 22302
Sabrina Mathis, Contracting Officer
Tel: (703) 305-2268 Fax: (703) 305-2071
Email: Sabrina.Mathis@fns.usda.gov
Web: www.fns.usda.gov

Contract and Management Branch
3101 Park Center Dr. #220
Alexandria, VA 22302
Patricia Palmer, Branch Chief, Contract Operations
Tel: (703) 305-2250 Fax: (703) 305-2071
Email: Patsy.Palmer@fns.usda.gov
Web: www.fns.usda.gov/fncs/

Forest Service
Rosslyn Plz. East #706, 1621 N. Kent St.
Arlington, VA 22209
James G. McDonald, Small Business Coordinator
Tel: (703) 605-5144 Fax: (703) 605-5100
Email: jmcdonald04@fs.fed.us
Web: www.fs.fed.us

COMMERCE, DEPT. OF

National Oceanic and Atmospheric Administration
Eastern Administrative Support Center, Acquisition & Grants Management, Acquisition Management Division
200 Granby St., Norfolk Federal Bldg, 8th Fl. #815
Norfolk, VA 23510
Jack O. Salmon, Director for Acquisition Management
Tel: (757) 441-6893 Fax: (757) 441-3786
Email: Jack.O.Salmon@noaa.gov
Web: www.rdc.noaa.gov

200 Granby St., Norfolk Federal Bldg, 8th Fl. #815
Norfolk, VA 23510
Michele A. McCoy, Small Business Specialist
Tel: (757) 441-6879 Fax: (757) 441-3786
Email: Michele.A.Mccoy@noaa.gov
Web: www.easc.noaa.gov

COMMERCE, DEPT. OF

Patent and Trademark

Office of Procurement
600 Dulany St., 7th Fl.
Alexandria, VA 22314
Muriel A. Brown, Small Business Liaison
Tel: (571) 272-6551 Fax: (571) 273-6551
Email: muriel.brown@uspto.gov
Web: www.uspto.gov

600 Dulany St., 7th Fl.
Alexandria, VA 22314
Kevin E. McGinn, Director
Tel: (571) 272-6550 Fax: (571) 273-0284
Email: kmcginn@uspto.gov
Web: www.uspto.gov

600 Dulaney Ave.
Alexandria, VA 22314
Page Etzel, Division Chief
Tel: (571) 272-6579 Fax: (571) 273-6579
Email: page.etzel@uspto.gov
Web: www.uspto.gov

Office of Procurement, Information
Technology Branch
2011 Crystal Dr., Crystal Park 1 #810
Arlington, VA 22202
Kate Kudrecwicv, Branch Chief
Tel: (571) 272-6575
Email: Kate.Kudrecwicv@uspto.gov
Web: www.uspto.gov

DEFENSE, DEPT. OF
Naval Facilities Engineering Command Atlantic
6506 Hampton Blvd.
Norfolk, VA 23508-1278
Barbara N. Taylor, Deputy for Small Business
Tel: (757) 322-4430 Fax: (757) 322-4615
Email: barbara.n.taylor@navy.mil
Web: www.navfac.navy.mil

Naval Surface Warfare Center/Dahlgren Division
17320 Dahlgren Rd.
Dahlgren, VA 22448-5100
Robert E. Ashley, Jr., Deputy for Small Business
Tel: (540) 653-4806 Fax: (540) 653-7088
Email: robert.e.ashley@navy.mil
Web: www.nswc.navy.mil

Office of Small and Disadvantaged Business Utilization
1777 N. Kent St. #9100
Arlington, VA 22209
Linda Oliver, Deputy Director
Tel: (703) 588-8631 Fax: (703) 588-7561
Email: linda.oliver@osd.mil
Web: www.acq.osd.mil

1777 N. Kent St. #9100
Arlington, VA 22209
Lee Renna, Women Business Representative
Tel: (703) 588-8631 Fax: (703) 588-7561
Email: lee.renna@osd.mil
Web: www.acq.osd.mil

Defense Advanced Research Projects Agency
3701 N. Fairfax Dr.,
Arlington, VA 22203-1714
Mark Swanstrom, Small Business Director
Tel: (571) 218-4675 Fax: (7571) 218-4680
Web: www.darpa.mil

Defense Commissary Agency
Small Business Office
1300 E. Ave.
Fort Lee, VA 23801-1800
Brian Kauffman, Small Business Specialist
Tel: (804) 734-8824 Fax: (804) 734-8619

Email: brian.kauffman@deca.mil
Web: www.commissaries.com

Defense Contract Management Agency,
Office of Small and Disadvantaged Business Utilization
6350 Walker Ln. DCMA-OCA
Alexandria, VA 22310
Barbara J. Little, Director of Small Business
Tel: (703) 428-0786 Fax: (703) 428-3578
Email: smallbusiness@hq.dcma.mil
Web: www.dcma.mil

Defense Energy Support Center
Small Business Office
8725 John J. Kingman Rd. #4943
Fort Belvoir, VA 22060-6222
Kathy S. Williams, Director
Tel: (703) 767-9400 Fax: (703) 767-9446
Email: kathy.s.williams@dla.mil
Web: www.desc.dla.mil

8725 John J. Kingman Rd. #4943
Fort Belvoir, VA 22060-6222
Dawn Gresham, Small Business Specialist
Tel: (703) 767-8530 Fax: (703) 767-9446
Email: dawn.gresham@dla.mil
Web: www.desc.dla.mil

Defense Logistics Agency
Office of Small and Disadvantaged Business Utilization
8725 John J. Kingman Rd.
Ft. Belvoir, VA 22060-6221
Thomas D. Ray, Director
Tel: (703) 767-1662 Fax: (703) 767-1670
Email: thomas.ray@dla.mil
Web: www.dla.mil/db

8725 John J. Kingman Rd. #2533
Ft. Belvoir, VA 22060-6221
Patricia A. Cleveland, Women Business Representative
Tel: (703) 767-1652 Fax: (703) 767-1670
Email: patricia.cleveland@dla.mil
Web: www.dla.mil/db

Fleet & Industrial Supply Center
1968 Gilbert St. #600 Code OOSB, Bldg. 143
Norfolk, VA 23511-3392
Linda Owen, Deputy for Small Business
Tel: (757) 443-1435 Fax: (757) 443-1355
Email: linda.owen@navy.mil
Web: www.nor.fisc.navy.mil

Office of Small and Disadvantaged Business Utilization
1777 N. Kent St. #9100
Arlington, VA 22209
Frank Ramos, Director
Tel: (703) 588-8631 Fax: (703) 588-7561
Email: frank.ramos@osd.mil
Web: www.acq.osd.mil/sadbu

US Air Force, 1st Contracting Squadron
Small Business Office
74 Nealy Ave. #100
Langley AFB, VA 23665-2088
Linda S. Greaves, Small Business Specialist
Tel: (757) 764-3246 Fax: (757) 764-7706
Email: linda.greaves@langley.af.mil
Web: www.langley.af.mil/1msg/1cons/lgcs_business.shtml

US Air Force, ACC Contracting Squadron/CCD-Air Combat Command
Small Business Office
130 Douglas St. #400
Langley AFB, VA 23665
Della Shelton, Small Business Specialist
Tel: (757) 764-4286 Fax: (757) 764-9773
Email: della.shelton@langley.af.mil
Web: www.selltoairforce.org

US Air Force, AFOSR/PK
Small Business Office
875 Randolph St., Bldg. 325 #3112
Arlington, VA 22203
Richard Pihl, Small Business Specialist
Tel: (703) 696-9728 Fax: (703) 696-9733
Email: richard.pihl@afosr.af.mil
Web: www.afosr.af.mil

US Marine Corps
Regional Contracting Office, NE
3250 Catlin Ave.
Quantico, VA 22134-5000
Greg Flaherty, Deputy Director
Tel: (703) 784-1921 Fax: (703) 784-3592
Email: gregory.flaherty@usmc.mil
Web: www.usmc.mil

ENERGY, DEPT. OF
Oak Ridge Operations Office, The Southeastern Universities Research Association
Small Business Office
Thomas Jefferson National Accelerator Facility, 12000 Jefferson Ave.
Newport News, VA 23606
Danny Lloyd, Small Business Program Manager
Tel: (757) 269-7121 Fax: (757) 269-7057
Email: lloyd@jlab.org
Web: www.jlab.org

INTERIOR, DEPT. OF THE
US Fish & Wildlife Service
Division of Contracting/Facilities Management
4401 N. Fairfax Dr. #210-A
Arlington, VA 22203
James W. McKoy, Jr., Business Utilization/Development Specialist
Tel: (703) 358-2225 Fax: (703) 358-2264
Email: jim_mckoy@fws.gov
Web: www.doi.gov

JUSTICE, DEPT. OF
Drug Enforcement Administration, Office of Procurement
700 Army-Navy Dr. #W-5140
Arlington, VA 22202
Cleopatra Allen, Small Business Specialist
Tel: (202) 307-7150 Fax: (202) 307-4877
Web: www.usdoj.gov

NATIONAL AERONAUTICS AND SPACE ADMINISTRATION
Langley Research Center/Office of Small and Disadvantaged Business Utilization
M/S 134
Hampton, VA 23681-2199
Vernon Vann, Small Business Specialist
Tel: (757) 864-2456 Fax: (757) 864-8541
Email: archer.v.vann@nasa.gov
Web: www.osdbu.nasa.gov

Langley Research Center
Small Business Office
M/S 144
Hampton, VA 23681-2199
Archer V. Vann, Jr., Small Business Specialist
Tel: (757) 864-2456
Email: a.v.vann@larc.nasa.gov
Web: http://op.larc.nasa.gov/

Wallops Flight Facility Goddard Space Flight Center
M/C 244.1
Wallops Island, VA 23337
Lisa B. Hall, Procurement Analyst
Tel: (757) 824-1420 Fax: (757) 824-1974
Email: lisa.b.hall@nasa.gov
Web: www.nasa.gov

NATIONAL SCIENCE FOUNDATION
Office of Small and Disadvantaged Business Utilization
4201 Wilson Blvd. #527
Arlington, VA 22230
Donald Senich, Director
Tel: (703) 292-7082 Fax: (703) 292-9055
Email: dsenich@nsf.gov
Web: www.nsf.gov

VETERANS AFFAIRS, DEPT. OF
Hampton VA Medical Center
100 Emancipation Dr.
Hampton, VA 23667
Nancy Bailey, Small Business Specialist
Tel: (757) 728-3113 Fax: (757) 728-3132
Email: nancy.bailey@med.va.gov
Web: www1.va.gov/midatlantic/facilities/hampton.htm

National Cemetery Administration
Operations Support Center/Centralized Contracting Division (402D3)
5105 Russell Rd.
Quantico, VA 22134
Marybeth Olexy, Small Business Specialist
Tel: (703) 441-4009 Fax: (703) 441-7025
Email: marybeth.olexy@cem.va.gov
Web: www.cem.va.gov

Richmond VA Medical Center
1201 Broad Rock Blvd.
Richmond, VA 23249
Kevin Buser, Small Business Specialist
Tel: (804) 675-5489 Fax: (804) 675-5502
Email: kevin.buser@med.va.gov
Web: www.va.gov

WASHINGTON

AGRICULTURE, DEPT. OF
Forest Service
Baker-Snoqualmie National Forest
21905 64th Ave. West
Mountlake Terrace, WA 98043-2278
Elizabeth Waits, Purchasing Agent
Tel: (425) 744-3338 Fax: (425) 744-3336
Email: ewaits@fs.fed.us
Web: www.fs.fed.us/r6/mbs

Colville National Forest
765 S. Main St.
Colville, WA 99114
Cathy E. Van Alyne, Contracting Specialist
Tel: (509) 684-7114 Fax: (509) 684-7280
Email: cvanalyne@fs.fed.us
Web: www.fs.fed.us/r6/colville

Okanogan National Forest
1240 S. 2nd Ave.
Okanogan, WA 98840-3275
Kris Bellini, Contract Specialist
Tel: (509) 826-3072 Fax: (509) 826-3789
Email: kbellini@fs.fed.us
Web: www.fs.fed.us/r6/okanogan

Olympic National Forest
1835 Black Lake Blvd. SW #A
Olympia, WA 98512-5623
Miley Sutherland, Contract Specialist
Tel: (360) 956-2471 Fax: (360) 956-2277
Email: msutherland@fs.fed.us
Web: www.fs.fed.us

Wenatchee National Forest
215 Melody Ln.
Wenatchee, WA 98801
Carl Erickson, Contract Specialist
Tel: (509) 664-9316 Fax: (509) 664-9281
Email: cerickson@fs.fed.us
Web: www.fs.fed.us/r6/wenatchee

COMMERCE, DEPT. OF
National and Oceanic and Atmospheric Administration
Western Administrative Support Center/
Acquisition Management Division
7600 Sand Point Way NE, M/C WC3
Seattle, WA 98115-6349
Heide Sickles, Chief
Tel: (206) 526-6033 Fax: (206) 526-6025
Web: www.ofa.noaa.gov

DEFENSE, DEPT. OF
US Air Force/62nd Contracting Squadron
Small Business Office
P.O. Box 4178
McChord AFB, WA 98438-0178
Lori Houghton, Small Business Specialist
Tel: (253) 982-3890 Fax: (253) 982-5207
Email: lori.houghton@mcchord.af.mil
Web: http://public.mcchord.amc.af.mil

US Air Force/LGC-Air Mobility Command
Small Business Office
110 W. Ent St. #200
Fairchild AFB, WA 99011-9403
Marion Nelson, Small Business Specialist
Tel: (509) 247-4880 Fax: (509) 247-9870
Email: marion.nelson@fairchild.af.mil
Web: www.selltoairforce.org

ENERGY, DEPT. OF

Environmental Management
Office of River Protection
CH2M Hill Hanford Group
P.O. Box 1500, MSIN H6-16
Richland, WA 99352
Leslie Wiberg, Small Business Program
Advocate
Tel: (509) 372-3457 Fax: (509) 372-8036
Email: Leslie_d_Wiberg@rl.gov
Web: www.hanford.gov/chgcp/

Office of River Protection
2440 Stevens Dr. #2321
Richland, WA 99353
Cloette Reid, Small Business Program
Manager
Tel: (509) 373-6140 Fax: (509) 376-8532
Email: cloette_b_reid@rl.gov
Web: www.hanford.gov/orp

Bechtel Corporation
Office of River Protection/Waste Treatment
Plant
2435 Stevens Center Pl. M/S 14-3A
Richland, WA 99354
Carrie Brittain, Small Business Program
Manager
Tel: (509) 371-2338 Fax: (509) 371-2286
Email: cjbritta@bechtel.com
Web: www.bechtel.com

Bonneville Power Administration
P.O. Box 491, TLOS
Vancouver, WA 98666
Hamid Habibi, Small Business Program
Manager
Tel: (360) 418-2696 Fax: (360) 418-2368
Email: hhabibi@bpa.gov
Web: www.bpa.gov/corporate

Pacific Northwest National Laboratory
P.O. Box 999
Richland, WA 99352
Andrea Melius, Small Business Program
Manager
Tel: (509) 376-4148 Fax: (509) 376-4149
Email: smallbusiness@pnl.gov
Web: www.pnl.gov/contracts

Richland Operations Office
Bechtel Hanford, Inc., 3070 George
Washington Way, M/S H0-04
Richland, WA 99354
Mary K. Funk, Small Business
Representative
Tel: (509) 372-9522 Fax: (509) 372-9049
Email: mkfunk@bhi-erc.com
Web: www.bhi-erc.com

Richland Operations Office
Fluor Hanford, Supplier Advocacy Office
P.O. Box 1000, M/S H7-10
Richland, WA 99354
V.J. Meadows, Small Business Advocate
Tel: (509) 376-4697 Fax: (509) 372-3668
Email: valjeanne_b_meadows@rl.gov
Web: www.hanford.gov/rl

Richland Operations Office
P.O. Box 550, A7-80
Richland, WA 99352
Melanie Fletcher, Small Business Program
Manager
Tel: (509) 376-4828 Fax: (509) 376-3703
Email: george_h_sanders@rl.gov
Web: www.hanford.gov/rl

ENVIRONMENTAL PROTECTION AGENCY
Region X-Office of Small and Disadvantaged
Business Utilization
1200 6th Ave. (OMP-145)
Seattle, WA 98101
Valerie Badon, Officer
Tel: (206) 553-1141 Fax: (206) 553-4957
Email: valerie.badon@epa.gov
Web: www.epa.gov/osdbu

GENERAL SERVICES ADMINISTRATION
Region X-Office of Small Business
Utilization
400 15th St. SW
Auburn, WA 98001-6599
Sheron Snyder, Small Business
Representative
Tel: (253) 931-7956 Fax: (253) 804-4887
Email: sheron.snyder@gsa.gov
Web: www.gsa.gov

HOMELAND SECURITY, DEPT. OF
US Coast Guard, Facilities Design & Construction Center
915 2nd Ave. #2664
Seattle, WA 98174-1011
Ed Rockenstire, Small Business Specialist
Tel: (206) 220-7420 Fax: (206) 220-7390
Email: erockenstire@pacnorwest.uscg.mil
Web: www.uscg.mil/mlcpac/fdccp/

VETERANS AFFAIRS, DEPT. OF
Jonathan M. Wainwright Memorial VA
Medical Center
77 Wainwright Dr.
Walla Walla, WA 99362
Steve Mallard, Small Business Specialist
Tel: (509) 525-5200 X22810 Fax: (509) 527-3474
Email: steve.mallard@med.va.gov
Web: www.va.gov

VA Medical Center
4815 N. Assembly St.
Spokane, WA 99205
Richard Hague, Small Business Specialist
Tel: (509) 434-7224 Fax: (509) 434-7101
Email: richard.hague@med.va.gov
Web: www.va.gov

VA Puget Sound Healthcare System
(S138P&C)
1660 S. Columbian Way
Seattle, WA 98108
Maria Boelter, Chief Logistics Officer
Tel: (206) 762-1010
Email: maria.boelter@med.va.gov
Web: www.va.gov/osdbu

WEST VIRGINIA

TREASURY, DEPT. OF THE
Bureau of the Public Debt
Small Business Office
200 3rd St. UNB, 4th Fl.
Parkersburg, WV 26101-1328
Jeff Stephenson, Small Business Specialist
Tel: (304) 480-7123 Fax: (304) 480-7203
Email: jeff.stephenson@bpd.treas.gov
Web: www.treas.gov

Internal Revenue Service
Martinsburg Computing Center
250 Murall Dr. M/S 250
Kearneysville, WV 25430
Linda Miller, Small Business Specialist
Tel: (304) 264-5589 Fax: (304) 264-7008
Email: linda.k.miller@irs.gov
Web: www.treas.gov

WISCONSIN

AGRICULTURE, DEPT. OF
Forest Service
Forest Products Laboratory
1 Gifford Pinchot Dr.
Madison, WI 53726
Mike Belovsky, Contract Specialist
Tel: (608) 231-9285 Fax: (608) 231-9585
Email: jbelovsky@fs.fed.us
Web: www.fpl.fs.fed.us

Natural Resources Conservation Service
Wisconsin State Office
8030 Excelsior Dr. #200
Madison, WI 53717
Rosabeth Garcia-Sais, Contracting
Specialist
Tel: (608) 662-4422 X220 Fax: (608) 662-4430
Email: rosabeth.garciasais@wi.usda.gov
Web: www.wi.nrcs.usda.gov

COMMERCE, DEPT. OF
Minority Business Development Agency
Wisconsin Minority Business Opportunity
Committee
235 W. Galena St. #102A
Milwaukee, WI 53212
Leni Siker, Executive Director
Tel: (414) 289-6767 Fax: (414) 289-8562
Email: information@wmboc.org
Web: www.wmboc.org

DEFENSE, DEPT. OF
US Air Force, 440th AW/LGC-Air Force Reserve Command
Small Business Office
Gen. Mitchell IAP-ARS, 300 E. College Ave.
Milwaukee, WI 53207-6299
Lonna Jonas, Small Business Specialist
Tel: (414) 482-5273 Fax: (414) 482-5901
Email: ljonas@generalmitchell.af.mil
Web: www.selltoairforce.org

WYOMING

AGRICULTURE, DEPT. OF
Natural Resources Conservation Service
Wyoming State Office
P.O. Box 33124
Casper, WY 82602
Joseph Kirkland, Contract Specialist
Tel: (307) 233-6787 Fax: (307) 233-6783
Email: joseph.kirkland@wy.usda.gov
Web: www.wy.nrcs.usda.gov

DEFENSE, DEPT. OF
US Air Force, 90th Contracting Squadron/ LGCD-Air Force Space Command
Small Business Office
7505 Marne Loop, Bldg. 208
Warren AFB, WY 82005-2860
Charles (Mel) Melvin, Director of Small
Business Operations
Tel: (307) 773-4737 Fax: (307) 773-3964
Email: charles.melvin@warren.af.mil
Web: www.warren.af.mil

ENERGY, DEPT. OF
Naval Petroleum Reserves
Rocky Mountain Oilfield Testing Center
907 N. Poplar #150
Casper, WY 82601
Neil Hauglend, Small Business Program
Manager
Tel: (307) 261-5000 X5017 Fax: (307) 261-5817
Email: neil.hauglend@rmotc.doe.gov
Web: www.rmotc.com

Rocky Mountain Oilfield Testing Center
907 N. Poplar #150
Casper, WY 82601
Janet Boulanger, Small Business Program
Manager
Tel: (307) 261-5000 X5076 Fax: (307) 261-5817
Email: janet.boulanger@rmotc.doe.gov
Web: www.rmotc.com

VETERANS AFFAIRS, DEPT. OF
Cheyenne VA Medical Center/Regional
Office Center
2360 E. Pershing Blvd.
Cheyenne, WY 82001
Robert O. Baker, Small Business Specialist
Tel: (307) 778-7326 Fax: (307) 778-7361
Email: bob.baker@med.va.gov
Web: www.va.gov

VA Medical Center
1898 Fort Rd. M/S 90C
Sheridan, WY 82801
James C. Wiltse, Contracting Specialist
Tel: (307) 672-1679 Fax: (307) 672-1901
Email: james.wiltse@med.va.gov
Web: www.va.gov

Private Sector Minority Business Opportunities

ALABAMA

REGIONS FINANCIAL
Corporate Heaquarters
471 N. 20th St.
Birmingham, AL 35203
Tel: (205) 944-1300
Web: www.regions.com

SAKS
Corporate Headquarters
750 Lakeshore Pkwy
Birmingham, AL 35211
Barbara Webb,
Tel: (205) 940-4010
Web: www.saksincorporated.com

ARIZONA

ALLIED WASTE INDUSTRIES
Procurement
15880 N. Greenway-Hayden Loop
Scottsdale, AZ 85260
Jennifer Bryant, Manager, Corporate Procurement
Tel: (480) 627-2700
Web: www.alliedwaste.com

KB HOME
Purchasing
432 N. 44th st #400
Pheonix, AZ 85008
Derek Bowen, Purchasing Manager
Tel: 602-567-4800

ARKANSAS

ALLTEL
Vendor Relations
1 Allied Dr.
Little Rock, AR 72202
Tel: (501) 905-8000
Email: corp.corporate.communications@alltel.com
Web: www.alltel.com

AVNET
Corporate Headquarters
2211 S. 47th St.
Phoenix, AR 85034
Greg Frazier, Executive Vice President, Supply Chain Services
Tel: (480) 643-2000
Web: www.avnet.com

DILLARD'S
Corporate Headquarters
1600 Cantrell Rd.
Little Rock, AR 72201

Tel: (501) 376-5200
Web: www.dillards.com

MURPHY OIL
Vendor Relations
200 Peach St.
El Dorado, AR 71731
Kelly Hammock, Manager, Purchasing
Tel: (870) 862-6411
Web: www.murphyoilcorp.com

PHELPS DODGE
Supply Chain Management
1 N. Central Ave.
Phoenix, AR 85004
Chuck Wargo, Global Supply Chain
Tel: (602) 366-8456
Web: www.phelpsdodge.com

TYSON FOODS
Corporate Headquarters
2210 W. Oaklawn Dr
Springdale, AR 72762
Donnie Smith, Senior Vice President Supply Chain Management
Tel: (479) 290-4000
Web: www.tysonfoodsinc.com

WAL-MART STORES
Arkansas
702 S.W. Eighth St.
Bentonville, AR 72716
Chris Rasche, Director, Supplier Diversity
Tel: (479) 277-2326
Web: www.walmartstores.com

CALIFORNIA

ADVANCED MICRO DEVICES
Corporate Headquarters
1 AMD Pl.
Sunnyvale, CA 94088
Tel: (408) 749-4000
Web: www.amd.com

AGILENT TECHNOLOGIES
Supplier Diversity
M/S 54L-BB, 5301 Stevens Creek Blvd.
Santa Clara, CA 95051-7295
Supplier Diversification Process Manager
Tel: (650) 752-5000
Email: supplier_diversity@agilent.com
Web: www.agilent.com

AMGEN
Corporate Headquarters
1 Amgen Center Dr.
Thousand Oaks, CA 91320
Tel: (805) 447-3600
Web: www.amgen.com

APPLE COMPUTER
Supplier Diversity
1 Infinite Loop
Cupertino, CA 95014
Tel: (408) 996-1010
Email: supplierdiversity@apple.com
Web: www.apple.com

APPLIED MATERIALS
Corporate Headquarters
3050 Bowers Ave.
Santa Clara, CA 95054
Mark R. Pinto, Chief Technology Officer and Senior Vice President New Business and New Product Group
Tel: (408) 727-5555
Web: www.appliedmaterials.com

AVERY DENNISON
Purchasing
150 N. Orange Grove Blvd
Pasadena, CA 91103
Juan Guerrero, Manager Purchasing
Tel: (626) 304-2000
Web: www.averydennison.com

CALPINE
Vendor Relations
50 W. San Fernando St.
San Jose, CA 95113
Tel: (408) 995-5115
Email: isvendor@calpine.com
Web: www.calpine.com

CHARLES SCHWAB
Procurement
120 Kearny St.
San Francisco, CA 94108
Ann Arhontes, Director, Procurement
Tel: (415) 627-7000
Web: www.schwab.com

CHEVRONTEXACO
Headquarters
6001 Bollinger Canyon Rd.
San Ramon, CA 94583
Audrey Goins Brichi, Supplier Diversity Manager
Tel: (925) 842-1000 Fax: (925) 790-3987
Web: www.chevrontexaco.com

CISCO SYSTEMS
Corporate Headquarters
170 W. Tasman Dr.
San Jose, CA 95134
Kate D'camp, Senior Vice President, Supplier Diversity and Human Resources
Tel: (408) 526-4000
Web: www.cisco.com

CLOROX
Corporate Headquarters
1221 Broadway

Oakland, CA 94612
Tel: (510) 271-7000
Web: www.clorox.com

CNF INC.
Purchasing
3240 Hillview Ave.
Palo Alto, CA 94304
D. Wayne Byerley, Jr., Vice President, Purchasing
Tel: (650) 424-2900
Web: www.cnf.com

COMPUTER SCIENCES
Corporate Headquarters
2100 E. Grand Ave.
El Segundo, CA 90245
Steve Goble, Manager Supply Chain
Tel: (214) 523-5552
Email: sgoble@csc.com
Web: www.csc.com

COUNTRYWIDE FINANCIAL
Corporate Headquarters
4500 Park Granada
Calabasas, CA 91302
Michael Keating, Senior Managing Director, Global Operations
Web: www.countrywide.com

DIRECTV GROUP
Corporate Headquarters
2250 E. Imperial Highway
El segundo, CA 90245
Tel: (310) 964-5000
Web: www.directv.com

DOLE FOOD
Corporate Headquarters
1 Dole Dr.
Westlake Village, CA 91362
Tel: (818) 879-6600
Web: www.dole.com

EDISON INTERNATIONAL
Corporate Headquarters
2244 Walnut Grove Ave.
Rosemead, CA 91770
Tel: (626) 302-2222
Web: www.edison.com

FIRST AMERICAN CORP.
Corporate Headquarters
1 First American Way
Santa Ana, CA 92707
Tel: (714) 800-3000
Web: www.firstam.com

FLUOR
Supplier Diversity
1 Enterprise Dr.
Aliso Viejo, CA 92656
Lisa Harley, Supplier Diversity Executive, Procurement

Tel: (949) 349-2000
Email: supplier.diveristy@fluor.com
Web: www.fluor.com

GAP
Corporate Headquarters
2 Folson St.
San Francisco, CA 94105
Nick J. Cullen, Executive Vice President, Supply Chain
Tel: (650) 952-4400
Web: www.gapinc.com

GATEWAY
New Vendor Relations
7565 Irvine Center Dr.
Irvine, CA 92618
Dan Stevenson, Vice President, Direct
Tel: (949) 491-7000
Web: www.gateway.com

GOLDEN WEST FINANCIAL
Corporate Headquarters
1901 Harrison St.
Oakland, CA 94612
Tel: (510) 446-3420
Web: www.worldsavings.com

HEALTH NET
Corporate Headquarters
26150 Oxnard St.
Woodland Hills, CA 91367
Strategic Sourcing and Procurement
Tel: (800) 590-1848
Email: supplierhotline@healthnet.com
Web: www.healthnet.com

HEWLETT-PACKARD
Headquarters
3000 Hanover St
Palo Alto, CA 94304
Jon Flaxman, Senior Vice President and Controller Accounting and Financial Reporting
Tel: (650) 857-1501 Fax: (650) 857-5518
Web: www.hp.com

INGRAM MICRO
1600 E. St. Andrews Pl.
Santa Ana, CA 92705
Terry Tysseland, Senior Vice President, Supply Chain
Tel: (714) 566-1000 x22040
Web: www.ingrammicro.com

INTEL
Corporate Headquarters
2200 Mission College Blvd
Santa Clara, CA 95052
Rosalin Hudnell, Director of Diversity
Tel: (408) 765-8080
Web: www.intel.com

JACOBS ENGINEERING GRP.
Corporate Headquarters
1111 S. Arroyo Pkwy
Pasadena, CA 91105
Tel: (865) 220-4800
Web: www.jacobs.com

LEVI STRAUSS
Corporate Headquarters
1155 Battery St.
San Francisco, CA 94111
Tel: (415) 501-6000
Web: www.levistrauss.com

LONGS DRUG STORES
Supplier Diversity
141 N. Civic Dr.
Walnut Creek, CA 94596
Tony Dickens, Supplier Diversity
Tel: (925) 937-1170
Web: www.longs.com

MATTEL
Corporate Headquarters
333 Continental Blvd
El Segundo, CA 90245
Tel: (310) 252-2000
Web: www.mattel.com

MAXTOR
Corporate Headquarters
500 McCarthy Blvd
Milpitas, CA 95035
Tel: (408) 894-5000
Web: www.maxtor.com

MCKESSON
Corporate Headquarters
1 Post St.
San Francisco, CA 94104
Susan Jee, Small Business Liaison Officer
Tel: (415) 983-7170
Email: supplier.diveresity@mckesson.com
Web: www.mckesson.com

NORTHROP GRUMMAN
Corporate Headquarters
1840 Century Park E.
Los Angeles, CA 90067
Katie Gray , Vice President, Materials Management and Procurement
Tel: (310) 553-6262 Fax: (310) 814-0660
Web: www.northropgrumman.com

OCCIDENTAL PETROLEUM
Corporate Headquarters
10889 Wilshire Blvd
Los Angeles, CA 90024
Tel: (310) 208-8800
Web: www.oxy.com

ORACLE
Corporate Headquarters
500 Oracle Pkwy
Redwood City, CA 94065
Tel: (650) 506-7200
Web: www.oracle.com

PACIFIC LIFE
Corporate Headquarters
700 Newport Center Dr.
Newport Beach, CA 92660
Tel: (949) 219-3011
Web: www.pacificlife.com

PACIFICARE HEALTH SYS.
Corporate Headquarters
5995 Plaza Dr.
Cypress, CA 90630
Tel: (714) 952-1121
Web: www.pacificare.com

PG&E CORP.
Supplier Diversity
1 Market St.
San Francisco, CA
Jane Jansen, Director Supplier Diversity
Tel: (415) 973-4853
Web: www.pgecorp.com

QUALCOMM
Diversity
5775 Morehouse Dr.
San Diego, CA 92121
Tel: (858) 587-1121
Email: diversity.info@qualcomm.com
Web: www.qualcomm.com

ROSS STORES
Purchasing
4440 Rosewood Dr.
Pleasanton, CA 94588
Rosanna Berger, Manager, Purchasing
Tel: (925) 965-4400
Web: www.rossstores.com

RYLAND GROUP
Purchasing
24025 park Sorrento
Calabasas, CA 91302
Steven M. Dwyer, Vice President, Purchasing
Tel: (818) 223-7500
Web: www.ryland.com

SAFEWAY
Corporate Headquarters
5918 Stoneridge Mall Rd.
Pleasanton, CA 94588
Sherrie Ysunza, Director, Supplier Diversity
Tel: (925) 467-3000 Fax: (925) 951-4709
Web: www.safeway.com

SANMINA-SCI
Corporate Headquarters
2700 N. First St
San Jose, CA 95143
Tel: (408) 964-3504 Fax: (408) 964-3636
Web: www.sanmina-sci.com

SCIENCE APPLICATIONS INTL.
Corporate Headquarters
10260 Campus Point Dr.
San Diego, CA 92121
George Otchere, Senior Vice President, Corporate Development and Small Business Development
Tel: (858) 826-6000
Web: www.saic.com

SEMPRA ENERGY
Corporate Headquarters
101 Ash St.
San Diego, CA 92101
Shawn Ferrar, Director, Diverse Business Enterprises
Tel: (877) 555-1212
Web: www.sempra.com

SOLECTRON
Corporate Headquarters
847 Gibraltar Dr.
Milpitas, CA 95053
Tel: (408) 957-8500
Web: www.solectron.com

STATER BROS. HOLDINGS
Purchasing
21700 Barton Rd.
Cotton, CA 92324
Ed Segura, Purchasing
Tel: (909) 783-5000
Web: www.starterbros.com

SUN MICROSYSTEMS
Supplier Diversity
4150 Network Circle
Santa Clara, CA 95054
Tel: (650) 960-1300 Fax: (510) 315-6072
Email: supplier_diversity@sun.com
Web: www.sun.com

UNOCAL CORPORATION
Vendor Relations
6001 Bollinger Canyon Rd. #H3040
San Ramon, CA 94583
Janet Winter Smith,
Tel: (925) 790-3947
Web: www.unocal.com

WALT DISNEY
Corporate Headquarters
500 S. Buena Vista Dr.
Burbank, CA 91521
Sandra Picaro, Director, Supplier Diversity
Tel: (818) 560-1000
Web: www.disney.com

WELLS FARGO
Corporate Headquarters
420 Montgomery Rd.
San Francisco, CA 94104
Tel: (800) 333-0343 Fax: (415) 975-6260
Email: www.suppdive@wellsfargo.com
Web: www.wellsfargo.com

COLORADO

BALL
Corporate Headquarters
10 Longs Peak Dr.
Broomfield, CO 80021
Tel: (303) 469-3131
Web: www.ball.com

ECHOSTAR COMMUNICATIONS
Procurement
9601 S. Meridian Blvd.
Englewood, CO 80112
Julie Peters
Tel: (303) 723-1000
Web: www.echostar.com

FIRST DATA
Corporate Procurement
6200 S. Quebec St.
Greenwood Village, CO 80111
Tel: (303) 488-8000
Email: corporate.procurement@firstdata.com
Web: www.firstdata.com

LEVEL 3 COMMUNICATIONS
Corporate Headquarters
1025 Eldorado Blvd.
Broomfield, CO 80021
Tel: (720) 888-1000 Fax: (720) 888-8296
Web: www.level3.com

LIBERTY MEDIA
12300 Liberty Blvd.
Englewood, CO 80112
Tel: (720) 875-5400
Web: www.libertymedia.com

MDC HOLDINGS
Purchasing
3600 S. Yosemite St.
Denver, CO 80237
Rob Wagner, Manager, Purchasing
Tel: (303) 773-1100
Web: www.richmondamerican.com

MOLSON COORS BREWING
Corporate Headquarters
311 Tenth St.
Golden, CO 80401
Tel: (303) 279-6565
Web: www.molsoncoors.com

NEWMONT MINING
Vendor Relations
1700 Lincoln St.
Denver, CO 80203
Debbie Robinson, Facilities Manager
Tel: (303) 863-7414
Web: www.newmont.com

QWEST COMMUNICATIONS
Supplier Diversity
1801 California St.
Denver, CO 80202
Angela Norris, Supplier Diversity
Tel: (303) 707-5572 Fax: (303) 707-9155
Email: supplier@qwest.com
Web: www.quest.com

TRANSMONTAIGNE
Corporate Headquarters
1670 Broadway
Denver, CO 80202
Tel: (303) 626-8200 Fax: (303) 626-8228
Web: www.transmontaigne.com

CONNECTICUT

AETNA
Corporate Headquarters
151 Farmington Ave
Hartford, CT 06156
Luz Calderon, Assistant Head of Diversity
Tel: (860) 273-0123
Email: supplierdiversity@aetna.com
Web: www.aetna.com

EMCOR GROUP
Corporate Headquarters
301 Merritt 7 Corporate Pk.
Norwalk, CT 06851
Tel: (203) 849-7800
Web: www.emcorpgroup.com

GENERAL ELECTRIC
Corporate Headquarters
3135 Easton Turnpike
Fairfield, CT 06828
Tel: (203) 373-2211
Email: newsuppliers@ge.com
Web: www.ge.com

HARTFORD FINANCIAL SERVICES
Corporate Headquarters
690 Asylum Ave.
Hartford, CT 06115
Tel: (860) 547-5000
Web: www.thehartford.com

INTERNATIONAL PAPER
Coporate Headquarters
400 Atlantic St.
Stamford, CT 06921
Deborah Wilson, Supplier Diversity
Tel: (901) 419-9000
Web: www.ipaper.com

NORTHEAST UTILITIES
Purchasing
107 Selden St.
Berlin, CT 06037
Cheryl Clark, Supplier Diversity Manager
Tel: (860) 665-5000
Web: www.nu.com

PITNEY BOWES
Business Diversity
1 Elmcroft Rd.
Stamford, CT 06926
Kevin Beirne, Manager, Business Diversity
Development
Tel: (203) 356-6265
Web: www.pb.com

PRAXAIR TECHNOLOGY INC.
Corporate Headquarters
39 Old Ridgebury Rd.
Danbury, CT 06810
John P. Stevens, Vice President,
Procurement and Material Management
Tel: (203) 837-2000
Web: www.praxair.com

PREMCOR
Corporate Headquarters
1700 E. Putnam Ave.
Old Greenwich, CT 06870
Tel: (203) 698-7500 Fax: (203) 698-7925
Web: www.premcor.com

TEREX
Supplier Services
500 Post Rd. E.
Westport, CT 06880
Edward Lutz, Corporate Supplier
Commodity Manager
Tel: (203) 222-7170 Fax: (203) 227-1647
Email: supplier@terex.com
Web: www.terex.com

UNITED TECHNOLOGIES
Corporate Headquarters
1 Financial Plaza
Hartford, CT 06103
Casandra Charles-Gerst, Minority Small
Business
Tel: (860) 678-4554
Web: www.utc.com

W.R. BERKLEY
Purchasing
475 Steamboat Rd.
Greenwich, CT 06830
Ann Thompson, Manager, Purchasing
Tel: (203) 629-3000
Web: www.wrbc.com

XEROX
Corporate Headquarters
800 Long Ridge Rd.
Stamford, CT 06904
Wim Appelo, Vice President, Paper,
Supplies and Supply Chain Operations
Business Group Operations
Tel: (203) 968-3000
Web: www.xerox.com

DELAWARE

DUPONT
Corporate Headquarters
1007 Market St.
Wilmington, DE 19898
Willie C. Martin, Vice President, Global
Diversity
Tel: (302) 774-1000
Web: www.dupont.com

MBNA
Corporate Headquarters
1100 N. King St.
Wilmington, DE 19884
Linda Dealing, Manager, Purchasing
Fax: (302) 458-1171
Web: www.mbna.com

DISTRICT OF COLUMBIA

DANAHER
Corporate Headquarters
2099 Pennsylvannia Ave, N.W
Washington, DC 20006
Tel: (202) 828-0850
Web: www.danaher.com

PEPCO HOLDINGS
Supplier Diversity
701 Ninth St. N.W.
Washington, DC 20068
Gerry Harsha, Coordinator of Supplier
Diversity
Tel: 202-872-2141
Web: www.pepcoholdings.com

FLORIDA

AUTONATION
Corporate Headquarters
110 S.E. Sixth St.
Fort Lauderdale, FL 33301
Lorraine Varese, Manager, Procurement
Tel: (954) 769-7000
Web: www.autonation.com

CSX
Corporate Headquarters
500 Water St.
Jacksonville, FL 32202

Fran Chinnici, Vice President, Purchasing
and Material
Tel: (904) 359-3109
Web: www.csx.com

DARDEN RESTAURANTS
Supplier Diversity
5900 Lake Ellenor Dr.
Orlando, FL 32809
Norma Sica, Supplier Diversity
Tel: (407) 245-5930
Email: nsica@darden.com
Web: www.darden.com

FIDELITY NATIONAL FINANCIAL
601 Riverside Ave.
Jacksonville, FL 32204
Pete Pennella, Staffing Manager
Tel: (904) 854-8100 Fax: (904) 854-4282
Web: www.fnf.com

FPL GROUP
Corporate Headquarters
700 Universe Blvd
Juno Beach, FL 33408
Tel: (561) 691-7827
Web: www.fplgroup.com

HUGHES SUPPLY
Supplier Diversity
1 Hughes Way
Orlando, FL 32805
Tamara V. Hall, Coordinator, Supplier
Diversity
Tel: (407) 822-2219 Fax: (407) 426-9173
Email: tamara.hall@hughessupply.com
Web: www.hughessupply.com

ITT INDUSTRIES
Corporate Purchasing
2 Corporate Dr.
Palm Coast, Fl 32137
Donna J. Bucci, Senior Buyer
Tel: (386) 446-6161 Fax: (386) 445-4012
Email: donna.bucci@itt.com
Web: www.itt-tds.com

JABIL CIRCUIT
Supply Chain
10560 Dr. Martin Luther King Jr. St. N.
St. Petersburg, FL 33716
Courtney J. Ryan, Senior Vice President,
Global Supply Chain
Tel: (727) 577-9749
Web: www.jabil.com

LENNAR
Corporate Headquarters
700 N.W. 107th Ave.
Miami, FL 33172
Kirk Younans, Manager, Purchasing
Tel: (305) 559-4000
Web: www.lennar.com

OFFICE DEPOT
Corporate Headquarters
2200 Old Germantown Rd.
Delray Beach, FL 33445
John Skinner, Director, Internal
Procurement Services
Tel: (561) 438-4800
Email: supplierdiversity@officedepot.com
Web: www.officedepot.com

PUBLIX SUPER MARKETS
Corporate Headquarters
3300 Publix Corporate Pkwy
Lakeland, FL 33811
Dave Duncan, Vice President, Facilities
Tel: (863) 688-1188
Web: www.publix.com

RYDER SYSTEM
Supplier Diversity

3600 N.W. 82nd Ave
Miami, FL 33166
Tel: (305) 500-3726
Email: supplier_diversity_program@ryder.
com
Web: www.ryder.com

TECH DATA
Corporate Headquarters
5350 Tech Data Dr.
Clearwater, FL 33760
William K. Todd Jr, Senior Vice President of
Logistics and Integration
Tel: (727) 539-7429
Web: www.techdata.com

WINN-DIXIE STORES
Corporate Headquarters
5050 Edgewood Ct
Jacksonville, FL 32254
Dick Judd, Senior Vice President, Sales and
Procurement
Tel: (904) 370-6890
Web: www.winn-dixie.com

WORLD FUEL SERVICES
Vendor Relations
9800 N.W. 41st St.
Miami, FL 33178
Tel: (305) 428-8000
Web: www.wfscorp.com

GEORGIA

AFLAC
Corporate Headquarters
1932 Wynnton Rd.
Columbus, GA 31999
Kay Mason, Director, Materials
Management
Tel: (706) 323-3431
Web: www.aflac.com

AGCO
Corporate Headquarters
4205 River Green Pkwy
Duluth, GA 30096
Greg Turnerman,
Tel: (770) 813-9200
Web: www.agcocorp.com

BEAZER HOMES USA
Corporate Headquarters
1000 Abernathy Rd
Atlanta, GA 30328
Tel: (770) 829-3700
Web: www.beazer.com

BELLSOUTH
Corporate Headquarters
1155 Peachtree St. NE
Atlanta, GA 30309
Valencia I. Adams, Vice President, Chief
Diversity Officer
Tel: (404) 249-2000
Email: supplier.qual@bellsouth.com
Web: www.bellsouth.com

COCA-COLA
Corporate Headquarters
1 Coca-Cola Plaza
Atlanta, GA 30313
Johnny B. Booker, Director, Supplier
Diversity
Tel: (404) 676-2121
Web: www.coca-cola.com

COCA-COLA ENTERPRISES
Corporate Headquarters
2500 Windy Ridge Pkwy.
Atlanta, GA 30339
Edward L. Sutter, Vice President
Tel: (770) 989-3000

Web: www.cokecce.com

COX COMMUNICATIONS
Purchasing
1400 Lake Hearn Dr.
Atlanta, GA 30319
Beverly Keith, Purchasing Coordinator
Tel: (404) 843-5000 Fax: (404) 269-1133
Web: www.cox.com

DELTA AIR LINES
Corporate Headquarters
1030 Delta Blvd
Atlanta, GA 30320
Lee Macenczak, Senior Vice President and
Chief Customer Service Officer
Tel: (404) 715-2600 Fax: (404) 677-1257
Email: supplier.diveresity@delta.com
Web: www.delta.com

GENUINE PARTS
Corporate Headquarters
2999 Circle 75 Pkwy.
Atlanta, GA 30339
Bob Thomley, Vice President, Wholesale
Management
Tel: (770) 953-1700
Web: www.genpt.com

GEORGIA-PACIFIC
Corporate Headquarters
133 Peachtree St. N.E.
Atlanta, GA 30303
Lissa J. Owens, Manager, Supplier Diversity
Tel: (404) 652-4000
Web: www.gp.com

HOME DEPOT
Corporate Headquarters
2455 Paces Ferry Rd., N.W.
Atlanta, GA 30339
John Costelo, Executive Vice President,
Marketing and Merchandising
Tel: (770) 433-8211
Web: www.homedepot.com

MIRANT
Procurement
1155 Perimeter Center W.
Atlanta, GA 30338
Tel: (678) 579-5000
Email: procurement@mirant.com
Web: www.mirant.com

MOHAWK INDUSTRIES
Purchasing
160 S. Industrial Blvd
Calhoun, GA 30701
Connie Layson, Manager, Purchasing
Tel: (800) 241-4072
Web: www.mohawkind.com

NEWELL RUBBERMAID
Purchasing
10 B GlenlakePkwy, #600
Atlanta, GA 30328
Paul Box, Vice President, Corporate
Purchasing
Tel: (770) 407-3800
Web: www.newellrubbermaid.com

SOUTHERN
Supplier Diversity
270 Peachtree St. N.W.
Atlanta, GA 30303
Tel: (404) 506-5000
Email: supplierdiversity@powersource.com
Web: www.southernco.com

SUNTRUST BANKS
Supplier Diversity
303 Peachtree St. N.E.
Atlanta, GA 30308

Tel: (404) 588-7711
Email: supplier.diversity@suntrust.com
Web: www.suntrust.com

UNITED PARCEL SERVICE
Corporate Headquarters
55 Glenlake Pkwy, N.E
Atlanta, GA 30328
Bob Stoffel, Senior Vice President, Supply
Chain Group
Tel: (404) 828-6000
Web: www.ups.com

IDAHO

ALBERTSON'S
Corporate Headquarters
250 Parkcenter Blvd.
Boise, ID 83642
Ana Marie Rodriguez, Supplier Diversity
Tel: (208) 914-3445
Web: www.albertsons.com

MICRON TECHNOLOGY
Corporate Headquarters
8000 S. Federal Way
Boise, ID 83716
Tel: (208) 368-4000
Web: www.micron.com

ILLINOIS

ABBOTT LABORATORIES
Corporate Headquarters
100 Abbott Park Rd.
Abbott Park, IL 60064
John Landgraf, Senior Vice President,
Pharmaceutical Supply
Tel: (847) 937-6100
Web: www.abbott.com

ALLSTATE
Corporate Headquarters
2775 Sanders Rd.
Northbrook, IL 60062
Erika Hatwig, Executive Assistant to the Vice
President
Tel: (847) 402-5600
Web: www.allstate.com

AON
Supplier Diversity
200 E. Randolph St.
Chicago, IL 60601
Jay Skiar, Director, Supplier Diversity
Tel: (312) 381-1000
Web: www.aon.com

ARCHER DANIELS MIDLAND
Corporate Headquarters
4666 Faries Pkwy
Decatur, IL 62525
John Taylor, Director, Corporate Supplier
Diversity
Tel: (800) 637-5843 Fax: (217) 451-4383
Email: supplier_diversity@admworld.com
Web: www.admworld.com

BAXTER INTERNATIONAL
Corporate Headquarters
1 Baxter Pkwy
Deerfield, IL 60015
Tel: (847) 948-2000
Web: www.baxter.com

BOEING
Corporate Headuarters
100 N. Riverside Park
Chicago, IL 60606
Walter Skowronski, Senior Vice President,
Boeing Capital Corporation

Tel: (312) 544-2000
Web: www.boeing.com

BRUNSWICK
Purchasing
1 N. Field Court
Lake Forest, IL 60045
Anna Baker, Manager, Purchasing
Tel: (847) 735-4700
Web: www.brunswick.com

CATERPILLAR
Corporate Headquarters
100 N.E. Adams St
Peoria, IL 61629
Mary H. Bell, Vice President, Logistics
Services and Supply Chain
Tel: (309) 675-1000
Web: www.cat.com

CDW
Purchasing
200 N. Milwaukee Ave.
Vernon Hills, IL 60061
Matthew A. Troka, Vice President,
Purchasing
Tel: (847) 465-6000
Web: www.cdw.com

EXELON
Corporate Headquarters
10 S. Dearborn St.
Chicago, IL 60680
Craig Adams, Chief Supply Officer
Tel: (312) 394-7398
Web: www.exeloncorp.com

FORTUNE BRANDS
Purchasing
300 Tower Pkwy
Lincolnshire, IL 60069
Christine Feltner, Manager, Purchasing
Tel: (847) 484-4400
Web: www.fortunebrands.com

ILLINOIS TOOL WORKS
Corporate Headquarters
3600 W. Lake Ave.
Glenview, IL 60026
Gary Anton, Vice President, Strategic
Sourcing
Tel: (847) 724-7500
Web: www.itw.com

JOHN DEERE
Corporate Headquarters
1 John Deere Pl.
Moline, IL 61265
William Norton, Senior VP/Worldwide
Supply Management
Tel: (309) 765-8000
Web: www.deere.com

LAIDLAW INTERNATIONAL
Corporate Headquarters
55 Shuman Blvd.
Naperville, IL 60563
Tel: (630) 848-3000
Web: www.laidlaw.com

MCDONALD'S
Corporate Headquarters
1 McDonald's Plaza
Oak Brook, IL 60523
Marcella Allen, Director, Supplier Diversity
Tel: (630) 623-3000
Web: www.mcdonalds.com

MOTOROLA
Corporate Headquarters
1303 E. Algonquin Rd.
Schaumburg, IL 60196
Theresa Metty, Senior VP and Chief
Procurement Officer

Tel: (847) 576-5000
Web: www.motorola.com

NAVISTAR INTERNATIONAL
Supplier Diversity
4201 Winfield Rd.
Warrenville, IL 60555
Tel: (630) 753-5000
Email: supplierdiversity@nav-international.
com
Web: www.navistar.com

OFFICEMAX
Corporate Headquarters
150 Pierce Rd.
Itasca, IL 60143
Reuben Slone, Executive Supply Chain
Tel: (630) 438-7800
Web: www.officemax.com

R.R. DONNELLEY & SONS
Supply Chain Management
3075 Highland Parkway
Downers Grove, IL 60515
Eva Chess, Supplier Diversity
Tel: 630-322-6335
Web: www.rrdonnelley.com

SARA LEE
Corporate Headquarters
3 First National Plaza
Chicago, IL 60602
Gary Berryman, Manager, Procurement
and Supply
Tel: (312) 726-2600
Web: www.saralee.com

SEARS ROEBUCK
Corporate Headquarters
3333 Beverly Rd.
Hoffman Estates, IL 60179
Carol Neltan, Supplier Diversity Director
Tel: (847) 286-2500
Web: www.sears.com

SERVICEMASTER
Corporate Headquarters
3250 Lacey Rd.
Downers Grove, IL 60515
Tel: (630) 663-2000
Web: www.svm.com

SMURFIT-STONE CONTAINER
Vendor Relations
150 N. Michigan Ave.
Chicago, IL 60601
Mark A. Polivka, Vice President,
Procurement
Tel: (312) 346-6600
Email: supplierzone@smurfit.com
Web: www.smurfit-stone.com

STATE FARM INSURANCE COS
Corporate Headquarters
1 State Farm Plz.
Bloomington, IL 61710
Leonard Bell, Manager, Supplier Diversity
Tel: (309) 766-2342
Web: www.statefarm.com

TELEPHONE & DATA SYS.
New Vendor Relations
30 N. LaSalle St.
Chicago, IL 60602
Meredith Roane, Legal Assistant, New
Vendor Relations
Tel: (312) 630-1990
Web: www.teldta.com

TENNECO AUTOMOTIVE
Supply Chain
500 N. Field Dr.
Lake Forest, IL 60045

Paul Schultz, Senior Vice President, Global
Supply Chain Management
Tel: (847) 482-5000
Web: www.tenneco-automotive.com

TRIBUNE
Purchasing
435 N. Michigan Ave.
Chicago, IL 60611
Andy Magaley, Purchasing Manager
Tel: (312) 222-9100
Web: www.tribune.com

UNITED AIRLINE INC.
Corporate Headquarters
1200 E. Algonquin Rd.
ElkGrove Township, IL 60007
Sandra Rand, Director Supplier Diversity
Tel: (847) 700-5121 Fax: (847) 700-5861
Email: sandra.rand@united.com
Web: www.united.com

UNITED STATIONERS
Purchasing
2200 E. Golf Rd.
Des Plaines, IL 60016
Doug Nash, Vice President, Purchasing
Tel: (847) 699-5000
Web: www.unitedstationers.com

USG
Purchasing
125 S. Franklin St.
Chicago, IL 60606
Michelle Shaw, Purchasing
Tel: (312) 606-4000
Web: www.usg.com

W.W. GRAINGER
Supplier Diversity
100 Grainger Pkwy
Lake Forest, IL 60045
Nancy Conner, Manager, Supplier Diversity
Tel: (847) 535-4471
Email: diversity.s@grainger.com
Web: www.grainger.com

WALGREENS
Corporate Headquarters
200 Wilmot Rd.
Deerfield, IL 60015
Roger Anderson, Director, Diversity Services
Tel: (847) 914-5165
Web: www.walgreens.com

WM. WRIGLEY JR.
Procurement
410 N. Michigan Ave.
Chicago, IL 60611
Patrick D. Mitchell, Vice President,
Procurement
Tel: (312) 644-1212
Web: www.wrigley.com

INDIANA

CONSECO
Corporate Headquarters
11825 N. Pennsylvania St.
Carmel, IN 46032
Tel: (317) 817-6100
Web: www.conseco.com

CUMMINS
Vendor Relations
500 Jackson St. M/C 6004
Columbus, IN 47201
Becky Speaker, Procurement Director
Tel: 812-377-5315

ELI LILLY
Corporate Headquarters

Lilly Corporate Center
Indianapolis, IN 46285
Steven R. Plump, Vice President, Global
Marketing and Sales
Tel: (317) 276-2000
Web: www.lilly.com

GUIDANT
Purchasing
111 Monument Circle
Indianapolis, IN 46204
Alice Gomez, Manager, Purchasing
Tel: (317) 971-2000
Web: www.guidant.com

NISOURCE
Supplier Diversity
801 E. 86th Ave.
Merrillville, IN 46410
Mike Law, Supplier Diversity
Tel: (219) 647-6200
Web: www.nisource.com

WELLPOINT
Supplier Diversity
120 Monument Circle
Indianapolis, IN 46204
Tel: (317) 488-6000
Email: supplierdiveresity@wellpoint.com
Web: www.wellpoint.com

IOWA

MAYTAG
Corporate Headquarters
403 W. Fourth St. N.
Newton, IA 50208
Tel: (641) 792-7000
Web: www.maytagcorp.com

PRINCIPAL FINANCIAL
Supplier Diversity
711 High St.
Des Moines, IA 50392
Lisa Sandos, Supplier Diversity
Tel: (515) 247-5111 Fax: (515) 248-4171
Web: www.principal.com

KANSAS

HUMANA
Supplier Diversity
500 W. Main St.
Louisville, KS 40202
Sandra Harper, Manager, Supplier Diversity
Tel: (502) 580-1000
Web: www.humana.com

SPRINT
Corporate Headquarters
6200 Sprint Pkwy
Overland Park, KS 66251
David P. Thomas, Vice President and Chief
Divesity Office
Tel: (800) 829-0965
Email: supplier.diversity@mail.sprint.com
Web: www.sprint.com

YELLOW ROADWAY
Supplier Diversity
10990 Roe Ave
Overland Park, KS 66211
Tel: (913) 696-6100
Email: supplier.diversity@yellowcorp.com
Web: www.yellowroadway.com

KENTUCKY

ASHLAND
Supplier Diversity
50 E. RiverCenter Blvd.
Covington, KY 41012
Mary Miller, Supplier Diversity
Tel: (859) 815-3333
Email: mmiller@ashland.com
Web: www.ashland.com

KINDRED HEALTHCARE
Purchasing
680 S. Fourth St.
Louisville, KY 40202
John Cowgill, Vice President, Facilities
Management
Tel: (502) 596-7300
Web: www.kindredhealthcare.com

LEXMARK INTERNATIONAL
Corporate Headquarters
740 W. New Circle Rd.
Lexington, KY 40550
Tel: (859) 232-2000
Web: www.lexmark.com

OMNICARE
Purchasing
100 E. RiverCenter Blvd
Covington, KY 41011
Daniel J. Maloney, R.Ph, Vice President,
Purchasing
Tel: (859) 392-3300
Web: www.omnicare.com

YUM BRANDS
Corporate Headquarters
1441 Gardiner Ln.
Louisville, KY 40213
Tel: (502) 874-2885 Fax: (502) 874-8662
Web: www.yum.com

LOUISIANA

ENTERGY
Corporate Headquarters
639 Loyola Ave.
New Orleans, LA 70113
Walter Rhodes, Vice President, Chief
Procurement
Tel: (504) 576-4000
Web: www.entergy.com

MARYLAND

BLACK & DECKER
Vendor Relations
701 E. Joppa Rd.
Towson, MD 21286
Tel: (410) 716-3900
Web: www.bdk.com

CONSTELLATION ENERGY
Corporate Headquarters
750 E. Pratt St.
Baltimore, MD 21202
Thomas F. Brady, Executive Vice President,
Corporate Strategy and Retail Competitive
Supply
Tel: (410) 783-2800
Web: www.constellation.com

COVENTRY HEALTH CARE
Purchasing
6705 Rockledge Dr.
Bethesda, MD 20817
Amy Nees, Manager, Purchasing
Tel: (301) 581-0600 Fax: (301) 493-0751
Web: www.cvty.com

HOST MARRIOTT
Purchasing
6903 Rockledge Rd.
Bethesda, MD 20817
Michelle Montano, Manager
Tel: (240) 744-1000
Web: www.hostmarriott.com

LOCKHEED MARTIN
Corporate Headquarters
6801 Rockledge Dr.
Bethesda, MD 20817
Meghan Mariman, Supplier Diversity
Tel: (301) 897-6195
Email: meghan.mariman@lmco.com
Web: www.lockheedmartin.com

MARRIOTT INTERNATIONAL
Corporate Headquarters
10400 Fernwwod Rd.
Bethesda, MD 20817
Tel: (877) 276-0249 Fax: (301) 380-1550
Web: www.marriott.com

MASSACHUSETTS

BJ'S WHOLESALE CLUB
Vendor Relations
1 Mercer Rd.
Natick, MA 01760
Tel: (508) 651-7400
Web: www.bjs.com

BOSTON SCIENTIFIC
Purchasing
1 Boston Scientific Pl.
Natick, MA 01760
Karen Winestin, Purchasing
Tel: (508) 650-8000
Web: www.bostonscientific.com

EMC
Supplier Diversity
176 South St.
Hopkinton, MA 01748
Aida Sabo, Senior Operations Manager
Tel: (508) 435-1000
Email: supplierdiversity@emc.com
Web: www.emc.com

LIBERTY MUTUAL INS. GROUP
Corporate Headquarters
175 Berkeley St.
Boston, MA 02116
Contract Manager
Tel: (617) 654-3950 Fax: (617) 574-5618
Email: supplier_contact@libertymutual.com
Web: www.libertymutual.com

MASSMUTUAL FINANCIAL GROUP
Corporate Headquarters
1295 State St.
Springfield, MA 01111
Tel: (413) 788-8411
Email: mmtechnology@massmutual.com
Web: www.massmutual.com

RAYTHEON
Corporate Headquarters
870 Winter St.
Waltham, MA 02451
Jim Schuster, Executive Director Diversity
Tel: (781) 522-3000
Web: www.raytheon.com

REEBOK INTERNATIONAL
Purchasing
1891 J.W. Foster Blvd
Cantori, MA 02021
Bill Bailey, Director, Purchasing
Tel: (781) 401-5000
Web: www.reebok.com

STAPLES
Corporate Headquarters
500 Staples Dr.
Framingham, MA 01702
Dorren Nichols, Director, Associate
Relations and Diversity
Tel: (508) 253-5000
Web: www.staples.com

STATE STREET CORPORATION
Purchasing
1 Lincoln St.
Boston, MA 02111
Tel: (617) 786-3000
Web: www.statestreet.com

THE GILLETTE COMPANY
Corporate Headquarters
Prudential Tower Bldg.
Boston, MA 02199
Jaime Van Celev-Troiano, Manager,
Strategic Sourcing/Supplier Diversity
Tel: (617) 421-8282 Fax: (617) 421-8002
Email: jamie_van_cleve@gillette.com
Web: www.gillette.com

THE TJX COMPANIES, INC.
Corporate Headquarters
770 Cochituate Rd.
Framingham, MA 01701
Ruth Johnson, Manager, Supplier Diversity
Tel: (508) 390-3043
Email: supplier_diversity@tjx.com
Web: www.tjx.com

MICHIGAN

ARVINMERITOR
Corporate Headquarters
2135 W. Maple Rd.
Troy, MI 48084
Tel: (248) 435-1000 Fax: (248) 435-1393
Web: www.arvinmeritor.com

AUTO-OWNERS INSURANCE
Procurement
6101 Anacapri Blvd
Lansing, MI 48917
Michael Storay, Manager
Tel: (517) 323-1200
Web: www.auto-owners.com

BORDERS GROUP
Corporate Headquarters
100 Phoenix Dr.
Ann Arbor, MI 48108
Tel: (734) 477-1100 Fax: (734) 477-1616
Web: www.bordersgroupinc.com

CMS ENERGY
Vendor Relations
1 Energy Plaza
Jackson, MI 49201
Eric Beda, New Vendor Relations
Tel: (517) 788-0550
Web: www.cmsenergy.com

COLLINS & AIKMAN
Corporate Headquarters
250 Stephenson Hwy
Troy, MI 48083
Tel: (248) 824-2500
Web: www.collinsaiken.com

DELPHI
Corporate Headquarters
5725 Delphi Dr.
Troy, MI 48098
R. David Nelson, Vice President Global
Supply Management
Tel: (248) 813-2000
Web: www.delphi.com

DOW CHEMICAL
Corporate Headquarters
2030 Dow Center
Midland, MI 48674
Tel: (989) 636-1000
Web: www.dow.com

DTE ENERGY
Diversity Management
2000 Second Ave.
Detroit, MI 48226
Nikki Moss
Tel: (313) 235-9363
Web: www.dteenergy.com

FEDERAL-MOGUL
Diversity
26555 Northwestern Hwy.
Southfield, MI 48034
Pam Mitchell, Director, Diversity
Web: www.federal-mogul.com

FORD MOTOR
Corporate Office
1 American Rd.,
Dearborn, MI 48126
Ray M. Jensen, Director, Supplier Diversity
Tel: (313) 390-3879 Fax: (313) 845-4713
Email: rjensen@ford.com
Web: www.ford.com

GENERAL MOTORS
Corporate Headquarters
300 Renaissance Center
Detriot, MI 48265
Bo I. Anderson, Vice President, Global
Purchasing and Supply Chain
Tel: (313) 556-5000 Fax: (517) 272-3709
Web: www.gm.com

KELLOGG
Supplier Diversity
1 Kellogg Square
Battle Creek, MI 49016
Cathy Kutch, Director, Supplier Diversity
Tel: (269) 961-2000 Fax: (269) 961-3687
Email: supplier.diversity@kellogg.com
Web: www.kelloggcompany.com

KELLY SERVICES
Supplier Diversity
999 W. Big Beaver Rd.
Troy, MI 48084
Amy Grudman, Supplier Diversity
Tel: (248) 244-5630
Web: www.kellyservices.com

KMART HOLDING
Corporate Headquarters
3100 W. Big Beaver Rd.
Troy, MI 48084
Tel: (248) 463-1000
Web: www.searsholdings.com

LEAR
Corporate Headquarters
21557 Telegraph Rd.
Southfield, MI 48034
Chuck White, Director, Supplier Diversity
Program
Tel: (248) 447-5137 Fax: (248) 447-5944
Web: www.lear.com

MASCO
Corporate Headquarters
21001 Van Born Rd.
Taylor, MI 48180
Tel: (313) 274-7400
Web: www.masco.com

PULTE HOMES
Corporate Headquarters
100 Bloomfield Hill Pkwy

Bloomfield, MI 48304
Tel: (248) 647-2750
Web: www.pulte.com

STRYKER
Purchasing
2725 Fairfield Rd.
Kalamazoo, MI 49002
Caroline Ridderman, Director, Purchasing
Tel: (269) 323-7700
Web: www.stryker.com

TRW AUTOMOTIVE HOLDINGS
Corporate Heaquarters
12025 Tech Center Dr.
Livonia, MI 48150
Renita Donladson, Cost Planning Manager
N.A. Procurement
Tel: (734) 855-2600
Email: MBE.diversity@trw.com
Web: www.trwauto.com

UNITED AUTO GROUP
Purchasing
2555 Telegraph Rd.
Bloomfield Hills, MI 48302
Jeff Edward, Vice President, Purchasing
Tel: (248) 648-2500
Web: www.unitedauto.com

VISTEON
Corporate Headquarters
1 Village Center Dr.
Van Buren Township, MI 48111
Henry Martin Jr., Associate Director,
Supplier Diversity Development
Tel: (800) 847-8366
Web: www.visteon.com

WHIRLPOOL
Corporate Headquarters
2000 North M-63
Benton Harbor, MI 49022
Tel: (269) 923-5000
Web: www.whirlpoolcorp.com

MINNESOTA

3M
Corporate Headquarters
3M Center
St. Paul, MN 55144
Tel: (888) 364-3577
Web: www.3m.com

BEST BUY
Corporate Headquarters
7601 Penn Ave., S.
Richfield, MN 55423
Susan Busch, Director, Corporate Public
Relations
Tel: (621) 291-1000
Web: www.bestbuy.com

C.H. ROBINSON WORLDWIDE
Purchasing
8100 Mitchell Rd.
Eden Prairie, MN 55344
Patrick Trombley, Manager, Purchasing
Tel: (952) 937-8500
Web: www.chrobinson.com

CHS INC.
Corporate Headquarters
5500 Cenex Cr.
Inver Grove Hghts., MN 55077
Tel: (651) 355-6000
Web: www.chsinc.com

ECOLAB
Supplier Diversity
370 Wabasha St. N.
St. Paul, MN 55102

Mitzy Lutz, Manager, Supplier Diversity
Tel: (651) 293-2233

GENERAL MILLS
Corporate Headquarters
1 General Mills Blvd
Minneapolis, MN 55426
Jana Goldenman, Supplier Diversity
Tel: (763) 764-7600
Web: www.generalmills.com

HORMEL FOODS
Purchasing
1 Hormel Place
Austin, MN 55912
Bradley Lindberg, Corporate Purchasing
Buyer
Tel: (507) 437-5611
Web: www.hormel.com

LAND O'LAKES
Purchasing
P.O. Box 64101
St. Paul, MN 55164
Tel: (651) 481-2222
Web: www.landolakesinc.com

MEDTRONIC
Supplier Diversity
710 Medtronic Pkwy.
Minneapolis, MN 55423
Gretchen Ebert, Manager, Supplier Diversity
Tel: (763) 514-4000
Email: gretchen.ebert@medtronic.com
Web: www.medtronic.com

NASH FINCH
Corporate Headquarters
7600 France Ave S.
Minneapolis, MN 55432
Tel: (952) 832-0534
Web: www.nashfinch.com

NORTHWEST AIRLINES
Corporate Headquarters
2700 Lone Oak Pkwy,
Eagan, MN 55121
Tel: (612) 726-2111
Email: general.purchasing@nwa.com
Web: www.nwa.com

ST. PAUL TRAVELERS COS.
Corporate Headquarters
385 Washington St.
St. Paul, MN 55102
Larry Gill, Personal Analyst, Supplier
Diversity
Tel: (860) 277-3220
Web: www.stpaultravelers.com

SUPERVALU
Corporate Headquarters
11840 valley View Rd
Eden Prairie, MN 55344
James Oesinger, Manager, Marketing
Tel: (717) 232-6821 X4006
Web: www.supervalu.com

TARGET
Corporate Headquarters
1000 Nicollet Mall
Minneapolis, MN 55403
Patricia Adams, Senior Vice President,
Merchandising
Tel: (612) 761-6500
Web: www.target.com

THRIVENT FINANCIAL FOR LUTHERANS
Corporate Headquarters
625 Fourth Ave S.
Minneapolis, MN 55415-1624
Tel: (800) 847-4836
Email: mail@thrivent.com
Web: www.thrivent.com

U.S. BANCORP
Supplier Diversity
800 Nicolett Mall
Minneapolis, MN 55402
Mary Andersen, Manager, Supplier Diversity
Tel: (651) 466-3000 Fax: (515) 245-6363
Web: www.usbank.com

UNITED HEALTH GROUP
Corporate Headquarters
9900 Bren Rd. E.
Minnetonla, MN 55343
Tel: (952) 936-1300
Web: www.unitedhealthgroup.com

XCEL ENERGY
Supplier Diversity
414 Nicollet Mall
Minneapolis, MN 55402
Ramona Wilson, Manager of Supplier Diversity
Tel: (612) 330-5500

MISSOURI

AMEREN
Minority Business Development
1901 Chouteua Ave.
St. Louis, MO 63103
Bran Montgomery, Minority Business Development Specialist
Tel: (314) 554-2709
Web: www.ameren.com

ANHEUSER-BUSCH
Corporate Headquarters
1 Busche Pl.
St. Louis, MO 63118
Arturo Corral, Director, Supplier Diversity
Tel: (314) 577-2000
Web: www.anheuser-busch.com

CHARTER COMMUNICATIONS
Purchasing
12405 Powerscourt Dr.
St. Louis, MO 63131
Dave Demming, Director, Purchasing
Tel: (314) 965-0555
Web: www.charter.com

EMERSON ELECTRIC
Corporate Headquarters
8000 W. Florissant Ave.
St. Louis, MO 63136
Larry Kremer, Vice President, Procurement
Tel: (314) 553-2000
Web: www.gotoemerson.com

EXPRESS SCRIPTS
Corporate Headquarters
13900 Riverport Rd.
Maryland Heights, MO 63043
Deborah Heck, Director Procurement
Tel: (314) 770-1666
Web: www.express-scripts.com

GRAYBAR ELECTRIC
Purchasing
34 N. Meramec Ave.
St. Louis, MO 63105
Mike Pooansky, Director, Purchasing
Tel: (314) 573-9200
Web: www.graybar.com

H&R BLOCK
Corporate Headquarters
4400 Main St.
Kansas City, MO 64111
Tel: (816) 753-6900
Web: www.hrblock.com

LEGGETT & PLATT
Purchasing
1 Leggett Rd.
Carthage, MO 64836
Kiley Williams, Contract Administration Manager
Tel: (417) 358-8131
Web: www.leggett.com

MAY DEPT. STORES
Corporate Headquarters
611 Olive St.
St. Louis, MO 63101
Judy Schultz, Director, Purchasing
Tel: (314) 554-7100
Web: www.mayco.com

MONSANTO
Diversity
800 N. Lindergh Blvd
St. Louis, MO 63167
Deborah Brick, Supplier Diversity
Tel: (314) 694-1000 Fax: (314) 694-4696
Email: monsanto.diversity@monsanto.com
Web: www.mosanto.com

PEABODY ENERGY
Purchasing
701 Market St.
St. Louis, MO 63101
Jennie Horton, Director, Purchasing
Tel: (314) 342-3400
Web: www.peabodyenergy.com

NEBRASKA

BERKSHIRE HATHAWAY
Corporate Headquarters
1440 Kiewit Plz.
Omaha, NE 68131
Tel: (402) 346-1400
Web: www.berkshirehathaway.com

CONAGRA FOODS
Corporate Headquarters
1 ConAgra Dr.
Omaha, NE 68102
Pam Reynolds, Manager, Supplier Diversity Program
Tel: (402) 595-4000 Fax: (402) 595-5304
Email: mwbe@conagrafoods.com
Web: www.conagrafoods.com

MUTUAL OF OMAHA INSURANCE
Procurement
Mutual of Omaha Plaza
Omaha, NE 38175
Gloria Raven, Manager, Procurement
Tel: (402) 342-7600
Web: www.mutualofomaha.com

UNION PACIFIC
Supplier Diversity
1400 Douglas St.
Omaha, NE 68179
Robert B. Morgan, Director, Supplier Diversity
Tel: (402) 271-3091
Web: www.up.com

NEVADA

CAESARS ENTERTAINMENT
Supplier Diversity
3930 Howard Hughes Pkwy
Las Vegas, NV 89109
Diane Michel, Supplier Diversity
Tel: (702) 699-5000
Web: www.caesars.com

HARRAH'S ENTERTAINMENT
Supplier Diversity
1 Harrah's Court
Las Vegas, NV 89119
Diane Michel, Supplier Diversity
Tel: (702) 407-6000 Fax: (706) 407-6079
Email: sshelpdesk@harrahs.com
Web: www.harrah's.com

MGM MIRAGE
Supplier Diversity
3600 las Vegas Blvd S.
Las Vegas, NV 89109
Tel: (702) 693-7120 Fax: (702) 891-1606
Email: supplierdiversity@mgmmirage.com
Web: www.mgmmirage.com

NEW HAMPSHIRE

FISHER SCIENTIFIC INTL.
New Business Services
1 Liberty Lane
Hampton, NH 03842
Dan Defelice, Manager, New Business Services
Tel: (412) 490-8300
Web: www.fisherscientific.com

NEW JERSEY

AMERICAN STANDARD
Corporate Headquarters
1 Centennial Ave.
Piscataway, NJ 08855
Tel: (732) 980-6000
Web: www.americanstandard.com

AT&T
Corporate Headquarters
1 AT&T
Bedminster, NJ 07921
Fred Lona, Manager, Supplier Diversity
Tel: (212) 944-2430
Email: flona@att.com
Web: www.att.com

AUTOMATIC DATA PROC.
Corporate Headquarters
1 ADP Blvd
Roseland, NJ 07068
Kathy Carpini, Corporate Purchasing
Tel: (973) 974-5000
Web: www.adp.com

AVAYA
Purchasing
211 Mount Airy Rd.
Basking Ridge, NJ 07920
Patricia R. Hume, Global Vice President, Small and Medium Business Solutions
Tel: (908) 953-6000
Web: www.avaya.com

BANK OF NEW YORK CO.
Procurement
925 Patterson Plank Rd.
Secaucus, NJ 07094
Thomas Raffa, VP for Procurement
Tel: (201) 325-7730
Web: www.bankofny.com

BECTON DICKINSON
Purchasing
1 Becton Dr.
Franklin Lakes, NJ 07417
Michael Pichano, Purchasing
Tel: (201) 847-6800
Web: www.bd.com

BED BATH & BEYOND
Purchasing
650 Liberty Ave
Union, NJ 07083
Teresa Miller, Vice President, Purchasing
Tel: (908) 688-0888
Web: www.bedbathandbeyond.com

CAMPBELL SOUP
Supplier Diversity
1 Campbell Place
Camden, NJ 08103
Harry Perales, Senior Procurement Manager
Tel: (856) 342-4800 Fax: (856) 342-3759
Email: Harry_perales@campbellsoup.com
Web: www.campbellsoupcompany.com

CHUBB
Corporate Headquarters
15 Mountain View Rd.
Warren, NJ 07061
Kathleen P. Marvel, Chief Diversity Officer
Tel: (908) 903-2000
Web: www.chubb.com

CIT GROUP
Vendor Relations
1 CIT Dr.
Livingston, NJ 07039
Tel: (973) 740-5000
Email: citcorporategiving@cit.org
Web: www.cit.com

ENGLEHARD
Corporate Headquarters
101 Wood Ave
Iselin, NJ 08830
Tel: (732) 205-5000
Web: www.englehard.com

HONEYWELL INTL.
Corporate Headquarters
101 Columbia Rd.
Morristown, NJ 07962
Mike Glass, Liaison Officer, SSEC Small Buiness
Tel: (973) 455-2000 Fax: (973) 455-4807
Web: www.honeywell.com

HOVNANIAN ENTERPRISES
Purchasing
10 Highway 35
Red Bank, NJ 07701
Lou Molinaro, Director, Purchasing
Tel: (732) 225-4001
Web: www.khov.com

JOHNSON & JOHNSON
Corporate Headquarters
1 Johnson & Johnson Plz.
New Brunswick, NJ 08933
Tel: (732) 524-0400
Email: purchasing@corus.jnj.com
Web: www.jnj.com

LUCENT TECHNOLOGIES
Diversity Business
600 Mountain Ave.
Murray Hill, NJ 07974
Jorge Valdes, Executive Director, Diversity Business Management
Tel: (908) 582-8500
Web: www.lucent.com

MEDCO HEALTH SOLUTIONS
Corporate Headquarters
100 Parsons Pond Dr.
Franklin Lakes, NJ 07417
Tel: (201) 269-3400
Web: www.medco.com

MERCK
Supplier Diversity
1 Merck Rd.
Whitehouse Station, NJ 08889
Silvana Demers, Procurement
Tel: (908) 423-4107
Email: supplier_diversity@merck.com

PATHMARK STORES
Corporate Headquarters
200 Milk St.
Carteret, NJ 07008
Tel: (732) 499-3000
Web: www.pathmark.com

PRUDENTIAL FINANCIAL
Corporate Headquarters
751 Broad st.
Newark, NJ 07102
Beth Canning, Manager, Supplier Diversity
Tel: (973) 367-7125 Fax: (973) 367-7138
Email: beth.canning@prudential.com
Web: www.prudential.com

PUBLIC SERVICE ENTERPRISE GROUP
Corporate Headquarters
80 Park Plaza
Newark, NJ 07102
Diane Stenburg, Supplier Diversity
Tel: (973) 430-5839
Web: www.pseg.com

QUEST DIAGNOSTICS
Supplier Diversity
1290 Wall St. W.
Lyndhurst, NJ 07071
Gladys Daniel, Director, Supplier Diversity
Tel: (610) 454-4158
Web: www.questdiagnostics.com

SCHERING-PLOUGH
Corporate Headquarters
2000 Galloping Hill Rd.
Kenilworth, NJ 07033
Tel: (908) 298-4000
Web: www.Schering-Plough.com

SEALED AIR
Corporate Headquarters
Park 80 E.
Saddle Brook, NJ 07663
Tel: (201) 791-7600
Web: www.sealedair.com

TOYS `R` US
Corporate Heaquarters
1 Geoffrey Way
Wayne, NJ 07470
Amanda Allen, Procurement
Tel: (973) 617-3500
Web: www.toyrusinc.com

WYETH
Corporate Headquarters
5 Giraida Farms
Madison, NJ 07940
Greg Bobyock, Vice President, Global New Products
Tel: (973) 660-5000
Web: www.wyeth.com

NEW YORK

ALTRIA GROUP
Corporate Headquarters
120 Park Ave.
New York, NY 10017
Corey Smith, ALCS Procurement
Tel: (917) 663-2358 Fax: (917) 663-5317
Web: www.altria.com

AMERADA HESS
Corporate Headquarters
1185 Sixth Ave.
New York, NY 10036
John Garbarino, Director, Procurement
Tel: (212) 997-8500
Web: www.hess.com

AMERICAN EXPRESS
Corporate Headquarters
200 Vesey St.
New York, NY 10285
Jeff Kaiser, Director, Procurement
Tel: (212) 640-2390
Web: www.americanexpress.com

AMERICAN INTL. GROUP
Corporate Headquarters
70 Pine St.,
New York, NY 10270
Tel: (212) 770-7000
Web: www.aig.com

ARROW ELECTRONICS
Corporate Headquarters
50 Marcus Dr.
Melville, NY 11747
Irene Staiton, Director, Purchasing
Tel: (631) 847-2000
Web: www.arrow.com

ASBURY AUTOMOTIVE GROUP
Vendor Relations
622 Third Ave
New York, NY 10017
Joe Moccia, New Vendor Relations
Tel: (212) 885-2500
Web: www.ashburyauto.com

ASSURANT
Corporate Headquarters
1 Chase Manhattan Center
New York, NY 10005
Tel: (212) 859-7000
Web: www.assurant.com

AVON PRODUCTS
Supplier Diversity
1345 Sixth Ave.
New York, NY 10105
Donna Westerman, Director, Supplier Diversity and Social Accountability North America
Tel: 212-282-7352
Web: www.avoncompany.com

BARNES & NOBLE
Corporate Headquarters
122 Fifth Ave
New York, NY 10011
Tel: (212) 633-3300
Web: www.barnesandnobleinc.com

BEAR STEARNS
Corporate Headquarters
383 Madison Ave.
New York, NY 10179
Tel: (212) 272-2000
Web: www.bearstearns.com

BRISTOL-MYERS SQUIBB
Corporate Headquarters
345 Park Ave.
New York, NY 10154
Ingrid M. Sheremeta, Associate Director, Supplier Diversity Procurement
Tel: (212) 546-4000
Email: Ingrid.Sheremeta@bms.com
Web: www.bms.com

CABLEVISION SYSTEMS
Corporate Headquarters
1111 Stewart Ave.
Bethpage, NY 11714

Tel: (516) 803-2300
Web: www.cablevision.com

CENDANT
Corporate Headquarters
9 W. 57th St.
New York, NY 10019
Scott Welsh, Cendant Corporation
Tel: (212) 413-1800
Email: Scott.Welsh@cendant.com
Web: www.cendant.com

CITIGROUP
Corporate Headquarters
399 Park Ave.,
New York, NY 10043
Simon Williams, Chief Risk Officer, Global Consumer Group
Tel: (212) 559-1000

COLGATE-PALMOLIVE
Product Supply Chain
300 Park Ave.
New York, NY 10022
David R. Groener, Vice President, Global Product Supply Chain
Tel: (212) 310-2000
Web: www.colgate.com

CONSOLIDATED EDISON
Supplier Diversity
4 Irving Pl.
New York, NY 10003
Joy Crichlow, Director, Supplier Diversity
Tel: (212) 460-4600
Web: www.conedison.com

CORNING
Diversity Program
1 Riverfront Plaza
Corning, NY 14831
Gail Baity, Manager, Diversity Programs
Tel: (607) 974-9000
Web: www.corning.com

DOVER
Vendor Relations
280 Park Ave.
New York, NY 10017
Tel: (212) 922-1640
Web: www.dovercorporation.com

EASTMAN KODAK
Corporate Headquarters
343 State St.
Rochester, NY 14650
Armond Kane, Supplier Diversity Manager
Tel: (585) 477-8288
Web: www.kodak.com

ENERGY EAST
Corporate Headquarters
Albany, NY 12212
Tel: (518) 434-3049
Web: www.energyeast.com

ESTÉE LAUDER
Corporate Headquarters
767 Fifth Ave.
New York, NY 10153
Tel: (212) 572-4200
Web: www.elcompanies.com

FOOT LOCKER
Corporate Headquarters
112 W. 34th St.
New York, NY 10120
Tel: (212) 720-3700
Web: www.footlocker-inc.com

GOLDMAN SACHS GROUP
Corporate Headquarters
85 Broad St.
New York, NY 10004

Liz Hyman, Supplier Diversity
Tel: (212) 902-1000 Fax: (212) 463-0220
Email: supplier.diversity@gm.com
Web: www.gs.com

GUARDIAN LIFE OF AMERICA
Human Resources Department
7 Hanover Square
New York, NY 10004
Steven Smith, Recruitment Manager
Tel: (212) 598-8000

HENRY SCHEIN
Purchasing
135 Duryea Rd.
Melville, NY 11747
Frank Audia, Manager, Purchasing
Tel: (631) 843-5500 Fax: (631) 843-5698
Web: www.henryschein.com

IAC/INTERACTIVE
Purchasing
152 W. 57th St.
New York, NY 10019
Joe Listo, Purchasing
Tel: (212) 314-7300
Web: www.iac.com

INTERPUBLIC GROUP
Human Resource
1114 Sixth Ave.
New York, NY 10036
James Simmons, Manager, Diversity Performance
Tel: (212) 704-1200
Web: www.interpublic.com

INTL. BUSINESS MACHINES (IBM)
Corporate Headquarters
New Orchard Rd.
Armock, NY 10504
I. Javette Jenkins, Minority Supplier Programs Director
Tel: (914) 499-1900
Email: javette@us.ibm.com
Web: www.ibm.com

J.P. MORGAN CHASE & CO.
Corporate Headquarters
270 Park Ave.,
New York, NY 10017
Harvey Butler, Vice President, Corporate Supplier Diversity
Tel: (201) 595-5264
Email: harvey.butler@jpmchase.com
Web: www.jpmorganchase.com

KEYSPAN
Diversity
1 Metro Tech Center
Brooklyn, NY 11201
Terrence McBeth, Diversity Manager
Tel: (718) 403-1000
Web: www.keyspanenergy.com

L-3 COMMUNICATIONS
Procurement
600 Third Ave
New York, NY 10016
Ralph DeNino, Vice President, Procurement
Tel: (212) 697-1111
Web: www.L-3com.com

LEHMAN BROTHERS HLDGS.
Supplier Diversity
745 Seventh Ave.
New York, NY 10019
Aaron Blumenthal, Manager, Supplier Diversity
Tel: (212) 526-7000 Fax: (646) 758-3146
Email: ablument@lehman.com
Web: www.lehman.com

LIZ CLAIBORNE
Corporate Headquarters
1441 Broadway
New York, NY 10018
Tel: (212) 354-4900
Web: www.lizclaiborne.com

LOEWS CORPORATION
Corporate Headquarters
667 Madison Ave
New York, NY 10021
Jackie Pineiro, Purchasing Manager,
National Program
Tel: (212) 521-2000 Fax: (212) 521-2996
Web: www.loews.com

MARSH & MCLENNAN
Corporate Headquarters
1166 Sixth Ave.
New York, NY 10036
Linda Creighton, Director, Purchasing
Tel: (212) 345-5000
Web: www.mmc.com

MCGRAW-HILL
Purchasing
1221 Sixth Ave.
New York, NY 10020
Evelyn Lowinsten, Manager, Purchasing
Tel: (212) 512-2000
Web: www.mcgraw-hill.com

MERRILL LYNCH
Corporate Headquarters
4 Financial Center
New York, NY 10080
Tamra Luckett, Supplier Diversity Director
Tel: (212) 449-1000 Fax: (609) 282-3557
Email: tamara_luckett@ml.com
Web: www.ml.com

METLIFE
Corporate Headquarters
200 Park Ave.
New York, NY 10166
Denise Singleton, Manager, Minority
Diversity
Tel: (908) 253-1068
Web: www.metlife.com

MORGAN STANLEY
Corporate Headquarters
1585 Broadway
New York, NY 10036
Jennifer Rosa, Executive Director, Supplier
Diversity
Tel: (212) 762-2034
Email: supdiversity@morganstanley.com
Web: www.morganstanley.com

NEW YORK LIFE INSURANCE
Supplier Diversity
51 Madison Ave
New York, NY 10010
Annette Fucucello, Director of Supplier
Diversity
Tel: (212) 576-7000
Email: nylsupplierdiversity@newyorklife.com
Web: www.newyorklife.com

NEWS CORP.
Corporate Headquarters
1211 Sixth Ave.
New York, NY 10036
Tel: (212) 852-7000
Web: www.newscorp.com

NTL
Corporate Headquarters
909 Third Ave
New York, NY 10022
Tel: (212) 906-8440
Web: www.ntl.com

OMNICOM GROUP
Vendor Relations
437 Madison Ave.
New York, NY 10022
Tel: (212) 415-3600 Fax: (212) 415-3530
Web: www.omnicompgroup.com

PEPSI BOTTLING
Corporate Headquarters
1 Pepsi Way
Somers, NY 10589
J. Frederick Canady, Director, Minority
Business
Tel: (914) 767-6000
Web: www.pbg.com

PEPSICO
700 Anderson Hill Rd.
Purchase, NY 10577
James Kozlowski, Senior Vice President,
Global Procurement
Tel: (914) 253-2000
Web: www.pepsico.com

PFIZER
235 E. 2nd St.
New York, NY 10017
Gwendolyn Turner, Supplier Diversity
Tel: (212) 573-2323
Web: www.pfizer.com

STARWOOD HOTELS & RSRTS.
Diversity
1111 Westchester Ave.
White Plains, NY 10604
Randal Tucker, Manager MBE and Diversity
Tel: (914) 640-8100
Web: www.starwoodhotels.com

TIAA-CREF
Corporate Headquarters
730 Third Ave.
New York, NY 10017
Joan Watson, Manager, Suppliers Diversity
Tel: (212) 490-9000 X3039 Fax: (212)
916-6030
Web: www.tiaa-cref.org

TIME WARNER
Corporate Headquarters
1 Time Warner Center
New York, NY 10019
Greta Davis, National Director, Supplier
Diversity
Tel: (212) 484-8000
Email: greta.davis@timewarner.com
Web: www.timewarner.com

VERIZON COMMUNICATIONS
Corporate Headquarters
1095 Sixth Ave.
New York, NY 10036
Lawrence T. Babbio, Jr., Vice Chairman and
President
Tel: (212) 395-2121 Fax: (212) 921-2917
Web: www.verizon.com

VIACOM
Corporate Headquarters
1515 Broadway
New York, NY 10036
Tel: (212) 258-6000
Web: www.viacom.com

WELLCHOICE
Vendor Relations
11 W. 42nd St.
New York, NY 10036
Tel: (888) 476-7245
Web: www.wellchoice.com

NORTH CAROLINA

BANK OF AMERICA CORP.
Corporate Headquarters
100 N. Tryon St.
Charlotte, NC 28255
Kim Yu, Supplier Diveristy Manager
Tel: (415) 241-3428 Fax: (415) 241-5386
Email: kim.t.vu@bankofamerica.com
Web: www.bankofamerica.com

BB&T CORP.
Vendor Relations
200 W. Second St.
Winston-Salem, NC 27101
Tel: (336) 733-2000
Web: www.bbandt.com

DUKE ENERGY
Corporate Headquarters
526 S. Church St.
Charlotte, NC 28202
Richard Williams, Vice President, Diversity
and Employment Services
Tel: (704) 594-6200
Web: www.duke-energy.com

FAMILY DOLLAR STORES
Supply Chain
10401 Monroe Rd.
Matthews, NC 28105
Charles S. Gibson Jr., Executive Vice
President, Supply Chain
Tel: (704) 847-6961
Web: www.familydollar.com

GOODRICH
Procurement
2730 W. Tyvola Rd.
Charlotte, NC 28217
Jim Burfield, Procurement Specialist
Tel: (704) 423-7000
Web: www.goodrich.com

JEFFERSON-PILOT
Purchasing
100 N. Greene St.
Greensboro, NC 27401
Theresa Darcy, Vice President,
Administrative Services
Tel: (336) 691-3000
Web: www.jpfinancial.com

LOWE'S
Supplier Diversity
100 Loews Blvd
Mooresville, NC 28117
Gil Galigos, Supplier Diversity Manager
Tel: (704) 758-2653
Web: www.loews.com

NUCOR
Corporate Headquarters
2100 Rexford Rd.
Charlotte, NC 28211
Tel: (704) 366-7000 Fax: (704) 362-4208
Web: www.nucor.com

PROGRESS ENERGY
Vendor Relations
410 S. Wilmington St.
Raleigh, NC 27601
Tel: (919) 546-6111
Email: psn-vendors@pgnmail.com
Web: www.progress-energy.com

REYNOLDS AMERICAN
Corporate Headquarters
401 N. Main St.
Winston-Salem, NC 27102
Tel: (336) 741-5500
Web: www.reynoldsamerican.com

SONIC AUTOMOTIVE
Corporate Headquarters
6415 Idlewild Rd
Charlotte, NC 28212
Tel: (704) 566-2400
Web: www.sonicautomotive.com

SPX CORPORATION
Corporate Headquarters
13515 Ballantyne Corporate Place
Charlotte, NC 28277
Tel: (704) 752-4400
Web: www.spx.com

VF CORPORATION
Corporate Headquarters
105 Corporate Center Blvd
Greensboro, NC 27408
Boyd Rogers, Vice President, Supply Chain
Tel: (336) 424-6000 Fax: (336) 424-7668
Web: www.vfc.vom

WACHOVIA CORP.
Corporate Headquarters
301 S. College St.
Charlotte, NC 28288
Ann Prock, Manager, Supplier Diversity
Tel: (704) 374-6807
Email: supplierdiversity@wachovia.com
Web: www.wachovia.com

OHIO

AK STEEL HOLDING
Supply Chain
703 Curtis St.
Middletown, OH 45043
John F. Kaloski, Senior Vice President,
Supply Chain
Tel: (513) 425-5000
Web: www.aksteel.com

AMERICAN ELECTRIC POWER
Corporate Headquarters
1 Riverside Rd
Columbus, OH 43215
Gloria Hines, Diversified Business
Coordinator
Tel: (614) 716-1955 Fax: (866) 705-9689
Web: www.aep.com

AMERICAN FINANCIAL GRP.
Purchasing
1 E. Fourth St.
Cincinnati, OH 45202
Fran Hall, Purchasing
Tel: (513) 579-2121
Web: www.afginc.com

BIG LOTS
Purchasing
300 Phillipi Rd.
Columbus, OH 43228
Debbie Sandol, Director, Purchasing
Tel: (614) 278-6800
Email: sell2us@biglots.com
Web: www.biglots.com

CARDINAL HEALTH
Corporate Headquarters
7000 Cardinal Pl.
Dublin, OH 43017
Kathy Benn, Vice President, Supplier
Diversity
Tel: (614) 757-5000
Web: www.cardinal.com

CINCINNATI FINANCIAL
Purchasing
6200 Gilmore Rd.
Fairfield, OH 45014

Stacey Hall, Manager, Purchasing
Tel: (513) 870-2000
Web: www.cinfin.com

CINERGY
Purchasing
139 E. Fourth St.
Cincinnati, OH 45202
April Collins, Purchasing
Tel: (513) 421-9500 X3018
Web: www.cinergy.com

COOPER TIRE & RUBBER
Supplier Relations
701 Lima Ave
Findlay, OH 45840
Lynn Maag, Manager, Supplier Performance
and Material Control
Tel: (419) 420-6161
Web: www.coopertire.com

DANA
Corporate Headquarters
4500 Dorr St.
Toledo, OH 43615
Felissa Parker, Director, Minority Supplier
Development
Tel: (248) 324-6762
Web: www.dana.com

EATON
Supplier Diversity
1111 Superior Ave
Cleveland, OH 44114
Deborah R. Pickens, Director, Supplier
Diversity
Tel: (216) 523-4226
Web: www.eaton.com

FEDERATED DEPT. STORES
Corporate Headquarters
7 W. Seventh St.
Cincinnati, OH 45202
Tom Knott, Director, Diversity Vendor
Relations
Tel: (513) 579-7803
Web: www.fds.com

FIFTH THIRD BANCORP
Diversity
38 Fountain Square Pl.
Cincinnati, OH 45263
Ann Lazarus-Barnes, Vice President,
Diversity
Tel: (513) 534-8204

FIRSTENERGY
Corporate Headquarters
76 S. Main St.
Akron, OH 44308
Michael J. Dowling, Chief Procurement
Officer, Vice President Supply Chain
Tel: (800) 736-3402
Web: www.firstenergycorp.com

GOODYEAR TIRE & RUBBER
Corporate Headquarters
1144 E. Market St.
Akron, OH 44316
Dave Stoltz, Global Diversity Initiatives
Manager
Tel: (330) 796-2121 Fax: (330) 796-2222
Web: www.goodyear.com

INTERNATIONAL STEEL GROUP
Corporate Headquarters
4020 Kinross Lakes Pkwy.
Richfield, OH 44286
Tel: (219) 399-1200
Web: www.intlsteel.com

KEYCORP
Vendor Relations
127 Public Square

Cleveland, OH 44114
Tel: (216) 689-6300
Web: www.key.com

KROGER
Corporate Headquarters
1014 Vine St.
Cincinnati, OH 45202
Denise Thomas, Director, Corporate
Supplier
Tel: (513) 762-4000
Web: www.kroger.com

LIMITED BRANDS
Corporate Headquarters
3 Limited Pkwy.
Columbus, OH 43230
Tel: (614) 415-7000
Web: www.limitedbrands.com

NATIONAL CITY CORP.
Vendor Diversity
1900 E. Ninth St.
Cleveland, OH 44114
Tel: (216) 222-2000
Email: vendordiversity@nationcity.com
Web: www.nationalcity.com

NATIONWIDE
Corporate Headquarters
1 Nationwide Plaza
Columbus, OH 43215
Tel: (614) 249-7111 X92977
Web: www.nationwide.com

NCR
Purchasing
1700 S. Patterson Blvd
Dayton, OH 45479
Tel: (937) 445-5000
Web: www.ncr.com

OWENS CORNING
Purchasing
1 Owens Corning Pkwy
Toledo, OH 43659
Doug Pontsler, Manager, Purchasing
Tel: (419) 248-8000
Web: www.owenscorning.com

OWENS-ILLINOIS
Procurement
1 SeaGate
Toledo, OH 43666
Ryan C. Schlaff, Vice President,
Procurement
Tel: (419) 247-5000
Web: www.o-i.com

PARKER HANNIFIN
Procurement
6035 Parkland Blvd.
Cleveland, OH 44124
John Dedinsky, VP Procurement
Tel: (216) 896-2761 Fax: (216) 896-4057
Web: www.parker.com

PROCTER & GAMBLE
1 Procter & Gamble Plz.
Cincinnati, OH 45202
Tel: (513) 983-1100
Email: hodnett.dm@pg.com
Web: www.pg.com

PROGRESSIVE
Corporate Headquarters
6300 Wilson Mills Rd.
Mayfield Village, OH 44143
Tel: (440) 461-5000
Web: www.progressive.com

SHERWIN-WILLIAMS
Purchasing
101 Prospect Ave. N.W.

Cleveland, OH 44115
Simi Gane, Manager, Purchasing
Tel: (216) 566-2000
Web: www.sherwin.com

TIMKEN
Supply Chain
1835 Dueber Ave S.W
Canton, OH 44706
Donna J. Demerling, Senior Vice President,
Supply Chain Transformation
Tel: (330) 438-3000
Web: www.timken.com

WENDY'S INTERNATIONAL, INC.
Corporate Headquarters
1 Dave Thomas Blvd.
Dublin, OH 43017
Tel: (614) 764-3100
Web: www.wendys.com

WESTERN & SOUTHERN FINANCIAL
Corporate Headquarters
400 Broadway
Cincinnati, OH 45202
Tel: (513) 629-1800
Web: www.westernsouthern.com

OKLAHOMA

DEVON ENERGY CORPORATION
Corporate Headquarters
20 N. Broadway
Oklahoma City, OK 73102
Tel: (405) 235-3611

KERR-MCGEE
Purchasing
Kerr-McGee Center
Oklahoma, OK 73125
Mat Thorton, Purchasing
Tel: (405) 270-1313
Web: www.kerr-mcgee.com

OGE ENERGY
Purchasing
321 N. Harvey Ave.
Oklahoma City, OK 73102
Earl Farmer, Purchasing
Tel: (405) 553-5868
Web: www.oge.com

ONEOK
Purchasing
100 W. Fifth St.
Tulsa, OK 74103
Gary Bradshaw, Manager, Purchasing
Tel: (918) 588-7000
Web: www.oneok.com

WILLIAMS
Corporate Headquarters
1 Williams Center
Tulsa, OK 74172
Kelly Swan, Purchasing
Tel: (918) 573-2000
Web: www.williams.com

OREGON

NIKE
Corporate Headquarters
1 Bowerman Dr.
Beaverton, OR 97005
Nicholas Athanasakos, Vice President,
Supply Chain
Web: www.nike.com

PENNSYLVANIA

AIR PRODUCTS & CHEM.
7201 Hamilton Blvd.
Allentown, PA 18195
Joe Troller
Tel: (610) 481-4911
Web: www.airproducts.com

ALCOA
Corporate Headquarters
201 Isabella St.
Pittsburgh, PA 15212
Mark Straszheim, Procurement
Tel: (213) 894-7395 Fax: (412) 553-4498
Web: www.alcoa.com

AMERISOURCEBERGEN
Corporate Headquarters
1300 Morris Dr.
Chesterbrook, PA 19087
Len Decandia, Manager, Procurement
Tel: (610) 727-7211
Email: pcerula@amerisourcebergen.com
Web: www.amerisourcebergen.com

ARAMARK
Corporate Headquarters
1101 Market St.
Philadelphia, PA 19107
John Orobono, Vice President, Vending
Services
Tel: (215) 238-3000
Web: www.aramark.com

CIGNA
Corporate Headquarters
1 Liberty Pl.
Philadelphia, PA 19192
Tel: (215) 761-1000
Email: vendorDA@cigna.com
Web: www.cigna.com/itvendors

COMCAST
Supplier Diversity
1500 Market St.
Philadelphia, PA 19102
Debbie Grossman, Vice President, Supplier
Diversity
Tel: (215) 665-1700 Fax: (215) 655-8113
Email: supplierinfo@cable.comcast.com
Web: www.comcast.com

CROWN HOLDINGS
Sourcing Department
1 Crown Way
Philadelphia, PA 19154
Alan Stott, Director of Sourcing Dept.
Tel: (215) 698-5100
Web: www.crowncork.com

ERIE INSURANCE GROUP
Corporate Headquarters
100 Erie Insurance Pl.
Erie, PA 16530
Cheryl Ferrie, Purchasing Director
Tel: (814) 870-2000
Web: www.erieinsurance.com

H.J. HEINZ
Supplier Diversity
Attn: Supplier Profile Questionnaire
P.O. Box 57
Pittsburgh, PA 15230
Tel: (412) 456-5700
Email: supplierdiversity@hjheinz.com
Web: www.heinz.com

HERSHEY FOODS
Purchasing
14 E. Chocolate Ave.
Hershey, PA 17033

Purchasing
Tel: (717) 534-6799
Web: www.hersheys.com

IKON OFFICE SOLUTIONS
Supplier Diversity
70 Valey Stream Pkwy
Malvern, PA 19355
Betsy Parrish, Diversity Program
Administrator
Tel: (610) 722-1520 Fax: (610) 727-2995
Email: supplierdiversity@ikon.com
Web: www.ikon.com

JONES APPAREL GROUP
Purchasing
250 Rittenhouse Circle
Bristol, PA 19007
Liz Raddi, Manager, Purchasing
Tel: (215) 785-4000
Web: www.jny.com

LINCOLN NATIONAL
Corporate Headquarters
1500 Market St.
Philadelphia, PA 19102
Tel: (215) 448-1400
Web: www.lfg.com

MELLON FINANCIAL CORP.
Corporate Headquarters
1 Melon Center
Pittsburgh, PA 15258
Tel: (412) 234-5530
Email: tech.info@mellon.com
Web: www.mellon.com

PILGRIM'S PRIDE
Purchasing
110 S. Texas St.
Pittsburg, PA 75686
Ron Pittington, Director, Purchasing
Tel: (903) 434-1122
Web: www.pilgrimspride.com

PNC FINANCIAL SERVICES
Purchasing
249 Fifth Ave
Pittsburgh, PA 15222
Tel: (412) 762-2000
Web: www.pnc.com

PPG INDUSTRIES
Corporate Headquarters
1 PPG St.
Pittsburgh, PA 15272
Kathleen A. McGuire, Vice President
Purchasing and Distribution
Tel: (412) 434-3131
Web: www.ppg.com

PPL CORPORATION
Supplier Diversity
2 N. Ninth St.
Allentwon, PA 18101
Gloria E. Collins, Administrator, Supplier
Diversity
Tel: (610) 774-5151
Web: www.pplweb.com

RITE AID
Corporate Headquarters
30 Hunter Lane
Camp Hill, PA 17011
Wilson A Lester, Jr., Senior Vice President
Supply Chain
Tel: (717) 761-2633
Web: www.riteaid.com

ROHM & HAAS
Vendor Relations
100 Independence Mall W.
Philadelphia, PA 19106

Jean-Francois Mayer, Vice President,
Procurement
Tel: (212) 592-3000 Fax: (212) 592-3377
Web: www.rohmhaas.com

SUNOCO
Corporate Headquarters
1801 Market Pl.
Philadlphia, PA 19103
Joel H. Maness, Senior Vice President,
Refining and Supply
Tel: (215) 977-6764
Web: www.sunocoinc.com

TOLL BROTHERS
Corporate Headquarters
250 Gibraltar Rd
Horsham, PA 19044
Tel: (215) 938-8000
Web: www.tollbrothers.com

UGI CORPORATION
Purchasing
460 N. Gulph Rd
King of Prussia, PA 19406
James Siege, Manager, Purchasing
Tel: (610) 337-1000
Web: www.unicorp.com

UNISYS
Supplier Diversity
Unisys Way
Blue Bell, PA 19424
Murray Schooner, Corporate Director,
Supplier Diversity
Tel: (703) 439-5098
Web: www.unisys.com

UNITED STATES STEEL
Corporate Headquarters
600 Grant St.
Philadelphia, PA 15219
Christopher J. Navetta, Senior Vice
President, Procurement, Logistics, and
Diversified Business
Tel: (412) 433-1121
Web: www.ussteel.com

UNIVERSAL HEALTH SVCS.
Purchasing
367 S. Gulph Rd.
King of Prussia, PA 19406
Clark Sailor, Director, Purchasing
Tel: (610) 768-3300
Web: www.uhsinc.com

WESCO INTERNATIONAL
Minority Business Relations
225 West Station Square Dr.
Pittsburgh, PA 15219
Mike Ludwig, Director, Minority Business
Relations
Tel: (412) 454-2200
Web: www.wesco.com

YORK INTERNATIONAL
Sourcing Dept.
631 S. Richland Ave.
York, PA 17403
Tel: (717) 771-7890
Email: sourcing@york.com
Web: www.york.com

RHODE ISLAND

CVS
Corporate Headquarters
1 CVS Dr.
Woonsocket, RI 02895
Tel: (401) 765-1500
Web: www.cvs.com

TEXTRON
Corporate Headquarters
40 Westminster St.
Providence, RI 02903
Tel: (401) 421-2800
Web: www.textron.com

SOUTH CAROLINA

SCANA
Procurement
1426 Main St.
Columbia, SC 29201
Sarena D. Burch, Senior Vice President,
Fuel Procurement and Asset Management
Tel: (803) 217-9000
Web: www.scana.com

TENNESSEE

AUTOZONE
Supply Chain
123 S. Front St.
Memphis, TN 38103
Michael E. Longo, Executive Vice President,
Supply Chain
Tel: (901) 495-6500
Web: www.autozone.com

CAREMARK RX
Corporate Headquarters
211 Commerce St.
Nashville, TN 37201
Ruben Hamilton, Director Procurement
and Supply
Tel: (847) 559-4700
Web: www.caremark.com

DOLLAR GENERAL
Supply Chain Management
100 Mission Ridge
Goodlettsville, TN 37072
Lloyd Davis, Senior Vice President, Supply
Chain Operations
Tel: (615) 855-4000
Web: www.dollargeneral.com

EASTMAN CHEMICAL
Vendor Relations
100 N. Eastman Rd.
Kingsport, TN 37660
Tom Mcpherson
Tel: (423) 229-2000
Web: www.eastman.com

FEDEX
Corporate Headquarters
924 S. Shady Grove Rd.
Memphis, TN 38120
Douglas E. Witt, President, Chief Executive
Officer Supply Chain Services
Tel: (901) 818-7500
Web: www.fedex.com

HOSPITAL CORPORATION OF AMERICA
Corporate Headquarters
1 Park Plz.
Nashville, TN 37203
James A. Fitzgerald , Senior Vice President,
Supply Chain Operations
Tel: (615) 344-9551
Web: www.hcahealthcare.com

UNUMPROVIDENT
Corporate Headquarters
1 Fountain Sq.
Chattanooga, TN 37402
Stacey Custeau, Director, Purchasing
Tel: (423) 755-1011
Web: www.unumprovident.com

TEXAS

AFFILIATED COMPUTER SVCS.
Purchasing
2828 N. Haskell Ave
Dallas, TX 75204
Brad Lawrenson, Manager, Purchasing
Tel: (214) 841-6111
Web: www.acs-inc.com

AMERICAN AIRLINES
Diversity Supplier Program
4333 Amon Carter Blvd.
Fort Worth, TX 76155-2664
Luis Gomez, Manager for Supplier Diversity
Tel: (817) 963-1234
Email: luis.gomez@aa.com
Web: www.aa.com/supplierdiversity

US Hispanic National Organizations and
Promotions
4255 Amon Carter Blvd. M/D 4412
Fort Worth, TX 76155
Juan J. Rios, Manager
Tel: (817) 931-4243
Email: juan.rios@aa.com
Web: www.aa-pro.com

ANADARKO PETROLEUM
Purchasing
1201 Lake Robbins Dr.
The Woodlands, TX 77380
Steve Englehardt, Manager, Purchasing
Tel: (832) 636-1000 Fax: (832) 636-5097
Email: steve_englehardt@anadarko.com
Web: www.anadarko.com

APACHE
Purchasing
2000 Post Oak Blvd
Houston, TX 77056
Joe Augustine, Corporate Purchasing,
Manager
Tel: (713) 296-6436
Web: www.apachecorp.com

BAKER HUGHES
Purchasing
3900 Essex Lane
Houston, TX 77027
Brenda Schelsteder, Manager, Purchasing
Tel: (713) 625-5700
Web: www.bakerhughes.com

BRINKER INTERNATIONAL
Purchasing
6820 L.B.J. Freeway
Dallas, TX 75240
Janine McShane, Director, Purchasing
Tel: (972) 980-9917
Web: www.brinker.com

BURLINGTON NO. SANTA FE
Corporate Headquarters
2650 Lou Menk Dr.
Fort Worth, TX 76131
Mary Escobar, Director, Procurement
Tel: (785) 676-3830 X31 Fax: (785)
676-3094
Web: www.bnsf.com

BURLINGTON RESOURCES
Purchasing
717 Texas Ave
Houston, TX 77002
Tel: (817) 347-2000
Web: www.br-inc.com

CENTERPOINT ENERGY
Supplier Diversity
1111 Louisiana St.
Houston, TX 77002
Jewel Smith, Manager, Supplier Diversity

Tel: (713) 207-6951 Fax: (713) 207-9347
Web: www.centerpointenergy.com

CLEAR CHANNEL COMMUNICATIONS
Diversity
200 E. Basse Rd.
San Antonio, TX 78209
M. Helen Cavazos, Diversity Manager
Tel: (210) 822-2828
Web: www.clearchannel.com

COMMERCIAL METALS
Corporate Headquarters
6565 N. MacArthur Blvd
Irving, TX 75039
Tel: (214) 689-4300
Web: www.commercialmetals.com

CONOCOPHILLIPS
Corporate Headquarters
600 N. Dairy Ashford Rd.
Houston, TX 77079
Jim W. Nokes, Executive Vice President
Refining, Marketing, Supply and
Transportation
Tel: (281) 293-1000
Web: www.conocophillips.com

CONTINENTAL AIRLINES
Supplier Diversity
1600 Smith St.
Houston, TX 77002
Phyllis Graham, Supplier Diversity Program
Liaison
Tel: (713) 324-5000
Email: sdp@coair.com
Web: www.continental.com

D.R. HORTON
Corporate Headquarters
301 Commerce St.
Fort Worth, TX 76102
Tel: (817) 390-8200
Web: www.drhorton.com

DEAN FOODS
Corporate Headquarters
2515 McKinney Ave.
Dallas, TX 75201
Tel: (214) 303-3400
Web: www.deanfoods.com

DELL
Corporate Headquarters
1 Dell Way
Round Rock, TX 78682
Fred Hayes, Supplier Diversity
Tel: (512) 338-4400 Fax: (512) 283-6161
Web: www.dell.com

DYNEGY
Purchasing
1000 Louisiana St.
Houston, TX 77002
Brenda Valladares, Manager, Purchasing
Tel: (713) 507-6400
Email: scm@dynegy.com
Web: www.dynegy.com

EL PASO
Materials and Contracts Management
1001 Louisiana St.
Houston, TX 77002
Helda Longoria, Coordinator, Supplier
Diversity Program
Tel: (713) 420-2600 Fax: (713) 420-7464
Web: www.elpaso.com

ELECTRONIC DATA SYSTEMS
Supplier Diversity
5400 Legacy Dr.
Plano, TX 75024

Mike Mussy, Manager, Supplier Diversity
Tel: (972) 604-6000
Web: www.eds.com

ENBRIDGE ENERGY PARTNERS
Corporate Headquarters
1100 Louisiana St.
Houston, TX 77002
Tel: (713) 821-2000
Web: www.enbridgepartners.com

ENTERPRISE PRODUCTS
Vendor Relations
2727 N. Loop West
Houston, TX 77008
Kim McKenny, Sourcing and Procurement
Tel: (713) 880-6500

EXXON MOBIL
Exxon Mobil Corporation
5959 Las Colinas Blvd
Irving, TX 75039-2298
Nancy Swartout, Supplier Diversity
Tel: (972) 444-1000 Fax: (972) 444-1883
Web: www.exxon.mobil.com

GROUP 1 AUTOMOTIVE
Corporate Headquarters
950 Echo Lane
Houston, TX 77024
Tel: (713) 647-5700
Web: www.group1auto.com

HALLIBURTON
Corporate Headquarters
1401 McKinney
Houston, TX 77010
len Cooper, Director, Procurement
Tel: (281) 575-3270
Web: www.haliburton.com

J.C. PENNEY
Corporate Headquarters
6501 Legacy Dr.
Plano, TX 75024
James W. LaBounty, Senior Vice President,
Director Supply Chain
Tel: (973) 431-1000
Web: www.jcpenney.net

KIMBERLY-CLARK
Corporate Headquarters
351 Phelps Dr.
Irving, TX 75038
Shannon Styker, Supplier Diversity and
Procurement
Tel: (920) 721-2000
Email: supplierdiversity@kcc.com
Web: www.kimberly-clark.com

KINDER MORGAN ENERGY
Contracting Department
500 Dallas St. #1000
Houston, TX 77002
Jenny Brown, Senior Contract Administrator
Tel: (713) 369-9296
Web: www.kindermorgan.com

LYONDELL CHEMICAL
Supply Management
1221 McKinney St.
Houston, TX 77010
Tel: (713) 652-7200
Web: www.lyondell.com

MARATHON OIL
Corporate Headquarters
5555 San Felipe Rd.
Houston, TX 77056
Donna Nichols-Carr, Supplier Diversity
Tel: (713) 296-4361
Email: dnicholscarr@marathon.com
Web: www.marathon.com

PLAINS ALL AMERICAN PIPELINE
Corporate Headquarters
333 Clay St.
Houston, TX 77002
Sky Cheney, Purchasing Manager
Tel: (713) 646-4100
Web: www.paalp.com

RADIOSHACK
Supply Chain
300 Radio Shack Circle
Fort Worth, TX 76102
Mike Kowal, Senior Vice President, Supply
Chain
Web: www.radioshackcorporation.com

RELIANT ENERGY
Corporate Headquarters
P.O. Box 4932
Houston, TX 77210-4932
Tel: (713) 497-3000
Web: www.reliantenergy.com

SBC COMMUNICATIONS
Corporate Headquarters
175 E. Houston St.
San Antonio, TX 78205
Tel: (210) 821-4105
Web: www.sbc.com

SMITH INTERNATIONAL
Supplier Diversity
411 N. Sam Houston Pkwy
Houston, TX 77060
Judy Fulton, Supplier Diversity
Tel: (281) 233-5582
Email: jfulton@smith.com
Web: www.smith.com

SOUTHWEST AIRLINES
Supplier Relations
2705 Love Field Dr.
Dallas, TX 75235
Lourdes Romero, Manager of Compliance
Tel: (214) 792-4000 Fax: (214) 792-5015
Email: lourdesromero@wnco.com
Web: www.southwest.com

SYSCO
Corporate Headquarters
1390 Enclave Pkwy
Houston, TX 77077
Cameron L. Blakely, Vice President,
eBusiness and BSCC Supplier Services
Tel: (281) 584-1390
Web: www.sysco.com

TEMPLE-INLAND
Supplier Diversity
1300 MoPac expressway S.
Austin, TX 78746
Novell Eustey, Director, Supplier Diversity
Tel: (512) 434-5800
Web: www.templeinland.com

TENET HEALTHCARE
Corporate Headquarters
13737 Noel Rd.
Dallas, TX 75240
Ken Newman, Manager, Purchasing
Tel: (469) 893-2200
Web: www.tenethealth.com

TESORO
Corporate Headquarters
300 Concord Plaza Dr.
San Antonio, TX 78216
C.A. Flagg, Senior Vice President, Supply
and Optimization
Tel: (210) 828-8484
Web: www.tsocorp.com

TEXAS INSTRUMENTS
Minority and Women supplier
12500 TI Blvd
Dallas, TX 75266
Shirely Smith, Minority and Women
Supplier Director
Tel: (972) 995-3773
Email: mwbd@list.ti.com
Web: www.ti.com

TRIAD HOSPITALS
Supply Chain
5800 Tennyson Pkwy
Plano, TX 75024
Corris Boyd, Vice President, Supply Chain
Optimization
Tel: (214) 473-7000
Web: www.triadhospitals.com

TXU
Supplier Diversity
1601 Bryan St.
Dallas, TX 75201
Sharon Rowlett, Procurement Specialist
Tel: (214) 812-6923 Fax: (214) 812-5597
Email: supplierdiversity@txu.com
Web: www.txucorp.com

USAA
Supplier Relations
9800 Fredericksburg Rd.
San Antonio, TX 78288
Tel: (210) 498-2211
Email: supplier.relations@usaa.com
Web: www.usaa.com

VALERO ENERGY
Corporate Headquarters
1 Valero Way
San Antonio, TX 78249
Tel: (210) 345-2000 Fax: (210) 345-2646
Web: www.valero.com

WASTE MANAGEMENT
Supplier Diversity
1001 Fannin St.
Houston, TX 77002
Betty Banks, Director, Supplier Diversity
Tel: (713) 265-1567 Fax: (713) 328-7604
Web: www.wm.com

WHOLE FOODS MARKET
Purchasing
550 Bowie St.
Austin, TX 78703
Tamara Gillary, Director, Purchasing
Tel: (512) 477-4455
Web: www.wholefoodsmarket.com

UTAH

AUTOLIV
Purchasing
3350 Airport Rd.
Ogden, UT 84405
Halvar Jonzon, Vice President, Purchasing
Tel: (801) 625-9200
Web: www.autoliv.com

VIRGINIA

ADVANCE AUTO PARTS
Corporate Headquarters
5673 Airport Rd.
Roanoke, VA 24012
Tel: (540) 362-4911 Fax: (540) 561-4104
Web: www.advanceautoparts.com

AES
Corporate Headquarters
4300 Wilson Blvd
Arlington, VA 22203
Ali Naqvi, Vice President, Chief
Procurement Officer
Tel: (703) 522-1315
Web: www.aes.com

BRINK'S
Corporate Headquarters
1801 Bayberry Ct.
Richmond, VA 23226
Tel: (804) 289-9700
Email: info@brinkscompany.com
Web: www.brinkscompany.com

CAPITAL ONE FINANCIAL
Corporate Headquarters
1680 Capital One Dr.
McLean, VA 22102
Tel: (703) 720-1000
Web: www.capitalone.com

CARMAX
Corporate Headquarters
4900 Cox Rd.
Glen Allen, VA 23060
Tel: (888) 601-5567
Web: www.carmax.com

CIRCUIT CITY STORES
Corporate Headquarters
9950 Maryland Dr.
Richmond, VA 23233
Ronald G. Cuthberton, Senior Vice
President, Supply Chain and Inventory
Management
Tel: (804) 527-4000
Web: www.circuitcity.com

DOMINION RESOURCES
Supplier Diversity
120 Tredegar St.
Richmond, VA 23219
Larry Taylor, Supplier Diversity
Tel: (804) 819-2000
Email: supplier_diversity@dom.com
Web: www.dom.com

GANNETT
Diversity
7950 Jones Branch Dr.
McLean, VA 22107
Jose Berrios, Vice President, Diversity
Tel: (703) 854-6000
Web: www.gannett.com

GENERAL DYNAMICS
Corporate Headquarters
2941 FairView Park Dr
Falls Church, VA 22042
Tel: (703) 876-3000 Fax: (703) 876-3125
Web: www.gd.com

MCI
Corporate Headquarters
22001 Loundon County Pkwy
Ashburn, VA 20147
John N. Marshall, Program Director,
Corporate Supplier Diversity
Tel: (703) 866-5600
Web: www.mci.com

MEADWESTVACO
Supplier Diversity
1011 Boulder Spring Dr
Richmond, VA 23225
Sally Crook, Manager, Supplier Diversity
Tel: (804) 327-7900 Fax: (804) 327-6334
Web: www.meadwestvaco.com

NEXTEL COMMUNICATIONS
Corporate Headquarters
2001 Edmund Halley Dr.
Reston, VA 20191
Ben Lusvy, Director, Purchasing
Tel: (703) 433-4000
Web: www.nextel.com

NORFOLK SOUTHERN
Corporate Headquarters
3 Commercial Pl.
Norfolk, VA 23510
Doug Clary, Manager, Purchasing
Tel: (540) 981-3086
Email: nsdbe@nscorp.com

NVR
Purchasing
7601 Lewinsville Rd
McLean, VA 22102
Paul Huber, Director, Purchasing
Tel: (703) 956-4000
Web: www.nvrinc.com

OWENS & MINOR
Supplier Diversity
4800 Cox Rd.
Glen Allen, VA 23060
Angela T. Wilkes, Director, Supplier Diversity
Tel: (804) 965-5874 Fax: (804) 965-5403
Email: angela.wilkes@owens-minor.com
Web: www.owens-minor.com

PERFORMANCE FOOD GROUP
Procurement
12500 W. Creek Pkwy.
Richmond, VA 23238
Scott Barnewolt, Director of Procurement
Tel: (804) 484-7700 Fax: (804) 484-7760
Email: sbarnewolt@pfgc.com
Web: www.pfgc.com

SALLIEMAE
Corporate Headquarters
12061 Bluemont Way
Reston, VA 20190
Tel: (703) 810-3000
Web: www.salliemae.com

SMITHFIELD FOODS
Purchasing
200 Commerce St.
Smithfield, VA 23430
Elaine C. Abicht, Vice President
Tel: (757) 365-3000
Web: www.smithfieldfoods.com

US AIRWAYS GROUP
Corporate Headquarters
2345 Crystal Dr.
Arlington, VA 22227
Jamie Jackson
Tel: (703) 872-7000
Web: www.usairways.com

AMAZON.COM
Corporate Headquarters
P. O. Box 81226
Seattle, WA 98108
Tel: (800) 201-7575
Web: www.amazon.com

COSTCO WHOLESALE
Corporate Headquarters
999 Lake Dr.
Issaquah, WA 98027
James P. Murphy, Senior Vice President,
International Operations
Tel: (425) 313-8100

Web: www.costco.com

MICROSOFT
Corporate Headquarters
1 Microsoft Way
Redmond, WA 98052
Tel: (425) 882-8080 Fax: (425) 936-7329
Web: www.microsoft.com

NORDSTROM
Supplier Diversity Program
1617 Sixth Ave.
Seattle, WA 98101
Chrinstine Young, Supplier Diversity Affairs
Tel: (206) 628-2111
Web: www.nordstrom.com

PACCAR
Corporate Headquarters
777 106th Ave.
Bellevue, WA 98004
Tel: (425) 468-7368 Fax: (425) 468-8235
Web: www.paccar.com

SAFECO
Diversity
Safeco Plaza
Seattle, WA 98185
Kevin Carter, Director of Diversity
Tel: (206) 545-5000 Fax: (206) 925-0165
Web: www.safeco.com

STARBUCKS
Vendor Relations
2401 Utah Ave.
Seattle, WA 98134
Dorothy Kim, Executive Vice President,
Supply Chain and Coffee Operations
Tel: (206) 447-1575
Web: www.starbucks.com

WASHINGTON MUTUAL
Corporate Headquarters
1201 Thrid Ave.
Seattle, WA 98101
Tel: (206) 461-2000
Web: www.wamu.com

WEYERHAEUSER
33633 Weyerhaeuser Way St.
Federal Way, WA 98063
Tel: (253) 924-4577 Fax: (253) 924-4692
Email: purchasing.contact@weyerhaeuser.com
Web: www.weyerhaeuser.com

AMERICAN FAMILY INSURANCE GROUP
Supplier Relations
6000 American Pkwy.
Madison, WI 53783
Tel: (608) 249-2111
Email: suppliercontact@amfam.com
Web: www.amfam.com

HARLEY-DAVIDSON
Purchasing
3700 Juneau Ave.
Milwaukee, WI 53208
Mary Evans, Purchasing
Tel: (414) 342-4680
Web: www.harley-davidson.com

JOHNSON CONTROLS
Corporate Headquarters
5757 N. Green Bay Ave
Milwaukee, WI 53201
Larry Alles, Vice President, Global Corporate
Procurement

Tel: (414) 524-1200
Email: diversitybusiness@jci.com
Web: www.johnsoncontrols.com

KOHL'S
Corporate Headquarters
N56 W. 17000 Ridewood Dr.
Menomonee Falls, WI 53051
Tel: (262) 703-7000 Fax: (262) 703-7115
Web: www.kohls.com

MANPOWER
Corporate Headquarters
5301 N. Ironwood Rd.
Milwaukee, WI 53217
Pico Senboutaraj, Manager Supplier
Diversity
Tel: (414) 961-1000
Web: www.manpower.com

NORTHWESTERN MUTUAL
Corporate Headquarters
720 E. Wisconsin Ave
Milwaukee, WI 53202
Tel: (414) 271-1444
Web: www.northwesternmutual.com

ROCKWELL AUTOMATION, INC.
Supplier Diversity
777 E. Wisconsin Ave.
Milwaukee, WI 53202
Dan Buecheo, Supplier Diversity
Tel: (414) 382-0510 Fax: (414) 382-0666
Email: rasupplierdiversity@ra.rockwell.com
Web: www.rockwellautomation.com

ROUNDY'S
Procurement
875 E. Wisconsin Ave
Milwaukee, WI 53202
Joe Becker, Director, Procurement
Tel: (414) 231-5000
Web: www.roundys.com

WISCONSIN ENERGY
Supplier Diversity
231 W. Michigan St.
Milwaukee, WI 53203
Jerry Fulmer, Director, Supplier Diversity
Tel: (414) 221-2345
Web: www.wisconsinenergy.com

WPS RESOURCES
Purchasing
700 N. Adams St.
Green Bay, WI 54307
Carrie Kugel, Manager, Purchasing
Tel: (920) 433-4901
Web: www.wpsr.com

Wondering how to pay for college?

The Coast Guard has the money to help.

Coast Guard Academy:

A free college education and guaranteed job after graduation as a Coast Guard officer.

College Student Pre-Commissioning Initiative:

Receive full tuition for your junior and senior years, books and educational fees, a monthly stipend of approximately $2,000, plus guaranteed job after graduation as a Coast Guard officer

Active Duty Montgomery GI Bill:

Up to $1034 per month for 36 months.

Reserve Montgomery GI Bill:

Up to $297 per month for 36 months.

Tuition Assistance:

Up to $297 per semester hour, up to $4,500 per year.

Coast Guard Foundation Grant:

$350 per student per year for books and other education-related expenses

Coast Guard Mutual Assistance:

Grants of $160 per student per year for the cost of college textbooks, plus interest free loans loans are available.

Servicemember's Opportunity College Coast Guard:

An affiliation of colleges, that assists members in earning an associate degree or a bachelor's degree, and allow Coast Guard members to transfer college credits between schools and reduce their requirements for residency.

For more information, call us toll-free at
1-877-NOW-USCG (1-877-669-8724).

or visit:

Active Duty & Reserve	Civilian
www.gocoastguard.com	www.uscg.mil.civilian jobs

These programs may have additional requirements for participation. Amounts and availability of programs are subject to change. Contact your local Coast Guard recruiter for more information.

A MESSAGE FROM THE COMMANDANT OF THE MARINE CORPS

It is an honor to congratulate TIYM Publishing on the sixth edition of the African American Yearbook. This publication is a valued resource that includes the many achievements of African Americans in our nation.

A number of the Corps' finest leaders are African American. Marines like Major General Cornell A. Wilson Jr., Director, Reserve Affairs, Headquarters Marine Corps, Brigadier General Ronald S. Coleman, Director, Personnel Management Division, HQMC, and Brig. Gen. Anthony L. Jackson, Deputy Commander, U.S. Marine Forces Central Command are but a few.

Another outstanding African American Marine is Captain Keystella Mitchell, a communications officer who was honored with the 2005 Roy Wilkins Renown Service Award during the NAACP's 30th Annual Armed Forces and Veteran Affairs Dinner this past summer.

The dedication and faithful service of these Marines and countless other African American Marines honor the proud heritage of African Americans.

Again, congratulations to the leadership of TIYM Publishing for developing this invaluable resource guide. The United States Marine Corps commends you for recognizing the accomplishments of African Americans throughout our nation. I wish you the very best for future success with this endeavor.

Semper Fidelis,

M. W. Hagee

General, U.S. Marine Corps

Heroes and Heritage
Captain Frederick C. Branch

Drafted into the Marine Corps in 1943, Frederick C. Branch went to boot camp at Camp Montford Point in North Carolina. Montford Point was a segregated Marine Corps training facility near Jacksonville, N.C., created in 1942 to train African American Marines.

Branch served with the 51st Defense Battalion in the South Pacific during World War II. On November 10th, 1945, the 170th birthday of the Marine Corps, Frederick Branch became the first African American to graduate from Officer Candidate School and receive his commission as a 2nd Lieutenant.

Though a reserve officer, Branch continued to serve on active duty and was a battery commander with an anti-aircraft unit at Camp Pendleton. Branch attained the rank of captain before leaving the service in 1952.

(Photos and text provided by the Montford Point Marine Association.)

eployed force designed for expeditionary operations by air, and or sea. It is our size and expertise that allow us to move aster and adapt to rapidly changing situations. Working to vercome disadvantage and turn conflict into victory, we accomplish great things, and we do it as a team.

While innovations and new technology are critical for improving readiness and combat and support capabilities, the Marine Corps never underestimates the importance and value f the individual Marine. We recognize that the individual Marine, with a diverse range of experiences and traditions, is he strength of our Corps.

veryone who joins the Marine Corps has chosen an extremely hallenging route. Marines — officer and enlisted — rise to hallenges, becoming more innovative and creative when aced with problems. Each Marine is encouraged to maximize eadership potential through practice and evaluation, leading o better decisions in real-world situations.

The common denominator is leadership. Marines are required to be leaders and advance based on their potential leadership qualities. Our training is tough. It has to be as Marines take on responsibilities well beyond their years.

As we move into the 21st century, we face a rapidly changing world with complex situations. Our focus must be on training people to make sound decisions under rapidly changing conditions. The Marine Corps must be prepared for what may be called a "three-block war." On one block we may deliver humanitarian assistance to help people survive. Moments later, on the next block, we may be called upon to take a harder line as a peacekeeping force. Finally, if hostilities do erupt, we must be able to win mid-intensity battles on a third block. To effectively make the right decision for the situations we face on each block requires a sharp and agile mind, and the ability to take charge.

HE BRAVE HAVE ALWAYS DEFINED WHAT THE REST OF US WISH TO BE. BUT BRAVERY IS MISUNDERSTOOD. IT IS NOT THE ABSENCE OF FEAR, **BUT THE WILL TO OVERCOME IT.**

Today's Marines

African Americans continue to find opportunities in the service of our Nation. From the lance corporal on the ground in Iraq to the most senior levels of leadership, more than 23,000 African Americans serve in today's Marine Corps.

If you are interested in developing your decision-making abilities and cultivating your leadership skills, consider joining the Marine Corps team. For more information about opportunities to serve in the United States Marine Corps, log on to Marines.com, MarineOfficer.com or call 1-800-MARINES. Keep an open mind. The Marine Corps is unlike anything you have ever experienced. We offer no excuses, and we take none. We make Marines and win battles. No compromises.

The Strength of Our Corps

"Our Marines have always been our greatest strength. Indeed, the Corps' enduring contribution to America is the development of Marines who embrace our service values and warrior culture, selflessly serve their country, and then return to society as outstanding private citizens."

— General Michael W. Hagee,

Commandant of the Marine Corps

Staff Sergeant John B. Noel
Drill Instructor
Marine Corps Recruit Depot, San Diego

Staff Sgt. John B. Noel, drill instructor, platoon 2079, Company H, overcame challenges and turned them into the passion that leads to winning in life.

"I learned people will help you, but you have to be willing to help yourself first. My decision to join the Corps was made with that in mind."

For many of the new recruits Noel trains, Marine Corps recruit training is the toughest challenge they've ever faced.

Captain Keystella Mitchell
Communications Officer
U.S.S. Blue Ridge (LCC-19)

Captain Mitchell was honored with the 2005 Roy Wilkins Renown Service Award from the NAACP.

As a mentor for Choices, a program designed for female Marines and sailors, Mitchell provides counseling on a variety of specific women's issues and concerns.

She is active in the Japanese community with weekly visits and volunteer work at nursing homes and elementary schools.

Major General Walter E. Gaskin
Commanding General
Marine Corps Recruiting Command

Major General Gaskin leads the organization responsible for finding young men and women willing to take up the challenge to become Marines. He entered the Marine Corps through the Naval ROTC program at Savannah State University and is the senior ranking African American Marine on active duty.

Over the course of his 31-year career, Gaskin has served in numerous billets around the world from Okinawa to Italy.

Colonel Ronald Bailey
Director
Expeditionary Warfare School

A native of St. Augustine, Fla., Colonel Bailey has commanded infantry Marine units at every level up to a regiment. He has contributed greatly to the training of young enlisted and officer Marines, with tours at the Marine Corps Recruit Depot, Parris Island, S.C. and in his current billet as the Director of the Expeditionary Warfare School, Quantico, Va. Notably, Bailey holds the distinction of representing the Marine Corps, and DoD, on the 2004-2005 Council on Foreign Relations.

Sergeant Major Barbara Titus
Sergeant Major
Marine Corps Systems Command

Sergeant Major Barbara J. Titus enlisted in the Marine Corps in March 1978. Throughout her career, she participated in various military operations and exercises and has served as a drill instructor, senior drill instructor and chief drill instructor.

She served in Operation Enduring Freedom and Operation Iraqi Freedom with Marine Tactical Air Command Squadron-38, 3rd Marine Air Wing out of Miramar, Calif.

Captain Vernice Armour
Helicopter Pilot
Marine Corps Air Staion Miramar, Calif.

Captain Vernice Armour is notable as the first-ever African American female combat pilot in the U.S. military.

Flying the AH-1W Super Cobra, Armour flew missions during Operation Iraqi Freedom.

"I don't look at this on the basis of gender or color. I'm a Marine Corps officer first, then I try to be the best officer that I can, and try to take care of the Marines in my charge the best way I can."

HEY CAME FROM SMALL TOWNS AND BIG CITIES **TO PROVE THEY BELONG IN THIS PROUD FAMILY**, WHOSE HERITAGE TRAVELS BACK MORE THAN TWO CENTURIES.

SILVER HAWK

rank Petersen, a man of firsts
ut always a Marine.

e following is an excerpt from an article in the Arpil 1998
ue of Marines Magazine.)

tten by Fred Carr Jr.

rank Petersen stood outside his home on the banks
of the Chesapeake Bay on Maryland's Eastern Shore
early February. Gazing upward, he pointed out one
he local landmarks to his visitors. There, high atop
ree, was a bald eagle's nest built strongly enough
defy the winds that sometimes close the nearby
esapeake Bay Bridge. His eyes were a reflection of
e and respect -- even kinship, for Frank Petersen is
"eagle" in his own right.

e bleached homes and wind-thinned pines that line
s area of the Chesapeake Bay are a long ways from
eka, Kansas, where Petersen was born in 1932.
t it is the place he has chosen to quietly enjoy the
ards of a life and career that will forever occupy
ne very notable pages of Marine Corps history.
ong the words that can best describe him are
st," "only," "hero," and "leader."

when asked how he feels about being recognized
the Marine Corps' first black aviator, its first black
eral, and the first African American Marine to wear
ee stars, he said, "We need to move forward to
ize, not capitalize on diversity. It's just a matter of
lizing peoples' talents."

d what talents Petersen had as a Marine! His retire-
nt as the commanding general of the Marine Corps
mbat Development Command at Quantico, Va., in
88 completed a saga that began in 1950 when he
ided to join the Navy.

ere wasn't much happening in Topeka. So when
e of my friends came home on leave from the
bees and started telling me about their travels and
entures, I decided it was time to go see the ocean
the first time in my life."

er recruit training at Naval Training Center San
go, Petersen was sent to school to become a Navy
ctronics technician. There, he heard about the Naval
ation Cadet program and suddenly found himself
a different path toward the adventure and travel
raved.

as sent to Pensacola, Fla., for flight training, and
t's where I met a man who would change my life."

t man was a former enlisted Marine, Dave Camp-
, also a Naval Aviation Cadet. And if things had
ked out a bit differently, the Corps' first African
erican aviator may have been Campbell, not
ersen.

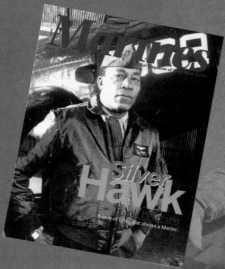

"I was only the fourth black cadet in the program,"
Petersen said. "It was tough training, and Dave ended
up washing out. But before he left, he advised me
there had never been a black aviator in the Corps,
something he had hoped to change. It was up to me to
carry that on."

Petersen persevered and, in October 1952, accepted
a commission as a second lieutenant in the Marine
Corps.

"They gave me orders to Marine Corps Air Station Cherry Point, N.C.," he recalled, "but I told them I would
prefer El Toro, Calif. I didn't know it at the time, but I
had just jumped from the frying pan into the fire."

Petersen got his "dream tour" to California, but it
ended up a short-lived one. The fire he had jumped
into turned out to be Korea where he flew Corsairs with
Marine Fighter Squadron 212 in 60 combat missions.
And it was there that he discovered the "eagle" in
himself, earning the Distinguished Flying Cross and 6
Air Medals.

"It was something, returning to El Toro as a lieutenant
wearing a DFC," he said. "You wouldn't believe some
of the looks I got."

But the attention leveled at Frank Petersen was just
beginning. He transitioned from prop fighters to jets,
while using his off-duty hours to attend night school
so he could qualify for the Bootstrap Program. He
knew he needed to finish college if he was going to be
competitive in the officer Corps.

His studies went more slowly than he preferred, inter-
rupted in part by assignments to Hawaii and Iwakuni,
Japan. Finally, he drew orders to the Amphibious
Warfare School at Quantico where he was able to finish
up his bachelor's degree at nearby George Washington
University. The year was now 1967 and fate was about
to create some new pages in the chronicles of Frank
Petersen.

"I went to Vietnam and took over Marine Fighter Attack
Squadron 314," he said. "It was one of the best as-

signments I had -- we took the title of Fighter Attack
Squadron of the Year in the Corps for 1968."

It was also one of Petersen's most dangerous assignments. In August 1968, his F-4 Phantom was shot
down.

"We had just taken off from Chu Lai," Petersen said,
"to provide close air support for a trapped recon unit.
I was leading the attack as we made a second run on
the target when my left engine was hit and caught fire.

"Both of us (Petersen and his radar intercept officer,
Maj. Ed Edelen) knew if we went down north of the
DMZ, we'd be guests at the Hanoi Hilton for a long
time, so we turned around. We were just about to the
DMZ when the second engine caught fire. We pressed
on. Then the fire crossed over our hydraulics and our
controls locked. We punched."

Petersen and Edelen were fortunate. Both were
rescued, but not before Petersen wrote a footnote to
his ordeal.

"As I was floating down on my chute, I could see the
Marine CH-46 (Sea Knight helicopter) about an eighth
of a mile away off to one side. Directly where I was
headed, though, I saw something else -- Vietnamese
running toward where I was going to land. I didn't
know it at the time, but they weren't interested in me,
they wanted my chute for silk pajamas."

Petersen's uncanny good fortune was illustrated again
before the week was out.

"I couldn't let my Marines think their "old man" was
having second thoughts, so we found another bird and
I was flying again in two days. When I found out what
our target was, I started muttering in my helmet. My
backseater said, 'Skipper, what's wrong?' I said, 'You
aren't gonna believe this, but we're headed right back
to where I got my ass shot down the other day!' But the
second time was a whole different story."

Vietnam safely behind him, Petersen continued his
upward spiral toward the eagle's nest. He commanded
a Marine Aircraft Group, a Marine Amphibious Brigade,
and a Marine Aircraft Wing, carving out many of his
successes during one of the Corps' most contentious
eras.

Petersen retired from the Marine Corps in 1988
and went to work for DuPont, where he rose to
become a vice president, teaching corporate
America about Marine Corps leadership. Retiring
from DuPont in 1997, Petersen now lives in his
home along the Chesapeake and donates his
time to his favorite causes.

COLOR DE HONOR
A COLOR OF HONOR

HONOR. DEBER. PATRI
HONOR. DUTY. COUNTR

From the Creator and Co-Executive Producer of award-winning "**Americanos**" – Latino Life in United States come stories of courage, patrioti and honor.

Author/Producer Manny Monterrey and the Hispa War Veterans of America are proud to present multimedia production "**A Color of Honor** **A Tribute To Latinos in the U.S. Military.**

PORQUE SU LEGADO DEBE CONTINUAF
BECAUSE THEIR LEGACY MUST LIVE ON

For more information about "**A Color of Honor**," or if y wish to send a contribution or become a corporate spon please visit us at:

www.acolorofhonor.org

"A Color of Honor" is a multimedia presentation by Monterrey Productions, Inc., P.O. Box 10425 Colorado Springs, CO 80923-1425. Tel (719) 761-1413.

FIG 1. Active Duty Military Personnel and Total U.S. Population by Race/Ethnicity: 2004

Across all branches of the United States military there are racial and ethnic disparities among active servicemen and women when compared with the total population. One of the most striking differences is the disproportionately high percentage of Black or African Americans currently serving in the Armed Forces. Despite making up about twelve percent of the total U.S. population, African Americans represent eighteen percent of active servicemen and women. Contrast this figure with the White population, which is actually underrepresented by over ten percent, and a picture of disproportion begins to emerge.

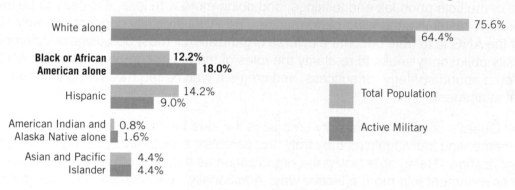

White alone — 75.6% / 64.4%
Black or African American alone — 12.2% / 18.0%
Hispanic — 14.2% / 9.0%
American Indian and Alaska Native alone — 0.8% / 1.6%
Asian and Pacific Islander — 4.4% / 4.4%

Total Population
Active Military

Source: U.S. Census Bureau, Current Population Survey, 2004 and Defense Manpower Data Center Report 3035EO

FIG 2. Active Duty Officers and Total Active Personnel by Race/Ethnicity:

The racial and ethnic distribution among active officers reveals a lack of equality in the Armed Forces. Looking at officer statistics is important because it indicates promotion trends, and likelihood, for each of the different groups. According to the U.S. Department of Defense's own figures, the percentage of officers that are White is over fourteen percent higher than that group's overall representation in the military. For African Americans, there is a nine percent swing in the other direction—only 8.9 percent of total officers are Black, despite making up eighteen percent of total active duty personnel.

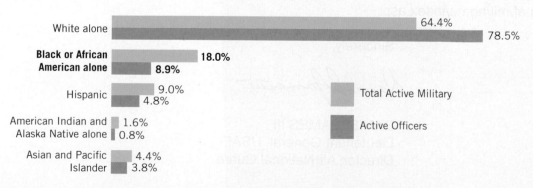

White alone — 64.4% / 78.5%
Black or African American alone — 18.0% / 8.9%
Hispanic — 9.0% / 4.8%
American Indian and Alaska Native alone — 1.6% / 0.8%
Asian and Pacific Islander — 4.4% / 3.8%

Total Active Military
Active Officers

Source: U.S. Census Bureau, Current Population Survey, 2004 and Defense Manpower Data Center Report 3035EO

DEPARTMENTS OF THE ARMY AND THE AIR FORCE
NATIONAL GUARD BUREAU
1411 JEFFERSON DAVIS HIGHWAY
ARLINGTON VA 22202-3231

A MESSAGE FROM THE DIRECTOR OF THE AIR NATIONAL GUARD

Embracing diversity at all levels in our organization will be the key to our success. We must continue to build upon a strong foundation, which entails vision, and demonstrated commitment from the Air National Guard's senior leadership. We must continue to win the war for talent by aggressively recruiting and retaining a high-quality military and civilian workforce that reflects the diverse talents of our citizenry, within key critical occupational skills.

In today's world of multiple priorities and taskings, and doing more with less, it is easy to be involved in activities that don't result in enhancing performance. The ANG diversity concept is a way of thinking that suggests if the ANG is to truly become a diverse organization it must do business differently. As such, our diversity philosophy seeks to re-clarify the roles of the major components of the ANG Diversity Initiative, develop a sound strategy for success, and create a web based measuring tool that indicates the level of goal attainment.

The Air National Guard's concept on diversity embraces the idea that it is critical to see the world, organizations, teams, and individuals as they truly are; complex, constantly adapting living systems that defy easy categorization. Being able to see the organization as it truly is provides agents the ability to navigate the environment in a more effective way. Additionally, collective collaboration between interested groups and enlightened guidance by ANG senior leadership can provide a sincere path toward effective objective achievement.

By thinking strategically about diversity and culture transformation, we can articulate, demonstrate, and detail the ANG commitment to achieving full participation to achieve the highest quality total defense and readiness: "Ready, Reliable, Relevant – Needed Now and in the Future". This strategy affirms our commitment to being at the vanguard of protecting and defending our communities, states and nation.

The Air National Guard's civilian and military personnel join me in congratulating your publication. I also send holiday greetings and best wishes for another successful milestone in your storied history. Establishing a climate that embraces diversity is a strategic goal the Air National Guard can not afford to miss. I invite you to learn more about the climate and transformation of our Air Guard at: http://angdiversity.ang.af.mil/home/index.asp.

Sincerely,

DANIEL JAMES III
Lieutenant General, USAF
Director, Air National Guard

TO ANGELA ZAVALA AND THE TEAM AT TIYM PUBLISHING

It is with great pleasure that I extend congratulations to you on the 20th anniversary of your publishing enterprise. Through hard work and diligence you have etched an indelible mark upon the African American, Hispanic, and Asian American communities by producing a quality resource. Your yearbooks not only inform and educate, but also strengthen and elevate the cause of diversity.

The value of diversity to the nation has always been important, perhaps more now than at any point in our history. The rapidly changing global economy requires us all to embrace people with different perspectives, backgrounds, and experiences in order to remain competitive. For our part, the Navy is making a concerted effort to seek out, challenge, and develop leaders from---and for---all parts of our great country. The Navy recognizes that diversity strengthens us as evidenced by the tremendous contributions of people like 1915 Medal of Honor recipient Fireman 1st Class Telesforo Trinidad, an Asian Pacific American who demonstrated extraordinary heroism despite severe personal injuries. Modern day achievers include Rear Admiral Cecil D. Haney, an African American submarine officer serving as Deputy Chief of Staff for Policy, Plans, and Requirements for the U.S. Pacific Fleet, and Captain Kathlene Contres, the highest ranking Latina on active duty in the United States Navy and who was selected to become Commandant of the Defense Equal Opportunity Management Institute, a joint service school.

These pioneers and so many others have shown us that like the motto engraved upon our coins--- *e pluribus unum* ---our rich diversity serves to truly strengthen the fabric of our nation, and bolsters our values of faith, freedom, family, work and country. They have taught us that while accommodating diversity is essential to ensure every citizen has the opportunity to excel, we gain so much more when we genuinely embrace and invest in the broad talents of all our people. Your yearbooks do a great service by highlighting those talents.

Again, congratulations on 20 terrific years. It is indicative of the esteem in which your company is held and the value accorded to your publications that you have not only survived in a highly competitive industry, but thrived. I wish you and your staff my very best and look forward to seeing you succeed for many years to come.

Sincerely,

M. G. MULLEN
Admiral, U. S. Navy

A Message From General Schoomaker, United States Army
For the TIYM 2006 African-American Yearbook

America is proud of its cultural and ethnic mix and has benefited from each group's contributions. Publications like this Yearbook help raise the awareness of the contributions of African-Americans in our Nation's history, while highlighting opportunities for personal and professional growth.

As an institution that embraces its diverse background, the Army salutes the early African-American Soldiers who courageously overcame obstacles to their service and who faced America's enemies on battlefields throughout the world. We honor them for their sacrifices and for their contributions to making the Army a pioneer institution with respect to racial equality. Because of their commitment, today, more than twenty percent of the Army's total force is African-American.

While diversity in our force fosters creativity and new ideas, the Army aspires to one set of unifying ideals--the seven Army Values of loyalty, duty, respect, selfless service, honor, integrity and personal courage. As we fight the war on terror, Soldiers of all religions, races, and creeds are now sacrificing to ensure the blessings of freedom for people around the world and to preserve America's limitless opportunities. Embodying the essence of our Nation, our Soldiers stand strongly together so that people around the world may benefit.

Thank you to TIYM Publishing Company for your continued programs to promote racial equality and for providing a comprehensive tool to serve members of diverse communities.

Sincerely,

Peter J. Schoomaker
General, United States Army

US Citizenship and Immigration Services

Contact information for the US Citizenship and Immigration Services (USCIS) within the Department of Homeland Security (DHS) is listed below.

ALABAMA

BIRMINGHAM APPLICATION SUPPORT CENTER
Beacon Ctr., 529 Beacon Pkwy. West #106
Birmingham, AL 35209
Tel: (800) 375-5283
Web: http://uscis.gov

ALASKA

ANCHORAGE DISTRICT OFFICE
620 E. 10th Ave. #102
Anchorage, AK 99501
Bernadette Nocerino-Doody, District Director
Tel: (800) 375-5283
Web: http://uscis.gov
Service Area: State of Alaska. The Anchorage District Office has offices at the ports-of-entry located in Ketchikan, Juneau, Fairbanks, Dutch Harbor, and Kodiak.

ARIZONA

PHOENIX APPLICATION SUPPORT CENTER
2545 E. Thomas Rd.
Phoenix, AZ 85016
Tel: (800) 375-5283
Web: http://uscis.gov

PHOENIX DISTRICT OFFICE
2035 N. Central Ave.
Phoenix, AZ 85004
Stephen L. Fickett, District Director
Tel: (800) 375-5283
Web: http://uscis.gov
Service Area: With respect to the submission of application for Service benefits, the Phoenix District Office has jurisdiction over all counties in Arizona with the exception of Cochise, Pima, Santa Cruz, Graham and Pinal, which are served by the Tucson Sub Office. To speak with an Immigration Information Officer, you may make an appointment via the Internet at www.infopass.uscis.gov.

TUCSON APPLICATION SUPPORT CENTER
1835 S. Alvernon #216
Tucson, AZ 85711
Tel: (800) 375-5283
Web: http://uscis.gov

TUCSON SUB OFFICE
6431 S. Country Club Rd.
Tucson, AZ 85706-5907

William N. Johnston, Officer In Charge
Tel: (800) 375-5283
Web: http://uscis.gov
Service Area: The Tucson Sub Office serves Southern Arizona: Pima, Santa Cruz, Cochise, Graham, and Pinal Counties.

YUMA APPLICATION SUPPORT CENTER
3250 S. 4th Ave. #E
Yuma, AZ 85365
Tel: (800) 375-5283
Web: http://uscis.gov

ARKANSAS

FORT SMITH APPLICATION SUPPORT CENTER
4977 Old Greenwood Rd.
Fort Smith, AR 72903
Carol A. Bellew, Officer in Charge
Tel: (800) 375-5283
Web: http://uscis.gov
Service Area: Western Arkansas: The counties of Ashley, Baxter, Benton, Boone, Bradley, Calhoun, Carroll, Clark, Columbia, Crawford, Franklin, Garland, Hempstead, Hot Spring, Howard, Johnson, Lafayette, Little River, Logan, Madison, Marion, Miller, Montegomery, Nevada, Newton, Ouchitta Pike, Polk, Seiver, Scott, Searcy, Sebastion, Union, Washington.
While the following counties generally fall under the responsibility of our Memphis office, persons residing in these counties may find it more convenient to use the information service and the Application Support Center at Fort Smth. From time to time application for persons residing in these counties may be processed in the Fort Smith Office: Arkansas, Chicot, Cleburne, Cleveland, Conway, Dallas Desha, Drew, Faulkner Fulton, Grant, Independence Izard, Jackson Jefferson, Lincoln, Lonoke, , Perry, Pope, Prairie, Pulaski, Saline, Sharp, Stone Van Buren, White, and Yell.

CALIFORNIA

BAKERSFIELD APPLICATION SUPPORT CENTER
4701 Planz Rd. A12
Bakersfield, CA 93309
Tel: (800) 375-5283
Web: http://uscis.gov

BELLFLOWER APPLICATION SUPPORT CENTER
Bellflower Plz., 17610 Bellflower Blvd. #A-110
Bellflower, CA 90706

Tel: (800) 375-5283
Web: http://uscis.gov

BUENA PARK APPLICATION SUPPORT CENTER
8381 La Palma Ave. #A
Buena Park, CA 90620
Tel: (800) 375-5283
Web: http://uscis.gov

CALEXICO APPLICATION SUPPORT CENTER
16 Heffernan Ave.
Calexico, CA 92231
Tel: (800) 375-5283
Web: http://uscis.gov

CALIFORNIA SERVICE CENTER
P.O. Box 30111
Laguna Niguel, CA 92607-0111
Christina Poulos, Acting Director
Tel: (800) 375-5283
Web: http://uscis.gov
Service Area: The CSC accepts and processes certain applications and petitions from locations across the country.

CHULA VISTA CUSTOMER SERVICE CENTER
1261 3rd Ave. #A
Chula Vista, CA 91911
Tel: (800) 375-5283
Web: http://uscis.gov
In order to improve service and shorten wait times, the San Diego District Information Office located in Room 1234 in the Federal Building in Downtown San Diego was merged with the Chula Vista Customer Service Center Information office on December 8, 2003. Customer service at the San Diego District Office will continue by appointment only. Customer service at the Chula Vista Customer Service Center is available only by INFOPASS appointment. You may make an appointment via the Internet at www.infopass.uscis.gov.

EL MONTE APPLICATION SUPPORT CENTER
Golden Vista Plz., 9251 Garvey Ave. #Q
South El Monte, CA 91733
Tel: (800) 375-5283
Web: http://uscis.gov

FAIRFAX APPLICATION SUPPORT CENTER
5949 W. Pico Blvd.
Los Angeles, CA 90035
Tel: (800) 375-5283
Web: http://uscis.gov

FRESNO APPLICATION SUPPORT CENTER
4893 E. Kings Canyon
Fresno, CA 93727
Tel: (800) 375-5283

Web: http://uscis.gov

FRESNO SUB OFFICE
1177 Fulton Mall
Fresno, CA 93721-1913
Don Riding, Officer In Charge
Tel: (800) 375-5283
Web: http://uscis.gov
Service Area: For all services: Fresno, Inyo, Kern, Kings, Madera, Mariposa, Merced, Mono,Tulare, and Stanislaus counties.

GARDENA APPLICATION SUPPORT CENTER, SOUTH LOS ANGELES
15715 Crenshaw Blvd. #B-112
Gardena, CA 90249
Tel: (800) 375-5283
Web: http://uscis.gov

GOLETA APPLICATION SUPPORT CENTER
6831-B Hollister Ave.
Goleta, CA 93117
Tel: (800) 375-5283
Web: http://uscis.gov

LOS ANGELES ASYLUM OFFICE
1585 S. Manchester Ave.
Anaheim, CA 92802
George S. Mihalko, Asylum Office Acting Director
Tel: (800) 375-5283 Fax: (714) 635-8707
Web: http://uscis.gov
Service Area: The Asylum Office in Los Angeles has jurisdiction over the States of Arizona and Hawaii, the Territory of Guam, the following counties in the State of California: Los Angeles, Orange, Riverside, San Bernardino, San Luis Obispo, Santa Barbara, Ventura, Imperial, and San Diego, and that southern portion of the State of Nevada currently within the jurisdiction of the Las Vegas Sub Office.

LOS ANGELES DISTRICT OFFICE
300 N. Los Angeles St. #1001
Los Angeles, CA 90012
Jane Arellano, Director
Tel: (800) 375-5283
Web: http://uscis.gov
Service Area: The Los Angeles District includes Los Angeles, Orange, Riverside, San Bernardino, Santa Barbara, San Luis Obispo, and Ventura counties. To speak with an Immigration Information Officer, you may make an appointment via the Internet at www.infopass.uscis.gov.

LOS ANGELES WILSHIRE APPLICATION SUPPORT CENTER
888 Wilshire Blvd.
Los Angeles, CA 90017
Tel: (800) 375-5283
Web: http://uscis.gov

Source: U.S. Department of Homeland Security, Citizenship and Immigration Services (USCIS).

MODESTO APPLICATION SUPPORT CENTER
901 N. Carpenter Rd. #14
Modesto, CA 95351
Tel: (800) 375-5283
Web: http://uscis.gov

OAKLAND APPLICATION SUPPORT CENTER
2040 Telegraph Ave.
Oakland, CA 94612
Tel: (800) 375-5283
Web: http://uscis.gov

OXNARD APPLICATION SUPPORT CENTER
Carriage Sq. Shopping Ctr.
250 Citrus Grove Ln. #100
Oxnard, CA 93036
Tel: (800) 375-5283
Web: http://uscis.gov

POMONA APPLICATION SUPPORT CENTER
435 W. Mission Blvd. #110
Pomona, CA 91766
Tel: (800) 375-5283
Web: http://uscis.gov

RIVERSIDE APPLICATION SUPPORT CENTER
10082 Magnolia Ave.
Riverside, CA 92503
Tel: (800) 375-5283
Web: http://uscis.gov

SACRAMENTO APPLICATION SUPPORT CENTER
731 K St. #100
Sacramento, CA 95814
Tel: (800) 375-5283
Web: http://uscis.gov

SACRAMENTO SUB OFFICE
650 Capitol Mall
Sacramento, CA 95814
Susan Curda, Officer In Charge
Tel: (800) 375-5283
Web: http://uscis.gov
Service Area: For all Services: The Sacramento Sub Office serves the counties of: Alpine, Amador, Butte, Calaveras, Colusa, El Dorado, Glenn, Lassen, Modoc, Nevada, Placer, Plumas, Sacramento, San Joaquin, Shasta, Sierra, Sutter, Siskiyou, Solano, Tehama, Tuolumne, Yolo, and Yuba. To speak with an Immigration Information Officer, you may make an appointment via the Internet at www.infopass.uscis.gov.

SALINAS APPLICATION SUPPORT CENTER
Santa Rita Plz., 1954 N. Main St.
Salinas, CA 93906
Tel: (800) 375-5283
Web: http://uscis.gov

SAN BERNARDINO SUB-OFFICE
655 W. Rialto Ave.
San Bernardino, CA 92410-3327
Irene Martin, Officer-in-Charge
Tel: (800) 375-5283
Web: http://uscis.gov
Service Area: Riverside and San Bernardino Counties. To speak with an Immigration Information Officer, you may make an appointment via the Internet at www.infopass.uscis.gov.

SAN DIEGO APPLICATION SUPPORT CENTER
2509 El Cajon Blvd.
San Diego, CA 92104
Tel: (800) 375-5283
Web: http://uscis.gov

SAN DIEGO DISTRICT OFFICE
880 Front St. #1234

San Diego, CA 92101
Debra A. Rogers, District Director
Tel: (800) 375-5283
Web: http://uscis.gov
Service Area: The San Diego District Office serves San Diego and Imperial Counties.

SAN FRANCISCO APPLICATION SUPPORT CENTER
250 Broadway
San Francisco, CA 94111
Tel: (800) 375-5283
Web: http://uscis.gov

SAN FRANCISCO ASYLUM OFFICE
75 Hawthorne St. #303S
San Francisco, CA 94107
Emilia Bardini, Asylum Office Director
Tel: (800) 375-5283
Web: http://uscis.gov
Service Area: The Asylum Office in San Francisco has jurisdiction over the following counties in the State of California: Alameda, Alpine, Amador, Butte, Calaveras, Colusa, Contra Costa, Del Norte, El Dorado, Fresno, Glenn, Humboldt, Inyo, Kern, Kings, Lake, Lassen, Madera, Marin, Mariposa, Mendocino, Merced, Modoc, Mono, Monterey, Napa, Nevada, Placer, Plumas, Sacramento, San Benito, San Francisco, San Joaquin, San Mateo, Santa Clara, Santa Cruz, Shasta, Sierra, Siskiyou, Solano, Sonoma, Stanislaus, Sutter, Tehama, Trinity, Tulare, Tuolumne, Yolo, and Yuba. The Asylum Office in San Francisco also has jurisdiction over the portion of Nevada currently under the jurisdiction of the Reno Sub Office, and the States of Oregon, Washington and Alaska.

SAN FRANCISCO DISTRICT OFFICE
630 Sansome St.
San Francisco, CA 94111
David N. Still, District Director
Tel: (800) 375-5283
Web: http://uscis.gov
Service Area: Alameda, Contra Costa, Del Norte, Humboldt, Lake, Marin, Mendocino, Napa, San Francisco, San Mateo, Sonoma, and Trinity Counties. To speak with an Immigration Information Officer, you may make an appointment via the Internet at www.infopass.uscis.gov.

SAN JOSE APPLICATION SUPPORT CENTER
122 Charcot Ave.
San Jose, CA 95131-1101
Tel: (800) 375-5283
Web: http://uscis.gov

SAN JOSE SUB OFFICE
1887 Monterey Rd.
San Jose, CA 95112
Warren Janssen, Officer-in-Charge
Tel: (800) 375-5283
Web: http://uscis.gov
Service Area: The San Jose Sub Office serves the following counties: Santa Clara, Santa Cruz, San Benito, and Monterey. To speak with an Immigration Information Officer, you may make an appointment via the Internet at www.infopass.uscis.gov.

SANTA ANA APPLICATION SUPPORT CENTER
1666 N. Main St. #100-A
Santa Ana, CA 92701
Tel: (800) 375-5283
Web: http://uscis.gov

SANTA ANA SUB OFFICE
34 Civic Ctr. Plz., Federal Bldg.
Santa Ana, CA 92701

Mary J. Kozlowski, Acting Officer-in-Charge
Tel: (800) 375-5283
Web: http://uscis.gov
Service Area: All of Orange County and a portion of South Los Angeles County. To speak with an Immigration Information Officer, you may make an appointment via the Internet at www.infopass.uscis.gov.

SANTA ROSA APPLICATION SUPPORT CENTER
1401 Guerneville Rd. #100
Santa Rosa, CA 95403
Tel: (800) 375-5283
Web: http://uscis.gov

VAN NUYS APPLICATION SUPPORT CENTER
14515 Hamlin St., 2nd Fl. #200
Van Nuys, CA 91411
Tel: (800) 375-5283
Web: http://uscis.gov

VISTA APPLICATION SUPPORT CENTER
727 W. San Marcos Blvd. #101-103
San Marcos, CA 92078
Tel: (800) 375-5283
Web: http://uscis.gov

COLORADO

DENVER APPLICATION SUPPORT CENTER
15037 E. Colfax Ave. #G
Aurora, CO 80011
Tel: (800) 375-5283
Web: http://uscis.gov

DENVER DISTRICT OFFICE
4730 Paris St.
Denver, CO 80239
Mario Ortiz, District Director
Tel: (800) 375-5283
Web: http://uscis.gov
Service Area: The Denver District serves the states of Colorado, Wyoming and Utah. The Denver District Office has a Sub Office in Salt Lake City, Utah; and a Satellite Office in Casper, Wyoming. To speak with an Immigration Information Officer, you may make an appointment via the Internet at www.infopass.uscis.gov.

GRAND JUNCTION APPLICATION SUPPORT CENTER
2454 Highway 6 and 50, Valley Plz. #115
Grand Junction, CO 81505
Tel: (800) 375-5283
Web: http://uscis.gov

CONNECTICUT

HARTFORD APPLICATION SUPPORT CENTER
249 Pearl St.
Hartford, CT 06103
Tel: (800) 375-5283
Web: http://uscis.gov

HARTFORD SUB OFFICE
450 Main St., 4th Fl.
Hartford, CT 06103-3060
Ethan Enzer, Officer In Charge
Tel: (800) 375-5283
Web: http://uscis.gov
Service Area: The State of Connecticut. To speak with an Immigration Information Officer, you may make an appointment via the Internet at www.infopass.uscis.gov.

DELAWARE

DOVER APPLICATION SUPPORT CENTER
Blue Hen Corporate Ctr., 655 S. Bay Rd. #4E
Dover, DE 19901-4699
Tel: (800) 375-5283
Web: http://uscis.gov

DOVER SATELLITE OFFICE
1305 McD Dr.
Dover, DE 19901
Donald Monica, District Director
Tel: (800) 375-5283
Web: http://uscis.gov
Service Area: State of Delaware. Customers are taken on a first-come, first-served basis.

FLORIDA

FT. LAUDERDALE APPLICATION SUPPORT CENTER
11690 State Rd. 84
Davie, FL 33325
Tel: (800) 375-5283
Web: http://uscis.gov

HIALEAH APPLICATION SUPPORT CENTER
Westland Promenade, 3700 W. 18th Ave. #110
Hialeah, FL 33012
Tel: (800) 375-5283
Web: http://uscis.gov

INFORMATION OFFICE
6445 NE 7th Ave.
Miami, FL 33138
Tel: (800) 375-5283
Web: http://uscis.gov
Located inside the American Legion Post.

JACKSONVILLE APPLICATION SUPPORT CENTER
4121 Southpoint Blvd.
Jacksonville, FL 32216
Tel: (800) 375-5283
Web: http://uscis.gov

JACKSONVILLE SUB OFFICE
4121 Southpoint Blvd.
Jacksonville, FL 32216
Louise Germain, Officer-in-Charge
Tel: (800) 375-5283
Web: http://uscis.gov
Service Area: For immigration-related matters, this office serves the following counties: Alachua, Baker, Bay, Bradford, Calhoun, Clay, Columbia, Dixie, Duval, Escambia, Franklin, Gadsden, Gilchrist, Gulf, Hamilton, Holmes, Jackson, Jefferson, Lafayette, Leon, Levy, Liberty, Madison, Nassau, Okaloosa, Putnam, SantaRosa, St. Johns, Suwanee, Taylor, Union, Wakulla, Walton, and Washington. To speak with an Immigration Information Officer, you may make an appointment via the Internet at www.infopass.uscis.gov.

MIAMI APPLICATION SUPPORT CENTER
11865 SW 26th St. (Coral Way) #J-6
Miami, FL 33175
Tel: (800) 375-5283
Web: http://uscis.gov

MIAMI ASYLUM OFFICE
77 SE 5th St., 3rd Fl.
Miami, FL 33131
Erich J. Cauller, Asylum Office Director
Tel: (800) 375-5283
Web: http://uscis.gov

Service Area: The Asylum Office in Miami has jurisdiction over the State of Florida, the Commonwealth of Puerto Rico, and the United States Virgin Islands.

MIAMI-BISCAYNE APPLICATION SUPPORT CENTER
Biscayne Plz., 521 NE 81st St., Bay 11
Miami, FL 33138
Tel: (800) 375-5283
Web: http://uscis.gov

MIAMI DISTRICT OFFICE
7880 Biscayne Blvd.
Miami, FL 33138
Jack Bulger, Director
Tel: (800) 375-5283
Web: http://uscis.gov
Service Area: State of Florida. To speak with an Immigration Information Officer, you may make an appointment via the Internet at www.infopass.uscis.gov.

NATURALIZATION OFFICE
77 SE 5th St., 2nd Fl.
Miami, FL 33131
Tel: (305) 415-6500
Web: http://uscis.gov
The Naturalization Office provides information on naturalization to persons in the Miami area. Scheduled naturalization interviews are conducted at this office.

ORLANDO APPLICATION SUPPORT CENTER
Terracotta Business Ctr., 5449 S Semoran Blvd. #18C
Orlando, FL 32822
Tel: (800) 375-5283
Web: http://uscis.gov

ORLANDO SUB OFFICE
9403 Tradeport Dr.
Orlando, FL 32827
Tel: (800) 375-5283
Web: http://uscis.gov
Service Area: The Orlando Sub Office serves the counties of Orange, Osceola, Seminole, Lake, Brevard, Flagler, Volusia, Marion, and Sumter. To speak with an Immigration Information Officer, you may make an appointment via the Internet at www.infopass.uscis.gov.

TAMPA APPLICATION SUPPORT CENTER
9280 Bay Plz. Blvd. #726
Tampa, FL 33619
Tel: (800) 375-5283
Web: http://uscis.gov

TAMPA SUB OFFICE
5524 W. Cypress St.
Tampa, FL 33607-1708
Kathy Redman, Officer in Charge
Tel: (800) 375-5283
Web: http://uscis.gov
Service Area: The Tampa Sub Office serves the counties of Citrus, Hernando, Pasco, Pinellas, Hillsborough, Polk, Hardee, Manatee, Sarasota, De Soto, Charlotte, and Lee. To speak with an Immigration Information Officer, you may make an appointment via the Internet at www.infopass.uscis.gov.

WEST PALM APPLICATION SUPPORT CENTER
2711 Exchange Ct.
West Palm Beach, FL 33409
Tel: (800) 375-5283
Web: http://uscis.gov

WEST PALM BEACH SATELLITE OFFICE
326 Fern St.
West Palm Beach, FL 33401

John Damone, Officer in Charge
Tel: (800) 375-5283
Web: http://uscis.gov
Service Area: Counties Served: Palm Beach, Martin, St. Lucie, Indian River, Okeechobee, Hendry, Glades, and Highland Counties. To speak with an Immigration Information Officer, you may make an appointment via the Internet at www.infopass.uscis.gov.

GEORGIA

ATLANTA APPLICATION SUPPORT CENTER
1255 Collier Rd.
Atlanta, GA 30318
Tel: (800) 375-5283
Web: http://uscis.gov

ATLANTA DISTRICT OFFICE
Martin Luther King Jr. Federal Bldg.,
77 Forsyth St. SW
Atlanta, GA 30303
Rosemary L. Melville, District Director
Tel: (800) 375-5283
Web: http://uscis.gov
Service Area: Alabama, North Carolina, South Carolina, and Georgia. To speak with an Immigration Information Officer, you may make an appointment via the Internet at www.infopass.uscis.gov.

US IMMIGRATION COURT, EXECUTIVE OFFICE FOR IMMIGRATION REVIEW
77 Forsyth St. SW #112
Atlanta, GA 30303
Tel: (800) 898-7180
Web: http://uscis.gov

GUAM

AGANA APPLICATION SUPPORT CENTER
Sirena Plz., 108 Hernan Cortez Ave. #100
Hagatna, GU 96910
Tel: (800) 375-5283
Web: http://uscis.gov

AGANA SUB OFFICE
Sirena Plz., 108 Hernan Cortez Ave. #100
Hagatna, GU 96910
Robert E. Johnson, Officer In Charge
Tel: (800) 375-5283
Web: http://uscis.gov
Service Area: Guam and the Northern Mariana Islands. To speak with an Immigration Information Officer, you must obtain a ticket, available on a first-come, first-served basis in the lobby of the office.

HAWAII

HONOLULU APPLICATION SUPPORT CENTER
677 Ala Moana Blvd. #102/103
Honolulu, HI 96813
Tel: (800) 375-5283
Web: http://uscis.gov

HONOLULU DISTRICT OFFICE
595 Ala Moana Blvd.
Honolulu, HI 96813
David Gulick , District Director
Tel: (800) 375-5283
Web: http://uscis.gov
Service Area: The Honolulu District Office serves the entire state of Hawaii, Territory of Guam, Commonwealth of Northern Marianas. To speak with an Immigration Information Officer, you may make an appointment via the Internet at www.infopass.uscis.gov.

IDAHO

BOISE APPLICATION SUPPORT CENTER
1185 S. Vinnell Way
Boise, ID 83709
Tel: (800) 375-5283
Web: http://uscis.gov

BOISE SUB OFFICE
1185 S. Vinnell Way
Boise, ID 83709
Robert Mather, Officer In Charge
Tel: (800) 375-5283
Web: http://uscis.gov
Service Area: The Boise Sub Office serves Southwest and South Central Idaho covering the counties of Ada, Gooding, Adams, Jerome, Blaine, Lincoln, Boise, Minidoka, Camas, Owyhee, Canyon, Payette, Cassia, Twin Falls, Elmore, Valley, Gem, and Washington. To speak with an Immigration Information Officer, you may make an appointment via the Internet at www.infopass.uscis.gov.

IDAHO FALLS APPLICATION SUPPORT CENTER
1820 E. 17th St. #190
Idaho Falls, ID 83404
Tel: (800) 375-5283
Web: http://uscis.gov

ILLINOIS

BROADWAY APPLICATION SUPPORT CENTER
4853 N. Broadway
Chicago, IL 60640
Tel: (800) 375-5283
Web: http://uscis.gov

CHICAGO APPLICATION SUPPORT CENTER
888 S. Route 59 #124
Naperville, IL 60540
Tel: (800) 375-5283
Web: http://uscis.gov

CHICAGO ASYLUM OFFICE
401 S. La Salle St., 8th Fl.
Chicago, IL 60605
Robert W. Esbrook, Asylum Office Director
Tel: (800) 375-5283/(312) 353-9607
Web: http://uscis.gov
Service Area: The Asylum Office in Chicago has jurisdiction over the States of Illinois, Indiana, Michigan, Wisconsin, Minnesota, North Dakota, South Dakota, Kansas, Missouri, Ohio, Iowa, Nebraska, Montana, Idaho, and Kentucky.

CHICAGO DISTRICT OFFICE
10 W. Jackson Blvd.
Chicago, IL 60604
Michael Comfort, District Director
Tel: (800) 375-5283
Web: http://uscis.gov
Service Area: The Chicago District includes the states of Illinois, Indiana, and Wisconsin. The Chicago Office serves the state of Illinois and the following counties in Northwest Indiana: Lake, Porter, LaPorte and St. Joseph. To speak with an Immigration Information Officer, you may make an appointment via the Internet at www.infopass.uscis.gov.

CHICAGO-NORRIDGE APPLICATION SUPPORT CENTER
4701 N. Cumberland Ave. #1-3 BCD
Chicago, IL 60706

Tel: (800) 375-5283
Web: http://uscis.gov

PULASKI APPLICATION SUPPORT CENTER
Super Mall, 5160 S. Pulaski Ave. #101
Chicago, IL 60632
Tel: (800) 375-5283
Web: http://uscis.gov

WAUKEGAN APPLICATION SUPPORT CENTER
25 S. Greenbay Rd.
Waukegan, IL 60085
Tel: (800) 375-5283
Web: http://uscis.gov

INDIANA

HAMMOND APPLICATION SUPPORT CENTER
Indianapolis Blvd. (RT. 41),
7852 Interstate Plz. Dr.
Hammond, IN 46324
Tel: (800) 375-5283
Web: http://uscis.gov

INDIANAPOLIS APPLICATION SUPPORT CENTER
950 N. Meridian St. #400
Indianapolis, IN 46204
Tel: (800) 375-5283
Web: http://uscis.gov

INDIANAPOLIS SUB OFFICE
950 N. Meridian St., #400
Indianapolis, IN 46204-3915
Donald Ferguson, Officer In Charge
Tel: (800) 375-5283
Web: http://uscis.gov
Service Area: The State of Indiana except Lake, Porter, LaPorte, and St. Joseph counties in Northwest Indiana. Residents of these four counties are served by the Chicago District Office. To speak with an Immigration Information Officer, you may make an appointment via the Internet at www.infopass.uscis.gov.

IOWA

DES MOINES APPLICATION SUPPORT CENTER
210 Walnut St. #371
Des Moines, IA 50309
Tel: (800) 375-5283
Web: http://uscis.gov

DES MOINES OFFICE
210 Walnut St., Federal Bldg. #369,
Des Moines, IA 50309
Conrad J. Zaragoza, Officer In Charge
Tel: (800) 375-5283
Web: http://uscis.gov
Service Area: This office serves the following counties: Adair, Adams, Allamakee, Appanoose, Benton, Blackhawk, Boone, Bremer, Buchanan, Butler, Calhoun, Cedar, Cerro Gordo, Chickasaw, Clarke, Clayton, Clinton, Dallas, Davis, Decatur, Delaware, Des Moines, Dubuque, Fayette, Floyd, Franklin, Grundy, Guthrie, Hamilton, Hancock, Hardin, Henry, Howard, Humboldt, Iowa, Jackson, Jasper, Jefferson, Johnson, Jones, Keokuk, Kossuth, Lee, Linn, Louisa, Lucas, Madison, Mahaska, Marion, Marshall, Mitchell, Monroe, Muscatine, Polk, Poweshiek, Scott, Story, Tama, Van Buren, Wapello, Warren, Washington, Wayne, Webster, Winnebago, Winneshiek, Worth, and Wright. Please note

that the Nebraska Service Center, located in Lincoln, Nebraska is a regional processing facility adjudicating applications and petitions for a number of states. All questions for the Nebraska Service Center must be directed to that office.

KANSAS

WICHITA APPLICATION SUPPORT CENTER & SATELLITE OFFICE
271 W. 3rd St. North #1050
Wichita, KS 67202-1212
Vacant, Officer In Charge
Tel: (800) 375-5283
Web: http://uscis.gov
Service Area: The Wichita Satellite Office serves the western two thirds of the state of Kansas. To speak with an Immigration Information Officer, you may make an appointment via the Internet at www.infopass.uscis.gov.

KENTUCKY

CHANGE OF ADDRESS
Gene Snyder US Courthouse & Customhouse,
601 W. Broadway #390
Louisville, KY 40202
Tel: (800) 375-5283
Web: http://uscis.gov
Form AR-11, Change of address.

LOUISVILLE APPLICATION SUPPORT CENTER & SUB OFFICE
Gene Snyder US Courthouse & Customhouse,
601 W. Broadway #390
Louisville, KY 40202
Michael J Conway, Officer In Charge
Tel: (800) 375-5283
Web: http://uscis.gov
Service Area: Kentucky for all applications.

LOUISIANA

NEW ORLEANS APPLICATION SUPPORT CENTER
701 Loyola Ave. #T-8011
New Orleans, LA 70113
Tel: (800) 375-5283
Web: http://uscis.gov

MAINE

HOULTON APPLICATION SUPPORT CENTER
Port Of Entry at end of Interstate 95,
POB 189
Houlton, ME 04730
Tel: (800) 375-5283
Web: http://uscis.gov

PORTLAND APPLICATION SUPPORT CENTER
176 Gannett Dr.
South Portland, ME 04106
Tel: (800) 375-5283
Web: http://uscis.gov

PORTLAND DISTRICT
176 Gannett Dr.
South Portland, ME 04106
Rodolfo Lara, District Director
Tel: (800) 375-5283
Web: http://uscis.gov
Service Area: The Portland District serves the States of Maine and Vermont and the Pittsburgh, NH Port of Entry. To speak with

an Immigration Information Officer, you may make an appointment via the Internet at www.infopass.uscis.gov.

MARYLAND

BALTIMORE DISTRICT
Fallon Federal Bldg.,
31 Hopkins Plz.
Baltimore, MD 21201
Richard Caterisano, District Director
Tel: (800) 375-5283
Web: http://uscis.gov
Service Area: The Baltimore District serves the state of Maryland. To speak with an Immigration Information Officer, you may make an appointment via the Internet at www.infopass.uscis.gov.

GLENMONT APPLICATION SUPPORT CENTER
Glenmont Plz., 12331-C Georgia Ave.
Wheaton, MD 20906
Tel: (800) 375-5283
Web: http://uscis.gov

SALISBURY APPLICATION SUPPORT CENTER
119 W. Naylor Mill Rd. #11
Salisbury, MD 21801
Tel: (800) 375-5283
Web: http://uscis.gov

MASSACHUSETTS

BOSTON APPLICATION SUPPORT CENTER
170 Portland St.
Boston, MA 02114
Tel: (800) 375-5283
Web: http://uscis.gov

BOSTON DISTRICT OFFICE
John F. Kennedy Federal Bldg.,
Government Ctr.
Boston, MA 02203
Denis Riordan, Director
Tel: (800) 375-5283
Web: http://uscis.gov
Service Area: The Boston District Office services the state of Massachusetts. To speak with an Immigration Information Officer, you may make an appointment via the Internet at www.infopass.uscis.gov.

MICHIGAN

DETROIT APPLICATION SUPPORT CENTER
2652 E. Jefferson Ave.
Detroit, MI 48207
Tel: (800) 375-5283
Web: http://uscis.gov

DETROIT DISTRICT OFFICE
333 Mt. Elliot
Detroit, MI 48207
Carol Jenifer, District Director
Tel: (800) 375-5283
Web: http://uscis.gov
Service Area: The Detroit District services the State of Michigan including the Upper Peninsula. To speak with an Immigration Information Officer, you may make an appointment via the Internet at www.infopass.uscis.gov.

GRAND RAPIDS APPLICATION SUPPORT CENTER
4484 Breton Rd.
Kentwood, MI 49508

Tel: (800) 375-5283
Web: http://uscis.gov

MINNESOTA

DULUTH APPLICATION SUPPORT CENTER
208 Federal Bldg., 515 W. 1st St.
Duluth, MN 55802
Tel: (800) 375-5283
Web: http://uscis.gov

ST. PAUL APPLICATION SUPPORT CENTER
1360 University Ave. #103
St. Paul, MN 55104
Tel: (800) 375-5283
Web: http://uscis.gov

ST. PAUL DISTRICT
2901 Metro Dr. #100
Bloomington, MN 55425
Denise Frazier, District Director
Tel: (800) 375-5283
Web: http://uscis.gov
Service Area: The St. Paul District serves Minnesota, North Dakota, and South Dakota. The following Wisconsin counties are serviced by the St. Paul USCIS office: Adams, Ashland, Barron, Bayfield, Buffalo, Burnett, Chippewa, Clark, Douglas, Dunn, Eau Claire, Iron, Jackson, Juneau, La Crosse, Lincoln, Marathon, Monroe, Oneida, Pepin, Pierce, Polk, Portage, Price, Rusk, Sawyer, St. Croix, Taylor, Trempealeau, Vernon, Vilas, Washburn, and Wood. To speak with an Immigration Information Officer, you may make an appointment via the Internet at www.infopass.uscis.gov.

MISSISSIPPI

JACKSON APPLICATION SUPPORT CENTER
McCoy Federal Bldg.,
100 W. Capitol St. #B8
Jackson, MS 39269
Tel: (800) 375-5283
Web: http://uscis.gov
Please be sure you have been scheduled to appear for fingerprinting by letter. Do not appear for fingerprinting without an appointment letter. Please note that this location cannot collect digital information for customers who wish to file their applications electronically.

JACKSON SATELLITE OFFICE
Dr. A. H. McCoy Federal Bldg.,
100 W. Capitol St. #727
Jackson, MS 39269
Tel: (800) 375-5283
Web: http://uscis.gov
Service Area: The Jackson office provides Information Services and Application Support Center Services to persons in the central area of Mississippi, consisting of the following counties: Bolivar, Calhoun, Carroll, Chickasaw, Choctaw, Clay, George, Hancock, Harrison, Humphreys, Jackson Leflore, Lowndes, Montgomery, Monroe, Oktibbeha, Pearl, Stone, Sunflower, Tallahatchie, Washington, Webster, Yalobusha Persons residing north of this service area are in the jurisdiction of the Memphis, Tennessee office and should go to that office for services and benefits related issues.

MISSOURI

KANSAS CITY APPLICATION SUPPORT CENTER & DISTRICT OFFICE
9747 NW Conant Ave.
Kansas City, MO 64153
Michael Jaromin, District Director
Tel: (800) 375-5283
Web: http://uscis.gov
Service Area: The Kansas City District includes the states of Missouri and Kansas. The Kansas City District Office serves western Missouri and eastern Kansas. The St. Louis Sub Office serves eastern Missouri. The Wichita Satellite Office serves western Kansas. To speak with an Immigration Information Officer, you may make an appointment via the Internet at www.infopass. uscis.gov.

ST. LOUIS APPLICATION SUPPORT CENTER
1222 Spruce St. #1.100, #1212
St. Louis, MO 63103
Tel: (800) 375-5283
Web: http://uscis.gov

ST. LOUIS SUB OFFICE
Robert A. Young Federal Bldg., 1222 Spruce St. #1.100
St. Louis, MO 63103-2815
Chester Moyer, Officer In Charge
Tel: (800) 375-5283
Web: http://uscis.gov
Service Area: The St. Louis Sub Office services eastern Missouri, which encompasses the Eastern Judicial District of the Federal District Court. To speak with an Immigration Information Officer, you must obtain a ticket, available on a first-come, first-served basis in the lobby of the office.

MONTANA

HELENA APPLICATION SUPPORT CENTER& DISTRICT OFFICE
2800 Skyway Dr.
Helena, MT 59602
Alan Puckett, District Director
Tel: (800) 375-5283
Web: http://uscis.gov
Service Area: We service the states of Montana and Idaho (except for the ten northernmost counties of Idaho, which fall under the jurisdiction of the Seattle District), and the Canadian Provinces of Alberta and Saskatchewan. The geographic area covers 700,000 square miles and includes a total population of over 3,500,000 people. To speak with an Immigration Information Officer, you may make an appointment via the Internet at www.infopass.uscis.gov.

NEBRASKA

INFORMATION OFFICE
1717 Ave. H E
Omaha, NE 68110-2752
Gerard Heinauer, District Director
Tel: (800) 375-5283
Web: http://uscis.gov
Employment Authorization Documents (work cards) and extensions are provided to eligible applicants from 8:00 AM to 12:00 PM at this office.

NEBRASKA SERVICE CENTER
P.O. Box 82521
Lincoln, NE 68501-2521

Evelyn Upchurch, Acting Director
Tel: (800) 375-5283
Web: http://uscis.gov
Form I-102, Application for Replacement/Initial Nonimmigrant Arrival-Departure Document.

P.O. Box 87130
Lincoln, NE 68501-7130
Tel: (800) 375-5283
Web: http://uscis.gov
Form I-129F, Petition for Fiance(e) (Not eligible for Premium Processing) and Form I-130, Petition for Alien Relative (note: those I-130s filed with an I-485 should be sent to the USCIS local office having jurisdiction over your place of residence)

P.O. Box 87131
Lincoln, NE 68501-7131
Tel: (800) 375-5283
Web: http://uscis.gov
Form I-131, Application for Travel Document (Note: If you are submitting Form I-131 and/or Form I-765 with your Form I-485, please send the entire package to the P.O. Box listed for Form I-485. If you are submitting Form I-485, Form I-131, and/or Form I-765 with your Form I-140, please send the entire package to the P.O. Box listed for concurrent filings for Form I-140.

P.O. Box 87485
Lincoln, NE 68501-7485
Tel: (800) 375-5283
Web: http://uscis.gov
Form I-140, Immigrant Petition for Alien Worker (if filed concurrently with Form I-485); Form I-485, Application to Register Permanent Residence or to Adjust Status

P.O. Box 87140
Lincoln, NE 68501-7140
Tel: (800) 375-5283
Web: http://uscis.gov
Form I-140, Immigrant Petition for Alien Worker (if filed alone); Form I-905, Application for Authorization to Issue Certification for Health Care Workers.

P.O. Box 87290
Lincoln, NE 68501-7290
Tel: (800) 375-5283
Web: http://uscis.gov
Form I-290, (Appeals & Motions)

P.O. Box 87360
Lincoln, NE 68501-7360
Tel: (800) 375-5283
Web: http://uscis.gov
Form I-360, Petition for Amerasian, Widow(er), or Special Immigrant (NOTE: Please see Form I-360 more information on where to file this petition.)

P.O. Box 87400
Lincoln, NE 68501-7400
Tel: (800) 375-5283
Web: http://uscis.gov
Service Area: Alaska. Form N-400, Application for Naturalization

P.O. Box 87209
Lincoln, NE 68501-7209
Tel: (800) 375-5283
Web: http://uscis.gov
Form I-485, (Refugee only)

P.O. Box 87589
Lincoln, NE 68501-7589
Tel: (800) 375-5283
Web: http://uscis.gov
Form I-589, Application for Asylum and Withholding of Deportation Fees.

P.O. Box 87698
Lincoln, NE 68501-7698
Tel: (800) 375-5283
Web: http://uscis.gov
Form I-694, Notice of Appeal of Decision; Form I-695, Application for Replacement of Form I-688A, Employment Authorization; or Form I-688, Temporary Resident Card (Under Public Law 99-603); Form I-698, Application to Adjust Status from Temporary to Permanent Resident (Under Section 245A of Public Law 99-603).

P.O. Box 87765
Lincoln, NE 68501-7765
Tel: (800) 375-5283
Web: http://uscis.gov
Form I-765, Application for Employment Authorization (NOTE: If you are submitting Form I-765 with another form, mail your applications to the P.O. Box for the other (principal) form. If you are submitting Form I-131 and/or Form I-765 with your Form I-485, or with your concurrently filed Forms I-140 and I-485, please send the entire package to the P.O. Box listed for concurrent filings for Form I-140.)

P.O. Box 87824
Lincoln, NE 68501-7824
Tel: (800) 375-5283
Web: http://uscis.gov
Form I-824, Application for Action on an Approved Application/Petition (NOTE: If you are submitting Form I-824 with another form, mail your package to the P.O. Box for the other (principal) form.)

P.O. Box 87865
Lincoln, NE 68501-7865
Tel: (800) 375-5283
Web: http://uscis.gov
Form I-865, Sponsor's Notice of Change of Address AND ALL OTHER Change of Address Requests.

P.O. Box 87426
Lincoln, NE 68501-7426
Tel: (800) 375-5283
Web: http://uscis.gov
Form N-426, Request for Certification of Military or Naval Services

P.O. Box 82521
Lincoln, NE 68501-2521
Tel: (800) 375-5283
Web: http://uscis.gov
General Correspondence (Inquiries) (Sending applications or petitions to this address will only delay their processing)

OMAHA APPLICATION SUPPORT CENTER & DISTRICT OFFICE
1717 Ave. H E
Omaha, NE 68110-2752
Gerard Heinauer, District Director
Tel: (800) 375-5283
Web: http://uscis.gov
Service Area: The Omaha District serves the states of Iowa and Nebraska. To speak with an Immigration Information Officer, you may make an appointment via the Internet at www.infopass.uscis.gov

NEVADA

LAS VEGAS APPLICATION SUPPORT CENTER
6175 S. Pecos Rd.
Las Vegas, NV 89120
Tel: (800) 375-5283
Web: http://uscis.gov

LAS VEGAS SUB OFFICE
3373 Pepper Ln.
Las Vegas, NV 89120-2739
Kathleen M. Banos, Acting Officer In Charge
Tel: (800) 375-5283
Web: http://uscis.gov
Service Area: The Las Vegas office serves the Nevada counties of Clark, Esmeralda, Nye, and Lincoln. All other counties in Nevada are serviced by the Reno office.

RENO SUB OFFICE
1351 Corporate Blvd.
Reno, NV 89502
Jerry Garcia, Officer In Charge
Tel: (800) 375-5283
Web: http://uscis.gov
Service Area: The Reno Sub Office serves people residing in Carson, Churchill, Douglas, Elko, Eureka, Humboldt, Lander, Lyon, Mineral, Pershing, Storey, Washoe and White Pine counties.

NEW HAMPSHIRE

MANCHESTER APPLICATION SUPPORT CENTER
803 Canal St.
Manchester, NH 03101
Tel: (800) 375-5283
Web: http://uscis.gov

MANCHESTER SATELLITE OFFICE
803 Canal St.
Manchester, NH 03101
Carole Donovan, Officer In Charge
Tel: (800) 375-5283
Web: http://uscis.gov
Service Area: The State of New Hampshire. To speak with an Immigration Information Officer, you may make an appointment via the Internet at www.infopass.uscis.gov

NEW JERSEY

CHERRY HILL SUB OFFICE
1886 Greentree Rd.
Cherry Hill, NJ 08003
Tel: (800) 375-5283
Web: http://uscis.gov
Service Area: Atlantic, Burlington, Camden, Cape May, Cumberland, Gloucester, Mercer, Monmouth, Ocean, and Salem Counties. To speak with an Immigration Information Officer, you may make an appointment via the Internet at www.infopass.uscis.gov.

HACKENSACK APPLICATION SUPPORT CENTER
116 Kansas St., Main Fl.
Hackensack, NJ 07601
Tel: (800) 375-5283
Web: http://uscis.gov

NEWARK ASYLUM OFFICE
1200 Wall St. West, 4th Fl.
Lyndhurst, NJ 07071
Susan Raufer, Asylum Office Director
Tel: (800) 375-5283
Web: http://uscis.gov
Service Area: The Newark Asylum Office in Lyndhurst, New Jersey, has jurisdiction over the State of New York within the boroughs of Manhattan and the Bronx in the City of New York; the Albany Sub Office; jurisdiction of the Buffalo District Office; the State of Pennsylvania, excluding the jurisdiction of the Pittsburgh Sub Office; and the States of Connecticut, Delaware, Maine, Massachusetts, New Hampshire, New Jersey, Rhode Island, and Vermont.

NEWARK DISTRICT OFFICE
970 Broad St.
Newark, NJ 07102
Andrea Quarantillo, District Director
Tel: (800) 375-5283
Web: http://uscis.gov
Service Area: Bergen, Essex, Hudson, Hunterdon, Middlesex, Morris, Passaic, Somerset, Sussex, Union, and Warren Counties. To speak with an Immigration Information Officer, you may make an appointment via the Internet at www.infopass.uscis.gov

NEW MEXICO

ALBUQUERQUE APPLICATION SUPPORT CENTER
1605 Isleta Blvd. SW #C
Albuquerque, NM 87105
Tel: (800) 375-5283
Web: http://uscis.gov

ALBUQUERQUE SUB OFFICE
1720 Randolph Rd. SE
Albuquerque, NM 87106
Betty Garcia, Officer In Charge
Tel: (800) 375-5283
Web: http://uscis.gov
Service Area: In Northern New Mexico, the counties of: Bernalillo, Catron, Cibola, Colfax, Curry, De Baca, Guadalupe, Harding, Los Alamos, McKinley, Mora, Quay, Rio Arriba, Roosevelt, San Miguel, Sandoval, San Juan, Santa Fe, Socorro, Taos, Torrance, Valencia, and Union. All other counties in New Mexico fall under the direct jurisdiction of the El Paso District Office.

NEW YORK

ALBANY APPLICATION SUPPORT CENTER
1086 Troy-Schenectady Rd.
Latham, NY 12110
Tel: (800) 375-5283
Web: http://uscis.gov

ALBANY SUB OFFICE
1086 Troy-Schenectady Rd.
Latham, NY 12110
Gary Hale, Officer in Charge
Tel: (800) 375-5283
Web: http://uscis.gov
Service Area: The Albany Sub Office serves the following counties in New York State: Albany, Broome, Chenango, Clinton, Columbia, Delaware, Essex, Franklin, Fulton, Greene, Hamilton, Herkimer, Madison, Montgomery, Oneida, Otsego, Rensselaer, Saint Lawrence, Saratoga, Schenectady, Schoharie, Tioga, Warren, and Washington. To speak with an Immigration Information Officer, you may make an appointment via the Internet at www.infopass.uscis.gov.

BUFFALO DISTRICT OFFICE
Federal Ctr., 130 Delaware Ave.
Buffalo, NY 14202
M. Frances Holmes, District Director
Tel: (800) 375-5283
Web: http://uscis.gov
Service Area: All of New York State with the

exception of the following counties: Bronx, Kings (Brooklyn), New York City (Manhattan), Queens, Staten Island, Richmond, Nassau, Suffolk, Dutchess, Orange, Putnam, Rockland, Sullivan, Ulster, and Westchester. To speak with an Immigration Information Officer, you may make an appointment via the Internet at www.infopass.uscis.gov.

NEW YORK ASYLUM OFFICE
1 Cross Island Plz., 3rd Fl.
Rosedale, NY 11422
Patricia Jackson, Asylum Office Director
Tel: (800) 375-5283
Web: http://uscis.gov
Service Area: The Asylum Office in New York has jurisdiction over the State of New York excluding the jurisdiction of the Albany Sub Office, the Buffalo District Office, and the boroughs of Manhattan and the Bronx.

NEW YORK CITY DISTRICT OFFICE
26 Federal Plz.
New York City, NY 10278
Mary Ann Gantner, District Director
Tel: (800) 375-5283
Web: http://uscis.gov
Service Area: New York City: We serve the following counties and 5 Boroughs: (Manhattan, Bronx, Brooklyn, Queens, Staten Island), Nassau, Orange, Suffolk, Westchester, Putnam, Rockland, Dutchess, Ulster, and Sullivan. To speak with an Immigration Information Officer, you may make an appointment via the Internet at www.infopass.uscis.gov

NORTH CAROLINA

CHARLOTTE APPLICATION SUPPORT CENTER
4801 Chastain Ave., Bldg. 10 #175
Charlotte, NC 28217
Tel: (800) 375-5283
Web: http://uscis.gov

CHARLOTTE SUB OFFICE
6130 Tyvola Centre Dr.
Charlotte, NC 28217
Richard Gottlieb, Officer In Charge
Tel: (800) 375-5283
Web: http://uscis.gov
Service Area: North Carolina. To speak with an Immigration Information Officer, you may make an appointment via the Internet at www.infopass.uscis.gov

NORTH DAKOTA

FARGO APPLICATION SUPPORT CENTER
657 2nd Ave. #248
North Fargo, ND 58102
Tel: (800) 375-5283
Web: http://uscis.gov

OHIO

CINCINNATI APPLICATION SUPPORT CENTER & SUB OFFICE
J.W. Peck Federal Bldg.,
550 Main St. #4001
Cincinnati, OH 45202
Helaine Tasch, Officer In Charge
Tel: (800) 375-5283
Web: http://uscis.gov
Service Area: Adams, Brown, Butler, Champaign, Clark, Clermont, Clinton, Darke, Greene, Hamilton, Highland, Lawrence, Miami, Montgomery, Preble, Scioto, Shelby,

and Warren. To speak with an Immigration Information Officer, you may make an appointment via the Internet at www.infopass.uscis.gov.

CLEVELAND APPLICATION SUPPORT CENTER & DISTRICT OFFICE
A.J.C. Federal Bldg., 1240 E. 9th St. #501
Cleveland, OH 44199
Mark B. Hansen, District Director
Tel: (800) 375-5283
Web: http://uscis.gov
Service Area: The Cleveland District Office has jurisdiction over the entire state of Ohio. The office services the following counties: Allen, Ashland, Ashtabula, Auglaize, Carroll, Columbiana, Crawford, Cuyahoga, Defiance, Erie, Fulton, Geauga, Hancock, Hardin, Henry, Holmes, Huron, Lake, Lorain, Lucas, Mahoning, Marion, Medina, Mercer, Ottawa, Paulding, Portage, Putnam, Richland, Ross, Sandusky, Seneca, Stark, Summit, Trumbull, Tuscarawas, Union, Van Wert, Wayne, Williams, Wood, and Wyandot. To speak with an Immigration Information Officer, you may make an appointment via the Internet at www.infopass.uscis.gov.

COLUMBUS APPLICATION SUPPORT CENTER & SATELLITE OFFICE
Leveque Tower, 50 W. Broad St. #306
Columbus, OH 43215
Cheryl Gallegos, Officer In Charge
Tel: (800) 375-5283
Web: http://uscis.gov
Service Area: Athens, Belmont, Coshocton, Delaware, Fairfield, Fayette, Franklin, Gallia, Guernsey, Harrison, Hocking, Jackson, Jefferson, Knox, Licking, Logan, Madison, Meigs, Monroe, Morgan, Morrow, Muskingum, Noble, Perry, Pickaway, Pike, Ross, Union, Vinton, and Washington. To speak with an Immigration Information Officer, you may make an appointment via the Internet at www.infopass.uscis.gov

OKLAHOMA

OKLAHOMA CITY APPLICATION SUPPORT CENTER
4400 SW 44th St. #A
Oklahoma City, OK 73119
Tel: (800) 375-5283
Web: http://uscis.gov

OKLAHOMA CITY SUB OFFICE
4400 SW 44th St. #A
Oklahoma City, OK 73119-2800
Barry C. Royce, Officer-In-Charge
Tel: (800) 375-5283
Web: http://uscis.gov
Service Area: The Oklahoma City Sub Office serves all of Oklahoma. To speak with an Immigration Information Officer, you may make an appointment via the Internet at www.infopass.uscis.gov

OREGON

PORTLAND APPLICATION SUPPORT CENTER
721 SW 14th Ave.
Portland, OR 97205
Tel: (800) 375-5283
Web: http://uscis.gov

PORTLAND, OREGON DISTRICT OFFICE
511 NW Broadway
Portland, OR 97209
William McNamee, District Director

Tel: (800) 375-5283
Web: http://uscis.gov
Service Area: The Portland District services the entire state of Oregon. To speak with an Immigration Information Officer, you may make an appointment via the Internet at www.infopass.uscis.gov

PENNSYLVANIA

PHILADELPHIA APPLICATION SUPPORT CENTER
120 N. 8th St.
Philadelphia, PA 19107
Tel: (800) 375-5283
Web: http://uscis.gov

PHILADELPHIA DISTRICT OFFICE
1600 Callowhill St.
Philadelphia, PA 19130
Donald Monica, District Director
Tel: (800) 375-5283
Web: http://uscis.gov
Service Area: The States of: Pennsylvania, Delaware, and West Virginia. The Philadelphia District Office serves the state of Delaware and the eastern Pennsylvania counties of: Adams, Berks, Bucks, Cameron, Carbon, Centre, Chester, Clinton, Columbia, Cumberland, Dauphin, Delaware, Franklin, Fulton, Huntingdon, Juniata, Lackawanna, Lancaster, Lebanon, Lehigh, Luzerne, Lycoming, Mifflin, Monroe, Montgomery, Montour, Northampton, Northumberland, Perry, Philadelphia, Pike, Potter, Schuykill, Snyder, Sullivan, Susquehanna, Tioga, Union, Wayne, Wyoming, and York. To speak with an Immigration Information Officer, you may make an appointment via the Internet at www.infopass.uscis.gov.

PITTSBURGH APPLICATION SUPPORT CENTER
800 Penn Ave. #101
Pittsburgh, PA 15222
Tel: (800) 375-5283
Web: http://uscis.gov

PITTSBURGH SUB OFFICE
3000 Sidney St. #241
Pittsburgh, PA 15203
Debra Zamberry, Officer in Charge
Tel: (800) 375-5283
Web: http://uscis.gov
Service Area: The Pittsburgh Sub Office serves the State of West Virginia and the western Pennsylvania counties of: Allegheny, Armstrong, Beaver, Bedford, Blair, Bradford, Butler, Cambria, Clarion, Clearfield, Crawford, Elk, Erie, Fayette, Forest, Greene, Indiana, Jefferson, Lawrence, McKean, Mercer, Somerset, Venango, Warren, Washington, and Westmoreland. To speak with an Immigration Information Officer, you may make an appointment via the Internet at www.infopass.uscis.gov.

YORK APPLICATION SUPPORT CENTER
3400 Concord Rd.
York, PA 17402
Tel: (800) 375-5283
Web: http://uscis.gov

PUERTO RICO

SAN JUAN DISTRICT OFFICE
San Patricio Office Ctr., 7
Tabonuco St. #100
Guaynabo, PR 00968
Maria Del Mar Arana, District Director

Tel: (800) 375-5283
Web: http://uscis.gov
Service Area: The San Juan District Office serves the entire island of Puerto Rico and the U.S. Virgin Islands. To speak with an Immigration Information Officer, you may make an appointment via the Internet at www.infopass.uscis.gov.

SAN JUAN, PR APPLICATION SUPPORT CENTER
458 Ing. Jose Canals St.
San Juan, PR 00918
Tel: (800) 375-5283
Web: http://uscis.gov

RHODE ISLAND

PROVIDENCE SUB OFFICE
200 Dyer St.
Providence, RI 02903
Jeffrey Trecartin, Officer In Charge
Tel: (800) 375-5283
Web: http://uscis.gov
Service Area: The State of Rhode Island. To speak with an Immigration Information Officer, you may make an appointment via the Internet at www.infopass.uscis.gov.

PROVIDENCE/CRANSTON, RI APPLICATION SUPPORT CENTER
Cross Roads Office Park, 105 Sockanosset Cross Rd. #210
Cranston, RI 02920
Tel: (800) 375-5283
Web: http://uscis.gov

SOUTH CAROLINA

CHARLESTON APPLICATION SUPPORT CENTER
Parkshore Ctr., 1 Poston Rd. #130
Charleston, SC 29407
Tel: (800) 375-5283
Web: http://uscis.gov
Please be sure you have been scheduled to appear for fingerprinting by letter. Do not appear for fingerprinting without an appointment letter. Please note that this location cannot collect digital information for customers who wish to file their applications electronically.

CHARLESTON OFFICE
Parkshore Ctr., 1 Poston Rd. #130
Charleston, SC 29407
Jerri Adair, Officer In Charge
Tel: (800) 375-5283
Web: http://uscis.gov
Service Area: Together with the satellite office in Greer, South Carolina, the Charleston Office services the entire state of South Carolina. To speak with an Immigration Information Officer, you must obtain a ticket, available on a first-come-first-served basis in the lobby of the office.

GREER, SC - SATELLITE OFFICE
142D W. Phillips Rd.
Greer, SC 29650
Tel: (800) 375-5283
Web: http://uscis.gov
Greer, SC - Satellite office (serves the "up-state" of South Carolina)

SOUTH DAKOTA

RAPID CITY APPLICATION SUPPORT CENTER
1675 Samco Rd.

Rapid City, SD 57702
Tel: (800) 375-5283
Web: http://uscis.gov

SIOUX FALLS APPLICATION SUPPORT CENTER
Riverside Station, 300 E. 8th St.
Sioux Falls, SD 57103
Tel: (800) 375-5283
Web: http://uscis.gov

TENNESSEE

MEMPHIS APPLICATION SUPPORT CENTER
1341 Sycamore View #100
Memphis, TN 38134
Tel: (800) 375-5283
Web: http://uscis.gov

MEMPHIS SUB OFFICE
842 Virginia Run Cove
Memphis, TN 38122
Tel: (800) 375-5283
Web: http://uscis.gov
Due to the devastation of Hurricane Katrina, the operations of the New Orleans District Office have been moved temporarily into this office. Service Area: Tennessee; The following counties in the State of Mississippi: Alcorn, Attala, Benton, Coahoma, Desoto, Grenada, Itawamba, Lafayette, Lee, Marshall, Panola, Pontotoc, Prentiss, Quitman, Tate, Tippah, Tishomingo, Tunica, Union, Winston. The following Counties in the State of Arkansas: Arkansas**, Chicot*, Clay, Cleburne**, Cleveland**, Conway**, Craighead, Crittenden, Cross, Dallas**, Desha*, Drew*, Faulkner**, Fulton**, Grant**, Greene, Independence**, Izard**, Jackson**, Jefferson**, Lawrence, Lee, Lincoln**, Lonoke**, Mississippi, Monroe, Perry**, Phillips, Poinsett, Pope**, Prairie**, Pulaski**, Randolph, St. Francis, Saline**, Sharp**, Stone**, Van Buren**, White**, Woodruff, and Yell**. Persons living in the counties marked with ** in the State of Arkansas may utilize our Fort Smith sub office for Information services or if they need to visit an Application Support Center. However applications which must be filed locally, except Form I-90, will be accepted at and processed through the Memphis Office.

NASHVILLE APPLICATION SUPPORT CENTER
247 Venture Cr.
Nashville, TN 37228
Tel: (800) 375-5283
Web: http://uscis.gov

NEW ORLEANS DISTRICT
842 Virginia Run Cove
Memphis, TN 38122
Tel: (800) 375-5283
Web: http://uscis.gov
Due to the devastation of Hurricane Katrina, the operations of this office have been moved temporarily into the Memphis, Tennessee Sub-Office. To speak with an Immigration Information Officer, you may make an appointment via the Internet at www.infopass.uscis.gov

TEXAS

BROWNSVILLE APPLICATION SUPPORT CENTER
Southwind Shopping Ctr., 943 N. Expressway 77 #23

Brownsville, TX 78520
Tel: (800) 375-5283
Web: http://uscis.gov

DALLAS APPLICATION SUPPORT CENTER
Village at Bachman Lake,
3701 W. Northwest Hwy. #211
Dallas, TX 75220
Tel: (800) 375-5283
Web: http://uscis.gov

DALLAS DISTRICT OFFICE
8101 N. Stemmons Freeway
Dallas, TX 75247
Angela Barrows, District Director
Tel: (800) 375-5283
Web: http://uscis.gov
Service Area: The Dallas District Office serves all of Dallas, Fort Worth, Irving, North and Central Texas (Panhandle and North of Waco). The following counties in Texas: Anderson, Andrews, Archer, Armstrong, Bailey, Baylor, Borden, Bosque, Bowie, Briscoe, Callahan, Camp, Carson, Cass, Castro, Cherokee, Childress, Clay, Cochran, Collin, Collingsworth, Comanche, Cooke, Cottle, Crosby, Dallam, Dallas, Dawson, Deaf Smith, Delta, Denton, Dickens, Donley, Eastland, Ellis, Erath, Fannin, Fisher, Floyd, Foard, Franklin, Freestone, Gaines, Garza, Gray, Grayson, Gregg, Hale, Hall, Hamilton, Hansford, Hardeman, Harison, Hartley, Haskell, Hemphill, Henderson, Hill, Hockley, Hood, Hopkins, Houston, Howard, Hunt, Hutchinson, Jack, Johnson, Jones, Kaufman, Kent, King, Knox, Lamar, Lamb, Leon, Limestone, Lipscomb, Lubbock, Lynn, Marion, Martin, Mitchell, Montague, Moore, Morris, Motley, Navarro, Nolan, Ochiltree, Oldham, Palo Pinto, Panola, Parker, Parmer, Potter, Rains, Randall, Red River, Roberts, Rockwall, Rusk, Scurry, Shackelford, Sherman, Smith, Somervell, Stephens, Stonewall, Swisher, Tarrant, Taylor, Terry, Throckmorton, Titus, Upshur, Van Zandt, Wheeler, Wichita, Willbarger, Wise, Wood, Yoakum, and Young. To speak with an Immigration Information Officer, you may make an appointment via the Internet at www.infopass.uscis.gov.

EL PASO DISTRICT OFFICE
1545 Hawkins Blvd. #167
El Paso, TX 79925
Raymond Adams, District Director
Tel: (800) 375-5283
Web: http://uscis.gov
Service Area: The El Paso District's area of operation includes the City and County of El Paso, 15 adjacent West Texas counties (Brewster, Crane, Culberson, Ector, Hudspeth, Jeff Davis, Loving, Midland, Pecos, Presidio, Reeves, Terrell, Upton, Ward and Winkler), and the state of New Mexico. To speak with an Immigration Information Officer, you may make an appointment via the Internet at www.infopass.uscis.gov.

FT. WORTH APPLICATION SUPPORT CENTER
Ft. Worth Town Ctr. Mall,
4200 S. Freeway #1309
Ft. Worth, TX 76115
Tel: (800) 375-5283
Web: http://uscis.gov

HARLINGEN DISTRICT OFFICE
1717 Zoy St.
Harlingen, TX 78552
Alfonso R. De Leon, District Director
Tel: (800) 375-5283
Web: http://uscis.gov
Service Area: The Harlingen District has

jurisdiction over the following counties located in the southernmost tip of the state of Texas: Brooks, Cameron, Hidalgo, Kennedy, Kleberg, Starr, and Willacy. To speak with an Immigration Information Officer, you may make an appointment via the Internet at www.infopass.uscis.gov.

HOUSTON APPLICATION SUPPORT CENTER
Corum Plz., 8505-D Gulf Freeway
Houston, TX 77017
Tel: (800) 375-5283
Web: http://uscis.gov

HOUSTON ASYLUM OFFICE
16630 Imperial Valley Dr. #200
Houston, TX 77060
Marie Hummert, Asylum Office Director
Tel: (800) 375-5283/(281) 774-4830
Web: http://uscis.gov
This Asylum Office serves the States of Louisiana, Arkansas, Mississippi, Tennessee, Texas, Oklahoma, New Mexico, Colorado, Utah, and Wyoming. Application status cannot be checked on a walk-in basis. Please submit your request in writing.

HOUSTON DISTRICT OFFICE
126 Northpoint Dr.
Houston, TX 77060
Sharon A. Hudson, District Director
Tel: (800) 375-5283
Web: http://uscis.gov
Service Area: 30 counties in southeastern Texas: Angelina, Austin, Brazoria, Chambers, Colorado, Fort Bend, Galveston, Grimes, Hardin, Harris, Jasper, Jefferson, Liberty, Madison, Matagorda, Montgomery, Nacogdoches, Newton, Orange, Polk, Sabine, San Augustine, San Jacinto, Shelby, Trinity, Tyler, Walker, Waller, Washington (for all services except Naturalization), and Wharton. Customers residing in Washington County who need assistance with naturalization issues or who are scheduled for naturalization interviews fall under the jurisdiction of the San Antonio District. To speak with an Immigration Information Officer, you may make an appointment via the Internet at www.infopass.uscis.gov.

HOUSTON NW APPLICATION SUPPORT CENTER
10555 NW Freeway #150
Houston, TX 77092
Tel: (800) 375-5283
Web: http://uscis.gov

LAREDO APPLICATION SUPPORT CENTER
707 E. Calton Rd. #301
Laredo, TX 78041
Tel: (800) 375-5283
Web: http://uscis.gov

LUBBOCK APPLICATION SUPPORT CENTER
3502 Slide Rd. #A-24
Lubbock, TX 79414
Tel: (800) 375-5283
Web: http://uscis.gov

MCALLEN APPLICATION SUPPORT CENTER
220 S. Bicentennial #C
McAllen, TX 78501
Tel: (800) 375-5283
Web: http://uscis.gov

SAN ANTONIO DISTRICT OFFICE
8940 Fourwinds Dr.
San Antonio, TX 78239
Kenneth Pasquarell, District Director
Tel: (800) 375-5283
Web: http://uscis.gov

Service Area: 78 counties of Central and South Texas, which includes major cities such as San Antonio, Austin, Waco, San Angelo, College Station/Bryan, Victoria, Corpus Christi, Kerrville, Uvalde, Del Rio, Eagle Pass, and Laredo. To speak with an Immigration Information Officer, you may make an appointment via the Internet at www.infopass.uscis.gov.

SOUTH DALLAS APPLICATION SUPPORT CENTER
7334 S. Westmoreland Rd.
Dallas, TX 75237
Tel: (800) 375-5283
Web: http://uscis.gov

SW HOUSTON APPLICATION SUPPORT CENTER
Fondren Rd. Plz., 7086 Bissonnet St.
Houston, TX 77074
Tel: (800) 375-5283
Web: http://uscis.gov

TEXAS SERVICE CENTER
P.O. Box 851488
Mesquite, TX 75185-1488
Lisa Kehl, Acting Director
Tel: (800) 375-5283
Web: http://uscis.gov
Service Area: The Texas Service Center accepts and processes certain applications and petitions from individuals residing in the following states: Alabama, Arkansas, Florida, Georgia, Kentucky, Louisiana, Mississippi, New Mexico, North Carolina, South Carolina, Oklahoma, Tennessee, and Texas.
P.O. Box 851204
Mesquite, TX 75185-1204
Tel: (800) 375-5283
Web: http://uscis.gov
Service area: Alabama.
Form N-400, Naturalization.

P.O. Box 851182
Mesquite, TX 75185-1182
Tel: (800) 375-5283
Web: http://uscis.gov
Form I-131, Application for Travel Document; Form I-824, Application for Action on an Approved Application/Petition; Form I-102, Application for Replacement/Initial Nonimmigrant Arrival-Departure Document; I-539, Application to Extend/Change Nonimmigrant.

P.O. Box 850997
Mesquite, TX 75185-0997
Tel: (800) 375-5283
Web: http://uscis.gov
Form I-765, Application for Employment; Form I-821, Application for Temporary Protected Status (El Salvador)

P.O. Box 853062
Mesquite, TX 75185-3062
Tel: (800) 375-5283
Web: http://uscis.gov
Form I-765, Application for Employment; Form I-821, Application for Temporary Protected Status (Mitch)

P.O. Box 851804
Mesquite, TX 75185-1804
Tel: (800) 375-5283
Web: http://uscis.gov
Form I-485, Application to Register Permanent Residence or to Adjust Status; I-181, Adjustment

P.O. Box 852211
Mesquite, TX 75185-2211
Tel: (800) 375-5283

US Citizenship and Immigration Services - Texas

Web: http://uscis.gov
Form I-129, Non-Immigrant Petition

P.O. Box 850919
Mesquite, TX 75185-0919
Tel: (800) 375-5283
Web: http://uscis.gov
Form I-130, Alien Relative Petition

P.O. Box 851892
Mesquite, TX 75185-1892
Tel: (800) 375-5283
Web: http://uscis.gov
Form I-589, Application For Asylum, I-213, FD258

P.O. Box 851391
Mesquite, TX 75185-1391
ATTN: E-Filed I-140,
Tel: (800) 375-5283
Web: http://uscis.gov
Form I-140, Immigrant Petition for Alien Worker (if filed alone); I-290 A&B, Notice of Appeal to the Administrative Appeals Unit (AAU); Form I-360, Petition for Amerasian, Widow(er), or Special Immigrant; Form I-526, Immigrant Petition By Alien Entrepreneur; Form I-829, Petition by Entrepreneur to Remove Conditions, Form I-140 Immigrant Petition for Alien Worker (if concurrently filed with I-485)

P.O. Box 851983
Mesquite, TX 75185-1983
Tel: (800) 375-5283
Web: http://uscis.gov
Form I-90, Application to Replace Permanent Resident - E-Filing

P.O. Box 850965
Mesquite, TX 75185-0965
Tel: (800) 375-5283
Web: http://uscis.gov
Form I-129F, Petition for Alien Fiance(e); Form I-212, Application for Permission to Reapply for Admission into the U.S. After Deportation or Removal; Form I-612, Application for Waiver of the Foreign Residence Requirement; Form I-751, Petition to Remove the Conditions on Residence; I-817, Application for Family Unity Benefits; All I-72 and RFE Responses

P.O. Box 279030
Dallas, TX 75227-0930
Tel: (800) 375-5283
Web: http://uscis.gov
Premium Processing

P.O. Box 851488
Mesquite, TX 75185-1488
Tel: (800) 375-5283
Web: http://uscis.gov
General Correspondence

UTAH

SALT LAKE CITY APPLICATION SUPPORT CENTER
5536 S. 1900 West St. #C
Taylorsville, UT 84118
Tel: (800) 375-5283
Web: http://uscis.gov

SALT LAKE CITY SUB OFFICE
5272 S. College Dr. #100
Murray, UT 84123
Allan Speirs, Officer In Charge
Tel: (800) 375-5283
Web: http://uscis.gov
Service Area: The Salt Lake City Sub Office serves the entire State of Utah. To speak with an Immigration Information Officer, you must obtain a ticket, available on a first-come, first-served basis in the lobby of the office.

VERMONT

CHARLOTTE AMALIE SUB OFFICE
8000 Nisky Ctr., 1st Fl. South #1A
Charlotte Amalie, St. Thomas, VI 00802
Jerome Kettles, Officer in Charge
Tel: (800) 375-5283
Web: http://uscis.gov
Service Area: The Charlotte Amalie Sub Office serves St. Thomas, St. John, and Walter Island, U.S. Virgin Islands.

ST. CROIX APPLICATION SUPPORT CENTER
Sunny Isles Shopping Ctr. #5-8A
Christiansted, St. Croix, VI 00820
Tel: (800) 375-5283
Web: http://uscis.gov
Please be sure you have been scheduled to appear for fingerprinting by letter. Do not appear for fingerprinting without an appointment letter. Please note that this location cannot collect digital information for customers who wish to file their applications electronically.

ST. CROIX SUB OFFICE
Sunny Isle Shopping Ctr. #5-A
Christiansted, St. Croix, VI 00823
Carol Harry, Officer in Charge
Tel: (800) 375-5283
Web: http://uscis.gov
Service Area: The St. Croix Sub Office serves the entire island of St. Croix, U.S. Virgin Islands.

ST. THOMAS APPLICATION SUPPORT CENTER
S. Nisky Ctr., 1st Fl. #1A
St. Thomas, VI 00802
Tel: (800) 375-5283
Web: http://uscis.gov

ST. ALBANS APPLICATION SUPPORT CENTER
64 Gricebrook Rd.
St. Albans, VT 05478
Tel: (800) 375-5283
Web: http://uscis.gov

ST. ALBANS SUB OFFICE
64 Gricebrook Rd.
Saint Albans, VT 05478
Pauline D. Smith, Officer In Charge
Tel: (800) 375-5283
Web: http://uscis.gov
An Immigration Information Officer is located at the front counter. It is not necessary to take a number for assistance.

VERMONT SERVICE CENTER
75 Lower Welden St.
Saint Albans, VT 05479
Paul Novak, Director
Tel: (800) 375-5283
Web: http://uscis.gov

VIRGINIA

ALEXANDRIA APPLICATION SUPPORT CENTER
8850 Richmond Hwy. #100
Alexandria, VA 22309-1586
Tel: (800) 375-5283
Web: http://uscis.gov

ARLINGTON ASYLUM OFFICE
1525 Wilson Blvd. #300
Arlington, VA 22209
Marla J. Belvedere, Asylum Office Director
Tel: (800) 375-5283
Web: http://uscis.gov
Service Area: The Asylum Office in Arlington has jurisdiction over the District of Columbia, the western portion of the State of Pennsylvania currently within the jurisdiction of the Pittsburgh Sub Office, and the States of Maryland, Virginia, West Virginia, North Carolina, Georgia, Alabama, and South Carolina.

NORFOLK SUB OFFICE
5280 Henneman Dr.
Norfolk, VA 23513
Mary Ann Russell, Officer In Charge
Tel: (800) 375-5283
Web: http://uscis.gov
Service Area: The Norfolk Sub Office serves the residents of southeastern Virginia including the cities and/or counties of Chesapeake, Fredericksburg, Richmond, Prince Edwards, Rockville, Williamsburg, Hampton Roads, Accomack, and Mecklenburg.

WASHINGTON DISTRICT OFFICE
2675 Prosperity Avenue
Fairfax, VA 22031
Phyllis Howard, District Director
Tel: (800) 375-5283
Web: http://uscis.gov
Service Area: District of Columbia and the Commonwealth of Virginia. This office is responsible for processing most immigration benefit applications (such as legal residence and naturalization), and enforcing US immigration law, for the entire state of Virginia and the District of Columbia. To speak with an Immigration Information Officer, you may make an appointment via the Internet at www.infopass.uscis.gov

WASHINGTON

SEATTLE APPLICATION SUPPORT CENTER
12500 Tukwila International Blvd.
Seattle, WA 98168
Tel: (800) 375-5283
Web: http://uscis.gov

SEATTLE DISTRICT OFFICE
815 Airport Way South
Seattle, WA 98134
Robert J. Okin, District Director
Tel: (800) 375-5283
Web: http://uscis.gov
Service Area: Seattle District Office: King, Pierce, Thurston, Clallam, Jefferson, Grays Harbor, Mason, Whatcom, Skagit, Snohomish, Lewis, Pacific, Wahkiakum, Cowlitz, Clark, Skamania, Kitsap counties. To speak with an Immigration Information Officer, you may make an appointment via the Internet at www.infopass.uscis.gov.

SPOKANE APPLICATION SUPPORT CENTER
920 W. Riverside #691
Spokane, WA 99201
Tel: (800) 375-5283
Web: http://uscis.gov

SPOKANE SUB OFFICE
US Courthouse, 920 W. Riverside #691
Spokane, WA 99201
Diana Wolder, Officer-In-Charge
Tel: (800) 375-5283
Web: http://uscis.gov
Service Area includes the following counties:

In Washington: Adams, Benton, Chelan, Asotin, Columbia, Douglas, Ferry, Franklin, Garfield, Grant, Lincoln, Okanogan, Pend O'reille, Spokane, Stevens, Walla Walla, and Whitman. In Idaho: Benewah, Bonner, Boundary, Clearwater, Idaho, Kootenai, Latah, Lewis, Nez Perce, and Shoshone. To speak with an Immigration Information Officer, you may make an appointment via the Internet at www.infopass.uscis.gov.

YAKIMA APPLICATION SUPPORT CENTER & SUB OFFICE
415 N. 3rd St.
Yakima, WA 98901
Keith Brown, Officer In Charge
Tel: (800) 375-5283
Web: http://uscis.gov
Service Area: Kittitas, Klickitat, and Yakima counties. To speak with an Immigration Information Officer, you may make an appointment via the Internet at www.infopass.uscis.gov

WEST VIRGINIA

CHARLESTON APPLICATION SUPPORT CENTER
210 Kanawha Blvd. West
Charleston, WV 25302
Tel: (800) 375-5283
Web: http://uscis.gov

CHARLESTON, WV SATELLITE OFFICE
210 Kanawha Blvd. West
Charleston, WV 25302
Debra Zamberry, Officer in Charge
Tel: (800) 375-5283
Web: http://uscis.gov
Service Area: The Charleston, WV Satellite office serves the State of West Virginia. It provides forms and information to the public and conducts naturalization interviews. To speak with an Immigration Information Officer, you may make an appointment via the Internet at www.infopass.uscis.gov

WISCONSIN

MILWAUKEE APPLICATION SUPPORT CENTER
310 E. Knapp, 1st Fl. #154
Milwaukee, WI 53202
Tel: (800) 375-5283
Web: http://uscis.gov

MILWAUKEE SUB OFFICE
310 E. Knapp St.
Milwaukee, WI 53202
Kay Leopold, Officer In Charge
Tel: (800) 375-5283
Web: http://uscis.gov
Service Area: Brown, Calumet, Columbia, Crawford, Dane, Dodge, Door, Florence, Fond Du Lac, Forest, Grant, Green, Green Lake, Iowa, Jefferson, Kenosha, Kewaunee, Lafayette, Langlade, Manitowoc, Marinette, Marquette, Menominee, Milwaukee, Oconto, Outgamie, Ozaukee, Racine, Richland, Rock, Sauk, Shawano, Sheboygan, Walworth, Washington, Waukesha, Waupaca, Waushara, and Winnebago.

WYOMING

CASPER APPLICATION SUPPORT CENTER
150 E. B St. #1014
Casper, WY 82601
Tel: (800) 375-5283
Web: http://uscis.gov

US Embassies and Consulates in African Countries

ALGERIA

ALGIERS (E)
4 Chemin Cheikh Bachir Ibrahimi
Algiers, Algeria
Tel: [213] (21) 69-12-55
Fax: [213] (21) 69-39-79
Web: http://algiers.usembassy.gov

AMB: Richard W. Erdman
AMB OMS: Nancy L. Graham
DCM: Marc J. Sievers
POL: Steven C. Rice
CON: Kristin Bongiovanni
MGT: Hugues P. Ogier
DAO: Daniel Doty
ECO: Michael E. Pignatello
FMO: Debra D. Taylor
GSO: Kim Shaw
IMO: Thomas S. Murray
ISO: Mark D. Raglin
ISSO: Daniel M. Childs
PAO: Linda M. Cowher
RSO: John C. Picardy

ANGOLA

LUANDA (E)
Rua Houari Boumedienne #32
Luanda, Angola
Tel: [244] (2) 445-481
Fax: [244] (2) 446-924
Web: http://luanda.usembassy.gov

AMB: Cynthia G. Efird
AMB OMS: Robin Welker
DCM: James A. Knight
POL: Joel R. Wiegert
POL/ECO/State ICASS: Edward G. Stafford
COM/CON: Inga Heemink
MGT: Mark J. Biedlingmaier
AFSA: Gail Spence
AID: Diana Swain
CLO: Vicki Heard
DAO: Ltc. Bernard Sparrow, USA
ECO/COM: Ruddy K. Wang
FMO: Neil P. Eynon
GSO: Frieda Martin
ICASS Chair/PAO: Kim F. Dubois
IMO/IPO: Harvey Heard
ISO: Anne Galchutt
ISSO: Harvey K. Heard
RSO: W. Gordon Hills

BENIN

COTONOU (E)
Rue Caporal Bernard Anani
Cotonou, Benin
Tel: [229] 30-06-50
Fax: [229] 30-19-74
Web: http://usembassy.state.gov/benin

AMB: Wayne E. Neill
DCM: Charles E. Luoma-Overstreet
POL/ECO: Shelly Dittmar
CON: Dan Hall
MGT: Ruth Wagoner
AID: Rudolph Thomas
CLO: Bryan Lunsford
GSO: Mozella Brown
ICASS Chair: Anne Martin
IMO/ISSO: David Ifversen
PAO/State ICASS: John Cushing
RSO: Tracey Lunsford

BOTSWANA

GABORONE (E)
P.O. Box 90
Gaborone, Botswana
Tel: [267] 395-3982
Fax: [267] 395-6947
Web: http://gaborone.usembassy.gov

AMB: Joseph Huggins
AMB OMS: Elizabeth Marker
DCM: Lois Aroian
DCM/OMS: Gun Wechsler
POL/AFSA: Judith Butterman
POL/ECO: Aaron Cope
COM: Hagen Maroney
CON: Michael Margolies
MGT: Jackie Holland-Craig
AID: Gerald Cashion
CLO: Sherry Knutelski
DAO: Lee Davis Butler
EEO/EST: Ted Pierce
FMO: Maureen Danzot
GSO: Harvey Weschler
IBB: William Martin
ICASS Chair: Eileen Devitt
IMO: Marv Adams
MLO: Andrew Overfield
PAO: Karen Morrissey
RSO: Douglas Marvin

BURKINA FASO

OUAGADOUGOU (E)
01 B.P. 35
602 Avenue Raoul Follereau
Ouagadougou, Burkina Faso
Tel: [226] 5030-6723
Fax: [226] 5030-3890
Web: http://ouagadougou.usembassy.gov

DCM OMS: Catherine Lawton
POL: Nausher Ali
CON: Jonathan Habjan
MGT: Jennifer Haskell
AFSA: Ali Nikooazm
CLO: Keri Johnston
ECO/COM: Sadie Okoko
EEO: Irvina Wallace
GSO: Nancy McCarthy
IMO/ISSO: Reginald Hopson
RSO/State ICASS: Todd Haskell
RSO: Brandon Lee

BURUNDI

BUJUMBURA (E)
Avenue des Etats-Unis
Bujumbura, Burundi
Tel: [257] 22-34-54
Fax: [257] 22-29-26
Web: http://bujumbura.usembassy.gov

AMB: James Yellin
AMB OMS: Brenda Moos
DCM: Alexander Laskaris
POL/State ICASS: Christopher Leslie
POL/ECO/CON/ECO/ICASS Chair: Robert Marks
MGT/EEO/FIN/FMO: Judes E. Stellingwerf
OTI: Tyrone Gaston
OFDA: Denise Gordon
REDSO: Robert Luneberg
DAO: Mark (Duke) Ellington
GSO: Matthew Blong
IMO: Harold Griffin
IPO: Donald Snead

CAMEROON

YAOUNDE (E)
B.P. 817
Rue Natchigale
Yaounde, Cameroon
Tel: [237] 223-0512
Fax: [237] 223-0753
Web: http://usembassy.state.gov/yaounde

AMB: R. Niels Marquardt
AMB OMS: Julie Harrison
DCM/CHG: Aric R. Schwan
DCM OMS: Monica Rancher
POL/ECO: Pauline Borderies (Acting Chief)
MGT: Jeffrey A. Spence
CLO: Martine McKinnie
DAO: Ross Clemons
FMO: Robert J. Gresbrink

GSO: Jadine R. Hill
IMO/ISO/ISSO: Leslie D. Oly
PAO: Jose Santacana
RSO: Wade Boston
State ICASS: Waran Ravindranath

CAPE VERDE

PRAIA (E)
Rua Abilio Macedo, No. 6
Plateau, Cape Verde
Tel: [238[(2) 61-56-16
Fax: [238] (2) 61-13-55
Web: http://capeverde.usembassy.gov

AMB: Donald C. Johnson
AMB OMS: Wendy F. Pelaez
DCM: Paul P. Pometto, II
CON: Frank DeParis
CLO: Karyn DeParis
State ICASS: Matthew Breman

CENTRAL AFRICAN REPUBLIC

BANGUI (E)
Blvd. David Dacko
Bangui, Central Africa Republic
Tel: [236] 61-02-00
Fax: [236] 61-44-94

DCM/CHG: A.J. Panos

CHAD

N'DJAMENA (E)
Ave. Felix Eboue
N'Djamena, Chad
Tel: [235] 516-211
Fax: [235] 515-654
Web: http://usembassy.state.gov/chad

AMB: Marc M. Wall
AMB OMS: Audrey J. Ley
DCM: Lucy Tamlyn
POL/ICASS Chair: Kathleen FitzGibbon
CON/ECO: Satrajit Sardar
MGT: Sharon D. James
DAO: Ltc. Tim Mitchell
EEO/GSO: Keiji Turner
FMO: Wally Eustis
IMO: Anthony James
IPO: Glenn Shellahammer
ISSO/RSO: Patrick Leonard
PAO: Arthur J. Bell

Source: U.S. Department of State. www.foia.state.gov

CONGO, DEMOCRATIC REPUBLIC OF THE

KINSHASA (E)
Unit 31550, APO AE 09828
498 Ave. Lukusa, Kin-Gombe
Kinshasa, Congo, Democratic Republic of the
Tel: [243] 81-225-5872
Fax: [243] 81-301-0531
Web: http://kinshasa.usembassy.gov

AMB: Roger A. Meece
AMB OMS/EEO: Wanda Wood
DCM: J. Thomas Dougherty
DCM OMS: Patti Hagopian
POL/State ICASS: Melissa M. Sanderson
CON: Laurie J. Meininger
MGT: Maureen E. Park
AID: Robert Hellyer
CLO: Julie Barnes
DAO: Roderic Jackson
ECO: Wendy Brafman
GSO: Barry F. Copenhaver
ICASS Chair: Karen Hawkins Reed
IMO: Floyd L. Wilson
ISSO/RSO: Christopher A. Bakken
PAO: Phillip E. Wright

CONGO

BRAZZAVILLE (E)
Unit 31550, APO AE 09828-1550
Rue Leon Jacob 70
Brazzaville, Congo, Republic of the
Tel: [243] (81) 225-5872
Fax: [243] (88) 40524

AMB: Robin Renee Sanders
AMB OMS: Judy Copenhaver
CON/ECO/LAB: Chelsea Bakken
DAO: Roderic Jackson (based in Kinshasa)
EEO: Eva L. Robinson (Embassy of Kinshasa)
RSO: Christopher A. Bakken (Embassy of Kinshas)

COTE D'IVOIRE

ABIDJAN (E)
B.P. 1712
Rue Jesse Owens
Abidjan, Cote D'Ivoire
Tel: [225] (22) 49-40-00
Fax: [225] (22) 49-43-23
Web: http://usembassy.state.gov/abidjan

AMB: Aubrey Hooks
AMB OMS: Carole Manley
DCM: Vicente Valle
DCM OMS: Wendy Bieber
POL: James Wojtasiewicz
CON: Lisa Conner
MGT: Robert Yamate
DAO: Peter Aubrey
ECO/ICASS Chair: Andrea Lewis
FMO: Francisco Lloret
GSO: Ayemere Okojie
IMO: Jon Woodley
ISO: Daniel Fern

ISSO: Scott Elston
PAO: Ergibe Boyd
RSO: Patrick Moore

DJIBOUTI, REPUBLIC OF

DJIBOUTI (E)
P.O. Box 185
Plateau du Serpent, Blvd. Marechal Joffre
Djibouti, Djibouti
Tel: [253] 35-39-95
Fax: [253] 35-39-40
Web: http://djibouti.usembassy.gov

AMB: Marguerita D. Ragsdale
AMB OMS: Diane Manago
DCM: David Ball
POL/ECO: Erinn Reed Stott
CON: Andrea K. Lewis
MGT: Howard McGowan
AFSA/IPO: Robert A. Nicholas
AID: Janet Schulman
EEO/IMO: Sweetie P. Lee Jones
GSO: Marissa D. Scott
ICASS Chair: Bryan Boyd
MLO: Brian Jenkins
PAO/State ICASS: Tiffany M. Bartish
RSO: Jeff Pursell

EGYPT

CAIRO (E)
APO/FPO Unit 64900, APO AE 09839
8 Kamal El Din Salah St., Garden City
Cairo, Egypt
Tel: [20] (2) 797-3300
Fax: [20] (2) 797-3200
Web: http://cairo.usembassy.gov

AMB: Francis J. Ricciardone
AMB OMS: Anissa A. Hanson
DCM/CHG: Gordon Gray
DCM OMS: Katrina Hourani
CG: Peter Kaestner
POL/ECO: Michael Corbin
COM/FCS: James Joy
MGT: Steven J. White
AFSA: Kevin M. Brady
AGR: Asif Chaudhry
AID: Kenneth Ellis
CLO: Kathryn Ramirez
DAO: Ted Seel
DEA: Donald Barnes
EEO: Colin Bucknor
EST: Michael Kidwell
FMO: Marilyn Ferdinand
GSO: Terry Leech
ICASS Chair: Trueman Sharp
IMO: James Vanderpool
IPO: James Williams

EQUATORIAL GUINEA

MALABO (E)
Carretera de Aeropuerto, Restaurante El Paraiso
Malabo, Equatorial Guinea
Tel: [240] 093-457
Fax: [240] 09-84-43

AMB: R. Niels Marquardt
DCM/CHG: Sarah Morrison

ERITREA

ASMARA (E)
P.O. Box 211
179 Alaa St.
Asmara, Eritrea
Tel: [291] (1) 120004
Fax: [291] (1) 127584
Web: http://asmara.usembassy.gov

AMB: Scott H. Delisi
AMB OMS: Ann E. Rehme
DCM: Sue K. Brown
POL/ECO/State ICASS: Joey R. Hood
CON/EEO: Elaine M. French
MGT: Michael A. McCarthy
AFSA: Daniel J. Cook
AID: Mike E. Sarhan
CLO: Sanny E. Wroblewski
IPO/ISSO: Roland D. Neiss
MLO: Maj. Tony B. Curtis
PAO: George W. Colvin
RSO: K. Andrew Wroblewski
SPSH: E. Holly O'Brien

ETHIOPIA

ADDIS ABABA (E)
14 Entoto Rd.
Addis Ababa, Ethiopia
Tel: [251] (1) 17-40-00
Fax: [251] (1) 24-24-01
Web: http://addisababa.usembassy.gov

AMB: Aurelia E. Brazeal
AMB OMS/EEO: Debra R. DeBose
DCM: Brian R. Moran, Acting
POL/State ICASS: Charles B. Gurney, Acting
COM: Elizabeth E. Jaffee
CON: Julie Stufft
MGT: Sherry Z. Sykes
AFSA/EST: Daniel K. Balzer
AID: William Hammink
CLO: Chris O'Connell
DAO: Richard Orth
FMO: Peggy D. Guttierrez
GSO: Ellen M. Rose
ICASS Chair: R. Douglas Arbuckle
IMO: Robert Lewis
PAO: Samuel S. Westgate, III
RSO: Ken Fisk

GABON

LIBREVILLE (E)
Blvd. du Bord de Mer
Libreville, Gabon
Tel: [241] 76-20-03/04
Fax: [241] 74-55-07
Web: http://libreville.usembassy.gov

AMB: Barrie R. Walkley
AMB OMS: Patricia B. Keller
DCM: Samuel Laeuchli
POL: Glenn Fedzer
CON: Michael Garcia
MGT/FIN: Barbara J. Martin
AFSA: Matthew Cassetta
CLO: Gabriella Codispoti
DAO: Neal Kringel
ECO: Lashandra Sullivan
GSO: Alexander Lipscomb
ICASS Chair/IMO/State ICASS: Dale Swedberg
ISSO/RSO: Aaron M. Codispoti

GAMBIA, THE

BANJUL (E)
P.M.B. 19
Kairaba Ave. Fajara
Banjul, The Gambia
Tel: [220] 439-2856
Fax: [220] 439-2475
Web: www.usembassybanjul.gm

AMB: Joseph D. Stafford, III
AMB OMS/State ICASS: Kevin M. Phillips
DCM/ICASS Chair: Vangala Ram
POL/ECO: Daniel M. Renna
CON: Elizabeth N. Schwefler
CLO: Adela Renna
EEO/GSO: Matthew Austin
IPO: Ross Klinger
RSO: Robert B. Kimbrough

GHANA

ACCRA (E)
P.O. Box 194
Ring Road East
Accra, Ghana
Tel: [233] (21) 775-347/8/9
Fax: [233] (21) 776-008
Web: http://accra.usembassy.gov

AMB: Mary C. Yates
AMB OMS: Carol V. Oakley
DCM: Jerry P. Lanier
DCM OMS: Vivian Kilgore
POL: Scott Ticknor
CON: Nan Stewart
MGT: Judith Francis
AGR: Ali Abdi
AID: Sharon Cromer
CLO: Jill Hankinson
DAO: Thomas Bruce
ECO: Chris Landberg
FAA: Edward X. Jones
FCS: Diane Jones
FMO: Kevin Doyle
IBB: Steve Lucas
ICASS Chair/State ICASS: Simon Hankinson
IMO/IPO/ISSO: A. Bryan Thibodeau

GUINEA

CONAKRY (E)
Rua Ka 38
Conakry, Guinea
Tel: [224] 41-15-20/21/23
Fax: [224] 41-15-22
Web: http://conakry.usembassy.gov

AMB: Jackson McDonald
AMB OMS: Judyann H. Dye
DCM: Frankie A. Reed
POL: Pete Davis
CON/State ICASS: Barbara Bartsch-Allen
MGT: Christopher D. Dye
AID: Annette Adams
CLO: Maria Rodriguez-Aybar
DAO: Maj. Christian Ramthun
ECO: Eric Turner
EEO/PAO: Louise Bedichek
FIN: Sharon Yang
FMO: Gary Rose
GSO: Jennifer McAlpine
ICASS Chair: Carrie Dailey
IPO/ISSO: Dwayne Taylor
RAMC: FSC Charleston
RSO: John Aybar

GUINEA-BISSAU

BISSAU (BO)
P.O. Box 297
Bissau Codex, Bairro de Penha, Rua
Ulysses Grant
Bissau, Guinea-Bissau
Tel: [245] 252-282
Fax: [245] 222-273

AMB: Richard Alan Roth
DCM: Robert Jackson
POL: Seiji T. Shiratori
MGT: Gary Mignano
DAO: Scott Womack
GSO: Frank Shields
PAO: Claud R. Young

KENYA

NAIROBI (E)
APO/FPO, Unit 64100, APO AE 09831
United Nations Ave., Gigiri
Nairobi, Kenya
Tel: [254] (20) 363-6000
Fax: [254] (20) 363-6157
Web: http://nairobi.usembassy.gov

AMB: William Bellamy
AMB OMS: Suzanne Lemandri
DCM: Leslie Rowe
DCM OMS: Evelyn Polidoro
CG: David Stone
POL: Michael Fitzpatrick
CON: Djenaba Kendrick
MGT: William Gaines
US PERM REP: Karen T. Levine
DEP PERM REP: Maya Han
AFSA/FMO: Mary Jo Rasing
AGR: Kevin Smith
AID: Dwight Smith
CLO: Abby Huck
DAO: Scott Rutherford
ECO: John Hoover
FSC: Edward Yagi
GSO: Melissa Coskuner
ICASS Chair: Tom Ray
IMO: Russell G. Le Clair, Jr.
INS: Michael Webster

LESOTHO

MASERU (E)
254 Kingsway Ave.
Maseru, Lesotho
Tel: [266] (22) 312-666
Fax: [266] (22) 310-116
Web: http://maseru.usembassy.gov

AMB: June Carter Perry
AMB OMS/State ICASS: Derlene Mazyck
DCM/POL/ECO: Karl P. Albrecht
CON: Jed Dornburg
MGT/FMO: Erica Renew
AGR: Richard Helm (Pretoria)
DEA: Larry W. Frye (Pretoria)
FAA: Edward Jones (Dakar)
GSO: Alison Blosser
IMO/ISSO: Daniel Siebert
IRS: James P. Beene (London)
LAB: Frederick J. Kaplan (Pretoria)
LEGATT: Gregory Groves (Pretoria)
PAO: Jed Dornburg
RSO: Doug Marvin (Gaborone)

LIBERIA

MONROVIA (E)
111 United Nations Dr.
Monrovia, Liberia
Tel: [231] 226-370
Fax: [231] 226-148/226-827
Web: http://monrovia.usembassy.gov

AMB: Donald E. Booth
AMB OMS: Terri L. Tedford
DCM: Duane E. Sams
POL: Alfreda E. Meyers
COM: John P. Marietti
MGT: John L. Thomas
AGR: Robert D. Simpson
AID: Wilbur Thomas
DAO: Ryan E. McMullen
DEA: Andre Kellum (resident in Lagos)
ECO/COM: Matt B. Chessen
FAA: Ronald L. Montgomery (resident in Dakar)
FMO: James Barber
ICASS CHAIR: Charles Colden
IMO: Anbes Keffelew
IRS: Marlene Sartipi (resident in Paris)
RSO: Norman C. Lisenbee

MADAGASCAR

ANTANANARIVO (E)
14-16 Rue Rainitovo
Antananarivo, Madagascar
Tel: [261] (20) 22-21257
Fax: [261] (20) 22-34539
Web: www.usmission.mg

AMB: James D. McGee
AMB OMS: Dorothy Dorsey
DCM: Zachary Z. Teich
DCM OMS: Carolyn D. Wachter
POL: Sarah O. Takats
CON/GSO: David J. Jea
MGT/ISSO: Vera Pauli-Widenhouse
AID: Stephen M. Haykin, Acting
DAO: Catherine D. Ripley
DEA: Jeffrey Wagner (Pretoria)
ECO/COM: Brian T. Neubert
EEO/ISO: Jose Savinon
FAA: Edward Jones (Dakar)
FMO: Victor Carbonell
IMO/IPO: James F. Lyne
PAO: William H. Cook
RSO: Christopher J. Gillis
State ICASS: Paul Cunningham

MALAWI

LILONGWE (E)
Area 40, Plot No. 24, Kenyatta Rd.
Lilongwe, Malawi
Tel: [265] (1) 773-166
Fax: [265] (1) 772-316
Web: http://lilongwe.usembassy.gov

AMB: Alan Eastham
DCM/CHG: David R. Gilmour
DCM OMS: Carol L. Grisham
POL: Tyler K. Sparks
CON: Pamnella Devolder
MGT: Craig L. Cloud
AFSA/ECO/COM: William R. Taliaferro
AGR: Kevin N. Smith
AID: Mary Lewellen
CLO: Angela Cloud
DAO: Dan Hampton (Harare)
EEO/GSO: Jessica N. Munson
FMO: Darcy M. Mercadante

ICASS Chair/PAO/State ICASS: Mitchell R. Moss
IMO: William J. Manuel
ISSO/RSO: Maureen I. McGeough

MALI

BAMAKO (E)
B.P. 34
Rue De Rochester NY and Rue Mohamed V
Bamako, Mali
Tel: [223] 222-54-70
Fax: [223] 222-37-12
Web: www.usa.org.ml

AMB: Terence McCulley
AMB OMS: Patricia Pidade
DCM/CHG: Steve Kraft
DCM OMS: Janelle Walker
PO/CON: Aaron Sampson
MGT: Dwight Rhoades
AFSA: Latanya Mapp
AID: Alex Newton
DAO: Argyrios Haritos
ECO: Matthew Miller
EEO: Laura Danylin
FMO: Shelton Haynie
IMO/ISSO: Barbara Darnielle
IPO: Wesley Pendergist
PAO: Mary Speer
RSO: Kevin Gilligan

MAURITANIA

NOUAKCHOTT (E)
Rue Abdallaye
Nouakchott, Mauritania
Tel: [222] 525-2660
Fax: [222] 525-1592
Web: http://mauritania.usembassy.gov

AMB: Joseph LeBaron
AMB OMS: Kathleen Donahue
DCM: Steven Koutsis
POL: Joshua Morris
CON: Anita Ghildyal
MGT: John K. Madden
CLO: Elizabeth H. Hilliard
DAO: James P. Sweeney
ECO/COM: Kay Moseley
FIN: Magida Safaoui
GSO: Michael Lampel
ICASS Chair/State ICASS: Christine Campbell
IMO/ISSO: Eddie H. Martin
RSO: David Groccia

MAURITIUS

PORT LOUIS (E)
Rogers House, John Kennedy Ave., 4th Fl.
Port Louis, Mauritius
Tel: [230] 202-4400
Fax: [230] 208-9534
Web: http://mauritius.usembassy.gov

DCM/CHG/ICASS Chair: Stephen Schwartz
DCM OMS: Ellen Brooks
POL: James Liddle
COM/CON/ECO: Dewitt Conklin
MGT: Judith Semilota
CUS: E.J. Chong
DAO: Cathy Ripley
DEA: Jeff Wagner
FAA: Ed Jones
FCS: Johnnie Brown
FMO: Victor Carbonell
IMO/ISSO: Hava Hegenbarth
INS: Robert Ballow

LEGATT: Mike Bonner
PAO: Victoria DeLong
RSO: David Walsh

MOROCCO

RABAT (E)
PSC 74 Box 021, APO AE 09718
2 Avenue Mohamed El Fassi
Rabat, Morocco
Tel: [212] (3) 776-2265
Fax: [212] (3) 776-5661
Web: http://rabat.usembassy.gov

AMB: Thomas T. Riley
AMB OMS: Nancy Rasari
DCM: Wayne J. Bush
DCM OMS: Jennifer Harrison
CG: Mary Pendleton (TDY)
CG OMS: Debra Tekin
POL/State ICASS: Timothy A. Lenderking
MGT: Catherine Ebert-Gray
AFSA: James Sallay
AGR: Michael Fay
AID: Monica Stein-Olson
CLO: Beth Koplovsky
DAO: David Solomon
ECO: Michael Koplovsky
EEO: Kerry Schnier
FMO: Christian Charette
GSO: Donald Hunt
IBB: David Strawman
ICASS Chair: Jean Loiseau
IMO: Kevin N. Bradshaw
IPO: Clinton Frith

CASABLANCA (CG)
PSC 74 Box 24, APO AE 09718
8 Moulay Youssef
Casablanca, Morocco
Tel: [212] (2) 226-4550
Fax: [212] (2) 220-8097

CG: Mary Pendleton
CG OMS: Debra Tekin
PO: Mary Pendleton
COM: Rick Ortiz
CON: Matt McKeever
MGT: Ray Rivera
CLO: Patricia Dlia
ECO: Jonathan A. Alan
EEO: Timothy Ponce
IPO: Marcellus D. Davis
ISSO: Zachery Smith
LAB: Amy Wilson
PAO: Charles Cole
RSO: Janet Fitzgerald

MOZAMBIQUE

MAPUTO (E)
P.O. Box 783
193 Kenneth Kaunda
Maputo, Mozambique
Tel: [258] (1) 492-797
Fax: [258] (1) 490-114
Web: www.usembassy-maputo.gov.mz

AMB: Helen R. Meagher La Lime
AMB OMS: Mary M. Mertz
DCM: James L. Dudley
DCM OMS: Sanya L. Hunsucker

POL: Cynthia A. Brown
POL/ECO: John A. Wysham
CON: Leyla L. Ones
MGT: John M. Kowalski
AFSA/PAO: Gregory L. Garland
AID: Jay Knott
CLO: Donald J. Heroux
DAO: Daniel M. Jones
ECO/COM: Brooke L. Williams
EEO/IMO: Mark E. Myelle
FMO: Martin B. Schwartz
GSO: Malia V. Heroux
ICASS Chair: Donna Stauffer
PAO/ADV: David J. Stephenson
RSO: Karen A. Lass

NAMIBIA

WINDHOEK (E)
P.B. 12029
14 Lossen St.
Windhoek, Namibia
Tel: [264] (61) 221-601
Fax: [264] (61) 229-792
Web: www.usembassy.namib.com

AMB: Joyce A. Barr
AMB OMS: Patricia C. Quinn
DCM: Eric D. Benjaminson
DCM OMS: Sally B. Lewis
POL: Mark J. Cassayre
CON: Aaron Daviet
MGT: Marja Verloop
AFSA/GSO: William J. McClure
AGR: Catherine Kay (Pretoria)
AID: Gary Newton
CLO: Henny M. Harsha
DAO: Michael J. Kelley
DEA: Jeffrey W. Wagner (resident in Pretoria)
ECO: Adrienne Galanek
EEO: Adriana Barel
FAA: Edward Jones (resident in Dakar)
FMO: Brian J. Peterson
ICASS Chair/PAO/State ICASS: Stanley Harsha
IMO/ISSO: Christopher House
IRS: Linda M. Garrard (resident in London)
LAB: Jeanine Collins (resident in Johannesburg)

NIGER

NIAMEY (E)
B.P. 11201
Rue Des Ambassades
Niamey, Niger
Tel: [227] 72-26-61
Fax: [227] 73-31-67
Web: http://niamey.usembassy.gov

AMB: Dennise G. Mathieu
AMB OMS: Sharon Rogers
DCM: John Davison
DCM OMS/EEO: Marcella Singleton
POL/State ICASS: Zachary V. Harkenrider
COM/CON/AFSA/ECO: Daniel L. Gage
MGT: Don D. Curtis
CLO: Susan E. McCarthy
DAO: Stephen A. Hughes
GSO: Alma M. Johnson
ICASS Chair: Roy Watson
IPO: Josetito Nakpil
ISSO: Kevin R. Kiah
PAO: Sita Chakrawarti
RSO: William McCarthy

NIGERIA

ABUJA (E)
9 Mambilla St., Off Aso Dr., Maitama District
Abuja, Nigeria
Tel: [234] (09) 523-0916
Fax: [234] (09) 523-0353
Web: http://abuja.usembassy.gov

AMB: John Campbell
AMB OMS: Diana Kniazuk
DCM: Thomas P. Furey
DCM OMS: Karen D. Miles
POL/AFSA: Russell Hanks
CON/EEO: Cristina Marko
MGT: Warrington E. Brown
AGR: Jamie Rothschild (resident in Lagos)
AID/ICASS Chair: Patrick Fleuret
CLO: Deborah George-Barnes
DAO: Sue Ann Sandusky
DEA: Sam Gaye (resident in Lagos)
ECO: Necia Quast
FCS: Michael McGee (resident in Lagos)
FMO: Tedla Yitna
GSO: Edward Burkhalter
IMO: Todd Roe
IPO: Glenwood R. Jarman
ISSO: Juan Brooks
LEGATT: Kevin Peterson (resident in Lagos)
PAO/State ICASS: Claudia E. Anyaso

LAGOS (CG)
2 Walter Carrington Crescent
Lagos, Nigeria
Tel: [234] (1) 261-0050/0078
Fax: [234] (1) 261-1863
Web: http://usembassy.state.gov/nigeria

AMB: John F. Campbell
DCM: Rick L. Roberts
CG/PO: Brian L. Browne
CG OMS/EEO: Carolyn O. Brooks
POL: position moved to Abuja
COM: John F. Campbell
CON: Ronald J. Kramer
MGT: Irvin Hicks, Jr.
AFSA: Jessica L. DavisBa
AGR: Jamie Rothschild
AID: Dawn Liberi
CLO: Felicia Wheeler
DAO: Timothy L. Lohof
DEA: Jeffrey A. Schoen
FCS: Michael L. McGee
FMO: Thea M. Wargowsky
GSO: Ayemere E. Okojie
ICASS Chair/State ICASS: AE Abuja
IPO: Griffith C. Murray

RWANDA

KIGALI (E)
P.O. Box 28
Blvd. de la Revolution
Kigali, Rwanda
Tel: [250] 505-601/2/3
Fax: [250] 572-128
Web: http://usembkigali.net

AMB: Charge Henderson Patrick
AMB OMS: Mary E. Parks
DCM: Janet Wilgus
POL/State ICASS: Eric M. Wong
POL/ECO: Maya Dietz
COM/CON: James Kay
MGT: Sally M. Walker
AFSA: John M. Jackson
AID: James Anderson
CLO: Christine Jones
DAO: John D. Ruffing
ECO/COM: James David Kay

EEO: Nan Mattingly
FMO: Margarita Halle
GSO: Aaron Thomas
ICASS Chair: Richard Warin
IMO/IPO/ISSO: Kim M. Long
PAO: Grace M. Brunton
RAMC: Charleston FSC
RSO: Gregory Anderson

SENEGAL

DAKAR (E)
P.O. Box 49
Ave. Jean XXIII
Dakar, Senegal
Tel: [221] 823-4296
Fax: [221] 822-2991
Web: http://dakar.usembassy.gov

AMB: Richard Alan Roth
AMB OMS: D. DaSilva
DCM: Robert P. Jackson
DCM OMS: B. Jensen
POL: Roy L. Whitaker
CON: Beth Payne
MGT: Gary S. Mignano
AFSA: Frank Shields
AID: Olivier C. Carduner
APHIS: Dr. Cheryl French
CLO: Sylvia Mathews
DAO: Scott Womack
ECO/LAB/State ICASS: Douglas Meurs
EEO: Barbara Jensen
FAA: Edward Jones
FCS: Cynthia A. Griffin-Greene
FMO: Reginald Whatley
GSO: Chanh T. Nguyen
ICASS Chair: Lee Jewell
IMO/ISO: Joel R. Rigby (Acting)
IPO: James D. Matthews

SIERRA LEONE

FREETOWN (E)
Siaka Stevens St.
Freetown, Sierra Leone
Tel: [232] (22) 226-481
Fax: [232] (22) 225-471
Web: http://freetown.usembassy.gov

AMB: Thomas N. Hul, III
AMB OMS: Mary Kay Beckwith
DCM: James A. Stewart
DCM OMS/EEO: Kathy Cavanagh
POL/ECO/CON/ECO/State ICASS: Rachael T. Doherty
MGT/AFSA/FMO: Salvatore Piazza
AID/ICASS Chair: Christine M. Sheckler
DAO: Patricia Parris
DEA: Sam Gaye (resident in Lagos)
GSO: Jennifer Bah
IMO: Joseph J. Hromatka
ISSO: Nicholas Brashich
PAO: Brenda C. Soya
RSO: Ezio Veloso

SOUTH AFRICA

PRETORIA (E)
877 Pretorius St.
Pretoria, South Africa
Tel: [27] (12) 431-4000
Fax: [27] (12) 342-2299
Web: http://pretoria.usembassy.gov

AMB: Jendayi E. Frazer
AMB OMS: Natasha Greer
DCM: Donald Teitelbaum
DCM OMS: Linda Ingalls
POL: Gayleatha Brown
CON: Cecilia Mulligan
MGT: Elizabeth Hinson
AFSA/ISO: William Walls
AGR: Scott Reynolds
AID: Carleene Dei
CLO: Lucy Neher/Linda Lockwood
CUS: William Thomas
DAO: Col. Michael Muolo
DEA: Jeff Wagner
ECO: Jeff Hartley
EEO: Diana McDowell/Daniel Stewart
EST: Nikki Brajevich
FMO: James Inder
GSO: Gerald Hanisch
IBB: Paula Caffey

SOUTH AFRICA

CAPE TOWN (CG)
Broadway Industries Ctr., 4th Fl.
Cape Town, South Africa
Tel: [27] (21) 421-4280
Fax: [27] (21) 418-1989

AMB: Jendayi E. Frazer
CG/PO: Moosa Valli
CG OMS: Phyllis M. Jones
DPO/POL: Randy Berry
CON: William D. Howard
MGT/GSO: Michael Toyryla
APHIS: Ken Nagata
CLO: Kendra Toyryla
ECO: John R. Walser
FCS: Tyrena Holley
IPO: John Adams
RSO: Patrick J. Keegan

DURBAN [CG]
303 W. 31st Fl.
Durban, South Africa 4001
Tel: [27] (31) 305-7600
Fax: [27] (31) 305-7650
Web: http://usembassy.state.gov/southafrica

DCM: Don Teitelbaum
PO: Eugene Young
POL/ECO: Amy Patel
COM: Tom Tanner
MGT/RSO: Jeremy M. Neitzke
IPO: Simon Guerrero
PAO: J. Riley Sever

JOHANNESBURG (CG)
1 River St., Killarney 2193
Johannesburg, South Africa
Tel: [27] (11) 644-8000
Fax: [27] (11) 646-6913

CG: David Dunn
PO: David B. Dunn
COM: Johnny Brown

CON: Raymond Baca
MGT: Matthew Cook
CLO: Virginia Merideth
EEO: Donald F. Mulligan
GSO: Charles Clegg
IBB: Paula Caffey
INS: Robert Ballow
IPO/ISSO: Bruce MacEwan
ISO/RSO: Tom Richardson
LAB: Bruce Neuling
PAO: Mary Jeffers

SUDAN

KHARTOUM (E)
Ali Abdel Latif St.
Khartoum, Sudan
Tel: [249] (183) 774-701/4
Fax: [249] (183) 774-137/775680
AMB OMS: Sandra McInturff
DCM: Robert Whitehead
POL/EEO: Janice L. Elmore
MGT: Michelle L. Stefanick
AID: Kate Farnsworth
DAO/ICASS Chair: William Godbout
FMO: Robert Watson
GSO: Dianna Chianis
IMO: Richard McInturff
ISO: Joseph Dalrymple
PAO: Elizabeth Colton
RSO: Richard Ingram

SWAZILAND

MBABANE (E)
2350 Mbabane Pl.
Mbabane, Swaziland
Tel: [268] 404-6441
Fax: [268] 404-5959
Web: http://mbabane.usembassy.gov

AMB: Lewis W. Lucke
AMB OMS: Nelda Villines
DCM/MGT/FIN: Lynn A. Allison
CON/POL/ECO: D. Shannon Dorsey
EEO/PAO: Peter Piness
GSO/State ICASS: Peter N. Van Eck
IMO: Michael McCowan
ISSO: Gaspar Guzman
RSO: J. Scott Mooneyham
SPSH: Des Diallo

TANZANIA

DAR ES SALAAM (E)
686 Old Bagamoyo Rd.
Dar Es Salaam, Tanzania
Tel: [255] (22) 266-8001
Fax: [255] (22) 266-8373
Web: http://tanzania.usembassy.gov

DCM: Daniel Purnell Delly
POL/State ICASS: Judith Buelow
COM: Katherine Bernsohn
CON/EEO: Elizabeth Jordan

MGT: Christopher L. Stillman
AFSA/PAO: John Haynes
AGR: Kevin Smith (NRB)
CLO: Candy Calvert
DAO: Laura Varhola
ECO: Brendan Salmon
FAA: Edward Jones (Dakar)
FMO: Charles McShane
GSO: Michael Davids
ICASS Chair: Art Lopez
IPO: Don James
RSO: Anne Brunn

TOGO

LOMÉ (E)
B.P. 852
Rue Kouenou and Beniglato Rue 15
Lomé, Togo
Tel: [228] 221-2991
Fax: [228] 221-7952/5391
Web: http://lome.usembassy.gov

DCM: J.A. Diffily
POL/ECO: Rona Rathod
CON: John Corrao
MGT: Barbara Martin
CLO: Clara Cates
DAO: Col. Thom Bruce (Accra)
GSO: Michelle N. Ward
IPO: Joellis Smith
PAO: Mary Daschbach
RSO: David Richeson

TUNISIA

TUNIS (E)
Les Berges du Lac 1053
Tunis, Tunisia
Tel: [216] (71) 107-000
Fax: [216] (71) 107-090
Web: http://tunis.usembassy.gov

AMB: William J. Hudson
AMB OMS: Karen Schoppl
DCM: David Ballard
DCM OMS: Paula J. Hart
POL/ECO: Elizabeth Hopkins
COM: Clark Ledger (ad interim)
CON/State ICASS: Nora Dempsey
MGT: Alan E. Greenfield
AFSA: D. Ashley Bagwell
AGR: Michael J. Fay (resident in Rabat)
CLO: Brigitte Campbell/Paul Bergen
DAO: Bradley Anderson
EEO: Stephanie Syptak
FAA: Lirio Liu (resident Paris)
FMO: Catherine Lienhart
GSO: Theodore Lienhart
IMO: Ross Campbell
IPO: Gerard Breton
IRS: Kathy J. Beck (resident in Paris)
ISO: M. Anne Borst
ISSO: Christina Bergen

UGANDA

KAMPALA (E)
1577 Ggaba Rd.
Kampala, Uganda
Tel: [256] (41) 259-791
Fax: [256] (41) 259-794
Web: http://kampala.usembassy.gov

AMB: Jimmy Kolker
AMB OMS: Marial Luisa N. Fotheringham
DCM: William Fitzgerald
DCM OMS: Courtney M. Preston
PO: Post One
POL: Nathan Holt
POL/ECO/STATE ICASS: Andrew Herrup
CON: Peter Hancon
MGT: Martina Flintrop
AFSA: Casey Mace
AID: Margot Ellis
CLO: Shawna Wentlandt
DAO: Richard Skow
ECO: Nathan Carter
FMO: Kevin Crews
GSO: Jan Sittel
ICASS Chair: Harold Rasmussen
IMO/ISO/ISSO: Stella Bulimo-Crews
IPO: Mike Fotheringham
PAO: Alyson Grunder

ZAMBIA

LUSAKA (E)
Corner of Independence and United
Nations Ave.
Lusaka, Zambia
Tel: [260] (1) 250-955
Fax: [260] (1) 252-225
Web: http://zambia.usembassy.gov

AMB: Martin G. Brennan
DCM: Andrew Passen
DCM OMS: Cynthia Hoof
POL/ECO/State ICASS: Katherine S. Dhanani
CON: Joshua Fischel
MGT: Ted D. Plosser
AFSA: Laura Gritz
AGR: Kevin N. Smith
AID: Jim Bednar
CLO: Judith Morris
DAO: Leslie M. Bryant
ECO: James Garry
EEO: Michelle Fulcher/Chris Gomes
FMO: Mike Wagoner
GSO: Craig Anderson
ICASS Chair: Allen Fulcher
IMO: Wayne Payton
ISSO: Robert Sadousky
LAB: Virginia Palmer
PAO: Dehab Ghebreab
RSO: Frank De Michele

ZIMBABWE

HARARE (E)
172 Herbert Chitepo Ave.
Harare, Zimbabwe
Tel: [263] (4) 250-593
Fax: [263] (4) 796-488

AMB: Christopher W. Dell
AMB OMS: Donna Mmoh
DCM: Eric T. Schultz
DCM OMS: Sonja Swamm
POL/EEO: Win Dayton
CON: Jayne Howell
MGT: Michael A. Rynor
AFSA/IMO: Aziz Ahmed
AGR: Scott Reynolds (resident in Pretoria)
AID: Paul Weisenfeld
CLO: Victoria Hougaard
DAO: K.D. Neal
FIN: Kevin Bohne
FMO: Curtis Hoyle
GSO: Jay Lykins
ICASS Chair: Virginia Bourassa
ISSO: George Westfall
LAB: Manav Jain
PAO/State ICASS: Tim Smith
PAO/ADV: Amy Moser
RSO: Raymond Yates

African Embassies in the US

ALGERIA

EMBASSY OF THE PEOPLE'S DEMOCRATIC REPUBLIC OF ALGERIA
2118 Kalorama Rd. NW
Washington, DC 20008
Tel: (202) 265-2800 Fax: (202) 667-2174
Email: ambassadoroffice@yahoo.com
Web: www.algeria-us.org

Ambassador E. and P.
His Excellency Amine KHERBI
Minister-Counsellor (Charge D'Affaires and Interim
Mr. Djamel MOKTEFI; Mrs. Sabah Moktefi
Minister (Consular)
Mr. Ahmed DJELLAL; Mrs. Salima Djellal
Counsellor (Press & Information)
Mr. Ameur BETKA; Mrs. Houria Betka
Counsellor (Political)
Mr. Abdelaziz DERDOURI;
Mrs. Zohra Derdouri
Counsellor (Congressional Liaison)
Mrs. Nadjia HAMDAD;
Mr. Abdelkader Hamdad
Counsellor (Political)
Mrs. Houria KHIARI; Mr. Kamel Khiari
Attaché (Administrative)
Mr. SAIDABDAT
Attaché
Mr. Mourad AMROUCHE;
Mrs. Houria Amrouche
Attaché (Financial)
Mr. Said BOUHDI;
Mrs. Baya Bouhdi
Attaché
Ms. Zakia IGHIL
Attaché
Mr. Abdelkader KOICHE; Mrs. Allala Koiche
Attaché (Administrative & Financial)
Mr. Salah MASSEL; Mrs. Aicha Massel
Defense, Military & Naval Attaché
Colonel Ahcene LAIMECHE;
Mrs. Nadia Laimeche
Air Attaché
Lieutenant Colonel Omar HARICHE;
Mrs. Nacira Hariche

Consular Office
2137 Wyoming Ave. NW
Washington, DC 20008

Economic & Administrative Office
2133 Wyoming Ave. NW
Washington, DC 20008

Military Office
2135 Wyoming Ave. NW
Washington, DC 20008

ANGOLA

EMBASSY OF THE REPUBLIC OF ANGOLA
2108 16th St. NW
Washington, DC 20009
Tel: (202) 785-1156 Fax: (202) 785-1258
Email: angola@angola.org
Web: www.angola.org

Ambassador E. and P.
Her Excellency Josefina Pitra DIAKITE;
Mr. Mamadou Diakite
Minister-Counsellor
Mr. Adao PINTO
Counsellor
Mrs. Maria Luisa Perdigao ABRANTES
Counsellor
Ms. Teresa SILVA
Counsellor (Commercial & Economic)
Mr. Agostinho A. Carvalho FERNANDES;
Mrs. Leopoldina M. Salvador Fernandes
First Secretary
Mr. Martinho Bachi CODO;
Mrs. Catarina Margarete Pinto
Second Secretary (Economic)
Mr. Joao Maria Teixeira FORTES
Second Secretary (Information)
Mr. Evaristo Antonio JOSE
Second Secretary
Mrs. Delfina Abel Cordeiro NASCIMENTO;
Mr. Manuel Goverffo Nascimento, Jr.
Third Secretary (Consular)
Mr. Luis Mateus Luis Dos SANTOS;
Mrs. Domingos Isabel Gaspar Dos Santos
Third Secretary
Mrs. Stela SANTIAGO;
Mr. Edielino Da Gama Dias De Elvas
Attaché (Administrative)
Mrs. Joana Nair S. Da C. Rosario ADAO;
Mr. Bernardo Venancio Adao
Attaché (Financial)
Mr. Fernando Fonseca Andrade CADETE;
Mrs. Ludovina Da Conceicao Cadete
Attaché
Ms. Silvia Prazeres Simoes Da CRUZ
Attaché (Financial)
Ms. Isabel Maria Simoes FARIA
Attaché
Mr. Fernando Das Chagas M. RANGEL;
Mrs. Paula Maria Laures B.M. Rangel
Defense, Military, Naval & Air Attaché
Lieutenant General Jacinto Pedro CAVUNGA;
Mrs. Maria H. Pinto De A. Cavunga
Asst. Defense & Military Attaché
Major Adao Eduardo SILVA;
Mrs. Adelia Flora Paulo Silva

Trade Office
1629 K St. NW #1100

Washington, DC 20006
Tel: (202) 785-6700 Fax: (202) 331-7605

BENIN

EMBASSY OF THE REPUBLIC OF BENIN
2124 Kalorama Rd. NW
Washington, DC 20008
Tel: (202) 232-6656 Fax: (202) 265-1996
Email: info@beninembassyus.org
Web: www.beninembassyus.org

Ambassador E. and P.
His Excellency Segbe Cyrille OGUIN;
Mrs. Hortense Dossa Oguin
Minister-Counsellor
Mr. Robert ZANTAN
Counsellor
Mr. Maurille Agenor Socrate de SOUZA;
Mrs. Esperance Abadagan de Souza
Counsellor (Finance & Administrative)
Mr. Egbonde Emmanuel OHIN;
Mrs. Josephine Adotanou Ohin
Counsellor
Mr. Robert Djimon ZANTAN;
Mrs. Claire Celine Hounkpatin Zantan
First Secretary (Finance & Administrative)
Mr. Yao Blaise AKOTCHENOUDE;
Mrs. Bai Clarisse Assogba Akotchenoude
Attaché
Mrs. Hisanatou Lai PIO
Attaché
Mr. Dimon Jean Marie WOROU;
Mrs. Bernadette Kemado Worou

Chancery Annex- Miscellaneous
2737 Cathedral Ave. NW
Washington, DC 20008

BOTSWANA

EMBASSY OF THE REPUBLIC OF BOTSWANA
1531-3 New Hampshire Ave. NW
Washington, DC 20036
Tel: (202) 244-4990 Fax: (202) 244-4164
Web: www.botswanaembassy.org

Ambassador E. and P.
His Excellency Lapologang Caesar LEKOA;
Mrs. Mpho Gloria Bojelo Lekoa
Counsellor
Mr. John G. Max MORETI;
Mrs. Segomotso Raseto Moreti
First Secretary (Administrative)
Mrs. Miriam Gagofele RADIKGOKONG

Third Secretary (Political)
Mr. Herold C. LUKE;
Mrs. Tiroyaone Tidoh Luke
Attaché (Education)
Mrs. Gloria Kerileng CHEBANNE
Attaché (Administrative)
Mrs. Kesolofetse C. Ratsiripe SEKGWA;
Mr. Kaboeamodimo Bernard Sekgwa
Attaché
Mr. Laly Laolang SEBOGISO

BURKINA FASO

EMBASSY OF BURKINA FASO
2340 Massachusetts Ave. NW
Washington, DC 20008
Tel: (202) 332-5577 Fax: (202) 667-1882
Email: ambawdc@verizon.net
Web: www.burkinaembassy-usa.org

Ambassador E. and P.
His Excellency Tertius ZONGO;
Mrs. Priscille Zongo Yanogo
Minister-Counsellor
Mr. Jacob Wenpayangda PASGO;
Mrs. Gnankan Pasgo
Counsellor (Economic)
Ms. Ma Ouedraogo DIALLO;
Mr. Amidou Ouedraogo
Counsellor (Legal)
Mrs. Priscille Zongo YANOGO;
His Excellency Tertius Zongo
First Secretary
Mr. Babou BAMA;
Mrs. Beatrice Bama Kando
Attaché (Press)
Ms. Jeanne Marie COULIBALY
Attaché (Financial)
Mr. Louis OUEDRAOGO;
Mrs. Eveline Ouedraogo
Attaché
Mrs. Rosine Mariam ZIDOUEMBA;
His Excellency Bruno Zidouemba

BURUNDI

EMBASSY OF THE REPUBLIC OF BURUNDI
2233 Wisconsin Ave. NW #212
Washington, DC 20007
Tel: (202) 342-2574 Fax: (202) 342-2578

Ambassador E. and P.
His Excellency Antoine NTAMOBWA;
Mrs. Rosette Ndereyimana
Counsellor
Mr. Zacharie RWAMAZA

Source: U.S. Department of State. www.state.gov

CAMEROON

EMBASSY OF THE REPUBLIC OF CAMEROON
2349 Massachusetts Ave. NW
Washington, DC 20008
Tel: (202) 265-8790 Fax: (202) 387-3826
Email: cdm@ambacam-usa.org
Web: www.ambacam-usa.org

Ambassador E. and P.
His Excellency Jerome MENDOUGA;
Mrs. Louisette M. R. Mendouga
Minister-Counsellor
Mr. Raymond Ebenezer EPOTE;
Ms. Madeleine Epote
Counsellor (Commercial)
Mr. Madou ABOUBAKAR;
Mrs. Boubakary Amadou Balkissou
Counsellor (Financial)
Mr. Francois NGOUBENE;
Mrs. Marie Therese Ngoubene Nken
Counsellor (Communication)
Mr. Richard Nyamboli NGWA;
Mrs. Patience N. Nyamboli Yancho
First Secretary
Mr. Modeste Michel ESSONO;
Mrs. Pulcherie Essono Chembou
First Secretary
Mr. Carson Ndongo EFEMBA;
Mrs. Therese Judith Ndongo
Second Secretary (Consular & Protocol)
Mrs. Regine Aicha BOUDJIHO
Second Secretary
Mr. Philippe Ondo ONDO;
Mrs. Felicite Ondo Andeme Engo
Attaché (Cultural)
Mr. Charles Di MINTYENE;
Mrs. Brigitte Nicole Di Mintyene
Military, Naval & Air Attaché
Captain Emmanuel BABOU;
Mrs. Esther Babou

CAPE VERDE

EMBASSY OF THE REPUBLIC OF CAPE VERDE
3415 Massachusetts Ave. NW
Washington, DC 20007
Tel: (202) 965-6820 Fax: (202) 965-1207

Ambassador E. and P.
His Excellency José BRITO;
Mrs. María Oliveira Santos
Second Secretary
Ms. Margarete Chantre LIMA
Second Secretary
Mr. Carlos Fernandes SEMEDO;
Mrs. Amalia Moniz

CENTRAL AFRICAN REPUBLIC

EMBASSY OF CENTRAL AFRICAN REPUBLIC
1618 22nd St. NW
Washington, DC 20008
Tel: (202) 483-7800 Fax: (202) 332-9893

Ambassador E. and P.
His Excellency Emmanuel TOUABOY;
Mrs. Mireille Nathalie Touaboy
Counsellor
Mr. Simon MAINA
Counsellor (Economic)
Mr. Honore Mba YE

Second Secretary (Financial & Administrative)
Mr. Sylvestre Edouard OLOFIO

CHAD

EMBASSY OF THE REPUBLIC OF CHAD
2002 R St. NW
Washington, DC 20009
Tel: (202) 462-4009 Fax: (202) 265-1937
Web: www.chadembassy.org

Ambassador E. and P.
His Excellency Bechir Mahamoud ADAM;
Mrs. Nouracham Bechir Niam
Counsellor
Mr. Abdoulaye BERI;
Mrs. Koudjo Celestine Beri
First Secretary
Mr. Tchouli GOMBO
Attaché
Mr. Hassane OUSMAN

COMOROS

EMBASSY OF THE FEDERAL AND ISLAMIC REPUBLIC OF THE COMOROS
866 United Nations Plz. #418
New York, NY 10017
Tel: (212) 750-1637 Fax: (212) 750-1637

Ambassador E. and P.
His Excellency Mahmoud Mohamed ABOUD

CONGO, DEMOCRATIC REPUBLIC OF THE

EMBASSY OF THE DEMOCRATIC REPUBLIC OF CONGO
1726 M St. NW #601
Washington, DC 20036
Tel: (202) 234-7690 Fax: (202) 234-2609

Ambassador E. and P.
Her Excellency Faida MITIFU
Minister-Counsellor
Mr. Tambo A. Kabila MUKENDI
Counsellor
Mr. Chiriji Celestin Chiza CHIVA
Counsellor
Mr. Thomas Siosi MBIMBA;
Mrs. Romaine Lazwe Mbimba
First Secretary
Mr. Serge TSHAMALA
Second Secretary
Mr. Yves Bashonga RUCHINAGIZA;
Mrs. Atifa Bashonga Shabani

CONGO, REPUBLIC OF

EMBASSY OF THE REPUBLIC OF THE CONGO
4891 Colorado Ave. NW
Washington, DC 20011
Tel: (202) 726-5500 Fax: (202) 726-1860

Ambassador E. and P.
His Excellency Serge MOMBOULI;
Mrs. Stella Corine Mombouli
First Secretary
Mr. Jean Christophe LINGOUA;
Mrs. Therese Lingoua
Second Secretary
Mr. Albert ONDONGO;
Mrs. Jeanine Ondongo

Third Secretary
Mr. Jean Mbossa MBOLLA;
Mrs. Roseline Isabelle Mbossa Mbolla
Attaché (Administrative)
Mr. Pascal ITOUA; Mrs. Georgine Itoua
Attaché (Administrative)
Commadant Daniel Mboussa AMPHA;
Mrs. Therese Mboussa Ampha Akouala
Attaché
Mrs. Elisabeth PEA
Defense Attaché
Colonel Pierre Parfait MANDZANDZA;
Mrs. Germaine Mandzandza Bomola
Asst. Defense Attaché
Colonel Georges ADDO;
Mrs. Charlotte Virginie Addo

Defense Attaché Office
4891 Colorado Ave. NW
Washington, DC 20011
Tel: (202) 726-5500 Fax: (202) 726-1860

COTE D'IVOIRE

EMBASSY OF THE REPUBLIC OF COTE D'IVOIRE
2424 Massachusetts Ave. NW
Washington, DC 20008
Tel: (202) 797-0300 Fax: (202) 462-9444

Ambassador E. and P.
His Excellency Daouda DIABATE;
Mrs. Cecile Diabate Nee Coffi
Counsellor (Communication & Press)
Mr. Mamadou BAMBA;
Mrs. Michelle Bamba
Counsellor
Mr. Fry KOUADIO;
Mrs. Kosso Nou Ama Cecile Kouadio Fry
Counsellor (Consular & Cultural)
Mr. Dja Kouadio DODIAR;
Mrs. Akissi Antoinette Dodiar
Counsellor
Miss Amena Catherine KOUASSI
Counsellor (Tourism)
Ms. Martine LIADE
Counsellor
Ms. Aya Georgette MBRAH
Counsellor (Economic)
Mr. John William Leon F. MORRISON;
Miss Nda Laetitia Desiree Morrisson
First Secretary
Mr. Abdoulaye ESSY
Second Secretary
Mr. Gilbert NENON
Attaché
Ms. Flore Lydie KOFFI
Attaché (Financial)
Mr. N'dri Julien KOFFI;
Mrs. Lea Sylvie Koffi Ahogny
Attaché (Financial)
Mr. Konin KOUADIO; Mrs. Ahou Kouadio
Defense, Military, Naval & Air Attaché
Lieutenant Colonel Gahodit Pierre OULATTA;
Mrs. Marie Louise Tcho Oulatta Kao

Chancery Annex:
2412 Massachusetts Ave. NW
Washington, DC 20008

DJIBOUTI

EMBASSY OF THE REPUBLIC OF DJIBOUTI
1156 15th St. NW #515
Washington, DC 20005
Tel: (202) 331-0270 Fax: (202) 331-0302

Ambassador E. and P.
His Excellency Roble OLHAYE;
Mrs. Amina Farah Ahmed Olhaye
First Secretary
Mr. Issa Daher BOURALEH;
Mrs. Fozia Ahmed Abaneh
First Secretary (Financial & Economic)
Mr. Mohamed Sikien KAYAD;
Mrs. Ayane Abass Ahmed
Second Secretary (Financial)
Mr. Mahdi A. GUIRREH

EGYPT

EMBASSY OF THE ARAB REPUBLIC OF EGYPT
3521 International Ct. NW
Washington, DC 20008
Tel: (202) 895-5400 Fax: (202) 244-4319
Email: embassy@egyptembdc.org
Web: www.egyptembassy.us

Ambassador E. and P.
His Excellency M. Nabil FAHMY;
Mrs. Nermin Abdel Nabil
Minister (Deputy Chief of Mission)
Dr. Walid Mahmoud ABDELNASSER;
Ms. Dahlia Mohamed Nazih M. Tawakol
Minister (Commercial & Economic)
Mr. Mohamed ZIDAN
Minister (Agricultural)
Dr. Hussein Mostafa Kamal MANSOUR;
Mrs. Zeinab M. Mostafa El Sayed Saadah
Minister
Mr. Mohamed I. ZIDAN;
Mrs. Shahinaz M. Abbas
Counsellor
Mr. Ayman Abdul Samie Zain ELDIN;
Mrs. Amal Mostafa K. Mourad
Counsellor
Mr. Wael Ahmed Kamal Aboul MAGD;
Mrs. Hanan Mohamed Aboul Magd
Counsellor
Mr. Hisham Ahmed Mamdouh Abdel HAKIM;
Mrs. Sahar Ibrahim Abdabuelgoud
Counsellor
Mr. Mohamed Amin Abou ELDAHAB
Counsellor
Mr. Mohamed A. DAWOOD
Counsellor (Press)
Dr. Hesham Moussa ELNAKIB;
Mrs. Dalia Sayed Awis Elkomi
Counsellor
Mr. Sameh Mohamed F. AHMED;
Mrs. Amal Mohamed Hassan Tantawy
Counsellor
Mr. Alaa Eldin Mohamed Hassan YOUSSEF;
Mrs. Amira Mahmoud Mohamed Aly
Counsellor
Mr. Hussein Abdel Karim MUBARAK;
Mrs. Hwaida Essam Abdel Rahman
Counsellor (Medical)
Dr. Mahmoud Abo Elnaser RASHEED;
Mrs. Suria Abdelmoeman
Counsellor (Cultural & Director)
Dr. Abdallah Sadik Said BAZARAA
First Secretary
Dr. Badr Ahmed Mohamed ABDELATTY;
Mrs. Naglaa Sobhy Kamal Elkhawanky

First Secretary
Mr. Hazem Hassan K. HASSANEIN
First Secretary
Mr. Mahmoud Mohamed Gamal Eldin ZAYED
Second Secretary
Mr. Tamer Mostafa Mohamed MOSTAFA;
Mrs. Nancy Ahmed A. Fattah Elsohafy
Third Secretary
Mr. Mohamed Abdelgawad E. Ahmed ALLAM;
Mrs. Mona Mohamed Ibrahim M. Youssif

Chancery Annex-Miscellaneous Press and
Information Office
1666 Connecticut Ave. NW #440
Washington, DC 20009
Tel: (202) 667-3402 Fax: (202) 234-6827

Chancery Annex-Procurement Office
5500 16th St. NW
Washington, DC 20011
Tel: (202) 726-8006 Fax: (202) 829-4909

Commercial and Economic Affairs Office
2232 Massachusetts Ave. NW
Washington, DC 20008
Tel: (202) 265-9111 Fax: (202) 328-4517

Cultural and Educational Bureau
1303 New Hampshire Ave. NW
Washington, DC 20036
Tel: (202) 296-3888 Fax: (202) 296-3891

Office of Defense, Military, Naval and Air
Attaché
2590 L St. NW
Washington, DC 20037
Tel: (202) 333-1283 Fax: (202) 333-7240

EQUATORIAL GUINEA

**EMBASSY OF THE REPUBLIC OF
EQUATORIAL GUINEA**
2020 16th St. NW
Washington, DC 20009
Tel: (202) 518-5700 Fax: (202) 518-5252

Ambassador E. and P.
His Excellency Teodoro Biyogo NSUE;
Mrs. Elena Mensa
First Secretary
Mr. Toribio Obiang Mbah MEYE
Third Secretary
Mrs. Paciencia Mata MOHOSE

ERITREA

EMBASSY OF THE STATE OF ERITREA
1708 New Hampshire Ave. NW
Washington, DC 20009
Tel: (202) 319-1991 Fax: (202) 319-1304

Ambassador E. and P.
His Excellency Girma ASMEROM
Counsellor (Deputy Chief of Mission)
Mr. Tsehaye FASSIL
First Secretary
Mr. Rezene Adonai HAILE;

Mrs. Abeba Ghebremicael Genzebu
Second Secretary (Consular)
Mr. Goitom Sium GHEBREZHABIHER;
Mrs. Tblez Abraha Asfaha
Second Secretary
Mr. Melake Tesfayohannes
HABTEMICHAEL
Second Secretary
Mr. Saleh Eman MAHMOUD;
Ms. Samia Ahmedin Mohammed Raki

ETHIOPIA

EMBASSY OF ETHIOPIA
3506 International Dr. NW
Washington, DC 20008
Tel: (202) 364-1200 Fax: (202) 587-0195
Email: info@ethiopiaembassy.org
Web: www.ethiopianembassy.org

Ambassador E. and P.
His Excellency Kassahun AYELE;
Mrs. Haregewoin Abebe Wondabeku
Minister
Mr. Fesseha Asghedom TESSEMA
Counsellor
Mr. Demeke Atnafu AMBULO;
Mrs. Wegayehu Mezene Mamo
Counsellor (Economic & Trade Affairs)
Mr. Gizachew Bizuayehu BEYENE;
Mrs. Nigatua Shibiru Hailemariam
Counsellor
Mr. Mesfin Endrias H. GEBRIEL;
Mrs. Kelemuwa Hailu Desta
Counsellor
Mr. Nebiyou Dagne TESSEMA;
Mrs. Haimanotteketel W. Gabriel
First Secretary
Mrs. Alganesh MESHESHA
First Secretary (Administrative & Finance)
Mr. Tilahun Woldesimon TEFERI;
Mrs. Azeb Abay Desta
Second Secretary
Mr. Tsegaye Edao GELGELU;
Mrs. Chaltu Edasa Shubo
Second Secretary
Mr. Fitsum Hailu ABRAHA;
Mrs. Mitslàl Girmay Berha
Attaché
Mr. Dejene Birru CHUCKO;
Mrs. Misrak Yimer Tessema

Consular Section
3506 International Dr. NW
Washington, DC 20008
Tel: (202) 274-4555 Fax: (202) 686-9621

Economic, Financial and Trade Office
3506 International Dr. NW
Washington, DC 20008
Tel: (202) 364-6385 Fax: (202) 364-6387

GABON

EMBASSY OF THE GABONESE REPUBLIC
2034 20th St. NW #200
Washington, DC 20009
Tel: (202) 797-1000 Fax: (202) 332-0668

Ambassador E. and P.

His Excellency Jules Marius
OGOUEBANDJA; Mrs. Blandine
Ogouebandja
Counsellor
Mrs. Helena Lydia Barro CHAMBRIER;
Mr. Alexandre Barro Chambrier
Counsellor
Mrs. Huguette Mboumba MOUSSODOU
Counsellor
Mr. Laurent NDONG; Mrs. Justine Ndong
Counsellor
Mr. Albert NGUIA
Counsellor
Mrs. Mireille Obame Nguema EKOMVONE;
Mr. Reginald Anthony Moore
Counsellor
Mrs. Eulalie Omanda NAMBO
Defense, Military, Naval & Air Attaché
Colonel Oudoki BOULINGUI;
Mrs. Rachel Moudoki

GAMBIA

EMBASSY OF THE GAMBIA
1156 15th St. NW #905
Washington, DC 20005
Tel: (202) 785-1379 Fax: (202) 785-1430

Ambassador E. and P.
His Excellency Dodou Bammy JAGNE;
Mrs. Begay Jagne
Minister-Counsellor (Deputy Chief of Mission)
Mr. Abdol Rahman COLE
First Secretary
Mr. Pa Njagga MENDY; Mrs. Jainaba Bojang
Attaché (Finance)
Mr. Lamin Binta SANYANG;
Mrs. Nyima Sanyang

GHANA

EMBASSY OF GHANA
3512 International Dr. NW
Washington, DC 20008
Tel: (202) 686-4520 Fax: (202) 686-4527
Web: www.ghana-embassy.org

Ambassador E. and P.
His Excellency Fritz POKU;
Mrs. Nana Efusa Salvo Poku
Minister (Deputy Chief of Mission)
Mr. Isaac AGGREY;
Mrs. Gloria Vivian Aggrey
Minister-Counsellor
Mr. Joseph Cudjoe ACKON; Mrs. Mary
Akuffo Ackon
Minister-Counsellor (Trade)
Mr. Johnson ADASI; Mrs. Georgina Adasi
Minister-Counsellor (Information)
Mr. Ivor Agyeman DUAH;
Mrs. Felicia Kufuor Agyeman Duah
Counsellor (Economic)
Mrs. Jennifer LARTEY; Mr. Steve Lartey
First Secretary (Administrative)
Ms. Adelaide Nana AGYEMAN
First Secretary (Administrative)
Mrs. Eleanor Afaribea DADEY
First Secretary

Ms. Elizabeth NYANTAKYI
First Secretary & Vice Consul
Mr. Chris OBENG
Second Secretary (Administrative)
Mr. Emmanuel Kwashi KPEMLI;
Mrs. Felicia Ameyo Kpemli
Attaché (Finance)
Ms. Ruth A.T. ABBAM
Defense, Military, Naval & Air Attaché
Colonel Emmanuel OKYERE

GUINEA

EMBASSY OF THE REPUBLIC OF GUINEA
2112 Leroy Pl. NW
Washington, DC 20008
Tel: (202) 986-4300 Fax: (202) 986-4800

Ambassador E. and P.
His Excellency Alpha Oumar Rafiou
BARRY; Mrs. Raye Diallo Barry
Counsellor
Mr. Elhadj Boubacar BARRY; Mrs. Hadja
Oussamatou Balde
Counsellor (Economic)
Ms. Bintou CONDE
Counsellor (Political)
Mr. Ibrahima Sory TRAORE; Mrs. Nyoula
Epse Traore Conte
First Secretary (Cultural)
Mr. Thierno Abdouramaman BALDE; Mrs.
Santou Balde
First Secretary (Finance & Consular)
Mr. Aly CAMARA; Mrs. Mabinty Camara
Attaché (Administrative)
Ms. Catherine SAGNO
Defense, Military, Naval & Air Attaché
Lieutenant Commander Mamadou Alimou
DIALLO; Mrs. Bokoum Binta Diallo

GUINEA-BISSAU

**EMBASSY OF THE REPUBLIC OF GUINEA-
BISSAU**
P.O. Box 33813
Washington, DC 20033
Tel: (301) 947-3958

Ambassador E. and P.
His Excellency Henrique Adriano DA SILVA;
Mrs. Maria Odilia Almeida Da Silva
**Minister-Counsellor (Charge D'Affaires Ad
Interim)**
Mr. Henrique Adriano DA SILVA;
Mrs. Maria Odilia Almeida Da Silva

KENYA

EMBASSY OF THE REPUBLIC OF KENYA
2249 R St. NW
Washington, DC 20008
Tel: (202) 387-6101 Fax: (202) 462-3829
Email: information@kenyaembassy.com
Web: www.kenyaembassy.com

Ambassador E. and P.
His Excellency Leonard NGAITHE;
Mrs. Susan Ngaithe
Counsellor
Mr. James Misasa WAKIAGA;
Mrs. Lucy Awuor Misasa Wakiaga
First Secretary (Political)
Mr. Mohamedabdi GELLO;
Mrs. Khadija Haji Issa

Counsellor (Political)
Mr. Philip LAGAT
Counsellor
Mr. James Misasa WAKIAGA;
Mrs. Lucy Awuor Misasa Wakiaga
First Secretary (Political)
Mr. Mohamed Abdi GELLO;
Mrs. Khadija Haj Issa
First Secretary (Finance)
Mr. Francis Ndiangui GITHIGI;
Mrs. Agnes Wanjiku Ndiangui
First Secretary (Legal)
Mrs. Beatrice Nyaboe KARAGO;
Mr. Paul Wamakima Karago
First Secretary (Economic)
Mr. Frank Lemiso KIRISWA;
Mrs. Sheila Hope Lemiso
First Secretary (Immigration)
Mr. Simon Moinkett Ole MEELI;
Mrs. Joyce Turaso Kipury Moinkett
Second Secretary (Political)
Mrs. Peris Wangari MURAGE;
Mr. Moses Murage Mugo
Attaché (Administrative)
Mr. James Nkonge KANANUA;
Mrs. Catherine Kaimuri Nkonge
Attaché (Administrative)
Mrs. Joyce Kambura MARETE;
Mr. Julius Willie Mareteh
Attaché (Commercial)
Mrs. Lina Osida OCHIENG;
Mr. Festus Jacob Ochieng
Attaché (Administrative)
Mr. Michael Siwa SUMUKWO;
Mrs. Salina Jemuge Sumukwo

LESOTHO

EMBASSY OF THE KINGDOM OF LESOTHO
2511 Massachusetts Ave. NW
Washington, DC 20008
Tel: (202) 797-5533 Fax: (202) 234-6815
Email: lesothoembassy@verizon.net
Web: www.lesothoemb-usa.gov.ls

Ambassador E. and P.
Her Excellency Molelekeng E. RAPOLAKI
Counsellor
Ms. Motheba Gwendoline MOELETSI
First Secretary
Mr. Tumelo Ephraim RABOLETSI;
Mrs. Maitumeleng Mpatlise Raboletsi
Third Secretary
Mr. E. Thabang LEPHEANA;
Mrs. Maphamotse M. Lepheana

LIBERIA

EMBASSY OF THE REPUBLIC OF LIBERIA
5201 16th St. NW
Washington, DC 20011
Tel: (202) 723-0437 Fax: (202) 723-0436
Email: info@embassyofliberia.org
Web: www.embassyofliberia.org

Ambassador E. and P.
His Excellency Charles A. MINOR;
Mrs. Comfort M. Minor
Minister
Mr. Abdulah K. DUNBAR;
Mrs. Beatrice M. Dunbar
Counsellor (Maritime)
Mr. George Massa ARKU;
Mrs. Kari H.J. Arku
Counsellor (Economic, Trade & Consul)
Mr. Alexander H.N. WALLACE, III;
Mrs. Miama L. Wallace

First Secretary & Consul
Mrs. Stataria Ethel COOPER
First Secretary & Consul
Mr. William Saima SALLEY;
Mrs. Jamah Salley
Second Secretary & Vice Consul
Mrs. Catherine J. NMAH

LIBYA

LIBYAN LIAISON OFFICE
2600 Virginia Ave. NW #705
Washington, DC 20037
Tel: (202) 944-9601 Fax: (202) 944-9606

Ambassador E. and P.
His Excellency Ali Suleiman AUJALI;
Mrs. Naima M. Bseikri
Counsellor
Mr. Mahmoud M.A. GHDORA;
Mrs. Ebtisam F.A. Ibrahim
Counsellor
Mr. Mawloud Ali SMIDA;
Mrs. Salma A.B. Yousef
Counsellor
Mr. Abdulhamed Othman YAHYA

MADAGASCAR

EMBASSY OF THE REPUBLIC OF MADAGASCAR
2374 Massachusetts Ave. NW
Washington, DC 20008
Tel: (202) 265-5525 Fax: (202) 265-3034
Web: www.embassy.org/madagascar

Ambassador E. and P.
His Excellency Rajaonarivony NARISOA;
Mrs. Ravaomalala Rondrosoa Narisoa
Counsellor (Deputy Chief of Mission)
Mrs. Eulalie Narisolo RAVELOSOA;
Mr. Jean De La Croix Rabemananjara
Counsellor (Economic)
Mr. Rasolozakanaly RAVONINJATOVO;
Mrs. Marie Constance Ranivomboahangy
Counsellor (Commercial)
Miss Josee Christiane RAZAFIJEMISA
Attaché (Financial)
Mr. Justin MANARINJARA;
Mrs. Georgine Manarinjara
Attaché (Protocol)
Mr. Robert Franck RAKOTOARIMANGA;
Mrs. Julie Euphrasie Rakotoarimanga

MALAWI

EMBASSY OF MALAWI
1156 15th St. NW #320
Washington, DC 20005
Tel: (202) 721-0270 Fax: (202) 721-0288

Ambassador E. and P.
His Excellency Bernard Herbert SANDE;
Mrs. Gladys Sande
Counsellor (Deputy Chief of Mission)
Mr. Victor Decio GEDDES;
Mrs. Jacqueline Wendy Geddes
Counsellor (Political)
Mrs. Roselyn MAKHUMULA;
Mr. Phillip Joseph Makhumula Nkhoma
First Secretary
Mrs. Jiddy Edith MALETA;
Mr. Robert Konzani Maleta

Second Secretary
Ms. Martha Thokozani Chikuni CHONGWE;
Mr. John John Chongwe
Second Secretary (Economic)
Ms. Jane Ngineriwa KAMBALAME

MALI

EMBASSY OF THE REPUBLIC OF MALI
2130 R St. NW
Washington, DC 20008
Tel: (202) 332-2249   Fax: (202) 332-6603
Email: infos@maliembassy.us
Web: www.maliembassy.us

Ambassador E. and P.
His Excellency Abdoulaye DIOP;
Mrs. Mariam Olga Linda Toure Epse Diop
Counsellor
Mr. Mamounou TOURE;
Mrs. Ouleymatou Toure
Second Secretary
Mr. Moustapha TRAORE;
Mrs. Nene Oumou Diallo Eps Traore
Attaché (Financial)
Mr. Mamadou CAMARA;
Mrs. Tenin Diakite Eps Camara

MAURITANIA

EMBASSY OF THE ISLAMIC REPUBLIC OF MAURITANIA
2129 Leroy Pl. NW
Washington, DC 20008
Tel: (202) 232-5700 Fax: (202) 319-2623

Ambassador E. and P.
His Excellency Tijani Ould M.E. KERIM;
Mrs. Marieme M'Bengue Ould Kerim
Minister-Counsellor
Mr. Abal Abbas BASS; Mrs. Marietou Bass
Counsellor
Mr. Kemal MOHAMEDOU;
Mrs. Fatimetou Mohamedou
Counsellor
Mr. Ahmed Ould BEKRINE

MAURITIUS

EMBASSY OF THE REPUBLIC OF MAURITIUS
4301 Connecticut Ave. NW #441
Washington, DC 20008
Tel: (202) 244-1491 Fax: (202) 966-0983
Email: mauritius.embassy@prodigy.net
Web: www.maurinet.com/embasydc.html

Minister-Counsellor (Deputy Chief of Mission)
Miss Shiu Ching Young Kim FAT
Minister-Counsellor (Trade)
Mr. Peter CRAIG; Mrs. Amrita Razya Craig
Second Secretary
Miss Shafeenaaz NURMAHOMED

MOROCCO

EMBASSY OF THE KINGDOM OF MOROCCO
1601 21st St. NW
Washington, DC 20009
Tel: (202) 462-7980 Fax: (202) 265-0161

Ambassador E. and P.
His Excellency Aziz MEKOUAR;
Mrs. Maria Felice Cittadini Cesi
Counsellor (Deputy Chief of Mission)
Mr. Mohammed ARIAD;
Mrs. Assia Temsamani
Minister (Consular)
Mr. Hassan KHANTACH
Minister-Counsellor (Administrative)
Mr. Abdelouahed BENMOUNA;
Mrs. Rachida Benmouna
Counsellor
Mr. Yahia A.F. AGOUMY
Counsellor (Paymaster General)
Mr. Mohamed El HAJJAJI
Counsellor (Economic)
Mr. Mohamed Adil EMBARCH;
Mrs. Aicha El Boukhari
Counsellor
Mr. Hakim JILALI
Counsellor (Consular Affairs)
Mr. Hassan KHANTACH;
Mrs. Maria Josefa Novalvosbaena
Counsellor (Economic)
Mr. Mourad LAYACHI;
Mrs. Sanae El Kadiri El Yamani
Counsellor
Mr. Driss OUKASSOU; Mrs. Nouzha Lhaiti
Counsellor
Ms. Fatiha REMH; Mr. Mostafa Terrab
First Secretary
Ms. Jamila ALAOUI
First Secretary
Mr. Abdelkader BOUMLIK
First Secretary
Ms. Lalla El Alaoui LAMDAGHRI
First Secretary
Mr. Rachid LAKHAL
Attaché (Army Supply)
Mr. Abdelkader OUAZZANI;
Mrs. Yamina Arfala
Defense, Military, Naval & Air Attaché
Colonel Ahmed ARARA; Mrs. Aicha Loutati

Chancery Annex
1821 Jefferson Pl. NW
Washington, DC 20036
Tel: (202) 462-7979 Fax: (202) 452-0106

MOZAMBIQUE

EMBASSY OF THE REPUBLIC OF MOZAMBIQUE
1990 M St. NW #570
Washington, DC 20036
Tel: (202) 293-7146 Fax: (202) 835-0245
Email: embamoc@aol.com
Web: www.embamoc-usa.org

Ambassador E. and P.
His Excellency Armando Alexandre
PANGUENE; Mrs. Teresa Panguene

First Secretary
Mr. Antonio Rodrigues JOSE;
Mrs. Emilia Helma Samuel Sengo
Second Secretary
Mr. Custodio Ferreira OSSIFO;
Ms. Jacinta De Jesus Fernandes
Attaché (Financial & Administrative)
Mr. Fernando GOENHA
Attaché (Financial)
Mr. Fernando GOENHA; Mrs. Faith Mbewe
Attaché (Administrative)
Mr. Maximiano MAXLHAEIA;
Mrs. Julia Augusto Guimaraes

NAMIBIA

EMBASSY OF THE REPUBLIC OF NAMIBIA
1605 New Hampshire Ave. NW
Washington, DC 20009
Tel: (202) 986-0540 Fax: (202) 986-0443
Email: info@namibiaembassyusa.org
Web: www.namibiaembassyusa.org

Ambassador E. and P.
Mr. Hopelong IPINGE
Minister-Counsellor (Charge D'Affaires Ad Interim)
Mrs. Selma Ashipala MUSAVYI;
Mr. Symphorien Musavyi
First Secretary
Mr. Pahukeni Paulus TITUS;
Mrs. Beatriz Maria Titus
Second Secretary
Mr. Dudley DELIE
Third Secretary
Ms. Renate Rosa Gorases GAES

NIGER

EMBASSY OF THE REPUBLIC OF NIGER
2204 R St. NW
Washington, DC 20008
Tel: (202) 483-4224 Fax: (202) 483-3169
Email: ambassadorniger@hotmail.com
Web: www.nigerembassyusa.org

Ambassador E. and P.
vacant
Counsellor
Mr. Amadou SOUNNA
First Secretary
Mr. Hassane TAHER; Mrs. Fadouma Sidi Taher
Attaché (Financial)
Mr. Bana MOUSSA; Mrs. Ramatou Moussa Bana Moussa
Defense, Military & Air Attaché
Lieutenant Colonel Soumana ZANGUINA;
Mrs. Fatima Zanguina

NIGERIA

EMBASSY OF THE FEDERAL REPUBLIC OF NIGERIA
3519 International Ct. NW
Washington, DC 20008
Tel: (202) 986-8400 Fax: (202) 362-6981
Web: www.nigeriaembassyusa.org

Ambassador E. and P.
His Excellency Professor George Achulike OBIOZOR; Mrs. Grace Clementine Obiozor
Minister (Deputy Chief of Mission)
Mr. Okon Ibanga UDOH
Minister (Economic & Commercial)

Mr. Enaruna E. IMOHE;
Mrs. Philomena O. Imohe
Minister
Mr. Umunna Humphrey ORJIAKO
Minister
Mr. Felix Yusufu PWOL;
Mrs. Angela Hwonghei Pwol
Minister
Mr. Albert Olakunle SOYOMBO;
Mrs. Folorunso Abeni Soyombo
Minister-Counsellor (Information)
Mr. Frederick Kehinde MARTINS;
Mrs. Ajibola Iyabode Martins
Minister-Counsellor
Mr. Ahmed UMAR; Mrs. Aisha Ahmed Umar
Counsellor (Communications)
Mr. Mohammed BELLO;
Mrs. Maimuna Mohammed Bello
Counsellor
Mr. James Thlau MEDUGU;
Mrs. Monica James Medugu
Counsellor
Mr. Ojemame Olusola OREVBA;
Mrs. Theresa Oluwayemisi Orevba
Attaché (Finance)
Colonel Cyril Uzoma AGULANNA
Attaché (Immigration)
Mr. Denen AKAA
Attaché (Communications)
Mr. Okechukwu Emmanuel IDEGWU;
Mrs. Blessing Idegwu
Attaché (Finance)
Mr. Ndubisi Anthony NJOKU;
Mrs. Nkechinyere Bertha Njoku
Defense, Military & Air Attaché
Group Captain Adebiyi Rasak OKANLAWON;
Mrs. Olawatoyin Aduke Okanlawon
Naval Attaché
Captain Gabriel Edmund OKOI;
Mrs. Ekaette Gabriel Okoi
Asst. Defense Attaché
Major James AKARAIWE;
Mrs. Rita Uluueme Akaraiwe

Chancery Annex
2201 M St. NW
Washington, DC

University Office
2010 Massachusetts Ave. NW, 4th Fl.
Washington, DC 20036
Tel: (202) 822-1520

RWANDA

EMBASSY OF THE REPUBLIC OF RWANDA
1714 New Hampshire Ave. NW
Washington, DC 20009
Tel: (202) 232-2882 Fax: (202) 232-4544
Email: rwandaemb@rwandaemb.org
Web: www.rwandaemb.org

Ambassador E. and P.
His Excellency Dr. Zac NSENGA;
Mrs. Eron Asimwe Nsenga
Counsellor
Mr. Kaliva KARURETWA
First Secretary
Ms. Violette UWAMUTARA
Second Secretary
Mr. Eugene Segore KAYIHURA;
Mrs. Nadia Ruyuki Shaza
Attaché (Commercial)
Miss Kaliza KARURETWA
Defense, Military, Naval & Air Attaché
Lieutenant Colonel Joseph NZABAMWITA

SENEGAL

EMBASSY OF THE REPUBLIC OF SENEGAL
2112 Wyoming Ave. NW
Washington, DC 20008
Tel: (202) 234-0540 Fax: (202) 332-6315

Ambassador E. and P.
His Excellency Dr. Amadou Lamine BA;
Mrs. Oulimata Gueye Ba
Minister-Counsellor
Mr. Mamadou DEME;
Mrs. Sallamata Diallo Deme
Minister-Counsellor
Mr. Mamadou Mountaga GUEYE;
Mrs. Ndeye Rokhaya Drame
Counsellor
Mr. Sadio CISSOKHO
Counsellor (Economic)
Mr. Amadou FALL;
Mrs. Coumba Wayrou Thiam Fall
Counsellor
Mr. Khassim MBACKE;
Mrs. Fatou Kebe Mbacke
Counsellor
Mrs. Fatoumata Binetou NDAO;
Mr. Daouda Ndao
Counsellor (Communication)
Mr. Alpha NDIAYE; Mrs. Aminata Ndiaye
Counsellor (Consular)
Mrs. Awa Ndiaye SYLLA; Mr. Tijane Sylla
First Secretary
Mr. Aliou DIOUF; Mrs. Sona Ndiaye Diouf
Second Secretary
Mr. El Hadji Mansour GUEYE;
Mrs. Aida Mbaye Epse Gueye
Attaché
Mr. Pierre DIOUF; Mrs. Anna Diouf
Defense, Military, Naval & Air Attaché
Colonel Oumar Baila KANE;
Mrs. Aissatou Toure Kane

Defense, Air & Military Attaché Office
1825 I St. NW #400
Washington, DC 20006
Tel: (202) 429-2098 Fax: (202) 332-6315

SEYCHELLES

EMBASSY OF THE REPUBLIC OF SEYCHELLES
800 2nd Ave. #400C
New York, NY 10017
Tel: (212) 972-1785 Fax: (212) 972-1786

Ambassador E. and P.
His Excellency Jeremie BONNELAME

SIERRA LEONE

EMBASSY OF SIERRA LEONE
1701 19th St. NW
Washington, DC 20009
Tel: (202) 939-9261 Fax: (202) 483-1793
Web: www.embassyofsierraleone.org

Ambassador E. and P.
His Excellency Ibrahim M. KAMARA;
Mrs. Memunatu A. Kamara
Counsellor
Mr. Hassan Mohamed CONTEH;
Mrs. Fatmata E. Conteh
First Secretary
Mr. Sheku MESALI;
Mrs. Bithadon Alice Mesali

SOUTH AFRICA

EMBASSY OF THE REPUBLIC OF SOUTH AFRICA
3051 Massachusetts Ave. NW
Washington, DC 20008
Tel: (202) 232-4400 Fax: (202) 265-1607
Web: www.saembassy.org

Ambassador E. and P.
Her Excellency Barbara Joyce Mosima MASEKELA
Minister (Economics)
Mr. Mdunwazi Robert BALOYI
Minister (Health)
Ms. Nobayeni Cecilia DLADLA
Minister (Agriculture)
Dr. Siphiwe Felix MKHIZE;
rs. Anna Sibongile Mkhize
Minister (Administration)
Mr. Pragalathan NAIDOO
Counsellor
Mr. Tshepo Lloyd MAZIBUKO
Counsellor (Political)
Mr. Daniel Thamaga NGWEPE
Counsellor
Mr. Gareth Edward REES;
Mrs. Nicole Anne Rees
First Secretary
Mr. David Charl BREWIS;
Mrs. Christina Johanna Susanna Brewis
First Secretary (Political)
Mr. Michael CANHAM;
Mrs. Teresa Sharon Louw
First Secretary (Administration)
Ms. Janette Fernanda Dos SANTOS
First Secretary
Mr. Andre Johannes GROENEWALD;
Mrs. Christina Maria Groenewald
Second Secretary
Mr. Montshioa Simon Prince CHOABI;
Mrs. Mapule Regina Mmisapitso
Second Secretary
Mr. Pieter Du PLESSIS;
Mrs. Heleen Du Plessis
Second Secretary
Mr. Jan Frederik JORDAAN
Third Secretary (Administrative)
Mr. Simon Lodewyk ACKERMANN;
Mrs. Janetta Debora Ackermann
Third Secretary (Political)
Ms. Joyce KALAOTE
Third Secretary (Political)
Mr. Rudzani Godfrey MULAUDZI;
Mrs. Sekao Tommy Mulaudzi
Third Secretary
Ms. Hema ODHAV
Third Secretary (Political)
Mr. Josiel Motumisi TAWANA
Attaché
Mr. Mashudu Elvis MAFUNE;
Mrs. Mmbulungeni Mafune

Agricultural Office
4301 Connecticut Ave. NW #200
Washington, DC 20008

Communication Section
3051 Massachusetts Ave. NW
Washington, DC 20008
Tel: (202) 232-4400 Fax: (202) 232-5370

Consular Office
4301 Connecticut Ave. NW
Washington, DC 20008
Tel: (202) 232-4400 Fax: (202) 232-3402

Department of Trade and Industry
4301 Connecticut Ave. NW

Washington, DC 20008
Tel: (202) 232-4400 Fax: (202) 232-4400

Public Affairs Office
4301 Connecticut Ave. NW #200
Washington, DC 20008

Technical Office
4301 Connecticut Ave. NW #200
Washington, DC 20008

Trade/Industry/Agricultural
4301 Connecticut Ave. NW #200
Washington, DC 20008
Tel: (202) 966-8910

SUDAN

EMBASSY OF THE REPUBLIC OF THE SUDAN
2210 Massachusetts Ave. NW
Washington, DC 20008
Tel: (202) 338-8565 Fax: (202) 667-2406
Email: info@sudanembassy.org
Web: www.sudanembassy.org

Ambassador E. and P.
Mr. Khidir Haroun AHMED
Minister (Charge D'Affaires Ad Interim)
vacant
Minister (Deputy Chief of Mission)
vacant
Minister
Mr. Salah Ahmed El Salih El GUNEID;
Mrs. Duria Mohamed Sharif Nour El Daim
Minister
vacant
Counsellor
Mr. Mohammed Abdallaali ELTOM;
Mrs. Amani Yousif Mukhtar
First Secretary
Mr. Maowai Osman Khalid MOHAMED;
Mrs. Ghada Abdel Dafie Abdel Gadir
Second Secretary (Consular)
Mr. Khalid Musa DAFALLA;
Mrs. Afaf Mohamed Mahamadani Hamid
Third Secretary
Mr. Gamal Malik Ahmed GORAISH; Mrs.
Mona M. Awadelkarim Mohamed
Attaché (Administrative)
Mr. Mubarak Osman Enan ALI; Mrs. Farida
Ibrahim Abdelrahman
Attaché (Financial)
Mr. Mooala Saeid Mooala SALAH; Mrs.
Hussna Hussein Elnour Gumaa

Information Attaché Office
2210 Massachusetts Ave. NW
Washington, DC 20008
Tel: (202) 797-8863 Fax: (202) 745-2615

Office of the Cultural Counsellor
2612 Woodley Pl.
Washington, DC 20008
Tel: (202) 387-8001

SWAZILAND

EMBASSY OF THE KINGDOM OF SWAZILAND
1712 New Hampshire Ave. NW
Washington, DC 20009
Tel: (202) 234-5002 Fax: (202) 234-8254

Counsellor
Mr. Christian M. NKAMBULE;

Mrs. Ncamsile Precious Nkambule
Third Secretary
Ms. Phindile Goodness NXUMALO
Attaché (Education)
Prince Gcina Samuel DLAMINI
Attaché (Administrative)
Mrs. Florence Shabangu HLOPHE

TANZANIA

EMBASSY OF THE UNITED REPUBLIC OF TANZANIA
2139 R St. NW
Washington, DC 20008
Tel: (202) 939-6125 Fax: (202) 797-7408
Email: balozi@tanzaniaembassy-us.org
Web: www.tanzaniaembassy-us.org

Ambassador E. and P.
His Excellency Andrew Mhando DARAJA;
Mrs. Anne M. Daraja
Minister
Mr. Ngosha Said MAGONYA
Minister (Head of Chancery)
Ms. Lily MUNANKA
Minister-Counsellor
Mr. Alan Steven MZENGI;
Mrs. Stella Alan Mzengi
Counsellor (Political)
Ms. Justa Matari NYANGE;
Mr. Herbert Herme Nyange
First Secretary
Mr. Joseph Edward SOKOINE;
Mrs. Christine Towo Sokoine
Attaché (Financial)
Mr. Halidi Juma LUSEKO;
Mrs. Margareth Nambuya Luseko

TOGO

EMBASSY OF THE REPUBLIC OF TOGO
2208 Massachusetts Ave. NW
Washington, DC 20008
Tel: (202) 234-4212 Fax: (202) 232-3190

Ambassador E. and P.
His Excellency Akoussoulelou BODJONA;
Mrs. Zaina Pierrette Bodjona
Minister-Counsellor
Mrs. B. Mayanendja Nonon Saa WOLOU
Counsellor (Press & Communication)
Mr. Bruno FINEL
Attaché (Financial)
Mr. Napo Bernard ALI-NAPO;
Mrs. Ayorkor Dope Ali Napo
Attaché
Mr. Azoguenou Komlanvi AMOUZOU;
Mrs. Ayoko Amouzou
Attaché (Cultural)
Ms. BEHEZAGNASSINGBE
Attaché (Financial)
Mr. Koffi TCHAOU;
Mrs. Ablavi Djreke Epse Tchaou

TUNISIA

EMBASSY OF TUNISIA
1515 Massachusetts Ave. NW
Washington, DC 20005
Tel: (202) 862-1850 Fax: (202) 862-1858

Ambassador E. and P.
Mr. Mohammed Nejib HACHANA
Counsellor
Mr. Mourad BELHASSEN
Counsellor (Consular)
Mr. Kamel Ben HASSINE;
Mrs. Hedia Briki Ben Hassine
Counsellor
Mr. Taoufik CHEBBI
Counsellor
Mr. Riadh DRIDI; Mrs. Faouzia Dridi
Counsellor
Mr. Mohamed Lamine LOURIMI;
Mrs. Najiba Lourimi
First Secretary
Mr. Ali Ben SAID; Mrs. Chahrazed Ben Said
Attaché (Administrative)
Mr. Abderrazak KOUKI
Attaché
Mr. Mourad TRABELSI
Defense, Military, Naval & Air Attaché
Colonel Taieb LAAJIMI;
Mrs. Fattouma Laajimi
Asst. Defense, Military, Naval & Air Attaché
Lieutenant Colonel Abdelkerim BAHRI;
Mrs. Hedia Cherif Ep Bahri

Defense Armed Forces Attaché
1515 Massachusetts Ave. NW
Washington, DC 20005
Tel: (202) 862-1850

Tunisian Information
1515 Massachusetts Ave. NW
Washington, DC 20005
Tel: (202) 446-2546

UGANDA

EMBASSY OF THE REPUBLIC OF UGANDA
5911 16th St. NW
Washington, DC 20011
Tel: (202) 726-7100 Fax: (202) 726-1727
Email: embassy@ugandaembassy.com
Web: www.ugandaembassy.com

Ambassador E. and P.
Her Excellency Edith Grace SSEMPALA
Minister-Counsellor
Mr. Joseph Kiiza KAHIIGWA;
Mrs. Olive Kahiigwa
First Secretary
Mr. Emmanuel Olobo BWOMONO;
Mrs. Olobo Christine Canrach
First Secretary
Mr. Tayebwa Philip KATUREEBE;

Mrs. Sheevon Katureebe
First Secretary (Public Relations & Commercial)
Mrs. Nimisha Jayant Madhvani-CHANDARIA;
Mr. Kapoor Chandaria
Second Secretary
Mr. Richard Tumusiime KABONERO;
Mrs. Grace Tumusiime Kabonero
Third Secretary (Assistant to Ambassador)
Ms. Jacinta KIIZA

ZAMBIA

EMBASSY OF THE REPUBLIC OF ZAMBIA
2419 Massachusetts Ave. NW
Washington, DC 20008
Tel: (202) 265-9717   Fax: (202) 332-0826
Email: info@zambiainfo.org
Web: www.zambiaembassy.org

Ambassador E. and P.
Her Excellency Dr. Inonge Mbikusita
LEWANIKA
Counsellor
Mr. Walubita IMAKANDO;
Mrs. Betty Imakando
First Secretary (Political & Consular)
Mr. Christopher Chiunje CHUNGU;
Mrs. Doreen Adamson Mbewe Changu
First Secretary
Mrs. Mataa Margaret MAKUNGO
First Secretary (Political)
Mr. Longa John MULUTULA;
Mrs. Chembe Irene Mulutula
Second Secretary (Accounts)
Mr. Frank MBEWE;
Mrs. Mtonga Febby Mbewe
Third Secretary (Administrative)
Mrs. Mable Kamoto IKACHANA;
Mr. Felix Akalalambili Ikachana
Defense, Military & Air Attaché
Brigadier General Jackson Dally NSOFU;
Mrs. Marjorie Nsofu

ZIMBABWE

EMBASSY OF REPUBLIC OF ZIMBABWE
1608 New Hampshire Ave. NW
Washington, DC 20009
Tel: (202) 332-7100 Fax: (202) 483-9326

Ambassador E. and P.
His Excellency Simbi Veke MUBAKO;
Mrs. Hazel Barbara Mubako
Minister-Counsellor
Mrs. Elita Tinoenda SAKUPWANYA
Counsellor (Political)
Mr. Chandavengerma GWASHAVANHU;
Counsellor (Political)
Mrs. Ruth Gwashavanhu
First Secretary (Financial)
Mr. Allan NCUBE; Mrs. Ollie Ncube
Third Secretary (Political & Administrative)
Ms. Loreta Evelyn MUTYORA
Defense, Military & Air Attaché
Lieutenant Colonel Romeo Daniel
MUTSVUNGUMA; Mrs. Miriam Mutsvunguma
Asst. Defense, Military & Air Attaché
Squadron Leader Felexio Alexio CHAGEZA;
Mrs. Placidity Chageza

ANGOLA

NEW YORK
New York (CG)
866 United Nations Plz. #552
New York, NY 10017
Tel: (212) 223-3588

Consul General
Ms. Julia MACHADO
Vice Consul
Mr. Jeronimo Gaspar de ALMEIDA
Consular Agent
Mr. Cristovao Da Paz JULIO
Consular Agent
Mr. Joao Jose Da ROCHA

TEXAS
Houston (CG)
3040 Post Oak Blvd. #780
Houston, TX 77056
Tel: (713) 212-3840 Fax: (713) 212-3841

Consul General
Mr. Clemente Pedro Francisco CAMENHA
Deputy Consular General
Mr. Horacio ULIENGUE
Vice Consul
Mr. Francisco BENTO
Consular Agent
Mrs. Francisca Pedro Augusto Da COSTA
Consular Agent
Mrs. Ines De Fatima Fragoso Da FONSECA

BOTSWANA

CALIFORNIA
Los Angeles (HC)
355 S. Grand Ave. #4000
Los Angeles, CA 90071
Tel: (213) 626-8484 Fax:

Honorary Consul
Mr. William Barnum RUDELL

TEXAS
Houston (HC)
10000 Memorial Dr. #400
Houston, TX 77024
Tel: (713) 680-1155 Fax: (713) 680-8055

Honorary Consul
Mr. Stephen V. VALLONE

BURKINA FASO

CALIFORNIA
Los Angeles (HCG)
214 23rd St.
Santa Monica, CA 90402
Tel: (310) 393-2531 Fax: (310) 393-0181

Honorary Consul General
Mr. Allen I. NEIMAN

LOUISIANA
New Orleans (HC)
1527 Robert E. Lee Blvd.
New Orleans, LA 70122
Tel: (504) 284-6351 Fax:

Honorary Consul
Mr. John William ORMOND

BURUNDI

CALIFORNIA
Los Angeles (HC)
532 S. Vermont Ave. #104
Los Angeles, CA 90020
Tel: (213) 637-1450

Honorary Consul
Dr. Nigisti Azebe TESFAI

CAMEROON

CALIFORNIA
San Francisco (HC)
147 Terra Vista Ave.
San Francisco, CA 94115
Tel: (415) 921-5372

Honorary Consul
Mr. Donald LOW

CAPE VERDE

MASSACHUSETTS
Boston (CG)
607 Boylston St., 4th Fl.
Boston, MA 02116
Tel: (617) 353-0014 Fax: (617) 859-9798

Consul General
Mr. Alfredo Amilcar MONTEIRO

CENTRAL AFRICAN REPUBLIC

CALIFORNIA
Los Angeles (HCG)
901 N. Camden Dr.
Beverly Hills, CA 90210
Tel: (310) 278-1095

Honorary Consul General
Mr. Clark E. PARKER, Sr.

NEW YORK
New York (HC)
51 E. 42nd St.
New York, NY 10017

Honorary Consul
Mr. Howard A. HIRSCHFELD

CONGO

LOUISIANA
New Orleans (HC)
201 St. Charles Ave. #2500
New Orleans, LA 70170
Tel: (504) 568-9376

Honorary Consul
Mr. Norbert A. SIMMONS

COTE D'IVOIRE

CALIFORNIA
San Francisco (HCG)
2670 Leavenworth St.
San Francisco, CA 94133
Tel: (415) 310-0812 Fax: (415) 440-0153

Honorary Consul General
Mr. Edgar De Pue OSGOOD

CONNECTICUT
Stamford (HC)
1055 Washington Blvd.
Stamford, CT 06901
Tel: (203) 348-7580 Fax: (203) 358-8423

Honorary Consul
Mr. George Ghassan TALISSE

MICHIGAN
Detroit (HC)
645 Griswold UN #444
Detroit, MI 48226
Tel: Fax:

Honorary Consul
Mr. Harold Richard VARNER

EGYPT

CALIFORNIA
San Francisco (CG)
3001 Pacific Ave.
San Francisco, CA 94115
Tel: (415) 346-9700 Fax: (415) 346-9480
Email: egypt@egy2000.com
Web: www.egy2000.com

Consul General
Mr. Abderahman SALAHELDIN
Deputy Consul General
Mr. Yasser ABED
Consul
Mr. Aldesouky YOUSSEF
Consul
Mr. Khaled ISMAIL
Vice Consul
Mr. Mahmoud SENOUSSI
Vice Consul
Mr. Hesham ELDAHSHAN
Vice Consul
Mr. Mohamed RADWAN
Vice Consul
Mr. Usama SALEH

CALIFORNIA
Egyptian Press Office
1255 Post St. #1034
San Francisco, CA 94109
Tel: (415) 346-3427 Fax: (415) 346-3430

Consul
Mr. Ahmed Mohamed Sharaf MORSY

CALIFORNIA
Egyptian Commercial Office
1255 Post St. #910
San Francisco, CA 94109
Tel: (415) 771-1995

Consul
Mr. Amin Sabry Abdel MEGUD

ILLINOIS
Chicago (CG)
500 N. Michigan Ave. #1900
Chicago, IL 60611
Tel: (312) 828-9162 Fax: (312) 828-9167

Consul General
Ms. Hoda Abdou Mohamed GOUDA
Deputy Consul General
Mrs. Nabila Makram A. WASSEF
Vice Consul
Mr. Adel Youssef Mohamed ABDALLAH
Vice Consul
Mr. Ahmed MOHAMED

Source: U.S. Department of State. www.state.gov

NEW YORK
New York (CG)

1110 2nd Ave. #201
New York, NY 10022
Tel: (212) 759-7120 Fax: (212) 308-7643

Consul General
Mr. Sherif Riad ELKHOLI
Deputy Consul General
Mr. Khaled Fathy YOUSSEF
Consul
Ms. Nelly Hassan Elorabi IBRAHIM
Consul
Mr. Ahmed Mohamed Hassan SHASH
Consul
Mr. Mahmoud A.M. ABOULFETOUH
Vice Consul
Mr. Atef Galal Abdel MAWGOOD
Vice Consul
Mr. Moanesa K. ALI
Vice Consul
Mr. Hussein A. HUSSEIN
Vice Consul
Mr. Hassan Mahmoud Hamed El DEEB
Vice Consul
Mr. Hosny A. SOLIMAN
Vice Consul
Mr. Hosni Mohamed ELGHARIB
Vice Consul
Mr. Magdi Sharaf Eldin Emam HASSAN
Vice Consul
Mr. Salah Mahmoud Mohamed MOUSTAFA
Vice Consul
Mrs. Soheir Said Ahmed GOUDA

NEW YORK
Tourist Office
630 5th Ave. #2305
New York, NY 10111
Tel: (212) 332-2570 Fax: (212) 956-6439

Consul
Mr. Aydens NOUR

NEW YORK
Economic and Commercial Office
10 Rockefeller Plz. #715
New York, NY 10020
Tel: (212) 399-9898 Fax: (212) 399-9899

Consul
Mr. Ahmed HOSNI
Vice Consul
Dr. Reda Mohamed Bayoumi BAKEER
Vice Consul
Mr. Mohamed Abdel KADER

TEXAS
Houston (CG)
1990 Post Oak Blvd. #2180
Houston, TX 77056
Tel: (713) 961-4915

Consul General
Mr. Omar Elfarouk Hassan MOHAMED
Consul
Mr. Khaled Mohamed Abdel RAHMAN
Consul
Mr. Khaled Ahmed Taha M. ABOUZEID
Vice Consul
Miss Mervat Abdel Gawad Ahmed
SOLIMAN
Vice Consul
Mr. Ossama Sayed M. ABDELMEGUID

GABON

NEW YORK
New York (C)
18 E. 41st St., 9th Fl.
New York, NY 10017
Tel: (212) 686-9720

Consular Agent
Mrs. Yvonne Walker BOROBO

GAMBIA

CALIFORNIA
Los Angeles (HCG)
10777 Bellagio Rd.
Los Angeles, CA 90077
Tel: (310) 476-0532

Honorary Consul General
Ms. Aimee KLAUS

GHANA

NEW YORK
New York (CG)
19 E. 47th St.
New York, NY 10017
Tel: (212) 832-1300

Consul General
Mr. Sidney Rudolph Yaw BIMPONG
Consul
Mr. Gilbert Tsatsu TAMAKLOE
Consul
Mr. Andrew BINEY
Vice Consul
Ms. Josephine AIDOO

TEXAS
Houston (HC)
3434 Locke Ln.
Houston, TX 77027-4139
Tel: (713) 960-8806 Fax: (713) 960-8833

Honorary Consul
Mr. Jack M. WEBB

GUINEA

DISTRICT OF COLUMBIA
Washington (EMB)
2112 Leroy Pl. NW
Washington, DC 20008
Tel: (202) 986-4300 Fax: (202) 986-4800

Consul
Mr. Aly CAMARA

PENNSYLVANIA
Philadelphia (HC)
24 W. Tupehocken St.
Philadelphia, PA 19144
Tel: (215) 842-0860

Honorary Consul
Mr. Stanley L. STRAUGHTER

LESOTHO

LOUISIANA
New Orleans (HCG)
4 Grand Teton Ct.
New Orleans, LA 70131
Tel: (504) 392-7949 Fax: (504) 392-1546

Honorary Consul General
Mr. Morris W. REED

TEXAS
Austin (HC)
7400 Valburn Dr.
Austin, TX 78731
Tel: (512) 345-0747 Fax: (512) 345-6422

Honorary Consul
Mrs. Bertha MEANS

LIBERIA

CALIFORNIA
Los Angeles (HCG)
P.O. Box 621
Malibu, CA 90265
Tel: (310) 457-1967 Fax: (310) 457-9122

Honorary Consul General
Mr. Andrew V. IPPOLITO

CALIFORNIA
San Francisco (HCG)
1101 Embarcadero West
Oakland, CA 94607
Tel: (510) 452-6373 Fax: (510) 444-3370

Honorary Consul General
Mr. Gary SCHNITZER

DISTRICT OF COLUMBIA
Washington (EMB)
5201 16th St. NW
Washington, DC 20011
Tel: (202) 723-0437 Fax: (202) 723-0436

Consul
Mr. Alexander H. WALLACE, III
Vice Consul
Mrs. Catherine J. NMAH

GEORGIA
Atlanta (HCG)
2265 Cascade Rd. SW
Atlanta, GA 30311
Tel: (404) 753-4753 Fax: (404) 753-4228

Honorary Consul General
Dr. Walter F.YOUNG

ILLINOIS
Chicago (HCG)
7342 S. Bennett Ave.
Chicago, IL 60649
Tel: (773) 643-8635 Fax:

Honorary Consul General
Mr. Alexander Poley GBAYEE

NEW YORK
New York (CG)
820 2nd Ave.
New York, NY 10017
Tel: (212) 687-1025

Consul General
Mr. Dorsey R. HANSFORD
Deputy Consul General
Mrs. Famatta DELINE
Consul
Mr. Victor E. DOUGBA, Sr.

PENNSYLVANIA
Philadelphia (HC)
2 Penn Ctr. #200
Philadelphia, PA 19102
Tel: (215) 854-6369

Consul General
Ms. Teta V. BANKS

MADAGASCAR

CALIFORNIA
Solana Beach (HC)
1318 Santa Luisa Dr.
Solana Beach, CA 92075
Tel: (858) 792-6999 Fax: (858) 481-7474

Honorary Consul
Ms. Monique RODRIGUEZ

NEW YORK
New York (CG)
820 2nd Ave. #800
New York, NY 10017
Tel: (212) 986-9491

Consul General
Mr. Zina ANDRIANARIVELO

PENNSYLVANIA
Philadelphia (HC)
400 Berwyn Park, 3rd Fl., 899 Cassatt Rd.
Berwyn, PA 19312
Tel: (610) 640-7832

Honorary Consul
Mr. John B. HUFFAKER

MALAWI

CALIFORNIA
Los Angeles (HC)
44970 Via Renaissance Unit
Temecula, CA 92590
Tel: (213) 223-2020

Honorary Consul
Dr. James F. CLEMENTS

MALI

FLORIDA
Ft. Lauderdale (HC)
1710 W. Cypress Creek Rd.
Ft. Lauderdale, FL 33309
Tel: (954) 771-1795 Fax: (954) 771-3281

Honorary Consul
Mr. Mayer SHIRAZIPOUR

LOUISIANA
New Orleans (HC)
4232 Williams Blvd. #101
Kenner, LA 70065
Tel: (504) 465-0765

Honorary Consul
Ms. Nancy Marinovic SUTHERLAND

MOROCCO

CALIFORNIA
Los Angeles (HC)
P.O. Box 80652
San Marino, CA 91118
Tel: (626) 570-0318
Email: asaoud@aol.com

Honorary Consul
Mr. Abdelhak SAOUD

KANSAS
Kansas City (HC)
10777 Barkley #200
Overland Park, KS 66211
Tel: (913) 649-8021

Honorary Consul
Mr. Harry MCLEAR

NEW YORK
New York (CG)
10 E. 40th St., 23rd Fl.
New York, NY 10016
Tel: (212) 758-2625 Fax: (212) 725-4198

Consul General
Mr. Abdeslam JAIDI
Deputy Consul General
Mr. Abderrahim BEYYOUDH
Vice Consul
Mr. Abdelouahab El BOUHALI
Vice Consul
Mr. Mohamed KARMOUNE
Vice Consul
Mr. MUSTAPHAELACHRAOUI

NAMIBIA

MICHIGAN
Detroit (HC)
400 Renaissance Ctr. #2400
Detroit, MI 48243

Honorary Consul
Mr. Don H. BARDEN

NIGERIA

GEORGIA
Atlanta (CG)
8060 Roswell Rd.
Dunwoody, GA 30350
Tel: (770) 394-6261 Fax: (770) 394-4671
Email: info@nigeria-consulate-atl.org
Web: www.nigeria-consulate-atl.org

Consul
Mrs. Folashikemi Victoria AIYEDUN
Consul
Mr. Henry Olasunkami SANDA
Consul
Mr. Aminu NABEGU
Consul
Mr. Hakeem DOSUNMU
Consul
Ms. Jadesola Adejumoke ADESUYI
Consul
Mr. RABIUSHEHU
Vice Consul

Mrs. Helen INYANGORU
Vice Consul
Ms. Nikechi Heleness EMEREONYE

NEW YORK
New York (CG)
828 2nd Ave.
New York, NY 10017
Tel: (212) 808-0301 Fax: (212) 687-1476
Email: info@nigeria-consulate-ny.org
Web: www.nigeria-consulate-ny.org

Consul General
Dr. F.R. ADERELE
Consul
Mr. N.M. AJANWACHUKU
Consul
Mr. I. AUWALI
Consul
Mr. O. FAMOYIN
Consul
Mrs. M.M. Hezekiah OKAA
Consul
Mr. Victor Onochie BOSAH
Consul
Ms. Vivian N.R. OKEKE
Consul
Mrs. Mary Margaret Hezekiah OKAA
Consul
Mr. Olusola Adegbite FAMOYIN
Consul
Mr. Buttler AMADU
Consul
Mr. Ibrahim AUWALU
Consul
Mr. Nwabueze Monk AJANWACHUKU
Consul
Mr. Edwin Enosakhare EDOBOR
Vice Consul
Mrs. Augustina Obiageli OKONKWO
Vice Consul
Ms. Mercy IJOHO

SAO TOME AND PRINCIPE

GEORGIA
Atlanta (HC)
245 Perimeter Center Pkwy. #610
Atlanta, GA 30346
Tel: (678) 904-2811 X235
Fax: (770) 454-0032

Honorary Consul
Mr. Gareth N. GENNER

ILLINOIS
Chicago (HC)
1320 Valley Ct.
Libertyville, IL 60048
Tel: (847) 362-5615

Honorary Consul
Mr. James KAO

SENEGAL

FLORIDA
Miami (HC)
4000 Ponce de Leon Blvd. #700
Coral Gables, FL 33146
Tel: (305) 371-4286 Fax: (305) 371-4288

Honorary Consul
Mr. Michael Stuart HACKER

LOUISIANA
New Orleans (HCG)
2144 World Trade Ctr.
New Orleans, LA 70130
Tel: (504) 529-7561

Honorary Consul General
Mr. William Manchester AYERS
Honorary Consul
Ms. Deborah Ann ADAMS

SEYCHELLES

ALASKA
Anchorage (HC)
7100 Hillside Way
Anchorage, AK 99516
Tel: (907) 244-5375 Fax: (907) 345-5607

Honorary Consul
Mr. Harold GREEN

WASHINGTON
Seattle (HCG)
3620 SW 309th St.
Federal Way, WA 98063
Tel: (253) 874-4579

Honorary Consul General
Mrs. Anne Lise M. CHURCH

SOUTH AFRICA

CALIFORNIA
Los Angeles (CG)
6300 Wilshire Blvd. #600
Los Angeles, CA 90048
Tel: (323) 651-0902 Fax: (323) 651-5969

Consul General
Ms. Jeanette T. NDHLOVU
Consul
Mr. Edward MPIYAKHE
Consul

Mr. Alan Graham MOORE
Vice Consul
Ms. Maria Elizabeth JOUBERT
Vice Consul
Mr. Simphiwe Paul MDINGI

ILLINOIS
Chicago (CG)
200 S. Michigan Ave., 6th Fl.
Chicago, IL 60604
Tel: (312) 939-7929

Consul General
Mr. YUSUFOMAR
Consul
Mr. Machiel Renier Van NIEKERK
Vice Consul
Mrs. Cilda PRETORIUS
Vice Consul
Mr. Azwifarwi Shadrack NEPFUMBADA

NEW YORK
New York (CG)
333 E. 38th St., 9th Fl.
New York, NY 10016
Tel: (212) 213-4880

Consul
Mr. Johannes Kgotso TIBA
Consul
Mr. Ivan Charles VOSLOO
Vice Consul
Ms. Sholeen P. MOOLJEE
Vice Consul
Mrs. Gertrude Nombeko SIKWEZA

UTAH
Salt Lake City (HC)
2272 S. Ridgewood Way
Bountiful, UT 84010
Tel: (801) 298-0824

Honorary Consul
Mr. Robert Paul THORN

TOGO

FLORIDA
Miami (HC)
4000 Ponce de Leon Blvd. #700
Coral Gables, FL 33146
Tel: (305) 371-4286 Fax: (305) 371-4288

Honorary Consul
Mr. Michael Stuart HACKER

Missions of African Countries to the United Nations

The United Nations works to maintain peace and provide humanitarian assistance throughout the world. It was founded on October 24, 1945 and includes 191 member states.

ALGERIA

PERMANENT MISSION OF ALGERIA TO THE UNITED NATIONS
326 E. 48th St.
New York, NY 10017
Tel: (212) 750-1960 Fax: (212) 759-9538
Email: algeria@un.int
Web: www.algeria-un.org

Ambassador E. and P.
His Excellency Abdallah Baali;
Mrs. Rafika Baali

ANGOLA

PERMANENT MISSION OF THE REPUBLIC OF ANGOLA TO THE UNITED NATIONS
125 E. 73rd St.
New York, NY 10021
Tel: (212) 861-5656 Fax: (212) 861-9295
Email: themission@angolaun.org
Web: www.angolamissionun.org

Ambassador E. and P.
His Excellency Ismael Abraao Gaspar Martins;
Mrs. Luiza de Jesus Gaspar Martins

BENIN

PERMANENT MISSION OF THE REPUBLIC OF BENIN TO THE UNITED NATIONS
125 E. 38th St.
New York, NY 10016
Tel: (212) 684-1339 Fax: (212) 684-2058
Email: benun@undp.org
Web: www.un.int/benin

Ambassador E. and P.
His Excellency Joel Adechi;
Mrs. Odile Adechi

BOTSWANA

PERMANENT MISSION OF BOTSWANA TO THE UNITED NATIONS
154 E. 46th St.
New York, NY 10017
Tel: (212) 889-2277 Fax: (212) 725-5061
Email: botswana@un.int

Ambassador E. and P.
His Excellency Alfred M. Dube;
Mrs. Elvyn Jones-Dube

BURKINA FASO

PERMANENT MISSION OF BURKINA FASO TO THE UNITED NATIONS
866 United Nations Plz. #326/327A
New York, NY 10017
Tel: (212) 308-4720 Fax: (212) 308-4690
Email: bfapm@un.int

Ambassador E. and P.
His Excellency Michel Kafando;
Mrs. Inny-Marie Kafando

BURUNDI

PERMANENT MISSION OF THE REPUBLIC OF BURUNDI TO THE UNITED NATIONS
336 E. 45th St., 12th Fl.
New York, NY 10017
Tel: (212) 499-0001 Fax: (212) 499-0006
Email: burundi@un.int

Ambassador E. and P.
Vacant

CAMEROON

PERMANENT MISSION OF THE REPUBLIC OF CAMEROON TO THE UNITED NATIONS
22 E. 73rd St.
New York, NY 10021
Tel: (212) 794-2295 Fax: (212) 249-0533

Ambassador E. and P.
His Excellency Martin Belinga-Eboutou;
Mrs. Chantal Belinga-Eboutou

CAPE VERDE

PERMANENT MISSION OF THE REPUBLIC OF CAPE VERDE TO THE UNITED NATIONS
27 E. 69th St.
New York, NY 10021
Tel: (212) 472-0333 Fax: (212) 794-1398
Email: capeverde@un.int

Ambassador E. and P.
Her Excellency Maria de Fatima Lima da Veiga

CENTRAL AFRICAN REPUBLIC

PERMANENT MISSION OF THE CENTRAL AFRICAN REPUBLIC TO THE UNITED NATIONS
51 Clifton Ave. #2008
Newark, NJ 07104
Tel: (973) 482-9161 Fax: (973) 350-1174
Email: caf@un.int

Ambassador E. and P.
His Excellency Fernand Poukre-Kono;
Mrs. Charlotte Poukre-Kono

CHAD

PERMANENT MISSION OF THE REPUBLIC OF CHAD TO THE UNITED NATIONS
211 E. 43rd St. #1703
New York, NY 10017
Tel: (212) 986-0980 Fax: (212) 986-0152
Email: tcdun@undp.org

Ambassador E. and P.
His Excellency Mahamat Ali Adoum;
Mrs. Fatima Adoum

COMOROS, UNION OF

PERMANENT MISSION OF THE UNION OF THE COMOROS TO THE UNITED NATIONS
866 United Nations Plz. #418
New York, NY 10017
Tel: (212) 750-1637 Fax: (212) 750-1657
Email: comoros@un.int
Web: www.un.int/comoros

Ambassador E. and P.
Vacant

CONGO

PERMANENT MISSION OF THE REPUBLIC OF THE CONGO TO THE UNITED NATIONS
2 Dag Hammarskjold Plz., 866 2nd Ave., 2nd Fl.
New York, NY 10017
Tel: (212) 832-6553 Fax: (212) 832-6558
Email: congo@un.int
Web: www.un.int/congo

Ambassador E. and P.
His Excellency Basile Ikouebe;
Mrs. Evelyne Ikouebe

CONGO, DEMOCRATIC REPUBLIC OF THE

PERMANENT MISSION OF THE DEMOCRATIC REPUBLIC OF THE CONGO TO THE UNITED NATIONS
866 United Nations Plz. #511
New York, NY 10017
Tel: (212) 319-8061 Fax: (212) 319-8232
Email: drcongo@un.int
Web: www.un.int/drcongo

Ambassador E. and P.
His Excellency Atoki Ileka; Mrs. Ileka

COTE D'IVOIRE

PERMANENT MISSION OF COTE D'IVOIRE TO THE UNITED NATIONS
46 E. 74th St.
New York, NY 10021
Tel: (212) 717-5555 Fax: (212) 717-4492

Ambassador E. and P.
His Excellency Philippe D. Djangoné-Bi;
Mrs. Bouzie Djangoné-Bi

DJIBOUTI

PERMANENT MISSION OF THE REPUBLIC OF DJIBOUTI TO THE UNITED NATIONS
866 United Nations Plz. #4011
New York, NY 10017
Tel: (212) 753-3163 Fax: (212) 223-1276
Email: djibouti@nyct.net

Ambassador E. and P.
His Excellency Roble Olhaye; Mrs. Olhaye

EGYPT

PERMANENT MISSION OF THE ARAB REPUBLIC OF EGYPT TO THE UNITED NATIONS
304 E. 44th St.
New York, NY 10017
Tel: (212) 503-0300 Fax: (212) 949-5999
Email: egypt@un.int

Ambassador E. and P.
His Excellency Maged Abdelfattah Abdelaziz; Mrs. Amira Kandil

Source: United Nations, www.un.org.

EQUATORIAL GUINEA

PERMANENT MISSION OF EQUATORIAL GUINEA TO THE UNITED NATIONS
242 E. 51st St.
New York, NY 10022
Tel: (212) 223-2324 Fax: (212) 223-2366
Email: gnqun@undp.org

Ambassador E. and P.
His Excellency Lino Sima Ekua Avomo;
Mrs. Mónica Salvador Obono Asu

ERITREA

PERMANENT MISSION OF ERITREA TO THE UNITED NATIONS
800 2nd Ave., 18th Fl.
New York, NY 10017
Tel: (212) 687-3390 Fax: (212) 687-3138
Email: mission@eritrea-un.org
Web: www.un.int/eritrea

Ambassador E. and P.
His Excellency Ahmed Tahir Baduri;
Mrs. Amna Hassen Naib

ETHIOPIA

PERMANENT MISSION OF THE FEDERAL DEMOCRATIC REPUBLIC OF ETHIOPIA TO THE UNITED NATIONS
866 2nd Ave., 3rd Fl.
New York, NY 10017
Tel: (212) 421-1830 Fax: (212) 754-0360
Email: ethiopia@un.int
Web: www.un.int/ethiopia

Ambassador E. and P.
Vacant

GABON

PERMANENT MISSION OF THE GABONESE REPUBLIC TO THE UNITED NATIONS
18 E. 41st St., 9th Fl.
New York, NY 10017
Tel: (212) 686-9720 Fax: (212) 689-5769
Web: www.un.int/gabon

Ambassador E. and P.
His Excellency Denis Dangue Réwaka; Mrs.
Meseret Adege Dangue Réwaka

GAMBIA

PERMANENT MISSION OF THE GAMBIA TO THE UNITED NATIONS
800 2nd Ave. #400F
New York, NY 10017
Tel: (212) 949-6640 Fax: (212) 856-9820
Email: gambia@un.int
Web: http:// gambia.un.int

Ambassador E. and P.
His Excellency Crispin Grey-Johnson;
Mrs. Sarah Grey-Johnson

GHANA

PERMANENT MISSION OF GHANA TO THE UNITED NATIONS
19 E. 47th St.
New York, NY 10017
Tel: (212) 832-1300 Fax: (212) 751-6743
Email: ghanaperm@aol.com
Web: www.un.int/ghana

Ambassador E. and P.
His Excellency Nana Effah-Apenteng;
Mrs. Christina Effah-Apenteng

GUINEA

PERMANENT MISSION OF THE REPUBLIC OF GUINEA TO THE UNITED NATIONS
140 E. 39th St.
New York, NY 10016
Tel: (212) 687-8115 Fax: (212) 687-8248
Email: missionofguinea@aol.com
Web: www.un.int/guinea

Ambassador E. and P.
His Excellency Alpha Ibrahima Sow;
Mrs. Adama Sow

GUINEA-BISSAU

PERMANENT MISSION OF THE REPUBLIC OF GUINEA-BISSAU TO THE UNITED NATIONS
800 2nd Ave. #400F
New York, NY 10017
Tel: (917) 770-5598 Fax: (212) 856-9820
Email: gnbun@undp.org

Ambassador E. and P.
His Excellency Alfredo Lopes Cabral;
Mrs. Maria Cabral

KENYA

PERMANENT MISSION OF THE REPUBLIC OF KENYA TO THE UNITED NATIONS
866 United Nations Plz. #304
New York, NY 10017
Tel: (212) 421-4741 Fax: (212) 486-1985
Email: kenya@un.int
Web: www.un.int/kenya

Ambassador E. and P.
His Excellency George Olago Owuor

LESOTHO

PERMANENT MISSION OF THE KINGDOM OF LESOTHO TO THE UNITED NATIONS
204 E. 39th St.
New York, NY 10016
Tel: (212) 661-1690 Fax: (212) 682-4388
Email: les@missions.un.org
Web: www.un.int/lesotho

Ambassador E. and P.
Vacant

LIBERIA

PERMANENT MISSION OF THE REPUBLIC OF LIBERIA TO THE UNITED NATIONS
820 2nd Ave., 13th Fl.
New York, NY 10017
Tel: (212) 687-1033 Fax: (212) 687-1035

Ambassador E. and P.
His Excellency Lami Kawah

HIRIYA

PERMANENT MISSION OF THE SOCIALIST PEOPLE'S LIBYAN ARAB JAMAHIRIYA TO THE UNITED NATIONS
309-315 E. 48th St.
New York, NY 10017
Tel: (212) 752-5775 Fax: (212) 593-4787
Web: www.libya-un.org

Ambassador E. and P.
Vacant

MADAGASCAR

PERMANENT MISSION OF THE REPUBLIC OF MADAGASCAR TO THE UNITED NATIONS
820 2nd Ave. #800
New York, NY 10017
Tel: (212) 986-9491 Fax: (212) 986-6271
Email: repermad@verizon.net

Ambassador E. and P.
His Excellency Zina Andrianarivelo-Razafy;
Mrs. Elise Bako Andrianarivelo-Razafy

MALAWI

PERMANENT MISSION OF THE REPUBLIC OF MALAWI TO THE UNITED NATIONS
866 Unites NAtions Plz. #444
New York, NY 10017
Tel: (212) 317-8738 Fax: (212) 317-8729
Email: felchan9@aol.com

Ambassador E. and P.
His Excellency Brown Beswick Chimphamba;
Mrs. Madeline Brown Chimphamba

MALI

PERMANENT MISSION OF THE REPUBLIC OF MALI TO THE UNITED NATIONS
111 E. 69th St.
New York, NY 10021
Tel: (212) 737-4150 Fax: (212) 472-3778
Email: malionu@aol.com
Web: www.un.int/mali

Ambassador E. and P.
His Excellency Cheick Sidi Diarra;
Mrs. Oumou Modibo Sangaré-Diarra

MAURITANIA

PERMANENT MISSION OF THE ISLAMIC REPUBLIC OF MAURITANIA TO THE UNITED NATIONS
116 E. 38th St.
New York, NY 10016
Tel: (212) 252-0113 Fax: (212) 252-0175
Email: mauritania@un.int

Ambassador E. and P.
His Excellency Mohamed Ould Tolba

MOROCCO

PERMANENT MISSION OF THE KINGDOM OF MOROCCO TO THE UNITED NATIONS
866 2nd Ave., 6th & 7th Fls.
New York, NY 10017
Tel: (212) 421-1580 Fax: (212) 980-1512
Email: marun@undp.org
Web: http://morocco-un.org

Ambassador E. and P.
His Excellency Mohamed Bennouna;
Mrs. Isabelle Bennouna

MOZAMBIQUE

PERMANENT MISSION OF THE REPUBLIC OF MOZAMBIQUE TO THE UNITED NATIONS
420 E. 50th St.
New York, NY 10022
Tel: (212) 644-6800 Fax: (212) 644-5972
Email: mozambique@un.int
Web: www.un.int/mozambique

Ambassador E. and P.
His Excellency Filipe Chidumo;
Mrs. Paula Chidumo

NAMIBIA

PERMANENT MISSION OF THE REPUBLIC OF NAMIBIA TO THE UNITED NATIONS
360 Lexington Ave. #1502
New York, NY 10017
Tel: (212) 685-2003 Fax: (212) 685-1561
Email: namibia@un.int
Web: www.un.int/namibia

Ambassador E. and P.
His Excellency Martin Andjaba;
Mrs. Rhona Andjaba

NIGER

PERMANENT MISSION OF NIGER TO THE
UNITED NATIONS
417 E. 50th St.
New York, NY 10022
Tel: (212) 421-3260 Fax: (212) 753-6931
Email: nigerun@aol.com
Web: www.un.int/niger

Ambassador E. and P.
Vacant

NIGERIA

PERMANENT MISSION OF NIGERIA TO
THE UNITED NATIONS
828 2nd Ave.
New York, NY 10017
Tel: (212) 953-9130 Fax: (212) 697-1970
Email: ngaun@undp.org

Ambassador E. and P.
His Excellency Aminu Bashir Wali;
Aisha Aminu Wali

RWANDA

PERMANENT MISSION OF THE REPUBLIC
OF RWANDA TO THE UNITED NATIONS
124 E. 39th St.
New York, NY 10016
Tel: (212) 679-9010 Fax: (212) 679-9133
Email: rwaun@un.int

Ambassador E. and P.
His Excellency Stanislas Kamanzi;
Mrs. Geneviève Mukarugwiza

SAO TOME AND PRINCIPE

PERMANENT MISSION OF SAO TOME AND
PRINCIPE TO THE UNITED NATIONS
400 Park Ave., 7th Fl.
New York, NY 10022
Tel: (212) 317-0533 Fax: (212) 317-0580
Email: stp1@attglobal.net

Ambassador E. and P.
Vacant

SENEGAL

PERMANENT MISSION OF THE REPUBLIC
OF SENEGAL TO THE UNITED NATIONS
238 E. 68th St.
New York, NY 10021
Tel: (212) 517-9030 Fax: (212) 517-3032
Web: www.un.int/senegal

Ambassador E. and P.
His Excellency Paul Badji;
Mrs. Désirée Juliette Tendeng Badji

SEYCHELLES

PERMANENT MISSION OF THE REPUBLIC
OF SEYCHELLES TO THE UNITED NATIONS
800 2nd Ave. #400C
New York, NY 10017
Tel: (212) 972-1785 Fax: (212) 972-1786
Email: seychelles@un.int

Ambassador E. and P.
His Excellency Jérémie Bonnelame

SIERRA LEONE

PERMANENT MISSION OF THE REPUBLIC
OF SIERRA LEONE TO THE UNITED
NATIONS
245 E. 49th St.
New York, NY 10017
Tel: (212) 688-1656   Fax: (212) 688-4924
Email: sierraleone@un.int
Web: www.un.int/sierraleone

Ambassador E. and P.
His Excellency Joe Robert Pemagbi

SOMALIA

PERMANENT MISSION OF THE SOMALI
REPUBLIC TO THE UNITED NATIONS
425 E. 61st St. #702
New York, NY 10021
Tel: (212) 688-9410 Fax: (212) 759-0651
Email: somalia@un.int

Ambassador E. and P.
His Excellency Ahmed Abdi Hashi

SOUTH AFRICA

PERMANENT MISSION OF THE REPUBLIC
OF SOUTH AFRICA TO THE UNITED
NATIONS
333 E. 38th St., 9th Fl.
New York, NY 10016
Tel: (212) 213-5583 Fax: (212) 692-2498
Email: soafun@worldnet.att.net
Web: www.southafrica-newyork.net/pmun

Ambassador E. and P.
His Excellency Dumisani Shadrack
Kumalo; Mrs. Ntombikayice Beatrice
Kumalo

SUDAN

PERMANENT MISSION OF THE REPUBLIC
OF THE SUDAN TO THE UNITED NATIONS
3 Dag Hammarskjold Plz., 4th Fl., 305 E.
47th St.
New York, NY 10017
Tel: (212) 573-6033 Fax: (212) 573-6160
Email: sudan@sudanmission.org

Ambassador E. and P.
His Excellency Elfatih Mohamed
Ahmed Erwa;Mrs. Erwa

SWAZILAND

PERMANENT MISSION OF THE KINGDOM
OF SWAZILAND TO THE UNITED NATIONS
408 E. 50th St.
New York, NY 10022
Tel: (212) 371-8910 Fax: (212) 754-2755
Email: swaziland@un.int

Ambassador E. and P.
Vacant

UNITED REPUBLIC OF TANZANIA

PERMANENT MISSION OF THE UNITED
REPUBLIC OF TANZANIA TO THE UNITED
NATIONS
201 E. 42nd St. #1700
New York, NY 10017
Tel: (212) 972-9160 Fax: (212) 682-5232
Email: tzrepny@aol.com

Ambassador E. and P.
His Excellency Augustine P. Mahiga;
Mrs. Elizabeth Mahiga

TOGO

PERMANENT MISSION OF TOGO TO THE
UNITED NATIONS
112 E. 40th St.
New York, NY 10016
Tel: (212) 490-3455 Fax: (212) 983-6684
Email: togun@mindspring.com

Ambassador E. and P.
Vacant

TUNISIA

PERMANENT MISSION OF TUNISIA TO
THE UNITED NATIONS
31 Beekman Pl.
New York, NY 10022
Tel: (212) 751-7503 Fax: (212) 751-0569
Email: tunisnyc@nyc.rr.com

Ambassador E. and P.
His Excellency Ali Hachani;
Mrs. Najet Hachani

UGANDA

PERMANENT MISSION OF THE REPUBLIC
OF UGANDA TO THE UNITED NATIONS
336 E. 45th St.
New York, NY 10017
Tel: (212) 949-0110 Fax: (212) 687-4517

Ambassador E. and P.
His Excellency Francis K. Butagira;
Mrs. Lydia Butagira

ZAMBIA

PERMANENT MISSION OF THE REPUBLIC
OF ZAMBIA TO THE UNITED NATIONS
237 E. 52nd St.
New York, NY 10022
Tel: (212) 888-5770 Fax: (212) 888-5213
Email: zambia@un.int
Web: www.un.int/zambia

Ambassador E. and P.
His Excellency Mr. Tens C. Kapoma;
Mrs. Rhoda Kapembwa Kapoma

ZIMBABWE

PERMANENT MISSION OF THE REPUBLIC
OF ZIMBABWE TO THE UNITED NATIONS
128 E. 56th St.
New York, NY 10022
Tel: (212) 980-9511 Fax: (212) 308-6705
Email: zimbabwe@un.int.org

Ambassador E. and P.
His Excellency His Excellency Boniface G.
Chidyausiku; Mrs. Evelyn Chidyausiku

Wondering how to pay for college?

The Coast Guard has the money to help.

Coast Guard Academy:

A free college education and guaranteed job after graduation as a Coast Guard officer.

College Student Pre-Commissioning Initiative:

Receive full tuition for your junior and senior years, books and educational fees, a monthly stipend of approximately $2,000, plus guaranteed job after graduation as a Coast Guard officer

Active Duty Montgomery GI Bill:

Up to $1034 per month for 36 months.

Reserve Montgomery GI Bill:

Up to $297 per month for 36 months.

Tuition Assistance:

Up to $297 per semester hour, up to $4,500 per year.

Coast Guard Foundation Grant:

$350 per student per year for books and other education-related expenses

Coast Guard Mutual Assistance:

Grants of $160 per student per year for the cost of college textbooks, plus interest free loans loans are available.

Servicemember's Opportunity College Coast Guard:

An affiliation of colleges, that assists members in earning an associate degree or a bachelor's degree, and allow Coast Guard members to transfer college credits between schools and reduce their requirements for residency.

For more information, call us toll-free at

1-877-NOW-USCG (1-877-669-8724).

or visit:

Active Duty & Reserve
www.gocoastguard.com

Civilian
www.uscg.mil.civilian jobs

These programs may have additional requirements for participation. Amounts and availability of programs are subject to change.
Contact your local Coast Guard recruiter for more information.

A MESSAGE FROM THE COMMANDANT OF THE COAST GUARD

Congratulations on the sixth edition of the African American Yearbook. Since its creation, this publication has been a valuable resource for Americans to obtain a better understanding of resources and leaders in the African American community nationwide. It also serves to broaden the interest of youth and to ensure success in advancing their academic aspirations…which ultimately serves our organization in meeting our mission to obtain and sustain a diverse workforce.

The Coast Guard is a military, multi-mission and maritime service. Though we are America's smallest armed service, we perform an astonishingly broad range of services for our country. Never was that more evident than in the preparation and response last year to the worst hurricane season on record. In the aftermath of Hurricane Katrina the Coast Guard saved more than 24,000 people and evacuated almost 9,500 hospital patients to safety. Take Lieutenant Marcus Canady, HH-65 Dolphin Helicopter Pilot, who flew for 13 consecutive days, logging 35 hours of flight time. Lieutenant Canady's actions were personally responsible for saving 28 lives and he assisted in saving 33 more. The Coast Guard also responded to more than 3800 marine pollution cases, and reopened affected waterways to restart commerce in most areas within a week. The Coast Guard's unique abilities and missions allowed us to respond quickly and decisively, balancing our simultaneous roles of lifesavers, environmental responders, and law enforcement officers within our military command and control structure.

The Coast Guard succeeds because of our terrific and diverse people. We seek the best talent America has to offer to keep our Service strong. We draw on the strengths of our differences and similarities to create an environment that places high value on individual dignity, respect, and professional growth so that all members can achieve their full potential and make their greatest contribution to the mission.

Coast Guard people are unsung heroes that make up our American community. They are your neighbors who make the extraordinary things look ordinary every day. They are active duty and reserve military personnel, civilian employees, and even volunteers from the Coast Guard Auxiliary. Our people are what make the Coast Guard great. We invite you to join us and share in a lifelong affiliation with a noble service.

Semper Paratus – Always Ready.

Thomas H Collins

THOMAS H. COLLINS
Admiral, United States Coast Guard

Education

FIG 1. Educational Attainment of the U.S. Population 25 Years and Over by Race, Hispanic Origin: 2004

In 2004, 36 percent of African Americans age 25 years and older held only a high school diploma. 17.6 percent held a bachelor's degree or more, up slightly from the previous year. Among all major ethnic/racial groups, African Americans had the second lowest percentage of bachelor's degrees, with only Hispanics faring worse.

[1] Some college includes respondents who have completed some college, but have no degree and those who have completed an associate's degree.

Source: U.S. Census Bureau, Current Population Survey, Annual Social and Economic Supplement, 2004

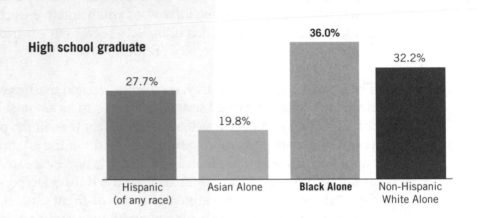

High school graduate

27.7% Hispanic (of any race) · 19.8% Asian Alone · **36.0% Black Alone** · 32.2% Non-Hispanic White Alone

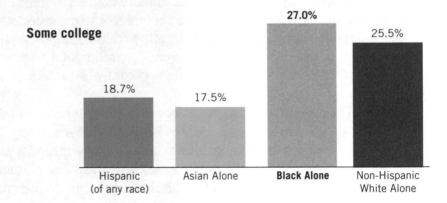

Some college

18.7% Hispanic (of any race) · 17.5% Asian Alone · **27.0% Black Alone** · 25.5% Non-Hispanic White Alone

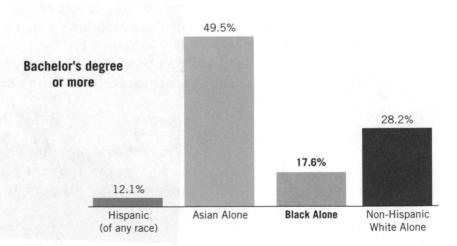

Bachelor's degree or more

12.1% Hispanic (of any race) · 49.5% Asian Alone · **17.6% Black Alone** · 28.2% Non-Hispanic White Alone

FIG 2. Educational Attainment of the Population 25 years and Over by Nativity and Hispanic Origin: 2004

Foreign-born African Americans, as of 2004 had a higher proportion of students with only a high school education and with some college.

[1]Some college includes respondents who have completed some college, but have no degree and those who have completed an associate's degree.

Source: U.S. Census Bureau, Current Population Survey, Annual Social and Economic Supplement, 2004

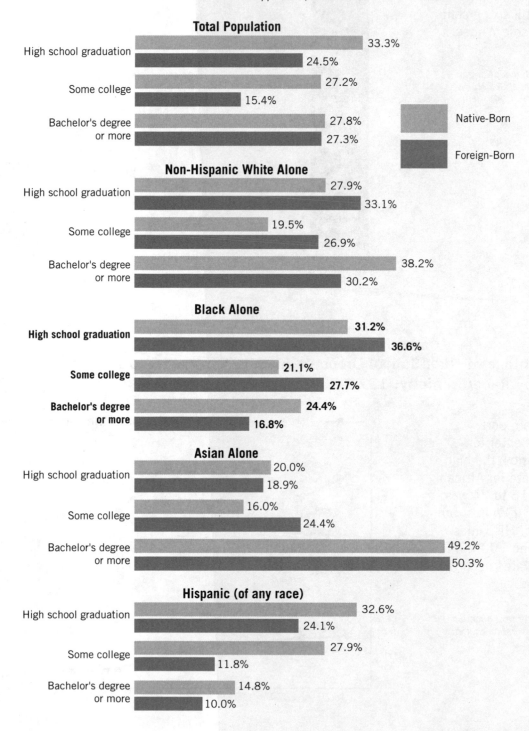

Total Population

High school graduation: 33.3% / 24.5%
Some college: 27.2% / 15.4%
Bachelor's degree or more: 27.8% / 27.3%

Native-Born
Foreign-Born

Non-Hispanic White Alone

High school graduation: 27.9% / 33.1%
Some college: 19.5% / 26.9%
Bachelor's degree or more: 38.2% / 30.2%

Black Alone

High school graduation: 31.2% / 36.6%
Some college: 21.1% / 27.7%
Bachelor's degree or more: 24.4% / 16.8%

Asian Alone

High school graduation: 20.0% / 18.9%
Some college: 16.0% / 24.4%
Bachelor's degree or more: 49.2% / 50.3%

Hispanic (of any race)

High school graduation: 32.6% / 24.1%
Some college: 27.9% / 11.8%
Bachelor's degree or more: 14.8% / 10.0%

FIG 3. Percentage of the Foreign-Born Population 25 Years and Older that has Attained a Bachelor's Degree or Higher, by Selected Race/Ethnicity: 2004

Among foreign-born people of the three largest racial and ethnic groups, the Black population ranked in the middle. This group was fourteen percent higher than Hispanics, but still six percent behind non-Hispanic Whites.

Source: U.S. Census Bureau, Current Population Survey, Annual Social and Economic Supplement, 2004

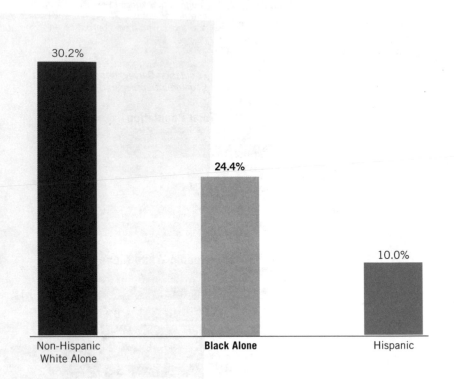

FIG 4. Percentage of High School Dropouts Among Persons 16 to 24 Years Old, by Race/Ethnicity: 1972-2003

According to a report by the National Center for Education Statistics, the high school dropout rate for African Americans ages 16 to 24 was higher than that of Whites, but lower than that of Hispanics between 1972 and 2003. All groups' dropout rates declined during this period.

Source: National Center for Education Statistics, Digest of Education Statistics, 2004

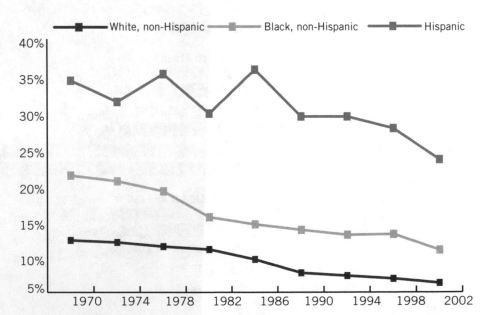

FIG 5. Percent of 9-Year-Old Students at or Above Selected Reading Score Level, by Race/Ethnicity: Selected Years, 1975 to 2004[1]

Nine-year-old African American students very nearly matched Hispanics on basic reading abilities from 1975 to 2004. The most recent figures from the National Center for Education Statistics still show Black students below Whites in reading skills, although the gains made over the last 30 years were much greater among African Americans.

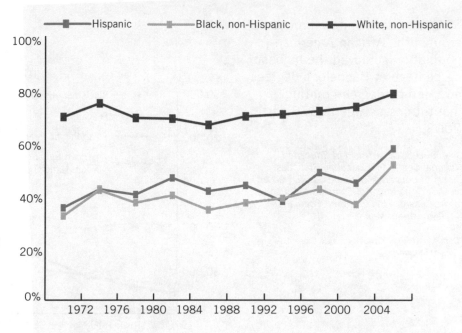

[1] The reading level selected for this figure is the U.S. Dept. Education's level 200, defined as students who are "able to understand, combine, and make inferences based on short uncomplicated passages about specific or sequentually related information."

Source: National Center for Education Statistics, Digest of Education Statistics, 2004

FIG 6. Percent of 9-Year-Old Students at or Above Selected Mathematics Proficiency Level, by Race/Ethnicity: 1978 and 2004[1]

Similar results can be found in the improvements made in math skills for African American students. The National Center for Education Statistics shows that from 1978 to 2004, Black students improved more than any other major ethnic/racial group, although overall still coming in last in this category.

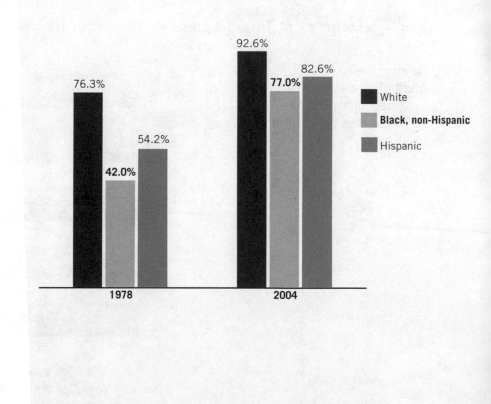

[1] The math level selected for this U.S. Dept. of Education's Level 150, defined as students who have "Begining skills and understanding" of mathematics.

Source: National Center for Education Statistics, Digest of Education Statistics, 2004

FIG 7. Bachelor's Degree Conferred by Degree-Granting Institutions, by non-White Racial/ Ethnic Group: Selected Years, 1976 to 2003

Among non-White ethnic/racial groups, the African American population achieved the highest percentage of Bachelor's degrees awarded by degree-granting institutions between 1976 and 2003.

Source: U.S. Department of Education, National Center for Education Statistics, Digest of Education Statistics, 2001, based on U.S. Department of Commerce, Bureau of the Census, March Current Population Surveys, various years.

[1]*Data for White and Black include those of Hispanic origin*

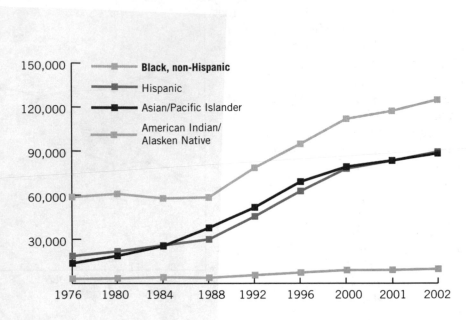

FIG 8. Percentage of Total Degrees Conferred by non-White Racial/Ethnic Group: 2003

Among the same groups, Black students had a higher percentage of post-secondary degrees in all categories except first professional.

Source: National Center for Education Statistics, Digest of Education Statistics, 2004

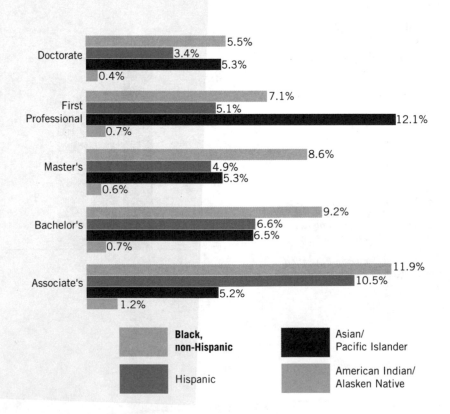

FIG 9. Percent Distribution of Enrollment in Colleges and Universities, by Sex and Race/Ethnicity: 2002

According to the U.S. Department of Education, African American females had the highest rate of enrollment in colleges and universities of any racial/ethnic group.

Source: U.S. Department of Education, National Center for Education Statistics, Integrated Postsecondary Education Data System (IPEDS), "Fall Enrollment Survey", October 2004

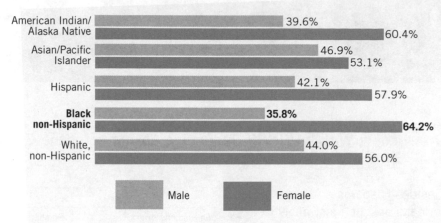

FIG 10. Number of Degrees Conferred to Black, non-Hispanics by All Colleges and Universities and by Historically Black Colleges and Universities (HBCUs), by Degree Level: 2001-2002

From 2000 to 2001, about one-fifth of all bachelors degrees earned by African Americans were from Historically Black Colleges and Universities.

Source: U.S. Department of Education, National Center for Education Statistics, Digest of Education Statistics, 2004

Degree Type	Degrees confered to Black, non-Hispanics by all colleges and universities	Degrees conferred to Black, non-Hispanics by HBCUs	Percent of degrees conferred by HBCUs
Associate	75,430	**1,875**	2.5%
Bachelor's	124,241	**25,122**	20.2%
Master's	44,272	**4,461**	10.1%
Doctor's	5,715	**256**	4.5%
First-professional	2,517	**977**	39.6%

FIG 11. Percentage of High School Completers Who Enrolled in College by Race/Ethnicity: Selected Years 1980 - 2003

African American gains in college enrollment were only outpaced by White, non-Hispanic increases from 1980 to 2003, according to the most recent figures from the US Department of Education.

Source: U.S. Department of Education, National Center for Education Statistics, Digest of Education Statistics, 2004

Year	White, Non-Hispanic	Black, Non-Hispanic	Hispanic
1980	49.8%	**42.7%**	52.3%
1985	60.1%	**42.2%**	51.0%
1990	63.0%	**46.8%**	42.7%
1995	64.3%	**51.2%**	53.7%
2000	65.7%	**54.9%**	52.9%
2001	64.3%	**55.0%**	51.7%
2002	69.1%	**59.4%**	53.6%
2003	66.2%	**57.5%**	58.6%

Health

FIG 1. People Without Health Insurance Coverage for the Entire Year by Race and Ethnicity: 2002 and 2004

Besides Hispanics, African Americans are the most likely to be uninsured. This figure has held more or less steady during the past few years, according to the U.S. Census Bureau.

Source: U.S. Census Bureau, Current Population Survey, Annual Social and Economic Supplement, 2004

Race and Hispanic origin	2002		2004	
	Number	Percent	Number	Percent
All races	43,574	15.2%	45,820	15.7%
White alone or in combination	33,320	14.2%	35,627	14.9%
White alone	32,706	14.2%	34,788	14.9%
White alone, not Hispanic	20,782	10.7%	21,983	11.3%
Black alone or in combination	7,429	19.2%	7,447	19.5%
Black alone	7,228	20.2%	7,186	19.7%
Asian alone or in combination	2,248	18.0%	2,217	16.6%
Asian alone	2,132	18.4%	2,070	16.8%
Hispanic (of any race)	12,756	32.4%	13,678	32.7%

FIG 2. Cancer Incidence per 100,000 Population by Race/Ethnicity: 2001

The likelihood of cancer among the Black population was higher than any other group, with an average of 465.1 cases reported per 100,000 members of the population.

Source: State Health Facts published by the Kaiser Family Foundation at www.statehealthfacts.org

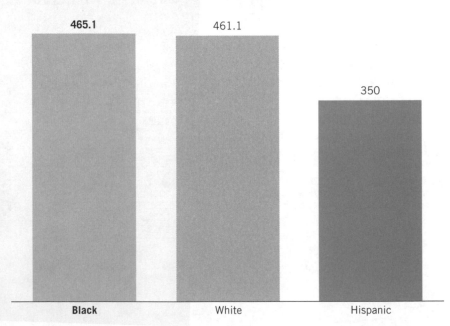

Black	White	Hispanic
465.1	461.1	350

WWW.AFRICANAMERICANYEARBOOK.COM **2006/2007**

FIG 3. Distribution of Cumulative AIDS Cases by Race/Ethnicity, Reported through 2003

According to the Kaiser Family Foundation, African Americans had the second highest number of reported AIDS cases through 2003.

Source: State Health Facts published by the Kaiser Family Foundation at www.statehealthfacts.org

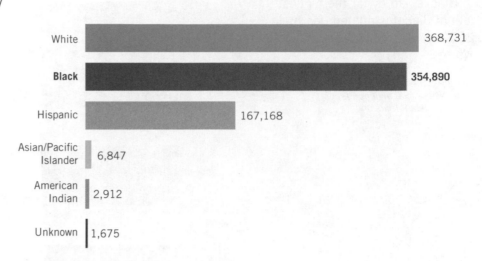

White — 368,731
Black — 354,890
Hispanic — 167,168
Asian/Pacific Islander — 6,847
American Indian — 2,912
Unknown — 1,675

FIG 4. Health Insurance Coverage for the Black Population: 2003 to 2004
(Numbers in thousands. People as of March of the following year.)

From 2003 to 2004, the rate of health insurance coverage among African Americans did not change much.

| | | Covered by private or government health insurance | | | | | | | | |
| | | Private health insurance | | | | Government health insurance | | | | |
	Total People	Total	Total	Employment based	Direct purchase	Total	Medicaid	Medicare	Military health care	Not covered
Black alone or in combination										
2004	38,161	30,714	20,457	18,885	1,825	13,501	9,451	4,000	1,446	7,447
2003	37,651	30,344	20,136	10,282	1,732	13,195	9,292	4,080	1,283	7,307
Percents										
2004	100	80.5	53.6	49.5	4.8	35.4	24.8	10.5	3.8	19.5
2003	100	80.6	53.5	49.6	4.6	35.1	24.7	10.8	3.4	19.4
Black alone										
2004	36,546	29,360	19,596	18,122	1,732	12,878	8,943	3,925	1,369	7,186
2003	36,121	29,041	19,320	17,924	1,663	12,585	8,797	3,989	1,225	7,080
Percents										
2004	100	80.3	53.6	49.6	4.7	35.2	24.5	10.7	3.7	19.7
2003	100	80.4	53.5	49.6	4.6	34.8	24.4	11.0	3.4	19.6

Source: U.S. Census Bureau, Income, Poverty and Health Insurance Coverage in the United States: 2004

FIG 5. Number of Diabetes Deaths per 100,000 Population by Race/Ethnicity: 2002

Blacks had by far the highest rate of diabetes-related deaths in 2002, more than double that of Whites.

Source: State Health Facts published by the Kaiser Family Foundation at www.statehealthfacts.org

FIG 6. Percent of Children Ages 19-35 Months Who Are Immunized by Race/Ethnicity: 2002-2003

Immunization numbers were also discouraging for African Americans. Seventy-one percent of Black children aged 19-35 months were immunized in 2002-2003, compared with eighty-one percent and seventy-six percent for Whites and Hispanics, respectively.

Source: State Health Facts published by the Kaiser Family Foundation at www.statehealthfacts.org

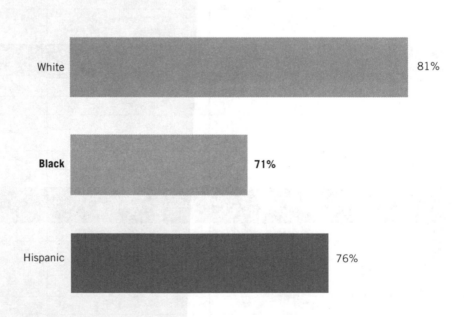

FIG 7. Uninsured Children by Poverty Status, Age, and Race and Hispanic Origin: 2004

According to the 2004 Census Bureau report, *Income, Poverty, and Health Insurance Coverage in the United States*, Black children were the second most likely group to be uninsured.

Source: U.S. Census Bureau, Income, Poverty and Health Insurance Coverage in the United States: 2004

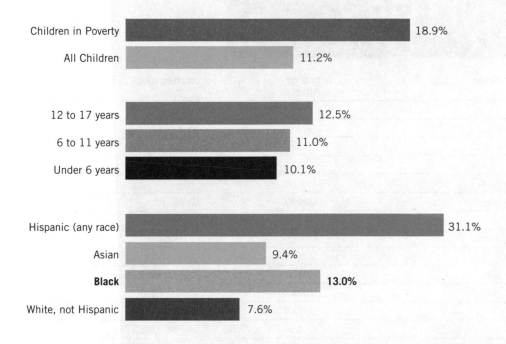

Children in Poverty	18.9%
All Children	11.2%
12 to 17 years	12.5%
6 to 11 years	11.0%
Under 6 years	10.1%
Hispanic (any race)	31.1%
Asian	9.4%
Black	**13.0%**
White, not Hispanic	7.6%

FIG 8. Ten Leading Causes of Death for African Americans: 2002

The top three leading causes of death for African Americans – heart disease, cancer and stroke – were the same as the general population. Diabetes and homicide, however, ranked much higher on the list for Black Americans than for the population overall.

Source: Center for Disease Control (CDC): Health, United States, 2004

African Americans All Ages/Both Sexes	African American Males All Ages	African American Females All Ages
Heart Disease 77,621	Heart Disease 37,094	Heart Disease 40,527
Cancer 62,617	Cancer 32,627	Cancer 29,990
Stroke 18,856	Accidents 8,612	Stroke 11,028
Diabetes 12,687	Stroke 7,828	Diabetes 7,480
Accidents 12,513	Homicide 6,896	Kidney Disease 4,061
Homicide 8,287	Human Immunodeficiency Virus (HIV) Disease 5,301	Accidents 3,901
Human Immunodeficiency Virus (HIV) Disease 7,835	Diabetes 5,207	Chronic Lower Respiratory disease 3,490
Chronic Lower Respiratory Disease 7,831	Chronic Lower Respiratory Disease 4,341	Septicema 3,434
Kidney Disease 7,488	Kidney Disease 3,427	Influenza and Pneumonia 3,103
Septicema 6,137	Influenza and Pneumonia 2,768	Human Immunodeficiency Virus (HIV) Disease 2,534

COUNTRY/RELIGION	TOTAL POP./ FOLLOWERS	%	COUNTRY/RELIGION	TOTAL POP./ FOLLOWERS	%
Algeria	32,531,853		Muslim	569,984	15.0%
Sunni Muslim	32,206,534	99.0%	**Chad**	9,826,419	
Christian and Jewish	325,318	1.0%	Muslim	5,011,473	51.0%
Angola	11,190,786		Christian	3,439,246	35.0%
Indigenous Beliefs	5,259,669	47.0%	Animist	687,849	7.0%
Roman Catholic	4,252,498	38.0%	Other	687,849	7.0%
Protestant	1,678,617	15.0%	**Comoros**	671,247	
Benin	7,460,025		Sunni Muslim	657,822	98.0%
Indigenous Beliefs	3,730,012	50.0%	Roman Catholic	13,424	2.0%
Christian	2,238,007	30.0%	**Congo, Democratic Republic**	60,085,804	
Muslim	1,492,005	20.0%	Roman Catholic	30,042,902	50.0%
Botswana	1,640,115		Protestant	12,017,160	20.0%
Christian	1,174,322	71.6%	Kimbanguist	6,008,580	10.0%
Badimo	98,406	6.0%	Muslim	6,008,580	10.0%
Other	22,961	1.4%	Syncretic/Indigenous Beliefs	6,008,580	10.0%
Unspecified	6,560	0.4%	**Congo, Republic of the**	3,039,126	
None	337,863	20.6%	Christian	1,519,563	50.0%
Burkina Faso	13,925,313		Animist	1,458,780	48.0%
Indigenous Beliefs	5,570,125	40.0%	Muslim	60,782	2.0%
Muslim	6,962,656	50.0%	**Cote d'Ivoire**	17,298,040	
Christian (mainly Roman Catholic)	1,392,531	10.0%	Christian		20-30%
Burundi	6,370,609		Muslim		35-40%
Christian (mainly Roman Catholic 62%, Protestant 5%)	4,268,308	67.0%	Indigenous		25-40%
Indigenous Beliefs	1,465,240	23.0%	**Djibouti**		
Muslim	637,060	10.0%	Total Population	476,703	
Cameroon	16,380,005		Muslim	448,100	94.0%
Indigenous Beliefs	6,552,002	40.0%	Christian	28,602	6.0%
Christian	6,552,002	40.0%	**Egypt**	77,505,756	
Muslim	3,276,001	20.0%	Muslim (mostly Sunni)	72,855,410	94.0%
Cape Verde	418,224		Coptic Christian and Other	4,650,345	6.0%
Roman Catholic (infused with indigenous beliefs)			**Equatorial Guinea**	535,881	
Protestant (mostly church of the Nazarene)			Nominally Christian and predominantly Roman Catholic, pagan practices		
Central African Republic	3,799,897		**Eritrea**	4,561,599	
Indigenous Beliefs	1,329,963	35.0%	Muslim		
Protestant	949,974	25.0%	Coptic Christian		
Roman Catholic	949,974	25.0%	Roman Catholic		

Source: Central Intelligence Agency. The World Factbook 2005, Internet edition. http://www.cia.gov/cia/publications/factbook

COUNTRY/RELIGION	TOTAL POP./ FOLLOWERS	%
Protestant		
Ethiopia	73,053,286	
Muslim		45-50%
Ethiopian Orthodox		35-40%
Animist	8,766,394	12.0%
Other		3-8%
Gabon	1,389,201	
Christian		55-75%
Animist, Muslim	13,892	1.0%
Gambia, The	1,593,256	
Muslim	1,433,930	90.0%
Christian	143,393	9.0%
Indigenous Beliefs	15,932	1.0%
Ghana	21,029,853	
Christian	13,248,807	63.0%
Muslim	3,364,776	16.0%
Indigenous Beliefs	4,416,269	21.0%
Guinea	9,467,866	
Muslim	8,047,686	85.0%
Christian	757,429	8.0%
Indigenous Beliefs	662,750	7.0%
Guinea-Bissau	1,416,027	
Indigenous Beliefs	708,013	50.0%
Muslim	637,212	45.0%
Christian	70,801	5.0%
Kenya	33,829,590	
Protestant	15,223,315	45.0%
Roman Catholic	11,163,764	33.0%
Indigenous Beliefs	3,382,959	10.0%
Muslim	3,382,959	10.0%
Other	676,591	2.0%
Lesotho	1,867,035	
Christian	1,493,628	80.0%
Indigenous Beliefs	373,407	20.0%
Liberia	3,482,211	
Indigenous Beliefs	1,392,884	40.0%
Christian	1,392,884	40.0%
Muslim	696,442	20.0%
Libya	5,765,563	
Sunni Muslim	5,592,596	97.0%
Madagascar	18,040,341	
Indigenous Beliefs	9,380,977	52.0%
Christian	7,396,539	41.0%
Muslim	1,262,823	7.0%
Malawi	12,158,924	
Christian	9,714,980	79.9%
Muslim	1,556,342	12.8%
Other	364,767	3.0%
None	522,833	4.3%

COUNTRY/RELIGION	TOTAL POP./ FOLLOWERS	%
Mali	12,291,529	
Muslim	11,062,376	90.0%
Indigenous Beliefs	1,106,237	9.0%
Christian	122,915	1.0%
Mauritania	3,086,859	
Muslim	3,086,859	100.0%
Morocco	32,725,847	
Muslim	32,300,410	98.7%
Christian	359,984	1.1%
Jewish	65,451	0.2%
Mozambique	19,406,703	
Catholic	4,618,795	23.8%
Zionist Christian	3,396,173	17.5%
Muslim	3,454,393	17.8%
Other	3,454,939	17.8%
None	4,482,948	23.1%
Namibia	2,030,692	
Christian (Lutheran 50% at least)		80-90%
Indigenous Beliefs		10-20%
Niger	11,665,937	
Muslim	9,332,749	80.0%
Indigenous Beliefs/Christian		
Nigeria	128,771,988	
Muslim	64,385,994	50.0%
Christian	51,508,795	40.0%
Indigenous Beliefs	12,877,198	10.0%
Rwanda	8,440,820	
Roman Catholic	4,769,063	56.5%
Protestant	2,194,613	26.0%
Adventists	936,931	11.1%
Muslim	388,277	4.6%
Indigenous Beliefs	8,440	0.1%
None	143,493	1.7%
Sao Tome and Principe	187,410	
Catholic	131,749	70.3%
Evangelical	6,371	3.4%
New Apostolic	3,748	2.0%
Adventists	3,373	1.8%
Other	5,809	3.1%
None	36,357	19.4%
Senegal	11,126,832	
Muslim	10,459,222	94.0%
Indigenous Beliefs	111,268	1.0%
Christian (mostly Roman Catholic)	556,341	5.0%
Seychelles	81,188	
Roman Catholic	66,817	82.3%
Anglican	5,196	6.4%
Seventh Day Adventist	893	1.1%
Other Christian	2,760	3.4%

Religion in African Countries

COUNTRY/RELIGION	TOTAL POP./FOLLOWERS	%	COUNTRY/RELIGION	TOTAL POP./FOLLOWERS	%
Hindu	1,704	2.1%	**Tanzania**	36,766,356	
Muslim	893	1.1%	Mainland, Christian	11,029,906	30.0%
Other non-Christian	1,217	1.5%	Muslim	12,868,224	35.0%
Unspecified	1,217	1.5%	Indigenous Beliefs	12,868,224	35.0%
None	487	0.6%	Zanzibar-more than Muslim	36,398,692	99.0%
Sierra Leone	6,017,643		**Togo**	5,681,519	
Muslim	3,610,585	60.0%	Indigenous Beliefs	2,897,574	51.0%
Indigenous Beliefs	1,805,292	30.0%	Christian	1,647,640	29.0%
Christian	601,764	10.0%	Muslim	1,136,303	20.0%
Somalia	8,591,629		**Tunisia**	10,074,951	
Sunni Muslim			Muslim	9,873,451	98.0%
South Africa	44,344,136		Christian	100,749	1.0%
Zion Christian	4,922,199	11.1%	Jewish and Other	100,749	1.0%
Pentecostal/Charismatic	3,636,219	8.2%	**Uganda**	27,269,482	
Catholic	3,148,433	7.1%	Roman Catholic	8,998,929	33.0%
Methodist	3,015,401	6.8%	Protestant	8,998,929	33.0%
Dutch Reformed	2,971,057	6.7%	Muslim	4,363,117	16.0%
Anglican	1,685,077	3.8%	Indigenous Beliefs	4,908,506	18.0%
Other Christian	15,963,888	36.0%	**Western Sahara**	273,008	
Islam	665,162	1.5%	Muslim		
Other	1,019,915	2.3%	**Yemen**	20,727,063	
Unspecified	620,817	1.4%	Muslim including Shaf'i (Sunni) and Zaydi (Shi'a), small numbers of Jewish, Christian, and Hindu		
None	6,695,964	15.1%	**Zambia**	11,261,795	
Sudan	40,187,486		Christian		50-75%
Sunni Muslim (in North)	28,131,240	70.0%	Muslim and Hindu		24-49%
Indigenous Beliefs	10,046,871	25.0%	Indigenous Beliefs	112,617	1.0%
Christian (mostly in South and Khartoum)	2,009,374	5.0%	**Zimbabwe**	12,746,990	
Swaziland	1,173,900		Syncretic (part Christian, part Indigenous Beliefs)	6,373,495	50.0%
Zionist (a blend of Christianity and indigenous ancestral worship)	469,560	40.0%	Christian	3,186,747	25.0%
Roman Catholic	234780	20.0%	Indigenous Beliefs	3,059,277	24.0%
Muslim	117,390	10.0%	Muslim and Other	127,469	1.0%
Anglican, Bahai, Methodist, Mormon, Jewish and Other	352,170	30.0%			

Federal and State Health Departments and Offices of Minority Health

ALABAMA

ALABAMA DEPARTMENT OF PUBLIC HEALTH
Minority Health Section
201 Monroe St. #710, RSA Tower
Montgomery, AL 36104
Tel: (334) 206-5396 Fax: (334) 206-5434
Web: www.adph.org/minorityhealth

AMERICAN SAMOA

AMERICAN SAMOAN GOVERNMENT
P.O. Box LBJ
LBJ Tropical Medical Ctr.
Pago Pago, AS 96799
Tel: (684) 633-1222 Fax: (684) 633-5379

ARIZONA

ARIZONA DEPARTMENT OF HEALTH SERVICES
Office of Health Systems Development, Center for Minority Health
1740 W. Adams St. #410
Phoenix, AZ 85007
Tel: (602) 542-1219 Fax: (602) 542-2011

ARKANSAS

ARKANSAS DEPARTMENT OF HEALTH
Arkansas Minority Health Commission
1123 S. University #312
Little Rock, AR 72204
Tel: (501) 686-2720 Fax: (501) 686-2722
Web: www.arminorityhealth.com

Office of Minority Health & Health Disparities
P.O. Box 1437, Slot H-22
Little Rock, AR 72203-1437
Tel: (501) 661-2193 Fax: (501) 661-2414
Web: www.healthyarkansas.com

CALIFORNIA

DEPARTMENT OF HEALTH SERVICES
Office of Multicultural Health
P.O. Box 997413, M/S 0022
Sacramento, CA 95899-7413
Tel: (916) 440-7562 Fax: (916) 440-7565

COLORADO

COLORADO DEPARTMENT OF PUBLIC HEALTH & ENVIRONMENT
Office of Health Disparities
4300 Cherry Creek Dr. South #B1
Denver, CO 80246-1530
Tel: (303) 692-2329 Fax: (303) 691-7746

CONNECTICUT

CONNECTICUT DEPARTMENT OF PUBLIC HEALTH
Office of Multicultural Health
410 Capitol Ave., MS-11GCT
Hartford, CT 06134
Tel: (860) 509-8098 Fax: (860) 508-7227

DELAWARE

DELAWARE DEPARTMENT OF HEALTH
Office of Minority Health, Division of Public Health
P.O. Box 637
Federal & Waters Sts.
Dover, DE 19903
Tel: (302) 744-4700 Fax: (302) 739-6659
Web: www.state.de.us/dhss/dph

DISTRICT OF COLUMBIA

DISTRICT OF COLUMBIA DEPARTMENT OF HEALTH
State Center for Health Statistics Administration, Research & Analysis Division
825 N. Capitol St. NE, 2nd Fl.
Washington, DC 20002
Tel: (202) 442-9039 Fax: (202) 442-4833
Web: www.dchealth.dc.gov

FLORIDA

FLORIDA STATE DEPARTMENT OF HEALTH
Office of Minority Health
4052 Bald Cypress Way, #A00
Tallahassee, FL 32399-1701
Tel: (850) 245-4012 Fax: (850) 487-2168

GEORGIA

GEORGIA DEPARTMENT OF COMMUNITY HEALTH
Office of Minority Health, Health Improvement Programs
2 Peachtree St. NW, 36th Fl.
Atlanta, GA 30303-3159
Tel: (404) 457-6707 Fax: (404) 657-2769

Georgia Department of Community Health Office of Minority Health
2 Peachtree St. NW, 38th Fl.
Atlanta, GA 30303-3159
Tel: (404) 463-3450 Fax: (404) 657-2769

GUAM

GOVERNMENT OF GUAM
Department of Public Health & Social Services
P.O. Box 2816
Agana, Guam 96932
Tel: (671) 734-7102 Fax: (671) 734-5910

HAWAII

HAWAII STATE DEPARTMENT OF HEALTH
Office of Health Equity
1250 Punchbowl St. #257
Honolulu, HI 96813
Tel: (808) 586-4673 Fax: (808) 586-8252

IDAHO

IDAHO DEPARTMENT OF HEALTH & WELFARE
State Office of Rural Health & Primary Care
450 W. State St., 4th Fl.
Boise, ID 83720
Tel: (208) 332-7212 Fax: (208) 332-7262

ILLINOIS

COOK COUNTY DEPARTMENT OF PUBLIC HEALTH
Health Promotion Unit
1010 Lake St. #300
Oak Park, IL 60301
Tel: (708) 492-2079 Fax: (708) 492-2913
Web: www.idph.state.il.us

ILLINOIS DEPARTMENT OF PUBLIC HEALTH
Center for Minority Health Services
535 W. Jefferson, 5th Fl.
Springfield, IL 62761
Tel: (217) 785-4311 Fax: (217) 558-7181
Web: www.idph.state.il.us

INDIANA

INDIANA MINORITY HEALTH COALITION, INC.
3737 N. Meridian St. #300
Indianapolis, IN 46208
Tel: (317) 926-4011 Fax: (317) 926-4012
Web: www.imhc.org

INDIANA STATE DEPARTMENT OF HEALTH
Office of Minority Health
2 N. Meridian St. #2-K
Indianapolis, IN 46204
Tel: (317) 233-3006 Fax: (317) 233-7943
Web: www.in.gov/isdh

IOWA

IOWA DEPARTMENT OF HEALTH
Office of Multicultural Health
321 E. 12th St., 4th Fl.
Des Moines, IA 50319-0075
Tel: (515) 281-4904 Fax: (515) 242-6384
Web: www.idph.state.ia.us

KANSAS

KANSAS DEPARTMENT OF HEALTH & ENVIRONMENT
1000 SW Jackson St. #540
Topeka, KS 66612-1368
Tel: (785) 291-3219 Fax: (785) 368-6368

LOUISIANA

LOUISIANA DEPARTMENT OF HEALTH & HOSPITALS
Bureau of Minority Health Access
1201 Capitol Access Rd., 3rd Fl.
Baton Rouge, LA 70821
Tel: (225) 342-9500 Fax: (225) 342-5568
Web: www.dhh.state.la.us/lamha

MAINE

MAINE DEPARTMENT HEALTH & HUMAN SERVICES
Office of Minority Health
161 Capitol St. #11
Augusta, ME 04333-0011
Tel: (207) 287-5503 Fax: (207) 287-5431

MARSHALL ISLANDS

REPUBLIC OF THE MARSHALL ISLANDS
Minister of Health & Environment
P.O. Box 16
Majuro, Marshall Islands 96960
Tel: (692) 625-3432 Fax: (692) 625-4543

MARYLAND

MARYLAND DEPARTMENT OF HEALTH & MENTAL HYGIENE
Office of Minority Health & Health Disparities
201 W. Preston St. #500
Baltimore, MD 21201
Tel: (410) 767-0094 Fax: (410) 333-5100
Web: www.dhmh.state.md.us

MASSACHUSETTS

MASSACHUSETTS DEPARTMENT OF PUBLIC HEALTH
Office of Multicultural Health
250 Washington St., 5th Fl.
Boston, MA 02108
Tel: (617) 624-5471 Fax: (617) 624-6062
Web: www.state.ma.us/dph/omh/omh.htm

MICHIGAN

MICHIGAN DEPARTMENT OF COMMUNITY HEALTH
Health Disparities Reduction & Minority Health Section, Division of Health, Wellness & Disease Control
109 Michigan Ave., 10th Fl.
Lansing, MI 48913
Tel: (517) 241-0854 Fax: (517) 241-0875

MICRONESIA

FEDERATED STATES OF MICRONESIA DEPARTMENT OF HEALTH, EDUCATION & SOCIAL SERVICES
P.S. 70
Palikir, Pohnpei State, FM 96941
Tel: (691) 320-2872 Fax: (691) 320-5263

MINNESOTA

MINNESOTA DEPARTMENT OF HEALTH
Office of Minority & Multicultural Health
625 Robert St. North
St. Paul, MN 55155-2538
Tel: (651) 201-5813 Fax: (651) 201-4986
Web: www.health.state.mn.us/ommh

MISSISSIPPI

MISSISSIPPI DEPARTMENT OF HEALTH
Office of Health Disparity
570 E. Woodrow Wilson Blvd. #120
Jackson, MS 39215
Tel: (601) 576-8102 Fax: (601) 576-7270
Web: www.msdh.state.ms.us

MISSOURI

MISSOURI DEPARTMENT OF HEALTH & SENIOR SERVICES
Office of Minority Health
P.O. Box 570
912 Wildwood Dr.
Jefferson City, MO 65102
Tel: (573) 751-6064 Fax: (573) 522-1599
Web: www.health.state.mo.us

MONTANA

MONTANA DEPARTMENT OF PUBLIC HEALTH & HUMAN SERVICES
1400 Broadway, #C202
Helena, MT 59620
Tel: (406) 444-3583 Fax: (406) 444-0272
Web: www.dphhs.state.mt.us

NEBRASKA

NEBRASKA HEALTH & HUMAN SERVICES SYSTEM
Nebraska Health & Human Services System, Office of Minority Health
P.O. Box 95044
301 Centennial Mall South
Lincoln, NE 68509-5007
Tel: (402) 471-0152 Fax: (402) 471-0383
Web: www.hhs.state.ne.us/omh

NEVADA

STATE DEPARTMENT OF HEALTH & HUMAN RESOURCES
Office of Minority Health
505 E. King St. #201
Carson City, NV 89701
Tel: (775) 684-4200 Fax: (775) 684-4046

NEW HAMPSHIRE

NEW HAMPSHIRE DEPARTMENT OF HEALTH & HUMAN SERVICES
Office of Minority Health
129 Pleasant St.
Concord, NH 03301
Tel: (603) 271-8459 Fax: (603) 271-4727
Web: www.dhhs.state.nh.us/DHHS/MHO/default.htm

NEW JERSEY

NEW JERSEY DEPARTMENT OF HEALTH & SENIOR SERVICES
Office of Minority & Multicultural Health
P.O. Box 360
Trenton, NJ 08625-0360
Tel: (609) 292-6962 Fax: (609) 292-8713
Web: www.state.nj.us/health/commiss/omh/index.html

NEW MEXICO

NEW MEXICO DEPARTMENT OF HEALTH
Office of Policy & Multicultural Health
1190 St. Francis Dr. #S-4260
Santa Fe, NM 87502-6110
Tel: (505) 827-2280 Fax: (505) 827-2942

NEW YORK

NEW YORK CITY DEPARTMENT OF HEALTH & MENTAL HYGIENE
Office of Minority Health Programs
485 Throop Ave. #1460
Brooklyn, NY 11221
Tel: (646) 253-5800 Fax: (646) 253-7502

NEW YORK STATE DEPARTMENT OF HEALTH
Office of Minority Health
ESP-Corning Tower Bldg. #780
Albany, NY 12237-0092
Tel: (518) 474-2180 Fax: (518) 473-4695

NORTH CAROLINA

NORTH CAROLINA DEPARTMENT OF HEALTH & HUMAN SERVICES
Office of Minority Health & Health Disparities
1110 Navaho Dr. #510, 1906 Mail Service Ctr.
Raleigh, NC 27699-1906
Tel: (919) 431-1613 Fax: (919) 850-2758
Web: http://www.ncminorityhealth.org/omhhd/index.html

NORTHERN MARIANA ISLANDS

COMMONWEALTH OF THE NORTHERN MARIANA ISLANDS
Secretary of Health
P.O. Box 500-409 CK
Saipan, MP 96950-0409
Tel: (670) 234-8950 Fax: (670) 234-8930

OHIO

COLUMBUS HEALTH DEPARTMENT
Office of Minority Health
240 Parsons Ave.
Columbus, OH 43215
Tel: (614) 645-7159 Fax: (614) 645-5888
Web: www.cmhhealth.org

COMBINED HEALTH DISTRICT OF MONTGOMERY COUNTY
117 S. Main St.
Dayton, OH 45402
Tel: (937) 225-4403

OHIO COMMISSION ON MINORITY HEALTH
Vern Riffe Center for Government and the Performing Arts, 77 S. High St. #745
Columbus, OH 43215
Tel: (614) 466-4000 Fax: (614) 752-9049
Web: www.state.oh.us/mih

OKLAHOMA

OKLAHOMA STATE DEPARTMENT OF HEALTH
Office of Minority Health
1000 NE 10th St. #211
Oklahoma City, OK 73117-1299
Tel: (405) 271-1337 Fax: (405) 271-9228
Web: www.health.state.ok.us

OREGON

DEPARTMENT OF HUMAN SERVICES
Office of Multicultural Health
800 NE Oregon St. #930
Portland, OR 97232
Tel: (971) 673-1285 Fax: (971) 673-1299
Web: www.healthoregon.org/omh/index.cfm

PENNSYLVANIA

PENNSYLVANIA DEPARTMENT OF HEALTH
7th and Forster Sts., Health & Welfare Bldg. #802
Harrisburg, PA 17102-0090
Tel: (717) 787-6436 Fax: (717) 7870191

PUERTO RICO

PUERTO RICO DEPARTMENT OF HEALTH
Office of Special Racial/Ethnic Health Issues
P.O. Box 70139
Bldg. A, Medical Center
San Juan, PR 00936
Tel: (787) 274-7735 Fax: (787) 759-6864

REPUBLIC OF PALAU

REPUBLIC OF PALAU
Minister of Health
P.O. Box 6027
Koror, Republic of Palau 96940
Tel: (680) 488-5552 Fax: (680) 488-1215

RHODE ISLAND

RHODE ISLAND DEPARTMENT OF HEALTH
Office of Minority Health, Ctr. for Healthy People
3 Capitol Hill #401
Providence, RI 02908
Tel: (401) 222-2901 Fax: (401) 273-4350

SOUTH CAROLINA

SOUTH CAROLINA DEPARTMENT OF HEALTH & ENVIRONMENT CONTROL
Office of Minority Health
2600 Bull St.
Columbia, SC 29201
Tel: (803) 898-3808 Fax: (803) 898-3810
Web: www.scdhec.gov/omh

SOUTH DAKOTA

SOUTH DAKOTA DEPARTMENT OF HEALTH
600 E. Capitol Ave.
Pierre, SD 57501
Tel: (605) 773-5303 Fax: (605) 773-5683

TENNESSEE

TENNESSEE DEPARTMENT OF HEALTH
Office of Minority Health
425 5th Ave. North, Cordell Hull Bldg., 3rd Fl.
Nashville, TN 37247
Tel: (615) 741-9443 Fax: (615) 253-1434
Web: www2.state.tn.us/health/minorityhealth

TEXAS

TEXAS DEPARTMENT OF STATE HEALTH SERVICES
Office for the Elimination of Health Disparities, Center for Program Coordination
1100 W. 49th St. #M-760
Austin, TX 78756
Tel: (512) 458-7629 Fax: (512) 458-7488
Web: www.dshs.state.tx.us

UTAH

UTAH DEPARTMENT OF HEALTH
Office of Multicultural Health
P.O. Box 142001
Salt Lake City, UT 84114-2001
Tel: (801) 538-9457 Fax: (801) 538-6591

VERMONT

VERMONT DEPARTMENT OF HEALTH
Office of Minority Health
P.O. Box 70
108 Cherry St.
Burlington, VT 05402
Tel: (802) 863-7273 Fax: (802) 651-1634

VIRGIN ISLANDS

VIRGIN ISLANDS DEPARTMENT OF HEALTH
Office of Minority Health
48 Sugar Estate
St. Thomas, VI 00802
Tel: (340) 776-8311 X5079 Fax: (340) 777-4001

VIRGINIA

VIRGINIA DEPARTMENT OF HEALTH
Office of Policy & Planning, Office of Minority Health
109 Governor St., Madison Bldg., 10th Fl.
Richmond, VA 23219

Tel: (804) 864-7432 Fax: (804) 864-7440
Web: www.vdh.state.va.us

WASHINGTON

WASHINGTON DEPARTMENT OF HEALTH
Office of Policy, Legislative & Constituent Relations
P.O. Box 47890
101 Israel Rd. SE, Town Ctr. 1
Olympia, WA 98501
Tel: (360) 236-4021 Fax: (360) 586-7424

WEST VIRGINIA

WEST VIRGINIA DEPARTMENT OF HEALTH & HUMAN RESOURCES
Bureau for Public Health, Office of Rural Health, Minority Health Programs
350 Capitol St. #515
Charleston, WV 25301-3716
Tel: (304) 558-7138 Fax: (304) 558-2183

WISCONSIN

DEPARTMENT OF HEALTH & FAMILY SERVICES
Division of Public Health, Minority Health Program
1 W. Wilson St. #665
Madison, WI 53701
Tel: (608) 267-2173 Fax: (608) 264-7720
Web: www.dhfs.state.wi.us/Health/MinorityHealth

WYOMING

WYOMING DEPARTMENT OF HEALTH
Office of Minority Health
6101 Yellowstone Rd. #510
Cheyenne, WY 82002
Tel: (307) 777-5601 Fax: (307) 777-8545
Web: http://wdh.state.wy.us

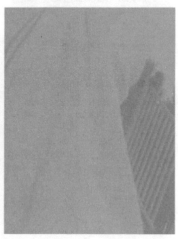

ScholarSite.com Financial Aid

Approximately 40 student financial aid opportunities are listed below. They were selected for their focus on African American students at the undergraduate level. For more detailed information on conditions and restrictions for these and thousands of other opportunities, please visit TIYM's financial aid website, www.scholarsite.com.

Award

W

WESTERN ILLINOIS UNIVERSITY
Office of Financial Aid
1 University Circle
Macomb, IL 61455-1396

Donald Poindexter Research Award Fund
Janice Owens, Director of University Scholarship Activities
Tel: (309) 298-2001 Fax: (309) 298-2432
Email: info@wiu.edu
Web: www.wiu.edu
Requirements: Student must be an American ethnic minority, and have a research proposal aproved. Priority will be given to undergraduates but graduate students are also eligible. Contact the Department of Psychology.
Disciplines: Psychology
Award: $150
Eligible Inst.: Western Illinois University

Fellowship

A

AMERICAN SOCIETY FOR MICROBIOLOGY
Office of Education & Training
1752 N St., N.W
Washington, DC 20036

ASM Undergraduate Research Fellowship
Tel: (202) 942-9283 Fax: (202) 942-9329
Email: fellowships-careerinformation@asmusa.org
Web: www.asm.org
Requirements: The ASM Undergraduate Research Fellowship (URF) is aimed at highly competitive students who wish to pursue graduate careers (Ph.D. or MD/Ph.D) in microbiology. Students will have the opportunity to conduct full time research at their home institution with an ASM member and present research results at the ASM General Meeting the following year. Students will conduct a research project for a minimum of 10 weeks beginning in the summer of 2005, work with a faculty mentor who is an ASM member and who is employed at the student's home institution, and submit a research abstract for presentation at the 2006 ASM General Meeting. Eligible student candidates for the fellowship must be enrolled as a full-time matriculating undergraduate student during the 2005-2006 academic year at an accredited U.S. Institution, be involved in a research project, have an ASM member at their home institution willing to serve as the mentor, and not receive financial support for research (i.e., Council for Undergraduate Research, Minority Access to Research Careers, Sigma Xi) during the fellowship.
Disciplines: Research, Biological Science, Biology
Eligible Inst.: US schools
Deadline: February 1

U

UNIVERSITY OF CALIFORNIA AT BERKELEY
Graduate Division
312 Mcluaghlin Hall #1702
Berkeley, CA 94720

UC-Berkeley Summer Research for Minority Undergraduates
Pamela D. Jennings, Coordinator
Tel: (510) 643-6443 Fax: (510) 643-5600
Email: cblf@berkeley.edu
Web: www.berkeley.edu
Requirements: A 10-week summer research and professional development program is available for disadvantaged and underrepresented minority students Interested in careers as physician scientists. The program is designed for students in their freshman, sophomore or junior years of college.
Disciplines: Natural Sciences, Social Sciences, Humanities & Liberal Arts, Biology
Award: $1,600
Eligible Inst.: University of California Berkeley

Grant

P

PAGE EDUCATION FOUNDATION
P.O. Box 581254
Minneapolis, MN 55458-1254

Page Education Foundation Grant
Ramona Harristhal, Administrative Director
Tel: (612) 332-0406 Fax: (612) 332-0403
Email: info@page-ed.org
Web: www.page-ed.org
Requirements: Are students of color, show financial aid, demonstrate a positive attitude toward education and community service, attend post secondary school in Minnesota, and be willing to complete 50 hours of service to children each year.
Disciplines: Any
Award: $1,000-2,500
Eligible Inst.: US schools

Deadline: May 1

Internship

N

NEWS JOURNAL
P.O. Box 15505
Wilmington, DE 19850

Internship Program
John Sweeney, Public Editor
Tel: (302) 324-2500 Fax: (302) 324-2578
Web: www.delawareonline.com/
Requirements: Internship programs are available in info graphics and layout/design. The internship is available for the summer. Send resume, sample of works, references, and a cover letter.
Disciplines: Graphic Communications, Design
Award: Varies

U.S. DEPARTMENT OF ENERGY

Historically Black Colleges and Universities and Minority Institutions Collaborative Research Project
Christina Budwine
Tel: (925) 422-5460
Web: www.doe.gov
Requirements: The program gives minority students valuable hands-on experience in developing technologies to promote the efficient and environmentally safe use of coal, oil and natural gas.
Disciplines: Natural Sciences
Award: Varies
Eligible Inst.: US schools

Scholarship

A

ALABAMA SPACE GRANT CONSORTIUM
c/o University of Alabama in Huntsville
Materials Science Bldg. #205
Huntsville, AL 35899

Teacher Education Scholarship Program
Tel: (256) 824-6800 Fax: (256) 890-6061
Web: www.uah.edu
Requirements: The Teacher Education Scholarship Program, is designed to attract and encourage talented individuals to enter a course of study leading to pre-college secondary teaching certification in the sciences, mathematics and technology education. Applications are solicited from high school seniors and community college students in their final year who have been accepted at one of the seven Alabama Space Grant Universities.
Disciplines: Education
Award: $1,000
Eligible Inst.: University of Alabama
Deadline: March 1

ALBERTUS MAGNUS COLLEGE
Financial Aid
700 Prospectus St.
New Haven, CT 06511

Nationwide Insurance Scholarship
Tel: (203) 773-8505 Fax: (203) 773-8972
Email: admissions@albertus.edu
Web: www.albertus.edu
Requirements: This scholarship is available to minority students who demonstrate financial need.
Disciplines: Any
Award: $1,250
Eligible Inst.: Albertus Magnus College
Deadline: April 15

AMERICAN NUCLEAR SOCIETY
555 N. Kensington Ave.
La Grange Park, IL 60525

Undergraduate Scholarship
Tony Bishop, Scholarship Coordinator
Tel: (708) 352-6611 Fax: (708) 352-0499
Email: tbishop@ans.org
Web: www.ans.org
Requirements: This scholarship is available to a sophomore student enrolled in a course of study relating to a degree in nuclear science or nuclear engineering in a U.S. institution and must be either a U.S citizen or permanent resident.
Disciplines: Nuclear Science, Engineering
Award: $2,000
Eligible Inst.: US schools
Deadline: February 1

ARKANSAS STATE UNIVERSITY
College of Communications
P.O. Box 540
State University, AR 72467

William Randolph Hearst Minority Scholarship in Journalism and Radio-Television
Tel: (870) 972-2310 Fax: (870) 972-2794
Email: admissions@chickasaw.astate.edu
Web: www.astate.edu
Requirements: This scholarship is available to the most outstanding recent graduate or graduate senior student and above majoring in journalism or radio-television.
Disciplines: Journalism, Radio Broadcasting, TV Broadcasting, Broadcasting, Communications
Eligible Inst.: Arkansas State University
Deadline: April 1

B

BENNETT COLLEGE
Financial Aid Office
900 E. Washington St.
Greensboro, NC 27401

African American Atelier/Miller Memorial Prize Scholarship
Monty Hickman, Director
Tel: (336) 370-8677 Fax: (336) 517-2204
Email: financial_aid@bennett.edu
Web: www.bennett.edu
Requirements: The African American Atelier/ Eva Hamlin Miller Memorial Prize awards $500 to a rising sophomore or junior major in Visual Arts or Visual Arts Management. The student must exhibit high academic ability and a commitment to the discipline. A minimum 3.0 grade point average is required. The prize is given in memory of Eva Hamlin Miller, the first curator of the African American Atelier Gallery.
Disciplines: Visual Arts, Fine Arts
Award: $500
Eligible Inst.: Bennett College

BIOLA UNIVERSITY
Office of Admissions
13800 Biola Ave.
La Mirada, CA 90639-4652

Scholarships for Underrepresented Groups of Ethnicity (SURGE)
Scholarship Administrator
Tel: (562) 903-4752 Fax: (562) 906-4541
Web: www.biola.edu
Requirements: These scholarships are available to African-American, Hispanic-American or Native American full time undergraduate students showing merit and involvement in cultural activities. Applicant must maintain GPA of 3.0.
Disciplines: Any
Award: $6,500
Eligible Inst.: Biola University
Deadline: February 15

BROWN FOUNDATION FOR EDUCATIONAL EQUITY, EXCELLENCE, AND RESEARCH
P.O. Box 4862
Zip Topeka, KS 66604

Brown Scholar
Chelsey Smith, Administrative Assistant
Tel: (785) 235-3939 Fax: (785) 235-1001
Email: brownfound@juno.com
Web: www.brownvboard.org
Requirements: Applicants must be a minority student and admitted to a teacher education program at a 4-year college or university. In addition, applicant must submit two letters of recommendation: one from a teacher, counselor, or other school official and one from a person familar with the applicant's skills and abilities who is not a family member.
Disciplines: Education
Award: $1,000
Eligible Inst.: US schools
Deadline: March 30

BUCKNELL UNIVERSITY
Financial Aid Office
621 St. George St.
Lewisburg, PA 17837

Berlin Family Scholarship
Andrea C.A. Leithner, Director
Tel: (570) 577-1331 Fax: (570) 577-1481
Email: finaid@bucknell.edu
Web: www.bucknell.edu

Requirements: The Berlin Family Scholarship was established by George R. Berlin, Class of 1965, his mother, Elizabeth Smith Berlin, Class of 1935, and his sons, Bradley J. Berlin, Class of 1993, and William B. Berlin, Class of 1993 (M.A.), in recognition of George R. Berlin's father, William H. Berlin, Class of 1935. Preference for the scholarship award shall be given to students whose racial, ethnic, cultural, economic or other characteristics enhance the diversity of Bucknell's student group.
Disciplines: Any
Award: Varies
Eligible Inst.: Bucknell University

C

Catherine Vaughan Hellerman Scholarship
Andrea C.A. Leithner, Director
Tel: (570) 577-1331 Fax: (570) 577-1481
Email: finaid@bucknell.edu
Web: www.bucknell.edu
Requirements: The Catherine Vaughan Hellerman Scholarship was established by Stephen W. Vittorini, Class of 1979, in memory of his grandmother and great-grandfather, Charles P. Vaughan, acting president of Bucknell University in 1931. Preference for the scholarship award shall be given to a student or students from the Philadelphia area whose ethnic and economic origins add to the diversity of the university. It is the donor's wish that the scholarship recipient(s), upon graduation, expect to use their learned skills and knowledge to enhance the economic and cultural well-being of communities similar to those from which they were selected.
Disciplines: Any
Award: Varies
Eligible Inst.: Bucknell University

John H. and Susan B. Mathias Scholarship
Andrea C.A. Leithner, Director
Tel: (570) 577-1331 Fax: (570) 577-1481
Email: finaid@bucknell.edu
Web: www.bucknell.edu
Requirements: The John H. and Susan B. Mathias Scholarship was established by John H. '69 and Susan B. Mathias '69, and honors the extensive ties of the Mathias family to Bucknell University. Preference for the scholarship award shall be given to students whose ethnic, racial, economic, or national origins add to the diversity of Bucknell.
Disciplines: Any
Award: Varies
Eligible Inst.: Bucknell University

Tague Family Scholarship
Andrea C.A. Leithner, Director
Tel: (570) 577-1331 Fax: (570) 577-1481
Email: finaid@bucknell.edu
Web: www.bucknell.edu
Requirements: The Tague Family Scholarship was established by Barry E. Tague, Class of 1960, and his wife, Dorothy Tague. Preference for the scholarship award shall be given to students from the greater Philadelphia area, with demonstrated financial need, whose ethnic, racial, economic or national origins add to the diversity of Bucknell.
Disciplines: Any
Award: Varies
Eligible Inst.: Bucknell University

D

DAVIDSON COLLEGE
Financial Aid Office
P.O. Box 7157
Davidson, NC 28035-7157

Romare Howard Bearden Scholarship
Christopher J. Gruber, Acting Dean of Admission/Financial Aid
Tel: (800) 768-0380 Fax: (704) 894-2845
Email: admission@davidson.edu
Web: www.davidson.edu
Requirements: This scholarship is available to African-American students who demonstrate exceptional ability and promise in studio art.
Disciplines: Arts
Award: $10,000
Eligible Inst.: Davidson College
Deadline: February 15

DUKE UNIVERSITY
Financial Aid Office
2122 Campus Dr.
Durham, NC 27708

United Methodist Minority Scholarship
James A. Belvin, Jr., Director
Tel: (919) 684-6225 Fax: (919) 660-9811
Email: finaid@duke.edu
Web: www.duke.edu
Requirements: This scholarship is available to Methodist students who have shown financial need and minority students.
Disciplines: Any
Award: $500
Eligible Inst.: Duke University

E

EASTERN ILLINOIS UNIVERSITY
Journalism Department
600 Lincoln Ave.
Charleston, IL 61920-3099

James C. Copley Foundation Award for Minority Students
James Tidwell, Acting Chair of Journalism Dept.
Tel: (217) 581-6003 Fax: (217) 581-2923
Email: admissns@eiu.edu
Web: www.eiu.edu
Requirements: This scholarship is available to a minority journalism major who intends to pursue a career in journalism. Candidates should have made a significant contribution to campus media.
Disciplines: Journalism
Eligible Inst.: Eastern Illinois University
Deadline: March 10

ELMHURST COLLEGE
Office of Admission and Financial Aid
190 Prospect Ave.
Elmhurst, IL 60126

Enrichment Scholarship
Ruth Pusich, Director, Financial Aid
Tel: (630) 617-3400 Fax: (630) 617-5501
Email: admit@elmhurst.edu
Web: www.elmhurst.edu
Requirements: This scholarship is available to academically eligible Asian, African American, Hispanic, or Native American students. Recipients are required to apply for financial aid.
Disciplines: Any
Award: $5,000
Eligible Inst.: Elmhurst College
Deadline: April 15

HERCULES, INC.
1313 N. Market St.
Wilmington, DE 19894-0001

Minority Engineering Development Program
Tel: (302) 594-5000 Fax: (302) 594-5400
Web: www.herc.com
Requirements: The Hercules MinD Program is designed to increase the availability of under-represented minority group members in professions found in the Chemical Industry, especially the engineering fields. The program involves a combination of student scholarships, work experiences and grants to participating institutions.
Disciplines: Engineering, Engineering
Eligible Inst.: US schools

I

IDAHO STATE BOARD OF EDUCATION
Scholarship Programs
P.O. Box 83720
Boise, ID 83720-0037

Idaho Minority and "At-Risk" Student Scholarship
Dana Kelly
Tel: (208) 334-2270 Fax: (208) 334-2632
Email: dkelly@osbe.state.id.us
Web: www.idahoboardofed.org
Requirements: Be a U.S. citizen and a resident of Idaho, be a graduate of an Idaho high school, be a first-generation college student, be disabled, be a migrant farm worker or the dependent of a migrant farm worker, have substantial financial need, be a member of an ethnic minority historically underrepresented in higher education in Idaho.
Disciplines: Any
Award: $3,000
Eligible Inst.: US schools

M

MARTIN LUTHER KING, JR. MEMORIAL SCHOLARSHIP FUND
P.O. Box 921
Burlingame, CA 94011

Martin Luther King, Jr. Memorial Scholarship
Tel: (949) 824-5461 Fax: (949) 824-2092
Email: scholarships@cta.org
Web: www.scholars.uci.edu
Requirements: In order to be eligible an applicant must be pursuing a teaching related career in public education and be a member of a defined ethnic minority group. Applicants must also be an active member of CTA, or a dependent child of an active, retired-life or deceased CTA member, or a member of Student CTA (SCTA).
Disciplines: Education
Award: Varies
Eligible Inst.: US schools
Deadline: March 15

METROPOLITAN STATE COLLEGE OF DENVER
Office of Financial Aid
P.O. Box 173362
Denver, CO 80217-3362

E.B. Jeppesen Endowed Memorial Scholarship
Tel: (303) 556-2983 Fax: (303) 556-4927
Web: www.mscd.edu
Requirements: Applicants must be full-time students with financial need, and have a

declared major in Aerospace Science, with a GPA of 3.0 in the major and overall. Student would need to write an essay.
Disciplines: Aerospace Science, Management, Technology
Eligible Inst.: Metropolitan State College of Denver
Deadline: March 1

William T. Blackburn, Jr. Endowed Memorial Scholarship
Tel: (303) 556-3130 Fax: (303) 556-4927
Web: www.mscd.edu
Requirements: Applicants must have a declared major in the Health Professions Department, have completed 12 credit hours in the department, carry 6 credit hours, show financial need.
Disciplines: Nursing
Eligible Inst.: Metropolitan State College of Denver
Deadline: March 1

N

NATIONAL ALLIANCE OF BLACK SCHOOL EDUCATORS
NABSE/LSAC Scholarship Committee
310 Pennsylvania ave, SE
Washington, DC 20003

President's Scholarship
Ms. Betty Collin, LSAC Chairperson
Tel: (202) 608-6310 Fax: (202) 608-6319
Web: http://nabse.org
Requirements: This grant is for students currently in their junior or senior year of high school.
Disciplines: Education
Award: varies
Eligible Inst.: US schools

NATIONAL MINORITY JUNIOR GOLF SCHOLARSHIP ASSOCIATION
4950 E. Thomas rd
Phoenix, AZ 85018

NMJGSA Scholarship
Tel: (602) 258-7851 Fax: (602) 258-3412
Web: www.nmjgsa.org/
Requirements: This scholarship is available to college-bound or continuing minority golfer who already exist in the database.
Disciplines: Athletics
Award: $1,000-$6,000
Eligible Inst.: US schools

NORTH CAROLINA CENTRAL UNIVERSITY
Office of Undergraduate Admissions
P.O. Box 19717
Durham, NC 27707

Glaxo Scholarship
Tel: (919) 560-6298 Fax: (919) 530-7625
Web: www.nccu.edu
Requirements: This scholarship is available to students majoring in biology, chemistry, or psychology.
Disciplines: Biological Science, Biology, Chemistry, Biochemistry, Psychology
Award: $1000/yr
Eligible Inst.: North Carolina Central University
Deadline: March 31

NOVA SOUTHEASTERN UNIVERSITY
Office of Student Financial Aid
3301 College Ave.
Fort Lauderdale, FL 33314-7796

Chancellor's Scholarship
Tel: (954) 262-3380 Fax: (954) 262-3533
Web: www.nova.edu
Requirements: Candidates must be currently

enrolled or accepted for enrollment. (Currently enrolled students must be in good academic standing and must be permanent residents of Florida.) Candidates must be from a disadvantaged background and demonstrate financial need. Consideration will be given to those from families where few or no members have previously attended college.
Disciplines: Medical Sciences, Medical Doctor, Health Care, Nursing
Award: Tuition
Eligible Inst.: Nova Southeastern University
Deadline: May 30

S

SAN DIEGO STATE UNIVERSITY
School of Communication
5500 Campanile Dr.
San Diego, CA 92182-4516

KFMB Scholarship
Tel: (619) 594-5200 Fax: (619) 594-4268
Web: www.sdsu.edu
Requirements: This scholarship is available to minority students in the fields of news-editorial and radio-TV news.
Disciplines: Editing/Reporting, TV Broadcasting, Broadcasting
Award: Varies
Eligible Inst.: San Diego State University
Deadline: March 1

SAN DIEGO STATE UNIVERSITY
Department of Journalism
5500 Campanile Dr.
San Diego, CA 92182-0116

Reggie Smith Memorial Scholarship
Dr. Glen Broom, Professor & Chair
Tel: (619) 594-5200 Fax: (619) 594-4268
Web: www.sdsu.edu
Requirements: Candidates must be in good academic standing. Preference is given to underrepresented minority students. For application materials, contact the Department of Communication.
Disciplines: Journalism
Award: Varies
Eligible Inst.: San Diego State University
Deadline: March 1

SAN FRANCISCO STATE UNIVERSITY
Student Financial Aid Office
HSS 120, 1600 Holloway Ave.
San Francisco, CA 94132

Rosa Parks Scholarship
Evelyn Hooker
Tel: (415) 338-2032 Fax: (415) 338-0949
Email: ehooker@sfsu.edu
Web: www.sfsu.edu
Requirements: This scholarship is available to student who has been accepted into a graduate or credential program at SFSU; Enrolled in at least 8 units. Applicant must be a U.S. citizen.
Disciplines: Any
Award: $750
Eligible Inst.: San Francisco State University

SAN JUAN COLLEGE
Financial Aid Office
4601 College Blvd.
Farmington, NM 87402

San Juan Generating Station of the Public Service Company of New Mexico Scholarship
Roger Evans, Director
Tel: (505) 566-3323 Fax: (505) 566-3568
Email: evansr@sanjuancollege.edu
Web: www.sanjuancollege.edu

Requirements: This scholarship is awarded to full-time students residing in San Juan County. Preference is given to students who are minority or female. Applicants must plan to enroll in a minimum of 12 credit hours; have obtained a minimum high school GPA of 2.8 (or college GPA of 3.0).
Disciplines: Any
Award: Varies
Eligible Inst.: San Juan College
Deadline: April 15

U

UNITED NEGRO COLLEGE FUND
229 Peachtree St. NE
Atlanta, GA 30303

11-Alive Community Service Scholarship Test
Web: www.uncf.org
Requirements: Student must plan to enroll full-time at Clark Atlanta University, Morehouse College or Spelman College. Student must have a cumulative GPA of 2.5 or higher on a 4.0 scale. Student must major in communications, journalism, or related majors. Student must demonstrate an unmet financial need. Student must be a 2002-03 graduating senior from a metropolitan Atlanta Public high school.
Disciplines: Communications, Journalism
Award: $3,000
Eligible Inst.: Clark Atlanta University, Morehouse College, Spelman College
Deadline: May 15

UNIVERSITY OF ALABAMA
College of Communication and Information Sciences
P.O. Box 870172
Tuscaloosa, AL 35487-0172

James T. and Joanne Lynagh Endowed Minority Scholarship
Jim Oakley
Tel: (205) 348-8594 Fax: (205) 348-6544
Email: joakley@ccom.ua.edu
Web: www.ua.edu
Requirements: This scholarship is available to outstanding minority students majoring in communication, freshman through junior enrolled full-time. Priority is given to telecommunication and film majors.
Disciplines: Communications
Award: $1,000/yr
Eligible Inst.: University of Alabama
Deadline: December 1

John S. and James L. Knight Minority Scholarship
Jim Oakley, Placement Director
Tel: (205) 348-8594 Fax: (205) 348-3836
Email: joakley@ua.edu
Web: www.ua.edu
Requirements: This scholarship is available to outstanding minority students majoring in journalism. Applicants must be full-time freshmen through juniors.
Disciplines: Journalism
Award: $1,000/Yr.
Eligible Inst.: University of Alabama
Deadline: December 1

UNIVERSITY OF IDAHO
Office of Student Financial Aid Services
875 Perimeter Dr.
Moscow, ID 83844-4291

Minority at Risk Scholarship
Tel: (208) 885-6312 Fax: (208) 885-4477
Email: finaid@uidaho.edu
Web: www.uidaho.edu/sfas/
Requirements: This scholarship is available to

a first generation college student who either has a disablity or has an ethnic background of Hispanic American, African American or Native American descent demonstrating substantial financial need or be a son or daughter of a migrant farm family. Must also be a graduate of a Idaho high school.
Disciplines: Any
Eligible Inst.: University of Idaho

Multi-Cultural Scholars in Agriculture Scholarship
Tel: (208) 885-6312 Fax: (208) 885-4477
Email: finaid@uidaho.edu
Web: www.uidaho.edu/sfas/
Requirements: This scholarship is available to undergraduate students in the field of agricultural and life sciences.
Disciplines: Agriculture
Eligible Inst.: University of Idaho

UNIVERSITY OF MIAMI
School of Business Administration
P.O. Box 248027
Coral Gables, FL 33146

Morgan-Stanley Scholarship/Internship
Tel: (305) 284-4643 Fax: (305) 284-2507
Email: admission@miami.edu
Web: www.miami.edu/admission-information/
Requirements: This scholarship is available to undergraduate juniors, with preference given to minorities.
Disciplines: Business
Award: Varies
Eligible Inst.: University of Miami
Deadline: April 11

UNIVERSITY OF SOUTHERN CALIFORNIA
Black Alumni Programs Office
700 Childs Way, JHH 324
Los Angeles, CA 90089-4890

Ebonics Support Group
Tel: (213) 740-8342 Fax: (213) 749-9781
Web: www.usc.edu
Requirements: Applicants must be undergraduate or graduate students attending USC who have completed at least one semester and are of African-American descent. Applicants must be U.S. citizens, and must apply for funding through the USC Financial Aid Office.
Disciplines: Any
Award: Varies
Eligible Inst.: University of Southern California

W

WESTERN CAROLINA UNIVERSITY
Financial Aid Office
242 H.F. Robinson Administration Bldg.
Cullowhee, NC 28723

C.D. Spangler Jr. Scholarship for Minority Students
Nancy B. Dillard, Director
Tel: (828) 227-7290 Fax: (828) 227-7042
Email: finaid@wcu.edu
Web: www.wcu.edu
Requirements: This endowed scholarship program's purpose is to provide financial support for deserving young minority students. Awards are based upon high academic achievement, successful participation in various school activities, overall social and civic contributions, and financial need. Contact the Office of Financial Aid.
Disciplines: Any
Award: Varies
Eligible Inst.: Western Carolina University
Deadline: March 31

Historically Black Colleges and Universities

ALABAMA

ALABAMA A&M UNIVERSITY
4900 Meridian St.
Normal, AL 35762
Virginia Caples, Interim President
Tel: (256) 372-5000 Fax: (256) 372-5249
Email: admissions@mail.aamu.edu
Web: www.aamu.edu

ALABAMA STATE UNIVERSITY
915 S. Jackson St.
Montgomery, AL 36101
Dr. Joe A. Lee, President
Tel: (800) 253-5037 Fax: (334) 229-4984
Email: admission@alasu.edu
Web: www.alasu.edu

BISHOP STATE COMMUNITY COLLEGE
351 N. Broad St.
Mobile, AL 36603-5898
Dr. Yvonne Kennedy, President
Tel: (251) 690-6801 Fax: (251) 438-5403
Email: info@bishop.edu
Web: www.bishop.edu

CONCORDIA COLLEGE
1804 Green St.
Selma, AL 36701
Dr. Julius Jenkins, President
Tel: (334) 874-5700 Fax: (334) 874-3728
Email: epickens@concordiacollegeselma.edu
Web: www.concordiaselma.edu

GADSDEN STATE COMMUNITY COLLEGE
P.O. Box 227
Gadsden, AL 35902-0227
Dr. Renee D. Culverhouse, President
Tel: (800) 746-6472 Fax: (256) 549-8205
Email: mpruitt@gadsdenstate.edu
Web: www.gadsdenst.cc.al.us

J.F. DRAKE STATE TECHNICAL COLLEGE
3421 Meridian St. North
Huntsville, AL 35810-7439
Dr. Helen McAlpine, President
Tel: (888) 413-7253 Fax: (256) 551-3142
Email: clemons@drakestate.edu
Web: www.dstc.cc.al.us

LAWSON STATE COMMUNITY COLLEGE
3060 Wilson Rd.
Birmingham, AL 35221
Dr. Perry Ward, President
Tel: (205) 929-6309 Fax: (205) 923-7106
Email: dallen@lawsonstate.edu
Web: www.ls.cc.al.us

MILES COLLEGE
5500 Myron Massey Blvd.
Fairfield, AL 35064
Albert J.H. Sloan, II, President
Tel: (205) 929-1000 Fax: (205) 929-1453
Email: info@mail.miles.edu
Web: www.miles.edu

OAKWOOD COLLEGE
7000 Adventist Blvd.
Huntsville, AL 35896
Dr. Delbert W. Baker, President
Tel: (800) 824-5312 Fax: (256) 726-7154
Email: admission@oakwood.edu
Web: www.oakwood.edu

SELMA UNIVERSITY
1501 Lapsley St.
Selma, AL 36701
Dr. Alvin Cleveland, President
Tel: (334) 872-2533 Fax: (334) 872-7746
Email: selmauniversity@bellsouth.net
Web: www.selmauniversity.org

SHELTON STATE COMMUNITY COLLEGE
9500 Old Greensboro Rd.
Tuscaloosa, AL 35405
Rick Rogers, President
Tel: (205) 391-2989 Fax: (205) 391-3910
Email: rrogers@sheltonstate.edu
Web: www.sheltonstate.edu

STILLMAN UNIVERSITY
P.O. Box 1430
Tuscaloosa, AL 35403
Dr. Ernest McNealey, President
Tel: (800) 841-5722 Fax: (205) 366-8941
Email: admissions@stillman.edu
Web: www.stillman.edu

TALLADEGA COLLEGE
627 W. Battle St.
Talladega, AL 35160
Dr. Oscar L. Prater, Interim President
Tel: (800) 540-3956 Fax: (256) 362-0274
Email: admissions@talladega.edu
Web: www.talladega.edu

TRENHOLM STATE TECHNICAL COLLEGE
1225 Air Base Blvd.
Montgomery, AL 36108
Dr. Anthony Molina, President
Tel: (334) 420-4310 Fax: (334) 420-4344
Email: information@trenholmtech.cc.al.us
Web: www.trenholmtech.cc.al.us

TUSKEGEE UNIVERSITY
102 Old Admin Bldg.
Tuskegee, AL 36088
Dr. Benjamin F. Payton, President
Tel: (800) 622-6531 Fax: (334) 727-5750
Email: admissions@tuskegee.edu
Web: www.tuskegee.edu

ARKANSAS

ARKANSAS BAPTIST COLLEGE
1600 Bishop St.
Little Rock, AR 72202
Mary Jarrett, Acting President
Tel: (501) 374-7856 Fax: (501) 374-6136
Web: www.arbaptcol.edu

PHILANDER SMITH COLLEGE
1 Trudie Kibbe Reed Dr.
Little Rock, AR 72202
Dr. Walter Kembrough, President
Tel: (501) 370-5221 Fax: (501) 370-5225
Email: sbeasley@philander.edu
Web: www.philander.edu

SHORTER COLLEGE
604 Locust St.
North Little Rock, AR 72114
Dr. Cora McHenry, President
Tel: (501) 374-6305 Fax: (501) 374-9333
Email: libekwe@hotmail.com
Web: www.shorter.edu

UNIVERSITY OF ARKANSAS AT PINE BLUFF
1200 N. University Dr.
Pine Bluff, AR 71601
Lawrence Davis, Chancellor
Tel: (870) 575-8000 Fax: (870) 575-4608
Email: sanders_d@uapb.edu
Web: www.uapb.edu

DELAWARE

DELAWARE STATE UNIVERSITY
1200 N. DuPont Hwy.
Dover, DE 19901
Dr. Allen L. Sessoms, President
Tel: (302) 857-6351 Fax: (302) 857-6352
Email: admissions@desu.edu
Web: www.desu.edu

DISTRICT OF COLUMBIA

HOWARD UNIVERSITY
2400 6th St. NW
Washington, DC 20059
H. Patrick Swygert, President
Tel: (800) 822-6363 Fax: (202) 806-4465
Email: admission@howard.edu
Web: www.howard.edu

UNIVERSITY OF THE DISTRICT OF COLUMBIA
4200 Connecticut Ave. NW
Washington, DC 20008
Dr. William L. Pollard, President
Tel: (202) 274-5100 Fax: (202) 274-6341
Email: mdouglas@udc.edu
Web: www.udc.edu

FLORIDA

BETHUNE-COOKMAN COLLEGE
640 Dr. Mary McLeod Bethune Blvd.
Daytona Beach, FL 32114-3099
Dr. Trudie Kibbie Reed , President
Tel: (800) 448-0228 Fax: (386) 481-2601
Email: admissions@cookman.edu
Web: www.cookman.edu

EDWARD WATERS COLLEGE
1658 Kings Rd.
Jacksonville, FL 32209
Dr. Oswald Bronson, President
Tel: (904) 470-8200 Fax: (904) 470-8048
Email: admissions@ewc.edu
Web: www.ewc.edu

FLORIDA A& M UNIVERSITY
Foote Hilyer Administration Ctr. #G9
Tallahassee, FL 32307
Dr. Castell Bryant, Interim President
Tel: (866) 642-1198 Fax: (850) 599-3069
Email: admissions@famu.edu
Web: www.famu.edu

FLORIDA MEMORIAL UNIVERSITY
15800 NW 42nd Ave.
Miami, FL 33054
Dr. Albert E. Smith, President
Tel: (305) 626-3600 Fax: (305) 623-1462
Email: pmartin@fmuniv.edu
Web: www.fmuniv.edu

GEORGIA

ALBANY STATE UNIVERSITY
504 College Dr.
Albany, GA 31705
Dr. Everette Freeman, President
Tel: (229) 430-4604 Fax: (229) 430-4105
Email: portia.shields@asurams.edu
Web: http://asuweb.asurams.edu/asu/

CLARK ATLANTA UNIVERSITY
223 James P. Brawley Dr. SW
Atlanta, GA 30314
Dr. Walter D. Broadnax, President
Tel: (800) 688-3228 Fax: (404) 880-6174
Email: cauadmissions@cau.edu
Web: www.cau.edu

FORT VALLEY STATE UNIVERSITY
1005 State University Dr.
Fort Valley, GA 31030-4313
William H. Harris, President
Tel: (877) 462-3878 Fax: (478) 825-6169
Email: admissap@fvsu.edu
Web: www.fvsu.edu

INTERDENOMINATIONAL THEOLOGICAL CENTER
700 Martin Luther King, Jr. Dr.
Atlanta, GA 30314-4143
Dr. Michael A. Battle, President
Tel: (404) 527-7792 Fax: (404) 527-0901
Email: info@itc.edu
Web: www.itc.edu

MOREHOUSE COLLEGE
830 Westview Dr. SW
Atlanta, GA 30314
Walter E. Massey, President
Tel: (404) 681-2800 Fax: (404) 215-2748
Email: admissions@morehouse.edu
Web: www.morehouse.edu

MOREHOUSE SCHOOL OF MEDICINE
720 Westview Dr. SW
Atlanta, GA 30310-1495
Dr. David Satcher, Interim President
Tel: (404) 752-1500 Fax: (404) 752-1512
Email: mdadmissions@msm.edu
Web: www.msm.edu

MORRIS BROWN COLLEGE
643 Martin Luther King, Jr. Dr.
Atlanta, GA 30314-4140
Dr. Samuel D. Jolley, President
Tel: (404) 739-1000 Fax: (404) 739-1075
Email: serena.wilson@morrisbrown.edu
Web: www.morrisbrown.edu

PAINE COLLEGE
1235 15th St.
Augusta, GA 30901
Dr. Shirley Lewis, President
Tel: (706) 821-8320 Fax: (706) 821-8648
Email: tinsleyj@mail.paine.edu
Web: www.paine.edu

SAVANNAH STATE UNIVERSITY
3219 College St.
Savannah, GA 31404
Dr. Carlton E. Brown, President
Tel: (912) 356-2181 Fax: (912) 356-2556
Email: admissions@savstate.edu
Web: www.savstate.edu

SPELMAN COLLEGE
350 Spelman Ln. SW
Atlanta, GA 30314-4399
Dr. Beverly Daniel Tatum, President
Tel: (404) 681-3643 Fax: (404) 270-5118
Email: admiss@spelman.edu
Web: www.spelman.edu

KENTUCKY

KENTUCKY STATE UNIVERSITY
400 E. Main St.
Frankfort, KY 40601
Mary Evans Sias, President
Tel: (502) 597-6813 Fax: (502) 597-6490
Email: admissions@kysu.edu
Web: www.kysu.edu

LOUISIANA

DILLARD UNIVERSITY
2601 Gentilly Blvd.
New Orleans, LA 70122
Dr. Marvalene Hughes, President
Tel: (504) 283-8822 Fax: (504) 816-4895
Email: admissions@dillard.edu
Web: www.dillard.edu

GRAMBLING STATE UNIVERSITY
100 Main St.
Grambling, LA 71245
Dr. Horace Judson, President
Tel: (800) 569-4714 Fax: (318) 274-3292
Email: admissions@gram.edu
Web: www.gram.edu

SOUTHERN UNIVERSITY AND A&M COLLEGE
P.O. Box 9901
Baton Rouge, LA 70813
Edward R. Jackson, Chancellor
Tel: (225) 771-2430 Fax: (225) 771-2500
Email: edward_jackson@subr.edu
Web: www.subr.edu

SOUTHERN UNIVERSITY AT NEW ORLEANS
6400 Press Dr.
New Orleans, LA 70126
Robert B. Gex, Chancellor
Tel: (504) 286-5311 Fax: (504) 284-5500
Web: www.suno.edu

SOUTHERN UNIVERSITY AT SHREVEPORT
3050 Martin Luther King, Jr. Dr.
Shreveport, LA 71107
Dr. Ray L. Belton, Chancellor
Tel: (318) 674-3300 Fax: (318) 674-3483
Email: admissions@susla.edu
Web: www.susla.edu

XAVIER UNIVERSITY
P.O. Box 29
Grambling, LA 71245
Dr. Norman Francis, President
Tel: (504) 486-7388 Fax: (504) 520-7941
Email: apply@xula.edu
Web: www.xula.edu

MARYLAND

BOWIE STATE UNIVERSITY
14000 Jericho Park Rd.
Bowie, MD 20715-9465
Calvin W. Lowe, President
Tel: (301) 860-4000 Fax: (301) 860-3518
Email: clowe@bowiestate.edu
Web: www.bowiestate.edu

COPPIN STATE UNIVERSITY
2500 W. North Ave.
Baltimore, MD 21216-3698
Dr. Stanley F. Battle, President
Tel: (800) 635-3674 Fax: (410) 333-5369
Email: mgross@coppin.edu
Web: www.coppin.edu

MORGAN STATE UNIVERSITY
1700 E. Cold Spring Ln.
Baltimore, MD 21251
Dr. Earl S. Richardson, President
Tel: (443) 885-3200 Fax: (443) 885-8260
Email: admissions@morgan.edu
Web: www.morgan.edu

UNIVERSITY OF MARYLAND EASTERN SHORE
11868 Academic Oval
Princess Anne, MD 21853
Dr. Thelma B. Thompson, President
Tel: (410) 651-2200 Fax: (410) 651-7922
Email: semorse@mail.umes.edu
Web: www.umes.edu

MICHIGAN

LEWIS COLLEGE OF BUSINESS
17370 Meyers
Detroit, MI 48235
Dr. Marjorie Harris, President
Tel: (313) 862-6300 Fax: (313) 341-7170
Email: cking@lewiscollege.edu
Web: www.lewiscollege.edu

MISSISSIPPI

ALCORN STATE UNIVERSITY
1000 ASU Dr. #300
Alcorn State, MS 39096-9900
Dr. Clinton Bristow, Jr., President
Tel: (800) 222-6790 Fax: (601) 877-6347
Email: ebarnes@lorman.alcorn.edu
Web: www.alcorn.edu

COAHOMA COMMUNITY COLLEGE
3240 Friars Point Rd.
Clarksdale, MS 38614
Dr. Vivian M. Presley, President
Tel: (662) 627-2571 Fax: (662) 621-4297
Email: wholmes@coahomacc.edu
Web: www.ccc.cc.ms.us

HINDS COMMUNITY COLLEGE, UTICA
P.O. Box 1007
Utica, MS 39154
Dr. Clyde Muse, President
Tel: (601) 885-7025 Fax: (601) 885-7134
Email: info@hindscc.edu
Web: http://lrc.hindscc.edu

JACKSON STATE UNIVERSITY
1400 John R. Lynch St.
Jackson, MS 39217
Ronald Mason, Jr., President
Tel: (601) 979-2323 Fax: (601) 979-2948
Email: rmason@jsums.edu
Web: www.jsums.edu

MISSISSIPPI VALLEY STATE UNIVERSITY
14000 Hwy. 82 West
Itta Bena, MS 38941
Dr. Lester C. Newman, President
Tel: (662) 254-3347 Fax: (662) 254-3759
Email: admsn@mvsu.edu
Web: www.mvsu.edu

RUST COLLEGE
150 Rust Ave.
Holly Springs, MS 38635
David L. Beckley, President
Tel: (662) 252-8000 Fax: (662) 252-7932
Email: admissions@rustcollege.edu
Web: www.rustcollege.edu

TOUGALOO COLLEGE
500 W. County Line Rd.
Tougaloo, MS 39174
Dr. Beverly Wade Hogan, President
Tel: (888) 424-2566 Fax: (601) 977-6185
Email: jjacobs@tougaloo.edu
Web: www.tougaloo.edu

MISSOURI

HARRIS-STOWE STATE UNIVERSITY
3026 Laclede Ave.
St. Louis, MO 63103
Dr. Henry Givens, Jr., President
Tel: (314) 340-3300 Fax: (314) 340-3555
Email: admissions@hssc.edu
Web: www.hssc.edu

LINCOLN UNIVERSITY OF MISSOURI
820 Chestnut St.
Jefferson City, MO 65101
David Henson, President
Tel: (800) 521-5052 Fax: (573) 681-5889
Email: enroll@lincolnu.edu
Web: www.lincolnu.edu

NORTH CAROLINA

BARBER-SCOTIA COLLEGE
145 Cabarrus Ave. West
Concord, NC 28025
Dr. Gloria Tinubu, President
Tel: (704) 789-2902 Fax: (704) 789-8907
Email: ealexander@b-sc.edu
Web: www.b-sc.edu

BENNETT COLLEGE
900 E. Washington St.
Greensboro, NC 27401
Dr. Johnnetta B. Cole, President
Tel: (800) 413-5323 Fax: (336) 517-2166
Email: admiss@bennett.edu
Web: www.bennett.edu

ELIZABETH CITY STATE UNIVERSITY
1704 Weeksville Rd.
Elizabeth City, NC 27909
Dr. Mickey L. Burnim, Chancellor
Tel: (252) 335-3081 Fax: (252) 335-3731
Email: admissions@mail.ecsu.edu
Web: www.ecsu.edu

FAYETTEVILLE STATE UNIVERSITY
1200 Murchison Rd.
Fayetteville, NC 28301
Dr. T.J. Bryan, Chancellor
Tel: (800) 222-2594 Fax: (910) 672-1414
Email: admissions@uncfsu.edu
Web: www.uncfsu.edu

JOHNSON C. SMITH UNIVERSITY
100 Beatties Ford Rd.
Charlotte, NC 28216
Dr. Dorothy Cowser Yancy, President
Tel: (800) 782-7303 Fax: (704) 378-1242
Email: admissions@jcsu.edu
Web: www.jcsu.edu

LIVINGSTONE COLLEGE
701 W. Monroe St.
Salisbury, NC 28144
Dr. Catrelia Hunter, President
Tel: (704) 216-6001 Fax: (704) 216-6215
Email: admissions@livingstone.edu
Web: www.livingstone.edu

NORTH CAROLINA A&T STATE UNIVERSITY
1601 E. Market St.
Greensboro, NC 27411
James C. Renick, Chancellor
Tel: (336) 334-7946 Fax: (336) 256-2145
Email: uadmit@ncat.edu
Web: www.ncat.edu

NORTH CAROLINA CENTRAL UNIVERSITY
1801 Fayetteville St.
Durham, NC 27707
Dr. James H. Ammons, Chancellor
Tel: (877) 667-7533 Fax: (919) 530-7625
Email: admissions@nccu.edu
Web: www.nccu.edu

SAINT AUGUSTINE'S COLLEGE
1315 Oakwood Ave.
Raleigh, NC 27610
Theresa Bennett-Wilkes, President
Tel: (919) 516-4000 Fax: (919) 516-5805
Email: admissions@st-aug.edu
Web: www.st-aug.edu

SHAW UNIVERSITY
118 E. South St.
Raleigh, NC 27601
Dr. Clarence G. Newsome, President
Tel: (919) 546-8275 Fax: (919) 546-8271
Email: admissions@shawu.edu
Web: www.shawuniversity.edu

WINSTON-SALEM STATE UNIVERSITY
601 Martin Luther King, Jr. Dr.
Winston-Salem, NC 27110
Dr. Harold L. Martin, Sr., Chancellor
Tel: (800) 257-4052 Fax: (336) 750-2079
Email: admissions@wssu.edu
Web: www.wssu.edu

OHIO

CENTRAL STATE UNIVERSITY
P.O. Box 1004
Wilberforce, OH 45384
John W. Garland, Esq., President
Tel: (937) 376-6011 Fax: (937) 376-6648
Email: info@csu.ces.edu
Web: www.centralstate.edu

WILBERFORCE UNIVERSITY
1055 N. Bickett Rd.
Wilberforce, OH 45384-1001
Rev. Dr. Floyd H. Flake, President
Tel: (800) 367-8568 Fax: (937) 376-4751
Email: admissions@wilberforce.edu
Web: www.wilberforce.edu

OKLAHOMA

LANGSTON UNIVERSITY
P.O. Box 728
Langston, OK 73050
JoAnn Haysbert, President
Tel: (405) 466-3428 Fax: (405) 466-3391
Email: admissions@lunet.edu
Web: www.lunet.edu

PENNSYLVANIA

CHEYNEY UNIVERSITY
1837 University Cir.
Cheyney, PA 19319-0200
Wallace C. Arnold, President
Tel: (610) 399-2275 Fax: (610) 399-2099
Email: gstemley@cheyney.edu
Web: www.cheyney.edu

LINCOLN UNIVERSITY
1570 Baltimore Pike
Lincoln, PA 19352
Dr. Ivory V. Nelson, President
Tel: (610) 932-8300 Fax: (610) 932-1209
Email: admiss@lu.lincoln.edu
Web: www.lincoln.edu

SOUTH CAROLINA

ALLEN UNIVERSITY
1530 Harden St.
Columbia, SC 29204
Dr. Charles E. Young, President
Tel: (803) 376-5735 Fax: (803) 376-5733
Email: admissions@allenuniversity.edu
Web: www.allenuniversity.edu

BENEDICT COLLEGE
1600 Harden St.
Columbia, SC 29204
Dr. David H. Swinton, President
Tel: (803) 253-5143 Fax: (803) 253-5167
Email: thompsop@benedict.edu
Web: www.benedict.edu

CLAFLIN COLLEGE
400 Magnolia St.
Orangeburg, SC 29115
Dr. Henry N. Tisdale, President
Tel: (803) 535-5000 Fax: (803) 535-5385
Email: mzeigler@claflin.ed
Web: www.claflin.edu

CLINTON JUNIOR COLLEGE
1029 Crawford Rd.
Rock Hill, SC 29730
Dr. Elaine Johnson Copeland, President
Tel: (877) 837-9645 Fax: (803) 327-3261
Email: rcopeland@clintonjuniorcollege.edu
Web: www.clintonjuniorcollege.edu

DENMARK TECHNICAL COLLEGE
500 Soloman Blatt Ave.
Denmark, SC 29042
Dr. Joann R. G. Boyd-Scotland, President
Tel: (803) 793-5176 Fax: (803) 793-5942
Email: thomast@denmarktech.edu
Web: www.denmarktech.edu

MORRIS COLLEGE
100 W. College St.
Sumter, SC 29150-3599
Luns C. Richardson, President
Tel: (803) 934-3225 Fax: (803) 773-8241
Email: webcomment@morris.edu
Web: www.morris.edu

SOUTH CAROLINA STATE UNIVERSITY
300 College St. NE
Orangeburg, SC 29117-0001
Dr. Andrew Hugine, Jr. , President
Tel: (803) 536-7185 Fax: (803) 536-8990
Email: admissions@scsu.edu
Web: www.scsu.edu

VOORHEES COLLEGE
P.O. Box 678
Denmark, SC 29042
Dr. Lee E. Monroe, Jr., President
Tel: (803) 793-3351 Fax: (803) 703-7124
Email: bwatson@voorhees.edu
Web: www.voorhees.edu

TENNESSEE

FISK UNIVERSITY
1000 17th Ave. North
Nashville, TN 37208-3051
Hazel O'Leary, President
Tel: (800) 443-3475 Fax: (615) 329-8774
Email: admit@fisk.edu
Web: www.fisk.edu

KNOXVILLE COLLEGE
901 Knoxville College Dr.
Knoxville, TN 37921
Dr. Barbara R. Hatton, President
Tel: (865) 524-6525 Fax: (865) 524-6686
Email: bhatton@knoxvillecollege.edu
Web: www.knoxvillecollege.edu

LANE COLLEGE
545 Lane Ave.
Jackson, TN 38301
Dr. Wesley Cornelious McClure, President
Tel: (800) 960-7533 Fax: (731) 426-7559
Email: admissions@lanecollege.edu
Web: www.lanecollege.edu

LEMOYNE OWEN COLLEGE
807 Walker Ave.
Memphis, TN 38126
Dr. James G. Wingate, President
Tel: (800) 737-7778 Fax: (901) 435-1524
Email: admission@loc.edu
Web: www.loc.edu

MEHARRY MEDICAL COLLEGE
1005 Dr. D.B. Todd, Jr. Blvd.
Nashville, TN 37208
Dr. John E. Maupin, Jr. , President
Tel: (615) 327-6000 Fax: (615) 327-6228
Email: admissions@mmc.edu
Web: www.mmc.edu

TENNESSEE STATE UNIVERSITY
P.O. Box 9609
Nashville, TN 37209-1561
Melvin N. Johnson, President
Tel: (888) 463-6878 Fax: (615) 963-2930
Email: gclark@tnstate.edu
Web: www.tnstate.edu

TEXAS

HUSTON-TILLOTSON UNIVERSITY
900 Chicon St.
Austin, TX 78702
Dr. Larry L. Earvin, President
Tel: (512) 505-3000 Fax: (512) 505-3192
Email: mennefee@htu.edu
Web: www.htu.edu

JARVIS CHRISTIAN COLLEGE
P.O. Box 1470
Hawkins, TX 75765
Dr. Sebetha Jenkins, President
Tel: (903) 769-5883 Fax: (903) 769-4842
Email: sebetha_jenkins@jarvis.edu
Web: www.jarvis.edu

PAUL QUINN COLLEGE
3837 Simpson Stuart
Dallas, TX 75241
Oswell Person, President
Tel: (800) 237-2648 Fax: (214) 302-3506
Email: nrichey@pqc.edu
Web: www.pqc.edu

PRAIRIE VIEW A&M UNIVERSITY
P.O. Box 519
Prairie View, TX 77446-0519
Dr. George C. Wright, President
Tel: (936) 857-3311 Fax: (936) 857-2699
Email: admissions@pvamu.edu
Web: www.pvamu.edu

SOUTHWESTERN CHRISTIAN COLLEGE
P.O. Box 10
Terrell, TX 75160
Dr. Jack Evans, President
Tel: (972) 524-3341 Fax: (972) 563-7133
Email: rhodr@swcc.edu
Web: www.swcc.edu

ST. PHILIP'S COLLEGE
1801 Martin Luther King Dr.
San Antonio, TX 78203
Dr. Angie Runnels, President
Tel: (210) 531-3200 Fax: (210) 568-3103
Email: spcrr@accd.edu
Web: www.accd.edu/spc/spcmain/spc.htm

TEXAS COLLEGE
2404 N. Grand Ave.
Tyler, TX 75702
Billy C. Hawkins, President
Tel: (800) 306-6299 Fax: (903) 596-0001
Email: afrancis@texascollege.edu
Web: www.texascollege.edu

TEXAS SOUTHERN UNIVERSITY
3100 Cleburne St.
Houston, TX 77004
Dr. Priscilla D. Slade, President
Tel: (713) 313-7011 Fax: (713) 313-7851
Web: www.tsu.edu

WILEY COLLEGE
711 Wiley Ave.
Marshall, TX 75670
Dr. Haywood Strickland, President
Tel: (800) 658-6889 Fax: (927) 927-3366
Email: lestes@wileyc.edu
Web: www.wileyc.edu

VIRGIN ISLANDS

UNIVERSITY OF THE VIRGIN ISLANDS
#2 John Brewer's Bay
St. Thomas, VI 00802-9990
Dr. LaVerne E. Ragster, President
Tel: (340) 693-1150 Fax: (340) 693-1005
Email: pr@uvi.edu
Web: www.uvi.edu

VIRGINIA

HAMPTON UNIVERSITY
Hampton University
Hampton, VA 23668
Dr. William R. Harvey, President
Tel: (757) 727-5328 Fax: (757) 727-5095
Email: admissions@hampton.edu
Web: www.hamptonu.edu

NORFOLK STATE UNIVERSITY
700 Park Ave.
Norfolk, VA 23504
Alvin J. Schexnider, Interim President
Tel: (757) 823-8600 Fax: (757) 823-2078
Email: president@nsu.edu
Web: www.nsu.edu

SAINT PAUL'S COLLEGE
115 College Dr.
Lawrenceville, VA 23868
Dr. John Kenneth Waddell, President
Tel: (800) 678-7071 Fax: (434) 848-1846
Email: vcrenshaw@saintpaulscollege.edu
Web: www.saintpauls.edu

VIRGINIA STATE UNIVERSITY
1 Hayden Dr.
Petersburg, VA 23806
Eddie N. Moore, Jr., President
Tel: (800) 871-7611 Fax: (804) 524-5055
Email: admiss@vsu.edu
Web: www.vsu.edu

VIRGINIA UNION UNIVERSITY
1500 N. Lombardy St.
Richmond, VA 23220
Dr. Belinda C. Anderson, President
Tel: (804) 257-5600 Fax: (804) 342-3511
Email: admissions@vuu.edu
Web: www.vuu.edu

WEST VIRGINIA

BLUEFIELD STATE COLLEGE
219 Rock St.
Bluefield, WV 24701-2198
Dr. Albert L. Walker, President
Tel: (304) 327-4000 Fax: (304) 327-4330
Email: bscadmit@bluefieldstate.edu
Web: www.bluefield.wvnet.edu

WEST VIRGINIA STATE UNIVERSITY
P.O. Box 1000
Institute, WV 25112-1000
Dr. Hazo W. Carter, Jr., President
Tel: (800) 987-2112 Fax: (304) 766-5182
Email: admissions@wvstateu.edu
Web: www.wvstateu.edu

African American Organizations

ALABAMA

BUSINESS

NATIONAL MINORITY SUPPLIER DEVELOPMENT COUNCIL, INC.
South Region Minority Business Council, Inc., Regional Council
4715 Alton Ct.
Birmingham, AL 35210
Chris Lewis, Interim Executive Director
Tel: (205) 957-1883 Fax: (205) 957-2114
Email: info@srmbc.org
Web: www.srmbc.org

CHAMBER OF COMMERCE

NORTH ALABAMA AFRICAN AMERICAN CHAMBER OF COMMERCE
225 Spragins St. #E
Huntsville, AL 35801
Jerry Mitchell, Executive Director
Tel: (256) 564-7574 Fax: (256) 564-7344
Email: info@thenaaacc.org
Web: www.thenaaacc.org

CULTURAL

AFRO-AMERICAN HISTORICAL AND GENEALOGICAL SOCIETY, INC.
North Alabama
P. O. Box 89
Normal, AL 35762
James Johnson, President
Tel: (256) 461-1955
Email: jwjkb@bellsouth.net
Web: www.aahgs.org

ENTERTAINMENT

NATIONAL AFRICAN AMERICAN RV'ERS ASSOCIATION
Alabama Black Campers Chapter
4121 Riverview Cove
Birmingham, AL 35243
Mitchell C. Baldwin, President
Tel: (205) 970-0231
Email: mcbaldwin@worldnet.att.net
Web: www.naarva.com

LAW ENFORCEMENT

NATIONAL ORGANIZATION OF BLACK LAW ENFORCEMENT EXECUTIVES
Alabama-Birmingham Chapter
FBI, 2121 8th Ave. North
Birmingham, AL 35203
Jimmie L. Brown, Supervisory Special Agent
Tel: (205) 715-0330 Fax: (205) 656-0714
Email: jaybrn5@aol.com
Web: www.noblenatl.org

South Alabama-Montgomery-Mobile
Prichard Police Department, 212 Bayview Dr.
Daphne, AL 36526
Sammie Brown, Chief of Police
Tel: (251) 452-7900 Fax: (251) 452-3707
Email: sbrown6694@aol.com
Web: www.noblenatl.org

POLITICAL ACTION

AMERICAN CIVIL LIBERTIES UNION
Alabama Chapter
207 Montgomery St. #825
Montgomery, AL 36104-3561

Olivia Turner, Executive Director
Tel: (334) 262-0304
Email: aclu@aclu.org
Web: www.aclu.org

BLACKS IN GOVERNMENT
Region IV-Columbia/Phoenix-Sin Chapter
1114 16th Ave.
Phoenix City, AL 36867
Laura P. Williams, Chapter President
Tel: (334) 297-2604 Fax: (334) 448-8876
Email: legalservice@bellsouth.net
Web: www.bignet.org

Region IV-General Chappie James Chapter
P.O. Box 20926
Montgomery, AL 36120-0926
Floyzell E. Stevenson, Chapter President
Tel: (334) 416-3486
Email: floyzell.stevenson@gunter.af.mil
Web: www.bignet.org

Region IV-Huntsville Madison Chapter
P.O. Box 505
Atlanta, AL 35811
James Foster, Chapter President (Interim)
Tel: (256) 852-2129
Email: huntsville-madison@bignet.org
Web: www.bignet.org

Region IV-Port City Chapter
4317 Eastview Dr.
Mobile, AL 36618
Gwendolyn P. McGrew, Chapter President
Tel: (334) 208-7794
Email: grewtoit@aol.com
Web: www.bignet.org

Region IV-Wiregrass Chapter
401 Antler Dr.
Enterprise, AL 36330
Edward M. Brown, Chapter President
Tel: (334) 348-2125
Email: breezeway@entercomp.com
Web: www.bignet.org

SOUTHERN POVERTY LAW CENTER
400 Washington Ave.
Montgomery, AL 36104
Richard Cohen, President/CEO
Tel: (334) 956-8200 Fax: (334) 956-8483
Web: www.splcenter.org

PROFESSIONAL

AMERICAN ASSOCIATION OF BLACKS IN ENERGY
Birmingham Chapter
P.O. Box 2563
c/o Southern Natural Gas, 1900 5th Ave. North
Birmingham, AL 35203
Corlene Williams, President
Tel: (205) 325-3559
Email: corlene.williams@elpaso.com
Web: www.aabe-bir.org

NATIONAL ASSOCIATION OF BLACK JOURNALISTS
Birmingham, Region IV
P.O. Box 185
Birmingham, AL 35201
Ronda Robinson, Chapter President
Tel: (205) 583-8413
Email: rrobinson@wbrc.com
Web: www.babj.net

NATIONAL BLACK MBA ASSOCIATION, INC.
P.O. Box 3009
Birmingham, AL 35202
Robert Hagler, President
Web: www.nbmbaa.org

NATIONAL FORUM FOR BLACK PUBLIC ADMINISTRATORS
East Central Alabama Chapter
365-A N. Donahue Dr.
Auburn, AL 63832
Timothy Woods, President
Tel: (334) 501-3080 Fax: (334) 826-6827
Email: twoody@auburnalabama.org
Web: www.nfbpa.org

Magic City Alabama Chapter
710 N. 20th St.
Birmingham, AL 35203
Vickie E. Reynolds, President
Tel: (205) 254-2840 Fax: (205) 254-2926
Email: vereyno@ci.birmingham.al.us
Web: www.nfbpa.org

NATIONAL SOCIETY OF BLACK ENGINEERS
Region 3-Auburn University Chapter (AUNSBE)
313 Ramsey Hall, Auburn University
Auburn, AL 36849
Brandy McKinney, President
Tel: (334) 844-2274 Fax: (334) 844-4203
Email: nsbe@eng.auburn.edu
Web: www.eng.auburn.edu/nsbe

Region 3-University of Alabama at Huntsville Chapter
P.O. Box 949
Huntsville, AL 35804
David Wright, President
Email: president@nsbe-northalabamaae.org
Web: www.nsbe.org

SPEC. INT., EMPLOYMENT

INROADS, INC.
Birmingham Affiliate
1608 13th Ave. South #115
Birmingham, AL 35205
Jacqueline M. Shepherd, Managing Director
Tel: (205) 939-3991 Fax: (205) 939-3910
Email: jshepherd@inroads.org
Web: www.inroads.org

SPEC. INT., HUMAN RELATIONS

BIRMINGHAM CIVIL RIGHTS INSTITUTE
520 16th St. North
Birmingham, AL 35203-1911
Dr. Lawrence J. Pijeaux, Jr., Executive Director
Tel: (205) 328-9696 Fax: (205) 251-6104
Email: bcri@bcri.org
Web: www.bcri.bham.al.us

SPEC. INT., SOCIAL INTEREST

100 BLACK MEN OF BIRMINGHAM, INC.
710 N. 20th St., 3rd Fl.
Birmingham, AL 35203
John Hudson, President
Tel: (205) 254-2294 Fax: (205) 254-2603
Email: johudson@southernco.com
Web: www.100blackmen.org

100 BLACK MEN OF GREATER HUNTSVILLE, INC.
3210 Hi-Lo Circle Ave.
Huntsville, AL 35811
Earnest L. Starks, President
Tel: (256) 532-1505 Fax: (256) 532-1515
Email: info@100ghc.org
Web: www.100ghc.org

100 BLACK MEN OF GREATER MOBILE, INC.
1107 Arlington St.
Mobile, AL 36605
Joe McCraw, President

Tel: (251) 432-7301 Fax: (251) 432-2935
Email: mobile100blackmen@mobilecan.org
Web: www.100blackmen.org

100 BLACK MEN OF GREATER MONTGOMERY, INC.
2924 Moorcroft Ln.
Montgomery, AL 36116
James L. Harrell, President
Tel: (334) 229-4305
Email: gmablackmen@knology.net
Web: www.100blackmen.org

FEDERATION OF SOUTHERN COOPERATIVES-LAND ASSISTANCE FUND
Rural Training & Research Center
P.O. Box 95
Epes, AL 35460
John Zippert, Director of Programs
Tel: (205) 652-9676 Fax: (205) 652-9678
Email: fscepes@mindspring.com
Web: www.federationsoutherncoop.com

NATIONAL URBAN LEAGUE, INC.
Birmingham Urban League
1229 3rd Ave. North
Birmingham, AL 35203
Elaine S. Jackson, President
Tel: (205) 326-0162 Fax: (205) 521-6951
Email: burbanleag@aol.com
Web: www.nul.org

STUDENT ORGANIZATION

ALPHA KAPPA ALPHA SORORITY, INC.
Beta Nu Omega Chapter
P.O. Box 250633
Montgomery, AL 36125
Lois Jenkins, Chapter President
Web: www.aka1908.com

Beta Xi Omega Chapter
P.O. Box 1342
Tuskeegee Institute, AL 36087
Beverly A. Ebo, Chapter President
Web: www.aka1908.com

Delta Sigma Chapter, Stillman College
P.O. Box 20397
Tuscaloosa, AL 35402
Genola Burke, Chapter President
Email: missy3e21@aol.com
Web: www.aka1908.com

Delta Theta Omega Chapter
9180 Cedar Ct.
Daphne, AL 36527
Ramona Marsalis Hill, Chapter President
Web: www.aka1908.com

Epsilon Gamma Omega Chapter
P.O. Box 3756
Huntsville, AL 35810
Annie Davis, Chapter President
Web: www.aka1908.com

Epsilon Upsilon Chapter, University of South Alabama
P.O. Box U-534
Mobile, AL 36688
Linda R. Stiell, Chapter Advisor
Email: windystiell@netscape.net
Web: www.aka1908.com

Eta Xi Omega Chapter
P.O. Box 1668
Tuscaloosa, AL 35403
Alice G. Thomas, Chapter President
Web: www.aka1908.com

Gamma Pi Chapter, Miles College
5500 Myron Massey Blvd.
Fairfield, AL 35208
Tammy Fincher, Chapter Advisor
Email: tfincher12@bellsouth.net
Web: www.aka1908.com

Iota Mu Omega Chapter
P.O. Box 2243
Anniston, AL 36202
Fannie M. Stockdale, Chapter President
Web: www.aka1908.com

Iota Phi Chapter, University of Alabama
P.O. Box 21, Hill University Ctr.
Birmingham, AL 35205
Dorothy Yvonne Wilson, Chapter Advisor
Email: akadkwilson@mindspring.com
Web: www.aka1908.com

Kappa Phi Omega Chapter
P.O. Box 2223
Muscle Shoals, AL 35661
Lenora L. Sheffey, Chapter President
Email: lsheffey@hiwaay.net
Web: www.aka1908.com

Kappa Pi Omega Chapter
117 Laurel Breeze Dr.
Enterprise, AL 36330
Ethel D. Simmons, Chapter President
Web: www.aka1908.com

Lambda Eta Omega Chapter
501 N. 4th Pl.
Gadsden, AL 35901
Mildred Woody, Chapter President
Web: www.aka1908.com

Lambda Zeta Omega Chapter
P.O. Box 670
Lanett, AL 36863
Glenda F.W. Brasfield, Chapter President
Email: glen3j20@charter.net
Web: www.aka1908.com

Mu Alpha Chapter, Troy State University
P.O. Box 820415
Troy, AL 36082
Tynisha Millender, Chapter President
Web: www.aka1908.com

Mu Mu Chapter, University of Montevallo
P.O. Box 1067
Montevallo, AL 35115
Trameca M. Roscoe, Chapter President
Web: www.aka1908.com

Mu Sigma Omega Chapter
P.O. Box 882
Opelika, AL 36803
Web: www.aka1908.com

Mu Tau Omega Chapter
390 Mays Bend Ln.
Talladega, AL 35128
Pell City, Chapter President
Web: www.aka1908.com

Nu Delta Chapter, Birmingham Southern College
P.O. Box 549112, BSC
Birmingham, AL 35254
Angela B. Day, Chapter Advisor
Email: daylittlebuddlie@aol.com
Web: www.aka1908.com

Nu Nu Omega Chapter
P.O. Box 1411
Livingston, AL 35470
Web: www.aka1908.com

Nu Omicron Chapter, University of North Alabama
P.O. Box 5356
Florence, AL 35632
Marlena Young, Chapter President
Web: www.aka1908.com

Omicron Mu Chapter, Samford University
P.O. Box 294028
Birmingham, AL 35229
Chitra Kirpalani, Chapter President
Email: crkirpalani@gmail.com
Web: www.aka1908.com

Omicron Omega Chapter
P.O. Box 12881
Birmingham, AL 35203
Gennia W. Baldwin, Chapter President
Web: www.aka1908.com

Omicron Zeta Chapter, University of Alabama
P.O. Box 11391
Huntsville, AL 35814
Tomeka Wilson, Chapter President
Web: www.aka1908.com

Phi Iota Omega Chapter
P.O. Box 1863
Birmingham, AL 35201
Barbara A. Franklin, Chapter President

Email: asubp13@aol.com
Web: www.aka1908.com

Phi Upsilon Omega Chapter
P.O. Box 372
Towncreek, AL 35672
Carrie Goode Warren, Chapter President
Web: www.aka1908.com

Pi Rho Chapter, Spring Hill College
4000 Dauphin St.
Mobile, AL 36608
Sinead Crandle, Chapter President
Web: www.aka1908.com

Rho Chi Chapter, Huntingdon College
P.O. Box 073
Montgomery, AL 36106
Djuana Taurette, Chapter Advisor
Web: www.aka1908.com

Rho Chi Omega Chapter
P.O. Box 611
Madison, AL 35758
Cheryl K. Johnson, Chapter President
Web: www.aka1908.com

Theta Sigma Chapter, University of Alabama
P.O. Box 11073
Tuscaloosa, AL 35846
Pamela Pruitt, Chapter Advisor
Email: pspruitts@aol.com

Upsilon Eta Omega Chapter
613 Glen Wood Dr.
Fairfield, AL 35064
Dontrelle R. Yo Foster, Chapter President
Web: www.aka1908.com

Zeta Eta Omega Chapter
103 Calvin Cir.
Selma, AL 36703
Helene T. Felton, Chapter President
Web: www.aka1908.com

ALPHA PHI ALPHA FRATERNITY, INC.
Alpha Beta Chapter, Talladega College
P.O. Box 325
Talladega, AL 35160
Web: www.alphaphialpha.net

Alpha Nu Lambda Chapter, Tuskegee Institute
P.O. Box 1242
Tuskegee, AL 36087
Web: www.alphaphialpha.net

Alpha Upsilon Lambda Chapter
P.O. Box 6058
Montgomery, AL 36106
Web: www.alphaphialpha.net

Beta Omicron Lambda Chapter
P.O. Box 2383
Mobile, AL 36652
Web: www.alphaphialpha.net

Beta Upsilon Chapter, Alabama State University
P.O. Box 28
Montgomery, AL 36195
Web: www.alphaphialpha.net

Delta Gamma Chapter, Alabama A&M University
P.O. Box 220
Normal, AL 35762
Web: www.alphaphialpha.net

Delta Phi Lambda Chapter
P.O. Box 20251
Tuscaloosa, AL 35402
Web: www.alphaphialpha.net

Delta Pi Lambda Chapter
P.O. Box 2486
Selma, AL 36702
Web: www.alphaphialpha.net

Delta Theta Lambda Chapter
P.O. Box 189
Normal, AL 35762
Web: www.alphaphialpha.net

Epsilon Delta Lambda Chapter
1728 Cooper Ave.
Anniston, AL 36201
Web: www.alphaphialpha.net

Epsilon Nu Chapter, Stillman College
P.O. Box 4198
Tuscaloosa, AL 35403
Web: www.alphaphialpha.net

Gamma Kappa Chapter, Miles College
P.O. Box 3800
Birmingham, AL 35208
Web: www.alphaphialpha.net

Gamma Phi Chapter, Tuskegee University
P.O. Box 36
Tuskegee, AL 36083
Web: www.alphaphialpha.net

Iota Nu Chapter, University of Alabama-Birmingham
P.O. Box 45
Birmingham, AL 35294
Web: www.alphaphialpha.net

Kappa Alpha Chapter, University of Alabama
P.O. Box 7368
Tuscaloosa, AL 35486
Web: www.alphaphialpha.net

Kappa Gamma Chapter, University of North Alabama
P.O. Box 5345
Florence, AL 35632
Web: www.alphaphialpha.net

Kappa Nu Lambda Chapter
P.O. Box 622
Sheffield, AL 35660
Web: www.alphaphialpha.net

Mu Psi Lambda Chapter
P.O. Box 2281
Birgmingham, AL 35202
Web: www.alphaphialpha.net

Omicron Alpha Chapter, Auburn University
P.O. Box 240053
Montgomery, AL 36117
Web: www.alphaphialpha.net

Omicron Kappa Chapter, Auburn University
P.O. Box 2843
Auburn, AL 36830
Web: www.alphaphialpha.net

Omircron Lambda Chapter
P.O. Box 3910
Birmingham, AL 35208
Web: www.alphaphialpha.net

Pi Delta Chapter, University of West Alabama
P.O. Box 34
Livingston, AL 35470
Web: www.alphaphialpha.net

Pi Epsilon Lambda Chapter
P.O. Box 925
Auburn, AL 36830
Web: www.alphaphialpha.net

Rho Chi Chapter, University of Alabama-Huntsville
P.O. Box 14476
Huntsville, AL 35815
Web: www.alphaphialpha.net

Theta Delta Chapter, University of South Alabama
P.O. Box U701
Mobile, AL 36688
Web: www.alphaphialpha.net

Theta Gamma Lambda Chapter
P.O. Box 6893
Dothan, AL 36302
Web: www.alphaphialpha.net

Xi Beta Chapter, Troy State University
P.O. Box 435
Troy, AL 36082
Web: www.alphaphialpha.net

Xi Xi Chapter, Jacksonville State University
P.O. Box 3018
Jacksonville, AL 36265
Web: www.alphaphialpha.net

BLACK STUDENT UNION OF AUBURN UNIVERSITY
Department of the Black Student Union
359 Foy Student Union, 3rd Fl.
Auburn, AL 36849
Charus Campbell, President
Tel: (334) 844-1389 Fax: (334) 844-0804
Email: bsu@mail.auburn.edu
Web: www.auburn.edu/student_info/bsu

NATIONAL BLACK LAW STUDENTS ASSOCIATION
Birmingham School of Law
205 20th St. North, 823 Frank Nelson Bldg.
Birmingham, AL 35203
Ginger Tomlin, Dean
Tel: (205) 322-6122 Fax: (205) 322-2822
Email: gtomlin@bsol.com
Web: www.nblsa.org

Jones School of Law
5345 Atlanta Hwy.
Montgomery, AL 36109
John Garman, Advisor
Tel: (334) 386-7210 Fax: (334) 386-7223
Email: jgarman@faulkner.edu

Samford University School of Law
800 Lakeshore Dr.
Birmingham, AL 35229
Tel: (205) 726-2701 Fax: (205) 726-2057
Web: www.nblsa.org

University of Alabama School of Law
P.O. Box 870382
Tuscaloosa, AL 35487
Tel: (205) 348-5440
Web: www.nblsa.org

ALASKA

POLITICAL ACTION

AMERICAN CIVIL LIBERTIES UNION
Region X-Alaska Chapter
P.O. Box 201844
Anchorage, AK 99520
Tel: (907) 276-2258 Fax: (907) 258-0288
Email: akclu@alaska.net
Web: www.aclu.org

BLACKS IN GOVERNMENT
Region X-Anchorage Chapter
P.O. Box 102056
Anchorage, AK 99510
John G. Youmans, Chapter President
Tel: (907) 272-0244
Email: region10.president@bignet.org
Web: www.bignet.org

Region X-Juneau Chapter
P.O. Box 21506
Juneau, AK 99802
Remond Henderson, Chapter President
Tel: (907) 465-5981
Email: region10.president@bignet.org
Web: www.bignet.org

STUDENT ORGANIZATION

ALPHA KAPPA ALPHA SORORITY, INC.
Xi Psi Omega Chapter
P.O. Box 140894
Anchorage, AK 99514
Margo Bellamy, Chapter President
Email: margobellamy@hotmail.com
Web: www.xipsiomega.com

ALPHA PHI ALPHA FRATERNITY, INC.
Rho Beta Chapter Ketchikan College
2600 7th St.
Ketchikan, AK 99901-5798
Clint Shultz, President
Tel: (907) 228-4544
Email: rhobeta@uaa.alaska.edu
Web: www.ptk.or

ARIZONA

BUSINESS

NATIONAL MINORITY SUPPLIER DEVELOPMENT COUNCIL, INC.
Grand Canyon Minority Supplier Development Council (GCMSDC), Regional Council
P.O. Box 1268
Phoenix, AZ 85001
Ron Williams, Executive Director
Tel: (602) 495-9950 Fax: (602) 495-9943
Web: www.gcmsdc.org

CHAMBER OF COMMERCE

GREATER PHOENIX BLACK CHAMBER OF COMMERCE
201 E. Washington St. #350
Phoenix, AZ 85004
Cody Williams, President/CEO
Tel: (602) 307-5200 Fax: (602) 307-5204
Email: cody@phoenixblackchamber.com
Web: www.phoenixblackchamber.com

TUCSON-SOUTHERN ARIZONA BLACK CHAMBER OF COMMERCE
1690 N. Stone Ave. #113
Tucson, AZ 85705
Clarence Boykins, Executive Director
Tel: (520) 623-0099 Fax: (520) 623-1930
Web: www.tucsonblackchamber.com

CULTURAL

AFRO-AMERICAN HISTORICAL AND GENEALOGICAL SOCIETY, INC.
Tucson Chapter
2011 W. Khaibar Pl.
Tucson, AZ 85704
Pearl Chandler, President
Tel: (520) 797-5537

POLITICAL ACTION

AMERICAN CIVIL LIBERTIES UNION
Arizona Civil Chapter
P.O. Box 17148
Phoenix, AZ 85011-0148
Eleanor Eisenberg, Executive Director
Tel: (602) 650-1967
Email: office@azclu.org
Web: www.azclu.org

PROFESSIONAL

NATIONAL BLACK MBA ASSOCIATION, INC.
Phoenix Chapter-West
P.O. Box 27601
Tempe, AZ 85285-7601
Kathryn J. Andrews, President
Tel: (602) 735-3958
Email: president@phoenixchapter.org
Web: www.phoenixchapter.org

NATIONAL SOCIETY OF BLACK ENGINEERS
Region 6: University of Arizona Chapter
Department of Engineering and Mines #200
Tucson, AZ 85719
Jeffery Goldberg, Associate Professor
Email: nsbe_listserv@listserv.arizona.edu
Web: http://clubs.asua.arizona.edu/~nsbe/ua_
information.htm

SPEC. INT., EDUCATION

NATIONAL ASSOCIATION FOR MULTICULTURAL EDUCATION
Arizona Chapter, Arizona State University
P.O. Box 1311
Tempe, AZ 87287
Victor Begay
Tel: (480) 727-7869
Email: vbegay@asu.edu
Web: www.nameorg.org

SPEC. INT., EMPLOYMENT

INROADS, INC.
Arizona Affiliate
10075 E. Via Linda Rd., 2nd Fl.
Scottsdale, AZ 85258-5325
Cristina Torres, Managing Director
Tel: (480) 767-5315 Fax: (480) 767-5320
Email: ctorres@inroads.org
Web: www.inroads.org

SPEC. INT., FAMILY PLANNING

NATIONAL HOOK-UP OF BLACK WOMEN, INC.
Phoenix Chapter
P.O. Box 7272
Surprise, AZ 85378
Toni Buggs, President
Tel: (602) 305-6775
Email: tonilb1@aol.com
Web: www.nhbwinc.com

SPEC. INT., HEALTH SERVICES

BLACK FAMILY & CHILD SERVICES, INC.
1522 E. Southern Ave.
Phoenix, AZ 85040
Mary Black, Executive Director
Tel: (602) 243-1773 Fax: (602) 253-4586
Email: mmb@bfcschoices.org

SPEC. INT., HOUSING

ASSOCIATION OF COMMUNITY ORGANIZATIONS FOR REFORM NOW
ACORN Housing Corporation, Inc.
1018 W. Roosevelt St.
Phoenix, AZ 85007
Helene O'Brien, National Field Director
Tel: (602) 254-5299 Fax: (602) 258-7143
Email: azacorn@acorn.org
Web: www.acorn.org

SPEC. INT., SOCIAL INTEREST

ARIZONA BLACK UNITED FUND, INC.
P.O. Box 24457
Phoenix, AZ 85074
Carolyn T. Lowery, Executive Director
Tel: (602) 268-0666 Fax: (606) 268-5776
Email: carolyntlowery@aol.com
Web: www.nbuf.org

INTERNATIONAL FOUNDATION FOR EDUCATION AND SELF-HELP
5040 E. Shea Blvd. #260
Scottsdale, AZ 85254-4687
DeJarnette Edwards, Executive VP/COO
Tel: (480) 443-1800 X615 Fax: (480) 443-1824
Email: dedwards@ifesh.org
Web: www.ifesh.org

NATIONAL URBAN LEAGUE, INC.
Greater Phoenix Urban League
1402 S. 7th Ave.
Phoenix, AZ 85007-3902
James Miller, Chairman
Tel: (602) 254-5611 Fax: (602) 253-7359
Email: info@greaterphxurbanleague.org
Web: www.greaterphxurbanleague.com

Tucson Urban League
2305 S. Park Ave.
Tucson, AZ 85713
Raymond Clarke, President/CEO
Tel: (520) 791-9522 Fax: (520) 623-9364
Email: rclarke@tucsonurbanleague.net
Web: www.tucsonurbanleague.com

STUDENT ORGANIZATION

ALPHA KAPPA ALPHA SORORITY, INC.
Delta Beta Omega Chapter
P.O. Box 64981
Phoenix, AZ 85082
Marlene Hannsberry, Chapter President
Web: www.aka1908.com

Eta Epsilon Omega Chapter
P.O. Box 42526
Tucson, AZ 85716
Anna M. Jolivet, Chapter President
Web: www.aka1908.com

Iota Tau Chapter
P.O. Box 44270
Tucson, AZ 85733
Tamara Sumler, Chapter President
Web: www.aka1908.com

Zeta Alpha Chapter
P.O. Box 1715
Tempe, AZ 85280
Elizabeth Adeola, Chapter President
Web: www.aka1908.com

ALPHA PHI ALPHA FRATERNITY, INC.
Delta Tau Lambda Chapter
P.O. Box 34471
Phoenix, AZ 85067
Antoine E. Stanford, Chapter President
Tel: (623) 570-7831
Email: stanford_a_06@yahoo.com
Web: www.deltataulambda.com

Eta Psi Lambda Chapter
P.O. Box 26791
Tucson, AZ 85726
Greg Williams, Chapter President
Tel: (520) 631-7725
Email: greg@1906.org
Web: www.1906.org

Zeta Theta Chapter, University of Arizona
P.O. Box 3431
Tucson, AZ 85722
Jomar Jenkins, Chapter President
Tel: (520) 471-0606
Email: jomar1bmoc@aol.com
Web: www.apa1906.org

BLACK & AFRICAN COALITION
Arizona State University
MU #304C
Tempe, AZ 85287
Rowland Tubi, Chair
Tel: (480) 965-9752
Email: asubac@yahoo.com
Web: www.asu.edu/clubs/bac/

NATIONAL BLACK LAW STUDENTS ASSOCIATION
Arizona State University
School of Law
P.O. Box 877906
Tempe, AZ 85287
Matthew Leathers, President
Tel: (480) 965-6181 Fax: (480) 965-5550
Email: blacklaw@asu.edu
Web: www.nblsa.org

ARKANSAS

BUSINESS

NATIONAL MINORITY SUPPLIER DEVELOPMENT COUNCIL, INC.
Arkansas Regional Minority Supplier Development Council (ARMSDC), Regional Council
ARMSDC/TEAM, 300 Spring Bldg. #415
Little Rock, AR 72201
Charles J. King, Executive Director
Tel: (501) 374-7026 Fax: (501) 371-0409
Email: info@armsdc.org
Web: www.armsdc.org

CULTURAL

AFRO-AMERICAN HISTORICAL AND GENEALOGICAL SOCIETY, INC.
Arkansas Chapter
P.O. Box 4294
Little Rock, AR 72214
Tamela Tenpenny-Lewis, President

Tel: (501) 425-5578 Fax: (501) 225-2029
Email: ttenplewis@aol.com
Web: www.rootsweb.com/~araahgs

SOUTHEAST ARKANSAS JUNETEENTH CELEBRATION
204 S. Maple St.
Dumas, AR 71639
Ignatius Higgins, III, President
Tel: (870) 382-5281 Fax: (870) 382-5281
Email: ignatius@seark.net

POLITICAL ACTION

AMERICAN CIVIL LIBERTIES UNION
Arkansas Chapter
904 W. 2nd St. #1
Little Rock, AR 72201
Rita Sklar, Executive Director
Tel: (501) 374-2660
Email: aclu@aclu.org
Web: www.aclu.org

ASSOCIATION OF COMMUNITY ORGANIZATIONS FOR REFORM NOW
Arkansas Broadcasting Foundation, Inc./KABF 88.3 FM
104 S. Main
Pine Bluff, AR 71601
Elena Giddings, Director for ACORN Radio Program
Tel: (870) 536-6300 Fax: (870) 543-4713
Email: aracornpb@acorn.org
Web: www.acorn.org

Little Rock Office
2101 S. Main St.
Little Rock, AR 72206
Tel: (501) 376-7151 Fax: (501) 376-3952
Email: aracorn@acorn.org
Web: www.acorn.org

BLACKS IN GOVERNMENT
Region VI-Central Arkansas Chapter
P.O. Box 72
Jefferson, AR 72079-0072
Cynthia Davis, Chapter President
Tel: (870) 543-7950
Email: cac@bignet.org
Web: www.bignet.org/regional/region6/index.htm

PROFESSIONAL

AMERICAN ASSOCIATION OF BLACKS IN ENERGY
Arkansas Chapter
P.O.Box 551, A9LA2E
c/o Entergy, 900 S. Louisiana Ave.
Little Rock, AR 72206
Leticia Finley, President
Tel: (501) 918-6518 Fax: (800) 223-3017
Email: lfinley@entergy.com
Web: www.aabe-ar.org

SPEC. INT., SOCIAL INTEREST

PRESERVATION OF AFRICAN AMERICAN CEMETERIES, INC.
P.O. Box 25923
Little Rock, AR 72221
Tamela Tenpenny Lewis, President
Tel: (501) 425-5578 Fax: (501) 225-2029
Email: ttenplewis@aol.com

STUDENT ORGANIZATION

ALPHA KAPPA ALPHA SORORITY, INC.
Alpha Rho Chapter, University of Arkansas
3910 Lincoln Green
Pine Bluff, AR 71603
Erica Akins, Chapter President
Web: www.aka1908.com

Epsilon Phi Chapter, University of Arkansas-Little Rock
13111 W. Markham St. #282
Little Rock, AR 72211
Kaneisha Robinson, Chapter President
Web: www.aka1908.com

Kappa Iota Chapter, University of Arkansas
Arkansas Union A6555
Fayetteville, AR 72701
Coretta Scott King, Chapter President
Web: www.aka1908.com

CALIFORNIA

ARTISTIC

AFRICAN-AMERICAN SHAKESPEARE COMPANY
Headquarters Office
762 Fulton St. #306
San Francisco, CA 94102

Sherri Young, Executive Director
Fax: (415) 762-2071
Email: syoung@african-americanshakes.org
Web: www.african-americanshakes.org

BAYVIEW OPERA HOUSE
4705 3rd St.
San Francisco, CA 94124
Shelley Bradford-Bell, Executive Director
Tel: (415) 824-0386 Fax: (415) 824-7124
Email: bvoh@pacbell.net
Web: www.bayviewoperahouse.org

BLACK AMERICAN CINEMA SOCIETY FILM SOCIETY
3617 Montclair St.
Los Angeles, CA 90018
Mayme Agnew Clayton Ph.D., Founder/Director
Tel: (323) 737-3292 Fax: (323) 737-2842
Email: mayneclayton@webtv.net

CULTURAL ODYSSEY
P.O. Box 156680
San Francisco, CA 94115
Idris Ackamoor, Executive Director
Tel: (415) 292-1850 Fax: (415) 346-9163
Email: idris@culturalodyssey.org
Web: www.culturalodyssey.org

LORRAINE HANSBERRY THEATER
710 Taylor St.
San Francisco, CA 94108
Quentin Easter, Executive Director
Tel: (415) 345-3980 Fax: (415) 345-3983
Email: lhtsf@aol.com
Web: www.lorrainehansberrytheatre.com

SAN DIEGO BLACK ENSEMBLE THEATRE
3710 Madison Ave. #C
San Diego, CA 92116
Rhys Green, Director
Tel: (619) 280-5650 Fax: (619) 280-5650
Email: sandiegobet@yahoo.com
Web: www.sdbet.com

BUSINESS

BLACK EXPO
P.O. Box 12456
Oakland, CA 94604
Dr. Diane Howell, Producer
Tel: (510) 839-0690 Fax: (510) 839-0565
Email: blackexpo@aol.com
Web: www.blackexpo2005.com

NATIONAL BLACK BUSINESS COUNCIL, INC.
600 Corporate Pointe #1010
Culver City, CA 90230
Rosalind Pennington, President/CEO
Tel: (310) 568-5000 Fax: (310) 417-7991
Email: rospennington@sbcglobal.net
Web: www.nbbc.org

NATIONAL MINORITY SUPPLIER DEVELOPMENT COUNCIL, INC.
Northern California Supplier Development Council
460 Hegenberger Rd. #730
Oakland, CA 94621
Michael Ruiz, President
Tel: (510) 686-2555 Fax: (510) 686-2552
Email: mruiz@ncsdc.org
Web: www.ncsdc.org

Southern California Minority Business Development Council, Inc.
515 S. Flower St. #1301
Los Angeles, CA 90071
John W. Murray, Jr., President
Tel: (213) 689-6960 Fax: (213) 689-1707
Email: info@scmbdc.org
Web: www.scmbdc.org

CHAMBER OF COMMERCE

CALIFORNIA BLACK CHAMBER OF COMMERCE
2951 Sunrise Blvd. #175
Rancho Cordova, CA 95742
Aubry L. Stone, President/CEO
Tel: (916) 463-0177 Fax: (916) 463-0190
Email: info@calbcc.org
Web: www.calbcc.org

SAN DIEGO REGIONAL AFRICAN AMERICAN CHAMBER OF COMMERCE
1727 N. Euclid Ave.
San Diego, CA 92105
Jerry Warren, President
Tel: (619) 262-2121 Fax: (619) 262-3841
Email: info@sdraacc.org
Web: www.sdraacc.org

SAN FRANCISCO BLACK CHAMBER OF COMMERCE
33 New Montgomery St. #210
San Francisco, CA 94105
Mel Washington, President

Tel: (415) 777-8550 Fax: (415) 777-8250
Email: mwashington@sfbcc.org

SILICON VALLEY BLACK CHAMBER OF COMMERCE
50 E. Saint John St. #103
San Jose, CA 95112-5596
Joel Wyrick, Executive Director
Tel: (408) 294-6583 Fax: (408) 297-5507
Email: info@blackchamber.com
Web: www.blackchamber.com

COMMUNICATIONS

MINORITIES IN BROADCASTING TRAINING PROGRAM
P.O. Box 67132
Century City, CA 90067
Patrice Williams, CEO
Tel: (323) 571-0766 Fax: (310) 388-1383
Email: emailus@thebroadcaster.com
Web: www.thebroadcaster.com

CULTURAL

AFRICAN AMERICAN ART & CULTURE COMPLEX
762 Fulton St.
San Francisco, CA 94102
London Breed, Executive Director
Tel: (415) 922-2049 Fax: (415) 922-5130
Email: info@aaacc.org
Web: www.aaacc.org

AFRICAN AMERICAN COMMUNITY SERVICE AGENCY
304 N. 6th St.
San Jose, CA 95112
Joanna Farris, President
Tel: (408) 292-3157 Fax: (408) 292-3276
Email: sjaacsa@hotmail.com
Web: www.sjaacsa.org

ASSOCIATION FOR THE STUDY OF CLASSICAL AFRICAN CIVILIZATIONS
2274 W. 20th St.
Los Angeles, CA 90018
Nzinga Ratibisha Heru, International President
Tel: (323) 730-1155 Fax: (323) 731-4998
Email: info@ascac.org
Web: www.ascac.org

BLACK NATIVE AMERICAN ASSOCIATION
San Antonio CDC
2228 E. 15th St.
Oakland, CA 94606
Don "Little Cloud" Davenport, Executive Director
Tel: (510) 536-1715 Fax: (510) 536-4066
Email: ltcloud@caliornia.com
Web: www.bnaa.org

CENTER FOR THE ARTS OF THE AFRICAN DIASPORA, INC.
P.O. Box 451102
Los Angeles, CA 90045-8510
Antoinette Johnson, President
Tel: (626) 296-9228 Fax: (323) 293-2332
Email: caadpr@aol.com
Web: www.caadweb.org

INSTITUTE FOR THE ADVANCED STUDIES OF BLACK FAMILY LIFE AND CULTURE
1012 Linden St.
Oakland, CA 94607
Dr. Wade Nobles, Executive Director
Tel: (510) 836-3245 Fax: (510) 836-3248
Web: www.iasbflc.org

ENTERTAINMENT

NATIONAL AFRICAN AMERICAN RV'ERS ASSOCIATION
California Sightseers Chapter
3631 Yorktown Rd.
Fremont, CA 94538-6119
William C. Smith, President
Tel: (510) 651-8323
Email: wcsmith@netzero.net
Web: www.naarva.com

THE PAN AFRICAN FILM FESTIVAL
P.O. Box 2418
Beverly Hills, CA 90213
Ayuko Babu, Founder/Executive Director
Tel: (323) 295-1706 Fax: (323) 295-1952
Email: lapaff@aol.com
Web: www.paff.org

LAW ENFORCEMENT

NATIONAL ORGANIZATION OF BLACK LAW ENFORCEMENT EXECUTIVES
Greater San Diego Chapter
P.O. Box 122769
San Diego, CA 92112

Melvin D. Maxwell, Lieutenant
Tel: (619) 533-5752 Fax: (619) 531-2713
Email: maenmax27@aol.com
Web: www.noblesandiego.homestead.com

Inland Empire Chapter
Rialto Police Department
P.O. Box 676
Rialto, CA 92377
Michael A. Meyers, Chief of Police
Tel: (909) 820-2555 Fax: (909) 421-7215
Email: mmeyers@rialtpd.com
Web: www.noblenatl.org

San Francisco Bay Area Chapter
4999 Gleason Dr.
Dublin, CA 94568
Stephen Bell, Captain
Tel: (415) 553-1145 Fax: (415) 553-1885
Email: noblesfbay@aol.com
Web: www.noblenatl.org

MULTI-PURPOSE

AFRICAN AMERICAN UNITY CENTER
944 W. 53rd St.
Los Angeles, CA 90037
Shariffe Bremond, Executive Director
Tel: (323) 789-7300 Fax: (323) 971-4188

MAGIC JOHNSON FOUNDATION, INC.
9100 Wilshire Blvd. #700-E
Beverly Hills, CA 90212
Kawanna Brown, President
Tel: (310) 246-4400 Fax: (310) 246-1106
Web: www.magicjohnson.org

NATIONAL ASSOCIATION FOR THE ADVANCEMENT OF COLORED PEOPLE
Los Angeles Chapter
3910 Martin Luther King Jr. Blvd. #202
Los Angeles, CA 90008
Geraldine Washington, Chapter President
Tel: (323) 296-2630 Fax: (323) 294-9435
Email: naacpla@sbcglobal.net
Web: www.naacp-losangeles.org

San Jose Branch
304 N. 6th St., African American Ctr.
San Jose, CA 95112
Rick L. Callender, Chapter President
Tel: (408) 295-3394 Fax: (408) 295-4355
Email: naacp@sanjosenaacp.org
Web: www.sanjosenaacp.org

POLITICAL ACTION

AMERICAN CIVIL LIBERTIES UNION
Northern California Chapter
1663 Mission St. #460
San Francisco, CA 94103
Dorothy M. Ehrlich, Executive Director
Tel: (415) 621-2493 Fax: (415) 255-1478
Web: www.aclunc.org

San Diego Chapter
P.O. Box 87131
San Diego, CA 92138
Katherine Nash, Administrative Director
Tel: (619) 232-2121
Email: info@aclusandiego.org
Web: www.aclusandiego.org

Southern California Chapter
1616 Beverly Blvd.
Los Angeles, CA 90026
Ramona Ripston, Executive Director
Tel: (213) 977-9500 Fax: (213) 250-3919
Email: acluinfo@aclu-sc.org
Web: www.aclu-sc.org

ASSOCIATION OF COMMUNITY ORGANIZATIONS FOR REFORM NOW
Los Angeles Office
3655 S. Grand Ave. #250
Los Angeles, CA 90007
Tel: (213) 747-4211 Fax: (213) 747-4221
Email: caacornlaro@acorn.org
Web: www.acorn.org

Oakland Office
3166 Fruitvale Ave.
Oakland, CA 94602
Tel: (510) 434-3110 Fax: (510) 434-3111
Email: caacornoaro@acorn.org
Web: www.acorn.org

Sacramento Office
4921 San Francisco Blvd.
Sacramento, CA 95820
Tel: (916) 455-1795 Fax: (916) 451-9660
Email: caacornsaro@acorn.org
Web: www.acorn.org

San Diego Office
1322 5th Ave. #1
San Diego, CA 92101
Tel: (619) 235-9593 Fax: (619) 235-9582
Email: caacornsd@acorn.org
Web: www.acorn.org

San Jose Office
540 Bird Ave. #100
San Jose, CA 95125
Tel: (408) 293-1520 Fax: (408) 293-1609
Email: caacornsj@acorn.org
Web: www.acorn.org

Contra Costa Office
132 Bailey Rd.
Bay Point, CA 94565
Tel: (925) 261-0233 Fax: (925) 261-0224
Email: caacornbpro@acorn.org
Web: www.acorn.org

San Bernardino Office
1726 N. D St. #A
San Bernardino, CA 92405
Tel: (909) 804-4004 Fax: (909) 804-4003
Email: caacornsb@acorn.org
Web: www.acorn.org

San Francisco Office
5319 Mission St.
San Francisco, CA 94112
Tel: (415) 587-9080 Fax: (415) 587-1778
Email: caacornsfro@acorn.org
Web: www.acorn.org

BLACK RADICAL CONGRESS
Sacramento Chapter
Freedom Bound Ctr.
4223 Assembly Ct. #19
Sacramento, CA 95823
Carl Pinkston, Chapter President
Tel: (916) 453-0190
Email: cpinkston@freedomboundcenter.org
Web: www.blackradicalcongress.com

BLACKS IN GOVERNMENT
Region IX-Central Valley Fresno Chapter
4580 W. Palo Alto #202
Fresno, CA 93722
J. Darnell Evans, Chapter President
Tel: (559) 438-8872
Email: region9.president@bignet.org
Web: http://bigfresno.tripod.com/home.html

Region IX-IMOJA Chapter
2977 School St.
Oakland, CA 94602
Lillie Zimmerman, Chapter President
Tel: (415) 436-2155
Web: www.bignet.org

Region IX-Long Beach Coastal Chapter
P.O. Box 15121
Long Beach, CA 90815
Harold D. Goings, Jr., Chapter President
Tel: (562) 826-5644

Region IX-Oakland Bay Area Chapter
4212 St. Andrew's Rd.
Oakland, CA 94605
Jo Robinson, Chapter President
Tel: (510) 639-1087
Web: www.bignet.org

Region IX-Sacramento Metro Area Chapter
19 Captain Ct.
Sacramento, CA 95831
Toni Y. Martin, Chapter President
Tel: (916) 974-5191
Email: sacramento@bignet.org
Web: www.bignet.org

Region IX-Solano County Chapter
P.O. Box 2225
Suisun City, CA 94585-5225
Toni Y. Martin, Chapter President
Tel: (415) 522-2897
Email: solano.county@bignet.org
Web: www.bignet.org

Region IX-Ventura County Chapter
P.O. Box 2152
Port Hueneme, CA 92044
Ken Pearson, Chapter President
Tel: (805) 228-8445
Web: www.bignet.org

CENTER FOR THIRD WORLD ORGANIZING
1218 E. 21st St.
Oakland, CA 94606
Danielle Mahones, Executive Director
Tel: (510) 533-7583 Fax: (510) 533-0923
Email: ctwo@ctwo.org
Web: www.ctwo.org

PROFESSIONAL

AMERICAN ASSOCIATION OF BLACKS IN ENERGY
Northern California Chapter
c/o AEST, 21565 Foothill Blvd.
Haywood, CA 94541
Demetria Summers, President
Tel: (510) 886-3501
Email: dsummers@aesti.com
Web: www.aabe-nocal.org

Southern California Chapter
c/o Sempra Energy, 555 W. 5th St., ML26F1
Los Angeles, CA 90013-1011
Charles Pulliam, President
Tel: (213) 244-5623 Fax: (213) 244-8261
Email: cpulliam@semprautilities.com
Web: www.aabe-socal.org

ASSOCIATION OF BLACK PSYCHOLOGISTS
San Diego Chapter
910 S. 41st St.
San Diego, CA 92113
Carrol Wayman, Ph.D., Chapter President
Tel: (619) 263-4929
Web: www.abpsi.org

Southern California Chapter
714 W. 109th St.
Los Angeles, CA 90044
Deirdre Yvette Sermons, PhD., Chapter President
Tel: (323) 732-4739
Email: deeisat1@aol.com
Web: www.abpsi.org

BLACK DATA PROCESSING ASSOCIATES
Bay Area Chapter
2625 Alcatraz Ave. #197
Berkeley, CA 94705
Christopher Epperson, Chapter President
Tel: (510) 868-8362
Email: president@bdpabac.org
Web: www.bdpabac.org

BLACK EMPLOYEES ASSOCIATION
4315-4317 Leimert Blvd.
Los Angeles, CA 90008
Adwoa Nyamekye, President
Tel: (323) 299-9562 Fax: (323) 292-6575
Email: infobea@blackemployees.org
Web: www.blackemployees.org

BLACK WOMEN LAWYERS ASSOCIATION OF LOS ANGELES, INC.
P.O. Box 8179
Los Angeles, CA 90008
Sharon K. Brown, President
Tel: (213) 538-0137
Email: president@blackwomenlawyersla.org
Web: www.blackwomenlawyersla.org

CALIFORNIA ASSOCIATION OF BLACK LAWYERS
20 Sunnyside Ave. #A-383
Mill Valley, CA 94941-1928
Nedra E. Austin, President
Tel: (510) 251-2864 X533 Fax: (818) 240-0270
Email: nedra.austin@ihopcorp.com
Web: www.calblacklawyers.com

CHARLES HOUSTON BAR ASSOCIATION
P.O. Box 1474
Oakland, CA 94612
Jennifer Madden, President
Tel: (415) 289-7004
Web: www.charleshoustonbar.org

CONFERENCE OF MINORITY TRANSPORTATION OFFICIALS
Northern California Chapter
300 Lakeside Dr.
Oakland, CA 94612
Lee L. Davis, President
Tel: (510) 464-6950 Fax: (510) 464-7587
Email: ldavis@bart.gov
Web: www.comto.org

Sacramento Chapter
P.O. Box 161507, Sacramento Regional Transit
Sacramento, CA 95816-161507
Brenda Lee, Chapter President
Tel: (916) 955-8004 Fax: (916) 689-6734
Email: ldylee2@aol.com
Web: www.comto.org

Southern California Chapter
Los Angeles County, MTA 1 Gateway Plz., M/S 99-13-6
Los Angeles, CA 90012
Marion J. Colston-Fayyaz, Manager/Human Resources
Tel: (213) 922-2260 Fax: (213) 922-5259
Email: colstonm@mta.net
Web: www.comto.org

LOS ANGELES COUNCIL OF BLACK PROFESSIONAL ENGINEERS
P.O. Box 881029
Los Angeles, CA 90009
Leroy Freelon, Jr., President
Tel: (310) 635-7734
Web: www.lablackengineers.org

NATIONAL ALLIANCE OF MARKET DEVELOPERS
Los Angeles Chapter
10736 Jefferson Blvd. #273
Culver City, CA 90230
Gale E. Harris, Chapter President
Tel: (323) 296-3681 Fax: (323) 293-1794
Web: www.namdntl.org/los_angeles.htm

NATIONAL ASSOCIATION OF BLACK JOURNALISTS
Region X- San Diego of Black Journalists
P.O. Box 880815
San Diego, CA 78250
Tim Carr, Chapter President
Tel: (858) 292-8403
Email: carrman_3@hotmail.com
Web: www.nabj.org

NATIONAL BLACK MBA ASSOCIATION, INC.
Los Angeles Chapter-West
2711 S. Robertson Blvd.
Los Angeles, CA 90034
Charles Clinton, President
Tel: (323) 964-3053
Email: labmba@labmba.org
Web: www.labmba.org

San Francisco Chapter
P.O. Box 193683
San Francisco, CA 94119-3683
Manuel Stevos, President
Tel: (510) 386-2622
Web: www.sfnbmbaa.org

NATIONAL BLACK PUBLIC RELATIONS SOCIETY
Tobin & Associates, Inc.
6565 Sunset Blvd. #425
Hollywood, CA 90028
Patricia Tobin, President/CEO
Tel: (323) 466-8221 Fax: (323) 856-9510
Email: nbprs@tobinpr.com
Web: www.nbprs.org

NATIONAL CONFERENCE OF BLACK LAWYERS
Bay Area Chapter
3130 Shattuck
Oakland, CA 94607
Bernida Reagan, Attorney
Tel: (510) 548-4040 X316 Fax: (510) 548-2566

NATIONAL FORUM FOR BLACK PUBLIC ADMINISTRATORS
Capitol City Chapter
9079 Brown Rd.
Elk Grove, CA 95624
Francine M. Douglas, President
Tel: (916) 464-5384 Fax: (916) 464-5212
Email: francine.douglas@dcss.ca.gov
Web: www.nfbpa.org

Southern California Chapter
City of Los Angeles, Office of Supervisor Yvonne Brathwaite Burke, 500 W. Temple St. #866
Los Angeles, CA 90012
John Hill, Chief of Staff
Tel: (213) 974-2222 Fax: (213) 680-3283
Email: jhill@bos.co.la.ca.us
Web: www.nfbpa.org

NATIONAL OPTOMETRIC ASSOCIATION
Region V-West Chapter
Kaiser Permanente, 3553 Whipple Rd., Bldg. B
Union City, CA 94587
Dr. Vicki L. Hughes, Trustee
Tel: (510) 675-2020 Fax: (510) 784-4782
Email: vladon@aol.com
Web: www.natoptassoc.org

NATIONAL SOCIETY OF BLACK ENGINEERS
California Polytechnic State University, San Luis Obispo Chapter
555 Ramona Dr.
San Luis Obispo, CA 93405
Clarice Dawson, Chapter President
Tel: (805) 593-0921
Web: www.calpoly.edu/~mep/sbes/home.html

Region 6: Black Alliance of Scientists and Engineers at San José State University Chapter
1 Washington Sq.
San Jose, CA 95192
David Piptman, Chapter President
Tel: (408) 924-3896 Fax: (408) 924-3818
Email: pnape57@yahoo.com
Web: http://web.innetix.com/~base/

Region 6: Cal Poly Ponoma Chapter
3801 W. Temple Ave., Bldg. 26 #124
Ponoma, CA 91768
Justin Troup, President
Tel: (909) 982-8863 Fax: (909) 869-4373
Email: juhjuh1@yahoo.com
Web: www.csupomona.edu/~jabrown5/all.htm

Region 6: California State University, Chico Chapter
400 W. 1st St.
Chico, CA 95929-0100
Carena Tate, Chapter President
Tel: (530) 898-4017
Email: ctate1@mail.csuchico.edu
Web: www.csuchico.edu/nsbes/

Region 6: California State University, Northridge Chapter
SDEC 18111 Nordhoff St.
Northridge, CA 91330
Christine Burton, Chapter President
Tel: (818) 677-2191 Fax: (818) 677-2191
Email: nsbe2@csun.edu
Web: www.csun.edu/~nsbe2/

Region 6: Computer Science University of California Chapter
MESA, College of Engineering University of California
Santa Barbara, CA 93106-5130
Ahmad Yamato, Chapter President
Tel: (805) 893-2809 Fax: (805) 893-4697
Email: uyamaa00@mcl.ucsb.edu
Web: www.geocities.com/SunsetStrip/Venue/7165/index2.htm

Region 6: DeVry University, Long Beach Campus Chapter
3880 Kilroy Airport Way #211
Long Beach, CA 90806
Portia Bacor, Student Development Coordinator
Tel: (562) 997-5422 Fax: (562) 997-5589
Email: pbacor@socal.devry.edu
Web: http://neptune.asee.org/sams/webprofiles9596/et99996_96.htm

Region 6: Loyola Marymount University Chapter
1 LMU Dr.
Los Angeles, CA 90045-8575
Nicolle Morris, Moderator
Tel: (310) 338-2833 Fax: (310) 338-5896

Region 6: University of California, Irvine Chapter
1027 W. Peltason Dr. #A
Irvine, CA 92617
Christopher Roberson, President
Tel: (714) 356-7671
Email: reeds@uci.edu
Web: http://spirit.dos.uci.edu/nsbe/mission.html

Region 6: University of California, La Jolla Chapter
9500 Gilman Dr. #C-19
La Jolla, CA 92093-0077
Stanley Calixte, Chapter President
Tel: (858) 361-5169
Email: scalixte@ucsd.edu
Web: http://acs.ucsd.edu/~nsbe/

THE BLACK FLIGHT ATTENDANTS OF AMERICA, INC.
1060 Crenshaw Blvd. #202
Los Angeles, CA 90019
Jaqueline Jacquet-Williams, National President
Tel: (323) 299-3406 Fax: (323) 299-7130
Email: bfaoa@aol.com
Web: www.bfaoa.com

THE ORGANIZATION OF BLACK SCREENWRITERS, INC.
1968 W. Adams Blvd.
Los Angeles, CA 90018
Sylvia Franklin, President
Tel: (323) 735-2050 Fax: (323) 735-2051
Email: sfranklin@obswriter.com
Web: www.obswriter.com

RELIGIOUS

AFRICAN ENTERPRISE
P.O. Box 727
Monrovia, CA 91017
Malcolm Graham, Executive Director
Tel: (800) 672-3742 Fax: (626) 359-2069
Email: info@aeusa.org
Web: www.africanenterprise.org

AFRICAN TEAM MINISTRIES
P.O. Box 115
Sierra Madre, CA 91025
Keith Jesson, Director
Tel: (626) 359-5075 Fax: (626) 359-8075
Email: atmm@earthlink.net
Web: www.africanteamministries.org

NATIONAL ASSOCIATION OF AFRICAN-AMERICAN CATHOLIC DEACONS
10125 Fabled Water Ct.
Spring Valley, CA 91977
Marvin Threatts, President
Tel: (619) 670-8339
Email: threatts@cox.net
Web: www.nccbuscc.org

RESEARCH

APPLIED RESEARCH CENTER
3781 Broadway
Oakland, CA 94611
Gary Delgado, Executive Director
Tel: (510) 653-3415 Fax: (510) 653-3427
Email: arc@arc.org
Web: www.arc.org

RALPH J. BUNCHE CENTER FOR AFRICAN AMERICAN STUDIES
University of California, Los Angeles
160 Haines Hall
Los Angeles, CA 90095
Darnell Hunt, Ph.D., Director
Tel: (310) 825-7403 Fax: (310) 825-5019
Web: www.bunchecenter.ucla.edu

SPEC. INT., AIDS

BLACK AIDS INSTITUTE
1833 W. 8th St. #200
Los Angeles, CA 90057
Phil Wilson, Founder/Executive Director
Tel: (213) 353-3610 X106 Fax: (213) 989-0181
Web: www.blackaids.org

BLACK COALITION ON AIDS
Head Office
2800 3rd St.
San Francisco, CA 94107
Perry Lang, Executive Director
Tel: (415) 615-9945 Fax: (415) 615-9943
Email: bcoa@bcoa.org
Web: www.bcoa.org

MINORITY AIDS PROJECT
5149 W. Jefferson Blvd.
Los Angeles, CA 90016
Victor McKamie, Executive Director
Tel: (323) 936-4949 Fax: (323) 936-4973
Email: cbowen@map-usa.org
Web: www.map-usa.org

THE AMASSI CENTER
160 S. La Brea Ave.
Inglewood, CA 90301
Cleo Manago, Founder/CEO
Tel: (310) 419-1969 Fax: (310) 419-1960
Email: amassi@amassi.com
Web: www.amassi.com

SPEC. INT., ALCOHOL/DRUG CTR.

SACRAMENTO BLACK ALCOHOLISM CENTER
3307 Broadway #200
Sacramento, CA 95817
Sandra Hill, Executive Director
Tel: (916) 454-4242 Fax: (916) 454-2930

SPEC. INT., CHILD CARE

NATIONAL CENTER FOR MISSING & EXPLOITED CHILDREN
California
18111 Irvine Blvd. #C
Tustin, CA 92780-3403
Shirley Goins, Director
Tel: (714) 508-0150 Fax: (714) 508-0154

SPEC. INT., EDUCATION

AFRICAN AMERICANS IN COMMUNICATION, MEDIA AND ENTERTAINMENT
University of California, Los Angeles
3130 Hershey Hall, 405 Hilgard Ave.
Los Angeles, CA 90095-1538
Michelle Turnage, President
Tel: (310) 839-1136
Email: aacme@ucla.edu
Web: www.ucla.edu

BLACK COMMUNITY SERVICES CENTER
Stanford University
P.O. Box 9546
418 Santa Teresa St.
Stanford, CA 94305-4009
Jan Baker Alexander, Director
Tel: (650) 723-1587 Fax: (650) 723-3107
Email: jbarker@stanford.edu
Web: www.stanford.edu/dept/bcsc

TPC FOUNDATION, INC.
4025 S. Bronson Ave.
Los Angeles, CA 90008
Patricia A. Means, President
Tel: (323) 299-6000 Fax: (323) 299-6006
Email: pmeans@turningpointmagazine.com
Web: www.turningpointmagazine.com

SPEC. INT., EMPLOYMENT

INROADS, INC.
Northern California Chapter
1970 Broadway #1100
Oakland, CA 94612
Reginald Duhe, Managing Director
Tel: (510) 238-8881 Fax: (510) 238-8883
Email: rduhe@inroads.org
Web: www.inroads.org

Southern California Chapter
12070 Telegraph Rd. #210
Santa Fe Springs, CA 90670
Hector LaFarga, Jr., Managing Director
Tel: (562) 777-1711 X213 Fax: (562) 777-1701
Email: hlafarga@inroads.org
Web: www.inroads.org

NATIONAL ASSOCIATION OF AFRICAN AMERICANS IN HUMAN RESOURCES
Los Angeles Chapter
P.O. Box 243
Inglewood, CA 90306
Katrina Anderson, President
Tel: (310) 330-0540 Fax: (310) 330-0540
Web: www.naaahr-la.org

SPEC. INT., FAMILY PLANNING

BLACK ADOPTION PLACEMENT AND RESEARCH CENTER
7801 Edgewater Dr. #2000
Oakland, CA 94621
Gloria King, Executive Director
Tel: (510) 430-3600 Fax: (510) 430-3615
Email: family@baprc.org
Web: www.baprc.org

DEPARTMENT OF CHILDREN AND FAMILY SERVICES
Adoption Division
695 S. Vermont Ave.
Los Angeles, CA 90005
Sari Grant, Manager
Tel: (213) 738-3268 Fax: (213) 639-3956
Email: gransa@dcfs.co.la.ca.us
Web: www.dcfs.co.la.ca.us

SPEC. INT., HEALTH SERVICES

SICKLE CELL DISEASE ASSOCIATION OF AMERICA, INC.
National Office
200 Corporate Pointe #495
Culver City, CA 90230-7633
Lynda K. Anderson, President/CEO
Tel: (800) 421-8453 Fax: (310) 215-3722
Email: scdaa@sicklecelldisease.org
Web: www.sicklecelldisease.org

SPEC. INT., IMMIGRATION

AFRICAN COMMUNITY RESOURCE CENTER
532 S. Vermont Ave. #104
Los Angeles, CA 90020
Dr. Nicki Tessai, Director
Tel: (213) 637-1450 Fax: (213) 382-6166
Email: ainfo@africancommunitycenter.org
Web: www.africancommunitycenter.org

AFRICAN IMMIGRANT AND REFUGEE RESOURCE CENTER
942 Market St. #305
San Francisco, CA 94102
Odis Cook, President
Tel: (415) 433-7300 Fax: (415) 433-7308
Email: airrc@pacbell.net
Web: www.ncccsf.org/airrc

SPEC. INT., LEGAL ASSISTANCE

MINORITY ASSISTANCE SERVICE
2601 Mission St. #212
San Francisco, CA 94110
Samy Baaghil, Attorney Representative
Tel: (415) 643-8866 Fax: (415) 643-8445

SPEC. INT., MENTAL HEALTH

LAMP COMMUNITY
627 Southsand Julien St.
Los Angeles, CA 90013
Mollie Lowery, Executive Director

Tel: (213) 488-0031 Fax: (213) 488-4934
Web: www.lamp.org

SPEC. INT., SOCIAL INTEREST

100 BLACK MEN OF ORANGE COUNTY, INC.
Spectrum 1 #200
Irvine, CA 92618
Austin Ray, President
Tel: (949) 623-8423 Fax: (949) 623-8305
Email: araz92@aol.com
Web: www.100bmoc.org

100 BLACK MEN OF SACRAMENTO
2251 Florin Rd. #140
Sacramento, CA 95822
Ronald Kelley, President
Tel: (916) 428-8203 Fax: (916) 428-3967
Email: sac100blkmen@sbcglobal.net
Web: www.sac100.com

100 BLACK MEN OF SAN DIEGO, INC.
P.O. Box 19037
San Diego, CA 92159
Larry Marion, President
Tel: (619) 589-5332 Fax: (619) 589-9060
Email: adjthomas@aol.com

100 BLACK MEN OF SILICON VALLEY, INC.
1101 S. Winchester Blvd. #H188
San Jose, CA 95128
Bill Kindricks, President
Tel: (408) 345-4831
Web: www.100bmsv.org

100 BLACK MEN OF SONOMA COUNTY
P.O. Box 1453
Rohnert Park, CA 94928
Andre Morrow, President
Tel: (707) 571-1003 Fax: (707) 571-1143
Email: djb@100blackmen.com
Web: www.100blackmen.com

100 BLACK MEN OF THE BAY AREA, INC.
P.O. Box 12123
Oakland, CA 94604-2123
Jake Sloan, President
Tel: (510) 763-3661 Fax: (510) 835-7613
Email: bayarea100blkmen@aol.com
Web: www.100blackmenba.org

100 BLACK MEN OF USC
University of Southern California Chapter
3601 Trousdale Pkwy., Student Union 1415
Los Angeles, CA 90089
Hiram Sims, President
Tel: (213) 740-8257 Fax: (213) 740-33298
Email: onehunbm@usc.edu
Web: www-scf.usc.edu/~onehunbm

BAY AREA BLACK UNITED FUND, INC.
1212 Broadway St. #730
Oalkland, CA 94612
Woody Carter, Executive Director
Tel: (510) 763-7270 Fax: (510) 763-3625
Email: information@babuf.org
Web: www.babuf.org

BLACK UNITED FUND OF SACRAMENTO VALLEY, INC.
5524 Assembly Ct. #19
Sacramento, CA 95823
Kakwasi Somadhi, President
Tel: (916) 422-6188 Fax: (916) 422-7925
Email: kakwasi.somadhi@prodigy.net
Web: www.nbuf.org

BROTHERHOOD CRUSADE BLACK UNITED FUND, INC.
200 E. Slauson Ave.
Los Angeles, CA 90011
Joseph Rouzan, Executive Vice President
Tel: (323) 231-2171 Fax: (323) 846-3324
Email: info@brotherhoodcrusade.org
Web: www.brotherhoodcrusade.org

COMMUNITY DEVELOPMENT INSTITUTE
P.O. Box 50099
East Palo Alto, CA 94303
Goro Mitchell, Executive Director
Tel: (650) 327-5846 Fax: (650) 327-4430
Email: goro@cdi-usa.org
Web: www.cdi-usa.org

IMOYASE GROUP, INC.
8939 S. Sepulveda Blvd. #208
Los Angeles, CA 90045
Cheryl N. Grills, Ph.D., President
Tel: (310) 568-9264 Fax: (310) 568-0070
Email: imoyase@imoyase.com
Web: www.imoyase.com

NATIONAL URBAN LEAGUE, INC.
Bay Area Urban League Chapter
2201 Broadway St.
Oakland, CA 94612
Tel: (510) 271-1846 Fax: (510) 839-8109
Web: www.richmondworks.org/rwmem/urb.htm

Greater Sacramento Urban League Chapter
3725 Marysville Blvd.
Sacramento, CA 95838
James C. Shelby, President/CEO
Tel: (916) 286-8600 Fax: (916) 561-0856
Email: jshelby@gsul.org
Web: www.gsul.org

Los Angeles Urban League Chapter
3450 Mount Vernon Dr.
Los Angeles, CA 90008
John W. Mack, President
Tel: (323) 299-9660 Fax: (323) 299-0618
Web: www.laul.org

San Diego Urban League Chapter
720 Gateway Center Dr.
San Diego, CA 92102
Cecil H. Steppe, President/CEO
Tel: (619) 263-3115 Fax: (619) 263-3660
Email: sdul@sdul.org
Web: www.sdul.org

RAINBOW/PUSH COALITION
Los Angeles Bureau
1968 W. Adams Blvd.
Los Angeles, CA 90018
Glenda Gill, Bureau Chief
Tel: (323) 734-3900 Fax: (323) 734-3913
Email: ggill@rainbowpush.org
Web: www.rainbowpush.org

SPEC. INT., WOMEN

AFRICAN AMERICAN WOMEN IN BUSINESS CONFERENCE
Headquarters Office
P.O. Box 881389
Los Angeles, CA 90009
Betty J. Price, CEO
Tel: (310) 680-0870 Fax: (310) 388-1341
Email: bjprice@sbcglobal.net
Web: www.aawibc.com

FEMINIST MAJORITY FOUNDATION
433 S. Beverly Dr.
Beverly Hills, CA 90212
Eleanor Smeal, President
Tel: (310) 556-2500 Fax: (310) 556-2509
Email: femmaj@feminist.org
Web: www.feminist.org

RADICAL WOMEN
2170 W. Washington Blvd., Solidarity Hall
Los Angeles, CA 90018
Wendy McPherson, President
Tel: (323) 732-6416 Fax: (323) 732-6410
Email: lafsprw6@aol.com
Web: www.radicalwomen.org

WOMEN'S INTERNATIONAL CENTER'S PILOT PROGRAM WOMEN FOR AFRICA
P.O. Box 880736
San Diego, CA 92168-0736
Gloria Lane, President
Tel: (619) 295-6446 Fax: (619) 296-1633
Email: gloria311@aol.com
Web: www.wic.org/orgs/wfa.htm

SPEC. INT., YOUTH

AFRICAN AMERICAN MALE ACHIEVERS NETWORK, INC.
6709 La Tijera Blvd. #261
Los Angeles, CA 90045
Hildreth Walker, Jr., Board Chairman/Co-Founder
Tel: (310) 412-2680 Fax: (310) 412-2632
Web: www.aman.org

CHILDREN'S DEFENSE FUND
Los Angeles Office
3655 S. Grand Ave. #270
Los Angeles, CA 90007-1068
Beth Osthimer, State Director
Tel: (213) 749-8787 Fax: (213) 749-4119
Email: bosthimer@www.cdfca.org
Web: www.cdfca.org

Oakland Office
2201 Broadway #705
Oakland, CA 94610
Deena Lahn, Policy Director
Tel: (510) 663-3224 Fax: (510) 663-1783
Email: dlahn@cdfca.org
Web: www.cdfca.org

GIRLS SCOUT COUNCIL OF ORANGE COUNTY
1620 Adams Ave.
Costa Mesa, CA 92626
Suzanne Huffmon Esber, Board Chair
Tel: (714) 979-7900 Fax: (714) 850-1299
Email: girlscouts@gscoc.org
Web: www.gscoc.org

GOLDEN STATE MINORITY FOUNDATION
8730 S. Vermont Ave., 2nd Fl.
Los Angeles, CA 90044
Ivan Abbott Houston, President/CEO
Tel: (866) 277-4763 Fax: (323) 751-5114
Email: education@gsmf.org
Web: www.gsmf.org

JACK & JILL OF AMERICA, INC.
Far West Region Chapter
2058 N. Mills Ave. PMB 247
Claremont, CA 91711
Regina M. Page, Regional Director
Tel: (909) 445-1247 Fax: (909) 626-0415
Email: rmpage.rmp@verizon.net
Web: www.jack-and-jill.org

North County San Diego Chapter
P.O. Box 502705
San Diego, CA 92150
Leslie Athill, Chapter President
Tel: (909) 445-1247 Fax: (909) 626-0415
Email: ncsd.membership@jjfarwest.org
Web: www.jjfarwest.org/ncsd

LOS ANGELES YOUTH NETWORK
1550 N. Gower St.
Los Angeles, CA 90028
Liz Gomez, Executive Director
Tel: (323) 957-7364 Fax: (323) 464-4357
Email: generalinfo@layn.org
Web: www.layn.org

STUDENT ORGANIZATION

ALPHA KAPPA ALPHA SORORITY, INC.
Alpha Gamma Omega Chapter
17104 Avenida de la Herradura
Pacific Palisades, CA 90272
Barbara Clayton Lake, Chapter President
Web: www.aka1908.com

Alpha Nu Chapter
5280 N. Jackson #36
Fresno, CA 93740
Kelly Boyer, Chapter President
Web: www.aka1908.com

Alpha Nu Omega Chapter
8745 Mountain Blvd.
Oakland, CA 94605
Denise Parker, Chapter President
Web: www.aka1908.com

Cerritos Chapter
P.O. Box 4176
Cerritos, CA 90703
Janet Turner Yarbrough, Chapter President
Web: www.aka1908.com

Delta Zeta Omega Chapter
P.O. Box 31370
San Francisco, CA 94131
Tel: (562) 402-1064
Jamie Jordan, Chapter President
Web: www.aka1908.com

Epsilon Eta Omega Chapter
27014 Karns Ct. #61001
Santa Clarita, CA 91387
April Dominique Scott-Goss, Chapter President
Web: www.aka1908.com

Epsilon Xi Omega Chapter
P.O. Box 880537
San Diego, CA 92114
Ida M. Williams, Chapter President
Web: www.aka1908.com

Eta Gamma Omega Chapter
4137 Sardinia Ct.
Elk Grove, CA 95758
Rita Abel, Chapter President
Web: www.aka1908.com

Eta Lambda Chapter
3926 Southport Dr.
Sacramento, CA 95826
Shanicka Bradley, Chapter President
Web: www.aka1908.com

Eta Lambda Omega Chapter
P.O. Box 90013
Pasadena, CA 90013
Clara P. Satterfield, Chapter President
Web: www.aka1908.com

Eta Nu Omega Chapter
P.O. Box 56067
Riverside, CA 92517

Elizabeth Thorn-Macon, Chapter President
Web: www.aka1908.com

Eta Rho Omega Chapter
P.O. Box 23302
San Jose, CA 95153
Susan G. Bishop, Chapter President
Web: www.aka1908.com

Iota Beta Chapter
2615 Ellendale Pl.
Los Angeles, CA 90004
Ifey Asiodu, Chapter President
Web: www.aka1908.com

Iota Omicron Omega Chapter
P.O. Box 1701
Fresno, CA 93717
Carolyn Odums, Chapter President
Web: www.aka1908.com

Kappa Beta Omega Chapter
P.O. Box 1092
Vallejo, CA 94590
Laverne C. Barbarin, Chapter President
Web: www.aka1908.com

Kappa Gamma Omega Chapter
P.O. Box 804
Seaside, CA 93955
Christine A. Burnett, Chapter President
Web: www.aka1908.com

Kappa Omega Omega Chapter
P.O. Box 40092
Bakersfield, CA 93384
Holly Mitchell, Chapter President
Web: www.aka1908.com

Lambda Alpha Chapter
P.O. Box 15456
Long Beach, CA 90815
Alisha Menzies, Chapter President
Web: www.aka1908.com

Lambda Sigma Chapter
P.O. Box 5534
Irvine, CA 92606
Tomeka Heglar, Chapter President
Web: www.aka1908.com

Mu Beta Omega Chapter
P.O. Box 0485
Inglewood, CA 90307
Carrie Crum, Chapter President
Web: www.aka1908.com

Mu Epsilon Omega Chapter
2380 S. Mira Ct. #167
Anaheim, CA 92802
Jeanette Burns, Chapter President
Web: www.aka1908.com

Mu Iota Chapter
P.O. Box 15719
San Diego, CA 92175
Alicia Moseby, Chapter President
Web: www.aka1908.com

Mu Kappa Chapter
9140 Los Lagos Cr. South
Granite Bay, CA 95746
Uzoamaka Frances Agu, Chapter President
Web: www.aka1908.com

Mu Lambda Omega Chapter
P.O. Box 4550
Culver City, CA 90230
Vivian Farr Cannon, Chapter President
Web: www.aka1908.com

Mu Zeta Omega Chapter
2708 Zarand Dr.
Modesto, CA 95355
Georgia Stinson, Chapter President
Web: www.aka1908.com

Nu Mu Omega Chapter
48 Carroll Dr.
Pittsburg, CA 94565
Bettye Burns, Chapter President
Web: www.aka1908.com

Nu Nu Chapter
P.O. Box 14784
Santa Barbara, CA 93106
Kelli Wilson, Chapter President
Web: www.aka1908.com

Pi Upsilon Chapter
P.O. Box 530
Seaside, CA 93955
Tatonia Taylor, Chapter President
Web: www.aka1908.com

Rho Chapter
102 Sproul Hall
Berkeley, CA 94720
Jennifer Jackson, Chapter President
Web: www.aka1908.com

Rho Delta Chapter
5500 University Pkwy.
San Bernadino, CA 92407
Kellina Lawrie, Chapter President
Web: www.aka1908.com

Rho Delta Omega Chapter
P.O. Box 50731
Palo Alto, CA 94303
Sharon Godbolt, Chapter President
Web: www.aka1908.com

Rho Epsilon Chapter
P.O. Box 90013
Pasadena, CA 90013
Web: www.aka1908.com

Rho Upsilon Omega Chapter
P.O. Box 1074
San Ramon, CA 94583
Patricia Lott, Chapter President
Web: www.aka1908.com

Sigma Delta Omega Chapter
P.O. Box 1294
Elk Grove, CA 95624
Gloria Clemons-White, Chapter President
Web: www.aka1908.com

Sigma Lambda Omega Chapter
15722 Sutton St.
Encino, CA 91436
Martha Jackie Ewing Ramos, Chapter President
Web: www.aka1908.com

Sigma Pi Omega Chapter
1212 Oakhorne Dr.
Harbor City, CA 90710
Willie Marie Malone, Chapter President
Web: www.aka1908.com

Tau Beta Omega Chapter
P.O. Box 9385
Marina Del Rey, CA 90295
Charmaine Scruggs-Robinson, Chapter President
Web: www.aka1908.com

Tau Tau Omega Chapter
3500-279 W. Manchester Blvd.
Inglewood, CA 90305
Catherine Cain Sumpter, Chapter President
Web: www.aka1908.com

Tau Upsilon Omega Chapter
P.O. Box 3119
Fairfield, CA 94533
Gwendolyn Lawton, Chapter President
Web: www.aka1908.com

Theta Alpha Omega Chapter
P.O. Box 92109
Long Beach, CA 90809
Abigail Hooker, Chapter President
Web: www.aka1908.com

Theta Mu Omega Chapter
4292 Don Luis Dr.
Los Angeles, CA 90008
Barbara Adelle Fields, Chapter President
Web: www.aka1908.com

Xi Beta Chapter
P.O. Box 19738
Stanford, CA 94309
Kelley Coleman, Chapter President
Web: www.aka1908.com

Xi Gamma Omega Chapter
P.O. Box 28136
Oakland, CA 94604
Erma Cobb, Chapter President
Web: www.aka1908.com

Xi Kappa Omega Chapter
P.O. Box 7732
Oxnard, CA 93031
Samwella King, Chapter President
Web: www.aka1908.com

Xi Pi Chapter
25800 Carlos Bee Blvd. #314
Hayward, CA 94542
Sanae Patton, Chapter President
Web: www.aka1908.com

Zeta Psi Chapter
P.O. Box 69
1 Washington Sq.
San Jose, CA 95192
Hayonna Ricks, Chapter President
Web: www.aka1908.com

ALPHA PHI ALPHA FRATERNITY, INC.
Gamma Chi Lambda Chapter
P.O. Box 883154
San Francisco, CA 94188
Web: www.alphaphialpha.net

Iota Psi Chapter, California Polytechnic Institute
Office of Student Life, 3560 Temple
Pomona, CA 91768

Web: www.alphaphialpha.net

Mu Chi Chapter, California State University
P.O. Box 92902
Long Beach, CA 90809
Web: www.alphaphialpha.net

Nu Sigma Chapter, Stanford University
P.O. Box 8297
Stanford, CA 94309
Web: www.alphaphialpha.net

Xi Rho Chapter, San Francisco State University
1600 Holloway Ave.
San Francisco, CA 94132
Web: www.alphaphialpha.net

Xi Upsilon Chapter, California Polytechnic Institute
P.O. Box 12004
San Luis Obispo, CA 93406
Web: www.alphaphialpha.net

BLACK ALUMNI ASSOCIATION OF THE UNIVERSITY OF SOUTHERN CALIFORNIA
USC Office of Black Alumni Programs
635 Childs Way, Widney Alumni House
Los Angeles, CA 90089-0461
Lura Ball, Director
Tel: (213) 740-8342 Fax: (213) 821-1527
Email: obap@usc.edu
Web: http://alumni.usc.edu/baa/

BLACK GRADUATE ENGINEERING AND SCIENCE STUDENTS
University of California at Berkeley Chapter
282 Cory Hall #1770
Berkeley, CA 94720-1770
Kofi Boakye, President
Tel: (510) 643-2026
Email: bgess@bgess.berkeley.edu
Web: http://bgess.berkeley.edu

BLACK STUDENT UNION
University of California, San Diego Chapter
9500 Gilman Dr. #D-41
La Jolla, CA 92093-0077
John Boatner, President
Tel: (858) 534-2499
Email: blacksu@ucsd.edu
Web: www-acs.ucsd.edu/~blacksu

CENTER OF BLACK CULTURAL AND STUDENTS AFFAIRS
University of Southern California
3601 Trousdale Pkwy., Student Union 415
Los Angeles, CA 90089
Corliss P. Bennett, Director
Tel: (213) 740-8257 Fax: (213) 740-3298
Email: cbcsa@usc.edu
Web: www.usc.edu/cbcsa

NATIONAL BLACK LAW STUDENTS ASSOCIATION
American College of Law
1717 S. State College Blvd. #100
Anaheim, CA 92806
Waleed Akleh, Dean
Tel: (714) 634-3699 Fax: (714) 634-3894
Email: info@aclaw.com
Web: www.aclaw.com

Cal Northern School of Law-Sudent Bar Association
1395 Ridgewood Dr. #100
Chico, CA 95973
Robert Hamilton, President
Tel: (530) 891-6900 Fax: (530) 891-3429
Email: info@calnorthern.edu
Web: www.calnorthern.edu

Humphreys College School of Law
536 Mission St.
San Fransico, CA 94105
Tel: (415) 442-6615 Fax: (415) 495-6756
Web: www.nblsa.org

Loyola University School of Law
919 S. Albany St.
Los Angeles, CA 90015
Demitria Graves, President
Tel: (213) 736-1000
Web: www.nblsa.org

New College of California School of Law
50 Fell St.
San Francisco, CA 94102
Tammy White, President
Tel: (415) 241-1374
Web: www.nblsa.org

Pepperdine University School of Law
24255 Pacific Coast Hwy.
Malibu, CA 90263
Tara Ferguson, President
Tel: (310) 506-4611 Fax: (310) 506-7668
Web: www.nblsa.org

San Francisco Law School
20 Haight St.
San Francisco, CA 94102

Bill Moore, President
Tel: (415) 626-5550 Fax: (415) 626-5584
Web: www.nblsa.org

San Joaquin College of Law
901 5th St.
Clovis, CA 93612
Cadee Ohanesian, President
Tel: (559) 323-2100 Fax: (559) 323-5566
Web: www.nblsa.org

Santa Clara School of Law
500 El Camino Real
Santa Clara, CA 95053
Keishonna Harper, President
Tel: (408) 554-5048 Fax: (408) 554-7897
Web: www.scu.edu/law/resources/organizations.html

Simon Greenleaf School of Law
2200 N. Grand Ave.
Santa Ana, CA 92705
Tel: (714) 836-7500
Web: www.nblsa.org

Southwestern University School of Law
675 S. Westmorland Ave.
Los Angeles, CA 90005
Joel Lofton, President
Tel: (213) 738-6716 Fax: (213) 383-1688
Email: stu_affairs@swlaw.edu
Web: www.swlaw.edu/contact/studentaffairs.html

University of California, Los Angeles, School of Law
405 Hilgard Ave.
Los Angeles, CA 90095
Robin F. Hazel, Co-Chair
Tel: (310) 206-8396
Email: blsa@orgs.law.ucla.edu
Web: www.law.ucla.edu/students/studentorgs/blsa/blsa.htm

University of California-Berkeley School of Law
289 Simon, Boalt Hall Berkeley
Berkeley, CA 94720-7200
Loren Raidmond, President
Tel: (510) 642-6403
Web: www.nblsa.org

University of California-Hastings College of Law
200 McAllister St.
San Francisco, CA 94102
Denise Butts, President
Tel: (415) 565-4600
Email: buttsd@uchastings.edu
Web: www.uchastings.edu/orgs_01/

Western State University College of Law
1111 N. State College Blvd.
Fullerton, CA 92831
Jocelyn Henderson, President
Tel: (714) 738-1000 X2470 Fax: (714) 738-8655
Web: www.wsulaw.edu/careersvcs/storgs/index.htm

Whittier Law School
3333 Harbor Blvd., Whittier Law School
Costa Mesa, CA 92626
Antoinette Robinson, President
Tel: (714) 444-4141 X407
Email: whittierblsa@yahoo.com
Web: www.nblsa.org

COLORADO

EDEN THEATRICAL WORKSHOP, INC.
1570 Gilpin St.
Denver, CO 80218-1631
Lucy M. Walker, President/Executive Director
Tel: (303) 321-2320

THE SPIRITUALS PROJECT
University of Denver, Sturm Hall #403
Denver, CO 80208
Connie Rule, Executive Director
Tel: (303) 871-7993 Fax: (303) 871-4262
Email: crule@spiritualsproject.org
Web: www.spiritualsproject.org

BUSINESS

NATIONAL MINORITY SUPPLIER DEVELOPMENT COUNCIL, INC.
Rocky Mountain Minority Supplier Development Council, Regional Council
1445 Market St. #310
Denver, CO 80202
Bonnie Freeman, Executive Director
Tel: (303) 623-3037 Fax: (303) 595-0027
Email: council@rmmsdc.org
Web: www.rmmsdc.org

POLITICAL ACTION

AMERICAN CIVIL LIBERTIES UNION
Boulder County Chapter
6341 Baseline Rd.
Boulder, CO 80303
Barry Satlow, Board Chair
Tel: (303) 494-3751
Email: worlock@infionline.net
Web: www.aclu-co.org/chapters/bld_aclu/boulder.htm

Colorado Chapter
400 Corona St.
Denver, CO 80218
Cathryn Hazouri, Executive Director
Tel: (303) 777-5482 Fax: (303) 777-1773
Email: info@aclu-co.org
Web: www.aclu-co.org

Colorado Springs Chapter
P.O. Box 519
Colorado Springs, CO 80901-0519
Bill Hochman, Board Chair
Tel: (719) 651-3001
Web: www.aclu-co.org/chapters/co_spngs/co_spngs.htm

ASSOCIATION OF COMMUNITY ORGANIZATIONS FOR REFORM NOW
ACORN Colorado
2854 Larimer St.
Denver, CO 80205
Tel: (303) 393-0773 Fax: (303) 388-0486
Email: coacorn@acorn.org
Web: www.acorn.org

BLACKS IN GOVERNMENT
Region VIII
17870 E. Gunnison Pl.
Aurora, CO 80017
Herber Baker, President
Tel: (303) 751-5705 Fax: (303) 751-0138
Email: hlbaker4@comcast.net
Web: www.bignet.org

Region VIII-Denver Federal Center Chapter
3363 Spotted Tail Dr.
Colorado Springs, CO 80916
James Foster, Chapter President
Tel: (719) 390-8759
Email: denver.federal-center@bignet.org
Web: www.bignet.org

Region VIII-Downtown Denver Chapter
P.O. Box 655
Denver, CO 80201
Rodney Whetspone, Chapter President
Tel: (303) 629-7171
Email: downtown.denver@bignet.org
Web: www.bignet.org

Region VIII-Mile High Chapter
P.O. Box 471747
Aurora, CO 80047
Sandra Jonson, Chapter President
Tel: (303) 346-2370 Fax: (888) 542-3990
Email: sandra_milehighchapter@comcast.net
Web: www.bignet.org

Region VIII-Colorado Springs Chapter
97 Easther Dr.
Colorado Springs, CO 80911-1470
Joyce V. Harrison, Chapter President
Tel: (719) 556-2001
Email: joyce.harrison@cisf.af.mil
Web: www.bignet.org

Region VIII-Denver Center Complex Chapter
4319 Dearborn St.
Denver, CO 80239
Gary Blackmon, Chapter President
Tel: (303) 676-3347
Web: www.bignet.org

Region VIII-Lakewood Area Chapter
17 Lakewood Heights Dr.
Lakewood, CO 80215
Marlette C. Lacey, Chapter President
Tel: (303) 275-5325 Fax: (303) 275-5671
Email: mlacey@fx.fed.us
Web: www.bignet.org

PROFESSIONAL

AMERICAN ASSOCIATION OF BLACKS IN ENERGY
Denver Chapter
c/o National Renewable Energy Lab, 1617 Cole Blvd.
Golden, CO 80401
Paul J. White, President
Tel: (303) 384-7575 Fax: (303) 384-7499
Email: paul_white@nrel.gov
Web: www.aabe-dv.org

ASSOCIATION OF BLACK PSYCHOLOGISTS
Denver-Rocky Mountain Chapter
P.O. Box 3171
Denver, CO 80201
Carnita M. Groves, M.A., Chapter President
Tel: (303) 534-3555
Web: www.dramabpsi.org

NATIONAL ASSOCIATION OF BLACK JOURNALISTS
Colorado Chapter-Region IX
P.O. Box 300736
Denver, CO 80237
Amani Ali, Chapter President
Tel: (303) 713-8500
Email: info@cabj-denver.org
Web: www.cabj-denver.org

NATIONAL BLACK MBA ASSOCIATION, INC.
Denver Chapter-West
P.O. Box 5926
Denver, CO 80217
Thomas Potter, President
Tel: (303) 328-3573
Email: mail@nbmbaa-denver.org
Web: www.nbmbaa-denver.org

NATIONAL MEDICAL ASSOCIATION
Region VI-Mile High Medical Society
2555 S. Downing #130
Denver, CO 80210
Johnny E. Johnson, Jr., M.D., President
Tel: (720) 570-8801 Fax: (720) 570-8805
Email: johnnydusty@ll.com
Web: www.nmanet.org

NATIONAL SOCIETY OF BLACK ENGINEERS
Region 6: University of Colorado at Denver
P.O. Box 173364
Denver, CO 80217-3364
Tishawna Kenneb, Chapter President
Tel: (303) 556-2701 Fax: (303) 556-2511

RESEARCH

BLACK BIOMEDICAL RESEARCH MOVEMENT
University of Colorado at Boulder
Campus Box 347
Department of Molecular, Cellular, and Developmental Biology
Boulder, CO 80309-0347
Patrick Allen, Founder
Tel: (888) 234-2495 Fax: (303) 492-7744
Email: blackhealth@colorado.edu
Web: www.bbrm.org

SPEC. INT., EMPLOYMENT

INROADS, INC.
Denver Affiliate
4601 DTC Blvd. #150A
Denver, CO 80237
Hollis E. Booker, Managing Director
Tel: (303) 607-0385 X24 Fax: (303) 607-0474
Email: hbooker@inroads.org
Web: www.inroads.org

SPEC. INT., SOCIAL INTEREST

100 BLACK MEN OF DENVER, INC.
P.O. Box 300188
Denver, CO 80203
Samuel Williams, Chapter President
Tel: (303) 864-0945
Email: zekunday@du.edu
Web: www.100bmdenver.org

METROPOLITAN DENVER BLACK UNITED FUND, INC.
3542 York St.
Denver, CO 80205
Mary McNeil-Jones, Executive Director
Tel: (303) 675-0583 Fax: (303) 675-0579
Web: www.nbuf.org

NATIONAL URBAN LEAGUE, INC.
Urban League of Metropolitan Denver
5900 E. 39th Ave.
Denver, CO 80207
Sharon Alexander-Holt, COO
Tel: (303) 388-5861 Fax: (303) 321-1245
Email: sholt@denverurbanleague.org
Web: www.denverurbanleague.org

Urban League of Pikes Peak Region
125 N. Parkside Dr.
Colorado Springs, CO 80909-1997
Deborah T. Wilson, President/CEO
Tel: (719) 634-1525 Fax: (719) 634-3357
Email: dwilson@ulcolospgs.org
Web: www.ulcolospgs.org

SPEC. INT., VOLUNTARY SERVICE

THE DENVER CENTER FOR CRIME VICTIMS
P.O. Box 18975
Denver, CO 80218
Cathy Phelps, M.A., M.S.W., Executive Director
Tel: (303) 860-0660 Fax: (303) 831-7282
Email: admin@denvervictims.org
Web: www.denvervictims.org

SPEC. INT., YOUTH

GIRLS INCORPORATED OF METRO DENVER
1499 Julian St.
Denver, CO 80204
Colleen Colarelli, President/CEO
Tel: (303) 893-4363 Fax: (303) 893-4352
Web: www.girlsincdenver.org

STUDENT ORGANIZATION

ALPHA KAPPA ALPHA SORORITY, INC.
Epsilon Nu Omega Chapter
P.O. Box 370753
Denver, CO 80237
Stacey Walker, Chapter President
Web: www.midwesternakas.com

Iota Beta Omega Chapter
P.O. Box 17452
Colorado Springs, CO 80935
Essie M. Bell, Chapter President
Web: www.midwesternakas.com

Mu Omega Omega Chapter
P.O. Box 471166
Aurora, CO 80047
Jacqueline Houston, Chapter President
Web: www.midwesternakas.com

ALPHA PHI ALPHA FRATERNITY, INC.
Delta Psi Lambda Chapter
P.O. Box 200296
Denver, CO 80220
Web: www.alphaphialpha.net

Iota Omicron Lambda Chapter
P.O. Box 15083
Colorado Springs, CO 80935
Web: www.alphaphialpha.net

Omicron Tau Chapter, University of Northern Colorado
Lory Student Ctr., Greek Life
Fort Collins, CO 80523
Web: www.alphaphialpha.net

BLACK LAW STUDENTS ASSOCIATION
University of Colorado School of Law
Campus Box 401
Boulder, CO 80309
Nikea Bleand, President
Tel: (303) 492-8412
Email: nikea.bleand@colorado.edu
Web: www.colorado.edu/law/elsa

BLACK STUDENT ORGANIZATION
Colorado State University Pueblo
2200 Bonforte Blvd.
Pueblo, CO 81001
Marjaneh Gross, President
Tel: (719) 549-2866 Fax: (719) 549-2293
Email: info@colostate-pueblo.edu
Web: www.colostate-pueblo.edu

BLACK STUDENTS ALLIANCE
University of Colorado
University Memorial Ctr. #207
Boulder, CO 80309
Mebraht Gebre-Michael, Director of Communications
Tel: (303) 492-1863
Email: blacksa@colorado.edu
Web: www.bsa-colorado.org

NATIONAL PAN-HELLENIC COUNCIL, INC.
Western Region
4330 Eugene Way
Denver, CO 80239
Jennifer Carter, Regional Director
Tel: (303) 576-9488
Email: westerndir@nphchq.org
Web: www.nphchq.org

CONNECTICUT

BUSINESS

NATIONAL MINORITY SUPPLIER DEVELOPMENT COUNCIL, INC.
Connecticut Minority Supplier Development Council, Inc., Regional Council
4133 Whitney Ave., Bldg. 4 Box 2
Hamden, CT 06518

Fred McKinney, President
Tel: (203) 288-9744 Fax: (203) 288-9310
Email: cmsdc@cmsdc.org
Web: www.cmsdc.org

COMMUNICATIONS

CONNECTICUT ASSOCIATION OF BLACK COMMUNICATORS
P.O. Box 599
Hartford, CT 06141-0535
Ann-Marie Adams, President
Tel: (860) 524-1977 X22
Email: aadams@ct-abc.org
Web: www.ct-abc.org

MULTI-PURPOSE

NATIONAL ASSOCIATION FOR THE ADVANCEMENT OF COLORED PEOPLE
Ansonia Branch
210 Goffe St.
New Haven, CT 06511
Greg Johnson, President
Web: www.naacpct.org

Bridgeport Branch
44 Lewis
Norwalk, CT 06601
Carolyn Nah, Branch President
Tel: (203) 334-3105
Web: www.naacpct.org

Greater Hartford Branch
P.O. Box 1012
Hartford, CT 06143
Carrie Saxon-Perry, Branch President
Tel: (860) 243-1937
Web: www.naacpct.org

Greater New Haven Branch
192 Dixwell Ave.
New Haven, CT 06515
Scot X Esdaile, Branch President
Tel: (203) 776-2662 Fax: (203) 752-1153
Email: scotx2001@yahoo.com
Web: www.naacpct.org

Meriden/Wallingford Branch
50 Rockledge Dr.
Meriden, CT 06416
Roland Cockfield, Branch President
Tel: (203) 235-3046
Email: roland.cockfield@snet.net
Web: www.naacpct.org

Middlesex County
P.O. Box 378
Middletown, CT 06457
Roxanne Aaron-Selph, Branch President
Tel: (860) 343-9467
Email: aaronselph@aol.com
Web: www.naacpct.org

New Britain Branch
P.O. Box 323
New Britain, CT 06050
Pauline Davis, Branch President
Tel: (203) 235-3046
Web: www.naacpct.org

New London Branch
P.O. Box 985
New London, CT 06320
Waldren Phillips, Branch President
Tel: (860) 444-2697
Web: www.naacpct.org

Norwalk Branch
P.O. Box 1647
Norwalk, CT 06852
Lindsay E. Curtis, Branch President
Tel: (203) 838-5717
Email: lecurtis@optonline.net
Web: www.naacpct.org

Norwich Branch
P.O. Box 24
Norwich, CT 06360
Jackie Owens, Branch President
Tel: (860) 886-1686
Email: aldenterprises@snet.net
Web: www.naacpct.org/norwich

Stamford Branch
P.O. Box 885
Stamford, CT 06904
John T. Brown, Branch President
Tel: (203) 323-0892 Fax: (203) 327-3695
Email: naacpstamford@optonline.net
Web: www.naacpct.org

Waterbury Branch
P.O. Box 1147
Waterbury, CT 06721
Jimmy Griffin, Branch President
Web: www.naacpct.org

POLITICAL ACTION

AMERICAN ASSOCIATION FOR AFFIRMATIVE ACTION
Region I
City of New London, 181 State St.
New London, CT 06320
Alvin Bingham, Alternate Regional Director/Affirmative Action Coordinator
Tel: (860) 447-5295
Email: abingham@ci.new-london.ct.us
Web: www.affirmativeaction.org

ASSOCIATION OF COMMUNITY ORGANIZATIONS FOR REFORM NOW
Connecticut
2310 Main St., 3rd Fl.
Bridgeport, CT 06606
Jeff Ordower
Tel: (203) 333-2676 Fax: (203) 366-0020
Email: ctacorn@acorn.org
Web: www.acorn.org

Hartford
621 Farmington Ave., 2nd Fl.
Hartford, CT 06105
David Lagstein, Head Organizer
Tel: (860) 523-1017 Fax: (860) 231-2419
Email: ctacorn@acorn.org
Web: www.acorn.org

BLACKS IN GOVERNMENT
Region I-Greater Hartford Chapter
31 Pershing St.
Hartford, CT 06112
Otis Mae Calloway, Chapter President
Tel: (203) 242-0101
Email: greater.boston@bignet.org
Web: www.bostonbig.org

CONNECTICUT CIVIL LIBERTIES UNION
Connecticut Chapter
32 Grand St.
Hartford, CT 06106
Roger V. Vann, Executive Director
Tel: (860) 247-9823 Fax: (860) 728-0227
Email: cclu@acluct.org
Web: www.cclu.org

NATIONAL ACTION NETWORK
Connecticut Chapter
1st Calvary Baptist Church, 605 Dixwell Ave.
New Haven, CT 06511
Rev. Boise Kimbert, Chair
Tel: (203) 624-1426 Fax: (203) 772-2959
Web: www.nationalactionnetwork.org

PROFESSIONAL

NATIONAL BLACK MBA ASSOCIATION, INC.
Hartford Chapter-East
P.O. Box 2332
Hartford, CT 06146
Kris Floyd, President
Tel: (860) 586-7002
Email: hartfordnbmbaa@yahoo.com
Web: www.nbmbaa-hartford.org

RESEARCH

GILDER LEHRMAN CENTER FOR THE STUDY OF SLAVERY, RESISTANCE, AND ABOLITION
Yale University
P.O. Box 208206
New Haven, CT 06520-8206
David W. Blight, Director
Tel: (203) 432-3339 Fax: (203) 432-6943
Email: gilder.lehrman.center@yale.edu
Web: www.yale.edu/glc

SPEC. INT., EDUCATION

AFRICAN STUDIES PROGRAM COMMITTEE
Central Connecticut State University
CCSU Psychology Dept., 1615 Stanley St.
New Britain, CT 06050
Charles Mate-Kole, Coordinator
Tel: (860) 832-3105 Fax: (860) 832-3123
Email: matekolec@ccsu.edu
Web: www.ccsu.edu

CONNECTICUT PRE-ENGINEERING PROGRAM
Central Office
45 Wintonbury Ave.
Bloomfield, CT 06002
Glenn A. Cassis, Executive Director
Tel: (860) 769-5285
Email: thomasj@cpep.org
Web: www.cpep.org

NATIONAL ASSOCIATION FOR MULTICULTURAL EDUCATION
Connecticut Chapter
Saint Joseph College, 1678 Asylum Ave.
West Hartford, CT 06117
Julie R. Alexandrin, President
Tel: (860) 231-5362 Fax: (860) 231-1691
Email: jalexandrin@sjc.edu
Web: www.ctname.org

THE NATIONAL AFRICAN AMERICAN SPEAKERS ASSOCIATION
Connecticut State Chapter
P.O. Box 592
New Milford, CT 06776
Daphne Clarke-Hudson, Chapter President
Tel: (860) 355-9838
Email: connecticut@4naasa.org
Web: www.4naasa.org

SPEC. INT., EMPLOYMENT

INROADS, INC.
Fairfield-Westchester Affiliate
111 Prospect St.
Stamford, CT 06901
Marcos A. Morales, Managing Director
Tel: (203) 358-0048 X236 Fax: (203) 975-1996
Email: mmorales@inroads.org
Web: www.inroads.org

Greater Hartford
750 Main St. #704
Hartford, CT 06103
C. Timothy Branner, II, Managing Director
Tel: (860) 278-9000 Fax: (860) 278-0570
Email: tbranner@inroads.org
Web: www.inroads.org

INSTITUTE FOR LIFE COPING SKILLS, INC.
Adkins Life Skills Program
141 Franklin St.
Stamford, CT 06901
Winthrop R. Adkins, PhD, President
Tel: (800)-783-2577 Fax: (203) 353-0699
Email: info@adkinslifeskills.org
Web: www.adkinslifeskills.org

SPEC. INT., SOCIAL INTEREST

100 BLACK MEN OF BRIDGEPORT, INC.
93 Holland Rd.
Bridgeport, CT 06610
James F. Morton, III, President
Tel: (203) 374-9743 Fax: (203) 371-7356
Email: revlee111@aol.com

NATIONAL URBAN LEAGUE, INC.
Urban League of Greater Hartford
140 Woodland St.
Hartford, CT 06105
James E. Willingham, Sr., President/CEO
Tel: (860) 527-0147 Fax: (860) 249-1563
Email: jwillingham@ulgh.org
Web: www.ulgh.org

Urban League of Southwestern Connecticut
46 Atlantic St.
Stamford, CT 06901
Rhetta Vinson, President
Tel: (203) 327-5810 Fax: (203) 406-0008
Email: admin@ulswc.org
Web: www.ulswc.org/start_low.htm

STUDENT ORGANIZATION

ALPHA KAPPA ALPHA SORORITY, INC.
Epsilon Omicron Omega Chapter
P.O. Box 1004
Hartford, CT 06143
Wanda Seldon, Chapter President
Web: www.aka1908.com

Omicron Upsilon Omega Chapter
P.O. Box 1136
Norwalk, CT 06856
Sandra Worrell, Chapter President
Web: www.aka1908.com

Tau Xi Omega Chapter
P.O. Box 6184
Hamden, CT 06517
Tracie R. Grimsley, Chapter President
Web: www.aka1908.com

Theta Epsilon Omega Chapter
P.O. Box 8298
New Haven, CT 06530
Katurah Abdul-Salaam, Chapter President
Web: www.aka1908.com

Theta Tau Omega Chapter
P.O. Box 256
Bridgeport, CT 06601
Vendette T. Thomas, Chapter President
Web: www.aka1908.com

Xi Omicron Chapter
40 Foxon Hill Rd. #36-J
New Haven, CT 06513
Audrey D. Holmes, Graduate Advisor
Email: audreyaka@cs.com
Web: http://akanorthatlantic.org

BLACK STUDENT ALLIANCE
Yale University
211 Park St.
New Haven, CT 06520
Rashayla Brown, President
Tel: (203) 432-4131 Fax: (203) 432-8138
Email: rashayla.brown@yale.edu
Web: www.yale.edu/bsay

DELTA SIGMA THETA SORORITY, INC.
Eastern Region
P.O. Box 598
Hartford, CT 06141-0598
Cheryl Hickmon, Regional Director
Tel: (202) 986-2400 Fax: (202) 986-2513
Email: easternregionrd@aol.com
Web: www.easternregiondst.org

NATIONAL BLACK LAW STUDENTS ASSOCIATION
Quinnipiac School of Law
275 Mt. Carmel Ave.
Hamden, CT 06518
Stacy Lynch, President
Tel: (203) 582-3215 Fax: (203) 582-3216
Web: www.nblsa.org

DELAWARE

LAW ENFORCEMENT

NATIONAL ORGANIZATION OF BLACK LAW ENFORCEMENT EXECUTIVES
Delaware Chapter
P.O. Box 2232
Virginia Union University PD
Wilmington, DE 19899
Renee Cannon, Chief of Police
Tel: (302) 857-7478 Fax: (302) 678-2113
Email: vuuchief@hotmail.com
Web: www.noblenatl.org

POLITICAL ACTION

AMERICAN CIVIL LIBERTIES UNION
Delaware Chapter
100 W. 10th St. #309
Wilmington, DE 19801
Drewery Nash Fennell, Executive Director
Tel: (302) 654-3966 Fax: (302) 654-3689
Email: aclu@acludelaware.org
Web: www.aclu-de.org

SCIENTIFIC

INTERNATIONAL SOCIETY OF AFRICAN SCIENTISTS
P.O. Box 9209
Wilmington, DE 19809
Cyril Broderick, President
Tel: (302) 857-6416 Fax: (302) 857-6455
Web: www.dca.net/isas

SPEC. INT., SOCIAL INTEREST

NATIONAL URBAN LEAGUE, INC.
Metropolitan Wilmington Urban League
100 W. 10th St. #710
Wilmington, DE 19801
James H. Gilliam, Sr., Chairman/CEO
Tel: (302) 622-4300 Fax: (302) 622-4303
Email: info@mwul.org
Web: www.mwul.org

STUDENT ORGANIZATION

ALPHA KAPPA ALPHA SORORITY, INC.
Delta Lambda Chapter, Delaware State College
804 Woodcrest Dr.
Dover, DE 19904
Karen Robinson, Chapter President
Email: krobinso@dsc.edu
Web: www.aka1908.com

Lambda Gamma Chapter, University of Delaware
2 Clipper Ct.
Bear, DE 19701
Sharon Bryant, Graduate Advisor
Email: bryant672@comcast.net
Web: www.aka1908.com

Theta Iota Chapter, West Chester State College
302 Victoria Blvd.
Newark, DE 19702
Karen Burnett, Graduate Advisor
Email: ksburnett@prodigy.net
Web: http://akanorthatlantic.org

DISTRICT OF COLUMBIA

ARTISTIC

AFRICAN HERITAGE DANCERS AND DRUMMERS
4018 Minnesota Ave. NE
Washington, DC 20019
Melvin Deal, Executive Director
Tel: (202) 399-5252 Fax: (202) 399-5252
Email: ahdd@interchange.org

PIN POINTS THEATRE
4353 Dubois Pl. SE
Washington, DC 20019-4264
Ersky Freeman, Director
Tel: (202) 582-0002 Fax: (301) 808-2398
Email: pinpoints@aol.com
Web: www.pinpoints.org

BUSINESS

CORPORATE COUNCIL ON AFRICA
1100 17th St. NW #1100
Washington, DC 20036
Stephen Hayes, President
Tel: (202) 835-1115 Fax: (202) 835-1117
Email: cca@africacncl.org
Web: www.africacncl.org

NATIONAL ASSOCIATION OF BLACK OWNED BROADCASTERS
1155 Connecticut Ave. NW #600
Washington, DC 20036
James Winston, Executive Director
Tel: (202) 463-8970 Fax: (202) 429-0657
Email: info@nabob.org
Web: www.nabob.org

NATIONAL ASSOCIATION OF INVESTMENT COMPANIES
1300 Pennsylvania Ave. NW #700
Washington, DC 20004
Robert L. Greene, President/CEO
Tel: (202) 204-3001 Fax: (202) 204-3022
Email: rgreene@naicvc.com
Web: www.naicvc.com

NATIONAL MINORITY SUPPLIER DEVELOPMENT COUNCIL, INC.
Maryland/Washington Minority Supplier Development Council, Regional Council
922 Pennsylvania Ave. SE
Washington, DC 20003
Sheila Dews-Johnson, Chairman
Tel: (202) 544-5700 Fax: (202) 544-5720
Email: info@mddccouncil.org
Web: www.mddccouncil.org

UNITED STATES SOUTH AFRICA BUSINESS COUNCIL
1625 K St. NW #200
Washington, DC 20006
J. Daniel O'Flaherty, Executive Director
Tel: (202) 887-0278 Fax: (202) 452-8160
Email: nftcinformation@nftc.org
Web: www.nftc.org

CHAMBER OF COMMERCE

NATIONAL BLACK CHAMBER OF COMMERCE, INC.
1350 Connecticut Ave. NW #405
Washington, DC 20036
Harry C. Alford, President/CEO
Tel: (202) 466-6888 Fax: (202) 466-4918
Email: info@nationalbcc.org
Web: www.nationalbcc.org

COMMUNICATIONS

MINORITY MEDIA AND TELECOMMUNICATIONS COUNCIL
3636 16th St. NW #B-366
Washington, DC 20010
Henry M. Rivera, Chair
Tel: (202) 332-0500 Fax: (202) 332-0503
Email: info@mmtconline.org
Web: www.mmtconline.org

CULTURAL

AFRICAN AMERICAN HERITAGE PRESERVATION FOUNDATION, INC.
420 7th St. NW #501
Washington, DC 20004
E. Renee Ingram, President/Founder
Tel: (202) 347-1149 Fax: (202) 248-0785
Email: reneei@aol.com
Web: www.aahpfdn.org

AFRO-AMERICAN HISTORICAL AND GENEALOGICAL SOCIETY, INC.
National Headquarters
P.O. Box 73067
Washington, DC 20056-3067
Carolyn Corpening Collins Rowe, National President
Tel: (202) 234-5350 Fax: (202) 829-8970
Email: info@aahgs.org
Web: www.aahgs.org

ASSOCIATION FOR THE STUDY OF AFRICAN-AMERICAN LIFE AND HISTORY
National Headquarters
CB Powell Bldg., 525 Bryant St. NW #C142
Washington, DC 20059
Sylvia Cyrus-Albriton, Executive Director
Tel: (202) 865-0053 Fax: (202) 265-7920
Email: executivedirector@asalh.net
Web: www.asalh.org

MEMORY OF AFRICAN CULTURE, INC.
P.O. Box 50042
Washington, DC 20091
Dijimo Kouyate, Director
Tel: (202) 726-1400 Fax: (202) 726-1400
Email: dialikouyate@aol.com
Web: www.memoryofafricanculture.org

THE BLACK PATRIOTS FOUNDATION
729 15th St. NW #500
Washington, DC 20005
Rhonda Roberson, President
Tel: (202) 452-1776 Fax: (202) 728-0770
Email: blackpatriots@blackpatriots.org
Web: www.blackpatriots.org

ENTERTAINMENT

NATIONAL AFRICAN AMERICAN RV'ERS ASSOCIATION
DC Ramblers
1208 Savannah St. SE
Washington, DC 20032
Lois Fletcher, President
Tel: (202) 561-0609
Web: www.naarva.com

GOVERNMENT

NATIONAL ASSOCIATION OF BLACK COUNTY OFFICIALS
440 1st St. NW #410
Washington, DC 20001
Joe Fuller, President
Tel: (202) 347-6953 Fax: (202) 393-6596
Email: nobco@naco.org

US GOVERNMENT AFRICAN DEVELOPMENT FOUNDATION
1400 I St. NW, 10th Fl.
Washington, DC 20005
Nathaniel Fields, President
Tel: (202) 673-3916 Fax: (202) 673-3810
Email: info@adf.gov
Web: www.adf.gov

LAW ENFORCEMENT

NATIONAL ORGANIZATION OF BLACK LAW ENFORCEMENT EXECUTIVES
Washington Metro Area Chapter
P.O. Box 64461
Washington, DC 20019-4461
Clarence Edwards, National President
Tel: (301) 352-0842
Email: president@noblewashingtondc.org
Web: www.noblewashingtondc.org

MULTI-PURPOSE

AFRICA-AMERICA INSTITUTE
1625 Massachusetts Ave. NW #400
Washington, DC 20036
Mora McLean, President/CEO
Tel: (202) 667-5636 Fax: (202) 265-6332
Web: www.aaionline.org

ALLIANCE FOR JUSTICE
11 Dupont Cr. NW, 2nd Fl.
Washington, DC 20036
Nan Aron, President
Tel: (202) 822-6070 Fax: (202) 822-6068
Email: alliance@afj.org
Web: www.afj.org

INTERNATIONAL ECONOMIC DEVELOPMENT COUNCIL
Head Office
734 15th St. NW #900
Washington, DC 20005
Jeffrey Finkle, President

Tel: (202) 223-7800 Fax: (202) 223-4745
Email: jfinkle@iedconline.org
Web: www.iedconline.org

NATIONAL ASSOCIATION FOR THE ADVANCEMENT OF COLORED PEOPLE
Washington Bureau
1025 Vermont Ave. NW #1120
Washington, DC 20005
Hilary Shelton, Director
Tel: (202) 638-2269 Fax: (202) 638-5936
Email: washingtonbureau@naacpnet.org
Web: www.naacp.org

NATIONAL BAR ASSOCIATION
1225 11th St. NW
Washington, DC 20001-4217
Kim M. Keenan, President
Tel: (202) 842-3900 Fax: (202) 289-6170
Email: headquarters@nationalbar.org
Web: www.nationalbar.org

URBAN FINANCIAL SERVICES COALITION
National Office
1300 L St. NW #825
Washington, DC 20005
Damita J. Barbee, President
Tel: (202) 289-8335 Fax: (202) 842-0567
Email: ufsc@ufscnet.org
Web: www.ufscnet.org

POLITICAL ACTION

A. PHILIP RANDOLPH INSTITUTE
1444 I St. NW #300
Washington, DC 20005
Norman Hill, President
Tel: (202) 289-2774 Fax: (202) 289-5289
Email: nhill@apri.org
Web: www.apri.org

AFRICA ACTION
1634 Eye St. NW #810
Washington, DC 20006
Salih Booker, Director
Tel: (202) 546-7961 Fax: (202) 546-1545
Email: africaaction@igc.org
Web: www.africaaction.org

AMERICAN CIVIL LIBERTIES UNION
National Capital Area Chapter
1400 20th St. NW #119
Washington, DC 20036-5920
Jonny Barnes, Executive Director
Tel: (202) 457-0800
Email: aclu@aclu.org
Web: www.aclu-nca.org

ASSOCIATION OF BLACK AMERICAN AMBASSADORS
1624 Crescent Pl. NW
Washington, DC 20009
Kenton W. Keith, President
Tel: (202) 939-5590 Fax: (202) 667-8980
Email: kkeith@meridian.org

ASSOCIATION OF COMMUNITY ORGANIZATIONS FOR REFORM NOW
DC Office
739 8th St. SE
Washington, DC 20003
Allison Conyers, Communications Coordinator
Tel: (202) 547-9292 Fax: (202) 546-2483
Email: dcacorn@acorn.org
Web: www.acorn.org

BLACK RADICAL CONGRESS
DC Chapter
P.O. Box 65814
Washington, DC 20035
Cameron Barron
Email: cameronbarron@hotmail.com
Web: www.blackradicalcongress.com

BLACKS IN GOVERNMENT
National Office
3005 Georgia Ave. NW
Washington, DC 20001
Darling H. Young, National President
Tel: (202) 667-3280 Fax: (202) 667-3705
Email: president@bignet.org
Web: www.bignet.org

Region XI
P.O. Box 2931
Washington, DC 20013-2931
Larry Phillips, President
Email: region11.president@bignet.org
Web: www.bigrxi.org

Region XI-Big Metro Chapter
P.O. Box 50172
Washington, DC 20091-0172
Robert Robertson, Chapter President

Tel: (202) 962-1475
Email: big.metro@bignet.org
Web: www.bignet.org

Region XI-Department of Education Chapter
P.O. Box 23612
Washington, DC 20026-0612
Avis R. McClenton Pasley-Martin, Chapter President
Tel: (202) 260-0958 Fax: (202) 260-7764
Email: avis.martin@ed.gov
Web: www.bignet.org

Region XI-Department of Energy Chapter
P.O. Box 23540
Washington, DC 20026-3540
Samuel V. Browne, Chapter President
Tel: (202) 586-8724
Email: energy@bignet.org
Web: www.bignet.org

Region XI-Ft. Belvoir Chapter
P.O. Box 78
Washington, DC 20206-0078
Ivory Stewart, Chapter President
Tel: (703) 602-1430
Email: ivory.stewart@army.mil
Web: www.bignet.org

Region XI-Housing and Urban Development Chapter
P.O. Box 44614
Washington, DC 20026-4614
Sandra A. Campbell, Chapter President
Tel: (202) 708-0614 X3791 Fax: (301) 436-2668
Email: sandra_a_campbell@hud.gov
Web: www.bignet.org

Region XI-National Transportation Safety Board Chapter
Steve Bennett, Chapter President
Tel: (202) 314-6228
Email: bennets@ntsb.gov
Web: www.bignet.org

Region XI-NAVSEA Chapter
1333 Isaac Hull Ave. SE, Washington Navy Yard
Washington, DC 20376-0001
Veradie L. Ore, Chapter President
Tel: (202) 781-1600
Web: www.bignet.org

Region XI-USAID Chapter
P.O. Box 14238, Ben Franklin Station
Washington, DC 20044-4238
Melvin Proter, Chapter President
Tel: (202) 712-5141 Fax: (703) 482-4199
Email: mporter@usaid.gov
Web: www.bignet.org

Region XI-ZAWADI Chapter
Washington, DC
Lautricia C. Bagley, Chapter President
Tel: (202) 745-8403
Email: bagley.lutricia_c@washington.va.gov
Web: www.bignet.org

Region XI-Benjamin Banneker Chapter
P.O. Box 23704
Washington, DC 20026-3704
Donald L. Smith, Chapter President
Tel: (202) 501-0981
Email: bbc@bignet.org
Web: www.bignet.org

Region XI-Carl T. Rowan Chapter
P.O. Box 44714
Washington, DC 20026
Darlene H. Young, National President
Tel: (202) 203-7533
Email: youngdh@state.gov
Web: www.bignet.org

Region XI-Coast Guard Chapter
P.O. Box 71055
Washington, DC 20024-1055
Larry R. Houstan, Chapter President
Tel: (202) 267-0641 Fax: (202) 267-4823
Email: cghc@bignet.org
Web: www.bignet.org

Region XI-Defense Intelligence Agency Chapter
P.O. Box 8585
Washington, DC 20332-8585
Jerry J. Jackson, Chapter President
Tel: (202) 231-3209 Fax: (202) 231-3244
Email: dia@bignet.org
Web: www.bignet.org

Region XI-Department of Labor Chapter
P.O. Box 2223
Washington, DC 20013-2223
Barbara Johnson Cox, Chapter President
Tel: (202) 691-6873 Fax: (202) 231-3244
Email: labor@bignet.org
Web: www.bignet.org

Region XI-Department of State Foreign Affairs Chapter
P.O. Box 58278, Watergate Station

Washington, DC 20037-9998
Barbara Fox, Chapter President
Tel: (202) 261-8368 Fax: (202) 261-8044
Email: foreign.affairs@bignet.org
Web: www.bignet.org

Region XI-Department of Transportation Chapter
P.O. Box 44226
Washington, DC 20026
Sharon A.H. Scott, Chapter President
Tel: (202) 366-4944 Fax: (202) 493-2833
Email: sscott@nhtsa.dot.gov
Web: www.bignet.org

Region XI-EPA William D. Barber, Jr. Chapter
P.O. Box 70396
Washington, DC 20024
Dione Bowlding, Chapter President
Tel: (202) 564-2088
Email: william.barber@bignet.org
Web: www.bignet.org

Region XI-FCC-Benjamin Hooks Chapter
Federal Communication Commission, 445 12th St. SW #6-C266
Washington, DC 20554
Wesley Jarmon, Chapter President
Tel: (202) 418-0815
Email: wjarmon@fcc.gov
Web: www.bignet.org

Region XI-Internal Revenue Service Chisholm-Hughes Chapter
P.O. Box 709
Washington, DC 20044
Samuel M. Farrow, Chapter President
Tel: (202) 622-5920
Email: chisholm.hughes@bignet.org
Web: www.bignet.org

Region XI-Internal Revenue Service New Carrollton Federal Bldg. Chapter
P.O. Box 2931
Washington, DC 20013
Afredia Jones, Regional Secretary
Tel: (202) 283-4160 Fax: (202) 283-4029
Email: alfredia.p.jones@irs.gov
Web: www.bignet.org

Region XI-Library of Congress Chapter
P.O. Box 15841
Washington, DC 20003-0841
Napoleon Jasper, Chapter President
Tel: (202) 707-6738
Email: loc@bignet.org
Web: www.bignet.org

Region XI-NASA HQTRS Chapter
300 E St. SW, Code CI
Washington, DC 20546
Brenda Williams, Chapter President
Tel: (202) 358-1479 Fax: (202) 358-2835
Email: bwilliam@hq.nasa.gov
Web: www.bignet.org

Region XI-Office of Personnel Management Chapter
1900 E. St. NW
Washington, DC 20415
Larry M. Stoner, Sr., Chapter President
Tel: (202) 606-2107 Fax: (202) 606-1674
Email: opm@bignet.org
Web: www.bignet.org

Region XI-Ronald H. Brown Center Chapter
P.O. Box 7824
Washington, DC 20044-7824
Mathew F. Fogg, Chapter President
Tel: (301) 423-9855 Fax: (866) 743-4522
Email: u.s.marshal@writeme.com
Web: www.bignet.org

Region XI-Sankofa Chapter
P.O. Box 7546
Washington, DC 20044-7546
Wanda Crowder, Chapter President
Tel: (202) 220-1092 Fax: (202) 220-1801
Web: www.bignet.org

Region XI-Treasury Chapter
1017 E St. NE
Washington, DC 20002-6131
Mary L. Yarborough, Chapter President
Tel: (202) 927-5755
Email: yarboroughm@oig.treas.gov
Web: www.bignet.org

Region XI-USDA Chapter
P.O. Box 23381
Washington, DC 20026
Charles Stouremire, Chapter President
Tel: (202) 690-1802 Fax: (202) 609-0681
Email: usda@bignet.org
Web: www.bignet.org

Region XI-Washington Navy Yard Chapter
PSC Box 339, NDW Anacostia Annex
Washington, DC 20373-0339

Joyce Ann Battle, Chapter President
Tel: (202) 433-2734 Fax: (202) 433-2748
Email: joyce.battle@ndw.navy.mil
Web: www.bignet.org

U.S. Coast Guard Headquarters Chapter
2100 2nd St. SW
Washington, DC 20593
Larry R. Houston, Chapter President
Tel: (202) 267-0641
Email: lhouston@comdt.uscg.mil
Web: www.bignet.org

COALITION OF BLACK TRADE UNIONISTS
National Office
P.O. Box 66268
Washington, DC 20035-6268
Gwend Johnson, Treasurer
Tel: (202) 429-1203 Fax: (202) 429-1102
Email: gwendjoh@cwa-union.org
Web: www.cbtu.org

CONGRESSIONAL BLACK CAUCUS
1632 Longworth Bldg.
Washington, DC 20515
Melvin L. Watt, Chairperson
Tel: (202) 226-9776 Fax: (202) 225-3178
Web: www.congressionalblackcaucus.net

CONGRESSIONAL BLACK CAUCUS FOUNDATION, INC.
Congressional Black Caucus
1720 Massachusetts Ave. NW
Washington, DC 20036
Don I. Tharpe, President/CEO
Tel: (202) 263-2800
Email: info@cbcfinc.org
Web: www.cbcfinc.org

GLOBAL COALITION FOR AFRICA
1919 Pennsylvania Ave. NW #550
Washington, DC 20006
Hage G. Geingob, Executive Secretary
Tel: (202) 458-4338 Fax: (202) 522-3259
Web: www.gcacma.org

HUMAN RIGHTS WATCH
Washington DC Office
1630 Connecticut Ave. NW #500
Washington, DC 20009
Kenneth Roth, Executive Director
Tel: (202) 612-4321 Fax: (202) 612-4333
Email: hrwdc@hrw.org
Web: www.hrw.org

LAWYERS COMMITTEE FOR CIVIL RIGHTS UNDER LAW
National Office
1401 New York Ave. NW #400
Washington, DC 20005
Barbara R. Arnwine, Executive Director
Tel: (202) 662-8600 Fax: (202) 783-0857
Email: barnwine@lawyerscomm.org
Web: www.lawyerscomm.org

LEADERSHIP CONFERENCE ON CIVIL RIGHTS
1629 K St. NW, 10th Fl.
Washington, DC 20006
Wade Henderson, Executive Director
Tel: (202) 466-3311 Fax: (202) 466-3435
Email: henderson@civilrights.org
Web: www.civilrights.org

NATIONAL ASSOCIATION FOR THE ADVANCEMENT OF COLORED PEOPLE
National Voter Fund
2001 L St. NW #1050
Washington, DC 20036
Greg Moore, Executive Director
Tel: (202) 898-0960 Fax: (202) 898-1397
Email: info@nvf-afe.org
Web: www.naacpnvf.org

NATIONAL BLACK CAUCUS OF LOCAL ELECTED OFFICIALS
c/o National League of Cities
1301 Pennsylvania Ave. NW #550
Washington, DC 20004-1763
Mary France Gordon, Director
Tel: (202) 626-3169 Fax: (202) 626-3043
Email: gordon@nlc.org
Web: www.nbc-leo.org

NATIONAL BLACK CAUCUS OF STATE LEGISLATORS
444 N. Capitol St. NW #622
Washington, DC 20001
LaKimba DeSadier Walker, Executive Director
Tel: (202) 624-5457 Fax: (202) 508-3826
Email: lakimba@nbcsl.com
Web: www.nbcsl.com

NATIONAL BLACK LEADERSHIP ROUNDTABLE
1242 Pennsylvania Ave. SE
Washington, DC 20003

Walter E. Fauntroy, President
Fax: (202) 544-8059
Web: www.nblr.org

NATIONAL SUMMIT ON AFRICA
1779 Massachusetts Ave. NW #510-A
Washington, DC 20036
Leonard H. Robinson, Jr., President/CEO
Tel: (202) 232-3862 Fax: (202) 232-3870
Email: fdoumbia@africasummit.org
Web: www.africasummit.org

TRANSAFRICA, INC./TRANSAFRICA FORUM
1426 21st St. NW, 2nd Fl.
Washington, DC 20036
Bill Fletcher, Jr., President
Tel: (202) 223-1960 Fax: (202) 223-1966
Email: info@transafricaforum.org
Web: www.transafricaforum.org

WASHINGTON OFFICE ON AFRICA
212 E. Capitol St. NE
Washington, DC 20003
Jennifer Davis, Interim Executive Director
Tel: (202) 547-7503 Fax: (202) 547-7505
Email: woa@igc.org
Web: www.woaafrica.org

PROFESSIONAL

AMERICAN ASSOCIATION OF BLACKS IN ENERGY
Philadelphia Chapter
3665 Eveline St.
Philadelphia, DC 19129
Pamela Moss, President
Tel: (215) 844-7527 Fax: (215) 844-7527
Email: dysolutions@aol.com
Web: www.aabe-phl.org

Washington, DC Metropolitan Chapter
927 15th St. NW #200
Washington, DC 20005
Joyce Hayes-Giles, Secretary
Tel: (202) 371-9530
Web: www.aabe.org

AMERICAN BLACK CHIROPRACTIC ASSOCIATION
1234 19th St. #801 NW
Washington, DC 20036
Alison Henderson, Committee Chairman
Tel: (202) 293-2225 Fax: (202) 293-7694
Web: www.abchiro.org

AMERICAN SOCIETY FOR PUBLIC ADMINISTRATION
Conference of Minority Public Administrators
1120 G St. NW #700
Washington, DC 20005
Antoinette Samuel, Executive Director
Tel: (202) 393-7878   Fax: (202) 638-4952
Email: info@aspanet.org
Web: www.aspanet.org

ASSOCIATION OF BLACK PSYCHOLOGISTS
National Office
P.O. Box 55999
Washington, DC 20040-5999
James Savage Jr., National President
Tel: (202) 722-0808 Fax: (202) 722-5941
Email: admin@abpsi.org
Web: www.abpsi.org

BLACK DATA PROCESSING ASSOCIATES
Washington Chapter
P.O. Box 2420
Washington, DC 20013-2420
Gwendolyn Hunnicutt, President
Tel: (202) 659-5367
Email: president@bdpa-dc.org
Web: www.bdpa-dc.org

CONFERENCE OF MINORITY TRANSPORTATION OFFICIALS
National Office
818 18th St. NW #850
Washington, DC 20006
Julie A. Cunningham, Executive Director/CEO
Tel: (202) 530-0551 X11 Fax: (202) 530-0617
Email: comto@comto.org
Web: www.comto.org

Washington, DC Chapter
WMATA, 600 5th St. NW
Washington, DC 20001
Bea Hicks, Chief Operations Liaison
Tel: (202) 962-1106 Fax: (202) 962-1436
Email: bhicks@wmata.com
Web: www.comto.org

IOTA PHI LAMBDA SORORITY, INC.
Gamma Chapter
P.O. Box 56293
Washington, DC 20040-6293
Leshaun Moy

Tel: (301) 603-0507
Email: mizziota1929@yahoo.com
Web: www.iota1929.org

NATIONAL ALLIANCE OF BLACK SCHOOL EDUCATORS
310 Pennsylvania Ave. SE
Washington, DC 20003
Quentin R. Lawson, Executive Director
Tel: (202) 608-6310 Fax: (202) 608-6319
Email: qlawson@nabse.org
Web: www.nabse.org

NATIONAL ALLIANCE OF POSTAL AND FEDERAL EMPLOYEES
1628 11th St. NW
Washington, DC 20001
James M. McGee, President
Tel: (202) 939-6325 Fax: (202) 939-6389
Email: headquarters@napfe.org
Web: www.napfe.com

NATIONAL ASSOCIATION OF BLACK JOURNALISTS
Washington Chapter, Region III
P.O. Box 77130
Washington, DC 20013
Theola Labbe, Chapter President
Tel: (202) 334-5191
Email: labbet@washpost.com
Web: http://nabj-proxy.nandomedia.com

NATIONAL ASSOCIATION OF BLACK TELECOMMUNICATIONS PROFESSIONALS
2020 Pennsylvania Ave. NW Box 735
Washington, DC 20006
Colin O' Garo, President
Tel: (800) 946-6228
Email: president@nabtp.org
Web: www.nabtp.org

NATIONAL ASSOCIATION OF MINORITY CONTRACTORS
666 11th St. NW #520
Washington, DC 20001
Owen Tonkins, Executive Director
Tel: (202) 347-8259 Fax: (202) 628-1876
Email: national@namcline.org
Web: www.namcline.org

NATIONAL ASSOCIATION OF SECURITIES PROFESSIONALS
1212 New York Ave. NW #210
Washington, DC 20005-3987
Pamela K. Anderson, Executive Director
Tel: (202) 371-5535 Fax: (202) 371-5536
Email: info@nasphq.com
Web: www.nasphq.com

NATIONAL BANKERS ASSOCIATION
1513 P St. NW
Washington, DC 20005
Norma Alexander Hart, President
Tel: (202) 588-5432 Fax: (202) 588-5443
Email: nahart@nationalbankers.org
Web: www.nationalbankers.org

NATIONAL BEAUTY CULTURISTS' LEAGUE
25 Logan Cir. NW
Washington, DC 20005
Wanda J. Nelson, President
Tel: (202) 332-2695
Email: info@nbcl.org
Web: www.nbcl.org

NATIONAL BLACK MBA ASSOCIATION, INC.
Washington DC Chapter-East
P.O. Box 14042
Washington, DC 20044
Angela Van Croft, President
Tel: (202) 628-0138
Email: info@dcbmbaa.org
Web: www.dcbmbaa.org

NATIONAL BLACK POLICE ASSOCIATION, INC.
3251 Mt. Pleasant St. NW, 2nd Fl.
Washington, DC 20010
Ronald E. Hampton, Executive Director
Tel: (202) 986-2070 Fax: (202) 986-0410
Email: nbpanatofc@worldnet.att.net
Web: www.blackpolice.org

NATIONAL COALITION OF BLACKS FOR REPARATIONS IN AMERICA
P.O. Box 90604
Washington, DC 20090-0604
Hannibal T. Afrik, Co-Chair
Tel: (202) 291-8400 Fax: (202) 291-4600
Email: nationalncobra@aol.com
Web: www.ncobra.org

NATIONAL COALITION ON BLACK CIVIC PARTICIPATION, INC.
1900 L St. NW #700

Washington, DC 20036
Melanie L. Campbell, Executive Director/CEO
Tel: (202) 659-4929 Fax: (202) 659-5025
Email: ncbcp@ncbcp.org
Web: www.bigvote.org

NATIONAL DENTAL ASSOCIATION
3517 16th St. NW
Washington, DC 20010
Robert S. Johns, Executive Director
Tel: (202) 588-1697 Fax: (202) 588-1244
Email: admin@ndaonline.org
Web: www.ndaonline.org

NATIONAL FORUM FOR BLACK PUBLIC ADMINISTRATORS
National Office
777 N. Capitol St. NE #807
Washington, DC 20744
John E. Saunders, III, Executive Director
Tel: (202) 408-9300 Fax: (202) 408-8558
Email: jsaunders@nfbpa.org
Web: www.nfbpa.org

NATIONAL MEDICAL ASSOCIATION
National Headquarters
1012 10th St. NW
Washington, DC 20001
Winston Price, President
Tel: (202) 347-1895 Fax: (202) 898-2510
Email: president@nmanet.org
Web: www.nmanet.org

NATIONAL NEWSPAPER PUBLISHERS ASSOCIATION
3200 13th St. NW
Washington, DC 20010
George E. Curry, Acting Executive Director
Tel: (202) 588-8764 Fax: (202) 588-8960
Email: webmaster@nnpa.org
Web: www.nnpa.org

NATIONAL ORGANIZATION FOR THE PROFESSIONAL ADVANCEMENT OF BLACK CHEMISTS AND CHEMICAL ENGINEERS
National Office
P.O. Box 77040
Washington, DC 20013
Dr. Marquita Qualls, President
Tel: (202) 667-1699 Fax: (202) 667-1705
Email: president@nobcche.org
Web: www.nobcche.org

NATIONAL SALES NETWORK
Washington/Baltimore Chapter
2117 L St. NW #317
Washington, DC 20037
Steven LaBroi, President
Tel: (202) 331-4407 Fax: (202) 544-7887
Email: nsn_dcbaltimore@hotmail.com
Web: www.nsndcbaltimore.org

ORGANIZATION OF BLACK DESIGNERS
300 M St. SW #N110
Washington, DC 20024-4019
Shauna Stallworth, Executive Director
Tel: (202) 488-1530 Fax: (202) 488-3838
Email: obdesign@aol.com
Web: www.core77.com/obd

RELIGIOUS

CATHOLICS FOR A FREE CHOICE
1436 U St. NW #301
Washington, DC 20009-3997
Frances Kissling, President
Tel: (202) 986-6093 Fax: (202) 332-7995
Email: cffc@catholicsforchoice.org
Web: www.catholicsforchoice.org

MISSIONARIES TO AFRICA
1624 21st St. NW
Washington, DC 20009
Rev. Richard Roy, Director
Tel: (202) 232-5154 Fax: (202) 332-8640

NATIONAL BLACK SISTERS CONFERENCE
101 Q St. NE
Washington, DC 20002-2166
Sr. Donna Banfield, SBS, President
Tel: (202) 529-9250 Fax: (202) 529-9370
Email: nbsc@igc.org
Web: http://nbsc68.tripod.com

NATIONAL UNITED CHURCH USHERS ASSOCIATION OF AMERICA, INC.
3298 Ft. Lincoln Dr. NE #1012
Washington, DC 20018-4342
Raymond W. Hall, Meetings/Conventions Coordinator
Tel: (202) 722-1192 Fax: (301) 588-0011
Email: ushers@ureach.com

PROGRESSIVE NATIONAL BAPTIST CONVENTION, INC.
601 50th St. NE

Washington, DC 20019
Dr. Major Lewis Jemison, President
Tel: (202) 396-0558 Fax: (202) 398-4998
Email: info@pnbc.org
Web: www.pnbc.org

UNITED STATES CONFERENCE OF CATHOLIC BISHOPS
Secretariat for African American Catholics
3211 4th St. NE
Washington, DC 20017-1194
Beverly A. Carroll, Executive Director
Tel: (202) 541-3177 Fax: (202) 541-3477
Email: saac@usccb.org
Web: www.nccbuscc.org/saac/index.htm

RESEARCH

AFRICA CENTER FOR STRATEGIC STUDIES
National Defense University, 300 5th Ave., Bldg. 62
Fort McNair
Washington, DC 20319-5066
General Carlton W. Fulford, Director
Tel: (202) 685-7300 Fax: (202) 685-3210
Web: www.africacenter.org

AMERICAN ASSOCIATION FOR THE ADVANCEMENT OF SCIENCE
Education and Human Resources
1200 New York Ave. NW
Washington, DC 20005
Dr. Shirley Ann Jackson, President
Tel: (202) 326-6640 Fax: (202) 371-9526
Email: membership@aaas.org
Web: www.aaas.org

CENTER FOR SICKLE CELL DISEASE
Howard University
2121 Georgia Ave. NW
Washington, DC 20059
Dr. Oswaldo Castro, Director
Tel: (202) 806-7930 Fax: (202) 806-4517
Email: ocastro@howard.edu

COUNCIL ON FOREIGN RELATIONS-A CENTER FOR THE STUDY AND PRACTICE OF INTERNATIONAL AFFAIRS AND U.S. FOREIGN POLICY
Washington Office
1779 Massachusetts Ave. NW #710
Washington, DC 20036
Nancy Roman, Vice President/Director
Tel: (202) 518-3400 Fax: (202) 986-2984
Email: dcmeetings@cfr.org
Web: www.cfr.org

JOINT CENTER FOR POLITICAL AND ECONOMIC STUDIES
1090 Vermont Ave. NW #1100
Washington, DC 20005
Togo Dennis West Jr., President/CEO
Tel: (202) 789-3500 Fax: (202) 789-6390
Email: jjoyner@jointcenter.org
Web: www.jointcenter.org

MOORLAND-SPINGARN RESEARCH CENTER
Howard University
500 Howard Pl. NW, #120, Founders Library
Washington, DC 20059
Dr. Thomas C. Battle, Director
Tel: (202) 806-7239 Fax: (202) 806-6405
Email: ranthony@howard.edu
Web: www.founders.howard.edu/moorland-spingarn

SCIENTIFIC

MEDICO-CHIRURGICAL SOCIETY OF THE DISTRICT OF COLUMBIA, INC.
P.O. Box 77013
Washington, DC 20013-8013
Theresa Greene Reed, MD, President
Tel: (202) 347-4170

SPEC. INT., AIDS

NATIONAL MINORITY AIDS COUNCIL
1931 13th St. NW
Washington, DC 20009
Paul Akio Kawata, Executive Director
Tel: (202) 483-6622 X321 Fax: (202) 483-1135
Email: pkawata@nmac.org
Web: www.nmac.org

SPEC. INT., ALCOHOL/DRUG CTR.

REGIONAL ADDICTION PREVENTION
1949 4th St. NE
Washington, DC 20002
Ron Clark, President
Tel: (202) 462-7500 Fax: (202) 526-8916
Email: rapinc2@bellatlantic.net

SPEC. INT., CHILD CARE

GAP COMMUNITY CHILD CARE CENTER
3636 16th St. NW #A131
Washington, DC 20010
Monica Guyot, Executive Director
Tel: (202) 462-3636
Email: guyotmonica@hotmail.com
Web: www.gapccc.org

SPEC. INT., EDUCATION

ACADEMY FOR EDUCATIONAL DEVELOPMENT
Headquarters, Public Policy and International
Affairs Fellowship Program
1825 Connecticut Ave. NW
Washington, DC 20009-5721
Stephen F. Moseley, President/CEO
Tel: (202) 884-8000 Fax: (202) 884-8400
Email: admindc@aed.org
Web: www.aed.org

AMERICAN COUNCIL ON EDUCATION
Center for Advancement of Racial and Ethnic Equity
1 Dupont Cir. NW #800
Washington, DC 20036
William B. Harvey, Vice President/Director
Tel: (202) 939-9395 Fax: (202) 785-2990
Email: career@ace.nche.edu
Web: www.acenet.edu

ASSOCIATION OF SCIENCE-TECHNOLOGY CENTERS
Partnership For Learning Program
1025 Vermont Ave. NW #500
Washington, DC 20005-6310
Bonnie Van Dorn, Executive Director
Tel: (202) 783-7200 Fax: (202) 783-7207
Email: bvandorn@astc.org
Web: www.astc.org

CITIWIDE COMPUTER TRAINING CENTER
3636 16th St. NW #BG-41
Washington, DC 20010
Anthony Chuukwu, Executive Director
Tel: (202) 667-3719 Fax: (202) 667-0554
Email: info@mycitiwide.com
Web: www.mycitiwide.com

COUNCIL OF INDEPENDENT BLACK INSTITUTIONS
770 Park Rd. NW
Washington, DC 20010-1518
Agyei Akota
Tel: (202) 291-5600
Email: contact@cibi.org
Web: www.cibi.org

DELTA RESEARCH AND EDUCATIONAL FOUNDATION
1707 New Hampshire Ave. NW
Washington, DC 20009
Mona H. Bailey, President
Tel: (202) 347-1337 Fax: (202) 347-5091
Email: dref@deltafoundation.net
Web: www.deltafoundation.net

EDUCATION AFRICA USA, INC.
1627 K St. NW #901
Washington, DC 20006
Walker Williams, Director
Tel: (202) 296-1974 Fax: (202) 296-7908
Email: ama3@idt.net
Web: www.educationafrica.org

METROPOLITAN CONSORTIUM FOR MINORITIES IN ENGINEERING
Howard University
College of Engineering, Architecture and Computer Science, 2400 6th St. NW #1114
Washington, DC 20059
Jean Louis Turner, Coordinator of Pre-College Programs
Tel: (202) 806-5524 Fax: (202) 806-4853
Email: j_turner@howard.edu
Web: www.howard.edu

NATIONAL ASSOCIATION FOR MULTICULTURAL EDUCATION
733 15th St. NW #430
Washington, DC 20005
Joyce E. Harris, Executive Director
Tel: (202) 628-6263 Fax: (202) 628-6264
Email: name@nameorg.org
Web: www.nameorg.org

NATIONAL ASSOCIATION OF STATE UNIVERSITIES AND LAND-GRANT COLLEGES
1307 New York Ave. NW #400
Washington, DC 20005-4722
C. Peter Magrath, President
Tel: (202) 478-6040 Fax: (202) 478-6046
Email: pmagrath@nasulgc.org
Web: www.nasulgc.org

NATIONAL MINORITY ORGAN TISSUE TRANSPLANT EDUCATION PROGRAM
National Office
2041 Georgia Ave. NW #3100
Washington, DC 20060
Clive O. Callender, M.D., FACS, Founder
Tel: (202) 865-4888 Fax: (202) 865-4880
Email: ccallender@nationalmottep.org
Web: www.nationalmottep.org

PHELPS-STOKES FUND
1420 K St. NW #800
Washington, DC 20005
Badi Foster, President
Tel: (202) 371-9544 Fax: (202) 371-9522
Email: contact@psfdc.org
Web: www.psfdc.org

THE BLACK STUDENT FUND
3636 16th St. NW, 4th Fl.
Washington, DC 20010
Barbara Patterson, President
Tel: (202) 387-1414 Fax: (202) 387-6237
Email: mail@blackstudentfund.org
Web: www.blackstudentfund.org

SPEC. INT., EMPLOYMENT

CONFERENCE OF MINORITY PUBLIC ADMINISTRATORS
1120 G St. NW #700
Washington, DC 20036
Antoinette Samuel, Executive Director
Tel: (202) 393-7878 Fax: (202) 639-4952
Web: www.natcompa.org

EMMA L. BOWEN FOUNDATION FOR MINORITY INTERESTS IN MEDIA, INC.
1299 Pennsylvania Ave. NW, 11th Fl.
Washington, DC 20004
Phylis Eagle-Oldson, President/CEO
Tel: (202) 637-4494 Fax: (202) 637-4495
Email: phylis.eagle-oldson@corporate.ge.com
Web: www.emmabowenfoundation.com

JUBILEE JOBS, INC.
2712 Ontario Rd. NW
Washington, DC 20009
Terry Flood, Executive Director
Tel: (202) 667-8970 Fax: (202) 667-8833
Email: info@jubileejobs.org
Web: www.jubileejobs.org

NATIONAL ASSOCIATION OF AFRICAN AMERICANS IN HUMAN RESOURCES
P.O. Box 11467
Washington, DC 20008
Joanne Robinson, President
Tel: (310) 330-0540 Fax: (310) 330-0540
Email: naaahr@naaahr.org
Web: www.naaahr.org

SPEC. INT., FAMILY PLANNING

NATIONAL HOOK-UP OF BLACK WOMEN, INC.
District of Columbia Chapter
P.O. Box 60640
Washington, DC 20019
Cathy Borris-Hale, President
Tel: (202) 271-3328
Email: cbhale@provhosp.org
Web: www.nhbwinc.com

SPEC. INT., HEALTH SERVICES

ASSOCIATION OF MINORITY HEALTH PROFESSIONS SCHOOLS
507 Capital Ct. NE #200
Washington, DC 20002
John Maupin, President
Tel: (202) 544-7499 Fax: (202) 546-7105

LUPUS FOUNDATION OF AMERICA, INC.
2000 L St. NW #710
Washington, DC 20036
Sandra Raymond, President
Tel: (202) 349-1155 Fax: (202) 349-1156
Email: info@lupus.org
Web: www.lupus.org

NATIONAL BLACK WOMEN'S HEALTH PROJECT
600 Pennsylvania Ave. SE #310
Washington, DC 20003
Lorraine Cole, President/CEO
Tel: (202) 543-9311 Fax: (202) 543-9743
Email: nbwhp@nbwhp.org
Web: www.blackwomenshealth.org

STUDENT NATIONAL MEDICAL ASSOCIATION
National Headquarters
5113 Georgia Ave. NW
Washington, DC 20011

Aaron Horne, Jr., National President
Tel: (202) 882-2881 Fax: (202) 882-2886
Email: snmamain@msn.com
Web: www.snma.org

WHITMAN-WALKER CLINIC
1407 S St. NW
Washington, DC 20009
A. Cornelius Baker, Executive Director
Tel: (202) 797-3500 Fax: (202) 797-3504
Email: wwcinfo@wwc.org
Web: www.wwc.org

SPEC. INT., HOUSING

NATIONAL HOUSING CONFERENCE
1801 K St. NW #M100
Washington, DC 20006-1306
Conrad Egen, President/CEO
Tel: (202) 466-2121 Fax: (202) 466-2122
Email: nhc@nhc.org
Web: www.nhc.org

NATIONAL LOW INCOME HOUSING COALITION
1012 14th St. NW #610
Washington, DC 20005
Sheila Crowley, President
Tel: (202) 662-1530 Fax: (202) 393-1973
Email: info@nlihc.org
Web: www.nlihc.org

SPEC. INT., HUMAN RELATIONS

AFRICAN AMERICAN REPUBLIC LEADERSHIP COUNCIL
1201 Pennsylvania Ave. NW #300
Washington, DC 20004
Alex St. James, Chairman
Tel: (202) 675-8338 Fax: (202) 661-4699
Email: info@aarlc.org
Web: www.aarlc.org

AMIDEAST
Headquarters
1730 M St. NW #1100
Washington, DC 20036-4505
Ambassador Theodore H. Kattouf, President/CEO
Tel: (202) 776-9600 Fax: (202) 776-7000
Email: inquiries@amideast.org
Web: www.amideast.org

CARNEGIE ENDOWMENT FOR INTERNATIONAL PEACE
1779 Massachusetts Ave. NW
Washington, DC 20036-2103
Jessica T. Mathews, President
Tel: (202) 483-7600 Fax: (202) 483-1840
Email: info@ceip.org
Web: www.ceip.org

INSTITUTE OF INTERNATIONAL EDUCATION
1400 K St. NW #650
Washington, DC 20005
Cheryl Sentino, Administrative Officer
Tel: (202) 898-0600 Fax: (202) 326-7835
Email: csentino@iie.org
Web: www.iie.org

SPEC. INT., LEGAL ASSISTANCE

MINORITY BUSINESS ENTERPRISE LEGAL DEFENSE AND EDUCATION FUND
419 New Jersey Ave. SE
Washington, DC 20003
Anthony W. Robinson, President
Tel: (202) 289-1700 Fax: (202) 289-1701
Email: arobinson@mbeldef.org
Web: www.mbeldef.org

SPEC. INT., SENIORS

NATIONAL CAUCUS AND CENTER ON BLACK AGED ESTATES
2801 14th St. NW
Washington, DC 20009
Neeve Wallace, Manager
Tel: (202) 387-4022 Fax: (202) 462-8403
Email: ncbahsng@aol.com

NATIONAL CAUCUS AND CENTER ON BLACK AGED, INC.
Headquarters
1220 L St. NW #800
Washington, DC 20005
Karyne Jones, President/CEO
Tel: (202) 637-8400 Fax: (202) 347-0895
Email: info@ncba-aged.org
Web: www.ncba-aged.org

SPEC. INT., SOCIAL INTEREST

100 BLACK MEN OF GREATER WASHINGTON, D.C.
P.O. Box 70558
Washington, DC 20024
Barry L. Hudson, Chapter President
Tel: (202) 289-8884
Email: info@100blackmendc.org
Web: www.100blackmendc.org

AFRICA FAITH AND JUSTICE NETWORK
3035 4th St. NE
Washington, DC 20017
Marcel Kitissou, Executive Director
Tel: (202) 832-3412 Fax: (202) 832-9051
Email: afjn@afjn.org
Web: http://afjn.cua.edu

AFRICAN WILDLIFE FOUNDATION
1400 16th St. NW #120
Washington, DC 20036
Patrick J. Bergin, President/CEO
Tel: (202) 939-3333 Fax: (202) 939-3332
Email: africanwildlife@awf.org
Web: www.awf.org

AFRICARE
440 R St. NW
Washington, DC 20001
Julius E. Coles, President
Tel: (202) 462-3614 Fax: (202) 387-1034
Email: africare@africare.org
Web: www.africare.org

ARK FOUNDATION OF AFRICA
5421 5th St. NW
Washington, DC 20011
Rhoi Wangila, Executive Director
Tel: (202) 832-5420 Fax: (202) 829-5596
Email: info@arkafrica.org
Web: www.arkafrica.org

BLACK LEADERSHIP FORUM, INC.
1900 L St. NW #405
Washington, DC 20036
Dr. Joe Leonard, Executive Director/COO
Tel: (202) 659-1881 Fax: (202) 659-1711
Email: info@blackleadershipforum.org
Web: www.blackleadershipforum.org

CONSTITUENCY FOR AFRICA
Headquarters
315 F St. NE #101
Washington, DC 20002
Melvin P. Foote, President/CEO
Tel: (202) 371-0588 Fax: (202) 371-9017
Email: mfoote2420@aol.com
Web: www.cfanet.org

DC HABITAT FOR HUMANITY
P.O. Box 43565
Washington, DC 20010-9998
Carol Casperson, Executive Director
Tel: (202) 882-4600 Fax: (202) 882-9343
Email: info@dchabitat.org
Web: www.dchabitat.org

FRIENDS OF LIBERIA
Head Office
4300 16th St. NW
Washington, DC 20011
Frank Ardaiolo, Chairman of the Board
Tel: (202) 545-0139 Fax: (202) 545-0139
Email: liberia@fol.org
Web: www.fol.org

FRIENDS OF SIERRA LEONE
P.O. Box 15875
Washington, DC 20003-0875
Mike Diliberti, President
Tel: (202) 544-5063 Fax: (703) 426-9580
Email: info@fosalone.org
Web: www.fosalone.org

NATIONAL ASSOCIATION OF BLACK SOCIAL WORKERS, INC.
Washington D.C. Chapter
1220 11th St. NW #2
Washington, DC 20001
Judith Jackson, President
Tel: (202) 589-1850 Fax: (202) 589-1853
Email: nabsw.harambee@verizon.net
Web: www.nabsw.org

NATIONAL ASSOCIATION OF NEIGHBORHOODS
1300 Pennsylvania Ave. NW #700
Washington, DC 20004
Ricardo C. Byrd, Executive Director
Tel: (202) 332-7766 Fax: (202) 332-2314
Email: staff@nanworld.org
Web: www.nanworld.org

NATIONAL BLACK CHILD DEVELOPMENT INSTITUTE
1101 15th St. NW #900
Washington, DC 20005
Evelyn K. Moore, President
Tel: (202) 833-2220 Fax: (202) 833-8222
Email: moreinfo@nbcdi.org
Web: www.nbcdi.org

NATIONAL MULTICULTURAL INSTITUTE
3000 Connecticut Ave. NW #438
Washington, DC 20008-2556
Elizabeth Pathy Salett, President
Tel: (202) 483-0700 Fax: (202) 483-5233
Email: nmci@nmci.org
Web: www.nmci.org

NATIONAL ORGANIZATION CONCERNED BLACK MEN, INC.
Washington, DC Chapter
1816 12th St. NW #204
Washington, DC 20009
George L. Garrow, Jr., Executive Director
Tel: (202) 783-6119 Fax: (202) 783-2480
Email: info@cbmnational.org
Web: www.cbmnational.org

NATIONAL URBAN LEAGUE
The Greater Washington Urban League
3501 14th St.
Washington, DC 20010
Maudine R. Cooper, President/CEO
Tel: (202) 265-8200 Fax: (202) 265-6122
Email: luwgdbs@aol.com
Web: www.gwul.org

RAINBOW/PUSH COALITION
Washington Bureau
1131 8th St. NE
Washington, DC 20002
Gary Flowers, Executive Director
Tel: (202) 547-3235 Fax: (202) 547-7397
Email: cgass@rainbowpush.org
Web: www.rainbowpush.org

UNITED BLACK FUND, INC.
P.O. Box 7051
Washington, DC 20032
Wilhelmina J. Rolark Esq., President/CEO
Tel: (202) 783-9300 Fax: (202) 347-2564
Email: unitedblackfund@ubfinc.org
Web: www.ubfinc.org

SPEC. INT., SPORTS

THE NATIONAL ASSOCIATION OF BLACK SCUBA DIVERS, INC.
P.O. Box 91630
Washington, DC 20090-1630
Sujon Low, President
Tel: (800) 521-6227 Fax: (202) 526-2907
Email: pres@nabsdivers.org
Web: www.nabsdivers.org

SPEC. INT., VOLUNTARY SERVICE

AUXILIARY TO THE NATIONAL MEDICAL ASSOCIATION, INC.
National Office
1012 10th St. NW
Washington, DC 20001
Dorothy Jean Smith, President
Tel: (202) 371-1674 Fax: (202) 289-2662
Email: anma2@earthlink.net
Web: www.anma-online.org

SPEC. INT., WOMEN

AFRICAN WOMEN'S MEDIA CENTER
Project of International Women's Media Center
1625 K St. NW #1275
Washington, DC 20006
Deborah Howell, Vice Chair
Tel: (202) 496-1992 Fax: (202) 496-1977
Email: info@awmc.com
Web: www.awmc.com

BLACK WOMEN'S AGENDA
1090 Vermont Ave. NW #800
Washington, DC 20005
Sonia Jarvis, President
Tel: (202) 216-5797 Fax: (202) 408-9888
Email: dottiebwa@aol.com
Web: www.blackwomensagenda.org

LINKS, INC.
1200 Massachusetts Ave. NW
Washington, DC 20005
Mary Clark, Executive Director
Tel: (202) 842-8686 Fax: (202) 842-4020
Email: mary.clark@linksinc.org
Web: www.linksinc.org

NATIONAL ASSOCIATION OF NEGRO BUSINESS AND PROFESSIONAL WOMEN'S CLUBS, INC.
1806 New Hampshire Ave. NW
Washington, DC 20009
Peola Smith-Smith, National President
Tel: (202) 483-4206 Fax: (202) 462-7253
Email: nanbpwc@aol.com
Web: www.nanbpwc.org

NATIONAL ASSOCIATION OF UNIVERSITY WOMEN
1001 E St. SE
Washington, DC 20003
Dr. Lenore R. Gall, President
Tel: (202) 547-3967 Fax: (202) 547-5226

NATIONAL ASSOCIATION OF WOMEN JUDGES
National Office
1112 16th St. NW #520
Washington, DC 20036
Sandra Thompson, President
Tel: (202) 393-0222 Fax: (202) 393-0125
Email: nawj@nawj.org
Web: www.nawj.org

NATIONAL WOMEN'S POLITICAL CAUCUS
National Headquarters
1634 Eye St. NW #310
Washington, DC 20006
Roselyn O' Connell, President
Tel: (202) 785-1100 Fax: (202) 785-3605
Email: info@nwpc.org
Web: www.nwpc.org

THE NATIONAL COUNCIL OF NEGRO WOMEN, INC.
633 Pennsylvania Ave. NW
Washington, DC 20004
Cheryl R. Cooper, Executive Director
Tel: (202) 737-0120 Fax: (202) 737-0476
Email: ccooper@ncnw.org
Web: www.ncnw.org

SPEC. INT., YOUTH

AMERICAN COUNCIL OF YOUNG POLITICAL LEADERS
1612 K St. NW #300
Washington, DC 20006
Brad Minnick, Executive Director
Tel: (202) 857-0999 Fax: (202) 857-0027
Email: info@acypl.org
Web: www.acypl.org

BLACK ADMINISTRATORS IN CHILD WELFARE, INC.
440 1st St. NW, 3rd Fl.
Washington, DC 20001
Sondra M. Jackson, Executive Director
Tel: (202) 662-4284 Fax: (202) 638-4004
Email: rgraham@cwla.org
Web: www.blackadministrators.org

CHILDREN'S DEFENSE FUND
National Headquarters
25 E St. NW
Washington, DC 20001
Marian Wright Edelman, President
Tel: (202) 628-8787 Fax: (202) 662-3580
Email: cdinfo@childrensdefense.org
Web: www.childrensdefense.org

JACK & JILL OF AMERICA, INC.
National Headquarters
1930 17th St. NW
Washington, DC 20009
Alice Leigh Peoples, National President
Tel: (202) 667-7010 Fax: (202) 667-6133
Email: jackandjill.inc@verizon.net
Web: www.jack-and-jill.org

NATIONAL CENTER FOR NEIGHBORHOOD ENTERPRISE
1424 16th St. NW #300
Washington, DC 20036
Robert L. Woodson, Sr., Founder/President
Tel: (202) 518-6500 Fax: (202) 588-0314
Email: info@ncne.com
Web: www.ncne.com

STUDENT ORGANIZATION

ALPHA KAPPA ALPHA SORORITY, INC.
Beta Lambda Chapter
4200 Connecticut Ave. NW
Washington, DC 20024
Kaya Keene, Chapter President
Web: www.aka1908.com

Omicron Pi Chapter
P.O. Box 77234
Washington, DC 20013
Lajwanne Lavergne, Chapter President
Web: www.aka1908.com

Rho Mu Omega Chapter
P.O. Box 91198
Washington, DC 20090
Mona Calhoun, Chapter President
Web: www.aka1908.com

Xi Omega Chapter
4411 14th St. NW
Washington, DC 20011
Phyllis E. Young, Chapter President
Web: www.aka1908.com

Xi Zeta Omega Chapter
P.O. Box 56492
Washington, DC 20011
Beverly Ann Fields, Esq., Chapter President
Tel: (202) 723-1111 Fax: (202) 723-1763
Web: www.aka1908.com

ALPHA PHI ALPHA FRATERNITY, INC.
Omicron Lambda Alpha Chapter, Howard University
P.O. Box 77422
Washington, DC 20013
Levonia C. Wiggins Jr., President
Email: ola_exec@yahoogroups.com
Web: www.ola1906.org

CHI ETA PHI SORORITY, INC.
National Headquarters
3029 13th St. NW
Washington, DC 20009
Carolyn W. Mosley, President
Tel: (202) 232-3858 Fax: (202) 232-3460
Email: chietaphi@erols.com
Web: www.chietaphi.com

DELTA SIGMA THETA SORORITY, INC.
Corporate Office
1707 New Hampshire Ave. NW
Washington, DC 20009
Dr. Louis A. Rice, National President
Tel: (202) 986-2400 Fax: (202) 986-2513
Email: dstemail@deltasigmatheta.org
Web: www.deltasigmatheta.org

LAMBDA KAPPA MU SORORITY, INC.
7302 Georgia Ave. NW #2
Washington, DC 20012
Catherine M. DeFord, Grand Basileus
Tel: (202) 829-2368
Email: admin@lkmsorority.org
Web: www.lkmsorority.org

NATIONAL BLACK GRADUATE STUDENT ASSOCIATION, INC.
Howard University Graduate School
MSC 590507 2400 6th St. NW
Washington, DC 20059
Marla Mitchell, President
Tel: (202) 806-7876 Fax: (202) 462-4053
Email: nationaloffice@nbgsa.org
Web: www.nbgsa.org

NATIONAL BLACK LAW STUDENTS ASSOCIATION
National Headquarters
1225 11th St. NW
Washington, DC 20001-4217
Christopher M. Chestnut, National Chair
Tel: (410) 486-6388 Fax: (202) 289-6170
Email: chair@nblsa.org
Web: www.nblsa.org

PHI BETA SIGMA FRATERNITY, INC.
National Office
145 Kennedy St. NW
Washington, DC 20011
Donald J. Jemison, National Executive Director
Tel: (202) 726-5434 Fax: (202) 882-1681
Email: president@pbs1914.org
Web: www.pbs1914.org

ZETA PHI BETA SORORITY, INC.
1734 New Hampshire Ave. NW
Washington, DC 20009
Lois H. Sylver, Executive Director
Tel: (202) 387-3103 Fax: (202) 232-4593
Email: info@zetaphibetasororityhq.org
Web: www.zphib1920.org

FLORIDA

BUSINESS

BLACK BUSINESS INVESTMENT FUND
315 E. Robinson St. #660
Orlando, FL 32801
Inez Long, President
Tel: (407) 649-4780 Fax: (407) 649-8688
Email: info@bbif.org
Web: www.bbif.org

NATIONAL MINORITY SUPPLIER DEVELOPMENT COUNCIL, INC.
National Minority Supplier Development Council of Florida, Inc., Regional Council
6880 Lake Ellenor Dr. #104A
Orlando, FL 32809
Malik Ali, Executive Director
Tel: (407) 245-6062 Fax: (407) 857-8647
Email: info@fmsdc.com
Web: www.nmsdcfl.com

NATIONAL MINORITY SUPPLIER DEVELOPMENT COUNCIL, INC.
The Florida Regional Minority Business Council, Inc.
600 NW 79th Ave. #136
Miami, FL 33126-4018
Beatrice Louissaint, President/CEO
Tel: (305) 260-9901 Fax: (305) 260-9902
Email: frmbc@frmbc.org
Web: www.frmbc.org

ENTERTAINMENT

NATIONAL AFRICAN AMERICAN RV'ERS ASSOCIATION
US Club
3982 SW 139th St.
Ocala, FL 34473
Naomi Atwater, President
Tel: (352) 245-1506
Email: jasperjbag@aol.com
Web: www.naarva.com

LAW ENFORCEMENT

NATIONAL ORGANIZATION OF BLACK LAW ENFORCEMENT EXECUTIVES
Central Florida Chapter
Palmetto Police Department 1115 10th St. West
Palmetto, FL 34221
Garry Lowe, President
Tel: (941) 737-1989
Email: chief@ypalmettopolice.com
Web: www.noblenatl.org

North Florida Chapter
FSU Police Department, 9110 Seafair Ln.
Tallahassee, FL 32311
Carey Drayton, President
Tel: (850) 644-1348 Fax: (850) 922-6598
Email: cdrayton@admin.fsu.edu
Web: www.noblenatl.org

South Florida Chapter
P.O. Box 521145
Miami-Dade Schools Police Department
Miami, FL 33152
Gerald L. Darling, President
Tel: (305) 795-2313
Email: gdarling@dadeschools.net
Web: www.noblenatl.org

MULTI-PURPOSE

AFRICAN FINANCE AND ECONOMICS ASSOCIATION
University of South Florida-Deparment of Economics
4202 E. Flower Ave. BSN 3432
Tampa, FL 33620
Sylvain Boko, President
Tel: (813) 974-6520 Fax: (813) 947-6510
Email: kgyimah@coba.usf.edu
Web: www.afea.org

NATIONAL ASSOCIATION FOR THE ADVANCEMENT OF COLORED PEOPLE
Fort Lauderdale Branch
1409 Sistrunk Blvd.
Fort Lauderdale, FL 33311
Marsha Allison, Chapter President
Tel: (954) 764-7604 Fax: (954) 467-8303
Email: info@ournaacp.com
Web: www.naacpftlaud.com

POLITICAL ACTION

AMERICAN CIVIL LIBERTIES UNION
Florida Chapter
4500 Biscayne Blvd. #340
Miami, FL 33137
Howard Simon, Executive Director
Tel: (305) 576-2336 Fax: (305) 576-1106
Email: aclufl@aclufl.org
Web: www.aclufl.org

ASSOCIATION OF COMMUNITY ORGANIZATIONS FOR REFORM NOW
Florida
1380 W. Flagler St.
Miami, FL 33135

Tel: (305) 644-3005 Fax: (305) 644-6091
Email: flacorn@acorn.org
Web: www.acornfl.org

1830 49th St. South
St. Petersburg, FL 33707
Tel: (727) 327-6869 Fax: (727) 327-7869
Email: flacornho@acorn.org
Web: www.acorn.org

1702 N. Avenida Republica de Cuba
Tampa, FL 33605
Tel: (813) 241-6333 Fax: (813) 241-6336
Email: flacorntaro@acorn.org
Web: www.acorn.org

BLACKS IN GOVERNMENT
Region IV-Central Florida Chapter
P.O. Box 140371
Orlando, FL 32814
Earlene Knight, Chapter President
Tel: (407) 646-4148
Email: earlene.l.knight@dfas.mil
Web: www.bignet.org

Region IV-Gainsville Metro Chapter
P.O. Box 373
Gainsville, FL 32602
Eddie Cummings, Chapter President
Tel: (352) 376-7414
Email: mreddiec@hotmail.com
Web: www.bignet.org

Region IV-Pensacola Chapter
502 N. Green St.
Pensacola, FL 32505
James Welcome, Chapter President
Tel: (850) 452-5990 X127
Email: jr.welcome@cnet.navy.mil
Web: www.bignet.org

NATIONAL ACTION NETWORK
Florida Chapter
3520 W. Broward Blvd. #218-B
Ft. Lauderdale, FL 33312
Andrew Ingraham, State Chair of Florida
Tel: (954) 792-9037 Fax: (954) 337-2877
Email: horizons@gate.net
Web: www.africanamericantravel.com

PROFESSIONAL

AMERICAN ASSOCIATION OF BLACKS IN ENERGY
Florida Chapter
P.O. Box 111
Tampa, FL 33601-0111
Darryl H. Scott, President
Tel: (813) 641-5102
Email: dhscott@tecoenergy.com
Web: www.aabe-fl.org

ASSOCIATION OF BLACK PSYCHOLOGISTS
Jacksonville Chapter
P.O. Box 61474
Jacksonville, FL 32236
Dr. Larry T. Richardson, Chapter President
Tel: (904) 378-9955 Fax: (904) 378-9922
Email: ibhcltr@aol.com
Web: www.abpsi.org

CONFERENCE OF MINORITY TRANSPORTATION OFFICIALS
Jacksonville Chapter
Austin & Austin, 1400 Prudential Dr. #1
Jacksonville, FL 32207
Cynthia B. Austin, Esq., Chairperson
Tel: (904) 346-3001 Fax: (904) 346-3940
Email: cbaustin@bellsouth.net
Web: www.comto.org

Miami Chapter
Miami-Dade Transit, 1103 NW 195th Ave.
Pembroke Pines, FL 33029
Fitz McLymont, Sr. Network Manager
Tel: (305) 375-3648 Fax: (305) 375-1192
Email: fitz@miamidade.gov
Web: www.comto.org

NATIONAL ASSOCIATION OF BLACK ACCOUNTANTS, INC.
Tallahassee Chapter
P.O. Box 20745
Tallahassee, FL 32316-0745
Jonhy F. Session, President
Tel: (850) 891-8867 Fax: (850) 386-8349
Email: sessionj@talgov.com
Web: www.nabainc.org

NATIONAL ASSOCIATION OF BLACK JOURNALISTS
Central Florida Chapter-Region IV
P.O. Box 745
Orlando, FL 32801-0745
Tammy Carter, President

Tel: (407) 251-3919 Fax: (407) 420-5350
Email: tcarter@orlandosentinel.com
Web: www.geocities.com/cfabj/

Palm Beach, Region IV
P.O. Box 19533
West Palm Beach, FL 33416
Lady Hereford, Chapter President
Tel: (561) 820-4790 Fax: (561) 837-8312
Email: lhereford@pbpost.com
Web: www.nabj.org

NATIONAL BLACK MBA ASSOCIATION, INC.
Central Florida Chapter-South
P.O. Box 692696
Orlando, FL 32869-2696
Eugene Campbell, President
Tel: (407) 518-1721
Web: www.nbmbaa.org

South Florida-South
P.O. Box 694154
Miami, FL 33169-3250
Sam Hines, President
Tel: (305) 264-9200
Email: info@sfmba.com
Web: www.sfmba.com

NATIONAL FORUM FOR BLACK PUBLIC ADMINISTRATORS
South Florida Chapter
100 S. Andrews Ave., 8th Fl.
Fort Lauderdale, FL 33304
Sharon Woods, Chapter President
Tel: (561) 659-8029
Email: swoods@broward.org
Web: www.nfbpasouthflorida.org

Tampa Bay Area Chapter
601 E. Kennedy Blvd., 34th Fl.
Tampa, FL 33602
Joyce A. Russell, African American Liaison
Tel: (813) 276-2637 Fax: (813) 272-5851
Email: russellj@hillsboroughcounty.org
Web: www.nfbpa.org

NATIONAL SOCIETY OF BLACK ENGINEERS
Region 3-Embry-Riddle Aeronautical University Chapter
600 S. Clyde Morris Blvd.
Daytona Beach, FL 32114
Romar Fraizel, Finance Chairperson
Tel: (386) 226-6000
Email: romar19@hotmail.com
Web: www.db.erau.edu/campus/student/clubs/nsbe/mainpage.html

RESEARCH

AFRICAN AMERICAN SUCCESS FOUNDATION
4330 W. Broward Blvd. #H
Fort Lauderdale, FL 33317-3753
Dr. E. Carol Webster, President/CEO
Tel: (954) 792-1117 Fax: (954) 792-9191
Email: info@blacksuccessfoundation.org
Web: http://blacksuccessfoundation.org

AFRICAN-AMERICAN RESEARCH LIBRARY AND CULTURAL CENTER
c/o Von D. Mizell Branch Library
2650 Sistrunk Blvd.
Fort Lauderdale, FL 33311
Robert E. Canon, Director
Tel: (954) 625-2800
Email: aarlcc@browardlibrary.org
Web: www.broward.org/library/aarlcc.htm

SPEC. INT., ALCOHOL/DRUG CTR.

NATIONAL BLACK ALCOHOLISM AND ADDICTIONS COUNCIL, INC.
5104 N. Orange Blossom Trail #111
Orlando, FL 32810
Ed Young, Director
Tel: (407) 532-2747 Fax: (407) 532-2815
Email: mail@nbacinc.org
Web: www.nbacinc.org

SPEC. INT., CHILD CARE

NATIONAL CENTER FOR MISSING & EXPLOITED CHILDREN
Florida Office
9176 Alternate A1A #100
Lake Park, FL 33403-1445
Nancy Mcbride, Executive Director
Tel: (561) 848-1900 Fax: (561) 848-0308
Email: flbranch@ncmec.org
Web: www.missingkids.com

SPEC. INT., EDUCATION

FLORIDA EDUCATION FUND
201 E. Kennedy Blvd. #1525
Tampa, FL 33602
Charles E. Jackson, Program Manager/Development Specialist
Tel: (813) 272-2772 Fax: (813) 272-2784
Email: office@fefonline.org
Web: www.fefonline.org

NATIONAL ASSOCIATION FOR MULTICULTURAL EDUCATION
Florida Chapter
Nova Southeastern University, 1750 NE 167th St.
North Miami Beach, FL 33162-3017
Edna Suarez-Columba
Tel: (954) 262-8545
Email: suareze@nova.edu
Web: www.nameorg.org

SPEC. INT., EMPLOYMENT

FARMWORKER ASSOCIATION OF FLORIDA, INC.
815 S. Park Ave.
Apopka, FL 32703
Louise Seay, Vice President
Tel: (407) 886-5151 Fax: (407) 884-6644
Email: apopkafwaf@aol.com
Web: www.charityadvantage.com/thefarmworkerassociationofflorida

SPEC. INT., FAMILY PLANNING

NATIONAL HOOK-UP OF BLACK WOMEN, INC.
Gadsden Chapter
404 S. Stewart St.
Quincy, FL 32351
Alice C. DuPont, President
Tel: (850) 627-3494
Email: alicedu@netquincy.com
Web: www.nhbwinc.com

Orlando Chapter
1172 Jessamine Lake Ct.
Orlando, FL 32839
Jennifer L. Quash, President
Tel: (407) 858-0488
Email: jennifer.l.quash@lmco.com
Web: www.nhbwinc.com

Tallahassee Chapter
P.O. Box 6647
Tallahassee, FL 32314
Dr. Shirley A. Jones, President
Tel: (850) 893-1926
Email: dr_sajones@hotmail.com
Web: www.nhbwinc.com

SPEC. INT., HEALTH SERVICES

FLORIDA BLOOD SERVICES
National Marrow Donor Program
10100 9th St. North
St. Petersburg, FL 33716
Glorea Sadler, Recruitment Specialist (African American community)
Tel: (727) 656-1790 Fax: (727) 568-2175
Email: gsadler@fbsblood.org
Web: www.fbsblood.org

SPEC. INT., SOCIAL INTEREST

100 BLACK MEN OF GREATER GAINESVILLE, INC.
P.O. Box 109
Gainesville, FL 132602
Tommie C. Howard, Jr., President
Tel: (352) 392-1308 Fax: (352) 392-1352
Email: thoward@ufl.edu

100 BLACK MEN OF JACKSONVILLE, INC.
1336 W. Edgewood Blvd.
Jacksonville, FL 32208
Kenneth M. Pinnix, President
Tel: (904) 924-2545 Fax: (904) 924-2545
Email: info@jax100.org
Web: www.jax100.org

100 BLACK MEN OF ORLANDO, INC.
P.O. Box 547683
Orlando, FL 32804
Ronald Rogers, President
Tel: (407) 839-3838 Fax: (407) 839-3828
Email: rrogers@wrjinc.com
Web: www.100blackmen.org

100 BLACK MEN OF SOUTH FLORIDA, INC.
P.O. Box 970997
Miami, FL 33197-0997
Jonathan L. Dotson, President
Tel: (305) 620-2260 Fax: (954) 442-3968

Email: info@100blackmensf.org
Web: www.100blackmensf.org

NATIONAL URBAN LEAGUE, INC.
Jacksonville Urban League
903 W. Union St.
Jacksonville, FL 32204
Richard D. Danford, Jr., Ph.D., President/CEO
Tel: (904) 356-8336 Fax: (904) 356-8369
Email: r.danford@jaxul.com
Web: www.jaxul.org

Pinellas County Urban League
333 31st St. North
St. Petersburg, FL 33713
Herman L. Lessard, Jr., President/CEO
Tel: (727) 327-2081 Fax: (727) 321-8349
Email: jospcul@aol.com
Web: www.pcul.org

Tallahassee Urban League
923 Old Bainbridge Rd.
Tallahassee, FL 32303
Rev. Ernest Ferrell, President
Tel: (850) 222-6111 Fax: (850) 561-8390
Email: turbanleague@yahoo.com
Web: www.nul.org

Tampa-Hillsborough Urban League, Inc.
1405 Tampa Park Plz.
Tampa, FL 33605
Joanna N. Tokley, President/CEO
Tel: (813) 229-8117 Fax: (813) 221-3947
Email: info@tampaurbanleague.org

Urban League of Broward County
11 NW 36th Ave.
Fort Lauderdale, FL 33311
Donald E. Bowen, President
Tel: (954) 584-0777 Fax: (954) 584-4413
Email: ulbcfl@aol.com
Web: www.campaignforchange.org

Urban League of Greater Miami
8500 NW 25th Ave.
Miami, FL 33147
T. Willard Fair, President/CEO
Tel: (305) 696-4450 Fax: (305) 696-4455
Web: www.urbanleague.org

Urban League of Palm Beach County, Inc.
1700 N. Australian Ave.
West Palm Beach, FL 33407
Patrick Franklin, President
Tel: (561) 833-1461 Fax: (561) 833-6050
Email: frankln@ulpbc.org
Web: www.ulpbc.org

REAL MEN COOK FOR CHARITY
Miami
1490 NW 3rd Ave.
Miami, FL 33136
Von Carol Kinchens
Tel: (305) 372-4550
Email: info@realmencook.com
Web: www.realmencook.com

SPEC. INT., WOMEN

BLACK WOMEN OF ESSENCE, INC.
P.O. Box 471001
Lake Monroe, FL 32747
Renee G. Ellis, Founder/President
Tel: (321) 279-8784 Fax: (866) 380-3737
Email: reneeellis@bwoe.org
Web: www.bwoe.org

STUDENT ORGANIZATION

ALPHA KAPPA ALPHA SORORITY, INC.
Beta Alpha Chapter
P.O. Box 6621
Tallahassee, FL 32314
Jennifer P. Twitty, Chapter President
Web: www.aka1908.com

Beta Gamma Chapter
7726 Herrington Dr.
Pensacola, FL 32534
Cherl Powell, Chapter President
Web: www.aka1908.com

Delta Eta Chapter
10711 SW 152nd St.
Miami, FL 33157
Chenique D. Whitney, Chapter President
Web: www.aka1908.com

Delta Iota Omega Chapter
4829 Birchwood Pl.
Pensacola, FL 32503
Corrie B. Mumford, Chapter President
Web: www.aka1908.com

Delta Kappa Omega Chapter
P.O. Box 6278
Tallahassee, FL 32314

Lerosa V. Brown, Chapter President
Web: www.aka1908.com

Delta Omicron Omega Chapter
P.O. Box 555036
Orlando, FL 32855
Jeraldine Coleman Sims, Chapter President
Web: www.aka1908.com

Eta Eta Omega Chapter
P.O. Box 1375
Fort Pierce, FL 34954
Narvelene Tory Lucas, Chapter President
Web: www.aka1908.com

Eta Tau Omega Chapter
P.O. Box 5864
Ocala, FL 34478
Kathlyn C. Kiner, Chapter President
Web: www.aka1908.com

Gamma Mu Omega Chapter
P.O. Box 9185
Daytona, FL 32120
Sheila Davis Jackson, Chapter President
Web: www.aka1908.com

Gamma Rho Omega Chapter
1836 W. 41st St.
Jacksonville, FL 32209
Mary Madison, Chapter President
Web: www.aka1908.com

Gamma Tau Chapter, Bethune Cookman College
640 Mary McLeod Bethune Blvd. #649
Daytona Beach, FL 32114
Chanelle Wong, Chapter President
Web: www.aka1908.com

Gamma Theta Omega Chapter
P.O. Box 1246
Tampa, FL 33601
Grace R. Jones, Chapter President
Web: www.aka1908.com

Gamma Zeta Omega Chapter
P.O. Box 914
Dania Beach, FL 33004
Geraline Gilyard Ingraham, Chapter President
Web: www.aka1908.com

Iota Lambda Chapter
P.O. Box 118505
300-19 Reitz Union
Gainesville, FL 32611
Nona C. Collins, Chapter President
Web: www.aka1908.com

Iota Nu Chapter
P.O. Box 430303
South Miami, FL 33243
Latisha Rowe, Chapter President
Web: www.aka1908.com

Iota Pi Omega Chapter
P.O. Box 865
Cocoa, FL 32922
Charlotte H. Owens, Chapter President
Web: www.aka1908.com

Kappa Kappa Omega Chapter
P.O. Box 1522
Pompano Beach, FL 33061
Allison Brooks, Chapter President
Web: www.aka1908.com

Kappa Omicron Omega Chapter
P.O. Box 1824
Bartow, FL 33831
Virginia Cummings-Lang, Chapter President
Web: www.aka1908.com

Kappa Sigma Omega Chapter
P.O. Box 896
Sanford, FL 32772
Geraldine Wright, Chapter President
Web: www.aka1908.com

Lambda Omicron Omega Chapter
P.O. Box 302
Bradenton, FL 34206
Edwina Stanley, Chapter President
Web: www.aka1908.com

Mu Rho Omega Chapter
P.O. Box 1258
Belle Glade, FL 33430
Sharon Brown, Chapter President
Web: www.aka1908.com

Mu Theta Chapter, University of North Florida
6455 Manhattan Dr.
Jacksonville, FL 32219
Shartrice S. Dunn, Chapter President
Web: www.aka1908.com

Mu Upsilon Omega Chapter
P.O. Box 140562
Gainesville, FL 32614

Shirley Green Brown, Chapter President
Web: www.aka1908.com

Nu Beta Omega Chapter
P.O. Box 923
Clearwater, FL 33757
Myra Mcnary, Chapter President
Web: www.aka1908.com

Nu Iota Chapter, Edward Waters College
5246 Locksley Ave.
Jacksonville, FL 32208
Web: www.aka1908.com

Nu Iota Omega Chapter
P.O. Box 941953
Maitland, FL 32751
Marnita Bland, Chapter President
Web: www.aka1908.com

Nu Omega Omega Chapter
P.O. Box 322
Madison, FL 32341
Deloris Jones, Chapter President
Web: www.aka1908.com

Omicron Delta Chapter, Jacksonville University
7939 E. Sweet Rose Ln.
Jacksonville, FL 32244
Falynne P. Correia, Chapter President
Web: www.aka1908.com

Omicron Kappa Omega Chapter
P.O. Box 135
Lakeland, FL 33802
Vivian B. Underwood, Chapter President
Web: www.aka1908.com

Pi Delta Omega Chapter
P.O. Box 571028
Miami, FL 33257
Elsie Hamler, Chapter President
Web: www.aka1908.com

Pi Eta Omega Chapter
P.O. Box 994
Orange Park, FL 32067
Gwendolyn L. Hunter, Chapter President
Web: www.aka1908.com

Pi Psi Chapter, University of Central Florida
P.O. Box 163245
Orlando, FL 32816
Shequilla D. Hall, Chapter President
Web: www.aka1908.com

Sigma Omicron Omega Chapter
P.O. Box 2702
Fort Walton Beach, FL 32548
Elinor Campbell, Chapter President
Web: www.aka1908.com

Tau Chi Omega Chapter
P.O. Box 4322
Deland, FL 32721
Juanita McNeil, Chapter President
Web: www.aka1908.com

Tau Theta Omega Chapter
P.O. Box 984
Quincy, FL 32351
Pauline Levon Gunn, Chapter President
Web: www.aka1908.com

Theta Nu Omega Chapter
P.O. Box 1591
Fort Meyers, FL 33902
Rose Eady Govan, Chapter President
Web: www.aka1908.com

Upsilon Xi Omega Chapter
301 N. Pine Island Rd. #257
Plantation, FL 33324
Edith Gooden Thompson, Chapter President
Web: www.aka1908.com

Xi Omicron Omega Chapter
P.O. Box 926
Lynn Haven, FL 32444
Yvette N. Griffin, Chapter President
Web: www.aka1908.com

Xi Pi Omega Chapter
P.O. Box 1642
Delrey Beach, FL 33447
Candace Fennell-Johnson, Chapter President
Web: www.aka1908.com

Zeta Omicron Chapter, Florida State University
FSU, Box 67009
Tallahassee, FL 32313
Deshaun Wise, Chapter President
Web: www.aka1908.com

Zeta Rho Omega Chapter
P.O. Box 9811
Fort Lauderdale, FL 33308
Patricia Carter, Chapter President
Web: www.aka1908.com

Zeta Tau Omega Chapter
P.O. Box 426
West Palm Beach, FL 33402
Charline Curtis, Chapter President
Web: www.aka1908.com

Zeta Upsilon Omega Chapter
P.O. Box 15004
St. Petersburg, FL 33733
Lena Wilfalk, Chapter President
Web: www.aka1908.com

ALPHA PHI ALPHA FRATERNITY, INC.

Beta Beta Lambda Chapter
P.O. Box 510027
Miami, FL 33151
Web: www.alphaphialpha.net

Beta Delta Lambda Chapter
P.O. Box 9443
Daytona Beach, FL 32118
Web: www.alphaphialpha.net

Beta Nu Chapter, Florida A&M University
P.O. Box 6784
Tallahassee, FL 32314
Web: www.alphaphialpha.net

Delta Beta Chapter, Bethune-Cookman College
P.O. Box 834
Daytona Beach, FL 32114
Web: www.alphaphialpha.net

Delta Delta Lambda Chapter
P.O. Box 866
West Palm Beach, FL 33402
Web: www.alphaphialpha.net

Delta Psi Chapter, Florida Memorial College
15800 NW 42nd Ave.
Miami, FL 33054
Web: www.alphaphialpha.net

Delta Xi Lambda Chapter
P.O. Box 555548
Orlando, FL 32855
George Ward, President
Email: mail@alphaorlando.org
Web: www.alphaorlando.org

Epsilon Mu Lambda Chapter
P.O. Box 2325
Pensacola, FL 32513
Web: www.alphaphialpha.net

Epsilon Pi Lambda Chapter
1822 SW 4th St.
Ocala, FL 34474
Web: www.alphaphialpha.net

Eta Delta Chapter, University of Miami
P.O. Box 248587
Coral Gables, FL 33146
Web: www.alphaphialpha.net

Eta Kappa Lambda Chapter
P.O. Box 1271
Fort Pierce, FL 34954
Web: www.alphaphialpha.net

Gamma Mu Lambda Chapter
P.O. Box 5474
Tallahassee, FL 32314
Web: www.alphaphialpha.net

Gamma Zeta Lambda Chapter
P.O. Box 82102
Tampa, FL 33612
Web: www.alphaphialpha.net

Iota Beta Lambda Chapter
P.O. Box 1275
Cocoa, FL 32923
Web: www.alphaphialpha.net

Iota Delta Chapter, Florida State University
FSU, Box 67002
Tallahassee, FL 32313
Web: www.alphaphialpha.net

Iota Pi Lambda Chapter
P.O. Box 571098
Miami, FL 33257
Web: www.alphaphialpha.net

Kappa Upsilon Chapter
1658 Kings Rd.
Jacksonville, FL 32208
Web: www.alphaphialpha.net

Mu Theta Chapter, University of West Florida
11000 University Pkwy.
Pensacola, FL 32514
Web: www.alphaphialpha.net

Mu Zeta Lambda Chapter
P.O. Box 7538
Winter Haven, FL 33883
Web: www.alphaphialpha.net

Nu Eta Lambda Chapter
P.O. Box 178
Gainesville, FL 32602
Web: www.alphaphialpha.net

Omicron Beta Lambda Chapter
P.O. Box 10595
Clearwater, FL 34617
Web: www.alphaphialpha.net

Omicron Upsilon Lambda Chapter
P.O. Box 2597
Delray Beach, FL 33447
Web: www.alphaphialpha.net

Pi Psi Lambda Chapter
P.O. Box 768
Gretna, FL 32332
Web: www.alphaphialpha.net

Sigma Upsilon Chapter, University of North Florida
4567 St. John's Bluff
Jacksonville, FL 32224
Web: www.alphaphialpha.net

Theta Eta Lambda Chapter
P.O. Box 15024
St. Petersburg, FL 33733
Web: www.alphaphialpha.net

Theta Gamma Chapter, University of South Florida
4202 E. Fowler Ave., Ctr. 2421
Tampa, FL 33620
Web: www.alphaphialpha.net

Theta Sigma Chapter, University of Florida
P.O. Box 15237
Gainesville, FL 32604
Web: www.alphaphialpha.net

Upsilon Lambda Chapter
P.O. Box 40081
Jacksonville, FL 32203
Web: www.alphaphialpha.net

Xi Iota Chapter, University of Central Florida
P.O. Box 168006
Orlando, FL 32816
Web: www.alphaphialpha.net

Xi Psi Lambda Chapter
P.O. Box 442
Bradenton, FL 34206
Web: www.alphaphialpha.net

Xi Rho Lambda Chapter
P.O. Box 0378
Bell Glade, FL 33430
Web: www.alphaphialpha.net

Xi Sigma Lambda Chapter
P.O. Box 16203
Panama City, FL 32406
Web: www.alphaphialpha.net

Zeta Alpha Lambda Chapter
P.O. Box 6072
Fort Lauderdale, FL 33310
Web: www.alphaphialpha.net

BLACK GRADUATE STUDENT ORGANIZATION OF THE UNIVERSITY OF FLORIDA
P.O. Box 34, J. W. Reitz Union
Gainesville, FL 32611-2042
Leah Evelyn Woodward, President
Tel: (352) 665-0505
Email: bgso@grove.ufl.edu
Web: http://grove.ufl.edu/~bgso

DELTA SIGMA THETA SORORITY, INC.
Tallahassee Alumnae Chapter
P.O. Box 5949
Tallahassee, FL 32314
Laurette Scott, President
Tel: (850) 915-9129
Email: laureatte.scott@famu.edu
Web: www.nettally.com/tac

NATIONAL BLACK LAW STUDENTS ASSOCIATION
Nova Southeastern University School of Law
3305 College Ave.
Ft. Lauderdale, FL 33314
Remigia Davis, President
Tel: (954) 262-6100
Email: davisr@nsu.law.nova.edu
Web: www.nblsa.org

University of Miami School of Law
1311 Miller Dr.
Coral Gables, FL 33146
Katrice Jenkins, President
Tel: (305) 284-2339
Web: www.nblsa.org

NATIONAL PAN-HELLENIC COUNCIL, INC.
College of Education, University of Florida
P.O. Box 117045, G415 Norman Hall
Gainsville, FL 32611-7045
Michael V. Bowie, National President

Tel: (352) 371-6453 Fax: (352) 846-3011
Email: president@nphchq.org
Web: www.nphchq.org

NATIONAL PAN-HELLENIC COUNCIL, INC.
Southern Region
P.O. Box 165503
Miami, FL 33116
Chester E. Fair, Jr., Director
Tel: (305) 256-3844 Fax: (305) 256-8145
Email: info@nphcsouthern.org
Web: www.nphcsouthern.org

GEORGIA

ARTISTIC

BALLETHNIC DANCE COMPANY
2587 Cheney St.
East Point, GA 30344
Earnestine Shuemake, Office Manager
Tel: (404) 762-1416 Fax: (404) 762-6319
Email: earnestine@ballethnic.org
Web: www.ballethnic.org

NATIONAL ASSOCIATION FOR THE STUDY AND PERFORMANCE OF AFRICAN-AMERICAN MUSIC
1140 Charleston Trace
Marietta, GA 30064
Orville Wright, President
Tel: (770) 426-5468 Fax: (770) 218-1586
Email: chicktaylo@comcast.net
Web: www.naspaam.org

NATIONAL BLACK ARTS FESTIVAL
659 Auburn Ave. #254, Studioplex Bldg.
Atlanta, GA 30312
Stephanie Hughley, Executive Producer
Tel: (404) 730-7315 Fax: (404) 730-7104
Email: info@nbaf.org
Web: www.nbaf.org

THE ALLIANCE THEATRE COMPANY
1280 Peachtree St. NE
Atlanta, GA 30309
Susan Booth, Artistic Director
Tel: (404) 733-4650 Fax: (404) 733-4625
Email: info@alliancetheatre.org
Web: www.alliancetheatre.org

BUSINESS

BLACK BUSINESS PROFESSIONALS & ENTREPRENEURS
P.O. Box 60561
Savannah, GA 31420
Jewel Daniels Radford, Executive Producer
Tel: (912) 354-7400 Fax: (501) 694-9220
Email: jewel@blackbusinessprofessionals.com
Web: www.blackbusinessprofessionals.com

NATIONAL MINORITY SUPPLIER DEVELOPMENT COUNCIL, INC.
Georgia Minority Supplier Development Council, Regional Council
100 Edgewood Ave. NE #1610
Atlanta, GA 30303
George Lottier, President/CEO
Tel: (404) 589-4929 Fax: (404) 589-4925
Email: info@gmsdc.org
Web: www.gmsdc.org

CHAMBER OF COMMERCE

THE GEORGIA BLACK CHAMBER OF COMMERCE
P.O. Box 370344
Decatur, GA 30037
Theresa Walker, Executive Director
Tel: (678) 437-6644 Fax: (404) 289-8257
Email: info@gablackchamberofcommerce.org
Web: www.gablackchamberofcommerce.org

COMMUNICATIONS

NATIONAL ASSOCIATION OF BLACK COLLEGE BROADCASTERS
P.O. Box 3191
Atlanta, GA 30302
Lo Jelks, Chairman
Tel: (404) 523-6136
Email: bcrmail@aol.com
Web: www.blackcollegeradio.com

ENTERTAINMENT

AMERICAN BRIDGE ASSOCIATION
Head Office
2828 Lakewood Ave. SW
Atlanta, GA 30315

Richard H. Bowling, National President
Tel: (404) 768-5517 Fax: (404) 767-1871
Email: trbowling@aol.com
Web: www.americanbridge.com

NATIONAL AFRICAN AMERICAN RV'ERS ASSOCIATION
Broward County Camper Club Chapter
4976 Moore Pond Rd.
Tallahassee, GA 32303
LeRoy Hill, President
Tel: (850) 562-8291
Web: www.naarva.com

Fun Seekers RV Club Chapter
3926 Murray St.
Augusta, GA 30909
Millie King, President
Tel: (864) 582-8181
Email: mjk615@cs.com
Web: www.naarva.com

Fun Seekers RV Club Chapter
4010 Harris Rd.
Albany, GA 31705
Benney Goettie, President
Tel: (229) 439-2741 Fax: (229) 439-2741
Email: mjk615@cs.com
Web: www.naarva.com

Merrimac Sams Chapter
2575 Tarian Dr.
Decator, GA 30034
Lamuel Horton, President
Tel: (404) 243-0888
Email: yhorton@aol.com
Web: www.naarva.com

LAW ENFORCEMENT

NATIONAL ORGANIZATION OF BLACK LAW ENFORCEMENT EXECUTIVES
Georgia Chapter
P.O. Box 50378
Fulton County Sheriff's Office
Atlanta, GA 30302
McArthur Holmes, Colonel
Tel: (404) 730-8142
Email: maholmes@chathamcounty.org
Web: www.noblegeorgiachapter.org

MULTI-PURPOSE

CARATS, INC.
2860 Oldknow Dr. NW
Atlanta, GA 30318
Virginia P. Stanley, President
Tel: (404) 794-3186 Fax: (404) 794-3186

FAMILIES FIRST, INC./CAPITAL AREA MOSAIC
P.O. Box 7948 Station C
1105 W. Peachtree St. NE
Atlanta, GA 30357
Pat Whatley Showell, President/CEO
Tel: (404) 853-2800
Email: pat@familiesfirst.org
Web: www.familiesfirst.org

MODERN FREE AND ACCEPTED MASONS OF THE WORLD, INC.
P.O. Box 1072
Columbus, GA 31902
Gregory Mccain, Supreme Grand Master
Tel: (706) 322-3326 Fax: (706) 322-3805
Email: modernfree@aol.com
Web: www.modernfree.com

NATIONAL ASSOCIATION FOR THE ADVANCEMENT OF COLORED PEOPLE
Atlanta Chapter
P.O. Box 115087
Atlanta, GA 30310
Dr. R.L. White, Chapter President
Tel: (404) 761-1266 Fax: (404) 762-9488
Email: naacpatlbr@aol.com
Web: www.atlantanaacp.org

NATIONAL EXCHANGE FOR URBAN LEADERSHIP
5300 Pamela Dr.
Douglasville, GA 30135
Mark E. Lawrence, President
Tel: (770) 852-6900 Fax: (770) 852-6953
Email: info@neulyouth.org
Web: www.neulyouth.org

POLITICAL ACTION

AMERICAN CIVIL LIBERTIES UNION
Georgia Chapter
70 Fairlie St. #340
Atlanta, GA 30303
Debbie Seagraves, Executive Director
Tel: (404) 523-5398

Email: info@acluga.org
Web: www.acluga.org

ASSOCIATION OF COMMUNITY ORGANIZATIONS FOR REFORM NOW
ACORN Georgia
250 Auburn Ave.
Atlanta, GA 30303
Tel: (404) 525-1013 Fax: (404) 525-1017
Email: gaacorn@acorn.org
Web: www.acorn.org

BLACKS IN GOVERNMENT
Region IV-Albany Area Chapter
P.O. Box 43205 MCLB
Albany, GA 31704
Billie J. Robinson, Chapter President
Tel: (229) 639-7134
Email: robinsonbj@matcom.usmc.mil
Web: www.bignet.org

Region IV-Atlanta Metro Chapter
2765 Da Vinci Crescent
Decatur, GA 30034-3122
Calvin Stevens, Chapter President
Tel: (404) 331-9616
Email: calvina.stevens@gsa.gov
Web: www.bignet.org

Region IV-Centers for Disease Control/ATSDR Chapter
1237 Hosea L. Williams Dr. SE
Atlanta, GA 30317
Shirley Holmes, Chapter President
Tel: (770) 488-8079
Email: cdc.atsdr@bignet.org
Web: www.bignet.org

Region IV-Fts. McPherson/Gillem Chapter
P.O. Box 91367
East Point, GA 30364
Caroline Wheat, Chapter President
Tel: (404) 464-6107
Email: wheatcar@usarc-emh2.army.mil
Web: www.bignet.org

Region IV-Greater Augusta Chapter
P.O. Box 8019
Ft. Gordon, GA 30905-5000
Harold F. Simon, Chapter President
Tel: (706) 863-3996
Email: h.f.simon@comcast.net
Web: www.bignet.org

Region IV-Greater Marietta Chapter
P.O. Box 1341
Power Springs, GA 30127-1341
William A. Ross, Chapter President
Tel: (678) 503-6466
Email: william.ross@dcma.mil
Web: www.bignet.org

Region IV-Middle Georgia Chapter
P.O. Box 158
Cochran, GA 31014
Fred Wilson, Chapter President
Tel: (478) 926-4951
Email: fred.wilson@robins.af.mil
Web: www.bignet.org

CENTER FOR DEMOCRATIC RENEWAL
P.O. Box 50469
Atlanta, GA 30303
Benetta Ivey, Executive Director
Tel: (404) 221-0025 Fax: (404) 221-0045
Email: info@thecdr.org
Web: www.thecdr.org

PROFESSIONAL

AMERICAN ASSOCIATION OF BLACKS IN ENERGY
Atlanta Chapter
P.O. Box 55216
Atlanta, GA 30308-5110
Wayne X. Young, President
Tel: (404) 965-3951 Fax: (404) 965-3952
Email: wayneyoung@htsenterprise.com
Web: www.aabe-atl.org

Savannah Chapter
P.O Box 2051
Savannah, GA 31402
Fred Tyson, President
Tel: (912) 238-2204 Fax: (912) 238-2236
Email: wftyson@southernco.com
Web: www.aabe.org

BLACK DATA PROCESSING ASSOCIATES
Atlanta Chapter
P.O. Box 50462
Atlanta, GA 30302-0998
Denise Wilmot, Chapter President
Tel: (770) 828-0603
Email: info@atlantabdpa.org
Web: www.atlantabdpa.org

BLACK FARMERS AND AGRICULTURALISTS ASSOCIATION
Georgia Chapter
2569 Southpoint Rd.
Bronwood, GA 39826
Ridgley Mu'Min, Vice President
Tel: (229) 995-6619 Fax: (229) 995-6771
Email: drridge@bellsouth.net
Web: www.bfaa-us.org

CONFERENCE OF MINORITY TRANSPORTATION OFFICIALS
Atlanta Chapter
Metropolitan Atlanta Rapid Transit Authority, 2424 Piedmont Rd. NE
Atlanta, GA 30324
Jonnie Keith, Manager/Operational Audit
Tel: (404) 848-5594 Fax: (404) 848-5094
Email: jkeith@itsmarta.com
Web: www.comto.org

NATIONAL ALLIANCE OF MARKET DEVELOPERS
Atlanta Chapter
4374 Lakeridge Cir. SW
Atlanta, GA 30331
Linda V. Brown, Ph.D., Chapter President
Tel: (404) 346-1388
Email: lvbconsulting@msn.com
Web: www.namdntl.org/atlanta.htm

NATIONAL BLACK MBA ASSOCIATION, INC.
Atlanta Chapter-South
P.O. Box 54656
Atlanta, GA 30308-0656
Jannet Thoms, President
Tel: (404) 572-8001
Web: www.atlbmba.org

NATIONAL CONFERENCE OF BLACK MAYORS, INC.
Georgia Conference of Black Mayors
P.O. Box 1900
Milledgeville, GA 31061
Floyd Griffin, President
Tel: (478) 414-4010
Email: info@ncbm.org
Web: www.ncbm.org

NATIONAL MEDICAL ASSOCIATION
Georgia State Medical Association
1330 W. Peachtree St. #500
Atlanta, GA 30309
Paul L. Douglass, M.D., President
Tel: (404) 897-1157 Fax: (404) 881-5021
Web: www.nmanet.org

NATIONAL OPTOMETRIC ASSOCIATION
Region III-South
801 W. Ponce de Leon Ave.
Decatur, GA 30030
Susan Primo, Trustee
Tel: (404) 778-3317 Fax: (770) 377-9324
Email: sprimo@emory.edu
Web: www.natoptassoc.org

NATIONAL ORGANIZATION OF MINORITY ARCHITECTS
Atlanta Chapter
250 E. Ponce de Leon Ave., 8th Fl.
Decatur, GA 30030
Johnny Edwards, Chapter President
Tel: (404) 377-2460 Fax: (404) 378-5833
Web: www.noma.net

NATIONAL SOCIETY OF BLACK ENGINEERS
Region 3: Georgia Institute of Technology Chapter
GTSBE, Student Organizations Space Georgia Tech
Atlanta, GA 30332-0283
Jessica Gordon, President
Tel: (404) 894-2444 Fax: (404) 872-0665
Email: nsbe@gatech.edu
Web: www.gtsbe.org

Region 3: Mercer University Chapter
Mercer University School of Engineering, 1400 Coleman Ave.
Macon, GA 31207
Tel: (478) 301-2700
Email: region3_src@yahoo.com
Web: www.mercer.edu/nsbe/index.html

RELIGIOUS

BLACK WOMEN IN CHURCH AND SOCIETY
700 Martin Luther King Jr., Dr. SW
Atlanta, GA 30314
Jacquelyn Grant, Founder/Director
Tel: (404) 527-7740 Fax: (404) 527-5715
Email: jgrant@itcitc.edu

SOUTHERN CHRISTIAN LEADERSHIP CONFERENCE
P.O. Box 89128
Atlanta, GA 30312
Charles Steele, Jr., President

Tel: (404) 522-1420 Fax: (404) 527-4333
Web: www.sclnational.org

SPEC. INT., EDUCATION

INSTITUTE FOR AFRICAN AMERICAN STUDIES
University of Georgia
Hunter Academic Bldg., 312 Holmes
Athens, GA 30602
Dr. R. Baxter Miller, Director
Tel: (706) 542-5197 Fax: (706) 542-3071
Email: rbmiller@uga.edu
Web: www.uga.edu/iaas

NATIONAL ASSOCIATION FOR MULTICULTURAL EDUCATION
Georgia Chapter
Clark Atlanta University, 103-D Clement Hall, 223
James P. Brawley Dr. SW
Atlanta, GA 30314
Francesina Jackson, President
Tel: (404) 880-8489 Fax: (404) 880-6997
Email: fjackson@cau.edu
Web: http://ganame.colstate.edu

Kennesaw State University Student Chapter
423 Pinhurst Dr.
Atlanta, GA 30339
LaToya Reeves, President
Tel: (678) 521-3274
Email: latoya_reeves@yahoo.com
Web: http://ganame.colstate.edu

NATIONAL BLACK COLLEGE ALUMNI HALL OF FAME FOUNDATION, INC.
230 Peachtree St. NW #530
Atlanta, GA 30303
Thomas W. Dortch, Jr., Chairman/Founder
Tel: (404) 524-1106 Fax: (404) 525-6226
Email: nbcahof@bellsouth.net
Web: www.nbcahof.org

NATIONAL CONFERENCE OF BLACK POLITICAL SCIENTISTS
3695-F Cascade Rd. SW #212
Atlanta, GA 30331
Marvin Haire, Ph.D., President
Tel: (404) 699-2032 Fax: (404) 215-9344
Email: mhaire8@tgow.com
Web: www.poli.ncat.edu/ncobps

NATIONAL COUNCIL FOR BLACK STUDIES
Georgia State University in Atlanta
P.O. Box 4109
Atlanta, GA 30302-4109
Summer L. Henry, Executive Director
Tel: (404) 463-9483 Fax: (404) 651-4883
Email: info@nationalcouncilforblackstudies.com
Web: www.nationalcouncilforblackstudies.com

SECME, INC.
c/o Georgia Institute of Technology, 151 6th St. NW
Atlanta, GA 30332-0270
Yvonne B. Freeman, Executive Director
Tel: (404) 894-6557 Fax: (404) 894-6553
Email: yvonne.freeman@coe.gatech.edu
Web: www.secme.org

SOUTHERN EDUCATION FOUNDATION, INC.
135 Auburn Ave. NE, 2nd Fl.
Atlanta, GA 30303
Lynn Huntley, President
Tel: (404) 523-0001 Fax: (404) 523-6904
Email: lhuntley@sefatl.org
Web: www.sefatl.org

SPEC. INT., EMPLOYMENT

MINORITY PROFESSIONAL NETWORK, INC.
P.O. Box 55399
Atlanta, GA 30308-5399
Thomas Brooks, Executive Vice President
Tel: (888) 676-6389
Web: www.minorityprofessionalnetwork.com

SPEC. INT., GAY&LESBIAN

ZAMI, INC.
P.O. Box 2502
Decatur, GA 30031
Mary Anne Adams, Executive Director
Tel: (404) 370-0920
Email: zami@zami.org
Web: www.zami.org

SPEC. INT., HEALTH SERVICES

ASSOCIATION OF BLACK CARDIOLOGISTS, INC.
6849-B2 Peachtree Dunwoody Rd. NE
Atlanta, GA 30328
B. Waine Kong, CEO
Tel: (678) 302-4222 Fax: (678) 302-4223

Email: abcardio@abcardio.org
Web: www.abcardio.org

INTERNATIONAL SOCIETY ON HYPERTENSION IN BLACKS
100 Auburn Ave. NE #401
Atlanta, GA 30303
Christopher T. Fitzpatrick, CEO
Tel: (404) 880-0343 Fax: (404) 880-0347
Email: inforequest@ishib.org
Web: www.ishib.org

MINORITY HEALTH PROFESSIONS FOUNDATION
100 Edgewood Ave. #1020
Atlanta, GA 30303
Phyllis Champion, Executive Director
Tel: (678) 904-4217 Fax: (678) 904-4518
Email: pchampion@minorityhealth.org
Web: www.minorityhealth.org

SICKLE CELL FOUNDATION OF GEORGIA, INC.
2391 Benjamin E. Mays Dr. SW
Atlanta, GA 30311
Jean Brannan, President/COO
Tel: (404) 755-1641 Fax: (404) 755-7955
Email: geninfo@sicklecellatlaga.org
Web: www.sicklecellatlaga.org

THE SICKLE CELL INFORMATION CENTER
Grady Memorial Hospital
P.O. Box 109
Atlanta, GA 30303
Allan Platt
Tel: (404) 616-3572 Fax: (404) 616-5998
Email: aplatt@emory.edu
Web: www.scinfo.org

SPEC. INT., HOUSING

ACORN HOUSING CORPORATION
Atlanta Office
250 Auburn Ave. NE #601
Atlanta, GA 30303
Kimberly Howard, Senior Loan Counselor
Tel: (404) 525-0033 Fax: (404) 525-2655
Email: ahclcgaat@acorn.org
Web: www.acornhousing.org

SPEC. INT., HUMAN RELATIONS

NATIONAL AFRICAN AMERICAN RELATIONSHIPS INSTITUTE
P.O. Box 372453
Decatur, GA 30037-2453
Patricia Dixon, Founding President/CEO
Tel: (877) 831-5258 Fax: (404) 241-5686
Email: inquiries@aarelationshipsinstitute.com
Web: www.aarelationshipsinstitute.com

SPEC. INT., SOCIAL INTEREST

100 BLACK MEN OF ALBANY, INC.
Albany State University
504 College Dr.
Albany, GA 31705
James L. Hill, President
Tel: (229) 430-1725
Email: jhill@asurams.edu
Web: www.100blackmen.com

100 BLACK MEN OF AMERICA, INC.
National Office
100 Auburn Ave.
Atlanta, GA 30303
John T. Grant, Executive Director
Tel: (404) 525-6200 Fax: (404) 525-6124
Email: jgrant@100blackmen-atlanta.org
Web: www.100blackmen-atlanta.org

100 BLACK MEN OF ATLANTA, INC.
Herndon Plz., 100 Auburn Ave. NE #301
Atlanta, GA 30303-2527
Robert G. Haley, President/Chairman
Tel: (404) 525-6220 Fax: (404) 525-6124
Email: rhaley@100blackmen-atlanta.org
Web: www.100blackmen-atlanta.org

100 BLACK MEN OF AUGUSTA, INC.
P.O. Box 3741
Augusta, GA 30914
Wayne Foster, President
Tel: (706) 737-6460 Fax: (706) 733-3060
Email: sanfordloyd@worldnet.att.net

100 BLACK MEN OF DEKALB, INC.
3951 Snapfinger Pkwy. #315
Decatur, GA 30035
Greg B. Levett, President/Chairman
Tel: (404) 288-2772 Fax: (404) 288-0107
Email: glevett@dekalb100blackmen.org
Web: www.dekalb100blackmen.com

100 BLACK MEN OF MACON-MIDDLE GEORGIA, INC.
1347 Georgia Ave.
Macon, GA 31201
Jimmie Samuels, President
Tel: (478) 738-3240 Fax: (478) 746-8076
Web: www.100blackmen-macon.com

100 BLACK MEN OF NORTH METRO, INC.
160 Stone Pond Ln.
Alpharetta, GA 30022
Marcel Henry, President
Tel: (770) 521-9404 Fax: (770) 521-8623
Email: marcel.henry@northmetro100.org
Web: www.northmetro100.org

100 BLACK MEN OF SOUTH METRO, INC.
6338 Church St.
Riverdale, GA 30274
Charles Reddick, President/Chairman
Tel: (770) 996-0314 Fax: (770) 996-0315
Email: 100blksm@bellsouth.net
Web: www.100blackmensouthmetro.org

AFRICAN AMERICAN SUMMIT
303 Peachtree St. NE #4420
Atlanta, GA 30308-3264
Andrew Young, Chairman
Tel: (404) 527-8484 Fax: (404) 527-3827
Email: info@gwiconsulting.com
Web: www.goodworksintl.com

FEDERATION OF SOUTHERN COOPERATIVES-LAND ASSISTANCE FUND
Administrative Office
2769 Church St.
East Point, GA 30344
Ralph Paige, Executive Director
Tel: (404) 765-0991 Fax: (404) 765-9178
Email: fsc@mindspring.com
Web: www.federationsoutherncoop.com

Georgia Field Office
P.O. Box 3092
Albany, GA 31706
Shirley Sherrod, State Director
Tel: (229) 432-5799 Fax: (229) 439-0894
Email: fscalbany@mindspring.com
Web: www.federationsoutherncoop.com

GEORGIA BLACK UNITED FUND, INC.
10 Park Pl. #505
Atlanta, GA 30303
Robert Davis, Executive Director
Tel: (404) 524-4003 Fax: (404) 524-6332
Email: gbuf-atlanta@mindspring.com
Web: www.nbuf.org/georgia

NATIONAL URBAN LEAGUE, INC.
Atlanta Urban League
100 Edgewood Ave. NE #600
Atlanta, GA 30303
Clinton E. Dye, President
Tel: (404) 659-1150 Fax: (404) 659-5771
Email: info@atlul.org
Web: www.atlul.org

Urban League of Greater Columbus, Inc.
802 1st Ave.
Columbus, GA 31901
Reginald L. Pugh, President/CEO
Tel: (706) 323-3687 Fax: (706) 596-2144
Email: ulgc@columbusurbanleague.org
Web: www.columbusurbanleague.org

RAINBOW PUSH COALITION
Atlanta Office
100 Auburn Ave. #101
Atlanta, GA 30303
Rev. Jesse L. Jackson, Sr., President
Tel: (404) 525-5663 Fax: (404) 525-5233
Email: info@rainbowpush.org
Web: www.rainbowpush.org

REAL MEN COOK FOR CHARITY
Atlanta Chapter
P.O. Box 311912
Atlanta, GA 31131
Diana Powell Larche, Event Manager
Tel: (404) 273-3227
Email: realmencookatl@yahoo.com
Web: www.realmencook.com

SOUTHERN REGIONAL COUNCIL
133 Carnegie Way NW #1030
Atlanta, GA 30303-1054
Toni Fannin, Interim Executive Director
Tel: (404) 522-8764 Fax: (404) 522-8791
Email: info@southerncouncil.org
Web: www.southerncouncil.org

THE MARTIN LUTHER KING, JR. CENTER FOR NONVIOLENT SOCIAL CHANGE, INC.
449 Auburn Ave. NE, Freedom Hall
Atlanta, GA 30312

Martin Luther King III, Chairman/CEO
Tel: (404) 526-8900 Fax: (404) 526-8969
Email: information@thekingcenter.org
Web: www.thekingcenter.org

SPEC. INT., YOUTH

JACK & JILL OF AMERICA, INC.
Southeastern Region
210 Dix-Lee'On Dr.
Fairburn, GA 30213
Marjorie Belton, Regional Director
Tel: (770) 461-4220 Fax: (770) 461-4220
Email: jnjserd@bellsouth.net
Web: www.jack-and-jill.org

STUDENT ORGANIZATION

ALPHA KAPPA ALPHA SORORITY, INC.
Alpha Pi Chapter, Clark Atlanta University
P.O. Box 324
J.P. Brawley at Fair
Atlanta, GA 30314
Larrisa Harvey, Chapter President
Web: www.aka1908.com

Delta Eta Omega Chapter
P.O. Box 3822
Albany, GA 31706
Linda Rogers Powers, Chapter President
Web: www.aka1908.com

Epsilon Omega Omega Chapter
P.O. Box 4823
Macon, GA 31208
Kelda Smith Cubit, Chapter President
Web: www.aka1908.com

Eta Iota Chapter, Columbus State University
c/o S Ellison 1, 1445 Bowie Ave.
Columbus, GA 31903
Kametria Bentley, Chapter President
Web: www.aka1908.com

Eta Mu Chapter
P.O. Box 93262
Atlanta, GA 30377
Sholonda Jackson, Chapter President
Web: www.aka1908.com

Gamma Gamma Chapter
3850 Stone Rd. SW
Atlanta, GA 30331
Kayrell Clark, Chapter President
Web: www.aka1908.com

Gamma Pi Omega Chapter
P.O. Box 1603
Fort Valley, GA 31030
Delores C. Thornton, Chapter President
Web: www.aka1908.com

Gamma Sigma Chapter, Albany State College
P.O. Box 30121
Albany, GA 31705
Jennifer Yolanda Edwards, Chapter President
Web: www.aka1908.com

Gamma Sigma Omega Chapter
P.O. Box 23292
Savannah, GA 31403
Carolyn Evelyn Bell, Chapter President
Web: www.aka1908.com

Gamma Tau Omega Chapter
P.O. Box 6238
Columbia, GA 31907
Carolyn G. Randolph, Chapter President
Tel: (773) 684-1282 Fax: (773) 288-8251
Web: www.aka1908.com

Iota Psi Omega Chapter
P.O. Box 303
Athens, GA 30603
Angela Jackson Nowell, Chapter President
Web: www.aka1908.com

Kappa Eta Chapter, Georgia College
P.O. Box 2416
Milledgeville, GA 31061
Rotonya Rhodes, Chapter President
Web: www.aka1908.com

Kappa Eta Omega Chapter
P.O. Box 2587
Valdosta, GA 31604
Sandra Edwards Monlyn, Chapter President
Web: www.aka1908.com

Kappa Omega Chapter
P.O. Box 50081
Atlanta, GA 30302
Alfredene Scott Cheely, Chapter President
Web: www.aka1908.com

Kappa Tau Chapter
P.O. Box 10009
Carrollton, GA 30118
Kristen Bowens, Chapter President

Web: www.aka1908.com

Kappa Upsilon Chapter, Valdosta State College
VSC, Box 7123
Valdosta, GA 31698
Tamika L. Stubbs, Chapter President
Web: www.aka1908.com

Lambda Epsilon Omega Chapter
P.O. Box 370337
Decatur, GA 30037
Peggy Lamar Smalls, Chapter President
Web: www.aka1908.com

Lambda Iota Omega Chapter
P.O. Box 5053
Gainesville, GA 30504
Lacrisia Larkin, Chapter President
Web: www.aka1908.com

Lambda Kappa Chapter, Georgia Southern University
P.O. Box 12453
Statesboro, GA 30460
Elishia Michelle Ingram, Chapter President
Web: www.aka1908.com

Lambda Xi Omega Chapter
P.O. Box 1001
Thomasville, GA 31799
Cheryl Conner-Mitchell, Chapter President
Web: www.aka1908.com

Mu Pi Chapter, Spelman College
350 Spellman Ln. #267
Atlanta, GA 30314
Aisha Jenelle McKnight, Chapter President
Web: www.aka1908.com

Mu Zeta Chapter, Augusta College
2500 Walton Way
Augusta, GA 30909
Lynthia Ross, Chapter President
Web: www.aka1908.com

Nu Alpha Chapter
Drawer G
Atlanta, GA 30322
Melissa Burroughs, Chapter President
Web: www.aka1908.com

Nu Beta Chapter
3771 Citation Dr.
Decatur, GA 30034
Alyssa Hughes, Chapter President
Web: www.aka1908.com

Nu Lambda Omega Chapter
P.O. Box 311-197
Atlanta, GA 31131
Markita Grant, Chapter President
Web: www.aka1908.com

Nu Rho Omega Chapter
P.O. Box 423
Hinesville, GA 31310
Yvonne Lambert, Chapter President
Web: www.aka1908.com

Nu Upsilon Omega Chapter
1113 King Circle Dr.
Swainsboro, GA 30401
Erma Jenkins, Chapter President
Web: www.aka1908.com

Nu Zeta Chapter, Georgia Southwestern College
GSW, Box 1188
Americus, GA 31709
Shannan N. Buckner, Chapter President
Web: www.aka1908.com

Phi Delta Omega Chapter
P.O. Box 1641
Vidala, GA 30475
Lillian Persha-Craig, Chapter President
Web: www.aka1908.com

Phi Phi Omega Chapter
P.O. Box 4012
Alpharetta, GA 30022
Bettye Lewis Maye, Chapter President
Web: www.aka1908.com

Phi Pi Omega Chapter
P.O. Box 125
Union City, GA 30291
Veronica G. Jones, Chapter President
Web: www.aka1908.com

Phi Tau Omega Chapter
P.O. Box 82306
Hapeville, GA 30354
Annette Dotson, Chapter President
Web: www.aka1908.com

Pi Alpha Omega Capter
P.O. Box 490760
College Park, GA 30349
Jacqueline Lawson Baker, Chapter President
Web: www.aka1908.com

Pi Phi Chapter, Kennesaw State College
1000 Chastain Rd.
Kennesaw, GA 30144
Crystal Dix Long, Chapter President
Web: www.aka1908.com

Rho Rho Omega Chapter
P.O. Box 6859
Columbus, GA 31907
Jaspconia Florence Moore, Chapter President
Web: www.aka1908.com

Rho Sigma Omega Chapter
P.O. Box 1711
Americus, GA 31709
Gwendolyn Wright, Chapter President
Web: www.aka1908.com

Rho Zeta Omega Chapter
P.O. Box 675499
Marietta, GA 30006
Brenda Lee Jordan, Chapter President
Web: www.aka1908.com

Sigma Alpha Omega Chapter
P.O. Box 7005
Tifton, GA 31793
Tonja Cummings Tift, Chapter President
Web: www.aka1908.com

Sigma Epsilon Omega Chapter
P.O. Box 852
Warner Robins, GA 31099
Myrtice Carolyn Jackson, Chapter President
Web: www.aka1908.com

Sigma Omega Omega Chapter
P.O. Box 162436
Atlanta, GA 30321
Candy Ynette Allen, Chapter President
Web: www.aka1908.com

Tau Epsilon Omega Chapter
P.O. Box 91084
East Point, GA 30364
Beverly R. Burks, Chapter President
Web: www.aka1908.com

Tau Omicron Omega Chapter
P.O. Box 1647
Dublin, GA 31040
Catherine Dixon Forrest, Chapter President
Web: www.aka1908.com

Tau Pi Omega Chapter
P.O. Box 1024
Stone Mountain, GA 30086
Gwendolyn Russell Green, Chapter President
Web: www.aka1908.com

Theta Omicron Omega Chapter
P.O. Box 1555
Cedartown, GA 30125
Daphnie Morrison, Chapter President
Web: www.aka1908.com

Theta Xi Omega Chapter
P.O. Box 2303
La Grange, GA 30241
Kathy Ellison, Chapter President
Web: www.aka1908.com

Upsilon Alpha Omega Chapter
P.O. Box 191
Lawrenceville, GA 30046
Debbie Payton, Chapter President
Web: www.aka1908.com

Xi Beta Omega Chapter
P.O. Box 273
Griffin, GA 30224
Cheryl Walker, Chapter President
Web: www.aka1908.com

Zeta Eta Chapter
1235 15th St.
Augusta, GA 30901
Carla Smith, Chapter President
Web: www.aka1908.com

Zeta Iota Omega Chapter
287 Oak Pointe Dr.
Richmond Hills, GA 31324
Cheryl Capers, President
Web: www.aka1908.com

Zeta Xi Omega Chapter
P.O. Box 1455
Augusta, GA 30903
Clemestine Williams, Chapter President
Web: www.aka1908.com

ALPHA PHI ALPHA FRATERNITY, INC.
Alpha Chi Lambda Chapter
P.O. Box 14752
Augusta, GA 30919
Web: www.alphaphialpha.net

Alpha Phi Chapter, Clark Atlanta University
P.O. Box 327
Atlanta, GA 30314
Web: www.alphaphialpha.net

Beta Phi Lambda Chapter
P.O. Box 1361
Savannah, GA 31402
Web: www.alphaphialpha.net

Delta Delta Chapter, Albany State University
P.O. Box 312900
Albany, GA 31705
Web: www.alphaphialpha.net

Delta Eta Chapter, Savannah State University
P.O. Box 20742
Savannah, GA 31404
Web: www.alphaphialpha.net

Delta Iota Lambda Chapter
P.O. Box 6344
Columbus, GA 31907
Web: www.alphaphialpha.net

Epsilon Beta Lambda Chapter
P.O. Box 5329
Macon, GA 31208
Web: www.alphaphialpha.net

Eta Iota Lambda Chapter
P.O. Box 902
Athens, GA 30603
Web: www.alphaphialpha.net

Eta Lambda Chapter
P.O. Box 92576
Atlanta, GA 30314
Web: www.alphaphialpha.net

Gamma Omicron Lambda Chapter
P.O. Box 4054
Albany, GA 31706
Web: www.alphaphialpha.net

Gamma Sigma Lambda Chapter
P.O. Box 415
Fort Valley, GA 31030
Web: www.alphaphialpha.net

Gamma Zeta Chapter, Fort Valley State University
P.O. Box 4326
Fort Valley, GA 31030
Web: www.alphaphialpha.net

Iota Chapter, Morris Brown College
3465 Somerset Trail
Atlanta, GA 30331
Web: www.alphaphialpha.net

Iota Eta Chapter, Mercer University
1842 Winship St.
Macon, GA 31204
Web: www.alphaphialpha.net

Iota Gamma Lambda Chapter
P.O. Box 2122
Brunswick, GA 31420
Web: www.alphaphialpha.net

Kappa Tau Lambda Chapter
P.O. Box 2981
Valdosta, GA 31604
Web: www.alphaphialpha.net

Mu Alpha Chapter, Emory University
Drawer N
Atlanta, GA 30322
Web: www.alphaphialpha.net

Mu Delta Chapter, Georgia Southwestern University
P.O. Box 1196
Americus, GA 31709
Web: www.alphaphialpha.net

Mu Gamma Chapter, Georgia College
P.O. Box 2423
Milledgeville, GA 31061
Web: www.alphaphialpha.net

Mu Omicron Chapter, Valdosta State College
P.O. Box 7114
Valdosta, GA 31698
Web: www.alphaphialpha.net

Nu Gamma Chapter, University of West Georgia
P.O. Box 10118
Carrollton, GA 30118
Andrew Weaver, President
Tel: (770) 830-8017
Web: www.alphaphialpha.net

Nu Mu Chapter, Georgia Institute of Technology
50223 Georgia Technology Station
Atlanta, GA 30332
Web: www.alphaphialpha.net

Nu Mu Lambda Chapter
P.O. Box 370275
Decatur, GA 30037
Web: www.alphaphialpha.net

Omicron Mu Lambda Chapter
P.O. Box 672832
Marietta, GA 30067
Web: www.alphaphialpha.net

Omicron Phi Lambda Chapter
P.O. Box 91393
East Point, GA 30364
Howard Kennedy, President
Email: rkreeves13@yahoo.com
Web: www.apa1906-ophilam.org

Pi Eta Lambda Chapter
Mall Station #378
Dublin, GA 31021
Web: www.alphaphialpha.net

Pi Gamma Lambda Chapter
P.O. Box 115386
Atlanta, GA 30310
Web: www.alphaphialpha.net

Pi Iota Lambda Chapter
P.O. Box 7153
Tifton, GA 31793
Web: www.alphaphialpha.net

Theta Beta Chapter, Columbus College
P.O. Box 6344
Columbus, GA 31907
Web: www.alphaphialpha.net

Theta Nu Lambda Chapter
P.O. Box 1818
Lagrange, GA 30241
Web: www.alphaphialpha.net

Xi Tau Chapter, Georgia Southern University
P.O. Box 8965
Statesboro, GA 30460
Web: www.alphaphialpha.net

Zeta Pi Chapter, University of Georgia
P.O. Box 2153
Athens, GA 30612
Web: www.alphaphialpha.net

NATIONAL BLACK LAW STUDENTS ASSOCIATION
Georgia State University College of Law
P.O. Box 4049
Atlanta, GA 30302-4049
Cassandre Galette, President
Tel: (404) 651-2048 Fax: (404) 651-1244
Email: georgiastatelbsa@yahoo.com
Web: http://law.gsu.edu/blsa/

John Marshall Law School
1422 W. Peachtree St. NW #400
Atlanta, GA 30309
Diangell Norris, President
Tel: (404) 872-3593 Fax: (404) 873-3802
Web: www.jmls.edu

Mercer University School of Law
1400 Coleman Ave.
Macon, GA 31207
Tel: (478) 301-2605 Fax: (478) 301-2828
Web: www.nblsa.org

OMEGA PSI PHI FRATERNITY, INC.
National Office
3951 Snapfinger Pkwy.
Decatur, GA 30035
George H. Grace, Grand Basileus
Tel: (404) 284-5533 Fax: (404) 284-0333
Email: omegagrace@oppf.com
Web: www.oppf.org

UNIVERSITY OF GEORGIA SCHOOL OF LAW
Black Law Student Association
Athens, GA 30602
Stephanie C. Anderson, President
Email: sca2006@uga.edu
Web: www.uga.edu/blsa

HAWAII

POLITICAL ACTION

AMERICAN CIVIL LIBERTIES UNION
Hawaii Chapter
P.O. Box 3410
Honolulu, HI 96801
Vanessa Y. Chong, Executive Director
Tel: (808) 522-5900 Fax: (808) 522-5909
Email: office@acluhawaii.org
Web: www.acluhawaii.org

STUDENT ORGANIZATION

ALPHA KAPPA ALPHA SORORITY, INC.
Lambda Chi Omega Chapter
P.O. Box 1792
Aiea, HI 96701

Barbara Perry, Chapter President
Web: www.aka1908.com

NATIONAL BLACK LAW STUDENTS ASSOCIATION
University of Hawaii School of Law
2515 Dole St.
Honolulu, HI 96822
Tel: (808) 956-7966 Fax: (800) 956-3813
Web: www.hawaii.edu/law

IDAHO

POLITICAL ACTION

AMERICAN CIVIL LIBERTIES UNION
Idaho Chapter
P.O. Box 1897
Boise, ID 83701
Jack Van Valkenburgh, Executive Director
Tel: (208) 344-9750 Fax: (208) 344-7201
Email: public@acluidaho.org
Web: www.acluidaho.org

ILLINOIS

ARTISTIC

BLACK ENSEMBLE THEATER CORPORATION
4520 N. Beacon St.
Chicago, IL 60640
Jackie Taylor, Executive Director
Tel: (773) 769-4451 Fax: (773) 769-4533
Email: blackensemble@aol.com
Web: www.blackensembletheater.org

CENTER FOR BLACK MUSIC RESEARCH
Columbia College Chicago, 600 S. Michigan Ave.
Chicago, IL 60605-1996
Rosita M. Sands, Director
Tel: (312) 344-7559 Fax: (312) 344-8029
Email: contact@cbmr.colum.edu
Web: www.cbmr.org

CONGO SQUARE THEATER COMPANY
2936 N. Southport Ave. #210
Chicago, IL 60657
Adam Thurman, Executive Director
Tel: (773) 296-1108 Fax: (773) 472-6634
Email: athurman@congosquaretheatre.org
Web: www.congosquaretheatre.org

ETA CREATIVE ARTS FOUNDATION, INC.
7558 S. South Chicago Ave.
Chicago, IL 60619-2644
Abena Joan P. Brown, President
Tel: (773) 752-3955 Fax: (773) 752-8727
Email: email@etacreativearts.org
Web: www.etacreativearts.org

JOEL HALL DANCE CENTER
1511 W. Berwyn Ave.
Chicago, IL 60640
Joel Hall, Artistic Director
Tel: (773) 293-0900 Fax: (773) 293-1130
Email: joelhall@joelhall.org
Web: www.joelhall.org

MA'AT PRODUCTION ASSOCIATION OF AFRIKAN CENTERED THEATER
P. O. Box 10039
Chicago, IL 60610-0039
Reginald Lawrence, Executive Director
Tel: (312) 409-6724
Email: information@mpaact.org
Web: www.mpaact.org

MUNTU DANCE THEATRE OF CHICAGO
6800 S. Wentworth Ave. #3E96
Chicago, IL 60621
Amaniyea Payne, Artistic Director
Tel: (773) 602-1135 Fax: (773) 602-1134
Email: info@muntu.com
Web: www.muntu.com

BUSINESS

BLACKS INTERESTED IN BUSINESS
SIU-Carbondale Chapter
Rehn Hall #119, College of Business &
Administration, SIUC
Carbondale, IL 62901
Michael Heywood, Director
Tel: (618) 453-7498 Fax: (618) 453-7961
Email: heywood@cba.siu.edu
Web: www.siu.edu/departments/rso/bib/

NATIONAL MINORITY SUPPLIER DEVELOPMENT COUNCIL, INC.
Chicago Minority Business Development Council
1 E. Wacker Dr. #1200
Chicago, IL 60601

Tracye E. Smith, Executive Director
Tel: (312) 755-8880 Fax: (312) 755-8890
Email: tsmith@cmbdc.org
Web: www.cmbdc.org

SOUTHEAST CHICAGO DEVELOPMENT COMMISSION
9204 S. Commercial Ave. #212
Chicago, IL 60617
Lynne Cunningham, President/CEO
Tel: (773) 731-8755 Fax: (773) 731-8618
Email: lcunningham@southeastchicago.org
Web: www.southeastchicago.org

CULTURAL

AFRICAN HERITAGE STUDIES ASSOCIATION AT CORNELL UNIVERSITY
Northern Illinois University
Center for Black Studies N. Illinois University
DeKalb, IL 60115
Laverne Gyant, Director of Black Studies
Tel: (815) 753-1423 Fax: (815) 753-9291
Email: lgyant@niu.edu
Web: www.niu.edu

ASSOCIATION FOR BLACK CULTURE CENTERS
2 E. South St.
Galesburg, IL 61401-4999
Dr. Fred Hord, Executive Director
Tel: (309) 341-7862 Fax: (309) 341-7079
Email: fhord@knox.edu
Web: www.abcc.net

ENTERTAINMENT

NATIONAL AFRICAN AMERICAN RV'ERS ASSOCIATION
Ebony Dream Makers Chapter
1246 Piner Ave.
Evanston, IL 60202
Alvin S. Keith, President
Tel: (773) 721-4877
Email: akeith1246@aol.com
Web: www.naarva.com

Windy City Travelers Chapter
3 Westwood Ct.
Park Forest, IL 60466
Frank Goodrich, President
Tel: (718) 748-4254
Web: www.naarva.com

LAW ENFORCEMENT

NATIONAL ORGANIZATION OF BLACK LAW ENFORCEMENT EXECUTIVES
Central Illinois "Land of Lincoln" Chapter
Urbana Police Department, 400 Vine St.
Urbana, IL 61801
Eddie B. Adair, Chief of Police
Tel: (217) 384-2321 Fax: (217) 384-2372
Email: adaireb@city.urbana.il.us
Web: www.landoflincoln.addr.com

Chicago Chapter
11223 S. Halsten St.
Chicago, IL 60620
Mitchell Ray Davis, III, President
Tel: (708) 388-3340 Fax: (708) 388-9981
Email: dixmoorchief@earthlink.net
Web: www.cmc.noblechapter.org

Northern Illinois Chapter
P.O. Box 1321
Dupage State's Attorney
Aurora, IL 60507
William M. Simmons, Chief of Investigations
Tel: (630) 682-7590 Fax: (630) 742-7018
Email: william.simmons@dupageco.org
Web: www.noblenatl.org

MULTI-PURPOSE

PEORIA CITIZENS COMMITTEE FOR ECONOMIC OPPORTUNITY, INC.
African-American Leadership Alliance
711 W. McBean St.
Peoria, IL 61605
McFarland A. Bragg, II, Director
Tel: (309) 671-3900 Fax: (309) 671-3913
Email: mabragg@pcceo.org
Web: www.pcceo.org

POLITICAL ACTION

AMERICAN CIVIL LIBERTIES UNION
Illinois Chapter
180 N. Michigan Ave. #2300
Chicago, IL 60601
Colleen K. Connell, Executive Director
Tel: (312) 201-9740 Fax: (312) 201-9760

Email: acluofillinois@aclu-il.org
Web: www.aclu-il.org

ASSOCIATION OF COMMUNITY ORGANIZATIONS FOR REFORM NOW
Chicago Office
650 S. Clark St. #200
Chicago, IL 60605
Tel: (312) 939-7488 Fax: (312) 939-6877
Email: ilacorn@acorn.org
Web: www.acorn.org

BLACKS IN GOVERNMENT
Region V-Chicago Midwest Chapter
P.O. Box A3948
Chicago, IL 60690
Mary J. Watkins, Chapter President
Tel: (312) 353-6236 X2552 Fax: (312) 353-9563
Email: chicago.midwest@bignet.org
Web: www.bignet.org/regional/region5/default.htm

Region V-Lake County Chapter
P.O. Box 25
Zion, IL 60099
Jacquelyn Pugh-Rodgers, Chapter President
Tel: (847) 688-1900 X84460 Fax: (847) 746-3068
Email: lake.county@bignet.org
Web: www.bignet.org/regional/region5/default.htm

Region V-New Kemet Harambee Chapter
P.O. Box 2732
Chicago, IL 60690
Vincent Saunders, III, Chapter President
Tel: (312) 353-9077
Email: kemet.harambe@bignet.org
Web: www.bignet.org/regional/region5/default.htm

Region V-Progressive Chapter
P.O. Box 2093
Danville, IL 61834-2093
David Groves, Chapter President
Tel: (217) 554-4200
Email: progressive.danville@bignet.org
Web: www.bignet.org/regional/region5/default.htm

Region V-Southern Illinois Chapter
P.O. Box 25372
Scott AFB, IL 62225-9998
Johnny Ware, Chapter President
Tel: (618) 292-2110
Email: southern.illinois@bignet.org
Web: www.bignet.org/regional/region5/default.htm

PROFESSIONAL

AFRICAN AMERICAN ASSOCIATION OF FORBES PROFESSIONALS
1507 E. 53rd St. #495
Chicago, IL 60615
Wendell Williams, Chair
Tel: (630) 268-7532
Email: aaafp93@hotmail.com
Web: www.aaafp.org

AMERICAN ASSOCIATION OF BLACKS IN ENERGY
Chicago Chapter
3 Lincoln Ctr.
Oakbrook Terrace, IL 60181-4260
Albert Cook, Executive Assistant
Tel: (630) 437-2910 Fax: (312) 394-5433
Email: albert.cook@exeloncorp.com
Web: www.aabe-chi.org

AMERICAN BAR ASSOCIATION
Commission of Racial and Ethnic Diversity in the Profession
321 N. Clark St.
Chicago, IL 60610
Sandra S. Yamate, Director of Commission of Racial
and Ethnic Diversity
Tel: (312) 988-5000 Fax: (312) 988-5647
Email: yamates@staff.abanet.org
Web: www.abanet.org/minorities

ASSOCIATION OF BLACK PSYCHOLOGISTS
Midwestern Region
8515 S. Constance
Chicago, IL 60617
Nkechi Townsend, Ph.D., Mid-West Regional
Representative
Tel: (773) 721-8334 Fax: (425) 699-6851
Email: nkechit2@aol.com
Web: www.abpsi.org

BLACK DATA PROCESSING ASSOCIATES
Chicago Chapter
215 N. Des Plaines Ave. #2S
Chicago, IL 60661
Reginald J. Gardner, President
Tel: (312) 575-8503
Email: bod@bdpa-chicago.org
Web: www.bdpa-chicago.org

CONFERENCE OF MINORITY TRANSPORTATION OFFICIALS
Chicago Chapter
P.O. Box 3555
Chicago Transit Authority
Chicago, IL 60654-0555
Joyce Coleman, Vice President of Human Resources
Tel: (312) 664-7200 X3440 Fax: (312) 494-6379
Email: jcoleman@transitchicago.com
Web: www.comto.com

NATIONAL ALLIANCE OF MARKET DEVELOPERS
Chicago Chapter
1507 E. 53rd St.
Chicago, IL 60615
Deborah J. Crable, Chapter President
Tel: (773) 548-7642
Email: dcrable1@sbcglobal.net
Web: www.namdchicago.com

NATIONAL ASSOCIATION OF BLACK ACCOUNTANTS, INC.
DePaul University Chapter
1 E. Jackson Blvd. #6008
Chicago, IL 60604
Rhonda Young, President
Tel: (312) 362-5051 Fax: (312) 362-6208
Email: naba@depaul.edu

NATIONAL ASSOCIATION OF BLACK JOURNALISTS
Chicago Chapter
P.O. Box 811132
Chicago, IL 60681
Vernon Jarrett, President
Tel: (773) 779-6936
Email: secretary@nabjchicago.org
Web: www.nabjchicago.org

NATIONAL BLACK MBA ASSOCIATION, INC.
Chicago Chapter-Midwest
P.O. Box 8513
Chicago, IL 60680
Kathy April-Barr, President
Tel: (312) 458-9161
Email: kathy@ccnbmbaa.org
Web: www.ccnbmbaa.org

National Headquarters
180 N. Michigan Ave. #1400
Chicago, IL 60601
Barbara Thomas, President/CEO
Tel: (312) 236-2622 Fax: (312) 236-0390
Email: mail@nbmbaa.org
Web: www.nbmbaa.org

NATIONAL CONFERENCE OF BLACK LAWYERS
Illinois Chapter
407 S. Dearborn #1395
Chicago, IL 60605
Standish Willis, Attorney
Tel: (312) 554-0005 Fax: (312) 554-1012
Email: swillis818@aol.com
Web: www.geocities.com/capitolhill/lobby/9470

NATIONAL FORUM FOR BLACK PUBLIC ADMINISTRATORS
Chicago Chapter
P.O. Box 64506
Chicago, IL 60664-0506
Darnetta K. Tyus, President
Tel: (312) 458-9281
Email: dtyus@thecha.org
Web: www.nfbpa.org

NATIONAL SALES NETWORK
Chicago Chapter
28 E. Jackson, 10th Fl. #N307
Chicago, IL 60604
Cliff Bailey, President
Tel: (312) 409-4660
Email: cbailey@worldvue.com
Web: www.nsnchicago.org

NATIONAL SOCIETY OF BLACK ENGINEERS
Region 4: DePaul University Chapter
243 S. Wabash Ave.
Chicago, IL 60604
Lloyd Hervey, President
Email: nsbe@cti.depaul.edu
Web: http://nsbe.cti.depaul.edu

Region 4: Illinois Institute of Technology Chapter
3255 S. Dearborn, Wishnick Hall #122
Chicago, IL 60616
Kalaida Holmes, Chair Emeritus
Tel: (312) 567-3184
Email: nsbe@hawk.cns.iit.edu
Web: www.iit.edu/~nsbe

Region 4: University of Illinois at Urbana-
Champaign Chapter
1308 W. Green St., Engineering Hall #103A
Urbana, IL 61801

Chris Jenkins, President
Tel: (217) 333-3558 Fax: (217) 244-4974
Email: cjenkins@uiuc.edu
Web: http://nsbe.ec.uiuc.edu/index.html

RELIGIOUS

CHRIST COMMUNITY CHURCH
1151 E. 170th St.
South Holland, IL 60473
Carl E. King, Sr., Senior Pastor
Tel: (708) 331-8389 Fax: (708) 331-8374
Email: cking46842@aol.com
Web: www.ccccogic.com

DIOCESE OF SPRINGFIELD IN ILLINOIS
Office for Social Concerns
1615 W. Washington St.
Springfield, IL 62702
Sr. Jane Boos, Director
Tel: (217) 698-8500 Fax: (217) 698-9581
Email: osc@dio.org
Web: www.dio.org

THE AFRICAN-AMERICAN YOUNG ADULTS ASSOCIATION
c/o St. Benedict the African-West Church
1818 W. 71st St.
Chicago, IL 60636
Tel: (773) 925-2535 Fax: (773) 925-5071
Email: st.benedictwest@yahoo.com

RESEARCH

APPLIED RESEARCH CENTER
Chicago Office
2125 W. North Ave.
Chicago, IL 60647
Terry Keleher, Director of the Action Education Program and the Racial Justice Policy Initiative
Tel: (773) 269-4062 Fax: (773) 278-3840
Email: arc@arc.org
Web: www.arc.org

SPEC. INT., EDUCATION

ALPHA KAPPA ALPHA EDUCATIONAL ADVANCEMENT FOUNDATION, INC.
5656 Stony Island Ave.
Chicago, IL 60637
Linda M. White, President
Tel: (773) 947-0026 Fax: (773) 947-0277
Email: akaeaf@aol.com
Web: www.akaeaf.org

NATIONAL ASSOCIATION FOR MULTICULTURAL EDUCATION
Illinois Chapter
Julian Middle School, 416 S. Richland
Oak Park, IL 60302
Lynn Allen, Chapter Organizer
Tel: (708) 524-7701 Fax: (708) 524 7703
Email: lallen@op97.org
Web: www.nameorg.org

SPEC. INT., EMPLOYMENT

ILLINOIS ASSOCIATION OF MINORITIES IN GOVERNMENT
110 W. Edwards
Springfield, IL 62704-0108
Roy Williams, Jr., Executive Director
Tel: (217) 753-1077 Fax: (217) 753-1277
Email: relations@iamg1.com
Web: www.iamg1.com

SPEC. INT., FAMILY PLANNING

NATIONAL HOOK-UP OF BLACK WOMEN, INC.
1809 E. 71st St. #205
Chicago, IL 60649
Dr. Wynetta Frazier, National President
Tel: (773) 667-7061 Fax: (773) 667-7064
Email: nhbwdir@aol.com
Web: www.nhbwinc.com

Joliet Chapter
P.O. Box 1084
Joliet, IL 60434
Bettye Gavin, President
Tel: (815) 724-0547
Email: g7349@sbcglobal.net
Web: www.nhbwinc.com

SPEC. INT., SOCIAL INTEREST

100 BLACK MEN OF ALTON, INC.
P.O. Box 321
Alton, IL 62002
Douglas Martin, Sr., President
Tel: (618) 462-5665 Fax: (618) 466-3447
Email: damart10@aol.com

Web: www.100bma.org

BLACK UNITED FUND OF ILLINOIS, INC.
1809 E. 71st St. #200
Chicago, IL 60649
Henry L. English, President/CEO
Tel: (773) 324-0494 Fax: (773) 324-6678
Email: english@bufi.org
Web: www.bufi.org

GHANA NATIONAL COUNCIL OF METROPOLITAN CHICAGO
1126 E. 101st St.
Chicago, IL 60628
Reuben Hadzide, President
Tel: (773) 425-7318 Fax: (866) 488-5495
Email: info@ghananationalcouncil.com
Web: www.ghananationalcouncil.com

NATIONAL BLACK ON BLACK LOVE CAMPAIGN
9535 S. Cottage Grove
Chicago, IL 60628
Francis Gutter-Wright, Executive Director
Tel: (773) 978-0868 Fax: (773) 978-7620
Email: blkonblklove@aol.com

NATIONAL BLACK UNITED FRONT
National Office
12817 S. Ashland Ave.
Calumet Park, IL 60827
Dr. Conrad W. Worrill, Chairman
Tel: (708) 389-9929 Fax: (708) 389-9819
Email: nbufchi@allways.net
Web: www.nbufront.org

NATIONAL URBAN LEAGUE, INC.
Chicago Urban League
4510 S. Michigan Ave.
Chicago, IL 60653
James W. Compton, President/CEO
Tel: (773) 285-5800 Fax: (773) 285-7772
Email: info@cul-chicago.org
Web: www.cul-chicago.org

Lake County Urban League
122 Madison St.
Waukegan, IL 60085
Patricia Handy, President
Tel: (847) 249-3770 Fax: (847) 249-4894
Web: www.nul.org

Madison County Urban League
P.O. Box 8093
210 William St.
Alton, IL 62002
Brenda Walker McCain, Interim President/CEO
Tel: (618) 463-1906 Fax: (618) 463-9021
Web: www.nul.org

Quad County Urban League
808 E. Galena Blvd. #B
Aurora, IL 60505
Theodia Gillespie, President/CEO
Tel: (630) 851-2203 Fax: (630) 851-2703
Email: qcul@aol.com
Web: www.qcul.org

Springfield Urban League, Inc.
100 N. 11th St.
Springfield, IL 62703
Nina Harris, Interim President
Tel: (217) 789-0830 Fax: (217) 789-9838
Email: nmh67@aol.com
Web: www.springfieldul.org

Tri-County Peoria Urban League
317 S. MacArthur Hwy.
Peoria, IL 61605-3892
Laraine E. Bryson, President
Tel: (309) 673-7474 Fax: (309) 672-4366
Email: uleague@tcpul.com
Web: www.tcpul.com

Urban League of Champaign County
314 S. Neil St.
Champaign, IL 61820
Tracy Parsons, President/CEO
Tel: (217) 363-3333 Fax: (217) 356-1310
Web: www.urbanleague.net

RAINBOW PUSH COALITION
National Headquarters
930 E. 50th St.
Chicago, IL 60615
Rev. Jesse L. Jackson, Sr., President
Tel: (773) 373-3366 Fax: (773) 373-3571
Email: info@rainbowpush.org
Web: www.rainbowpush.org

REAL MEN COOK FOR CHARITY, INC.
Chicago Chapter
47 W. Polk St. #100-261
Chicago, IL 60605
Yvette Moyo, President/CEO
Tel: (773) 651-8008
Email: info@realmencook.com

Web: www.realmencook.com

SPEC. INT., SPORTS

NATIONAL BROTHERHOOD OF SKIERS
Corporate Office
1525 E. 53rd St. #418
Chicago, IL 60615
Andrea Yowman, National President
Tel: (866) 280-4184
Email: andrea@nbs.org
Web: www.nbs.org

SPEC. INT., WOMEN

HOUSE OF THE GOOD SHEPHERD
P.O. Box 13453
Chicago, IL 60613
Sister Dorothy Renckens, Administrator
Tel: (773) 935-3434 Fax: (773) 935-3523

SPEC. INT., YOUTH

THE JESSE OWENS FOUNDATION
333 N. Michigan Ave. #932
Chicago, IL 60601
Marlene Owens Rankin, Executive Director
Tel: (312) 263-8222 Fax: (773) 538-4560
Email: owens@jesse-owens.org
Web: www.jesse-owens.org

TOP LADIES OF DISTINCTION, INC.
212 Bunker Hill Rd.
Belleville, IL 62221
Peggy Lewis LeCompte, National President
Tel: (618) 277-1754 Fax: (618) 277-0731
Email: tlodpresident@aol.com
Web: www.tlod.org

STUDENT ORGANIZATION

ALPHA KAPPA ALPHA SORORITY, INC.
Beta Chapter
P.O. Box 7253
Chicago, IL 60680
Jamari Trent, Chapter President
Web: www.aka1908.com

Chi Alpha Omega Chapter
P.O. Box 59493
Schaumburg, IL 60159
Jamel Ivory Penn, Chapter President
Web: www.aka1908.com

Delta Beta Chapter
P.O. Box 4042
Carbondale, IL 62902
Nancy Hanks, Chapter President
Web: www.aka1908.com

Delta Chi Omega Chapter
P.O. Box 5648
Evanston, IL 60204
Vickie J. Brown, Chapter President
Web: www.aka1908.com

Delta Delta Omega Chapter
P.O. Box 245
East St. Louis, IL 62201
Donna Bender, Chapter President
Web: www.aka1908.com

Delta Omicron Chapter
8016 S. Ellis Ave.
Chicago, IL 60619
Gina M. Jones, Chapter President
Web: www.aka1908.com

Epsilon Epsilon Omega Chapter
P.O. Box 971
Champaign, IL 61820
Murial Denise Bondurant, Chapter President
Web: www.aka1908.com

Epsilon Eta Chapter
1501 W. Bradley Ave.
Peoria, IL 61606
Nekeya Herrion, Chapter President
Web: www.aka1908.com

Epsilon Iota Chapter
P.O. Box 1168
Edwardsville, IL 62025
Shanita Smith, Chapter President
Web: www.aka1908.com

Epsilon Lambda Omega Chapter
P.O. Box 264
Cairo, IL 62914
Constance L.I. Williams, Chapter President
Web: www.aka1908.com

Gamma Chapter
P.O. Box 2747
Champaign, IL 61825
Nehanda Loiseau, Chapter President
Web: www.aka1908.com

Gamma Chi Chapter
P.O. Box 1055
Evanston, IL 60201
Allison Tucker, Chapter President
Web: www.aka1908.com

Gamma Kappa Omega Chapter
P.O. Box 519
Carbondale, IL 62903
Deborah Walton McCoy, Chapter President
Web: www.aka1908.com

Kappa Mu Omega
P.O. Box 213
Joliet, IL 60434
Thelma Kirkland, Chapter President
Web: www.aka1908.com

Lambda Alpha Omega Chapter
P.O. Box 2735
Naperville, IL 60567
Barbara Wade, Chapter President
Web: www.aka1908.com

Lambda Mu Omega Chapter
P.O. Box 437005
Chicago, IL 60643
Simona Haqq, Chapter President
Web: www.aka1908.com

Lambda Nu Omega Chapter
P.O. Box 8528
Waukegan, IL 60079
Pamela M. Foster-Stith, Chapter President
Web: www.aka1908.com

Lambda Psi Chapter
P.O. Box 5, Rt. 53
Romeoville, IL 60446
Symara Michelle Hearon, Chapter President
Web: www.aka1908.com

Lambda Tau Omega Chapter
P.O. Box 467
Matteson, IL 60443
Toya Tinette Harvey, Chapter President
Web: www.aka1908.com

National Office
5656 S. Stony Island Ave.
Chicago, IL 60637
Dr. Betty N. James, Executive Director
Tel: (773) 684-1282 Fax: (773) 288-8251
Email: exec@aka1908.com
Web: www.aka1908.com

Nu Omicron Omega Chapter
P.O. Box 5815
Springfield, IL 62705-5815
Pat A. Carpenter, Chapter President
Tel: (217) 787-1387 Fax: (217) 787-3972
Email: pac3524@sbcglobal.net
Web: www.nuomicronomega1908.tripod.com

Nu Pi Omega Chapter
P.O. Box 6068
Peoria, IL 61601
Wanda Higgins, Chapter President
Web: www.aka1908.com

Omicron Alpha Chapter
207 Hayes Ave.
Lagrange, IL 60525
Web: www.aka1908.com

Omicron Delta Omega Chapter
P.O. Box 1871
Bloomington, IL 61702
Marcia R. Thompkins, Chapter President
Web: www.aka1908.com

Phi Epsilon Omega Chapter
8636 S. Maryland
Chicago, IL 60619
Tanya Cherie Foucher, Chapter President
Web: www.aka1908.com

Phi Kappa Omega Chapter
P.O. Box 428437
Evergreen Park, IL 60805
Marianne C. Stallworth, Chapter President
Web: www.aka1908.com

Pi Gamma Omega Chapter
P.O. Box 5865
Rockford, IL 61125
Carol Lynn Craig, Chapter President
Web: www.aka1908.com

Sigma Gamma Chapter
P.O. Box C-1
555 N. Sheridan Rd.
Lake Forest, IL 60045
Catherine Calloway, Chapter President
Web: www.aka1908.com

Tau Gamma Omega Chapter
P.O. Box 802272
Chicago, IL 60680
Shari Johnson, Chapter President
Web: www.aka1908.com

Theta Omega Chapter
7741 S. Paxton
Chicago, IL 60649
Bette Reid, Chapter President
Web: www.aka1908.com

Theta Rho Omega Chapter
P.O. Box 152
Markham, IL 60426
Patricia A. Jones-Banks, Chapter President
Web: www.aka1908.com

Upsilon Phi Omega Chapter
P.O. Box 146
Edwardsville, IL 62025
Jimmie Ruth Cooper, Chapter President
Web: www.aka1908.com

Xi Eta Omega Chapter
P.O. Box 1316
Moline, IL 61265
Mattelyn Pritchett-Joplin, Chapter President
Web: www.aka1908.com

Xi Kappa Chapter
P.O. Box 438615
Chicago, IL 60643
Tamlyn Wright, Chapter President
Web: www.aka1908.com

Xi Nu Omega Chapter
P.O. Box 19166
Chicago, IL 60619
Nancy Banks, Chapter President
Web: www.aka1908.com

Zeta Iota Chapter
P.O. Box 6108
Macomb, IL 61455
Natasha D. Rochelle, Chapter President
Web: www.aka1908.com

ALPHA PHI ALPHA FRATERNITY, INC.
Alpha Mu Chapter, Northwestern University
P.O. Box 5684
Evanston, IL 60204
Web: www.alphaphialpha.net

Beta Eta Chapter, Southern Illinois University
Office of Student Development, Student Ctr.
Carbondale, IL 62901
Web: www.alphaphialpha.net

Delta Epsilon Lambda Chapter
P.O. Box 265
East St. Louis, IL 62201
Web: www.alphaphialpha.net

Epsilon Kappa Chapter, Bradley University
P.O. Box 1293
Peoria, IL 61606
Web: www.alphaphialpha.net

Epsilon Phi Chapter, Northern Illinois University
Campus Life Bldg.
Dekalb, IL 60115
Web: www.alphaphialpha.net

Eta Eta Chapter, Western Illinois University
Greek Council Office, University Union
Macomb, IL 61455
Web: www.alphaphialpha.net

Eta Tau Chapter, Illinois State University
P.O. Box 604
Normal, IL 61761
Web: www.alphaphialpha.net

Iota Delta Lambda Chapter
P.O. Box 805527
Chicago, IL 60680-4116
Jerald Knox, President
Web: www.idl1906.com

Iota Pi Chapter, Southern Illnois University
P.O. Box 1168
Edwardsville, IL 62025
Web: www.alphaphialpha.net

Kappa Chi Lambda Chapter
P.O. Box 512
North Chicago, IL 60064
Herschel A. Rayles, President
Tel: (262) 654-5145 Fax: (262) 654-5145
Email: haryales@juno.com

Kappa Pi Lambda Chapter
P.O. Box 1293
Peoria, IL 61602
Web: www.alphaphialpha.net

Mu Alpha Lambda Chapter
P.O. Box 438661
Chicago, IL 60643
Web: www.alphaphialpha.net

Mu Chi Lambda Chapter
P.O. Box 4993
Rock Island, IL 61201
Web: www.alphaphialpha.net

Mu Delta Lambda Chapter
P.O. Box 6191
Springfield, IL 62708
Web: www.alphaphialpha.net

Mu Mu Chapter, Elmhurst College
P.O. Box 2138
Chicago, IL 60126
Web: www.alphaphialpha.net

Mu Mu Lambda Chapter
P.O. Box 2815
Glen Ellyn, IL 60138
Michael J. Bates, President
Email: info@mumulambda.org
Web: http://mumulambda.org

Nu Psi Lambda Chapter
P.O. Box 1712
Bloomington, IL 61702
Web: www.alphaphialpha.net

Nu Rho Chapter, Illinois Institute of Technology
3300 S. Wabash Box #7
Chicago, IL 60617
Web: www.alphaphialpha.net

Omicron Lambda Beta Chapter
205 N. Matthews #412, M/C 250
Urbana, IL 61801
Web: www.alphaphialpha.net

Omicron Xi Chapter, Roosevelt University
P.O. Box 1
Chicago, IL 60605
Web: www.alphaphialpha.net

Pi Sigma Chapter, Aurora University
P.O. Box 6083
Aurora, IL 60598
Web: www.alphaphialpha.net

Tau Chapter, University of Illinois
P.O. Box 2066
Champaign, IL 61820
Web: www.alphaphialpha.net

Theta Mu Lambda Chapter
P.O. Box 1157
Calumet City, IL 60409
Web: www.alphaphialpha.net

Xi Lambda Chapter
P.O. Box 87529
Chicago, IL 60680
Web: www.alphaphialpha.net

Zeta Nu Chapter, Eastern Illinois University
P.O. Box 432
Charleston, IL 61920
Web: www.alphaphialpha.net

Zeta Xi Lambda Chapter
P.O. Box 5470
Evanston, IL 60201
Web: www.alphaphialpha.net

BLACK STUDENTS UNION
University of Illinois at Chicago
750 S. Halsted St. #340S
Chicago, IL 60607-7043
Annette Wright, Director of Student Activities
Tel: (312) 413-5070 Fax: (312) 413-5074
Web: www.uic.edu/depts/chcc/programs

NATIONAL BLACK LAW STUDENTS ASSOCIATION
Depaul University College of Law
25 E. Jackson Blvd.
Chicago, IL 60604
Michelle Duff, President
Tel: (312) 362-8701 Fax: (312) 362-5448
Email: blsa_depaul@yahoo.com
Web: www.law.depaul.edu

INDIANA

AFRICAN AMERICAN ARTS INSTITUTE
Indiana University-Bloomington
275 N. Jordan Ave. #310
Bloomington, IN 47405-1101
Dr. Charles E. Sykes, Director
Tel: (812) 855-9501 Fax: (812) 855-5168
Email: aaai@indiana.edu
Web: www.indiana.edu/~aaai

BUSINESS

INDIANA BLACK EXPO, INC.
3145 N. Meridian St.
Indianapolis, IN 46208
Joyce Rogers, President/CEO
Tel: (317) 925-2702 Fax: (317) 925-6624
Web: www.indianablackexpo.com

NATIONAL MINORITY SUPPLIER DEVELOPMENT COUNCIL, INC.
Indiana Regional Minority Supplier Development Council
2126 N. Meridian St.
Indianapolis, IN 46202
Reginald K. Henderson, President
Tel: (317) 923-2110 Fax: (317) 923-2204
Email: rkhenderson@irmsdc.com
Web: www.irmsdc.com

CHAMBER OF COMMERCE

INDIANAPOLIS BLACK CHAMBER OF COMMERCE
P.O. Box 88287
Indianapolis, IN 46208-0287
Charles Montgomery, Executive Director
Tel: (317) 924-9840 Fax: (317) 924-2513
Email: ibcc@sbcglobal.net
Web: www.indianapolisbcc.org

CULTURAL

AFRICAN/AFRICAN-AMERICAN HISTORICAL MUSEUM
436 E. Douglas Ave.
Fort Wayne, IN 46802
Jacqueline J. Patterson, Office Manager
Tel: (260) 420-0765 Fax: (260) 426-9773
Email: fwaahm@aol.com
Web: www.african-americanfw.com

BLACK CULTURAL CENTER
Purdue University, 1100 3rd St.
West Lafayette, IN 47906
Renee Thomas, Director
Tel: (765) 494-3092 Fax: (765) 496-1915
Email: rathomas@purdue.edu
Web: www.purdue.edu/bcc

ENTERTAINMENT

NATIONAL AFRICAN AMERICAN RV'ERS ASSOCIATION
Indiana Soul Journers RV Club Chapter
5116 Chatham Pl.
Indianapolis, IN 46626
Charles Kinslow, President
Tel: (317) 542-0245
Email: c_kinslow@hotmail.com
Web: www.naarva.com

Steel City Cruisers Chapter
2300 Ellsworth St.
Gary, IN 46404
Charles Barbour, President
Tel: (219) 949-2227
Email: cbarbour37@hotmail.com
Web: www.naarva.com

LAW ENFORCEMENT

NATIONAL ORGANIZATION OF BLACK LAW ENFORCEMENT EXECUTIVES
Northern Indiana Chapter
P.O. Box 64006
US Postal Inspection Service
Gary, IN 46401-0006
Richard Ligon, Postal Inspector/Team Leader
Tel: (219) 886-8239 Fax: (219) 886-8230
Email: richarddligon@aol.com
Web: www.noblenatl.org

Southern Indiana Chapter
P.O. Box 441784
Indianapolis, IN 46204-1784
Frank Anderson, Sheriff
Tel: (317) 231-8200 Fax: (317) 231-8596
Email: sh20728@indygov.org
Web: www.noblenatl.org

MULTI-PURPOSE

NATIONAL ASSOCIATION FOR THE ADVANCEMENT OF COLORED PEOPLE
Monroe County Branch
P.O. Box 243
Bloomington, IN 47402
William Vance, Jr., Chapter President
Tel: (812) 332-1513 Fax: (812) 332-8451
Email: wavdlv@sbcglobal.net
Web: www.bloomington.in.us/~mcbnaacp

POLITICAL ACTION

AMERICAN CIVIL LIBERTIES UNION
Indiana Chapter
Price Bldg., 1031 E. Washington St.
Indianapolis, IN 46202
Fran Quigley, Executive Director
Tel: (317) 635-4056

Web: www.iclu.org

BLACKS IN GOVERNMENT
Region V
2946 N. Park Ave.
Indianapolis, IN 46205-4149
Thomas A. Walton, President
Tel: (317) 925-6159
Email: region5.president@bignet.org
Web: www.bignet.org/regional/region5/default.htm

Region V-Crane Chapter
Unit One, P.O. Box 677
Crane, IN 47522
Tel: (757) 836-3564
Web: www.bignet.org/regional/region5/default.htm

Region V-Greater Indianapolis Chapter
P.O. Box 502038
Indianapolis, IN 46250
William Murray, Corresponding Secretary
Tel: (317) 510-4893
Email: bill.murray@defas.mil
Web: www.bignet.org/regional/region5/default.htm

PROFESSIONAL

AMERICAN ASSOCIATION OF BLACKS IN ENERGY
Indiana Chapter
c/o NIPSCO,1501 Hale Ave.
Fort Wayne, IN 46802
Lafayette Jordan, President
Tel: (260) 439-1237 Fax: (260) 439-1230
Email: ljordan@nisource.com
Web: www.aabe-ind.org

BLACK COACHES ASSOCIATION
Headquarters
201 S. Capital Ave. #495, Pan American Plz.
Indianapolis, IN 46225
Floyd Keith, Executive Director
Tel: (317) 829-5600 Fax: (317) 829-6601
Email: nationaloffice@bcasports.org
Web: www.bcasports.org

CONFERENCE OF MINORITY TRANSPORTATION OFFICIALS
Gary Chapter
Gary Public Transportation Corporation, 100 W. 4th Ave.
Gary, IN 46402
Jani Gant, Board Member
Tel: (219) 885-7555 Fax: (219) 881-2551
Email: jgantgha@aol.com
Web: www.comto.org

NATIONAL BLACK MBA ASSOCIATION, INC.
Indianapolis Chapter
P.O. Box 2325
Indianapolis, IN 46206-2325
Michael Florence, President
Tel: (317) 308-6447
Email: information@nbmbaa-indy.org
Web: www.nbmbaa-indy.org

NATIONAL OPTOMETRIC ASSOCIATION
National Headquarters
3723 Main St.
East Chicago, IN 46312
Dr. Charles Comer, Association Manager/Meeting Planner
Tel: (877) 394-2020 Fax: (219) 398-1077
Email: ccomer2@aol.com
Web: www.natoptassoc.org

SPEC. INT., EDUCATION

NATIONAL ASSOCIATION FOR MULTICULTURAL EDUCATION
Indiana Chapter
Indianapolis Public Schools, Office of Multicultural Education, 1140 Dr. Martin Luther King Jr. St.
Indianapolis, IN 46202
Patricia Payne, Chapter Organizer
Tel: (317) 226-2431 Fax: (317) 226-4611
Email: paynep@mail.ips.k12.in.us
Web: www.ips.k12.in.us

THE NATIONAL GEM CONSORTIUM
P.O. Box 537
Notre Dame, IN 46556
Leigh Hayden, Director of Marketing
Tel: (574) 631-7771 Fax: (574) 287-1486
Email: gem.1@nd.edu
Web: www.gemfellowship.org

SPEC. INT., SOCIAL INTEREST

100 BLACK MEN OF INDIANAPOLIS, INC.
3901 N. Meridian St.
Indianapolis, IN 46208
Clarence Crain, Chapter President

Tel: (317) 921-1276 Fax: (317) 920-2502
Email: info@100blackmenindy.org
Web: www.100blackmenindy.org

NATIONAL URBAN LEAGUE, INC.
Fort Wayne Urban League
227 E. Washington Blvd. #300
Fort Wayne, IN 46802
A. V. Fleming, President/CEO
Tel: (260) 745-3100 Fax: (260) 745-0405
Email: ftwuleague@aol.com
Web: www.nul.org

Indianapolis Urban League
777 Indiana Ave.
Indianapolis, IN 46202
Joseph Slash, President/CEO
Tel: (317) 693-7603 Fax: (317) 693-7613
Email: jslash@indplsul.org
Web: www.indplsul.org

Urban League of Madison County, Inc.
1210 W. 10th St.
Anderson, IN 46016
William Raymore, President
Tel: (765) 649-7126 Fax: (765) 644-6809
Email: wraymore@sbcglobal.net
Web: www.nul.org

Urban League of Northwest Indiana, Inc.
3101 Broadway
Gary, IN 46408
Eloise Gentry, President
Tel: (219) 887-9621 Fax: (219) 887-0020
Web: www.nul.org

Urban League of South Bend and St. Joseph County
1555 W. Western Ave.
South Bend, IN 46619
Seabe Gavin, Director of Operations
Tel: (574) 287-2800 Fax: (574) 287-6073
Email: sburbanleague@aol.com
Web: www.sburbanleague.com

ALPHA KAPPA ALPHA SORORITY, INC.
Alpha Eta Omega Chapter
P.O. Box 10421
Terre Haute, IN 47802
Tamara M. Ramey-Carter, Chapter President
Web: www.aka1908.com

Alpha Mu Omega Chapter
P.O. Box 88097
Indianapolis, IN 46208
Esther Bowman, Chapter President
Web: www.aka1908.com

Beta Phi Chapter
P.O. Box 250, Student Ctr.
Muncie, IN 47306
Mia A. Fields, Chapter President
Web: www.aka1908.com

Epsilon Rho Chapter
P.O. Box 696, Stewart Ctr.
W. Lafayette, IN 47906
Shalisa Sanderlin, Chapter President
Web: www.aka1908.com

Epsilon Xi Chapter
Pickeral Hall #16
Terre Haute, IN 47809
Afton Simpson, Chapter President
Web: www.aka1908.com

Eta Kappa Omega Chapter
P.O. Box 724
East Chicago, IN 46312
Paulina M. Johnson, Chapter President
Web: www.aka1908.com

Eta Mu Omega Chapter
P.O. Box 11647
South Bend, IN 46634
Giovanni Edwards, Chapter President
Web: www.aka1908.com

Gamma Psi Omega Chapter
P.O. Box 4575
Gary, IN 46404
Lori Benford-Bryant, Chapter President
Web: www.aka1908.com

Iota Chi Omega Chapter
P.O. Box 11136
Fort Wayne, IN 46805
Anita Nevils, Chapter President
Web: www.aka1908.com

Kappa Chapter
5227 Nob Ln.
Indianapolis, IN 46226
Susan Francis Brown, Chapter President
Web: www.aka1908.com

Kappa Epsilon Omega
P.O. Box 2148
Anderson, IN 46018
An'jou Connie Johnson, Chapter President
Web: www.aka1908.com

Kappa Tau Omega Chapter
P.O. Box 5007
Bloomington, IN 47407
Yolanda G. Raby, Chapter President
Web: www.aka1908.com

Nu Lambda Chapter
P.O. Box 1116
Gary, IN 46407
Kimberly Veal, Chapter President
Web: www.aka1908.com

Omicron Phi Omega Chapter
P.O. Box 2574
Kokomo, IN 46904
Alessia Renee Harrell, Chapter President
Web: www.aka1908.com

Pi Lambda Chapter
408 S. Locust St. UB #100
Greencastle, IN 46135
Deonna Nykole Craig, Chapter President
Web: www.aka1908.com

Sigma Phi Omega Chapter
P.O. Box 2908
Gary, IN 46403
Malline Morris, Chapter President
Web: www.aka1908.com

Zeta Zeta Omega Chapter
P.O. Box 15651
Evansville, IN 47716
Kimberly Lee Redding, Chapter President
Web: www.aka1908.com

ALPHA PHI ALPHA FRATERNITY, INC.
Gamma Eta Chapter, Indiana University
P.O. Box 5202
Bloomington, IN 47407
Email: apa1906@indiana.edu
Web: www.alphaphialpha.net

Gamma Rho Lambda Chapter
P.O. Box 4320
Gary, IN 46404
Web: www.alphaphialpha.net

Iota Lambda Chapter
P.O. Box 88131
Indianapolis, IN 46208
Web: www.alphaphialpha.net

Kappa Rho Lambda Chapter
P.O. Box 15031
Evansville, IN 47716
Web: www.alphaphialpha.net

Nu Nu Lambda Chapter
P.O. Box 5813
Bloomington, IN 47403
Web: www.alphaphialpha.net

Sigma Phi Chapter, University of Indiana/Depawl University
P.O. Box 441631
Indianapolis, IN 46244
Web: www.alphaphialpha.net

Theta Upsilon Lambda Chapter
P.O. Box 10757
Fort Wayne, IN 46853
Web: www.alphaphialpha.net

Theta Xi Chapter, Ball State University
P.O. Box 87
Muncie, IN 47306
Web: www.alphaphialpha.net

Theta Xi Lambda Chapter
P.O. Box 11396
Southbend, IN 46601
Web: www.alphaphialpha.net

BLACK STUDENT UNION
Indiana University Northwest
Dept. of Minority Studies, 3400 Broadway
Gary, IN 46408-1197
John Gunn, President
Tel: (219) 980-6629 Fax: (219) 980-6866
Email: jwgunn@iun.edu
Web: www.iun.edu/~bsunw

Indiana University, Purdue University Indianapolis
815 W. Michigan St. #UC-002
Indianapolis, IN 46202-5199
Marsha Currin, Advisor
Tel: (317) 274-3931 Fax: (317) 274-7099
Email: iupuibsu@iupui.edu
Web: www.iupui.edu

NATIONAL BLACK LAW STUDENTS ASSOCIATION
Indiana University School of Law
530 W. New York St.

Indianapolis, IN 46202
Cedric D'Hue, President
Tel: (317) 274-8523
Email: cdhue@iupui.edu
Web: http://indylaw.indiana.edu

Indiana University School of Law-Bloomington
211 S. Indiana Ave.
Bloomington, IN 47405
Tel: (812) 855-7995 Fax: (812) 855-0555
Web: www.law.indiana.edu

University of Notre Dame Law School
P.O. Box R
Notre Dame, IN 46556
Bobby Brown, President
Tel: (574) 631-6627 Fax: (574) 631-3980
Email: ndblsa@nd.edu
Web: www.nd.edu/~ndlaw

NATIONAL PAN-HELLENIC COUNCIL, INC.
National Headquarters-Indiana University
Eigenmann Ctr., 635, 1900 E. 10th St.
Bloomington, IN 47406
Virginia M. Le Blanc, Executive Director/CEO
Tel: (812) 855-8820 Fax: (812) 856-6742
Email: execdirector@nphchq.org
Web: www.nphchq.org

IOWA

GATEWAY DANCE THEATER
1225 Stephenson Way
Des Moines, IA 50314
Penny Furgerson, Director
Tel: (515) 283-8383 Fax: (515) 282-9262
Email: gdt@gatewaydance.org
Web: www.gatewaydance.org

AMERICAN CIVIL LIBERTIES UNION
Iowa Civil Liberties Union
505 5th Ave. #901
Des Moines, IA 50309
Ben Stone, Executive Director
Tel: (515) 243-3576
Email: iclu@iowaclu.org
Web: www.iowaclu.org

NATIONAL MEDICAL ASSOCIATION
The Central Iowa Chapter
Methodist Medical Plz. II, 1215 Pleasant St. #116
Des Moines, IA 50309-1426
Paula Mahone, M.D., President
Tel: (515) 241-8383 Fax: (515) 241-8386
Web: www.nmanet.org

NATIONAL SOCIETY OF BLACK ENGINEERS
Region 5: Iowa State University Chapter
Departmental-Engineering, 110 Marston Hall
Ames, IA 50011
Krystle J. Carr, President
Tel: (515) 572-7976
Email: kcarr@iastate.edu
Web: www.stuorg.iastate.edu/nsbe/

Region 5: University of Iowa
4133 Seamans Ctr. University of Iowa College of Engineering
Iowa City, IA 52242-1527
Victor Rodgers, Advisor
Tel: (319) 335-1401 Fax: (319) 335-1415
Email: victor-rodgers@uiowa.edu
Web: www.icaen.uiowa.edu/~mesa/

ALPHA KAPPA ALPHA SORORITY, INC.
Eta Tau Chapter
P.O. Box 41094
Des Moines, IA 50311
Nichelle Dawkins, Chapter President
Web: www.aka1908.com

Iota Zeta Omega Chapter
P.O. Box 8431
Des Moines, IA 50309
Margo Steele-Holland, Chapter President
Web: www.midwesternakas.com

Tau Psi Omega Chapter
P.O. Box 690
Iowa City, IA 52244
Hope Williams, Chapter President
Web: www.midwesternakas.com

ALPHA PHI ALPHA FRATERNITY, INC.
Omicron Pi Chapter, Iowa State University
Memorial Union #64

Ames, IA 50010
Web: www.alphaphialpha.net

Zeta Kappa Lambda Chapter
P.O. Box 5006
Des Moines, IA 50306
Web: www.alphaphialpha.net

CONCERNED BLACK STUDENTS
Grinnell College
1119 6th Ave.
Grinnell, IA 50112-1690
Michael Sams, Director Multicultura Affairs
Tel: (641) 269-3703 Fax: (641) 269-3710
Email: cbs@grinnell.edu
Web: www.grinnell.edu/cbs/

KANSAS

MINORITY SUPPLIER COUNCIL
9300 Metcalf #350
Overland Park, KS 66212
Lonnie C. Scott, President
Tel: (913) 534-2704 Fax: (913) 534-2047
Email: info@m-s-c.org
Web: www.m-s-c.org

NATIONAL ORGANIZATION OF BLACK LAW ENFORCEMENT EXECUTIVES
Kansas City Chapter
P.O. Box 338
Washburn University
Shawnee, KS 66203
Charles Lenoir, Ph.D., Associate Professor
Tel: (913) 962-4112 Fax: (913) 962-4130
Email: cclenoir@gbronline.com
Web: www.noblenatl.org

AMERICAN ASSOCIATION OF BLACKS IN ENERGY
University of Kansas/Student Chapter
4010 Learned Hall
Lawrence, KS 66045
Florence E. Boldridge, Advisor
Tel: (785) 864-3620 Fax: (785) 864-5445
Email: fboldridge@ukans.edu
Web: www.aabe-ks-stu.org

NATIONAL MEDICAL ASSOCIATION
Kaw Valley Medical Society
3550 S. 4th St. #120
Leavenworth, KS 66048-5061
Vernon Mills, M.D., President
Tel: (913) 772-6046 Fax: (913) 758-0500
Web: www.nmanet.org

NATIONAL SOCIETY OF BLACK ENGINEERS
Region 5: Kansas University Chapter
University of Kansas, School of Engineering, 1520 W. 15th St., Eaton Hall #1
Lawrence, KS 66045-7621
Florence Boldridge, Director of Diversity Programs
Tel: (785) 864-3620 Fax: (785) 864-5445
Email: fboldridge@ku.edu
Web: http://www.ku.edu/~nsbe/about.html

BROWN FOUNDATION FOR EDUCATIONAL EQUITY, EXCELLENCE AND RESEARCH
1515 SE Monroe
Topeka, KS 66612
Cheryl Brown Henderson, President
Tel: (785) 235-3939 Fax: (785) 235-1001
Email: brownfound@juno.com
Web: http://brownvboard.org/foundatn/foundatn.htm

NATIONAL ASSOCIATION FOR MULTICULTURAL EDUCATION
Wichita International Affiliate
Special Education, USD 373, 619 Boyd
Newton, KS 67114
Sharon Landrum, Co-President
Tel: (316) 284-6570 X318
Email: slandrum@newton.k12.ks.us
Web: www.nameorg.org

INTERNATIONAL BLACK STUDENT ALLIANCE, INC.
629 SE Quincy #102
Topeka, KS 66603
W. Lazone Grays, President/CEO
Tel: (785) 232-4272
Email: ibsa@myway.com

Web: www.ibsa-inc.org

SPEC. INT., HUMAN RELATIONS

KANSAS HUMAN RIGHTS COMMISSION
900 SW Jackson #568-S
Topeka, KS 66612-1258
William V. Minner, Executive Director
Tel: (785) 296-3206 Fax: (785) 296-0589
Email: khrc@ink.org
Web: www.khrc.net

SPEC. INT., SOCIAL INTEREST

NATIONAL URBAN LEAGUE, INC.
Urban League of Wichita, Inc.
1802 E. 13th St.
Wichita, KS 67214
Prentice Lewis, Interim President
Tel: (316) 262-2463 Fax: (316) 262-8841
Email: plewisulow@sbcglobal.net
Web: www.nul.org

STUDENT ORGANIZATION

ALPHA KAPPA ALPHA SORORITY, INC.
Alpha Iota Omega Chapter
P.O. Box 1994
Topeka, KS 66601
Kimberly Scott, Chapter President
Web: www.midwesternakas.com

Beta Kappa Omega Chapter
P.O. Box 8155
Wichita, KS 67208
Crystal Turner, Chapter President
Web: www.midwesternakas.com

Mu Eta Omega Chapter
805 Skyline Dr.
Junction City, KS 66414
Rosa Carter, Chapter President
Web: www.midwesternakas.com

Upsilon Rho Omega Chapter
P.O. Box 14252
Overland Park, KS 66285
Betty Hunter, Chapter President
Web: www.midwesternakas.com

ALPHA PHI ALPHA FRATERNITY, INC.
Delta Eta Lambda Chapter
P.O. Box 1692
Topeka, KS 66601
Web: www.alphaphialpha.net

Delta Mu Chapter, Wichita State University
P.O. Box 8781
Wichita, KS 67208
Web: www.alphaphialpha.net

Eta Beta Lambda Chapter
P.O. Box 68
Kechi, KS 67067
Web: www.alphaphialpha.net

Kappa Tau Chapter, Kansas State University
Holton Hall #202
Manhattan, KS 66506
Web: www.alphaphialpha.net

Pi Omicron Lambda Chapter
P.O. Box 3084
Fort Leavenworth, KS 66027
Web: www.alphaphialpha.net

Upsilon Chapter, University of Kansas
P.O. Box 1692
Lawrence, KS 66044
Web: www.alphaphialpha.net

BLACK STUDENTS UNION
University of Kansas
1301 Jayhawk Blvd., Kansas Union #400
Lawrence, KS 66045
Sam Allen, President
Tel: (785) 864-3984
Web: www.ku.edu

NATIONAL BLACK LAW STUDENTS ASSOCIATION
University of Kansas School of Law
1535 W. 15th St.
Lawrence, KS 66045
Daniel Dye, President
Tel: (785) 864-4550 Fax: (785) 864-5054
Web: www.nblsa.org

Washburn University School of Law
1700 College Ave.
Topeka, KS 66621-1140
Tel: (785) 231-1060 Fax: (785) 232- 8087
Email: onyi.ekwegwalu@washburn.edu
Web: www.nblsa.org

KENTUCKY

BUSINESS

NATIONAL MINORITY SUPPLIER DEVELOPMENT COUNCIL, INC.
Kentuckiana Minority Business Council
614 W. Main St. #5500
Louisville, KY 40202
Derwin L. Webb, President/CEO
Tel: (502) 625-0135 Fax: (502) 625-0082
Email: dwebb@kmbc.biz
Web: www.kmbc.biz

CULTURAL

JUNETEENTH THEATRE FESTIVAL
2314 S. Floyd St.
Louisville, KY 40292
Lundeana Thomas, Director
Tel: (502) 852-7682 Fax: (502) 852-7235
Email: lmthom01@athena.louisville.edu
Web: www.louisville.edu/a-s/ta

ENTERTAINMENT

NATIONAL AFRICAN AMERICAN RV'ERS ASSOCIATION
Kentuckiana RVers Chapter
1321 Cecil Ave.
Louisville, KY 40211
Luscious Green, President
Tel: (502) 778-9912
Email: luciousdina4@aol.com
Web: www.naarva.com

LAW ENFORCEMENT

NATIONAL ORGANIZATION OF BLACK LAW ENFORCEMENT EXECUTIVES
Kentucky Chapter
P.O. Box 1502
Jefferson County Police Department
Louisville, KY 40201
Jacqueline M. Cooper, President
Tel: (502) 239-6400
Email: jmc3@insightbb.com
Web: www.noblenatl.org

MULTI-PURPOSE

NATIONAL ASSOCIATION FOR THE ADVANCEMENT OF COLORED PEOPLE
Louisville Branch
1300 S. 4th St.
Louisville, KY 40208
Janice E. Carter, President
Tel: (502) 776-7608 Fax: (502) 634-8745
Email: jc40218@aol.com
Web: www.louisville-naacp.org

POLITICAL ACTION

AMERICAN CIVIL LIBERTIES UNION
Kentucky Chapter
315 Guthrie St. #300
Louisville, KY 40202-3820
Beth Wilson, Executive Director
Tel: (502) 581-1181 Fax: (502) 589-9687
Email: info@aclu-ky.org
Web: www.aclu-ky.org

BLACKS IN GOVERNMENT
Region IV-Blacks in Kentucky State Chapter
156 Tupelo Trail
Frankfort, KY 40601
Gwen Buffington, Chapter President
Tel: (502) 875-8105 Fax: (502) 564-6721
Email: gbuffing@kde.state.ky.us
Web: www.bignet.org

Region IV-Derby City Chapter
4207 W. Broadway
Louisville, KY 40211
Regina Morris, Chapter President
Tel: (502) 582-6123 Fax: (502) 582-6456
Email: vsdrmorr@vba.va.gov
Web: www.bignet.org

Region V-Greater Cincinnati/Miami Valley Chapter
763 Horse Branch Rd.
Edgewood, KY 41017-9691
Melvin Boyd, Chapter President
Tel: (513) 648-3412
Email: greater.cincinnati@bignet.org
Web: www.bignet.org/regional/region5/default.htm

PROFESSIONAL

NATIONAL ASSOCIATION OF BLACK ACCOUNTANTS, INC.
Greater Louisville Chapter
P.O. Box 715
Louisville, KY 40201-0715
Freida Winkfield, President
Email: nabaglc@hotmail.com
Web: www.nabainc.org

NATIONAL BLACK MBA ASSOCIATION, INC.
Louisville Chapter-Mideast
P.O. Box 2953
Louisville, KY 40201
Gerald Joiner, President
Tel: (502) 540-5946
Email: info@kyblackmba.com
Web: www.kyblackmba.com

NATIONAL MEDICAL ASSOCIATION
Kentucky State Medical Association
305 W. Broadway #104
Louisville, KY 40202
Beverly Gaines, M.D., State President
Tel: (502) 852-2924 Fax: (502) 585-2931
Email: bev0264@aol.com
Web: www.nmanet.org

SCIENTIFIC

THE INSTITUTE FOR CLINICAL RESEARCH AND COMMUNITY OUTREACH
305 W. Broadway #104
Louisville, KY 40202
Dr. Beverly Gaines, Founder/President
Tel: (502) 568-8800 Fax: (502) 585-2931
Email: bgicrco@aol.com

SPEC. INT., SOCIAL INTEREST

LOUISVILLE URBAN LEAGUE
1535 W. Broadway
Louisville, KY 40203
Benjamin K. Richmond, President/CEO
Tel: (502) 561-6830 Fax: (502) 585-2335
Email: brichmond@lul.org
Web: www.lul.org

NATIONAL URBAN LEAGUE, INC.
Louisville Urban League
1535 W. Broadway
Louisville, KY 40203
Benjamin K. Richmond, President/CEO
Tel: (502) 561-6830 Fax: (502) 585-2335
Email: brichmond@lul.org
Web: www.lul.org

Urban League of Lexington-Fayette County
148 DeWeese St.
Lexington, KY 40507
Porter G. Peeples, CEO
Tel: (859) 233-1561 Fax: (859) 233-7260
Email: admin@urbanleaguelexington.com
Web: www.nul.org

STUDENT ORGANIZATION

ALPHA KAPPA ALPHA SORORITY, INC.
Beta Gamma Omega Chapter
P.O. Box 11405
Lexington, KY 40575
Eugenia Johnson-Smith, Chapter President
Web: www.aka1908.com

Beta Omega Omega Chapter
P.O. Box 7171
Paducah, KY 42001
Erna Boykin, Chapter President
Web: www.aka1908.com

Beta Rho Omega Chapter
P.O. Box 196
Hopkinsville, KY 42240
Teresa Gore Moss, Chapter President
Web: www.aka1908.com

Beta Upsilon Omega Chapter
P.O. Box 845
Frankfort, KY 40602
Sheila Stuckey, Chapter President
Web: www.aka1908.com

Epsilon Zeta Chapter
P.O. Box 8304, College Heights
Bowling Green, KY 42101
April M. White, Chapter President
Web: www.aka1908.com

Eta Rho Chapter
P.O. Box 1248
Morehead, KY 40351
Yolonda Elaine Stone, Chapter President
Web: www.aka1908.com

Iota Sigma Chapter
3395 Spangler Dr. #152
Lexington, KY 40517
Ahlishia Shipley, Chapter President
Web: www.aka1908.com

Omicron Sigma Omega Chapter
P.O. Box 61
Bowling Green, KY 42101
Cheryl Lewis-Smith, Chapter President
Web: www.aka1908.com

Pi Lambda Omega Chapter
P.O. Box 99446
Louisville, KY 40299
Antoinette Davis-Jones, Chapter President
Web: www.aka1908.com

Zeta Zeta Chapter
University Station
Murray, KY 42071
Kimberly Joy Browning, Chapter President
Web: www.aka1908.com

ALPHA PHI ALPHA FRATERNITY, INC.
Alpha Beta Lambda Chapter
P.O. Box 1248
Lexington, KY 40590
Web: www.alphaphialpha.net

Alpha Lambda Chapter
P.O. Box 2963
Louisville, KY 40201
Web: www.alphaphialpha.net

Alpha Pi Chapter, University of Louisville
P.O. Box 12, Student Activities Ctr.
Louisville, KY 40292
Web: www.alphaphialpha.net

Beta Mu Chapter, Kentucky State University
P.O. Box 1545
Frankfort, KY 40601
Web: www.alphaphialpha.net

Epsilon Chi Chapter, University of Kentucky
P.O. Box 575
Lexington, KY 40526
Web: www.alphaphialpha.net

Eta Rho Chapter, Western Kentucky University
P.O. Box U-321
Bowling Green, KY 42101
Web: www.alphaphialpha.net

Gamma Beta Lambda Chapter
512 Grama Dr.
Frankfort, KY 40601
William Bearden
Web: www.alphaphialpha.net

Omicron Nu Lambda Chapter
P.O. Box 1053
Radcliff, KY 40159
Web: www.alphaphialpha.net

Rho Gamma Chapter, Northern Kentucky University
P.O. Box 239
Highland Heights, KY 41099
Web: www.alphaphialpha.net

Xi Alpha Chapter, Morehead State University
P.O. Box 2414
Morehead, KY 40351
Web: www.alphaphialpha.net

Xi Pi Lambda Chapter
P.O. Box 1612
Paducah, KY 42002
Web: www.alphaphialpha.net

Zeta Omicron Chapter, Murray State University
2309 State University
Murray, KY 42071
Ravon Shephard, President
Tel: (502) 762-6836
Email: don.cook@murraystate.edu
Web: http://campus.murraystate.edu/org/alpha_phi_alpha/alphazohome.htm

NATIONAL BLACK LAW STUDENTS ASSOCIATION
Salmon P. Chase College of Law-Northern Kentucky University
Nunn Hall #530
Highland Heights, KY 41099
Kimberly Blissett, President
Tel: (859) 572-6475
Email: blsa@nku.edu
Web: www.nku.edu/~chase/studentorgs.htm

LOUISIANA

BUSINESS

NATIONAL MINORITY SUPPLIER DEVELOPMENT COUNCIL, INC.
Louisiana Minority Business Council
935 Gravier St., 20th Fl.

New Orleans, LA 70112
Phala K. Mire, Executive Director
Tel: (504) 523-7110 Fax: (504) 592-6645
Email: info@lambc.org
Web: www.lambc.org

THE TUESDAY MORNING BREAKFAST GROUP
P.O. Box 3083
Spout, LA 71133
Lloyd Thompson, President
Tel: (318) 221-2344 Fax: (318) 635-9735
Email: thompson1856@yahoo.com

CULTURAL

AFRICAN AMERICAN MUSEUM
538 S. Blvd.
Baton Rouge, LA 70802
Sadie Roberts-Joseph, Founder/Curator
Tel: (225) 343-4411 Fax: (225) 343-4431
Email: sadierobertsjoseph@yahoo.com

BATON ROUGE JUNETEENTH CELEBRATION CADAV, INC.
538 S. Blvd.
Baton Rouge, LA 70802
Sadie Roberts-Joseph, State Coordinator
Tel: (225) 343-4411 Fax: (225) 343-4411

BLACK ARTS NATIONAL DIASPORA, INC.
1530 N. Claiborne Ave.
New Orleans, LA 70116
Fred Chambers
Tel: (504) 949-2263
Email: blkarts@bellsouth.net
Web: www.bandinc.org

ENTERTAINMENT

NATIONAL AFRICAN AMERICAN RV'ERS ASSOCIATION
Louisiana Gators RV Club
4843 Main HiWay
St. Martinvlle, LA 70582
Raymond Vavasseur, President
Tel: (337) 382-2035
Web: www.naarva.com

POLITICAL ACTION

AMERICAN CIVIL LIBERTIES UNION
Louisiana Chapter
P.O. Box 56157
New Orleans, LA 70156-6157
Joe Cook, Executive Director
Tel: (504) 522-0617
Email: admin@laaclu.org
Web: www.laaclu.org

ASSOCIATION OF COMMUNITY ORGANIZATIONS FOR REFORM NOW
Baton Rouge Office
5177 Greenwell Springs Rd.
Baton Rouge, LA 70806
Tel: (225) 925-5558 Fax: (225) 923-3144
Email: laacorn@acorn.org
Web: www.acorn.org

Lake Charles Office
1721 Jake St.
Lake Charles, LA 70601
Tel: (337) 436-0245 Fax: (337) 494-6273
Email: laacorn@acorn.org
Web: www.acorn.org

New Orleans National Office
1024 Elysian Fields Ave.
New Orleans, LA 70117
Tel: (504) 943-0044 Fax: (504) 943-3842
Email: chieforg@acorn.org
Web: www.acorn.org

BLACKS IN GOVERNMENT
Region VI-Central Louisiana Chapter
P.O. Box 3133
Fort Polk, LA 71459
Kevin J. Williams, Chapter President
Tel: (337) 531-2731
Web: www.bignet.org/regional/region6/index.htm

Region VI-Greater New Orleans Chapter
749 Mercedes Pl.
Terry Town, LA 70056
Trudy Criddle, Chapter President
Tel: (504) 481-0292
Email: trudy1102000@yahoo.com
Web: www.bignet.org/regional/region6/index.htm

Region VI-Lower Mississippi River Chapter
P.O. Box 60267
New Orleans, LA 70160-0267
Gwen Johnson, Chapter President
Tel: (504) 862-2510
Web: www.bignet.org/regional/region6/index.htm

PROFESSIONAL

AMERICAN ASSOCIATION OF BLACKS IN ENERGY
Central SW Louisiana Chapter
P.O. Box 5000
Pineville, LA 71361-5000
Jeffrey Hall, President
Tel: (318) 484-7400 Fax: (318) 484-7161
Email: jeff.hall@cleco.com
Web: www.aabe-c-swla.org

Louisiana Chapter
P.O. Box 51371
c/o Entergy Services, Inc., 639 Loyola Ave. (L-ENT-11B)
New Orleans, LA 70151
Eula Brown-Lynch, President
Tel: (504) 512-1104 Fax: (504) 576-4103
Email: e7cs@aol.com
Web: www.aabe-la.org

NATIONAL ALLIANCE OF MARKET DEVELOPERS
New Orleans Chapter
1600 Canal St.
New Orleans, LA 70112
Tierney DeCuir, Chapter President
Tel: (504) 539-9222 Fax: (504) 539-9228
Web: www.namdntl.org/new_orleans.htm

NATIONAL ASSOCIATION OF BLACK ACCOUNTANTS, INC.
Baton Rouge Chapter
P.O. Box 67022
Baton Rouge, LA 70896
Gwen B. Johnson, President
Tel: (225) 342-6920
Email: gbjohnso@dhh.la.gov
Web: www.nabainc.org

NATIONAL BLACK MBA ASSOCIATION, INC.
New Orleans Chapter-South
P.O. Box 57978
New Orleans, LA 70157-7978
Darryl Julian Ward, President
Tel: (504) 246-0694
Email: dward@jeffparish.net
Web: www.nonbmbaa.org

NATIONAL MEDICAL ASSOCIATION
7820 Chef Menteur Hwy.
New Orleans, LA 70126
Leonard Weather, M.D.
Tel: (504) 241-0413 Fax: (504) 241-1292
Email: drwea041@bellsouth.net
Web: www.nmanet.org

NATIONAL SOCIETY OF BLACK ENGINEERS
Region 5: University of New Orleans Chapter
2000 Lakeshore Dr.
New Orleans, LA 70148
Carsie Hall, Professor
Tel: (504) 280-6073 Fax: (504) 280-7413
Email: chall@uno.edu
Web: www.uno.edu/~nsbe/

RELIGIOUS

CONGREGATION OF THE SISTER OF THE HOLY FAMILY
6901 Chef Menteur Hwy.
New Orleans, LA 70126
Sister Sylvia Thibodeaux, Superior General
Tel: (504) 242-8315 Fax: (504) 241-3957
Email: sylviathib@aol.com
Web: www.sistersoftheholyfamily.org

KNIGHTS OF PETER CLAVER, INC.
1825 Orleans Ave.
New Orleans, LA 70116
Arthur McFarland, President
Tel: (504) 821-4225 Fax: (504) 821-4253
Email: execdir@knightsofpeterclaver.com
Web: www.knightsofpeterclaver.com

RESEARCH

AMISTAD RESEARCH CENTER
Tilton Hall, Tulane University
6823 St. Charles Ave.
New Orleans, LA 70118-5698
Leonce Hampton, Executive Director
Tel: (504) 865-5535 Fax: (504) 865-5580
Email: arc@tulane.edu
Web: www.amistadresearchcenter.org

SPEC. INT., EDUCATION

LOUISIANA ENGINEERING ADVANCEMENT PROGRAM
University of New Orleans

2000 Lake Shore Dr.
New Orleans, LA 70148
Vernard Henley, Jr., Executive Director
Tel: (504) 280-6073 Fax: (504) 280-5585
Email: vhenley@uno.edu
Web: www.leap1.org

NATIONAL ASSOCIATION FOR MULTICULTURAL EDUCATION
Florida Parishes Chapter
College of Education and Human Development, SLU
Box 749
Hammond, LA 70402
Paul Simoneaux, President
Tel: (504) 549-5244
Email: psimoneaux@selu.edu
Web: www.nameorg.org

SPEC. INT., HEALTH SERVICES

FRIENDLY MEMBERS MINISTRY
1009 Wilker Neal Ave.
Metairie, LA 70003
Rev. Frederick F. Batiste, Jr., President
Tel: (504) 464-9610 Fax: (504) 712-0830
Email: friendlymembers@ecofaith.com

SPEC. INT., SOCIAL INTEREST

100 BLACK MEN OF EAST FELICIANA PARISH, INC.
P.O. Box 8181
Clinton, LA 70722
Oliver Wingfield, President
Tel: (225) 634-7298

100 BLACK MEN OF METRO BATON ROUGE, INC.
P.O. Box 2286
Baton Rouge, LA 70821
Brace B. Godfrey, President
Tel: (225) 356-9444 Fax: (225) 356-9453
Email: info@100bmbr.brcoxmail.com
Web: www.100blackmenbr.org

NATIONAL URBAN LEAGUE, INC.
Urban League of Greater New Orleans
2322 Canal St.
New Orleans, LA 70119
Edith G. Jones, President/CEO
Tel: (504) 620-2332 Fax: (504) 620-9654
Email: ejones@urbanleagueneworleans.org
Web: www.urbanleagueneworleans.org

STUDENT ORGANIZATION

ALPHA KAPPA ALPHA SORORITY, INC.
Alpha Beta Omega Chapter
P.O. Box 50219
New Orleans, LA 70150
Carolyn Bryant, Chapter President
Web: www.aka1908.com

Beta Psi Chapter, Southern University
P.O. Box 11033
Baton Rouge, LA 70813
Nathalie N. Godfrey, Chapter President
Web: www.aka1908.com

Beta Upsilon Chapter, Dillard University
P.O. Box 820265
New Orleans, LA 70182
Krysten D. Jones, Chapter President
Web: www.aka1908.com

Delta Lambda Omega Chapter
6624 Venus Dr.
Shreveport, LA 71119
Margaret Thompson Hudson, Chapter President
Web: www.aka1908.com

Epsilon Beta Chapter, University of Southwestern Louisiana
USL, P.O. Box 43105
Lafayette, LA 70504
Evon Larae Hogan, Chapter President
Web: www.aka1908.com

Epsilon Psi Omega Chapter
P.O. Box 861
Grambling, LA 71245
Betty Jackson, Chapter President
Web: www.aka1908.com

Epsilon Tau Chapter, Xavier University
2707 Havana St.
New Orleans, LA 70125
Meisha Kristen Graham, Chapter President
Web: www.aka1908.com

Eta Chi Chapter, Northwestern State University
NSU, P.O. Box 3679
Natchitoches, LA 71497
Kalprina Williams, Chapter President
Web: www.aka1908.com

Eta Chi Omega Chapter

P.O. Box 90815
Lafayette, LA 70509
Stephanie A. Finley, Chapter President
Web: www.aka1908.com

Eta Eta Chapter
P.O. Box 791
New Orleans, LA 70148
Erin Freeman, Chapter President
Web: www.aka1908.com

Eta Kappa Chapter, Louisiana State University
P.O. Box 19189 LSU
Baton Rouge, LA 70893
Emilia P. Gilbert, Chapter President
Web: www.aka1908.com

Eta Theta Chapter, Loyola University
P.O. Box 1
6363 St. Charles Ave.
New Orleans, LA 70118
Reanda Fields, Chapter President
Web: www.aka1908.com

Gamma Eta Omega Chapter
P.O. Box 3902
Baton Rouge, LA 70821
Lovenia Deconge Watson, Chapter President
Web: www.aka1908.com

Iota Eta Omega Chapter
726 Leona St.
Morgan City, LA 70380
Dolores Charles Henderson, Chapter President
Web: www.aka1908.com

Iota Rho Omega Chapter
P.O. Box 1093
Minden, LA 71055
Adell Cosby Oliver, Chapter President
Web: www.aka1908.com

Lambda Beta Omega Chapter
P.O. Box 2028
Opelousa, LA 70571
Donna M. Fontenot, Chapter President
Web: www.aka1908.com

Lambda Omicron Chapter, Southeastern Louisiana University
SLU 12778
Hammond, LA 70402
Monica L. Jackson, Chapter President
Web: www.aka1908.com

Nu Gamma Omega Chapter
P.O. Box 4726
Baton Rouge, LA 70821
Linda C. Joseph, Chapter President
Web: www.aka1908.com

Omicron Iota Omega Chapter
P.O. Box 1236
West Monroe, LA 71294
Jackie Slack, Chapter President
Web: www.aka1908.com

Omicron Lambda Omega Chapter
P.O. Box 870403
New Orleans, LA 70127
Currita Waddy, Chapter President
Web: www.aka1908.com

Omicron Psi Chapter, Tulane University
P.O. Box 50845
New Orleans, LA 70150
Erin M. Steib, Chapter President
Web: www.aka1908.com

Phi Gamma Omega Chapter
5840 Poole St.
Alexandria, LA 71302
Maxine Pickens, Chapter President
Web: www.aka1908.com

Phi Rho Omega Chapter
P.O. Box 887
Franklin, LA 70538
Debra McClarity, Chapter President
Web: www.aka1908.com

Phi Sigma Omega Chapter
P.O. Box 1784
Gonzales, LA 70737
Toni Booker, Chapter President
Web: www.aka1908.com

Pi Alpha Chapter, Nicholls State University
P.O. Box 1065
Thibodaux, LA 70302
Shanedolyn Grover, Chapter President
Web: www.aka1908.com

Rho Beta Omega Chapter
P.O. Box 1191
Natchitoches, LA 71457
Celia Cannon, Chapter President
Web: www.aka1908.com

Rho Pi Omega Chapter
P.O. Box 285
Harvey, LA 70059
Vanessa B. Carter, Chapter President
Web: www.aka1908.com

Sigma Rho Omega Chapter
P.O. Box 3056
Shreveport, LA 71133
Pamela Levy, Chapter President
Web: www.aka1908.com

Tau Iota Omega Chapter
P.O. Box 1388
Slidell, LA 70459
Shai Lyn Menina, Chapter President
Web: www.aka1908.com

Tau Kappa Omega Chapter
P.O. Box 261
Plaquemine, LA 70765
Eunice Frank-Trent, Chapter President
Web: www.aka1908.com

Theta Lambda Chapter, Louisiana Tech University
P.O. Box 3139 T.S.
Ruston, LA 71272
Ashley Nicole Fort, Chapter President
Web: www.aka1908.com

Theta Zeta Chapter, Northeast Louisiana University
P.O. Box 5198
Monroe, LA 71209
Keinisha Bullard, Chapter President
Web: www.aka1908.com

Zeta Lambda Omega Chapter
P.O. Box 1147
Alexandria, LA 71309
Linda Valley Mccobbie, Chapter President
Web: www.aka1908.com

Zeta Phi Omega Chapter
P.O. Box 4712
Monroe, LA 71211
Sharilynn Loche, Chapter President
Web: www.aka1908.com

Zeta Pi Chapter, McNeese State University
P.O. Box 91457
Lake Charles, LA 70609
Keena Michelle Rossyion, Chapter President
Web: www.aka1908.com

Zeta Psi Omega Chapter
P.O. Box 321
Lake Charles, LA 70602
Judith W. Washington, Chapter President
Web: www.aka1908.com

Zeta Theta Chapter, Southern University-New Orleans
5350 Vermillion Blvd.
New Orleans, LA 70122
Paula Johnson, Chapter President
Web: www.aka1908.com

NATIONAL BLACK LAW STUDENTS ASSOCIATION
Louisiana State University Law Center
Paul M. Herbert Law Ctr. #202
Baton Rouge, LA 70803
Ronald Haley Jr., President
Tel: (225) 578-8646 Fax: (225) 578-8647
Email: rhaley1@lsu.edu
Web: http://students.law.lsu.edu/blsa/

Tulane Law School
6329 Freret St.
New Orleans, LA 70118
Tel: (504) 865-5939
Web: www.nblsa.org

MAINE

POLITICAL ACTION

AMERICAN CIVIL LIBERTIES UNION
Maine Chapter
401 Cumberland Ave.
Portland, ME 04101
Shenna Bellows, Executive Director
Tel: (207) 774-5444 Fax: (207) 774-1103
Email: info@mclu.org
Web: www.mclu.org

SPEC. INT., EDUCATION

NATIONAL ASSOCIATION OF AFRICAN AMERICAN STUDIES
P.O. Box 325
Biddeford, ME 04005
Dr. Lemuel Berry, Jr., Executive Director
Tel: (207) 839-8004 Fax: (207) 839-3776
Email: naaasconference@earthlink.net
Web: www.naaas.org

STUDENT ORGANIZATION

NATIONAL BLACK LAW STUDENTS ASSOCIATION
University of Maine School of Law
246 Deering Ave., 115 Law Bldg. Z
Portland, ME 04102
Natasha Baker, President
Tel: (207) 780-4309
Web: www.nblsa.org

MARYLAND

ARTISTIC

SOUL IN MOTION PLAYERS, INC.
P.O. Box 5374
Rockville, MD 20848-5374
Michael Friend, Artistic Director/Founder
Tel: (800) 355-1090
Email: info@soulinmotionplayers.org
Web: www.simpinc.org

BUSINESS

NATIONAL MINORITY SUPPLIER DEVELOPMENT COUNCIL, INC.
Maryland/Washington Minority Supplier Development Council, Regional Council
10770 Columbia Pike #L100
Silver Spring, MD 20901
Kenneth E. Clark, President/CEO
Tel: (301) 592-6700 Fax: (301) 592-6704
Email: jamaine.taylor@mddccouncil.org
Web: www.mddccouncil.org

CULTURAL

AFRICAN AMERICAN TOURISM COUNCIL OF MARYLAND
P.O. Box 3014
Baltimore, MD 21229
Louis C. Fields, Executive Director
Tel: (410) 783-5469 Fax: (410) 566-5254
Email: bbhtours@aol.com
Web: www.baltimoreblackheritagetours.com

AFRO-AMERICAN HISTORICAL AND GENEALOGICAL SOCIETY, INC.
Prince George's County, Maryland Chapter
P.O. Box 44252
Fort Washington, MD 20744-4252
William Shelton, President
Tel: (301) 248-9624
Email: quinns12@att.net
Web: pgcm.aahgs.org

THE GREAT BLACKS IN WAX MUSEUM, INC.
1601-03 E. North Ave.
Baltimore, MD 21213
Liz Byrd, Public Relation Coordinator
Tel: (410) 563-3404 Fax: (410) 563-7806
Email: lbyrd@greatblacksinwax.org
Web: www.greatblacksinwax.org

ENTERTAINMENT

NATIONAL AFRICAN AMERICAN RV'ERS ASSOCIATION
DC Connection RV Club
10306 Birwood Ct.
Largo, MD 20774
Anita Robinson, President
Tel: (301) 336-3912
Email: rustysplace@aol.com
Web: www.naarva.com

GOVERNMENT

GOVERNOR'S OFFICE OF MINORITY AFFAIRS
Maryland State Government
6 St. Paul St. #1502
Baltimore, MD 21202
Sharon Roberson Pinder, Special Secretary
Tel: (410) 767-8232 Fax: (410) 333-7568
Email: info@oma.state.md.us
Web: www.oma.state.md.us

LAW ENFORCEMENT

NATIONAL ORGANIZATION OF BLACK LAW ENFORCEMENT EXECUTIVES
Maryland Chapter
P.O. Box 23731
Baltimore, MD 21203
Raymond Grisset, Lieutenant
Tel: (410) 686-3101 Fax: (410) 780-0830
Email: ltgrissett@comcast.net
Web: www.noblemaryland.homestead.com

MULTI-PURPOSE

NATIONAL ASSOCIATION FOR THE ADVANCEMENT OF COLORED PEOPLE
Baltimore Branch
8 W. 26th St.
Baltimore, MD 21218
Marvin L. Cheatham Sr., President
Tel: (410) 366-3300 Fax: (410) 366-3304
Email: info@naacpbaltimore.org
Web: www.naacpbaltimore.org

National Headquarters
4805 Mt. Hope Dr.
Baltimore, MD 21215
Nelson B. Rivers, COO
Tel: (410) 521-4939
Web: www.naacp.org

Montgomery County
P.O. Box 2165
Rockville, MD 20847-2165
Henry Hailstock, President
Tel: (301) 657-2062 Fax: (301) 657-3401
Email: info@naacp-mc.org
Web: www.naacp-mc.org

NATIONAL TRUST FOR THE DEVELOPMENT OF AFRICAN AMERICAN MEN
6811 Kenilworth Ave. #501
Riverdale, MD 20737
Garry A. Mendez, Executive Director
Tel: (301) 887-0100 Fax: (301) 887-0405
Email: mendez2us@yahoo.com
Web: www.keepthetrust.org

POLITICAL ACTION

AMERICAN CIVIL LIBERTIES UNION OF MARYLAND
3600 Clipper Mill Rd. #350
Baltimore, MD 21211
Susan Goering, Executive Director
Tel: (410) 889-8555 Fax: (410) 366-7838
Email: aclu@aclu-md.org
Web: www.aclu-md.org

ASSOCIATION OF COMMUNITY ORGANIZATIONS FOR REFORM NOW
ACORN Maryland
16 W. 25th St.
Baltimore, MD 21218
Willie Ray, President
Tel: (410) 735-3360 Fax: (410) 735-3375
Email: mdacorn@acorn.org
Web: www.acorn.org

Prince George's County ACORN
3404 Kenilworth Ave.
Hyattsville, MD 20781
Jessica Lehman, Head Organizer
Tel: (301) 699-8000
Email: mdacornpgro@acorn.org
Web: www.acorn.org

BLACKS IN GOVERNMENT
Region III
525 Oak St.
Aberdeen, MD 21001
Carol Bruce, Council President
Tel: (410) 273-7940
Email: region3.president@bignet.org
Web: www.bignet.org

Region III-Agape Chapter
P.O. Box 23841
Baltimore, MD 21203-5841
Regina Lewis-Gordon, Chapter President
Tel: (410) 605-7125
Email: region3.president@bignet.org
Web: www.bignet.org

Region III-City Crescent Chapter
1740 Wentworth St.
Baltimore, MD 21234
Errigh Laboo, Chapter President
Tel: (410) 962-5670
Email: region3.president@bignet.org
Web: www.bignet.org

Region III-Health Care Finance Admin. Chapter
2917 Fendall Rd.
Baltimore, MD 21207
Anita A. Pinder, Chapter President
Tel: (410) 786-5493
Email: hcfa@bignet.org
Web: www.bignet.org

Region III-Patuxent River II Chapter
47244 Silver Slate
Lexington Park, MD 20653
Sheila A. Milburn, Chapter President
Tel: (301) 995-7939 Fax: (301) 737-4272
Email: samilburn64@hotmail.com
Web: www.bignet.org

Region III-Susquehanna Chapter
P.O. Box 827

Aberdeen Proving Ground, MD 21005
Carol Bruce, Chapter President
Tel: (410) 278-3176
Email: region3.president@bignet.org
Web: www.bignet.org

Region XI-Big Hoffman Chapter
13405 Tamarack Rd.
Silver Springs, MD 20904
Elise Johnson, Chapter President
Tel: (301) 384-7246 Fax: (703) 384-3057
Web: www.bignet.org

Region XI-Congressional Chapter
6495 New Hampshire Ave. #LL100-2
Hyattsville, MD 20783
Mary J. Rhone, Chapter President
Tel: (202) 228-5464 Fax: (202) 267-4823
Web: www.bignet.org

Region XI-FMS Chapter
P.O. Box 1753
Hyattsville, MD 20788-1683
Patricia M. Lee, Chapter President
Tel: (202) 874-6693 Fax: (202) 874-7991
Email: pat.lee@fms.treas.gov
Web: www.bignet.org

Region XI-NASA's Goddard Space Flight Center/WFF Chapter
P.O. Box 512
Glenn Dale, MD 20769
Merle E. Robbins, Chapter President
Tel: (301) 286-7819 Fax: (301) 286-0339
Email: merle.e.robbins@nasa.gov
Web: www.bignet.org

Region XI-National Maritime Intelligence Center Chapter
P.O. Box 1034
Suitland, MD 20752-1034
Paula Davis, Chapter President
Tel: (301) 669-3890 Fax: (301) 669-3895
Email: pedavis@nmic.navy.mil
Web: www.bignet.org

Region XI-National Oceanic and Atmospheric Administration Chapter
P.O. Box 14361
Silver Spring, MD 20911
Michael J. Washington, Chapter President
Tel: (301) 713-3379 Fax: (301) 713-1239
Email: michael.j.washington@noaa.gov
Web: www.bignet.org

Region XI-Navy Metro Chapter
P.O. Box 321
Cabin John, MD 20818
Cyd Johnson, Chapter President
Tel: (301) 227-4934
Email: charmarq@hotmail.com
Web: www.bignet.org

Region XI-Parklawn Center Chapter
5600 Fishers Ln.
Rockville, MD 20857
Dr. Patrick C. Wilson, Chapter President
Tel: (301) 827-3097 Fax: (301) 827-0003
Email: pwilson@oc.fda.gov
Web: www.bignet.org

NATIONAL ORGANIZATION FOR THE ADVANCEMENT OF HAITIANS
1400 East-West Hwy. #G
Silver Spring, MD 20910
Dr. Joseph Baptiste, Chairman
Tel: (301) 585-1235
Email: jbaptiste@aol.com
Web: www.noahhaiti.org

THE NATIONAL POLITICAL CONGRESS OF BLACK WOMEN, INC.
Bethune-DuBois Institute
8484 Georgia Ave. #420
Silver Spring, MD 20910
Dr. C. DeLores Tucker, Chair
Tel: (301) 562-8000 Fax: (301) 562-8303
Email: info@npcbw.org
Web: www.npcbw.org

PROFESSIONAL

ASSOCIATION OF BLACK MEDIA WORKERS
P.O. Box 1795
Baltimore, MD 21203-1795
Charles Robinson, President
Tel: (410) 837-2269
Email: info@abmw-md.org
Web: www.abmw-md.org

BLACK DATA PROCESSING ASSOCIATES
Baltimore Chapter
P.O. Box 22571
Baltimore, MD 21203

Denise Holland, Chapter President
Tel: (410) 347-1404
Email: baltimore@bdpa.org
Web: www.bdpa-baltimore.org

National Headquarters
6301 Ivy Ln. #700
Greenbelt, MD 20770-3343
Vercilla A. Brown, Executive Director
Tel: (301) 220-2180 Fax: (301) 220-2185
Email: info@bdpa.org
Web: www.bdpa.org

BLACK ENTERTAINMENT AND SPORTS LAWYERS ASSOCIATION
P.O. Box 441485
Fort Washington, MD 20749-1485
Phyllicia M. Hattom, Administrative Director
Tel: (301) 248-1818 Fax: (301) 248-0700
Email: beslamailbox@aol.com
Web: www.besla.org

CONFERENCE OF MINORITY TRANSPORTATION OFFICIALS
Maryland Chapter
Abel Woman Bldg. #800
Baltimore, MD 21202
Keith Scroggins, Bureau Head
Tel: (410) 396-3704 Fax: (410) 396-3498
Email: jj.keith.scroggins@baltimorecity.gov
Web: www.comto.org

CONSORTIUM OF INFORMATION AND TELECOMMUNICATION EXECUTIVES
Association of Telecommunications Managers and Associates, Inc.-Washington Metro Chapter
P.O. Box 3354
Capitol Heights, MD 20791-3354
Tillmon Figgs, Chapter President
Tel: (410) 707-2700
Email: president@cite-dcmetro.org
Web: www.cite-dcmetro.org

INTERNATIONAL ORGANIZATION OF BLACK SECURITY EXECUTIVES
International Headquarters
P.O. Box 4436
Upper Marlboro, MD 20775
Earl Watson, President
Tel: (888) 884-6273 Fax: (301) 352-7807
Email: earl_watson@gap.com
Web: www.iobse.com

NATIONAL ALLIANCE OF MARKET DEVELOPERS
Washington Chapter
P.O. Box 4984
Silver Spring, MD 20914
Paula L. Ralph, Chapter President
Tel: (301) 622-4145 Fax: (301) 622-2457
Email: namd_dc@yahoo.com
Web: www.namdntl.org/washington_dc.htm

NATIONAL ASSOCIATION OF BLACK ACCOUNTANTS, INC.
Maryland National Chapter
7249 Hanover Pkwy. #A
Greenbelt, MD 20770
Darryl R. Matthews, Sr., Executive Director
Tel: (301) 474-6222 Fax: (301) 474-3114
Email: dmatthews@nabainc.org
Web: www.nabainc.org

Metro-Washington, D.C. Chapter
7249-A Hanover Pkwy
Greenbelt, MD 20770
Norman Jenkins, National President
Tel: (301) 474-NABA Fax: (301) 474-3114
Web: www.nabainc.org

NATIONAL ASSOCIATION OF BLACK JOURNALISTS
University of Maryland
8701-A Adelphi Rd.
Adelphi, MD 20783-1716
Herbert Lowe, President
Tel: (301) 445-7100 x103 Fax: (301) 445-7101
Email: nabj@nabj.org
Web: www.nabj.org

NATIONAL BLACK NURSES ASSOCIATION, INC.
8630 Fenton St. #330
Silver Spring, MD 20910-3803
Bettye Davis-Lewis, President
Tel: (301) 589-3200 Fax: (301) 589-3223
Email: nbna@erols.com
Web: www.nbna.org

NATIONAL COALITION OF BLACK MEETING PLANNERS
8630 Fenton St. #126
Silver Spring, MD 20910
Beverly A. Bryant, President
Tel: (202) 628-3952 Fax: (301) 588-0011

Email: ncbmp@compuserve.com
Web: www.ncbmp.com

NATIONAL FORUM FOR BLACK PUBLIC ADMINISTRATORS
Maryland Chapter
512 N Paca St.
Baltimore, MD 21201
Nancy K. Pleasant, President
Tel: (410) 523-7506
Email: npleas413@aol.com
Web: www.nfbpa.org

NATIONAL SOCIETY OF BLACK ENGINEERS
Region 2: Bowie State University Chapter
1400 Jericho Park Rd.
Bowie, MD 20715-9465
Joan Langdon, Advisor
Tel: (301) 860-4036
Web: www.bowiestate.edu/students/nsbe.htm

ORGANIZATION OF BLACK AIRLINE PILOTS, INC.
National Office
8630 Fenton St. #126
Silver Spring, MD 20910
Karl Minter, President
Tel: (800) 538-6227 Fax: (301) 588-4660
Email: nationaloffice@obap.org
Web: www.obap.org

NATIONAL BLACK CATHOLIC CONGRESS
320 Cathedral St.
Baltimore, MD 21201
Valerie E. Washington, Executive Director
Tel: (410) 547-8496 Fax: (410) 727-5432
Email: nbcc@nbccongress.org
Web: www.nbccongress.org

DAVID C. DRISKELL CENTER FOR THE STUDY OF THE AFRICAN DIASPORA
University of Maryland
2114 Tawes Fine Arts Bldg.
College Park, MD 20742-1211
Daryle Williams, Director
Tel: (301) 314-2615 Fax: (301) 314-0679
Email: driskellcenter@umail.umd.edu
Web: www.driskellcenter.umd.edu

NATIONAL INSTITUTES OF HEALTH-BLACK SCIENTISTS ASSOCIATION
P.O. Box 2262
Kensington, MD 20891-2262
Janie Smith, President
Tel: (301) 435-4568
Email: smithj@mail.nih.gov
Web: http://bsa.od.nih.gov

THE EARTHMAP FOUNDATION
P.O. Box 3074
Silver Spring, MD 20918
Egondu Rosemary Onyejekwe, President/CEO
Fax: (614) 457-9079
Email: info@earthmap.org
Web: www.earthmap.org

BDPA-BLACK EDUCATION AND TECHNOLOGY FOUNDATION
4423 Lehigh Rd. #277
College Park, MD 20740
Ann Robinson, Executive Director
Tel: (202) 258-3252 Fax: (202) 318-2194
Web: www.betf.org

BLACK FACULTY AND STAFF ASSOCIATION
University of Maryland, College Park
1118 Patuxent Bldg.
College Park, MD 20742
Willie L. Brown, President
Tel: (301) 405-2951 Fax: (301) 314-6691
Email: wbrown@umd.edu
Web: www.bfsa.umd.edu

KUNTA KINTE-ALEX HALEY FOUNDATION
31 Old Solomons Island #102
Annapolis, MD 21401
Leonard A. Blackshear, President
Tel: (410) 841-6920 Fax: (410) 841-6505
Email: info@kintehaley.org
Web: www.kintehaley.org

MINORITY ACCESS, INC.
5214 Baltimore Ave.

Hyattsville, MD 20871
Andrea D. Mickle, President/CEO
Tel: (301) 779-7100 Fax: (301) 779-9812
Email: amickle@minorityaccess.org
Web: www.minorityaccess.org

NATIONAL ASSOCIATION FOR EQUAL OPPORTUNITY IN HIGHER EDUCATION
8701 Georgia Ave. #200
Silver Spring, MD 20910
William R. Harvey, Chairman
Tel: (301) 650-2440 Fax: (301) 495-3306
Email: ccollins@nafeo.org
Web: www.nafeo.org

NATIONAL ASSOCIATION FOR MULTICULTURAL EDUCATION
Maryland Chapter
312 E. Belcrest Rd.
Bel Air, MD 21014
Cathy R. Price, Interim President
Email: cathyprice@aol.com
Web: www.nameorg.org

NATIONAL COMMISSION FOR AFRICAN AMERICAN EDUCATION
2141 Industrial Pkwy. #202
Silver Spring, MD 20904
Claude Mayberry, Chairman
Tel: (301) 680-0148 Fax: (301) 680-9240
Email: scienceweekly@erols.com
Web: www.dogonvillage.com/ncaae/

NATIONAL HOOK-UP OF BLACK WOMEN, INC.
Greater Metropolitan Capital Area Chapter
511 Moat Way
Fort Washington, MD 20744
Bertha R. Thomas, President
Tel: (301) 567-3319
Email: berthom@comcast.net
Web: www.nhbwinc.com

Southern Maryland Chapter
8600 Shorthills Ct.
Clinton, MD 20735
Elaine Davis-Nickens, President
Tel: (301) 877-1392
Email: edavisnickens@msn.com
Web: www.nhbwinc.com

NATIONAL ASSOCIATION OF HEALTH SERVICES EXECUTIVES
Headquarters
8630 Fenton St. #126
Silver Spring, MD 20910
Patricia Webb, President
Tel: (202) 628-3953 Fax: (301) 588-0011
Email: nahse.hq@verizon.net
Web: www.nahse.org

100 BLACK MEN OF MARYLAND, INC.
2901 Druid Park Dr.
Baltimore, MD 21215
Roderick Larry, President
Tel: (410) 225-0601 Fax: (410) 225-0603
Email: info@100blackmenofmd.org
Web: www.100blackmenofmd.org

BLACK UNITED FUND OF MARYLAND, INC.
Dashiell and Associates
813 E. Baltimore St. #101
Baltimore, MD 21202
Robert Fulton Dashiell, Interim President
Tel: (410) 547-8820 Fax: (410) 547-8822
Email: dashielllaw@aol.com
Web: www.nbuf.org

INSTITUTE FOR BLACK CHARITIES
8605 Cameron St. #M6
Silver Spring, MD 20910
Charlene Taylor, President/CEO
Tel: (301) 563-6250 Fax: (301) 563-6251
Email: info@blackcharities.net
Web: www.blackcharities.net

MARYLAND BLACK CAUCUS FOUNDATION, INC.
P.O. Box 253
Annapolis, MD 21404
Michael L. Vaughn, President
Tel: (410) 626-9788
Web: www.blacklegislatormd.org

NATIONAL URBAN LEAGUE, INC.
Greater Baltimore Urban League
512 Orchard St.

Baltimore, MD 21201
J. Howard Henderson, Interim President
Tel: (410) 523-8150 Fax: (410) 523-4022
Email: mwelcome@bul.org
Web: www.bul.org

THE BLACK WORLD TODAY
P.O. Box 328
Randallstown, MD 21133
Gelvin Stevenson, Vice Chairman
Tel: (410) 659-8298 Fax: (410) 521-9993
Web: www.tbwt.org

BIG BROTHERS BIG SISTERS OF THE NATIONAL CAPITAL AREA
10210 Greenbelt Rd. #900, Aerospace Bldg.
Lanham, MD 20706
Paul Bliss, President
Tel: (301) 794-9170 Fax: (301) 794-9180
Email: pbliss@bbbsnca.org
Web: www.bbbsnca.org

ASSOCIATION OF AFRICAN AMERICAN WOMEN BUSINESS OWNERS
P.O. Box 13858
8604 2nd Ave. #125
Silver Spring, MD 20911
Brenda Alford, President/CEO
Tel: (301) 585-8051 Fax: (301) 681-3681
Email: aaawbo@yahoo.com

NATIONAL BLACK WOMEN'S CONSCIOUSNESS RAISING ASSOCIATION
1906 N. Charles St.
Baltimore, MD 21218
Dr. Elaine C. Simon, Executive Director
Tel: (410) 727-8900 Fax: (410) 230-2964
Email: elainesimon1@aol.com

ALPHA KAPPA ALPHA SORORITY, INC.
Alpha Delta Chapter, Morgan State University
1110 N. Central Ave.
Baltimore, MD 21202
Lois Knight-Harrison, Graduate Advisor
Email: akacscsp87@aol.com
Web: http://akanorthatlantic.org

Epsilon Kappa Chapter, Coppin State College
17 Tentmill Ln. #K
Baltimore, MD 21208
Nikisha L. Blackmon, Graduate Advisor
Email: nikiivy8@aol.com
Web: http://akanorthatlantic.org

Eta Chapter, Bowie State University
6103 Talles Rd.
Gwynn Oak, MD 21207
Marlena Colleton, Graduate Advisor
Email: ms_colleton@yahoo.com
Web: http://akanorthatlantic.org

Lambda Zeta Chapter, American University
14920 Cherrywood Dr.
Laurel, MD 20707
Kendra L. Riley, Graduate Advisor
Email: charade93@yahoo.com
Web: http://akanorthatlantic.org

Theta Nu Chapter, University of Maryland
5107 Southern Ave. #203
Capitol Heights, MD 20743
Kathy Keyes-Waymmann, Graduate Advisor
Email: kkway_78@hotmail.com
Web: http://akanorthatlantic.org

Upsilon Tau Omega Chapter
P.O. Box 44974
Ft. Washington, MD 20744
Lezell W. Murphy, Chapter President
Tel: (301) 292-0670
Email: lwmuraka@hotmail.com
Web: www.aka1908.com

Xi Tau Chapter, Johns Hopkins University
3511 Orchard Shade Rd.
Randallstown, MD 21133
Deneen Hamlin, Graduate Advisor
Web: http://akanorthatlantic.org

ALPHA PHI ALPHA FRATERNITY, INC.
Corporate Headquarters
2313 Saint Paul St.
Baltimore, MD 21218
Darryl R. Matthews, General President
Tel: (410) 554-0040 Fax: (410) 554-0054
Email: admin@apa1906.net
Web: www.alphaphialpha.net

Delta Lambda Chapter
9241 Sealed Message Rd.
Columbia, MD 21045
Ralph Johnson, Chapter President
Web: www.alphaphialpha.net

Main Headquarters
2313 St. Paul St.
Baltimore, MD 21218-5234
Darryl R. Matthews, Sr., General President
Tel: (410) 554-0040 Fax: (410) 554-0054
Web: www.alphaphialpha.net

BLACK STUDENT UNION
Towson University
8000 York Rd.
Towson, MD 21252
Jonathan Jones, President
Tel: (410) 704-3277 Fax: (410) 704-2713
Email: muzicman_2003@hotmail.com

BLACK STUDENTS ALLIANCE
Frostburg State University
Lane Ctr. 233, LC Mailbox 263
Frostburg, MD 21532
Ravyn Hall, President
Tel: (301) 687-7402

MASSACHUSETTS

ARTISTIC

NATIONAL CENTER OF AFRO-AMERICAN ARTISTS
300 Walnut Ave.
Boston, MA 02119
Edmund Barry Gaither, Director
Tel: (617) 442-8014 Fax: (617) 445-5525
Email: bgaither@mfa.org
Web: www.ncaaa.org

BUSINESS

NATIONAL MINORITY SUPPLIER DEVELOPMENT COUNCIL, INC.
New England Minority Supplier Development Council, Inc., Regional Council
100 Huntington Ave., Dartmouth Shops
Boston, MA 02116
Tina Andrews, President
Tel: (617) 578-8900 Fax: (617) 578-8902
Email: tandrews@nemsdc.org
Web: www.nemsdc.org

CULTURAL

AFRO-AMERICAN HISTORICAL AND GENEALOGICAL SOCIETY, INC.
New England Chapter
42 Laurelwood Dr.
Stoughton, MA 02072
Roland F. Stead, Archivist
Tel: (781) 341-1029
Email: irvrevallion@aol.com
Web: www.aahgs-ne.org

AMHERST HISTORY MUSEUM
African American History
67 Amity St.
Amherst, MA 01002
Fiona Russell, Museum Director
Tel: (413) 256-0678 Fax: (413) 256-0672
Email: amhersthistory@yahoo.com
Web: www.amhersthistory.org

ENTERTAINMENT

NATIONAL AFRICAN AMERICAN RV'ERS ASSOCIATION
New England Lighthouse Beamers
93 Abington Ave.
Holbrook, MA 02121
Delories Thompson, President
Tel: (781) 767-5518
Email: evthomp@aol.com
Web: www.naarva.com

LAW ENFORCEMENT

NATIONAL ORGANIZATION OF BLACK LAW ENFORCEMENT EXECUTIVES
New England Chapter
P.O. Box 1250
DEA
Boston, MA 02205-1250
Paul L.D. Russell, Jr., Special Agent
Tel: (617) 557-2100 Fax: (617) 357-2135
Web: www.noblenatl.org

POLITICAL ACTION

AMERICAN CIVIL LIBERTIES UNION
Massachusetts Chapter
99 Chauncy St. #310
Boston, MA 02111
Carol Rose, Executive Director
Tel: (617) 482-3170 Fax: (617) 451-0009
Web: www.aclu-mass.org

ASSOCIATION OF COMMUNITY ORGANIZATIONS FOR REFORM NOW
Boston Office
1486 Dorchester Ave.
Boston, MA 02122
Jen Kern, Living Wage Resource Center
Tel: (617) 436-7100 Fax: (617) 436-4878
Email: maacorn@acorn.org
Web: www.acorn.org

Springfield Office
1655 Main St. #402
Springfield, MA 01109
Email: maacornsp@acorn.org
Web: www.acorn.org

BLACKS IN GOVERNMENT
Region I-Greater Boston Chapter
P.O. Box 6064
Boston, MA 02114-6064
Palmer T. Doiley, Chapter President
Tel: (617) 445-0073
Email: info@bostonbig.org
Web: www.bostonbig.org

Region I-Middlesex County Chapter
15 Dickenson Way #81H
Marlborough, MA 01752
Willena Rosemond, Chapter President
Tel: (508) 233-5990
Email: willena.rosemond@natick.army.mil
Web: www.bostonbig.org

Region I-Positive Chapter
P.O. Box 190037
Boston, MA 02119
Steven E. Osborn, Chapter President
Tel: (617) 427-4898
Email: greater.boston@bignet.org
Web: www.bostonbig.org

Region I-Western Massachusetts Chapter
58 Greenlawn St.
Springfield, MA 01119
Leo Foster, Chapter President
Tel: (413) 557-3981
Email: greater.boston@bignet.org
Web: www.bostonbig.org

PROFESSIONAL

AMERICAN ASSOCIATION OF BLACKS IN ENERGY
Connecticut Chapter
P.O. Box 2010
West Springfield, MA 01090-2010
Rodney O. Powell, Chapter President
Tel: (413) 787-9292 Fax: (413) 787-9363
Email: powelro@nu.com
Web: www.aabe-ct.org

CONFERENCE OF MINORITY TRANSPORTATION OFFICIALS
Boston Chapter
AMTRAK, 2 S. Station, 5th Fl.
Boston, MA 02100
Prince Reid, Jr., Program Manager/Special Advisor to GM AMTRAK
Tel: (617) 345-7739 Fax: (617) 345-7780
Email: reidp@amtrak.com
Web: www.comto.org

CONSORTIUM OF INFORMATION AND TELECOMMUNICATION EXECUTIVES
CITE-New England
P.O. Box 960275
Boston, MA 02196
Brenda Mutcherson, Chapter President
Tel: (800) 996-3662
Email: cite-ne@cite-newengland.org
Web: www.cite-newengland.org

NATIONAL ASSOCIATION OF BLACK JOURNALISTS
Boston Herald Chapter
1 Harold Sq.
Boston, MA 02106
Howard Manly, President
Tel: (617) 619-6666 Fax: (617) 619-6388
Email: hmanly@bostonherald.com
Web: www.babj.org

NATIONAL BLACK MBA ASSOCIATION, INC.
Boston Chapter-East
P.O. Box 181188
Boston, MA 02118-0010
Renee Malbranche, President

Tel: (617) 989-0331
Email: info@bostonblackmba.org
Web: www.bostonblackmba.org

NATIONAL FORUM FOR BLACK PUBLIC ADMINISTRATORS
Boston Chapter
P.O. Box 132
Boston, MA 02133
Arnold E. Sapenter, Chapter President
Tel: (617) 292-5944 Fax: (617) 236-0158
Email: arnold.sapenter@state.ma.us
Web: www.nfbpa.org

RESEARCH

WEST AFRICAN RESEARCH ASSOCIATION
Boston University-African Studies Center
Boston University, 270 Bay State Rd.
Boston, MA 02215
Jennifer Yanco, US Director
Tel: (617) 353-8902 Fax: (617) 353-4975
Email: wara@bu.edu
Web: www.africa.ufl.edu/wara

SCIENTIFIC

COMPREHENSIVE SICKLE CELL CENTER
Boston Medical Center
1 Boston Medical Center Pl. FGH-2
Boston, MA 02118
Martin Steinberg, Director
Tel: (617) 414-1020 Fax: (617) 414-1021
Email: msteinberg@medicine.bumc.bu.edu
Web: www.rhofed.com/sickle/index.htm

SPEC. INT., EDUCATION

AFRICAN STUDIES CENTER
Boston University
270 Bay State Rd.
Boston, MA 02215
Dr. James A. Pritchett, Director
Tel: (617) 353-7308 Fax: (617) 353-4975
Email: pritchet@bu.edu
Web: www.bu.edu/africa/

MASSACHUSETTS PRE-ENGINEERING PROGRAM, INC.
Northern University
360 Huntington Ave.
Boston, MA 02115-5000
Bonita M. McAllister, President/CEO
Tel: (617) 373-3839
Email: masspepinc@earthlink.net
Web: www.masspepinc.org

NATIONAL ASSOCIATION FOR MULTICULTURAL EDUCATION
Massachusetts Chapter
Mount Wachusett Community College, 444 Green St. #135
Gardner, MA 01440
Michael J. Sidoti, Counselor for Students with Disabilities
Tel: (978) 630-9120
Email: msidoti@mwcc.mass.edu
Web: www.nameorg.org

TERI COLLEGE ACCESS
Boston Public Library
700 Boylston St.
Boston, MA 02116
Jane Horton, Director of Counseling/Community Services
Tel: (617) 536-0200 Fax: (617) 536-4737
Email: horton@teri.org
Web: www.tericollegeaccess.org

SPEC. INT., HEALTH SERVICES

COMMUNITY SICKLE CELL SUPPORT GROUP, INC.
1542 Tremont St.
Roxbury, MA 02120
Rev. Ronald Stephenson, President
Tel: (617) 427-4100 Fax: (617) 262-3190
Email: cscsginc@aol.com
Web: www.cscsginc.org

SPEC. INT., SOCIAL INTEREST

AFRICAN AMERICAN FEDERATION OF GREATER BOSTON, INC.
6 Roxbury St. #4
Roxbury, MA 02119
David Wright, President
Tel: (617) 523-2261 Fax: (617) 442-6532
Email: david@aafederation.org
Web: www.massagenda.com/afamfed/index.cfm

BLACK UNITED FUND OF MASSACHUSETTS, INC.
130 Dartmouth St. #1202
Boston, MA 02116-5140
John Marshall, President/CEO
Tel: (617) 536-2666 Fax: (617) 536-2218
Email: buf-mass@msn.com
Web: www.nbuf.org

NATIONAL URBAN LEAGUE, INC.
Urban League of Eastern Massachusetts
88 Warren St.
Roxbury, MA 02119
Darnell L. Williams, President/CEO
Tel: (617) 442-4519 Fax: (617) 442-0562
Email: dwilliams@ulem.org
Web: www.ulem.org

Urban League of Springfield
756 State St.
Springfield, MA 01109
Henry M. Thomas, III, President/CEO
Tel: (413) 739-7211 Fax: (413) 732-9364
Email: info@ulspringfield.org
Web: www.ulspringfield.org

STUDENT ORGANIZATION

ALPHA KAPPA ALPHA SORORITY, INC.
Epsilon Chapter
P.O. Box 15500
Boston, MA 02215
Bianca M. Gomez, Chapter President
Web: www.aka1908.com

Lambda Upsilon Chapter
Cambridge, MA 02139
Elizabeth Burr, Chapter President
Web: www.aka1908.com

Psi Omega Chapter
P.O. Box 191416
Boston, MA 02119
Roxbury Station
Helyn C. Hall, Chapter President
Web: www.aka1908.com

Rho Epsilon Omega Chapter
P.O. Box 812351
Wellesley, MA 02181
Sheilah Horton, Chapter President
Web: www.aka1908.com

Rho Kappa Chapter, University of Massachusetts-Amherst
227 Whitmore Bldg.
Amherst, MA 01002
Tuere McIntyre, Chapter President
Web: www.aka1908.com

Xi Nu Chapter
248 Amherst Rd. #F2
Sunderland, MA 01375
Catherine L. Adams, Graduate Advisor
Email: cadams@smith.edu
Web: http://akanorthatlantic.org

Xi Xi Omega Chapter
P.O. Box 91331
Springfield, MA 01139
Mentha Hynes, Chapter President
Web: www.aka1908.com

NATIONAL BLACK LAW STUDENTS ASSOCIATION
Harvard Law School
Hastings Hall Basement
Cambridge, MA 02138
Inez Cananda, President
Tel: (617) 495-4556
Email: blsa@law.harvard.edu
Web: www.law.harvard.edu/studorgs/blsa/

Massachusetts School of Law-Student Bar Association
500 Federal St., Woodland Park
Andover, MA 01810
Garnet Dacosta, President
Tel: (978) 681-0800
Web: www.nblsa.org

New England School of Law
154 Steward St.
Boston, MA 02116
Nikki Harris, President
Tel: (617) 422-7279 Fax: (617) 422-7224
Email: nikkibharris@hotmail.com
Web: www.nblsa.org

Suffolk University, School of Law
120 Tremont St. #450 F
Boston, MA 02108-4977
Tamela Bailey, President
Tel: (617) 305-6280 Fax: (617) 305-6281
Email: blsa@suffolk.edu
Web: www.law.suffolk.edu/stuservices/blsa/index.html

Western New England College of Law
1215 Wilbraham Rd.

Springfield, MA 01119
Muriel Mompoint, President
Tel: (413) 782-1465 Fax: (413) 796-2067
Web: www.nblsa.org

MICHIGAN

ARTISTIC

DETROIT REPERTORY THEATRE
13103 Woodrow Wilson St.
Detroit, MI 48238-3686
Bruce E. Millan, Artistic/Managing Director
Tel: (313) 868-1347 Fax: (313) 868-1705
Email: detrepth@aol.com
Web: www.detroitreptheater.com

GOSPEL MUSIC WORKSHOP OF AMERICA, INC.
3908 W. Warren Ave.
Detroit, MI 48208
Shelia Smith, Director of Operations
Tel: (313) 898-6900 Fax: (313) 898-4520
Email: manager@gmwa.org
Web: www.gmwa.org

PLOWSHARES THEATRE COMPANY
2870 E. Grand Blvd. #600
Detroit, MI 48202
Gary Anderson, Producing Artistic Director
Tel: (313) 872-0279 Fax: (313) 872-0067
Email: info@plowshares.org
Web: www.plowshares.org

BUSINESS

NATIONAL MINORITY SUPPLIER DEVELOPMENT COUNCIL, INC.
Michigan Minority Business Development Council, Flint Office
328 S. Saginaw #101
Flint, MI 48502
James Franklin, Regional Director
Tel: (810) 235-4542 Fax: (810) 235-0591
Email: jfranklin@mmbdc.com
Web: www.mmbdc.com

Michigan Minority Business Development Council, Grand Rapids Office
143 Bostwick NE Main Bldg. #208M
Grand Rapids, MI 49503
Valencia Cooper, Assistant Regional Director/West Michigan
Tel: (616) 776-1724 Fax: (616) 776-7772
Email: vrcooper@mmbdc.com
Web: www.mmbdc.com

The Michigan Minority Business Development Council, Regional Council
3011 W. Grand Blvd. #230
Detroit, MI 48202
Delbert Gray, President/CEO
Tel: (313) 873-3200 Fax: (313) 873-4783
Email: mail@mmbdc.com
Web: www.mmbdc.com

COMMUNICATIONS

BLACK AWARENESS IN TELEVISION
30 Josephine St., 3rd Fl.
Detroit, MI 48202-1810
David Rambeau, Director
Tel: (313) 871-3333 Fax: (313) 871-1449
Email: davidrambeau@hotmail.com
Web: www.projectbait.blakgold.net

PROJECT BAIT
30 Josephine, 3rd Fl.
Detroit, MI 48202-1810
David Rambeau, Executive Producer
Tel: (313) 871-3333
Email: davidrambeau@hotmail.com
Web: http://projectbait.blakgold.net

CULTURAL

BLACK POETS SOCIETY
Michigan State University
338 Student Services Bldg.
East Lansing, MI 48824
Murray Edwards, Senior Coordinator
Tel: (517) 353-7745 Fax: (517) 432-1495
Email: oresa@msu.edu
Web: www.oresa.msu.edu

LANSING JUNETEENTH CELEBRATION
Michigan State University
209 Bessey Hall
East Lansing, MI 48824
Nattavia D. Curry, Coordinator
Tel: (517) 353-5210 Fax: (517) 432-2962
Email: curry@msu.edu

Web: www.msu.edu/~oss/

MOTOWN HISTORICAL MUSEUM
2648 W. Grand Blvd.
Detroit, MI 48208
Robin R. Terry, Executive Director
Tel: (313) 875-2264 Fax: (313) 875-2267
Email: info@motownmuseum.com
Web: www.motownmuseum.org

ENTERTAINMENT

NATIONAL AFRICAN AMERICAN RV'ERS ASSOCIATION
Campers for Jesus Chapter
21620 Kenosha
Oak Park, MI 48237
Bennie Phipps, President
Tel: (248) 559-6608
Email: northern@naarva.com
Web: www.naarva.com

Free Rollers of Michigan Chapter
28155 Elwell Rd.
Belleville, MI 48111
Howard Harris, President
Tel: (734) 587-3485
Email: diplomat@gatecom.com
Web: www.naarva.com

Interstate Nomads Chapter
38875 Laurenwood Dr.
Wayne, MI 48184
Walter Durant, President
Tel: (734) 595-4473
Email: lady_durant@webtv.net
Web: www.naarva.com

Northwest Sunseekers Chapter
3549 Farnum
Inkster, MI 48184
Theopolius Baker, President
Tel: (734) 595-8125
Web: www.naarva.com

Sankofa Camping Club of Michigan Chapter
P.O. Box 38654
Detroit, MI 48238
Connie Wilson, President
Tel: (313) 204-7304
Email: mustang1995@msn.com
Web: www.naarva.com

Weekenders Camping Club Chapter
P.O. Box 23703
Detroit, MI 48223
Morline Wilson, President
Tel: (313) 836-1361
Email: northern@naarva.com
Web: www.naarva.com

LAW ENFORCEMENT

NATIONAL ORGANIZATION OF BLACK LAW ENFORCEMENT EXECUTIVES
Detroit Chapter
27301 S. River Park Dr.
Inkster, MI 48141
Gregory Gaskin, Deputy Chief
Tel: (313) 563-9850 Fax: (313) 561-1077
Email: ggaskin@inksterpd.com
Web: www.noblenatl.org

MULTI-PURPOSE

NATIONAL ASSOCIATION FOR THE ADVANCEMENT OF COLORED PEOPLE
Detroit Branch
2990 E. Grand Blvd.
Detroit, MI 48202
Rev. Wendell Anthony, Chapter President
Tel: (313) 871-2087 Fax: (313) 871-7745
Email: info@detroitnaacp.org
Web: www.detroitnaacp.org

NATIONAL ASSOCIATION FOR THE ADVANCEMENT OF COLORED PEOPLE
Region III: Mid-West
17 Ford Ave.
Highland Park, MI 48203
Shirley Pratt-Miles, Director
Tel: (313) 869-3717 Fax: (313) 869-3763
Email: milesregion3@aol.com
Web: www.naacp.org

POLITICAL ACTION

AMERICAN ASSOCIATION FOR AFFIRMATIVE ACTION
Region V

5700 Cass Ave. #3660-AAB
Detroit, MI 48202
Marjorie Powell, Regional Director/Affirmative Action Officer
Tel: (317) 274-2306 Fax: (313) 577-7738
Email: mkeyes@wayne.edu
Web: www.affirmativeaction.org

AMERICAN CIVIL LIBERTIES UNION
Michigan Chapter
60 W. Hancock
Detroit, MI 48201-1324
Kary L. Moss, Executive Director
Tel: (313) 578-6800 Fax: (313) 578-6811
Email: kmoss@aclumich.org
Web: www.aclumich.org

ASSOCIATION OF COMMUNITY ORGANIZATIONS FOR REFORM NOW
Detroit Office
1249 Washington Blvd. #1303
Detroit, MI 48226
Tel: (313) 963-1840 Fax: (313) 963-4268
Email: miacornde@acorn.org
Web: www.acorn.org

BLACKS IN GOVERNMENT
Region V-Cereal City Chapter
P.O. Box 1253
Battle Creek, MI 49016-1253
Sandra E. Kennedy, Chapter President
Tel: (269) 961-5425
Email: cereal.city@bignet.org
Web: www.bignet.org/regional/region5/default.htm

NATIONAL ACTION NETWORK
Michigan Chapter
11241 Gunston St.
Detroit, MI 48213
Rev. Horace L. Sheffield, III, President
Tel: (313) 521-2076 Fax: (313) 521-1707
Email: sheffield3@aol.com
Web: www.nationalactionnetwork.org

PROFESSIONAL

AMERICAN ASSOCIATION OF BLACKS IN ENERGY
Michigan Chapter
1945 W. Parnell
Jackson, MI 49201
Eugene Hurd, President
Tel: (517) 788-2296
Email: ehurd@cmsenergy.com
Web: www.aabe-mich.org

Michigan State University/Student Chapter
1528 C Spartan Village
East Lansing, MI 48910
Eric Beda, President
Tel: (517) 355-2858
Email: bedaeric@msu.edu
Web: www.aabe.org

CONFERENCE OF MINORITY TRANSPORTATION OFFICIALS
Detroit Chapter
Burbank, Inc., 34 Rhode Island
Highland Park, MI 48203
Byron Burbank
Tel: (313) 883-5254 Fax: (313) 883-9720
Email: burbank_inc@hotmail.com
Web: www.comto.org

NATIONAL ASSOCIATION OF BLACK ACCOUNTANTS, INC.
Greater Flint Chapter
P.O. Box 13583
125 E. Union
Flint, MI 48502
Patricia O'Neal, President
Tel: (810) 760-2852 Fax: (810) 760-2984
Email: onealdp@aol.com
Web: www.nabainc.org

Lansing Chapter
1448 Ivywood Dr.
Okemos, MI 48864
Darryl Horton, Treasurer
Tel: (517) 241-2636 Fax: (517) 381-0421
Email: dhorto@michigan.gov
Web: www.nabainc.org

NATIONAL BLACK MBA ASSOCIATION, INC.
Detroit Chapter- Mideast
P.O. Box 02398
Detroit, MI 48202
Corrie Patton, President
Tel: (313) 972-4832
Web: www.detblackmba.org

NATIONAL MEDICAL ASSOCIATION
Wolverine State Medical Society
P.O. Box 21489
10730 W. 7 Mile Rd.
Detroit, MI 48221
Alma Rose George, M.D., President
Tel: (313) 342-5189 Fax: (313) 342-2772
Web: www.nmanet.org

RELIGIOUS

UNION OF BLACK EPISCOPALIANS
Midwest Region
235 Welthy SE
Grand Rapids, MI 49503
Alice Webley, Director
Tel: (616) 454-1819 Fax: (616) 454-3939
Email: yelbew@aol.com
Web: www.angloafrican.org/ube

SPEC. INT., EDUCATION

NATIONAL ASSOCIATION FOR MULTICULTURAL EDUCATION
Michigan Chapter
Detroit Public Schools, 1760 David Ct.
Ann Arbor, MI 48105
Thomas Hoetger
Tel: (734) 663-3911
Email: tomhoetger@yahoo.com
Web: www.nameorg.org

SPEC. INT., LEGAL ASSISTANCE

MICHIGAN ACORN, ACORN USA
1249 Washington Blvd. #1303
Detroit, MI 48226
Richard Winshaw, Director
Tel: (313) 963-1840 Fax: (313) 963-4268
Email: miacorn@acorn.org
Web: www.acorn.org

SPEC. INT., SOCIAL INTEREST

100 BLACK MEN OF GREATER DETROIT, INC.
P.O. Box 231361
Detroit, MI 48223-1361
Thomas Worford, Chapter President
Tel: (866) 670-4110 Fax: (313) 874-1678
Email: 100bmdetroit@comcast.net
Web: www.100bmdetroit.org

BLACK UNITED FUND OF MICHIGAN, INC.
2187 West Grand Blvd.
Detroit, MI 48208
Brenda L. Rayford, Executive Director
Tel: (313) 894-2200 Fax: (313) 894-7562
Email: bufbr@aol.com
Web: www.bufmi.org

CHARMS, INC.
2241 Charms Revene Dr.
Wixom, MI 48393
Dr. Patricia Johnson, President
Tel: (248) 669-0102
Email: president@charmsincorporated.com
Web: www.charmsincorporated.com

NATIONAL BLACK UNITED FRONT
Detroit Chapter
10100 Harper
Detroit, MI 48213
Makini Reeder, Chair
Tel: (313) 921-9422 Fax: (313) 921-9214
Email: alkebu@aol.com
Web: www.nbufront.org

NATIONAL BLACK UNITED FRONT
Muskegon Chapter
P.O. Box 1309
Muskegon, MI 49443
Betty Warfield, Chair
Tel: (616) 728-4570
Web: www.nbufront.org

NATIONAL URBAN LEAGUE, INC.
Detroit Urban League
208 Mack Ave.
Detroit, MI 48201
N. Charles Anderson, President/CEO
Tel: (313) 832-4600 Fax: (313) 832-3222
Email: gmitchell@deturbanleague.org
Web: www.detroiturbanleague.org

Grand Rapids Urban League
745 Eastern Ave. SE
Grand Rapids, MI 49503
Walter M. Brame, President
Tel: (616) 245-2207 Fax: (616) 245-7026
Email: ceogrul@aol.com
Web: www.nul.org

Southwestern Michigan Urban League

172 W. Van Buren
Battle Creek, MI 49017
Kenneth F. Little, President
Tel: (269) 962-5553 Fax: (616) 962-2228
Email: klittle@ulbc.org
Web: www.nul.org

Urban League of Flint
5005 Cloverlawn Dr.
Flint, MI 48504
Paul Newman, President/ CEO
Tel: (810) 789-7611 Fax: (810) 787-4518
Email: ulflint@aol.com
Web: www.nul.org

Urban League of Greater Muskegon
425 Catawba Ave.
Muskegon, MI 49442-5140
Rodney D. Brown, Interim President
Tel: (231) 726-6019 Fax: (231) 722-2728
Email: ggulgm@aol.com
Web: www.urbanleaguegm.org

RAINBOW/PUSH COALITION
Detroit Bureau
First National Bldg., 660 Woodward Ave. #1433
Detroit, MI 48226
Glenda Gill, Bureau Chief
Tel: (313) 963-9005 Fax: (313) 963-9012
Email: ggill@rainbowpush.org
Web: www.rainbowpush.org

STUDENT ORGANIZATION

ALPHA KAPPA ALPHA SORORITY, INC.
Alpha Rho Omega Chapter
P.O. Box 441013
Detroit, MI 48244
Altha Steen, Chapter President
Web: www.aka1908.com

Beta Mu Chapter
211 Student Ctr., Bldg. 5
Detroit, MI 48202
Linita N. Harlan, Chapter President
Web: www.aka1908.com

Delta Psi Omega Chapter
1483 McCarthy
Ypsilanti, MI 48198
W. Frances Dekard, Chapter President
Web: www.aka1908.com

Delta Tau Omega Chapter
P.O. Box 25153
Lansing, MI 48909
Esther Norton, Chapter President
Web: www.aka1908.com

Delta Zeta Chapter
P.O. Box 6346
Lansing, MI 48826
Web: www.aka1908.com

Eta Iota Omega Chapter
P.O. Box 187
Inkster, MI 48141
Patricia Eileen Jenkins, Chapter President
Web: www.aka1908.com

Eta Upsilon Omega Chapter
P.O. Box 14380
Saginaw, MI 48601
Carrie Jackson-Zackrie, Chapter President
Web: www.aka1908.com

Iota Iota Omega Chapter
P.O. Box 1564
Benton Harbor, MI 49023
Sinie Elizabeth Bass, Chapter President
Web: www.aka1908.com

Iota Sigma Omega Chapter
P.O. Box 3413
Kalamazoo, MI 49003
Angela Reed, Chapter President
Web: www.aka1908.com

Lambda Pi Omega Chapter
P.O. Box 28182
Detroit, MI 48228
Angelina Gallant, Chapter President
Web: www.aka1908.com

Mu Alpha Omega Chapter
P.O. Box 1374
Midland, MI 48640
Janice Wallace, Chapter President
Web: www.aka1908.com

Mu Phi Chapter
7400 Bay Rd.
University Center, MI 48710
Kenyatta Hurd, Chapter President
Web: www.aka1908.com

Nu Phi Omega Chapter
P.O. Box 946

Muskegon, MI 49442
Marchelle I. Latin, Chapter President
Web: www.aka1908.com

Nu Theta Chapter
Kirkhof Ctr., Student Life Office
Allendale, MI 49401
Tanisha Bowman, Chapter President
Web: www.aka1908.com

Pi Delta Chapter
21000 W. 10 Mile Rd.
Southfield, MI 48075
Tiffany Atchinson, Chapter President
Web: www.aka1908.com

Pi Tau Omega Chapter
P.O. Box 0794
Southfield, MI 48037
Joletta V. McCormick, Chapter President
Web: www.aka1908.com

Sigma Zeta Chapter
4680 Kellogg Ctr.
Albion, MI 49224
Salina Baldwin, Chapter President
Web: www.aka1908.com

Tau Alpha Omega Chapter
P.O. Box 40508
Redford, MI 48239
Doris Taylor Turner, Chapter President
Web: www.aka1908.com

Theta Chi Omega Chapter
3073 Plainfield Ave. NE
Grand Rapids, MI 49505
Billijean C. Johnson, Chapter President
Web: www.aka1908.com

Theta Lambda Omega Chapter
25839 Farmington Rd.
Farmington Hills, MI 48336
Earnestine Malcheff, Chapter President
Web: www.aka1908.com

Theta Tau Chapter
20034 Fenmore
Detroit, MI 48235
Ella Moore, Chapter President
Web: www.aka1908.com

Xi Chi Chapter
P.O. Box 13457
Flint, MI 48501
Kimberly Brantley, Chapter President
Web: www.aka1908.com

Xi Phi Chapter
P.O. Box 216
4901 Evergreen Rd.
Dearborn, MI 18216
Angelina Belinda Richardson, Chapter President
Web: www.aka1908.com

Zeta Beta Omega Chapter
P.O. Box 77
Flint, MI 48501
Shirley W. Johnson, Chapter President
Web: www.aka1908.com

Zeta Rho Chapter
P.O. Box 75
University Ctr.
Mt Pleasant, MI 48858
Angel Pringle, Chapter President
Web: www.aka1908.com

ALPHA PHI ALPHA FRATERNITY, INC.
Alpha Upsilon Chapter, Wayne State University
Gullen Mall, Box 7
Detroit, MI 48202
Web: www.alphaphialpha.net

Epsilon Eta Chapter, Eastern Michigan University
McKenny Union, Campus Life Box 2
Ypsilanti, MI 48197
Daniel Mahoney, President
Tel: (734) 487-1760
Email: dmahone2@emich.edu
Web: www.alphaphialpha.net

Epsilon Upsilon Lambda Chapter
P.O. Box 1218
Flint, MI 48501
Web: www.alphaphialpha.net

Epsilon Xi Chapter, Western Michigan University
P.O. Box 29
Kalamazoo, MI 49008
Web: www.alphaphialpha.net

Eta Nu Lambda Chapter
P.O. Box 8276
Grand Rapids, MI 49518
Web: www.alphaphialpha.net

Gamma Lambda Chapter
P.O. Box 441763
Detroit, MI 48244

Web: www.alphaphialpha.net

Iota Chi Lambda Chapter
P.O. Box 14836
Saginaw, MI 48601
Web: www.alphaphialpha.net

Iota Epsilon Chapter, Grand Valley State University
1 Campus Dr., Kirkhof Ctr.
Allendale, MI 49401
Web: www.alphaphialpha.net

Iota Phi Lambda Chapter
P.O. Box 44033
Muskegon Heights, MI 49444
Web: www.alphaphialpha.net

Iota Rho Lambda Chapter
P.O. Box 332
Southfield, MI 48037
Web: www.alphaphialpha.net

Kappa Delta Lambda Chapter
P.O. Box 14303
Lansing, MI 48901
Web: www.alphaphialpha.net

Kappa Psi Lambda Chapter
P.O. Box 191
Portage, MI 49081
Web: www.alphaphialpha.net

Pi Upsilon Chapter, University of Michigan
4901 Evergreen Rd.
Dearborn, MI 48128
Web: www.alphaphialpha.net

Theta Tau Chapter, GMI Engineering and Management Institute
1700 W. 3rd Ave.
Flint, MI 48503
Web: www.alphaphialpha.net

Theta Zeta Lambda Chapter
P.O. Box 15321
Ann Arbor, MI 48104
Web: www.alphaphialpha.net

Zeta Beta Chapter, Ferris State University
Rankin Ctr.
P.O. Box 6
Big Rapids, MI 49307
Web: www.alphaphialpha.net

Zeta Delta Chapter, Michigan State University
P.O. Box 6806
East Lansing, MI 48826
Keith Redmond, President
Email: aphia@msu.edu
Web: www.msu.edu/~aphia

ETA PHI BETA SORORITY, INC.
16815 James Couzens Fwy.
Detroit, MI 48235
Louise Hoskins Broadnax, National President
Tel: (313) 862-0600 Fax: (313) 862-6245
Email: nationaloffice@etaphibetanatl.org
Web: www.etaphibetanatl.org

MINNESOTA

ARTISTIC

PENUMBRA THEATER COMPANY, INC.
270 N. Kent St.
Saint Paul, MN 55102
Lou Bellamy, Artistic Director/Founder
Tel: (651) 224-4601 Fax: (651) 224-7074
Email: bellamylou@hotmail.com
Web: www.penumbratheatre.org

BUSINESS

NATIONAL MINORITY SUPPLIER DEVELOPMENT COUNCIL, INC.
Minnesota Minority Supplier Diversity Council
2855 Anthony Ln. South #215
St. Anthony, MN 55418
Norman Harrington, President
Tel: (612) 465-8881 Fax: (612) 465-8887
Email: info@mmsdc.org
Web: www.mmsdc.org

LAW ENFORCEMENT

NATIONAL ORGANIZATION OF BLACK LAW ENFORCEMENT EXECUTIVES
Minnesota Regional Chapter
St. Paul Police Department, 100 E. 11th St.
St. Paul, MN 55101
John Harrington, Chief of Police
Tel: (651) 292-3526 Fax: (651) 292-3600
Email: john.harrington@ci.stpaul.mn.us
Web: www.noblenatl.org

POLITICAL ACTION

AMERICAN CIVIL LIBERTIES UNION
Minnesota Chapter
450 N. Syndicate #230
St. Paul, MN 55104
Charles Samuelson, Executive Director
Tel: (651) 645-4097 Fax: (651) 647-5948
Email: csamuelson@aclu-mn.org
Web: www.aclu-mn.org

ASSOCIATION OF COMMUNITY ORGANIZATIONS FOR REFORM NOW
St. Paul Office
757 Raymond Ave.
St. Paul, MN 55114
Tel: (651) 642-9639 Fax: (651) 642-0060
Email: mnacorn@acorn.org
Web: www.acorn.org

PROFESSIONAL

MINNESOTA ASSOCIATION OF BLACK LAWYERS
P.O. Box 582892
Minneapolis, MN 55458-2892
Harvey D. Rupert, President
Tel: (612) 766-7246
Email: president@mabl.org
Web: www.mabl.org

NATIONAL ASSOCIATION OF BLACK JOURNALISTS
Region VIII-Twin Cities Chapter
Star Tribune, 425 Portland Ave.
Minneapolis, MN 55488
Greg Patterson, Chapter President
Tel: (612) 673-7287
Email: gpatterson@startribune.com
Web: www.nabj.org

NATIONAL BLACK MBA ASSOCIATION, INC.
Twin Cities Chapter-Midwest
P.O. Box 2709
Minneapolis, MN 55402
Linda Sloan, President
Tel: (651) 223-7373
Email: info@nbmbaatc.org
Web: www.nbmbaatc.org

NATIONAL FORUM FOR BLACK PUBLIC ADMINISTRATORS
Metro-Area Chapter
Community Action of Minneapolis, 401 2nd Ave.
South, #500 NW Midland Bldg.
Minneapolis, MN 55401
William J. Davis, President
Tel: (612) 348-8858 Fax: (612) 348-9384
Email: lkurth@campls.org
Web: www.nfbpa.org

NATIONAL MEDICAL ASSOCIATION
Minnesota Association of Black Physicians
393 N. Dunlap St. #600
St. Paul, MN 55104
Inell C. Rosario, M.D., President
Tel: (651) 645-0691 Fax: (651) 603-8100
Email: inellr@yahoo.com
Web: www.nmanet.org

SPEC. INT., AIDS

THE CITY, INC.
HAS (HIV/AID/STD) Prevention and Awareness Program
1545 E. Lake St.
Minneapolis, MN 55407
Charlnitta "Chi" Ellis, Program Director
Tel: (612) 728-9110 Fax: (612) 724-0692
Email: thehasprogram@thecityinc.org
Web: www.checkyoself.20m.com

SPEC. INT., EDUCATION

NATIONAL ASSOCIATION FOR MULTICULTURAL EDUCATION
Minnesota Chapter
Graduate School of Education, Hamline University,
300 4th St. #709 East
St. Paul, MN 55101
Paul C. Gorski, Chapter Organizer
Tel: (651) 523-2584
Email: gorski@earthlink.net
Web: www.nameorg.org

SPEC. INT., HUMAN RELATIONS

MINNESOTA DEPARTMENT OF HUMAN RIGHTS
190 E. 5th St. #700
St. Paul, MN 55101
Velma Korbel, Commissioner
Tel: (651) 296-5663 Fax: (651) 296-9055
Email: velma.korbel@state.mn.us
Web: www.humanrights.state.mn.us

Kansas City, MO 64108
Gwendolyn Grant, President/CEO
Tel: (816) 471-0550 Fax: (816) 471-3064
Email: ggrant@ulkc.org
Web: www.ulkc.org

Urban League of Metropolitan St. Louis
3701 Grandel Sq.
St. Louis, MO 63108
James H. Buford, President
Tel: (314) 615-3600 Fax: (314) 531-4849
Email: mlawrence@urbanleague-stl.org
Web: www.stlouis.missouri.org/urbanleagu

STUDENT ORGANIZATION

ALPHA KAPPA ALPHA SORORITY, INC.
Beta Delta Chapter
P.O. Box 50
Contract Station 24
St. Louis, MO 63130
De-Andrea Blaylock, Chapter President
Web: www.aka1908.com

Beta Omega Chapter
P.O. Box 411762
Kansas City, MO 64141
Helen Harrington, Chapter President
Web: www.midwesternakas.com

Delta Tau Chapter
A022 Brady Commons
Columbia, MO 65201
Sharita K. Wright, Chapter President
Web: www.aka1908.com

Gamma Epsilon Omega Chapter
P.O. Box 882
Jefferson City, MO 65101
Donna White, Chapter President
Web: www.midwesternakas.com

Gamma Omega Chapter
P.O. Box 170042
St. Louis, MO 63117
Gale Greene Hardeman, Chapter President
Web: www.aka1908.com

Kappa Chi Omega Chapter
P.O. Box 635
Columbia, MO 65201
Maria Dixon, Chapter President
Web: www.midwesternakas.com

Mu Omega Chapter
P.O. Box 171253
Kansas City, MO 66117
Phyllis Collins, Chapter President
Web: www.midwesternakas.com

Omicron Eta Omega Chapter
P.O. Box 24257
University City, MO 63130
Colette M. Cummings, Chapter President
Web: www.aka1908.com

Omicron Theta Omega Chapter
Weathers Station
P.O. Box 24800
St. Louis, MO 63115
Elaine Flipping, Chapter President
Web: www.aka1908.com

Rho Alpha Chapter
5100 Rockhill, University Ctr. #G-7
Kansas City, MO 64110
Amber Smith, Chapter President
Web: www.aka1908.com

Rho Iota Chapter Chapter
P.O. Box 8362
St. Louis, MO 64508
Kamita Shelby, Chapter President
Web: www.aka1908.com

Xi Tau Omega Chapter
P.O. Box 411433
Kansas City, MO 64141
Claudia Smith, Chapter President
Web: www.midwesternakas.com

ALPHA PHI ALPHA FRATERNITY, INC.
Alpha Eta Chapter, Washington University
325 Debaliviere
St. Louis, MO 63112
Antoine Brown, President
Email: ah1906@hotmail.com
Web: www.geocities.com/CollegePark/Housing/4196/

Alpha Psi Chapter, Lincoln University
P.O. Box 292
Jefferson City, MO 65102
Cameron Hardy, President
Web: www.geocities.com/Colosseum/8213/

Beta Lambda Chapter
P.O. Box 300221
Kansas City, MO 64130
Ivan Smith, President

Tel: (816) 921-6161
Email: events@betalambda.org
Web: www.betalambda.org

Beta Zeta Lambda Chapter
1503 Chestnut St.
Jefferson City, MO 65101
Web: www.alphaphialpha.net

Epsilon Lambda Chapter
P.O. Box 11971
St. Louis, MO 63112
Web: www.alphaphialpha.net

Epsilon Psi Chapter, University of Missouri
P.O. Box V
Rolla, MO 65402
Web: www.alphaphialpha.net

Iota Xi Chapter, Northeast Missouri State University
Student Union Bldg.
Kirksville, MO 63501
Web: www.alphaphialpha.net

Rho Theta Chapter, Northwest Missouri State University
800 University Dr., Student Union
Maryville, MO 64468
Email: rho_theta@hotmail.com
Web: www.alphaphialpha.net

Sigma Kappa Chapter, Missouri Western State College
P.O. Box 1579
St. Joseph, MO 64502
Web: www.alphaphialpha.net

Zeta Alpha Chapter, University of Missouri/Central Methodist College
A022 Brady Commons
Columbia, MO 65203
Web: www.alphaphialpha.net

Zeta Gamma Chapter, Central Missouri State University
SAC, P.O. Box 12
Warrensburg, MO 64093
Web: www.alphaphialpha.net

NATIONAL PAN-HELLENIC COUNCIL, INC.
North Central Region
4624 W. Rosalie St.
St. Louis, MO 63115-2224
Garvenya Lockhart, Regional Director
Tel: (314) 381-7547
Email: ncentraldir@nphchq.org
Web: www.nphchq.org

MONTANA

POLITICAL ACTION

AMERICAN CIVIL LIBERTIES UNION
Montana Chapter
P.O. Box 1317
7 W. 6th Ave. #518, Power Block Bldg.
Helena, MT 59601
Scott Crichton, Executive Director
Tel: (406) 443-8590 Fax: (406) 457-5484
Email: aclu@aclumontana.org
Web: www.aclumontana.org

NEBRASKA

ARTISTIC

OMAHA THEATER COMPANY FOR YOUNG PEOPLE
2001 Farnam St.
Omaha, NE 68102
Vic Gutman, Executive Director
Tel: (402) 345-4849
Email: vicg@rosetheater.org
Web: www.rosetheater.org

BUSINESS

NATIONAL MINORITY SUPPLIER DEVELOPMENT COUNCIL, INC.
Greater Omaha Economic Development Council
1301 Harney St.
Omaha, NE 68102
Rod Moseman
Tel: (800) 852-2622 Fax: (402) 346-7050
Email: rmoseman@accessomaha.com
Web: www.accessomaha.com

POLITICAL ACTION

AMERICAN ASSOCIATION FOR AFFIRMATIVE ACTION
Region VII
University of Nebraska at Omaha, 6001 Dodge St.
Omaha, NE 68182

Sharon Ulmar, Regional Director
Tel: (402) 554-2311
Email: sulmar@mail.unomaha.edu
Web: www.affirmativeaction.org

AMERICAN CIVIL LIBERTIES UNION
Nebraska Chapter
941 O St. #706
Lincoln, NE 68508
Tim Butz, Executive Director
Tel: (402) 476-8091 Fax: (402) 476-8135
Email: info@aclunebraska.org
Web: www.aclunebraska.org

SPEC. INT., SOCIAL INTEREST

100 BLACK MEN OF OMAHA, INC.
P.O. Box 20125
Omaha, NE 68110
Greg Johnson, President
Tel: (402) 390-2480 Fax: (402) 390-0885
Email: gjohnson@hayes-cpa.com
Web: www.100blackmen.org

URBAN LEAGUE OF NEBRASKA
3022 N. 24th St.
Omaha, NE 68110
Marilyn McGary, President/CEO
Tel: (402) 453-9730 Fax: (402) 453-9676
Email: mmcgary@urbanleagueneb.org
Web: www.urbanleagueneb.org

STUDENT ORGANIZATION

ALPHA KAPPA ALPHA SORORITY, INC.
Delta Epsilon Omega Chapter
P.O. Box 3322
Omaha, NE 68103
LaVon Stennis-Williams, Chapter President
Web: www.midwesternakas.com

ALPHA PHI ALPHA FRATERNITY, INC.
Beta Xi Lambda Chapter
P.O. Box 1425
Bellevue, NE 68005
Web: www.alphaphialpha.net

NEVADA

BUSINESS

NATIONAL MINORITY SUPPLIER DEVELOPMENT COUNCIL, INC.
Nevada Minority Business Council
1785 E. Sahara Ave. #360
Las Vegas, NV 89104
Diane Fontes, President
Tel: (702) 894-4477 Fax: (702) 894-9474
Email: nvminority@aol.com
Web: www.nvmpc.com

LAW ENFORCEMENT

NATIONAL ORGANIZATION OF BLACK LAW ENFORCEMENT EXECUTIVES
Southern Nevada Chapter
P.O. Box 1252
U.S. Postal Inspection Service
Las Vegas, NV 89101
Gregory D. Boyakins, President
Tel: (702) 796-2965X28 Fax: (702) 796-6780
Email: gdboyakins@uspis.gov
Web: www.noblenatl.org

Washoe County Chapter
P.O. Box 8031
Washoe County Sheriff's Office
Reno, NV 89510
Gregory D. Boyakins, President
Tel: (702) 328-2954
Email: patrickpwee@aol.com
Web: www.noblenatl.org

POLITICAL ACTION

AMERICAN CIVIL LIBERTIES UNION
Northern Nevada Office
1101 Riverside Dr.
Reno, NV 89503
Gary Peck, Executive Director
Tel: (775) 786-6757
Email: aclunv@anv.net
Web: www.aclunv.org

Southern Nevada Chapter
1700 E. Desert Inn Rd. #113
Las Vegas, NV 89109
Gary Peck, Executive Director
Tel: (702) 366-1226
Email: aclunv@anv.net
Web: www.aclunv.org

NATIONAL ACTION NETWORK
Nevada Chapter
3925 MLK #213
North Las Vegas, NV 89032
Gene Collins, Chair
Tel: (702) 646-9720 Fax: (702) 646-9842
Email: nanlv@ureach.com
Web: www.nationalactionnetworklv.org

PROFESSIONAL

NATIONAL FORUM FOR BLACK PUBLIC ADMINISTRATORS
Las Vegas Chapter
4425 W. Tropicana Ave.
Las Vegas, NV 89103
Kevin Chapman, President
Tel: (702) 455-7700 Fax: (702) 455-8349
Email: klc@co.clark.nv.us
Web: www.nfbpa.org

NATIONAL MEDICAL ASSOCIATION
Region VI-INAMI Health Center
1701 W. Charleston #215
Las Vegas, NV 89102
James S. Tate, Jr., M.D., Director
Tel: (702) 388-4292 Fax: (702) 388-2922
Web: www.nmanet.org

NATIONAL SOCIETY OF BLACK ENGINEERS
Region 6: University of Nevada, Las Vegas
4505 Maryland Pkwy.
Las Vegas, NV 89154
Crystar Jorge
Tel: (702) 895-3221 Fax: (702) 895-4103
Web: www.unlv.edu/studentserv/ccd/activities.html#organizations

SPEC. INT., EDUCATION

NATIONAL ASSOCIATION FOR MULTICULTURAL EDUCATION
Nevada Chapter
University of Nevada, 4505 Maryland Pkwy.
Las Vegas, NV 89154-3005
Dr. Porter L. Troutman, Jr., Professor
Tel: (702) 895-4407 Fax: (702) 895-4898
Email: porter@nevada.edu
Web: www.unlv.edu/faculty/troutman/NAME/index.html

Nevada-University of Reno Chapter
University of Nevada Reno, Department of Educational Specialty, M/S 299
Reno, NV 89557
Tel: (775) 784-4961X2006 Fax: (775) 784-4384
Web: www.nameorg.org

SPEC. INT., SOCIAL INTEREST

100 BLACK MEN OF LAS VEGAS, INC.
71 Casa Del Fuego St.
Henderson, NV 89012
Larry J. Mosley, President
Tel: (702) 567-0366 Fax: (702) 567-1284
Email: larryjmosley@msn.com
Web: www.100blackmenlasvegas.org

STUDENT ORGANIZATION

ALPHA KAPPA ALPHA SORORITY, INC.
Kappa Xi Chapter
P.O. Box 73175
Las Vegas, NV 89170
Andrea Cox, Chapter President
Web: www.aka1908.com

Theta Theta Omega Chapter
2816 N. Jones Blvd.
Las Vegas, NV 89018
Billie Knight Rayford, Chapter President
Web: www.aka1908.com

ALPHA PHI ALPHA FRATERNITY, INC.
Sigma Psi Chapter, University of Las Vegas
P.O. Box 452
Las Vegas, NV 89154
Web: www.alphaphialpha.net

Theta Pi Lambda Chapter
P.O. Box 93716
Las Vegas, NV 89193
Web: www.alphaphialpha.net

THE BROTHERHOOD/SISTER SOL
512 W. 143rd St.
New York, NY 10031
Valery J. Jean, Development Coordinator
Tel: (212) 283-7044 Fax: (212) 283-3700
Email: vj@brotherhood-sistersol.org
Web: www.brotherhood-sistersol.org

NEW HAMPSHIRE

POLITICAL ACTION

AMERICAN CIVIL LIBERTIES UNION
New Hampshire Chapter
18 Low Ave.
Concord, NH 03301
Claire Ebel, Executive Director
Tel: (603) 225-3080
Email: aclu@aclu.org
Web: www.nhclu.org

STUDENT ORGANIZATION

ALPHA KAPPA ALPHA SORORITY, INC.
Xi Lambda Chapter, Dartmouth College
5228 Parkhurst
Hanover, NH 03755
Leah Wright, Chapter President
Email: 1908@dartmouth.edu
Web: www.aka1908.com

NEW JERSEY

ARTISTIC

**AFRICAN GLOBE STUDIOS, ARTS &
ENTERTAINMENT CORPORATION**
1028 Broad St.
Newark, NJ 07102
Kabu Okai-Davies, Executive Director/Founder
Tel: (973) 624-1584 Fax: (973) 624-6333
Email: afglobe@aol.com
Web: www.africanglobe.com

BUSINESS

**NATIONAL MINORITY SUPPLIER DEVELOPMENT
COUNCIL, INC.**
**New York/New Jersey Minority Purchasing Council,
Regional Council Satellite Office**
80 Park Plz., M/C P2M
Newark, NJ 07102
Lynda Ireland, President
Tel: (973) 430-6320 Fax: (973) 286-0023
Email: council@nynjmpc.org
Web: www.nynjmpc.org

ENTERTAINMENT

**NATIONAL AFRICAN AMERICAN RV'ERS
ASSOCIATION**
Leisure Travelers
27 Walden Dr.
Bridgeton, NJ 08302
John Robinson, President
Tel: (856) 455-6745
Web: www.naarva.com

The Group Camping Club Chapter
11 Hawley Pl.
Willingboro, NJ 08046
John Robinson, President
Tel: (609) 871-1365
Email: jrob46@msn.com
Web: www.naarva.com

LAW ENFORCEMENT

**NATIONAL ORGANIZATION OF BLACK LAW
ENFORCEMENT EXECUTIVES**
Northern Jersey Chapter
P.O. Box 9
Fanwood, NJ 07023
Siddeeq W. El-Amin, Captain
Tel: (908) 753-3088 Fax: (908) 753-3476
Email: selamin35@aol.com
Web: www.nnj.noblechapter.org

South Jersey Chapter
P.O. Box 965
Bellmawr, NJ 08099
David Owens, Deputy County Administrator for Public
Safety
Tel: (856) 225-7632 Fax: (856) 225-5319
Email: dowens@camdencounty.com
Web: www.sjc.noblechapter.org

POLITICAL ACTION

AMERICAN CIVIL LIBERTIES UNION
New Jersey Chapter
P.O. Box 750
Newark, NJ 07101
Deborah Jacobs, Executive Director
Tel: (973) 642-2084
Email: info@aclu-nj.org
Web: www.aclu-nj.org

**ASSOCIATION OF COMMUNITY ORGANIZATIONS
FOR REFORM NOW**
Newark Office
972 Broad St., 7th Fl.
Newark, NJ 07102
Tel: (973) 645-1377
Email: njacorn@acorn.org
Web: www.acorn.org

Paterson Office
175 Market St. #211
Paterson, NJ 07504
Tel: (973) 684-8880 Fax: (973) 684-8890
Email: njacornpa@acorn.org
Web: www.acorn.org

BLACKS IN GOVERNMENT
Region II-Mentors Chapter
P.O. Box 89
Ft. Monmouth, NJ 07703
Phillipe Atwell, Chapter President
Tel: (732) 532-3531 Fax: (732) 532-1204
Email: region2.president@bignet.org
Web: www.bignet.org/regional/region2/index.htm

NATIONAL ACTION NETWORK
New Jersey Chapter
155 Ellison St.
Paterson, NJ 07505
Rev. Ronald Tuff, Chair of Newark
Tel: (973) 279-2333 Fax: (973) 279-2334
Email: paterson.taskforce@verizon.net

PROFESSIONAL

AMERICAN ASSOCIATION OF BLACKS IN ENERGY
New Jersey Chapter
c/o PSE&G, 20 Commerce Dr.
Cranford, NJ 07016
W. Darryl Brittingham, President
Tel: (908) 709-2200 Fax: (908) 272-1443
Email: weymouth.brittingham@pseg.com
Web: www.aabe-nj.org

ASSOCIATION OF BLACK PSYCHOLOGISTS
New Jersey Chapter
659 Eaglerock Ave.
West Orange, NJ 07052
Phyllis Bolling, Chapter President
Tel: (973) 677-1148 Fax: (973) 596-3419
Web: www.abpsi.org

**CONFERENCE OF MINORITY TRANSPORTATION
OFFICIALS**
New Jersey Chapter
P.O. Box 22968
Newark, NJ 07101
Larry Hamm, President
Tel: (973) 491-8068
Email: chrmlxh@njtransit.com
Web: www.comtonj.org

**CONSORTIUM OF INFORMATION AND
TELECOMMUNICATION EXECUTIVES
CITE-NJ**
1000 Cellar Ave.
Scotchplane, NJ 07076
Doris Bryant, Chapter President
Tel: (973) 649-0095
Email: gail.e.baskerville-norris@verizon.com
Web: www.cite-nj.org

NATIONAL ALLIANCE OF MARKET DEVELOPERS
National Office
620 Sheridan Ave.
Plainfield, NJ 07060
Deborah J. Crable, National President
Tel: (908) 561-4062 Fax: (908) 561-6827
Email: dcrable1@sbcglobal.net
Web: www.namdntl.org

NATIONAL BLACK MBA ASSOCIATION, INC.
New Jersey Chapter-East
P.O. Box 28023
Newark, NJ 07101
Kevin B. McMillan, President
Tel: (732) 246-2878
Email: info@nbmbaa-newjersey.org
Web: www.nbmbaa-newjersey.org

NATIONAL OPTOMETRIC ASSOCIATION
Region I-Northeast
311 Main St.
Orange, NJ 07050
Stella Marie Korieccha, Trustee
Tel: (973) 673-5773 Fax: (973) 673-5794
Web: www.natoptassoc.org

NATIONAL SALES NETWORK
National Office
1075 Easton Ave. #11, PMB 316
Somerset, NJ 08873

Michael Davis, National President
Tel: (732) 246-5236 Fax: (201) 836-3103
Email: national@salesnetwork.org
Web: www.salesnetwork.org

SOUTH JERSEY MEDICAL ASSOCIATION
141 S. Black Horse Pike #104
Blackwood, NJ 08012
William E. Johnston, M.D., President
Tel: (856) 228-2451 Fax: (856) 227-0195
Web: www.southjerseymedical.com

RELIGIOUS

THE SOCIETY OF AFRICAN MISSIONS
Headquarters-SAM American Provincial
23 Bliss Ave.
Tenafly, NJ 07670
Rev. Thomas Wright, Provincial Superior
Tel: (201) 567-0450 Fax: (201) 541-1280
Email: smausa-c@smafathers.org
Web: www.smafathers.org

UNION OF BLACK EPISCOPALIANS
Mid-Atlantic Region
1 Sunnyfield Terrace.
Neptune, NJ 07753
Annette Buchanan, Regional Director
Tel: (732) 918-8023 Fax: (732) 957-7977
Email: annette.buchanan@lucent.com
Web: www.ube.org

UNION OF BLACK EPISCOPALIANS
Northeast Region
75 Lafayette Ave.
East Orange, NJ 07017
Bert Jones, Director
Tel: (973) 674-1931
Email: bjones9234@aol.com
Web: www.ube.org

SPEC. INT., EDUCATION

AFRICAN STUDIES ASSOCIATION
Rutgers, The State University of New Jersey
Douglass Campus, 132 George St.
New Brunswick, NJ 08901-1400
Carol L. Martin, Ph.D., Executive Director
Tel: (732) 932-8173 Fax: (732) 932-3394
Email: clmasa@rci.rutgers.edu
Web: www.africanstudies.org

**NATIONAL ASSOCIATION FOR MULTICULTURAL
EDUCATION**
New Jersey Chapter
College of Education, William Paterson University, 300
Pompton Rd.
Wayne, NJ 07470
Djanna Hill, Chapter President
Tel: (973) 720-2260
Email: hilld@wpunj.edu
Web: www.nameorg.org

SPEC. INT., FAMILY PLANNING

NATIONAL HOOK-UP OF BLACK WOMEN, INC.
Camden-Philadelphia Chapter
1045 Haddon Ave.
Camden, NJ 08103
Kathryn E. Gaines, President
Tel: (856) 541-7239
Email: divarubykathy@aol.com
Web: www.nhbwinc.com

Cherry Hill Chapter
18 Stoneybridge Rd.
Laurel Springs, NJ 08021
Dianne P. Hood, President
Tel: (856) 228-6985
Email: dphood@aol.com
Web: www.nhbwinc.com

SPEC. INT., SOCIAL INTEREST

BLACK UNITED FUND OF NEW JERSEY, INC.
132 S. Harrison St.
East Orange, NJ 07018
Sondra Clark, President/CEO
Tel: (973) 676-5283 Fax: (973) 672-5030
Email: bufnj132@aol.com
Web: www.bufnj.org

CONCERNED BLACK MEN, INC.
Burlington County Chapter
Burlington County, NJ
Tel: (888) 395-7816
Email: lhughes@cbmnational.org
Web: www.cbmnational.org

NATIONAL BLACK UNITED FRONT
Jersey City Chapter

P.O. Box 15073
Jersey City, NJ 07305
Tel: (201) 920-0653
Web: www.nbufront.org

NATIONAL BLACK UNITED FUND, INC.
40 Clinton St.
Newark, NJ 07102
William Merritt, President
Tel: (973) 643-3767 Fax: (973) 648-8350
Email: nbuf@nbuf.org
Web: www.nbuf.org

NATIONAL URBAN AFFAIRS COUNCIL
P.O. Box 51
Plainfield, NJ 07061-0051
Arnold K. Hamm, President
Tel: (908) 561-6989 Fax: (908) 561-1901

NATIONAL URBAN LEAGUE, INC.
Morris County Urban League
13 1/2 James St.
Morristown, NJ 07960
William D. Primus, President/CEO
Tel: (973) 539-2121 Fax: (973) 644-9496
Email: adminsup@ulmcnj.org
Web: www.ulmcnj.org

Urban League for Bergen County
106 W. Palisade Ave.
Englewood, NJ 07631
Eddie Raynord Hadden, President/CEO
Tel: (201) 568-4988 Fax: (201) 568-3192
Email: ulbc@conversent.net
Web: www.urbanleaguebc.org

Urban League of Essex County
508 Central Ave.
Newark, NJ 07107-1430
Vivian Fox, President
Tel: (973) 624-9535 Fax: (973) 624-1103
Email: information@ulec.org
Web: www.ulec.org

Urban League of Hudson County
253 Martin Luther King Dr.
Jersey City, NJ 07305
Elnora Watson, President/CEO
Tel: (201) 451-8888 Fax: (201) 451-4158
Email: info@ulohc.org
Web: www.urbanleaguehudsonnj.org

Urban League of Metro Trenton
235 E. Hanover St.
Trenton, NJ 08616
Paul P. Pintella, President
Tel: (609) 393-1512 Fax: (609) 396-8893
Web: www.nul.org

Urban League of Union County
288 N. Broad St.
Elizabeth, NJ 07207
Ella S. Teal, President
Tel: (908) 351-7200 Fax: (908) 527-9881
Web: www.nul.org

SPEC. INT., SPORTS

10TH CALVERY GUN CLUB
New Jersey Chapter
P.O. Box 582
Newton, NJ 07860
Jerry Martin, President
Tel: (973) 989-8916

SPEC. INT., YOUTH

JACK & JILL OF AMERICA, INC.
Eastern Region
P.O. Box 586
Brigantine, NJ 08203
Vivian M. J. Darkes, Regional Director
Tel: (609) 348-1081 Fax: (609) 348-1082
Email: regionaldirector@hotmail.com
Web: www.jack-and-jill.org

STUDENT ORGANIZATION

ALPHA KAPPA ALPHA SORORITY, INC.
Beta Alpha Omega Chapter
P.O. Box 2005
Newark, NJ 07114
Carline Hill, Chapter President
Web: www.aka1908.com

Epsilon Upsilon Omega Chapter
P.O. Box 1324
Trenton, NJ 08607
Shirley Tyler, Chapter President
Web: www.aka1908.com

**Gamma Zeta Chapter, Rutger University & New
Jersey Institute of Technology**
120 Rutgers St. #C9

Belleville, NJ 07109
Lucie Thibeaud, Graduate Advisor
Email: gzgradadv@netscape.net
Web: http://akanorthatlantic.org

Iota Epsilon Omega Chapter
P.O. Box 1126
Teaneck, NJ 07666
Sandra Waite, Chapter President
Web: www.aka1908.com

Lambda Omega Omega Chapter
P.O. Box 778
Oakhurst, NJ 07755
Tracy Marie Simmons-Hart, Chapter President
Web: www.aka1908.com

Lambda Rho Chapter, Rowan University
25 Raintree Dr.
Erial, NJ 08081
Minretta B. McFadden, Graduate Advisor
Email: minnielb@comcast.net
Web: http://akanorthatlantic.org

Nu Kappa Chapter, Fairleigh Dickinson University
325 Windsor Rd.
Englewood, NJ 07631
Eudella Grant, Graduate Advisor
Email: dellegee2001@yahoo.com
Web: http://akanorthatlantic.org

Nu Xi Omega Chapter
P.O. Box 446
Piscataway, NJ 08855
Constance Pizarro, Chapter President
Web: www.aka1908.com

Omicron Xi Omega Chapter
P.O. Box 509
Montclair, NJ 07042
Mary Lamar, Chapter President
Web: www.aka1908.com

Phi Eta Omega Chapter
P.O. Box 854
Scotch Plains, NJ 07076
Joyce R. Hobbs, Chapter President
Web: www.aka1908.com

Pi Chi Chapter, Richard Stockton College of New Jersey
126 Bernard Ave.
Egg Harbor Township, NJ 08234
Andrea Atkins, Graduate Advisor
Email: aatkins957@aol.com
Web: http://akanorthatlantic.org

Pi Mu Omega Chapter
P.O. Box 2055
Willingboro, NJ 08046
Ann Giles, Chapter President
Web: www.aka1908.com

Pi Theta Omega Chapter
P.O. Box 1548
Morristown, NJ 07962
Tammy Williams-Blackwell, Chapter President
Tel: (973) 731-4714
Email: twmsblackwell@comcast.net
Web: www.pithetaomega.net

Pi Xi Omega Chapter
P.O. Box 6852
Patterson, NJ 07509
Kim Daniel-Robinson, Chapter President
Web: www.aka1908.com

Rho Gamma Omega Chapter
P.O. Box 1064
South Orange, NJ 07079
Zaundria May, Chapter President
Web: www.aka1908.com

Rho Kappa Omega Chapter
32 Bentley Ave.
Jersey City, NJ 07304
Rasheeda Bennett, Chapter President
Web: www.aka1908.com

Rho Phi Chapter
459 Willow St.
Orange, NJ 07050
Rachel Archelus, Graduate Advisor
Email: hookie459@aol.com
Web: http://akanorthatlantic.org

Tau Nu Omega Chapter
1686 Fairfield St.
Teaneck, NJ 07666
Marselle Heywood-Julian, Chapter President
Web: www.aka1908.com

Theta Kappa Omega Chapter
P.O. Box 7866
Atlantic City, NJ 08441
Dianne L. Hill, Chapter President
Web: www.aka1908.com

Theta Phi Omega Chapter

P.O. Box 5259
Plainfield, NJ 07060
Joan Evelyn, Chapter President
Web: www.aka1908.com

Theta Pi Omega Chapter
9102 Bishop's View Cir.
Cherry Hill, NJ 08002
Marie Kersey Brown, Chapter Presient
Web: www.aka1908.com

Upsilon Delta Omega Chapter
P.O. Box 3607
Cherry Hill, NJ 08034
Norma R. Evans, Chapter President
Web: www.aka1908.com

Zeta Sigma Chapter, Trenton State College
108 Irick Rd.
Westhampton, NJ 08060
Deirdre Pearson, Graduate Advisor
Email: lincoln1972@hotmail.com
Web: http://akanorthatlantic.org

NEW MEXICO

POLITICAL ACTION

AMERICAN CIVIL LIBERTIES UNION
New Mexico Chapter
P.O. Box 80915
Albuquerque, NM 87198
Peter Simonson, Executive Director
Tel: (800) 773-5706 Fax: (505) 266-5916
Email: info@aclu-nm.org
Web: www.aclu-nm.org

ASSOCIATION OF COMMUNITY ORGANIZATIONS FOR REFORM NOW
Albuquerque Office
411 Bellamah NW
Albuquerque, NM 87102
Tel: (505) 242-7411 Fax: (505) 244-1090
Email: nmacorn@acorn.org
Web: www.acorn.org

BLACKS IN GOVERNMENT
Region VI-New Mexico Chapter
P.O. Box 91833
Albuquerque, NM 87199-1833
A. Mae Harris, Chapter President
Tel: (505) 846-2074 Fax: (505) 846-1766
Email: boydnya@comcast.net
Web: www.bignet.org/regional/region6/index.htm

PROFESSIONAL

NATIONAL SOCIETY OF BLACK ENGINEERS
New Mexico State University Chapter
P.O. Box 30001
Las Cruces, NM 88003
Carlos Curry, Chamber President
Tel: (505) 646-7784 Fax: (505) 646-1984

STUDENT ORGANIZATION

ALPHA KAPPA ALPHA SORORITY, INC.
Iota Xi Omega Chapter
P.O. Box 30694
Albuquerque, NM 87190
Brenda Chandler, Chapter President
Web: www.aka1908.com

ALPHA PHI ALPHA FRATERNITY, INC.
Iota Psi Lambda Chapter
P.O. Box 5435
Albuquerque, NM 87185
Web: www.alphaphialpha.net

Pi Zeta Lambda Chapter
P.O. Box 15066
Las Cruces, NM 88004
Web: www.alphaphialpha.net

BLACK ALLIED STUDENT ORGANIZATION
New Mexico State University
P.O. Box 30001, #4188
Las Cruces, NM 88003
Rachael Jones, President
Tel: (505) 646-4208 Fax: (505) 646-1984
Email: racjones@nmsu.edu

NEW YORK

ARTISTIC

AFRIKAN POETRY THEATRE, INC.
176-03 Jamaica Ave.
Jamaica, NY 11432-5503

John Watusi Branch, Executive Director
Tel: (718) 523-3312 Fax: (718) 523-1054
Email: jwatusi@aol.com
Web: www.afrikapoetrytheatre.com

ALVIN AILEY AMERICAN DANCE THEATER
405 W. 55th St.
New York, NY 10019
Sharon Gersten Luckman, Executive Director
Tel: (212) 767-0590 Fax: (212) 405-9001
Email: info@alvinailey.org
Web: www.alvinailey.org

ARTS ALLIANCE OF HAVERSTRAW
91 Broadway
Haverstraw, NY 10927
Jessica Otero, Director
Tel: (845) 786-0253 Fax: (845) 786-3288
Email: aaharts@aol.com
Web: www.arts-alliance.org

AUDIENCE DEVELOPMENT COMMITTEE, INC.
Head Office
Manhattan Bill Station
P.O. Box 30
New York, NY 10027
Grace Jones, Chairman
Tel: (212) 222-0206 Fax: (212) 368-6906
Email: audelco@aol.com

BLACK FILMMAKER FOUNDATION DV LAB
11 W. 42nd St., 9th Fl.
New York, NY 10036
Warrington Hudlin, Founder/Chief
Tel: (212) 253-1690
Email: hudlin@dvrepublic.org
Web: www.dvrepublic.org

BLACK SPECTRUM THEATER
119-07 Merrick Blvd.
Jamaica, NY 11434
Carl Clay, Founder/Executive Producer
Tel: (718) 723-1800 Fax: (718) 723-1806
Web: www.blackspectrum.com

DANCE THEATRE OF HARLEM SCHOOL
School of Dance
466 W. 152nd St.
New York, NY 10031
Laveen Naidu, Director
Tel: (212) 690-2800 Fax: (212) 690-8736
Email: lnaidu@dancetheatreofharlem.org
Web: www.dancetheatreofharlem.org

EN FOCO, INC.
32 E. Kingsbridge Rd.
Bronx, NY 10468
Charles Biasiny-Rivera, Executive Director
Tel: (718) 584-7718 Fax: (718) 584-7718
Email: info@enfoco.org
Web: www.enfoco.org

FREDERICK DOUGLASS CREATIVE ARTS CENTER
270 W. 96th St.
New York, NY 10025
Fred Hudson, Founder/President
Tel: (212) 864-3375 Fax: (212) 864-3474
Email: fdcac@aol.com
Web: www.fdcac.org

HARLEM JAZZ SCENE, INC.
P.O. Box 0551
New York, NY 10025
William E. Saxton, President/CEO
Tel: (212) 662-3463 Fax: (212) 666-7383
Email: hjscene@hotmail.com

HARLEM SCHOOL OF THE ARTS
645 St. Nicholas Ave.
New York, NY 10030
Camille Giraud Akeju, President/CEO
Tel: (212) 926-4100 Fax: (212) 491-6913
Email: info@harlemschoolofthearts.org
Web: www.harlemschoolofthearts.org

HENRY STREET SETTLEMENT
Abrons Arts Center
466 Grand St.
New York, NY 10002
Jane Delgado-Semidei, Chief Administrator
Tel: (212) 598-0400 Fax: (212) 505-8329
Email: info@henrystreet.org
Web: www.henrystreet.org

INTERNATIONAL AGENCY FOR MINORITY ARTIST AFFAIRS, INC.
163 W. 125th St. #909
New York, NY 10027
Percy E. Sutton, President
Tel: (212) 749-5298 Fax: (212) 749-3745
Email: iamaa@pipeline.com
Web: www.charityadvantage.com/aboutharlemarts

MULTICULTURAL MUSIC GROUP, INC.
114 Briggs Ave.
Yonkers, NY 10701
Luis Mojica, Executive Director
Tel: (718) 884-5495 Fax: (914) 375-0945
Email: mmg@multiculturalmusic.org
Web: www.multiculturalmusic.org

NATIONAL BLACK THEATER INSTITUTE
2031 5th Ave.
New York, NY 10035
Barbara Ann Teer, Director
Tel: (212) 722-3800 Fax: (212) 860-8004
Email: nabitca@aol.com
Web: www.nationalblacktheatre.org

NEGRO ENSEMBLE COMPANY, INC.
303 W. 42nd St. #501
New York, NY 10036
O.L. Duke, Artistic Director
Tel: (212) 582-5860 Fax: (212) 582-9639
Email: info@necinc.org
Web: http://necinc.org

NEW FEDERAL THEATER
292 Henry St.
New York, NY 10002
Woodie King, Jr., Director
Tel: (212) 353-1176 Fax: (212) 353-1088
Email: newfederal@aol.com
Web: www.newfederaltheatre.org

NEW PROFESSIONAL THEATER
229 W. 42nd St. #501
New York, NY 10036
Sheila Kay Davis, Founder/Artistic Director
Tel: (212) 398-2666 Fax: (212) 398-2924
Email: newprof@aol.com
Web: www.newprofessionaltheatre.org

THE BILLIE HOLIDAY THEATER
P.O. Box 470131
Brooklyn, NY 11247-0131
Marjorie A. Moon, Executive Director
Tel: (718) 636-0918 Fax: (718) 636-2165
Email: billieholidaytheatre@yahoo.com
Web: www.thebillieholiday.org

THE BOYS CHOIR OF HARLEM
2005 Madison Ave.
New York, NY 10035
Dr. Walter Turnbull, Founder/Director
Tel: (212) 289-1815 Fax: (212) 289-4195
Email: info@boyschoirofharlem.org
Web: www.boyschoirofharlem.org

THE STUDIO MUSEUM IN HARLEM
144 W. 125th St.
New York, NY 10027
Ali Evans, Public Relations Manager
Tel: (212) 864-4500 Fax: (212) 864-4800
Email: aevans@studiomuseum.org
Web: www.studiomuseuminharlem.org

UJIMA COMPANY, INC.
545 Elmwood Ave.
Buffalo, NY 14222
Lorna C. Hill, Artistic Director
Tel: (716) 883-4232 Fax: (716) 882-4960
Email: ujimacoinc@aol.com
Web: www.ujimatheatre.org

BUSINESS

AFRICAN HERITAGE NETWORK
307 W. 38th St. #1510
New York, NY 10018
Chase Walker, CEO
Tel: (212) 480-0777 Fax: (212) 227-8391

ASSOCIATION OF MINORITY ENTERPRISES OF NEW YORK, INC.
135-20 Liberty Ave.
Richmond Hill, NY 11419
James Hyliger, President
Tel: (718) 291-1641 Fax: (718) 291-1887
Email: heyligerj@aol.com
Web: www.ameny.org

BUFFALO ECONOMIC RENAISSANCE CORPORATION
Women and Minority and Small Business Development
65 Niagara Sq. #920
Buffalo, NY 14202
Timothy Wanamaker, President
Tel: (716) 842-6923 Fax: (716) 842-6942
Email: twanamaker@city-buffalo.org
Web: www.berc.org

MANHATTAN/BRONX MINORITY BUSINESS DEVELOPMENT CENTER
Minority Business Development Agency

350 5th Ave. #2202
New York, NY 10118
Lorraine Kelsey, Executive Director
Tel: (212) 947-5351 Fax: (212) 947-1506
Email: mbmbdc@manhattan-bronx-mbdc.com
Web: www.manhattan-bronx-mbdc.com

NATIONAL MINORITY BUSINESS COUNCIL, INC.
25 W. 45th St. #301
New York, NY 10036
John F. Robinson, President/CEO
Tel: (212) 997-4753 Fax: (212) 997-5102
Email: nmbc@msn.com
Web: www.nmbc.org

NATIONAL MINORITY SUPPLIER DEVELOPMENT COUNCIL, INC.
Headquarters
1040 Ave. of the Americas, 2nd Fl.
New York, NY 10018
Harriet R. Michel, President
Tel: (212) 944-2430 Fax: (212) 719-9611
Email: nmsdc1@aol.com
Web: www.nmsdcus.org

Minority Supplier Development Council of NY & NJ
330 7th Ave., 8th Fl.
New York, NY 10001
Lynda Ireland, President
Tel: (212) 502-5663 Fax: (212) 502-5807
Email: council@nynjmpc.org
Web: www.nynjmsdc.org

Upstate New York Regional Minority Purchasing Council
85 River Rock Dr. #113
Buffalo, NY 14207
Darlene M. Graves, Executive Director
Tel: (716) 871-4120 Fax: (716) 871-3725
Email: unyrmpci@unyrmpci.org
Web: www.unyrmpci.org

THE BUSINESS CONSORTIUM FUND, INC.
305 7th Ave., 20th Fl.
New York, NY 10001
Marcial E. Robiou, President
Tel: (212) 243-7360 Fax: (212) 243-7647
Email: mrobiou@bcfcapital.com
Web: www.bcfcapital.com

CHAMBER OF COMMERCE

AFRICAN AMERICAN CHAMBER OF COMMERCE OF WESTCHESTER AND ROCKLAND COUNTIES, INC.
Westchester Office
100 Stevens Ave. #202
Mount Vernon, NY 10550
Robin L. Douglas, President/CEO
Tel: (914) 699-9050 Fax: (914) 699-6279
Email: robinlisadouglas@cs.com
Web: www.africanamericanchamberofcommercenys.org

CARIBBEAN AMERICAN CHAMBER OF COMMERCE AND INDUSTRY, INC.
Brooklyn Navy Yard, 63 Flushing Ave., Bldg. #5
Brooklyn, NY 11205
Roy A. Hastick, Sr., President/CEO
Tel: (718) 834-4544 Fax: (718) 834-9774
Email: rahastick@msn.com
Web: www.caribbeantradecenter.com

COMMUNICATIONS

NATIONAL BLACK PROGRAMMING CONSORTIUM,
New York Office
68 E. 131st St., 7th Fl.
New York, NY 10037
Mable Haddock, President/CEO
Tel: (212) 234-8200 Fax: (212) 234-7032
Email: info@nbpc.tv
Web: www.nbpc.tv

WEST AFRICAN DISCUSSION AGREEMENT
1200 Midland Ave.
Bronxville, NY 10708
Harold J. Moran, Executive Administrator
Tel: (914) 779-1622 Fax: (914) 779-3841

CULTURAL

AFRICA TRAVEL ASSOCIATION
Head Office
347 5th Ave. #610
New York, NY 10016
Mira Berman, Director
Tel: (212) 447-1926 Fax: (212) 725-8253
Email: africatravelasso@aol.com
Web: www.africa-ata.org

AFRICAN AMERICAN CULTURAL CENTER, INC.
Paul Robeson Theater
350 Masten Ave.
Buffalo, NY 14209
Paulette D. Harris, Artistic Director
Tel: (716) 884-2013 Fax: (716) 885-2590
Email: aacc@wzrd.com
Web: www.paulrobesontheatre.com

ASSOCIATION FOR THE STUDY OF AFRICAN-AMERICAN LIFE AND HISTORY
Bronx Branch
4127 Montecello Ave.
Bronx, NY 10466
Bessy Jackson, Chapter President
Tel: (718) 994-4149
Web: www.asalh.com

THE FRANKLIN H. WILLIAMS CARIBBEAN CULTURAL CENTER AFRICAN DIASPORA INSTITUTE
408 W. 58th St.
New York, NY 10019
Marta Moreno, Founder
Tel: (212) 307- 7420 Fax: (212) 315-1086
Email: mail@caribecenter.org
Web: www.caribecenter.org

ENTERTAINMENT

NATIONAL AFRICAN AMERICAN RV'ERS ASSOCIATION
Long Island Travelers Chapter
6 Greg Ln.
Brentwood, NY 11717
Clifford Dubois, President
Tel: (631) 273-3027
Email: cwdej@optonline.net
Web: www.naarva.com

New York Ravens Chapter
1153 W. River Rd.
Grand Island, NY 14072
Meredith Anding, President
Tel: (716) 773-2465
Email: maumer@netzero.net
Web: www.naarva.com

The Royal Campers Chapter
P.O. Box 130-167
Springfield Gardens, NY 11413
Reginald L. Braithwaite, President
Tel: (718) 344-4718
Email: theroyalcampers@aol.com
Web: www.naarva.com

LAW ENFORCEMENT

NATIONAL ORGANIZATION OF BLACK LAW ENFORCEMENT EXECUTIVES
Buffalo & Niagara Frontier Chapter
Buffalo Police Department, District B
Buffalo, NY 14209
John Battle, Inspector
Tel: (716) 851-5602
Web: www.noblenatl.org

Central New York Chapter
P.O. Box 13162
New York State Police
Albany, NY 12212
Pedro Perez, Lt. Colonel
Tel: (518) 457-9579 Fax: (518) 485-5495
Email: pperez@troopers.state.ny.us
Web: www.noblenatl.org

MULTI-PURPOSE

CONGRESS OF RACIAL EQUALITY
817 Broadway, 3rd Fl.
New York, NY 10003
Roy Innis, National Chairman/CEO
Tel: (212) 598-4000 Fax: (212) 982-0184
Email: corenyc@aol.com
Web: www.core-online.org

DAVIDSON COMMUNITY CENTER
2038 Davidson Ave.
Bronx, NY 10453
Angel Caballero, Executive Director
Tel: (718) 731-6360 Fax: (718) 731-8580
Email: angel.dcc@verizon.net

GODDARD RIVERSIDE COMMUNITY CENTER
Main Administrative Office
593 Columbus Ave.
New York, NY 10024
Stephan Russo, Executive Director
Tel: (212) 873-6600 Fax: (212) 595-6498
Email: srusso@goddard.org
Web: www.goddard.org

NATIONAL ASSOCIATION FOR THE ADVANCEMENT OF COLORED PEOPLE
Islip Town
67 Harrison Ave.
Bay Shore, NY 11706-6721
Yvonne M. Patterson-Quirk, President
Tel: (631) 581-4741 Fax: (631) 581-4741
Email: islipnaacp@juno.com
Web: www.naacp-islip.org

Region II: Northeastern
39 Broadway #2221, 22nd Fl.
New York, NY 10006
Hilda Rodgers, Director
Tel: (212) 344-7474X102 Fax: (212) 344-1212
Email: hrodgers@naacp.net
Web: www.naacp.org

State University of New York at Buffalo
1490 Jefferson Ave.
Buffalo, NY 14208-1518
Frank B. Mesiah, President
Tel: (716) 884-7242 Fax: (716) 884-7243
Email: naacp@apollo3.com
Web: www.apollo3.com/~naacp/

THE JACKIE ROBINSON FOUNDATION
3 W. 35th St., 11th Fl.
New York, NY 10001
Allison Davis, Vice President
Tel: (212) 290-8600 Fax: (212) 290-8081
Email: info@jackierobinson.org
Web: www.jackierobinson.org

POLITICAL ACTION

AMERICAN CIVIL LIBERTIES UNION
Capital Region Chapter
90 State St. #518
Albany, NY 12207
Stephen E. Gottlieb, President
Tel: (518) 436-8594 Fax: (518) 426-9341
Email: e-d@nyclu-crc.org
Web: www.nyclu-crc.org

Central New York Chapter
753 James St. #8
Syracuse, NY 13203
Barrie Gawanter, Executive Director
Tel: (315) 471-2821 Fax: (315) 471-1077
Email: director@cnyclu.org
Web: www.aclu.org

Lower Hudson Valley Chapter
2 William St. #200
White Plains, NY 10601
Arlene R. Popkin, Chair
Tel: (914) 997-7479 Fax: (914) 997-2936
Email: wclu@wclu.org
Web: www.nycluhv.org

Nassau Chapter
33 Willis Ave. #100
Mineola, NY 11501
Barbara Bernstein, Executive Director
Tel: (516) 741-8520 Fax: (516) 741-8534
Email: nyclunas@aol.com
Web: www.nyclu.org/nassau

National Headquarters
125 Broad St., 18th Fl.
New York, NY 10004
Anthony Romero, Executive Director
Tel: (212) 549-2500 Fax: (212) 549-2658
Email: aclu@aclu.org
Web: www.aclu.org

New York Chapter
125 Broad St., 17th Fl.
New York, NY 10004
Donna Lieberman, Executive Director
Tel: (212) 344-3005 Fax: (212) 334-3318
Web: www.nyclu.org

New York, Rochester and Genesee Valley Chapter
121 N. Fitzhugh St.
Rochester, NY 14614
Barbara de Leeuw, Executive Director
Tel: (585) 454-4334 Fax: (585) 454-0516
Email: info@gvclu.org
Web: www.gvclu.org

Suffolk Chapter
P.O. Box 488
Greenlawn, NY 11740
Jared Feuer, Executive Director
Tel: (631) 423-3846 Fax: (631) 423-3847
Web: www.suffolknyclu.org

Western Regional Office
100 S. Elmwood Ave., 2nd Fl.
Buffalo, NY 14202
Jeanne-Noel Mahoney, Executive Director
Tel: (716) 852-4033 Fax: (716) 852-4034
Email: wro@nyclubuffalo.org
Web: www.nyclubuffalo.org

ASSOCIATION OF COMMUNITY ORGANIZATIONS FOR REFORM NOW
ACORN New York
88 3rd Ave., 3rd Fl.
Brooklyn, NY 11217
Tel: (718) 246-7900 Fax: (718) 246-7939
Email: nyacorn@acorn.org
Web: www.acorn.org

Bronx Office
597 E. 139th St.
Bronx, NY 10451
Heather Appel, Head Organizer
Tel: (718) 292-0070 Fax: (718) 292-8846
Email: nyacornbrxro@acorn.org
Web: www.acorn.org

Hempstead Office
91 N. Franklin #209A
Hempstead, NY 11550
Atlanta Cockrell, President
Tel: (516) 481-6769 Fax: (516) 481-6781
Email: nyacornliro@acorn.org
Web: www.acorn.org

National Office
88 3rd Ave.
Brooklyn, NY 11217
Steve Kest, Executive Director
Tel: (718) 246-7900 Fax: (718) 246-7939
Email: natexdirect@acorn.org
Web: www.acorn.org

BLACKS IN GOVERNMENT
Region II
44 Hillside Dr.
Marlboro, NY 12542-5000
Phillipe Atwell, President
Tel: (845) 938-5940 Fax: (845) 938-1061
Email: region2.president@bignet.org
Web: www.bignet.org/regional/region2/index.htm

Region II- Brooklyn/Jamaica Chapter
40 Pkwy. South
Mount Vernon, NY 10552
Ella S. Walker, Chapter President
Tel: (718) 340-7008
Email: region2.president@bignet.org
Web: www.bignet.org/regional/region2/index.htm

Region II-Joseph Riley Chapter
Brooklyn, NY 11210
Deborah Toussant, Chapter President
Email: region2.president@bignet.org
Web: www.bignet.org/regional/region2/index.htm

Region II-Lower Manhattan Chapter
290 Broadway, 23rd Fl.
New York, NY 10007-1866
Sandra Jackson, President
Tel: (212) 637-3328 Fax: (212) 637-3354
Email: jackson.sandra@epa.gov
Web: www.bignet.org/regional/region2/index.htm

Region II-Midtown Manhattan Chapter
P.O. Box G
New York, NY 10159
Joyce M. Jones, Chapter President
Tel: (212) 686-7500 X4123
Email: region2.president@bignet.org
Web: www.bignet.org/regional/region2/index.htm

Region II-NY Elite Chapter
1595 Odell St. #1D
Bronx, NY 10462
Barbara Johnson, Chapter President
Tel: (212) 637-4431
Email: johnson.barbaraj@epa.gov
Web: www.bignet.org/regional/region2/index.htm

Region II-NYC Municipal Chapter
225 Clermont Ave.
Brooklyn, NY 11205
Brandon Ward, Chapter President
Tel: (212) 788-1720
Email: region2.president@bignet.org
Web: www.bignet.org/regional/region2/index.htm

Region II-Upstate NY Albany Chapter
295 Sheridan Ave.
Albany, NY 12206
Merton Simpson, Chapter President
Tel: (518) 432-3521
Email: khalil395@cs.com
Web: www.bignet.org/regional/region2/index.htm

CENTER FOR CONSTITUTIONAL RIGHTS
666 Broadway, 7th Fl.

New York, NY 10012
Michael Ratner, President
Tel: (212) 614-6464 Fax: (212) 614-6499
Email: info@ccr-ny.org
Web: www.ccr-ny.org

PROFESSIONAL

AMERICAN ASSOCIATION OF BLACKS IN ENERGY
New York Metropolitan Chapter
c/o Consolidated Edison Co. of NY, 4 Irving Pl. #1638
New York, NY 10017
Debra Smallwood, President
Tel: (212) 460-4736 Fax: (212) 614-1453
Email: smallwood@coded.com
Web: www.aabe-nymac.org

BLACK AMERICANS IN PUBLISHING, INC.
FDR Station
P.O. Box 6275
New York, NY 10150
Lynnette Velasco, President
Email: president@baip.org
Web: www.baip.org

BLACK CAUCUS OF THE AMERICAN LIBRARY ASSOCIATION, INC.
Langston Hughes Community Library and Cultural Center-QPL
100-01 Northern Blvd.
Corona, NY 11368
Andrew P. Jackson, President
Tel: (718) 651-1100 Fax: (718) 651-6258
Email: andrew.p.jackson@queenslibrary.org
Web: www.bcala.org

BLACK DATA PROCESSING ASSOCIATES
New York Chapter
Murray Hill Station
P.O. Box 808
New York, NY 10156
Jeffry Kimble, Chapter President
Tel: (212) 802-5341
Email: info@bdpany.org
Web: www.bdpany.org

BLACK FARMERS AND AGRICULTURALISTS ASSOCIATION
New York Chapter
150 W. 96th St. #4A
New York, NY 10025
Barry Crumbley, President
Tel: (212) 369-7410
Email: barry@intactcdc.org
Web: www.bfaa-us.org

BLACK PSYCHIATRISTS OF GREATER NEW YORK
331 W. 57th St. #522
New York, NY 10019
Dr. Phyllis Harrison-Ross, Founder/Managing Director
Tel: (212) 969-0417 Fax: (212) 898-1145
Email: info@bpgny.com
Web: www.bpgny.com

BLACK RETAIL ACTION GROUP
P.O. Box 1192, Rockefeller Center Station
New York, NY 10185
Gail Monroe-Perry, President
Tel: (212) 319-7751 Fax: (212) 997-5102
Email: info@bragusa.org
Web: www.bragusa.org

CONSORTIUM OF INFORMATION AND TELECOMMUNICATIONS EXECUTIVES
CITE-New York
P.O. Box 3452
New York, NY 10008
Darrie Scott, Chapter President
Tel: (212) 395-2912 Fax: (516) 222-7083
Email: darrie.g.scott@verizon.net
Web: www.citeny.org

NATIONAL ALLIANCE OF BLACK SALESMEN AND SALESWOMEN/BLACK SALES INSTITUTE
Manhattanville Station
P.O. Box 2814
New York, NY 10027
Franklyn Bryant, President
Tel: (718) 409-4925
Email: itwaseid@aol.com

NATIONAL ALLIANCE OF MARKET DEVELOPERS
New York Chapter
29 E. 31st St., 6th Fl.
New York, NY 10016
Christopher Mack, Chapter President
Tel: (212) 685-4033 Fax: (212) 685-3114
Email: cmack@ncgonline.com
Web: www.namdnyc.com

NATIONAL ASSOCIATION OF BLACK JOURNALISTS
Region II-Buffalo Chapter

P.O. Box 736
Buffalo, NY 14205
Rod Watson, Chapter President
Tel: (716) 849-5598 Fax: (716) 847-0207
Email: rwatson@buffnews.com
Web: www.nabj.org

Region II-New York Chapter
P.O. Box 107
Brooklyn, NY 11238
Matthew Scott, Chapter President
Tel: (212) 886-9589 Fax: (212) 886-9610
Email: nyabj@yahoo.com
Web: www.nyabj.org

NATIONAL ASSOCIATION OF BLACK SOCIAL WORKERS, INC.
New York City Chapter
1969 Madison Ave.
New York, NY 10035
Robert Knox, President
Tel: (212) 348-0035 Fax: (212) 831-5350
Web: www.nabsw.org

NATIONAL BLACK MBA ASSOCIATION, INC.
New York Chapter-East
P.O. Box 8138
New York, NY 10116
Frances W. Ferguson, President
Tel: (212) 439-5100
Email: president@nyblackmba.org
Web: www.nyblackmba.org

Westchester/Greater Connecticut Chapter-East
P.O. Box 552
White Plains, NY 10602
D. Dayneen Preston, President
Tel: (914) 882-8881 Fax: (718) 634 4958
Email: info@nationalblackmba.org
Web: www.nationalblackmba.org

Western New York Chapter-Mideast
P.O. Box 20581
Rochester, NY 14602
Marie Y. Phillipe, President
Tel: (716) 234-4412
Email: wnychapter@wnyblackmba.org
Web: www.wnyblackmba.org

NATIONAL CONFERENCE OF BLACK LAWYERS
New York Chapter
P.O. Box 240583
Borough, NY 10424
Florence Morgan, Attorney
Tel: (718) 286-2161
Web: www.ncbl.org

NATIONAL SOCIETY OF BLACK ENGINEERS
Region I: State University of New York at Buffalo Chapter
303 Student Union
Buffalo, NY 14260-1605
Trisha Atkins, Regional Chairperson
Tel: (716) 645-6643
Email: nsbe.eng@buffalo.edu
Web: www.nsbe.org

RELIGIOUS

AFRICA INLAND MISSION INTERNATIONAL
P.O. Box 178
Pearl River, NY 10965
Ted Barnett, US Director
Tel: (845) 735-4014 Fax: (845) 735-1814
Email: go@aimint.net
Web: www.aim-us.org

AFRICAN PEOPLES' CHRISTIAN ORGANIZATION
415 Atlantic Ave.
Brooklyn, NY 11217
Hubert Daughtry, Executive Director
Tel: (718) 596-1991 Fax: (718) 625-3410
Email: hol.church@verizon.net

INTERRELIGIOUS FOUNDATION FOR COMMUNITY ORGANIZATION
402 W. 145th St.
New York, NY 10031
Rev. Lucius Walker, Jr., Founder/Executive Director
Tel: (212) 926-5757 Fax: (212) 926-5842
Email: ifco@igc.org
Web: www.ifconews.org

OFFICE OF BLACK MINISTRIES
Episcopal Church Center
815 2nd Ave., 8th Fl.
New York, NY 10017
Valerie Harris, Executive Assistance
Tel: (212) 922-5343 Fax: (212) 867-7652
Web: www.episcopalchurch.org

SOCIETY OF THE HOLY CHILD JESUS
African Province Development Office
Dalton Center 6135 Liebig Ave.
Bronx, NY 10471-1007

Sister Margret Rogers, Director
Tel: (718) 601-2289 Fax: (718) 601-2227
Email: mrogers@shcj.org
Web: www.shcj.org/shcj.nsf/pages/HCIAC

RESEARCH

AFRICAN AMERICAN INSTITUTE
State University of New York
41 State St.
Albany, NY 12207
Anne Pope, Director
Tel: (518) 443-5798 Fax: (518) 443-5803
Email: popean@spo.rf.suny.edu.

AFRICAN DEVELOPMENT INSTITUTE, INC.
P.O. Box 1644
New York, NY 10185
Kwame Akonor, Executive Director
Tel: (888) 619-7535 Fax: (201) 944-773
Email: ca498@bfn.org
Web: www.africainstitute.com

AFRICANA STUDIES PROGRAM
New York University
269 Mercer St. #601
New York, NY 10003-6687
Robert Hinton, Associate Director
Tel: (212) 998-2130 Fax: (212) 995-4109
Email: robert.hinton@nyu.edu
Web: www.nyu.edu/gsas/dept//africana

APPLIED RESEARCH CENTER
New York Office
11 Park Pl. #914
New York, NY 10007
Rinku Sen, Communications Director
Tel: (212) 513-7925 Fax: (212) 513-1367
Email: rsen@arc.org
Web: www.arc.org

INSTITUTE FOR RESEARCH IN AFRICAN-AMERICAN STUDIES
Columbia University
758 Schermerhorn Extension, 1200 Amsterdam Ave.
M/C 5512
New York, NY 10027
Manning Marable, Founding Director
Tel: (212) 854-7080 Fax: (212) 854-7060
Email: iraas@columbia.edu
Web: www.columbia.edu/cu/iraas/

SCHOMBURG CENTER FOR RESEARCH IN BLACK CULTURE
515 Malcolm X Blvd.
New York, NY 10037-1801
Howard Dodson, Director
Tel: (212) 491-2263 Fax: (212) 491-2011
Email: hdodson@nypl.org
Web: www.schomburgcenter.org

SPEC. INT., AIDS

LONG ISLAND MINORITY AIDS COALITION, INC.
1045 Rt. 109 #101
Lindenhurst, NY 11757
La-keshia Dandy, Executive Director
Tel: (631) 225-5500 Fax: (631) 225-5501

MINORITY TASK FORCE ON AIDS
Head Office
123 W. 115th St.
New York, NY 10026
Nyron Pringles, Program Director
Tel: (212) 663-7772 Fax: (212) 663-2436
Web: www.mtfany.org

NATIONAL BLACK LEADERSHIP COMMISSION ON AIDS, INC.
105 E. 22nd St. #711
New York, NY 10010
Debra Fraser-Howze, President/CEO
Tel: (212) 614-0023 Fax: (212) 614-0508
Email: info@nblca.org
Web: www.nblca.org

THE BALM IN GILEAD, INC.
130 W. 42nd St. #450
New York, NY 10036
Pernessa C. Seele, Founder/CEO
Tel: (212) 730-7381 Fax: (212) 730-2551
Email: info@balmingilead.org
Web: www.balmingilead.org

THE MOMENTUM AIDS PROJECT, INC.
322 8th Ave., 3rd Fl.
New York, NY 10001
Dawn Bryan, President/CEO
Tel: (212) 691-8100 Fax: (212) 691-2960
Email: momentum@momentumaidsproject.org
Web: www.momentumaidsproject.org

SPEC. INT., CHILD CARE

NATIONAL CENTER FOR MISSING & EXPLOITED CHILDREN
New York
275 Lake Ave.
Rochester, NY 14608
Ed Suk, Executive Director
Tel: (585) 242-0900 Fax: (585) 242-0717
Email: nybranch@ncmec.org
Web: www.missingkids.com

New York/Manhattan Affiliate
395 Hudson St. 10th Fl.
New York, NY 10014
Tel: (212) 366-7880 Fax: (212) 366-7881
Web: www.missingkids.com

New York/Metropolitan New York
769 Elmont Rd.
Elmont, NY 11003
Tel: (718) 222-5888 Fax: (718) 222-5889
Web: www.missingkids.com

New York/Mohawk Valley
934 York St.
Utica, NY 13502
Katherine Slocum, Director
Tel: (315) 732-7233 Fax: (315) 732-2465
Email: kslocum@ncmec.org
Web: www.missingkids.com

SPEC. INT., EDUCATION

A BETTER CHANCE, INC.
National Office
240 W. 35th St., 9th Fl.
New York, NY 10001-2506
Sandra Timmons, President
Tel: (646) 346-1310 Fax: (646) 346-1311
Email: stimmons@abetterchance.org
Web: www.abetterchance.org

ACADEMY FOR EDUCATIONAL DEVELOPMENT
New York Office, Center for School and Community Services
100 5th Ave., 8th Fl.
New York, NY 10011
Patrick Montesano, Vice President/Director
Tel: (212) 243-1110 Fax: (212) 627-0407
Email: pmontesa@aed.org
Web: www.aed.org/scs/

AESTHETIC REALISM FOUNDATION
141 Greene St.
New York, NY 10012
Margot Carpenter, Executive Director
Tel: (212) 777-4490 Fax: (212) 777-4426
Web: www.aestheticrealism.org

AFRICA STUDY GROUP, INC.
YOUTH TRAVEL AND STUDY PROGRAM
405 Tarrytown Rd. #1217
White Plains, NY 10607
Barbara Ann Glover, Executive Director
Tel: (914) 714-3424 Fax: (914) 997-0670
Email: africais@usa.net

BUFFALO AREA ENGINEERING AWARENESS FOR MINORITIES
206 Fronczak Hall
Buffalo, NY 14260
Marilyn Helenbrook, Executive Director
Tel: (716) 645-3066 Fax: (716) 645-3951
Email: helenbrk@eng.buffalo.edu

NATIONAL ASSOCIATION FOR MULTICULTURAL EDUCATION
New York Chapter
State University of New York at Oswego, 217 Edgemont Dr.
Syracuse, NY 13214
Arcenia P. London, Visiting Professor
Tel: (315) 446-2714
Email: london@oswego.edu
Web: www.nameorg.org

OFFICE OF PUBLIC EDUCATION AND INTERPRETATION OF THE AFRICAN BURIAL GROUND
201 Varick St. #1021
New York, NY 10014
Dr. Sherrill D. Wilson, Director
Tel: (212) 337-2001 Fax: (212) 337-1447
Email: nyabg@att.net
Web: www.africanburialground.com

SOCIETY OF BLACK AMERICANS AWARENESS
Lenox Terr., 10 W. 135th St. #K
New York, NY 10037
Dr. Dolores Bernadette Grier, President
Tel: (212) 283-7111
Email: dolores.grier@att.net

THURGOOD MARSHALL SCHOLARSHIP FUND
90 William St. #1203
New York, NY 10038
Dwayne Ashley, President
Tel: (212) 573-8888 Fax: (212) 573-8497
Email: dashley@tmsf.org
Web: www.thurgoodmarshallfund.org

SPEC. INT., EMPLOYMENT

EMMA L. BOWEN FOUNDATION FOR MINORITY INTERESTS IN MEDIA, INC.
New York Office
524 W. 57th St.
New York, NY 10019
Sandra Dorsey Rice, Vice President-Eastern Region
Tel: (212) 975-2545 Fax: (212) 975-5884
Email: sdrice@cbs.com
Web: www.emmabowenfoundation.com

MINORITY MANAGEMENT SOCIETY
State University of New York at Buffalo
542 Capen Hall, 350 Student Union
Buffalo, NY 14260-1605
Shanell Parker, President
Email: sdparker@buffalo.edu
Web: www.sa.buffalo.edu

SPEC. INT., GAY&LESBIAN

GAY MEN OF AFRICAN DESCENT
103 E. 125th St. #503
New York, NY 10035
Tokes Osubu, Executive Director
Tel: (212) 828-1697 Fax: (212) 828-9602
Email: gmad@gmad.org
Web: www.gmad.org

MEN OF ALL COLORS TOGETHER
New York
Ansonia Station
P.O. Box 237107
New York, NY 10023
Gregory Terry, Secretary
Tel: (212) 330-7678
Email: secretary@mactny.org
Web: www.mactny.org

SPEC. INT., HEALTH SERVICES

GUINEA DEVELOPMENT FOUNDATION, INC.
140 W. End Ave. #17G
New York, NY 10023
Sekou M. Sylla, M.D., MPH, President
Tel: (212) 874-2911 Fax: (212) 874-2911
Email: gdf@guineadev.org
Web: www.guineadev.org

SPEC. INT., IMMIGRATION

MULTICULTURAL IMMIGRANT SERVICES
2703 Church Ave., 2nd Fl.
Brooklyn, NY 11226
Anthony Williams, Director
Tel: (718) 282-0978 Fax: (718) 941-4970

SPEC. INT., LEGAL ASSISTANCE

NATIONAL ASSOCIATION FOR THE ADVANCEMENT OF COLORED PEOPLE
Legal Defense and Educational Fund, Inc.
99 Hudson St., 16th Fl.
New York, NY 10013
Theodore M. Shaw, President/Director-Counsel
Tel: (212) 965-2200 Fax: (212) 226-7592
Web: www.naacpldf.org

SPEC. INT., MENTAL HEALTH

STEINWAY CHILD & FAMILY SERVICES, INC.
Associated Black Charities
41-36 27th St.
Long Island City, NY 11101
Mary Redd, President/CEO
Tel: (718) 389-5100 Fax: (718) 784-2920
Email: info@assocblackcharities.org
Web: www.assocblackcharities.org

SPEC. INT., SENIORS

RIDGEWOOD BUSHWICK SENIOR CITIZENS COUNCIL, INC.
217 Wyckoff Ave.
Brooklyn, NY 11237
Christiana M. Fisher, CEO
Tel: (718) 821-0254 Fax: (718) 417-9056
Email: rbscc@rbscc.org
Web: www.rbscc.org

SPEC. INT., SOCIAL INTEREST

100 BLACK MEN OF LONG ISLAND, INC.
9 Centre St.
Hempstead, NY 11550
Henry Holley, President
Tel: (516) 538-6318 Fax: (516) 538-6318
Email: obmli@cs.com
Web: www.100blackmen.org

100 BLACK MEN OF NEW YORK, INC.
105 E. 22nd St.
New York, NY 10010
Paul T. Williams, Jr., President
Tel: (212) 777-7070 Fax: (212) 995-5145
Email: info@ohbmny.org
Web: www.ohbmny.org

AFRICAN AMERICAN MEN OF WESTCHESTER
333 Mamaroneck Ave., PMB 29
White Plains, NY 10605
Melvin Burruss, President
Tel: (914) 949-9463 Fax: (914) 949-9473
Email: info@aamw.com
Web: www.aamw.com

AFRICAN AMERICAN PLANNING COMMISSION, INC.
Central Office
647A DeGraw St.
Brooklyn, NY 11217-3111
Matthew Okebiyi, Executive Director
Tel: (718) 218-7254 Fax: (718) 218-7115
Email: mokebiyi@aapci.org
Web: www.aapci.org

ASSOCIATED BLACK CHARITIES
105 E. 22nd St. #915
New York, NY 10010
Rayton Gerald, Chairman
Tel: (212) 777-6060 Fax: (212) 777-7904
Email: info@assocblackcharities.org
Web: www.associatedblackcharities.org

BLACK VETERANS FOR SOCIAL JUSTICE, INC.
665 Willoughby Ave.
Brooklyn, NY 11206
Job Mashariki, President/CEO
Tel: (718) 935-1116 Fax: (718) 852-4805
Email: admin@bvsj.org
Web: www.bvsj.org

EDUCATIONAL EQUITY CONCEPTS, INC.
Head Office
100 5th Ave., 8th Fl.
New York, NY 10011
Merle Froschl, Co-Founder
Tel: (212) 243-1110 Fax: (212) 627-0407
Email: information@edequity.org
Web: www.edequity.org

NATIONAL BLACK UNITED FRONT
New York Chapter
P.O. Box 401336
Brooklyn, NY 11240
Jitu Weusi, Chair
Tel: (718) 857-1427 Fax: (718) 778-8630
Email: jweusi@aol.com
Web: www.nbufront.org

NATIONAL URBAN LEAGUE, INC.
Broome County Urban League
43-45 Carroll St.
Binghamton, NY 13901
Jennifer Cubic, Interim Director
Tel: (607) 723-7303 Fax: (607) 723-5827
Email: jcubic@bcul.org
Web: www.bcul.org

Buffalo Urban League
15 E. Genesee St.
Buffalo, NY 14203
Brenda McDuffie, President/CEO
Tel: (716) 854-7625 Fax: (716) 854-8960
Email: bmcduffie@buffalourbanleague.org
Web: www.buffalourbanleague.org

Headquarters
120 Wall St., 8th Fl.
New York, NY 10005
Marc H. Morial, President/CEO
Tel: (212) 558-5300 Fax: (212) 344-5332
Email: info@nul.org
Web: www.nul.org

New York Urban League
204 W. 136th St.
New York, NY 10030
Darwin M. Davis, President/CEO
Tel: (212) 926-8000 Fax: (212) 283-2736
Email: nyuldmd@aol.com
Web: www.nyul.org

Urban League of Long Island
219 Carleton Ave.
Central Islip, NY 11722
Theresa Sanders, President
Tel: (631) 232-2482 Fax: (631) 232-3849
Email: tsanders@urbanleagueoflongisland.org
Web: www.urbanleaguelongisland.org

Urban League of Rochester
265 N. Clinton Ave.
Rochester, NY 14605
William G. Clark, President/CEO
Tel: (585) 325-6530 Fax: (585) 325-4864
Email: wclark@ulr.org
Web: www.ulr.org

Urban League of Westchester County
61 Mitchell Pl.
White Plains, NY 10601
Ernest S. Prince, President/CEO
Tel: (914) 428-6300 Fax: (914) 428-6358
Email: ulwesp@aol.com
Web: www.nul.org

NEW YORK CITY MISSION SOCIETY
105 E. 22nd St.
New York, NY 10010-5494
Stephanie Palmer, Executive Director
Tel: (212) 674-3500 Fax: (212) 979-5764
Email: spalmer@nycmissionsociety.org
Web: www.nycmissionsociety.org

RAINBOW/PUSH COALITION
New York-Wall Street Project
Empire State Bldg., 350 5th Ave. #2701
New York, NY 10118
Andrew Carr, Executive Director
Tel: (212) 425-7874 Fax: (212) 968-1412
Email: info@rainbowpush.org
Web: www.rainbowpush.org

THE AFRICAN-AMERICAN INSTITUTE
420 Lexington Ave. #1706
New York, NY 10170-0002
Mora McLean, President
Tel: (212) 949-5666 Fax: (212) 682-3920
Email: aainy@aaionline.org
Web: www.aaionline.org

TWENTY-FIRST CENTURY FOUNDATION
271 W. 125th St. #303
New York, NY 10027-4424
Erica Hunt, President
Tel: (212) 662-3700 Fax: (212) 662-6690
Email: info@21cf.org
Web: www.21cf.org

SPEC. INT., SPORTS

NATIONAL BOWLING ASSOCIATION, INC.
377 Park Ave., 7th Fl. South
New York, NY 10016
Alesia A. Bryant, President
Tel: (212) 689-8308 Fax: (212) 725-5063
Email: president@tnbainc.org
Web: www.tnbainc.org

SPEC. INT., WOMEN

NATIONAL COALITION OF 100 BLACK WOMEN
National Office
38 W. 32nd St. #1610
New York, NY 10001
Shirley L. Poole, Executive Director
Tel: (212) 947-2196 Fax: (212) 947-2477
Email: nc100bw@aol.com
Web: www.ncbw.org

THE NEW YORK ASSOCIATION OF BLACK WOMEN OWNED ENTERPRISES, INC.
730 Fulton Ave.
Hempstead, NY 11550
Gina Slater Parker, President/CEO
Tel: (516) 485-5900 Fax: (516) 706-9470
Email: info@blackwomenenterprises.org
Web: www.blackwomenenterprises.org

THE SEASONED WOMAN, INC.
Park West Finance Station
P.O. Box 20616
New York, NY 10025
Dr. Theda Palmar Saxton, President
Tel: (212) 662-0952 Fax: (212) 666-7382
Email: swoman4@juno.com

SPEC. INT., YOUTH

CHILDREN'S DEFENSE FUND
Albany Office
119 Washington Ave.
Albany, NY 12210
Donna Lawrence, Director
Tel: (518) 449-2830 Fax: (518) 449-2846
Web: www.cdfny.org

New York City Office
420 Lexington Ave.
New York, NY 10070
Donna Lawrence, Director
Tel: (212) 697-2323 Fax: (212) 697-0566
Email: messages@cdfny.org
Web: www.cdfny.org

NEIGHBORHOOD YOUTH & FAMILY SERVICES
601 E. Tremont Ave., 2nd Fl.
Bronx, NY 10457
Lael Telseyan, Marketing/Fundraising Coordinator
Tel: (718) 299-2340 Fax: (718) 299-2343
Email: nyfsmarketing@aol.com

STUDENT ORGANIZATION

ALPHA KAPPA ALPHA SORORITY, INC.
Alpha Mu Chapter
176 Monroe St.
Brooklyn, NY 11216
Beryl Miles, Graduate Advisor
Email: babysis445@aol.com
Web: http://akanorthatlantic.org

Delta Mu Omega Chapter
223 Vincenza Ln.
Schenectady, NY 12309
Betty Shadrick, Chapter President
Web: www.aka1908.org

Delta Rho Omega Chapter
309 Lafayette Ave. #19I
Brooklyn, NY 11238
Carole Brinkley, Chapter President
Web: www.aka1908.com

Epsilon Pi Omega Chapter
P.O. Box 120553
St. Albans, NY 11412
Elizabeth A. Hooks, Chapter President
Web: www.aka1908.com

Eta Omega Omega Chapter
1019 E. 22nd St.
Bronx, NY 10469
Laverne Yard, Chapter President
Web: www.aka1908.com

Iota Alpha Omega Chapter
P.O. Box 1682
Poughkeepsie, NY 12601
Velda Brown, Chapter President
Web: www.aka1908.com

Iota Rho Chapter
184 Victoria Dr.
Utica, NY 13501
Carla Anderson, Chapter President
Web: www.aka1908.com

Iota Upsilon Chapter
P.O. Box 37163
Syracuse, NY 13235
Jeanelle Degraffenreid, Chapter President
Web: www.aka1908.com

Kappa Epsilon Chapter, Adelphi University
22 Sherman St.
Roosevelt, NY 11575
Valerie Smith, Graduate Advisor
Email: marvalous1@aol.com
Web: http://akanorthatlantic.org

Kappa Phi Chapter
150 Washington St. #6U
Hempstead, NY 11550
Tameka Wharwood, Chapter President
Web: www.aka1908.com

Lambda Chapter
P.O. Box 101
New York, NY 10018
Reena Nicole Goldthree, Chapter President
Web: www.aka1908.com

Mu Upsilon Chapter
R. Purcell Community Ctr.
P.O. Box H13B
Ithaca, NY 14853
Mariangela P. Mosley, Chapter President
Web: www.aka1908.com

Nu Mu Chapter, St. Johns University, Queens College and York College
245-25 77th St.
Bellrose, NY 11426
Lynn C. Landeau, Graduate Advisor
Email: protocol@mail.com
Web: http://akanorthatlantic.org

Omicron Beta Chapter
23 Bru-Mar Dr.
Rochester, NY 14606
Michee Holland, Chapter President
Web: www.aka1908.com

Omicron Eta Chapter
P.O. Box 518
New Rochelle, NY 10801
Veneek M. Linton, Chapter President
Web: www.aka1908.com

Omicron Nu Omega Chapter
P.O. Box 4754
Ithaca, NY 14852
Millicent Clarke-Maynard, Chapter President
Web: www.aka1908.com

Omicron Theta Chapter
221 E. 71st St.
New York, NY 10021
Cheryl Tyson, Chapter President
Web: www.aka1908.com

Pi Iota Omega Chapter
Main Station
P.O. Box 1636
White Plains, NY 10606
Lonnette Tuck, Chapter President
Web: www.aka1908.com

Pi Kappa Omega Chapter
3 Dussenbury Dr.
Florida, NY 10921
Michele Clayton, Chapter President
Web: www.aka1908.com

Pi Phi Omega Chapter
219-23 100 Ave.
Queens Village, NY 11429
Tonya Pearson, Chapter President
Tel: (718) 465-6742
Web: www.aka1908.com

Pi Pi Omega Chapter
42 Cherry St.
Central Islip, NY 11722
Janice Smith, Chapter President
Web: www.aka1908.com

Pi Psi Omega Chapter
P. O. Box 1748
Spring Valley, NY 10977
Alexandreena Dixon, Chapter President
Web: www.aka1908.com

Rho Theta Chapter, Pace University
80 Gold St. #3F
New York, NY 10038
Charlotte E. Banks, Graduate Advisor
Email: cevans6@nyc.rr.com
Web: http://akanorthatlantic.org

Sigma Psi Omega Chapter
1705 Nicole Dr.
Port Jefferson St. NY 11722
Hughette N. Clarke, Chapter President
Web: www.aka1908.com

Tau Omega Chapter
310 W. 138th St.
New York, NY 10030
Rosalyn Graves-Baker, Chapter President
Web: www.aka1908.com

Theta Iota Omega Chapter
21 Summer Ln.
Amityville, NY 11701
Hazel Palmore, Chapter President
Web: www.aka1908.com

Upsilon Nu Omega Chapter
P.O. Box 3303
Binghamton, NY 13902
Pamela Hatchett-Rogers, Chapter President
Web: www.aka1908.com

Xi Chi Omega Chapter
P.O. Box 191
Chappaqua, NY 10514
Linda Helm, Chapter President
Web: www.aka1908.com

Xi Epsilon Omega Chapter
P.O. Box 1861
Amherst, NY 14226
Rita Fraiser, Chapter President
Web: www.aka1908.com

Xi Mu Chapter
17 Marsdale Ct.
Selkirk, NY 12158
Meredith Henderson, Graduate Advisor
Email: meredithaka@aol.com
Web: http://akanorthatlantic.org

Xi Xi Chapter, Lehman College
135 W. 138th St. #5B
New York, NY 10030
Pauline L. Monsanto, Graduate Advisor
Email: plmsilverstar@aol.com
Web: http://akanorthatlantic.org

Zeta Nu Omega Chapter
P.O. Box 1159
New Rochelle, NY 10802

Fay L. Fagan, Chapter President
Web: www.aka1908.com

ALPHA PHI ALPHA FRATERNITY, INC.
Beta Pi Lambda Chapter
P.O. Box 14164
Albany, NY 12212
Email: betapilambda@alphaeast.com
Web: www.alphaphialpha.net

BLACK STUDENT SCIENCE ORGANIZATION
202 Stewart St.
Elmont, NY 11003
Darcie Joseph, President
Tel: (917) 554-3820
Email: dj336@nyu.edu
Web: www.nyu.edu/clubs/bsso

BLACK STUDENT UNION
New York State University
125 Hewitt Union, State University of New York
Oswego, NY 13126
Kendra Jordan, President
Tel: (315) 312-2945 Fax: (315) 312-5410
Email: blcksgdnt@yahoo.com

BLACK STUDENTS SCIENCE ORGANIZATION
New York University
60 Washington Sq. South, 7th Fl. #38
New York, NY 10012
Tel: (212) 998-4703 Fax: (212) 995-4116
Email: jl839@nyu.edu
Web: www.nyu.edu/clubs/bsso

NATIONAL BLACK LAW STUDENTS ASSOCIATION
Albany Law School
80 New Scotland Ave.
Albany, NY 12208
Tel: (518) 472-5830
Email: blsa@mail.als.edu

Benjamin N. Cardozo School of Law
55 5th Ave.
New York, NY 10003
Richard Joel, President
Tel: (212) 790-0353
Web: www.cardozo.yu.edu

Brooklyn Law School
250 Joralemon St.
Brooklyn, NY 11201
Annette Gill, President
Tel: (718) 780-7962
Email: raqui79@yahoo.com
Web: www.nblsa.org

City University of New York Law School at Queens College
65-21 Main St.
Flushing, NY 11367
Rogi Patel, Director
Tel: (718) 340-4207 Fax: (718) 340-4372
Email: blsa@mail.law.cuny.edu
Web: www.nblsa.org

Fordham University School of Law
140 W. 62nd St.
New York, NY 10023
BLSA President
Tel: (212) 636-6800
Web: www.nblsa.org

Touro College Law Center
300 Nassau Rd. Attn: Black Law Students Association
Huntington, NY 11743
Jameelah Hayes
Tel: (631) 421-2244 X413
Email: jameelahhayes@hotmail.com
Web: www.nblsa.org

NORTH CAROLINA

ARTISTIC

NORTH CAROLINA BLACK REPERTORY COMPANY
610 Coliseum Dr.
Winston-Salem, NC 27106
Larry Leon Hamlin, Artistic Director/Producer
Tel: (336) 723-2266 Fax: (336) 723-2223
Email: llhamlin@bellsouth.net
Web: www.nbtf.org

BUSINESS

NATIONAL MINORITY SUPPLIER DEVELOPMENT COUNCIL, INC.
Carolinas Minority Supplier Development Councils, Inc.
Lincoln Ctr., 10400 Mallard Creek Rd. #340
Charlotte, NC 28262
Julian Brown, President
Tel: (704) 549-1000 Fax: (704) 549-1616

Email: cmsdcinc@bellsouth.net
Web: www.carolinasmsdc.net

NORTH CAROLINA INSTITUTE OF MINORITY ECONOMIC DEVELOPMENT
114 W. Parrish St.
Durham, NC 27701
Andrea Harris, President
Tel: (919) 956-8889 Fax: (919) 688-7668
Email: info@ncimed.com
Web: www.ncimed.com

CULTURAL

AFRO-AMERICAN CULTURAL CENTER
401 N. Myers St.
Charlotte, NC 28202
Beverly A. Cureton, Executive Director
Tel: (704) 374-1565 Fax: (704) 374-9273
Email: beverly@aacc-charlotte.org
Web: www.aacc-charlotte.org

CONCERNED CITIZENS OF TILLERY
P.O. Box 61
Tillery, NC 27887
Gary R. Grant, National President
Tel: (252) 826-3017 Fax: (252) 826-3244
Email: tillery@aol.com
Web: http://members.aol.com/tillery

LEDONIA WRIGHT CULTURAL CENTER
East Carolina University
Bloxton House
Greenville, NC 27858-4353
Dr. Lathan E. Turner, Director
Tel: (252) 328-6495 Fax: (252) 328-0370
Email: akd0129@mail.ecu.edu
Web: www.ecu.edu/lwcc

MARY LOU WILLIAMS CENTER FOR BLACK CULTURE
Duke University
P.O. Box 90880
02 W. Union Bldg.
Durham, NC 27708
Andrea Caldwell, Interim Director
Tel: (919) 684-3814 Fax: (919) 681-7472
Web: http://mlw.studentaffairs.duke.edu

ST. JOSEPH HISTORIC FOUNDATION, INC.
804 Old Fayetteville St.
Durham, NC 27702
V. Dianne Pledger, President/CEO
Tel: (919) 683-1709 Fax: (919) 682-5869
Email: info@hayti.org
Web: www.hayti.org

ENTERTAINMENT

NATIONAL AFRICAN AMERICAN RV'ERS ASSOCIATION
The Innovators Chapter
P.O. Box 3432
Wilmington, NC 28406
James Smith, President
Tel: (910) 262-2387
Email: smithje@aol.com
Web: www.naarva.com

The Triangle RVers Chapter
3121 Deichester Ct.
Durham, NC 27713
Naomi Atwater, President
Tel: (919) 544-5589
Email: naomi_atwater@msn.com
Web: www.naarva.com

LAW ENFORCEMENT

NATIONAL ORGANIZATION OF BLACK LAW ENFORCEMENT EXECUTIVES
Greater Charlotte Chapter
P.O. Box 472262
North Carolina A&T State University
Charlotte, NC 28247
Marlon C. Lynch, President
Tel: (336) 334-7289 Fax: (336) 334-7230
Email: mclynch@ncat.edu
Web: www.gcc.noblechapter.org

POLITICAL ACTION

AMERICAN CIVIL LIBERTIES UNION
North Carolina Chapter
P.O. Box 28004
Raleigh, NC 27611
Jennifer Rudinger, Executive Director
Tel: (919) 834-3390 Fax: (919) 828-3265
Email: aclunc@z-wave.net
Web: www.acluofnorthcarolina.org

BLACK RADICAL CONGRESS
Central-East, North Carolina Chapter
2316 Keith Dr.
Raleigh, NC 27610
Ajamu Dillahunt
Tel: (919) 829-0957
Email: ardillahunt@igc.org
Web: www.blackradicalcongress.com

BLACKS IN GOVERNMENT
Region IV-Research Triangle Park Chapter
P.O. Box 8
Morrisville, NC 27560
Kimberly Peterson, Chapter President
Tel: (919) 541-3120
Email: research.triangle@bignet.org
Web: www.bignet.org

PROFESSIONAL

ASSOCIATION OF BLACK PSYCHOLOGISTS
North Carolina Chapter
2515 Apex Hwy. #A
Durham, NC 27713
Anthony Smith, Chapter President
Tel: (919) 957-7357 Fax: (919) 957-9359
Email: dranthonysmith@alase.net
Web: www.abpsi.org

BLACK DATA PROCESSING ASSOCIATES
Charlotte Chapter
P.O. Box 620787
Charlotte, NC 28262
Email: charlotte@bdpa.org
Web: www.bdpa-charlotte.org

BLACK FARMERS & AGRICULTURALISTS ASSOCIATION
Head Office
P.O. Box 61
Tillery, NC 27887
Gary R. Grant, National President
Tel: (252) 826-2800 Fax: (252) 826-3244
Email: tillery@aol.com
Web: http://www.coax.net/people/lwf/bfaa.htm

NATIONAL BLACK MBA ASSOCIATION, INC.
Charlotte Chapter-South
P.O. Box 34613
Charlotte, NC 28234
Stewart Hubbard, President
Tel: (800) 925-1312
Web: www.nbmbaa.org

Piedmont-Triad
P.O. Box 4182
Winston -Salem, NC 27115
Charles H. Horton Jr., President
Tel: (336) 779-6222
Email: c.m.horton@earthlink.net
Web: www.nbmbaa.org

Raleigh/Durham Chapter-South
P.O. Box 13614
Durham, NC 27709
Sandra Thompson, President
Tel: (919) 990-2351
Email: rdumba@rdumba.org
Web: www.rdumba.org

NATIONAL FORUM FOR BLACK PUBLIC ADMINISTRATORS
North Carolina Triad Chapter
P.O. Box 3136
Greensboro, NC 27402
Calvin O. Foster, President
Tel: (336) 373-2876 Fax: (336) 373-2338
Email: calvin.foster@greensboro-nc.gov
Web: www.nfbpa.org

NATIONAL PHARMACEUTICAL ASSOCIATION
107 Kilmayne Dr. #C
Cary, NC 27511
Alex Taylor, President
Tel: (800) 944-6742 Fax: (919) 469-5870
Email: npha@npha.net
Web: www.npha.net

NATIONAL SOCIETY OF BLACK ENGINEERS
Region 2: North Carolina A&T Chapter
NC A&T #5150,1601 E. Market St.
Greensboro, NC 27411
Dr. Lee Parrish, Advisor
Tel: (336) 334-7589 Fax: (336) 334-7540
Email: parrishl@ncat.edu
Web: www.ncatnsbe.com

NATIONAL SOCIETY OF BLACK PHYSICISTS
North Carolina A&T State University Chapter
Department of Physics, 1601 E. Market St.
Greensboro, NC 27411
Floyd James, Contact Representative

Tel: (336) 334-7646 Fax: (336) 334-7283
Email: president@nsbp.org
Web: www.nsbp.org

AFRICAN & AFRICAN AMERICAN STUDIES
Duke University, John Hope Franklin Center
2204 Erwin Rd., Box 90252
Durham, NC 27708
Charles M. Payne, Director
Tel: (919) 684-2830 Fax: (919) 684-2832
Email: cmpayne@duke.edu
Web: www.duke.edu/web/africanameric/

AFRICAN AMERICAN STUDENT AFFAIRS
NC State University
Campus Box 7314, 1107 Pullen Hall
Raleigh, NC 27695-7314
Stacie S. Solomon, Assistant Director
Tel: (919) 515-3835 Fax: (919) 515-8078
Email: stacie_solomon@ncsu.edu
Web: www.ncsu.edu/for_students/aasac/

UNIVERSITY OF NORTH CAROLINA MATHEMATICS AND SCIENCE EDUCATION NETWORK
Center for Leadership Development
P.O. Box 2688
140 Friday Center Dr.
Chapel Hill, NC 27515-2688
Dr. Verna Holoman, Executive Director
Tel: (919) 966-3256 Fax: (919) 962-1316
Email: holomanv@northcarolina.edu
Web: www.unc.edu/depts/msen

100 BLACK MEN OF AMERICA, INC.
Greater Charlotte Chapter
740 W. 5th St. #208
Charlotte, NC 28202
Jacquelin C. Peters, Acting Executive Director
Tel: (704) 375-7300 Fax: (704) 375-5151
Email: charlottethe100@aol.com
Web: www.100blackmenofcharlotte.org

100 BLACK MEN OF CAPE FEAR REGION, INC.
P.O. Box 912
Fayetteville, NC 28302
Ladelle Olion, Chapter President
Tel: (910) 672-1074 Fax: (910) 672-1782
Email: lolion@uncfsu.edu
Web: www.100blackmen.org

IMPROVED BENEVOLENT PROTECTIVE ORDER OF THE ELKS OF THE WORLD
Headquarters
P.O. Box 159
Winton, NC 27986
Dr. Donald P. Wilson, Grand Exalted Ruler
Tel: (252) 358-7661 Fax: (252) 358-7681

NATIONAL URBAN LEAGUE, INC.
Triangle Urban League
150 Fayetteville St. Mall #220
Raleigh, NC 27601
Keith Sutton, President/CEO
Tel: (919) 834-7252 Fax: (919) 834-5717
Web: www.triangleul.org

Urban League of Central Carolinas
740 W. 5th St.
Charlotte, NC 28202
Madine Fails, President/CEO
Tel: (704) 373-2256 Fax: (704) 373-2262
Email: sbyoung@urbanleaguecc.org
Web: www.urbanleaguecc.org

Winston-Salem Urban League
740 W. 5th St.
Charlotte, NC 28202
Madine Fails, President/CEO
Tel: (704) 373-2256 Fax: (704) 373-2262
Email: wsyoung@urbanleaguecc.org
Web: www.urbanleaguecc.org

THUG MINISTRY NANCOM-COMMUNICATION
256 1st St.
Charlotte, NC 28208
Shelton J. Boyd, Executive Director
Tel: (704) 713-3616 Fax: (803) 327-8067
Email: thugministry_2000@yahoo.com
Web: www.freedomtempleministries.org

ALPHA KAPPA ALPHA SORORITY, INC.
Alpha Chi Chapter
P.O. Box 19834-C
Durham, NC 27707
Keosha McKoy, Chapter President
Web: www.aka1908.com

Alpha Lambda Omega Chapter
P.O. Box 31624
Charlotte, NC 28231
Barbara Atwater, Chapter President

Alpha Phi Chapter
1601 E. Market St. #5079
Greensboro, NC 27411
Tanya Wheeler, Chapter President
Web: www.aka1908.com

Alpha Psi Omega Chapter
2535-11 Costmary Ln.
Wilmington, NC 28412
Ivy Lori Murrain, Chapter President
Web: www.aka1908.com

Alpha Theta Omega Chapter
P.O. Box 25578
Raleigh, NC 27611
Linda B. Gill, Chapter President
Web: www.aka1908.com

Alpha Xi Chapter
P.O. Box 983
Salisbury, NC 28145
Tamika Greene, Chapter President
Web: www.aka1908.com

Alpha Zeta Omega Chapter
P.O. Box 52465
Durham, NC 27717
Tara Lynne Fikes, Chapter President
Web: www.aka1908.com

Beta Iota Omega Chapter
P.O. Box 20724
Greensboro, NC 27420
Simone B. Langley, Chapter President
Web: www.aka1908.com

Beta Rho Chapter
P.O. Box 722
Raleigh, NC 27602
Tanesha L. Haynes, Chapter President
Web: www.aka1908.com

Chi Omega Chapter
P.O. Box 6211
Rocky Mount, NC 27802
Josie Davis, Chapter President
Web: www.aka1908.com

Delta Alpha Chapter
1200 Murchison Rd.
Fayetteville, NC 28301
Kendra White, Chapter President
Web: www.aka1908.com

Delta Psi Chapter
145 Cabarrus Ave. West
Concord, NC 28025
Tamasheika Baker, Chapter President
Web: www.aka1908.com

Delta Theta Chapter
P.O. Box 736, ECSU
Elizabeth City, NC 27909
Kimberly W. Bond, Chapter President
Web: www.aka1908.com

Delta Xi Omega Chapter
P.O. Box 983
Salisbury, NC 28145
Marsha D. Pruitt, Chapter President
Web: www.aka1908.com

Epsilon Phi Omega Chapter
P.O. Box 1421
Goldsboro, NC 27533
Renita D. Allen, Chapter President
Web: www.aka1908.com

Eta Omicron Omega Chapter
P.O. Box 147
High Point, NC 27261
Jocelyn Z. Hollowell, Chapter President
Web: www.aka1908.com

Gamma Beta Omega Chapter
P.O. Box 4217
Wilson, NC 27893
Shlondra P. Amacker, Chapter President
Web: www.aka1908.com

Gamma Gamma Omega Chapter
P.O. Box 3152
Asheville, NC 28802
Willie Vincent, Chapter President
Web: www.aka1908.com

Gamma Lambda Chapter
133 Winterbrook Ct.
Winston-Salem, NC 27105
Karen Smith, Chapter President
Web: www.aka1908.com

Iota Kappa Omega Chapter
P.O. Box 7012
Greenville, NC 27834

Laura W. Carmon, Chapter President
Web: www.aka1908.com

Kappa Iota Omega Chapter
P.O. Box G
Garysburg, NC 27831
Elease Frederick, Chapter President
Web: www.aka1908.com

Kappa Omicron Chapter
P.O. Box 5831
Raleigh, NC 27606
Davida S. Jones, Chapter President
Web: www.aka1908.com

Lambda Delta Omega Chapter
P.O. Box 89
Williamston, NC 27892
Shirley Hodges Council, Chapter President
Web: www.aka1908.com

Lambda Upsilon Omega Chapter
4316 Stonefield Dr.
Charlotte, NC 28269
Ruth Davis Berry, Chapter President
Web: www.aka1908.com

Mu Omicron Omega Chapter
P.O. Box 16486
Chapel Hill, NC 27514
Valerie Celeste Jones, Chapter President
Web: www.aka1908.com

Nu Chi Omega Chapter
P.O. Box 69
Creedmoor, NC 27522
Shirley Holliday, Chapter President
Web: www.aka1908.com

Nu Eta Omega Chapter
P.O. Box 244
Edenton, NC 27932
Jolyquin Belfield, Chapter President
Web: www.aka1908.com

Omicron Epsilon Chapter
7020 Campus Box
Elon College, NC 27244
Royce Evans, Chapter President
Web: www.aka1908.com

Omicron Lambda Chapter
22761 Old Lumberton Rd.
Maxton, NC 28364
Demetrice McMillan, Chapter President
Web: www.aka1908.com

Omicron Omega Omega Chapter
P.O. Box 848
Southern Pines, NC 28388
Nancy Wooten Coor, Chapter President
Web: www.aka1908.com

Omicron Phi Chapter
601 S. College Rd., C/O Greek Aff.
Wilmington, NC 28405
Shaunita Monique Wallace, Chapter President
Web: www.aka1908.com

Omicron Psi Omega Chapter
P.O. Box 1111
Lexington, NC 27293
Cynthia Elizabeth Mosley, Chapter President
Web: www.aka1908.com

Phi Omega Chapter
P.O. Box 16065
Winston-Salem, NC 27115
Susie Nance, Chapter President
Web: www.aka1908.com

Phi Theta Omega Chapter
P.O. Box 2576
Washington, NC 27889
Sharon Evans, Chapter President
Web: www.aka1908.com

Pi Beta Chapter
P.O. Box 7381
Winston-Salem, NC 27109
Kendra Danika Stewart, Chapter President
Web: www.aka1908.com

Pi Omicron Omega Chapter
P.O. Box 2006
Burlington, NC 27216
Clara T. Foriest, Chapter President
Web: www.aka1908.com

Rho Alpha Omega Chapter
1001 Heather Ln.
Laurinburg, NC 28352
Bernice James, Chapter President
Web: www.aka1908.com

Rho Omega Omega Chapter
P.O. Box 623
Clinton, NC 28328
Marion Delores Phillips, Chapter President
Web: www.aka1908.com

Rho Psi Omega Chapter
P.O. Box 30833
Charlotte, NC 28230
Valerie Patterson, Chapter President
Web: www.aka1908.com

Rho Tau Omega Chapter
P.O. Box 852, Warren County
Norlina, NC 27563
Jennie Franklin, Chapter President
Web: www.aka1908.com

Sigma Iota Omega Chapter
P.O. Box 223
Fairmont, NC 28340
Anita Powell-McDowell, Chapter President
Web: www.aka1908.com

Sigma Kappa Omega Chapter
P.O. Box 2427
Greensboro, NC 27402
Marvette Artis, Chapter President
Web: www.aka1908.com

Sigma Nu Omega Chapter
P.O. Box 3407
Roxboro, NC 27573
Eulonda Lea Booker, Chapter President
Web: www.aka1908.com

Sigma Tau Omega Chapter
P.O. Box 667
Cary, NC 27512
Kim Smith Deck, Chapter President
Web: www.aka1908.com

Tau Omega Omega Chapter
P.O. Box 352
Jacksonville, NC 28540
Dolores Faison, Chapter President
Web: www.aka1908.com

Theta Alpha Chapter
P.O. Box 2886
Greenville, NC 27858
Crystal Frye, Chapter President
Web: www.aka1908.com

Theta Beta Omega Chapter
P.O. Box 15426
New Bern, NC 28561
Ernell Fonville Thompkins, Chapter President
Web: www.aka1908.com

Theta Pi Chapter
P.O. Box 1107
Chapel Hill, NC 27514
Shannon Eaves, Chapter President
Web: www.aka1908.com

Upsilon Kappa Omega Chapter
P.O. Box 53241
Fayetteville, NC 28305
Arrie Mcallister, Chapter President
Web: www.aka1908.com

Xi Phi Omega Chapter
P.O. Box 486
Hickory, NC 28603
Felicia Culbreath-Setzer, Chapter President
Web: www.aka1908.com

Xi Rho Omega Chapter
P.O. Box 965
Ahoskie, NC 27910
Linda Davis Pierce, Chapter President
Web: www.aka1908.com

Zeta Kappa Omega Chapter
P.O. Box 2063
Elizabeth City, NC 27909
Delphine Walton, Chapter President
Web: www.aka1908.com

Zeta Mu Omega Chapter
P.O. Box 1771
Gastonia, NC 28053
Valerie Boyd, Chapter President
Web: www.aka1908.com

Zeta Omicron Omega Chapter
P.O. Box 1692
Kinston, NC 28502
Betty B. Little, Chapter President
Web: www.aka1908.com

Zeta Pi Omega Chapter
P.O. Box 395
Fayetteville, NC 28302
Sharon Alexander, Chapter President
Web: www.aka1908.com

Zeta Xi Chapter
900 E. Washington St.
Greensboro, NC 27401
Monya Tomlinson, Chapter President
Web: www.aka1908.com

ALPHA PHI ALPHA FRATERNITY, INC.
Alpha Omicron Chapter, Johnson C. Smith University

P.O. Box 1035
Charlotte, NC 28216
Web: www.alphaphialpha.net

Alpha Pi Lambda Chapter
P.O. Box 11316
Winston-Salem, NC 27116
Web: www.alphaphialpha.net

Beta Epsilon Chapter, North Carolina A&T State University
P.O. Box 20566
Greensboro, NC 27402
Web: www.alphaphialpha.net

Beta Iota Chapter, Winston-Salem State University
601 Martin Luther King Jr., Dr.
Winston-Salem, NC 27110
Jeffery Purcell, President
Email: black_alpha@hotmail.com
Web: www.geocities.com/CollegePark/8864/

Beta Nu Lambda Chapter
P.O. Box 562663
Charlotte, NC 28256
Jonathan L. Lindsay, President
Email: jlindsay@carolina.rr.com
Web: www.betanulambda.org

Beta Rho Chapter, Shaw University
P.O. Box 28721
Raleigh, NC 27601
Web: www.alphaphialpha.net

Beta Theta Lambda Chapter
P.O. Box 3522
Durham, NC 27702
Web: www.alphaphialpha.net

Beta Zeta Chapter, Elizabeth City State University
P.O. Box 762
Elizabeth City, NC 27909
Web: www.alphaphialpha.net

Epsilon Chi Lambda Chapter
P.O. Box 802
Elizabeth City, NC 27909
Web: www.alphaphialpha.net

Epsilon Rho Lambda Chapter
P.O. Box 1572
Fayetteville, NC 28302
Web: www.alphaphialpha.net

Epsilon Sigma Lambda Chapter
P.O. Box 1762
Rocky Mount, NC 27802
Web: www.alphaphialpha.net

Epsilon Zeta Chapter, Fayetteville State University
P.O. Box 14906
Fayetteville, NC 28301
Web: www.alphaphialpha.net

Eta Mu Lambda Chapter
P.O. Box 141
Gastonia, NC 28053
Web: www.alphaphialpha.net

Eta Omicron Chapter, North Carolina State University
P.O. Box 5963
Raleigh, NC 27695
Web: www.alphaphialpha.net

Gamma Kappa Lambda Chapter
P.O. Box 1552
Wilmington, NC 28402
Web: www.alphaphialpha.net

Gamma Mu Chapter, Livingstone College
P.O. Box 14
Salisbury, NC 28145
Web: www.alphaphialpha.net

Gamma Psi Chapter, St. Augustine's College
P.O. Box 28012
Raleigh, NC 27610
Web: www.alphaphialpha.net

Kappa Lambda Chapter
P.O. Box 21052
Greensboro, NC 27420
Web: www.alphaphialpha.net

Kappa Omicron Chapter, Duke University
P.O. Box 99347
Durham, NC 27708
Web: www.alphaphialpha.net

Mu Zeta Chapter, University of North Carolina
P.O. Box 1031
Chapel Hill, NC 27514
Web: www.alphaphialpha.net

Nu Iota Lambda Chapter
P.O. Box 205
Kinston, NC 28502
Web: www.alphaphialpha.net

Nu Kappa Lambda Chapter
P.O. Box 2655
Lumberton, NC 28359
Web: www.alphaphialpha.net

Omicron Gamma Lambda Chapter
P.O. Box 681
Winston-Salem, NC 27102
Web: www.alphaphialpha.net

Phi Lambda Chapter
P.O. Box 28797
Raleigh, NC 27611
Web: www.alphaphialpha.net

Pi Chi Lambda Chapter
P.O. Box 2023
Clinton, NC 28328
Web: www.alphaphialpha.net

Pi Nu Chapter, Appalachian State University
P.O. Box 8984
Boone, NC 28608
Web: www.alphaphialpha.net

Pi Zeta Chapter, University of North Carolina -Greensboro
P.O. Box 1061
Greensboro, NC 27412
Web: www.alphaphialpha.net

Sigma Delta Chapter, Elon College
Campus Box 5431
Elon College, NC 27244
Web: www.alphaphialpha.net

Theta Omicron Lambda Chapter
P.O. Box 824
Goldsboro, NC 27533
Web: www.alphaphialpha.net

Xi Eta Chapter, Wake Forest University
P.O. Box 7322
Winston-Salem, NC 27109
Web: www.alphaphialpha.net

Zeta Epsilon Chapter, Barber Scotia College
145 Cabarrus Ave.
Concord, NC 28025
Web: www.alphaphialpha.net

Zeta Eta Lambda Chapter
P.O. Box 1187
Greenville, NC 27835
Web: www.alphaphialpha.net

BLACK STUDENT ALLIANCE
Duke University
101-3 Bryan Ctr. #90834
Durham, NC 27708
Pascale Thomas, President
Tel: (919) 684-4154 Fax: (919) 684-8395
Email: mmj2@duke.edu
Web: www.duke.edu/web/bsa

NATIONAL BLACK LAW STUDENTS ASSOCIATION
Campbell University-Norman Adrian Wiggins School of Law
423 Lenoxplace Cir.
Raleigh, NC 27603
Kia Scott, President
Tel: (704) 467-3166
Email: kia_n_scott@hotmail.com
Web: http://law.campbell.edu

University of North Carolina School of Law Van-Hecke Wettach Hall
CB #3380
Chapel Hill, NC 27599
Wilson White, President
Tel: (919) 962-5106 Fax: (919) 843-7939
Email: wlwhite@email.com
Web: www.unc.edu/student/orgs/blsa/

SIGMA GAMMA RHO SORORITY, INC.
1000 Southhill Dr. #200
Cary, NC 27513-8630
Jennifer Jones, Executive Director
Tel: (919) 678-9720 Fax: (919) 678-9721
Email: executivedirector@sgrho1922.org
Web: www.sgrho1922.org

SIGMA GAMMA RHO SORORITY, INC.
International Headquarters
1000 Southhill Dr. #200
Cary, NC 27513
Dr. Mynora J. Bryant, International Grand Basileus
Tel: (888) 747-1922 Fax: (919) 678-9721
Email: executivedirector@sgrho1922.org
Web: www.sgrho1922.org

NORTH DAKOTA

CULTURAL

GRAND FOLKS JUNETEENTH CELEBRATION
Multicultural Student Services Box 70902 , University of North Dakota
Grand Folks, ND 58202
MC Diop, State Coordinator
Tel: (701) 777-4362 Fax: (701) 777-4119

Email: mcdiop@hotmail.com
Web: www.und.edu

POLITICAL ACTION

AMERICAN CIVIL LIBERTIES UNION
The Dakotas Chapter
Manchester Bldg., 112 N. University Dr. #301
Fargo, ND 58102-4661
Jennifer Ring, Executive Director
Tel: (701) 461-7290 Fax: (701) 461-7291
Email: dakaclu@cs.com
Web: www.aclu.org

OHIO

ARTISTIC

ARTS CONSORTIUM OF CINCINNATI
Cincinnati Museum Center
1301 Western Ave.
Cincinnati, OH 45203
Paula Sherman, Associate Director
Tel: (513) 381-0645 Fax: (513) 381-0915
Email: psherman@nattiarts.org
Web: www.artsconsortiumcincy.org

KARAMU HOUSE, INC.
2355 E. 89th St.
Cleveland, OH 44106
Gerry McClamy, Executive Director
Tel: (216) 795-7070 Fax: (216) 795-7073
Email: info@karamu.com
Web: www.karamu.com

BUSINESS

CINCINNATI BDS, INC.
Ohio Statewide Minority Business Development Center
7162 Reading Rd. #630
Cincinnati, OH 45237
Onnie R. Martin, Executive Director
Tel: (513) 631-7666 Fax: (513) 631-7613
Email: omartin@ohiostatewidembdc.org
Web: www.ohiostatewidembdc.org

MINORITY CONTRACTORS AND BUSINESS ASSISTANCE PROGRAM
Division of Minority Business Affairs
P.O. Box 1001
Columbus, OH 43216
Frank Watson, President
Tel: (800) 848-1300 Fax: (614) 466-4172
Web: www.odod.state.oh.us/dmba/mcbap.htm

NATIONAL MINORITY SUPPLIER DEVELOPMENT COUNCIL, INC.
Northern Ohio Minority Business Council
Tower City Ctr., 50 Public Square #200
Cleveland, OH 44113-2291
Wyatt Brownlee, Executive Director
Tel: (216) 621-3300 Fax: (216) 621-5461
Email: nombc@gcpartnership.com
Web: www.nombconline.org

South Central Ohio Minority Business Council, Cincinnati Office
300 Carew Tower, 441 Vine St.
Cincinnati, OH 45202-2812
Crystal Davis, Area Manager
Tel: (513) 579-3104 Fax: (513) 579-3101
Email: cdavis@gccc.com
Web: www.scombc.com

South Central Ohio Minority Business Council, Dayton Office
1 Chamber Plz.
Dayton, OH 45402
Kellye Hickman, Area Manager
Tel: (937) 226-8265 Fax: (937) 226-8221
Email: khickman@dacc.org
Web: www.scombc.com

South Central Ohio Minority Business Council, Headquarter Office
37 N. High St.
Columbus, OH 43215
Cathy Mock, President
Tel: (614) 225-6959 Fax: (614) 221-1669
Email: cathy_mock@scombc.org
Web: www.scombc.com

OHIO VALLEY MINORITY BUSINESS ASSOCIATION,
P.O. Box 847
1206 Waller St.
Portsmouth, OH 45662
Scott Tyler, Executive Director
Tel: (740) 353-8395 Fax: (740) 353-2695

CHAMBER OF COMMERCE

GREATER CINCINNATI NORTHERN KENTUCKY AFRICAN AMERICAN CHAMBER OF COMMERCE
2945 Gilbert Ave.
Cincinnati, OH 45206
Arlene Koth, Chair
Tel: (513) 751-9900 Fax: (513) 751-9100
Email: info@gcaacc.com
Web: www.gcaacc.com

CULTURAL

A CULTURAL EXCHANGE
12624 Larchmere Blvd.
Cleveland, OH 44120
Deborah McHamm, President/CEO
Tel: (216) 229-8300 Fax: (216) 795-5302
Email: demc.ace@juno.com

ASSOCIATION OF AFRICAN AMERICAN MUSEUMS
P.O. Box 578
Wilberforce, OH 45384
William Billingsley, Executive Director
Tel: (937) 376-4944 X123 Fax: (937) 376-2007
Email: wbillingsley@ohiohistory.org
Web: www.blackmuseums.org

BLACK POETIC SOCIETY
Cleveland State Univesity
2121 Euclid Ave.
Cleveland, OH 44115
Tel: (216) 687-2048 Fax: (216) 687-5441

JUNETEENTH OHIO
1206 N. High St.
Columbus, OH 43201
Mustafaa Shabazz, CEO
Tel: (614) 299-4488 Fax: (614) 252-8052
Email: smustafaa@aol.com
Web: www.juneteenthohio.net

ENTERTAINMENT

NATIONAL AFRICAN AMERICAN RV'ERS ASSOCIATION
Akron Adventures Kamper Club Chapter
593 Doorchester Rd.
Akron, OH 44320
John Davison, President
Tel: (330) 867-3940
Email: jroller@aol.com
Web: www.naarva.co

Buckeye Explorers Chapter
4801 Little Richmond Rd.
Trotwood, OH 45426
Curtis Johnson, President
Tel: (937) 854-3251
Email: jrob46@msn.com
Web: www.naarva.com

Columbus Camper Club Chapter
P.O. Box 356
Worthington, OH 43085
Richard Macer, President
Tel: (614) 846-3667
Email: bpor98@juno.com
Web: www.naarva.com

Lake Erie Travelers Chapter
P.O. Box 201663
Cleveland, OH 04120
Ed Brown, President
Tel: (216) 921-0937
Web: www.naarva.com

Ohio Buckeye Road Runners Chapter
3725 Congreve Ave.
Cincinnati, OH 45213
Norman L. Ellis, President
Tel: (513) 637-7753
Email: lyna.norman@att.worldnet.com
Web: www.naarva.com

LAW ENFORCEMENT

NATIONAL ORGANIZATION OF BLACK LAW ENFORCEMENT EXECUTIVES
Cleveland Chapter
P.O. Box 5541
Cuyahoga Community College
Cleveland, OH 44101-0531
Clayton Harris, President
Tel: (216) 987-4425 Fax: (216) 987-4223
Email: clayton.harris@tri-c.edu
Web: www.noblenatl.org

Greater Cincinnati Chapter
P.O. Box 1773
Lincoln Heights Police Dept, 1201 Steffens Ave.

Cincinnati, OH 45202
Gregory C. Hutchins, Probation Officer
Tel: (513) 564-7562 Fax: (513) 564-7587
Email: greg_c_hutchins@ohsp.uscourts.gov
Web: www.noblenatl.org

POLITICAL ACTION

AMERICAN CIVIL LIBERTIES UNION
Ohio Chapter
Max Wohl Civil Liberties Ctr., 4506 Chester Ave.
Cleveland, OH 44103
Christine Link, Executive Director
Tel: (216) 472-2200 Fax: (216) 472-2210
Email: contact@acluohio.org
Web: www.acluohio.org

ASSOCIATION OF COMMUNITY ORGANIZATIONS FOR REFORM NOW
Cleveland Office
3615 Superior Ave., 4th Fl.
Cleveland, OH 44114
Tel: (216) 431-0573 Fax: (216) 431-6077
Email: ohacorncv@acorn.org
Web: www.acorn.org

Toledo Office
454 Delaware
Toledo, OH 43610
Tel: (419) 244-7250 Fax: (419) 243-3151
Email: ohacornto@acorn.org
Web: www.acorn.org

BLACKS IN GOVERNMENT
Region V-Columbus Area Chapter
P.O. Box 09084
Columbus, OH 43209
Yolanda Brown-Harris, Chapter President
Tel: (614) 692-0742
Email: columbus.area@bignet.org
Web: www.bignet.org/regional/region5/default.htm

Region V-Dayton VAMC Chapter
P.O. Box 28099
Dayton, OH 45428
Barbara J. Walker, Chapter President
Tel: (937) 262-2118
Email: dayton.vamc@bignet.org
Web: www.bignet.org/regional/region5/default.htm

Region V-Greater Cleveland Chapter
P.O. Box 811071
Cleveland, OH 44181-1071
James F. Travis, Chapter President
Tel: (216) 433-9338
Email: greater.cleveland@bignet.org
Web: www.bignet.org/regional/region5/default.htm

Region V-Greater Dayton Chapter
P.O. Box 33684
Dayton, OH 45433-0684
Rodrick Waldron, Chapter President
Tel: (937) 257-2349
Email: greater.dayton@bignet.org
Web: www.bignet.org/regional/greater.dayton/index.htm

Region V-Lake Erie Chapter
3600 E. 105th St.
Cleveland, OH 44105
Elizabeth F. Harris, Chapter President
Tel: (216) 204-9159
Email: lake.erie@bignet.org
Web: www.bignet.org/regional/region5/default.htm

Region V-Southwest Ohio Chapter
9 Peachtree Ct.
Fairfield, OH 45014
Ollie Darby, Chapter President
Tel: (513) 829-4270
Web: www.bignet.org/regional/region5/default.htm

OHIO LEGISLATIVE BLACK CAUCUS
271 E. State St.
Columbus, OH 43215
Barbara Sykes, President
Tel: (614) 341-6912 Fax: (614) 221-0721
Email: staff@olbc1967.org
Web: www.olbc1967.org

OPERATION STEP UP, INC.
2081 Seymour Ave.
Cincinnati, OH 45237
Steven Reece, President
Tel: (513) 731-6308 Fax: (513) 731-6307
Email: reeceevents@aol.com
Web: www.sreece.com

PROFESSIONAL

ADVANCE
Student Activities and Leadership Develpment, University of Cincinnati
P.O. Box 210136
150 Student Life Pavilion North

Cincinnati, OH 45221-0136
Jamie Dinwiddle, President
Fax: (513) 556-6077
Email: jdinwiddle@fuse.net
Web: www.soa.uc.edu

AMERICAN ASSOCIATION OF BLACKS IN ENERGY
Cincinnati Chapter
c/o Cinergy Corp., 426 Gest St. #304
Cincinnati, OH 45203
Charles L. Sessions, Jr., President
Tel: (513) 287-5748
Email: csession@cinergy.com
Web: www.aabe-cin.com

ASSOCIATION OF BLACK PSYCHOLOGISTS
Central Ohio Chapter
33 S. James Rd. #233
Columbus, OH 43219
Dr. Dennis Alexander, Vice President
Tel: (614) 292-5766
Email: alexander.16@osu.edu
Web: www.abpsi.org

Cincinnati Chapter
130 Wellington Pl.
Cincinnati, OH 45219
Dr. Kenneth Washington, Chairperson
Web: www.abpsi.org

Cleveland Chapter
20310 Chagrin Blvd.
Shaker Heights, OH 44122
Dr. Willie Williams, Chapter President
Tel: (216) 491-9406 Fax: (216) 491-8025
Email: wmsIII@aol.com
Web: www.abpsi.org

BLACK DATA PROCESSING ASSOCIATES
Cincinnati Chapter
P.O. Box 429215
Cincinnati, OH 45242-9215
Frank Hill, Chapter President
Tel: (513) 956-0636 Fax: (513) 777-0323
Email: info@bdpa-cincy.org
Web: www.bdpa-cincy.org

Cleveland Chapter
4415 Euclid Ave. #201F
Cleveland, OH 44103
Willard J. Brown, Chapter President
Tel: (216) 577-0600
Email: president@bdpa-cleveland.org
Web: www.bdpa-cleveland.org

Dayton Chapter
P.O. Box 33346
Dayton, OH 45433-0346
Clifford Hall, President
Email: president@bdpadayton.org
Web: www.bdpadayton.org

CONFERENCE OF MINORITY TRANSPORTATION OFFICIALS
Cleveland Northeast Ohio Chapter
Greater Cleveland RTA, 1240 W. 6th St.
Cleveland, OH 44113
Richard Newell, President
Tel: (216) 566-5055 Fax: (216) 566-5017
Email: rnewell@gcrta.org
Web: www.comto.org

Columbus Chapter
Central Ohio Transit Authority, 1600 McKinley Ave.
Columbus, OH 43222-1093
Carol Perkins, President
Tel: (614) 275-5800 Fax: (614) 275-5894
Email: perkinscl@cota.com
Web: www.comto.org

Dayton Chapter
Miami Valley Regional Transit Authority, 600 Longworth
Dayton, OH 45401
John W. Brown, Chief Transportation Officer
Tel: (937) 425-8590 Fax: (937) 443-3124
Email: jbrown4241@aol.com
Web: www.comto.org

NATIONAL ASSOCIATION OF BLACK ACCOUNTANTS,
Cleveland Chapter
P.O. 201686
Shaker Heights, OH 44120
Lennon Taylor
Tel: (216) 267-7100 Fax: (216) 475-1300
Email: ltaylor@oatey.com
Web: www.nabainc.org

University of Akron Chapter
259 S. Broadway
Akron, OH 44325
Dr. Emeka Ofobike, Advisor
Tel: (330) 972-7586 Fax: (330) 972-8597
Email: ofobike@uakron.edu

Web: www.uakron.edu/studdev/orgs.html

NATIONAL ASSOCIATION OF BLACK JOURNALISTS
Columbus Chapter
P.O. Box 1924
Columbus, OH 43216
Kirk Richards, Chapter President
Tel: (614) 559-1751
Email: krichards@dispatch.com
Web: www.cabjcolumbus.org

Region VI
P.O. Box 93134
Cleveland, OH 44103
Sandy Scott, Chapter President
Tel: (216) 344-3300
Email: sscott@wkyc.com
Web: www.nabj.org

NATIONAL BLACK MBA ASSOCIATION, INC.
Cincinnati Chapter-Mideast
P.O. Box 14656
Cincinnati, OH 45250
Vanessa Enoch, President
Tel: (513) 787-4451
Email: nbmbaa_cinn@yahoo.com
Web: www.nbmbaa-cincinnati.org

Cleveland Chapter
P.O. Box 22839
Beachwood, OH 44122
Alton A. Tinker, President
Tel: (440) 439-2548
Email: clevelandblackmbas@yahoo.com
Web: www.clevelandblackmbas.org

Columbus Chapter-Mideast
P.O. Box 163575
Columbus, OH 43216-3575
Oyauma Garrison, President
Tel: (614) 470-1683
Email: nbmbaa_columbus@yahoo.com
Web: www.columbusbma.org

Dayton Chapter-Mideast
P.O. Box 3709
Dayton, OH 45401-3709
Dwight Johnson, President
Tel: (937) 285-0113
Web: www.nbmbaa.org

Piedmont-Triad
P.O. Box 22839
Beachwood, OH 44122
Alton Tinker, President
Tel: (216) 556-3633
Email: clevelandblackmbas@yahoo.com
Web: www.clevelandblackmbas.org

NATIONAL MEDICAL ASSOCIATION
Buckeye State Medical Association
270 S. Grant Ave.
Columbus, OH 43215
George Barnett
Tel: (614) 221-3141 Fax: (614) 221-4870
Email: gmedman1@aol.com
Web: www.nmanet.org

NATIONAL SOCIETY OF BLACK ENGINEERS
Region 4: Case Western Reserve University Chapter
10900 Euclid Ave.
Cleveland, OH 44104-7103
Chris Burrell, President
Tel: (216) 368-2679
Email: cmb22@po.cwru.edu
Web: www.cwru.edu/orgs/nsbe/info.html

Region 4: Central State University-Manufacturing Engineering
P.O. Box 1004
1400 Brush Row Rd.
Wilberforce, OH 45384-1004
Irvin Gonzales, President
Tel: (937) 376-6348 Fax: (937) 376-6679
Web: www.centralstate.edu/academics/maneng.html

Region 4: University of Akron
302 E. Buchtel Mall
Akron, OH 44325
Malik Elbuluk, Advisor
Tel: (330) 972-6531
Email: melbuluk@uakron.edu
Web: www.uakron.edu/nsbe/

University of Cincinnati
P.O. Box 210018
Cincinnati, OH 45221-0018
Christopher Jelks, Chapter President
Tel: (513) 556-5435
Email: jelksc@email.uc.edu
Web: www.nsbe.uc.edu

NATIONAL SOCIETY OF REAL ESTATE APPRAISERS, INC.
1265 E. 105th St.
Cleveland, OH 44108

Lytle Davis, President
Tel: (216) 561-2900 Fax: (216) 721-3336

NATIONAL TECHNICAL ASSOCIATION, INC.
P.O. Box 91934
Cleveland, OH 44114
Mark Sorrells, President
Tel: (216) 298-4425 Fax: (216) 289-3015
Email: cleveland@ntaonline.org
Web: www.ntaonline.org

SOCIETY OF URBAN PROFESSIONALS
5951 Sunset Dr.
Bedford, OH 44146
Tel: (440) 439-2548
Email: altinker123@yahoo.com
Web: www.souplunch.org

RELIGIOUS

UNITED CHURCH OF CHRIST, RACIAL JUSTICE MINISTRY
700 Prospect Ave.
Cleveland, OH 44115
Ferne Clements, Aministrative Assistant
Tel: (216) 736-3721 Fax: (216) 736-3703
Email: clementf@ucc.org
Web: www.ucc.org

INTEREST, ALCOHOL/DRUG CENTER

AFRICENTRIC PERSONAL DEVELOPMENT SHOP, INC.
1409 E. Livingston Ave.
Columbus, OH 43205
Jerry Saunders, President/CEO
Tel: (614) 253-4448 Fax: (614) 253-5005
Email: apds@apdsinc.org
Web: www.apdsinc.org

LORAIN URBAN MINORITY ALCOHOLISM DRUG ABUSE OUTREACH
2314 Kelly Pl.
Lorain, OH 44052
Ruth Williams-Clark, Executive Director
Tel: (440) 246-4616 Fax: (440) 246-1997
Email: lor_umadaop@yahoo.com
Web: www.umadaops.com

URBAN MINORITY ALCOHOLISM AND DRUG ABUSE OUTREACH PROGRAM
625 Salem Ave.
Dayton, OH 45406
Deborah E. Styles, Executive Manager
Tel: (937) 276-2176 Fax: (937) 276-2048
Email: umadaop@aol.com
Web: www.umadaops.com

2447 Nebraska Ave.
Toledo, OH 43607
John Edwards, Executive Director
Tel: (419) 255-4444 Fax: (419) 531-1596
Email: u4444@amplex.net
Web: www.umadaops.com

4015 Cherry St. #1
Cincinnati, OH 45223
Sedara Burson, Executive Director
Tel: (513) 541-7099 Fax: (513) 541-0989
Email: cinumadaop@aol.com
Web: www.umadaops.com

665 W. Market St. #2D
Akron, OH 44303
Janice Bourda Mercier, CEO
Tel: (330) 379-3467 Fax: (330) 379-3465
Email: info@akronumadaop.org
Web: www.umadaops.com

1215 E. 79th St.
Cleveland, OH 44103
Jessica B. Horne, Executive Director
Tel: (216) 361-2040 Fax: (216) 361-1856
Web: www.umadaops.com

4087 Youngstown Rd. SE
Warren, OH 44484
Beverly-Jean Pollard, Executive Director
Tel: (330) 393-3044 Fax: (330) 393-3048
Email: umadaop@onecom.com
Web: www.umadaops.com

YOUNGSTOWN URBAN MINORITY ALCOHOLISM AND DRUG ABUSE OUTREACH PROGRAM, INC.
496 Glenwood Ave. #120
Youngstown, OH 44502
Darryl Alexander, Executive Director
Tel: (330) 743-2772 Fax: (330) 743-2238
Email: yumadaop@aol.com
Web: www.yumadaop.org

SPEC. INT., EDUCATION

CLEVELAND AFRO-AMERICAN LIBRARY ASSOCIATION
14101 Euclid Ave.
East Cleveland, OH 44112
Lainey Westbrooks, President
Tel: (216) 541-4128 Fax: (216) 541-1790
Email: lainey@ecpl.lib.oh.us
Web: www.caala.us

DUKE E. ELLIS HUMAN DEVELOPMENT INSTITUTE
School of Professional Psychology, Wright State University
9 N. Edwin C. Moses Blvd.
Dayton, OH 45407
Emmett Orr, Executive Director
Tel: (937) 775-4300 Fax: (937) 775-4323
Email: emmett.orr@wright.edu
Web: www.wright.edu/sopp/ellis

NATIONAL ASSOCIATION FOR MULTICULTURAL EDUCATION
Ohio Chapter
P.O. Box 5190
Kent State University, 306 White Hall
Kent, OH 44242
Roberto Chavez, Student Development Coordinator
Tel: (330) 672-0739 Fax: (330) 672-3549
Email: rchavez@kent.edu
Web: www.nameorg.org

THE SANKOFA EDUCATIONAL ENRICHMENT PROGRAM
2240 Raeburn Dr.
Cincinnati, OH 45223
Kimya Moyo, Founder/Director
Tel: (513) 541-3364
Email: moyokim@cps-k12.org

SPEC. INT., EMPLOYMENT

MINORITY EXECUTIVE SEARCH
2490 Lee Blvd. #301
Cleveland, OH 44118
Eral Burks, President/CEO
Tel: (216) 932-2022 Fax: (216) 932-7988
Email: eral@minorityexecsearch.com
Web: www.minorityexecsearch.com

SPEC. INT., FAMILY PLANNING

DAYTON AREA MINORITY ADOPTIVE PARENTS, INC.
191 Coddington Ave.
Xenia, OH 45395-5439
Raymond Moore, President
Fax: (937) 372-8894
Email: rmoore@dayton.net
Web: www.damap.org

SPEC. INT., HEALTH SERVICES

JUNETEENTH OF OHIO, ALKEBULAND INC.
Alkebulan Health & Wellness Center
1206 N. High St.
Columbus, OH 43201
Mustafaa Shabazz, CEO
Tel: (614) 299-4488 Fax: (614) 299-4483
Email: smustafaa@aol.com
Web: www.juneteenthohio.net

SPEC. INT., SOCIAL INTEREST

100 BLACK MEN OF CENTRAL OHIO, INC.
P.O. Box 091235
Columbus, OH 43209
Jerry Saunders, President
Tel: (614) 341-7004 Fax: (614) 253-8781
Email: info@100bmco.org
Web: www.100bmco.org

100 BLACK MEN OF GREATER CLEVELAND, INC.
3530 Warrensville Center Rd. #209
Cleveland, OH 44122
Michael L. Nelson, Sr., Chapter President
Tel: (216) 491-3072 Fax: (216) 472-0226
Email: info@100blackmencleveland.org
Web: www.100blackmencleveland.org

BLACK UNITED FUND OF CENTRAL OHIO, INC.
1561 Leonard Ave.
Columbus, OH 43219
Hazel Williams, President
Tel: (614) 252-0888 Fax: (614) 252-4520
Web: www.nbuf.org

NATIONAL URBAN LEAGUE, INC.
Akron Urban League
250 E. Market St.
Akron, OH 44308
Bernett L. Williams, President/CEO
Tel: (330) 434-3101 Fax: (330) 434-2716

Email: aul250@aol.com
Web: www.akronul.org

Canton Urban League
1400 Sherrick Rd.
Canton, OH 44707
Janet M. Gordon, Acting President/CEO
Tel: (330) 456-3479 Fax: (330) 456-3307
Email: jgordon@cantonul.org
Web: www.cantonul.org

Columbus Urban League
788 Mount Vernon Ave.
Columbus, OH 43203-1408
Samuel Gresham, Jr., President/CEO
Tel: (614) 257-6300 Fax: (614) 257-6327
Email: sgresham@cul.org
Web: www.cul.org

Dayton Urban League
907 W. 5th St.
Dayton, OH 45402
Willie F. Walker, President
Tel: (937) 220-6650 Fax: (937) 220-6666
Email: williewalker@earthlink.net
Web: www.daytonurbanleague.org

Greater Toledo Urban League
608 Madison Ave. #1525
Toledo, OH 43604
Johnny McDuffy Mickler, Sr., President/CEO
Tel: (419) 243-3343 Fax: (419) 243-5445
Email: gtul557@aol.com

Lorain County Urban League
401 Broad St. #205
Elyria, OH 44035
Fred Wright, President/CEO
Tel: (440) 323-3364 Fax: (440) 323-5299
Email: kgroner@lcul.org
Web: www.lcul.org

Massillon Urban League
35 Erie St. North
Massillon, OH 44646
Rev. Beverly Lewis, Interim President
Tel: (330) 833-2804 Fax: (330) 833-0126
Web: www.nul.org

Urban League of Greater Cincinnati
3458 Reading Rd.
Cincinnati, OH 45229-3128
Donna Jones Stanley, President/CEO
Tel: (513) 281-9955 Fax: (513) 281-0455
Email: djstanley@gcul.org
Web: www.gcul.org

Urban League of Greater Cleveland
2930 Prospect Ave.
Cleveland, OH 44115
Myron Robinson, President/CEO
Tel: (216) 622-0999 Fax: (216) 622-0997
Email: info@ulcleveland.org
Web: www.ulcleveland.org

Warren-Trumbull Urban League
290 W. Market St.
Warren, OH 44481
Thomas Conley, President/CEO
Tel: (330) 394-4316 Fax: (330) 394-3167
Email: lwarrentrumbull@neo.rr.com
Web: www.nul.org

Youngstown Area Urban League
1350 5th Ave. #112
Youngstown, OH 44504
William Ronald Miller, Esq., President/CEO
Tel: (330) 744-4111 Fax: (330) 744-1140
Email: line1588@aol.com
Web: www.nul.org

SPEC. INT., WOMEN

ASSOCIATION FOR THE ADVANCEMENT OF AFRICAN-AMERICAN WOMEN
2503 Student Union
Toledo, OH 43606-3390
Tel: (419) 530-4728 Fax: (419) 530-4638
Web: www.utoledo.edu/~blkorg/4aw/4aw.html

BLACK CAREER WOMEN
P.O. Box 19332
Cincinnati, OH 45219-0332
Linda Bates Parker, President
Tel: (513) 531-1932 Fax: (513) 531-2166
Email: linda.parker@uc.edu
Web: www.bcw.org

SPEC. INT., YOUTH

CHILDREN'S DEFENSE FUND
Cincinnati Office
629 Oak St. #400
Cincinnati, OH 45206
Eileen Cooper Reed, Director
Tel: (513) 751-2332 Fax: (513) 751-2003
Email: cdfinfo@childrensdefense.org
Web: www.cdfcinti.org

Columbus Office
52 E. Lynn St. #400
Columbus, OH 43215-3507
Ronald Browder, Director
Tel: (614) 221-2244 Fax: (614) 221-2247
Email: cdfohio@cdfohio.org
Web: www.cdfohio.org

JACK & JILL OF AMERICA, INC.
The Associates Group
13415 Buckthorne Cir.
Highland Heights, OH 44143
James Murphy Spigner, National Associate Chair
Tel: (972) 644-6349 Fax: (972) 644-4945
Email: mspigner@airmail.net
Web: www.jack-and-jill.org

STUDENT ORGANIZATION

ALPHA KAPPA ALPHA SORORITY, INC.
Alpha Lambda Chapter
6233 W. Bancroft
Toledo, OH 43615
Jeanna E. Odoms, Chapter President
Web: www.aka1908.com

Alpha Omega Chapter
P.O. Box 93717
Cleveland, OH 44101
Tillie Colter, Chapter President
Web: www.aka1908.com

Alpha Sigma Omega Chapter
P.O. Box 09866
Columbus, OH 43209
Lenita Bunch, Chapter President
Web: www.aka1908.com

Beta Eta Omega Chapter
P.O. Box 31411
Dayton, OH 45424
Jone L. West, Chapter President
Web: www.aka1908.com

Delta Delta Chapter
1 Univ. Plz.
Younstown, OH 44555
Darlene P. Taylor, Chapter President
Web: www.aka1908.com

Delta Phi Chapter
P.O. Box 2410
Columbus, OH 45701
Larae Booker, Chapter President
Web: www.aka1908.com

Delta Pi Chapter
229 Spicer St.
Akron, OH 44304
Web: www.aka1908.com

Epsilon Chi Chapter
P.O. Box 3016
Dayton, OH 45401
Ashley L. Scott, Chapter President
Web: www.aka1908.com

Epsilon Mu Omega Chapter
P.O. Box 1352
Youngstown, OH 44501
Alnita Bryant-Russell, Chapter President
Web: www.aka1908.com

Iota Iota Chapter
424 Saddlemire Bldg. BGSU
Bowling Green, OH 43403
Paris Tyler, Chapter President
Web: www.aka1908.com

Iota Phi Omega Chapter
1046 Alpine Dr.
Sandusky, OH 44870
Betty Irby, Chapter President
Web: www.aka1908.com

Lambda Mu Chapter
112 Richard Hall
Oxford, OH 45056
Jennifer Ryan Johnson, Chapter President
Web: www.aka1908.com

Lambda Phi Omega Chapter
25286 Concord Dr.
Beachwood, OH 44122
Reba Denmark, Chapter President
Web: www.aka1908.com

Omega Chapter
1897 Penrose Ave.
East Cleveland, OH 44112
Nicole D. Radford, Chapter President
Web: www.aka1908.com

Omicron Chapter
5123 Grafton
Cincinnati, OH 45237
Diana Jones, Chapter President
Web: www.aka1908.com

Pi Gamma Chapter
2285 Meadow Spring Cir.
Columbus, OH 43235
Antoinette Necole Greene, Chapter President
Web: www.aka1908.com

Pi Omicron Chapter
4401 Payn Down Ave.
Euclid, OH 44103
Sherrell M. Jackson, Chapter President
Web: www.aka1908.com

Rho Omega Chapter
P.O. Box 461
Wilberforce, OH 45324
Ela Powell, Chapter President
Tel: (937) 879-4287
Web: www.aka1908.com

Rho Psi Chapter
587 Beaufort Ct.
Cincinnati, OH 45240
Lawanna Baker, Chapter President
Web: www.aka1908.com

Sigma Mu Omega Chapter
P.O. Box 216
Lima, OH 45802
Brenda Ellis, Chapter President
Web: www.aka1908.com

Sigma Omega Chapter
P.O. Box 17194
Cincinnati, OH 45217
Jeanette McGee, Chapter President
Web: www.aka1908.com

Tau Lambda Omega Chapter
P.O. Box 26397
Trotwood, OH 45426
Lynnette M. Heard, Chapter President
Tel: (513) 870-0312 Fax: (513) 870-0507
Email: president@trotwoodaka.org
Web: www.trotwoodaka.org

Theta Chapter
P.O. Box 3074
Columbus, OH 43210
Armada M. Stevens, Chapter President
Web: www.aka1908.com

Zeta Alpha Omega Chapter
44 Melody Ln.
Toledo, OH 43615
Denise Black-Poon, Chapter President
Web: www.aka1908.com

Zeta Chapter
P.O. Box 127
Wilberforce, OH 45384
Arniesa M. Wilson, Chapter President
Web: www.aka1908.com

Zeta Theta Omega Chapter
P.O. Box 4
Akron, OH 44309
Joyce Frances Rowland, Chapter President
Web: www.aka1908.com

ALPHA PHI ALPHA FRATERNITY, INC.
Alpha Alpha Chapter, University of Cincinnati
P.O. Box 9096
Cincinnati, OH 45221
Web: www.alphaphialpha.net

Alpha Rho Lambda Chapter
P.O. Box 360464
Columbus, OH 43236
Web: www.alphaphialpha.net

Alpha Tau Chapter, University of Akron
657 Sumner St. #2B
Akron, OH 44311
Web: www.alphaphialpha.net

Alpha Xi Lambda Chapter
525 E. Woodruff #311
Toledo, OH 43624
Silas Tarver, President
Email: silas_tarver@usa.net
Web: http://members.tripod.com/alpha_xi_lambda/

Chi Lambda Chapter
P.O. Box 351
Wilberforce, OH 45384
Web: www.alphaphialpha.net

Delta Alpha Lambda Chapter
P.O. Box 99551
Cleveland, OH 44199
Web: www.alphaphialpha.net

Delta Gamma Lambda Chapter
P.O. Box 2951
Cincinnati, OH 45201
Web: www.alphaphialpha.net

Delta Upsilon Chapter, Miami University
P.O. Box 731
Oxford, OH 45056

Web: www.alphaphialpha.net

Delta Xi Chapter, Central State University
P.O. Box 441
Wilberforce, OH 45384
Web: www.alphaphialpha.net

Epsilon Alpha Chapter, University of Toledo
P.O. Box 3292
Toledo, OH 43607
Web: www.alphaphialpha.net

Epsilon Delta Chapter, Kent State University
Student Activities Box
Kent, OH 44240
Web: www.alphaphialpha.net

Epsilon Theta Chapter, Bowling Green State University
603 E. Reed St.
Bowling Green, OH 43402
Web: www.alphaphialpha.net

Eta Tau Lambda Chapter
P.O. Box 582
Akron, OH 44309
Web: www.alphaphialpha.net

Gamma Theta Chapter, University of Dayton
331 Kiefaber St.
Dayton, OH 45409
Web: www.alphaphialpha.net

Iota Phi Chapter, Mount Union College
P.O. Box 126
Alliance, OH 44601
Web: www.alphaphialpha.net

Kappa Chapter, Ohio State University
Ohio Union, 1739 High St.
Columbus, OH 43210
Keith Foster, President
Email: foster.346@osu.edu
Web: http://apa.org.ohio-state.edu

Omicron Epsilon Chapter, Youngstown State University
Student Government Office
Youngstown, OH 44503
Web: www.alphaphialpha.net

Omicron Rho Chapter, Otterbein College
P.O. Box 1651
Delaware, OH 43015
Web: www.alphaphialpha.net

Phi Chapter, Ohio University
P.O. Box 2311
Athens, OH 45701
Web: www.alphaphialpha.net

Pi Chapter, Cleveland State University
2631 New Hampshire
Cleveland, OH 44106
Web: www.alphaphialpha.net

Rho Upsilon Chapter, Denison University
P.O. Box 2426
Granville, OH 43023
Web: www.alphaphialpha.net

Sigma Gamma Chapter, Xavier University
3800 Victory Pkwy.
Cincinnati, OH 45207
Web: www.alphaphialpha.net

Theta Lambda Chapter
P.O. Box 468
Paul Lawrence Dunbar Station
Dayton, OH 45417
Web: www.alphaphialpha.net

Xi Chapter
P.O. Box 21
Wilberforce, OH 45384
Web: www.geocities.com/alphaland

Zeta Delta Lambda Chapter
P.O. Box 1952
Springfield, OH 45502
Web: www.alphaphialpha.net

BLACK GRADUATE AND PROFESSIONAL STUDENT CAUCUS
Ohio State University
153 W. 12th Ave.
Columbus, OH 43210
Esther Jones, Primary Leader
Tel: (614) 292-8763
Email: jones.1669@osu.edu
Web: www.osu.edu/students/bgpsc/

BLACK GRADUATE STUDENT ORGANIZATION
Cleveland State University
2121 Euclid Ave.
Cleveland, OH 44115
Eric King, Executive Officer
Tel: (216) 687-3656
Email: eking1914@hotmail.com

BLACK LAW STUDENTS ASSOCIATION
Toledo University
University of Toledo, College of Law, 2801 W. Bankcroft
Toledo, OH 43606-3390
Caleen Sullivan, President
Tel: (419) 530-4125
Email: sullivan_caleen@hotmail.com
Web: www.utoledo.edu/~blkorg/blaw/blacklawstudents.htm

University of Akron School of Law
302 University Ave.
Akron, OH 44325-2901
Malina Coleman, Advisor
Tel: (330) 972-6797
Email: mcoleman@uakron.edu

BLACK STUDENT UNION
Toledo University
University of Toledo, Student Union 2801 Westban Cross
Toledo, OH 43606
Verónica Callaway, President
Tel: (419) 530-4291 Fax: (419) 539-2908
Web: www.utoledo.edu/~blkorg/bsu/bsu.html

BLACK UNITED STUDENTS
Kent University
Kent University, Office of Campus Life #6
Kent, OH 44242
Damareo Cooper, President
Tel: (330) 672-7985
Web: http://dept.kent.edu/stuorg/bus

KAPPA ALPHA PSI FRATERNITY, INC.
Toledo University
M/S 105, 2801 Westbancroft
Toledo, OH 43606
Lance Johnson, President
Tel: (419) 530-7221 Fax: (419) 530-2908
Email: betaxinupes@yahoo.com

SIGMA LAMBDA BETA FRANTERNITY, INC.
Toledo University
1042 Kipling Dr.
Toledo, OH 43612
Ed Willis, Advisor
Tel: (419) 478-1907
Web: www.utoledo.edu/~blkorg/greeks/sigmalb/sigmalamdabeta.html

OKLAHOMA

ARTISTIC

OKLAHOMA JAZZ HALL OF FAME
322 N. Greenwood Ave.
Tulsa, OK 74120
Charles "Chuck" Cissel, CEO
Tel: (800) 348-9336 Fax: (918) 596-1005
Email: info@okjazz.org
Web: www.okjazz.org

BUSINESS

NATIONAL MINORITY SUPPLIER DEVELOPMENT COUNCIL, INC.
Oklahoma Minority Supplier Development Council
The Pavilion Bldg., 6701 N. Broadway #216
Oklahoma City, OK 73116
Debra Ponder-Nelson, Executive Director
Tel: (405) 767-9900 Fax: (405) 767-9901
Email: oklamsdc@aol.com
Web: www.omsdc.org

POLITICAL ACTION

AMERICAN CIVIL LIBERTIES UNION
Oklahoma Chapter
3000 Paseo Dr.
Oklahoma City, OK 73103
Joann Bell, Executive Director
Tel: (405) 524-8511 Fax: (405) 524-2296
Email: acluok@mindspring.com
Web: www.acluok.org

BLACKS IN GOVERNMENT
Region VI-Green County Chapter
1301 W. Woodrow St.
Tulsa, OK 74127
Wendy Williams, Chapter President
Tel: (918) 764-7286
Web: www.bignet.org/regional/region6/index.htm

PROFESSIONAL

AMERICAN ASSOCIATION OF BLACKS IN ENERGY
Oklahoma Chapter

P.O. Box 401
c/o Oklahoma Natural Gas Company
Oklahoma City, OK 73101-0401
Wayne Williams, President
Tel: (405) 556-6409 Fax: (405) 566-6422
Email: wcwilliams@ong.com
Web: www.aabe-ok.org

University of Tulsa/Student Chapter
600 S. College, Holmes Student Ctr. #51
Tulsa, OK 74104
Yolanda Taylor, President
Tel: (918) 631-2327 Fax: (918) 631-3459
Web: www.aabe-tul-stu.org

NATIONAL ASSOCIATION OF BLACK JOURNALISTS
Region VII- Tulsa Chapter
P.O. Box 2904
Tulsa, OK 74101-2904
Russell LaCour, Chapter President
Tel: (800) 999-6397 Fax: (918) 581-8353
Email: russell.lacour@tulsaworld.com
Web: www.nabj.org

NATIONAL FORUM FOR BLACK PUBLIC ADMINISTRATORS
Sooner Chapter
City of Oklahoma City, 621 N. Pennsylvania Ave.
Oklahoma City, OK 73107
Gayle Owens, President
Tel: (405) 297-2609 Fax: (405) 264-2429
Email: gayle.owens@okc.gov
Web: www.nfbpa.org

SOCIETY OF BLACK ENGINEERS, ARCHITECTS AND TECHS
Oklahoma State University
101 Engineering North, Oklahoma University Campus
Stillwater, OK 74078
Ira Smith, President
Tel: (405) 744-5276 Fax: (405) 744-6066

SPEC. INT., SOCIAL INTEREST

NATIONAL URBAN LEAGUE, INC.
Metropolitan Tulsa Urban League
240 E. Apache St.
Tulsa, OK 74106
James (Gerry) Goodwin, President
Tel: (918) 584-0001 Fax: (918) 584-0569
Email: jgoodwin@mtul.org
Web: www.nul.org

SPEC. INT., WOMEN

SISTERFRIENDS ORGANIZATION
Oklahoma City
P.O Box 75423
Oklahoma City, OK 73147
Gayle Thomas, Chapter President
Tel: (405) 848-5448 Fax: (405) 848-3518
Email: okcsisterfriends@yahoo.com
Web: www.sisterfriends.org

SPEC. INT., YOUTH

JACK & JILL OF AMERICA, INC.
Central Region
4529 NE 38th St.
Oklahoma City, OK 73121
Tara Ravnell Bradley, Regional Director
Tel: (405) 427-1218 Fax: (405) 427-1205
Email: tbradley@ong.com
Web: www.jack-and-jill.org

STUDENT ORGANIZATION

AFRICAN AMERICAN STUDENT ASSOCIATION
Oklahoma State University
320 Student Union, Oklahoma State University
Stillwater, OK 74078
Bryan Calvin, President
Tel: (405) 744-5481 Fax: (405) 744-8380
Email: lbelind@okst.edu
Web: http://you.okstate.edu/core/services/orgs/findorg.asp

ALPHA KAPPA ALPHA SORORITY, INC.
Alpha Chi Omega Chapter
P.O. Box 27033
Tulsa, OK 74127
Felicia Jones-Moncrief, Chapter President
Web: www.midwesternakas.com

Alpha Epsilon Omega Chapter
114 S. David Ln. #614
Muskogee, OK 74401
Remonica Hughes, Chapter President
Web: www.midwesternakas.com

Alpha Upsilon Omega Chapter
1101 NE 14th St.
Oklahoma City, OK 73117
Thelma Wallace, Chapter President

Web: www.midwesternakas.com

Alpha Zeta Chapter, Langston University
210 W. Sanford Hall
Langston, OK 73050
Latisha Hishaw, Chapter President
Web: www.midwesternakas.com

Beta Beta Chapter, University of Central Oklahoma
2545 NW 34th St.
Oklahoma City, OK 73112
Amelia Perkins, Chapter President
Web: www.aka1908.com

Beta Omicron Omega Chapter
P.O. Box 461
Okmulgee, OK 74447
Gladys Overstreet, Chapter President
Web: www.midwesternakas.com

Beta Sigma Omega Chapter
P.O. Box 796
Oklahoma City, OK 73101
Vickie Miles-LaGrange, Chapter President
Web: www.midwesternakas.com

Epsilon Rho Omega Chapter
P.O. Box 267
Boley, OK 74829
Dora Wilson, Chapter President
Web: www.midwesternakas.com

Kappa Psi Chapter, University of Oklahoma
P.O. Box 2242
Norman, OK 73070
Maria T. Massey, Chapter President
Tel: (773) 684-1282 Fax: (773) 288-8251
Web: www.aka1908.com

Sigma Eta Omega Chapter
904 Cambridge Dr.
Altus, OK 73521
Fannie E. Johnson, Chapter President
Web: www.midwesternakas.com

Sigma Sigma Omega Chapter
P.O. Box 13354
Oklahoma City, OK 73113
Armisha Walker-Harrison, Chapter President
Web: www.midwesternakas.com

Theta Beta Chapter, Oklahoma State University
211 B Friends
Stillwater, OK 74078
Tiffany Scott, Chapter President
Web: www.midwesternakas.com

Theta Upsilon Omega Chapter
P.O. Box 2843
Lawton, OK 73502
Arlie Hampton, Chapter President
Web: www.midwesternakas.com

Theta Xi Chapter
600 S. College Ave. HSC51
Tulsa, OK 74104
Mesha Griffin, Chapter President
Web: www.aka1908.com

Upsilon Theta Omega Chapter
P.O. Box 2392
Stillwater, OK 74075
Claire Echols, Chapter President
Web: www.midwesternakas.com

Xi Iota Chapter, Cameron University
625 SW Arbuckle St.
Lawton, OK 73501
Melissa Williams, Chapter President
Web: www.midwesternakas.com

ALPHA PHI ALPHA FRATERNITY, INC.
Beta Chi Lambda Chapter
704 Anthony
Muskogee, OK 74403
Web: www.alphaphialpha.net

Beta Eta Lambda Chapter
P.O. Box 11105
Oklahoma City, OK 73136
Web: www.alphaphialpha.net

Beta Kappa Chapter, Langston University
P.O. Box 58
Langston, OK 73050
Web: www.alphaphialpha.net

Epsilon Epsilon Chapter, Oklahoma State University
050 Student Union
Stillwater, OK 74077
Web: www.alphaphialpha.net

Eta Xi Lambda Chapter
P.O. Box 6752
Lawton, OK 73506
Web: www.alphaphialpha.net

Omicron Nu Chapter, University of Tulsa
Student Affairs, 600 S. College Ave.
Tulsa, OK 74104
Web: www.alphaphialpha.net

Pi Kappa Lambda Chapter
P.O. Box 48667
Tulsa, OK 74148
Web: www.alphaphialpha.net

Zeta Gamma Lambda Chapter
P.O. Box 180
Langston, OK 73050
Web: www.alphaphialpha.net

Zeta Sigma Chapter, University of Central Oklahoma
P.O. Box 341208
Edmond, OK 73034
Web: www.alphaphialpha.net

Zeta Zeta Chapter, University of Oklahoma
P.O. Box 2863
Norman, OK 73072
Web: www.alphaphialpha.net

BLACK STUDENT ASSOCIATION
University of Oklahoma
900 Asp Ave. #391
Norman, OK 73019-4058
Adrian D. Templeton, President
Tel: (405) 325 -0167 Fax: (405) 325-7493
Web: www.ou.edu/student/bsa/index.htm

DELTA SIGMA THETA SORORITY, INC.
Central Region
6106 Mason's Dr.
Oklahoma City, OK 73142
Gayona L. Washington, Regional Director
Tel: (202) 986-2400 Fax: (202) 986-2513
Email: dstcentralregion@aol.com
Web: www.dstcentralregion.org

NATIONAL BLACK LAW STUDENTS ASSOCIATION
Oklahoma City University School of Law
2501 N. Blackwelder St.
Oklahoma City, OK 73106
Tel: (405) 521-5354 Fax: (405) 521-5802
Web: www.nblsa.org

OREGON

CULTURAL

HOMOWO AFRICAN ARTS AND CULTURES
4839 NE Martin Luther King Blvd. #209
Portland, OR 97211
Susan Addy, President
Tel: (503) 288-3025
Email: info@homowo.org
Web: www.homowo.org

ENTERTAINMENT

NATIONAL AFRICAN AMERICAN RV'ERS ASSOCIATION
Ebony Rose City Chapter
222 NE 197th Ave.
Portland, OR 97230
James Thomas, President
Tel: (503) 661-1730
Email: mywayrv@aol.com
Web: www.naarva.com

LAW ENFORCEMENT

NATIONAL ORGANIZATION OF BLACK LAW ENFORCEMENT EXECUTIVES
Northwest Chapter
Multnomah County Sheriff's Department, 1120 SW 3rd Ave.
Portland, OR 97204
Dorothy Elmore, Lieutenant
Tel: (503) 988-3397
Email: vloop1uponx@msn.com
Web: www.noblenatl.org

POLITICAL ACTION

ASSOCIATION OF COMMUNITY ORGANIZATIONS FOR REFORM NOW
Portland Office
5112 SE Powell Blvd.
Portland, OR 97206
Tel: (503) 788-4362 Fax: (503) 788-4723
Email: oracorn@acorn.org
Web: www.acorn.org

BLACKS IN GOVERNMENT
Region X-Greater Portland Chapter
12200 SE McLoughlin Blvd. #6101
Milwaukie, OR 97222
James C. Mack, Chapter President
Tel: (503) 731-4012
Email: greater.portland@bignet.org

Web: www.bignet.org

Region X-Southwest Washington Chapter
P.O. Box 6643
Portland, OR 97228-66439
Diane Storey-Taylor, Chapter President
Tel: (503) 220-8262
Web: www.bignet.org

Region X-Williamette River Chapter
P.O. Box 40120
Portland, OR 97240
Odell Sanders, III, Chapter President
Tel: (541) 465-6563
Web: www.bignet.org

PROFESSIONAL

AMERICAN ASSOCIATION OF BLACKS IN ENERGY
Seattle Chapter
P.O. Box 3621
Portland, OR 97208-3621
Margaret Lewis, President
Tel: (503) 230-7552 Fax: (206) 220-6803
Email: mllewis@bpa.gov
Web: www.aabe-sea-por.org

CONFERENCE OF MINORITY TRANSPORTATION OFFICIALS
SW Washington/Oregon Chapter
Tri-Met, 710 NE Holladay St.
Portland, OR 97232-2168
Rockchild Scott, Director
Tel: (503) 962-2460 Fax: (503) 962-2488
Email: scottr@trimet.org
Web: www.comto.org

NATIONAL BLACK MBA ASSOCIATION, INC.
Seattle/Portland Chapter
P.O. Box 4143
Portland, OR 97208
Leon Augustine, President
Tel: (503) 327-4420
Email: mail@nbmba-portland.org
Web: www.nbmba-portland.org

NATIONAL FORUM FOR BLACK PUBLIC ADMINISTRATORS
Oregon Chapter
Portland Housing & Community Development, 421 SW 6th St. #1100
Portland, OR 97204
Deena Pierott, President
Tel: (503) 823-2377 Fax: (503) 823-2387
Email: dpierott@ci.portland.or.us
Web: www.nfbpa.org

RELIGIOUS

FULL GOSPEL PENTECOSTAL CHURCH INTERNATIONAL
Emmanuel Temple Church
1033 N. Sumner Ave.
Portland, OR 97217
Pastor C.T. Wells, Senior Pastor
Tel: (503) 287-2223 Fax: (503) 287-7990
Web: www.etchurch.com

SPEC. INT., EDUCATION

NATIONAL ASSOCIATION FOR MULTICULTURAL EDUCATION
Oregon Chapter
Education Department Linfield College, 900 SE Baker St.
McMinnville, OR 97128 ·
Jioanna Carjuzaa
Tel: (503) 883-2238
Email: jcarjuz@linfield.edu
Web: www.nameorg.org

SPEC. INT., SOCIAL INTEREST

BLACK UNITED FUND OF OREGON, INC.
2828 NE Alberta St.
Portland, OR 97211
Amina Anderson, President
Tel: (503) 282-7973 Fax: (503) 282-3482
Email: bufor@teleport.com
Web: www.bufor.org

NATIONAL URBAN LEAGUE, INC.
Urban League of Portland
10 N. Russell St.
Portland, OR 97227
Vanessa Gaston, President/CEO
Tel: (503) 280-2600 Fax: (503) 281-2612
Email: vgaston@ulpdx.org
Web: www.ulpdx.org

SPEC. INT., YOUTH

EMMANUEL COMMUNITY SERVICES
Emmanuel Temple Church
1033 N. Sumner Ave., 2nd Fl.
Portland, OR 97217
Robert Richardson, Executive Director
Tel: (503) 287-2223 Fax: (503) 287-7990

STUDENT ORGANIZATION

ALPHA KAPPA ALPHA SORORITY, INC.
Pi Sigma Chapter
P.O. Box 751
Portland, OR 97207
Katrina Sartin, Chapter President
Web: www.aka1908.com

Sigma Delta Chapter
3888 Century Dr.
Eugene, OR 97402
Nicole Johnson, Chapter President
Web: www.aka1908.com

Upsilon Gamma Omega Chapter
P.O. Box 70765
Eugene, OR 97401
Kellie Coleman-Johnson, Chapter President
Web: www.aka1908.com

Zeta Sigma Omega Chapter
P.O. Box 5631
Portland, OR 97228
Joy Fowler, Chapter President
Web: www.aka1908.com

PENNSYLVANIA

ARTISTIC

ART SANCTUARY
Church of Advocate
1801 W. Diamond St.
Philadelphia, PA 19121
Mirenda Watkins, Office Manager
Tel: (215) 232-4485 Fax: (215) 232-4088
Email: info@artsanctuary.org
Web: www.artsanctuary.org

FREEDOM THEATER
1346 N. Broad St.
Philadelphia, PA 19121
Dr. Walter Dallas, Producing Artistic Director
Tel: (215) 765-2793 Fax: (215) 765-4191
Web: www.freedomtheatre.org

INTERNATIONAL ASSOCIATION OF AFRICAN-AMERICAN MUSIC
Corporate Office
P.O. Box 382
Gladwyne, PA 19035
Dyana Williams, President
Tel: (610) 664-8292 Fax: (610) 664-5940
Email: iaaam1@aol.com
Web: www.iaaam.com

KUNTU REPERTORY THEATER
University of Pittsburgh, Department of Africana Studies
4140 Wesley W. Posvar Hall, 230 S. Bouquet St.
Pittsburgh, PA 15260
Vernell A. Lillie, Director
Tel: (412) 624-7298 Fax: (412) 648-7214
Email: info@kuntu.org
Web: www.kuntu.org

MANCHESTER CRAFTSMEN'S GUILD
1815 Metropolitan St.
Pittsburgh, PA 15233
William E. Strickland, Jr., President/CEO
Tel: (412) 322-1773 Fax: (412) 321-2120
Email: wstricklandjr@mcg-btc.org
Web: www.manchesterguild.org

BUSINESS

AFRICARIBE MICROENTERPRISE NETWORK
8320 Lynnwood Rd.
Philadelphia, PA 19150
Agatha C. Johnson, Founder/CEO
Tel: (267) 257-8581 Fax: (215) 843-1992
Email: africaribe@aol.com

NATIONAL MINORITY SUPPLIER DEVELOPMENT COUNCIL, INC.
Minority Supplier Development Council of PA-NJ-DE
42 S. 15th St. #1060
Philadelphia, PA 19102
Darlene Jenkins, President
Tel: (215) 569-1005 Fax: (215) 569-2667
Email: msdc.panjde@verizon.net
Web: http://msdc-panjde.org

Pittsburgh Regional Minority Purchasing Council
425 6th Ave. #2690

Pittsburgh, PA 15219
Alexander Nichols, Executive Director
Tel: (412) 391-4423 Fax: (412) 391-3132
Email: info@prmpc.org
Web: www.prmpc.org

NATIONAL UNITED MERCHANTS BEVERAGE ASSOCIATION, INC.
609 Ann St.
Homestead, PA 15120
Melvin Cornelious, National President
Tel: (412) 678-9583 Fax: (412) 678-9584

CULTURAL

AFRO-AMERICAN HISTORICAL AND GENEALOGICAL SOCIETY, INC.
Pittsburgh
P. O. Box 2272
Bala Cynwyd, PA 19004
Ernestine Kinsey Marshall, President
Tel: (215) 927-1202
Email: aahgsfamilyquest@aol.com
Web: http://pittsburgh.aahgs.org

BLACK CULTURAL CENTER
Swarthmore College
500 College Ave.
Swarthmore, PA 19081
Timothy E. Sams, Director
Tel: (610) 328-8455 Fax: (610) 690-5711
Email: tsams1@swarthmnore.edu
Web: www.swarthmore.edu/admin/bcc

PHILADELPHIA BLACK FAMILY REUNION CULTURAL CENTER
2233 N. Broad St.
Philadelphia, PA 19132
Barbara Daniel-Cox, President
Tel: (215) 684-1008 Fax: (215) 684-2448
Email: bdclove@aol.com

UMOJA AFRICAN ARTS COMPANY
601 Wood St. #9
Pittsburgh, PA 15222
LaVette Malloy Smith, Managing Director
Tel: (412) 471-1121 Fax: (412) 232-3262
Email: umoja@umojacompany.com
Web: www.umojacompany.com

ENTERTAINMENT

NATIONAL AFRICAN AMERICAN RV'ERS ASSOCIATION
Roxie Ramblers Chapter
P.O. Box 166
Latrobe, PA 15650
Clyde Eddins, President
Tel: (724) 537-4050
Email: eddinlat@aol.com
Web: www.naarva.com

GOVERNMENT

GOVERNOR'S ADVISORY COMMISSION ON AFRICAN AMERICAN AFFAIRS
Finance Bldg. #506
Harrisburg, PA 17120
Mannwell Glenn, Executive Director
Tel: (717) 772-5085 Fax: (717) 787-4015
Email: gacaaa@state.pa.us
Web: www.africanam.state.pa.us/africanamaff/site/default.asp

LAW ENFORCEMENT

NATIONAL ORGANIZATION OF BLACK LAW ENFORCEMENT EXECUTIVES
Central Pennsylvania Chapter
P.O. Box 10745
Harrisburg, PA 17105-0745
Marcenia M. Robinson, Lieutenant
Tel: (717) 787-7220 Fax: (717) 705-2185
Email: marcrobins83@hotmail.com
Web: www.noblecentralpa.homestead.com

Philadelphia Chapter
P.O. Box 34040 TSA
Philadelphia, PA 19101-4040
Darrell G. O'Connor, Principal
Tel: (202) 385-1073 Fax: (202) 744-8750
Email: doc2443@aol.com
Web: http://gpc.noblechapter.org

Pittsburgh Chapter
P.O. Box 5296
Pittsburgh, PA 15206
Maurita Bryant, Commander
Pittsburgh Bureau of Police
Pittsburgh, PA 15206
Maurita Bryant, Commander
Tel: (412) 665-3605 Fax: (412) 665-3669
Email: maurita.bryant@verizon.net
Web: www.noblepittsburgh.org

MULTI-PURPOSE

FRONTIERS INTERNATIONAL FOUNDATION, INC.
6301 Crittenden St.
Philadelphia, PA 19138
Johny Moutry, Chairman
Tel: (215) 549-4550 Fax: (215) 549-4589

NATIONAL ASSOCIATION FOR THE ADVANCEMENT OF COLORED PEOPLE
Allegheny East Branch
P.O. Box 8
Monroeville, PA 15146
Loraine P. White, President
Tel: (412) 856-7127
Web: www.naacp.org

Allegheny-Kiski Valley Branch
P.O. Box 215
Leechburg, PA 15656
John C. Lovelace, President
Tel: (724) 842-5061
Web: http://paweb.bizland.com/NAACP2.htm

Beaver County Branch
116 Boyana Dr.
Industry, PA 15052
Willie Sallis, President
Tel: (724) 378-6690 Fax: (724) 378-6870
Email: bcnaacp@access995.com
Web: www.naacp.org

Clairton Branch
P.O. Box 33
Clairton, PA 15025
Gregory E. Stewart, President
Tel: (814) 233-3400 Fax: (814) 233-7909
Web: http://paweb.bizland.com/naacp2.htm

East Boroughs Branch
P.O. Box 0741
Braddock, PA 15104
Gregory Pierce, President
Tel: (412) 271-3579
Web: http://paweb.bizland.com/naacp2.htm

Fayette County Chapter
137 N. Beeson St. #113
Union Town, PA 15401
Clinton Anderson, President
Tel: (724) 430-0771 Fax: (724) 430-0771
Web: http://paweb.bizland.com/naacp2.htm

Greensburg/Jeannette Branch
1011 Old Salem Rd. #207, Human Services Bldg.
Greensburg, PA 15601
Ruth Tolbert, President
Tel: (724) 838-9146 Fax: (724) 838-0894
Web: http://paweb.bizland.com/naacp.htm

Indiana Branch
P.O. Box 7
Indiana, PA 15701
Edwina Vold, President
Tel: (724) 463-0631
Web: www.naacp.org

McKeesport Branch
P.O. Box 394
McKeesport, PA 15132
V. Schnel Simmons, President
Tel: (412) 673-7993
Web: www.naacp.org

Mon Valley Branch
Eastgate 11 #50
Monessen, PA 15062
George Burroughs, Jr., President
Tel: (724) 684-8545 Fax: (724) 684-3196
Email: naacp@midmon.com
Web: http://paweb.bizland.com/naacp2.htm

Pittsburgh Branch
2203 Wylie Ave.
Pittsburgh, PA 15219
Tim Stevens, President
Tel: (412) 471-1024 Fax: (412) 471-1313
Email: naacp.pittsburg@verizon.net
Web: www.naacp.org

Steel Valley Branch
11219 E. 15th Ave.
Homestead, PA 15120
Marlaine Robinson, President
Tel: (412) 462-9475
Web: www.naacp.org

Wilkinsburg Branch
P.O. Box 86036
Wilkinsburg, PA 15221
Kara Whitfield, President
Tel: (412) 880-0317
Web: www.naacp.org

ONYX ALLIANCE, INC.
625 Liberty Ave. #2800
Pittsburgh, PA 15222
Marimba Milliones, President
Tel: (412) 255-3751 Fax: (412) 255-3701
Email: info@onyxalliance.com
Web: www.onyxalliance.com

OPPORTUNITIES INDUSTRIALIZATION CENTERS OF AMERICA, INC.
1415 N. Broad St.
Philadelphia, PA 19122-3323
Thomasenia G. Cotton, President/COO
Tel: (215) 236-4500 Fax: (215) 236-7480
Email: info@oicofamerica.org
Web: www.oicofamerica.org

POLITICAL ACTION

AMERICAN CIVIL LIBERTIES UNION
Central Pennsylvania Chapter
500 E. Maryland Ave., Foxdale Village #112
State College, PA 16801
Tel: (814) 355-7175
Web: www.aclupa.org

Greater Philadelphia Chapter
P.O. Box 1161
Philadelphia, PA 19105-1161
Tel: (215) 923-4357 X118 Fax: (215) 592-1343
Web: www.aclupa.org

Greater Pittsburgh Chapter
313 Atwood St.
Pittsburgh, PA 15213-4090
Susan McIntosh, Intake Co-ordinator
Tel: (412) 681-7736 Fax: (412) 681-8707
Web: www.aclupa.org

Keystone Chapter
P.O. Box 53
Altoona, PA 16603
Tel: (814) 696-8688
Web: www.aclupa.org

Lancaster County Chapter
P.O. Box 693
Lancaster, PA 17608
John Lefever
Tel: (717) 391-6502
Web: www.aclupa.org

Philadelphia Office
P.O. Box 1161
Philadelphia, PA 19105-1161
Susan Sheppard, Interim Executive Director
Tel: (215) 592-1513
Email: info@aclupa.org
Web: www.aclupa.org

ASSOCIATION OF COMMUNITY ORGANIZATIONS FOR REFORM NOW
Philadelphia Office
846 N. Broad St., 2nd Fl.
Philadelphia, PA 19130
Piper Stanton, Fund Raiser
Tel: (215) 765-0042 Fax: (215) 765-1073
Email: paacorn@acorn.org
Web: www.acorn.org

Pittsburgh Office
5907 Penn Ave. #300
Pittsburgh, PA 15206
Tel: (412) 441-6551 Fax: (412) 441-6317
Email: paacornpiho@acorn.org
Web: www.acorn.org

BLACK RADICAL CONGRESS
Philadelphia Chapter
P.O. Box 23743
Philadelphia, PA 19118
Debbie Bell
Tel: (215) 242-9066 Fax: (215) 242-8220
Email: damisbell@aol.com
Web: www.blackradicalcongress.com

BLACKS IN GOVERNMENT
Region III-ALMECH Chapter
P.O. Box 7083
Mechanisburg, PA 17055
Beatrice U. Gallatin, Chapter President
Tel: (717) 605-7125
Email: region3.president@bignet.org
Web: www.bignet.org

Region III-Greater Pittsburgh Area Chapter
P.O. Box 10895
Pittsburgh, PA 15236
Otis Mills, Jr., Chapter President
Tel: (412) 386-5890
Email: region3.president@bignet.org
Web: www.bignet.org

Region III-Independence Chapter
P.O. Box 45252
Pittsburgh, PA 19124-8252
Tel: (215) 737-2740
Email: independence@bignet.org
Web: www.bignet.org

NATIONAL ACTION NETWORK
Pennsylvania Chapter
230 N. 57th St. #G4
Philadelphia, PA 19139
Sister D. Baxter, Chair
Tel: (215) 474-2826
Web: www.nationalactionnetwork.org

PHILADELPHIA MARTIN LUTHER KING, JR. ASSOCIATION FOR NONVIOLENCE, INC.
1809 Spring Garden St.
Philadelphia, PA 19130-3916
Dr. Dolores Tucker, President
Tel: (215) 751-9300 Fax: (215) 751-9141
Email: info@philamlk.org
Web: www.philamlk.org

PROFESSIONAL

BLACK DATA PROCESSING ASSOCIATES
Greater Philadelphia Chapter
P.O. Box 42611
Philadelphia, PA 19101-2611
Donald X. Campbell, Chapter President
Tel: (215) 844-3235
Email: president@bdpaphilly.org
Web: www.bdpaphilly.org

CONFERENCE OF MINORITY TRANSPORTATION OFFICIALS
Philadelphia Chapter-Southeastern Pennsylvania Transportation Authority
P.O. Box 53728
Philadelphia, PA 19105-3728
Warren S. Montague, Chapter President
Tel: (215) 580-3423 Fax: (215) 580-3475
Email: wmontague@septa.org
Web: www.comto.org

Pittsburgh Chapter
Port Authority Allegheny County, 2235 Beaver Ave.
Pittsburgh, PA 15233
Edward Greene, DBE Contract Compliance Coordinator
Tel: (412) 237-7326 Fax: (412) 237-7289
Email: egreene@portauthority.org
Web: www.comto.org

CONSORTIUM OF INFORMATION AND TELECOMMUNICATIONS EXECUTIVES
CITE PA/DE
201 Stanwix St., 6th Fl.
Pittsburgh, PA 15222
Bonnie Adams, Chapter President
Tel: (412) 633-5729 Fax: (412) 633-5729
Email: bonnie.k.adams@verizon.com
Web: www.cite-pade.org

NATIONAL ALLIANCE OF MARKET DEVELOPERS
Philadelphia Chapter
1427 Catherine St. #406
Philadelphia, PA 19146
Norm Bond, Chapter President
Tel: (215) 724-8099 Fax: (215) 387-2367
Email: norm@normbond.com
Web: www.namdntl.org/philadelphia.htm

NATIONAL ASSOCIATION OF BLACK JOURNALISTS
Philadelphia Chapter
P.O. Box 8232
Philadelphia, PA 19101
Keith Herbert, President
Tel: (610) 272-7184
Email: pabj@pabj.org
Web: www.pabj.org

NATIONAL ASSOCIATION OF MINORITY CONTRACTORS
Coady Sous Bldg., 7249 Frankstown Ave.
Pittsburgh, PA 15208
Linda M. Couchs, Director
Tel: (412) 247-4822 Fax: (412) 247-4471
Web: www.namcline.org

NATIONAL BLACK MBA ASSOCIATION, INC.
Philadelphia Chapter
P.O. Box 1384
Philadelphia, PA 19105
Venetta S. Larry, President
Tel: (215) 472-2622
Email: info@nbmbaa-philly.org
Web: www.nbmbaa-philly.org

Piedmont-Triad
P.O. Box 3502
Pittsburgh, PA 15230
James Beach, President
Tel: (412) 402-2622
Email: natlblackmbapgh@mailcity.com
Web: www.nbmbaa.org

RELIGIOUS

CHRISTIAN LIFE SKILLS, INC.
P.O. Box 56958
Pittsburgh, PA 15208
Barbara Rogers, Executive Director
Tel: (412) 889-4065
Email: clsmp@aol.com
Web: www.christianlifeskills.net

SOCIETY OF THE HOLY CHILD JESUS
P.O. Box 364
West Point, PA 19486
Kathy Gibbons, Director of International Marketing
Tel: (215) 699-6661 Fax: (215) 699-9766
Email: kgibbons@shcj.org
Web: www.shcj.org/shcj.nsf.pages/hciac

ST. FRANCIS OF ASSISI CHURCH
1439 Market St.
Harrisburg, PA 17103
Father Daniel Mitzel
Tel: (717) 232-1003 Fax: (717) 232-4536

RESEARCH

AFRICAN AMERICAN UNITED FUND
2227 N. Broad St.
Philadelphia, PA 19132
Linda Richardson, President
Tel: (215) 236-2100 Fax: (215) 236-9077
Email: alrbuffer@aol.com

BRADY ENTERPRISE ASSOCIATION, INC.
P.O. Box 14455
Pittsburgh, PA 15239-9998
Mary Lee Brady, Ph.D., President
Tel: (412) 793-0489 Fax: (412) 793-2547
Email: suzyq8@adelphia.net
Web: www.bradyenterprises.org

CENTER FOR AFRICAN AMERICAN URBAN STUDIES AND THE ECONOMY
The Department of History
Baker Hall 244, Carnegie Mellon University
Pittsburgh, PA 15213
Joe W. Trotter, Director
Tel: (412) 268-8928 Fax: (412) 268-1019
Email: na28@andrew.cmu.edu
Web: www.hss.cmu.edu/cause

SPEC. INT., CHILD CARE

FATHERS RAISING CHILDREN PROJECT
Hill House Association
1835 Centre Ave.
Pittsburgh, PA 15219
Tel: (412) 392-4410 Fax: (412) 291-1771
Email: webmaster@frcpgh.org
Web: www.frcpgh.org

SPEC. INT., EDUCATION

AMERICAN FOUNDATION FOR NEGRO AFFAIRS
117 S. 17th St. #1200
Philadelphia, PA 19103
Samuel Evans, Founder
Tel: (215) 854-1470 Fax: (215) 854-1487

NATIONAL ASSOCIATION FOR MULTICULTURAL EDUCATION
Pennsylvania Chapter
Pennsylvania State University, College of Education
University Park, PA 16801
Andrew Jackson, Sr., Academic Advisor
Tel: (814) 865-1499 Fax: (814) 865-0489
Email: axj119@psu.edu
Web: www.ed.psu.edu/multicultural-ed

NEGRO EDUCATIONAL EMERGENCY DRIVE
425 6th Ave. #2790
Pittsburgh, PA 15219
Sylvester Pace, M. Ed., Executive Director
Tel: (412) 566-2760
Web: www.needld.org

SPEC. INT., FAMILY PLANNING

CENTER FOR FAMILY EXCELLENCE, INC.
409 Dinwiddie St.
Pittsburgh, PA 15219-3367
Jerome Taylor, Executive Director
Tel: (412) 232-0322 Fax: (412) 232-0331
Web: www.cffei.org

THE FAMILY REUNION INSTITUTE
Temple University
School of Social Administration, 1301 Cecil B. Moore Ave.
Philadelphia, PA 19122

Dr. Ione D. Vargus, Founder
Tel: (215) 204-6244 Fax: (215) 204-9606
Email: ivargus@temple.edu
Web: www.temple.edu/fri/familyreunion

SPEC. INT., HOUSING

HILL HOUSE ASSOCIATION
1835 Centre Ave.
Philadelphia, PA 15219
Evan Fraizer, Executive Director
Tel: (412) 392-4400 Fax: (412) 932-4462
Email: contactus@hillhouse.org
Web: www.hillhouse.org

SPEC. INT., SOCIAL INTEREST

100 BLACK MEN OF GREATER PHILADELPHIA, INC.
730 E. Rittenhouse St.
Philadelphia, PA 19144-1248
Ken Lassister, President
Tel: (215) 848-5105 Fax: (800) 892-1898
Email: ceo@thelassitergroup.com
Web: www.100blackmen.org

BLACK UNITED FUND OF PENNSYLVANIA, INC.
2227 N. Broad St.
Philadelphia, PA 19132
Tel: (215) 236-2100 Fax: (215) 236-7539
Email: bufpa@aol.com
Web: www.hometown.aol.com/bufpa

CONCERNED BLACK MEN, INC.
Philadelphia Chapter
7200 N. 21st St.
Philadelphia, PA 19138
Charles Patton, Executive Director
Tel: (215) 276-2260 Fax: (215) 276-4734
Email: info@cbmphilly.org
Web: www.cbmphilly.org

MULTICULTURAL HEALTH EDUCATION DEVELOPMENT
2928 Peach St.
Erie, PA 16508
Agnes Piscaro, Director
Tel: (814) 453-6229 Fax: (814) 456-7362

NATIONAL ASSOCIATION OF AFRICAN AMERICANS FOR POSITIVE IMAGERY
1231 N. Broad St.
Philadelphia, PA 19122
Rev. Jesse W. Brown, Jr., Executive Director
Tel: (215) 235-6488 Fax: (215) 235-6491
Email: naaapi@msn.com
Web: www.naaapi.org

NATIONAL URBAN LEAGUE, INC.
Urban League of Lancaster County
502 S. Duke St.
Lancaster, PA 17602
Phyllis L. Campbell, President/CEO
Tel: (717) 394-1966 Fax: (717) 295-5044
Email: ullcplc@aol.com
Web: www.nul.org

Urban League of Philadelphia
Ten Penn Ctr. #250, 1801 Market St.
Philadelphia, PA 19103
Patricia A. Coulter, President/CEO
Tel: (215) 561-6070 Fax: (215) 561-4524
Email: coulterulp@aol.com
Web: www.urbanleaguephila.org

Urban League of Pittsburgh
1 Smithfield St., 3rd Fl.
Pittsburgh, PA 15222-2222
Esther L. Bush, President/CEO
Tel: (412) 227-4802 Fax: (412) 227-4870
Web: www.ulpgh.org

Urban League of Shenango Valley
601 Indiana Ave.
Farrell, PA 16121
James A. Long, President
Tel: (724) 981-5310 Fax: (724) 981-1544
Email: jlong2@earthlink.net
Web: www.nul.org

PROGRAM TO AID CITIZEN ENTERPRISE
1 Gateway Ctr. #500, 420 Fort Duquesen Blvd.
Pittsburgh, PA 15222
Lucille E. Dabney, Executive Director
Tel: (412) 562-0290 Fax: (412) 562-0292
Web: www.pacepgh.com

REAL MEN COOK FOR CHARITY
Philadelphia Chapter
7901 Fayette St., 1st Fl.
Philadelphia, PA 19150
Bruce B. Rush, Event Manager

Tel: (215) 924-6263
Email: rmcphila@aol.com
Web: www.realmencook.com

UNIVERSAL NEGRO IMPROVEMENT ASSOCIATION AND AFRICAN COMMUNITIES LEAGUE
Thomas W. Harvey Memorial Division #121, 1609-11
Cecil B. Moore Ave.
Philadelphia, PA 19121
Hon. Marcus Garvey, Founder
Tel: (215) 236-0782
Email: info@unia-acl.org
Web: www.unia-acl.org

SPEC. INT., SPORTS

WEST PENN MINORITY JR. GOLF ASSOCIATION, INC.
322 Mall Blvd. #165
Monroeville, PA 15146
Robert "Rock" Robinson, President
Tel: (412) 292-8175 Fax: (412) 371-7577
Email: wpmjga@aol.com
Web: www.wpmjga.org

SPEC. INT., VOLUNTARY SERVICE

BIG BROTHERS BIG SISTERS OF GREATER PITTSBURGH
Allegheny County Office
5989 Penn Cir. South
Pittsburgh, PA 15206-3828
Walter Jenkins, Executive Director
Tel: (412) 363-6100 Fax: (412) 363-6801
Email: wjenkins@bbbspittsburgh.org
Web: www.bbbspittsburgh.org

Greene County
P.O. Box 185
Jefferson, PA 15344
Walter F. Jenkins, Executive Director
Tel: (724) 883-2118 Fax: (412) 363-6801
Email: wjenkins@bbbspgh.org
Web: www.bbbspgh.org

SPEC. INT., WOMEN

AMERICAN WOMEN'S HERITAGE SOCIETY, INC.
West Fairmount Park, 2000 Belmont Mansion Dr.
Philadelphia, PA 19131
Audrey R. Johnson-Thornton, President
Tel: (215) 878-8844
Email: bthorn1653@aol.com
Web: www.awhsinc.org

SISTERFRIENDS ORGANIZATION
Pottsville Area Metro Chapter
P.O.Box 1293
Pottsville, PA 17901
De'Edra Lewis-Johnson, President
Tel: (570) 365-9739
Email: dlewisjohn@aol.com
Web: www.sisterfriends.org

THE BLACK WOMEN HEALTH ALLIANCE
1231 N. Broad St., 2nd Fl.
Philadelphia, PA 19122
Tarren Gaddy, Executive Director
Tel: (215) 232-1115 Fax: (215) 232-2847
Email: sistersintouch@yahoo.com
Web: www.blackwomenshealthproject.org

SPEC. INT., YOUTH

CONTINENTAL SOCIETIES, INC.
4323 Haverford Ave.
Philadelphia, PA 19104-1355
E. Tonya Greenwood, National President
Tel: (215) 473-8635 Fax: (215) 473-8635
Web: www.continentalsocietiesinc.org

THE CARING PLACE
931 Hamilton St.
Allentown, PA 18101
Mary Ellen Griffin, Executive Director
Tel: (610) 433-5683 Fax: (610) 433-9165
Email: cplace200@aol.com

STUDENT ORGANIZATION

ALPHA KAPPA ALPHA SORORITY, INC.
Alpha Alpha Omega Chapter
P. O. Box 5044
Pittsburgh, PA 15206
Denyse G. Littles-Cullens, Chapter President
Web: www.aka1908.com

Alpha Sigma Chapter
P.O. Box 4790
Pittsburgh, PA 15206
Amanda J. Williams, Chapter President
Web: www.aka1908.com

Delta Gamma Chapter, Penn State University
204 Wild Cherry Ln.
Marietta, PA 17547
Melissa Oden, Graduate Advisor
Email: mssy@aol.com
Web: http://akanorthatlantic.org

Delta Mu Chapter, Temple University
628 E. Allens Ln.
Philadelphia, PA 19119
Mary A. Jones, Graduate Advisor
Email: mryjns@aol.com
Web: http://akanorthatlantic.org

Epsilon Sigma Omega Chapter
P.O. Box 1924
Harrisburg, PA 17105
Elsie L. Caldwell, Chapter President
Web: www.aka1908.com

Gamma Chi Omega Chapter
152 Ruble Run Rd.
Lake Lynn, PA 15451
Angela Marie Metheney, Chapter President
Web: www.aka1908.com

Gamma Epsilon Chapter
6821 Walnut Park Dr.
Upper Darby, PA 19082
Charlene Collins, Graduate Advisor
Email: ccollins1908@comcast.net
Web: http://akanorthatlantic.org

Iota Chapter
100 Oakville Dr. #2-B
Pittsburgh, PA 15213
Joy Jones, Chapter President
Web: www.aka1908.com

Iota Tau Omega Chapter
25 Grist Mill Ln.
West Grove, PA 19063
Tracy L. Wise, Chapter President
Web: www.aka1908.com

Kappa Beta Chapter
P.O. Box 285
California, PA 15419
Violet Michaux, Chapter President
Web: www.aka1908.com

Kappa Zeta Chapter
P.O. Box 442
Gemmell Complex
Clarion, PA 16214
Wanda F. Nesbitt, Chapter President
Web: www.aka1908.com

Mu Nu Omega Chapter
P.O. Box 10694
Erie, PA 16514
Charlise Moore, Chapter President
Web: www.aka1908.com

Mu Omicron Chapter
008 Old Maine
Slippery Rock, PA 16057
Web: www.aka1908.com

Omega Omega Chapter
P.O. Box 13056
Philadelphia, PA 19101
Delores M. Arrington, Chapter President
Web: www.aka1908.com

Phi Beta Omega Chapter
P.O. Box 1385
North Wales, PA 19454
Wanda Lewis-Campbell, Chapter President
Web: www.aka1908.com

Pi Epsilon Chapter, Rutgers University
922 E. McPherson St.
Philadelphia, PA 19150-3212
Shirley Turpin Parham, Graduate Advisor
Email: partyham@aol.com
Web: http://akanorthatlantic.org

Pi Pi Chapter
P.O. Box 10694
Erie, PA 16514
Leela M. Barney, Chapter President
Web: www.aka1908.com

Rho Theta Omega Chapter
P.O. Box 27147
Philadelphia, PA 19118
Evelyn R. Sample-Oates, Chapter President
Web: www.aka1908.com

Sigma Lambda Chapter
5643 Gainor Rd.
Philadelphia, PA 19131
Pamela Galloway, Graduate Advisor
Email: pamgllwy@msn.com
Web: http://akanorthatlantic.org

Tau Delta Omega Chapter
P.O. Box 323
Chester, PA 19016
Adrienne Gordy, Chapter President

Web: www.aka1908.com

Theta Iota Chapter
Sykes Student Union
West Chester, PA 19383
April Grant, Chapter President
Web: www.aka1908.com

BLACK LAW STUDENTS ASSOCIATION
Temple University, Beasley School of Law
1719 N. Broad St.
Philadelphia, PA 19122
Tel: (215) 204-7861 Fax: (215) 204-1185
Email: law@astro.temple.edu
Web: www2.law.temple.edu

KAPPA ALPHA PSI FRATERNITY, INC.
National Office
2322-24 N. Broad St.
Philadelphia, PA 19132-4590
Richard L. Snow, Executive Director
Tel: (215) 228-7184 Fax: (215) 228-7181
Email: executive_director@kappaalphapsi1911.com
Web: www.kappaalphapsi1911.com

NATIONAL BLACK LAW STUDENTS ASSOCIATION
Duquesne University School of Law
900 Locust St.
Pittsburgh, PA 15282
Michelle Joiner
Tel: (412) 396-6300 Fax: (412) 396-1073
Web: www.law.duq.edu/sba/sba.html

The Dickinson School of Law, The Pennsylvania State University
150 S. College St.
Carlisle, PA 17013
Angela D. Hall, President
Tel: (717) 240-5149
Email: dslblsa@psu.edu
Web: www.dsl.psu.edu/groups/blsa.cfm

PUERTO RICO

BUSINESS

NATIONAL MINORITY SUPPLIER DEVELOPMENT COUNCIL, INC.
Puerto Rico Supplier Development Council, Inc., **Regional Council**
P.O. Box 192410
San Juan, PR 00919-2410
Jacqueline Matos, Executive Director
Tel: (787) 759-9445 Fax: (787) 756-7670
Email: sdc@sdcpr.org
Web: www.sdcpr.org

RHODE ISLAND

ARTISTIC

RITES AND REASON THEATER
Brown University
P.O. Box 1148
Providence, RI 02912
Elmo Terry-Morgan, Artistic Director
Tel: (401) 863-3558 Fax: (401) 863-3559
Email: elmo_terry-morgan@brown.edu

BUSINESS

MULTICULTURAL FOODSERVICE & HOSPITALITY ALLIANCE
1144 Narragansett Blvd.
Cranston, RI 02905
Eddy Barea, President
Tel: (401) 461-6342 Fax: (401) 461-9004
Email: mfhainfo@mfha.net
Web: www.mfha.net

POLITICAL ACTION

AMERICAN CIVIL LIBERTIES UNION
Rhode Island Chapter
128 Dorrance St. #220
Providence, RI 02903
Steve Brown, Executive Director
Tel: (401) 831-7171 Fax: (401) 831-7175
Email: riaclu@aol.com
Web: www.riaclu.org

ASSOCIATION OF COMMUNITY ORGANIZATIONS FOR REFORM NOW
Rhode Island Chapter
807 Broad St. #220
Providence, RI 02907
Aimee Olin, Head Organizer
Tel: (401) 780-0500 Fax: (401) 780-0826
Email: riacorn@acorn.org
Web: www.acorn.org

BLACKS IN GOVERNMENT
Region 1
P.O. Box 5024
Newport, RI 02841
Elijah Drew, President
Tel: (401) 832-1337 Fax: (401) 832-1061
Email: region1.president@bignet.org
Web: www.bignet.org

Region I-NUWC DIV. Newport Chapter
P.O. Box 3282
Newport, RI 02840
Elijah Drew, Chapter President
Tel: (401) 832-1337
Email: info@bostonbig.org
Web: www.bostonbig.org

Region I-Rhode Island Chapter
130 Mayflower St.
East Providence, RI 02914
Dan R. Corria, Chapter President
Tel: (617) 565-5842 Fax: (617) 565-5842
Email: dcorria@cox.net
Web: www.bostonbig.org

SPEC. INT., EDUCATION

SUDAN STUDIES ASSOCIATION
Rhode Island College
Dept. of Anthropology
Providence, RI 02908
Dr. Richard Lobban, Executive Director
Tel: (401) 456-8784 Fax: (401) 461-0907
Email: rlobban@ric.edu
Web: www.sudanstudies.org

SPEC. INT., SOCIAL INTEREST

NATIONAL URBAN LEAGUE, INC.
Urban League of Rhode Island
246 Prairie Ave.
Providence, RI 02905
Dennis B. Langley, Executive Director
Tel: (401) 351-5000 Fax: (401) 545-1946
Email: mj@ulri.org

URBAN LEAGUE OF RHODE ISLAND, INC.
246 Prairie Ave.
Providence, RI 02905-2397
Dennis B. Langley
Tel: (401) 351-5000 Fax: (401) 454-1946
Web: www.ulri.org

STUDENT ORGANIZATION

ALPHA KAPPA ALPHA SORORITY, INC.
Iota Alpha Chapter, Brown University
P.O. Box 1157
Providence, RI 02912
Andrea O'Neal, Chapter President
Web: www.aka1908.com

Theta Psi Omega Chapter
P.O. Box 2382
Providence, RI 02906
Deborah Pierce Kanston, Chapter President
Web: www.aka1908.com

SOUTH CAROLINA

ENTERTAINMENT

NATIONAL AFRICAN AMERICAN RV'ERS ASSOCIATION
Columbia Travelers RV Club
1006 E. Sherwood
Sumter, SC 29153
John Reed, President
Tel: (803) 778-0907
Web: www.naarva.com

LAW ENFORCEMENT

NATIONAL ORGANIZATION OF BLACK LAW ENFORCEMENT EXECUTIVES
South Carolina Chapter
P.O. Box 30882
Charleston Police Department
Charleston, SC 29417
George A. Brisbon, President
Tel: (843) 720-2408 Fax: (843) 722-4085
Email: brisbong@ci.charleston.sc.us
Web: www.noblenatl.org

POLITICAL ACTION

AMERICAN CIVIL LIBERTIES UNION
Beaufort County Chapter
1519 Main St.
Hilton Head, SC 29926
John M. King, President

Tel: (843) 682-3191
Email: kingjf@hargray.com
Web: www.aclusc.org

Midlands Chapter
P.O. Box 7814
Columbia, SC 29202
Katherine E. Macedon, President
Tel: (803) 798-2278 Fax: (803) 254-7374
Email: kem1@usit.net
Web: www.aclusc.org

South Carolina Chapter
2712 Middleburg Dr. #104
Columbia, SC 29204
Denyse Williams, Executive Director
Fax: (803) 254-7374
Email: aclusc@aol.com
Web: www.aclusc.org

BLACKS IN GOVERNMENT
Region IV
410 Forest Cir.
New Ellenton, SC 29809
Alice D. Mercer, President
Tel: (803) 652-7996
Email: region4.president@bignet.org
Web: www.bignet.org

Region IV-East Central Savannah River Chapter
P.O. Box 1142
Jackson, SC 29831-1142
Morris James, Chapter President
Tel: (803) 725-5960
Email: morris.james@srs.gov
Web: www.bignet.org

Region IV-NIA Chapter
1449 Swamp Angel Ct.
Charleston, SC 29412
John McQueen, Chapter President
Email: bob.brown@dfas.mil
Web: www.bignet.org

NATIONAL ACTION NETWORK
South Carolina Chapter
125 Hampton St. #201
Rock Hill, SC 29730
John Barnett, Chair
Tel: (803) 327-7888 Fax: (803) 327-8067
Email: nansc@yahoo.com
Web: www.nationalactionnetwork.org

PROFESSIONAL

AMERICAN ASSOCIATION OF BLACKS IN ENERGY
South Carolina Chapter
c/o SCANA, 1426 Main St. MC 123
Columbia, SC 29201
Jimmy Duncan, President
Tel: (803) 217-9537 Fax: (803) 217-9568
Email: jduncan@scana.com
Web: www.aabe-sc.org

CONFERENCE OF MINORITY TRANSPORTATION OFFICIALS
South Carolina Chapter
P.O. Box 8144
Orangeburg, SC 29117
James L. Gordon, Construction Project Coordinator
Tel: (803) 536-8863 Fax: (803) 533-3955
Email: jlgordon@scsu.edu
Web: www.comto.us

NATIONAL ASSOCIATION OF BLACK JOURNALISTS
South Carolina Upstate-The Greenville News
305 S. Main St.
Greenville, SC 29602
E. Richard Walton, Chapter President
Tel: (864) 298-4317 Fax: (864) 298-4395
Email: rwalton@greenvillenews.com
Web: www.nabj.org

SPEC. INT., CHILD CARE

NATIONAL CENTER FOR MISSING & EXPLOITED CHILDREN
South Carolina Office
2008 Marion St. #1
Columbia, SC 29201-2151
Tel: (803) 254-2326 Fax: (803) 254-4299
Web: www.missingkids.com

SPEC. INT., SOCIAL INTEREST

100 BLACK MEN OF CHARLESTON, INC.
P.O. Box 42134
Charleston, SC 29423
Lee Moultrie, Chairman
Tel: (843) 767-1957 Fax: (843) 760-6584
Email: lhmassc@aol.com

Web: www.charleston.net/org/100blackmen

100 BLACK MEN OF PEE DEE, INC.
159 N. Court St.
Florence, SC 29501
Spencer R. Scott, President
Tel: (843) 629-0202

NATIONAL URBAN LEAGUE, INC.
Trident Urban League
656 King St.
Charleston, SC 29403
Luther W.C. Brook, President
Tel: (843) 965-4037 Fax: (843) 965-4039
Email: tul@bellsouth.net
Web: www.tuw.org

Urban League of the Upstate
15 Regency Hill Dr.
Greenville, SC 29607
William B. Whitney, President/CEO
Tel: (864) 244-3862 Fax: (864) 244-6134
Email: aclusc@urbanleagueoftheupstate.org
Web: www.urbanleagueoftheupstate.org

SPEC. INT., YOUTH

CHILDREN'S DEFENSE FUND
Bennettsville Office
117 Cheraw St.
Bennettsville, SC 29512
Robin Sally, Director
Tel: (843) 479-5310 Fax: (843) 479-0605
Email: rsally@childrensdefense.org
Web: www.childrensdefense.org

STUDENT ORGANIZATION

ALPHA KAPPA ALPHA SORORITY, INC.
Beta Sigma Chapter, South Carolina State University
P.O. Box 7481
300 College St. NE
Orangeburg, SC 29117
Kristina N. Stroud, Chapter President
Web: www.aka1908.com

Beta Zeta Omega Chapter
P.O. Box 241
Orangeburg, SC 29116
Rowena G. Loadholt, Chapter President
Web: www.aka1908.com

Epsilon Beta Omega Chapter
P.O. Box 1427
Spartanburg, SC 29304
English J. Gibbs, Chapter President
Web: www.aka1908.com

Epsilon Chi Omega Chapter
P.O. Box 2421
Florence, SC 29503
Marlene Williams, Chapter President
Web: www.aka1908.com

Epsilon Tau Omega Chapter
P.O. Box 17034
Greenville, SC 29606
Barbara Hawkins, Chapter President
Web: www.aka1908.com

Eta Alpha Omega Chapter
P.O. Box 11192
Rock Hill, SC 29731
Tanzella Gaither, Chapter President
Web: www.aka1908.com

Eta Nu Chapter, Voorhees College
P.O. Box 678
Denmark, SC 29042
Latonya Mills, Chapter President
Web: www.aka1908.com

Gamma Nu Chapter, Claflin College
400 College Ave.
Orangeburg, SC 29115
Waverly Gordon, Chapter President
Web: www.aka1908.com

Gamma Nu Omega Chapter
P.O. Box 3385
Columbia, SC 29203
Mazie Dell Lewis, Chapter President
Web: www.aka1908.com

Gamma Xi Omega Chapter
P.O. Box 20792
Charleston, SC 29413
Vanessa Turner-Maybank, Chapter President
Web: www.aka1908.com

Iota Omega Omega Chapter
P.O. Box 267
Camden, SC 29020
Mary L. Clinton, Chapter President
Tel: (803) 424-1667
Email: emelcee@charter.net

Web: www.aka1908.com

Iota Omicron Chapter, College of Charleston
66 George St.
Charleston, SC 29424
Kiana A. Sullivan, Chapter President
Web: www.aka1908.com

Iota Theta Omega Chapter
P.O. Box 478
Lancaster, SC 29720
Vera Witherspoon, Chapter President
Web: www.aka1908.com

Iota Upsilon Omega Chapter
P.O. Box 779
Greenwood, SC 29648
Rosella Quarles, Chapter President
Web: www.aka1908.com

Iota Xi Chapter, Francis Marion University
P.O. Box 4131
Florence, SC 29502
Shaquantia Harrison, Chapter President
Web: www.aka1908.com

Kappa Upsilon Omega Chapter
P.O. Box 1467
Aiken, SC 29802
Betty Ann Butler, Chapter President
Web: www.aka1908.com

Kappa Zeta Omega Chapter
P.O. Box 2831
Anderson, SC 29622
Jean Holloway, Chapter President
Web: www.aka1908.com

Lambda Lambda Chapter, Lander College
CPO 6186
Greenwood, SC 29649
Tanisha Marie Graves, Chapter President
Web: www.aka1908.com

Lambda Rho Omega Chapter
P.O. Box 1951
Gaffney, SC 29342
Ola Copeland, Chapter President
Web: www.aka1908.com

Lambda Theta Omega Chapter
P.O. Box 941
Kingstree, SC 29556
Wanda Strong, Chapter President
Web: www.aka1908.com

Mu Chapter
101 Kempshire Blvd.
Hopkins, SC 29061
Ventryce D. Hampton, Chapter President
Web: www.aka1908.com

Mu Iota Omega Chapter
P.O. Box 1642
Conway, SC 29526
Ballery Skipper, Chapter President
Web: www.aka1908.com

Mu Lambda Chapter, University of South Carolina-Aiken
471 University Pkwy.
Aiken, SC 29801
Datra Natasha Singleton, Chapter President
Web: www.aka1908.com

Mu Phi Omega Chapter
P.O. Box 169
Georgetown, SC 29442
Patricia G. Matthews, Chapter President
Web: www.aka1908.com

Mu Xi Chapter, Winthrop College
WPO 5121
Rock Hill, SC 29733
Atiya McPherson, Chapter President
Web: www.aka1908.com

Nu Alpha Omega Chapter
P.O. Box 1106
Moncks Corner, SC 29461
Nathlyn Jenkins, Chapter President
Web: www.aka1908.com

Nu Delta Omega Chapter
P.O. Box 1501
Beaufort, SC 29901
Constance Smith Gardner, Chapter President
Web: www.aka1908.com

Nu Tau Omega Chapter
P.O. Box 764
Denmark, SC 29042
Alzena Robinson, Chapter President
Web: www.aka1908.com

Nu Theta Omega Chapter
P.O. Box 1303
Clinton, SC 29325
Janet L. Sullivan Thompson, Chapter President
Web: www.aka1908.com

Omicron Omicron Omega Chapter
P.O. Box 338
Marion, SC 29571
Lauretha Tart Hodge, Chapter President
Web: www.aka1908.com

Omicron Rho Omega Chapter
P.O. Box 71431
North Charleston, SC 29405
Audrey Wilder, Chapter President
Web: www.aka1908.com

Omicron Zeta Omega Chapter
P.O. Box 1453
Cheraw, SC 29520
Camalah Ashe Bittle, Chapter President
Web: www.aka1908.com

Phi Omega Omega Chapter
1222 Ocean Rd.
Alcolu, SC 29001
Gwendolyn Elease Hudson, Chapter President
Web: www.aka1908.com

Pi Beta Omega Chapter
P.O. Box 1065
Newberry, SC 29108
Bennie M. Brown, Chapter President
Web: www.aka1908.com

Pi Zeta Omega Chapter
P.O. Box 2761
Greenville, SC 29602
Randolyn Harmon, Chapter President
Web: www.aka1908.com

Psi Chapter
c/o AKA, 1600 Harden St.
Columbia, SC 29204
Tiara V. Bryant, Chapter President
Web: www.aka1908.com

Rho Pi Chapter, Coastal Carolina University
P.O. Box 261954
Conway, SC 29528
Jessica Greene, Chapter President
Web: www.aka1908.com

Rho Tau Chapter, University of South Carolina
800 University Way
Spartanburg, SC 29303
Deniela M. Sherard, Chapter President
Web: www.aka1908.com

Rho Zeta Chapter, Furman University
P.O. Box 28533
3300 Poinsett Hwy.
Greenville, SC 29613
Natasha N. Murray, Chapter President
Web: www.aka1908.com

Sigma Upsilon Omega Chapter
P.O. Box 2516
Summerville, SC 29484
Ruth Nelson McFadden, Chapter President
Web: www.aka1908.com

Theta Gamma Chapter, University of South Carolina
1400 Greene St., RHUU 044
Columbia, SC 29208
Shequeita T. Orr, Chapter President
Web: www.aka1908.com

Upsilon Omega Omega Chapter
P.O. Box 2012
Irmo, SC 29063
Joann Moore Thompson, Chapter President
Web: www.aka1908.com

Upsilon Sigma Omega Chapter
P.O. Box 536
Bennetsville, SC 29512
Eva S. Johnson, Chapter President
Web: www.aka1908.com

Xi Omega Omega Chapter
P.O. Box 192
Walterboro, SC 29488
Vennie Mitchell, Chapter President
Web: www.aka1908.com

ALPHA PHI ALPHA FRATERNITY, INC.
Alpha Psi Lambda Chapter
P.O. Box 2107
Columbia, SC 29202
Web: www.alphaphialpha.net

Beta Delta Chapter, South Carolina State College
P.O. Box 7454
Orangeburg, SC 29117
Web: www.alphaphialpha.net

Beta Delta Chapter, South Carolina State University
300 College St. NE
Orangeburg, SC 29117
Web: www.alphaphialpha.net

Beta Kappa Lambda Chapter
P.O. Box 22096
Charleston, SC 29413
Web: www.alphaphialpha.net

Delta Alpha Chapter, Claflin College
P.O. Box 1682
Orangeburg, SC 29115
Web: www.alphaphialpha.net

Delta Kappa Lambda Chapter
P.O. Box 384
Florence, SC 29503
Web: www.alphaphialpha.net

Delta Zeta Lambda Chapter
P.O. Box 152
Orangeburg, SC 29116
Web: www.alphaphialpha.net

Eta Iota Chapter, Voorhees College
P.O. Box 448
Denmark, SC 29042
Web: www.alphaphialpha.net

Eta Omicron Lambda Chapter
P.O. Box 81
Lancaster, SC 29721
Web: www.alphaphialpha.net

Gamma Gamma Lambda Chapter
P.O. Box 5244
Greenville, SC 29606
Web: www.alphaphialpha.net

Gamma Pi Chapter, Benedict College
P.O. Box 851
Columbia, SC 29204
Web: www.alphaphialpha.net

Iota Eta Lambda Chapter
P.O. Box 452
Orangeburg, SC 29116
Web: www.alphaphialpha.net

Kappa Chi Chapter, Francis Marion College
P.O. Box 384
Florence, SC 29503
Web: www.alphaphialpha.net

Mu Epsilon Lambda Chapter
P.O. Box 64
Conway, SC 29526
Web: www.alphaphialpha.net

Mu Pi Chapter, Charleston Southern University
P.O. Box 299
Charleston, SC 29423
Web: www.alphaphialpha.net

Omicron Iota Lambda Chapter
P.O. Box 12522
Columbia, SC 29211
Web: www.alphaphialpha.net

Omicron Kappa Lambda Chapter
100 W. College St.
Sumter, SC 29150
Web: www.alphaphialpha.net

Omicron Tau Lambda Chapter
P.O. Box 2722
Aiken, SC 29803
Web: www.alphaphialpha.net

Pi Alpha Chapter, Clemson University
P.O. Box 7182
Clemson, SC 29632
Web: www.alphaphialpha.net

Pi Delta Lambda Chapter
P.O. Box 437
Georgetown, SC 29442
Web: www.alphaphialpha.net

Sigma Tau Chapter, University of South Carolina
P.O. Box 801
Aiken, SC 29802
Web: www.alphaphialpha.net

Theta Nu Chapter, University of South Carolina
P.O. Box 85128
Columbia, SC 29225
Web: www.alphaphialpha.net

Theta Phi Lambda Chapter
P.O. Box 1522
Bennettsville, SC 29512
Web: www.alphaphialpha.net

Xi Epsilon Chapter, Morris College
100 W. College St.
Sumter, SC 29150
Web: www.alphaphialpha.net

Xi Gamma Lambda Chapter
P.O. Box 2044
Beaufort, SC 29901
Web: www.alphaphialpha.net

Xi Phi Chapter, Winthrop University
P.O. Box 5018
Rock Hill, SC 29733
Web: www.alphaphialpha.net

Xi Phi Lambda Chapter
138 Elker Dr.
Summerville, SC 29483
Web: www.alphaphialpha.net

Xi Theta Lambda Chapter
132 Oxford Rd.
Spartanburg, SC 29301
Web: www.alphaphialpha.net

TENNESSEE

BUSINESS

NATIONAL MINORITY SUPPLIER DEVELOPMENT COUNCIL, INC.
Tennessee Minority Supplier Development Council, Knoxville Branch Office
1545 Western Ave. #210
Knoxville, TN 37921
Cheri Henderson, Executive Director
Tel: (865) 637-6966 Fax: (865) 524-3437
Email: info@tmsdc.net
Web: www.tmsdc.net

Tennessee Minority Supplier Development Council, Nashville State Office
Metro Center Plaza Bldg. 1, 220 Athens Way #105
Nashville, TN 37228
Cheri Henderson, Executive Director
Tel: (615) 259-4699 Fax: (615) 259-9480
Email: info@tmsdc.net
Web: www.tmsdc.net

CULTURAL

AFRICAN AMERICAN CULTURAL ALLIANCE
P.O. Box 22173
Nashville, TN 37202
Kwame Lillard, President
Tel: (615) 251-0007
Email: aaca1983@bellsouth.net
Web: www.africanamericanculturalalliance.com

AFRICAN AMERICAN CULTURAL CENTER
Austin Peay State University
P.O. Box 4715
Clarksville, TN 37044
Dr. Valerie Barnes, Director
Tel: (931) 221-7120 Fax: (931) 221-7952
Email: barnes@apsu.edu
Web: www.apsu.edu/aacc

JUNETEENTH FREEDOM FESTIVAL
P.O. Box 80001
Memphis, TN 38108-0001
Glynn Reed,
Tel: (901) 385-4943 Fax: (901) 385-4876
Email: juneteenthmemphis@msn.com
Web: www.juneteenthmemphis.org

MEMPHIS BLACK ARTS ALLIANCE, INC.
Fire House Community Arts Center
P.O. Box 40854
Memphis, TN 38174-0854
Bennie Nelson-West, Executive Director
Tel: (901) 948-9522 Fax: (901) 948-9936
Email: memphisarts@bellsouth.net
Web: www.webspawner.com/users/mbaa

ENTERTAINMENT

NATIONAL AFRICAN AMERICAN RV'ERS ASSOCIATION
Tennessee RV 2 Plus RV Club Chapter
1633 Nellie Rd.
Memphis, TN 38116
Odell Nathaniel, President
Tel: (615) 794-1457
Email: onate1633@aol.com
Web: www.naarva.com

LAW ENFORCEMENT

NATIONAL ORGANIZATION OF BLACK LAW ENFORCEMENT EXECUTIVES
Chattanooga Chapter
P.O. Box 8098
Chattanooga Police Department
Chattanooga, TN 37414
Charles Cooke, Deputy Chief of Police
Tel: (423) 698-9520 Fax: (423) 697-1361
Email: cooke_chas@mail.chattanooga.gov
Web: www.noblenatl.org

West Tennessee Chapter
Shelby County Sheriff's Office, 5705 Shelby Oaks Dr.
Memphis, TN 38134
Terry Yarbrough, President
Tel: (901) 867-1413 Fax: (901) 752-6582
Email: yart@bellsouth.net
Web: www.noblenatl.org

POLITICAL ACTION

AMERICAN CIVIL LIBERTIES UNION
Tennessee Chapter
P.O. Box 120160
Nashville, TN 37212
Hedy Weinberg, Executive Director
Tel: (615) 320-7142
Web: www.aclu-tn.org

ASSOCIATION OF COMMUNITY ORGANIZATIONS FOR REFORM NOW
Memphis Office
1000 S. Cooper St.
Memphis, TN 38104
Tel: (901) 272-0056 Fax: (901) 276-0008
Email: fieldrdso@acorn.org
Web: www.acorn.org

BLACKS IN GOVERNMENT
Region IV- Greater Memphis Chapter
P.O. Box 3041
Memphis, TN 38173-0041
Jeanette Owens, Chapter President (Interim)
Tel: (901) 544-3190
Email: jeanetteowens@earthlink.net
Web: www.bignet.org

Region IV-Oak Ridge Chapter
P.O. Box 2001
Oak Ridge, TN 37831
Tanisha Smith-Wimes, Chapter President
Tel: (865) 576-1025
Email: smithwimestl@oro.doe.gov
Web: www.bignet.org

Region IV-TVA-Chattanooga Area Chapter
Tennessee Valley Authority, 101 Market St., Missionary Ridge Pl. #3B
Chattanooga, TN 37401
Jennelle Archie, Chapter President
Tel: (423) 751-6195
Email: tva.chattanooga@bignet.org
Web: www.bignet.org

PROFESSIONAL

AMERICAN ASSOCIATION OF BLACKS IN ENERGY
Tenessee Chapter
P.O. Box 430
c/o Memphis Light, Gas & Water Division
Memphis, TN 38103
Alonzo Weaver, President
Tel: (901) 528-4481 Fax: (901) 528-4086
Email: aweaver@mlgw.org
Web: www.aabe-tn.org

NATIONAL ASSOCIATION OF BLACK ACCOUNTANTS, INC.
Nashville Chapter
3525 Dove Creek Rd.
Antioch, TN 37013
Wallace Barber
Tel: (615) 749-1170
Web: www.nabainc.org

NATIONAL ASSOCIATION OF BLACK JOURNALISTS
Region VI- Nashville Chapter
474 James Robertson Pkwy.
Nashville, TN 37219
Lelan A. Statom, Chapter President
Tel: (615) 248-5372 Fax: (615) 244-5883
Email: lstatom@newschannel5.com
Web: www.nabj.org

NATIONAL BLACK MBA ASSOCIATION, INC.
Nashville Chapter-South
P.O. Box 25131
Nashville, TN 37202
Lolita Toney, President
Tel: (615) 255-0172
Web: www.blackmbanashville.org

NATIONAL MEDICAL ASSOCIATION
Volunteer State Medical Association
4124 Melinda Dr.
Chattanooga, TN 37416-3005
John Arrandando, President
Fax: (423) 892-0340
Web: www.nmanet.org

RELIGIOUS

NATIONAL BAPTIST CONVENTION USA, INC.
1700 Baptist World Center Dr.
Nashville, TN 37207
Dr. William Shaw, President
Tel: (615) 228-6292 Fax: (615) 262-3917
Email: info.nbcusa@verizon.net
Web: www.nationalbaptist.com

SPEC. INT., EDUCATION

THE NATIONAL AFRICAN AMERICAN SPEAKERS ASSOCIATION
Nashville Chapter
1215 North Ave.
Nashville, TN
Terry Richards, Chapter President
Tel: (615) 847-8335
Email: tennessee@4naasa.org
Web: www.4naasa.org

SPEC. INT., FAMILY PLANNING

NATIONAL HOOK-UP OF BLACK WOMEN, INC.
Nashville Chapter
4001 Anderson Rd. #A-138
Nashville, TN 37217
Barbara Biggers-Matthews, President
Tel: (615) 254-3856
Web: www.nhbwinc.com

SPEC. INT., SOCIAL INTEREST

100 BLACK MEN OF CHATTANOOGA, INC.
P.O. Box 1201
Chattanooga, TN 37401
Rose Martin, Chapter President
Tel: (423) 756-0790 Fax: (423) 756-2976
Web: www.100blackmen.org

100 BLACK MEN OF MIDDLE TENNESSEE, INC.
1 Vantage Way #E200
Nashville, TN 37228
Darrell Freeman, President
Tel: (615) 248-2721 Fax: (615) 248-3156
Email: info@the100.org
Web: www.the100.org

100 BLACK MEN OF WEST TENNESSEE, INC.
153 Cheyenne Dr.
Jackson, TN 38305
Ernest T. Brooks, President
Tel: (731) 668-1425

BLACK UNITED FUND OF MEMPHIS
283 N. Bellevue St.
Memphis, TN 38105
Garry Rowe, President
Tel: (901) 726-5353 Fax: (901) 726-5355
Email: mphisbuf@aol.com
Web: http://tenn.nbuf.org

NATIONAL BLACK UNITED FRONT
Memphis Chapter
5369 Scottsdale Ave.
Memphis, TN 38115
Kamau Omondi, Chair
Tel: (901) 351-8669
Email: memphisnbuf@hotmail.com
Web: www.nbufront.org

NATIONAL URBAN LEAGUE, INC.
Knoxville Area Urban League
P.O. Box 1911
Knoxville, TN 37917
Phyllis Y. Nicholas, President/CEO
Tel: (865) 524-5511 Fax: (865) 525-5154
Email: info@thekaul.org
Web: www.thekaul.org

Memphis Urban League
413 N. Cleveland St.
Memphis, TN 38104-7012
Darryl S. Tukufu, President
Tel: (901) 272-2491 Fax: (901) 272-1673
Email: dtukufu@mphsurbanleague.org
Web: www.mphsurbanleague.org

Urban League of Greater Chattanooga
730 Martin Luther King Blvd.
Chattanooga, TN 37403
Warren E. Logan, President/CEO
Tel: (423) 756-1762 Fax: (423) 756-7255
Email: info@ulchatt.net
Web: www.ulchatt.org

Urban League of Middle Tennessee
1219 9th Ave. North
Nashville, TN 37208
Rosalyn Carpenter, President/CEO
Tel: (615) 254-0525 Fax: (615) 254-0636
Email: rcarpenter@urbanleagueofmidtn.org
Web: www.urbanleagueofmidtn.org

SPEC. INT., YOUTH

CHILDREN'S DEFENSE FUND
Clinton Office
P.O. Box 840
Clinton, TN 37717-0840
Rev. Dr. Joan S. Parrott, Director
Tel: (865) 457-6466 Fax: (865) 457-6464
Email: cdfhaley@childrensdefense.org
Web: www.childrensdefense.org

STUDENT ORGANIZATION

ALPHA KAPPA ALPHA SORORITY, INC.
Alpha Delta Omega Chapter
6760 Cold Stream Dr.
Nashville, TN 37221
Francene Gilmer, Chapter President
Web: www.aka1908.com

Alpha Pi Omega Chapter
P.O. Box 2013
Knoxville, TN 37901
Rosalyn Tillman, Chapter President
Web: www.aka1908.com

Beta Epsilon Omega Chapter
1269 N. Lion's Gate
Memphis, TN 38116
Marilyn Evans, Chapter President
Web: www.aka1908.com

Epsilon Epsilon Chapter, University of Memphis
Office of Greek Affairs, University Ctr. #427
Memphis, TN 38152
Mary Wilson, Chapter President
Web: www.aka1908.com

Eta Beta Chapter, Vanderbilt University
Station B
P.O. Box 357093
Nashville, TN 37235
Laurie Michelle Durham, Chapter President
Web: www.aka1908.com

Eta Psi Chapter, Middle Tennessee State University
P.O. Box 609, MTSU
Murfreesboro, TN 37132
Kelly Alexander, Chapter President
Web: www.aka1908.com

Gamma Alpha Omega Chapter
P.O. Box 516
Jackson, TN 38302
Mary J. Platt, Chapter President
Web: www.aka1908.com

Kappa Lambda Omega Chapter
P.O. Box 23526
Nashville, TN 37202-3526
Cleatrice T. Mctorry, Chapter President
Tel: (615) 373-0050
Email: cleamctorry@aol.com
Web: www.aka1908.com

Kappa Rho Chapter, Austin Peay State University
P.O. Box 8345
Clarksville, TN 37044
Kimberly N. Quinn, Chapter President
Web: www.aka1908.com

Mu Epsilon Chapter, Christian Brothers University
650 E. Pkwy. South #T-2
Memphis, TN 38104
Tequilla Parson, Chapter President
Web: www.aka1908.com

Omicron Chi Chapter, Rhodes College
P.O. Box 3051
2000 N Pkwy.
Memphis, TN 38112
Takeisha T. Moses, Chapter President
Web: www.aka1908.com

Omicron Rho Chapter, East Tennessee State University
P.O. Box 70253
Johnson City, TN 37614
Leslee R. Phillips, Chapter President
Web: www.aka1908.com

Phi Lambda Omega Chapter
P.O. Box 752282
Memphis, TN 38175
Lasherrie McKinnie Bates, Chapter President
Web: www.aka1908.com

Pi Nu Omega Chapter
P.O. Box 8009
Murfreesboro, TN 37133
Debbie Baird Pumphrey, Chapter President
Web: www.aka1908.com

Pi Omega Chapter
P.O. Box 3543
Chattanooga, TN 37404
Audra Dean Ingram, Chapter President
Web: www.aka1908.com

Pi Omega Omega Chapter
2109 Hickory Springs Rd. #14
Johnson City, TN 37604
Marian Hassell Whitson, Chapter President
Web: www.aka1908.com

Tau Eta Omega Chapter
P.O. Box 585
Cleveland, TN 37364
Cynthia Humes, Chapter President
Web: www.aka1908.com

Theta Eta Omega Chapter
P.O. Box 11837
Jackson, TN 38305
Victoria E. Brooks, Chapter President
Web: www.aka1908.com

Upsilon Psi Omega Chapter
P.O. Box 23463
Nashville, TN 37202
LaRhonda Williams, Chapter President
Web: www.aka1908.com

Xi Alpha Chpter
P.O. Box 5234
Cookeville, TN 38505
Ca'trecha B. Butts, Chapter President
Web: www.aka1908.com

Xi Iota Omega Chapter
P.O. Box 5064
Oak Ridge, TN 37831
Estella Simmons, Chapter President
Web: www.aka1908.com

Xi Lambda Omega Chapter
P.O. Box 15
Ripley, TN 38063
Shirley Smith, Chapter President
Web: www.aka1908.com

Zeta Delta Chapter, University of Tennessee-Knoxville
1531 W. Cumberland #108
Knoxville, TN 37996
Roshaunda Ross, Chapter President
Web: www.aka1908.com

Zeta Kappa Chapter, University of Tennessee-Chattanooga
818 University St., UTC #3227
Chattanooga, TN 37403
Tiffany Conner, Chapter President
Web: www.aka1908.com

Zeta Lambda Chapter, University of Tennessee-Martin
P.O. Box 106
Martin, TN 38238
Darla D. Young, Chapter President
Web: www.aka1908.com

Alpha Delta Lambda Chapter
P.O. Box 1906
Memphis, TN 38101
Web: www.alphaphialpha.net

Alpha Mu Lambda Chapter
P.O. Box 2091
Knoxville, TN 37901
Web: www.alphaphialpha.net

Beta Omicron Chapter, Tennessee State University
P.O. Box 1234
Nashville, TN 37209
Web: www.alphaphialpha.net

Beta Pi Chapter, Lane College
P.O. Box 3284
Jackson, TN 38301
Web: www.alphaphialpha.net

Beta Upsilon Lambda Chapter
P.O. Box 216
Jackson, TN 38301
Web: www.alphaphialpha.net

Beta Xi Chapter, Lemoyne Owen College
P.O. Box 76
Memphis, TN 38126
Web: www.alphaphialpha.net

Chi Chapter, Meharry Medical College
P.O. Box 229
Nashville, TN 37208
Web: www.alphaphialpha.net

Kappa Xi Chapter, Middle Tennessee State University
P.O. Box 655
Murfreesboro, TN 37132
Web: www.alphaphialpha.net

Mu Iota Chapter, University of Tennessee
1810 Lake Ave.
Knoxville, TN 37916
Web: www.alphaphialpha.net

Mu Nu Lambda Chapter
P.O. Box 3463
Kingsport, TN 37664
Web: www.alphaphialpha.net

Omicron Phi Chapter, Tennessee Technological University
P.O. Box 5231
Cookeville, TN 38505
Web: www.alphaphialpha.net

Omicron Sigma Lambda Chapter
P.O. Box 2685
Murfreesboro, TN 37133
Web: www.alphaphialpha.net

Psi Lambda Chapter
P.O. Box 334
Chattanooga, TN 37401
Web: www.alphaphialpha.net

Sigma Beta Chapter, East Tennessee State University
P.O. Box 23026
Johnson City, TN 37614
Web: www.alphaphialpha.net

Tau Lambda Chapter
P.O. Box 80646
Nashville, TN 37208
Email: taulambda@edonline.com
Web: www.alphaphialpha.net

NATIONAL BLACK LAW STUDENTS ASSOCIATION
University of Tennessee School of Law
1505 W. Cumberland Ave.
Knoxville, TN 37996
Tel: (865) 974-4241
Web: www.law.utk.edu

Vanderbilt University School of Law
131 21st. Ave., South
Nashville, TN 37203
BLSA President
Tel: (615) 322-2615 Fax: (615) 322-6631
Web: http://law.vanderbilt.edu

TEXAS

ARTISTIC

BLACKEN BLUES THEATER
P.O. Box 151334
Dallas, TX 75315
Willie Holmes, Founder/Executive Director
Tel: (214) 618-4522
Email: info@blackenblues.com
Web: www.blackenblues.com

NATIONAL ASSOCIATION OF NEGRO MUSICIANS, INC.
Southern Region
1264 Whispering Trail
Dallas, TX 75241
Jowanda E. Jordan, Vice President/Regional Director
Tel: (214) 374-6037 Fax: (214) 374-2763
Email: jej1264@sbcglobal.net

THE BLACK ACADEMY OF ARTS AND LETTERS, INC.
650 S. Griffin St.
Dallas, TX 75202
Curtis King, Founder/President
Tel: (214) 743-2440 Fax: (214) 743-2450
Email: info@tbaal.org
Web: www.tbaal.org

BUSINESS

HOUSTON MINORITY BUSINESS COUNCIL
6671 SW Fwy. #110
Houston, TX 77074
Richard Huebner, Executive Director
Tel: (713) 271-7805 Fax: (713) 271-9770
Email: info@hmbc.org
Web: www.hmbc.org

NATIONAL MINORITY SUPPLIER DEVELOPMENT COUNCIL, INC.
Central & South Texas Minority Business Council
912 Bastrop Hwy. #101
Austin, TX 78741
Dinah Lovett, President
Tel: (512) 386-8766 Fax: (512) 386-8988
Email: cstmbc@aol.com
Web: www.cstmbc.org

Dallas/Fort Worth Minority Business Development Council
1000 Stemmons Tower South, 2720 Stemmons Frwy.
Dallas, TX 75207-2212
Margo J. Posey, Council President
Tel: (214) 630-0747 Fax: (214) 637-2241
Email: info@dfwmbdc.com
Web: www.dfwmbdc.com

Houston Minority Business Council
6671 SW Fwy. #110
Houston, TX 77074
Richard Huebner, Executive Director
Tel: (713) 271-7805 Fax: (713) 271-9770
Email: info@hmbc.org
Web: www.hmbc.org

CHAMBER OF COMMERCE

ALAMO CITY CHAMBER OF COMMERCE
600 Hemisfair Plz. Way, Bldg. 406-10
San Antonio, TX 78205
Llew Frankambles, President
Tel: (210) 226-9055 Fax: (210) 226-0524
Email: info@alamocitychamber.org
Web: www.alamocitychamber.org

BLACK CHAMBER OF COMMERCE OF THE PERMIAN BASIN
700 N. Grant St. #200
Odessa, TX 79761
Odel Crawford, President/CEO
Tel: (432) 332-5812 Fax: (432) 333-7858
Email: odel.crawford@sbcglobal.net

CAPITAL CITY AFRICAN-AMERICAN CHAMBER OF COMMERCE
5407 N. IH 35 #304
Austin, TX 78723
Greg Marshall, President/CEO
Tel: (512) 459-1182 Fax: (512) 459-1183
Email: admin@capcitychamber.org
Web: www.capcitychamber.org

FORT WORTH METROPOLITAN BLACK CHAMBER OF COMMERCE
1150 South Fwy. #211
Fort Worth, TX 76104
Devoyd Jennings, President/CEO
Tel: (817) 871-6538 Fax: (817) 332-6438
Email: djennings@fwmbcc.org
Web: www.fwmbcc.org

TEXAS ASSOCIATION OF AFRICAN AMERICAN CHAMBERS OF COMMERCE
Abilene Black Chamber of Commerce
P.O. Box 661
Abilene, TX 79604
Leon Petty
Tel: (915) 673-4741 Fax: (915) 673-4743
Web: www.taaacc.com

African-American Chamber of Commerce of San Antonio
1717 N. Loop 1604 East #220
San Antonio, TX 78232-1553
Lou Miller, President
Tel: (210) 490-1624
Email: blackchamber@aol.com
Web: www.aaccsa.com

Atlanta Negro Chamber of Commerce
P.O. Box 194
Atlanta, TX 75551
Waylon Jackson, President
Tel: (903) 796-9647 Fax: (903) 796-9647
Web: www.taaacc.com

Corpus Christi Black Chamber of Commerce
5658 Bear Ln.
Corpus Christi, TX 78405
Lamont Taylor, President
Tel: (361) 289-2712 Fax: (361) 289-3006
Email: ltaylor@pattymont.com
Web: www.taaacc.com

Dallas Black Chamber of Commerce
2838 Martin Luther King, Jr. Blvd.
Dallas, TX 75215
Reginald Gates, President
Tel: (214) 421-5200 Fax: (214) 421-5510
Email: rgates@dbcc.org
Web: www.dbcc.org

Denton Black Chamber of Commerce
P.O. Box 51026
Denton, TX 76206
Elihu Gillespie, Chairman
Tel: (972) 347-3252 Fax: (940) 382-9695
Email: info@dentonblackchamber.com
Web: www.dentonblackchamber.com

Ennis Negro Chamber of Commerce
P.O. Box 1036
Ennis, TX 75120
Ernest Bradley, Secretary
Tel: (972) 878-0068 Fax: (972) 878-0068
Email: ebrad683@aol.com

Headquarters
807 Brazos St. #316
Austin, TX 78701
Tel: (512) 457-0370 Fax: (512) 457-1078
Web: www.taaacc.org

Heart of Texas Chamber of Commerce
P.O. Box 1485
Waco, TX 76703
Mac F. Florence, President

Tel: (254) 235-5538 Fax: (254) 751-1057
Web: www.taaacc.com

Houston Citizens Chamber of Commerce
2808 Wheeler St.
Houston, TX 77004
Earl Loggins, Board Chairman
Tel: (713) 522-9745 Fax: (713) 522-5965
Web: www.hccoc.org

Longview Metro Black Chamber of Commerce
303 Webb St.
Daingerfield, TX 75638
Roderick Mitchell
Tel: (903) 645-3932 Fax: (903) 645-7565
Web: www.taaacc.org

CULTURAL

AFRICAN AMERICAN CULTURE COMMITTEE
University of Texas at Austin
P.O. Box 7338
Austin, TX 78713-7338
Tamika R. Stevenson, President
Tel: (512) 475-6645 Fax: (512) 475-6414
Email: melliott@union.utexas.edu
Web: www.sec.union.utexas.edu

ASSOCIATION FOR THE STUDY OF AFRICAN-AMERICAN LIFE AND HISTORY
Houston Branch
P.O. Box 2558
Houston, TX 77252-8093
Algenita Scott-Davis, Chapter President
Tel: (713) 216-4057
Web: www.asalh.com

AUSTIN AREA HERITAGE COUNCIL, INC.
P.O. Box 81807
Austin, TX 78708
Carol Wright, Chair
Tel: (512) 478-4655 Fax: (512) 498-4655
Email: carol@aahc.org
Web: www.aahc.org

MIDLAND AFRICAN-AMERICAN ROOTS HISTORICAL /CULTURAL ARTS COUNCIL, INC.
P.O. Box 50473
Midland, TX 79710
Robbyne Hocker Fuller, Founder & Chairwoman of the Board
Tel: (432) 682-2864 Fax: (432) 684-7346
Email: mbce@swbell.net

ENTERTAINMENT

NATIONAL AFRICAN AMERICAN RV'ERS ASSOCIATION
Texas Sojourners Chapter
4507 Kushla
Dallas, TX 75216
Elbert D. Smith, President
Tel: (214) 374-8014
Email: e999ds@sbcglobal.net
Web: www.naarva.com

LAW ENFORCEMENT

NATIONAL ORGANIZATION OF BLACK LAW ENFORCEMENT EXECUTIVES
Central Texas Chapter
Texas Department of Public Safety, 5805 N. Lamar
Austin, TX 78773
Curly W. Colquitt, Captain
Tel: (512) 424-5903 Fax: (512) 424-7211
Email: nobell53@msn.com
Web: www.noblecentraltxchapter.homestead.com

Greater North Texas Chapter
P.O. Box 750334
Dallas Police Department
Dallas, TX 75275-0034
Floyd Simpson, Deputy Chief of Police
Tel: (214) 670-8595 Fax: (214) 670-8608
Email: fsimpson@mail.ci.dallas.tx.us
Web: www.noblengntc.com

Houston Chapter
P.O. Box 3083
Houston Metro Police Department
Houston, TX 77253-3083
Vera Bumpers-Pentecost, Lieutenant
Tel: (281) 403-8010 Fax: (713) 881-3028
Email: region5vp@noblenational.net
Web: www.noblenatl.org

MULTI-PURPOSE

NATIONAL ASSOCIATION FOR THE ADVANCEMENT OF COLORED PEOPLE
Region VI: Southwestern
3003 S. Loop W #500
Houston, TX 77054
Georgia Noone, Director
Tel: (713) 662-2727 Fax: (713) 661-5982
Email: gnoone@naacpnet.org
Web: www.naacp.org

POLITICAL ACTION

AMERICAN ASSOCIATION FOR AFFIRMATIVE ACTION
Region VI
Office of Equal Opportunity & Diversity, UTMB at Galveston, 301 University Blvd.
Galveston, TX 77555-0106
Melvin William, Regional Director
Tel: (409) 747-8823 Fax: (409) 747-8836
Email: mwilliam@utmb.edu
Web: www.affirmativeaction.org

AMERICAN CIVIL LIBERTIES UNION
Central Texas Chapter
P.O. Box 12905
Austin, TX 78711
Kathy Mitchell, President
Tel: (512) 478-7309 Fax: (512) 478-7303
Email: info@aclutx.org
Web: www.aclutx.org

Collin/Grayson Counties Chapter
P.O. Box 865010
Plano, TX 75086-5010
David M. Smith, President
Tel: (972) 398-9847
Web: www.aclutx.org

Dallas Chapter
P.O. Box 710356
Dallas, TX 75371
Mike Howard, President
Tel: (214) 939-8089 Fax: (214) 939-8089
Email: mhoward@acludallas.org
Web: www.acludallas.org

Greater Denton Chapter
P.O. Box 424354, TWU Station
Denton, TX 76203
Jim Baird, President
Tel: (940) 382-3028
Web: www.aclutx.org

Greater Fort Worth Civil Liberties Chapter
P.O. Box 8772
Fort Worth, TX 76124
Reed Bilz, President
Tel: (817) 534-6883
Email: rbilz@earthlink.net
Web: www.aclutx.org

High Plains Chapter
P.O. Box 2468
Amarillo, TX 79105
Michael Walsh, President
Tel: (806) 352-9401
Email: info@aclutx.org
Web: www.aclutx.org

Houston Chapter
P.O. Box 132047
Houston, TX 77219-2047
George Barnstone, President
Tel: (713) 942-8146 Fax: (713) 942-8146
Web: www.aclu-houston.org

Lubbock Chapter
P.O. Box 4033
Lubbock, TX 79409
Harvey Madison, President
Tel: (806) 793-3754
Web: www.aclutx.org

San Antonio & Southwest Region Chapter
P.O. Box 276286
San Antonio, TX 78227-6286
Michael White, President
Tel: (210) 226-8707 Fax: (210) 226-9059
Email: aclu_t@sbcglobal.net
Web: www.aclutx.org

Texas Chapter
P.O. Box 12905
Austin, TX 78711
Will Harrell, Executive Director
Tel: (512) 478-7309 Fax: (512) 478-7303
Email: info@aclutx.org
Web: www.aclutx.org

Arlington Office
714 N. Watson #304C
Arlington, TX 76006
Tel: (817) 649-8256
Email: txacornar@acorn.org
Web: www.acorn.org

Dallas Office
5353 Maple #200
Dallas, TX 75235
Tel: (214) 823-4580 Fax: (214) 823-1090
Email: txacorndaro@acorn.org
Web: www.acorn.org

Ft. Worth Office
3722 Decatur Ave.
Ft. Worth, TX 76106
Tel: (817) 626-0251
Email: txacornfwro@acorn.org
Web: www.acorn.org

San Antonio Office
2300 W. Commerce #105
San Antonio, TX 78207
Tel: (210) 226-2584 Fax: (210) 226-3604
Email: txacornsaro@acorn.org
Web: www.acorn.org

BLACKS IN GOVERNMENT
Region VI
434 Rifleman Trail
Arlington, TX 76002
Duane Braxton, President
Tel: (817) 223-4251
Email: region6.president@bignet.org
Web: www.bignet.org

Region VI- Dallas Metroplex Chapter
P.O. Box 223583
Dallas, TX 75222-3583
Terry L. Branch, Chapter President
Email: dallas.metroplex@bignet.org
Web: www.bignet.org/regional/dallas-metroplex/index. htm

Region VI-Austin Chapter
P.O. Box 19423
Austin, TX 78760
Trikes Britton, Chapter President
Email: austin@bignet.org
Web: www.bignet.org/regional/region6/index.htm

Region VI-Houston Area Chapter
19502 Sweetgum Forest
Humble, TX 77346
Faye Stewart-Henderson, Chapter President
Tel: (281) 987-6825 Fax: (281) 987-6808
Email: faye.stewart@mms.gov
Web: www.bignet.org

Region VI-Houston VAMC Chapter
3803 Cherry Forest Dr.
Houston, TX 77088
Patricia Limbrick, Chapter President
Tel: (713) 336-4320 Fax: (713) 224-6812
Email: plimbrick@yahoo.com
Web: www.bignet.org/regional/houston.area/index.htm

Region VI-North Texas Chapter
P.O. Box 17006
Fort Worth, TX 76102-0006
Janice Teddleton, Chapter President
Tel: (817) 978-5577 Fax: (817) 978-5748
Email: north.texas@bignet.org
Web: www.bignet.org/regional/region6/index.htm

Region VI-White Sands Missile Range
5116 Garland Ln.
El Paso, TX 79924-2315
Felicia Chamberlain, Chapter President
Tel: (505) 678-8139
Email: white.sands@bignet.org
Web: www.bignet.org/regional/region6/index.htm

NATIONAL ACTION NETWORK
Texas Chapter
Northwest Community Baptist Church, 1023 Pinemont Dr.
Houston, TX 77018
Rev. James W.E. Dixon, II, Chair
Tel: (713) 688-2900 Fax: (713) 688-3682
Web: www.nationalactionnetwork.org

PROFESSIONAL

AMERICAN ASSOCIATION OF BLACKS IN ENERGY
Dallas/Fort Worth Chapter
P.O. Box 1002, Mail Zone M35
6332 N. FM 56
Geln Rose, TX 76043
Tony Marvray, President
Tel: (254) 897-0821 Fax: (254) 897-0710
Email: hmarv1@txu.com
Web: www.aabe-dal-ftw.org

ASSOCIATION OF BLACK PSYCHOLOGISTS
Dallas Chapter
424 S. Corinth Street Rd.
Dallas, TX 75203
Donald Chandler, Ph.D., Chapter President
Tel: (214) 941-0578 Fax: (214) 941-0579
Email: donaldchandler@email.msn.com
Web: www.abpsi.org

Houston Chapter
2225 Herman Dr.
Houston, TX 77004
Dr. Xyna Bell, Chapter President
Tel: (713) 522-3015 Fax: (713) 522-3016
Email: xynabell@aol.com
Web: www.abpsi.org

BLACK DATA PROCESSING ASSOCIATES
Dallas Chapter
P.O. Box 815783
Dallas, TX 75381
DJ Washington, Chapter President
Tel: (972) 407-6895
Email: dallas@bdpa.org
Web: www.bdpa-dallas.org

Houston Chapter
P.O. Box 1266
Missouri City, TX 77459
Aaron Jones, Chapter President
Email: president@bdpahouston.org
Web: www.bdpahouston.org

CONFERENCE OF MINORITY TRANSPORTATION OFFICIALS
Dallas Chapter
Dallas Area Rapid Transit, 1401 Pacific Ave.
Dallas, TX 75266-7202
Frank Cortez, President
Tel: (214) 749-3841 Fax: (214) 749-3615
Email: fcortez@dart.org
Web: www.comto.org

Fort Worth Chapter
Fort Worth Transportation Authority, 1600 E. Lancaster Ave.
Fort Worth, TX 76102-6720
Betty Battles, Marketing Administrator
Tel: (817) 215-8623 Fax: (817) 215-8709
Email: bbattles@the-t.com
Web: www.comto.org

Houston Chapter
5100 Westheimer #580
Houston, TX 77056
Mary Ann Collier, VP, Communications/Marketing
Tel: (713) 850-0444 Fax: (713) 850-7901
Email: mc18@ridemetro.org
Web: www.comto.org

San Antonio Chapter
VIA Metro Transit Authority, 1720 N. Flores
San Antonio, TX 78212
James E. Hudson, Manager/Material Distribution Division
Tel: (210) 362-2400 Fax: (210) 362-2547
Email: james.hudson@viainfo.net
Web: www.comto.org

NATIONAL ASSOCIATION OF BLACK ACCOUNTANTS, INC.
Austin Central Texas Chapter
P.O. Box 142572
Austin, TX 78714
Brian Williams, President
Tel: (513) 385-5559
Email: brian.williams@ci.austin.tx.us

Houston Chapter
P.O. Box 3433
Houston, TX 77253
Erskine Payne, President
Tel: (713) 801-3547
Email: nabahouston@yahoo.com
Web: www.nabahouston.org

NATIONAL ASSOCIATION OF BLACK JOURNALISTS
Region VII-Austin Chapter
3201 Steck Ave.
Austin, TX 78767
Shelton Green, Chapter President
Tel: (512) 459-2086
Email: sgreen@kvue.com
Web: www.nabj.org

Region VII-Houston Chapter
P.O. Box 565
Houston, TX 77001-0565
Anthony Ogbo, Chapter President
Tel: (713) 953-0155 Fax: (281) 643-9520
Email: internationalguardian@pdq.net
Web: www.nabj.org

NATIONAL BLACK MBA ASSOCIATION, INC.
Dallas Chapter-West

P.O. Box 797174
Dallas, TX 75379-7174
Kevin Davis, President
Tel: (214) 853-4497
Email: mail@dallasmbas.org
Web: www.dallasmbas.org

Houston Chapter-West
P.O. Box 56509
Houston, TX 77256
Paul Charles, President
Tel: (713) 866-6573
Email: email@houstonblackmba.org
Web: www.houstonblackmba.org

Memphis Chapter-South
P.O. Box 181099
Memphis, TX 38181-1099
Kathy O. Lofton, Chapter President
Tel: (901) 725-4166
Email: nbmbaamemphis@nbmbaamemphis.org
Web: www.nbmbaamemphis.org

NATIONAL FORUM FOR BLACK PUBLIC ADMINISTRATORS
Houston Chapter
P.O. Box 301092
Houston, TX 77230-1092
Bonita Cade, President
Tel: (713) 837-0815
Email: information@nfbpahouston.org
Web: www.nfbpahouston.org

North Texas Chapter
P.O. Box 17092
Fort Worth, TX 76102
Anthony J. Snipes, President
Tel: (817) 392-6123 Fax: (817) 392-6134
Email: anthony.snipes@fortworthgov.org
Web: www.northtexasnfbpa.org

San Antonio Chapter
P.O. Box 2449
San Antonio, TX 78298
Veronica Godley, President
Tel: (210) 704-7353 Fax: (210) 704-8135
Email: vgodley@saws.org
Web: www.nfbpa.org

NATIONAL MEDICAL ASSOCIATION
Lone Star State Medical Association
12602 Toepperwein Rd. #211
San Antonio, TX 78233
Jesse Moss, Jr.,M.D., President
Tel: (210) 656-8888 Fax: (210) 656-2608
Email: doc@jmossjr.com
Web: www.nmanet.org

NATIONAL OPTOMETRIC ASSOCIATION
Region IV
6207 Shady Timbers Dr.
Houston, TX 77016
Ouida C. Middleton, Trustee
Tel: (713) 442-2627
Email: omiddleton.2000@alumni.opt.uh.edu
Web: www.natoptassoc.org

NATIONAL SOCIETY OF BLACK ENGINEERS
Region 5: University of Texas at Austin Chapter
College of Engineering, Ernest Cockrell, Jr. ECJ 1.224
Austin, TX 78712
Chrystal Tyler, Chapter President
Tel: (512) 471-7112
Email: keylolot2@msn.com
Web: www.engr.utexas.edu/nsbe

RELIGIOUS

NATIONAL ASSOCIATION OF BLACK CATHOLIC ADMINISTRATORS
800 W. Loop, 820 South
Ft. Worth, TX 76108
Ralph McLoud, President
Tel: (817) 560-3300 Fax: (817) 244-8839

SPEC. INT., EDUCATION

NATIONAL ASSOCIATION FOR MULTICULTURAL EDUCATION
Texas Chapter
Texas Tech University, 3008 18th St.
Lubbock, TX 79401
Sheryl Linda Santos, Dean
Tel: (806) 742-1837 Fax: (806) 742-2179
Email: sheryl.santos@ttu.edu
Web: www.coe.unt.edu/texas_name

PROJECT GRAD HOUSTON
6700 W. Loop South #500
Bellaire, TX 77401
Roy Hughes, Executive Director
Tel: (832) 325-0325 Fax: (832) 325-0455
Email: rhughes@projectgradhouston.org

Web: www.projectgradhouston.org

THE AFRICAN OVERSEAS UNION
8700 Commerce Park #409
Houston, TX 77074
Tel: (713) 541-1414
Email: aouevent@aanhr.com
Web: http://houstonprogressive.org/africanoverseasunion/

SPEC. INT., HEALTH SERVICES

AFRICAN-AMERICAN PRE-HEALTH ASSOCIATION
University of Houston
Campus Activities Box #237, 51 University Ctr.
Houston, TX 77204
Sepideh Shirali, President
Email: mudelta@uh.edu
Web: www.uh.edu/mudelta

SPEC. INT., HUMAN RELATIONS

GIRL FRIENDS, INC.
5215 Lobello Dr.
Dallas, TX 75229-5514
Veronica M. Frazier, Advisory Board Chairman
Tel: (214) 373-8513 Fax: (214) 739-4691

SPEC. INT., SOCIAL INTEREST

100 BLACK MEN OF AUSTIN & CENTRAL TEXAS, INC.
P.O. Box 202017
Austin, TX 78720
Vincent McElhaney, President
Tel: (512) 728-4692
Email: dchubbs@austin.rr.com
Web: www.100blackmen.org

100 BLACK MEN OF CORPUS CHRISTI, INC.
P.O. Box 271329
Corpus Christi, TX 78427
Charles Tryon, President
Tel: (361) 877-0230 Fax: (361) 884-0601
Email: sirpryon@aol.com
Web: www.100blackmen.org

100 BLACK MEN OF GREATER DALLAS, INC.
P.O. Box 226081
Dallas, TX 75222
Robert Tapley, President
Tel: (972) 898-0186

100 BLACK MEN OF SAN ANTONIO, INC.
4302 Jarbet Dr.
San Antonio, TX 78220
Ira Smith, Jr., President
Tel: (210) 359-8762 Fax: (210) 337-2008
Web: www.100blackmenofsanantonio.com

BLACK UNITED FUND OF TEXAS, INC.
5407 Chenevert St. #101
Houston, TX 77004
Cleo Glenn-Johnson, President
Tel: (713) 524-5767 Fax: (713) 524-5769
Email: buftx@buftx.org
Web: www.blackunitedfundoftexas.org

NATIONAL BLACK UNITED FRONT
Houston Chapter
2428 Southmore
Houston, TX 77004
Tel: (713) 942-0365
Email: omowale32@aol.com
Web: www.nbufhouston.org

NATIONAL URBAN LEAGUE, INC.
Austin Area Urban League
1033 La Posada Dr. #150
Austin, TX 78752
Grova Jones, Interim President/CEO
Tel: (512) 478-7176 Fax: (512) 478-1239
Email: info@aaul.org
Web: www.aaul.org

Houston Area Urban League
1301 Texas Ave.
Houston, TX 77002
Sylvia K. Brooks, President/CEO
Tel: (713) 393-8700 Fax: (713) 393-8701
Email: sbrooks@haul.org
Web: www.haul.org

Urban League of Greater Dallas and North Central Texas
4315 S. Lancaster Rd.
Dallas, TX 75216
Dr. Beverly Mitchell-Brooks, CEO
Tel: (214) 915-4600 Fax: (214) 915-4601
Email: donnahwoods@ulgdnctx.com
Web: www.dallasurbanleague.com

REAL MEN COOK FOR CHARITY
Dallas Chapter

6932 Greenville #162
Dallas, TX 75231
Terry Allen, Chief Development Planner
Tel: (214) 376-6530 Fax: (214) 376-6535
Web: www.realmencook.com

SPEC. INT., YOUTH

CHILDREN'S DEFENSE FUND
Austin Office
316 W. 12th St. #105
Austin, TX 78701
Patti Everett, Executive Director
Tel: (512) 480-0990 Fax: (512) 480-0995
Email: peveritt@childrensdefense.org
Web: www.childrensdefense.org

Bellaire Office
4500 Bissonnet #260
Bellaire, TX 77401
Barbra Best, Health Project Manager
Tel: (713) 664-4080 Fax: (713) 664-1975
Email: cdfinfo@childrensdefense.org
Web: www.childrensdefense.org

Rio Grande Valley Office
944 A. W. Nolana Loop
Pahrr, TX 78577
Olga Gabriel, Director
Tel: (956) 782-4000 Fax: (956) 283-7975
Email: ogabriel@childrensdefense.org
Web: www.childrensdefense.org

JACK & JILL OF AMERICA, INC.
South Central Region
907 Tangle Briar Dr.
Seabrook, TX 77586
Izella M. Dornell, Regional Director
Tel: (281) 532-3457 Fax: (281) 532-3863
Email: ldornell@houston.rr.com
Web: www.jack-and-jill.org

RITES OF PASSAGE PROGRAM FOR GIRLS, INC.
P.O. Box 398908
Dallas, TX 75339
Rheta D. Norman, Founder/Executive Director
Tel: (214) 467-4411 Fax: (214) 330-0212
Email: ropp4girls@sbcglobal.net
Web: www.roppforgirls.org

STUDENT ORGANIZATION

AFRICAN AMERICAN NURSING STUDENT ASSOCIATION
University of Texas at Austin
Center Box #044
Austin, TX 78701
Tracie Jones, President
Tel: (281) 773-5884
Email: tjones0882@mail.utexas.edu

AFRICAN AMERICAN STAFF ADVOCATING PROGRESS
University of Texas at Austin
P.O. Box 7755
Austin, TX 78713
Stella Smith, President
Tel: (512) 232-4850
Email: stella_smith@mail.utexas.edu
Web: http://dpweb1.dp.utexas.edu/dsorg/detail.wb?code=99999

ALPHA KAPPA ALPHA SORORITY, INC.
Alpha Kappa Omega Chapter
7710 Candlegreen Ln.
Houston, TX 77071
Patricia Roberts, Chapter President
Web: www.aka1908.com

Alpha Omega Omega Chapter
4175 Crow Rd. #15
Beaumont, TX 77706
Sophia Perkins, Chapter President
Web: www.aka1908.com

Alpha Tau Chapter, Texas College
2404 N. Grand Ave.
Tyler, TX 75702
Keitha Ray, Chapter President
Web: www.aka1908.com

Alpha Tau Omega Chapter
P.O. Box 200954
San Antonio, TX 78220
Mary Taylor, Chapter President
Web: www.aka1908.com

P.O. Box 50654
Dallas, TX 75250
Jacqueline Waiters-Lee, Chapter President
Tel: (214) 924-0390
Web: www.aka1908.com

Beta Kappa Chapter, Houston-Tilliston College

900 Chicon
P.O. Box 160
Austin, TX 78702
Katrina Sterling, Chapter President
Web: www.aka1908.com

Beta Mu Omega Chapter
P.O. Box 15726
Fort Worth, TX 76119
Charlotte Christopher, Chapter President
Web: www.aka1908.com

Beta Phi Omega Chapter
P.O. Box 3133
Galveston, TX 77552
Barbara McIlveen, Chapter President
Web: www.aka1908.com

Beta Psi Omega Chapter
P.O. Box 80055
Austin, TX 78708
Debra Franklin-Owens, President
Email: info@betapsiomega.org
Web: www.betapsiomega.org

Delta Alpha Omega Chapter
4324 N. 23rd St.
Waco, TX 76708
Cynthia Courtney, Chapter President
Web: www.aka1908.com

Delta Gamma Omega Chapter
P.O. Box 6192
Corpus Christi, TX 78466
Cynthia Bunton, Chapter President
Web: www.aka1908.com

Delta Rho Chapter
6626 Honey Ridge Ln.
San Antonio, TX 78239
Tiffany Fluellen, Chapter President
Web: www.aka1908.com

Delta Xi Chapter, University of Texas-Austin
100-C. W. Dean Keaton, SOC #211
Austin, TX 78712
Jearine Willoughby, Chapter President
Web: www.aka1908.com

Epsilon Lambda Chapter
4800 Calhoun Blvd.
P.O. Box 101
Houston, TX 77204
Elecia Brown, Chapter President
Web: www.aka1908.com

Epsilon Lambda Chapter
51 University Dr.
P.O. Box 101
Houston, TX 77204
Tunu Tenede, President
Tel: (832) 338-6222
Email: tunu04@aol.com
Web: www.uh.edu/aka/

Epsilon Mu Chapter
UNT, P.O. Box 305207
Denton, TX 76203
Lyndsay Levingston, Chapter President
Web: www.aka1908.com

Epsilon Sigma Chapter, Texas A&M University-Commerce
AKA Student Life Office
Commerce, TX 75429
Jacqueline Goffney, Chapter President
Web: www.aka1908.com

Epsilon Zeta Omega Chapter
P.O. Box 3442
Longview, TX 75606
Geryl D. Tucker, Chapter President
Web: www.aka1908.com

Eta Delta Chapter, University of Texas-El Paso
P.O. Box 82
El Paso, TX 79968
Jackie Beard, Chapter President
Web: www.aka1908.com

Eta Pi Omega Chapter
P.O. Box 971845
El Paso, TX 79997
Karen C. Linen, Chapter President
Web: www.aka1908.com

Gamma Omega Omega Chapter
P.O. Box 875
Lamarque, TX 77568
Winifred Gilmore, Chapter President
Web: www.aka1908.com

Gamma Omicron Omega Chapter
1722 Northridge Dr.
Tyler, TX 75702
Joan Brooks, Chapter President
Web: www.aka1908.com

Gamma Psi Chapter, Texas Southern University

3100 Clebuene
P.O. Box 1445
Houston, TX 77004
Bianca Roberts, Chapter President
Web: www.aka1908.com

Kappa Lambda Chapter, Texas Christian University
P.O. Box 296955
Forth Worth, TX 76129
Shanika Brooks, Chapter President
Web: www.aka1908.com

Kappa Mu Chapter, Southern Methodist University
3105 Fondren Dr.
Dallas, TX 75205
Jarie Antoinette Bradley, Chapter President
Web: www.aka1908.com

Kappa Nu Chapter
P.O. Box 424942
Denton, TX 76204
Hope S. Hayes, Chapter President
Web: www.aka1908.com

Kappa Xi Omega Chapter
P.O. Box 5762
Texarkana, TX 75501
Tonya R. Nelson, Chapter President
Web: www.aka1908.com

Mu Kappa Omega Chapter
P.O. Box 1097
Missouri City, TX 77459
Kechia V. Warren, Chapter President
Web: www.aka1908.com

Mu Mu Omega Chapter
P.O. Box 1091
Huntsville, TX 77342
Jacklyn Merchant, Chapter President
Web: www.aka1908.com

Mu Theta Omega Chapter
P.O. Box 1315
Killeen, TX 76540
Patricia Lyons, Chapter President
Web: www.aka1908.com

Nu Omega Chapter
503 Wain Ct.
Longview, TX 75604
Beverly Hanon, Chapter President
Web: www.aka1908.com

Omicron Epsilon Omega Chapter
P.O. Box 8172
Wichita Falls, TX 76307
Olga Roberts, Chapter President
Web: www.aka1908.com

Omicron Gamma Chapter
8403 Claiborne
Houston, TX 77078
Kaimiccia Patterson, Chapter President
Web: www.aka1908.com

Omicron Mu Omega Chapter
P.O. Box 227203
Dallas, TX 75222
Bonnie Adams Barrett, Chapter President
Web: www.aka1908.com

Omicron Tau Chapter, University of Texas-San Antonio
5310 Stormy Sunset
San Antonio, TX 78247
Latanya N. Ward, Chapter President
Web: www.aka1908.com

Omicron Tau Omega Chapter
P.O. Box 690973
Houston, TX 77269
Shirley Alford Benn, Chapter President
Web: www.aka1908.com

Phi Chapter, Wiley College
P.O. Box 8112
Marshall, TX 75670
Jennifer Alexander, Chapter President
Web: www.aka1908.com

Phi Xi Omega Chapter
P.O. Box 328
San Marcos, TX 78666
Sherri H. Benn, Chapter President
Web: www.aka1908.com

Pi Mu Chapter, Baylor University
P.O. Box 85609
Waco, TX 76798
Christiana Onita, Chapter President
Tel: (254) 710-2371
Web: www.aka1908.com

Rho Iota Omega Chapter
P.O. Box 372
Odessa, TX 79760

Dorothy Greene Jackson, Chapter President
Web: www.aka1908.com

Rho Nu Chapter, Mid Western State University
3410 Taft Blvd.
P.O. Box 12802
Wichita Falls, TX 76308
Ashley N. Dennis, Chapter President
Web: www.aka1908.com

Rho Omicron Omega Chapter
P.O. Box 2814
Baytown, TX 77522
Lola Robinson, Chapter President
Web: www.aka1908.com

Rho Phi Omega Chapter
P.O. Box 6274
Bryan, TX 77805
Maria G. Pitre, Chapter President
Web: www.aka1908.com

Sigma Beta Chapter
6300 Ocean Dr.
Corpus Christi, TX 78412
Evbu Joan Osawaru, Chapter President
Web: www.aka1908.com

Sigma Epsilon Chapter
601 University Dr., LBJ Student Ctr.
San Marcos, TX 78666
Yolanda R. Washington, Chapter President
Web: www.aka1908.com

Sigma Kappa Chapter
P.O. Box 830454
Richardson, TX 75083
Erica Lewis, Chapter President
Web: www.aka1908.com

Sigma Theta Chapter
7502 Fondren Rd.
Houston, TX 77074
Courtney Smith, Chapter President
Web: www.aka1908.com

Tau Rho Omega Chapter
P.O. Box 116820
Carrollton, TX 75011
Beverly Terry Bolden, Chapter President
Web: www.aka1908.com

Tau Zeta Omega Chapter
P.O. Box 58592
Webster, TX 77598
Noreen Khan-Mayberry, Chapter President
Web: www.aka1908.com

Theta Delta Omega Chapter
716 W. Pine
Midland, TX 79705
Emma Threat, Chapter President
Web: www.aka1908.com

Theta Epsilon Chapter, Sam Houston State University
P.O. Box 2476
Huntsville, TX 77341
Rhonda King, Chapter President
Web: www.aka1908.com

Theta Gamma Omega Chapter
4710 Carrie Ann Ln.
Abilene, TX 79606
Terrenia M. Fitts, Chapter President
Web: www.aka1908.com

Theta Theta Chapter, Paul Quinn College
3837 Simpson Stuart
P.O. Box 191
Dallas, TX 75241
Zakkyya Watson, Chapter President
Web: www.aka1908.com

Upsilon Lambda Omega Chapter
P.O. Box 461
Desoto, TX 75123
Nona Eath, Chapter President
Web: www.aka1908.com

Upsilon Zeta Omega Chapter
P.O. Box 632754
Nacogdoches, TX 75963
Lawanda Alexander, Chapter President
Web: www.aka1908.com

Xi Alpha Omega Chapter
P.O. Box 70068
Houston, TX 77270
Shawn Simmons, Chapter President
Web: www.aka1908.com

Xi Psi Chapter, Texas A&M University
P.O. Box 2388
College Station, TX 77841
Shanee' D. Stewart, Chapter President

Web: www.aka1908.com

Xi Theta Omega Chapter
P.O. Box 151534
Arlington, TX 76015
Stephanie Craig Phillips, Chapter President
Web: www.aka1908.com

Zeta Beta Chapter, Lamar University
P.O. Box 10018
Beaumont, TX 77710
Kimosha Seastrunk, Chapter President
Web: www.aka1908.com

Zeta Chi Chapter, Jarvis Christian College
P.O. Box 1203
Hawkins, TX 75765
Ne'Keisha King, Chapter President
Web: www.aka1908.com

Zeta Gamma Chapter, Prairie View A&M University
P.O. Box 2531
Prairie View, TX 77446
Bridget Dew, Chapter President
Web: www.aka1908.com

Zeta Gamma Omega Chapter
P.O. Box 3028
Prairie View, TX 77446
Veronica Hines, Chapter President
Web: www.aka1908.com

Zeta Mu Chapter, University of Texas
P.O. Box 190887
Arlington, TX 76019
Marina Valley, Chapter President
Web: www.aka1908.com

Zeta Tau Chapter, Texas Tech University
Student Union
P.O. Box 54
Lubbock, TX 79406
Gwendolyn Y. Williams, Chapter President
Web: www.aka1908.com

ALPHA PHI ALPHA FRATERNITY, INC.
Alpha Sigma Lambda Chapter
P.O. Box 150303
Dallas, TX 75215
David W. Griffin, President
Tel: (214) 565-1907
Email: dwgriffin06@yahoo.com
Web: www.houseofalpha.com

BLACK GRADUATE STUDENTS ASSOCIATION
University of Texas at Austin
100-B W. Dean Keeton St.
Austin, TX 78712
Michael Stewart,,Chair
Tel: (512) 448-4922
Email: michael.stewart@mba04.mccombs.utexas.edu
Web: www.utexas.edu/students/bgsa/

BLACK STUDENT NURSES ASSOCIATION
University of Texas at Arlington
UTA Box 19407, 411 South Medderman
Arlington, TX 76019-0407
Elizabeth Poster, Dean
Tel: (817) 272-2776 Fax: (817) 272-5006
Web: www.uta.edu/nursing/bsna.htm

NATIONAL BLACK LAW STUDENTS ASSOCIATION
University of Texas Law School
727 E. 26th St.
Austin, TX 78705
Keith Smith, President
Tel: (512) 232-1393 Fax: (512) 232-1494
Email: mithkd@mail.utexas.edu
Web: www.utexas.edu/students/tmls

NATIONAL PAN-HELLENIC COUNCIL, INC.
Southwestern Region
P.O. Box 600751
Dallas, TX 75360
Candace E. Wicks, Regional Director
Tel: (214) 376-2061
Email: swesterndir@nphchq.org
Web: http://swnphc.tripod.com/southwesternregional/

TEXAS ALLIANCE FOR MINORITIES IN ENGINEERING, INC.
10100 Burnet Rd., University of Texas at Austin
#9200 Bldg. 16 #10
Austin, TX 78758
Shari Getz, Executive Director
Tel: (512) 471-6100 Fax: (512) 471-6797
Email: shari.getz@mail.utexas.edu
Web: www.tame.org

UTAH

POLITICAL ACTION

AMERICAN CIVIL LIBERTIES UNION
Utah Chapter
355 N. 300 West #1
Salt Lake City, UT 84103
Dani Eyer, Executive Director
Tel: (801) 521-9862 Fax: (801) 532-2850
Email: aclu@acluutah.org
Web: www.acluutah.org

STUDENT ORGANIZATION

ALPHA KAPPA ALPHA SORORITY, INC.
Upsilon Beta Omega Chapter
5106 Honey Clover Ct.
Murray, UT 84123
Frances Battle, Chapter President
Web: www.aka1908.com

ALPHA PHI ALPHA FRATERNITY, INC.
Iota Upsilon Chapter, Utah State University
UMC 0105
Logan, UT 84322
Web: www.alphaphialpha.net

Pi Xi Lambda Chapter
P.O. Box 973
Clearfield, UT 84015
Web: www.alphaphialpha.net

NATIONAL BLACK LAW STUDENTS ASSOCIATION
Brigham Young University Law School
P.O. Box 28000
Provo, UT 84602
Tel: (801) 378-4274 Fax: (801) 422-0389
Web: www.nblsa.org

LADIES OF AFRICA
8340 Greensboro Dr. #1001
McLean, VA 22102
Angie Zepal, President

VERMONT

POLITICAL ACTION

AMERICAN CIVIL LIBERTIES UNION
Vermont Chapter
137 Elm St.
Montpelier, VT 05602
Allen Gilbert, Executive Director
Tel: (802) 223-6304
Email: info@acluvt.org
Web: www.acluvt.org

VIRGIN ISLANDS

SPEC. INT., SOCIAL INTEREST

100 BLACK MEN OF US VIRGIN ISLANDS, INC.
P.O. Box 224605
Christiansted, St. Croix, VI 00822-4605
Gerard Luz James, President
Tel: (340) 778-8663 Fax: (340) 778-8661
Email: fdinhouse@aol.com

VIRGINIA

BUSINESS

AIRPORT MINORITY ADVISORY COUNCIL
2800 Shirlington Rd. #940
Arlington, VA 22206
William H. Swift, Chair
Tel: (703) 379-5701 Fax: (703) 379-5703
Email: wswift3703@aol.com
Web: www.amac-org.com

METROPOLITAN BUSINESS LEAGUE
115 E. Marshall St.
Richmond, VA 23219
Oliver R. Hun Singleton, Jr., President/CEO
Tel: (804) 649-7473 Fax: (804) 649-7474
Email: website@thembl.com
Web: www.thembl.com

NATIONAL BLACK FARMERS ASSOCIATION
Integrated Farmer
68 Wind Rd.
Bakerville, VA 23915
John W. Boyd, Jr., President
Tel: (434) 848-1865 Fax: (434) 848-3111
Email: johnwboyd2000@yahoo.com
Web: www.blackfarmers.org

NATIONAL MINORITY SUPPLIER DEVELOPMENT COUNCIL, INC.
Virginia Minority Supplier Development Council, Headquarters & Central Virginia Office
9210 Arboretum Pkwy. #150
Richmond, VA 23236
Sylvia B. Thomas, Director
Tel: (804) 320-2100 Fax: (804) 320-3966
Email: sylvia.thomas@vmsdc.org
Web: www.vmsdc.org

NATIONAL MINORITY SUPPLIER DEVELOPMENT COUNCIL, INC.
Virginia Regional Minority Supplier Development Council, Regional Council. Staunton Regional Office
SunTrust Bank Bldg., 2-14 W. Beverley St.
Staunton, VA 24401-4201
Neslon Grabes, Western Virginia Director
Tel: (540) 885-6748 Fax: (540) 885-9216
Email: nelson.graves@vmsdc.org
Web: www.vmsdc.org

PAINTER BLACK UNITED FUND, INC.
Rural Route 178, RFD Box 533
Painter, VA 23420
Bedford Rogers, President
Tel: (757) 442-7820

PRIDE AFRICA
100 N. Pitt St. #202
Alexandria, VA 22314
Jonathan Campaigne, Executive Director
Tel: (703) 519-7778 Fax: (703) 519-7557
Email: jfc@prideafrica.com
Web: www.prideafrica.com

CULTURAL

AFRICAN AMERICAN HISTORIC ASSOCIATION
P.O. Box 340
4243 Loudoun Ave.
The Plains, VA 20198-0340
Karen Hughes White, President/Executive Director
Tel: (540) 253-7488 Fax: (540) 253-5126
Email: aaha@infionline.net
Web: www.afro-americanofva.org

ALEXANDRIA BLACK HISTORY MUSEUM
902 Wythe St.
Alexandria, VA 22314
Louis Hicks, Director
Tel: (703) 838-4356 Fax: (703) 706-3999
Email: black.history@alexandriava.gov
Web: www.alexblackhistory.org

ASSOCIATION FOR THE STUDY OF AFRICAN AMERICAN LIFE AND HISTORY
Luther P. Jackson Chapter-Northern Virginia
8200 Greensboro Dr. #500
McLean, VA 22102
Lou Phillips, Chapter President
Tel: (703) 821-3300 Fax: (703) 821-3996
Email: louphillips@mtba.org
Web: www.asalh.org

BLACK CULTURAL CENTER
Virginia Polytechnic Institute and State University
126 Squires Student Ctr., Multicultural Programs, Dean of Students Office
Blacksburg, VA 24061-0138
Kimberly Philpott, Assistant Director of Student Life and Advocacy
Tel: (540) 231-6023 Fax: (540) 231-4035
Email: multprog@vt.edu
Web: www.mcp.vt.edu/culturalcenters/bcc.shtml

VIRGINIA FOUNDATION FOR THE HUMANITIES
African American Heritage Program
145 Ednam Dr.
Charlottesville, VA 22903-4749
Christina Draper, Director
Tel: (434) 243-5528 Fax: (434) 296-4714
Email: vfhinfo@virginia.edu
Web: www.virginiafoundation.org

ENTERTAINMENT

NATIONAL AFRICAN AMERICAN RV'ERS ASSOCIATION
Virginia Camping Cardinals
1548 Lauren Ashleigh Dr.
Chesapeake, VA 23321
Irvin Askew, President
Tel: (757) 465-3315
Email: askewbrdg@aol.com
Web: www.naarva.com

LAW ENFORCEMENT

NATIONAL ORGANIZATION OF BLACK LAW ENFORCEMENT EXECUTIVES
Central Virginia Chapter
P.O. Box 26851
U.S. Postal Inspection Service
Richmond, VA 23261-6851
Morris E. Roberson, President
Tel: (804) 598-1537 Fax: (804) 598-1569
Email: morris.roberson@worldnet.att.net
Web: www.noblecvc.org

Hampton Roads Virginia Chapter
P.O. Box 85
Virginia Department of Alcoholic Beverage Control
Norfolk, VA 23501-0085
Joseph S. Johnson, Assistant Special Agent in Charge
Tel: (757) 825-7832 Fax: (757) 825-7884
Email: noblehrva@homestead.com
Web: www.noblehrva.homestead.com

National Office
4609 Pinecrest Office Park Dr. #F
Alexandria, VA 22312-1442
Jessie Lee, Executive Director
Tel: (703) 658-1529 Fax: (703) 658-9479
Email: noble@noblenatl.org
Web: www.noblenational.org

Northern Virginia Chapter
P.O. Box 5096
Omniplex, International
Herndon, VA 22070
Patsy Bennett, Supervisory Viewer
Tel: (703) 652-3440
Email: pfayben@hotmail.com
Web: www.noblenorthernvirginia.org

MULTI-PURPOSE

ETHIOPIAN COMMUNITY DEVELOPMENT COUNCIL, INC.
901 S. Highland St.
Arlington, VA 22204
Dr. Tsehayi Teserra, President
Tel: (703) 685-0510 Fax: (703) 685-0529
Email: info@ecdcinternational.org
Web: www.ecdcinternational.org

NATIONAL ASSOCIATION FOR THE ADVANCEMENT OF COLORED PEOPLE
Alexandria Branch
P.O. Box 1740
Alexandria, VA 22312
S. Howard Woodson, President
Tel: (703) 684-6190 Fax: (703) 619-0450
Email: naacp@naacpalexandria.org
Web: www.naacpalexandria.org

Norfolk State University Chapter
700 Park Ave.
Norfolk, VA 23504
Rudolph Wilson, Director
Tel: (757) 823-8999 Fax: (757) 823-9413
Web: www.naacp.virginia.com

Virginia State Conference NAACP
P.O. Box 27212
Richmond, VA 23261
Linda Thomas, President
Tel: (804) 321-5678 Fax: (804) 321-5687
Email: statenaacp@aol.com

POLITICAL ACTION

AMERICAN ASSOCIATION FOR AFFIRMATIVE ACTION
12100 Sunset Hills Rd. #130
Reston, VA 20190
Laura Garcia Hacek, Executive Director
Tel: (800) 252-8952 Fax: (703) 435-4390
Email: execdir@affirmativeaction.org
Web: www.affirmativeaction.org

AMERICAN CIVIL LIBERTIES UNION
Virginia Chapter
6 N. 6th St. #400
Richmond, VA 23219
Kent Willis, Executive Director
Tel: (804) 644-8022 Fax: (804) 649-2733
Email: acluva@acluva.org
Web: www.acluva.org

BLACKS IN GOVERNMENT
Region III-Central Virginia Chapter
P.O. Box 5651
Fort Lee, VA 23801-0651
Tony F. Gaines, Chapter President
Tel: (804) 765-2835
Email: central.virginia@bignet.org

Region III-Hampton Roads Ebonact Chapter
P.O. Box 4350
Ft. Eustis, VA 23604
Tanya Garrett, Chapter President

Tel: (757) 878-7606
Email: hampton.roads@bignet.org
Web: www.bignet.org

Region III-Tidewater Chapter
3813 Headwind Ln.
Portsmouth, VA 23703
Valarie Jones, Chapter President
Tel: (757) 396-7165
Email: tidewater@bignet.org
Web: www.bignet.org

Region XI-Big IMPACT Chapter
P.O. Box 3444
Arlington, VA 22203
William Spencer, Chapter President
Tel: (703) 882-0332 Fax: (703) 882-2880
Email: big.impact@bignet.org
Web: www.bignet.org

Region XI-Big Pentagon Chapter
P.O. Box 2332
Arlington, VA 22202-0332
Dolores Richards, Chapter President
Tel: (703) 602-1713
Email: deloisrichards@hqda.army.mil
Web: www.bignet.org

Region XI-KHALFANI Chapter
P.O. Box 222341
Chantilly, VA 20153-2341
Kenneth D. Phillips, Chapter President
Tel: (703) 808-1019
Web: www.bignet.org

Region XI-UMOJA Chapter
P.O. Box 259
McLean, VA 22101
Morgann J. Royster, Chapter President
Tel: (703) 874-4338 Fax: (703) 874-4351
Email: jrsygryll@aol.com
Web: www.bignet.org

PROFESSIONAL

AMERICAN ANTHROPOLOGICAL ASSOCIATION
Association of Black Anthropologist
2200 Wilson Blvd. #600
Arlington, VA 22201
Bill Davis, Executive Director
Tel: (703) 528-1902 Fax: (703) 528-3546
Web: www.aaanet.org

AMERICAN ASSOCIATION OF BLACKS IN ENERGY
North Carolina Chapter
P.O. Box 1551
c/o Progress Energy
Raleigh, VA 27602
Carl L. Wilkins, President
Tel: (919) 857-9008 Fax: (919) 832-2696
Email: cwilkins@advancedenergy.org
Web: www.aabe-nc.org

BLACK DATA PROCESSING ASSOCIATES
Richmond Metropolitan Area Chapter
P.O. Box 26243
Richmond, VA 23260
Maurisa L. Westbury, Chapter President
Tel: (804) 751-5171
Email: president@bdparichmond.org
Web: www.bdparichmond.org

NATIONAL ASSOCIATION OF MINORITY MEDIA EXECUTIVES
1921 Gallows Rd. #600
Vienna, VA 22182-3900
Toni F. Laws, Executive Director
Tel: (703) 893-2410 Fax: (703) 893-2414
Email: tlaws@namme.org
Web: www.namme.org

NATIONAL BLACK MBA ASSOCIATION, INC.
Richmond Chapter-East
P.O. Box 15492
Richmond, VA 23227
Jeanette S. Barnes, President
Tel: (804) 222-2005
Email: membership@ricbmbaa.org
Web: www.ricbmbaa.org

NATIONAL FORUM FOR BLACK PUBLIC ADMINISTRATORS
Northern Virginia Chapter
2419 S. 1st St.
Arlington, VA 22204
James L. Younger, Deputy Chief of Police
Tel: (703) 228-4095 Fax: (703) 228-4128
Web: www.nfbpa.org

NATIONAL MEDICAL ASSOCIATION
Hopewell Medical Group
354 Suiry ,VA 23883
401-405 Hopewell St.
Hopewell, VA 23860
June Tunstall, M.D., President

Tel: (757) 294-3188 Fax: (757) 294-0108
Email: jtunst3611@aol.com
Web: www.nmanet.org

NATIONAL SOCIETY OF BLACK ENGINEERS
National Office
1454 Duke St.
Alexandria, VA 22314
Gary S. May, Chairperson
Tel: (703) 549-2207 Fax: (703) 683-5312
Email: info@nsbe.org
Web: www.nsbe.org

NATIONAL SOCIETY OF BLACK PHYSICISTS
6704G Lee Hwy.
Arlington, VA 22205
Tel: (703) 536-4207 Fax: (703) 536-4203
Email: headquarters@nsbp.org
Web: www.nsbp.org

UNITY: JOURNALISTS OF COLOR, INC.
1601 N. Kent St. #1003
Arlington, VA 22209
Anna M. Lopez, Executive Director
Tel: (703) 469-2100 Fax: (703) 469-2108
Email: info@unityjournalists.org
Web: www.unityjournalists.org

RELIGIOUS

FIRST AFRICAN METHODIST EPISCOPAL CHURCH
10313 S. Grant Ave.
Manassas, VA 20110
Retha M. Fulmore, Director/Public Relations
Tel: (703) 361-8791 Fax: (703) 361-3440
Email: firstamechurch@msn.com
Web: www.famechurch.com

SPEC. INT., ALCOHOL/DRUG CTR.

ONE CHURCH-ONE ADDICT, INC.
805 King St. #400
Alexandria, VA 22314
Father George Clements, President
Tel: (703) 299-0088 Fax: (703) 299-3089
Email: ocoaocoi@aol.com

SPEC. INT., CHILD CARE

NATIONAL CENTER FOR MISSING & EXPLOITED CHILDREN
National Headquarters
Charles B. Wang Intl. Children's Bldg., 699 Prince St.
Alexandria, VA 22314-3175
Herb Jones, Vice President of External Affairs
Tel: (703) 274-3900 Fax: (703) 274-2200
Web: www.missingkids.com

SPEC. INT., EDUCATION

BLACK FACULTY AND STAFF FORUM
College of William and Mary
P.O. Box 8795
Williamsburg, VA 23187-8795
Jacqueline Smith, Chair
Tel: (757) 221-7546
Email: jxsmit@wm.edu
Web: http://web.wm.edu/bfsf/

NATIONAL ASSOCIATION FOR MULTICULTURAL EDUCATION
Virginia Chapter
James Madison University, Dept. of Social Work
MCS-4303
Harrisonburg, VA 22807
Marilyn Osborne Wakefield, Contact
Tel: (540) 568-2925
Email: wakefimo@jmu.edu
Web: www.nameorg.org

UNITED NEGRO COLLEGE FUND
8260 Willow Oaks Corporate Dr.
Fairfax, VA 22031
Dr. Michael L. Lomax, President/CEO
Tel: (703) 205-3400
Web: www.uncf.org

SPEC. INT., EMPLOYMENT

NATIONAL NAVAL OFFICERS ASSOCIATION, INC.
Washington DC Chapter
P.O. Box 30850
Alexandria, VA 22310
CAPT Willie Evans, Treasurer
Tel: (202) 874-4994
Web: www.dcnnoa.org

SPEC. INT., HEALTH SERVICES

AMERICAN DIABETES ASSOCIATION NATIONAL OFFICE
African American Program
1701 N. Beauregard St.
Alexandria, VA 22311
Gaynell Bowden-Diaz, Director
Tel: (703) 549-2047 Fax: (703) 253-4358
Email: customerservice@diabetes.org
Web: www.diabetes.org

SPEC. INT., HUMAN RELATIONS

TINNER HILL HERITAGE FOUNDATION
105 N. Virginia Ave.
Falls Church, VA 22046
Edwin Bancroft Henderson, II, President
Tel: (703) 241-4109 Fax: (703) 241-4169
Email: info@tinnerhill.org
Web: www.tinnerhill.org

SPEC. INT., SOCIAL INTEREST

100 BLACK MEN OF VIRGINIA PENINSULA, INC.
P.O. Box 2400
Newport News, VA 23609
Thaddeus B. Holloman, President
Tel: (757) 930-3012

BLACK UNITED FUND OF HAMPTON ROADS , INC.
555 Fenchurch St. #106
Norfolk, VA 23510
Douglas Johnson, President
Tel: (757) 627-2585 Fax: (757) 627-8010
Web: www.nbuf.org

CONCERNED BLACK MEN, INC.
Richmond Chapter
P.O. Box 4747
Richmond, VA 23220
William Nelson, President
Tel: (804) 343-2680 Fax: (804) 646-1573
Email: cannonth@ci.richmond.va.us
Web: www.cbmnational.org

FREEDOM FORUM WORLD CENTER
International Division
1101 Wilson Blvd.
Arlington, VA 22209-2248
Charles L. Overby, Chairman/CEO
Tel: (703) 528-0800 Fax: (703) 284-2836
Email: news@freedomforum.org
Web: www.freedomforum.org

NATIONAL URBAN LEAGUE, INC.
Northern Virginia Urban League
1315 Duke St.
Alexandria, VA 22314
Lavern J. Chatman, President/CEO
Tel: (703) 836-2858 Fax: (703) 836-8948
Email: chatmanlj@aol.com
Web: www.nvul.org

Urban League of Greater Richmond, Inc.
511 W. Grace St.
Richmond, VA 23220
Thomas J. Victory, Interim President/CEO
Tel: (804) 649-8407 Fax: (804) 649-1745
Email: tvictory@urbanleaguerichmond.org
Web: www.urbanleaguerichmond.org

Urban League of Hampton Roads
840 Church St. #I
Norfolk, VA 23510
Edith G. White, President
Tel: (757) 627-0864 Fax: (757) 627-8016
Email: ewhite@ulhr.org
Web: www.ulhr.org

TUSKEGEE AIRMEN, INC.
National Office
1501 Lee Hwy. #130
Arlington, VA 22209-1109
Brian R. Smith, President
Tel: (703) 522-8590 Fax: (703) 522-8542
Email: hqtai@tuskegeeairmen.org
Web: www.tuskegeeairmen.org

SPEC. INT., VOLUNTARY SERVICE

AMERICA'S DEVELOPMENT FOUNDATION
101 N. Union St. #200
Alexandria, VA 22314
Michael D. Miller, President
Tel: (703) 836-2717 Fax: (703) 836-3379
Email: mmiller@adfusa.org
Web: www.adfusa.org

SPEC. INT., WOMEN

BLACK WOMEN UNITED FOR ACTION
6551 Loisdale Ct. #218
Springfield, VA 22150
Sheila B. Coates, President
Tel: (703) 922-5757 Fax: (703) 922-7681
Email: bwufa@hotmail.com
Web: www.bwufa.org

FEMINIST MAJORITY FOUNDATION
1600 Wilson Blvd. #801
Arlington, VA 22209
Eleanor Smeal, President
Tel: (703) 522-2214 Fax: (703) 522-2219
Email: femmaj@feminist.org
Web: www.feminist.org

INTERNATIONAL BLACK WOMEN'S CONGRESS
555 Fenchurch St. #102
Norfolk, VA 23510
Dr. Sahron R. Brownbailey, President
Tel: (757) 625-0500 Fax: (757) 625-1905
Email: ibwc1609@cs.com
Web: www.ibwc.info

RAPE AGRESSION DEFENSE SYSTEM
Falls Church City Police Department
300 Park Ave.
Falls Church, VA 22046
Officer Stephanie Jones, Instructor
Tel: (757) 868-4400 Fax: (757) 868-4401
Email: radinfo@rad-systems.com
Web: www.rad-systems.com

WOMEN IN COMMUNITY SERVICE, INC.
1900 N. Beauregard St. #103
Alexandria, VA 22311
Jacquelyn L. Lendsey, President/CEO
Tel: (800) 442-9427 Fax: (703) 671-4489
Email: wicsnatl@wics.org
Web: www.wics.org

SPEC. INT., YOUTH

JACK & JILL OF AMERICA, INC.
Mid-Atlantic Region
13912 Sunrise Bluff Rd.
Midlothian, VA 23112
Kyle R. Grinnage, Regional Director
Tel: (804) 608-8386 Fax: (804) 608-8387
Email: regionaldirector@comcast.net
Web: www.jack-and-jill.org

STUDENT ORGANIZATION

ALPHA KAPPA ALPHA SORORITY, INC.
Alpha Epsilon Chapter
P.O. Box 9076
Petersburg, VA 23803
Valary T. Rawlings, Chapter President
Web: www.aka1908.com

Alpha Eta Chapter
5008 Sandpiper Dr.
Richmond, VA 23227
Lolita D. Cobbs, Chapter President
Web: www.aka1908.com

Alpha Phi Omega Chapter
P.O. Box 3406
Danville, VA 24543
Gwendolyn Edwards, Chapter President
Web: www.aka1908.com

Alpha Upsilon Chapter
115 College Dr.
Lawrenceville, VA 23868
Renee L. McKeever, Chapter President
Web: www.aka1908.com

Beta Chi Omega Chapter
P.O. Box 13891
Roanoke, VA 24038
Demetria Tucker, Chapter President
Web: www.aka1908.com

Chi Beta Omega Chapter
P.O. Box 145
Falls Church, VA 22040
Sheila Y. Harvey, Chapter President
Web: www.aka1908.com

Delta Epsilon Chapter
P.O. Box 2068
700 Park Ave.
Norfolk, VA 23504
Kristal S. Whitehead, Chapter President
Web: www.aka1908.com

Delta Omega Chapter
P.O. Box 2224
Petersburg, VA 23804
Julia W. Pope, Chapter President

Web: www.aka1908.com

Eta Phi Omega Chapter
P.O. Box 5783
Charlottesville, VA 22905
Jacquelyn Cecelia Perry, Chapter President
Web: www.aka1908.com

Gamma Delta Omega Chapter
P.O. Box 7393
Portsmouth, VA 23707
Wendy A. Hunter, Chapter President
Web: www.aka1908.com

Gamma Iota Omega Chapter
P.O. Box 11842
Lynchburg, VA 24506
Mable Hamlette-Franklin, Chapter President
Web: www.aka1908.com

Gamma Lambda Omega Chapter
P.O. Box 905
Lawrenceville, VA 23868
Leorie Kenyatta Mallory, Chapter President
Web: www.aka1908.com

Gamma Theta Chapter
P.O. Box 7066
Hampton, VA 23666
Dawna Anne Bonne, Chapter President
Web: www.aka1908.com

Gamma Upsilon Omega Chapter
305 Shoreline Dr.
Hampton, VA 23664
Jeanette Clarey, Chapter President
Web: www.aka1908.com

Iota Omega Chapter
P.O. Box 2732
Norfolk, VA 23501
Mamie Ratliff, Chapter President
Web: www.aka1908.com

Kappa Delta Omega Chapter
P.O. Box 726
Martinsville, VA 24114
Jean I Hairston, Chapter President
Web: www.aka1908.com

Kappa Rho Omega Chapter
P.O. Box 788
Farmville, VA 23901
Avis Gresby, Chapter President
Web: www.aka1908.com

Lambda Delta Chapter
P.O. Box 2994
Farmville, VA 23909
Teneka Trent, Chapter President
Web: www.aka1908.com

Lambda Gamma Omega Chapter
P.O. Box 65124
Virginia Beach, VA 23467
Annie M. Parker, Chapter President
Web: www.aka1908.com

Lambda Kappa Omega Chapter
P.O. Box 2323
Fairfax, VA 22031
Ruth Laverne Buchanan, Chapter President
Web: www.aka1908.com

Lambda Lambda Omega Chapter
P.O. Box 918
Williamsburg, VA 23187
Dorothy L. Moore-Moyler, Chapter President
Web: www.aka1908.com

Lambda Omega Chapter
P.O. Box 120273
Newport News, VA 23612
Joan Spratley, Chapter President
Web: www.aka1908.com

Lambda Psi Omega Chapter
P.O. Box 702
Franklin, VA 23851
Diane Harris, Chapter President
Web: www.aka1908.com

Omicron Chi Omega Chapter
P.O. Box 1905
Woodbridge, VA 22195
Leona Johnson, Chapter President
Web: www.aka1908.com

Omicron Iota Chapter
4400 University Dr.
Fairfax, VA 22030
DeJuan Stroman, Chapter President
Web: www.aka1908.com

Omicron Pi Omega Chapter
P.O. Box 3079
Chesapeake, VA 23327
Wilberta G. Mccoy, Chapter President
Web: www.aka1908.com

Omicron Sigma Chapter
P.O. Box 11732
Lynchburg, VA 24506
Aba E. Mills-Robertson, Chapter President
Web: www.aka1908.com

Phi Chi Omega Chapter
P.O. Box 341
Smithfield, VA 23431
Joanne Wilkerson Jones, Chapter President
Web: www.aka1908.com

Phi Nu Omega Chapter
P.O. Box 9270
Alexandria, VA 22304
Sharon H. Worthy, Chapter President
Web: www.aka1908.com

Pi Epsilon Omega Chapter
P.O. Box 544
Exmore, VA 23350
Sheila T. Walker, Chapter President
Web: www.aka1908.com

Pi Rho Omega Chapter
P.O. Box 35593
Richmond, VA 23235
Carolyn Walker, Chapter President
Web: www.aka1908.com

Rho Eta Omega Chapter
P.O. Box 6562
Richmond, VA 23230
Linda Curry Brown, Chapter President
Web: www.aka1908.com

Rho Mu Chapter
P.O. Box 51
28 Westhampton Way
Richmond, VA 23173
Jacqueline Alycia Gordon, Chapter President
Web: www.aka1908.com

Sigma Alpha Chapter
P.O. Box 3369
Arlington, VA 22203
La Sha Crosby, Chapter President
Web: www.aka1908.com

Sigma Gamma Omega Chapter
P.O. Box 688
Harrisonburg, VA 22801
Joanne Veal Gabbin, Chapter President
Web: www.aka1908.com

Tau Mu Omega Chapter
P.O. Box 397
Christiansburg, VA 24073
Carlotta Lewis, Chapter President
Web: www.aka1908.com

Tau Phi Omega Chapter
1978 N. Westchester Dr.
Richmond, VA 23805
Rolaunda H. Miles, Chapter President
Web: www.aka1908.com

Theta Chi Chapter
P.O. Box 6989
Radford, VA 24142
Angela Gravely, Chapter President
Web: www.aka1908.com

Theta Kappa Chapter
P.O. Box 415
Newcomb Hall Station
Charlottesville, VA 22904
Elisa Dobbins, Chapter President
Web: www.aka1908.com

Upsilon Omega Chapter
P.O. Box 25306
Richmond, VA 23260
Lillie Mae Taylor, Chapter President
Web: www.aka1908.com

Upsilon Omicron Omega Chapter
P.O. Box 12832
Norfolk, VA 23541
Delores E. Wilson, Chapter President
Web: www.aka1908.com

Xi Upsilon Omega Chapter
P.O. Box 8363
Frederickburg, VA 22404
Brenda Collymore, Chapter President
Web: www.aka1908.com

Zeta Chi Omega Chapter
P.O. Box 10627
Alexandria, VA 22310
Theresa L. Shannon, Chapter President
Web: www.aka1908.com

Zeta Epsilon Omega Chapter
P.O. Box 3276
Suffolk, VA 23434
Dorothy Shelton Diggs, Chapter President
Web: www.aka1908.com

ALPHA PHI ALPHA FRATERNITY, INC.
Alpha Phi Lambda Chapter
P.O. Box 816
Norfolk, VA 23510
Email: alphaphilambda@alphaeast.com
Web: www.alphaphialpha.net

Delta Beta Lambda Chapter
P.O. Box 7239
Hampton, VA 23666
Email: deltabetalambda@alphaeast.com
Web: www.alphaphialpha.net

Gamma Chapter, Virginia Union University
P.O. Box 25097
Richmond, VA 23260
Laurence E.E. Whitney, President
Email: gamma07@hotmail.com
Web: www.geocities.com/gamma1907

Iota Tau Lambda Chapter
P.O. Box 202
Charlotte Court House, VA 23923
Email: iotataulambda@alphaeast.com
Web: www.alphaphialpha.net

Sigma Pi Chapter, Lynchburg College
Office of Student Activities, 1501 Lakeside Dr.
Lynchburg, VA 24501
Email: sigmapi@alphaeast.com
Web: www.alphaphialpha.net

Xi Delta Chapter, James Madison University
P.O. Box 8041
Harrisonburg, VA 22807
Email: xidelta@alphaeast.com
Web: www.alphaphialpha.net

Zeta Upsilon Lamda Chapter
P.O. Box 8234
Reston, VA 20190
Email: zetaupsilonlambda@alphaeast.com
Web: www.alphaphialpha.net

BLACK STUDENT ALLIANCE
James Madison University
800 S. Main St. #8067
Harrisonburg, VA 22807
Rasheeda Miller, President
Tel: (540) 568-6361
Email: jmubsa@hotmail.com
Web: http://orgs.jmu.edu/bsa

NATIONAL BLACK LAW STUDENTS ASSOCIATION
University of Virginia School of Law
580 Massie Rd.
Charlottesville, VA 22903
Archie L. Alston, II, President
Tel: (434) 924-7632
Email: uvablsa@virginia.edu
Web: www.student.virginia.edu/~uvablsa

NATIONAL PAN-HELLENIC COUNCIL, INC.
Eastern Region
P.O. Box 25358
Richmond, VA 23260-5358
Francine P. Young, Regional Director
Tel: (804) 257-7285 Fax: (804) 358-7283
Email: easterndir@nphchq.org
Web: www.nphchq.org

WASHINGTON

ENTERTAINMENT

NATIONAL AFRICAN AMERICAN RV'ERS ASSOCIATION
Emerald City Rolling Roadsters Chapter
4550 SE Basswood Ln.
Port Orchard, WA 98366
Louis J. Henderson, President
Tel: (360) 871-0984
Email: hendoo5@msn.com
Web: www.naarva.com

NATIONAL AFRICAN AMERICAN RV'ERS ASSOCIATION
Funseekers/Rain City Travelers Chapter
300 25th Ave.
Seattle, WA 98122
Jerelene T. Armstead, President
Tel: (206) 322-3461
Email: jerrytrv@aol.com
Web: www.naarva.com

NATIONAL AFRICAN AMERICAN RV'ERS ASSOCIATION
The Northwest Travelers Chapter
P.O. Box 111658
Tacoma, WA 98411
Chico McClatcher, President
Email: mcclathcer@aol.com
Web: www.naarva.com

POLITICAL ACTION

AMERICAN CIVIL LIBERTIES UNION
Washington State Chapter
705 2nd Ave. #300
Seattle, WA 98104
Kathleen Taylor, Executive Director
Tel: (206) 624-2184
Email: administration@aclu-wa.org
Web: www.aclu-wa.org

ASSOCIATION OF COMMUNITY ORGANIZATIONS FOR REFORM NOW
Burien Office
134 SW 153rd St. #D
Burien, WA 98166
Tel: (206) 723-5845 Fax: (206) 246-1841
Email: waacorn@acorn.org
Web: www.acorn.org

BLACKS IN GOVERNMENT
Region X
22443 Foss Rd. NE
Paulsbo, WA 98370
Walter E. Washington, President
Tel: (360) 697-0026
Email: region10.president@bignet.org
Web: www.bignet.org

Region X-Federal Center South Chapter
21507 84th Ave., West
Edmonds, WA 98026
Theola Hall-Austin, Chapter President
Tel: (206) 764-3777
Email: region10.president@bignet.org
Web: www.bignet.org

Region X-Port of Seattle Chapter
P.O. Box 68727
Seattle, WA 98003
Tina Bush, Chapter President
Tel: (206) 988-5598 Fax: (206) 439-7725
Email: bush.t@portseattle.org
Web: www.bignet.org

Region X-Seattle Chapter
P.O. Box 21005
Seattle, WA 9811-3974
Freddie Curry, Chapter President
Tel: (206) 220-5669
Email: seattle@bignet.org
Web: www.bignet.org

Region X-Southeast Chapter
P.O. Box 69782
Seattle, WA 98168
Lloyd Dow, Chapter President
Tel: (206) 684-0620
Email: southeast@bignet.org
Web: www.bignet.org

Region X-Tacoma/Pierce County Chapter
P.O. Box 5105
Tacoma, WA 98405-0105
Ellen R. Smith, Chapter President
Tel: (206) 753-3397
Web: www.bignet.org

Region X-Yakima Valley Chapter
P.O. Box 2571
Yakima, WA 98907
Ghanneyatun Hadee, Chapter President
Tel: (509) 575-2677
Web: www.bignet.org

PROFESSIONAL

NATIONAL ASSOCIATION OF BLACK ACCOUNTANTS, INC.
Seattle Chapter
2301 S. Jackson St. #101G
Seattle, WA 98144
George Stewart, Contact
Tel: (206) 328-8554 Fax: (206) 328-0383
Email: stewcpasea@aol.com
Web: www.nabainc.org

NATIONAL MEDICAL ASSOCIATION
Region VI-Washington State Medical Society
1511 40th Ave.
Seattle, WA 98122
Gail N. Morgan, M.D., Chapter President
Tel: (206) 860-1063 Fax: (206) 320-8697
Email: gnmorganmd@qwest.net
Web: www.nmanet.org

SPEC. INT., AIDS

PEOPLE OF COLOR AGAINST AIDS NETWORK
2200 Rainier Ave., South
Seattle, WA 98144
Kiande Jakada, Operations Manager
Tel: (206) 322-7061 Fax: (206) 322-7204
Email: kiande@pocaan.org
Web: www.pocaan.org

SPEC. INT., SOCIAL INTEREST

NATIONAL BLACK UNITED FRONT
Seattle Chapter
930 24th South
Seattle, WA 98144
Charles Rolland, Chair
Tel: (206) 325-9456 Fax: (206) 323-0458
Email: rolland@wolfenet.com
Web: www.nbufront.org

NATIONAL URBAN LEAGUE, INC.
Tacoma Urban League
2550 S. Yakima Ave.
Tacoma, WA 98405
Steven P. Ellis, President/CEO
Tel: (253) 383-2007 Fax: (253) 383-4818
Web: www.tacomaurbanleague.org

Urban League of Metropolitan Seattle
105 14th Ave.
Seattle, WA 98122
James Kelly, President/CEO
Tel: (206) 461-3792 Fax: (206) 461-8425
Email: info@urbanleague.org
Web: www.urbanleague.org

SPEC. INT., WOMEN

FREEDOM SOCIALIST PARTY/RADICAL WOMEN
Seattle Office
New Freeway Hall, 5018 Rainier Ave., South
Seattle, WA 98118
Luma Nichol, Organizer
Tel: (206) 722-2453 Fax: (206) 723-7691
Email: fspseattle@mindspring.com
Web: www.socialism.com

NORTHWEST WOMEN'S LAW CENTER
3161 Elliott Ave. #101
Seattle, WA 98121
Lisa M. Stone, Executive Director
Tel: (206) 682-9552 Fax: (206) 521-4317
Email: nwwlc@nwwlc.org
Web: www.nwwlc.org

STUDENT ORGANIZATION

ALPHA KAPPA ALPHA SORORITY, INC.
Delta Upsilon Omega Chapter
P.O. Box 28656
Seattle, WA 98118
Annette Schley, Chapter President
Web: www.aka1908.com

Kappa Sigma Chapter
P.O. Box 3003
Pullman, WA 99165
Carolyn Wright, Chapter President
Web: www.aka1908.com

Zeta Omega Omega Chapter
P.O. Box 11072
Tacoma, WA 98411
Regina Tyner Glenn, Chapter President
Web: www.aka1908.com

NATIONAL BLACK LAW STUDENTS ASSOCIATION
Gonzaga University School of Law
P.O. Box 3528
Spokane, WA 99220
BLSA President
Tel: (509) 323-5824
Web: www.nblsa.org

WEST VIRGINIA

POLITICAL ACTION

AMERICAN CIVIL LIBERTIES UNION
West Virginia Chapter
P.O. Box 3952
Charleston, WV 25339-3952

Andrew Schneider, Executive Director
Tel: (304) 345-9246 Fax: (304) 345-9262
Email: wvaclu@aol.com
Web: www.aclu-wv.org

BLACKS IN GOVERNMENT
Region III-Mandela Chapter
Veteran Affairs Medical Ctr.
Martinsburg, WV 25401
Charles Kidrick, Chapter President
Tel: (304) 263-0811
Email: region3.president@bignet.org
Web: www.bignet.org

STUDENT ORGANIZATION

ALPHA KAPPA ALPHA SORORITY, INC.
Alpha Omicron Omega Chapter
P.O. Box 181
Institute, WV 25112
Ralpheal Hill, Chapter President
Web: www.aka1908.com

Beta Beta Omega Chapter
1032 Temple St.
South Charleston, WV 25312
Sherrie Lynn Davis, Chapter President
Web: www.aka1908.com

Beta Lambda Omega Chapter
P.O. Box 385
Bluefield, WV 24701
Robin Rosenbalm Powell, Chapter President
Web: www.aka1908.com

Beta Omicron Chapter
219 Rock St.
Bluefield, WV 24701
Timitra Spencer, Chapter President
Web: www.aka1908.com

Beta Tau Omega Chapter
P.O. Box 1934
Huntington, WV 25720
Cheryl Lynne Henderson, Chapter President
Web: www.aka1908.com

Beta Theta Omega Chapter
Box 117A
Rd. #3
New Cumberland, WV 26047
Patricia Easterling, Chapter President
Web: www.aka1908.com

Epsilon Alpha Omega Chapter
P.O. Box 864
Logan, WV 25601
Ora Hagood, Chapter President
Web: www.aka1908.com

Epsilon Delta Omega Chapter
P.O. Box 743
Beckley, WV 25802
Anita Law, Chapter President
Web: www.aka1908.com

Eta Zeta Chapter
2W38 Memorial Student Ctr.
Huntington, WV 25701
Adrienne Smith, Chapter President
Web: www.aka1908.com

Nu Chapter
P.O. Box 751
Institute, WV 25112
Autumn Melinda Anderson, Chapter President
Web: www.aka1908.com

Nu Pi Chapter
105 Harriet
Dunbar, WV 25064
Mikael Joy Terry, Chapter President
Web: www.aka1908.com

ALPHA PHI ALPHA FRATERNITY, INC.
Alpha Iota Lambda Chapter
P.O. Box 904
Institute, WV 25112
Web: www.alphaphialpha.net

Alpha Zeta Chapter, West Virginia State College
P.O. Box 415
Institute, WV 25112
Web: www.alphaphialpha.net

Alpha Zeta Lambda Chapter
P.O. Box 671
Bluefield, WV 24701
Web: www.alphaphialpha.net

Beta Theta Chapter, Bluefield State College
P.O. Box 506
Bluefield, WV 24701
Web: www.alphaphialpha.net

Nu Nu Chapter, Marshall University
P.O. Box 1116
Huntington, WV 25713
Web: www.alphaphialpha.net

Pi Mu Chapter, West Virginia University
P.O. Box 1262
Morgantown, WV 26505
Web: www.alphaphialpha.net

Rho Tau Chapter, West Virginia Wesleyan College
P.O. Box 155
Buckhannon, WV 26201
Web: www.alphaphialpha.net

NATIONAL BLACK LAW STUDENTS ASSOCIATION
West Virginia University College of Law
P.O. Box 6130
Morgantown, WV 26506-6130
Brandolyn Felton, President
Tel: (304) 291-5576
Email: bfelton2@mix.wvu.edu
Web: www.wvu.edu/~law/student/BLSA.htm

WISCONSIN

ARTISTIC

KO-THI DANCE COMPANY
P.O. Box 1093
Milwaukee, WI 53201
Ferne Caulker, Director
Tel: (414) 273-0676 Fax: (414) 273-0727
Email: kkothi@aol.com
Web: www.ko-thi.org

BUSINESS

NATIONAL MINORITY SUPPLIER DEVELOPMENT COUNCIL, INC.
Wisconsin Supplier Development Council
P.O. Box 8577
Madison, WI 53708-8577
Floyd Rose, Executive Director
Tel: (608) 241-5858 Fax: (608) 241-9100
Email: wsdcrose@aol.com
Web: www.suppliercouncil.org

CULTURAL

MILWAUKEE JUNETEENTH CELEBRATION
2460 N. 6th St.
Milwaukee, WI 53212
Mac Weddle, Director
Tel: (414) 372-3770 Fax: (414) 372-3619
Email: macweddle@hotmail.com

POLITICAL ACTION

ASSOCIATION OF COMMUNITY ORGANIZATIONS FOR REFORM NOW
Milwaukee Office
152 W. Wisconsin Ave. #731
Milwaukee, WI 53203
Tel: (414) 276-8181 Fax: (414) 342-1998
Email: wiacornmi@acorn.org
Web: www.acorn.org

BLACKS IN GOVERNMENT
Region V-Milwaukee Chapter
P.O. Box 1088
Milwaukee, WI 53201
Dennis Williams, Chapter President
Tel: (414) 384-2000 x42180
Email: milwaukee@bignet.org
Web: www.bignet.org/regional/region5/default.htm

Region V-New Detroit Chapter
P.O. Box 44195
Detroit, WI 48244
Sharon Watson, Chapter President
Tel: (313) 234-1344
Email: sharon.watson@irs.gov
Web: www.bignet.org

PROFESSIONAL

AMERICAN ASSOCIATION OF BLACKS IN ENERGY
Wisconsin Chapter
1035 W. Canal St.
Milwaukee, WI 53233
Sandra Camberos, President
Tel: (414) 221-3518 Fax: (414) 221-3799
Email: sandracamberos@we-energies.com
Web: www.aabe-wi.org

NATIONAL BLACK MBA ASSOCIATION, INC.
MIlwaukee Chapter- Midwest
P.O. Box 1472

Milwaukee, WI 53201
Brenda Pegues, President
Web: www.nbmbaa.org

NATIONAL FORUM FOR BLACK PUBLIC ADMINISTRATORS
Milwaukee Chapter
Department of Employee Relations, City of Milwaukee,
200 E. Wells St. #707
Milwaukee, WI 53202
Florence J. Dukes, President
Tel: (414) 935-7991 Fax: (414) 286-2106
Email: fdukes@ci.mil.wi.us
Web: www.nfbpa.org

SPEC. INT., SOCIAL INTEREST

CENTER FOR VETERANS ISSUES, LTD.
3312 W. Wells
Milwaukee, WI 53208
Thomas Wynn, Sr, President/CEO
Tel: (414) 342-4284 Fax: (414) 342-1073

NATIONAL ASSOCIATION FOR BLACK VETERANS, INC.
P.O. Box 11432
Milwaukee, WI 53211
Richard Rodgers, Director of Management Services
Tel: (877) 622-8387 Fax: (414) 342-1073
Email: nabvets@nabvets.com
Web: www.nabvets.com

NATIONAL URBAN LEAGUE, INC.
Milwaukee Urban League
2800 W. Wright St.
Milwaukee, WI 53210
Ralph E. Hollmon, President/CEO
Tel: (414) 374-5850 Fax: (414) 562-8620
Email: rhollmon@wi.rr.com
Web: www.tmul.org

Urban League of Greater Madison
151 E. Gorham St.
Madison, WI 53703
Stephen L. Braunginn, President/CEO
Tel: (608) 251-8550 Fax: (608) 251-0944
Email: ulgm@ulgm.org
Web: www.ulgm.org

Urban League of Racine and Kenosha
718 N. Memorial Dr.
Racine, WI 53404
Honey Renaue, President
Tel: (262) 637-8532 Fax: (262) 637-8634
Web: www.nul.org

NEW CONCEPT SELF DEVELOPMENT CENTER, INC.
4828 W. Fond Du Lac Ave.
Milwaukee, WI 53216
June Perry, CEO
Tel: (414) 444-1952 Fax: (414) 444-5557
Email: junifer@aol.com
Web: www.ncsdc-inc.org

VETS PLACE CENTRAL
3330 W. Wells St.
Milwaukee, WI 53208
Robert Cocroft, President/CEO
Tel: (414) 342-5000 Fax: (414) 342-4999

SPEC. INT., YOUTH

JACK & JILL OF AMERICA, INC.
Mid-Western Region
P.O. Box 1285
Milwaukee, WI 53201
Jacqueline Moore Bowles, Regional Director
Email: jacquebowles@aol.com
Web: www.jack-and-jill.org

STUDENT ORGANIZATION

ALPHA KAPPA ALPHA SORORITY, INC.
Iota Delta Chapter
P.O. Box 162
2200 E. Kenwd Blvd.
Milwaukee, WI 53201
Lakeshia Exum, Chapter President
Web: www.aka1908.com

Kappa Psi Omega Chapter
P.O. Box 2347
Madison, WI 53701
T. Ella Strother, Chapter President
Web: www.aka1908.com

Mu Beta Chapter
4529 N. 58th St.
Milwaukee, WI 53218

Audia Lawanda Dobson, Chapter President
Web: www.aka1908.com

Omicron Xi Chapter
8608 W. Hemlock St.
Milwaukee, WI 53224
Erica Horton, Chapter President
Web: www.aka1908.com

Upsilon Mu Omega Chapter
6019 W. Calumet Rd
Milwaukee, WI 53223
Sandra Bokamba Lockett, Chapter President
Web: www.aka1908.com

ALPHA PHI ALPHA FRATERNITY, INC.
Delta Chi Lambda Chapter
P.O. Box 83205
Milwaukee, WI 53223
Web: www.alphaphialpha.net

Epsilon Tau Chapter, University of Wisconsin
2200 Kenwood Blvd.
Milwaukee, WI 53211
Web: www.alphaphialpha.net

Eta Pi Chapter, University of Wisconsin
Multicultural Education Ctr., 751 Algoma Blvd.
Oshkosh, WI 54901
Web: www.alphaphialpha.net

Gamma Epsilon Chapter, University of Wisconsin
1606 Fordem Ave. #115
Madison, WI 53704
Lyntrel Smith, Contact
Tel: (608) 242-1751
Web: www.alphaphialpha.net

Zeta Iota Chapter, University of Wisconsin
P.O. Box 181
Whitewater, WI 53190
Web: www.alphaphialpha.net

WYOMING

POLITICAL ACTION

AMERICAN CIVIL LIBERTIES UNION
Wyoming Chapter
P.O. Box 20706
Cheyenne, WY 82003
Linda Burt, Executive Director
Tel: (307) 637-4565 Fax: (307) 637-4565
Email: wyoaclu@aol.com
Web: www.aclu-wy.org

STUDENT ORGANIZATION

MINORITY LAW STUDENT ASSOCIATION
University of Wyoming College of Law
P.O. Box 3035
Laramie, WY 82071
Rob Ingram, President
Tel: (307) 766-6416
Web: www.nblsa.org

3 ISSUES/YEAR

ACHIEVE
National Association of Black Accountants, Inc.
7249 Hanover Pkwy. #A
Greenbelt, MD 20770
Johnetta Boseman Hardy, Deputy Executive Director
Tel: (301) 474-6222 **Fax:** (301) 474-3114
Email: jbhardy@nabainc.org
Web: www.nabainc.org
Circ.: 5,000
Price: Free **Subscription:** $20.00/year
Publication description: To provide an opportunity for accounting, finance, and business students to have access to timely updates on accounting and finance-related matters.

INTERNATIONAL JOURNAL OF AFRICAN HISTORICAL STUDIES
Boston University
270 Bay State Rd.
Boston, MA 02215
Jean Hay, Editor
Tel: (617) 353-7306 **Fax:** (617) 353-4975
Email: jhay@bu.edu
Web: www.bu.edu/africa/publications/ijahs/index.html
Circ.: 800
Subscription: $50.00/year
Date established: 1968

LEGISLATOR, THE
National Black Caucus of State Legislators
444 N. Capitol St. NW #622
Washington, DC 20001
LaKimba DeSadier Walker, Executive Director
Tel: (202) 624-5457 **Fax:** (202) 508-3826
Email: lakimba@nbcsl.com
Web: www.nbcsl.com
Circ.: 700
Price: Free
Publication description: The primary mission is to develop, conduct and promote educational, research and training programs designed to enhance the effectiveness of its members, as they consider legislation and issues of public policy which impact, either directly or indirectly upon "the general welfare" of African American constituents within their respective jurisdictions.
Date established: 1977

NUEVA LUZ
En Foco, Inc.
32 E. Kingsbridge Rd.
Bronx, NY 10468
Charles Biasiny-Rivera, Publisher
Tel: (718) 584-7718 **Fax:** (718) 584-7718
Email: info@enfoco.org

Web: www.enfoco.org
Circ.: 3,000
Price: $7.00 **Subscription:** $30.00/year
Publication description: To promote photographers of color, Hispanic, African American, Asian and other minorities.
Date established: 1974

SPECTRUM
National Association of Black Accountants, Inc.
7249 Hanover Pkwy. #A
Greenbelt, MD 20770
Johnetta Boseman Hardy, Deputy Executive Director
Tel: (301) 474-6222 **Fax:** (301) 474-3114
Email: jbhardy@nabainc.org
Web: www.nabainc.org
Price: Free **Subscription:** $20.00/year
Publication description: To provide a communication mechanism whereby readers are kept abreast of key topics of interest within the accounting, finance, and business professions.

USAID IN AFRICA
Africa Bureau Information Center
1001 Pennsylvania Ave. NW #300 South
Washington, DC 20004
Christine Chumbler, Senior Writer/Editor
Tel: (202) 661-5827 **Fax:** (202) 661-5890
Email: abic@dis.cdie.org
Web: www.usaid.gov/locations/sub-saharan_africa/newsletters/
Circ.: 4,500
Price: Free
Publication description: African Voices is published by the Africa Bureau Information Center, operated by the Academy for Educational Development under contract to the U.S. Agency for International Development (USAID), and is part of the Development Information Services project of USAID's Center for Development Information and Evaluation.
Date established: 1995

5 ISSUES/YEAR

FOOTSTEPS: AFRICAN AMERICAN HISTORY
Cobblestone Publishing
30 Grove St. #C
Peterborough, NH 03458
Charlis Baker, Editor
Tel: (603) 924-7209 **Fax:** (603) 924-7380
Email: cbaker@cobblestonepub.com
Web: www.cobblestonepub.com
Price: $4.97 **Subscription:** $23.95/year
Publication description: Footsteps is designed for young people, their parents, and other individuals interested in discovering the

scope, substance, and many often unheralded facts of African American history. An excellent classroom resource for teachers, a valuable research tool for students, and an important vehicle for bringing this rich history to people of all backgrounds.
Date established: 1975

NSBE BRIDGE & NSBE MAGAZINE
National Society of Black Engineers
1454 Duke St.
Alexandria, VA 22314
Pamela Sharif, Publisher
Tel: (703) 549-2208 **Fax:** (703) 683-5312
Email: publications@nsbe.org
Web: www.nsbe.org
Circ.: 15,000
Price: Free
Publication description: Offers regular sections and exciting feature articles of interest in a variety of engineering and technology disciplines.
Date established: 1971

PATHFINDERS TRAVEL
6325 Germantown Ave.
Philadelphia, PA 19144
Weller Thomas, Publisher/CEO
Tel: (215) 438-2140 **Fax:** (215) 438-2144
Email: info@pathfinderstravel.com
Web: www.pathfinderstravel.com
Circ.: 100,000
Price: $3.95 **Subscription:** $18.00/year
Date established: 1997

MED-CHI NEWSLETTER
Medico-Chirurgical Society of the District of Columbia, Inc.
P.O. Box 77013
Washington, DC 20013-8013
Theresa Greene Reed, MD, President
Tel: (202) 347-4170
Price: Free
Publication description: To promote the public health and the protection of the common interest of its members and the public.
Date established: 1884

6 ISSUES/YEAR

ABOUT...TIME
About...Time Magazine, Inc.
283 Genesee St.
Rochester, NY 14611-3496
Carolyne Blount, Editor
Tel: (585) 235-7150 **Fax:** (585) 235-7195
Email: atmag@abouttimemag.com
Web: www.abouttimemag.com
Circ.: 65,500
Price: $3.00 **Subscription:** $15.00/year
Date established: 1972

AFRICA JOURNAL, THE
Corporate Council on Africa
1100 17th St. NW #1100
Washington, DC 20036
Stephen Hayes, President
Tel: (202) 835-1115 **Fax:** (202) 835-1117
Email: cca@africacncl.org
Web: www.africacncl.org
Circ.: 5,000
Date established: 1993

CRISIS MAGAZINE, THE
National Association for the Advancement of Colored People
7600 Georgia Ave. NW
Washington, DC 20012
Victoria Valentine, Editor
Tel: (202) 829-5700
Email: thecrisiseditorial@naacpnet.org
Web: www.thecrisismagazine.com
Circ.: 250,000
Price: $3.00 **Subscription:** $12.00/year
Publication description: The Crisis magazine is dedicated to being an open and honest forum for discussing critical issues confronting people of color, American society and the world in addition to highlighting the historical and cultural achievements of these diverse peoples.
Date established: 1910

FREEDOM SOCIALIST NEWSPAPER
Freedom Socialist Party/Radical Women
5018 Rainier Ave. South, New Freeway Hall
Seattle, WA 98118
Andrea Bauer, Managing Editor
Tel: (206) 722-2453 **Fax:** (206) 723-7691
Email: fsnews@mindspring.com
Web: www.socialism.com
Price: $1.00 **Subscription:** $8.00/year
Publication description: Socialist Feminist political party dedicated to eradicating injustice and inequality and bigotry for all people.
Date established: 1965

LINCOLN REVIEW
The Lincoln Institute for Research and Education, Inc.
10315 Georgetown Pike
Great Falls, VA 22066-2415
Jay A. Parker, President/Editor
Tel: (202) 223-5112 **Fax:** (703) 759-7308
Circ.: 6,700
Price: $3.00 **Subscription:** $12.00/year
Date established: 1979

OUT OF AFRICA
African Enterprise
128 E. Palm Ave.
Monrovia, CA 91016
Malcolm Graham, Executive Director
Tel: (626) 357-8811 **Fax:** (626) 359-2069

Email: info@aeusa.org
Web: www.africanenterprise.org
Circ.: 13,000
Price: Free
Date established: 1961

7 ISSUES/YEAR

BLACK DIASPORA
Black Diaspora Comm., Ltd.
350 5th Ave.
New York, NY 10118
Rene John-Sandy, Publisher
Tel: (212) 268-8348 **Fax:** (212) 268-8370
Email: blackdias@earthlink.net
Circ.: 215,000
Price: $4.95 **Subscription:** $15.00-18.00/year
Publication description: Hispanic and African American publication.
Date established: 1979

8 ISSUES/YEAR

SOPHISTICATE'S BLACK HAIRSTYLES & CARE GUIDE
Associated Publications, Inc.
875 N. Michigan Ave. #3434
Chicago, IL 60611
Jocelyn Amador, Editor
Tel: (312) 573-3038 **Fax:** (312) 573-3020
Web: www.associatepub.com
Circ.: 158,000
Price: $4.99 **Subscription:** $31.90/year
Date established: 1984

10 ISSUES/YEAR

CITY FLIGHT MAGAZINE
Flight Community Services
P.O. Box 1484
San Jose, CA 95109
Tim Hilton, Executive Director
Tel: (888) 564-2108 **Fax:** (510) 291-2831
Email: info@cityflight.com
Web: www.cityflight.com
Date established: 1995

11 ISSUES/YEAR

CHICAGO REPORTER, THE
The Community Renewal Society
332 S. Michigan Ave. #500
Chicago, IL 60604
Alysia Tate, Editor/Publisher
Tel: (312) 427-4830 **Fax:** (312) 427-6130
Email: tcr@chicagoreporter.com
Web: www.chicagoreporter.com
Circ.: 5,000
Price: $5.00 **Subscription:** $10.00/year
Publication description: The Chicago Reporter is an investigative magazine that identifies, analyzes and reports on the social, economic and political issues in metropolitan Chicago with a special focus on race and poverty.
Date established: 1972

ANNUALLY

AFRICAN DEVELOPMENT INDICATORS 2005
The World Bank Publications
P.O. Box 960
Herndon, VA 20172-0960
The World Bank, Publisher

Tel: (800) 645-7247 **Fax:** (703) 661-1501
Email: books@worldbank.org
Web: www.worldbank.org
Price: $50.00

AFRICAN-AMERICAN YEARBOOK
TIYM Publishing Company, Inc.
6718 Whittier Ave. #130
McLean, VA 22101
Angela E. Zavala, Editor
Tel: (703) 734-1632 **Fax:** (703) 356-0787
Email: africanamericanyearbook@tiym.com
Web: www.africanamericanyearbook.com
Circ.: 50,000
Price: $29.95
Publication description: The most comprehensive reference guide for and about African-Americans. The Yearbook is a unique resource in the areas of employment, business, education, and health, as well as a powerful tool for organizations seeking to reach the large African-American market.
Date established: 2001

BLACK BUSINESS DIRECTORY
Renaissance Publications, Inc.
1516 5th Ave.
Pittsburgh, PA 15219
Connie Portis, President/Publisher
Tel: (412) 391-8208 **Fax:** (412) 391-8006
Email: renpub@earthlink.net
Circ.: 20,000
Price: $9.95
Date established: 1984

BLACK PAGES OF AMERICA
The Black Pages of America
221 Ruthers Rd. #203
Richmond, VA 23235
David Walton, Publisher
Tel: (804) 314-3090 **Fax:** (703) 997-0852
Email: support@blackpages.com
Web: www.blackpages.com
Circ.: 50,000
Price: $5.00
Publication description: Business directory designed to target African-American consumers and businesses.
Date established: 1988

BLACK PAGES USA
Thomas-McCants Media, Inc.
355 Crawford St. #402
Portsmouth, VA 23704
Gerry McCants, Publisher
Tel: (757) 399-4153 **Fax:** (757) 399-0969
Email: gerry@blackpagesusa.com
Web: www.blackpagesusa.com
Circ.: 50,000
Subscription: Free
Publication description: The mission of Thomas-McCants Media, Inc. is to encourage, support and facilitate economic empowerment of the African-American community through the development of a strategic local business network, educational initiatives and communications ventures.

CHATTANOOGA BLACK PAGES
Chattanooga Black Pages
P.O. Box 508
Chattanooga, TN 37401
Veronica Dunson, Publisher
Tel: (423) 697-0020 **Fax:** (423) 697-0804
Email: chatblkpge@aol.com
Web: www.chattanoogablackpages.com
Circ.: 20,000
Price: Free
Date established: 1993

CLEVELAND BLACK PAGES
1814 E. 40th St.
Cleveland, OH 44103

Bob Lanier, Publisher
Tel: (216) 391-7735 **Fax:** (216) 391-8541
Email: blackpages@blackpagesohio.com
Web: www.blackpagesohio.com
Circ.: 85,000
Price: Free
Publication description: The Black Pages is a free business listing and information guide established in 1991 to support, encourage, and act as an advocate for African-American owned businesses and entrepreneurs. Voted the "Minority Business Advocate of the Year" by the city of Cleveland, the mission of the Black Pages is the economic revitalization of African-American communities in Northeast Ohio.
Date established: 1991

CONTINUING SIGNIFICANCE OF RACISM: US COLLEGES AND UNIVERSITIES, THE
American Council of Education
1 DuPont Cir. NW
Washington, DC 20036
William B. Harvey, Vice President/Director
Tel: (301) 632-6757 **Fax:** (301) 843-0159
Email: pubs@ace.nche.edu
Web: www.acenet.edu
Price: $15.00
Publication description: The paper provides a compelling, and not altogether complimentary analysis of the atmosphere on some college and university campuses as seen by the students and faculty of color who participated in interviews and focus groups.
Date established: 1985

EMPHASIS MAGAZINE
National Alliance of Market Developers
620 Sheradan Ave.
Plainfield, NJ 07060
Clyde Allen, Executive Director
Tel: (908) 561-4062 **Fax:** (908) 561-6827
Email: allenpartner@earthlink.net
Web: www.namdntl.org
Circ.: 2,500
Price: Free
Publication description: To be a catalyst for positive and progressive changes for African-Americans in marketing, public relations, advertising, sales, and urban affairs.
Date established: 1952

GREATER LOS ANGELES BLACK PAGES
3717 LaBrea Ave. #479
Los Angeles, CA 90016
Stephan Buckley, Editor
Tel: (323) 296-4075 **Fax:** (323) 290-1430
Email: glabd@attbi.com
Web: www.lablackdirectory.com
Circ.: 100,000
Price: Free
Date established: 1980

JARVISONIAN MAGAZINE, THE
Jarvis Christian College
P.O. Box 1470
Hawkins, TX 75765
Dr. Sebetha Jenkins, President
Tel: (903) 769-5883 **Fax:** (903) 769-4842
Email: sebetha_jenkins@jarvis.edu
Web: www.jarvis.edu
Circ.: 5,000
Date established: 1912

MAKING COLLEGE AFFORDABLE
The Education Resources Institute/TERI
700 Boylston St.
Boston, MA 02116
Jane Horton, Director of Counseling
Tel: (617) 536-0200 **Fax:** (617) 536-4737
Web: www.edinfo.org
Circ.: 10,000
Price: $3.50
Publication description: A workbook on

financial aid, loans and scholarships for college bound students and their families.
Date established: 1984

MINORITIES IN HIGHER EDUCATION ANNUAL STATUS REPORT
American Council of Education
1 DuPont Cir. NW
Washington, DC 20036
William B. Harvey, Vice President/Director
Tel: (301) 632-6757 **Fax:** (301) 843-0159
Email: pubs@ace.nche.edu
Web: www.acenet.edu
Price: $29.95
Publication description: Widely recognized as the national source of information on current trends and issues related to minorities in higher education, this annual study summarizes high school completion and college participation rates, college enrollments by race/ethnicity, educational attainment, and degrees conferred by field of study and race/ethnicity.
Date established: 1985

MINORITY BUSINESS & CONSUMER RESOURCE DIRECTORY
Minority Business and Consumer Resource Directory
P.O. Box 3726
Baltimore, MD 21217
Michael A. Graham, Publisher
Tel: (410) 669-6641 **Fax:** (410) 383-2677
Email: mbcrd@mbcrd.com
Web: www.mbcrd.com
Circ.: 50,000
Price: Free
Date established: 1995

N'COBRA
National Coalition of Blacks for Reparations in America
P.O. Box 90604
Washington, DC 20090-0604
Wautella Yusuf, Publisher
Tel: (202) 466-1622 **Fax:** (202) 291-4600
Email: nationalncobra@aol.com
Web: www.ncobra.com
Price: $5.00
Publication description: Annual Magazine/journal.
Date established: 1990

N'DIGO MAGAPAPER
Hartman Publishing
19 N. Sangamon St.
Chicago, IL 60607
Hermene D. Hartman, Publisher
Tel: (312) 822-0202 **Fax:** (312) 822-0288
Web: www.ndigo.com
Circ.: 160,000
Price: Free **Subscription:** $63.00/year
Publication description: Published each year in March, N'DIGO Profiles is a special edition of N'DIGO that focuses on a specific theme. The highly visual publication is the largest African American-distributed publication in Chicago and a must-read for consumers who want a new view of contemporary culture.
Date established: 1995

OPPORTUNITY JOURNAL
National Urban League, Inc.
120 Wall St., 8th Fl.
New York, NY 10005
Marc H. Morial, President/CEO
Tel: (212) 558-5300 **Fax:** (212) 344-5189
Email: info@nul.org
Web: www.nul.org
Circ.: 85,000
Price: $4.95
Publication description: Opportunity Journal, the official publication of the Urban League

movement, examines some of today's issues affecting African-Americans, and offers a look back at some of the unexplored challenges and successes that have touched their lives.
Date established: 1976

PAY YOURSELF FIRST-THE AFRICAN AMERICAN GUIDE TO FINANCIAL SUCCESS
Amber Communications Group, Inc.
1334 E. Chandler Blvd. #5-D67
Phoenix, AZ 85048
Tony Rose, Publisher/CEO
Tel: (602) 243-3144 **Fax:** (480) 283-0991
Email: amberbk@aol.com
Web: www.amberbooks.com
Circ.: 48,000
Price: $14.95
Date established: 1998

SOURCE BOOK OF MULTICULTURAL EXPERTS, THE
Multicultural Marketing Resources, Inc.
286 Spring St. #201
New York, NY 10013
Melanie Eisenberg, Editor
Tel: (212) 242-3351 **Fax:** (212) 691-5969
Email: marketing@multicultural.com
Web: www.multiculturalmarketingresources.com
Circ.: 14,000
Price: $59.95
Publication description: The Source Book of Multicultural Experts is a desktop reference guide to experts on many different cultural and lifestyle markets such as Hispanic, Asian American, African American, women, and gay/lesbian.
Date established: 1998

STATE OF BLACK AMERICA, THE
National Urban League, Inc.
120 Wall St., 8th Fl.
New York, NY 10005
Marc H. Morial, President/CEO
Tel: (212) 558-5300 **Fax:** (212) 344-5189
Email: info@nul.org
Web: www.nul.org
Circ.: 16,000
Price: $29.95
Publication description: A compilation of essays and papers about the progress and plight of African-Americans in our society. As is the tradition of The State of Black America, each edition also proposes solutions to the problems it reveals.
Date established: 1976

BIANNUALLY

ANNUAL REPORT
National Urban Fellows, Inc.
102 W. 38th St. #700
New York, NY 10018
Luis Alvarez, President
Tel: (212) 730-1700 **Fax:** (212) 730-1823
Email: luisalvarez@nuf.org
Web: www.nuf.org
Circ.: 3,000
Price: Free
Date established: 1969

BIG BULLETIN, THE
Blacks In Government
3005 Georgia Ave. NW
Washington, DC 20001
Willis Lewis, Editor
Tel: (571) 437-9473 **Fax:** (202) 667-3705
Email: lewischill@aol.com
Web: www.bignet.org

Price: Free
Publication description: Brief publication with membership update information.

BIG REPORTER, THE
Blacks In Government
3005 Georgia Ave. NW
Washington, DC 20001
Willis Lewis, Editor
Tel: (571) 437-9473 **Fax:** (202) 667-3705
Email: lewischill@aol.com
Web: www.bignet.org
Price: Free
Publication description: Member focus magazine that provides information on programs and initiatives throughout the entire organization.

BLACK COLLEGIAN MAGAZINE, THE
IMDiversity, Inc.
140 Carondelat St.
New Orleans, LA 70130
James Perry, Editor
Tel: (504) 523-0154 **Fax:** (504) 523-0271
Email: pres@imdiversity.com
Web: www.black-collegian.com
Circ.: 891,000
Price: $4.00 **Subscription:** $8.00/year
Publication description: The Black Collegian Magazine is a career and self development magazine targeted to African-American students seeking information on careers, job opportunities, graduate/professional school, internships/co-ops, study abroad programs, etc.
Date established: 1970

BLACK PERSPECTIVE, THE
EM Publishing Enterprises, Inc.
13351 Riverside Dr. #514
Sherman Oaks, CA 91423
Jeff Palmatier, President/CEO
Tel: (818) 654-0870 **Fax:** (818) 654-0874
Email: jp@equalitymagazines.com
Web: www.blackperspective.com
Circ.: online format
Publication description: The Black Perspective is a publication dedicated to informing the African-American community about opportunities in the worlds of business, technology, and education. In addition to reporting on these subjects, The Black Perspective reports on historical, civil rights, and societal issues as they affect the community. Ultimately, our goal is to level the playing field and make it possible for African-Americans to succeed, and to make equal opportunity a reality.
Date established: 1990

GODDARD RIVERSIDE NEWS
Goddard Riverside Community Center
593 Columbus Ave.
New York, NY 10024
Stephan Russo, Executive Director
Tel: (212) 873-6600 **Fax:** (212) 595-6498
Email: response@goddard.org
Web: www.goddard.org
Circ.: 10,000
Price: Free
Date established: 1959

KUUMBA
BLK Publishing Co., Inc.
P.O. Box 83912
Los Angeles, CA 90083-0912
Alan Bell, Publisher
Tel: (310) 410-0808 **Fax:** (310) 410-9250
Email: newsroom@blk.com
Web: www.blk.com
Circ.: 35,000
Price: $4.50 **Subscription:** $14.00/year
Publication description: Kuumba publishes poetry and drawings dedicated to the

celebration of the lives, culture, and experiences of black people in the life.
Date established: 1992

LIBERTY
American Civil Liberties Union of Idaho
P.O. Box 1897
Boise, ID 83701-1897
Jack Van Valkenburgh, Director
Tel: (208) 344-5243 **Fax:** (208) 344-7201
Email: aclu-id@acluidaho.org
Web: www.acluidaho.org
Circ.: 1,500
Price: Free
Date established: 1993

MINORITY STUDENT OPPORTUNITIES IN UNITED STATES MEDICAL SCHOOLS
Association of American Medical Colleges
2450 North St. NW
Washington, DC 20037
Laly May Johnson, Editor
Tel: (202) 828-0416 **Fax:** (202) 828-1123
Email: publications@aamc.org
Web: www.aamc.org
Circ.: 500
Price: $12.00
Publication description: The data published show the number of minority applicants, the number offered an acceptance, the number of matriculants, and the number of graduates by gender and racial/ethnic groups.
Date established: 1987

NABSE NEWSBRIEFS NEWSLETTER
National Alliance of Black School Educators
310 Pennsylvania Ave. SE
Washington, DC 20003
Quentin R. Lawson, Executive Director
Tel: (202) 608-6310 **Fax:** (202) 608-6319
Email: qlawson@nabse.org
Web: www.nabse.org
Circ.: 8,000
Price: Free
Publication description: The official newsletter of the National Alliance of Black School Educators
Date established: 1971

NOA NEWSLETTER
National Optometric Association
3723 Main St.
East Chicago, IN 46312
Dr. Charles Comer, Association Manager
Tel: (877) 394-2020 **Fax:** (219) 398-1077
Email: ccomer2@aol.com
Web: www.natoptassoc.org
Date established: 1969

PHILADELPHIA TRIBUNE
The Philadelphia Tribune Co.
520 S. 16th St.
Philadelphia, PA 19146
Robert W. Bogle, CEO
Tel: (215) 893-4050 **Fax:** (215) 893-5767
Email: info@phila-tribune.com
Web: www.phila-tribune.com
Circ.: 203,000
Price: $0.60-1.00 **Subscription:** $90.00/year
Date established: 1884

BIMONTHLY

AARP MAGAZINE
601 East St. NW
Washington, DC 20049
Steven Slon, Editor
Tel: (202) 434-6880
Email: member@aarp.org

Web: www.aarp.org
Circ.: 35,000,000
Price: $3.50 **Subscription:** $12.50/year
Date established: 1950

ABC DIGEST OF URBAN CARDIOLOGY, THE
Association of Black Cardiologists, Inc.
6849-B2 Peachtree Dunwoody Rd. NE
Atlanta, GA 30328
Elizabeth Ofili, Editor In Chief
Tel: (678) 302-4222 **Fax:** (678) 302-4223
Email: abcardio@abcardio.org
Web: www.abcardio.org
Publication description: The ABC Digest of Urban Cardiology, published bimonthly, is an official publication of the Association of Black Cardiologists, Inc.

AFRICAN ABROAD NEWSPAPER
Gioku Communications, Inc.
110-39 157th St.
Jamaica, NY 11433
Alex Kabba, Editor/Publisher
Tel: (718) 843-1429 **Fax:** (718) 843-1935
Email: apoye@aol.com
Web: www.africanabroadonline.com
Circ.: 50,000
Price: Free **Subscription:** $48.00/year
Publication description: Covers news on African Americans and also news on the African Continent.

AFRICAN AMERICANS ON WHEELS
On Wheels, Inc.
585 E. Larned St. #100
Detroit, MI 48226
Lyndon Conrad Bell, Editor
Tel: (313) 963-2209 **Fax:** (313) 963-7778
Email: lyndon@onwheelsinc.com
Web: www.onwheelsinc.com
Circ.: 800,000
Price: Free **Subscription:** $13.97/year
Publication description: AAWM magazine serves as a consumer magazine featuring auto-related lifestyle trends, a guide to the historical contributions of African Americans to the auto industry, and a guide to the automotive products, personnel and related industries.
Date established: 1995

BLACK ISSUES BOOK REVIEW
Empire State Bldg., 350 5th Ave. #1522
New York, NY 10118-0165
Clarence Reynolds, Managing Editor
Tel: (212) 947-8515 **Fax:** (212) 947-5674
Email: bibredit@cmapublishing.com
Web: www.bibookreview.com
Circ.: 75,000
Price: $2.49 **Subscription:** $14.95/year
Publication description: Covers reading, writing and publishing in the black community.
Date established: 1984

BLACKGIRL MAGAZINE
P.O. Box 90729
Atlanta, GA 30364
Kenya Jordana James, Founder/Editor
Tel: (404) 762-0282 **Fax:** (404) 762-0283
Email: editor@blackgirlmagazine.com
Web: www.blackgirlmagazine.com
Subscription: $24.00/6 issues
Publication description: Blackgirl Magazine focuses on promoting positive messages and imagery among African American teens, while offering insightful coverage of history, culture, lifestyle, and entertainment news.
Date established: 2002

CABLE EXPRESS, THE
The Conference of Minority Transportation Officials

818 18th St. NW #850
Washington, DC 20006
Julie A. Cunningham, Executive Director/
CEO
Tel: (202) 530-0551 **Fax:** (202) 530-0617
Email: comto@comto.org
Web: www.comto.org
Circ.: 2,200
Price: Free
Publication description: COMTO was founded
in 1971 at Howard University in Washington,
D.C. and was created to provide a forum
for senior minority professionals in the
transportation industry. With over 28 chapters
and 2200 members, and 50 business
partners worldwide, COMTO's mandate
has evolved to include not only public
transportation industry executives, but also
professionals at every level.
Date established: 1971

COUNTY NEWS

Iredell Publishing
P.O. Box 407
Statesville, NC 28687
Mason McCullough, Publisher
Tel: (704) 873-1054 **Fax:** (704) 873-1054
Email: countynews4you@aol.com
Circ.: 2,500
Price: Free **Subscription:** $25.00/year
Date established: 1980

FAMILY HEALTH GUIDE, THE

3325 Wilshire Blvd. #768
Los Angeles, CA 90010
Martin L. Jimpson, Publisher/CEO
Tel: (213) 733-6834 **Fax:** (213) 382-5428
Email: mljfhg@sbcglobal.net
Web: www.thefamilyhealthguide.com
Circ.: 50,000
Price: Free **Subscription:** $19.95/year
Publication description: Provides the African-
American community with vital information on
health and social issues that particularly affect
African Americans.
Date established: 2001

FLOSSLINE NEWSLETTER

National Dental Association
3517 16th St. NW
Washington, DC 20010
Robert S. Johns, Executive Director
Tel: (202) 588-1697 **Fax:** (202) 588-1244
Email: admin@ndaonline.org
Web: www.ndaonline.org
Circ.: 4,700
Price: Free
Date established: 1913

FLOSS MAGAZINE

373 Broadway, 3rd Fl. #C8
New York, NY 10013
Paris Sawundu, Publisher
Tel: (212) 343-8154 **Fax:** (212) 941-1744
Web: www.flossmagazine.com
Price: $3.99
Publication description:: Floss is the fashion,
entertainment and lifestyle magazine for
trendy young men and women of the hip-
hop generation.

JOURNAL OF BLACK STUDIES

Sage Publications
2455 Teller Rd.
Thousand Oaks, CA 91320
Molefi Kete Asante, Editor
Tel: (805) 499-0721 **Fax:** (805) 499-0871
Email: journals@sagepub.com
Web: www.sagepub.com
Circ.: 1,650
Price: $25.00 **Subscription:** $91.00-
117.00/year

MAOA NETWORK

Minority Apartment Owners Association
11215 S. Western
Los Angeles, CA 90047
Ruth Hayles, Executive Director
Tel: (323) 754-2818 **Fax:** (323) 754-0540
Email: maoa87@aol.com
Web: www.intlrealtyinvestment.com
Subscription: $35.00/year
Date established: 1987

MESSAGE MAGAZINE

Review and Herald Publishing Association
55 W. Oak Ridge Dr.
Hagerstown, MD 21740
Dr. Ronald Smith, Editor
Tel: (301) 393-3000 **Fax:** (301) 393-4103
Email: ronsmith@rhpa.org
Web: www.rhpa.org
Circ.: 75,000
Price: $4.00 **Subscription:** $14.95/year
Publication description: The magazine with
a contemporary Christian perspective and
an urban feel.
Date established: 1898

MINORITY BUSINESS ENTREPRENEUR
MAGAZINE

3528 Torrance Blvd. #101
Torrance, CA 90503
Ginger Conrad, Publisher
Tel: (310) 540-9398 **Fax:** (310) 792-8263
Email: gconrad@mbemag.com
Web: www.mbemag.com
Price: $5.00 **Subscription:** $18.00/year
Publication description: The development of
minority and women owned businesses is
the cornerstone of building strong, healthy
communities in which each individual has
the opportunity to contribute, to his or her
fullest potential.
Date established: 1984

MINORITY VOICE NEWSPAPER, THE

Jim Rouse Communications Group
P.O. Box 8361
Greenville, NC 27835
Jim Rouse, President/CEO
Tel: (252) 757-0365 **Fax:** (252) 757-1793
Email: woow.1@juno.com
Circ.: 18,000
Price: Free **Subscription:** $68.00/year
Publication description: To educate, entertain,
inform and communicate the view of the
African American communities.
Date established: 1981

MOTHER JONES MAGAZINE

Foundation for National Progress
222 Sutter St., 6th Fl.
San Francisco, CA 94108
Jay Harris, Publisher
Tel: (415) 321-1770 **Fax:** (415) 321-1772
Email: ellis@motherjones.com
Web: www.motherjones.com
Circ.: 250,000
Price: $4.50 **Subscription:** $24.00/year
Publication description: Mother Jones is an
independent nonprofit whose roots lie in a
commitment to social justice implemented
through first rate investigative reporting.
Date established: 1976

MULTICULTURAL MARKETING NEWS

Multicultural Marketing Resources, Inc.
286 Spring St. #201
New York, NY 10013
Melanie Eisenberg, Editor
Tel: (212) 242-3351 **Fax:** (212) 691-5969
Email: marketing@multicultural.com
Web: www.multiculturalmarketingresources.
com

Circ.: 8,500
Subscription: $125.00/year
Publication description: Newsletter specializing
in promoting corporate multicultural news and
news from companies owned by women and
minorities.
Date established: 1998

SALAD BOWL, THE

Multicultural Education Department
416 South Ridgeland # A213
Oak Park, IL 60302
Pearl Hall, Assistant to the Director
Tel: (708) 524-7700 **Fax:** (708) 524-7703
Circ.: 500

SMITH COUNTY HERALD

P.O. Box 8252
Tyler, TX 75701
Stephanie Pierce, Publisher
Tel: (903) 593-3558 **Fax:** (903) 593-1668
Email: theherald@tyler.net
Circ.: 5,000
Price: Free **Subscription:** $30.00/year
Date established: 1989

TURNING POINT MAGAZINE

Turning Point Communications, Inc.
P.O. Box 8746
Los Angeles, CA 90008
Patricia A. Means, Publisher
Tel: (323) 299-6000 **Fax:** (310) 299-6006
Email: pmeans@turningpointmagazine.com
Web: www.turningpointmagazine.com
Circ.: 50,000
Price: $4.50 **Subscription:** $16.95/year
Date established: 1992

URBAN INFLUENCE

National Urban League, Inc.
19900 Governors Dr., Bldg. 5 #14
Olympia Fields, IL 60461
Pamela Tamara-Brown, Publisher
Tel: (708) 481-9160 **Fax:** (708) 481-9163
Email: info@urbaninfluencemagazine.com
Web: www.urbaninfluencemagazine.com
Circ.: 90,000
Price: $3.99 **Subscription:** $16.00/6 issues
Publication description: A nationally distributed
publication targeting progressive African
American professionals with a message of
building wealth through social change.
Date established: 2004

VILLAGE BEAT, THE

The Village Beat
1030 S. Federal Hwy. #118
Delray Beach, FL 33483
Charlotte G. Durante, Publisher
Tel: (561) 265-4701 **Fax:** (561) 265-3536
Email: thevillagebeat@aol.com
Circ.: 7,000
Price: Free
Date established: 1997

BIWEEKLY

ATLANTA NEWSLEADER NEWSPAPER

Positive Publications, Inc.
4405 Mall Blvd. #521
Union City, GA 30291
Creed W. Pannell, Jr., Publisher
Tel: (770) 969-7711 **Fax:** (770) 969-7811
Email: atlmet@bellsouth.net
Circ.: 16,700
Price: $0.50 **Subscription:** $26.00/year
Date established: 1984

BLACK VOICE/CARTA LATINA

Rutgers University
Paul Robeson Cultural Ctr., 600

Bartholomew Rd.
Piscataway, NJ 08854
RaVal Davis, Editor-in-Chief
Tel: (732) 445-7025
Email: bvcl_submission@yahoo.com
Web: www.eden.rutgers.edu/~bvcl/
Circ.: 3,000
Price: Free
Publication description: The Black Voice/Carta
Latina is a student-run campus newspaper
dedicated to keeping the Rutgers University
community informed about issues pertinent to
the African American Communities.
Date established: 1969

BLUFF CITY POST

Bluff City Post Newspaper and Printing
719 Franklin St.
Natchez, MS 39120
William Terrell, Publisher
Tel: (601) 446-5218 **Fax:** (601) 446-5218
Email: wilterrell@hotmail.com
Circ.: 2,500
Price: $0.50 **Subscription:** $22.00-24.00/
year
Date established: 1978

CAROLINIAN, THE

P.O. Box 25308
Raleigh, NC 27611
Paul R. Jervay, Publisher
Tel: (919) 834-5558 **Fax:** (919) 832-3243
Email: carolinian@mindspring.com
Circ.: 14,468
Price: $0.50 **Subscription:** $30.00/year
Date established: 1940

COMMUNITY COLLEGE WEEK

10520 Warwick Ave. #B-8
Fairfax, VA 22030
Margaret Miller, Editor
Tel: (703) 385-2981 **Fax:** (703) 385-1839
Email: kristinal@cmabiccw.com
Web: www.ccweek.com
Circ.: 18,000
Price: $2.75 **Subscription:** $26.00/year
Publication description: Community College
Week has been the independent source of
in-depth information for and about two-year
college faculty, administrators and trustees.
Published biweekly, Community College
Week's readers include college presidents,
chief academic officers, faculty, student
service professionals, librarians and other
educators.
Date established: 1988

COMMUNITY VOICE, THE

TCV Publishing, Inc.
P.O. Box 20804
Wichita, KS 67208
Bonita Gooch, General Manager
Tel: (316) 681-1155 **Fax:** (316) 681-0360
Email: adcopy@tcvtub.com
Circ.: 1,000
Price: $0.75 **Subscription:** $22.95-29.95/
year
Date established: 1995

DIVERSE ISSUES IN HIGHER EDUCATION

10520 Warwick Ave. #B-8
Fairfax, VA 22030-3136
Margaret Miller, Editor
Tel: (703) 385-2981 **Fax:** (703) 385-1839
Email: editor@cmapublishing.com
Web: www.blackissues.com
Circ.: 40,000
Subscription: $26.00/year
Publication description: The only biweekly
newsmagazine that covers minority issues in
higher education.
Date established: 1984

FLORIDA SENTINEL BULLETIN

Florida Sentinel-Bulletin
2207 21st Ave.
Tampa, FL 33605
Gwen Hayes, Editor
Tel: (813) 248-1921 **Fax:** (813) 248-4507
Email: ghayes@flsentinel.com
Web: www.flsentinel.com
Circ.: 28,000
Price: $0.50 **Subscription:** $60.00/year
Date established: 1945

GULLAH SENTINEL NEWSPAPER, THE

The Gullah Sentinel
2303 Boundary St. #1
Beaufort, SC 29902
Jabari Moketsi, Publisher/Editor-in-Chief
Tel: (843) 982-0500 **Fax:** (843) 982-0285
Email: thegullah@charter.net
Circ.: 8,000
Price: $0.50 **Subscription:** $45.00/year
Publication description: To educate and inform African American readers about events and issues that impact their communities.
Date established: 1996

INSIDE MOREHOUSE

Morehouse College, Office of Communications
830 Westview Dr. SW
Atlanta, GA 30314
Vikie Hampton, Editor
Tel: (404) 215-2680 **Fax:** (404) 215-2729
Email: vhampton@morehouse.edu
Web: www.morehouse.edu/communications/publications.html
Circ.: 3,000
Price: Free
Publication description: Biweekly campus newsletter for students, faculty and staff during the regular academic year.

INSIDER NEWS

Insider, Inc.
1661 Douglas Ave.
Racine, WI 53404
Ken Lumpkin, Publisher
Tel: (262) 632-9370 **Fax:** (262) 619-3135
Email: insider@wi.net
Web: www.racineinsider.com
Circ.: 10,000
Price: Free
Date established: 1993

KIP BUSINESS REPORT, THE

KIP Communications
P.O. Box 20789, Columbus Cir. Station
New York, NY 10023
Lloyd C. Grant, Publisher
Tel: (646) 546-5974 **Fax:** (646) 403-9825
Email: info@kipbusinessreport.com
Web: www.kipbusinessreport.com
Circ.: 13,500
Price: $2.00 **Subscription:** $39.00/year
Publication description: The KIP Business Report, provides readers with the business and financial intelligence they need to grow their companies and advance their careers.
Date established: 1998

MILWAUKEE COMMUNITY JOURNAL

Community Journal, Inc.
3612 N. Martin Luther King Dr.
Milwaukee, WI 53212
Thomas Mitchell, Editor
Tel: (414) 265-5300 **Fax:** (414) 265-1536
Email: editorial@communityjournal.net
Web: www.communityjournal.net
Circ.: 75,000
Price: Free **Subscription:** $90.00/year
Date established: 1976

MILWAUKEE WEEKEND EDITION

Community Journal, Inc.
3612 N. Martin Luther King Dr.
Milwaukee, WI 53212
Thomas Mitchell, Editor
Tel: (414) 265-5300 **Fax:** (414) 265-1536
Email: editorial@communityjournal.net
Web: www.communityjournal.net
Circ.: 75,000
Price: Free **Subscription:** $55.00/year
Date established: 1976

MUNCIE TIMES, THE

1304 N. Broadway St.
Muncie, IN 47303
Bea-Moten Foster, Publisher
Tel: (765) 741-0037 **Fax:** (765) 741-0040
Email: themancietimes@comcast.net
Circ.: 10,000
Price: Free **Subscription:** $15.00/year
Date established: 1990

NEW PITTSBURGH COURIER

315 E. Carson St.
Pittsburgh, PA 15219
Rod Doss, Publisher/Editor
Tel: (412) 481-8302 **Fax:** (412) 481-1360
Email: rdoss@newpittsburghcourier.com
Web: www.newpittsburghcourier.com
Circ.: 31,000
Price: $0.50 **Subscription:** $45.00/year
Date established: 1910

NEW YORK TREND

TTW Associates, Inc.
14 Bond St. #176
Great Neck, NY 11021
Dr. Teresa Taylor Williams, Publisher
Tel: (516) 466-0028 **Fax:** (516) 466-0062
Email: nytrend@aol.com
Circ.: 42,000
Price: $1.00 **Subscription:** $40.00/year
Publication description: It is an urban publication with coverage of business, finance, political, social and health issues that are prevalent in the African and Caribbean American communities.
Date established: 1989

SOUTHEAST CHICAGO OBSERVER

Southeast Chicago Development Commission
9204 S. Commercial Ave. #307
Chicago, IL 60617
Jerome A. Jajchik, General Manager
Tel: (773) 768-4386 **Fax:** (773) 768-4394
Email: jjajchik@southeastchicagoobserver.com
Web: www.southeastchicagoobserver.com
Circ.: 17,000
Price: Free **Subscription:** $27.00/year
Publication description: To inform residents, promote business and encourage community growth and development.
Date established: 1998

TODAY'S CHRONICLE

1333 S. Wabash #52
Chicago, IL 60605
Betty Furcron, Publisher
Tel: (773) 291-6976 **Fax:** (708) 849-8679
Email: todayschronicle@worldnet.att.net
Subscription: $35.00/year

UNITY FIRST NEWS

682 Sumner Ave.
Springfield, MA 01108
Janine Fondon, Publisher
Tel: (413) 734-6444 **Fax:** (413) 737-1458
Email: jfondon@unityfirst.com
Web: www.unityfirst.com
Circ.: 60,000

Price: Free **Subscription:** $35.00/year
Date established: 1996

DAILY

CHICAGO DEFENDER

Sengstacke Enterprises
2400 S. Michigan Ave.
Chicago, IL 60616
Ronald Martin, Executive Editor
Tel: (312) 225-2400 **Fax:** (312) 225-5659
Web: www.chicagodefender.com
Circ.: 18,000
Price: $0.35 **Subscription:** $159.80/year
Date established: 1905

DAILY CHALLENGE, THE

The Challenge Group
1195 Atlantic Ave.
Brooklyn, NY 11216
Thomas H. Watkins, Jr., Publisher/CEO
Tel: (718) 636-9500 **Fax:** (718) 857-9115
Email: challengegroup@yahoo.com
Web: www.challenge-group.com
Circ.: 81,000
Price: $0.35 **Subscription:** $125.00/year
Publication description: The Daily Challenge is the only daily newspaper serving the Black community in the New York Metropolitan area. Over the past 30 years the Challenge has come to be the daily that African Americans and Caribbean and African immigrants look to for the truth about issues confronting them in their daily lives. Each day Monday through Friday the Challenge features local, national and international news from the Caribbean, Latin America and Africa and from wherever issues confronting Africans throughout the Diaspora are unfolding.
Date established: 1975

DAILY JOURNAL

General Media Strategies, Inc.
303 W. 42nd St. #515
New York, NY 10036
Steve Mallory, Publisher
Tel: (212) 586-4141 **Fax:** (212) 586-4272
Email: blacknewswatch@aol.com
Circ.: 62,000
Price: $0.35 **Subscription:** $125.00/year
Publication description: To cover local, national and international news as well as issues an events of particular significance to blacks.
Date established: 2001

NATIONAL MEDIA LIMITED SOUTH AFRICA

Media 24, Inc.
National Press Bldg. 1113
Washington, DC 20045
Deon Lamprecht, Washington Bureau Chief
Tel: (202) 638-0399 **Fax:** (202) 393-5647
Email: dlamprec@aol.com
Web: www.news24.com
Publication description: Newspaper Bureau representative of South Africa newspapers: Die Beeld, Die Burger, Die Volksblad, Rapport, City Press.

WINSTON-SALEM JOURNAL

P.O. Box 3159
Winston-Salem, NC 27102
John Witherspoon, President/Publisher
Tel: (336) 727-7211 **Fax:** (336) 727-7315
Email: blackissues@wsjournal.com
Web: www.journalnow.com
Circ.: 85,463
Price: $0.50 **Subscription:** $119.60/year
Publication description: Daily newspaper with a primary coverage area of, nine counties in Northwest North Carolina: Alleghany, Ashe, Davidson, Davie, Forsyth, Stokes, Surry, Watuaga, Wilkes and Yadkin.
Date established: 1897

IRREGULAR

KUJIONA MAGAZINE

White's Art Gallery
2080 Hayes St.
San Francisco, CA 94117
Eugene E. White, Publisher
Tel: (415) 752-3663
Email: eugene_lynnette@sbcglobal.net
Web: www.eugenewhite.com

MONTHLY

AFFIRMATIVE ACTION REGISTER

Affirmative Action, Inc.
8356 Olive Blvd.
St. Louis, MO 63132
Joyce Green, Editor
Tel: (314) 991-1335 **Fax:** (314) 997-1788
Email: aareeo@concentric.net
Web: www.aar-eeo.com
Circ.: 65,000
Price: Free **Subscription:** $15.00/year
Publication description: A national resource for equal opportunity/affirmative action recruitment of professional, managerial, technical and administrative personnel for positions in business, academia, healthcare, government and non-governmental organizations. AAR publishes information to the general population and to a highly targeted audience of minority, female, disabled and veteran candidates.
Date established: 1973

ALAMO CITY CHAMBER NEWS JOURNAL

Alamo City Chamber of Commerce
600 Hemisfair Plz. Way, Bldg. 406-10
San Antonio, TX 78205
Valarie Toller, Publisher
Tel: (210) 226-9055 **Fax:** (210) 226-0524
Email: info@alamocitychamber.org
Web: www.alamocitychamber.org
Circ.: 100
Price: Free
Publication description: Newsletter of the Alamo City Chamber of Commerce.
Date established: 1938

ATLANTA GOODLIFE

Ace III Communications, Inc.
P.O. Box 1347
Decatur, GA 30031-1347
Carolyn Glenn, Publisher
Tel: (404) 373-7779 **Fax:** (404) 373-7721
Email: cfjglenn@hotmail.com
Web: www.atlantagoodlifemagazine.com
Circ.: 25,000
Price: $2.00 **Subscription:** $24.00/year
Publication description: Atlanta goodlife is metro Atlanta's only life and style magazine featuring the city's affluent African-American residents up close and in person. Revealing, entertaining, and thought provoking, we focus on culture, fashion, style, home, health, relationships and spirituality.
Date established: 1999

ATLANTA METRO MAGAZINE

Positive Publications, Inc.
4405 Mall Blvd. #521
Union City, GA 30291
Creed W. Pannell, Jr., Publisher
Tel: (770) 969-7711 **Fax:** (770) 969-7811
Email: atlmet@bellsouth.net

Circ.: 29,000
Price: $1.00 Subscription: $12.00/year
Date established: 1984

ATLANTA TRIBUNE MAGAZINE

L&L Communications, Inc.
875 Old Roswell Rd. #C-100
Roswell, GA 30076-1660
Pat Lottier, Publisher
Tel: (770) 587-0501 Fax: (770) 642-6501
Email: info@atlantatribune.com
Web: www.atlantatribune.com
Circ.: 30,000
Price: $3.95 Subscription: $24.00/year
Publication description: The magazine is
Black Atlanta's leading source for relevant,
thought-provoking news and information
on business, careers, technology, wealth-
building, politics and education.
Date established: 1987

BLACK BUSINESS JOURNAL, THE

The Black Business Journal
8303 SW Fwy. #100
Houston, TX 77074
Chido Nwangwu, Founder/Publisher
Tel: (713) 270-5500 Fax: (713) 270-8131
Email: founder@bbjonline.com
Web: http://bbjonline.com
Price: Free
Publication description: The Black Business
Journal contains diversity issues, technology
insight and financial information magazine
for African-Americans an non-Blacks who
do business in the community.
Date established: 1998

BLACK BUSINESS LISTINGS NEWSPAPER

Black Business Listings Newspaper
P.O. Box 12456
Oakland, CA 94604
C. Diane Howell, Ph.D., Publisher
Tel: (510) 839-0690 Fax: (510) 839-0565
Email: blackexpo@aol.com
Web: www.blackexpo2004.com
Circ.: 35,000
Price: Free Subscription: $15.00/year
Publication description: Monthly newspaper
featuring listings of businesses, African-
Americans in major corporations and public
agencies, an extensive calendar of events,
business and job opportunities.
Date established: 1989

BLACK ENTERPRISE MAGAZINE

Earl G. Graves Publishing Company, Inc.
130 5th Ave.
New York, NY 10011-4399
Earl G. Graves, Publisher
Tel: (212) 242-8000 Fax: (212) 886-9610
Email: benyc_ads@blackenterprise.com
Web: www.blackenterprise.com
Price: $3.99 Subscription: $17.95/year
Date established: 1970

BLACK SUBURBAN JOURNAL, THE

The Black Suburban Journal Publishing
P.O. Box 277
Paoli, PA 19301
Robert Booker, Publisher
Tel: (610) 827-1499 Fax: (610) 827-1479
Email: booker@voicenet.com
Circ.: 80,000
Price: $0.50 Subscription: $30.00/year
Date established: 1996

BLK

BLK Publishing Co., Inc.
P.O. Box 83912
Los Angeles, CA 90083-0912
Alan Bell, Publisher
Tel: (310) 410-0808 Fax: (310) 410-9250
Email: newsroom@blk.com

Web: www.blk.com
Circ.: 35,000
Price: $2.95 Subscription: $18.00/year
Publication description: BLK includes in-
depth feature articles, profiles, interviews,
analysis, controversy and commentary as
well as news from across the nation, the
arts, a media watch column and an irreverent
gossip column.
Date established: 1988

CAMPUS DIGEST

Tuskegee University
223 Kresge Ctr.
Tuskegee, AL 36088
Denise Berkhalter, Director of Public Media
Affairs
Tel: (334) 727-8263 Fax: (334) 724-4586
Email: campusdigest@tuskegee.edu
Web: www.tuskegee.edu/campusdigest
Circ.: 3,000
Price: Free
Publication description: Student newspaper.

COLORSNW MAGAZINE

1319 Dexter Ave. North #250
Seattle, WA 98109
Robert Jeffrey, Jr., Publisher/CEO
Tel: (206) 444-9251 Fax: (206) 281-7490
Email: info@colorsnw.com
Web: www.colorsnw.com
Circ.: 25,000
Price: Free Subscription: $30.00/year
Date established: 2002

EBONY MAGAZINE

Johnson Publishing, Inc.
820 S. Michigan Ave.
Chicago, IL 60605
John H. Johnson, Publisher
Tel: (312) 322-9200 Fax: (312) 322-0951
Web: www.ebony.com
Circ.: 16,248,000
Price: $3.50 Subscription: $22.00/year
Date established: 1945

ESSENCE MAGAZINE

Essence Communications
1500 Broadway, 6th Fl.
New York, NY 10036
Angela Burt-Murry, Editor
Tel: (212) 642-0600 Fax: (212) 921-5173
Email: info@essence.com
Web: www.essence.com
Circ.: 1,000,000
Price: $6.00 Subscription: $18.96/year

EVERYBODY'S MAGAZINE

Herman Hall Communications, Inc.
1630 Nostrand Ave.
Brooklyn, NY 11226
Herman Hall, Publisher
Tel: (718) 941-1879 Fax: (718) 941-1886
Email: everybodys@msn.com
Web: www.everybodysmag.com
Circ.: 90,000
Price: $3.00 Subscription: $15.00/year
Publication description: To serves Caribbean-
American consumers from Alaska to Louisiana
to New York. It is the most influential of
Caribbean-American publications. It covers
performings arts, concerts, politics, sports,
technology, music, fashion, food and
restaurants, theater reviews and more.
Date established: 1977

FLORIDA TREND

490 1st Ave. South
St. Petersburg, FL 33701
Lynda Keever, Publisher/COO
Tel: (727) 821-5800
Email: lkeever@floridatrend.com
Web: www.floridatrend.com

Subscription: $29.95-$39.95/year
Date established: 1960

FORT VALLEY HERALD

P.O. Box 2066
Savannah, GA 31402
Robert James, Publisher
Tel: (912) 233-6128 Fax: (912) 233-6140
Email: sharon@savannahtribune.com
Web: www.savannahtribune.com
Circ.: 6,000
Price: Free Subscription: $30.00/year
Date established: 1985

GUYANA MONITOR

P.O. Box 190222
Richmond Hill, NY 11419
Mustak Rasul, Publisher
Tel: (718) 835-5708 Fax: (718) 835-5708
Email: mrasul821@aol.com
Web: www.acgusa.us
Circ.: 15,000
Price: Free
Publication description: Covers news from
Guyana, development in the Caribbean, and
some local and national current events.
Date established: 1992

HMBC NETWORK NEWSLETTER

Houston Minority Business Council,
Regional Council
6671 SW Fwy. #110
Houston, TX 77074
Richard Huebner, Executive Director
Tel: (713) 271-7805 Fax: (713) 271-9770
Email: info@hmbc.org
Web: www.hmbc.org
Circ.: 2,000
Price: Free
Date established: 1973

MARKETING TO THE EMERGING MAJORITIES

EPM Communications, Inc.
160 Mercer St., 3rd Fl.
New York, NY 10012-3212
Ira Mayer, Publisher
Tel: (212) 941-0099 Fax: (212) 941-1622
Email: info@epmcom.com
Web: www.epmcom.com
Price: $35.00 Subscription: $325.00/year
Publication description: Publish information
on marketing to Black, Hispanic and Asian
Americans.
Date established: 1988

MINORITY CAREER JOURNAL

C.L. Lovick and Associates, Inc.
5777 W. Century Blvd. #1480
Los Angeles, CA 90045
Calvin Lovick, Publisher
Tel: (310) 410-7220 Fax: (310) 410-7225
Email: minoritycareer@sbcglobal.net
Web: www.minoritycareer.com
Circ.: 40,000
Price: $2.95
Date established: 1990

NETWORK JOURNAL, THE

39 Broadway #2120
New York, NY 10006
Rosalind McLymont, Editor
Tel: (212) 962-3791 Fax: (212) 962-3537
Email: editors@tnj.com
Web: www.tnj.com
Circ.: 22,000
Price: $3.00 Subscription: $15.00/year
Publication description: The Network Journal
reaches professionals, small business owners
and upwardly mobile individuals. Readers are
provided with motivating articles on innovative
business techniques that are essential
for today's entrepreneurs and corporate

employees. Each issue gives business owners
new ideas in areas such as management,
marketing, legal matters, taxes, and office
technology.
Date established: 1993

NUBIAN NEWS

324 S. Broad St.
Trenton, NJ 08608
Kamau Kujichagulia, Publisher
Tel: (609) 858-2785 Fax: (609) 394-0075
Email: nubiannews@nubiannews.com
Web: www.nubiannews.com
Circ.: 10,000
Price: Free Subscription: $39.00/year
Date established: 1989

OUR TIME PRESS

DBG Media
679 Lafayette Ave.
Brooklyn, NY 11216-1009
David Mark Greaves, Publisher
Tel: (718) 599-6828 Fax: (718) 599-6825
Email: editors@ourtimepress.com
Web: www.ourtimepress.com
Circ.: 30,000
Price: Free Subscription: $35.00/year
Publication description: Our Time Press is
one of the largest African-American owned
and operated free tabloid-sized papers in
New York.
Date established: 1995

PURE-NEWS USA

1701 S. College Ave.
Springfield, IL 62704
T.C. Christian, Jr., CEO/Publisher
Tel: (217) 528-5588 Fax: (217) 528-6777
Email: tellit@pure-news-usa.com
Web: www.pure-news-usa.com
Circ.: 55,000
Price: Free Subscription: $10.00/year
Publication description: The purpose of Pure-
News USA is a free monthly newspaper, which
is of high quality, informative, newsworthy, and
entertaining. Their mission is to target the vast
diverse market of readers and consumers who
would welcome a free national newspaper.
Pure-News USA is available at churches,
colleges, government offices, restaurants,
retail stores, and airports.
Date established: 1983

RENAISSANCE NEWS IN PITTSBURGH

Renaissance Publications, Inc.
1516 5th Ave.
Pittsburgh, PA 15219
Connie Portis, President/Publisher
Tel: (412) 391-8208 Fax: (412) 391-8006
Email: renpub@earthlink.net
Circ.: 30,000
Price: Free Subscription: $25.00/year
Date established: 1965

SAN JOSE SILICON VALLEY NAACP

San Jose Silicon Valley NAACP
304 N. 6th St.
San Jose, CA 95112
Rick L. Callender, Deputy Executive Director
Tel: (408) 295-3394 Fax: (408) 295-4355
Email: rick@sanjosenaacp.org
Web: www.sanjosenaacp.org
Publication description: The aim of the San
Jose Silicon Valley NAACP for the past 50
years has been and continues to be the
protection and the enhancement of the
civil rights of African Americans and other
minorities.
Date established: 1952

SCOOP MAGAZINE

2021 E. 52nd St. #204
Indianapolis, IN 46205

Clifford Robinson, Publisher
Tel: (317) 748-5261
Web: www.scoopmagazine.info
Price: Free

SISTER 2 SISTER MAGAZINE
P.O. Box 41148
Jamie Foster Brown, Publisher
Tel: (301) 270-5999
Web: www.s2smagazine.com
Price: $14.99/year
Date established: 1988

SOURCE, THE
28 W. 23rd St.
New York, NY 10010
David Mays, Publisher
Tel: (212) 253-3700 **Fax:** (212) 253-9344
Email: subscription@thesource.com
Web: www.thesource.com
Circ.: 500,000
Price: $2.99 **Subscription:** $19.95/year
Publication description: Hip-hop music, culture & politics.
Date established: 1988

TAKE PRIDE COMMUNITY MAGAZINE
1014 Franklin St. SE
Grand Rapids, MI 49507-1327
Walter L. Mathis, Sr., Founder
Tel: (616) 243-4114
Email: wmathis@oneblood-onerace.org
Web: www.oneblood-onerace.org
Circ.: 10,000
Price: Free **Subscription:** $26.00/year
Date established: 1991

URBAN SPECTRUM, THE
2499 Washington St.
Denver, CO 80205
Rosalind "Bee" J. Harris-Diaw, Publisher
Tel: (303) 292-6446 **Fax:** (303) 292-6543
Email: urbanspectrum@qwest.net
Web: www.urbanspectrum.net
Circ.: 25,000
Price: Free **Subscription:** $42.00/year
Publication description: The Urban Spectrum's mission is to spread the news about people of color.
Date established: 1987

UPSCALE MAGAZINE
600 Bronner Brothers
Atlanta, GA 30310
Bernard Bronner Publisher
Tel: (404) 758-7467
Web: www.upscalemagazine.com
Price:$12.00/year

VIBE MAGAZINE
Miller Publishing Group, LLC
215 Lexington Ave., 6th Fl.
New York, NY 10016
Len Burnette, Publisher
Tel: (212) 448-7300 **Fax:** (212) 448-7400
Email: info@vibe.com
Web: www.vibe.com
Price: $3.50 **Subscription:** $11.95/year

WORD UP!
Great Eastern Publications, Inc.
210 Rt. 4 East #211
Paramus, NJ 07652
Mary Ann Cassatta, Editor
Tel: (201) 843-4004 X150 **Fax:** (201) 843-8636
Circ.: 150,000
Price: $3.00
Publication description: Urban Music publication.

YO! YOUTH OUTLOOK
Pacific News Service
275 9th St.
San Francisco, CA 94103
Kevin Weston, Editor
Tel: (415) 503-4170 **Fax:** (415) 503-0970
Email: kweston@pacificnews.org
Web: www.youthoutlook.org
Circ.: 25,000
Subscription: $15.00/10 issues
Publication description: YO! Youth Outlook is an award-winning literary monthly journal of youth life in the Bay Area. Featuring in-depth reporting pieces and first-person essays, comic strips and poetry pages, YO! is the communication outlet for youth who feel their voice and visions need to be seen and heard. YO! is a bridge to the world of youth expression.
Date established: 1991

PERIODICALLY

BAYVIEW HERITAGE
Bayview Opera House, Inc.
4705 3rd St.
San Francisco, CA 94124
Sheila Bradford-Bell, Editor
Tel: (415) 824-0386 **Fax:** (415) 824-7124
Email: bvoh@pacbell.net
Web: www.bayviewoperahouse.org
Price: Free
Publication description: To provide cultural enrichment by promoting community arts and education to ensure economic and employment development in the Bayview Hunters Point Community.
Date established: 1991

MOSAIC MAGAZINE
314 W. 231st St. #470
Bronx, NY 10463
Ron Kavanaugh, Publisher/Editor in Chief
Tel: (718) 530-9132 **Fax:** (718) 504-9600
Email: magazine@mosaicbooks.com
Web: www.mosaicbooks.com
Subscription: $17.00/ 8 issues
Publication description: Launched in 1998, with a desire to showcase and honestly critique African American and Hispanic literature, Mosaic is proud to be in the forefront of literature.
Date established: 1998

SISTA
The National Council of Negro Women
633 Pennsylvania Ave. NW
Washington, DC 20004
Cheryl R. Cooper, Executive Director
Tel: (202) 737-0120 **Fax:** (202) 737-0476
Email: ccooper@ncnw.org
Web: www.ncnw.org
Price: Free
Publication description: The newsletter focuses on the advocacy process.
Date established: 1935

VANGUARD
Minority Business Enterprise Legal Defense and Education Fund
1100 Mercantile Ln. #115-A
Largo, MD 20774
Anthony W. Robinson, Editor
Tel: (301) 583-4648 **Fax:** (301) 772-8392
Email: staff@mbeldef.org
Web: www.mbeldef.org
Price: Free
Publication description: Minority Business Enterprise Legal Defense and Education Fund newsletter.
Date established: 1980

QUARTERLY

AABE ENERGY NEWS
American Association of Blacks in Energy
927 15th St. NW #200
Washington, DC 20005
Lakeesha Wilson, Executive Assistant
Tel: (202) 371-9530 **Fax:** (202) 371-9218
Email: lwilson@aabe.org
Web: www.aabe-dcmet.org
Circ.: 1,200
Price: Free
Publication description: Newsletter that offers a variety of news items about the recent AABE events, as well as information about chapter's activities.

ABC NEWSLETTER
Association of Black Cardiologists, Inc.
6849-B2 Peachtree Dunwoody Rd. NE
Atlanta, GA 30328
Elizabeth Ofili, Editor In Chief
Tel: (678) 302-4222 **Fax:** (678) 302-4223
Email: abcardio@abcardio.org
Web: www.abcardio.org
Circ.: 15,000
Price: Free
Publication description: This publication highlights new and innovative medical events and accomplishments of our members.

AFRICA RENEWAL
United Nations
United Nations, #DC1-550
New York, NY 10017
Ernest Harsch, Managing Editor
Tel: (212) 963-6857 **Fax:** (212) 963-4556
Email: africa_renewal@un.org
Web: www.africarecovery.org
Circ.: 35,000
Price: Free **Subscription:** $20.00/year
Publication description: Africa Recovery magazine seeks to provide timely and accurate news and analysis on the critical economic and development challenges facing the African continent.
Date established: 2004

AFRICAN AMERICAN GOLFER'S DIGEST
139 Fulton St. #209
New York, NY 10038
Debert Cook, Publisher
Tel: (212) 571-6559 **Fax:** (212) 571-1943
Email: debertcook@aol.com
Web: www.africanamericangolfersdigest.com
Circ.: 20,000
Price: $4.50 **Subscription:** $18.00/year
Date established: 2002

AFRICAN AMERICAN REVIEW
Saint Louis University
3800 Lindell Blvd., Humanities #317
St. Louis, MO 63108
Aileen M. Keenan, Managing Editor
Tel: (314) 977-3688 **Fax:** (314) 977-1514
Email: keenanam@slu.edu
Web: http://aar.slu.edu
Circ.: 2,000
Price: $12.00 **Subscription:** $40.00-80.00/year
Publication description: Official publication of the Division on Black American Literature and Culture of the Modern Language Association, the magazine promotes a lively exchange among writers and scholars in the arts, humanities, and social sciences who hold diverse perspectives on African American Literature and culture.
Date established: 1967

AFRICAN VOICES MAGAZINE
African Voices Communications, Inc.
270 W. 96th St.
New York, NY 10025
Carolyn Butts, Publisher/Editor
Tel: (212) 865-2982 **Fax:** (212) 316-3335
Email: cbutts@africanvoices.com
Web: www.africanvoices.com
Subscription: $12.00/year
Publication description: An art and literary magazine, founded by and established for African and African-American artists and writers.
Date established: 1992

AFRICA UPDATE NEWSLETTER
Central Connecticut State University African Studies Program History Department, CCSU
1615 Stanley St.
New Britain, CT 06050
Gloria T. Emeagwali, Chief Editor
Tel: (860) 832-2815 **Fax:** (860) 832-7804
Email: emeagwali@ccsu.edu
Web: www.ccsu.edu/afstudy
Price: Free
Publication description: Africa Update is the quarterly newsletter of the Central Connecticut State University African Studies Program.
Date established: 1993

ALTERNATIVE PRESS INDEX
Alternative Press Center
P.O. Box 33109
Baltimore, MD 21218
Chuck D'Adamo, Editor
Tel: (410) 243-2471 **Fax:** (410) 235-5325
Email: altpress@altpress.org
Web: www.altpress.org
Circ.: 750,000
Subscription: $425.00-print /$825.00-electronic/year
Date established: 1969

ATLANTA BUSINESS JOURNAL
Positive Publications, Inc.
4405 Mall Blvd. #521
Union City, GA 30291
Creed W. Pannell, Jr., Publisher
Tel: (770) 969-7711 **Fax:** (770) 969-7811
Email: atlmet@bellsouth.net
Circ.: 45,000
Price: $2.95 **Subscription:** $25.00/year
Date established: 1984

AMERICAN LEGACY MAGAZINE
60th Ave.
New York, NY 10011
Rodney J. Reynolds, Publisher
Tel: (212) 367-3107
Email: apeterson@forbes.com
Web: www.americanlegacygacymag.com

BAPRC'S NEWSLETTER
Black Adoption Placement and Research Center
7801 Edgewater Dr. #2000
Oakland, CA 94621
Gloria King, Executive Director
Tel: (510) 430-3600 **Fax:** (510) 430-3615
Email: family@baprc.org
Web: www.baprc.org
Price: Free
Publication description: Presents news and information of interest to BAPRC.
Date established: 1990

BEAVER COUNTY NAACP NEWSLETTER
Beaver County NAACP
392 Franklin Ave. #25
Aliquippa, PA 15001
Willie Sallis, President
Tel: (724) 378-6690 **Fax:** (724) 378-6870

Email: bcnaacp@access995.com
Circ.: 100
Price: Free
Publication description: Newsletter for the Beaver County NAACP.
Date established: 1911

BIHA NEWSLETTER

Black, Indian, Hispanic, and Asian Women in Action
1830 James Ave. North
Minneapolis, MN 55411
Alice O. Lynch, Executive Director
Tel: (612) 521-2986 **Fax:** (612) 529-6745
Email: info@biha.org
Web: www.biha.org
Circ.: 2,000
Price: Free
Publication description: BIHA was created to provide education, information and advocacy for and by Communities of Color and to serve as a forum for translating current concerns (family violence, racism, ageism, AIDS, chemical abuse) within communities of color for presentation to society as a whole.
Date established: 1983

BLACK COLLEGE RADIO NEWS

National Association of Black College Broadcasters
P.O. Box 3191
Atlanta, GA 30302
Lo Jelks, Chairman
Tel: (404) 523-6136 **Fax:** (404) 523-5467
Email: bcrmail@blackcollegeradio.com
Web: www.blackcollegeradio.com
Circ.: 25,000
Price: Free **Subscription:** $42.00/year
Publication description: The newspaper is distributed free to more than 100 black colleges and universities throughout the US.
Date established: 1978

BLACK EOE JOURNAL

6845 Indiana Ave. #200
Riverside, CA 92506
Pamela Burke, Senior Account Representative
Tel: (800) 487-5099 **Fax:** (951) 276-1700
Email: pburke@blackeoejournal.com
Web: www.blackeoejournal.com
Circ.: 125,000
Price: $3.65 **Subscription:** $16.00/year
Publication description: The Black Equal Opportunity Employment Journal is one of the nation's largest and longest established publications supporting the minority community and addressing the needs of employers as they relate to workforce diversity.
Date established: 1990

BLACK FORTUNE MAGAZINE

Niche Lab
415 Washington Ave. #22
Brooklyn, NY 11238
Dora Thomas, Editor
Tel: (516) 292-2438 **Fax:** (516) 292-2442
Email: sheilanevins@yahoo.com
Circ.: 10,000
Price: $19.95
Publication description: Black Fortune Magazine was founded through the need to provide sound investment information to the growing number of African American families that wish to improve their "quality of life."
Date established: 2001

BLACK HISTORY BULLETIN, THE

Association for the Study of African-American Life and History
CB Powell Bldg., 525 Bryant St. NW #C142
Washington, DC 20059
Daryl Michael Scott, Publication Chair

Tel: (202) 865-0053 **Fax:** (202) 265-7920
Email: executivedirector@asalh.net
Web: www.asalh.org
Circ.: 2,000
Price: $4.50 **Subscription:** $40.00/year
Publication description: To provide those who instruct youth with innovative materials, which teach Black history and conform to national history standards.
Date established: 1937

BLACK MEDIA NEWS

Life Media Publishing, Inc.
7657 Winnetka Ave. #504
Winnetka, CA 91306
Sandy Gentry, Editor
Tel: (818) 776-2500 **Fax:** (818) 776-2562
Email: bmnmedia@aol.com
Web: www.blackmedianews.com
Price: Free
Date established: 1988

BLACK REPARATIONS TIMES

National Coalition of Blacks for Reparations in America
P.O. Box 90604
Washington, DC 20090-0604
Wautella Yusuf, Publisher
Tel: (202) 466-1622 **Fax:** (202) 291-4600
Email: nationalncobra@aol.com
Web: www.ncobra.com
Price: $5.00 **Subscription:** $25.00/year
Publication description: Newspaper
Date established: 2000

BLACK TENNIS MAGAZINE

P.O. Box 210767
Dallas, TX 75211
Marcus A. Freeman, Jr., Editor
Tel: (214) 339-7370 **Fax:** (214) 339-7370
Email: marcus.freeman.tennis@airmail.net
Web: www.btmag.com
Circ.: 9,000
Price: $6.00 **Subscription:** $15.00/year
Publication description: To inform the public about the outstanding achievements of minority tennis players, organizations, and programs in all parts of the world.
Date established: 1977

BRIDGE, THE

Opportunities Minority News Network
P.O. Box 11064
Portland, ME 04104
Leonard Cummings, Publisher
Tel: (207) 772-7767
Circ.: 4,000
Price: Free
Date established: 1994

CBCF NEWSLETTER

Congressional Black Caucus Foundation, Inc.
1720 Massachusetts Ave. NW
Washington, DC 20036
Patty Rice, Director of Media Relations/Communications
Tel: (301) 405-8893 **Fax:** (202) 263-0847
Email: harrell@emd.edu
Web: www.cbcfinc.org
Price: Free
Publication description: CBCF's mission is to assist the leaders of today, while helping to prepare a new generation of leaders for the future. To that end, the CBCF has worked to broaden and elevate the influence of African Americans in the political, legislative and public policy arenas.
Date established: 1976

COLOR OF SERVICE MAGAZINE

P.O. Box 45589
Los Angeles, CA 90045

Shawn Lindsey, CEO/Publisher
Tel: (800) 598-6111 **Fax:** (323) 294-3313
Email: ctt3navy@aol.com
Web: www.colorofservice.com
Subscription: $11.00/year
Publication description: Color of Service Magazine is the first multicultural military magazine.

COLORLINES MAGAZINE

Applied Research Ctr.
4096 Piedmont Ave. PMB 319
Oakland, CA 94611-9924
Tram Nguyen, Executive Editor
Tel: (510) 653-3415 **Fax:** (510) 653-3427
Email: colorlines@arc.org
Web: www.colorlines.com
Circ.: 5,000
Price: $4.95 **Subscription:** $16.00/year
Publication description: ColorLines is the first national, multiracial magazine devoted to covering the politics and creations of communities of color.
Date established: 1998

CON BRIO NEWSLETTER

National Association for the Study and Performance of African American Music
1201 Mary Jane
Memphis, TN 38116
Frank Suggs, Editor
Tel: (901) 396-2913
Email: fsuggs@ilstu.edu
Web: www.naspaam.org
Circ.: 700
Price: Free
Publication description: Publication with an emphasis on African American Music. It reaches urban school systems; Historically Black Colleges and Universities; African American Non Profit Music Organizations; professional African American Music Educators; teachers, composers and arrangers; and end users of African American music related products.
Date established: 1990

ECLIPSE MAGAZINE

National Association for Black Veterans, Inc.
P.O. Box 11432
Milwaukee, WI 53211
Richard Rodgers, Director of Management Services
Tel: (877) 622-8387 **Fax:** (414) 342-1073
Email: nabvets@nabvets.com
Web: www.nabvets.com
Circ.: 5,000
Date established: 1973

ENTREPRENEUR MAGAZINE

African American Chamber of Commerce of Westchester and Rockland Counties, Inc.
100 Stevens Ave. #202
Mount Vernon, NY 10550
Robin L. Douglas, President/CEO/Founder
Tel: (914) 699-9050 **Fax:** (914) 699-6279
Email: robinlisadouglas@cs.com
Web: www.africanamericanchamberofcommercenys.org/entreprenuer.asp
Circ.: 15,000
Price: Free
Publication description: The Entrepreneur is designed to give exposure to new members of the chamber, in addition to an opportunity for members to advertise. Readers will get updates on community and chamber events, financial tips and current news within the business community via print media.
Date established: 1996

ETHNICITY AND DISEASE JOURNAL

International Society of Hypertension in Blacks, Inc.
100 Auburn Ave. NE #401
Atlanta, GA 30303
Christopher T. Fitzpatrick, CEO
Tel: (404) 880-0343 **Fax:** (404) 880-0347
Email: inforequest@ishib.org
Web: www.ishib.org
Circ.: 375,000
Subscription: $115.00-$207.00/year
Publication description: Dedicated to improving the health and life expectancy of Ethnic Minority population around the world.
Date established: 1991

FAMILY DIGEST

Family Digest Media Group
P.O. Box 1900-E
Danville, CA 94526
Tel: (888) 923-7673
Web: www.familydigest.com
Price: $3.99

FOR MY PEOPLE

Project Bait
30 Josephine, 3rd Fl.
Detroit, MI 48202-1810
David Rambeau, Executive Producer
Tel: (313) 871-3333
Email: davidrambeau@hotmail.com
Web: http://projectbait.blakgold.net
Circ.: 1,000
Date established: 1970

FORUM, THE

National Forum for Black Administrators
777 N. Capitol St. NE #807
Washington, DC 20002
John E. Saunders, III, CAE, Executive Director
Tel: (202) 408-9300 **Fax:** (202) 408-8558
Email: jsaunders@nfbpa.org
Web: www.nfbpa.org
Circ.: 2,500
Price: Free
Publication description: The mission of the NFBPA is embodied in the organization's commitment to strengthen the position of Blacks within the field of public administration; to increase the number of Blacks appointed to executive positions in public service organizations; and, to groom and prepare younger, aspiring administrators for senior public management posts in the years ahead.
Date established: 1983

FUSION

Newspaper Association of America
1921 Gallows Rd. #600
Vienna, VA 22182-3900
Jeanne Fox-Alston, Publisher
Tel: (703) 902-1725 **Fax:** (703) 917-0636
Email: jeanne.foxalston@naa.org
Web: www.naa.org
Price: Free
Date established: 1992

GLOBAL WOMAN MAGAZINE

Global Black Woman
P.O. Box 8089
Cherry Hill, NJ 08002
Dana Marniche, Editor/Publisher
Tel: (856) 482-0833 **Fax:** (856) 667-1078
Email: gbwoman@aol.com
Circ.: 90,000-110,000
Price: $3.95 **Subscription:** $15.95/year
Date established: 2001

ILLINOIS BRIEF, THE
American Civil Liberties Union
180 N. Michigan Ave. #2300
Chicago, IL 60601
Edwin C. Yohnka, Director of
Communications
Tel: (312) 201-9740 **Fax:** (312) 201-9760
Email: acluofillinois@aclu-il.org
Web: www.aclu-il.org
Circ.: 18,000
Price: Free **Subscription:** $25.00/year
Publication description: Newsletter
Date established: 1920

INFORMATION PLUS
Fort Worth Metropolitan Black Chamber of
Commerce
1150 S. Fwy #211
Fort Worth, TX 76104
Glenda Thompson, Editor
Tel: (817) 871-6538 **Fax:** (817) 332-6438
Email: gthompson@fwmbcc.org
Web: www.fwmbcc.org
Circ.: 500
Price: Free
Publication description: Metropolitan Black
Chamber of Commerce's Newsletter.
Date established: 2002

IRINKERINDO: A JOURNAL OF AFRICAN MIGRATION
Brooklyn College, CUNY
Department of Political Science, 2900
Bedford Ave., James Hall #3409
Brooklyn, NY 11210
Mojabaolu Olufunke Okeme, Ph.D., Editor
Tel: (718) 951-4318 **Fax:** (718) 951-4833
Email: mokome@princeton.edu
Web: www.africamigration.com
Circ.: 5,000
Price: Free
Date established: 2003

IVY LEAF
Alpha Kappa Alpha Sorority, Inc.
5656 S. Stony Island Ave.
Chicago, IL 60637
Connie Cochran Toole, Ivy Leaf Media
Relations
Tel: (773) 684-1282 **Fax:** (773) 288-8251
Email: ctoole@aka1908.com
Web: www.aka1908.com
Circ.: 40,000
Price: $4.00
Date established: 1908

JOURNAL OF AFRICAN AMERICAN HISTORY
Association for the Study of African
American Life and History
CB Powell Bldg., 525 Bryant St. NW #C142
Washington, DC 20059
VP Franklin, Editor
Tel: (202) 865-0053 **Fax:** (202) 265-7920
Email: executivedirector@asalh.net
Web: www.asalh.org
Circ.: 3,000
Price: $10.00 **Subscription:** $35.00-75.00/
year
Publication description: To promote, research,
preserve, interpret, and disseminate
information about black life, history and
culture to the global community.
Date established: 1916

JOURNAL OF NEGRO EDUCATION, THE
Howard University
2900 Van Ness St. NW #116, Holy Cross Hall
Washington, DC 20008
Frederick D. Harper, Editor
Tel: (202) 806-8120 **Fax:** (202) 806-8434
Email: jne@howard.edu
Web: www.journalnegroed.org

Circ.: 1,500
Price: $30.00 **Subscription:** $55.00/year
Publication description: To stimulate the
collection and facilitate the dissemination of
facts about the education of Black people.
Date established: 1932

MCKINLEY MEDALLION
Ada S. Mckinley Community Services, Inc.
725 S. Wells #1-A
Chicago, IL 60607
George Jones, Jr., Executive Director
Tel: (312) 554-0600 **Fax:** (312) 554-0292
Web: www.adasmckinley.org
Circ.: 2,500
Price: Free
Publication description: To serve those who,
because of disabilities or other limiting
conditions, need help in finding and pursuing
paths leading to healthy, productive, and
fulfilling lives.
Date established: 1978

MOREHOUSE MAGAZINE
Morehouse College, Office of
Communications
830 Westview Dr. SW
Atlanta, GA 30314
Vikie Hampton, Editor
Tel: (404) 215-2680 **Fax:** (404) 215-2729
Email: vhampton@morehouse.edu
Web: www.morehouse.edu/
communications/publications.html
Price: Free
Publication description: Monthly newsletter
for students, faculty, staff and friends of
the College.

NEWS LETTER
Black Administrators in Child Welfare, Inc.
440 1st St. NW, 3rd Fl.
Washington, DC 20001
Sondra M. Jackson, Executive Director
Tel: (202) 662-4284 **Fax:** (202) 638-4004
Email: rgraham@cwla.org
Web: www.blackadministrators.org
Date established: 1971

NEWSLETTER
National Organization for the Advancement
of Haitians
1400 E. West Hwy. #G
Silver Spring, MD 20910
Dr. Joseph Baptiste, Chairman
Tel: (301) 585-1235
Email: jbaptiste@aol.com
Web: www.noahhaiti.org
Date established: 1991

NEWSPLUS
National Association of Black Accountants,
Inc.
7249 Hanover Pkwy. #A
Greenbelt, MD 20770
Johnetta Boseman Hardy, Deputy Executive
Director
Tel: (301) 474-6222 **Fax:** (301) 474-3114
Email: jbhardy@nabainc.org
Web: www.nabainc.org
Circ.: 20,000
Price: Free **Subscription:** $20.00/year
Publication description: To provide a
communication mechanism whereby readers
are kept abreast of key topics of interest
within the accounting, finance, and business
professions.
Date established: 1984

OPEN FORUM
American Civil Liberties Union of Southern
California
1616 W. Beverly Blvd.
Los Angeles, CA 90026

Michelle Matthews, Editor
Tel: (213) 977-9500 **Fax:** (213) 250-3919
Email: acluinfo@aclu-sc.org
Web: www.aclu-sc.org
Circ.: 45,000
Price: Free
Date established: 1923

PURE HEART MAGAZINE
Triumph Publications, Inc.
P.O. Box 11130
Birmingham, AL 35202
Nicol King, Publisher
Tel: (205) 862-1488 **Fax:** (205) 520-5138
Publication description: The nation's premiere
publication for and about African-American
Christian Singles.
Date established: 1998

REGINE MAGAZINE
Regine Magazine, LLC
P.O. Box 1930
New York, NY 10025
Regine Lopez-Pierre, Editor
Tel: (212) 961-9371
Email: reginemagazine@aol.com
Circ.: 25,000
Subscription: $36.00/year
Publication description: To celebrate the
affluence and social consciousness of urban
professionals. It will also report on the social
scene for black-tie dinners, conferences,
book signings, art exhibits and fundraisers.
Date established: 2003

REPARATIONS NOW
National Coalition of Blacks for Reparations
in America
P.O. Box 90604
Washington, DC 20090-0604
Wautella Yusuf, Publisher
Tel: (202) 466-1622 **Fax:** (202) 291-4600
Email: nationalncobra@aol.com
Web: www.ncobra.com
Price: Free
Publication description: Quarterly membership
newsletter.
Date established: 1995

TRANSITION MAGAZINE
Soft Skull Press of Brooklyn
69 Dunster St.
Cambridge, MA 02138
Michael C. Vazquez, Executive Editor
Tel: (617) 496-2847 **Fax:** (617) 496-2877
Email: transition@fas.harvard.edu
Web: www.transitionmagazine.com
Circ.: 3,500
Price: $10.00 **Subscription:** $30.00-90.00/
year
Publication description: Transition Magazine
is published by Duke University Press.
Date established: 1961

US BLACK ENGINEER
Career Communications Group, Inc.
729 E. Pratt St. #504
Baltimore, MD 21202
Tyrone Taborn, Publisher
Tel: (410) 244-7101 **Fax:** (410) 752-1837
Email: tyrone.taborn@ccgmag.com
Web: www.blackengineer.com
Circ.: 15,300
Price: $6.95 **Subscription:** $26.00/year
Date established: 1986

WESTERN JOURNAL OF BLACK STUDIES, THE
70C Cleveland Hall
Pullman, WA 99164-2103
E. Lincoln James, Editor
Tel: (509) 335-8681 **Fax:** (509) 335-8338

Email: wjbs@mail.wsu.edu
Web: www.wsu.edu/~wjbs
Circ.: 400
Price: $12.00
Publication description: Devoted to publishing
scholarly articles, from a wide range of
disciplines that focus mainly on the experience
of African Americans in the United States of
America.
Date established: 1997

WOMEN'S POLITICAL TIMES
National Women's Political Caucus
1634 I St. NW #310
Washington, DC 20006
Kristin Carter, Editor
Tel: (202) 785-1100 **Fax:** (202) 785-3605
Email: info@nwpc.org
Web: www.nwpc.org
Circ.: 4,000
Price: Free **Subscription:** $20.00/year
Publication description: The purpose of the
National Women's Political Caucus is to
increase women's participation in the political
process and to identify, recruit, train and
support pro-choice women for election and
appointment to public office.
Date established: 1971

SEMIANNUALLY

JOURNAL OF INTERCULTURAL DISCIPLINES
National Association of African American
Studies
P.O. Box 325
Biddeford, ME 04005
Dr. Lemuel Berry, Jr., Executive Director
Tel: (207) 839-8004 **Fax:** (207) 839-3776
Email: naaasconference@earthlink.net
Web: www.naaas.org
Circ.: 700
Date established: 1993

AFRO-AMERICANS IN NEW YORK LIFE AND HISTORY JOURNAL
Afro-American Historical Association of the
Niagara Frontier, Inc.
P.O. Box 63
Buffalo, NY 14207
Sharon Holly, Board Member
Tel: (716) 858-7151
Email: fordham@adelphi.net
Web: www.nyhistory.com/aanylh
Price: $6.00 **Subscription:** $12.00/year
Publication description: The journal will
publish analytical, historical, and descriptive
articles dealing with the life and history of
Afro-Americans in New York State.
Date established: 1974

TRIWEEKLY

FAMUAN, THE
Florida A&M University
510 Orr Dr. #381
Tallahassee, FL 32307-4800
Alexia Robinson, Editor in Chief
Tel: (850) 599-3159 **Fax:** (850) 561-2570
Email: thefamuaneditor@hotmail.com
Web: www.thefamuanonline.com
Circ.: 5,000
Subscription: $50.00/year
Date established: 1900

AFRICAN SUN TIMES
African Sun Times
463 N. Arlington Ave. #17
East Orange, NJ 07017-3927
Chika Onyeani, Publisher
Tel: (973) 675-9919 Fax: (973) 675-5704
Email: afrstime@aol.com
Web: www.africansuntimes.com
Circ.: 45,000
Price: $1.00 Subscription: $60.00/year
Publication description: The largest and only weekly African newspaper with national distribution, printing African news and analysis.
Date established: 1989

AFRICAN-AMERICAN OBSERVER
General Media Strategies, Inc.
303 W. 42nd St. #515
New York, NY 10036
Steve Mallory, Publisher
Tel: (212) 586-4141 Fax: (212) 586-4272
Email: blacknewswatch@aol.com
Circ.: 55,000
Price: $0.75 Subscription: $40.00/year
Publication description: To cover local, national and international news as well as issues an events of particular significance to blacks.
Date established: 1992

AFRO-AMERICAN NEWSPAPER
Afro-American Newspapers Co.
1612 14th St. NW
Washington, DC 20009
Reggie William, Editor
Tel: (202) 332-0080 Fax: (202) 939-7461
Email: dceditor@afro.com
Web: www.afro.com
Circ.: 45,000
Price: $0.50 Subscription: $27.48/year
Date established: 1892

AFRO-AMERICAN NEWSPAPERS, THE
Afro-American Newspapers Co.
2519 N. Charles St.
Baltimore, MD 21218
John J. Oliver, Jr., Publisher
Tel: (410) 554-8200 Fax: (410) 554-8213
Email: dboulware@afro.com
Web: www.afro.com
Circ.: 25,000
Price: $0.50 Subscription: $15.00/year
Publication description: Published weekly in Baltimore and Washington, DC.
Date established: 1892

ALBEMARLE TRIBUNE
P.O. Box 3428
Charlottesville, VA 22903
Agnes White, Publisher
Tel: (434) 979-0373 Fax: (434) 971-5821
Email: awhitehsd01@earthlink.net
Circ.: 8,500
Price: $0.50 Subscription: $40.00/year
Date established: 1954

ANNAPOLIS TIMES, THE
BlackPressUSA Network, The Baltimore Times, Inc.
2513 N. Charles St.
Baltimore, MD 21218
Dena Wane, Managing Editor
Tel: (410) 366-3900 Fax: (410) 243-1627
Email: info@btimes.com
Web: www.btimes.com
Circ.: 32,000
Price: Free Subscription: $60.00/year
Publication description: The Baltimore Times, Inc., publisher of The Baltimore Times, The Annapolis Times, The Shore Times, and The Prince George's County Times weekly newspapers. The Baltimore Times newspapers focus on local and community events, as well as personal finance, health, religion, business, education, sports, entertainment and real estate. Collectively, our publications provide information that enhances the quality of life of our readers.
Date established: 1986

AUC DIGEST, THE
Atlanta University Center
P.O. Box 3191
Atlanta, GA 30302
Lo Jelks, Publisher
Tel: (404) 523-6136
Email: aucdigestmail@aol.com
Web: www.aucdigest.com
Circ.: 25,000
Price: Free Subscription: $42.00/year
Publication description: Weekly newspaper serving the Atlanta University Center. Newspaper served the largest independent group of black colleges and universities in the world.
Date established: 1972

AUGUSTA FOCUS
Walker Group
1143 Laney Walker Blvd.
Augusta, GA 30901
Charles W. Walker, Publisher
Tel: (706) 724-7855 Fax: (706) 724-8432
Email: ads@augustafocus.com
Web: www.augustafocus.com
Circ.: 5,000
Price: $0.50 Subscription: $24.95/year
Publication description: The Augusta Focus has over 21 years experience in developing a news source relied upon for its insight on local and national news, political affairs, commentary and cutting-edge cultural features.
Date established: 1981

BALTIMORE TIMES, THE
BlackPressUSA Network, The Baltimore Times, Inc.
2513 N. Charles St.
Baltimore, MD 21218
Joiy Bramble, Publisher
Tel: (410) 366-3900 Fax: (410) 243-1627
Email: info@btimes.com
Web: www.btimes.com
Circ.: 32,000
Price: Free Subscription: $60.00/year
Publication description: The Baltimore Times, Inc., is the publisher of The Baltimore Times, The Annapolis Times, The Shore Times, and The Prince George's County Times weekly newspapers. The Baltimore Times newspapers focus on local and community events, as well as personal finance, health, religion, business, education, sports, entertainment and real estate. Collectively, our publications provide information that enhances the quality of life of our readers.
Date established: 1986

BEAT WITHIN, THE
Pacific News Service
275 9th St.
San Francisco, CA 94103
David Inocencio, Director/Lead Editor
Tel: (415) 503-4170 Fax: (415) 503-0970
Email: davidi@pacificnews.org
Web: www.thebeatwithin.org/news
Circ.: 1,500
Subscription: $50.00/year
Publication description: The Beat Within is a publication of writing and art from juvenile hall and beyond. Started with one writing and conversation workshop in San Francisco Youth Guidance Center, we now conduct over 40 weekly workshops in 8 county juvenile halls. We produce two weekly editions of the Beat Within, totaling between 120-160 pages, and a Best of The Beat monthly edition.
Date established: 1996

BERKELEY TRI-CITY POST
Post Newspaper Group
405 14th St. #400
Oakland, CA 94612
Paul Cobb, Publisher
Tel: (510) 287-8200 Fax: (510) 287-8247
Email: ads@postnewsgroup.com
Web: www.postnewsgroup.com
Circ.: 50,000
Price: Free Subscription: $99.50/year
Date established: 1963

BLACK ECONOMIC TIMES, THE
1846 E. Rosemeade Pkwy. #193
Carrollton, TX 75007
Chevis King, Jr., Publisher
Tel: (214) 549-4195 Fax: (972) 317-2522
Email: bet@blackeconomictimes.com
Web: www.blackeconomictimes.com
Circ.: 12,000
Price: $1.00
Publication description: The Black Economic Times is a weekly newspaper written and edited solely for the purpose of providing information about retail economic development, market share, job creation and community wealth building.
Date established: 1992

BROOKLYN NEW YORK RECORDER
Brooklyn New York Recorder
86 Bainbridge St.
Brooklyn, NY 11233
Dale Watkins, Editor
Tel: (718) 493-4616 Fax: (718) 493-4616
Email: dtw@blackhup.com
Circ.: 54,000
Subscription: $455.00/year

BROWARD TIMES, THE
The Broward Times, Inc.
3301 NW 55th St.
Fort Lauderdale, FL 33309
Keith A. Clayborne, Publisher
Tel: (954) 497-3190 Fax: (954) 497-3193
Email: browardtimes@aol.com
Web: www.browardtimes.com
Circ.: 24,000
Price: $0.25 Subscription: $52.00/year
Date established: 1990

BUFFALO CRITERION
Buffalo Criterion
623-625 William St.
Buffalo, NY 14206
Frances J. Merriweather, Publisher
Fax: (716) 882-9570
Email: criterion@apollo3.com
Web: www.buffalocriterion.com
Circ.: 10,000
Price: $0.50 Subscription: $24.95/year
Date established: 1925

CALIFORNIA ADVOCATE, THE
Kimber Kimber & Associates
P.O. Box 11826
Fresno, CA 93775
Mark Kimber, Publisher
Tel: (559) 268-0941 Fax: (559) 268-0943
Email: info@caladvocate.com
Web: www.caladvocate.com
Circ.: 52,013
Price: $0.50 Subscription: $20.00/year
Date established: 1967

CALIFORNIA VOICE
Sun Reporter Publishing Co.
1791 Bancroft Ave.
San Francisco, CA 94111
Amelia Ashley-Ward, Publisher
Tel: (415) 671-1000 Fax: (415) 671-1005
Email: sunmedia97@aol.com
Web: www.sunreporter.com
Circ.: 38,000
Price: Free Subscription: $20.00/year
Publication description: Northern California's oldest, largest, and most influential Black Press. Key local source for information on what is happening in the schools, churches and community happenings.
Date established: 1919

CALL & POST
King Media Enterprises, Inc.
109 Hamilton Park.
Columbus, OH 43203
Don King, Publisher
Tel: (614) 224-8123 Fax: (614) 224-8517
Email: cbusnews@aol.com
Web: www.callandpost.com
Circ.: 55,000
Price: $0.75 Subscription: $39.00/year
Date established: 1962

CALL, THE
The Kansas City Call Co., Inc.
1715 E. 18th St.
Kansas City, MO 64108
Donna Steward, Publisher
Tel: (816) 842-3804 Fax: (816) 842-4420
Email: kccallnewspaper@hotmail.com
Web: www.kccall.com
Circ.: 17,500
Price: $0.50 Subscription: $26.00/year
Date established: 1919

CARIBBEAN DAYLIGHT
Caribbean Daylight, Inc.
P.O. Box 25, Valley Stream
New York, NY 11582-0025
Rohit Kanhai, Editor
Tel: (516) 285-1965 Fax: (516) 285-0037
Email: caribbeandaylight@worldnet.att.net
Circ.: 25,000
Price: Free
Publication description: Caribbean News
Date established: 1992

CAROLINA PANORAMA NEWSPAPER
T&N Publishing Co.
2346B Two Notch Rd. #E
Columbia, SC 29204
Nathaniel Abraham, Jr., Publisher
Tel: (803) 256-4015 Fax: (803) 256-6732
Email: cpanorama@aol.com
Circ.: 16,000
Price: $0.50 Subscription: $26.00/year
Date established: 1984

CENTRAL FLORIDA ADVOCATE, THE
Trexel Communications and Publishing Group
218 S. Lime Ave.
Orlando, FL 32805
Louise Seraaj, Editor
Tel: (407) 648-1162 Fax: (407) 649-8702
Email: newsdesk@cfadvocate.com
Web: www.cfadvocate.com
Circ.: 10,000
Price: Free Subscription: $34.50/year
Publication description: The Central Florida Advocate is the fastest growing weekly newspaper in Central Florida targeting the African- and Caribbean-American communities. With a decided emphasis on local news, business features, and investigative reporting, it is the undisputed

leader in its community sphere in political, social and business circles.
Date established: 1993

CHARLESTON CHRONICLE
P.O. Box 20548
Charleston, SC 29403
Nanette French-Smalls, Publisher
Tel: (843) 723-2785 **Fax:** (843) 577-6099
Email: chaschron@aol.com
Circ.: 6,000
Price: $0.50 **Subscription:** $45.00/year
Date established: 1971

CHATTANOOGA COURIER
Pride Newspaper Group
625 Main St.
Nashville, TN 37206
Larry Davis, Publisher
Tel: (615) 292-9150 **Fax:** (615) 292-9056
Email: mpnews@comcast.net
Circ.: 17,000
Price: $0.50 **Subscription:** $18.00/year
Publication description: Service and news for the African American community.
Date established: 1994

CHICAGO SOUTH SHORE SCENE
South Shore Commission
P.O. Box 490085
Chicago, IL 60649
Claudette McFarland, Publisher
Tel: (773) 363-0441 **Fax:** (773) 363-2911
Circ.: 80,000
Price: Free **Subscription:** $25.00/year
Date established: 1954

CHICAGO WESTSIDE JOURNAL
Chicago Westside Journal
16618 S. Hermitage St.
Markham, IL 60428
Heruanita McIlvaine, Publisher
Tel: (708) 333-2210 **Fax:** (708) 339-8769
Email: wstjournal@aol.com
Web: www.wstjournal.com
Circ.: 30,000
Price: Free
Date established: 1972

CLARKSVILLE PRESS
Pride Newspaper Group
625 Main St.
Nashville, TN 37206
Larry Davis, Publisher
Tel: (615) 292-9150 **Fax:** (615) 292-9056
Email: mpnews@comcast.net
Circ.: 14,782
Price: $0.50 **Subscription:** $18.00/year
Publication description: Service and news for the African American community.
Date established: 1991

COLUMBUS POST NEWSPAPER
Lynch Communications, Ltd.
172 E. State St., 6th Fl.
Columbus, OH 43215
Kim Tolley, Editor
Tel: (614) 224-6723 **Fax:** (614) 224-7998
Email: news@columbuspost.com
Web: www.columbuspost.com
Circ.: 4,500
Price: $0.50 **Subscription:** $25.00/year
Publication description: A weekly newspaper boasting several columns including editorials, opinions, health, youth, lifestyles, fashion, religion, business, entertainment, classifieds, sports.
Date established: 1995

DATA NEWS WEEKLY
Data Enterprise, Inc.
P.O. Box 51933
New Orleans, LA 70151

Terry B. Jones, Publisher
Tel: (504) 822-0306 **Fax:** (504) 821-0320
Email: datanews@bellsouth.net
Circ.: 20,000
Price: Free **Subscription:** $22.00/year
Date established: 1966

DAYTON DEFENDER, THE
SESH Communications
354 Hearne Ave.
Cincinnati, OH 45229
Eric H. Kearney, Publisher
Tel: (513) 961-3331 **Fax:** (513) 961-0304
Email: seshadsd@fuse.net
Circ.: 6,000
Price: $0.50 **Subscription:** $25.00/year
Date established: 1995

DISPATCH, THE
P.O. Box 1833
Walterboro, SC 29488
Melissa Buckn, Editor
Tel: (843) 549-1754 **Fax:** (843) 549-9181
Email: editor@ctdispatch.com
Circ.: 1,000
Price: $0.25 **Subscription:** $17.00/year
Date established: 1996

DRUM, THE
P.O. Box 1399
Ponchatoula, LA 70454
Eddie Ponds, Publisher
Tel: (985) 386-6532 **Fax:** (985) 386-4446
Email: thedrum@bellsouth.net
Circ.: 2,000
Price: Free **Subscription:** $23.00/year
Date established: 1986

EAST TEXAS REVIEW
517 S. Mobberly Ave.
Longview, TX 75607-2473
Robert Fadojutimi, Publisher
Tel: (903) 236-0406 **Fax:** (903) 757-7527
Email: joycelyne@easttexasreview.com
Web: www.easttexasreview.com
Circ.: 10,000
Price: Free **Subscription:** $60.00/year

EBONY VOICE, THE
12000 Westhiemer St. #302
Houston, TX 77077
Johnetta Norberg, Editor
Tel: (281) 589-8950 **Fax:** (281) 589-8995
Email: fblavida@swbell.net
Circ.: 30,000
Price: Free **Subscription:** $32.00/year
Date established: 1997

FINE PRINT NEWS
806 Fillmore Ave.
Buffalo, NY 14212
Ronald H. Fleming, Publisher
Tel: (716) 855-3810 **Fax:** (716) 855-3810
Email: fineprintnews2@juno.com
Circ.: 10,000
Price: Free
Date established: 1970

FLORIDA COURIER
605 N. 7th St.
Ft. Pierce, FL 34950
Charles W. Cherry, II, Publisher/Editor
Tel: (772) 489-2766 **Fax:** (772) 489-2729
Email: ccherry2@bellsouth.net
Circ.: 10,000
Price: $0.50 **Subscription:** $45.00/year
Date established: 1994

FLORIDA DOLLAR STRETCHER
P.O. Box 8205
Tampa, FL 33674
Nathaniel Hanna, Publisher
Tel: (813) 930-9599 **Fax:** (813) 930-9698

Email: dollarstretcher1@aol.com
Circ.: 9,000
Price: Free

FROST ILLUSTRATED
The News Sun
3121 S. Calhoun St.
Fort Wayne, IN 46807
Edward N. Smith, Publisher
Tel: (260) 745-0552 **Fax:** (260) 745-9503
Email: frostnews@aol.com
Web: www.frostillustrated.com
Circ.: 8,500
Price: $0.50 **Subscription:** $25.00-30.00/year
Date established: 1968

GRAND RAPIDS TIMES
Grand Rapids Times
2016 Eastern Ave. SE
Grand Rapids, MI 49507
Patricia Pulliam, Publisher
Tel: (616) 245-8737 **Fax:** (616) 245-1026
Email: staff@grtimes.com
Circ.: 24,000
Price: $0.50 **Subscription:** $20.00/year
Date established: 1957

GREENE COUNTY DEMOCRAT
P.O. Box 598
Eutaw, AL 35462
John Zippert, Co-Publisher/Editor
Tel: (205) 372-3373 **Fax:** (205) 372-2243
Email: jzippert@aol.com
Circ.: 3,500
Price: $0.50 **Subscription:** $25.00/year
Publication description: Weekly newspaper serving Greene County.
Date established: 1985

HOUSTON DEFENDER
3003 S. Loop West #320
Houston, TX 77054
Sonny Messiah-Jiles, Publisher
Tel: (713) 663-6996 **Fax:** (713) 663-7116
Email: news@houstondefender.com
Web: www.houstondefender.com
Circ.: 35,768
Price: Free **Subscription:** $40.00/year
Date established: 1930

HOUSTON FORWARD TIMES
Forward Times Publishing Co.
P.O. Box 8346
Houston, TX 77288-8346
Lenora Carter, Publisher
Tel: (713) 526-4727 **Fax:** (713) 526-3170
Email: forwardtimes@forwardtimes.com
Web: www.forwardtimes.com
Circ.: 63,000
Price: $0.50 **Subscription:** $30.00/year
Publication description: The Houston Forward Times is the largest independently owned and operated African-American newspaper published in the South/Southwest area. The Houston Forward Times is a major source of positive news about accomplishments of African-Americans.
Date established: 1960

HOUSTON STYLE
2646 S. Loop West #375
Houston, TX 77054-2676
Francis Page, Publisher
Tel: (713) 748-6300 **Fax:** (713) 748-6320
Email: editorial@stylemagazine.com
Web: www.stylemagazine.com
Circ.: 46,500
Subscription: $30.00/year
Date established: 1989

HOUSTON SUN, THE
Sun News Group, The
1520 Isabella St.
Houston, TX 77004
Dorris Ellis, Publisher/Editor
Tel: (713) 528-4786 **Fax:** (713) 524-6786
Email: info@houstonsun.com
Web: www.houstonsun.com
Circ.: 80,000
Publication description: To publish news and information you can use and trust.
Date established: 1983

INFORMER & TEXAS FREEMAN NEWSPAPER
2646 S. Loop West #375
Houston, TX 77054
Pluria Marshall, Jr., Publisher
Tel: (713) 218-7400 **Fax:** (713) 218-7077
Email: houstoninformer@yahoo.com
Circ.: 30,000
Subscription: $50.00/year
Date established: 1893

INNER-CITY NEWSPAPER, THE
Penfield Communication
50 Fitch St.
New Haven, CT 06515
John Thomas, Jr., Publisher
Tel: (203) 387-0354 **Fax:** (203) 387-2684
Email: jthomas@penfieldcomm.com
Circ.: 35,000
Price: Free **Subscription:** $30.00/year
Publication description: A weekly newspaper focusing on the African-American community in New Haven.
Date established: 1990

INSIGHT NEWS
Insight News, Inc.
1815 Bryant Ave. North
Minneapolis, MN 55411
Al McFarlane, Publisher
Tel: (612) 588-1313 **Fax:** (612) 588-2031
Email: info@insightnews.com
Web: www.insightnews.com
Circ.: 35,000
Price: Free **Subscription:** $42.00/year
Date established: 1974

JERSEY CITY DAILY CHALLENGE
BlackPressUSA Network, The Challenge Group
1195 Atlantic Ave.
Brooklyn, NY 11216
Thomas H. Watkins, Jr., Publisher
Tel: (718) 636-9119 **Fax:** (718) 857-9115
Email: challengegroup@yahoo.com
Web: www.challenge-group.com
Circ.: 81,000
Price: $0.35 **Subscription:** $125.00/year
Date established: 1972

JET MAGAZINE
Johnson Publishing, Inc.
820 S. Michigan Ave.
Chicago, IL 60605
John H. Johnson, Publisher
Tel: (312) 322-9200 **Fax:** (312) 322-0951
Web: www.jetmag.com
Circ.: 954,259
Price: $1.50 **Subscription:** $26.00/year
Date established: 1951

KANSAS STATE GLOBE
P.O. Box 12462
Kansas City, KS 66112
Doretha C. Jordon, Editor
Tel: (913) 299-0001 **Fax:** (913) 287-4506
Email: ksglobe@sbcglobal.net
Circ.: 25,600
Price: $0.50 **Subscription:** $30.00/year
Date established: 1972

KNOXVILLE ENLIGHTENER

Pride Newspaper Group
625 Main St.
Nashville, TN 37206
Larry Davis, Publisher
Tel: (615) 292-9150 **Fax:** (615) 292-9056
Email: mpnews@comcast.net
Circ.: 18,275
Price: $0.50 **Subscription:** $18.00/year
Publication description: Service and news for the African American community.
Date established: 1991

LA VIDA NEWS, THE BLACK VOICE

P.O. Box 751
Fort Worth, TX 76101
Ted Pruitt, Publisher
Tel: (817) 543-2095 **Fax:** (817) 274-8023
Email: newsdesk@lavidanewstheblackvoice.com
Circ.: 18,000
Price: Free **Subscription:** $85.00/year
Date established: 1957

LADIES OF AFRICA NEWSLETTER

8370 Greensboro Dr. #1007
McLean, VA 22102

LONG BEACH TIMES

Long Beach Times
121 Linden Ave.
Long Beach, CA 90802
Richard A. Love, Publisher
Tel: (562) 436-8221 **Fax:** (562) 628-1907
Email: lbtimes@aol.com
Web: www.lbtimesnews.com
Circ.: 43,000
Price: $0.25 **Subscription:** $55.00/year
Date established: 1987

LOUISIANA WEEKLY

Louisiana Weekly
P.O. Box 8628
New Orleans, LA 70182
Henry B. Dejoie, Sr., Publisher
Tel: (504) 282-3705 **Fax:** (504) 282-3773
Email: info@louisianaweekly.com
Web: www.louisianaweekly.com
Circ.: 10,000
Price: $0.50 **Subscription:** $24.00/year
Publication description: Our goal is to add value to people's lives by delivering economic, social and scientific "new information" from business, culture, and the natural and social sciences, which enhances personal and community growth.
Date established: 1930

MACON COURIER

Jodd Publishing, Inc.
P.O. 52201
Macon, GA 31208
Melvyn J. Williams, Publisher/Editor
Tel: (478) 746-5605 **Fax:** (478) 742-4274
Email: info@themaconcourier.com
Web: www.themaconcourier.com
Circ.: 17,300
Price: $0.50 **Subscription:** $46.00/year
Date established: 1976

MADISON TIMES WEEKLY, THE

The Madison Times Weekly
931 E. Main St. #7
Madison, WI 53703
David Hammons, Publisher
Tel: (608) 256-2185 **Fax:** (608) 256-2215
Email: news@madtimes.com
Web: www.madtimes.com
Circ.: 8,500
Price: Free **Subscription:** $35.00/year
Publication description: The Madison Times focuses on positive and success stories in the African American, Latino, Southeast Asian, and American Indian communities, and in other communities of color. It delivers fresh reports on current events and features interviews about various issues impacting communities of color, particularly in the Madison area. The paper also stresses positive social and personal values, education, and economic empowerment and encourages minority youth to aim high and make a difference.
Date established: 1991

MEMPHIS SILVER STAR NEWS

Memphis Silver Star News
3019 Park Ave.
Memphis, TN 38114
J. Delnoah Williams, Publisher
Tel: (901) 452-8828 **Fax:** (901) 452-1656
Email: silverst@bellsouth.net
Circ.: 84,000
Price: $0.50 **Subscription:** $27.50/year
Date established: 1986

METRO HERALD, THE

Davis Communications Group, Inc.
901 N. Washington St. #603
Alexandria, VA 22314
Paris D. Davis, Publisher/Executive Director
Tel: (703) 548-8891 **Fax:** (703) 739-1542
Email: pjr@metroherald.com
Web: www.metroherald.com
Circ.: 42,000
Price: $0.75 **Subscription:** $75.00/year
Publication description: In Maryland, The Metro Herald is the only black-owned newspaper in Anne Arundel, Carroll, Charles, Howard, and Montgomery counties. It shares readership with one other minority-owned newspaper in Prince George's County.

METRO REPORTER

Sun Reporter Publishing Co.
1791 Bancroft Ave.
San Francisco, CA 94111
Amelia Ashley-Ward, Publisher
Tel: (415) 671-1000 **Fax:** (415) 671-1005
Email: sunmedia97@aol.com
Web: www.sunreporter.com
Circ.: 11,000
Price: Free **Subscription:** $20.00/year
Publication description: Northern California's oldest, largest, and most influential Black Press. Key local source for information on what is happening in the schools, churches and community happenings.
Date established: 1919

MICHIGAN FRONT PAGE

479 Ledyard St.
Detroit, MI 48201-2687
Sam Logan, Publisher
Tel: (313) 963-5522 **Fax:** (313) 963-8788
Email: publisher@michchronicle.com
Web: www.michchronicle.com
Circ.: 75,000
Price: $0.50 **Subscription:** $25.00/year
Date established: 1936

MILITANT, THE

306 W. 37th St., 10th Fl.
New York, NY 10018
Argiris Malapanis, Editor
Tel: (212) 244-4899 **Fax:** (212) 244-4947
Email: themilitant@verizon.net
Web: www.themilitant.com
Circ.: 2,000
Price: $1.00 **Subscription:** $35.00/year
Publication description: While not an African American publication, this publication covers news regarding the African American struggle in the USA and in the world.
Date established: 1928

MILWAUKEE COURIER

BlackPressUSA Network
2003 W. Capital Dr.
Milwaukee, WI 53206
Faithe Colas, Publisher
Tel: (414) 449-4864 **Fax:** (414) 449-4872
Email: milwaukeecourier@aol.com
Web: www.milwaukeecourier.org
Circ.: 40,000
Price: Free **Subscription:** $25.00/year
Publication description: The Milwaukee Courier is Wisconsin's Original News Source for the African American Community.

MINORITY CONSTRUCTION NEWS BULLETIN

Kern Minority Contractors Association
P.O. Box 2367
Bakersfield, CA 93303
Marvin Dean, Publisher
Tel: (661) 324-7535 **Fax:** (661) 323-9287
Email: marvindean@sbcglobal.net
Web: www.minoritynews.info
Circ.: 3,000
Subscription: $45.00/6 months
Publication description: The Minority Construction News Bulletin is a trade and focus publication, published weekly since 1993.
Date established: 1993

MINORITY RESOURCE GUIDE, THE

The Columbus Times
2230 Buena Vista Rd.
Columbus, GA 31906
Opelia Mitchell, Publisher
Tel: (706) 324-2404 **Fax:** (706) 596-0657
Email: columbustimes@knology.net
Web: www.columbustimes.com
Circ.: 10,000
Price: $1.00 **Subscription:** $65.48/year
Date established: 1995

MISSISSIPPI LINK, THE

Mississippi Link, Inc.
2659 Livingston Rd.
Jackson, MS 39213
Socrates Garrett, Publisher
Tel: (601) 896-0084 X207 **Fax:** (601) 896-0091
Email: mslink@misnet.com
Web: www.mississippilink.com
Circ.: 17,080
Price: $0.50 **Subscription:** $32.00/year
Date established: 1993

MUSLIM JOURNAL

Muslim Journal Enterprises, Inc.
1141 W. 175th St.
Homewood, IL 60430
Ayesha K. Mustafaa, Publisher/Editor
Tel: (708) 647-9600 **Fax:** (708) 647-0754
Email: muslimjrnl@aol.com
Web: www.muslimjournal.com
Circ.: 20,000
Price: $1.75 **Subscription:** $52.00/year
Publication description: The Muslim Journal is a 27-year-old weekly newspaper serving the Muslim community throughout the United States and abroad.
Date established: 1975

NASHVILLE PRIDE

Pride Newspaper Group
625 Main St.
Nashville, TN 37206
Larry Davis, Publisher
Tel: (615) 292-9150 **Fax:** (615) 292-9056
Email: mpnews@comcast.net
Circ.: 30,000
Price: $0.50 **Subscription:** $18.00/year
Publication description: Service and news for the African American community.
Date established: 1988

OAKLAND POST

Post Newspaper Group
405 14th St. #400
Oakland, CA 94612
Paul Cobb, Publisher
Tel: (510) 287-8200 **Fax:** (510) 287-8247
Email: ads@postnewsgroup.com
Web: www.postnewsgroup.com
Circ.: 50,000
Price: Free **Subscription:** $99.50/year
Date established: 1963

PHILADELPHIA SUNDAY SUN, THE

Phila Sun Group, Inc.
6661 Germantown Ave.
Philadelphia, PA 19119
J. Whyatt Mondesire, Publisher/Editor
Tel: (215) 848-7864 **Fax:** (215) 848-7893
Email: infosundaysun@yahoo.com
Web: www.philasun.com
Circ.: 20,000
Price: $0.75 **Subscription:** $36.00/year
Date established: 1992

PORTLAND MEDIUM, THE

The Seattle Medium Newspaper Group
P.O. Box 22047
Seattle, WA 22047
Christopher B. Bennett, Publisher
Tel: (206) 323-3070 **Fax:** (206) 322-6518
Email: mediumnews@aol.com
Web: www.seattlemedium.com
Circ.: 16,500
Price: Free
Date established: 1970

PRINCE GEORGE'S POST

15207 Marlboro Pike
Marlboro, MD 20772
David Zirin, Publisher
Tel: (301) 627-0900 **Fax:** (301) 627-8147
Email: pgpost@gmail.com
Web: www.pgpost.com
Circ.: 10,000
Price: $0.25 **Subscription:** $15.00/year
Date established: 1932

RICHMOND POST

Post Newspaper Group
405 14th St. #400
Oakland, CA 94612
Paul Cobb, Publisher
Tel: (510) 287-8200 **Fax:** (510) 287-8247
Email: ads@postnewsgroup.com
Web: www.postnewsgroup.com
Circ.: 50,000
Price: Free **Subscription:** $99.50/year
Date established: 1963

RICHMOND VOICE

South Side Voice, Inc.
205 E. Clay St.
Richmond, VA 23219
Jack Green, Publisher
Tel: (804) 644-9060 **Fax:** (804) 644-5617
Email: richmond.voice@verizon.net
Web: www.voicenewspaper.com
Circ.: 44,000
Price: Free **Subscription:** $30.00/year
Date established: 1985

SAN ANTONIO OBSERVER

P.O. Box 200226
San Antonio, TX 78220
LaNell M. Taylor, Editor-in-Chief
Tel: (210) 212-6397 **Fax:** (210) 271-0441
Email: taylor2039@aol.com
Web: www.saobserver.com
Circ.: 60,000

Price: $5.00 **Subscription:** $50.00/year
Date established: 1985

SAN ANTONIO REGISTER NEWSPAPER
3427 Belgium Ln.
San Antonio, TX 78219
Sherry L. Logan, Owner
Tel: (210) 212-6397 **Fax:** (210) 271-0441
Email: taylor2039@aol.com
Web: www.saregister.com
Circ.: 60,000
Price: Free
Date established: 1931

SAN FRANCISCO POST
Post Newspaper Group
405 14th St. #400
Oakland, CA 94612
Paul Cobb, Publisher
Tel: (510) 287-8200 **Fax:** (510) 287-8247
Email: ads@postnewsgroup.com
Web: www.postnewsgroup.com
Circ.: 50,000
Price: Free **Subscription:** $99.50/year
Date established: 1963

SEATTLE MEDIUM, THE
The Seattle Medium Newspaper Group
P.O. Box 22047
Seattle, WA 22047
Christopher B. Bennett, Publisher
Tel: (206) 323-3070 **Fax:** (206) 323-6518
Email: mediumnews@aol.com
Web: www.seattlemedium.com
Circ.: 37,500
Price: Free **Subscription:** $34.00/year
Date established: 1970

SEATTLE METRO HOMEMAKER
The Seattle Medium Newspaper Group
P.O. Box 22047
Seattle, WA 22047
Christopher B. Bennett, Publisher
Tel: (206) 323-3070 **Fax:** (206) 323-6518
Email: mediumnews@aol.com
Web: www.seattlemedium.com
Circ.: 24,000
Price: Free
Date established: 1970

SKANNER, THE
The Skanner News Group
P.O. Box 94473
Seattle, WA 98124
Monica Foster, Office Manager
Tel: (206) 233-9888 **Fax:** (206) 233-9795
Email: seattle@theskanner.com
Web: www.theskanner.com
Price: Free **Subscription:** $59.00/year
Publication description: The Skanner is a weekly newspaper published in Portland, Oregon, and Seattle, Washington. Established in 1975, The Skanner News Group has advanced the cause of the Black Press in the North Western United States.
Date established: 1975

SOUTHWEST DIGEST
1302 Ave. Q
Lubbock, TX 79401
Eddie P. Richardson, Co-Publisher
Tel: (806) 762-3612 **Fax:** (806) 741-0000
Email: swdigest@sbcglobal.net
Circ.: 4,000
Price: $0.50 **Subscription:** $20.00/year
Date established: 1977

ST. LOUIS AMERICAN NEWSPAPER
Tribune Publishing
4242 Lindell Blvd.
St. Louis, MO 63108
Kevin Jones, COO
Tel: (314) 533-8000 **Fax:** (314) 533-0038

Email: kjones@stlamerican.com
Web: www.stlamerican.com
Circ.: 70,000
Price: Free **Subscription:** $40.00/year
Date established: 1928

ST. LOUIS METRO EVENING WHIRL
Thomas Publishing Co., Inc.
P.O. Box 5088
St. Louis, MO 63115-0088
Barry R. Thomas, Publisher/CEO
Tel: (314) 535-4033 **Fax:** (314) 535-4280
Email: tpcwhirl@aol.com
Circ.: 49,500
Price: $0.50 **Subscription:** $50.00/year
Publication description: The world's greatest and most popular crime fighting community newspaper in the United States.
Date established: 1938

TACOMA TRUE CITIZEN
The Seattle Medium Newspaper Group
P.O. Box 22047
Seattle, WA 22047
Christopher B. Bennett, Publisher
Tel: (206) 323-3070 **Fax:** (206) 322-6518
Email: mediumnews@aol.com
Web: www.seattlemedium.com
Circ.: 16,500
Price: Free
Date established: 1970

TENNESSEE TRIBUNE
BlackPressUSA Network, Perry & Perry & Associates, Inc.
1501 Jefferson St.
Nashville, TN 37208
Rosetta Miller Perry, Publisher
Tel: (615) 321-3268 **Fax:** (615) 321-0409
Email: sales1501@aol.com
Web: www.thetennesseetribune.com
Circ.: 45,000
Price: $1.00 **Subscription:** $35.00/year
Date established: 1990

TIMES WEEKLY NEWSPAPER, THE
254 E. Cass St.
Joliet, IL 60432
Jayme Cain, Publisher
Tel: (815) 723-0325 **Fax:** (815) 723-0326
Email: timesweekly@sbcglobal.net
Circ.: 30,000
Price: $0.35 **Subscription:** $55.00/year
Date established: 1987

TRI-COUNTY SENTRY
Hunt Communications
P.O. Box 20515
Oxnard, CA 93034
Debbie Hunt, Publisher
Tel: (805) 486-8430 **Fax:** (805) 486-3650
Email: sentry1234@aol.com
Circ.: 10,000
Price: Free **Subscription:** $45.00/year
Publication description: Serves as newspaper media.
Date established: 1991

TRIANGLE TRIBUNE, THE
DBA The Triangle Tribune
115 Market St. #211
Durham, NC 27701
Bonitta Best, Editor
Tel: (919) 688-9408 **Fax:** (919) 688-2740
Email: duredt@mindspring.com
Circ.: 20,000
Price: $1.00 **Subscription:** $60.00/year
Publication description: To provide information vital to the black community.
Date established: 1998

URBAN JOURNAL, THE
Latham Publishing Co.
1310 Clinton St. #204
Nashville, TN 37203
Sam Latham, Editor
Tel: (615) 321-3533 **Fax:** (615) 321-6433
Email: news@urbanjournal-nash.com
Web: www.urbanjournalonline.com
Circ.: 30,000
Price: Free
Publication description: African American newspaper.
Date established: 1980

VILLAGER NEWSPAPER, THE
The Villager
1223-A Rosewood Ave.
Austin, TX 78702
T.L. Wyatt, Publisher
Tel: (512) 476-0082 **Fax:** (512) 476-0179
Email: vil3202@aol.com
Circ.: 6,000
Price: Free **Subscription:** $20.00/year
Publication description: A community newspaper.
Date established: 1973

WASHINGTON AFRO-AMERICAN
The Afro-American Newspaper Company of Baltimore, Inc.
1612 14th St. NW
Washington, DC 20009
Reggie William, Editor
Tel: (202) 332-0080 **Fax:** (202) 939-7461
Email: dceditor@afro.com
Web: www.afro.com
Circ.: 13,200
Price: $0.50 **Subscription:** $27.48/year
Date established: 1892

WEEKLY STAR
17211 Hillside Ave.
Jamaica, NY 11432
Moveta Munroe, Editor
Tel: (718) 657-0788 **Fax:** (718) 657-0857
Email: gleanerstar@aol.com
Web: www.jamaica-gleaner.com
Circ.: 65,000
Price: $1.25 **Subscription:** $51.00/year
Date established: 1840

WOMEN OF AFRICA NEWSLETTER
8370 Greensboro Dr. #1007
McLean, VA 22102

WEEKLY-THURSDAY

AFRO TIMES
The Challenge Group
1195 Atlantic Ave.
Brooklyn, NY 11216
Thomas H. Watkins, Jr., Publisher/CEO
Tel: (718) 636-9500 **Fax:** (718) 857-9115
Email: afronewseditor@aol.com
Web: www.challenge-group.com
Circ.: 60,000
Price: $0.50 **Subscription:** $55.00/year
Publication description: The Afro Times is a family oriented, general interest newspaper covering current news and events taking place in our region and around the world. It is designed to enlighten the African American community about the issues confronting them. Special features include arts & entertainment where readers learn the latest in theater, art, and entertainment as well as the current news surrounding various genres of music and art.
Date established: 1987

ALBANY SOUTHWEST GEORGIAN
P.O. Box 1943
Albany, GA 31702
Art Searles, Publisher/Editor
Tel: (229) 436-2156 **Fax:** (229) 435-6860
Email: advertise@albanysouthwestgeorgian.com
Web: www.albanysouthwestgeorgian.com
Circ.: 19,700
Price: $0.50 **Subscription:** $30.00/year
Publication description: The Albany Southwest Georgian was founded in August of 1938 to serve the Black community in Albany, Georgia and the surrounding area. Since that time this newspaper has been in continuous operation each week.
Date established: 1938

ALEXANDRIA NEWS WEEKLY
1746 Mason St.
Alexandria, LA 71301
Leon Coleman, Sr., Publisher
Tel: (318) 443-7664 **Fax:** (318) 487-1827
Circ.: 10,000
Price: $0.50 **Subscription:** $59.00/year
Date established: 1963

AMERICAN NEWS, THE
The American News
1583 W. Baseline St.
San Bernardino, CA 92411
Samuel Martin, Publisher
Tel: (909) 889-7677 **Fax:** (909) 889-2882
Email: samerisam1@earthlink.net
Circ.: 7,000
Price: $0.25 **Subscription:** $18.00-20.00/year
Date established: 1969

AMSTERDAM NEWS
BlackPressUSA Network
2340 Frederick Douglas Blvd.
New York, NY 10027
Elinor Tatum, Publisher
Tel: (212) 932-7400 **Fax:** (212) 932-7467
Email: info@amsterdamnews.org
Web: www.amsterdamnews.org
Circ.: 30,000
Price: $0.75 **Subscription:** $35.00/year
Publication description: The New York Amsterdam News has been one of the leading black weekly newspapers for most of the 20th century.
Date established: 1909

ATLANTA DAILY WORLD
145 Auburn Ave. NE
Atlanta, GA 30303-1201
Alexis Scott, Publisher/CEO
Tel: (404) 659-1110 X18 **Fax:** (404) 659-4988
Email: publisher@atlantadailyworld.com
Web: www.atlantadailyworld.com
Circ.: 18,000
Price: $0.50 **Subscription:** $40.00/year
Date established: 1928

ATLANTA INQUIRER, THE
BlackPressUSA Network
947 Martin Luther King, Jr. Dr. NW
Atlanta, GA 30314-0367
John B. Smith, Jr., Editor
Tel: (404) 523-6086 **Fax:** (404) 523-6088
Email: news@atlinq.com
Web: www.atlinq.com
Circ.: 59,904
Price: $0.40 **Subscription:** $26.00/year
Date established: 1960

ATLANTA VOICE, THE
BlackPressUSA Network
633 Pryor St. SW
Atlanta, GA 30312
Janis L. Ware, Publisher
Tel: (404) 524-6426 **Fax:** (404) 523-7853
Email: jlware@theatlantavoice.com
Web: www.atlantavoice.com
Circ.: 40,000
Price: Free **Subscription:** $49.00/year
Date established: 1966

BAY STATE BANNER, THE
Banner Publications, Inc.
23 Drydock Ave.
Boston, MA 02210
Melvin B. Miller, Publisher/Editor
Tel: (617) 261-4600 **Fax:** (617) 261-2346
Email: mbm@b-banner.com
Web: www.baystatebanner.com
Circ.: 25,000
Price: Free **Subscription:** $20.00/year
Date established: 1965

BIRMINGHAM TIMES
BlackPressUSA Network
115 3rd Ave. West
Birmingham, AL 35204
James E. Lewis, Publisher
Tel: (205) 251-5158 **Fax:** (205) 323-2294
Email: celdridge@birminghamtimes.com
Web: www.thebirminghamtimes.com
Circ.: 16,500
Price: $0.50 **Subscription:** $30.00/year
Date established: 1964

BLACK CHRONICLE, THE
Perry Publishing and Broadcasting
1457 NE 23rd St.
Oklahoma City, OK 73111
Russell M. Perry, Publisher/Editor
Tel: (405) 425-4100 **Fax:** (405) 424-8811
Email: tcooper@blackchronicle.com
Web: www.blackchronicle.com
Circ.: 30,000
Price: $0.50 **Subscription:** $19.95/year
Date established: 1979

BLACK NEWS
South Carolina Black Media Group
P.O. Box 11128
Columbia, SC 29211
Isaac Washington, Publisher
Tel: (803) 799-5252 **Fax:** (803) 799-7709
Email: scbnews@aol.com
Web: www.scblacknews.com
Circ.: 75,000
Price: $0.50 **Subscription:** $25.00/year
Publication description: South Carolina
Black Media Group is designed to meet the
informational needs of the Black population
in South Carolina. The weekly publication
encompasses the forty-six (46) counties,
reaching a mixture of rural, suburban and
metropolitan areas.
Date established: 1973

BLACK STAR NEWS
234 5th Ave., 5th Fl.
New York, NY 10001
Milton Allimadi, Publisher/CEO
Tel: (212) 481-7745
Email: milton@blackstarnews.com
Web: www.blackstarnews.com
Circ.: 50,000
Price: $1.00 **Subscription:** $65.00/year
Publication description: Aims to reach African
American, Caribbean and African immigrant
New Yorkers. Covers news as well as sports
and entertainment.
Date established: 1997

CALL & POST
King Media Enterprises, Inc.
11800 Shaker Blvd.
Cleveland, OH 44120
Don King, Publisher
Tel: (216) 791-7600 **Fax:** (216) 451-0404
Email: cbusnews@aol.com
Web: www.callandpost.com
Circ.: 38,000
Price: $0.75 **Subscription:** $39.00/year
Date established: 1902

CAPITAL OUTLOOK
Capital Outlook
225 E. Jennings St.
Tallahassee, FL 32301-1114
Roosevelt Wilson, President/Publisher
Tel: (850) 681-1852 **Fax:** (850) 681-1093
Email: coutlook@aol.com
Web: www.capitaloutlook.com
Circ.: 15,000
Price: $0.25 **Subscription:** $30.00/year
Date established: 1975

CAROLINA PEACEMAKER
BlackPressUSA Network, Carolina
Newspapers, Inc.
400 Summit Ave.
Greensboro, NC 27405
John M. Kilimanjaro, Publisher
Tel: (336) 274-6210 **Fax:** (336) 273-5103
Email: cpnews@bellsouth.net
Web: www.carolinapeacemaker.com
Circ.: 8,500
Price: $0.50 **Subscription:** $35.00-$45.00/
year
Publication description: The Carolina
Peacemaker has been an important part of
Greensboro History since 1967, particularly
in the areas of economic development, civil
rights, and human relations.
Date established: 1967

CAROLINA TIMES
United Publishers, Inc.
P.O. Box 3825
Durham, NC 27702
Kenneth Edmonds, Publisher
Tel: (919) 682-2913 **Fax:** (919) 688-8434
Email: thecarolinatimes@cs.com
Circ.: 6,000
Price: $0.30 **Subscription:** $22.00/year
Date established: 1926

CHAMPION, THE
Ace III Communications, Inc.
P.O. Box 1347
Decatur, GA 30031-1347
Carolyn Glenn, Publisher
Tel: (404) 373-7779 **Fax:** (404) 373-7721
Email: cfjglenn@hotmail.com
Web: www.championnewspaper.com
Circ.: 18,900
Price: $0.50 **Subscription:** $26.00/year
Date established: 1991

CHARLOTTE POST
Consolidated Media Group
1531 Camden Rd.
Charlotte, NC 28203
Gerald O. Johnson, Publisher
Tel: (704) 376-0496 **Fax:** (704) 342-2160
Email: advertising@thecharlottepost.com
Web: www.thecharlottepost.com
Circ.: 23,438
Price: $1.00 **Subscription:** $40.00/year
Date established: 1878

CHICAGO CRUSADER
Chicago Crusader
6429 S. Martin Luther King Dr.
Chicago, IL 60637

Dorothy R. Leavell, Publisher
Tel: (773) 752-2500 **Fax:** (773) 752-2817
Email: crusaderil@aol.com
Web: www.chgocrusader.com
Circ.: 73,000
Price: $0.25 **Subscription:** $22.00/year
Date established: 1940

CHICAGO INDEPENDENT BULLETIN
1550 W. 88th St. #107
Chicago, IL 60620
Hurley Green, Jr., Publisher
Tel: (773) 233-6210 **Fax:** (773) 233-6245
Circ.: 62,000
Price: Free **Subscription:** $25.00/year
Date established: 1972

CHICAGO SOUTH SUBURBAN STANDARD
BlackPressUSA Network
615 S. Halsted St.
Chicago Heights, IL 60411
Lorenzo Martin, Publisher
Tel: (708) 755-5021 **Fax:** (708) 755-5020
Email: standardnewspapers@sbcglobal.net
Web: www.standardnewspapers.com
Circ.: 15,000
Price: Free **Subscription:** $25.00/year
Date established: 1979

CHICAGO STANDARD NEWSPAPER
BlackPressUSA Network
615 S. Halsted St.
Chicago Heights, IL 60411
Lorenzo Martin, Publisher
Tel: (708) 755-5021 **Fax:** (708) 755-5020
Email: standardnewspapers@sbcglobal.net
Web: www.standardnewspapers.com
Circ.: 15,000
Price: $0.20 **Subscription:** $30.00/year
Date established: 1979

CHRONICLE NEWSROOM, THE
617 N. Liberty St.
Winston-Salem, NC 27101
Ernest H. Pitt, Publisher
Tel: (336) 722-8624 **Fax:** (336) 723-9173
Email: news@wschronicle.com
Web: www.wschronicle.com
Circ.: 10,500
Price: $0.75 **Subscription:** $30.72/year
Date established: 1974

CINCINNATI HERALD, THE
SESH Communications
354 Hearne Ave.
Cincinnati, OH 45229
Eric H. Kearney, Publisher
Tel: (513) 961-3331 **Fax:** (513) 961-0304
Email: sesh@fuse.net
Circ.: 16,000
Price: $0.75 **Subscription:** $20.00/year
Date established: 1945

CITY NEWS OHIO
BlackPressUSA Network, Crosby Media
News
1419 E. 40th St.
Cleveland, OH 44103
James R. Crosby, Publisher
Tel: (216) 881-0799 **Fax:** (216) 881-1019
Email: ads@citynewsohio.com
Web: www.citynewsohio.com
Circ.: 75,000
Price: Free
Publication description: They are dedicated
to improving the financial and social lives of
blacks as well as giving all Clevelanders the
opportunity to be represented by an honest,
hardworking group of individuals.
Date established: 1998

COLUMBUS TIMES, THE
The Columbus Times
2230 Buena Vista Rd.
Columbus, GA 31906
Carol Gertigerdes, Publisher
Tel: (706) 324-2404 **Fax:** (706) 596-0657
Email: columbustimes@knology.net
Web: www.columbustimes.com
Circ.: 10,000
Price: $0.50 **Subscription:** $65.48/year
Publication description: The Columbus Times
Newspaper proudly carries the weight of
that respected role. We pride ourselves on
locating and reporting the positive aspects of
our community, the success stories and the
achievements. At the same time, we keep our
reader informed of those issues and events
of importance on the local, regional, national
and international levels.
Date established: 1958

COMMUNITY VOICE
3046 La Fayette St.
Fort Myers, FL 33916
Charles P. Weaver, Publisher
Tel: (239) 337-4444 **Fax:** (239) 334-8289
Email: commuvoice@aol.com
Circ.: 10,000
Price: Free **Subscription:** $20.00/year
Date established: 1987

COMPTON METROPOLITAN GAZETTE
LA Metro Publications
14621 Titus St. #228
Van Nuys, CA 91402
Beverly Hamm, Publisher
Tel: (818) 782-8695 **Fax:** (818) 782-2924
Email: lametroinc@aol.com
Circ.: 5,000
Price: $0.25 **Subscription:** $12.50/year
Date established: 1966

DALLAS EXAMINER
Dallas Examiner
1516 Corinth St.
Dallas, TX 75215
Mollie Finch Belt, Publisher
Tel: (214) 428-3446 **Fax:** (214) 428-3451
Email: editor@dallasexaminer.com
Web: www.dallasexaminer.com
Circ.: 10,000
Price: $0.50 **Subscription:** $40.00/year
Date established: 1986

DALLAS POST TRIBUNE
Tribune Publishing, Inc.
2726 S. Beckley Ave.
Dallas, TX 75224
Theodore Lee, Jr., Publisher
Tel: (214) 946-7678 **Fax:** (214) 946-6823
Email: posttrib@airmail.net
Web: www.dallaspost.com
Circ.: 18,500
Price: $0.50 **Subscription:** $65.00/year
Publication description: The Dallas Post
Tribune, a weekly newspaper serving the
Dallas area for half a century.
Date established: 1957

DAYTONA TIMES
The Observer Publishing Co.
427 S. Dr. Martin Luther King Jr. Blvd.
Daytona Beach, FL 32114
Charles W. Cherry II, General Manager
Tel: (386) 253-0321 **Fax:** (386) 254-7510
Email: info@daytonatimes.com
Web: www.daytonatimes.com
Circ.: 10,000
Price: $0.50 **Subscription:** $45.00/year
Publication description: To provide pertinent
news to the African-American community.
Date established: 1978

DENVER WEEKLY NEWS
Denver Weekly News
2937 Welton St.
Denver, CO 80205
Lenora Alexander, Publisher
Tel: (303) 292-5158 **Fax:** (303) 292-5344
Email: dwnews@qwest.net
Circ.: 10,000
Price: $0.50 **Subscription:** $30.00/year
Date established: 1971

E SCENE MAGAZINE
Wave Newspaper Group
4201 Wilshire Blvd. #600
Los Angeles, CA 90010
Pluria Marshall, Jr., Publisher
Tel: (323) 290-3000 **Fax:** (323) 556-5704
Email: voices@wavenewspapers.com
Web: www.wavenewspapers.com
Circ.: 57,500
Price: Free **Subscription:** $90.00/year

EAST ST. LOUIS MONITOR
East St. Louis Monitor Publishing, Inc.
1501 State St.
East St. Louis, IL 62205
Anne Jordan, Publisher
Tel: (618) 271-0468 **Fax:** (618) 271-8443
Circ.: 12,500
Price: $0.50 **Subscription:** $100.00/year
Date established: 1963

FIRESTONE PARK NEWS
Herald Dispatch Publishing Co.
P.O. Box 191727
Los Angeles, CA 90019
John Holoman, Publisher
Tel: (323) 291-9486 **Fax:** (323) 291-2123
Circ.: 22,000
Price: $0.50 **Subscription:** $40.00/year
Date established: 1924

FLORIDA STAR, THE
P.O. Box 40629
Jacksonville, FL 32203
Clara McLaughlin Criswell, Publisher/Editor
in Chief
Tel: (904) 766-8834 **Fax:** (904) 765-1673
Email: floridastar@fdn.com
Web: www.thefloridastar.com
Circ.: 7,500
Price: $0.50 **Subscription:** $33.00/year
Publication description: Northeast Florida's
largest and oldest African American Owned
Newspaper serving North/Central Florida and
Southern Georgia for over 50 years.
Date established: 1952

FREE PRESS
Free Press
216 Collier St.
Monroe, LA 71211-4717
Roosevelt Wright, Jr., Publisher/Editor
Tel: (318) 388-1310 **Fax:** (318) 388-2911
Email: rooseveltwright@prodigy.net
Web: www.monroefreepress.com
Circ.: 15,000
Price: $1.00 **Subscription:** $25.00/year
Publication description: To serve as an
advocate for minorities, working people, and
women's issues.
Date established: 1969

GARY CRUSADER
1549 Broadway
Gary, IN 46407
Dorothy R. Leavell, Publisher
Tel: (219) 885-4357 **Fax:** (219) 883-3317
Email: crusaderil@aol.com
Web: www.chgocrusader.com
Circ.: 33,700
Price: $0.25 **Subscription:** $20.00/year
Date established: 1940

GAZETTE, THE
Minority Opportunity News
P.O. Box 940226
Plano, TX 75074
Thurman R. Jones, Publisher
Tel: (972) 516-4191 **Fax:** (972) 516-9058
Email: editor@monthegazette.com
Web: www.monthegazette.com
Circ.: 30,000
Price: Free **Subscription:** $97.00/year
Publication description: To promote economic
development in the areas of housing, career
and business opportunities from an African
American perspective by reaching out to
women and other minority cultures and
building coalitions by providing information
and discussion to help our readers address
political, economic and community
opportunities.
Date established: 1991

GREATER DIVERSITY NEWS
P.O. Box 1679
Wilmington, NC 28402
Kathy Grear, Publisher
Tel: (800) 462-0738 **Fax:** (910) 763-6304
Email: kgrear@greaterdiversity.com
Web: www.greaterdiversity.com
Circ.: 5,000
Price: $0.50 **Subscription:** $35.00/year
Date established: 1987

HERALD AMERICA
Wave Newspaper Group
4201 Wilshire Blvd. #600
Los Angeles, CA 90010
Pluria Marshall, Jr., Publisher
Tel: (323) 290-3000 **Fax:** (323) 556-5704
Email: voices@wavenewspapers.com
Web: www.wavenewspapers.com
Circ.: 57,500
Price: Free **Subscription:** $90.00/year

HERALD DISPATCH
Herald Dispatch Publishing Co.
P.O. Box 191727
Los Angeles, CA 90019
John Holoman, Publisher
Tel: (323) 291-9486 **Fax:** (323) 291-2123
Circ.: 22,000
Price: $0.50 **Subscription:** $40.00/year
Date established: 1952

HYDE PARK CITIZEN
Chicago Citizen Newspaper Group
806 E. 78th St.
Chicago, IL 60619
William A. Garth, Publisher
Tel: (773) 783-1251 **Fax:** (773) 783-1301
Email: chall628@yahoo.com
Circ.: 17,000
Price: $0.25 **Subscription:** $50.00/year
Date established: 1968

INDEPENDENT BULLETIN
1550 W. 88th St. #107
Chicago, IL 60620
Hurley Green, III, Publisher
Tel: (773) 233-6210 **Fax:** (773) 233-6245
Email: bulletinnewspaper@comcast.net
Circ.: 62,000
Price: $0.25 **Subscription:** $25.00/year
Date established: 1972

INDIANA HERALD, THE
2170 N. Illinois St.
Indianapolis, IN 46202-1334
Mary Tandy, Publisher/Editor
Tel: (317) 923-8291 **Fax:** (317) 923-8292
Email: herald1@earthlink.net
Web: www.indianaherald.com
Circ.: 25,000
Price: $0.50 **Subscription:** $27.00/year

Publication description: The African American
and multiethnic newspaper serving Indiana
and nationally for over 46 years.
Date established: 1958

INDIANAPOLIS RECORDER
Indianapolis Recorder
2901 N. Tacoma Ave.
Indianapolis, IN 46218
Carolene Mays, Publisher/General Manager
Tel: (317) 924-5143 **Fax:** (317) 921-6653
Email: advertising@indyrecorder.com
Web: www.indianapolisrecorder.com
Circ.: 13,000
Price: $0.75 **Subscription:** $39.00/year
Date established: 1895

INLAND VALLEY NEWS
Inland Valley News, Inc.
2249 N. Garey Ave.
Pomona, CA 91767
Gloria Morrow, Ph.D., Publisher
Tel: (909) 392-6907 **Fax:** (909) 392-6917
Email: ivnews@aol.com
Web: www.inlandvalleynews.com
Circ.: 15,000
Price: Free **Subscription:** $35.00/year
Publication description: The Inland Valley
News is the only African American owned
newspaper between the cities of Los Angeles
and San Bernardino.
Date established: 1992

JACKSON ADVOCATE
438 N. Mill St.
Jackson, MS 39202
Charles Tisdale, Publisher
Tel: (601) 948-4122 **Fax:** (601) 948-4125
Email: jadvocat@aol.com
Web: www.jacksonadvocate.com
Circ.: 17,500
Price: $0.50 **Subscription:** $30.00/year
Publication description: The Jackson
Advocate is Mississippi's oldest African
American newspaper, and the largest weekly
newspaper in the state.
Date established: 1938

JACKSONVILLE ADVOCATE
BlackPressUSA Network
1284 W. 20th St.
Jacksonville, FL 32209
Isiah J. Williams, III, Publisher/Editor
Tel: (904) 358-8522 **Fax:** (904) 358-8592
Email: jaxadvocat@aol.com
Web: www.jacksonvilleadvocate.com
Circ.: 17,500
Price: $0.50 **Subscription:** $40.00/year
Publication description: The Jacksonville
Advocate is a Black-owned community
newspaper, published by the Florida Advocate
Publishing Company. It is an issue-oriented
newspaper that seeks not only to inform, but
to educate.
Date established: 1976

JACKSONVILLE FREE PRESS
Jacksonville Free Press
903 W. Edgewood Ave.
Jacksonville, FL 32208
Rita Perry, Publisher
Tel: (904) 634-1993 **Fax:** (904) 384-0235
Email: jfreepress@aol.com
Web: www.jacksonvillefreepress.com
Circ.: 43,500
Price: $0.50 **Subscription:** $35.50-$45.50/
year
Date established: 1985

L.A. WATTS TIMES
L.A. Watts Times, Inc.
3540 Wilshire Blvd. #PH3
Los Angeles, CA 90010

Melanie Polk, Publisher
Tel: (213) 251-5700 **Fax:** (213) 251-5720
Circ.: 25,500
Price: Free **Subscription:** $49.50/year
Publication description: To provide uplifting and
informative news on issues, events, and people
often overlooked by mainstream media.
Date established: 1976

LA METROPOLITAN GAZETTE
LA Metro Publications
14621 Titus St. #228
Van Nuys, CA 91402
Beverly Hamm, Publisher
Tel: (818) 782-8695 **Fax:** (818) 782-2924
Email: lametroinc@aol.com
Circ.: 20,000
Price: $0.25 **Subscription:** $12.50/year
Date established: 1966

LA VIDA NEWS
12000 Westhiemer St. #214
Houston, TX 77077
William Hadnot, Publisher
Tel: (281) 589-8950 **Fax:** (281) 589-8995
Email: fblavida@swbell.net
Circ.: 30,000
Price: Free **Subscription:** $32.00/year
Date established: 1957

LAS VEGAS SENTINEL-VOICE
Griot Communications Group
900 E. Charleston Blvd.
Las Vegas, NV 89104
Ramon Savoy, Publisher/Editor
Tel: (702) 380-8100 **Fax:** (702) 380-8102
Email: lvsentinelvoice@earthlink.net
Circ.: 6,000
Price: Free **Subscription:** $78.00/year
Publication description: The Sentinel Voice
newspaper consists of local and national
news, business, entertainment briefs, point
of view, commentary, international news,
community billboard, legal notices, news
briefs, employment, and sports.
Date established: 1980

LONG BEACH EXPRESS GAZETTE
LA Metro Publications
14621 Titus St. #228
Van Nuys, CA 91402
Beverly Hamm, Publisher
Tel: (818) 782-8695 **Fax:** (818) 782-2924
Email: lametroinc@aol.com
Circ.: 7,000
Price: $0.25 **Subscription:** $25.00/year
Date established: 1966

LOS ANGELES INDEPENDENT
L.A. Independent Newspaper Group
4201 Wilshire Blvd. #600
Los Angeles, CA 90010
Pluria Marshall, Jr., Publisher
Tel: (323) 290-3000 **Fax:** (323) 556-5704
Email: reynolds@laindependent.com
Web: www.laindependent.com
Price: Free **Subscription:** $90.00/year

LOS ANGELES SENTINEL
3800 Crenshaw Blvd.
Los Angeles, CA 90008
Jennifer Thomas, Publisher
Tel: (323) 299-9800 **Fax:** (323) 299-3896
Email: jamesbolden@losangelessentinel.
com
Circ.: 30,000
Price: $0.35 **Subscription:** $25.00/year
Date established: 1933

LOUISVILLE DEFENDER, THE
The Louisville Defender Newspaper
1720 Dixie Hwy.
Louisville, KY 40210

Clarence Leslie, Vice President/General Manager
Tel: (502) 772-2591 **Fax:** (502) 775-8655
Email: loudefender@aol.com
Circ.: 8,500
Price: $0.50 **Subscription:** $19.50/year
Date established: 1933

LYNWOOD PRESS
Wave Newspaper Group
4201 Wilshire Blvd. #600
Los Angeles, CA 90010
Pluria Marshall, Jr., Publisher
Tel: (323) 290-3000 **Fax:** (323) 556-5704
Email: voices@wavenewspapers.com
Web: www.wavenewspapers.com
Circ.: 57,500
Price: Free **Subscription:** $90.00/year

METRO COURIER, THE
The Metro Courier
P.O. Box 2385
Augusta, GA 30901
Barbara A. Gordon, Editor
Tel: (706) 724-6556 **Fax:** (706) 722-7104
Circ.: 28,780
Price: $0.50 **Subscription:** $40.00-50.00/year
Date established: 1983

MICHIGAN CITIZEN
Daily Telegraph
2669 Bagley St.
Detroit, MI 48216
Charles Kelly, Publisher
Tel: (313) 963-8282 **Fax:** (313) 963-8285
Email: editor@michigancitizen.com
Web: www.michigancitizen.com
Circ.: 58,000
Price: $0.50 **Subscription:** $26.00/year
Date established: 1978

MILWAUKEE TIMES WEEKLY
BlackPressUSA Network
1938 N. Dr. Martin Luther King Jr., Dr.
Milwaukee, WI 53212
Linda Jackson, Senior Account Executive
Tel: (414) 263-5088 **Fax:** (414) 263-4445
Email: miltimes@execpc.com
Web: www.themilwaukeetimesweekly.com
Circ.: 15,000
Price: $0.50 **Subscription:** $55.00/year
Date established: 1981

MINNESOTA SPOKESMAN-RECORDER
BlackPressUSA Network, Spokesman Recorder Publishing Co.
3744 4th Ave. South
Minneapolis, MN 55409
Tracey Williams, President
Tel: (612) 827-4021 **Fax:** (612) 827-0577
Email: twilliams@spokesman-recorder.com
Web: www.spokesman-recorder.com
Circ.: 26,000
Price: $0.50 **Subscription:** $30.00-35.00/year
Publication description: Cecil E. Newman established the Minnesota Spokesman-Recorder in 1934. Today, celebrating 69 years of publishing, the Minnesota Spokesman-Recorder newspaper is a minority and woman owned company led by publisher Launa Q. Newman.
Date established: 1934

MINORITY COMMUNICATOR NEWS
90 W. Campus View Blvd.
Columbus, OH 43235
Jack Harris, Publisher
Tel: (614) 781-1160
Email: communicatornew@aol.com
Circ.: 126,000
Publication description: The Communicator

News is Columbus' leading African American weekly newspaper that serves central Ohio. It is dedicated to providing its readers timely, thought-provoking and targeted news in a professional manner.
Date established: 1989

MONTGOMERY-TUSKEGEE TIMES
P.O. Box 9133
Montgomery, AL 36108
Rev. Al Dixon, Publisher
Tel: (334) 280-2444 **Fax:** (334) 280-2454
Email: adixon711@aol.com
Web: www.montgomerytuskegeetimes.com
Circ.: 10,000
Price: $0.50 **Subscription:** $50.00/year
Date established: 1977

N'DIGO
Hartman Publishing
19 N. Sangamon St.
Chicago, IL 60607
Hermene D. Hartman, Publisher
Tel: (312) 822-0202 **Fax:** (312) 822-0288
Web: www.ndigo.com
Circ.: 160,000
Price: Free **Subscription:** $63.00/year
Publication description: N'DIGO is Chicago's largest African American weekly publication and offers its diverse readers a new view on contemporary culture.
Date established: 1989

NEW AMERICAN, THE
The Challenge Group
1195 Atlantic Ave.
Brooklyn, NY 11216
Thomas H. Watkins, Jr., Publisher/CEO
Tel: (718) 636-9500 **Fax:** (718) 857-9115
Email: thenewamerican@hotmail.com
Web: www.challenge-group.com
Circ.: 67,000
Subscription: $55.00/year
Publication description: The New American maintains a unique position in New York as the only weekly newspaper focusing primarily on art, culture and entertainment for the Black community. Each week the New American features reviews, interviews, in depth articles and even the latest gossip to keep those with a need to know, aware of what's happening in the worlds of movies, books, music, theater, nightlife, art and more.
Date established: 1966

NEW VOICE OF NEW YORK, THE
The New Voice of New York
108-18 Queens Blvd., 8th Fl. #1
Forest Hills, NY 11375
Kenneth Drew, Publisher
Tel: (718) 459-5717 **Fax:** (718) 459-0030
Email: newvoiceny@aol.com
Circ.: 90,000
Price: $0.75 **Subscription:** $80.00/year
Date established: 1959

NEW YORK BEACON
BlackPressUSA Network, Smith Haj Group, Inc.
341 38th St., 8th Fl.
New York, NY 10018
Walter Smith, Jr., Publisher
Tel: (212) 213-8585 **Fax:** (212) 213-6291
Email: nybeacon@hotmail.com
Web: www.newyorkbeacon.com
Circ.: 71,750
Price: $0.75 **Subscription:** $35.00/year
Date established: 1975

NOKOA (THE OBSERVER) NEWSPAPER
Nokoa News
1154-B Angelina St.
Austin, TX 78702

Akwasi Evans, Publisher/Founder
Tel: (512) 499-8713 **Fax:** (512) 499-8740
Email: akwasievans@hotmail.com
Circ.: 8,000
Price: Free **Subscription:** $50.00/year
Date established: 1987

OKLAHOMA EAGLE, THE
P.O. Box 3267
Tulsa, OK 74101
Joseph Goodwin, Publisher
Tel: (918) 582-7124 **Fax:** (918) 582-8905
Email: newsokeagle@newbox.net
Circ.: 4,000
Price: $0.50 **Subscription:** $28.00/year
Date established: 1921

OMAHA STAR, THE
The Omaha Star, Inc.
P.O. Box 11128
Omaha, NE 68111
Marguerita L. Washington, Publisher
Tel: (402) 346-4041 **Fax:** (402) 346-4064
Email: marguerita@omahastar.omhcoxmail.com
Circ.: 33,000
Price: $0.35 **Subscription:** $28.00/year
Date established: 1938

ORLANDO TIMES, THE
4403 Vineland Rd. #B-5
Orlando, FL 32811-7362
Dr. Calvin Collins, Publisher
Tel: (407) 841-3710 **Fax:** (407) 849-0434
Email: news@orlando-times.com
Web: www.orlando-times.com
Circ.: 70,000
Price: $0.50 **Subscription:** $30.00-34.00/year
Publication description: Central Florida's quality, African-American newspaper, is published every Thursday and has a larger circulation than any other African-American newspaper in Orange county.
Date established: 1975

PALM BEACH GAZETTE
Paper Clips, Inc.
P.O. Box 18469
West Palm Beach, FL 33416
Gwen Ivory, Publisher
Tel: (561) 844-5501 **Fax:** (561) 844-5551
Email: paperclips1@hotmail.com
Circ.: 3,000
Date established: 1989

PASADENA GAZETTE
LA Metro Publications
14621 Titus St. #228
Van Nuys, CA 91402
Beverly Hamm, Publisher
Tel: (818) 782-8695 **Fax:** (818) 782-2924
Email: lametroinc@aol.com
Circ.: 20,000
Price: $0.25 **Subscription:** $12.50/year
Date established: 1966

PASADENA/SAN GABRIEL VALLEY JOURNAL, THE
1541 N. Lake Ave.
Pasadena, CA 91104
Ruthie Hopkins, Publisher/Managing Editor
Tel: (626) 798-3972 **Fax:** (626) 798-3282
Email: pasjour@pacbell.net
Web: www.pasadenajournal.com
Circ.: 7,000
Price: Free **Subscription:** $40.00/year
Publication description: The only newspaper serving the African-American and Latino communities of Pasadena, Altadena, Monrovia, Duarte and the West San Gabriel Valley.
Date established: 1989

PENSACOLA VOICE, THE
The Pensacola Voice
213 E. Yonge St.
Pensacola, FL 32503
LaDonna Spivey, Publisher
Tel: (850) 434-6963 **Fax:** (850) 469-8745
Email: info@pensacolavoice.com
Web: www.pensacolavoice.com
Circ.: 38,275
Price: $0.50 **Subscription:** $20.00/year
Publication description: The Pensacola Voice was established in 1963 to serve as the voice of the African American community. Pensacola Voice strives to provide exemplary coverage of news items affecting the lives of African Americans.
Date established: 1963

PRECINCT REPORTER
Precinct Reporter Group
1677 W. Baseline St.
San Bernardino, CA 92411
Brian Townsend, Publisher
Tel: (909) 889-0597 **Fax:** (909) 889-1706
Email: prgroupnews@adelphi.net
Circ.: 55,000
Price: Free **Subscription:** $20.00/year
Date established: 1965

PRESS, THE
Wave Newspaper Group
4201 Wilshire Blvd. #600
Los Angeles, CA 90010
Pluria Marshall, Jr., Publisher
Tel: (323) 290-3000 **Fax:** (323) 556-5704
Email: voices@wavenewspapers.com
Web: www.wavenewspapers.com
Circ.: 57,500
Price: Free **Subscription:** $90.00/year

PROVIDENCE AMERICAN, THE
The Amerzine Company
131 Washington St. #212
Providence, RI 02903
Frank Graham, CEO/Publisher
Tel: (401) 351-8860 **Fax:** (401) 351-8865
Email: amerzine@ix.netcom.com
Web: www.providence.edu/afro/students/bresnahan/amerzine.htm
Circ.: 5,000
Price: $0.50 **Subscription:** $30.00/year
Publication description: The Providence American is a community newspaper that serves the African American population. The paper provides a minority perspective for persons of color living within the Providence community. Due to the city's diverse minority population, the paper covers local and national issues that affect African Americans, Cape Verdeans, Latinos, Asians, and Native Americans.
Date established: 1986

RICHMOND FREE PRESS
Paradigm Communications, Inc.
P.O. Box 27709
Richmond, VA 23261
Raymond H. Boone, Publisher
Tel: (804) 644-0496 **Fax:** (804) 643-7519
Email: news@richmondfreepress.com
Circ.: 30,000
Price: Free **Subscription:** $40.00/year
Date established: 1992

ROANOKE TRIBUNE
Salem Times Register
P.O. Box 6021
Roanoke, VA 24017
Claudia A. Whitworth, Publisher/Editor
Tel: (540) 343-0326 **Fax:** (540) 343-7366
Circ.: 6,200
Price: $0.40 **Subscription:** $18.00/year
Date established: 1939

SACRAMENTO OBSERVER
2330 Alhambra Blvd.
Sacramento, CA 95817
William H. Lee, Publisher
Tel: (916) 452-4781 **Fax:** (916) 452-7744
Email: whlee@sacobserver.com
Web: www.sacobserver.com
Circ.: 50,000
Price: $0.75 **Subscription:** $130.00/year
Date established: 1962

SAN ANTONIO INFORMER
Urban Communications
333 S. Hackberry St.
San Antonio, TX 78203
Tommy Moore, Publisher
Tel: (210) 227-8300 **Fax:** (210) 223-4111
Email: sainformer@sbcglobal.net
Circ.: 5,000
Price: $1.00 **Subscription:** $30.00/year
Date established: 1988

SAN FERNANDO VALLEY GAZETTE
LA Metro Publications
14621 Titus St. #228
Van Nuys, CA 91402
Beverly Hamm, Publisher
Tel: (818) 782-8695 **Fax:** (818) 782-2924
Email: lametroinc@aol.com
Circ.: 10,000
Price: $0.25 **Subscription:** $12.50/year
Date established: 1966

SHREVEPORT SUN
Shreveport Sun, Inc.
P.O. Box 38357
Shreveport, LA 71133-8357
Sonya C. Landry, Publisher
Tel: (318) 631-6222 **Fax:** (318) 635-2822
Email: sunweekly@aol.com
Circ.: 5,000
Price: $0.50 **Subscription:** $23.69/year
Date established: 1920

SNAP NEWS
Snap News
1609 E. Houston St.
San Antonio, TX 78202
Eugene Coleman, Publisher
Tel: (210) 224-0706 **Fax:** (210) 223-1500
Email: snap.coleman@whoo.com
Circ.: 7,000
Price: $0.50 **Subscription:** $50.00/year
Date established: 1949

SOUTH END CITIZEN
Chicago Citizen Newspaper Group
806 E. 78th St.
Chicago, IL 60619
William A. Garth, Publisher
Tel: (773) 783-1251 **Fax:** (773) 783-1301
Email: chall628@yahoo.com
Circ.: 28,707
Price: $0.25 **Subscription:** $50.00/year
Date established: 1968

SOUTHEAST NEWSPRESS
Herald Dispatch Publishing Co.
P.O. Box 191727
Los Angeles, CA 90019
John Holoman, Publisher
Tel: (323) 291-9486 **Fax:** (323) 291-2123
Circ.: 22,000
Price: $0.50 **Subscription:** $40.00/year
Date established: 1924

SOUTHEASTERN STAR
BlackPressUSA Network
2003 W. Capital Dr.
Milwaukee, WI 53206
Faithe Colas, Publisher
Tel: (414) 449-4864 **Fax:** (414) 449-4872

Email: milwaukeecourier@aol.com
Web: www.milwaukeecourier.org
Circ.: 40,000
Price: Free **Subscription:** $25.00/year

ST. LOUIS ARGUS
4595 Martin Luther King Dr.
St. Louis, MO 63113
Eddie Hasan, Publisher
Tel: (314) 531-1323 **Fax:** (314) 531-1324
Email: media@stlouisargus.com
Web: www.stlargus.com
Circ.: 44,000
Price: Free **Subscription:** $58.00/year
Date established: 1912

ST. LOUIS METRO SENTINEL JOURNAL
2900 N. Market St.
St. Louis, MO 63106
Michael Williams, Publisher
Tel: (314) 531-2101 **Fax:** (314) 531-4442
Email: stlsentinelnews@aol.com
Circ.: 10,000
Price: Free **Subscription:** $50.00/year
Date established: 1968

SUN JOURNAL
LA Metro Publications
14621 Titus St. #228
Van Nuys, CA 91402
Beverly Hamm, Publisher
Tel: (818) 782-8695 **Fax:** (818) 782-2924
Email: lametroinc@aol.com
Circ.: 5,000
Price: $0.25 **Subscription:** $12.50/year
Date established: 1966

SUN REPORTER
Sun Reporter Publishing Co.
1791 Bancroft Ave.
San Francisco, CA 94111
Amelia Ashley-Ward, Publisher
Tel: (415) 671-1000 **Fax:** (415) 671-1005
Email: sunmedia97@aol.com
Web: www.sunreporter.com
Circ.: 11,000
Price: $0.30 **Subscription:** $20.00/year
Date established: 1944

TELEGRAM NEWS
The Telegram Publishing Co.
3920 W. Jefferson Ave.
Ecorse, MI 48229
Ben Wade, Publisher
Tel: (313) 928-2955 **Fax:** (313) 928-3014
Email: telegramnews@aol.com
Circ.: 12,000
Price: $0.25 **Subscription:** $30.00/year
Date established: 1945

TRI STATE DEFENDER
Real Times, Inc.
124 G.E. Patterson Ave.
Memphis, TN 38103
Marcie Thomas, Publisher
Tel: (901) 523-1818 **Fax:** (901) 523-1820
Email: editorial@tri-statedefender.com
Web: www.tri-statedefender.com
Circ.: 38,500
Price: $0.75 **Subscription:** $28.00/year
Date established: 1951

VOICE & VIEWPOINT
Warren Communications
1729 N. Euclid Ave.
San Diego, CA 92112
John E. Warren, Publisher
Tel: (619) 266-2233 **Fax:** (619) 266-0533
Email: sdvoice@pacbell.net
Circ.: 25,000
Price: $0.50 **Subscription:** $30.00/year
Date established: 1961

WASHINGTON INFORMER
3117 Martin Luther King Jr. Ave. SE
Washington, DC 20032
Denise Rolark Barnes, Publisher
Tel: (202) 561-4100 **Fax:** (202) 574-3785
Email: washington.informer@verizon.net
Web: www.washingtoninformer.com
Circ.: 15,000
Price: Free **Subscription:** $20.00/year
Date established: 1964

WASHINGTON SUN, THE
830 Kennedy St. NW
Washington, DC 20011
J.C. Cooke, Publisher
Tel: (202) 882-1021 **Fax:** (202) 882-9817
Email: thewashingtonsun@aol.com
Circ.: 55,000
Price: $0.20 **Subscription:** $50.00/year
Date established: 1967

WATTS STAR REVIEW
Herald Dispatch Publishing Co.
P.O. Box 191727
Los Angeles, CA 90019
John Holoman, Publisher
Tel: (323) 291-9486 **Fax:** (323) 291-2123
Circ.: 22,000
Price: $0.50 **Subscription:** $40.00/year
Date established: 1875

WAVE-EAST EDITION
BlackPressUSA Network
4201 Wilshire Blvd. #600
Los Angeles, CA 90010
Pluria Marshall, Jr., Publisher
Tel: (323) 290-3000 **Fax:** (323) 556-5704
Email: voices@wavenewspaper.com
Web: www.wavenewspaper.com
Circ.: 150,000
Price: Free **Subscription:** $90.00/year
Publication description: Wave Newspapers includes 14 weekly publications covering more than 39 cities and communities in South Los Angeles, the Los Angeles Eastside and Northeast, East Los Angeles, the San Gabriel Valley and communities in Southeast Los Angeles County.
Date established: 1898

WAVE-NORTHEAST EDITION
BlackPressUSA Network
4201 Wilshire Blvd. #600
Los Angeles, CA 90010
Pluria Marshall, Jr., Publisher
Tel: (323) 290-3000 **Fax:** (323) 556-5704
Email: voices@wavenewspaper.com
Web: www.wavenewspaper.com
Circ.: 150,000
Price: Free **Subscription:** $90.00/year
Publication description: Wave Newspapers includes 14 weekly publications covering more than 39 cities and communities in South Los Angeles, the Los Angeles Eastside and Northeast, East Los Angeles, the San Gabriel Valley and communities in Southeast Los Angeles County.
Date established: 1898

WAVE-WEST EDITION
BlackPressUSA Network
4201 Wilshire Blvd. #600
Los Angeles, CA 90010
Pluria Marshall, Jr., Publisher
Tel: (323) 290-3000 **Fax:** (323) 556-5704
Email: voices@wavenewspaper.com
Web: www.wavenewspaper.com
Circ.: 150,000
Price: $1.50 **Subscription:** $90.00/year
Publication description: Wave Newspapers includes 14 weekly publications covering more than 39 cities and communities in

South Los Angeles, the Los Angeles Eastside and Northeast, East Los Angeles, the San Gabriel Valley and communities in Southeast Los Angeles County.
Date established: 1898

WEEKLY CHALLENGER, THE
BlackPressUSA Network
2500 Dr. Martin Luther King Jr. St. South
St. Petersburg, FL 33705
loretta Cleveland, Officer Manager
Tel: (727) 822-8996 **Fax:** (727) 823-2568
Email: tchallen@tampabay.rr.com
Web: www.theweeklychallenger.com
Circ.: 20,000
Price: $0.25 **Subscription:** $30.00/year
Publication description: Newspaper
Date established: 1967

WESTCHESTER COUNTY PRESS, THE
The Westchester County Press
29 W. 4th St.
Mt. Vernon, NY 10550
M. Paul Redd, President/Publisher
Tel: (914) 684-0006 **Fax:** (914) 699-2633
Circ.: 10,000
Price: $0.40 **Subscription:** $25.00/year
Date established: 1930

WESTSIDE GAZETTE
BlackPressUSA Network
545 NW 7th Terrace
Fort Lauderdale, FL 33311
Bobby R. Henry, Sr., Publisher
Tel: (954) 525-1489 **Fax:** (954) 525-1489
Email: wgazette@bellsouth.net
Web: www.thewestsidegazette.com
Circ.: 50,000
Price: $0.50 **Subscription:** $35.00/year
Publication description: Broward County's oldest and largest African-American owned and operated newspaper. Distributed in Dade, Broward and Palm beach Counties with a circulation of 50,000. Focuses on positive African American community news.
Date established: 1971

WILMINGTON JOURNAL, THE
BlackPressUSA Network
P.O. Box 1020
Wilmington, NC 28402
Mary Thatch, Publisher
Tel: (910) 762-5502 **Fax:** (910) 343-1334
Email: wilmjourn@aol.com
Web: www.wilmingtonjournal.com
Circ.: 10,000
Price: $0.50 **Subscription:** $32.00/year
Date established: 1927

WINDY CITY WORD, THE
The Windy City Word
5090 W. Harrison St.
Chicago, IL 60644
Mary Denson, Publisher
Tel: (773) 378-0261 **Fax:** (773) 378-2408
Email: windycityword02@yahoo.com
Web: www.windycityword.com
Circ.: 20,000
Price: Free **Subscription:** $39.00/year
Publication description: A weekly newspaper serving the Greater West Side of Chicago distributed every Thursday since July 1, 1991. Was created after an outcry from the community of constant negative reporting of West Side news by TV and major media of Chicago.
Date established: 1991

WEEKLY-WEDNESDAY

AFRICAN-AMERICAN NEWS & ISSUES
Malonson Co., Inc.
6130 Wheatley St.
Houston, TX 77091-3947
Fred Smith, Publisher
Tel: (713) 692-1892 **Fax:** (713) 692-1183
Email: aframnews@pdq.net
Web: www.aframnews.com
Circ.: 380,000
Price: Free **Subscription:** $60.00/year
Date established: 1996

AFRICAN-AMERICAN VOICE
625 E. Wood St.
Decatur, IL 62523
Horace Livingston, Jr., Editor/Publisher
Tel: (217) 423-2231 **Fax:** (217) 423-5860
Email: decaturvoice1@aol.com
Circ.: 18,000
Price: $0.60 **Subscription:** $28.00/year
Publication description: The African-American Voice is a tabloid published in Decatur, Illinois and Bloomington.
Date established: 1973

ARIZONA INFORMANT
Arizona Informant Publishing Co.
1746 E. Madison St. #2
Phoenix, AZ 85034
Dr. Charles Campbell, Publisher
Tel: (602) 257-9300 **Fax:** (602) 257-0547
Email: advertise@azinformant.com
Web: www.arizonainformantnewspaper.com
Circ.: 50,000
Price: $0.50 **Subscription:** $27.50/year
Date established: 1971

BAKERSFIELD NEWS OBSERVER
Observer Group Newspapers of Southern California
1219 20th St.
Bakersfield, CA 93301
Ellen Coley, Publisher
Tel: (661) 324-9466 **Fax:** (661) 324-9472
Email: ellencoley@sbcglobal.net
Circ.: 21,000
Price: $0.50 **Subscription:** $50.00/year
Date established: 1977

BLAZER NEWS
New City Resources, Inc.
P.O. Box 806
Jackson, MI 49204
Edith Davis, Publisher
Tel: (517) 788-4600 **Fax:** (517) 788-5300
Email: theblazernews@yahoo.com
Circ.: 3,000
Price: $0.50 **Subscription:** $50.00-75.00/year
Date established: 1962

BRIDGEPORT INQUIRER, THE
Inquirer Newspaper Group
P.O. Box 1260
Hartford, CT 06143
William R. Hales, Publisher
Tel: (860) 522-1462 **Fax:** (860) 522-3014
Email: info@inqnews.com
Web: www.inqnews.com
Circ.: 120,000
Price: Free **Subscription:** $30.00/year
Publication description: The Hartford Inquirer is the largest African-American newspaper organization in New England.
Date established: 1975

BUCKEYE REVIEW
Buckeye Review Publishing, LLC
1201 Belmont Ave.
Youngstown, OH 44504

Linda McNair, Publisher/Editor
Tel: (330) 743-2250 **Fax:** (330) 746-2340
Email: mike@buckeyereview.com
Web: www.buckeyereview.com
Circ.: 5,300
Price: $0.50 **Subscription:** $30.00/year
Publication description: To provide customers with another forum where the African American can tell their side of any story. To aide in diversity training and give the other cultures/races an opportunity to learn more about the African American.
Date established: 1937

CHALLENGER, THE
1337 Jefferson Ave.
Buffalo, NY 14204
Al-Nisa Barbara Banks, Publisher
Tel: (716) 897-0442 **Fax:** (716) 897-3307
Circ.: 10,000
Price: $0.50 **Subscription:** $25.00/year
Date established: 1962

CHATMAN-SOUTHEAST CITIZEN
Chicago Citizen Newspaper Group
806 E. 78th St.
Chicago, IL 60619
William A. Garth, Publisher
Tel: (773) 783-1251 **Fax:** (773) 783-1301
Email: chall628@yahoo.com
Circ.: 29,000
Price: $0.25 **Subscription:** $50.00/year
Date established: 1968

CHICAGO WEEKEND
Chicago Citizen Newspaper Group
806 E. 78th St.
Chicago, IL 60619
William A. Garth, Publisher
Tel: (773) 783-1251 **Fax:** (773) 783-1301
Email: chall628@yahoo.com
Circ.: 24,636
Price: $0.25 **Subscription:** $50.00/year
Date established: 1968

DALLAS WEEKLY
Ad Mast Publishing, Inc.
P.O. Box 151789
Dallas, TX 75315
James Washington, Publisher
Tel: (214) 428-8958 **Fax:** (214) 428-2807
Email: sriley@dallasweekly.com
Web: www.dallasweekly.com
Circ.: 11,500
Price: Free **Subscription:** $60.00/year
Date established: 1953

FACTS NEWSPAPER, THE
The Facts Newspaper
2765 E. Cherry St.
Seattle, WA 98122
Elizabeth Beaver, Publisher
Tel: (206) 324-0552 **Fax:** (206) 324-1007
Email: thefactsnewspaper@excite.com
Circ.: 100,000
Price: Free **Subscription:** $60.00/year
Date established: 1961

FINAL CALL, THE
FCN Publishing
734 W. 79th St.
Chicago, IL 60620
Dora Muhammad, Managing Editor
Tel: (773) 602-1230 **Fax:** (773) 602-1013
Email: fcnprod@aol.com
Web: www.finalcall.com
Circ.: 900,000
Price: $1.00 **Subscription:** $45.00/year
Date established: 1930

HARTFORD INQUIRER, THE
Inquirer Newspaper Group
P.O. Box 1260
Hartford, CT 06143
William R. Hales, Publisher
Tel: (860) 522-1462 **Fax:** (860) 522-3014
Email: info@inqnews.com
Web: www.inqnews.com
Circ.: 120,000
Price: Free **Subscription:** $30.00/year
Publication description: The Hartford Inquirer is the largest African-American newspaper organization in New England.
Date established: 1975

HUDSON VALLEY PRESS
Hudson Valley Black Press
P.O. Box 2160
Newburgh, NY 12550
Chuck Stewart, Publisher
Tel: (845) 562-1313 **Fax:** (845) 562-1348
Price: $0.50 **Subscription:** $35.00/year
Date established: 1983

LEADER, THE
Journal Register Company, The New Hope Gazette
2385 W. Cheltenham Ave. #182
Philadelphia, PA 19150
Skip Henry, Publisher
Tel: (215) 885-4111 **Fax:** (215) 885-0226
Email: leader@ingnews.com
Web: www.wolleader.com
Circ.: 29,000
Price: Free **Subscription:** $78.00/year
Date established: 1972

MIAMI TIMES, THE
900 NW 54th St.
Miami, FL 33127
Rachel J. Reeves, Publisher
Tel: (305) 757-1147 **Fax:** (305) 757-5770
Email: info@miamitimesonline.com
Web: www.miamitimesonline.com
Circ.: 50,000
Price: $0.50 **Subscription:** $35.00/year
Publication description: The Miami Times, Miami's largest Black Community Newspaper represents the pinnacle of community relations.
Date established: 1923

MICHIGAN CHRONICLE
479 Ledyard St.
Detroit, MI 48201-2687
Sam Logan, Publisher
Tel: (313) 963-5522 **Fax:** (313) 963-8788
Email: publisher@michchronicle.com
Web: www.michchronicle.com
Circ.: 75,000
Price: $0.50 **Subscription:** $25.00/year
Publication description: The Michigan Chronicle is the state's most respected African American publication. This award-winning weekly newspaper received the prestigious John B. Russworm for the "Best Black Newspaper in the Country" (voted by the National Newspaper Publishers Association), a recognition the Michigan Chronicle held six times last year.
Date established: 1936

MOBILE BEACON-CITIZEN
Mobile Beacon
2311 Costarides St.
Mobile, AL 36617
Cleretta T. Blackmon, Publisher/CEO
Tel: (251) 479-0629 **Fax:** (251) 479-0610
Email: mobeaconinc@bellsouth.net
Circ.: 5,000
Price: $0.50 **Subscription:** $30.00/year
Date established: 1943

NEW HAVEN INQUIRER, THE
Inquirer Newspaper Group
P.O. Box 1260
Hartford, CT 06143
William R. Hales, Publisher
Tel: (860) 522-1462 **Fax:** (860) 522-3014
Email: info@inqnews.com
Web: www.inqnews.com
Circ.: 120,000
Price: Free **Subscription:** $30.00/year
Publication description: The Hartford Inquirer is the largest African-American newspaper organization in New England.
Date established: 1975

NEW JOURNAL & GUIDE
974 Norforlk Sq.
Norfolk, VA 23502
Brenda H. Andrews, Publisher/Owner
Tel: (757) 543-6531 **Fax:** (757) 543-7620
Email: andrews@njournalg.com
Web: www.njournalg.com
Circ.: 25,000
Price: $0.75 **Subscription:** $29.99/year
Date established: 1900

NEW YORK CARIB NEWS, THE
New York Carib News
7 W. 36th St., 8th Fl.
New York, NY 10018
Karl Rodney, Publisher
Tel: (212) 944-1991 **Fax:** (212) 944-2089
Email: nycarib@aol.com
Web: www.nycaribnews.com
Circ.: 76,000
Price: $0.50 **Subscription:** $40.00/year
Date established: 1982

PHILADELPHIA NEWS OBSERVER, THE
BlackPressUSA Network, Black Minority Paper
1520 Locust St. #700
Philadelphia, PA 19102
J. H. Warren, III, Publisher/Editor
Tel: (215) 545-7500 **Fax:** (215) 545-5548
Email: media@pnonews.com
Web: www.pnonews.com
Circ.: 80,000
Price: Free **Subscription:** $30.00/year
Publication description: The Philadelphia News Observer is dedicated to the human rights of all people giving objective news, and presenting a variety of thoughts that will bring about a better understanding of each other.
Date established: 1975

PORTLAND OBSERVER, THE
Coray Publications, Inc.
P.O. Box 3137
Portland, OR 97208
Charles Washington, Publisher
Tel: (503) 288-0033 **Fax:** (503) 288-0015
Email: news@portlandobserver.com
Web: www.portlandobserver.com
Circ.: 40,000
Price: Free **Subscription:** $60.00/year
Date established: 1970

SAN FRANCISCO BAY VIEW
Bay View, Inc.
4917 3rd St.
San Francisco, CA 94124
Willie Ratcliff, Publisher
Tel: (415) 671-0789 **Fax:** (415) 671-0316
Email: editor@sfbayview.com
Web: www.sfbayview.com
Circ.: 20,000
Price: Free **Subscription:** $39.00/year
Publication description: A weekly African American newspaper with a Bay Area readership. To encourage, enlighten and empower the African American Community.
Date established: 1976

SAVANNAH HERALD
The Herald of Savannah, Inc.
P.O. Box 486
Savannah, GA 31402
Floyd Adams, Jr., Publisher
Tel: (912) 232-4505 **Fax:** (912) 231-0018
Email: savher@aol.com
Web: www.savannahherald.com
Circ.: 9,000
Price: $0.35 **Subscription:** $26.50/year
Publication description: The Savannah Herald is Savannah's Black Voice published weekly. Our readership consists of professionals, educators, clergy, etc. with an age range of 21-75. The Savannah Herald is distributed through paid subscription, boxes and newsstands. We are the most read African American weekly newspaper in the Savannah area.
Date established: 1945

SAVANNAH TRIBUNE, THE
916 Montgomery St.
Savannah, GA 31402
Shirley B. James, Publisher
Tel: (912) 233-6128 **Fax:** (912) 233-6140
Email: sharon@savannahtribune.com
Web: www.savannahtribune.com
Circ.: 8,000
Price: Free **Subscription:** $28.00-30.00/year
Publication description: Savannah's first minority owned newspaper.
Date established: 1875

SOUTH SUBURBAN CITIZEN
Chicago Citizen Newspaper Group
806 E. 78th St.
Chicago, IL 60619
William A. Garth, Publisher
Tel: (773) 783-1251 **Fax:** (773) 783-1301
Email: chall628@yahoo.com
Circ.: 21,500
Price: $0.25 **Subscription:** $50.00/year
Date established: 1968

SPEAKIN' OUT NEWS
P.O. Box 2826
Huntsville, AL 35804
William Smothers, Publisher
Tel: (256) 551-1020 **Fax:** (256) 551-0607
Email: wsmoth3193@aol.com

Web: www.speakinoutnews.com
Circ.: 26,000
Price: $0.50 **Subscription:** $25.00/year
Date established: 1980

SPRINGFIELD INQUIRER, THE
Inquirer Newspaper Group
P.O. Box 1260
Hartford, CT 06143
William R. Hales, Publisher
Tel: (860) 522-1462 **Fax:** (860) 522-3014
Email: info@inqnews.com
Web: www.inqnews.com
Circ.: 120,000
Price: Free **Subscription:** $30.00/year
Publication description: The Hartford Inquirer is the largest African-American newspaper organization in New England.
Date established: 1975

TOLEDO JOURNAL, THE
BlackPressUSA Network
3021 Douglas Rd.
Toledo, OH 43606
Sandra S. Stewart, Publisher

Tel: (419) 472-4521
Email: toledo411@aol.com
Web: www.thetoledojournal.com
Circ.: 22,500
Price: Free **Subscription:** $50.00/year
Date established: 1975

WATERBURY INQUIRER, THE
Inquirer Newspaper Group
P.O. Box 1260
Hartford, CT 06143
William R. Hales, Publisher
Tel: (860) 522-1462 **Fax:** (860) 522-3014
Email: info@inqnews.com
Web: www.inqnews.com
Circ.: 120,000
Price: Free **Subscription:** $30.00/year
Publication description: The Hartford Inquirer is the largest African-American newspaper organization in New England.
Date established: 1975

African American Radio Stations

ALABAMA

WACT-AM (1420-AM KHZ)
Clear Channel Communications
3900 11th Ave. South
Tuscaloosa, AL 35401
Lori Moore, General Manager
Tel: (205) 344-4589 Fax: (205) 752-9269

WAGF-FM (101.3-FM MHZ)
Wilson Broadcast
805 N. Lena St. #13
Dothan, AL 36303
J.R. Wilson, General Manager
Tel: (334) 671-1753 Fax: (334) 677-6923

WAGG-AM (610-AM KHZ)
950 22nd St. North #1000
Birmingham, AL 35203
David Dubose, General Manager
Tel: (205) 322-2987 Fax: (205) 324-6329

WAPZ-AM (1250-AM KHZ)
WAPZ Broadcasting Corp.
2821 US Hwy. 231
Wetumpka, AL 36093
Robert Henderson, General Manager
Tel: (334) 567-2251 Fax: (334) 567-7971
Email: rh5672@aol.com

WATV-AM (900-AM KHZ)
Birmingham Ebony Broadcasting
3025 Ensley Ave.
Birmingham, AL 35208
James Locklin, General Manager
Tel: (205) 780-2014 Fax: (205) 780-4034

WAYE-AM (1220-AM KHZ)
Wliss Broadcasting, Inc.
836 Lomb Ave. SW
Birmingham, AL 35211
Mary Agee, General Manager
Tel: (205) 786-9293 Fax: (205) 786-9296

WBHJ-FM (95.7-FM MHZ)
950 22nd St. North #1000
Birmingham, AL 35203
David Dubose, General Manager
Tel: (205) 322-2987 Fax: (205) 324-6329

WBHK-FM (98.7-FM MHZ)
950 22nd St. North #1000
Birmingham, AL 35203
David Dubose, General Manager
Tel: (205) 322-2987 Fax: (205) 324-6329

WBLX-FM (92.9-FM MHZ)
Cumulus Broadcasting
2800 Dauphin St. #104
Mobile, AL 36606
Gary Pizzati, General Manager
Tel: (251) 652-2000 Fax: (251) 652-2001

WDLT-AM (660-AM KHZ)
Cumulus Broadcasting
2800 Dauphin St. #104
Mobile, AL 36606
Gary Pizzati, General Manager
Tel: (251) 652-2000 Fax: (251) 652-2001

WDLT-FM (98.3-FM MHZ)
Cumulus Broadcasting
2800 Dauphin St. #104
Mobile, AL 36606
Gary Pizzati, General Manager
Tel: (251) 652-2000 Fax: (251) 652-2001

WENN-FM (105.9-FM MHZ)
Clear Channel Communications
600 Beacon Pkwy. West #400
Birmingham, AL 35209
Jimmy Vineyard, General Manager
Tel: (205) 439-9600 Fax: (205) 439-8390
Web: www.hallelujah1059.com

WERC-AM (960-AM KHZ)
Clear Channel Communications
600 Beacon Pkwy. West #400
Birmingham, AL 35209
Jimmy Vineyard, General Manager
Tel: (205) 439-9600 Fax: (205) 439-8390

WEUP-FM (103.1-FM MHZ)
WEUP Radio Station
2609 Jordan Ln. NW
Huntsville, AL 35816
Hundley Batts, General Manager
Tel: (256) 837-9387 Fax: (256) 837-9404
Email: hundley@103weup.com
Web: www.103weup.com

WGOK-AM (900-AM KHZ)
Cumulus Broadcasting
2800 Dauphin St. #104
Mobile, AL 36606
Gary Pizzati, General Manager
Tel: (251) 652-2000 Fax: (251) 652-2001

WIJK-AM (1470-AM KHZ)
Gulf Coast Broadcasting Corp.
P.O. Box 705
Evergreen, AL 36401
Luther Upton, General Manager
Tel: (251) 578-2780 Fax: (251) 578-5399
Email: powerpig@bellsouth.net

WJAM-FM (97.3-FM MHZ)
Scott Communications, Inc.
273 Persimmon Tree Rd.
Selma, AL 36701
Scott Alexander, General Manager
Tel: (334) 875-9360 Fax: (334) 875-1340
Email: walx@charterinternet.com

WJJN-FM (92.1-FM MHZ)
Wilson Broadcast
805 N. Lena St. #13

Dothan, AL 36303
J.R. Wilson, General Manager
Tel: (334) 671-1753 Fax: (334) 677-6923

WJLD-AM (1400-AM KHZ)
Richardson Broadcasting
P.O. Box 19123
Birmingham, AL 35219
Gary Richardson, General Manager
Tel: (205) 942-1776 Fax: (205) 942-4814
Email: wjld@juno.com
Web: www.wjld1400.com

WJLQ-FM (100.7-FM MHZ)
Cumulus Broadcasting
2800 Dauphin St. #104
Mobile, AL 36606
Gary Pizzati, General Manager
Tel: (251) 652-2000 Fax: (251) 652-2001

WKXN-FM (95.9-FM MHZ)
Autaugaville Radio, Inc.
P.O. Box 369
Greenville, AL 36037
Roscoe Miller, General Manager
Tel: (334) 382-6555 Fax: (334) 382-7770
Email: wkxn@wkxn.com
Web: www.wkxn.com

WMJJ-FM (96.5-FM MHZ)
Clear Channel Communications
600 Beacon Pkwy. West #400
Birmingham, AL 35209
Jimmy Vineyard, General Manager
Tel: (205) 439-9600 Fax: (205) 439-8390
Web: www.magic96fm.com

WQEN-FM (103.7-FM MHZ)
Clear Channel Communications
600 Beacon Pkwy. West #400
Birmingham, AL 35209
Jimmy Vineyard, General Manager
Tel: (205) 439-9600 Fax: (205) 439-8390
Web: www.1037theq.com

WSBM-AM (1340-AM KHZ)
Big-River Broadcasting Corp.
624 Sam Phillips St.
Florence, AL 35630
Nick Martin, General Manager
Tel: (256) 764-8121 Fax: (256) 764-8169
Web: www.wsbm.com

WSLY-FM (104.9-FM MHZ)
Grantell Broadcasting Co.
11474 US Hwy. 11
York, AL 36925
Tim Craddock, General Manager
Tel: (205) 392-5234 Fax: (205) 392-5536

WTSK-AM (790-AM KHZ)
Citadel Broadcasting
142 Skyland Blvd.
Tuscaloosa, AL 35405

Gigi South, General Manager
Tel: (205) 345-7200 Fax: (205) 349-1715
Web: www.musicalsoulfood.com

WTUG-FM (92.9-FM MHZ)
Citadel Broadcasting, Inc.
142 Skyland Blvd.
Tuscaloosa, AL 35405
Gigi South, General Manager
Tel: (205) 345-7200 Fax: (205) 349-1715
Web: www.wtug.com

WVAS-FM (90.7-FM MHZ)
Alabama State University
915 S. Jackson St.
Montgomery, AL 36104
Rick Hall, Station Manager
Tel: (334) 229-4287 Fax: (334) 269-4995

WWMG-FM (97.1-FM MHZ)
Clear Channel Communications
203 Gunn Rd.
Montgomery , AL 36117
Arnessa Leverett, General Manager
Tel: (334) 274-6464 Fax: (334) 274-6465
Web: mymagic97.com

WXFL-FM (96.1-FM MHZ)
Big-River Broadcasting Corp.
624 Sam Phillips St.
Florence, AL 35630
Nick Martin, General Manager
Tel: (256) 764-8121 Fax: (256) 764-8169
Web: www.wxfl.com

WXVI-AM (1600-AM KHZ)
New Life Radio Ministries
912 S. Perry St.
Montgomery, AL 36104
Glenda Perkins, Program Director
Tel: (334) 263-4141 Fax: (334) 263-9191
Email: faythnGod@yahoo.com

WYLS-AM (670-AM KHZ)
Grantell Broadcasting Co.
11474 US Hwy. 11
York, AL 36925
Tim Craddock, General Manager
Tel: (205) 392-5234 Fax: (205) 392-5536

WYOK-FM (104.1-FM MHZ)
Cumulus Broadcasting
2800 Dauphin St. #104
Mobile, AL 36606
Gary Pizzati, General Manager
Tel: (251) 652-2000 Fax: (251) 652-2001
Web: www.hot104mobile.com

WZHT-FM (105.7-FM MHZ)
Clear Channel Communications
203 Gunn Rd.
Montgomery, AL 36117
Arnessa Leverett, General Manager
Tel: (334) 274-6464 Fax: (334) 274-6465
Web: myhot105.com

WZMG-AM (910-AM KHZ)
Qantum Communications
P.O. Box 2329
Opelika, AL 36803
Jim Powell, General Manager
Tel: (334) 745-4656 Fax: (334) 749-1520
Web: intouch910am.com

WZZA-AM (1410-AM KHZ)
Muscle Shows Broadcasting
1570 Woodmont Dr.
Tuscumbia, AL 35674
Tori Baeley, General Manager
Tel: (256) 383-5810 Fax: (256) 381-6006
Email: wzzaradio@aol.com

ARIZONA

KAJM-FM (104.3-FM MHZ)
Mega and Energy Radio
7434 E. Stetson Dr. #255
Scottsdale, AZ 85251
Michael Mallace, General Manager
Tel: (480) 994-9100 Fax: (480) 423-8770
Web: www.mega1043.com

KOHT-FM (98.3-FM MHZ)
Clear Channel Communications
3202 N. Oracle Rd.
Tucson, AZ 85705
Debbie Wagner, General Manager
Tel: (520) 618-2100 Fax: (520) 618-2165
Email: comments@hot983.com
Web: www.hot983.com

ARKANSAS

KAKJ-FM (105.3-FM MHZ)
Delta Force II Radio
P.O. Box 2870
West Helena, AR 72390
Raymond Fimes, General Manager
Tel: (870) 572-9506 Fax: (870) 572-1845
Email: force2@sbcglobal.net
Web: www.force2radio.com

KCLT-FM (104.9-FM MHZ)
Delta Force II Radio
P.O. Box 2870
West Helena, AR 72390
Raymond Fimes, General Manager
Tel: (870) 572-9506 Fax: (870) 572-1845
Email: force2@sbcglobal.net
Web: www.force2radio.com

KIPR-FM (92.3-FM MHZ)
Citadel Broadcasting Company
700 Wellington Hills Rd.
Little Rock, AR 72211
Jim Beard, General Manager
Tel: (501) 401-0200 Fax: (501) 401-0366
Web: www.power923.com

KITA-AM (1440-AM KHZ)
KITA, Inc.
723 Daisy L. Bates Dr.
Little Rock, AR 72202
Kaysie Rusk, General Manager
Tel: (501) 375-1440 Fax: (501) 375-1440
Email: kita1440@earthlink.com

KLIH-AM (1250-AM KHZ)
Citadel Broadcasting Company
700 Wellington Hills Rd.
Little Rock, AR 72211
Jim Beard, General Manager
Tel: (501) 401-0200 Fax: (501) 401-0366

KOKY-FM (102.1-FM MHZ)
Citadel Broadcasting Company
700 Wellington Hills Rd.

Little Rock, AR 72211
Jim Beard, General Manager
Tel: (501) 401-0200 Fax: (501) 401-0366
Web: www.koky.com

KYFX-FM (99.5-FM MHZ)
Nameloc Inc.
415 N. McKinley #505, Plz. West Bldg.
Little Rock, AR 72205
Loretta Lever, General Manager
Tel: (501) 666-9499 Fax: (501) 666-9699

CALIFORNIA

KBLX-FM (102.9-FM MHZ)
ICBC Broadcast Holdings-CA, Inc.
55 Hawthorne St. #900
San Francisco, CA 94105
Harvey Stone, General Manager
Tel: (415) 284-1029 Fax: (415) 764-1029
Email: info@kblx.com
Web: www.kblx.com

KBOS-FM (94.9-FM MHZ)
Clear Channel Communications
83 E. Shaw Ave. #150
Fresno, CA 93710
Jeff Negrete, General Manager
Tel: (559) 230-4300 Fax: (559) 243-4301
Email: jeffnegrete@clearchannel.com
Web: www.b954life.com

KDYA-AM (1190-AM KHZ)
1190 AM, LLC
3260 Blume Dr. #520
Richmond, CA 94806
Andy Santamaria, General Manager
Tel: (510) 222-4242 Fax: (510) 262-9054
Web: www.gospel1190.net

KEST-AM (1450-AM KHZ)
Multicultural Radio Broadcasting
145 Natoma St., 4th Fl.
San Francisco, CA 94105
Andrea Yamazaki, General Manager
Tel: (415) 978-5378 Fax: (415) 978-5380
Email: kest1450@sbcglobal.net
Web: www.kestradio.com

KFCF-FM (88.1-FM MHZ)
KFCF, Inc.
P.O. Box 4364
Fresno, CA 93744
Roy Campanella, II, General Manager
Tel: (559) 233-2221 Fax: (559) 233-5776
Email: kfcf@kfcf.org
Web: www.kfcf.org

KFSR-FM (90.7-FM MHZ)
California State University
5201 N. Maple St., M/S 119
Fresno, CA 93740
Joe Moore, Station Manager
Tel: (559) 278-2598 Fax: (559) 278-6985
Email: kfsrfresno@hotmail.com
Web: www.kfsr.org

KHYL-FM (101.1-FM MHZ)
Clear Channel Communications
1440 Ethan Way
Sacramento, CA 95825
Jeff Holden, General Manager
Tel: (916) 929-5325 Fax: (916) 925-0118
Email: jeffholden@clearchannel.com
Web: www.v1011fm.com

KISQ-FM (98.1-FM MHZ)
Clear Channel Communications
340 Towsend St.
San Francisco, CA 94107
Kim Bryant, Vice President
Tel: (415) 356-0949 Fax: (415) 808-9494
Web: www.981kissfm.com

KJLH-FM (102.3-FM MHZ)
Taxi Productions, Inc.
161 N. LaBrea Ave.
Inglewood, CA 90301
Karen E. Slade, General Manager
Tel: (310) 330-2200 Fax: (310) 330-2244
Web: www.kjlhradio.com

KKBT-FM (100.3-FM MHZ)
Radio One Broadcasting, Inc.
5900 Wilshire Blvd. #1900
Los Angeles, CA 90036
Sue Freund, General Manager
Tel: (323) 634-1800 Fax: (323) 931-0262

KMEL-FM (106.1-FM MHZ)
Clear Channel Communications
340 Towsend St.
San Francisco, CA 94107
Kim Bryant, Vice President
Tel: (415) 356-0949 Fax: (415) 808-9494
Web: www.106kmel.com

KNGV-FM (97.9-FM MHZ)
Infinity Broadcasting
1071 W. Shaw Ave.
Fresno, CA 93711
Patty Hixson, General Manager
Tel: (559) 490-9800 Fax: (559) 490-4199
Email: pbhixson@cbs.com
Web: www.mega979.com

KPFA-FM (94.1-FM MHZ)
KPFA, Inc.
1929 Martin Luther King, Jr. Way
Berkeley, CA 94704
Roy Campanella, II, General Manager
Tel: (510) 848-6767 Fax: (510) 848-3812
Email: info@kpfa.org
Web: www.kpfa.org

KPOO-FM (89.5-FM MHZ)
KPOO, Inc.
P.O. Box 423030
San Francisco, CA 94142
Jerome Parsons, General Manager
Tel: (415) 346-5373 Fax: (415) 346-5173
Email: info@kpoo.com
Web: www.kpoo.com

KPWR-FM (105.9-FM MHZ)
Emmis Communications
2600 W. Olive Ave., 8th Fl.
Burbank, CA 91505
Val Maki, General Manager
Tel: (818) 953-4200 Fax: (818) 848-0961
Web: www.power106.fm

KQOD-FM (100.1-FM MHZ)
Clear Channel Communications
2121 Lancey Dr.
Modesto, CA 95355
Gary Granger, General Manager
Tel: (209) 551-1306 Fax: (209) 551-1351
Web: www.mega100online.com

KVTO-AM (1400-AM KHZ)
ICBC Broadcast Holdings-CA, Inc.
55 Hawthorne St. #900
San Francisco, CA 94105
Harvey Stone, General Manager
Tel: (415) 284-1029 Fax: (415) 764-1029

KVVN-AM (1410-AM KHZ)
ICBC Broadcast Holdings-CA, Inc.
55 Hawthorne St. #900
San Francisco, CA 94105
Harvey Stone, General Manager
Tel: (415) 284-1029 Fax: (415) 764-1029

KYLD-FM (94.9-FM MHZ)
Clear Channel Communications
340 Towsend St.

San Francisco, CA 94107
Kim Bryant, Vice President
Tel: (415) 356-0949 Fax: (415) 808-9494
Web: www.wild949.com

XHRM-FM (92.5-FM MHZ)
Clear Channel Communications
9660 Granite Ridge Dr.
San Diego, CA 92123
Bob Bolinger, General Manager
Tel: (619) 291-9191 Fax: (619) 477-1925
Web: www.magic925.com

CONNECTICUT

WQTQ-FM (89.9-FM MHZ)
Hartford Board of Education
Weaver High School, 415 Granby St.
Hartford, CT 06112
Tom Smith, General Manager
Tel: (860) 722-8660 Fax: (860) 286-9909
Email: wqtqfm@yahoo.com

WYBC-AM (1340-AM KHZ)
Yale Broadcasting Company
142 Temple St. #203
New Haven, CT 06510
Vivian Hsu, General Manager
Tel: (203) 776-4118 Fax: (203) 776-2446
Web: www.wybc.com

WYBC-FM (94.3-FM MHZ)
Yale Broadcasting Company
142 Temple St. #203
New Haven, CT 06510
Vivian Hsu, General Manager
Tel: (203) 776-4118 Fax: (203) 776-2446
Web: www.wybc.com

DELAWARE

WFAI-AM (1510-AM KHZ)
QC Communications
704 King St. #604, 1st Federal Plz., Bldg.
Wilmington, DE 19801
Tony Quartarone, General Manager
Tel: (302) 622-8895 Fax: (302) 622-8678
Email: tonyg@faith1510.com
Web: www.faith1510.com

WJKS-FM (101.7-FM MHZ)
QC Communications
704 King St. #604, 1st Federal Plz., Bldg.
Wilmington, DE 19801
Tony Quartarone, General Manager
Tel: (302) 622-8895 Fax: (302) 622-8678
Web: www.wjks1017.com

DISTRICT OF COLUMBIA

WHUR-FM (96.3-FM MHZ)
Howard University
529 Bryant St. NW
Washington, DC 20059
Millard J. Watkins, III, General Manager
Tel: (202) 806-3500 Fax: (202) 806-3522

FLORIDA

WANM-FM (90.5-FM MHZ)
Florida A&M University
P.O. Box 6202
Tallahassee, FL 32312
Keith Males, General Manager
Tel: (850) 599-3083 Fax: (850) 561-2829
Email: theflavastation@hotmail.com

WCFB-FM (94.5-FM MHZ)
Cox Radio
4192 John Young Pkwy.
Orlando, FL 32804
Brian Elam, General Manager
Tel: (407) 297-0945 Fax: (407) 297-7595

WEBZ-FM (93.5-FM MHZ)
Clear Channel Communications
1834 Lisenby Ave.
Panama City, FL 32405
Peter Norden, General Manager
Tel: (850) 769-1408 Fax: (850) 769-0659
Web: www.935thebeat.com

WEDR-FM (99.1-FM MHZ)
2741 N. 29th Ave.
Hollywood, FL 33020
Gerry Rushin, General Manager
Tel: (954) 584-7117 Fax: (954) 847-3218
Web: www.wedr.com

WEXY-AM (1520-AM KHZ)
Multicultural Broadcasting
412 W. Oakland Park Blvd.
Fort Lauderdale, FL 33311-1712
Doug Adevos, Station Manager
Tel: (954) 561-1520 Fax: (954) 561-9830

WHQT-FM (105.1-FM MHZ)
2741 N. 29th Ave.
Hollywood, FL 33020
Gerry Rushin, General Manager
Tel: (954) 584-7117 Fax: (954) 847-3223
Web: www.hot105fm.com

WJBT-FM (92.7-FM MHZ)
Clear Channel Communications
11700 Central Pkwy.
Jacksonville, FL 32224
Norman Feuer , General Manager
Tel: (904) 642-3030 Fax: (904) 997-7758
Web: www.wjbt.com

WJHM-FM (101.9-FM MHZ)
Infinity Broadcasting
1800 Pembrook Dr. #400
Orlando, FL 32810
Earnest James, General Manager
Tel: (407) 919-1000 Fax: (407) 919-1136

WRNE-AM (980-AM KHZ)
Media One Broadcasting
312 E. Nine Mile Rd. #29D
Pensacola, FL 32514
Robert Hill, General Manager
Tel: (850) 478-6000 Fax: (850) 484-8080
Email: hill@wrne980.com
Web: www.wrne980.com

WRXB-AM (1590-AM KHZ)
Metropolitan Radio Group
2060 1st Ave. North
St. Petersburg, FL 33713
Nita Dials, General Manger
Tel: (727) 327-9792 Fax: (727) 321-3025
Email: wrxb@juno.com

WSOL-FM (101.5-FM MHZ)
Clear Channel Communications
11700 Central Pkwy.
Jacksonville, FL 32224
Norman Feuer , General Manager
Tel: (904) 642-3030 Fax: (904) 997-7708
Web: www.v1015.com

WSRF-AM (1580-AM KHZ)
Urban Radio of Florida, LLC
4431 Rock Island Rd.
Ft. Lauderdale, FL 33319
Lynda Hudson, General Manager
Tel: (954) 731-1855 Fax: (954) 731-1833
Email: lhudson@wsrf.com
Web: www.wsrf.com

WSVE-AM (1280-AM KHZ)
The Emily Timmons Show
6814 Bogota
Jacksonville, FL 32210
Emily Simmons, Host & Reseacher
Tel: (904) 571-4525 Fax: (904) 778-7335

WSWN-AM (900-AM KHZ)
BGI Broadcasting
P.O. Box 1505
Belle Glade, FL 33430
Phil Haire, General Manager
Tel: (561) 996-2063 Fax: (561) 996-1852

WTCL-AM (1580-AM KHZ)
Metz Broadcasting
P.O. Box 36
Chattaahoochee, FL 32324
Chris Starr, General Manager
Tel: (850) 663-3857 Fax: (850) 663-8543

WTMG-FM (101.3-FM MHZ)
Connecticut Broadcasting
249 W. University Ave. #B
Gainesville, FL 32601
Dan Hill, General Manager
Tel: (352) 371-1980 Fax: (352) 338-0560
Web: www.magic1013.com

WTMP-AM (1150-AM KHZ)
Tama Broadcasting
5207 Washington Blvd.
Tampa, FL 33619
Dr Glenn Cherry, General Manager
Tel: (813) 620-1300 Fax: (813) 628-0713
Email: wtmpjamz@wtmp.com
Web: www.wtmp.com

WVCG-AM (1080-AM KHZ)
Radio One
2828 W. Flagler St.
Miami, FL 33135
Eunice Haness, Business Manager
Tel: (305) 644-0800 Fax: (305) 644-9512

WWAB-AM (1330-AM KHZ)
WWAB, Corp.
1203 Chase St.
Lakeland, FL 33801
Gerry Hughes, General Manager
Tel: (863) 682-2998

WZAZ-AM (1400-AM KHZ)
Salem Communications
4190 Belfort Rd. #450
Jacksonville, FL 32216
Steve Griffin, General Manager
Tel: (904) 470-4615 Fax: (904) 296-1683
Web: www.1400wzaz.com

GEORGIA

KISS-FM (104.1-FM MHZ)
Cox Radio
1601 W. Peachtree St. NE
Atlanta, GA 30309
Tony Kidd, General Manager
Tel: (404) 897-7500 Fax: (404) 897-6495
Web: www.kiss1041fm.com

WAGH-FM (98.3-FM MHZ)
Clear Channel Communications
1501 13th Ave.
Columbus, GA 31901
Jim Martin, General Manager
Tel: (706) 576-3000 Fax: (706) 576-3010
Web: www.magic98.3online.com

WAMJ-FM (102.5-FM MHZ)
Radio One
75 Piedmont Ave., 10th Fl.
Atlanta, GA 30303
Wayne Brown, General Manager

Tel: (404) 765-9750 Fax: (404) 688-7686
Web: www.classicsoul1025.com

WAOK-AM (1380-AM KHZ)
Infinity Broadcasting
1201 Peachtree St. #800
Atlanta, GA 30361
Rick Caffey, General Manager
Tel: (404) 898-8900 Fax: (404) 898-8909
Web: www.waok.com

WCLA-AM (1470-AM KHZ)
Progressive United Communication
316 N. River St.
Claxton, GA 30417
Don Jones, General Manager
Tel: (912) 739-9252 Fax: (912) 739-0050
Email: orchard41@bellsouth.net

WFXM-FM (107.1-FM MHZ)
Roberts Communications, Inc.
6174 Hwy. 57
Macon, GA 31217
Mike Roberts, President
Tel: (478) 745-3301 Fax: (478) 742-2293
Email: robertsrci@aol.com

WGOV-AM (950-AM KHZ)
GRAM Corp.
P.O. Box 1207
Valdosta, GA 31603
Rick Humphrey, General Manager
Tel: (229) 242-4513 Fax: (229) 247-7676
Email: mail@wgovradio.com
Web: www.wgovradio.com

WGOV-FM (96.7-FM MHZ)
GRAM Corp.
P.O. Box 1207
Valdosta, GA 31603
Rick Humphrey, General Manager
Tel: (229) 242-4513 Fax: (229) 247-7676
Email: mail@wgovradio.com
Web: www.wgovradio.com

WHCJ-FM (90.3-FM MHZ)
Savannah State University
P.O. Box 20484
Savannah, GA 31404
Ike Carter, General Manager
Tel: (912) 356-2399 Fax: (912) 356-2041
Email: cartert@savstate.edu
Web: www.savstate.edu/whcj/whcj.htm

WHGH-AM (840-AM KHZ)
Goss Broadcasting
P.O. Box 2218
Thomasville, GA 31799
Lisa Register, General Manager
Tel: (229) 228-4124 Fax: (229) 225-9508
Email: cos2k@hotmail.com

WHTA-FM (107.9-FM MHZ)
Radio One
75 Piedmont Ave., 10th Fl.
Atlanta, GA 30303
Wayne Brown, General Manager
Tel: (404) 765-9750 Fax: (404) 688-7686
Web: www.hot1079atl.com

WIBB-FM (97.9-FM MHZ)
Clear Channel Communications
7080 Industrial Hwy.
Macon, GA 31216
Bill Clark, General Manager
Tel: (478) 781-1063 Fax: (478) 781-6711
Web: www.wibb.com

WJAT-AM (800-AM KHZ)
Radio Jones
2 Radio Loop
Swainsboro, GA 30401
Jolly Martin, General Manager
Tel: (478) 237-1590 Fax: (478) 237-3559
Email: jmartin@radiojones.com

WJGA-FM (92.1-FM MHZ)
Earnhart Broadcasting
P.O. Box 878
Jackson, GA 30233
Don Earnhart, General Manager
Tel: (770) 775-3151 Fax: (770) 775-3153

WJIZ-FM (96.3-FM MHZ)
Clear Channel Communications
809 S. Westover Blvd.
Albany, GA 31707
John Richards, General Manager
Tel: (229) 439-9704 Fax: (229) 439-1509
Web: www.wjiz.com

WJZZ-FM (107.5-FM MHZ)
Radio One
75 Piedmont Ave., 10th Fl.
Atlanta, GA 30303
Wayne Brown, General Manager
Tel: (404) 765-9750 Fax: (404) 688-7686
Web: www.smoothjazzWJZZ.com

WLVH-FM (101.1-FM MHZ)
Clear Channel Communications
245 Alfred St.
Savanah, GA 31408
Jeff Story, General Manager
Tel: (843) 784-6994 Fax: (912) 964-9414
Web: www.love1011.com

WMOC-FM (88.7-FM MHZ)
Full Gospel Church of God
P.O. Box 520
Lumber City, GA 31549
Eddy Conaway, General Manager
Tel: (912) 363-2203 Fax: (912) 363-4502
Web: www.wmoc887fm.com

WPRW-FM (107.7-FM MHZ)
Clear Channel Communications
2743 Perimeter Pkwy., Bldg. 100 #300
Augusta, GA 30909
Barry Kay, General Manager
Tel: (706) 396-6000 Fax: (706) 396-6010
Web: www.power107.net

WRBV-FM (101.7-FM MHZ)
Clear Channel Communications
7080 Industrial Hwy.
Macon, GA 31216
Bill Clark, General Manager
Tel: (478) 781-1063 Fax: (478) 781-6711
Web: www.v1017.com

WTZE-FM (97.5-FM MHZ)
Radio One
75 Piedmont Ave., 10th Fl.
Atlanta, GA 30303
Wayne Brown, General Manager
Tel: (404) 765-9750 Fax: (404) 688-7686
Web: www.praise975.com

WVEE-FM (103.3-FM MHZ)
Infinity Broadcasting
1201 Peachtree St. #800
Atlanta, GA 30361
Rick Caffey, General Manager
Tel: (404) 898-8900 Fax: (404) 898-8909
Web: www.v-103.com

ILLINOIS

WBCP-AM (1580-AM KHZ)
WBCP, Inc.
904 N. 4th St. #D
Champaign, IL 61820
Lonnie Clark, General Manager
Tel: (217) 359-1580 Fax: (217) 359-1583
Email: wbcpradio@sbcglobal.net

WESL-AM (1490-AM KHZ)
WESL Radio, Inc.

149 S. 8th St.
East St. Louis, IL 62201
Dave Green, General Manager
Tel: (618) 271-7687 Fax: (618) 875-4315
Email: frank@1490wesl.com

WGCI-AM (1390-AM KHZ)
Clear Channel Communications
233 N. Michigan Ave. #2800
Chicago, IL 60601
John Gehron, General Manager
Tel: (312) 540-2000 Fax: (312) 938-4477
Web: www.gospel1390.com

WGCI-FM (107.5-FM MHZ)
Clear Channel Communications
233 N. Michigan Ave. #2800
Chicago, IL 60601
John Gehron, General Manager
Tel: (312) 540-2000 Fax: (312) 938-4477
Web: www.wgci.com

WSSD-FM (88.1-FM MHZ)
Lakeside Telecommunications
515 W. 111th St.
Chicago, IL 60628
Steven McKinney, Station Manager
Tel: (773) 928-8800 Fax: (773) 928-9009

WVAZ-FM (102.7-FM MHZ)
Clear Channel Communications
233 N. Michigan Ave.
Chicago, IL 60601
John Gehron, General Manager
Tel: (312) 540-2000 Fax: (312) 938-0111
Web: www.wvaz.com

WVON-AM (1450-AM KHZ)
Midway Broadcasting Co.
3350 S. Kedzie St.
Chicago, IL 60623
Melody Spann Cooper, General Manager
Tel: (773) 247-6200 Fax: (773) 247-5336
Web: www.wvon.com

INDIANA

WHHH-FM (96.3-FM MHZ)
Radio One
21 E. St. Joseph St.
Indianapolis, IN 46204
Linda O'Conner, General Manager
Tel: (317) 266-9600 Fax: (317) 328-3870
Web: www.hot963.com

WJFX-FM (107.9-FM MHZ)
Fort Wayne Radio Corp.
5936 E. State Blvd.
Fort Wayne, IN 46815
Roger Diehn, General Manager
Tel: (260) 493-9539 Fax: (260) 749-5151
Web: www.hot1079online.com

WTLC-FM (106.7-FM MHZ)
Radio One
21 E. St. Joseph St.
Indianapolis, IN 46204
Linda O'Conner, General Manager
Tel: (317) 266-9600 Fax: (317) 328-3870
Web: www.wtcl.com

WYCA-FM (106.3-FM MHZ)
Crawford Broadcasting Co.
6336 Calumet Ave.
Hammond, IN 46234
Taft Harris, General Manager
Tel: (219) 933-4455 Fax: (219) 933-0323

WYJZ-FM (100.9-FM MHZ)
Radio One
21 E. St. Joseph St.
Indianapolis, IN 46204

Linda O'Conner, General Manager
Tel: (317) 266-9600 Fax: (317) 328-3870
Web: www.wyjzradio.com

IOWA

KBBG-FM (88.1-FM MHZ)
African American Community Broadcasting, Inc.
918 Newell St.
Waterloo, IA 50703
Lou Porter, Development Director
Tel: (319) 234-1441 Fax: (319) 234-6182
Email: management@kbbg.org
Web: www.kbbgfm.org

KENTUCKY

WEGK-FM (104.3-FM MHZ)
Radio One
520 S. 4th Ave., 2nd Fl.
Louisville, KY 40202
Dale Schaeifer, General Manager
Tel: (502) 625-1220 Fax: (502) 625-1253
Web: www.eagle1043.com

WGZB-FM (96.5-FM MHZ)
Radio One
520 S. 4th Ave., 2nd Fl.
Louisville, KY 40202
Dale Schaeifer, General Manager
Tel: (502) 625-1220 Fax: (502) 625-1253
Web: www.b96jams.com

WMJM-FM (101.3-FM MHZ)
Radio One
520 S. 4th Ave., 2nd Fl.
Louisville, KY 40202
Dale Schaeifer, General Manager
Tel: (502) 625-1220 Fax: (502) 625-1253
Web: www.1013online.com

LOUISIANA

KBCE-FM (102.3-FM MHZ)
Urban Radio Network
1605 Murray St. #216
Alexandria, LA 71301
Kevin Wagner, CEO
Tel: (318) 793-4202 Fax: (318) 793-8888
Web: www.urbanradio.fm

KBTT-FM (103.7-FM MHZ)
Access One
208 N. Thomas Dr.
Shreveport, LA 71107
Cary Camp, General Manager
Tel: (318) 222-0636 Fax: (318) 222-2957
Web: k103thebeat@shreve.net

KDKS-FM (102.1-FM MHZ)
Access One
208 N. Thomas Dr.
Shreveport, LA 71107
Cary Camp, General Manager
Tel: (318) 222-0636 Fax: (318) 222-2957
Web: kdkshot102@shreve.net

KFXZ-FM (106.3-FM MHZ)
Citadel Broadcasting Company
3225 Ambassador Caffery Pkwy.
Lafayette, LA 70506-7214
Mary Galyean, General Manager
Tel: (337) 981-0106 Fax: (337) 988-0443

KJCB-AM (770-AM KHZ)
RNN Broadcasting, Inc.
604 St. John's St.
Lafayette, LA 70501-7057

Jenelle Chargois, General Manager
Tel: (337) 233-4262 Fax: (337) 235-9681

KJMG-FM (97.3-FM MHZ)
Holliday Broadcasting
1109 Hudson Ln.
Monroe, LA 71201
Bob Holliday, General Manager
Tel: (318) 322-1914 Fax: (318) 388-0569
Web: www.majic97.com

KJMH-FM (107.5-FM MHZ)
Apex Broadcasting
900 N. Lake Shore Dr.
Lake Charles, LA 70601
Bill May, General Manager
Tel: (337) 433-1641 Fax: (337) 433-2999
Web: www.107jamz.com

KLCL-AM (1470-AM KHZ)
Apex Broadcasting
900 N. Lake Shore Dr.
Lake Charles, LA 70601
Bill May, General Manager
Tel: (337) 433-1641 Fax: (337) 433-2999

KNEK-FM (104.7-FM MHZ)
Citadel Broadcasting Company
202 Galbert Rd.
Lafayette, LA 70506
Mary Galyean, General Manager
Tel: (337) 232-1311 Fax: (337) 233-3779

KOKA-AM (980-AM KHZ)
Access One
208 N. Thomas Dr.
Shreveport, LA 71107
Cary Camp, General Manager
Tel: (318) 222-0636 Fax: (318) 222-2957

KQXL-FM (106.5-FM MHZ)
Citadel Broadcasting Company
650 Wooddale Blvd.
Baton Rouge, LA 70806
Donnie Picou, General Manager
Tel: (225) 926-1106 Fax: (225) 928-1606

KRRQ-FM (95.5-FM MHZ)
Citadel Broadcasting Company
202 Galbert Rd.
Lafayette, LA 70506
Mary Galyean, General Manager
Tel: (337) 232-1311 Fax: (337) 233-3779
Web: www.krrq.com

KRUS-AM (1490-AM KHZ)
Ruston Broadcasting
500 N. Monroe St., Box 430
Ruston, LA 71270
Gary McKenney, General Manager
Tel: (318) 255-2530 Fax: (318) 255-5084
Email: z1075fm@bayou.com

KRVV-FM (100.1-FM MHZ)
Holliday Broadcasting
1109 Hudson Ln.
Monroe, LA 71201
Bob Holliday, General Manager
Tel: (318) 322-1914 Fax: (318) 388-0569

KXZZ-AM (1580-AM KHZ)
Cumulus Broadcasting
425 Broad St.
Lake Charles, LA 70601
Susan Lucchesi, General Manager
Tel: (337) 436-7277 Fax: (337) 433-7701

KZWA-FM (104.9-FM MHZ)
B&C Broadcasting of LC
305 Enterprise Blvd.
Lake Charles, LA 70601
Faye Blackwell, General Manager
Tel: (337) 491-9955 Fax: (337) 437-8097
Web: www.kzwa.com

WEMX-FM (94.1-FM MHZ)
Citadel Broadcasting Company
650 Wooddale Blvd.
Baton Rouge, LA 70806
Donnie Picou, General Manager
Tel: (225) 926-1106 Fax: (225) 928-1606

WODT-AM (1280-AM KHZ)
Clear Channel Communications
929 Howard Ave.
New Orleans, LA 70113
Muriel R. Funches, General Manager
Tel: (504) 679-7300 Fax: (504) 827-6045

WQUE-FM (93.3-FM MHZ)
Clear Channel Communications
929 Howard Ave.
New Orleans, LA 70113
Muriel R. Funches, General Manager
Tel: (504) 679-7300 Fax: (504) 827-6045

WWOZ-FM (90.7-FM MHZ)
WWOZ, Inc.
P.O. Box 51840
New Orleans, LA 70151
David Freedman, General Manager
Tel: (504) 568-1239 Fax: (504) 568-9267
Web: www.wwoz.com

WXOK-AM (1460-AM KHZ)
Citadel Broadcasting Company
650 Wooddale Blvd.
Baton Rouge, LA 70806
Donnie Picou, General Manager
Tel: (225) 926-1106 Fax: (225) 928-1606

WYLD-AM (940-AM KHZ)
Clear Channel Communications
929 Howard Ave.
New Orleans, LA 70113
Muriel R. Funches, General Manager
Tel: (504) 679-7300 Fax: (504) 827-6045

WYLD-FM (98.5-FM MHZ)
Clear Channel Communications
929 Howard Ave.
New Orleans, LA 70113
Muriel R. Funches, General Manager
Tel: (504) 679-7300 Fax: (504) 827-6045
Web: www.wyldfm.com

MARYLAND

WCAO-AM (600-AM KHZ)
Clear Channel Radio
711 W. 40th St. #350
Baltimore, MD 21211
Jim Dolan, General Manager
Tel: (410) 366-7600 Fax: (410) 467-0011
Web: www.heaven600.com

WERQ-FM (92.3-FM MHZ)
Radio One
1705 Whitehead Rd.
Baltimore, MD 21207
Howard Mazer, Station Manager
Tel: (410) 332-8200 Fax: (410) 944-7989
Web: www.92qjams.com

WESM-FM (91.3-FM MHZ)
University of Maryland, Eastern Shore
Backbone Rd.
Princess Anne, MD 21853
Marva Lovett, General Manager
Tel: (410) 651-8001 Fax: (410) 651-8005
Email: wesm913@mail.umes.edu
Web: www.wsm913.org

WFBR-AM (1590-AM KHZ)
Metro Radio, Inc.
159 8th Ave. NW
Glen Burnie, MD 21061-2800

Keith Baldwin, General Manager
Tel: (410) 761-1590 Fax: (410) 761-9220
Email: keithb4@verizon.net

WKYS-FM (93.9-FM MHZ)
Radio One
5900 Princess Garden Pkwy., 8th Fl.
Lanham, MD 20706
Michele Williams, General Manager
Tel: (301) 306-1111 Fax: (301) 306-9540
Web: www.939wkys.com

WMMJ-FM (102.3-FM MHZ)
5900 Princess Garden Pkwy., 8th Fl.
Lanham, MD 20706
Michele Williams, General Manager
Tel: (301) 306-1111 Fax: (301) 306-9540

WOLB-AM (1010-AM KHZ)
1705 Whitehead Rd.
Baltimore, MD 21207
Howard Mazer, Station Manager
Tel: (410) 332-8200 Fax: (410) 944-7989
Web: www.wolb1010.com

WPGC-FM (95.5-FM MHZ)
Infinity Broadcasting
4200 Parliament Pl.
Lanham, MD 20706
Sam Rogers, General Manager
Tel: (301) 918-0955 Fax: (301) 459-9557
Web: www.wpgc955.com

WSBY-FM (98.9-FM MHZ)
Clear Channel Communications
351 Tillman Rd.
Salisbury, MD 21804
Frank Hamilton, General Manager
Tel: (410) 742-1923 Fax: (410) 742-2329

WTGM-AM (960-AM KHZ)
351 Tillman Rd.
Salisbury, MD 21804
Frank Hamilton, General Manager
Tel: (410) 742-1923 Fax: (410) 742-2329

WWIN-AM (1400-AM KHZ)
Radio One
1705 Whitehead Rd.
Baltimore, MD 21207
Howard Mazer, Station Manager
Tel: (410) 332-8200 Fax: (410) 944-7989
Web: www.spirit1400.com

WWIN-FM (95.9-FM MHZ)
Radio One
1705 Whitehead Rd.
Baltimore, MD 21207
Howard Mazer, Station Manager
Tel: (410) 332-8200 Fax: (410) 944-7989
Web: www.magic95baltimore.com

WXYV-FM (105.7-FM MHZ)
Infinity Broadcasting
600 Washington Ave. #201
Baltimore, MD 21204
Bob Phillips, General Manager
Tel: (410) 828-7722 Fax: (410) 821-8256
Web: www.live1057.com

WYCB-AM (1340-AM KHZ)
Radio One
5900 Princess Garden Pkwy., 8th Fl.
Lanham, MD 20706
Michele Williams, General Manager
Tel: (301) 306-1111 Fax: (301) 306-9540

MASSACHUSETTS

WAIC-FM (91.9-FM MHZ)
American International College
1000 State St.
Springfield, MA 01109

Doc Holiday, General Manager
Tel: (413) 205-3288 Fax: (413) 205-3943
Email: jbernst@acad.aic.edu

WBOT-FM (97.7-FM MHZ)
Radio One
500 Victory Rd.
Quincy, MA 02171
Frank Kelley, General Manager
Tel: (617) 472-9447 Fax: (617) 472-9474
Web: www.wbothot977.com

WILD-AM (1090-AM KHZ)
Radio One
500 Victory Rd.
Quincy, MA 02171
Frank Kelley, General Manager
Tel: (617) 472-9447 Fax: (617) 472-9474
Web: www.wild1090.com

WJMN-FM (94.5-FM MHZ)
Clear Channel Broadcasting
10 Cabot Rd.
Medford, MA 02155
Jake Karger, General Manager
Tel: (781) 290-0009 Fax: (781) 290-0722
Web: www.jamn.com

MICHIGAN

WCHB-AM (1200-AM KHZ)
Radio One
3250 Franklin St.
Detroit, MI 48207
Carol Lawrence, General Manager
Tel: (313) 259-2000 Fax: (313) 259-7011
Web: www.wchb1200.com

WDMK-FM (102.7-FM MHZ)
Radio One
3250 Franklin Rd.
Detroit, MI 48207
Carol Lawrence, General Manager
Tel: (313) 259-2000 Fax: (313) 259-7011
Web: www.hot1027detroit.com

WDTJ-FM (105.9-FM MHZ)
Radio One
3250 Franklin Rd.
Detroit, MI 48207
Carol Lawrence, General Manager
Tel: (313) 259-2000 Fax: (313) 259-7011
Web: www.kissdetroit.com

WDZZ-FM (92.7-FM MHZ)
Cumulus Broadcasting
6317 Taylor Dr.
Flint, MI 48507
Mike Chiref, General Manager
Tel: (810) 238-7300 Fax: (810) 238-7310
Email: wdzz@wdzz.com
Web: www.wdzz.com

WGPR-FM (107.5-FM MHZ)
WGPR Broadcasting
3146 E. Jefferson Ave.
Detroit, MI 48207
George Mathews, President
Tel: (313) 259-8862 Fax: (313) 259-6662
Web: www.wgprdetroit.com

WHPR-FM (88.1-FM MHZ)
Watkins Broadcasting
15851 Woodward Ave.
Highland Park, MI 48203
R.J. Watkins, General Manager
Tel: (313) 868-6612 Fax: (313) 868-8725
Web: www.whprtv33.com

WJLB-FM (97.9-FM MHZ)
Clear Channel Broadcasting
645 Griswold St. #633

Detroit, MI 48226-4177
David Pugh, Station Manager
Tel: (313) 965-2000 Fax: (313) 965-9970
Web: www.wjlb.com

WJMZ-AM (1140-AM KHZ)
Goodrich Radio Group
3777 44th St. SE
Grand Rapids, MI 49512
Ross Pettinga, General Manager
Tel: (616) 698-7733 Fax: (616) 656-9326
Email: mstcyr@wjnz.ocm
Web: www.wjnz.ocm

WJNZ-AM (1140-AM KHZ)
WJNZ Radio, LLC
1919 Eastern Ave. SE
Grand Rapids, MI 49507
Mike St. Cyr, President/General Manager
Tel: (616) 475-4299 Fax: (616) 475-4335
Email: mjs@wjnz.com
Web: www.wjnz.com

WMFN-AM (640-AM KHZ)
TB&J Consultants, Inc., LLC
2422 Burton St. SE
Grand Rapids, MI 49546
Tyrone Bynum, General Manager
Tel: (616) 949-8585 Fax: (619) 949-9262
Email: tyrone@hottalk640.com
Web: www.hottalk640.com

WMXD-FM (92.3-FM MHZ)
Clear Channel Broadcasting
645 Griswold St. #633
Detroit, MI 48226-4177
David Pugh, Station Manager
Tel: (313) 965-2000 Fax: (313) 965-9970

WNWN-AM (1560-AM KHZ)
Midwest Radio Group
6021 S. Westnedge Ave.
Kalamazoo, MI 49002
Peter Tanz, General Manager
Tel: (269) 327-7600 Fax: (269) 327-0726
Web: www.1560radio.com

WQHH-FM (96.5-FM MHZ)
Mid Michigan FM, Inc.
1011 Northcrest Rd. #4
Lansing, MI 48906-1262
Helena Dubose, General Manager
Tel: (517) 484-9600 Fax: (517) 484-9699
Email: mmfmtraffick@comcast.net

WXLA-AM (1180-AM KHZ)
Mid Michigan FM, Inc.
1011 Northcrest Rd. #4
Lansing, MI 48906-1262
Helena Dubose, General Manager
Tel: (517) 484-9600 Fax: (517) 484-9699
Email: mmfmtraffick@comcast.net

MINNESOTA

KMOJ-FM (89.9-FM MHZ)
Center for Communications and
Development
555 Girard Terr.
Minneapolis, MN 55405
RC Williams, Operations Manager
Tel: (612) 377-0594 Fax: (612) 377-6919
Email: kelvinquarles@hotmail.com

KTTB-FM (96.3-FM MHZ)
Blue Chip Broadcasting
5300 Edina Industrial Blvd. #200
Edina, MN 55439
Steve Woodbury, General Manager
Tel: (952) 842-7200 Fax: (952) 842-1048
Web: www.b96online.com

WGVX-FM (105.1-FM MHZ)
ABC Radio
2000 SE Elm St.
Minneapolis, MN 55414
Susan Larkin, Manager
Tel: (612) 617-4000 Fax: (612) 676-8292
Email: comments@drive105.com
Web: www.drive105.com

WGVY-FM (105.3-FM MHZ)
2000 SE Elm St.
Minneapolis, MN 55414
Susan Larkin, Manager
Tel: (612) 617-4000 Fax: (612) 676-8292
Email: comments@drive105.com
Web: www.drive105.com

WGVZ-FM (105.7-FM MHZ)
2000 SE Elm St.
Minneapolis, MN 55414
Susan Larkin, Manager
Tel: (612) 617-4000 Fax: (612) 676-8292
Email: comments@drive105.com
Web: www.drive105.com

MISSISSIPPI

WACR-FM (103.9-FM MHZ)
TNW Communications
1910 14th Ave. North
Columbus, MS 39701
Edna Turner, General Manger
Tel: (662) 328-1050 Fax: (662) 328-1054
Email: wacr1039@yahoo.com

WAID-FM (106.5-FM MHZ)
Radio Cleveland, Inc.
P.O. Box 780
Cleveland, MS 38732
Clint Webster, General Manager
Tel: (662) 843-4091 Fax: (662) 843-9805
Email: waid@techinfo.com
Web: www.missradio.com

WALT-AM (910-AM KHZ)
New South Broadcasting Company
P.O. Box 5797
Meridian, MS 39302
Scott Stevens, General Manager
Tel: (601) 693-2661 Fax: (601) 483-0826
Email: scottstevens@spots.com

WBAD-FM (94.3-FM MHZ)
Interchange Communications
P.O. Box 4426
Greenville, MS 38704
Bill Jackson, President
Tel: (662) 335-9265 Fax: (662) 335-5538
Email: wbad.radio@cox-internet.com

WCLD-AM (1490-AM KHZ)
Radio Cleveland, Inc.
P.O. Box 780
Cleveland, MS 38732
Clint Webster, General Manager
Tel: (662) 843-4091 Fax: (662) 843-9805
Email: wcld@techinfo.com
Web: www.missradio.com

WCLD-FM (103.9-FM MHZ)
Radio Cleveland, Inc.
P.O. Box 780
Cleveland, MS 38732
Clint Webster, General Manager
Tel: (662) 843-4091 Fax: (662) 843-9805
Email: wcld@tchinfo.com
Web: www.missradio.com

WESE-FM (92.5-FM MHZ)
Clear Channel Radio
5026 Cliff Gookin Blvd.
Tupelo, MS 38801

Jeff Lee, Program Director
Tel: (662) 842-1067 Fax: (662) 842-0725
Email: myradiojamz@aol.com
Web: www.925jams.com

WESY-AM (1580-AM KHZ)
East Delta Communications
P.O. Box 5804
Greenville, MS 38704-5804
Stanley Sherman, General Manager
Tel: (662) 378-9405 Fax: (662) 335-5538
Email: wbad.radio@cox-internet.com

WJKX-FM (102.5-FM MHZ)
Clear Channel Communications
6555 Hwy. 98 West #8
Hattiesburg, MS 39402
Mike Comfort, General Manager
Tel: (601) 296-9800 Fax: (601) 296-9838
Web: www.102jkx.com

WJMI-FM (99.7-FM MHZ)
ICBC Broadcast Holding-MS, Inc.
731 S. Pear Orchard #27
Ridgeland, MS 39157
Kevin Webb, General Manager
Tel: (601) 957-1300 Fax: (601) 956-0516
Email: kwebb1234@aol.com
Web: www.wjmi.com

WJXM-FM (105.7-FM MHZ)
New South Broadcasting Company
3436 Hwy. 45 North
Meridian, MS 39301
Scott Stevens, General Manager
Tel: (601) 485-1057 Fax: (601) 483-0826
Email: scottstevens@spots.com

WKRA-AM (1110-AM KHZ)
WKRA Radio Station
P.O. Box 398
Holly Springs, MS 38635
Von Autry, General Manager
Tel: (662) 252-6692 Fax: (662) 252-2739
Email: wkra@bellsouth.com

WKRA-FM (92.7-FM MHZ)
WKRA Radio Station
P.O. Box 398
Holly Springs, MS 38635
Von Autry, General Manager
Tel: (662) 252-6692 Fax: (662) 252-2739
Email: wkra@bellsouth.com

WKXG-AM (1540-AM KHZ)
Telesouth Communications
P.O. Box 1686
Greenwood, MS 38935
Charlotte Baglan, General Manager
Tel: (662) 453-2174 Fax: (662) 455-5733
Email: cbaglan@adelphia.net

WKXI-AM (1400-AM KHZ)
ICBC Broadcast Holding-MS, Inc.
731 S. Pear Orchard Rd. #27
Ridgeland, MS 39157
Kevin Webb, General Manager
Tel: (601) 957-1300 Fax: (601) 956-0516
Email: kwebb1234@aol.com
Web: www.wkxi.com

WKXI-FM (107.5-FM MHZ)
ICBC Broadcast Holding-MS, Inc.
731 S. Pear Orchard #27
Ridgeland, MS 39157
Kevin Webb, General Manager
Tel: (601) 957-1300 Fax: (601) 956-0516
Email: kwebb1234@aol.com
Web: www.wkxi.com

WMIS-AM (1240-AM KHZ)
Natchez Broadcasting Company
20 E. Franklin St.
Natchez, MS 39120

Lijuna Grennell Weir, Station Manager
Tel: (601) 442-2522 Fax: (601) 446-9918
Email: wmiswtyj@aol.com

WMXU-FM (106.1-FM MHZ)
Cumulus Broadcasting
601 2nd Ave. North
Columbus, MS 39701
Greg Benefield, General Manager
Tel: (662) 327-1183 Fax: (662) 328-1122

WNBN-AM (1290-AM KHZ)
Rackley Broadcasting
266 23rd St.
Meridian, MS 39301
Frank Rackley, General Manager
Tel: (601) 483-3401 Fax: (601) 483-3411

WOAD-AM (1300-AM KHZ)
ICBC Broadcast Holding-MS, Inc.
731 S. Pear Orchard Rd. #27
Ridgeland, MS 39157
Kevin Webb, General Manager
Tel: (601) 957-1300 Fax: (601) 956-0516
Email: kwebb1234@aol.com
Web: www.woad.com

WOAD-FM (105.9-FM MHZ)
ICBC Broadcast Holding-MS, Inc.
731 S. Pear Orchard Rd. #27
Ridgeland, MS 39157
Kevin Webb, General Manager
Tel: (601) 957-1300 Fax: (601) 956-0516
Email: kwebb1234@aol.com
Web: www.woad.com

WONG-AM (1150-AM KHZ)
Southern Gulf Broadcasting
126 E. Sowell Rd.
Canton, MS 39046
K. Hill, General Manager
Tel: (601) 855-2035 Fax: (601) 855-2094

WQJQ-FM (105.1-FM MHZ)
Clear Channel Communications
1375 Beasley Rd.
Jackson, MS 39206
Kenneth Windham, General Manager
Tel: (601) 982-1062 Fax: (601) 362-8270
Web: www.usa@clearchannel.com

WTYJ-FM (97.7-FM MHZ)
Natchez Broadcasting Company
20 E. Franklin St.
Natchez, MS 39120
Lijuna Grennell Weir, Station Manager
Tel: (601) 442-2522 Fax: (601) 446-9918
Email: wmiswtyj@aol.com

WZKS-FM (104.1-FM MHZ)
Clear Channel Communications
4307 Hwy. 39 North
Meridian, MS 39301
Ron Harper, General Manager
Tel: (601) 693-2381 Fax: (601) 485-2792

WZLD-FM (106.3-FM MHZ)
Clear Channel Communications
6555 Hwy. 98 West #8
Hattiesburg, MS 39402
Mike Comfort, General Manager
Tel: (601) 296-9800 Fax: (601) 296-9838
Web: www.wzldfm.com

MISSOURI

KATZ-AM (1600-AM KHZ)
Clear Channel Communications
10001 Highland Plaza Dr. West #100
St. Louis, MO 63132
Lee Clear, General Manager
Tel: (314) 333-8000 Fax: (314) 333-8883

KATZ-FM (100.3-FM MHZ)
Clear Channel Communications
10001 Highland Plaza Dr. West #100
St. Louis, MO 63132
Lee Clear, General Manager
Tel: (314) 333-8000 Fax: (314) 333-8883

KMJM-FM (104.9-FM MHZ)
Clear Channel Communications
10001 Highland Plaza Dr. West #100
St. Louis, MO 63132
Lee Clear, General Manager
Tel: (314) 333-8000 Fax: (314) 333-8883

WFUN-FM (95.5-FM MHZ)
Radio One
9666 Olive Blvd. #610
St. Louis, MO 63132
Linda O'Conner, General Manager
Tel: (314) 989-9550 Fax: (314) 989-9551
Web: www.foxy955.net

NEVADA

KCEP-FM (88.1-FM MHZ)
Economic Opportunity Board of CC
330 W. Washington St.
Las Vegas, NV 89106
Billy Thompson, Program Director
Tel: (702) 648-0104 Fax: (702) 647-0803
Email: power88@power88lv.com
Web: www.power88lv.com

NEW MEXICO

KAGM-FM (106.3-FM MHZ)
AGM Radio
4125 Carlisle NE
Albuquerque, NM 87107
Scott Hutton, General Manager
Tel: (505) 878-0980 Fax: (505) 878-0098
Web: www.kgm.com

NEW YORK

WAJZ-FM (96.3-FM MHZ)
Albany Broadcasting Company
6 Johnson Rd.
Latham, NY 12110
Dan Austin, General Manager
Tel: (518) 786-6600 Fax: (518) 786-6610
Web: www.jamz963.com

WBLK-FM (93.7-FM MHZ)
Infinity Broadcasting
14 Lafayette Sq. #1300
Buffalo, NY 14203
Jeff Silver, General Manager
Tel: (716) 852-9393 Fax: (716) 852-9390
Web: www.wblk.com

WBLS-FM (107.5-FM MHZ)
ICBC Broadcast Holdings-NY, Inc.
3 Park Ave., 41st Fl.
New York, NY 10016
Deon Levingson, General Manager
Tel: (212) 447-1000 Fax: (212) 447-5211
Email: deon@wbls.com
Web: www.wbls.com

WDKX-FM (103.9-FM MHZ)
Monroe County Broadcasting Company, Ltd.
683 E. Main St.
Rochester, NY 14605
Andrew E. Langston, General Manager
Tel: (585) 262-2050 Fax: (585) 262-2626
Web: www.wdkx.com

WGMC-FM (90.1-FM MHZ)
Community Education of Greece
1139 Maiden Ln
Rochester, NY 14615
Rob Linton, Station Manager
Tel: (585) 966-2660 Fax: (585) 581-8185
Email: rob@jazz901.org
Web: www.jazz901.org

WLIB-AM (1190-AM KHZ)
ICBC Broadcast Holdings-NY, Inc.
3 Park Ave., 41st Fl.
New York, NY 10016
Deon Levingson, General Manager
Tel: (212) 447-1000 Fax: (212) 447-5211
Email: deon@wbls.com

WRKS-FM (98.7-FM MHZ)
Emmis Communications
395 Hudson St.
New York, NY 10014
Barry Mayo, General Manager
Tel: (212) 242-9870 Fax: (212) 242-0706
Email: 987kissfm@987kissfm.com
Web: www.987kissfm.com

WVCR-FM (88.3-FM MHZ)
Siena College
515 Loudon Rd.
Loudonville, NY 12211
Bombay, General Manager
Tel: (518) 782-6751 Fax: (518) 782-6498
Web: www.wvcr.com

WWPR-FM (105.1-FM MHZ)
Clear Channel Communications
1120 Ave. of the Americas
New York, NY 10036
Andy Rosen, General Manager
Tel: (212) 704-1051 Fax: (212) 869-3299
Email: power1051fm@clearchannel.com
Web: www.power1051fm.com

WWRL-AM (1600-AM KHZ)
Access One
333 7th Ave., 14th Fl.
New York, NY 10001
Adrian Gaines, General Manager
Tel: (212) 631-0800 Fax: (212) 239-7203
Web: www.wwrl1600.com

NORTH CAROLINA

WBAV-FM (101.9-FM MHZ)
Infinity Broadcasting
1520 South Blvd. #300
Charlotte, NC 28203
Bill Schoening, General Manager
Tel: (704) 342-2644 Fax: (704) 227-8979
Web: www.v1019.com

WEAL-AM (1510-AM KHZ)
Intercom
7819 National Service Rd. #401
Greensboro, NC 27409
Brad Millar, General Manager
Tel: (336) 605-5200 Fax: (336) 605-0138
Web: www.1510weal.com

WFSS-FM (91.9-FM MHZ)
WFSS Public Radio Station
1200 Murchison Rd.
Fayetteville, NC 28301
Joseph Ross, General Manager
Tel: (910) 672-2030 Fax: (910) 672-1964
Email: jross@uncfsu.edu
Web: www.wfss.org

WFXC-FM (107.1-FM MHZ)
Radio One
8001-101 Creedmoor Rd.
Raleigh, NC 27613

Gary Weiss, General Manager
Tel: (919) 848-9736 Fax: (919) 848-4724
Web: www.foxyhits.com

WFXK-FM (104.3-FM MHZ)
Radio One
8001-101 Creedmoor Rd.
Raleigh, NC 27613
Gary Weiss, General Manager
Tel: (919) 848-9736 Fax: (919) 848-4724
Web: www.foxyhits.com

WIDU-AM (1600-AM KHZ)
WIDU Broadcasting, Inc.
P.O. Box 2247
Fayetteville, NC 28302
Sandy Loston, General Manager
Tel: (910) 483-6111 Fax: (910) 483-6601

WIKS-FM (101.9-FM MHZ)
Beasley Broadcasting Group, Inc.
207 Glenburnie Dr.
New Bern, NC 28560
Bruce Simel, General Manager
Tel: (252) 633-1500 Fax: (252) 633-0718
Email: bruce@wsfl.com
Web: www.kiss102.com

WKXB-FM (99.9-FM MHZ)
Next Media
25 N. Kerr Ave.
Wilmington, NC 28405
Bea Raybourne, General Manager
Tel: (910) 791-3088 Fax: (910) 791-0112
Web: www.b999fm.com

WMNX-FM (97.3-FM MHZ)
Cumulus Broadcasting
3233 Burnt Mill Rd. #4
Wilmington, NC 28403
Jim Principi, Market Manager
Tel: (910) 763-9977 Fax: (910) 763-0201
Web: www.coast973.com

WNAA-FM (90.1-FM MHZ)
NC A&T State University
200 Price Hall
Greensboro, NC 27411
Mamie Johnson, Production/Station Ad-
ministration
Tel: (336) 334-7936 Fax: (336) 334-7960
Email: mamiej@ncat.edu
Web: www.wnaalive.ncat.edu

WNNL-FM (103.9-FM MHZ)
Radio One
8001-101 Creedmoor Rd.
Raleigh, NC 27613
Gary Weiss, General Manager
Tel: (919) 848-9736 Fax: (919) 848-4724
Web: www.thelight1039.com

WOOW-AM (1340-AM KHZ)
Jim Rouse Communications Group
P.O. Box 8361
Greenville, NC 27834
Jim Rouse, President/CEO
Tel: (252) 757-0365 Fax: (252) 757-1793
Email: woow.1@juno.com

WPEG-FM (97.9-FM MHZ)
Infinity Broadcasting
1520 South Blvd. #300
Charlotte, NC 28203
Bill Schoening, General Manager
Tel: (704) 342-2644 Fax: (704) 227-8979
Web: www.powerfm.com

WQNC-FM (92.7-FM MHZ)
Radio One
2303 W. Morehead St.
Charlotte, NC 28208
Debbie Kwei, General Manager
Tel: (704) 358-0211 Fax: (704) 358-3752

Email: dkwei@radio-one.com
Web: www.q927fm.com

WQOK-FM (97.5-FM MHZ)
Radio One
8001-101 Creedmoor Rd.
Raleigh, NC 27613
Gary Weiss, General Manager
Tel: (919) 848-9736 Fax: (919) 848-4724

WSMY-AM (1400-AM KHZ)
First Media Radio, LLC
P.O. Box 910
Roanoke Rapids, NC 27870
John Green , Program Director
Tel: (252) 536-3115 Fax: (252) 538-0378
Email: info@wsmy1400.com
Web: www.wsmy1400.com

WSNC-FM (90.5-FM MHZ)
Winston-Salem State University
601 Martin Luther King Jr. Dr., Hall Pat-
terson Bldg.
Winston-Salem, NC 27110
Elvin Jenkins, General Manager
Tel: (336) 750-2324 Fax: (336) 750-2329
Email: jenkinse@wssu.edu
Web: www.wsncfm.org

WTOW-AM (1320-AM KHZ)
Jim Rouse Communications Group
P.O. Box 8361
Greenville, NC 27834
Jim Rouse, President/CEO
Tel: (252) 757-0365 Fax: (252) 757-1793
Email: woow.1@juno.com

WZFX-FM (99.1-FM MHZ)
Beasley Broadcasting Group, Inc.
508 Person St.
Fayetteville, NC 28301
Danny Highsmith, General Manager
Tel: (910) 486-4114 Fax: (910) 486-6720
Web: www.foxy99.com

OHIO

WCIN-AM (1480-AM KHZ)
J4 Broadcasting
3540 Reading Rd.
Cincinnati, OH 45229
John Thomas, General Manager
Tel: (513) 281-7180 Fax: (513) 281-6125
Web: www.1480wcin.com

WCKX-FM (107.5-FM MHZ)
Radio One
1500 W. 3rd Ave. #300
Columbus, OH 43212
Jeff Wilson, General Manager
Tel: (614) 487-1444 Fax: (614) 487-5863
Web: www.power1075.com

WDBZ-AM (1230-AM KHZ)
1 Centennel Plz., 705 Central Ave. #200
Cincinnati, OH 45202
Rick Porter, General Manager
Tel: (513) 679-6000 Fax: (513) 679-6014
Web: www.1230thebuzz.com

WENZ-FM (107.9-FM MHZ)
2510 St. Claire Ave. NE
Cleveland, OH 44114-4013
David Bevins, General Manager
Tel: (216) 579-1111 Fax: (216) 621-2176
Web: www.z1079fm.com

WERE-AM (1300-AM KHZ)
2510 St. Claire Ave. NE
Cleveland, OH 44114-4013
David Bevins, General Manager
Tel: (216) 579-1111 Fax: (216) 621-2176
Web: www.1300were.com

WIMX-FM (95.7-FM MHZ)
Urban Radio Broadcasting
5744 Southwyck Blvd. #200
Toledo, OH 43614
Barbara Hubley, Business Manger
Tel: (419) 868-7914 Fax: (419) 868-8765
Web: www.mix957.fm

WIZF-FM (100.9-FM MHZ)
Radio One
705 Central Ave. #200
Cincinnati, OH 45202
Rick Porter, General Manager
Tel: (513) 679-6000 Fax: (513) 679-6014
Web: www.wizfm.com

WJMO-AM (1490-AM KHZ)
2510 St. Claire Ave. NE
Cleveland, OH 44114-4013
David Bevins, General Manager
Tel: (216) 579-1111 Fax: (216) 621-2176
Web: www.1490wjmo.com

WJTB-AM (1040-AM KHZ)
Taylor Broadcast
105 Lake Ave.
Elyria, OH 44035
Jay Taylor, General Manager
Tel: (440) 327-1844 Fax: (440) 322-8942

WJYD-FM (106.3-FM MHZ)
Radio One
1500 W. 3rd Ave. #300
Columbus, OH 43212
Jeff Wilson, General Manager
Tel: (614) 487-1444 Fax: (614) 487-5863
Web: www.joy106.com

WMOJ-FM (94.9-FM MHZ)
Radio Cincinnati
895 Central Ave. #900
Cincinnati, OH 45202
Dan Swensson, General Manager
Tel: (513) 241-9898 Fax: (513) 241-6689
Web: www.mojo949.com

WXMG-FM (98.9-FM MHZ)
Radio One
1500 W. 3rd Ave. #300
Columbus, OH 43212
Jeff Wilson, General Manager
Tel: (614) 487-1444 Fax: (614) 487-5863
Web: www.magic989.com

WXTM-FM (92.3-FM MHZ)
Extreme Radio
1041 Huron Rd.
Cleveland, OH 44115
Tom Herschel, General Manager
Tel: (216) 861-0100 Fax: (216) 696-3710
Web: www.923xtreme.com

WZAK-FM (93.1-FM MHZ)
Radio One
2510 St. Claire Ave. NE
Cleveland, OH 44114-4013
David Bevins, General Manager
Tel: (216) 579-1111 Fax: (216) 621-2176
Web: www.931wzale.com

WZIP-FM (88.1-FM MHZ)
University of Akron
302 E. Buchtel Ave.
Akron, OH 44325
Tom Beck, General Manager
Tel: (330) 972-7105 Fax: (330) 972-5521
Web: www.uakron.edu/wzip

OKLAHOMA

KJMM-FM (105.3-FM MHZ)
Perry Publishing and Broadcasting Co.

7030 S. Yale St. #302
Tulsa, OK 74136
Brian Robinson, General Manager
Tel: (918) 494-9886 Fax: (918) 494-9683
Web: www.1053kjamz.com

KJMZ-FM (98.1-FM MHZ)
**Perry Publishing and Broadcasting
Company**
1525 SE Flower Mound Rd.
Lawton, OK 73501
Joy Chapman, General Manager
Tel: (580) 355-1050 Fax: (580) 355-1056
Email: joyc@kjmz.com
Web: www.perry-pub-broadcasting.com

KKRX-AM (1050-AM KHZ)
**Perry Publishing and Broadcasting
Company**
1525 SE Flower Mound Rd.
Lawton, OK 73501
Joy Chapman, General Manager
Tel: (580) 355-1050 Fax: (580) 355-1056
Email: joyc@kjmz.com

KRMP-AM (1140-AM KHZ)
**Perry Publishing and Broadcasting
Company**
1528 NE 23rd St.
Oklahoma City, OK 73111
Russell Perry, General Manager
Tel: (405) 425-4100 Fax: (405) 424-8811
Email: kperry@kvsp.com
Web: www.perry-pub-broadcasting.com

PENNSYLVANIA

WAMO-FM (106.7-FM MHZ)
Sheridan Broadcasting
960 Penn Ave. #200
Pittsburgh, PA 15222
Ronald R. Davenport, Jr., Chairman
Tel: (412) 471-2181 Fax: (412) 391-3559
Email: rdavenportjr@sbcol.com
Web: www.wamo.com

WAMO-AM (860-AM KHZ)
Sheridan Broadcasting
960 Penn Ave. #200
Pittsburgh, PA 15222
Ronald R. Davenport, Jr., Chairman
Tel: (412) 471-2181 Fax: (412) 391-3559
Email: rdavenportjr@sbcol.com

WJJJ-FM (104.7-FM MHZ)
Sheridan Broadcasting
960 Penn Ave. #200
Pittsburgh, PA 15222
Ronald R. Davenport, Jr., Chairman
Tel: (412) 471-2181 Fax: (412) 391-3559
Email: rdavenportjr@sbcol.com

WPGB-FM (104.7-FM MHZ)
Clear Channel Communications
200 Fleet St.
Pittsburgh, PA 15220
John Rohm, General Manager
Tel: (412) 937-1441 Fax: (412) 937-0323
Web: www.wpgb.com

WPGR-AM (1050-AM KHZ)
Sheridan Broadcasting
960 Penn Ave. #200
Pittsburgh, PA 15222
Ronald R. Davenport, Jr., Chairman
Tel: (412) 471-2181 Fax: (412) 391-3559
Email: rdavenportjr@sbcol.com

WPHI-FM (100.3-FM MHZ)
Radio One
1000 River Rd. #400
Conshohocken, PA 19428

Chester Schofield, General Manager
Tel: (610) 276-1100 Fax: (610) 276-1139
Email: cschofield@radio-one.com
Web: www.1003thebeatphilly.com

WPPZ-FM (103.9-FM MHZ)
Radio One
1000 River Rd. #400
Conshohocken, PA 19428
Chester Schofield, Vice President
Tel: (610) 276-1100 Fax: (610) 276-1139
Email: cschofield@radio-one.com
Web: www.radio-one.com

WTCY-AM (1400-AM KHZ)
Cumulus Broadcasting
2300 Vartan Way
Harrisburg, PA 17110
Ron Giovanniello, General Manager
Tel: (717) 238-1041 Fax: (717) 238-1454
Email: harrisburg.production@cumulus.com
Web: www.1400thetouch.com

WURP-AM (1550-AM KHZ)
Urban Radio of Pennsylvania, LLC
4736 Penn Ave.
Pittsburgh, PA 15224
Chris Squire, General Manager
Tel: (412) 942-0076
Web: www.edge1550.com

WUSL-FM (98.9-FM MHZ)
Clear Channel Communications
440 Domino Ln.
Philadelphia, PA 19128
Richard Lewis, General Manager
Tel: (215) 483-8900 Fax: (215) 483-5930
Web: www.power99.com

RHODE ISLAND

WRIB-AM (1220-AM KHZ)
Carter Broadcasting, Inc.
200 Water St.
East Providence, RI 02914
John Pierce, General Manager
Tel: (401) 434-0406 Fax: (401) 434-0409
Web: www.wrib.com

SOUTH CAROLINA

WAEG-AM (1550-AM KHZ)
Radio One
104 Bennett Ln.
North Augusta, SC 29841
Dennis Jackson, General Manager
Tel: (803) 279-2330 Fax: (803) 819-3759
Web: www.wthbgospelalive.com

WAEG-FM (92.3-FM MHZ)
104 Bennett Ln.
North Augusta, SC 29841
Dennis Jackson, General Manager
Tel: (803) 279-2330 Fax: (803) 819-3759
Web: www.waeg92.3.com

WAEJ-FM (100.9-FM MHZ)
104 Bennett Ln.
North Augusta, SC 29841
Dennis Jackson, General Manager
Tel: (803) 279-2330 Fax: (803) 819-3759
Web: www.wthbgospelalive.com

WAKB-FM (96.6-FM MHZ)
104 Bennett Ln.
North Augusta, SC 29841
Dennis Jackson, General Manager
Tel: (803) 279-2330 Fax: (803) 819-3759
Web: www.magic969.com

WARQ-FM (93.5-FM MHZ)
Urban Radio of South Carolina
1900 Pineview Dr.
Columbia, SC 29209
Steve Patterson, General Manager
Tel: (803) 776-1013 Fax: (803) 695-8605
Email: spatterson@innercitysc.com
Web: www.warq.com

WASC-AM (1530-AM KHZ)
New South Broadcasting
P.O. Box 5686
Spartanburg, SC 29304
Joe Sessoms, General Manager
Tel: (864) 585-1530 Fax: (864) 573-7790

WBAW-FM (99.1-FM MHZ)
JMB Broadcasting
P.O. Box 685
Barnwell, SC 29812
Belinda Parker, General Manager
Tel: (803) 541-9989 Fax: (803) 541-6215

WDOG-AM (1460-AM KHZ)
Good Radio Broadcasting
P.O. Box 442
Allendale, SC 29810
Carl Gooding, General Manager
Tel: (803) 584-3500
Email: wdog935@aol.com

WDOG-FM (93.5-FM MHZ)
Good Radio Broadcasting
P.O. Box 442
Allendale, SC 29810
Carl Gooding, General Manager
Tel: (803) 584-3500
Email: wdog935@aol.com

WFXA-FM (103.1-FM MHZ)
Radio One
104 Bennett Ln.
North Augusta, SC 29841
Dennis Jackson, General Manager
Tel: (803) 279-2330 Fax: (803) 819-3759
Web: www.wfxa103.1.com

WIGL-FM (93.9-FM MHZ)
Miller Communications, Inc.
200 Regional Pkwy., Bldg. C #200
Orangeburg, SC 29118
Theresa Miller, General Manager
Tel: (803) 536-1710 Fax: (803) 531-1089
Email: tmiller55@aol.com
Web: www.miller.fm

WLBG-AM (860-AM KHZ)
South Eastern Broadcast Associates
P.O. Box 1289
Laurens, SC 29360
Emil Finley, General Manager
Tel: (864) 984-3544 Fax: (864) 984-3545

WLXC-FM (98.5-FM MHZ)
Citadel Broadcasting
P.O. Box 5106
Columbia, SC 29250
William McElveen, General Manager
Tel: (803) 796-9975 Fax: (803) 796-5502
Email: bill.mcelveen@citcom.com
Web: www.kiss985fm.com

WMFX-FM (102.3-FM MHZ)
Urban Radio of South Carolina
1900 Pineview Dr.
Columbia, SC 29209
Steve Patterson, General Manager
Tel: (803) 776-1013 Fax: (803) 695-8605
Email: spatterson@innercitysc.com
Web: www.fox102.com

WMGL-FM (101.7-FM MHZ)
Citadel Broadcasting Company

4230 Faber Place Dr. #100
North Charleston, SC 29405
Paul O'Malley, General Manager
Tel: (843) 277-1200 Fax: (843) 277-1212
Email: paul.omalley@citcomm.com
Web: www.magic1017.com

WOIC-AM (1230-AM KHZ)
Urban Radio of South Carolina
1900 Pineview Rd.
Columbia, SC 29209
Steve Patterson, General Manager
Tel: (803) 776-1013 Fax: (803) 695-8605
Email: spatterson@innercitysc.com
Web: www.wico.com

WWDM-FM (101.3-FM MHZ)
Urban Radio of South Carolina
1900 Pineview Rd.
Columbia, SC 29209
Steve Patterson, General Manager
Tel: (803) 776-1013 Fax: (803) 695-8605
Email: spatterson@innercitysc.com
Web: www.thebigdm.com

WWWZ-FM (93.3-FM MHZ)
Citadel Broadcasting Company
4230 Faber Place Dr. #100
North Charleston, SC 29405
Paul O'Malley, General Manager
Tel: (843) 277-1200 Fax: (843) 277-1212
Email: paul.omalley@citcomm.com

WXBT-FM (100.1-FM MHZ)
Clear Channel Communications
316 Greystone Blvd.
Columbia, SC 29210
Bob Huntley, General Manager
Tel: (803) 343-1100 Fax: (803) 779-9727
Web: www.wxbt.com

WXTC-AM (1390-AM KHZ)
Citadel Broadcasting Company
4230 Faber Place Dr. #100
North Charleston, SC 29405
Paul O'Malley, General Manager
Tel: (843) 277-1200 Fax: (843) 277-1212
Email: paul.omalley@citcomm.com
Web: www.heaven1390.com

TENNESSEE

KWAM-AM (990-AM KHZ)
Clear Channel Communications
2650 Thousand Oaks Blvd. #4100
Memphis, TN 38118
Brece Temps, General Manager
Tel: (901) 529-4300 Fax: (901) 259-6449
Web: www.am990.com

WDBL-AM (1590-AM KHZ)
Lightning Broadcasting
P.O. Box 909
Springfield, TN 37172
Neil Peterson, General Manager
Tel: (615) 384-5541 Fax: (615) 384-9746

WDIA-AM (1070-AM KHZ)
Clear Channel Communications
2650 Thousand Oaks Blvd. #4100
Memphis, TN 38118
Brece Temps, General Manager
Tel: (901) 529-4300 Fax: (901) 259-6449
Web: www.am1070wdia.com

WFKX-FM (95.7-FM MHZ)
Thomas Media
111 W. Main St.
Jackson, TN 38301
Chip Thomas, General Manager
Tel: (731) 427-9616 Fax: (731) 424-2473
Web: www.96kix.fm

WHRK-FM (97.1-FM MHZ)
Clear Channel Communications
2650 Thousand Oaks Blvd. #4100
Memphis, TN 38118
Brece Temps, General Manager
Tel: (901) 529-4300 Fax: (901) 259-6449
Web: www.k97fm.com

WJTT-FM (94.3-FM MHZ)
Brewer Broadcasting
1305 Carter St.
Chattanooga, TN 37402
Jim Brewer, II, General Manager
Tel: (423) 265-9494 Fax: (423) 266-2335
Web: www.power94.com

WKFN-AM (1370-AM KHZ)
Five Star Radio Group
1640 Old Russellville Pike
Clarksville, TN 37043
Susan Quesenberry, General Manager
Tel: (931) 431-4984 Fax: (931) 648-7769

WKXJ-FM (98.1-FM MHZ)
Clear Channel Communications
7413 Old Lee Hwy.
Chattanooga, TN 37421
Sammy George, General Manager
Tel: (423) 892-3333 Fax: (423) 642-0096
Web: www.wkxj.com

WQQK-FM (92.1-FM MHZ)
Cumulus Media
10 Music Cir. East
Nashville, TN 37203
Michael Dickey, General Manager
Tel: (615) 321-1067 Fax: (615) 321-5771

WVOL-AM (1470-AM KHZ)
Headelberg Broadcasting
1320 Brick Church Pike
Nashville, TN 37207
John Headelberg, Owner
Tel: (615) 227-1470 Fax: (615) 226-0709
Email: wvol1470@wvol1470.com
Web: www.wvol1470.com

TEXAS

KAZE-FM (106.9-FM MHZ)
The Blaze
212 Grande Blvd. #C120
Tyler, TX 75703
Rick Reynolds, General Manager
Tel: (903) 845-2259 Fax: (903) 939-3473
Email: rick@theblaze.cc
Web: www.theblaze.cc

KAZI-FM (88.7-FM MHZ)
Austin Community Radio
8906 Wall St. #203
Austin, TX 78754
Steve Savage, General Manager
Tel: (512) 836-9544 Fax: (512) 836-9563
Email: steve@kazifm.com
Web: www.kazifm.com

KBFB-FM (97.9-FM MHZ)
Radio One Dallas
13331 Preston Rd. #1180
Dallas, TX 75240
Shawn Nunn, General Manager
Tel: (972) 331-5400 Fax: (972) 331-5560
Web: www.979thebeat.com

KBLZ-FM (102.7-FM MHZ)
The Blaze
212 Grande Blvd. #C120
Tyler, TX 75703
Rick Reynolds, General Manager
Tel: (903) 845-2259 Fax: (903) 939-3473
Email: rick@theblaze.cc
Web: www.theblaze.cc

KBXX-FM (97.9-FM MHZ)
Radio One
24 Greenway Plz. #900
Houston, TX 77046
Doug Abermethy, General Manager
Tel: (713) 623-2108 Fax: (713) 622-6066
Web: www.kbxx.com

KCHX-FM (106.7-FM MHZ)
Clear Channel Communications
1330 E. 8th St. #207
Odessa, TX 79761
Gloria Apolinario, General Manager
Tel: (432) 563-9102 Fax: (432) 580-9102
Web: www.mymix1067.com

KCOH-AM (1430-AM KHZ)
KCOH, Inc.
5011 Alameda Rd.
Houston, TX 77004
Mike Petrizzo, Executive VP/General Manager
Tel: (713) 522-1001 Fax: (713) 521-0769
Email: mpetrizzo@kcohradio.com
Web: www.kcohradio.com

KELZ-FM (106.7-FM MHZ)
Cox Radio
8122 Datapoint Dr. #500
San Antonio, TX 78229
Marty Choate, General Manager
Tel: (210) 615-5400 Fax: (210) 615-5300

KFMK-FM (105.9-FM MHZ)
Clear Channel Communications
3601 S. Congress Ave.
Austin, TX 78704
Dusty Black, General Manager
Tel: (512) 495-1300 Fax: (512) 684-7441
Web: www.jammin1059.com

KHVN-AM (970-AM KHZ)
Mortenson Broadcasting Company
5787 S. Hampton Rd. #285
Dallas, TX 75232
Deon Mortenson, General Manager
Tel: (214) 331-5486 Fax: (214) 331-1908
Email: Heaven97@khvam.com
Web: www.khvnam.com

KIIZ-FM (92.3-FM MHZ)
Clear Channel Communications
100 W. Central Texas Expwy. #306
Harker Heights, TX 76548
Evan Armstrong, General Manager
Tel: (254) 699-5000 Fax: (254) 680-4211
Web: www.kiiz.com

KJCE-AM (1370-AM KHZ)
Infinity Broadcasting
4301 Westbank Dr., Escalade-B, 3rd Fl.
Austin, TX 78746
John Hiatt, General Manager
Tel: (512) 327-9595 Fax: (512) 329-6257
Email: feedback@talkradio1370am.com
Web: www.kjuice.com

KKDA-AM (730-AM KHZ)
KKDA Broadcasting, Inc.
P.O. Box 530860
Grand Prairie, TX 75053
Chuck Smith, General Manager
Tel: (972) 263-9911 Fax: (972) 558-0010

KKDA-FM (104.5-FM MHZ)
P.O. Box 530860
Grand Prairie, TX 75053
Chuck Smith, General Manager
Tel: (972) 263-9911 Fax: (972) 558-0010
Web: www.k104fm.com

KMJQ-FM (102.1-FM MHZ)
Radio One
24 Greenway Plz. #900

Houston, TX 77046
Doug Abermethy, General Manager
Tel: (713) 623-2108 Fax: (713) 622-6066
Web: www.kmjq.com

KMRK-FM (96.1-FM MHZ)
Clear Channel Communications
1330 E. 8th St. #207
Odessa , TX 79761
Gloria Apolinario, General Manager
Tel: (432) 563-9102 Fax: (432) 580-9102
Web: www.wild961.com

KPVU-FM (91.3-FM MHZ)
Prairie View A&M University
P.O. Box 156
Prairie View, TX 77446
Larry Coleman, General Manager
Tel: (936) 857-4511 Fax: (936) 857-2729
Email: kpvu_fm@pvamu.edu
Web: www.pvamu.edu/kpvu

KRNB-FM (105.7-FM MHZ)
KKDA Broadcasting, Inc.
P.O. Box 530860
Grand Prairie, TX 75053
Chuck Smith, General Manager
Tel: (972) 263-9911 Fax: (972) 558-0010
Web: www.krnb.com

KRPX-FM (107.3-FM MHZ)
Convergent Broadcasting
826 S. Padre Island Dr.
Corpus Christi, TX 78416
Mark White, General Manager
Tel: (361) 814-3800 Fax: (361) 855-3770
Web: www.1073thex.com

KSJL-AM (810-AM KHZ)
Clear Channel Communications
6222 NW IH-10
San Antonio, TX 78201
Tom Glade, General Manager
Tel: (210) 736-9700 Fax: (210) 735-8811
Web: www.ksjl.com

KSJL-FM (92.5-FM MHZ)
Clear Channel Communications
6222 NW IH-10
San Antonio, TX 78201
Tom Glade, General Manager
Tel: (210) 736-9700 Fax: (210) 735-8811
Web: www.ksjl.com

KSOC-FM (94.5-FM MHZ)
Radio One Dallas
13331 Preston Rd. #1180
Dallas, TX 75240
Shawn Nunn, General Manager
Tel: (972) 331-5400 Fax: (972) 331-5560
Web: www.945ksoul.com

KTHT-FM (97.1-FM MHZ)
Cox Radio
1990 Post Oak Blvd. #2300
Houston, TX 77056
Carolyn Devine, General Manager
Tel: (713) 622-5533 Fax: (713) 993-9300
Web: www.countrylegens971.com

KTYL-FM (93.1-FM MHZ)
Clear Channel Communications
3810 Brookside Dr.
Tyler, TX 75701
Craig Reininger, General Manager
Tel: (903) 581-0606 Fax: (903) 581-2011
Web: www.mix931fm.com

KVJM-FM (103.1-FM MHZ)
Equal Access Media
219 N. Main St. #600
Bryan, TX 77803
Edward Sanchez, General Manager
Tel: (979) 779-3337 Fax: (979) 779-3444

Email: edwardz103fm@hotmail.com

KZEY-AM (690-AM KHZ)
Community Broadcast Group
P.O. Box 4248
Tyler, TX 75712
Esther Milton, General Manager
Tel: (903) 593-1744 Fax: (903) 593-2666

KZRB-FM (103.5-FM MHZ)
B&H Broadcasting Systems, Inc.
710 W. Ave. A
Hooks, TX 75561
Ray Bursey, Jr., General Manager
Tel: (903) 547-3223 Fax: (903) 547-3095
Web: www.kzrb.com

VIRGIN ISLANDS

WVJZ-FM (105.3-FM MHZ)
Knight Quality Stations
P.O. Box 305678
St. Thomas, VI 00803-5678
Mark Bastin, General Manager
Tel: (340) 776-1000 Fax: (340) 776-5357
Email: kqsgmgsm@hotmail.com
Web: www.wvjz.net

WVVI-AM (1000-AM KHZ)
Knight Quality Stations
P.O. Box 305678
St. Thomas, VI 00803-5678
Mark Bastin, General Manager
Tel: (340) 776-1000 Fax: (340) 776-5357
Email: kqsgmgsm@hotmail.com
Web: www.wvvi.net

WWKS-FM (101.3-FM MHZ)
Knight Quality Stations
P.O. Box 305678
St. Thomas, VI 00803-5678
Mark Bastin, General Manager
Tel: (340) 776-1000 Fax: (340) 776-5357
Email: kqsgmgsm@hotmail.com
Web: www.wwks.net

VIRGINIA

WCDG-FM (92.1-FM MHZ)
Clear Channel Communications
1003 Norfolk Sq.
Norfolk, VA 23502
Reggie Jordan, General Manager
Tel: (757) 466-0009 Fax: (757) 466-9523

WCDX-FM (92.1-FM MHZ)
Radio One
2809 Emerywood Pkwy. #300
Richmond, VA 23294
Linda Forem, General Manager
Tel: (804) 672-9299 Fax: (804) 672-9316
Email: lforem@radio-one.com
Web: www.power921jamz.com

WHOV-FM (88.1-FM MHZ)
Hampton University
Script Howard Ctr., Hampton University
Hampton, VA 23668
Rob Dixon, General Manager
Tel: (757) 727-5407 Fax: (757) 727-5427
Email: whovfm@go.com
Web: www.whovfm.com

WILA-AM (1580-AM KHZ)
Tol-Tol Communications, Inc.
P.O. Box 3444
Danville, VA 24543
Lawrence A. Toller, General Manager
Tel: (434) 792-2133 Fax: (434) 792-2134
Email: wilaradio@gamewood.net

WKBY-AM (1080-AM KHZ)
WKBY, Inc.
12932 US Hwy. 29
Chatham, VA 24531
Vickie Pritchett, General Manager
Tel: (434) 432-8108 Fax: (434) 432-1523
Email: WKBY1080@ganewood.net

WKJM-FM (99.3-FM MHZ)
Radio One
2809 Emerywood Pkwy. #300
Richmond, VA 23294
Linda Forem, General Manager
Tel: (804) 672-9299 Fax: (804) 672-9316
Email: lforem@radio-one.com
Web: www.praise1047.com

WKJS-FM (105.7-FM MHZ)
Radio One
2809 Emerywood Pkwy. #300
Richmond , VA 23294
Linda Forem, General Manager
Tel: (804) 672-9299 Fax: (804) 672-9316
Email: lforem@radio-one.com
Web: www.yestokiss.com

WKUS-FM (105.3-FM MHZ)
Clear Channel Communications
1003 Norfolk Sq.
Norfolk, VA 23502
Reggie Jordan, General Manager
Tel: (757) 466-0009 Fax: (757) 466-9523
Web: www.vibezone.com

WOWI-FM (102.9-FM MHZ)
Clear Channel Communications
1003 Norfolk Sq.
Norfolk, VA 23502
Reggie Jordan, General Manager
Tel: (757) 466-0009 Fax: (757) 466-9523

WPAK-AM (1490-AM KHZ)
Great Virginia Ventures
446 Old Plank Rd.
Farmville, VA 23901
Dr. Steveson Bynom, General Manager
Tel: (434) 392-8114 Fax: (434) 392-8114

WPZZ-FM (104.7-FM MHZ)
Radio One
2809 Emerywood Pkwy. #300
Richmond, VA 23294
Linda Forem, General Manager
Tel: (804) 672-9299 Fax: (804) 672-9316
Email: lforem@radio-one.com
Web: www.praise1047.com

WSHV-AM (1370-AM KHZ)
Sun Up Until Sun Down Broadcasting
P.O. Box 216
South Hill, VA 23970
Greg Trift, General Manager
Tel: (434) 447-8997 Fax: (434) 447-4789
Email: gregtrift@lakesmediallc.com

WTJZ-AM (1270-AM KHZ)
Chesapeake Port Smith Broadcasting Company
553 Michigan Dr.
Hampton, VA 23669
Gerome Barber, General Manager
Tel: (757) 723-1270
Email: wtjz@msn.com

WVKL-FM (95.7-FM MHZ)
Entercom Communications Corp.
236 Clearfield Ave. #206
Virginia Beach, VA 23462

continued on p. 286

African American TV Stations

Other states have African-American oriented stations that are not necessarily specifically targeted to that community and so were omitted.

CALIFORNIA

KNTV-TV CHANNEL 11
Granite Broadcasting, Inc.
645 Park Ave.
San Jose, CA 95110
Bob Franklin, General Manager
Tel: (408) 286-1111 Fax: (408) 286-1530
Web: www.newschannel11.com

KSEE-TV CHANNEL 24
Granite Broadcasting Station
5035 E. McKinley Ave.
Fresno, CA 93727
Todd McWilliams, General Manager
Tel: (559) 454-2424 Fax: (559) 454-2485
Web: www.ksee24.com

KPST-TV
Golden Link TV Incorporated
832 Folsom St. #700
Vallejo, CA 94107
Eddie L. Whitehead, President
Tel: (415) 243-8866 Fax: (415) 547-1428
Web: www.kpst.com

CONNECTICUT

WHPX-TV CHANNEL 26
Paxson Communications, Inc.
3 Shaws Cove #226
New London, CT 06320

vacant, General Manager
Tel: (860) 444-2626 Fax: (860) 440-2601

DISTRICT OF COLUMBIA

WHUT-TV CHANNEL 32
Howard University Television
2222 4th St. NW
Washington, DC 20059
Jennifer Lawson, General Manager
Tel: (202) 806-3200 Fax: (202) 806-3300
Web: www.whut.org

ILLINOIS

WEEK-TV CHANNEL 25
Granite Broadcasting Station
2907 Springfield Rd.
E. Peoria, IL 61611
Mark DeSantis, General Manager
Tel: (309) 698-2525 Fax: (309) 698-2070
Web: www.week.com

WJYS-TV CHANNEL 62
Jovon Broadcasting Corporation
18600 S. Oak Park Ave.
Tinley Park, IL 60477
Joseph Stroud, General Manager
Tel: (708) 633-0001 Fax: (708) 633-0040
Email: wjys62@aol.com

INDIANA

WPTA-TV CHANNEL 21
Malara Broadcasting Group
3401 Butler Rd.
Fort Wayne, IN 46808
Chris Fedle, General Manager
Tel: (260) 483-0584 Fax: (260) 483-2568
Email: wpta@wpta.com
Web: www.wpta.com

MINNESOTA

KBJR-TV CHANNEL 6
Granite Broadcasting Station
246 S. Lake Ave.
Duluth, MN 55802
Bob Wilmers, General Manager
Tel: (218) 727-8484 Fax: (218) 727-9660
Email: comments@kbjr.com
Web: www.kbjr.com

MISSOURI

WRBU-TV CHANNEL 46
Roberts Broadcasting, Inc.
1408 N. Kings Hwy.
St. Louis, MO 53113
Greg Filandrinos, General Manager

Tel: (314) 367-4600 Fax: (314) 367-0174
Web: www.upn46stl.com

NEW YORK

WKBW-TV CHANNEL 7
Granite Broadcasting Station
7 Broadcast Plz.
Buffalo, NY 14202
Bill Ransom, General Manager
Tel: (716) 845-6100 Fax: (716) 842-1855
Email: ransomb@wkbw.com
Web: www.wkbw.com

WTVH-TV CHANNEL 5
Granite Broadcasting Station
980 James St.
Syracuse, NY 13203
Les Vann, General Manager
Tel: (315) 425-5555 Fax: (315) 425-5513
Web: www.wtvh.com

WISCONSIN

WJJA-TV CHANNEL 49
TV 49, Inc.
P.O. Box 92
Oakcreek, WI 53154
Joel J. Kinlow, General Manager
Tel: (414) 764-4953 Fax: (414) 764-5190

African American Radio Stations *continued from p. 285*

Skip Schmidt, General Manager
Tel: (757) 497-2000 Fax: (757) 456-5458
Email: ddaconti@entercom.com
Web: www.957rnb.com

WASHINGTON

KKNW-AM (1150-AM KHZ)
Sandusky Radio
3650 131st Ave. SE #550
Bellevue, WA 98006
Marc Kaye, General Manager
Tel: (425) 373-5536 Fax: (425) 373-5507
Email: marck@sanduskyseattle.com
Web: www.1150kknw.com

KRIZ-AM (1420-AM KHZ)
The Seattle Media Newspaper Group
2600 S. Jackson St.
Seattle, WA 98144

Chris Bennett, General Manager
Tel: (206) 329-7880 Fax: (206) 322-6518
Email: ztwins@aol.com
Web: www.ztwins.com

KUBE-FM (93.0-FM MHZ)
Clear Channel Communications
351 Elliott Ave. #300
Seattle , WA 98119
Michelle Grosenick, General Manager
Tel: (206) 285-2295 Fax: (206) 286-2376

KYIZ-AM (1620-AM KHZ)
The Seattle Media Newspaper Group
2600 S. Jackson St.
Seattle, WA 98144
Chris Bennett, General Manager
Tel: (206) 329-7880 Fax: (206) 322-6518
Email: ztwins@aol.com
Web: www.ztwins.com

KZIZ-AM (1560-AM KHZ)
The Seattle Media Newspaper Group
2600 S. Jackson St.
Seattle, WA 98144
Chris Bennett, General Manager
Tel: (206) 329-7880 Fax: (206) 322-6518
Email: ztwins@aol.com
Web: www.ztwins.com

WISCONSIN

WKKV-FM (100.7-FM MHZ)
Clear Channel Milwaukee
12100 W. Howard Ave.
Greenfield, WI 53228
Cindy McDowell, General Manager
Tel: (414) 321-1007 Fax: (414) 327-3200
Web: www.v100.com

WMCS-AM (1290-AM KHZ)
Milwaukee Radio Alliance
4222 W. Capitol Dr.
Milwaukee, WI 53216
Don Rosette, General Manager
Tel: (414) 444-1290 Fax: (414) 444-1409
Email: drosette@milwaukeeradio.com
Web: www.1290wmcs.com

WNOV-AM (860-AM KHZ)
Courrer Communications
3815 N. Teutonia Ave.
Milwaukee, WI 53206
Sandra Robinson, General Manager
Tel: (414) 449-9668 Fax: (414) 449-9945
Web: www.wnov.com

Readership Survey

By completing this survey, you will automatically receive a 50% discount on the 2007/2008 AFRICAN-AMERICAN YEARBOOK.

Name: _____

☐ Male ☐ Female

DOB: _____

Address: _____

City, State, Zip: _____

Phone (optional): _____

E-mail (optional): _____

Profession/Occupation: _____

Salary (approximately):
☐ Under 24,000   ☐ 25-40,000   ☐ 41-55,000
☐ 56-75,000   ☐ 76-100,000   ☐ over 100,000

Educational Attainment:
☐ High School   ☐ Undergraduate
☐ Graduate Degree   ☐ Post-Graduate Degree
☐ Other

Languages: _____

I utilize the Yearbook to _____

I think the Yearbook should include more information about _____

_____

I learned about the Yearbook through:

☐ Library   ☐ Bookstore   ☐ Internet   ☐ Friend   ☐ Employer   ☐ Conference/Convention
☐ Other _____

Please feel free to provide additional comments in the space below:

_____

_____

Thank you for your valuable feedback.
TIYM Publishing Co., Inc.
6718 Whittier Ave., #130 McLean, VA 22101 - Tel: (703) 734-1632 - Fax: (703) 356-0787
E-mail: tiym@tiym.com

Information Update

If your organization, agency, or publication has made changes during the past year, or if you know of one that does not appear within this edition, please take a few moments to let us know by filling out the form below and faxing to us at **(703) 356-0787** or mailing it to: TIYM Publishing Co., Inc. 6718 Whittier Ave., #130, McLean, VA 22101.

You may also e-mail the updated information by visiting **www.africanamericanyearbook.com.**

Please indicate listing preference:

- ☐ Career Opportunities for African Americans ☐ Federal/State   ☐ Private Sector
- ☐ Minority Business Opportunities
- ☐ Institution Offering Scholastic Financial Aid
- ☐ African American Company
- ☐ African American Organization
- ☐ African American Publication
- ☐ African American Radio Station
- ☐ African American TV Station
- ☐ Other

Agency/ Company/ Organization Name: _____

Date Founded: _____

If it is a ☐ Branch or ☐   Affiliate of a larger organization, What is the name of that organization?_____

Address: _____

City: _____ State: _____ Zip Code: _____

Telephone 1: _____ Telephone 2: _____ Fax: _____

E-mail: _____ Web: _____

Name of the Principal Contact: _____

Title of the Principal Contact: _____

Chief Purpose of the Organization (☐ attached is a separate sheet with a detailed description, or organization brochure): _____

Publication/Station Name: _____

Circulation: _____ Verified: _____

No. of Members: _____ Most Important Meeting: _____ Date Held: _____

How often is the Publication Produced: _____

Language: ☐ English   ☐ Other: _____

Other Specifications: _____

Thank you for helping us keep the **AFRICAN-AMERICAN YEARBOOK** up-to-date.